Italy

Italy

A Phaidon Cultural Guide

With over 750 color illustrations
and 13 pages of maps

PRENTICE-HALL, INC.
Englewood Cliffs
New Jersey 07632

Editor: Franz N. Mehling

Contributors: Dr Emma Ceppo, Michael Foster, Maximilian Gand, Gernot Kachel, Dr Marianne Mehling, Dr Gerhard Pauli, Dr Edith Prochazka, Dr Brigitte Regler, Dr Albin Rohrmoser, Dr Christa Svoboda, Dr Gerlinde Werner

Photographs: Fratelli Fabbri Editori S.p.A., Milan; Löbl/Schreyer, Ellbach/Obb.; SCALA Istituto Fotografico Editoriale, Florence; Armin M. Boerne, Dr Hermann Götz, Dr Gerhard Pauli

Maps: Huber & Oberländer, Munich

Ground-plans: Satzstudio Lidl + Pfeifer, Munich

Library of Congress Cataloging in Publication Data

Knaurs Kulturführer in Farbe: Italien. English.
  Italy, a Phaidon cultural guide.

  Translation of: Knaurs Kulturführer in Farbe: Italien.
  Includes index.
  1. Art—Italy—Guide-books. 2. Architecture—
  Italy—Guide-books. 3. Italy—Antiquities—Guide-books.
  4. Italy—Description and travel—Guide-books. I. Title.
  N6911.K5413 1985   914.5'04928   84-18109
  ISBN 0-13-506734-0 (case)

This book is available at a special discount when ordered in bulk quantities. Contact Prentice-Hall, Inc., General Publishing Division, Special Sales, Englewood Cliffs. N.J. 07632.

This edition published in the United States and Canada 1985 by Prentice-Hall Inc., Englewood Cliffs, New Jersey 07632

Originally published as *Knaurs Kulturführer in Farbe: Italien*
© Droemersche Verlagsanstalt Th. Knaur Nachf. Munich/Zurich 1978
Translation © Phaidon Press Limited, Oxford, 1985

ISBN 0-13-506734-0

Translated and edited by Babel Translations, London
Typeset by Electronic Village Limited, Richmond, Surrey
Printed in Spain by H. Fournier, S.A.—Vitoria

Cover illustration: interior of the Basilica of San Marco, Venice
(Angelo Hornak Photograph Library, London)

Preface

Italia! oh Italia! thou who hast
The fatal gift of beauty

BYRON

The feeling of well-being which the foreigner experiences when in Italy is caused not only by the appealing climate and the free, informal style of living, but also by the country's unique and ancient culture, which the traveller finds everywhere.

The temples of the Greeks have survived, as have traces of the Etruscan civilization, exemplified best by their tomb art. The ruins of the Forum Romanum are evidence of the culture of the Roman Empire. The country's museums contain some of the most famous artistic monuments of all time. The traveller can acquaint himself fully with the buildings of the Middle Ages, with the Byzantine influence in Ravenna and Venice, and with the birth and culmination of the Renaissance, the Baroque and Neoclassicism.

Over the centuries Italy has preserved a rich cultural heritage, and it is an impossible task adequately to describe all the cultural monuments within the confines of this volume. Although the guide sets out to be comprehensive, it has to be selective, but it is hoped that what is included will give the observer an impression of the essential characteristics of this remarkable country.

As with the other guides in this series, the entries are arranged in alphabetical order for easy reference. The illustrations—which are all in colour—are placed next to the relevant text. More than 750 churches, castles, forts, museums, theatres and works of art are shown, including many ground-plans of important buildings.

The heading to each entry gives the town and postal code in bold type and, immediately below, the province and region and a reference to the map section (pp. 410–22), giving page number and grid reference. (Since each map covers two pages and the system of grid squares runs across both pages, only even-numbered page numbers are given.)

Within each entry the sights are generally given in the following order: sacred buildings, secular buildings, particularly significant objects of interest, theatres, museums, less significant objects of interest (under the heading **Also worth seeing**) and places of interest in the immediate vicinity (**Environs**). The appendices consist of a glossary of technical terms, an index of major artists whose works are mentioned, and a list of places cross-referred to the entries under which they are discussed.

The Publishers would be grateful for notification of any errors or omissions.

Abano Terme 35031

Padua/Veneto   p.410☐G 4

The town's thermal springs (*Aquae Pata-vinae*) were used by the Romans. They are the result of volcanic activity in the surrounding Euganean Hills.

S.Lorenzo (Piazza S.Lorenzo): Frequent rebuilding (12,14,18,20C) on the church's old foundation (971). It has a beautiful *campanile* (14C) with arched cornice, two-arched windows, pillars, peaked roof and surmounting battlement.

Abbasanta 09030

Cágliari/Sardinia   p.422☐C 12

Apart from the parish church, the highly ornamented, single-storey houses are particularly interesting. Essentially Gothic, they have a Catalan flavour, and their projecting stone arcades suggest Spanish models of the 16&17C.

Environs: In **Ghilarza** (2 km.), the early Romanesque church, *S. Palmerio*, stands amid the narrowest of alleyways. Built of tachylite (basalt) in alternately coloured bands, it has striking blind arcades in the three-arched facade. Beneath the church is an ancient crypt. Nearby the stone ruins of a square Catalan watch-tower, built in the 15C, are conspicuously alien and are

most impressive. The *Nuraghe Orgono* stands 1 km. NE. Its strange overhanging form is probably the result of the NW portion having been built too steeply. 8 km. SE (on the way N. out of **Zuri**) stands the famous dark-red tachylite church of *S. Pietro*. Built in 1291 in Lombard Romanesque style by Anselmo de Como, it originally stood in the Tirso valley. However, when in 1922 the village was rebuilt 500 ft. higher up because of a rise in Lake

Roman bridge near Busachi (Abbasanta)

Omodeo's water level, the church was carefully reconstructed on its present site. It is long and low with a nave and a Gothic apse (*c.* 1240); there is a Gothic niche, the priest's 'lavabo', with two columns which twine strangely around one another. The façade has three clear arches; on the architrave above the portal there are well preserved reliefs on the external capitals of the pillars. The relief on the NE pillar, with its depiction of a procession performing the 'ballo sardo' (Sardinian folk-dance), is famous. The campanile close to the church is notable for the unusual arcading (15C). On a patch of land in the middle of the market place there are some tree stumps from the Tertiary. Petrified by the action of silicic acid they stand as a token of ancient Zuri. Below **Busachi** there are several *domus de janas* ('fairy houses', prenuraghic grave hollows). 1300 yards below the dam is the old *Roman bridge*. At **Aidomaggiore** (8 km.) there are some strange and rather forbidding houses, built of dark basalt. Nearby there are many nuraghic remains, the best to have survived being the *Nuraghe Sanilo*; the *barrows* at the *Nuraghe Uras* are worth visiting. **Sedilo:** The village church, *S.Giovanni*,

unchanged late Gothic design (15–16C). *Perda fitta*, a site 500 ft. SE, near the small country church of *S.Antine* is probably prenuraghic in origin. Tradition has it that this is a petrified woman. There are many small nuraghi in the general neighbourhood. 2 km. SW is the *Nuraghe Losa*, the most impressive in the entire area and the main bastion in an extensive system of defensive works. In about 1000 BC the middle tower had three storeys, today, only the lower vault remains. Other parts to have survived include: the tuckstone; some side passages; and the rising spiral staircase (which turns off at right angles and leads to the ruined wall of the second vault). Smaller side towers from the 8&7C BC have survived only as walls of half their former height. Excavations carried out recently have uncovered an extensive complex inside the cyclops wall (6C BC, watch-towers, arrow slits). There are also some Roman graves on the SE perimeter. Travelling 5 km. SW, in the direction of **Paulilátino**, then 6 km. W., and finally 1200 m N., on a cart-track, the traveller reaches the *Nuraghe Lugheras*, which today is overrun by mighty oak trees. Construction began about 1000 BC, and by the

Santa Cristina (Abbasanta), holy well

7C BC it had been expanded into a fort with three central towers and four at the periphery. The Carthaginians destroyed it as early as the 5C BC, but it was subseqently rebuilt as the centre of a Carthaginian fertility cult (excavations have uncovered many consecration gifts, sacrificial lamps and a fine bronze head). This unusual monument has been wrecked by shepherds over the centuries. Some 600 yards NW, the three famous *baetyls* (images of deities) *of Perdu Pes* stand as 'guardians' before a giants' tomb *(Tomba di giganti)*. Shepherds overturned the middle figure and 'redesigned' it as an animal trough. About 3.5 km. SW of Paulilátino, road signs point to **Santa Cristina**. Next to this little shepherds' village there stands what is probably Sardinia's most beautiful and largest well shrine; it is impressive for the astonishing precision in the construction of its steps.

Abbazia di S.Maria di Vezzolano
Turin/Piedmont   p.412☐B 4

Abbazia di S.Maria di Vezzolano: Legend has it that this was founded by Charlemagne. The church, which has a nave and two aisles, was built on the remains of a building whose existence is documented from 1095 onwards. Completed in the 13C, it possesses a Romanesque *façade* with blind arcades and decorative figures. The S. aisle forms part of the *cloisters*, which are decorated with Gothic frescos. The main feature is the *choir screen*, which dates from 1189 and is decorated with reliefs; it displays the first Italian Lamentation of the Virgin (Burgundian Gothic style). There is also a coloured late Gothic *terracotta triptych* (1490).

Abbiategrasso 20081
Milan/Lombardy   p.412☐C 3

The history of this town is closely linked to that of Milan. Giovanni Maria Visconti was born here in 1388, and Gian Galeazzo Sforza in 1469.

S.Maria Nuova: To the front of the church there is a courtyard of irregular shape, which is surrounded by arcades on all four sides and decorated with busts and

Abbiategrasso, S.Maria Nuova

terracottas. One row of arcades is interrupted by the massive *pronaos* of the church. The church façade forms the arcade's rear wall and this is divided visually into three horizontal sections by the use of tiers of pilasters; the wall itself bears figures in niches and paintings. Cloisters and pronaos were built by Bramante in 1497. The church dates from 1395 and was altered in the baroque style by Francesco Croce in 1740.

Also worth seeing: *Castello* (Piazza Garibaldi): built in 1382 by order of Gian Galeazzo Visconti. In Corso Matteoti: façade of the Banca Populare di Abbiategrasso by Portaluppi. Piazza Marconi: houses with porticoes of the 14–18C and *Palazzo Comunale* by Francesco Croce, 1750.

Environs: *L'Abbazia di Morimondo* (6 km. towards Pavia). Founded in 1136 by monks from Morimond, one of the original Cistercian monasteries in France. Dissolved under Napoleon in 1798.
Today the village consists of the ruins of what was once an extensive monastery. *Santa Maria* (1182–1296), the former abbey church, is in the village square. Its portico dates from 1736. It was restored 1948–50. In the church there is an interesting *holy-water stoup* from the 14C. There are *cloisters* and a *chapterhouse*.

Acerenza 85011
Potenza/Basilicata   p.418□M 11

The town was inhabited in prehistoric times and stands on a tufa rock to the N. of Potenza, from which there is a beautiful panoramic view.

Cathedral of Assunta e S.Canio: One of the most interesting buildings in Basilicata. Founded in 1080, there were originally three entrances in the façade. The one on the right was lost when towers were added to that side. The central portal is in the local (Apulian) Romanesque style of the 12C. The cylindrical dome is a modern addition. Inside, nave and two aisles separated by stout pillars. There are

3 apsidioles and numerous *spolia* (e.g. an Ionic capital used as a holy-water stoup). Notable features include two 16C panels, a *Pietà* and *Madonna of the Rosary*, and also the two *Renaissance portals* leading to the crypt. *Sacristy:* Only surviving *bust of Julian the Apostate*.

Acerra 80011
Naples/Campania   p.416□K 11

An Oscan-Etruscan foundation, *Acerrae*, became Samnite in the 5C BC. In Roman times it was a so-called 'civitas sine suffragio' (i.e. the inhabitants had a limited Roman civil legal system). Andrea Ciuccio, a well-known Pulcinella (commedia dell' arte figure), was born here around 1656.

Cathedral of S.Maria Assunta (Piazza del Duomo): Probably built on the foundations of an ancient temple; pulled down and completely rebuilt in the 19C. In front of the façade (1874) there is an *atrium* with Ionic columns. Nave and two aisles. Features worth seeing inside: a Renaissance *bishop's throne* in marble and a 16C *marble relief* on the holy-water stoup beside the entrance. This depicts the Ascension and was part of the old church.

Chiesa dell'Annunziata (Via Annunziata): Baroque, with a fine *dome*. The first chapel on the right contains a 12C *wooden crucifix* in the Franco-Iberian style. The high altar has a 15C *Annunciation*.

Also worth seeing: *Castle* (Piazza Castello) with a massive round tower.

Environs: Cancello (c. 6 km. NE): Ruins of the ancient Italic town of *Suéssula* (burial ground, remains of wall) are to be found near Cancello, close to the *La Pagliara* quarter.

Acireale 95024
Catania/Sicily   p.420□L 17

Cathedral of the Annunziata e S.Venera (Piazza del Duomo): Built

1597–1618 in the baroque style, and rebuilt in the 18C. The *façade*, particularly the marble entrance, is well worth seeing. Nave and two aisles with dome. The ground plan is a Latin cross. The *Cappella di S.Venera* (right transept) contains fine *frescos* and a 17C silver figure of S.Venera, the town's patroness. The left aisle has a *holy-water stoup* (1525), attributed to Antonello Gagini.

S.Sebastiano (Piazza L.Vigo): Baroque, with splendid 17C façade. The interior (nave, two aisles, dome) was painted by the local artist P.P. Vasta (1697–1760).

Biblioteca e Pinacoteca Zelantea (Via Marchese di S.Giuliano): Built in 1915, it contains an extensive *library*, a *picture gallery* and an *archaeological museum*. An ancient *bust of Julius Caesar* in room II is of interest.

Also worth seeing: *Church of SS.Pietro e Paolo*, beside the cathedral, dates from the 17C and has a fine baroque façade. *Chiesa dei Crociferi* (Via Galatea), also 17C with some fine frescos. *Palazzo Comunale* (Piazza del Duomo), dating from 1659 with a *Madonna and Child* by G.Sciuti (1900; on the ground floor). *Palazzo Pennisi di Floristella* (Piazza L.Vigo) with a valuable collection of ancient Sicilian-Greek coins; *Terme di S.Venera* (Via delle Terme) dating from 1873, with a neoclassical façade.

Environs: Aci Castello with a Norman castle (1076), built of black lava.

Acquapendente 01021
Viterbo/Latium   p.414☐G 8

Probably the *Aquesium, Acula* or *Aquula* of the Faliscans. In the 8C, it was an Ottonian and Swabian fortress. Formerly part of Tuscany, as the inheritance of Matilda of Canossa, it became the possession of the Holy See. Municipal charter from the time of Nicholas V.

Cathedral of S.Sepolcro: The Benedic-

Acerenza, cathedral

tine basilica was reconstructed in its original Romanesque form after severe bomb damage in World War 2. Massive façade with twin towers. On the right side of the church there is a cloister with Romanesque remains. Of the three semicircular apsidioles, only the middle one is original. Inside: an impressive nave and two aisles with raised eastern section. The first two pillars on the right still have original capitals. The restored ambones by the stairs up to the sanctuary have reliefs by Agostino di Duccio (*St. Michael Defeating the Dragon; Tobias and the Angel Raphael*). The *bust of Pope Innocent X* by Alessandro Algardi stands by the stairs in the right transept. This transept also contains the sumptuous *altar of the sacraments* (1522) by Jacopo Beneventano. The *choir stalls* are richly inlaid. Especially noteworthy: the *crypt* with a ribbed vault, which is supported on low pillars with Romanesque capitals. 13C frescos. One of the chapels on the left contains supposed fragments of the pillar on which Christ was scourged. A relic of the atrium of the praetorium of Jerusalem is in a *sacellum* lower down.

Also worth seeing: (In the Via Battisti) the *Palazzo Viscontini* (1582) with a richly decorated entrance. (In the nearby piazza) the Church of *S.Maria* (also called S.Francesco): A Gothic hall church with 13C wooden crucifix; 17&18C frescos.

Acquasparta 05021
Terni/Umbria   p.414□H 8

This town lies in the Naja valley, 1,000 ft. above sea level, and is known as a spa because of its mineral waters (used to treat catarrh and a disturbed metabolism). In medieval times the town was an important stronghold near to the ruined Roman town of Carsulae.
In 1588 Acquasparta became the seat of the Dukes of Cesi, having previously been in the possession of the town of Todi and of the Church. It was the home of Cardinal Matteo d'Acquasparta, the papal ambas-

Acqui Terme, Roman Aqueduct

sador in Florence when the poet Dante Alighieri (1265–1321) was exiled. Prince Federico Cesi founded the famous 'Accademia dei Lincei' here in 1603.

Worth seeing: *The Palace of the Dukes of Cesi* (designed by Domenico Bianchi, 2nd half of the 16C), with its magnificent courtyard; the rooms have frescos by Zuccaro and his school. The church of *S.Francesco* (end of 13C) has a 15C wooden crucifix. The church of *S.Cecilia* is notable for its chapel (1581). The medieval *town wall* is also worth seeing. Outside the town there is the Fondaia, a very fine *ancient Roman bridge*.

Acqui Terme 15011
Alessandria/Piedmont   p.412□C 5

Acqui Terme (the Roman *Aquae Statiellae*), a famous thermal bath which, because of its springs, was frequently visited as far back as the days of the Roman Empire. It was a diocesan town from the end of the 4C onwards and, as the main town of a Franconian province, it was a member of the Lombard league of cities. From 1277 – 1708, with some interruptions, it belonged to the Duchy of Monferrato, and thereafter to Savoy.

Cathedral (Piazza Duomo): Founded in 1067; three Romanesque *apses* have survived. The *main entrance* dates from 1481; façade 17C. Some Romanesque features in the 14C *cloisters*. Late Gothic *Palazzo Vescovile* (Bishop's Palace) (1444–60) stands beside the cathedral.

Basilica di S.Pietro (Piazza Addolorata): The first cathedral was built in 989–1018 on the ground plan of an early Christian basilica.

Also worth seeing: *Roman Aqueduct*, on the bank of the river Bormida, facing the town. The *Antiche Terme* have been incorporated in the modern thermal baths. The *Castello dei Paleologhi* lies above the town (11C; destroyed in 1646 and rebuilt shortly after).

Adrano 95031
Catania/Sicily   p.420□L 17

Founded by Syracuse about 400 BC, on the site of a much older settlement (inter alia, a shrine for the Siculan god Adranos). Until 1929 it bore the Norman name ('Adernò'). Badly damaged in 1943 during fighting between American and German troops.

Castle, also an **Archaeological Museum** (Piazza Umberto I): Built by the Normans under Count Roger in the 11C; rebuilt in the 14C. Has four wings and is about 110 ft. high. It is surrounded by a square of defensive walls with corner turrets. On the 2nd floor, the Norman *chapel* has a fine entrance and is worth seeing. **Museum:** Good selection of finds from the Etna district.

Also worth seeing: *Chiesa Madre* (to the left of the castle): Norman, converted in the 17C. Inside there are 16 basalt columns, possibly of ancient origin. Church of *S.Lucia* (Via Roma): on the site of the former monastery of the same name. Founded 1158, rebuilt 1596, and again in the 18C (with oval interior). Church of *S.Francesco* (Via Catena) with a fine 17C wooden cross by Fra Umile da Petralia (first altar on the right). *Remains of Greek Wall* (4C BC) in the Contrada Cartalemi. 10 columns from a *Temple of Demeter* (4C BC, in a garden on the Via Buglio).

Environs: The *remains of a Siculan town* from the 5–4C BC can be found to the NW of Adrano (Mendolito district); parts of the town fortifications have survived. Also in the NW is the so-called *Saracen bridge* which is probably 14C.

Adria 45011
Rovigo/Veneto   p.410□G 4

This ancient Graeco-Etruscan port was used by the Veneti as a naval base before the 6C BC. Having given its name to this part of the Mediterranean, Adria is now some 25 km. from the Adriatic coast.

New Cathedral (Piazza Garibaldi): The interior of this comparatively modern, 19C building has some interesting art. The 3rd pillar on the left has a Byzantine bas relief from Ephesus (6C); it depicts Mary between the Archangels Michael and Gabriel, and has a Greek inscription. *Marble sculptures* on the altar in the left transept are the work of Antonio Bonazza (18C). In the sacristy there are some splendid *cabinets* decorated with caryatids (Giac. Piazzetta, 1683). An entrance in the left aisle leads to the:

Old Cathedral, today the **parish church of S.Giovanni.** An octagonal *marble font* and the *remains of a crypt* date from the time of the cathedral's foundation. 8C Byzantine frescos.

S. Maria Assunta della Tomba (Via Angeli): This church has been altered several times in the past. The bricks of the middle entrance come from Roman thermal springs, and an inscription on the campanile, mentioning the town's sea-

Adria, Archaeological Museum

men's guild, is also Roman. The campanile dates from 1931. Inside, the chapel to the left of the entrance has an octogonal *font* with an episcopal inscription from the 9C. There is also a *holy water stoup* from the Middle Ages with symbols of the Evangelists. In the *Cappella della Madonna* (to the right of the entrance), there is a fine 15C terracotta, 'Dormition of the Virgin', possibly by Michele da Firenze. There are also two terracotta figures representing *The Virgin Mary* and *Gabriel*, Venetian school (15C).

Archaeological museum (Piazza degli Etruschi): This collection is worth seeing and contains relics of the town's earliest period (*c.* 8C BC up to 5C AD). Among the ceramic vessels, glasses, bronze statues, and Etruscan gold work, the *Biga del Lucumone*, an iron chariot from the grave of a Gallic warrior, (4C BC) is particularly splendid.

Biblioteca Civica (Corso Vittorio Emanuele II. No. 35): Attached to the library there is an archive housing the famous Tintoretto painting The Blind Man

Agordo, Palazzo Crotta

of Adria (1582). The man in the picture is Luigi Groto, a humanist.

Agira 94011
Enna/Sicily   p.420□K 17

During the 4–3C BC, this was a flourishing Siculan town known as Argyrion. It was the home of Diodorus Siculus (1C BC), a Greek historian who wrote a history of the world.

S. Filippo (also *S. Maria Latina*, Via Vitt. Emanuele): Founded in the late Middle Ages and rebuilt in the rococo style of the 18C. Modern façade. Nave and two aisles. The painting, 'Madonna Enthroned', by Giuseppe Velasquez is worth seeing, and there is a fine 15C *triptych*. Splendid *church treasure*.

S.Salvatore (Piazza Roma): Built in the 14C; *baroque façade*, 1556. Remains of the building's original structure e.g. pillars are discernible in the nave, aisles and *campanile*. The *church treasure* is interesting and includes a richly ornamented 14C mitre and a 14C bishop's crook.

Also worth seeing: *S.Antonio da Padova* (Piazza Garibaldi), 1549, with a fine baroque façade of 1754. *S. Maria Maggiore* (below the castle) has Norman features. In *S.Antonio Abate* there is a picture of St. Andrew, ascribed to Polidoro da Caravaggio. *S.Margherita* with fine baroque interior. *Biblioteca Comunale* (Via Diodorea) has a valuable collection of manuscripts and early printed books. Medieval *castle*.

Agordo 32021
Beluno/Veneto   p.410□G 2

Palazzo Crotta (now *Manzoni;* Piazza della Libertà): Elements of several architectural styles (17&18C) have been brought together in this palace with extraordinary success. Stone sculptures on columns enliven the little garden. Inside there are fine rooms with frescos by Pietro Paoletti, from Belluno, and others.

Agrigento 92100

Agrigento/Sicily   p.420☐I 17

Founded by people from Gela in 582 BC, when it was called 'Akragas'. The Greek poet Pindar called it, 'man's finest town'. Under Empedocles (*c.* 500–430 BC) it attained the height of its power as a trading centre. In 406 BC the town was destroyed by the Carthaginians and was unimportant for several centuries thereafter. Under the Norman, Roger I, the town enjoyed a renaissance and a wealthy diocese was founded in 1086. Since 1927, the town has borne its own name again, Agrigento replacing the Arabic 'Girgenti'. Its ancient buildings make it one of the most interesting sights in Sicily.

Ancient temple area (in the south of the town): The so-called **Temple of 'Juno Lacinia'**, the Greek temple of Hera, was built in the classical Doric style (460–40 BC) on a splendid site; it was destroyed in 406 BC. 125 x 56 ft., it is a *peripteros*, with 6 x 13 columns (all survive upright on the N. side). The *pronaos* and *cella* are divided by *pylons*, which have spiral staircases leading up to the roof. To the E. of the temple are the remains of a large *altar*.

The so-called **Temple of Concord** was possibly a dioscuran temple (the Dioscuri were the sons of Zeus). This is the best-preserved Greek temple in Italy; it was in use as a church from the 7C AD onwards. In date and style it is practically identical to the Temple of Hera above. 131 x 56 ft., *peripteros* with 6 x 13 columns, *pronaos* and *opisthodomos*. Both *pediments* and the two *pylons*, which give access to the roof, have survived intact. Inside there are indications of its former use as a church with nave and two aisles, e.g. the round arches in the cella.

Temple of Hercules: Oldest of Agrigento's temples; much ruined. Built in the late Archaic-Doric style at the end of the 6C BC. 220 x 79 ft., *peripteros* with 6 x 15 columns (this means that the temple is very long, a typically Archaic feature). *Pronaos* and *opisthodomos; cella* converted in the Roman period. In 1924, *8 columns* were erected on the S. side.

Temple of Olympian Zeus: Third

Agrigento, Temple of Castor and Pollux

largest temple of the ancient world (after Ephesus and Miletus); 367 x 184 ft. In the Doric style. Building began in 510 BC, continuing until 480 BC, using Carthaginian prisoners of war; never completed. Destroyed by the Carthaginians in 406 BC. Today, it is in very bad condition, having been used as a quarry in the 18C for the construction of the moles in Porto Empedocle. Nave and two aisles, *Pseudoperipteros* (7 x 14 half-columns on the outside). Originally there were 'telamones' between the semi-columns; these have a human shape, are 25 ft. high and are the bearers of the entablature. One of them has been reconstructed in front of the temple; the museum contains parts of some others. Previously the *pediments* depicted 'the battle of the giants' and 'the conquest of Troy'—ruined fragments can be found in the museum. There is a large *altar* in front of the museum.

Shrine of the Chthonic deities: 6C BC; shrine of Demeter Malophoros and Persephone. *Parts of the exterior wall* have survived, as have the remains of *12 altars* and of eight small *temples*.

So-called **temple of Castor and Pollux:** Probably a temple of Demeter and Persephone. Built in the Doric style around 470 BC. 128 x 56 ft., *peripteros* with 6 x 13 columns. The entablature and pediment are not original but are the result of a disputed reconstruction undertaken in 1836.

To the S., some remains of a Hellenistic building (the so-called *Temple L*). Beyond the river Ipsas, to the W. are the remains of the so-called *Temple of Hephaistos* (5C BC). The building is almost square with two columns still standing.

Remains of the town's ancient fortifications are to the S. of the temple area; the gates *Porta Aurea and Porta di Gela* are worth visiting.

Remains of the Graeco-Roman town (Quartiere ellenistico-romano): Building began in the 4C BC and continued up to the Imperial period. The streets are at right-angles, in the style of Hippodamos

(the first town planner). Fine *floor mosaics* have survived in some houses (motifs include left-winged swastikas). The *House of the abstract master* is particularly fine.

Temple of Demeter and Persephone (just off the Via F. Crispi): Built in 480–60 BC; 98 x 43 ft. Today a Norman church, *S. Biagio*, occupies the site of the cella. An apse has been built over part of the *pronaos* of the ancient temple. Nearby is the descent to the **rock shrine to Demeter**, which is, in fact, just outside the old town walls. It is Agrigento's oldest shrine, from the pre-Grecian period and consists of two caves and in front of them an L-shaped building, which serves as an ante-room. Numerous votive offerings have been found.

Museo Nazionale Archeologico (close to S.Nicola, between the new town and the site of the ancient temples): Among other things, it houses excavation finds from the temples. The following exhibits are particularly notable: *Room 3*, fine vases (Attic, Italic, 6–4C BC); *Room 5*, 'telamone' from the temple of Zeus; *Room 7*, finds from the Graeco-Roman town; *Room 9*, coin collection; *Room 10*, the 'Ephebus of Agrigento' (a statue of Apollo, 470 BC). Adjoining the museum is the church of *S. Nicola*, a 13C Cistercian building, at present containing the famous *Phaedra sarcophagus*, 2–3C AD. To the W. is the *Oratory of Phalaris*, a Hellenistic temple building from the 1C BC.

Also worth seeing: Cathedral of *S.Gerlando* (Via Duomo): 11C, rebuilt 14C, with the *Museo Diocesano*. *S.Maria dei Greci*, built on the site of a Doric temple. *S.Spirito* (13C) with fine stucco work by Giac. Serpotta. The *Rupe Atenea* (Rock of Athena) with magnificent view of the temples. *Tomba di Terone* (to the S. outside the city wall), an ancient tomb. The *Temple of Asklepios* (S. of the above tomb), 5C BC.

Agrigento, Temple of Concord ▷

Ala 38061
Trento/South Tyrol-Trentino   p.410□F 3

The name of this southernmost town of the former Tyrol—first mentioned in documents in 814—developed from the Latin 'ad palatium'. The little town owes the fine baroque palaces to its important position as a centre of the velvet and silk industry in the 17–19C.

Particularly worth seeing: *Palazzo Angelini*, where Emperor Josef II spent the night; rich fresco and stucco decorations. *Palazzo Pizzini* and *Palazzo Malfatti* are both 18C. *S. Maria Assunta* dates from the 18C. *S. Giovanni* contains paintings by Alessandro Turchi and G. Craffonara.

Alatri 03011
Frosinone/Latium   p.416□I 10

Alatrium or *Aletrium* was one of the main towns of the Hernici. It became an important Roman colony, and was later a municipium. Destroyed by Totila in the 6C AD, it later became a Civita Nova. Both Henry VI of Swabia (1186) and Frederick II (1243) besieged it in vain. From 547 it was a diocesan town, and from 1389 a church possession. Numerous Gothic and even Romanesque houses have survived; above them stands the mighty acropolis. Alatri also possesses an impressive Cyclops wall which was extended in the Middle Ages. All these features contribute to making Alatri one of the most interesting examples of a medieval town in Italy.

S.Maria Maggiore: Dates from the period of transition from Romanesque to Gothic (13C). Façade with three entrances and original rose window (the tracery spreads from a square in the middle of the window). Fine campanile, subdivided vertically by successive levels of two-arched windows. The lunette above an entrance to the tower (now blocked up) has a 15C fresco of the *Madonna and Child*. Remains of frescoes in the lunettes above the entrances in the façade date from the same period. There is an inner narthex. Nave and two aisles are divided by massive pillars. In the 18C a row of chapels along the left aisle was completely renovated. The first chapel contains a Romanesque *font*, borne by two male figures. Behind it is the *Madonna of Constantinople*, the church's most important work. The painted frame dates from the time the figures were installed in a winged shrine (end of the 13C). The *Fonte Pia*, a fountain given by Pius IX (1846–78) stands in the picturesque *Piazza Santa Maria Maggiore*. Here too is *Santa Maria dei Padri Scolopi* (mid-18C). The influence of Francesco Borromini can be seen in the design of the façade and in the interior.

Acropolis: Fortifications have survived from the 4C BC; trapezoidal ground plan. Its former impressiveness is most apparent in the SW corner, with its 14 mighty pillars. Nearby is the main gate, the *Porta di Civita*, with monolithic door lintels. A

Agrigento, Ephebus, Museo Archeologico

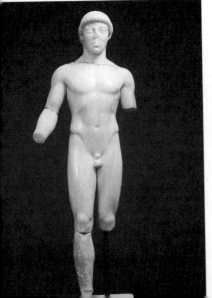

Agrigento, red figure vase ▷

staircase covered with mighty monoliths leads from the entrance within to an extensive plateau-like area. On the N. is the *Porta Minore*, a gate with a portcullis, which has a phallic motif.

Cathedral: 17C façade. Simple building with a nave and two aisles. Tombstone of Pope Sixtus I whose body was brought to Alatri in 1132. To the right of the cathedral is the *Casa del Sacristano* (sacristan's house), whose polygonal stonework may be a remnant of a sacrificial altar.

Also worth seeing: Church of *S. Francesco* (12C), with a fine rose window and remains of frescos from the 14&15C. *San Sylvestro* has two aisles, and in the crypt there are frescos from the 13&14C. The Gothic *Palazzo Casegrandi* (13C) and the Romanesque *residential tower* house the *Museo Civico* which has numerous Roman epigraphs and late medieval works from the region. The foundations of the so-called *Temple of Alatri* are a short distance from the town (1 km. towards Fiuggi).

Environs: Certosa di Trisulti (about 10 km): A new monastery was erected by the Carthusians (at the behest of Pope Innocent III), beside the ruins of the *Benedictine Abbey*, which had been abandoned in 1204. In turn, the new building was greatly enlarged and altered in the 18C. Since 1947 it has been in the possession of the Cistercians of Casamari. The old *pharmacy*, with its 17C fittings, is of especial interest. Pope Innocent's house (13C) is in front of the church. The monastery has a large cloister with monks' cells and a fine *refectory*.

Alba 12051
Cuneo/Piedmont   p.412☐B 4

Alba's origin lies in prehistory. The town, named *Alba Pompeia* in honour of Gnaius Pompeius Strabo, was first conquered by the Gauls and then by the Romans. In the 4C it was a diocesan town, and later, in the Carolingian period, the seat of a count. The Saracens conquered it in 892. Having become a free town in the 11C, it came into the possession of the Marquis of Monferrato in 1283. In 1347 it was taken over by the Visconti, then by the Gonzaga, and, in 1631, by Savoy.

Alatri, S.Maria Maggiore, Madonna of Constantinople

Cathedral of S.Lorenzo (Piazza Risorgimento): Lombard- Gothic building, begun in 1486, and altered several times before the 18C, restored by A. Mella in 1867–72. The *portals* are of fine quality, as are the *choir stalls* (1501), which are decorated with inlaid work.

Also worth seeing: *S. Giovanni Battista* (Piazza Pertinace), with a picture of the Madonna by Barnaba di Modena (1377) on the first altar on the left. *S.Domenico* (Via Teobaldo Calissano) a 14C Gothic church; rather wide; nave and two aisles, are decorated with frescos, some of them by Macrino d'Alba (15–16C). *S.Maddalena* (Via P. Belli) was rebuilt by Bernardo Vittone in 1749. The adjacent Dominican convent was founded in 1446 by Margherita di Savoy. In the *Palazzo Comunale* (Piazza Risorgimento), the 'Sala del Consiglio' contains valuable paintings, including some by Macrino d'Alba and Mattia Preti. *Museo Archeologico 'Frederico Eusebio'* (Via Teobaldo Calissano), has archaeological finds from the Stone Age up until the Roman period.

Albano Laziale 00041

Rome/Latium   p.414☐H 10

The name Albano indicates that the area belongs to Alba Longa. Between the Via Appia and the Lake of Albano, the Emperor Domitian built a villa, the grounds of which became the site of the *Castra Albana*. This was a military camp built by the Emperor Septimius Severus for the II Legion ('Parthica') which was loyally devoted to him. At the end of the 13C the town was in the possession of the Savelli family from Ariccia, who built their castle above the ruins of a Roman watch-tower. In 1697 the Church again took over the town.

Porta Pretoria (Via del Plebiscito): Mighty fortress-like main gate of Severus's 'Castra Albana' (brought to light in 1944 when the town was bombed). Two towers, with a complex of three gates 118 ft. wide.

Santa Maria della Rotonda (nearby):

formerly a nymphaeum to an ancient villa; later adapted as a Christian church. Small rotunda made bigger by the addition of niches. The dome dates from 1670. Restoration work carried out in 1937 largely recreated the ancient form of the building. The Romanesque tower added to the church dates from the 13C.

Cisternone: Formerly the reservoir for Severus's camp. Cut out of the rock, the vaulted room is subdivided by 3 rows of mighty pillars, and had a capacity of about 10,000 cu. m. of water. Architecturally, it is one of the most impressive of Roman functional buildings.

Monument to the Horatii and Curiatii (at the end of the Borgo Garibaldi): The ruins reveal a complex necropolis, very like the Etruscan open-air grave. The burial area, which is diamond-shaped, is surrounded by conical pillars on short buttresses. Tradition has it that the necropolis—which was not built until the end of the Roman Republic—is the grave not only of the Horatii, triplet brothers from Rome, but also of the Curiatii, triplet brothers from Alba Longa.

Albano Laziale, tomb of the Horatii

These brothers are said to have been killed around 600 BC, during the reign of Tullus Hostilius, in duels for the supremacy over their towns.

Also worth seeing: Ruins of the *thermal baths* which are up to 100 ft. high and divided into three storeys. The church of *S.Pietro*, built of ancient material, is very near to the baths.

Environs: Ariccia: Like Albano Laziale, the site of a Roman camp. The ancient *Aricia* was one of the leading Latin towns and took part in all the wars between the Latins and the Romans. From 1661 onwards Ariccia was in the hands of the Chigi family.

The *Piazza della Republica*, which has two fountains and is dominated by the magnificent *Palazzo Chigi*, owes its design mainly to Gian Lorenzo Bernini. The main body of the church of *S.Maria dell'Assunzione* is crowned by a dome and has a 17C fresco by Borgognone of the Assumption. Outside the town is the pilgrim church of *S.Maria di Galloro* (enlarged in 1624 and 1661); the façade is based on a design by G.Bernini.

Albe 67050
L'Aquilia/Abruzzi   p.416□ I 9

The Ancient *Alba Fucens* was founded as a Roman colony to oppose the Sabines. Excavations, carried out systematically since 1949 have revealed a square of streets, surrounded by a town wall, dating from the 3–2C BC. In the middle of the town, along the narrow side of the forum, there is a *basilica* with a speaker's tribune, and shops beneath. Behind this building is the market, the *baths* and the *Hall of Hercules* (the colossal figure of Hercules found here is in the Museo Provinciale in Chieti). To the E. of Hercules Square is the *theatre*, and to the S., outside the square of streets, is the *amphitheatre*.

S.Pietro. Built in the early 13C; badly damaged in the earthquake of 1915, and rebuilt in 1955–57. The walls of a *temple of Apollo* were included in the new building, as were some columns from surrounding buildings. The *pulpit* with its Cosmati work (coloured inlays) is by Giovanni di Guido (early 13C), while the *iconostasis* is the work of Andrea, his assistant. The *Easter candelabra* is an ancient pillar, with a medieval capital. The church's carved *wooden doors* are preserved in the Museo Nazionale in L'Aquila.

Albenga 17031
Savona/Liguria   p.412□ B 6

Together with Ventimiglia and Savona, Albenga is one of the oldest settlements on the Ligurian coast. Called *Albium Ingaunum* (Albingaunum), it already existed in pre-Roman times. The medieval town centre, built above Roman houses, has remained admirably intact. It is chiefly remarkable for its many towers of reddish brick.

Cathedral of San Michele: Originally built in the 5C, it has been rebuilt several times. The *campanile* dates from the end of the 11C, but was altered in 1391; the addition of an octagonal spire is more recent. In the first half of the 14C two side aisles were added and, in 1669, the baroque portal was built. From 1964–6, alterations were made inside to bring it as near as possible into line with its medieval proportions.

Baptistry (beside the cathedral): This is the most important early Christian monument in Liguria. Outside, it is ten-sided with an octagonal drum. Inside it is an octagon; 8 arcaded arches of Corsican granite, and above, a row of 16 smaller arches, half of which are window openings; wooden ceiling. Inside there are the remains of an octagonal *font*. In the niche opposite the entrance there is a delightful *mosaic* (5–6C) with a Christ monogram, doves and lambs.

Palazzo Vecchio del Comune and tower: The palace, which is crowned with battlements, is a reconstruction (it was

Albenga, medieval tower

Albenga, amphorae, Museo Navale

originally built in 1387). Frescos and sculptures from the 15C have survived, as has a Byzantine sarcophagus. The *Museo Civico Ingauno* can be found here too. The town's tallest *tower* (197 ft.), dates from the early 14C and has a good view of the town.

Museo Navale Romano (Piazza San Michele 12): 13C tower. Since 1950, the fine rooms of this palace have housed a most interesting display, consisting of the finds from a Roman ship from the 1C BC, which was found just off shore and brought out of the sea. In addition to over 1000 amphorae, there are also exhibits which provide information on Roman shipping.

Also worth seeing: *S.Maria in Fontibus:* Early Romanesque, rebuilt several times, with a charming Gothic entrance. Inside is a painting by Domenico Fiasella *(Cosmas and Damian).* Opposite this, is the *Torre Cazzulini,* a 13C tower.

Environs: *S.Giorgio di Campochièsa* (12C), with an interesting fresco in the sanctuary *(Last Judgement,* 1446).

Alberobello 70011
Bari/ Apulia   p.418□O 11

Centre and highlight of the 'Zona dei Trulli': Gian Girolamo III, Duke of Aquaviva, founded the town in the 17C, (in the 12C, it was known as 'Silva Arboris Belli'). At this time the king of the Two Sicilies levied taxes from each new town. Thus the citizens built Alberobello in the trulli style. When the royal tax collectors appeared, the citizens would quickly tear down the houses and later they would rebuild them. In this ancient building style, the conical roof is layered as a dummy vault, without mortar, each stone jutting above the one underneath (similar to the

Mycenean dome-shaped graves). Even when Murat, King of Naples (1808–15) finally officially recognized the town, and also permitted the use of mortar, building, nevertheless, continued in the traditional manner. In Alberobello today there is still an entire quarter of the town with over 1000 *trulli* (signposts refer to 'Zona Monumentale').

S.Antonio: The church of S. Antonio combines elements from the local (Apulian) neo-Romanesque style with the trulli style. In recent years Alberobello has developed into a major tourist attraction, and thereby, unfortunately, has lost much of its originality.

Environs: SE of Alberobello, on the hills of the Murge (the Apulian plateau), we find three of the finest 'white towns of the Murge': **Locorotondo, Martina Franca** and **Cisternino,** all of which offer a splendid panoramic view of the uplands. The journey from Locorotondo to Martina Franca leads through the *Valle d'Itria,* a valley studded with innumerable trulli (see signposts).

Alcamo 91011
Trapani/Sicily   p.420☐H 16

Chiesa Matrice (S.Maria Assunta, Piazza IV Novembre): Built in the 14C, but completely altered in 1669 in the baroque style. The façade is late 18C; the campanile of the original building has a fine *marble portal* from the late 15C. The ground plan is a Latin cross. Nave and two aisles. In the apse and around the dome are *frescos* by the Flemish artist W. Borremans (1736 – 7). The church contains numerous works by the Gagini family: the 2nd altar on the right has a *crucifix* by Antonello Gagini (1523); an altar to the left has a *Figure of Peter,* by Giacomo Gagini, (1556); and there are other works.

S.Francesco di Paola (also Badia Nuova, Via Caruso): 18C, with tower-like façade. No aisles. Some *stucco figures* of 1724 by Giacomo Serpotta on the walls of the nave, are particularly worth seeing; they include Peace, St. Peter, St. Paul and Bravery). The 2nd chapel on the left has another group

Alberobello, Trulli

by Serpotta *(Crucifix with Mary the Virgin and Mary Magdalene).*

Also worth seeing: *S. Francesco d'Assisi* (Corso 6. Aprile), built about 1625. Nave, no aisles. Two fine figures by Antonello Gagini dated 1520 (S.Mark and Mary Magdalene). *S. Oliva Piazza* (Piazza Ciullo), with works by A. and G.Gagini. *Castle* (1430), a four-winged building with two round towers. *SS.Cosma e Damiano* (Corso 6 Aprile), early 18C with works by Serpotta and Borremans.

Alessandria 15100

Alessandria/Piedmont   p. 412□C 4

Alessandria was founded by the Guelphs in 1168 and given its name in honour of Pope Alexander III. Frederick Barbarossa besieged the town several times until its surrender in 1183. As a new imperial foundation, Alessandria took the name of Cesaria. After 1198, it became a free town. In 1348 it fell to the Visconti, and in 1707, to Savoy. It was an important fortress in the war against Austria (1849).

Cathedral (Piazza della Cattedrale): Built in 1810 on the site of the first cathedral (1170); altered in the classical style by Edoardo Arbori Mella.

Also worth seeing: *S.Maria di Castello* (Via S.Maria di Castello); Gothic, (14&15C), on the site of the original 11C Rovereto fortress. The 15C Gothic church of *S.Maria del Carmine.* The *Palazzo della Prefettura e della Provincia*, formerly the Palazzo Ghilini (Piazza d. Libertà), a beginner's work in an early classical style by Benedetto Alfieri. The *Pinacoteca Civica* is in the same building as the municipal library (Via Tripoli 8), and houses pictures from the 16-20C. The *Citadel*, built in 1726-1859, stands opposite the town on the other side of the Tánaro. *Marengo*, a former Lombard settlement—today incorporated into Alessandria—was the scene of Napoleon's victory over the Austrians in the War of the Second Coalition on 14 June 1800.

Environs: Bosco Marengo, birthplace of Pope Pius V (1505-72). *Santa Croce,* the former church of the Dominican monastery (abolished by the French in 1802), was built by Ignazio Danti (1563-72) under Pius V. Danti also built the monastery. The façade is subdivided by pilasters and was built on the model of S.Vittorio Grande in Milan. Its ground plan is a Latin cross with a dome over the crossing. Nave and two aisles, the side aisles divided into chapels.

The splendid interior includes: the *mausoleum of Pope Pius V,* east wall of the south transept (an architectonic marble edifice with sculptures, probably by Giovanni Antonio Buzzi); *picture cycle* by Giorgio Vasari; and the *choir stalls* by Angelo Siciliano and Giovanni Gargioli.

The former monastery contains a fine *Renaissance library* and cloisters.

Alghero 07041

Sássari/Sardinia   p.422□B 12

The name of the present-day town literally means 'seaweed beach' after the 'Neptune

Alcamo, S. Francesco di Paola

grass' washed up by the sea swell. As a result of this contamination of the beach, the Romans built a harbour further west along the coast, at Portus Nympharum, where there was more shelter from the wind. It was only in 1102 that the Genoese Doria family built a harbour, which was protected by a fortress; this was soon followed by a fishing village. After the sea battle off Porto Conte (AD1353), the victorious Catalans drove all Sardinians and Genoese out of Alghero and the surrounding area, settling their own countrymen—as fishermen and peasants—there instead. In 1355 Pedro IV of Aragon declared Alghero Catalan. Since that time Spanish influences on the language, cultural life and architecture have been preserved; witness also the inhabitants' pride in their non-Sardinian origin, although the settlement has long since extended beyond the narrow limits of the walls and towers, some of which are still visible today (Torre La Maddalena at the harbour, Torre di Porta a Terra in the town centre, in the S.Torre Sulis, and, in the SW, Torre San Giacomo).

Cathedral: Today rather cramped by the surrounding buildings. It was originally built in 1562, in Catalan-Gothic style, and received a classical façade in the 19C. During its long period of construction (up until 1730), the body of the hall, which is subdivided into a nave and two aisles by pillars and Doric columns, was provided with 4 chapels on a right-angled ground plan with cross-arched vaults adjoining the barrel vault of the nave. All that has remained of the original exterior is the peculiar octagonal tower—with tiled conical spire rising above Gothic decorations — and the magnificent *Gothic portal*. This opens into a narrow alley, the Via Prinzipe Umberto, which is typically Catalan.

Also worth seeing: No. 7, Via Prinzipe Umberto is the *Casa Doria* (16C) with Renaissance portal and Catalan window. Almost opposite, two alleys further along in the Via Carlo Alberto, is the Gothic church of *S.Francesco* (15-16C), famous for the following features: *stellar vault*, above the sanctuary, which has survived despite reconstruction work; a Gothic apse; the oc-

tagonal tower; and the *Chiostro*, an inner courtyard surrounded by a two-storeyed cloister. The baroque church of *S.Michele* (1612) has a conspicuous dome of coloured tiles. Immediately next to it is the *Liceo Azuni* with the municipal library (more than 12,000 books, including numerous valuable Catalan manuscripts).

Environs: Fertilia: The remains of an ancient bridge variously described as Roman or medieval. Within sight of **Porto Conte** is the *Nuraghe Palmavera*. This was carefully restored in 1963 and has a central tower with forecourt, smaller protective towers and a large circular wall, (also the remains of stone rings). The *Porto Conte* watch-tower dates from the Aragonese occupation and is one of the many Saracen towers on the Sardinian coast. From the S. end of the street, a gentle descent leads W. down the 'deer stairs' (Escala del Cabirol), between the sheer walls of the Capo Caccia to the *Neptune grotto*, which is probably the finest grotto in Sardinia. From the upper car park, a guide (!) must be used to find the E. descent to the *grotta verde*. Here there are ruined walls, which were probably part of nuraghi (altar grottoes) and also tall, moss-covered stalagmites. The route continues to the small *grotta dei Ricami* where the stalactites glisten with a white crystal covering. **Olmedo:** The route W. leads to the burial site, *Anghelu Ruju*. Over the centuries this had fallen into disrepair, but was re-excavated after 1974, and has provided us with a detailed reference board for the 36 main graves. The beginnings of the Ozieri culture developed here about 3000 BC. Important finds from Anghelu Ruju of a mechanical nature can be seen in the museums in Sássari and Cágliari. The only visible elements *in situ* are some stairs at the entrances, structures made to look like wood and some badly weather-beaten decorations, which include bulls' heads. From Olmedo the traveller climbs 2.5 km. past the dam and on to a ridge. On the descent S. from the ridge, half of a mighty *nuraghe* is visible; the rest has fallen into the valley below. In front of this is a wide *megalithic dam*, built up in flat layers both outside and inside. From Olmedo the route leads 5 km. S. and then

Anghelu Ruju near Olmedo (Alghero), tomb entrance

2 km. E., to the burial chamber of *Santu Pedru*. This is reached via a long corridor just N. of the road. From the front hall the traveller passes through a narrow window into the main hall, which has 2 columns and 7 small adjoining chambers. Above the first chamber on the right is a stylized symbol of a bull. Some 165 ft. above, under a fig bush, there is another burial vault with pillars—although it not recorded anywhere.

Alife 81011
Caserta/Campania   p.416☐K 10

The ancient town of 'Allifae' (Roman since 326 BC) struck its own coins in the 4C BC.

Cathedral of S.Maria Assunta e Sisto I. Papa: Built in the 13C, but completely altered in the 17C. The campanile bears *Roman inscriptions* and two *Romanesque lions*. Nave and two aisles. Inside, on the rear wall of the first chapel on the right, there are some remains of *Romanesque portals* from the 12C. The entrances to the *crypt* are in the side aisles. This is part of the original structure and has three semi-circular apses and 20 columns (some ancient).

Also worth seeing: Roman *cryptoporticus*, a gallery with 30 arches. Remains of the *ancient town wall* from the 1C BC, with medieval additions. *Roman mausoleum* (today it is a chapel to commemorate war dead). Just outside the town, to the NW, on the ancient *Via Latina*, there are the remains of two *Roman tombs*.

Alseno 29010
Piacenza/Emilia-Romagna   p.412☐E 4

Abbazia di Chiaravalle della Colomba
The abbey is 4 km. from Alseno, a small

agricultural town which has a poorly preserved fort and a rebuilt 14C Gothic church (S.Martino, Via Emilia). Founded in 1135 at the suggestion of St. Bernhard of Clairvaux, the monastery was plundered several times in 1214 and devastated by Frederick II's soldiers in 1248. In 1441 Pope Eugene IV granted it to Giovanni Landriani, from Milan, as a prebend. It was turned into a hospital for the citizens of Piacenza by Napoleon in 1810. In contrast to the monastery building —most of which was redesigned in the 17C — the *church* has retained its original form. The brickwork façade is tripartite with three rose-windows and a portico, mirroring the arrangement of the aisles. To the left of the Romanesque entrance is a *Gothic tomb,* probably by Oberto Pallavicino (d. 1148) with a fresco depicting Abbot Giovanni I. The *campanile* dates from the 16C. Inside, the oldest section is the south transept. In the nave, half columns, which end on consoles at half the normal height, are characteristic of Cistercian church architecture. *Frescos* decorate the second column on the left, the chapel by the vestry (both 14C), and also the North transept (15C). The sanctuary has a *marble altar* (1771). There

are, among other items, some prized Romanesque capitals, which have survived and these are to be found in the Gothic cloister adjoining the last bay of the S.aisle.

Altamura 70022
Bari/Apulia   p.416☐ N 11

This town's ancient name is not known. It is still surrounded by a town wall which dates from the 5C BC, and was once four kilometres long. Destroyed by Saracens in the 9C AD, the town was founded anew in about 1230 by order of Emperor Frederick II Hohenstaufen.

Cathedral of S.Assunta: This is the only church in Italy whose construction was both ordered and financed by Frederick II. It was an 'Ecclesia Palatina' and subordinate only to the Pope. Completed by about 1232, it was destroyed by an earthquake in 1316. The cathedral's finest features are the portal and rose-window. The *portal* is of a type traditional in Apulia. The outer arch has scenes from the Life of Jesus; the architrave has the Last Supper (Judas is shown as the traitor); and in the *tympanum*, Mary appears as the Queen of Heaven with the Christ Child on her arm. The splendid *rose-window* probably dates from the same period as the portal. The cathedral was altered under the Spanish viceroys, in the 16C.

Also worth seeing: *S.Nicolò dei Greci* (Corso Federico II di Svevia), the last surviving church built by Greek colonists during the time of Hohenstaufen domination; the Romanesque portal is impressive.

Alviano 05020
Terni/Umbria   p.414☐ G 8

This small town enjoyed a period of moderate political importance under the d'Alviano family, who built the Alviano fortress in the 15C, (it is now in the possession of the Doria-Pamphili family). Rectangular layout with towers and fine

Alghero, cathedral

Renaissance courtyard. The 15C *parish church* has a 'Transfiguration of Mary' by Niccolò di Liberatore (1430–1502) and a fresco by Pordenone. The 11C hermitage, *Eremo di S.Illuminata*, lies outside the town.

Alzano Lombardo 24022
Bergamo/Lombardy   p.412☐D 3

Basilica of S.Martino: Rebuilding began in 1659 to plans by Girolomo Quadrios; work was not completed until the early 19C. Nave and both aisles are richly adorned with painting: the *Martyrdom of St.Christopher*, 1st altar on the right; the *Cappella del Rosario* by G.B. Piazzetta on the left side, has sumptuous decoration including the *Madonna and St.Christopher* by J.Tintoretto; the 1st altar on the left has the *Martyrdom of S.Peter of Verona* by Lorenzo Lotto and a splendid *pulpit*, by Andrea Fantoni (1712). The two *sacristies* are of particular interest. The first sacristy has 6 wall cupboards by Grazioso Fantoni; the second has inlaid sideboards by Andrea Fantoni.

Amalfi 84011
Salerno/Campania   p.418☐K 12

Amalfi was once one of Italy's most powerful maritime republics, at its zenith around the turn of the millennium. Conquered by the Normans in 1073, it was plundered by Pisa in 1135. The so-called 'Tavole amalfitane' (see below)—used as the maritime laws of that time—are famous. Tradition has it that the town was the home of Flavio Gioia, the (European) inventor of the compass. Amalfi has a most picturesque townscape, which makes it particularly worth a visit.

Cathedral of S.Andrea (Piazza del Duomo): Mentioned from the 9C onwards; rebuilt around 1200 in the Arab-Norman style and altered many times since then. The façade was reconstructed in the style of the 13C, while the *campanile* has not been altered (1180–1276). The main portal with its famous *bronze door* (executed by Master Simon in Constantinople, 1066) is particularly fine. Nave and two aisles.

Alseno, cloister of the abbey church

Altamura, cathedral portal

The inside is completely baroque with many fine features. There are two impressive *ancient columns* (monoliths) near the entrance to the choir; on each side of the high altar, two 12–13C *ambones* with mosaic decoration; the 1st chapel on the left has an ancient *font* of red porphyry. The entrance to the 13C *crypt* is in the N. aisle. Here, under the altar, are the *relics of Andrew the Apostle* (in Amalfi since 1208) and marble sculptures of St.Lawrence and St.Stephen by Pietro Bernini. The entrance hall of the cathedral leads into the magnificent *Chiostro del Paradiso*, (pointed-arched, overlapping arcades on double columns). Built as a graveyard in 1266–68, today it contains a small *Lapidarium*).

Also worth seeing: *Town hall* (Municipio) with a small *Museum* whose main treasure is the above-mentioned 'Tavole amalfitane' (medieval text on a 16C codex). *Remains of the Arsenal* (at the beginning of the Via M. Camera). Excursion to the *Grotta di Smeraldo* (near Positano) with magnificent stalactite formations.

Environs: The church of *S.Maria Maddalena* (1274) stands in **Atrani**, just to the E. of Amalfi. Originally Gothic, it was later altered in the baroque style. In *S.Salvatore de'Bireto* the Doges of Amalfi were crowned. It has a portal with a fine bronzè door (1087) (cf. Amalfi Cathedral). *c.* 5 km. to the NE is **Minori**, where excavations of a *Roman villa* from the 1C AD are worth seeing. *c.* 7 km. to the NE is **Maiori** and the church of *S.Maria a Mare*. Originally Romanesque, it has been completely altered. On the High Altar, there is a fine 14C wooden 'Madonna and Child'. **Positano** is *c.* 17 km. to the W. in a picturesque location. The 13C parish church, *S.Maria Assunta*, has a fine 13C picture of the Madonna (in the Byzantine style), above the High Altar.

Amalfi, painting by G.Giganti

Amatrice 02012
Rieti/Latium   p.416☐I 8

Small mountain town, picturesquely located. Its appearance has changed little
throughout history.

At the time of the Lombard invasion Amatrice belonged to the Duchy of Spoleto. In
1529 it was destroyed by the troops of
Philip of Chalon and was subsequently
rebuilt according to Renaissance ideas of
town planning. The new planner is
thought to have been Nicola Filotesio,
known as Cola dell'Amatrice, an architect
and painter who was born here and active
from 1509 until *c.* 1547. Renaissance and
baroque houses and palaces predominate,
but there are also some medieval buildings.
The Romanesque church of *S.Maria
Lauretana* (or *S.Emidio*), was altered in the
15C; it has tall flanking campaniles. Inside
are two aisles and a row of Romanesque
columns. *Apse frescos* by Dionisio Cappelli
(*c.* 1510) and Cola dell'Amatrice.

S.Francesco: Built with early Gothic
proportions, which were old-fashioned
even then (late 14C). The façade is divided
into horizontal strips and adorned by a fine
marble portal. Tympanum of multicoloured terracotta has a *Madonna and
Child between two angels*. The interior is
wide and simple, with a single aisle. There
are numerous frescos from the 15C school
of the Marches. Frescos in the apse
(15&16C) were influenced by the Rimini
school. A *bust of Camillo Orsini* by Alessandro Leopardi can be found in a wall
niche. On the altar there is a fine Gothic
reliquary (1472), attributed to Pietro di
Vannino.

S.Agostino: Façade divided into horizontal bands. Portal (1428) has a pointed arch

Positano (Amalfi)

Amalfi, Chiostro del Paradiso ▷

and a sculpture of the *Annunciation* in the tympanum. The interior is baroque and has frescos by the master of the Madonna della Misericordia (Annunciation, 1491); Madonna with Child and Angels (1492).

Amella 05022
Terni/Umbria   p.414☐H 8

Amella is surrounded by a massive cyclops wall dating from pre-Roman times.

Worth seeing: The *Cathedral* has an 11C Romanesque campanile, which was destroyed, then rebuilt in 1640. Inside: Turkish flags captured during the battle of Lepanto; also pictures by Pomarancio and some from the school of Agostino di Duccio. *Palazzo Ferratini* (16C) by Sangallo the younger. *Palazzo Petrignani*, (16C) with frescos by pupils of the Zuccari; the medi-

eval pulpit is also of interest. *S. Agostino* (14–15C) has a fine Gothic portal. *Municipal tower* (11C). *S. Filippo e Giacomo* (S. Francesco; 13C): tombs of Matteo and Elisabetta Geraldini, by Agostino di Duccio.

Anagni 03012
Frosinone/Latium   p.414☐H 10

The ancient *Anagnia* was the main town of the Hernici. It was conquered by the Romans in 306 BC. After the 8C AD it became a Papal possession. Birthplace of numerous medieval Popes (Innocent III, Gregory IX, Alexander IV, Boniface VIII, 1294–1303).

Cathedral of S.Maria: The cathedral was built by Bishop Pietro in 1077–1104, on the site of the ancient acropolis. The ar-

chitecture and church furnishings make this building one of the most fascinating Romanesque monuments in Italy. It was partly altered in the Gothic style in the 13C. Alexander II pronounced the excommunication of the Emperor, Frederick Barbarossa, here in 1160. *Exterior:* The N. side, which faces the town, is richly articulated. A statue of Boniface VIII seated, (1295), occupies a dominant position. Beyond the transept the eastern section has three apses and is decorated with pilasters and blind arches. The upper part of the dominating middle apse has a dwarf gallery for decoration. The 12C Romanesque *campanile* is remarkable for its wealth of windows, and, standing in front of the façade, it makes a severe impression. Despite the Gothic alterations, the *interior* owes much to the Romanesque. Basilica arrangement with nave and two aisles, separated by alternating columns and pillars. The body of the church is not very long, and contains the nave, with its open roof truss, and the side aisles with groined vaults. Towards the transept, the columns become massive and clustered. Particularly notable is the *floor* (1227), designed by Cosma di Jacopo in Cosmati work. A low choir screen divides the nave from the transept, whose middle bay passes into the chancel. The altar has a Romanesque *pyx* on four Corinthian columns. To the right of the altar is a splendid monumental *Easter candelabra* which has a turned shaft and is decorated in Cosmati work. The bowl of the candelabra is borne by a kneeling Atlas, executed in 1263 by Vassalletto—who also made the *bishop's throne* in the apse. This marble throne has arm-rests in the form of recumbent lions, and a disc-shaped top section above its back-rest. The *family chapel of the Caetani* (the family of Boniface VIII) is in the N. aisle. The tombs of three members of the family—the work of Cosma de Jacopo and his sons Luca and Jacopo—are along the left wall, under a Gothic baldachino. The back wall has a fresco in the style of Pietro Cavallini (1325). The *crypt* is mentioned in documents as early as 1112, in connection with an altar consecration. Relics of S.Magnus, buried here in 1130. Cosma and his sons Luca and Jacopo laid the floor in 1231. The walls, the 21 bays of the crypt (nave and two aisles) and the apses are decorated with one of the richest fresco cycles in Italy—and one of the most interesting from the iconographical point of view. Work on this cycle must have begun no later than 1231 and ended by the final consecration in 1255. The work on these extensive decorations was shared by three anonymous masters, whose style and quality of work differ; artistically they seem to have their roots in the Roman tradition. There are four main themes: 1. *The Legend of S.Magnus* and the depiction of individual saints (E. apses, W. wall); 2. *Theophany* and *Subjects from the Apocalypse* (vault); 3. *Old Testament*, in particular the *History of the Ark of the Covenant* (vault); 4. *Cosmology* (W. wall). Beside the crypt is the *chapel of St.Thomas à Becket*, which is decorated with crude Romanesque frescos. *Treasure chamber*, important mainly for a magnificent collection of 13C *paraments* owned by Innocent III. Also noteworthy: the *reliquary of St.Thomas à Becket* (enamel from Limoges).

This town is rich in medieval buildings; two of the most important being the **Palazzo Comunale** and the **Palazzo Bonifaz VIII**.

Anagni, cathedral

Ancona 60100
Ancona/Marches   p.414□I 6

Main town of the province of the same name. A Greek colony in the 4C BC; conquered by the Romans in 239 BC and independent in the Middle Ages; from 1532 onwards it belonged to the Papal States. A major port, formerly a point of departure for the Crusades.

Cathedral of S.Ciriaco: on Monte Guasco, on the site of a former Temple of Venus. The church of *S.Lorenzo* was built in the 6C; destroyed by Saracens in 840; rebuilt in the 9C, and renamed when the remains of S.Cyriacus were moved here. The present building, erected on the ground plan of a Greek cross, was built mainly between the 11&13C. The main entrance, whose arches become progressively more pointed towards the inside of the archivolt, was built c. 1200; the portico—with columns resting on lions—and also the cupola, are late 13C. Within, just inside the right transept, are two panels (probably formerly framed in colour) depicting animals and saints. In the left transept there is an *Altar with a Madonna* by Luigi Vanvitelli.

S.Domenico: Built by Carlo Marchioni in 1763–88. Inside, a *Crucifixion* (1558) by Titian and an *Annunciation* (1662) by Guercino.

S.Francesco delle Scale: Built in 1323, and altered in the baroque style in the 18C. Secularized in 1860, it returned to its original function in 1953. The *portal* with numerous reliefs and statues was designed by Giorgio Orsini (1455). Inside there is an *Assumption* by Lorenzo Lotto.

S.Maria della Piazza Probably 12C. The portal in the façade is by Master Filippo, and is decorated with reliefs (1210–25). Inside, remains of the 6C floor are set into the wall.

Loggia dei Mercanti: Built by Giovanni Pace in 1443. The *façade*, with *statues* representing the virtues, is the work of Giorgio Orsini (1451–9); the lower sections were restored by Pellegrino Tibaldi in the 16C. The wooden door dates from c. 1600.

Anagni, cathedral, 13C frescos

Palazzo Ferretti: Probably built by Pellegrino Tibaldi *c.* 1560; he also painted some of the rooms. It houses the *Museo Nazionale delle Marche,* which has an archaeological collection.

Palazzo degli Anziani: Built by Margaritone d' Arezzo in 1270; the portal dates from 1571 and the façade from 1647 (upper sections still have some 13C reliefs). Inside is the *Pinacoteca Comunale Podesti:* Madonna with Saints by Titian (1520); paintings by Lorenzo Lotto, Carlo Crivelli, Guercino.

Also worth seeing: In the harbour below Monte Guasco is *Trajan's Arch,* on which the emperor's equestrian statue originally stood. The *Arco Clementino* was built by Luigi Vanvitelli in 1733 in honour of Pope Clement XII. On the other side of the harbour are the *Porta Pia* (1787–9) and the former *quarantine hospital,* a pentagonal building on an island.

Andria 70031
Bari/Apulia   p.416□N 10

In the Middle Ages, this was the favourite residence of the Hohenstaufen Emperor, Frederick II.

Cathedral of S.Riccardo (with crypt): The *crypt,* originally a separate 10C structure, was integrated into the Norman cathedral (begun in 1024). Entrance to the crypt is at the front of the right aisle. Two consorts of the above-mentioned emperor are buried here — Yolande of Jerusalem, through whom Frederick II gained the title of King of Jerusalem and who died in 1228 after giving birth to a son, Conrad IV and Isabella of England, who died in Foggia in 1241. Used as a charnel-house (place for bones or dead bodies), from the 15C onwards, the crypt was re-opened in 1904. Despite much research the position of the graves cannot be determined with certainty. Hardly anything remains of the original appearance of the cathedral, either inside or outside.

Also worth seeing: *S.Agostino,* with a fine 14C portal (Piazza S.Agostino). *S.Maria di Porta Santa* with Renaissance portal, where, tradition has it, Frederick II and his son Manfred are depicted in the medallions on the pilasters. *S.Domenico,* with the re-

Ancona, Loggia dei Mercanti

mains of a 14C cloister, and a bust of Francesco II del Balzo by Francesco Laureana in the sacristy. *Porta S.Andrea*, on the way to the Castel del Monte, with an inscription of thanks by Frederick II for the loyalty of the people of Andria, 15C. *Palazzo Ducale* (18C).

Angera 21021

Varese/Lombardy   p.412□C 3

Excavations carried out near the cemetery have revealed traces of Roman temples and burial grounds.

Environs: *Rocca di Angera:* The Lombard fortress was much altered in the 14, 16&17C. The E. part of the palace was originally built on the orders of Giovanni Visconti (14C). Inside, in the *Sala della Giustizia*, there are Early Gothic frescos (pre-1325).

Anzù 32032

Belluno/Veneto   p.410□G 2

Pilgrim church of SS. Vittore e Co-rona: *c.* 1060 relics of saints, who were much venerated in the Middle Ages, were removed from the former mausoleum in Venice and placed in this church, which stands 1, 100 ft. above sea-level. The church was endowed by a knight who received the relics as a gift from the Doge. Except for the choir, the Romanesque building (Byzantine dome), was given its present shape in the 12C. The sacristy, an apse, was only added in the 19C. The façade is severe, built of heavy stones, although the upper part has 16C chiaroscuro frescos. Steps lead from the portico to the interior, which is quite stunning. Nave and two aisles. Pillars and walls are covered with well-preserved 14C frescos. Next to the walls of the choir, and at half their height, is a very fine *gallery* with elegant columns; the capitals display niello work. In the middle of this lies the *Sarcophagus of the Martyrs*; endowed by Emperor Charles IV in 1335, it stands on a fine base of columns. To the left of the altar is a fine Gothic *tabernacle*. Near the second pillar on the right there is a red marble *bishop's chair*. The *tomb of the donor*, Giovanni da Vidor, rests on two columns (tomb: end of 11C), in the sacristy, behind the choir. The

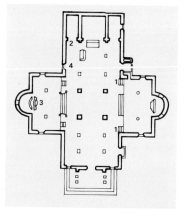

Ancona, cathedral 1 slabs from the former pulpit **2** tomb of G.Dalmata, 1509 **3** Madonna by V.Vitelli **4** entrance to the sacristy (Museo Diocesano)

Ancona, S. Domenico

reconstructed monastery building and cloister (1495) are to the right of the church.

Aosta 11100

Aosta/Piedmont   p.412☐A 3

The Roman name of Aosta was *Augusta Praetoria Salassorum*. After the conquest of the Gallic Salassi in 25 BC, the town was established as a military colony to secure the Alpine road. During the Franco-Burgundian period, it was the main town of a region (the Valle d'Aosta). In 1032, it came into the possession of the Counts of Savoy. Their vassals, the Lords of Challant, made it their residence in the Middle Ages. Today it is the main town of the province of the same name, and also a diocesan town. St. Anselm of Canterbury (1033–1109) was born in Aosta.

Collegiata dei Santi Pietro e Orso (Piazza S.Orso): Formerly a collegiate church founded by Bishop Anselm II (994–1026). The church, as it is today, was built under Prior Giorgio di Challant (1468–1509) in typical Late Gothic Piedmont style. The *crypt*, which has a nave and four aisles, with twelve Roman columns, survives from the previous building, as does an important 11C fresco cycle on the roof of the nave; it shows scenes from the life of Christ and the Apostles. The *campanile* is 12C, and the *cloister*, on the S. side of the church, has wonderful Romanesque capitals decorated with figures (2nd quarter of the 12C). The *church treasure* includes the 13C arm reliquary of S.Orso.

Priorato di S.Orso: The priory is to the S. of the church, and was built in 1494–1509, under Giorgio di Challant. It is remarkable for an octagonal tower and terracotta window frames and friezes. The chapel is decorated with a Late Gothic *fresco cycle* in Franco-Flemish style with Lombard influence and it depicts the story of St.George.

Cathedral (Piazza Cattedrale): Originally built in the 11C, today this essentially Late Gothic church dates from the end of the 15C; Renaissance façade 1522–6 and neoclassical portal in 1848. 12C *mosaic floor*

Ancona, S. Ciriaco

survives in the choir, where there are splendid *choir stalls*, with carved figures (*c.* 1500). The *windows* of the nave are much-prized 12&13C French glass paintings. The Cathedral's great treasure includes a *horn-book* with an Augustan cameo and Venetian filigree work.

Also worth seeing: Roman buildings: The *Porta Pretoria* (Via Torre Pretoriane), 24 BC; originally a double gate, its base is now 8 ft. below *ground level*. Nearby is the square *medieval tower* of the castle of the lords of Quant. The *Arco di Augusto* (Piazza Arco di Augusto), 24 BC, well restored in 1912-14. The *theatre* (Via di Teatro Romano), formerly four-storeyed, with a stage wall which is still 72 ft. high today. The *Roman town wall* and the remains of the Roman *amphitheatre* in the convent of S. Caterina (Via Baillage).

Archaeological Museum (Via S.Orso): many valuable exhibits, including the very fine *Bust of Jupiter* by a native artist of the early 2C.

Environs: Fenis: Well-preserved castle on the right bank of the Dora Baltea; founded by Aymont Challant in 1340. With battlements, towers and arrow-slits, it looks like a fortress. Splendid inner courtyard. 15C wall paintings inside the castle are worth seeing. Today it contains a *museum of local history* (Museo dell'Arredamento valdostano) with various notable exhibits.

Appiano/Eppan 39057
Bolzano/South Tyrol-Trentino   p.410□F 2

A widely scattered group of villages devoted to cultivating vines, on a plateau in the Upper Adige. Interesting 16&17C houses characteristic of the region, built joined on to one another, exhibit a mixture of German Gothic and Lombard Renaissance architectural styles.

Parish church of St. Paul/S.Paolo: This immense church in the St. Paul quarter was built 1461-1552. The choir dates from the 2nd half of the 16C. The Late Gothic façade was executed by Master Philip in 1514 to designs by Master Jakob Zwiesel. The upper part of the tower is by Master Hans Lutz (1520-33), while the ba-

Aosta, Collegiata dei Santi Pietro e Orso, cloister

Aosta, Arco di Augusto

roque dome and the dome support were added in the 1st half of the 17C. Hall church with a nave and two aisles; inside the ribbed vaults were designed by Andrea Crivelli and Marco della Bolla, in 1550. The W. gallery (1609) is by Pietro de Bosio. *Furnishings* from the 15&16C are interesting and include: a wooden *pietà*, on the right side altar (1430); a *crucifix* on the inner wall of the nave (1st half 16C); and the marble half-length reliefs of the *Apostles (c.* 1575) on the outer walls of the nave.

Also worth seeing: Near the parish church is the *cemetery* (1571) with the Chapel of *St.Lucia*, built in 1593. *St.Nikolaus in Unterrain*: Late Gothic structure of 1512 with winged altar (*c.* 1500) and statue of St. Nicholas (1450). *St.Michael/S.Michele* (in the St.Michael quarter, in the S. of the town): Built *c.* 1530, in Late Gothic style. Also in the St.Michael quarter are the 16C church of

St.Anna and the *Gleif Chapel of the Lamentation of the Blessed Virgin*, a building from the 1st half of the 18C. The Gothic chapel of *St.Sebastian in Englar*, attached to a *residence of the same name*, (15–16C), is also worth mentioning. The chapel was built in 1475 and has elegant fan vaults and arabesque-type painting. The 16C residence *Gandegg/Castel Ganda*, with the *Maria-Schnee Kapelle* (10 min. from S.Anna) is interesting. The chapel of *St.Valentin* (attached to the 16C *residence of the same name*) was built in 1510; a side altar has a winged shrine dated 1500. 17C *Schloss Reinsberg/Castel Monteriva*, near to St.Michael, with the *Hl. Kreuz Kapelle/S.Croce. Freudenstein/Castel Lodrone*: this castle was built in the 13C and reconstructed in the 16&17C; it includes the castle chapel of *St.Andreas*, dating from the 1st half of the 16C. Above S.Paolo are the 13C *Schloss Korb/Castel Corba* and the ruined 13C castle, *Boimont/Castel Bel-*

Aosta, Roman theatre

monte. Behind it, the picturesque ruined *Burg Hocheppan/Castel d'Appiano* (originally 12C), stands on a steep rock above and to the NW of the town of Missian. This — the former ancestral seat of the Counts of Eppan—is one of the most important medieval castles in the South Tyrol. The complex, extended in the 13&16C, has a simple *Romanesque chapel* (castle courtyard), decorated both inside and out with the South Tyrol's most important Romanesque frescos (*c.* 1170–80). To the S.of S.Paolo, towards the Mendel pass, are the ruins of the *Altenburg/Castel Vecchio* (11C?, the original ancestral seat of the Counts of Eppan) and the 13C *Burg Warth/Castel Guardia.*

Environs: The **Burg Sigmundskron/Castel Firmiano** is E. of Eppan (St.Paul), on a steep cliff, near the confluence of the Adige and the Isarco. This site was inhabited even in prehistoric

Fenis castle (Aosta)

times, and its strategic location meant that it often had an important role to play. The extensive ruins date from the 12C—when the Bishops of Trento resided in the castle and used it as a base against the Counts of the Tyrol—and also from the 15C, when Archduke Sigmund extended the castle (called Sigmundskron since then) for use as a fortress against the Venetians. **Caldaro/Kaltern** This well-known wine-growing town lies S. of Appiano on the Southern Tyrolean wine route in the direction of Salorno (near Trento). Like Appiano, Caldaro also has Gothic- and Renaissance-style houses joined on to one another, in the typical Alto Adige style. *Parish church, Mariae Himmelfahrt:* The neoclassical church, built in 1791–2, has a tower dated 1500. Ceiling frescos inside the church are by Jos. Schöpf (1792). The *Kalvarienbergkirche* (Church of the Holy Cross) is a massive bodied building, dating from 1720–3. Altarpiece by P.Troger (1722). The Gothic church of *St.Katharina* (1st half of 16C) is in Mitterdorf which, together with St.Anton, Pfus and St.Nikolaus are part of Caldaro. Inside: net vault and some good frescos—those in the left side chapel date from 1414, those from

the chapel on the right, 1519, and those in the choir c. 1400. *St.Nikolaus*, has a tower (*c.* 1300), with a late Gothic helm roof. When the church was rebuilt, in 1521, in late Gothic style, the original W. façade (1300) was preserved. The paintings (1528–36), in the vault, are by Bartlme Dill Riemenschneider, son of Tilman Riemenschneider. The church of *St.Anton* (1470) has a Romanesque tower with a Gothic helm roof; the choir has fine frescos dated 1470. *Schloss Kampan*(13&16C), has a fine arcaded courtyard (1600). The 17C *Schloss Ringberg* houses the *South Tyrolean wine museum* and also fascinating model castles. **Termeno/Tramin** This village, further S. along the wine route, has typical Alto Adige houses, some of which have outside staircases, vaulted porches and, within, old frescos. *Parish church of St.Julitta and Quiricus.* Built in 1466–92, the tower is one of the finest examples of Southern Tyrolean Gothic. A neo-Gothic nave, dated 1910, was added to the Gothic choir built by Master Konrad in *c.* 1400. Inside: the outer walls of the nave have very fine frescos (Last Judgement, *c.* 1500, Coronation of the Virgin and Crucifixion, *c.* 1400). There are frescos from the early

Tramin with St. Jakob in the background (Eppan)

15C in the arch of the choir, on the inner choir walls and in the choir vault. The altarpiece (1790) is by M.Knoller. *St.Jakob in Kastellaz* is a small flat-roofed church, built *c.* 1200, on a steep hill to the N. of the village (on the site of a former castle); groin vaulted aisle added *c.* 1400. Superb Romanesque frescos from the 2nd half of the 13C in the apse. The aisle vault was painted in 1441. *St.Valentin* (by the cemetery): a Romanesque church, with 13C tower and helm roof; the nave has frescos of the Bolzano school, dated 1390–1420.

Aquileia 33051
Udine/Friuli   p.411☐I 13

Aquileia was founded as a Roman colony in 181 BC and from the 1C BC onwards it developed into the chief town in NE Italy. It was a patriarchal seat from early Christian times until 1751. The town began to decline in importance in the 13C.

Cathedral of S.Maria (Piazza Capitolo): First built under the Patriarch Theodosius (4C); rebuilt after the invasion of the Huns (5C). Subsequently repeatedly extended—

the apses, transept and Chiesa dei Pagani, etc., were added in the 9C. Altered to its present Romanesque form in the 11C under the Patriarch Poppo. The choir was rebuilt in the Renaissance, and restored to its original form in the 18C. Simple external structure: fine *double window* in the façade; portico with some ancient columns (9C). Inside the basilica (nave and two aisles), there is a mixture of different styles (Romanesque, Gothic, Renaissance). Fine *ancient columns* are on unusually thick bases because of the excavation of the floor. The apse is an 11C addition and has a *fresco of the Madonna* of the same date, which is in poor condition. In the right transept, the *Chapel of S.Pietro* has fine frescos, and a 'Santo Sepolcro', a copy of the Holy Sepulchre in Jerusalem, also 11C. The church's main decoration is the *mosaic floor c.* 4C (approx. 7,500 sq.ft.), discovered in 1909, when the church's floor was excavated. The mosaics depict human figures, animals and plants, all framed by geometrical patterns. The *Crypt* has 13C frescos of great interest. (Entry by a door at the side of the choir.) In the left aisle there is the entrance to the *Cripta degli Scavi*, the excavations of an *early Christian religious*

Eppan, St.Pauls

Sigmundskron castle (Eppan)

Tramin (Eppan), frescos in St. Jakob

building, beneath the cathedral (4C church, see above). Three levels of superb *mosaic floors* have been uncovered, two from the 4C and one pre-4C. In front of the cathedral is the ruined 5C *baptistery*, connected to the cathedral by the so-called *Chiesa dei Pagani* (9C), where those awaiting baptism lived. The 11C *campanile* is to the left of the cathedral and stands *c.* 240 ft. high.

The **Archaeological Museum** (Via Roma): contains archaeological finds from Aquileia. Rooms 1–5 have *fragments of sculptures and buildings* (Room 2 includes Aquileia's foundation inscription). Room 6 has fine *objects of precious stone and amber, and also cameos.* Room 10 has good examples of *Roman glass.* In the garden there are interesting *architectural fragments and funeral urns.*

Also worth seeing: *Roman Forum* (left off the Via Guilia). Remains of the *ancient river port*, along the *Via Sacra*, with architectural fragments. *Roman family graves* (accessible via the Via XXIV Maggio). *Ruins of the amphitheatre* (Via XXIV Maggio). Remains of *Roman houses* with *floor mosaics* (N. of the cathedral). Two *early Christian oratories* (4C, between Piazza Capitolo and Via Sacra). Ruins of the *circus* (right, off the Via Giulia). *Roman Basilica* (on the Via Giulia). Remains of the ancient *town wall* (S. of the cathedral). *Basilica of Monastero* (Piazza Principe Umberto) from the early Christian period; fine floor mosaics. In the same complex is the *Museo Palaeocristiano* (the Early Christian museum), with funeral urns, choir screens and fragments of mosaic floors.

Aquino 03031
Frosinone/Latium   p.416□I 10

Ancient *Aquinum* was an important Volsci town on the Via Latina. Destroyed by the Lombards in 577, Aquino became their most forward outpost against Byzantine Gaeta. From the mid-10C, it was the seat of a count. Decimus Junius Juvenalis — Juvenal — (c. AD 60 – 140), the last Roman satirist of importance, came from Aquino. Thomas Aquinas (1226 – 74), one of the most important medieval theologians, was related to the Counts of Aquino.

S.Maria della Libera: Built in 1125, on the ruins of the Temple of Hercules Liberatrix, using ancient *spolia*. The church was restored after being damaged in World War 2. There is a pleasant walk to the *ruins of Aquinum*.

Arcevia 60011
Ancona/Marches   p.414□H 7

S.Medardo: In the apse there are paintings by L. Signorelli (1507), *Madonna and Child with 8 Saints* and *God the Father*; in the Baptistery, *The Baptism of Christ* (1508), by the same artist. In the left transept there is an altarpiece from the Della Robbia workshop (1513). The 1st chapel on the right has a *Mary Magdalene* by Guercino. The *choir stalls* (1490) were carved by a German craftsman called Konrad.

Ardara 07010
Sassari/Sardinia   p.422□C 12

The former 'main town of Logudoro' (Golden Water Meadow). When the seat of government was threatened by enemy raids and malaria, the Giudicati of Porto Torres moved here. Walls and a tower are all that remain of the ancient fortifications.

Santa Maria del Regno: Begun in 1170. Built predominantly of dark basalt, the building is strictly Romanesque, and was to became a model for other, later churches in Sardinia. Inside, the nave and two aisles are divided by massive columns; these are close together and have frescos, which are

Aquileia, Sepolcreto Romano

in poor condition. An interesting *altarpiece* in the choir is composed of 31 individual panels. In the main it is the work of Giovanni Muru in 1515 but it was completed by a Spaniard from the Valencia school (possibly Martin Torner).

Environs: Sant'Antioco di Bisarcio: The country church of *Sant'Antioco di Bisarcio* is older than Santa Maria del Regno, but has been altered several times. It was built in 1150 – 90 as a cathedral for the whole of Logudoro, on the site of an earlier church, dating from 1090, which had burnt down. A mighty Romanesque church of red tachylite and greenish basalt, it was erected by builders from Santa Giusta (Oristano), who had been trained in Pisa. Some 100 years later, masons from Burgundy added a portico of three arches, a staircase and many decorative motifs. During the Aragonese rule, the upper left part of the façade, which had almost com-

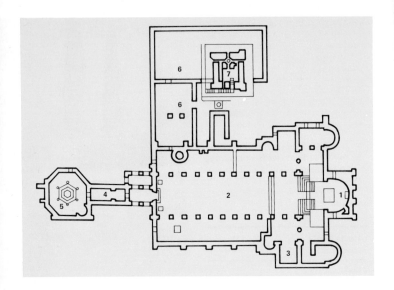

Aquileia, cathedral 1 11C fresco of the Madonna **2** mosaic pavement **3** Cappella di S.Pietro **4** Chiesa dei Pagani **5** baptistery **6** early Christian religious site **7** campanile

pletely collapsed, was replaced by simple masonry; the only surviving parts of the original decoration include arches with supporting columns, and a frieze of

Aquileia, cathedral of S.Maria

pointed arches, on the right, under the stepped roof. The massive square tower has blind arcading. Inside, the nave is divided from the two aisles by red tachylite columns, each hewn from a single block of stone, and possessing particularly fine capitals. In 1114, further W., monks from Camaldoli began work on an extensive monastery, with a country church, in Pisan-Romanesque style. Along with some ruins of the above-mentioned monastery, the *Santissima Trinità di Saccargia* has survived as Sardinia's finest sacred architectural monument. The gloriously colourful frescos in the middle apse, from the early 13C, are particularly famous; despite obvious Byzantine influence, they are attributed to an unknown Pisan artist. Towards the end of the 12C, the basilica was extended by the addition of a portico with three rounded arches and, on the N. side, a chapel with pointed-arch windows. It was also at this time that the church received its striking decorative colouring, achieved by facing the masonry with horizontal strips of dark basalt and almost white limestone. The E. and W. fronts in particular were enriched by decorative façades and ornamental panels, based on

Tuscan models. At this time too, the campanile rose to 130 ft. and acquired its two- and three-arched windows. **Salvénero:** 5 km. E. with the church of *San Michele di Salvénero*. Built in 1110–30 in the old Pisan style. It was extended and a campanile was added from 1200–25 (of the latter only the foundations survive); decorative features were added, blind arcades on the front façade and apses, and the striped ornamentation of basalt bars and limestone slabs. Today the church has fallen into complete disrepair. The typically Pisan striped pattern is also seen in the small shepherds' church of *Sant'Antonio di Salvénero*, 1,000 yards to the S., squeezed between a sheepfold and another small ruined church. S.Antonio is built of pale limestone and red porphyry, and is a complete, almost unadorned, building in the Romanesque style (1220–5). Large standing stone with superimposed cross. **Ploaghe:** This, possibly pre-Carthaginian, settlement was a diocesan town in the Middle Ages. In the sacristy of the simple *parish church* there is a small *picture gallery*. It was a gift of the geologist and historian Giovanni Spanno (1803–78), and includes works by F.Lippi (15C). The

Aquileia, cathedral of S.Maria, interior with nave and two aisles

Aquino, S.Maria della Libera, portal

Sant'Antioco di Bisarcio (Ardara), façade

gravestones carry inscriptions in the dialect of Logudoro.

Arezzo 52100

Arezzo/Tuscany   p.414☐G 7

Chief town in the E. of the Tuscan province of the same name. Situated on the slope of a hill in the midst of a beautiful, fertile region. An old Etruscan city (one of the confederation of 12 cities). Alliance with Rome in the 4C, prevented the town's destruction. After a varied history the town fell to Florence in 1384. Birthplace of some of Italy's most famous men: G.Maecenas (died 8 BC), patron of Virgil and Horace; Francesco Petrarch (1304–74) poet; Pietro Aretino (1492–1556) writer; the painter, architect, and writer, Giorgio Vasari (1511 –74) and Guido von Arezzo, a Benedictine monk (*c.* 990–1050) who introduced the interval-type musical notation still used today.

The predominantly medieval townscape is a tribute to Arezzo's artistic heyday in the Middle Ages and the Renaissance. The *Giostra del Saracino*, a Saracen tournament held each year in the Piazza Grande on the first Sunday in September, is documented as dating back to 1593 and may possibly be even older. 8 knights, 2 from each of the old town quarters (Porta S.Andrea, Porta Crucifera, Porta del Foro, Porta S.Spirito), charge in turn with their lances, aiming to hit the centre of a shield on a turning quintain.

Cathedral: A building with both Romanesque and Gothic features. Begun in 1277, and continued in 1313, with additions in 1510. The *façade* is Gothic, but was actually completed in 1900–14. 3 *portals* from the early 15C and a *rose- window* by Guillaume de Marcillat (early 16C). In the right aisle there is a portal from the 14C building, with tympanum and peaked arches (terracotta by Nicolo d'Arezzo, *Madonna and Child with Saints*). Inside: behind the high altar, is the *Arca di S.Donato,* a marble tomb (white sarcophagus on 12 pilasters with reliefs depicting the lives of saints) by various artists (*c.* 1369). The monumen-

Santissima Trinità di Saccargia (Ardara)

tal *tomb of Bishop Tarlati* was executed in 1330 to Giotto's designs. To the left of the sacristy door is a *fresco by Piero della Francesca* (Mary Magdalene). *Capella della Madonna del Conforto* (entrance from the north transept): an almost independent small church with nave and two aisles; beautiful terracotta altars and reliefs by Andrea della Robbia (Christ Crucified with Saints, Assumption of the Virgin) and (Madonna Enthroned with Saints) by his school. The *Baptistery* has a 15C hexagonal font with 3 marble reliefs.

S.Maria della Pieve, or **Pieve di S.Maria:** Familiarly known as *Pieve.* The town's oldest and most famous church and one of the finest Romanesque churches in Tuscany. Dates from 1140, built on the site of a simple temple. It is consecrated to the Assumption of the Virgin and to S.Donatus, the town's patron, whose *relics* are inside the church in a fine gilded silver bust

of local manufacture. The Romanesque façade reflects Pisan influence in its three tiers of arcades with horizontal border (newly restored a few years ago). Of the three *portals*, the middle one with reliefs of the months by an unknown 13C artist, is the finest. *The interior* is austere and has a nave and two aisles. The sanctuary is part of the original Romanesque structure and is elevated by the crypt; light enters through 18 two-arched windows. There is an 11C *font* and a charming *polyptych* (1320) by P.Lorenzetti (Madonna and Child, Annunciation and other figures). The *campanile* of 1330 is tall (194 ft.) and its striking appearance—the 'cento buche' (100 holes) and 40 Romanesque, two-arched windows—makes it stand out on the town's skyline.

S.Francesco Brick building from the end of the 13C; vast single-aisled interior. Numerous *frescos*, the most famous being the *cycle in the sanctuary* by Piero della Francesca. These pictures, painted between 1453 and 1466, show clarity of line, mastery of perspective, and understanding of the use of light. The subject of the cycle is the *Legend of the True Cross*, which begins chronologically with the death of Adam. The seed of the Tree of Knowledge grew into a tree on Adam's grave and this tree provided the wood for Christ's cross. In the picture the *Dream of Emperor Constantine*, where he is promised victory through the Cross, the light is very realistic; it is one of the earliest paintings of a night scene. The *Cappella Tarlati* has a fresco of the *Annunciation* by the young Luca Signorelli, which was painted when he was still under the influence of Piero della Francesca. To the right of the sanctuary is the *Cappella Cuascani*, with frescos by Spinello Aretino dated 1400. There is an interesting holy-water stoup made of a Roman urn standing on a 14C column, to the right of the sacristy.

More churches worth seeing:
S.Domenico: According to Vasari, built in 1275 to a design by Nicolo Pisano. Inside: Christ on the Cross, an early work by Cimabue, still rooted in Byzantine art. *SS.Annunziata* is a Renaissance building, of 1490–1, built above an older building and completed by Antonio da Sangallo the elder.

Palaces: *Palazzo Pretorio* (on the Corso Italia): 16C with coats of arms from the 15–18C carved in stone. *Palazzo della Fraternita dei Laici*: built in the 14–15C during the time of Francis of Assisi. In the façade Gothic forms harmonize with those of the Renaissance. *Palazzo Bruni-Ciocchi*, also known as *Palazzo della Dogana* (Via S.Lorentino 8): Renaissance building from the mid-15C, extended over the centuries. It houses the *picture gallery* and the *museum* of medieval art *(Galleria e Museo Medioevale e Moderno)*, with works by Spinello Aretino, Luca Signorelli, Andrea della Robbia, Giorgio Vasari, etc; fine ceramics collection. The **Palazzo delle Logge** is based on a design by Giorgio Vasari (1573–81).

Museo Archeologico Mecenate (Via Margaritone 10): Etruscan finds from the neighbourhood, Roman tombstones, coins from the Etruscan and Roman periods, and

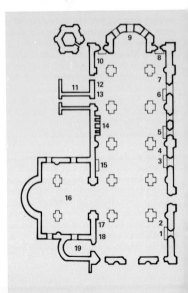

Arezzo, cathedral 1 stained-glass window, De Marcillat, 1520 (Calling of Matthew) **2** tomb of Gregory X **3** stained-glass window, De Marcillat, 1519 (Baptism of Christ) **4** frescos attributed to Buffalmacca, 14C **5** fresco by Lippo Fiorentino, early-14C (Madonna and Child and 6 scenes from the life of Christ and Jacob); stained-glass window, De Marcillat, 1520 **6** Capp.di Ciuccio Tarlati, 1334, frescos of the Siennese school, c. 1380 **7** stained-glass windows, De Marcillat, 1520 (Driving the money-changers from the Temple) **8** chapel, stained-glass window, mid-15C **9** sanctuary, Arco di S.Donato, Giov. and Betto di Francesco and others, 1369 **10** Capp. del B.Gregorio, stained-glass windows, De Marcillat (St.Lucy and St.Sylvester) **11** sacristy, detached fresco, Bart. della Gatta (St. Jerome) **12** fresco, Piero della Francesca (Magdalene) **13** tomb of bishop Guido Tarlati, designed Giotto, by Agost. di Giovanni and Angiolo da Siena, 1330 **14** organ, Vasari, 1535; wooden sculpture, late 13C (Madonna and Child) **15** altarpiece, P.Benvenuti, 1794 (martyrdom of St.Donatus) **16** Capp. della Madonna del Conforto, decoration by Gius. del. Rosso, 1796; wrought-iron grille, 18C; terracotta, Andrea della Robbia (Madonna); at the altar is a work by Andrea della Robbia (Crucifixion and St.Donatus and St.Francis) **17** tomb of Francesco Redi, late 17C; wooden crucifix, 13C **18** altar, 17C **19** baptistery, marble font

Arretine pottery. The latter uses the local soil to make red earthenware vessels—the famous collection of the so-called *'vasi corallini'.*

Casa di Giorgio Vasari (Via XX Settembre 55): The famous painter, architect and art historian was born here. His biographies of Italian artists, 'Le Vite de' piu eccelenti Pittori, Scultori e Architettori' (1550), made him the father of art history. The *Museo e Archivio Vasariano* is on the first floor of the building, where frescos by the artist, dated 1542, can be seen (mainly portraits of contemporary artists).

Casa Petrarca (Via nell'Orto 28): The poet Francesco Petrarch was born here. Today it houses the Petrarch Academy.

Roman Amphitheatre (in the S. of the town): A brick edifice from the 1C AD, most of the best building material—such as marble blocks—have been re-used in the construction of the nearby church of *S.Bernardo.* In former times the amphitheatre was capable of holding 8,000 people. There is also an *Archaeological museum*, with a collection of 'vasi arretini'—red glazed clay with fine reliefs.

Environs: *S.Maria delle Grazie* (15C), with elegant early Renaissance colonnaded loggia by Benedetto da Maiano. **Camáldoli**, monastery and hermitage of the Camaldolensian monks. The name derives from Conte Maldolo d' Arezzo. He presented the site to St.Romuald, who built the first cell of the hermitage here, on the remains of the ancient castle of Fontebuona. Work on the monastery (at a height of 2,677 ft.) began in 1012. It is still inhabited by monks. The church of this extensive monastery was built in 1509–24, on the foundations of the 1st building (mid-11C). Inside: *paintings by G.Vasari.* Between the monastery and the hermitage (3,622 ft.), there is a huge wood with many different types of trees. The *Eremo di Camaldoli*, the first house of the order, was founded by S.Romuald in 1012. Its 20 cells can be visited. The church, consecrated in 1027, has been rebuilt many times; today it has a baroque façade with two towers. The monks take their meals together in the monastery refectory 12 times a year. **Anghiari** is a charming little town lying between Arezzo and Sansepolcro. The ancient city centre is surrounded by a wall. It was first mentioned in 1048 as the 'Cas-

Arezzo, cathedral

Arezzo, S. Maria della Pieve, polyptych by P. Lorenzetti

trum Angulare'. Since 1440, it has belonged to Florence (Leonardo da Vinci's 'Battle of Anghiari', of which the cartoon alone has survived shows Florence defeating Milan). **Sansepolcro** is on the road from Arezzo, at the Foce di Scopetone, where there is a wonderful view of the upper Tiber valley. It is on the left bank of the Tiber, at the foot of the Alpe della Luna (4,770 ft.) and on the border of Umbria. It was the birthplace of Piero della Francesca and is surrounded by an old wall. *Cathedral*: formerly the abbey of the Camaldolensians (1012–49); extended in the 13&14C. A simple façade with 3 portals and a splendid *rose-window*. Inside: *St.Romuald* and *St.Benedict*, terracotta figures in the style of the della Robbia school, as is the elegant *tabernacle* in the sacristy; an Ascension attributed to Perugino. *Picture gallery* (in the Palazzo Comunale), a much-restored building, which was originally 14C. It houses a collection of former Church possessions, a fresco by Piero della Francesca (Resurrection, 1463) and a *polyptych* (post 1445) in the predella (Madonna and Saints, Annunciation, Crucifixion and 5 scenes from the Passion), also by Piero and assistants as well as works by della Robbia and others.

Ariano Irpino 83031

Avellino/Campania   p.416☐L 11

A settlement even in prehistoric times; the present town was founded in the early medieval period.

Cathedral of S.Maria Assunta (Piazza del Duomo): Original building probably 11C; often rebuilt since then (mainly after earthquakes). Façade 1502–12; three fine *portals*. Inside, a *font* dated 1070.

Arezzo, S. Francesco

Arezzo, S. Francesco

Also worth seeing: *Collegiata S.Michele,* restored in the 18C, with fine Late Catalan abbot's chair (1563). *S.Pietro Apostolo* with Gothic portals dated 1358. *S.Anna* with a 14C Gothic porch. S.Francesco (16C, with Gothic elements in the apse). From the *ruins of the Norman castle* there is a fine view.

Environs: *c.* 13 km NW is **Montecalvo Irpino** with the 14C *Collegiata S.Maria Assunta;* to the right is the *Cappella Carafa* which has a fine old font.

Aritzo 08031
Nuoro/Sardinia   p.422□C 13

The position of this town, high on the edge of the Gennargentu massif, makes it a popular summer resort. The completed extension of the road to Arcu Guddetorgiu

(3,678 ft. and panoramic views), which continues to Arcu Tascusi (4,091 ft.), makes for easy access to the highest vantage points in Sardinia (Bruncu Spina, 5,997 ft, and Punta La Marmore, 6,017 ft). Aritzo itself is famous for its folk art (wood carvings, weaving, both fabrics and carpets). The Late Gothic 16C *parish church has a fine Passion cross* by a silversmith from Cagliari (late 14C) and two polychrome wooden statues by native artists (*Pietà*, 18C, and St.Christophorus, 17C).

Environs: The somewhat tiring drive along the lonely mountain road via Seúlo to **Sádali**, is one of the finest in Sardinia from the scenic point of view. Sádali has a *parish church* with an impressive Gothic portal. Just S.of the town are archaeological remains and the well-preserved, small *Nuraghe Mannu.* The strawberry tree, a botanical rarity, still grows in the mountain forests between Monte Orrù and

Monte Tónnefi. The church of Sant'Antonio in **Désulo** contains numerous carvings with popular ornamental motifs, some of which are painted (crucifix, statues of saints, and a pulpit dated 1682). Here, as everywhere else in the mountains, there is a long tradition of carving chestnut wood, examples include some 'bridal chests' and the splendid cupboards seen in Tonara.
Sórgono (23 km.): The tower and sanctuary of the *parish church* still have parts of the original 16C Aragonese-Gothic building. Some 7 km. W., in a secluded spot, is *San Mauro di Sórgono*, a Catalan-Gothic country church, also 16C, whose simple rectangular façade is adorned by a splendid rosette. The *parish church* of nearby **Atzara** not only has 16C Late Gothic structural elements but also some early Renaissance features; in the sacristy there is a crucifix of the Cagliarai school. This also applies to the 16C *San Bartolomeo in* **Meana Sardo**, with attached campanile.
Láconi (25 km.): birthplace of S.Ignatius of Láconi, a Capuchin monk. The splendid Catalan-Gothic church tower is 16C, while the massive tower of *Aymerich*, a ruined castle formerly inhabited by the Giudicati of Arborea, dates from the 11C.

The historical *park* of Láconi is extensive and famous for its grottoes, rocks, waterfalls and rare, even exotic, flora. The unique *tachylite standing stone* of Genna 'e Arrele was also discovered near Láconi.

Arona 28041
Novara/Piedmont   p.412□C 3

An ancient town of Roman origin on the SW shore of Lake Maggiore; terraced layout. Site of ruins of the Borromeo castle. Elevated to the status of a town in the 10C, it was taken over by the archbishops of Milan in the 11C, and subsequently by the Visconti. From 1439–1743 it was under the dominion of the Borromei. From 1743 onwards it belonged to the kingdom of Sardinia. Arona is the birthplace of St. Carlo Borromeo (1538–84), one of Milan's most important archbishops and a significant figure in the Counter-Reformation.

S.Maria Nascente (Via S.Carlo): Building of the collegiate church began in the 15C and was completed by Cardinal Federico Borromeo in the 17C; restored 1856

Arezzo, S. Francesco, frescos by Piero della Francesca

-7. The 10C Romanesque tower with its baroque upper part was originally part of the castle, which was destroyed. The upper part of the church was rebuilt in the baroque style. Inside, a *polyptych* by Gaudenzio Ferrari (1511).

SS. Martiri (Piazza S. Graziano): Single-aisled church from the 15&16C, with 18C baroque façade. Marble *high altar* and *Sacra Conversazione* by Bergognone.

Madonna di Piazza (Piazza del Popolo): Built in 1592 to plans by Pellegrino Tibaldi in fine Mannerist style.

Environs: *Spectacular statue of S. Carlo Borromeo* (1694), 75 ft. tall with a pedestal of 39 ft.; erected in bronze to plans by G.B.Crespi. Popularly known as 'San Carlone'.

Arqua Petrarca 35032
Padua/Veneto   p.410□G 4

This town, picturesquely located in the Euganean Hills, has by and large retained its medieval character. The poet Francesco Petrarch spent the last years of his life here, where he was a friend of the ruling Carrara family (1370–4).

Tomb of Francesco Petrarch (main square): The sarcophagus, which rests on stout columns, was built in 1380 on the orders of Petrarch's son-in-law; restored in the 19C. Petrarch is said to have written his own epigraph. The bronze bust (1547) — the original is in Petrarch's house—was donated by Pietro Paolo Valdezocco.

Petrarch's house (Piazzetta S.Marco): The house was built in the 14C and extended in the 16C. The poet wrote his last verses here. Small museum; the visitors book has interesting entries, e.g. Lord Byron.

Also worth seeing: The *parish church of S. Maria*, a simple, aisleless church from the 11C, which was extended in the 17C and altered again in 1926. Frescos from 11,13&14C; painting in the apse *Assumption of the Virgin* by Palma il Giovane; *Madonna of the Rosary* by Damini in the

S. Maria delle Grazie (Arezzo)

sacristy. In the Piazzetta S.Marco, a Lion of St.Mark on a column (1612; restored); the *Oratorio della Trinità* (12C, extended in the 14C), with a late work by Palma il Giovane, *Holy Trinity with Saints* (1626), above the high altar; in front of the oratory, the *Loggia dei Vicari*.

Arrone 05031
Terni/Umbria   p.414☐H 8

This small community has a 15C church, *S.Maria*, with a fine portal. Inside, good frescos by Vincenzo Tamagni and Giovanni da Spoleto. The Terra quarter has an old *fortress* and the small church of *S.Giovanni* (13&14C). The frescos in this chapel show the influence of Piero della Francesca.

Arzachena 07021
Sássari/Sardinia   p.422☐D 11

To the W. of the Costa Smeralda. Originally no more than a peasant village in the

Arqua Petrarca, Petrarch's house

Arzachena, stone tombs

mountains, it has grown into a large settlement with no particular cultural features of its own; such features are to be found in the surroundings.

Environs People of the Arzachena culture (from 3000 BC onwards) lived in hollows in the granite rocks, which are typical of the area. The technique of using stone walls to protect natural rock holes from wind and weather is still employed by shepherds of the Gallura. The tombs of this period are square *box graves* with a round covering hill and upright granite rocks; the finest of them can still be seen at **Li Muri**. They differ from the usual burial chambers of the time (domus de janas in Anghelu Ruju, cf. Alghero, Sant' Andrea Priu) in the more widespread Ozieri culture. The characteristic *stone rings*, circular Cyclops walls of unhewn blocks of stone, are concentrated on the heights in the NE of the area. Recently, in the SW, a truly gigantic tomb, the *tomba di gigante* was discovered. The *Nuraghe Malchittu* is to the E., near the road. It is typical of Arzachena, half is built on high steep rocks (*c.* 7C BC). The console stones that survive on the N side are impressive,

as too is the cella—accessible from an outer courtyard—with side passages and a flight of stairs ascending inwards with five massive architraves. Some 15 km. to the N. is the wild and rugged Capo d'Orso, and, 6 km. further on, Palau, a fishing village of little interest. Cars can be shipped to **La Maddalena** (2 km.), the chief island of the archipelago of the same name (old Genoese tower, 'La Guardia Vecchia'). This connects by bridge to **Caprera** where *Garibaldi*'s simple house (a national monument) stands amid a magnificent garden. On the small neighbouring island of **Santo Stéfano**—Napoleon once installed cannons in the NE for defence—the *Cala di Vela Marina* has some prehistoric finds; at present they are thought to be the oldest evidence of human habitation in Sardinia. The port of **Santa Teresa Gallura** was founded by Victor Emmanuel of Sardinia-Piedmont on 12 August 1808. Here, centuries before, Pisan sailors had sought refuge from storms in the 'Long Harbour' ('Longosardo') and busily pursued their smuggling together with Sardinian shepherds. In a granite quarry which has been left open on the nearby rocky island of **Manica**, there are still some half-

Arzachena, tomba di gigante

Ascoli Piceno, SS. Vincenzo e A.

finished columns after an ancient model. **Marmorata**, the main island, has similar remains.

Ascoli Piceno 63100
Ascoli Piceno/Marches   p.416 ☐ I 8

The ancient *Asculum* became a Roman colony in the 3C BC. After periods of relative freedom in the Middle Ages, it came under the dominion of the Sforza in the 14C; they were followed by other princes and finally by the Papacy.

Cathedral of S.Emidio Built in the 12C on the ruins of an early Christian building; extended and altered in the following centuries. Cola dell'Amatrice drew up a new design with colossal columns for the incomplete façade. On the left there is a Renaissance portal with a door by Francesco di Giovanni (1496). The *Chapel of the Sacrament* has a polyptych by Carlo Crivelli (1473)—the Madonna in the middle, a Pietà above her, to the side the Saints and the apostles below. The *choir stalls* in the apse are by Francesco and Paolino di Giovanni d'Ascoli. *Baptistery*, a 12C building, with a 13C *font*.

S.Francesco: The foundation stone was laid in 1258 but work on building the church continued until 1464. In 1521–67 the church was vaulted; the façade was only completed in the 17C. The side portal has a statue of Pope Julius II (1506).

SS.Vincenzo e Anastasio: The church dates from the 11–14C, the portal is 14C and at one time it was probably painted. The campanile is from an earlier building.

Palazzo Comunale: The 12C Palazzo dell'Arringo and the 13C Palazzo Comunale were joined together in 1683 by a common front. Inside, the *Pinacoteca Civica*: St.Francis receiving the stigmata by Titian (1561); Crucifixion by Taddeo Zuccari; *Mantle of Pope Nicholas IV*, an English embroidery from the 2nd half of the 13C.

Also worth seeing: The 13C *Palazzo dei Capitani del Popolo*, altered in the 16C. Above the mighty portal is a statue of Paul III, attributed to Cola dell'Amatrice. The *Porta Gemina* is Roman.

Ascoli Piceno, Piazza del Popolo   *Ascoli Piceno, cathedral, Crivelli* ▷

Asola 46041
Mantua / Lombardy   p.410 □ E 4

S.Andrea (1472 – 1514): Characteristic Lombard late Gothic building. The transept adjoins the third bay of the nave and the two aisles. The organ gallery and pulpit in the nave have paintings by Romanino (1525–36)—*scenes from the Old Testament* and *prophets, sibyls* and *saints*.

Asolo 31011
Treviso / Veneto   p.410 □ G 3

This magnificently situated town has been inhabited since prehistoric times. It became a Roman municipium and joined the Republic of Venice in the early 14C. Some centuries later, the town was a favourite resort of the English poet Robert Browning; the legendary actress Eleonara Duse is buried here.

Cathedral of S.Maria di Breda (Piazza Maggiore): This building, erected on the site of Roman baths, was rebuilt in 1747 and completed in the 19C. It has some valuable paintings in the left aisle, including an *Assumption* by L. Lotto (1506).

Castello della Regina (Via Regina Cornaro): Parts of the wall and of the *Torre dell'Orologio* are all that survive of this once splendid Queen's Palace.

Loggia del Capitano (Piazza Maggiore): A fine, though severe, 15C building, with frescos by A. Contarini, 1560. Today it houses the **Museo Civico** with archaeological finds and records of Eleonara Duse.

Casa Lombarda (Via S.Caterina): This small palace, built around 1500, derives its name from an inscription on the unusual, divided façade.

Assisi 06081
Perugia / Umbria   p.414 □ H 7

This small medieval town lies in a peaceful landscape on the slope of Monte Subasio and has an atmosphere of serene mysticism and deep inner peace.

Assisi, view with S. Francesco and the castle

History The town may have originated as an old Umbrian and Etruscan settlement. Under Rome it was a flourishing municipium, where the poet Propertius had his home. King Totila destroyed Assisi in 545. The free community suffered several times under Perugia in the Middle Ages. Despite Assisi's bloody history, it was the birthplace of one of the greatest of religious movements, initiated by St. Francis of Assisi (actually Francesco di Pietro Bernardone, 1182–1226). In the 15C, however, Assisi was occupied and destroyed by various rulers. Peace was not re-established until the 16C.

S.Francesco (Basilica and monastery): Work on this imposing building—which has two churches, one above the other owing to the slope, began in 1228. Today, the architect is thought to have been Frate Elia, but he must have had helpers familiar with the French Gothic style. S.Francesco must thus be regarded as one of the very first Italian interpretations of the Gothic style. The soaring arches, which serve as an artificial base for the building, are a stunning feature. The portico (from the Piazza delle Logge) and part of the monastery were built in the 15C.

Lower church: The visitor passes from the Piazza delle Logge through a fine portal (late 13C) into the lower church. The 2 wooden portals are 16C Umbrian. The massive architecture of the low interior is largely Romanesque and provides an atmosphere of security and devotion. The small *Chapel of St.Sebastian* is on the left, by the entrance. On the right, there are

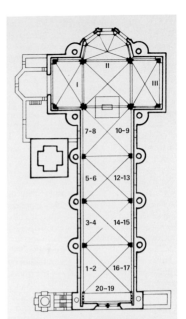

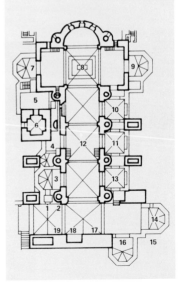

Assisi, S.Francesco, upper church 1, 3, 5, 7, 9, 13, 15, 17 (above) scenes from the Old and New Testaments 2, 4, 6, 8, 10, 12, 14, 16, 20 (below) Giotto's fresco cycle I, II, III Cimabue's frescos

Assisi, S.Francesco, lower church 1 chapel of St. Sebastian 2 15C Madonna and Child with Saints 3 chapel of St.Martin 4 chapel of St.Peter of Alcantara 5 sacristy 6 relic sacristy 7 chapel of St.John the Baptist 8 high altar 9 chapel of St. Nicholas 10 chapel of Mary Magdalene 11 chapel of St.Antony of Padua 12 tomb of St.Francis 13 chapel of St.Louis or St.Stephen 14 chapel of St.Catherine 15 cemetery 16 chapel of St.Antony 17, 18, 19 tombs

tombs by Giovanni de Cerchi (with a large porphyry vessel, a gift of the Queen of Cyprus), by an unknown 14C artist and by Jean de Brienne. Next, there is the *Chapel of St.Antony* and the entrance to the monks' cemetery. The *Chapel of St.Catherine*, with frescos by Andrea da Bologna, is opposite the church entrance. Remains of the church's oldest frescos can be seen on the walls of the nave: on the right, the story of Christ's Passion; on the left, the life of St.Francis; both are the work of the so-called 'Maestro di S.Francesco'.

Chapels on the right side of the nave: Chapel of St.Louis and St.Stephen with 16C frescos by Dono Doni (life of St.Stephen, prophets and sibyls) and fine window painting (14C Siennese). *Chapel of St.Antony* with 17C frescos by Sermei; Life of the Saint and fine 14C window painting by a pupil of Giotto. Chapel of Mary Magdalene with frescos by Giotto and his school (Life of the Saint, etc.).

Chapels on left side of nave: Chapel of St. Martin with frescos by Simone Martini (life of St.Martin and portraits of other saints), one of this artist's best works. Fa-

mous details include a musician with two pipes and St.Clare. The *Chapel of St.Peter of Alcantara* is simple and irregular. Two *sacristies*, the last but one housing valuable objects from the time of St.Francis. *Crypt:* A double stairway in the nave leads to the crypt, which houses the tomb of St.Francis. His companions—Fra Angelo, Fra Leone, Fra Masseo and Fra Rufino—are buried with him. Also interred here is Jacopa de' Settesoli, the saint's benefactress and friend, whom he called 'Brother Jacopa'.

Transept and high altar: This part of the church is rich in excellent painting. The central vaults above the sumptuous Gothic high altar have frescos by a pupil of Giotto, executed to designs by Giotto (allegory of chastity, obedience and poverty; triumph of St.Francis). Left transept: The *Chapel of St.Nicholas* has frescos by Giotto (Childhood of Jesus, Miracle of St.Francis) and Simone Martini (saints); the '5 companions of St.Francis' are by Pietro Lorenzetti; 'Mary and Child on the throne' (this fresco is thought to contain a portrait of St. Francis). Right transept: near the *Chapel of John the Baptist*, there are frescos by

Assisi, S.Francesco, lower church   *Assisi, S.Francesco, fresco by Giotto* ▷

P.Lorenzetti (story of Christ's passion; Mary and Child with two saints).

Upper church: In contrast to the Lower church, this interior is airy, bright and delicate. It has frescos by Cimabue (transept and choir) and Giotto (28 paintings from the life of St.Francis on the lower section of the nave walls). Some of the stories from the Old Testament (upper part of the right wall) and from the New Testament (upper part of the left wall) are by Giotto, others are by unknown artists (Roman and Tuscan schools, end of the 13C). The windows of the crossing, and the first two windows in the nave, are French (late 13C). The wooden choir stalls in the apse are late 15C.

Via San Francesco: The Piazza del Comune is linked to the Piazza S.Francesco by the Via S.Francesco, a fascinating Medieval street, which continues as the Via del Seminario and Via Portica. There are a number of interesting buildings along its length: the *Casa dei maestri comancini*, at No. 14 (13C); the *Palazzo Giacobetti* (No. 162); housing the municipal library and the International Society for Franciscan Studies (the library has old manuscripts);

opposite the latter, the *Oratorio dei Pellegrini*, which houses some important Umbrian paintings; across from the *Palazzo Bindangoli*, No. 8 (13–16C) is the *Portico del Monte Frumentario* (13&16C); next to this there is a fountain (Fonte Oliviera); opposite, at No. 9, the 11C *crypt of S. Nicolo*, housing the municipal museum and the entrance to the Roman forum.

Piazza del Comune: The *Temple of Minerva* dating from the first years of the Roman Empire; the interior has 17&18C decorations. Next to it stands the *Torre Comunale* (1275–1305), then the *Palazzo del Podestà* (1212–82); the *Palazzo dei Priori* (begun in 1337) is opposite. The city council meets here and it houses the municipal picture gallery (Umbrian painting). Near the Piazza, in the Vicolo S.Antonio, is the *Oratorio di S.Francesco Piccolino*, where St.Francis was born. The *Chiesa Nuova* stands on the Piazza itself. Begun in 1615, it is the only church built in Assisi after the 15C.

Cathedral of S.Rufino: Begun in the mid-12C and designed by Giovanni da Gubbio. The façade is one of the finest in

Assisi, S.Francesco, upper church

S. Francesco, St. Francis preaching to the ▷ birds, Giotto

S. Francesco, St. Clare by S. Martini

the Romanesque style of Umbria; Pisan influence is visible in the small loggia. The interior was altered by G.Alessi in 1571. Frederick II, St.Clare and St.Francis were baptized in the *font*. Frescos by A.Carlone in the *Chapel of the Sacrament*. The apse contains *wooden choir stalls* (1520). There is a 15C German wooden pietà on the right of the sanctuary. Beneath the campanile, there is a Roman cistern. The *crypt* (entrance in the Piazza), part of a former 11C basilica, is also worth seeing (11C frescos, 3C sarcophagus). *Cathedral museum.*

S.Chiara: Begun in 1257. The façade is an imitation of the upper church. Inside: The left transept has frescos by the school of Cimabue and Giotto and an Umbrian-Siennese 'Birth of Christ'. There are also frescos by Giotto's school in the middle vaults above the high altar and in the right transept (one exception is the 'Life of St.Clare', a panel by the anonymous 'Maes-

tro di S.Chiara', (1283)—the large cross in the apse is attributed to the same artist). The 'Crucifix' which spoke to St. Francis in the church of S.Damiano can be found in the *Cappella del Crocefisso*. Adjoining this, the *Chapel of the Sacrament* (frescos by the Giotto school) is part of the former church of S.Giorgio, in which St.Francis was buried and canonized. The body of St.Clare can be seen in the crypt (built in 1850).

Continuing along the route, you pass along the Via S.Agnese and the Via S.Antonio to the *Piazza del Vescovado*, where St. Francis renounced his father's riches. *S.Maria Maggiore* (begun in 1163) is near the Piazza. This church was built above an early Christian church (7 or 9C), which in turn was erected on the site of a pagan temple of Apollo. The interior (one nave, two aisles), is irregular and sober in style. 12&14C frescos. The ciborium is noteworthy (probably after a Provençal model and unique in Italy).

S.Damiano: Along a country road, is a typical Franciscan building, which still has its original atmosphere. S.Damiano is thought to be where St.Francis worked and prayed (it was here that the crucifix spoke to the young man). This was the first house of the Poor Clares. Beneath the three arches of the portico there are 15&16C frescos. The small, single-aisled church has 14C frescos of scenes from the life of St.Francis. Impressive features include the *choir of the Poor Clares* (scenes from St.Clare's life), the convent courtyard and the nuns' *refectory* with frescos by Dono Doni.

S.Maria degli Angeli (on the plain): Begun in 1569, designed by G.Alessi. The campanile was built in 1678–84. In 1832 the basilica was damaged by an earthquake. The present façade dates from 1928. There is a fountain (1610) on the left. Inside, nave and two aisles, with Doric friezes, and a small 4C chapel (the *Cappella della Porziuncola*) where St.Francis established himself with his monks in 1211. Here, on 19.3.1212, the young Chiara had her hair cut by the saint and became a nun. There is a fresco by Johann Friedrich Overbeck

Assisi, cathedral

on the façade of the chapel. The interior is very simple, the only decoration being a large painted panel on the high altar (1393) by Ilario da Viterbo. The *Cappella del Transito*, where St.Francis died, is behind the right-hand column of the cupola. The statue on the altar is by Andrea della Robbia. A fresco depicts the basilica as it was before the earthquake of 1832 (5th chapel on the right from the entrance). Next to it, in the right transept, there is a splendid late 17C altar. The *rose garden*, entry via the sacristy, is also worth seeing.

Castle of Rocca Maggiore: Built before the 11C and destroyed in 1198. In the 14C rebuilding work began on the orders of Cardinal Egidio Albornoz but completion was delayed until the 16C.

Also worth seeing: The remains of the Roman amphitheatre at the Porta Perlici. Nearby, the picturesque *Via S.Maria delle Rose* with 13&14C buildings, including the *Palazzo dei Consoli*.

Environs: Eremo delle Carceri (5 km. from the Porta dei Cappuccini): This spot, in a densely wooded area, is where Francis used to meditate. It is a convenient base for excursions into the countryside. The monastery was built in the first half of the 16C. **Tugurio di Rivotorto** (on the autostrada to Rome): the Franciscan order was founded here. The church (rebuilt after the earthquake in 1854) contains the hovel (tugurio) where the monks lived after the order was founded (1209–11).

Asti 14100
Asti/Piedmont   p.412☐ B 4

Asti, originally a Ligurian, then a Roman settlement, became the seat of a Lombard

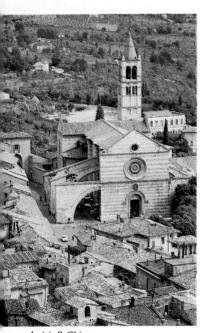

Assisi, S. Chiara

Assisi, Temple of Minerva

duchy in 569 and a diocesan town in 932. It was a free imperial town in the Middle Ages, and fell to Savoy in 1529. Asti is the birthplace of Vittorio Alfieri (1749–1803), the most important 18C Italian tragedian.

Cathedral of S.Maria Assunta and S.Gottardo (Piazza Cattedrale): The Gothic cathedral was built in 1309–54 in alternating colours of bricks. The 13C Romanesque campanile is from the previous building.

Also worth seeing: *S. Secondo* (Piazzo S. Secondo), a Romanesque hall church with a nave and two aisles, built in the 12C Lombard Romanesque style with a 10C crypt; in 1462 it was given a Late Gothic façade on the model of that of the cathedral. The Romanesque *baptistery of S. Pietro in Consavia*; the so-called *Rotonda* (Piazza Medici); the *Palazzo Alfieri*, where Vittorio Alfieri was born; and the *Palazzo*

Bellino and *Museo del Risorgimento*, both rebuilt by Benedetto Alfieri (Corso Vittorio Alfieri).

Atri 64032
Teramo/Abruzzi   p.416□I 8

The ancient town of *Hadria Picena* is said to have given the Adriatic Sea its name. The autonomous city-republic was conquered by Rome in 269 BC. From 1395–1760 it was in the possession of the Counts Acquaviva.

Cathedral of S.Maria Assunta: A new building was erected at the end of the 13C above the earlier 9&10C ones. The façade and campanile were completed by Rainaldo da Atri in 1305, and the frieze on the façade was replaced after the earthquake of 1563. The rectangular façade—

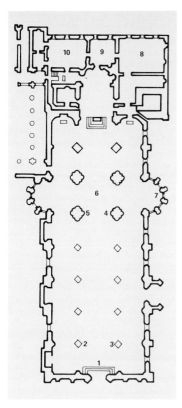

Atri, cathedral

Asti cathedral 1 Urban II consecrating the third cathedral in 1096, fresco by A. Pozzo **2** and **3** holy-water stoups made from capitals from the Romanesque cathedral **4** 12C bas relief of a knight **5** Gothic bas relief of Bishop Baldraco Malabayla giving his blessing **6** frescos of Paradise and the Evangelists in the dome by Bianchi and Milloco **7** chapel of St.Philip Neri or of the Sacrament **8** sacristy with paintings **9** sacristy of the Cappellani **10** chapterhouse with intarsia work, above the entrance is a commemoration of the mass held by Pius VII in the cathedral on 28.4.1805

typical of this area—is divided by two pilaster strips. There is a *rose window* in the middle section and, in a niche above this, a *Madonna*. The frescos on both sides are 15C. Raimondo di Poggio built the middle of the three southern portals in 1288 and the right-hand one in 1302; the one on the left—the Porta Santa—dates from 1305 and is by Rainaldo da Atri. Nave and two aisles. In the *sanctuary* there are frescos by Andrea Delitio (1450). The *mosaic floor*, which has been uncovered, is from the 3/2C BC. The end wall of the N. aisle has a fresco, the *Encounter of the Living and the Dead*, dated 1260. In the S. aisle there are 14&15C frescos, *Madonna lactans*, *Madonna with Goldfinch* and various saints. The *Cappella Acquaviva* and the *font*, which is surmounted by a baldachino and was built from medieval remains, date from 1503. The *cloister* is E. of the church and is used in summer to get to the *crypt* (nave and four aisles). In the middle of the cloister there is a fountain (1763).

Cathedral museum: Liturgical items, valuable paintings, a *Madonna* by Luca della Robbia.

Also worth seeing: *S.Agostino*—portal

probably by Andrea Lombardo, 1470; *Palazzo Ducale*, today the town hall, built by Antonio Acquaviva in the 14C.

Augusta 96011
Syracuse/Sicily   p.420□L 17

The present-day town was founded in 1232 by Emperor ('Augustus') Frederick II of Hohenstaufen, but in Antiquity it was known as 'Xiphonia'. It became important as a naval port in the following years. Completely destroyed by earthquake in 1693 and partly destroyed by an air raid in 1943, today it is an important oil port with refineries.

Cathedral of S.M.Assunta (Via Principe Umberto): Begun in 1644 and only finished in 1769. Inside, nave and two aisles, Latin cross ground plan. A series of 13 paintings in the nave, depicting *Christ and the Apostles*, by an unknown artist is particularly worth seeing.

Castle: Built between 1232–42; bastions from the 16&17C. Today used as prison.

Also worth seeing: *Palazzo del Municipio* (Via Principe Umberto), built in 1699, with a fine Hohenstaufen eagle at the front.

Environs. Some 13 km. SW, the excavations of the ancient town of **Megara Hyblaia**, which was probably founded in 728 BC by Greeks from Megara. The excavations include *remains of the town fortifications* (7&3C BC) as well as *remains of houses, temples* and the *agora*. By the sea (near the remains of the heraion, or temple to Hera) there is a small *museum*. *Fort Avalos* (1569) stands on a small island S. of the town.

Avellino 83100
Avellino/Campania   p.416□L 11

In 1130, the investiture of Roger the Norman as King of Sicily by Anti-Pope Anacletus took place here. Avellino has been the main town of the province since 1806.

Cathedral of S.Maria Assunta (Piazza del Duomo): Founded in the 12C, and subsequently altered many times (most recently in 1868). Classical façade. Inside there are a nave and two aisles; altered in classical style. The following furnishings stand out: a *tabernacle* by Giovanni da Nola (1488–1558) in the chapel to the right of the choir; in the apse, some fine, carved 16C *choir stalls*. The *Cripta dell' Addolorata*, altered in the 18C, lies beneath the church; on the site of a former Roman temple.

Museo Irpino *(Villa Comunale;* Via Roma): The chief exhibits are the *archaeological finds* from the area occupied by the Hirpini (Province of Avellino), from prehistoric times up to the Roman era (notable collection of Italic ceramics and wooden figures). A 1C AD marble *altar* from the ancient Abellinum is particularly worth seeing.

Also worth seeing: 18C church of *S.Maria di Costantinopoli* (Via Umberto I) with a fine 15C fresco, (Madonna and Child) on the high altar. The medieval *Palazzo della Dogana* (Piazza Amendola). A fine *baroque fountain* on the Corso Umberto I. Remains of the medieval *castle*.

Environs: Some 5 km. to the W., **Mercogliano:** From here the road leads up to the most famous pilgrimage church in the Campania, the **Santuario di Montevergine,** founded in 1114 by St.William of Vercelli. The complex consists of the new *basilica* (built 1952 – 61; the sanctuary houses the 13C painting, the 'Madonna di Montevergine'); the adjoining *Chiesa Vecchia* (13C wooden bishop's throne in the sanctuary); and the *monastery* (which also has a small *museum* with ancient and medieval exhibits, including a 13C wooden crucifix).

Aversa 81031
Caserta/Campania   p.416□K 11

Founded by the Normans in 1030, it developed into the main town of the first

Norman fiefdom in Italy. Aversa was the home town of the composer Domenico Cimarosa (1749–1801).

Cathedral of S.Paolo (Piazza del Duomo): Begun in 1053 under the Norman Richard I of Aversa; completed in 1090; rebuilt for the last time in the 18C, after fire and earthquake damage. The apse and the *dome* were part of the original building. The dome is in the Arab-Norman style (octagonal drum, 128 marble columns in two orders, lantern borne by four columns). The left transept has a *Romanesque portal*. Nave and two aisles. Interesting features: a fine *Renaissance altar* (1563) on the right wall of the right transept; a magnificent 11C *Romanesque ambulatory* in the choir; fine vaults; remains of Romanesque sculptures; Three semi-circular apses; 9&10C reliefs on the wall by the altar.

Chiesa l'Annunciata (by the Porta Napoli): Built in the 14C. Reached through a marble *Renaissance arch* (1518). The church façade is baroque, with a three-arched *portico* (cipolin columns) in front of it. Massive 15C *campanile* (beyond the

Porta Napoli). Single-aisled interior. Features of interest: a painting of *John the Evangelist* by Angelillo Arcuccio (1464–92) on the right wall of the 1st side chapel to the right; *Adoration of the Shepherds* by Franco Solimena (1657–1747) on the altar in the left transept.

Also worth seeing: Church of *S.Maria a Piazza* (Piazza Trieste e Trento), 14C, with fine pointed-arch portal. 11C church of *S.Biagio* (Strada S.Biagio), with a fine cloister, partly Romanesque. Church of *S.Francesco* (Strada S.Francesco), founded in the 11C, with 11C portico, in the monks' choir, a fine 13C Madonna in the Byzantine style. The former *monastery of S.Lorenzo*, with Renaissance cloister, lies a short way outside the town. Norman *Castle*.

Avigliana 10051

Turin/Piedmont   p.412☐A 4

Two former glacial lakes lie a few km. to the S. of this picturesque small town. The castle ruins look down on the town. Prob-

La Sacra di S.Michele (Avigliana)

ably founded by the Celts, Avigliana was a camp under the Romans and fell to the Saracens in the 10C. A favourite residence of the house of Savoy (11–15C).

Places of interest: *S.Giovanni Battista* (Piazzetta S.Giovanni); this Romanesque-Gothic parish church, founded in 1284 and completed in 1320, has a 15C Renaissance façade. Inside, paintings by D.Ferrari from the early 15C are the main feature of the decorations. *S.Pietro*, a Romanesque-Gothic church, was built in the 9&10C. It has a fresco depicting the castle. The castle was built from the 10C on, and destroyed first in 1536 and then finally in 1692. 13&14C *Torre dell'Orologio* (Via dell'Orologio). The *Porta Ferronia* (Via Oscar Borgesa), fine Gothic gate.

Environs: Abbazia di S.Antonio di Ranverso. The abbey was founded in 1188 for the Antonites who cared for pa-tients suffering from 'St.Antony's fire'. The church is a typical example of those Gothic buildings in Piedmont which were influenced by the French Gothic style. The present 14&15C structure has a façade topped by projecting high gables. Notable features inside include: the Gothic *frescos* (1426) in the choir and the *altar-piece* of the high altar, *c.* 1520, one of the main works of D.Ferrari. **La Sacra di S.Michele** *Abbazia della Chiusa:* This massive, partly ruined monastery, one of the most important artistic monuments in Piedmont, stands on the slope of Monte Pirchiriano (fine view). Under the Lombards it was a shrine of St.Michael, and in 998 a fortified place of pilgrimage. Rebuilt *c.* 1050, badly damaged by fire in 1339. The church has a nave, two aisles, and a *crypt* with three chapels from different centuries. Inside, just to the right of the entrance, there is a fine 15C *fresco cycle* by Secondo del Bosco da Poirino. The *sanctuary* has splendid 15C frescos. The *altarpiece* of the high altar was painted by D.Ferrari.

Baceno 28031
Novara/Piedmont   p.412□C 2

S.Gaudenzio: The parish church was built in the early 14C with a nave and two aisles. In the 16C the number of aisles was increased to four. There is a fresco showing the *Adoration of the Magi* (1505) in the tympanum of the portal in the façade. Beside the portal is a fresco depicting *St.Christopher* (1542) by Antonio Zanetti. The inside of the church is also decorated with frescos, mostly by Antonio Zanetti.

Badia Polesine 45021
Rovigo/Veneto   p.410□F 4

Abbazia della Vangadizza: Founded in the 10C and later handed over to the Camaldolensians. Certain parts are open to the public: *cloister*, with *loggia*; 15C *well*; *refectory* (1466), and also other remains dating from the same time. An overall impression of the once imposing complex is gained from the following: traces of three apses; the campanile (late 12C) with a bas-relief of Hellenistic-Roman origin; and a large chapel dated 1490, the *Cappella della Madonna*.

Bagheria 90011
Palermo/Sicily   p.420□I 16

Villa Palagonia: This, the best-known of Bagheria's villas, is in serious disrepair. Built in 1715, by Tomaso di Napoli and Agatino Daidone, it is late baroque in style. Both villa and garden house a collection of curiosities; Goethe, during his Italian

Bagheria, Villa Palagonia

journey in 1787, called them 'Fantastically crazy works of art'. The park wall bears figures of musicians, dancers, horsemen, ancient heroes, gods, dwarfs, headless monsters, dragons and chimerae.

Also worth seeing: *Villa Butera* (1656), with a waxwork collection; the splendidly situated *Villa Valguarnera* (1721); *Villa Ramacca* and *Villa S.Isidoro*, both 17C.

Environs: To the N. of Bagheria (near S.Flavia), there are excavations of the ancient town of **Soluntum** (at the foot of M.Catalfano). It was founded by Carthaginians in the 4C BC, conquered by Romans *c.* 250 BC and rebuilt on a Hellenistic, *i.e.* chequered, ground plan. Later, abandoned by the inhabitants, it was finally destroyed by Saracens. Excavation work began in 1826, but has only been carried out systematically since 1951. Of the so-called *Gymnasium*, some Doric columns are still standing; remains of *paved roads* have survived. Other excavated finds include the Hellenistic *theatre* (partly built into the side of a mountain), and *Roman residential buildings* (in the typically Roman style, with an atrium and peristyle). There is a small *museum*.

Bagnacavallo 48012
Ravenna/Emilia-Romagna   p.410☐G 5

S.Michele (Via Mazzini): The collegiata is 15C; a polygonal apse survives from the original building. Façade, nave and aisles were rebuilt in 1584–1622. Paintings inside include: *Saviour with Saints* (1542) by Bagnacavallo, and *Sacra Conversazione with Peter and Paul* by his school.

S.Pietro in Sylvis (Via Garibaldi): Brick building of a type found in Ravenna; perhaps as late as the early 7C. The church was extensively restored in 1932–3. The apse has good frescos (painted in 1320–5 under the influence of Pietro da Rimini and well restored at the end of the 1960s): in the semicircular vault, *Christ enthroned between the Apostles*; underneath it *Crucifixion with Mary* and *John*, in the middle of a series of apostles.

S.Francesco (Via Ramenghi): Built above a 14C structure. A 14C *painted cross possibly by Giovanni da Rimini*, and a 15C *Dutch panel* are particularly fine.

Bagheria, Villa Valguarnera

Also worth seeing: The *market place* (Piazza Nuova, Via Cesare Battisti), 1759. The *Istituto delle Opere Pie Raggruparte* (Via Mazzini 3), with 15&16C paintings. The *Piazza Libertà* with clock tower (15C), town hall (No. 12), and next to it, the 18C Teatro Comunale Goldoni, and Biblioteca Civica Taroni (No. 5).

Bagno di Romagna 47021
Forlì/Emilia-Romagna   p.414☐G 6

S.Maria Assunta: From the 2nd half of the 11C; given its present form in the 15C. In 1874 it was restored and slightly altered. Parts of the façade, which has a fine 15C portal, are Romanesque. Mainly 15C furnishings; a particularly interesting *triptych of the Ascension and Saints* (1468) by Neri di Bicci (1419–91), and *Mother of God with John the Evangelist and John the Baptist* by the school of Andrea del Sarto.

Palazzo Pretorio: The façade of this 16C palace has numerous *coats of arms* from the Florentine period. Inside, there is a fresco from the school of Luca Signorelli.

Bagnoli Irpino 83043
Avellino/Campania   p.418☐L 11

Parish church of S.Maria Assunta: Built in the 17C, in the baroque style; double stairway in front of the façade. Inside, the *choir stalls* have fine 17C carvings (scenes from the Old and New Testaments) by craftsmen from a local wood-carving school.

S.Domenico: Renovated in the 16C. A portico with fine old columns stands in front of the façade. The inside is rather neglected but there are interesting *paintings*, and carved *choir stalls*. The *Cloister* is part of the Renaissance remains of the monastery.

Also worth seeing: The *Pinacoteca Comunale* in the town hall.

Environs: Some 30 km. NE, **S.Angelo dei Lombardi,** an old Lombard settlement: The *cathedral* (originally 11C, with a fine Renaissance portal) is worth a visit. Some 7 km. SW of S.Angelo, the old 12C *S.Guglielmo di Goleto*; the 'Chiesa Piccola' and the campanile of 1152 are worth seeing.

Bari 70100
Bari/Apulia   p.416☐N 11

Bari, today the second largest city in Southern Italy after Naples, was utterly unimportant in ancient times (when it was known as Barium). The town was the centre of Byzantine power in Southern Italy in the early Middle Ages, and was conquered by the Norman Duke, Robert Guiscard, in 1070. From 1324–1558 it was the main town of a virtually independent fiefdom, falling once again to the Kingdom of Naples when its rulers died out.

Basilica of S.Nicola (road from the Lungomare Imperatore Augusto is signposted): The 'mother' of all the Romanesque

Bagnacavallo, Madonna (Dürer)

churches in Apulia. In 1087, sailors from Bari took the remains of St.Nicholas of Myra from Asia Minor to Bari. The basilica containing these remains was built on the ruins of the palace of the Byzantine governor. The crypt was consecrated in 1089, and the church completed in 1197. Most of the medieval obstructions have been removed. The *W.façade* is magnificent, and the use of bulls as stylophores for a Romanesque portal, is unique in Apulia. The apse contains the most astonishing of Apulian Romanesque works of art, the *throne of Bishop Elia*, who was Archbishop of Bari at the time the church was built. In front of it there is the only *pyx* to have survived undamaged in Apulia.

Cathedral of S.Sabino (at the end of the Strada di Carmine): A site formerly occupied by a Byzantine building, which was altered and extended by Archbishop Bisanzius in 1024–40. In 1156 the entire complex was destroyed by the Norman king, William I. Rebuilt *c.* 1160 on the model of the basilica of St.Nicholas. The apse is adorned by a magnificent *window*. In the 18C the portals were rebuilt in the baroque style. Inside there are the first *false galleries* (openings only serving to vary the appearance of the masses of masonry) to be found in an Apulian pillared basilica. Only a few of the original church furnishings survive, e.g. bishop's throne, pyx, pulpit and choir screens. In the sacristy there are parts of an 11C *exsultet roll* (the eulogy in the Catholic Easter liturgy), and in the crypt, a Byzantine *painting of the Madonna*.

Castle (Corso Trieste): Probably formerly a Byzantine building, taken over and extended by the Normans. In 1233 Emperor Frederick II had the building rebuilt and extended still further (particularly the basement in the N. wing). Frederick II is said to have met Francis of Assisi here. The appearance of the building was subsequently changed considerably; Charles I of Anjou added to it, and, in 1501, Isabella Sforza began the fortifications which today surround the Norman central section. After being used alternately as a barracks and a prison, it is today a *museum for copies of Apulian-Romanesque sculpture*.

Also worth seeing: 11C *S.Gregorio*, with fine windows (next door to S.Nicola). 19C *Teatro Petruzelli*, one of Italy's largest theatres (Corso Cavour). *Lungomare Nazario Sauro*, the seaside road with many buildings from the Fascist period. The *Archaeological Museum* (Piazza Battisti), which includes a collection of antique vases and finds from Canusium. The *Pinacoteca Provinciale* (Lungomare N.Sauro) has a collection of medieval paintings, and sculpture and pictures by Giovanni Bellini and others.

Environs: Bitetto, with the 14C cathedral of *S.Michele*, a late Romanesque-Apulian building with a fine portal (about 15 km. SW).

Barletta 70051

Bari/Apulia   p.416☐N 10

Cathedral of S.Maria Maggiore (Via del Duomo): Begun *c.* 1140, in Romanesque style. Of the oldest section only the 4 W. bays of the nave are now standing. The walls of the original apse were discovered in the crypt. After 1307 the E. section of the cathedral was extended in the Gothic style and given two more bays, but with only two storeys; two further bays were added at the end of the 14C. Inside, the *pyx* and *pulpit* are partly 13C. The middle chapel of the five apsidal chapels contains the *'Madonna della Disfida'*, painted by P.Serafini, in 1387.

S.Sepolcro (Corso V.Emanuele): In 1162, the town walls were extended and the church was included within the town. It was rebuilt in Burgundian-Cistercian style. On the W. side, there is an inner narthex, with a chapel above. There are also 13C frescos above the narthex.

Colossus of Barletta (immediately in front of S.Sepolcro): According to prevail-

Bari, S.Nicola, bishop's throne of Elia ▷

Bari, castle

ing opinion, this statue, 14 ft. 9 in. high, is the only original ancient bronze statue and depicts the Late Roman Emperor Valentinian I (AD 364–75). This statue was to be taken from Constantinople to Venice, in 1204, as the booty of the Venetians, but it arrived in Barletta. In 1309 monks cast bells from its arms and legs; since 1491 the restored figure has stood in the same place.

Also worth seeing: *S.Andrea*, with fine 13–14C portal. 13C Hohenstaufen *Castle* (not open). *Museo Comunale* (Corso Garibaldi), with the famous 'Bust of Barletta' (long regarded as a likeness of Emperor Frederick II). *Palazzo di Monte di Pietà* with *Jesuit church*, a fine Baroque ensemble (near the Piazza della Sfida). *Cantina della Disfida.*

Environs: Italy's largest salt-works are some 15 km. N., up the coast, at **Margerita di Savoia.**

Barúmini 09051
Cágliari/Sardinia   p.422☐C 13

It is still possible to see Romanesque features in the Late Gothic parish church (begun 1541). The altarpiece is by the school of P.Cavaro (16C). The colourfully painted 15C wooden shrine is based on Catalan models. Barúmini is known around the world for its nuraghi fortifications.

Su Nuraxi: A nuraghi fortification with a late nuraghi settlement (from the 8–6C BC), and buildings from an earlier time. Since 1951, as a result of excavations, mill chambers, baking ovens, storage houses, wells and even a bathing area have been on view. The main stronghold, with a central tower (1500–1450 BC, originally three-storeyed), together with corner towers (added later, in 9–8C BC) and the well, with

Barletta, colossus of Barletta

Barúmini, nuraghic settlement

its deep ground water, forms a complete unit in itself. During the 8–6C BC, an additional external wall was added, with 7 round towers and a NE outwork. It was captured by Carthage at the end of the 6C BC, and partially destroyed.

Environs: Remains of *small nuraghi* lie hidden at the place where the Giara di Géxturi breaks off (there are still wild asses and small reddish-brown wild horses living here). These nuraghi probably date from after the capture of Su Nuraxi by Carthage. The church of *San Pietro* in **Tuili** has an altarpiece of the Trinity, by the anonymous master of Castelsardo (late 15C). *Las Plassas*, a 12C ruined castle and former border fortification of the Giudicato of Arborea stands on a nearby mountain. In the *village church* of **Mándas**, parts of the original Gothic–Catalan building have survived, e.g. the stellar vault; there are also some 15C

painted, wooden statues. The 15C Gothic-Aragon building style is still apparent in the *parish church* of **Gergei**; 16C altarpiece by a pupil of P.Cavaro. In the SW, there is a fine *giant grave*, near Nuraghe Preganti; in the S., as far as the Rio Murera valley, there are several remains of *nuraghi*. A paved road leads from Serri, via the Giara di Serri, to the restored small, medieval church, *Sante Vittoria*, and to the like-named Nuraghe *spring temple*, in front of a spacious shrine. The spring temple is built from skilfully-hewn blocks of basalt and, in layout, is probably the finest of any of the similar old complexes. Around it there is an oval Cyclops wall, with a crescent-shaped opening; then a moat and a drainage gutter (for sacrificial blood?); finally, an elevated ante-room and a stairwell with 13 steps into the hollow cone of the spring—all of which is surmounted by a dome. To the W. there are two altars and guardrooms, which are screened off by a defensive complex with a jumble of walkways. To the E. is the sacred precinct, which is a broad oval, with a leafed corridor, several 'houses' and functional buildings. The importance of this complex extended over a large area and, apart from the Carthaginians (whose presence is documented by finds), it must later have held Byzantine troops (soldiers' graves exist) to protect the communications from Caralis into the island's interior. The *Nuraghe Is Paras* is near the road N. out of the town; it has been restored since 1975 and possesses splendid imitation vaulting. Some 3 km. N., near the road, perched on a crag of stratified rock, are the ruins of the Romanesque *Chiesetta di San Sebastiano*. In the little church of *Maria 'e Aleanza* in Nuragus, the holy-water stoup rests on a Roman milestone. The *Nuraghe Serra Illici* has bronze bars from Crete (Cyprus?), dated from the 14C BC.

Bassano del Grappa 36061

Vicenza/Veneto   p.410☐G 3

Known as *Fundus Baxianus* in the late antique period. A succession of rulers (including the Scaligeri and Visconti); Venetian since 1404. Famous for its independent school of painters (chief representative, Jacopo da Ponte). Home of the baroque sculptor Orazio Marinali.

Cathedral of S.Maria in Colle: Begun in the 11C, rebuilt several times in the 15C and thereafter. Hall church, nave no aisles, barrel-vaulted sanctuary. 12C Romanesque *wooden crucifix* on the altar ; fine marble statues by Marinali on the so-called *Altare del Rosario*. A *Nativity* by Jacopo da Ponte — known as *Bassano* — graces the chapel to the left of the sanctuary.

S.Francesco (Piazza Garibaldi): Built by Franciscans in the 12C; a portico, in the form of a baldachino, was added in 1306. Inside, the structure is very sober, embellished solely by pilaster-strips with a pointed-arch frieze above. A fresco of the *Annunciation, c.* 1400 to the right of the entrance. Nave with open timbering; choir apse with ribbed vaults. 15C *painted crucifix* in the sanctuary. The *tomb of Francesco da Ponte*, the painter (d.1592), is to the left of the entrance.

Bassano del Grappa, view with the bridge over the Brenta (1569)

S.Giovanni Battista (Piazza Libertà): Begun in 1308, rebuilt by Giovanni Miazzi in 1747–82; monumental façade. Within, the *Cappella del Sacramento* has fine statues of angels by Orazio Marinali. There is a 15C *Pietà* in the chapel opposite the main door.

Museo Civico (Via del Museo): Gives a good overall idea of the works of Jacopo Bassano and his school; many drawings by Antonio Canova.

Ponte degli Alpini: The bridge across the Brenta is one of the town's landmarks. First mentioned in 1209. Covered with an open roof truss. Rebuilt in 1569 to Palladio's plans after successive destructions and reconstructions.

Environs: Some 7 km. to the SW, **Maróstica**, which has a fine medieval townscape. In the parish church there is a masterpiece by Jacopo and Francesco Bassano, entitled *St.Paul in Athens*, (1574). *Cartigliano:* Magnificent *fresco-cycle* by Jacopo Bassano in the *Cappella della Madonna* of the parish church.

Bastia 06083
Perugia/Umbria   p.414☐H 7

S.Croce: Building began at the end of the 12C; redesigned in the 15C. Inside: a fresco by Tiberio d'Assisi, depicting the Passion of St.Luke, and a triptych by Nicola da Foligno.

Also worth seeing: Remains of medieval *town wall*. The former fortress now houses a Benedictine monastery; some fine 15C *houses*.

Battaglia Terme 35041
Padua/Veneto   p.410☐G 4

Villa Emo Capodilista: A flight of 142 steps leads to the villa up on the *Hill of S.Elena*. Begun in 1593 and completed in the mid 17C. Heinrich Heine was a guest

here. The *dome* (inspired by Oriental examples) is a striking feature between battlemented corner turrets. The *main façade*, in the style of Andrea Palladio, faces S.and is most imposing. On the first floor there are four large frescos by Luca Ferrari (1650).

Belluno 32100
Belluno/Veneto   p.410☐G 2

At the confluence of the rivers Ardo and Piave and surrounded by mountains. A provincial town, it can look back upon a long history, beginning in the pre-Roman period. It was a Roman municipium, then fell into the hands of the Lombards; later governed by the Church and the Carrara, Scaligeri and Visconti families. The town allied with Venice in 1404.

Cathedral of S.Maria Assunta (Piazza del Duomo): Designed by Tullio Lombardo in the early 16C, it replaced an earlier 13C structure. (Apse and dome restored.) The rough, rather sober façade accentuates the nave. Two rather plain aisles are covered by lean-to roofs. Each has a portal (1578) and is lit by a round window. On the right, outer wall there is a fine, 15C *Crucifixion*, which, regrettably, is much damaged. To the left, a baroque tower by Filippo Juvarra (1732–43), 226 ft. tall has a massive pedestal. The interior, with nave and two aisles, is impressive for its simplicity and its beautiful 18C *marble altars*. Good paintings by Jac. Bassano, *Martyrdom of St.Lawrence* and *Entombment* by Palma il Giovane (4th altar on the right). The two 16C *marble sculptures of St.Lucanus* and *St.Jonathan* are attributed to Tullio Lombardo. In the crypt, which has two aisles, a *sarcophagus* with fine 14C reliefs is used as an altar table.

Palazzo dei Rettori (Piazza del Duomo, No. 38): Former seat of the Venetian Governor. Splendid Renaissance façade; ground floor with arcades, and two upper floors of arched windows and ornate balconies, (shields and busts were added later).

Bassano del Grappa, Flight into Egypt, Bassano

Belluno, Palazzo dei Rettori

S.Stefano (Piazza S.Stefano): Essentially Gothic in form and detail, this church was built in 1468. Fine 14C *portal*, in front of which there is an interesting Roman *sarcophagus* with hunting scenes. Inside, nave, two aisles, high Gothic arcades and ribbed vault. The chapel to the left of the sanctuary has a carving, the *Madonna della Salute* by A. di Foro; set in gold, it is full of colour and figures. In the left side aisle there is a carving of the *Crucified Christ*, by Andrea Brustolon.

Also worth seeing: The *Museo Civico* in the Palazzo dei Giuristi (Via Duomo): The museum contains a number of fine paintings, especially those on the 1st floor, e.g. paintings by S.Ricci (born in Belluno), Matteo Cesa, Palma il Giovane, B.Montagna etc. The *Piazza del Mercato* is very picturesque, with a charming *fountain* (1410), Renaissance buildings, and arbours. From the *Via Mezzaterra*, which passes through old Belluno, a walk to the *Porta Rugo* (12C; restored, 1622), is rewarded with a fine view.

Benevagienna 12041
Cuneo/Piedmont   p.412□B 5

S. Assunta (Piazza Botero): A 15C parish church, restored in the 17&18C; Gothic campanile.

Also worth seeing: *Chiesa della Misericordia* (Via XX Settembre): built in 1713–34 to plans by Francesco Gallo. The campanile was built in 1671. *Castle* (Via Vittorio Emanuele II), today a hospital. A fine, square 14C building. *Museo Civico* (Via Roma) has items from Augusta Bagiennorum.

Environs: *Augusta Bagiennorum:* A Roman town from 1C BC; destroyed in the 4C AD.

Benevento 82100
Benevento/Campania   p.416□L 11

Until Pyrrhus's victory over the Romans, in 275 BC, the town was known as 'Maleventum' (bad outcome). In 268 BC, a military colony was founded and the town was renamed Beneventum (good outcome). It was an important ancient centre of communications (junction of Via Appia with other Roman roads). From the 6–11C, Benevento was the residence of Lombard Dukes, and until 1860 it was part of the Papal States.

Cathedral (Piazza del Duomo): First built in the 7C and expanded into a building with a nave and two aisles in the 11C; in the 12C, enlarged again into a nave and five aisles. Rebuilt in the baroque style in the 18C. Restored extensively after damage in World War 2. Fine 13C Pisan-Tuscan *façade* (fragments of the main portal's famous *bronze door*, dating from the 1st half of the 13C, can be found in the Biblioteca Capitolare). The walls of the *Campanile* (1279) incorporate ancient Roman reliefs.

On entering the church proper, there is a baptism chapel on the right. In the left aisle, the 'Cappella del Sacramento' has 18 *marble columns* from the original building.

S. Sofia (Piazza Matteotti): Founded by the Lombards in the 8C and rebuilt after the earthquake of 1688. Today, well restored to its original form. Fine 13C *portal*. Very interesting interior with unusual ground plan. There are remains of an 8C *fresco cycle* (scenes from the story of Zacharias) in the two smaller apses. Picturesque 12C *cloister* (with horseshoe arches above) adjoins the church. Behind the church is the Museo del Sannio, see below.

Arco di Traiano (Via Traiano): Also known as *Porta Aurea*, it is the town's landmark, and one of the best-preserved of Roman triumphal arches. 51 ft. tall, it was made from Greek marble, in honour of the Emperor Trajan (inscription on the attic) in AD 114. Famous for *reliefs* glorifying the Emperor's deeds.

Teatro Romano (Via Port'Arsa): Built under the Emperor Hadrian (AD 117–38) and extended under Caracalla in AD 200–10. A stand for spectators, with room for some

Benevento, S. Sofia

20,000 people, has survived in excellent condition.

Rocca dei Rettori (Piazza IV Novembre): Built in 1321 on the ruins of a Lombard (or earlier) fortification; used as a prison until the 19C. Consists of 2 complexes. On the left, the *castle* itself, with fine pointed-arch windows and a polygonal ground plan. On the right, the former *seat of the 'Delegazione Apostolica'*. Ancient Roman buildings, including a strong gate, have been uncovered in the S. of the complex. The Rocca houses the *Department of History and Folklore* of the 'Museo del Sannio'.

Museo del Sannio (near S.Sofia, see above): Houses notable *Prehistoric and Archaeological Collection*. Room XI has Graeco-Italian ceramics; fine Greek, Roman and Egyptian statues. Room XXII has a large *collection of mainly ancient coins*, with particularly fine examples from Magna Graecia and from the Roman and Lombard periods. The top floor houses the *picture gallery* (three paintings by Luca Giordano).

Also worth seeing: *S.Bartolomeo* (Piazza F. Torre): 18C, with richly decorated interior. *S.Domenico* (Piazza F.D. Guerazzi) in the baroque style (rebuilt after being destroyed in World War 2). *Chiesa dell' Annunziata* (Via Pellegrini): built in the 17&18C, with fine stucco work inside. Basilica of the *Madonna delle Grazie* (Viala S.Lorenzo): a 19C neoclassical building; on the high altar a fine carved figure of the Madonna, probably by Giovanni da Nola (1488–1558). The Roman *Ponte Leproso*, reached from the Port'Arsa, carries the ancient Via Appia across the river Sabato. The *Biblioteca Capitolare* (in the Archbishop's Palace, Piazza Orsini) has a large collection of manuscripts. The Egyptian *obelisk* of unhewn granite was raised in AD 88 (Corso Garibaldi).

Bergamo 24100
Bergamo/Lombardy   p.412☐D 3

The old Gallic foundation of the Orobians fell to Rome in 197 BC, and in 49 BC it became a municipium. A diocesan town from the mid-4C onwards. Destroyed by the Visigoths under Alaric in 408, and again

Benevento, Arco di Traiano   *Benevento, cathedral, the bronze door* ▷

by Attila's hordes in 452. From 575 it was the main town of a Lombard duchy, which had its heyday under Theodolinda's government. In 776 it was made a free commune. During the 10&11C, power was in the hands of the bishops. The commune took shape at the beginning of the 12C (consuls are documented as early as 1112). In 1166 the town successfully resisted Barbarossa. Bergamo became one of the most active members of the First Lombard League of Towns. The dispute between Guelphs (Colleoni family) and Ghibellines (Suardi family), who were the representatives of the aristocracy, was increased by their clashes with the representatives of the people. It was mainly the Visconti (of Milan) who harassed the town from outside. In 1408–9 it came under the dominion of Pandolfo Malatesta, followed by the Visconti. In 1428, after the battle of Maclodio, the Visconti ceded it to Venice, under whose power Bergamo remained until 1797.

Città alta: The town consists of the *Città alta* (upper town) and the mainly 19C *Città bassa* (lower town). The Città alta is still completely surrounded by its wall and

Bergamo, city square

gives an impressive picture of medieval town building. The main axis (Via Gombuto and Via B.Colleoni) begins in the Piazza Mercato delle Scarpe and runs fairly precisely through the middle of the upper town. Halfway along, on the left, it opens into the Piazza Vecchia, the old centre of Bergamo, with the Biblioteca, the Pal. del Podestà and the Pal. della Ragione, which forms the link with the Piazza del Duomo behind it (Cathedral, S.Maria Maggiore with Cappella Colleoni, and the Baptistery).

Piazza Vecchia: This square was given its clear, regular shape in 1440–93 when several houses were removed. In the middle it has a *fountain* (1780).

Palazzo della Ragione: The building, dating from 1198, was burned down in 1513. It was restored in 1538–54, in the style of the early 12C. On the ground floor there is an open arcade, which leads to the cathedral square; above the hall is the council chamber. A Venetian window, surmounted by the lions of St.Mark, forms the central opening of the triforium, on the side facing the Piazza Vecchia. On one of the arcade's pillars there is a statue of Torquato Tasso (1681). To the right of the Palazzo della Ragione there is a roofed staircase leading to the *council chamber*. Behind it is the 12C *Torre de Comune*, also known as Torre del Campanone, which was originally the Suardi's fortified tower. The building occupying the NE side of the square was formerly the residence of the Podestà of Venice. The SE side of the square is has the *Palazzo della Biblioteca*, begun in 1604 to A.Vanone's plans and completed by V.Scamozzi in 1611. This building, in a style characteristic of Venetian State buildings, was used as a town hall from 1648–1873, and now houses the municipal library.

Piazza del Duomo: A narrow square surrounded by tall buildings which, despite the disparity between them, make a harmonious overall impression. The group formed by S.Maria Maggiore with the Colleoni chapel dominates the NW side with its exuberant façade.

S.Maria Maggiore: On the site of a church dating back to 774. Building began in 1137 and was completed c. 1200. A basilica with a nave, two aisles and a tower over the crossing; the transepts originally had 2 apses each, 3 of which still survive. Nave and transept are of equal length, thereby giving the impression of a centrally planned building. The exterior is Lombard-Romanesque, with an octagonal stepped-back tower over the crossing, dwarf galleries on the apse and a decorative band running around the whole building. The entrance in the SE transept functions as the main door. It has a delightful portico by Giovanni da Campione (1350–3): an arch carved with an animal frieze is supported by two columns, themselves resting on two lions. Above the arch is a little loggia with four columns and the figures of St.Barbara, St.Alexander (mounted) and St.Vincent; the whole is surmounted by a pyramidal canopy with statues of the Madonna and Child and of St.Esteria and St.Grata. The portal proper has richly worked jambs. The other (N.) transept has a simpler portico of 1360, also by G.da Campione. The *interior* was completely redecorated with stucco from the end of the 16C to the mid-17C. Remains of 14C *frescos*: 'Last Supper', on the wall next to the main entrance; on the opposite transept wall, 'St.Bonaventure's Tree of Life' (1347). Sumptuous Flemish *tapestries* hang in all parts of the church. Against pillars, in front of the choir, there are two *marble pulpits* (1591–1602) with bronze staircases and 6 magnificent *candelabras* (1597). The choir opening itself is closed off by a choir screen with a triumphal arch, above which is a 14C *triumphal cross*. The choir screen's balustrade forms the rear of the choir stalls, and has remarkable *intarsia panels*, with Old Testament scenes, after models by L.Lotto. The *choir stalls* were carved and inlaid by Bergamasque craftsmen in 1522–55. Frescos in the apse (1595) and in the dome (angels and prophets) are by Cavagna. At the end of the nave there are monuments to the composer G.Donizetti (1855) and the musician Simon Mayr (1852). The painting 'Crossing of the Red Sea' by Luca Giordano, 1681, is also here. At the side of the nave, next to the monument to Simon Mayr, is that to Cardinal Longhi (1320, Ugo Campione). On the other side of the nave there is a richly carved confessional.

Bergamo, view

88   Bergamo

Cappella Colleoni: Built in 1472–6 by sculptor and architect Giovanni Antonio Amadeo. The chapel is part of S.Maria Maggiore's transept—by order of Colleoni, a transept apse (the sacristy) was broken off for this purpose. In the 15C, the chapel was known as the Cappella sepulchri (burial chapel), in the 16&17C, as the Cappella della Pietà (devotional chapel) and in the 19C, as Mausoleo del Capitano. Architecturally, the chapel is modelled on the Florentine example of the Old Sacristy of S.Lorenzo, one of the Medici burial chapels. *Façade:* Decoratively, rather than architecturally subdivided. Around the base there are Old Testament scenes and the story of Hercules. Pilaster strips bear heads of famous men of antiquity and heads of the apostles. On a pediment above the door, there is the mourning motif of a curtain, with guardian angel. The statue of a warrior, Colleoni, as the new Joshua, stands above the wheel window. **Inside:** On the main wall, is the *monument to Colleoni*, with two sarcophagi above one another. The lower one contains the remains of the condottiere, the upper serves as the base for the equestrian monument spanned by a triumphal arch. The whole is rich in symbolism. The gilded *equestrian statue* of Colleoni as Captain-General of the Venetian Republic, is flanked by the Virtues. On the wall leading to the transept is the tomb of Colleoni's daughter Medea (1470), who died young. Some of the remaining decoration was restored in the 18C, including the paintings in the lunettes (G.B.Tiepolo) and on the entrance wall (Pittoni). The sanctuary has paintings by Tiepolo in the lunettes and a 'Holy Family' by Angelica Kaufmann.

Duomo S.Alessandro: Dedicated to St.Vincent until 1688, the date of rebuilding. The previous buildings date from the 8,13&15C. In the 19C, parts of Carlo Fontana's design were greatly altered (dome 1853, façade 1886). The 18C interior is single-aisled, has a Latin cross groundplan and is richly decorated. *Church Furnishings:* Elegant choir stalls. On the left of the transept is the Martyrdom of Saint John the Bishop by Tiepolo, 1743. On the front wall of the left transept is a bas-relief by

Andrea Fantoni. The *Cappella del SS. Sacramento* (1855) is on the left of the nave. The altar has a panel by Moroni (1576).

Baptistery: A small octagonal structure. Built in 1340 by Giovanni da Campione and inside S.Maria Maggiore since 1898. On the upper floor, going all around the building, there is a delicate loggia enclosed by bars.

Also worth seeing in the Città alta (old town): *Ateneo,* W. of the cathedral, built for the Accademia degli Ecitati at the end of the 18C. Since 1810 it has housed the Academy of Fine Arts. *S.Croce* (on the W. side of S.Maria Maggiore), small 11C centrally-planned building with 4 apses. *S.Grata:* built in 1591, with a late (baroque) portal. The 2nd altar on the left has a painting, Madonna with saints, by G.P.Cavagna. Beside S.Grata, is the *Museo Donizetti* (Donizetti was born in Bergamo). The *Ginnaseo Liceo* (1846) is a massive complex of buildings. *Palazzo Terzi* (Piazza Terzi), has a façade of 1631 with colonnaded passage and large terrace (fine panorama). The *Porta S. Giacomo* is a typical town gate with Tuscan-Doric order (1561 –98). *Casa del Arciprete* (Via Donizetti) of 1520, with decorative window frames. *Mura:* the ramparts of the upper town, built by the Venetians in 1561–85, in place of the medieval wall there are 4 gates and 16 bastions or platforms. *S.Pancrazio* (Via Gombito): 10C, completely rebuilt in the 16C. 14C *Carmelite church* (Via B.Colleoni): restored in 1451 and 1730. Cloister with two-storeyed galleries (15–16C). The *Luogo Pio della Pietà* (Via B.Colleoni No. 9–11) was the former town house of Colleoni who, in 1475, turned it into a charitable establishment; interesting decoration. *Rocca:* fortification begun in 1331 by John of Luxemburg, further expanded by the Visconti, then by the Venetians, and once again in 1850, by the Austrians. *S. Andrea* (Via Porta Dipinta), completely rebuilt in 1840–7. Inside, a Madonna Enthroned with Saints by Moretto (2nd chapel on the right). *S.Michele al Pozzo Bi-*

S.Maria Maggiore (Capp. Colleoni) ▷

Capp. Colleoni, tomb of Colleoni

anco (Via Porta Dipinta): 12–13C, with 14C frescos in the choir. *S.Agostino* (by the Porta S.Agostino): a secularized monastery, founded in the late 12C; a church from the first half of the 14C. Two cloisters on the N. side. *Porta S.Agostino:* town gate (1575).

Città bassa: The Borgo (town quarter) of S.Lorenzo (S. of the upper town) and the Borgi of S.Antonio, Pignolo and S.Caterina (SE of the upper town) developed very rapidly during the 19C, as a result of increasing industrialization. In 1909, a competition was announced for an urban plan covering the area in the middle of these quarters, which even at the beginning of the 20C had hardly any buildings on it; (since the 10C, it had been used as a fairground). The Porta Nuova, (a former customs post) at that time an isolated building, was now to be included in the plan. The contract went to Marcello Piacentini. Work began in 1914 and continued until 1927. The centre of the Città bassa today comprises *five squares* connected by monumental buildings which make a grand impression. These squares are among the most interesting urban developments of the first half of the 20C. The *Vi-*

Trescore Balneario (Bergamo)

Accademia Carrara, Montegua

ale Giovanni XXIII leads into the *Porta Nuova*, built in 1837 in a cool classical style, as an imposing town gate. Behind it, the *Piazza Matteotti* with the *town hall* (formerly Palazzo Frizzoni, 1825–40): fine courtyard and staircase, good interior decoration. The Piazza Matteotti passes into the smaller, arcaded *Piazza Vittorio Veneto*. To the left is the *Torre dei Caduti* (memorial to the fallen). Between the Piazza Vittorio Veneto and the Piazza Matteotti is the so-called *Sentirone*, a broad promenade extending NE; arcades on one side and the dominating façade of the Teatro Donizetti on the other. The Sentirone ends with the façade (1897) of the 17C S.Bartolomeo as its backdrop. Inside: behind the high altar, there is a panel by L.Lotto dated 1516 (Madonna and Child with Saints). The Teatro Donizetti stands beside the small Piazza Cavour and the *Prefettura*, 1867, is behind it (Via Torquato Tasso). The visitor passes through the arcades of the Sentirone in order to turn into the *Piazza Dante*, which has an 18C fountain in the centre. The square is surrounded by administrative buildings; to the N., the Palace of Justice. Behind it is the *Piazza della Libertà*, the newest of the squares (1930–

Pontida (Bergamo), Benedictine abbey

Bergamo, Accademia Carrara, Moroni

Accademia Carrara, Bellini

5), with the monumental Palazzo della Libertà (spectacular portico).

Churches of the lower town: *S.Marta* (behind the Torre dei Caduti): cloister with two-storeyed gallery. *S.Alessandro in Colonna* (Via S.Alessandro): probably founded as early as the 6C; the existing building is 18C. Spacious interior; in the sacristy there is an Entombment by L.Lotto. *S.Benedetto* (Via S.Alessandro/Via C.Botta): 15C; interesting cloister, brick ornamentation, dated 1522. *S.Spirito* (Via Torquato Tasso/Via Pignola): by Isabello (1530–5); single-aisled with tunnel vault, decorated in Early Renaissance style. Some good paintings: Virgin with four saints, by L.Lotto, 1521 (4th chapel on the right); John the Baptist and other Saints, by A.Previtali, 1515 (1st chapel on the left); and a polyptych by Bergognone, 1507 (2nd chapel on the left). *S.Bernardino in Pignolo* (Via Pignolo): Built 1593; single-aisled. In the sanctuary there is another work by L.Lotto, dated 1521. *S.Alessandro della Croce* (Via Pignolo/Via Masone): 1st half of 17C, single-aisled, with good paintings etc. Coronation of the Virgin, by Moroni (entrance wall); Saviour with St.Roch and St.Sebastian, by Palma il Giovane (1st chapel on right); an altar by A.Fantoni in the 2nd chapel; Madonna with Saints, by Pittoni (3rd chapel); Ascension, by J.Bassano (4th chapel); in the sacristies, to the right of the sanctuary, The Holy Trinity, by L.Lotto, Christ bearing the Cross, by L.Costa, and The Christ Crucified, by Previtali.

Palazzo Grataroli-De Beni (Via Pignolo): 1515, by P.Isabello. This palace, with portico, loggia and elegant inner courtyard, is the most interesting of a number of palaces built along this street in the 16–18C.

Museums: (Piazza Citadella): The former Hospitium Magnum is a large complex located on the N. edge of the upper town; it was fortified under the Visconti in 1355, and today houses the *Archaeological* and *Natural History Museum.*

Accademia Carrara: Founded by Count Giacomo Carrara in 1795. The gallery's main exhibits have come from the Carrara (1796), Lochis (1859) and Morelli (1891) bequests. An important picture gallery, with one of the most comprehensive collections of Bergamasque, Lombard and Venetian artists. *Teatro Donizetti:* Built in 1783–91, rebuilt in 1797 after a fire; radically restored and expanded in 1964; façade dates from 1897/8.

Environs: Pontida (15 km. towards Lecco): *Benedictine abbey,* founded in the 2nd half of the 11C. Almost completely devastated by Bernabo Visconti in 1373, it was restored in the 15C. In the 18C it was at the height of its importance, but was abolished in 1798. Since 1910 it has again been occupied by monks. *Church of S.Giacomo:* Building completed in 1310, and despite later refacing, its old structure is still quite visible. Façade with portico built in 1830–2. Inside (nave and two aisles), the decorations are chiefly baroque. The choir has a relief of the Weighing of Souls, which dates from the early 12C and shows strong Burgundian influence. *Monastery building:* Completely rebuilt from 1485 onwards; two cloisters, the Chiostro superiore (1510), in Venetian form, and the Chiostro inferiore (1490). **Trescore Balneario** (15 km E): important for its baths under the Romans and in the Middle Ages. *S.Barbara* (Villa Suardi) has frescos by L.Lotto. The church itself was built in the 14C and rather badly restored in the late 19C. Lotto painted his fresco cycle, illustrating the legend of St.Barbara, in 1524; he also painted the ceiling. **S.Paolo d'Argon** (12 km. E.): *Former monastery* (founded by Cluny in the 11C), with two lovely cloisters (15C & early 16C); and the former *refectory.* The former monastery church (with fine baroque decoration) is today in use as a *parish church.* **Cavernago** (12 km. towards Cremona): *Castello Mazzotti* (formerly Martinengo): Late 16C; the elegant inner courtyard is surrounded by a two-storeyed Palladian loggia. *Malpaga*

Bergamo, Accademia Carrara (Carpaccio) ▷

Castle (2 km. S.of Cavernago), built as a simple castle in 1383, acquired and extended by B.Colleoni 1456. Fresco on the portico in the central courtyard. In the ceremonial hall there is a fresco cycle of 1474 depicting the visit of King Christian of Denmark. Frescos of *c.* 1520 are by Romanino. **Ghisalba** (16 km. towards Cremona): The parish church of *S.Lorenzo* is a classical building by Cagnola. Consecrated in 1834, it is modelled on Canova's rotunda in Possagno (Veneto). **Romano di Lombardia** (25 km towards Cremona): *Parish church of S.Maria Assunta* with interesting twin-towered façade; consecrated in 1735. Inside (4th altar on the left), a Last Supper by G.B.Moroni and an inlaid antependium (1697) by G.B.Caniana (2nd altar on the left). **Cassano d'Adda:** The *Castello Borromeo d'Adda* towers above the Adda in picturesque fashion; originally dating back to before 1000, the present building is from the 13–15C. Fine arcaded courtyard. The *Villa Borromeo* (Via Vittorio Veneto), built in the mid-18C to plans by Francesco Croce, was completely rebuilt in classical style in 1781. Elegant, grilled gate. **Vaprio d'Adda:** The small 12–13C church of *S.*

Colombano (restored in 1970) lies on the outskirts of the town. The left-hand portal is decorated with simple sculpture, including *St.Colomban giving his blessing* and a *siren*. The style of these suggests southern French models, which is rather unusual for Lombardy. *Palazzo Melzi d'Eril:* Built in the 15C on the site of a medieval castle, extended in the 17C. Redesigned in the 19C. The main building, above the Adda, is connected to the garden by terraces. Inside, there is a fresco *(Il Madonnone)* attributed to Leonardo. **Trezzo sull'Adda:** Remains of a medieval castle, the *Castello di Trezzo*, of Lombard or Carolingian origin. **Almenno S.Bartolomeo:** The church of *S.Tomé,* some 1.5 km. outside the town, is regarded as the purest example of a centrally planned Romanesque building in Lombardy. Probably built *c.* 1000 (some evidence points to the early 12C) on the site of a baptistery. The circular ground plan is only broken by the projecting apse. On the outside there are half-columns and Lombard band. The portal has remains of Romanesque sculpture. Inside, the central area is separated from the ambulatory by an arcade (round pillars with capitals of various

Bevagna, Piazza Filippo Silvestri

styles). There is a gallery above the ambulatory. **Almenno S.Salvatore:** The church of the *Madonna del Castello* dates from the 10C (crypt). The main parts of the present-day building are 16&17C. Renaissance portal (1578). Decoration: 11 –16C *frescos*, 13C Romanesque *pulpit* with figures of the four Evangelists; a late 16C fresco of John the Baptist and a richly painted 16C octagonal tempietto.

Bettona 06084
Perugia/Umbria   p.414 □ H 7/8

Originally an Etruscan settlement. From 1516–1648 Bettona was held as a fief by the Baglioni family from Perugia.

Necropolis: Fine Etruscan burial chamber from the 2C BC. (Interior from same period.)

Also worth seeing: 13C church of *S.Maria Maggiore* with a fresco by Perugino. The *picture gallery* has panel paintings, frescos, Etruscan bronzes and local historical documents, as well as important works by the painters Fiorenzo di Lorenzo (St.Michael), Perugino (Madonna with St.Maurus St.Jerome and St.Antony) and Tiberio d'Assisi (St.Roch).

Bevagna 06031
Perugia/Umbria   p.414 □ H 8

Piazza Filippo Silvestri /Piazza della Libertà: The old town centre, surrounded by well-preserved medieval buildings. The two churches are gems of Umbrian-Romanesque architecture. The fountain dates from 1889.

S.Silvestro: Built by Binello in 1195; inside, the nave has a tunnel vault and the two aisles half-tunnel vaults.

S.Michele: Built in 1200 to plans by Binello and Rudolfo, and partly rebuilt in the 18C.

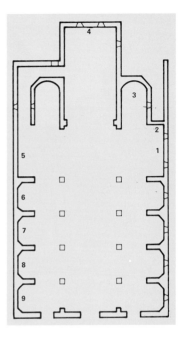

Biella, S.Sebastiano 1 Statue of Giovanna Bertie Mathew in prayer by O.Tabacchi, 1877, and a bust of her husband A.Lamarmora by V.Vela 2 door to Lamarmora family tomb 3 altar by B.Lanino, 1534 4 choir stalls by Gerolamo Mellis da Vespolate, 1546 5 polyptych by Martino Spanzotti 6 fresco by the school of G.Ferrari 7 Madonna with Saints, Bolognese school 8 painting by Grammorsea 9 frescos attributed to G.Ferrari

Palazzo dei Consoli: Italian-Gothic from the late 13C. Gives the piazza the appearance of a stage set, with its great external staircase. Massive hall on the ground floor.

Also worth seeing: Well-preserved mosaics from the *Roman baths*; remains of a Roman *amphitheatre* and *temple*. Archaeological finds and paintings by Dono Doni are exhibited in the *town hall*. The church of *S.Francesco* has pictures by Dono Doni and a fresco by Fantino, a painter from Bevagna. The church of *S.Michele Arcangelo* has frescos by the painter Andrea Camassei.

Biella, baptistery (cathedral)

Biella 13051
Vercelli/Piedmont   p.412☐B 3

Biella, the medieval *Bugella*, comprises 'Biella Piano', the old town, and 'Biella Piazzo', the new town. First mentioned in 826, it was a diocesan town from the 10C onwards. It fell under the sway of the bishops of Vercelli in 1377, and under that of Savoy in 1379.

Cathedral of S.Maria Maggiore (Biella Piano, Piazza del Duomo): The Gothic cathedral, begun in 1402, was altered in the 15&18C; the façade dates from 1825. The *pulpit*, decorated with intarsia work, is particularly fine. The pre-Romanesque *baptistery* (9–10C) is quatrefoil in form, with a polygonal base, along the lines of S.Vitale in Ravenna and S.Lorenzo in Milan. Fine 12C Romanesque *campanile* beside it.

S.Sebastiano (Via S.Sebastiano): Begun in 1502, and completed in 1551 as a Renaissance church with a nave and two aisles. The neoclassical façade was built in 1882. The following are worth seeing: *frescos* by Gaudenzio Ferrari, the *choir stalls* (1546), the monumental *burial chapels* and an *Ascension* by Bernardino Lanino (1543).

Chiesa della Trinità (Via Italia): Built 1626-1750, with fine frescos by Vincenzo Costantino (1640) and Antonio Ciancia Perrone (1865).

Museo Civico (Via Pietro Micca): Roman finds, medieval frescos and a small collection of paintings.

S.Giacomo (Bella Piazza, Via Avogadro): Lombard-Gothic, 13C, with fine *Madonna and Saints* (1497) by Daniele De Bosis. The *Roman Necropolis* (2C AD) was uncovered in 1951. The *Palazzo d.Cisterna* (Via Avogadro) from the 2nd half of the 16C, and the 15C *Palazzo Ferrero-Lamarmora* (Corso del Piazzo) are also worth seeing.

Environs: Santuario della Madonna di Oropa: one of Italy's most important places of pilgrimage, the oldest shrine to the Virgin Mary in the West. Legend has it that the shrine was founded by St. Eusebius, Bishop of Vercelli, who brought the wooden figure of the Virgin Mary (supposedly by St.Luke) from Palestine in 369. Along a road leading to the shrine there are 19 chapels dedicated to the Virgin. Tower-like corner pavilions on the access road give the impression of a castle. The focal point of the complex is formed by the Renaissance church of *Basilica di Oropa*, with a nave, two aisles and an octagonal dome (1500-1600). On the S.side of the courtyard there is an arcaded building (1644-54). Work on the completion of the wing between church and riverside began in 1653; the W. wing opposite the church portal was completed from 1690 onwards. Filippo Juvarra designed the decorations for the jubilee festivities in 1720. Following this, the façade of the complex was rebuilt to plans by F. Juvarra and others. In addition, in 1885, the new

Bitonto, cathedral, pulpit of 1229, with Frederick II

domed church (Chiesa Nuova) was built over the baroque shrine to existing plans by Ignazio Galleti (1774). **Santuario di Graglia:** (1659–1760), dedicated to the Madonna di Loreto. The church was built to plans by Pietro Arduzzi. There is a hospice (1735) beside the church. **Castello di Gaglianico:** a well preserved castle. Built on a square ground plan with a fine 14C inner courtyard and a 17C park by André Le Nôtre, who designed the park at Versailles. The 15C **Castle of Verrone** is one of Piedmont's finest castles.

Bitonto 70032
Bari/Apulia   p.416 □ N 11

Cathedral of S.Valentino (Piazza Cattedrale): Regarded as the most mature creation of the Apulian Romanesque style, it is highly uniform and was completed in only 25 years (1175–1200). *Exterior:* Splendid *rose window* on the W. façade. The richly decorated *main portal* is a gem of the Apulian Romanesque style. Fine *dwarf gallery* on the S. side of the nave. *Inside:* The ambo (1229) is by the first pillar on the right of the crossing. It is the finest piece of work in the cathedral and is probably by the same Nicola who designed the campanile of the cathedral in Trani (inscription on the marble lectern). The ambo steps, at the rear, may show the Emperor Frederick II and his family but this is uncertain. 13C font. Beneath the cathedral there is a *crypt* with 24 columns and splendid capitals; also, the remains of 14C frescos.

Also worth seeing: *Palazzo Sylos* (Via Planelli 51) Catalan-Gothic in style, with a fine Renaissance courtyard (*c.* 1500); the old *town walls* of Bitonto, which still completely surround the town.

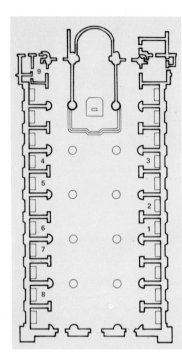

Bologna, Palazzo Comunale

Bologna, S.Petronio 1 Pietà by Aspertini, 1519 **2** St.Jerome by Lorenzo Costa *c.* 1500 **3** pews by Raffaele da Brescia, 1521 **4** St. Roch by Parmagianino **5** Sacra Conversazione by L.Costa, 1492 **6** Martyrdom of St. Sebastian, mid-15C **7** wall paintings by Giovanni da Modena, 1410–15 **8** wall paintings by Torreggiani, 1743 – 50 **9** museum

---

Blera 01010

Viterbo/ Latium   p.414☐G 9

This town's picturesque location makes it a fascinating spot. It stands on the site of an Etruscan settlement which had its heyday in the 7/6C BC. Some 1000 rock tombs survive in the environs of Blera. A *burial house* near the Etruscan *Ponte della Rocca* (2C BC) is of particular interest.

Bologna 40100

Bologna/ Emilia-Romagna   p.410☐F 5

Bologna had a flourishing culture as long ago as 1000 BC under the Umbrians. In the 6C BC the Etruscans conquered the town and named it *Felsina*. Towards the middle of the 4C BC it fell to the Gallic Boii tribe, under whom it became *Bononia*. It was under this name that the town became a Roman province in 189 BC and rose to great commercial importance as the intersection of various trade routes. In 89 BC it was a municipium (free city), and in AD 53 the Emperor Claudius caused the town (which had been burned down), to be rebuilt. Destroyed by the Lombards in 727–28, it then became a dependency of the Franconians. The University (Europe's oldest) was founded in 1119. From 1167 onwards Bologna was a member of the Lombard League and took part in the fight against the Hohenstaufens. It reached its peak as a free city state in the late Middle Ages. The campaigns waged by various noble families against the Popes, and also to gain possession of the town, ended in victory for the Pope in 1512. The last Imperial coronation (that of Charles V) took place here in 1530. The Council of Trent was moved here in 1547. Captured by the French in 1796, the town became part of the Kingdom of Italy, until in 1815 it once again fell to the Pope.

S.Petronio (Piazza Maggiore): One of the largest places of worship in Christendom. Begun in 1390. 1st phase of construction until 1400. The architect, Antonio di Vincenzo, was advised in his work by Fra Andrea Manfredi, the Servite general. A 2nd, intensive phase of construction took place in 1445-1525. However, the building was not finished until 1659. The campanile (1481-92) is by Giovanni da Brensa. The completed church differs greatly from the original plan, owing to the length of time building took. The marble facing of the façade was begun in 1538 but extends only to the height of the three portals; the rest is still brick. The *central portal* (1425-38), one of Jacopo della Quercia's masterpieces, was completed by other artists in the early 16C. The *side portals* were conceived by Domenico da Varignana in 1518 as part of the new façade, and were built in 1524-7 to plans by Seccadinari. The inside is richly furnished and very like a Gothic basilica. Of particular interest are: a *Pietà* of 1519 by Amico Aspertini (altar in the 5th chapel on the right); *St.Girolamo* (*c.* 1500)

by Lorenzo Costa (altar in the 6th chapel on the right); *stalls* (1521) by Raffaele da Brescia (8th chapel on the right); *St.Roch* by Parmigianino (altar in 8th chapel on the left); *Sacra Conversazione* (1492) by Lorenzo Costa (altar in the 7th chapel on the left); *Martyrdom of St.Sebastian* (mid 15C) by an Emilian artist (altar in the 5th chapel on the left); *wall paintings* from 1410 - 15 by Giovanni da Modena (4th chapel on the left); the 2nd chapel on the left has *wall paintings* (1743-50) by Torreggiani. The *museum* (end of the left aisle) has designs for the church façade, sacred utensils, illustrated liturgical books and editions of musical texts.

Palazzo Comunale (Piazza Maggiore): A brick building which developed after 1287 around the centre of an older house. On the right of the façade (1425-8, by Fieravanti) there is a portal of 1555 by Alessi, a *sculpture of the seated Pope Gregory XIII* (1580) by Manganti and a signed Madonna in relief (1478) by Niccolò dell'Arca. At the side of the 1st, Gothic façade there is a corner tower (1441) with clock (1773). In the large courtyard, the staircase (said to have been designed by Bramante in 1507) leads to the

Bologna, S.Petronio, fresco by Giovanni da Modena

State chambers, which are worth seeing, and to the city art collections in rooms with 16&17C ceilings. Important exhibits: *Portrait of an old man* by Canova; *Crucifixion* by a follower of Pisano; *Crucifixion (c.* 1470) by Francia; *Maria Magdalena* by Signorelli; *Portrait of an old man* by Tintoretto; *St.Peter* by Alcantara; and *St.Antony* and *Portrait of Cardinal Lambertini* by G.M.Crespi.

Fontana del Nettuno (also known as *del Gigante,* Piazza del Nettuno): The fountain is to a design by Laurenti. The bronzes (1566) are the work of Giovanni Bologna, who also supplied the model for the main figure. Restoration work was carried out in 1726, 1762, 1888, 1907 and after World War 2.

Museo Civico Archeologico (Portico del Pavaglione 2) is in the former 15C Ospedale of *S.Maria della Morte.* It contains prehistoric finds from the town and round about, a notable Egyptian department (especially 5 relief slabs from Memphis), fine Greek sculptures and vessels, and a comprehensive Roman collection (tombstones, reliefs, work in marble, portraits of emperors etc.) and the largest collection of inscriptions in N. Italy. The most important department is devoted to the finds excavated from the region's Etruscan burial grounds.

Pinacoteca Nazionale (Via delle Belle Arti 56): The picture gallery gives an unrivalled overall view of Bolognese painting of the 14–18C. The most important exhibits include works by the following artists: Vitale da Bologna, Giotto *(Madonna Enthroned),* Jacopino da Bologna, L.Costa, Ercole Roberti, Raphael *(Annunciation of St.Cecilia),* Franciabigio, Perugino, Nicolo Pisano, Parmigianino, Schongauer, the Carracci, G.M.Crespi, Reni, Tintoretto, Piazetta, Domenichino and Guercino.

S.Giacomo Maggiore (Piazza Rossini): The building dates from 1267–1315; the façade, the side with pilaster strips, and part of the campanile (upper part, 1471) survive from this time. The apse and some ambulatory chapels were built in 1343.

The side portico was built in 1477–81. From 1492–1505 the church was rebuilt by Pietro da Brescia in Renaissance style, the roof being replaced by a domical vault. Shortly after, Tibaldi built the main dome and the *Cappella Poggi.* One of the four recesses for tombs which flank the portal contains a 14C *sarcophagus.* The inside of the church was altered in the 18C and gives a good overall view of art in Bologna. The following are outstanding: *St. Roch comforted by an angel* by L.Carracci (10th chapel on the right). The *Cappella Poggi* of 1527–96 is by Tibaldi (11th chapel on the right). The 2nd ambulatory chapel has a *Polyptych* by Paolo Veneziano. The *Bentivoglio tomb* of 1435 by Jacopo della Quercia is on the right wall of choir, opposite the 4th chapel (1445–86) which itself has an altarpiece (*c.* 1494) by Francia and 2 allegories (1490) by L.Costa (left wall). The entrance to the **Oratorio di S.Cecilia** (Via Zamboni 15) is found in the arched passageway along the side of the church. The history of the oratory is uncertain but it goes back to *c.* 1300 at the latest. Thoroughly restored in 1359; the vault was added in 1483. When the Bentivoglio chapel was built, the oratory was shortened and the arched passageway added. Inside there are some of Bologna's finest frescos —the *10 scenes from the lives of St.Cecilia and St.Valerian* (1504 – 6) by Francia, L.Costa, Aspertini and other artists from Bologna.

S.Maria dei Servi (Strada Maggiore 43): Begun in 1346, probably by Antonio di Vincenzo; outer walls and nave arcade completed in 1396. Work restarted in 1425, but the main apse was not completed until 1437. The two side apses were torn down in 1470 to make way for two chapels. The nave vault was not completed until 1504. The campanile of 1453 was rebuilt in 1725. Interesting paintings: *Madonna with the seven founders of the Servite order* by G.M.Crespi (sanctuary, left wall); *fresco fragments* by Vitale da Bologna (ambulatory wall on the right); *Madonna enthroned,*

Bologna, picture gallery, St. George by Vitale da Bologna

ascribed to Cimabue (left-hand chapel of ambulatory).

S.Stefano (Piazza S.Stefano): A large complex of five sacred buildings, greatly restored in 1880 and 1924. The nave walls and the crypt (with some original capitals) survive from the original 11C *Chiesa del Crocifisso*. The sanctuary dates from 1637. The central structure, the *Chiesa del Sepolcro* (or *del Calvario*), dates from a baptistery (possibly 5C) destroyed in 903, and rebult in the early 12C. This central structure contains the *tomb of St.Petronius*, the town's patron, with 14C reliefs. *SS.Vitale e Agricola* perhaps orginates from the 5C, but was altered in the 8&11C. The basilica contains 2 ancient *sarcophagi* (behind the high altar) and the *tombs of St.Vitalis and Agricola* (left and right side apses). The visitor passes through the *Cortile di Pilato* (12C with an 8C marble vase in the middle) into the *Chiesa della Trinità*, an early 13C building. The columns and capitals of the arcade are Romanesque, and traces of 14C frescos survive. On the right side of the cortile di Pilato is the *Cappella della Consolazione* with a 12C fresco by the altar. A portal dating from 1574 to the left of the chapel leads into the fine *cloister*, whose lower walk is 11C. The upper (12C) one leads into the *museum*, with paintings from the 13–17C.

S.Domenico (Piazza S.Domenico): consists of two buildings, one behind the other: the front one, *(S.Nicolò della Vigna)*, completed *c.* 1233, was intended for the congregation, the rear one (1298), for the friars. The apse and numerous chapels are 14–16C. The interior (1728–32) was designed by C.F.Dotti. In 1909/10 the present-day façade was built and the *Cappella Ghisilandi*, built to Peruzzi's plans, was restored. The *Arca di S.Domenico* in the chapel of the same name (6th on the right) is a key work in the development of Italian sculpture. Nicola Pisano received the commission for it in 1265–7, but it was mostly executed by his pupils. After the sarcophagus was transferred from the crypt to the chapel in 1411, a number of additions were made by Niccolò dell' Arca (1469–73; cover), Michelangelo (1495; light-bearing angels, St.Petronius and Proculus, and a figure of a youth), Alfonso Lombardi (1532; reliefs on altar and plinth) and Coltellini (1539; John the Baptist). Below the altar there is a *reliquary* of St. Dominic (1383). Other features: *Apotheosis of St.Dominic* (1615) by Reni (apse). The *Cappella Bolignini* (added to right transept) has an altarpiece by Guercino. *Marriage of St. Catherine* (1501) by Filippino Lippi (chapel to the right of the sanctuary). *Choir stalls* (1541–51) by Damiano da Bergamo (apse). *Crucifixion* (*c.* 1240) by Giunta Pisano (7th chapel on left). 15 paintings by Calvaert, Cesi, A. and L.Carracci, Reni and Albani (5th chapel on left, around the niche of the Madonna on the altar). Altarpiece by L.Carracci (2nd chapel on left). The sacristy leads into the *museum*. Note

Bologna, S. Francesco 1 Cappella S. Bernardino, 15C **2** tomb for Lodovico Boccadiferro (d. 1545), to a design attributed to Giulio Romano

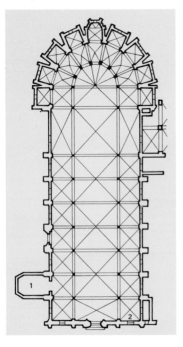

the following in the 1st room: A *bust of St. Dominic* (1474) by Niccolò dell'Arca and 2 frescos, *Charity* and *St. Francis*, by L.Carracci. The 2nd room has reliquaries, liturgical manuscripts and vestments. The 1st cloister, the *Chiostro dei Morti*, was built in various phases—14C (E.), 1446 (S) and 15C (W). The 2nd cloister, the *Chiostro Maggiore* (1551) is by Terribilia.

S.Francesco (Piazza S.Francesco): One of the prime examples of the influence of the French Gothic style in Italy (the ring of chapels is one of the first in Italy); it was begun in 1236, consecrated in 1254 and largely completed in 1263. The sacristy (1397; restored in 1950) and the large campanile (1397–*c*.1402) are by Antonio di Vincenzo. Finally, in the 15C, the *Cappella S.Bernardino* was added on the left side of the church (restored in 1928). The façade, completed in 1250, is still Romanesque and is out of keeping with the Gothic church. Note: the *marble reredos* (1388–92) by Jacobello and Pier Paolo dalle Masegne (sanctuary) and the *Monument to Lodovico Boccadiferro* (d. 1545), to a design thought to be by Giulio Romano (façade wall, including the right door).

Cathedral of S.Pietro, known as Metropolitana, (Via dell'Indipendenza). Remains of a 10C church were discovered in 1905; however, the church was probably founded at a still earlier date. Destroyed by a fire in the town in 1141, the church was rebuilt in 1165–75 and consecrated in 1184. The church was demolished in 1605, and a new building was constructed to plans by Floriano Ambrosini (Domenico Tibaldi's choir of 1575 was retained). The present form of the church—single-aisled and interconnecting side chapels—is based on plans by Nicola Donati. In 1754–5 Alfonso Torreggiani built the façade (altered in 1776). The campanile (1184) and the crypt have survived from the Romanesque building. The most significant decorations are: 2 *marble lions* (*c*. 1220) from the portal of the Romanesque building (main portal); *Lamentation* by L.Carracci (vault of the chapterhouse); 18C *tapestries* to designs by Anton Raphael Mengs (treasury); *Annunciation* (1618/19), the last work of L.Carracci (inner arch of choir); wooden 12C *crucifixion group* (1st altar on left in crypt); also in the crypt, on the third altar on the left, is an early 16C *terracotta pietà* by Alfonso Lombardi.

Bologna, Palazzo Accursio

Bologna, Torre degli Asinelli and Torre Garisenda

Santuario della Madonna di S. Lucca

Also worth seeing: The two surviving *towers* (Strada Maggiore), the *Torre degli Asinelli* (1109–19) and the late 11C *Torre Garisenda*. The *Palazzo Bevilacqua* (Via D'Azeglio 31–33), built 1477–82 and the most elegant palace in Bologna, with superb courtyard and fine façade. The *Palazzo del Podestà* (Piazza Maggiore): a complex of several connected palaces cut through by two intersecting roads. Work on building began in the early 13C. The tower (1212) also dates from this period. *S.Bartolomeo* (Strada Maggiore 4): finished in its present form in 1653–84. The portal survives from an earlier, 16C building. The campanile dates from 1694. Two notable paintings: *Annunciation* (1632) by Albani (4th altar on right) and a small *Madonna and Child* by Guido Reni (chapel in left transept). The *Palazzo della Mercanzia* (Piazza della Mercanzia): A brick building begun in 1382 and one of the finest Gothic buildings in Northern Italy. The *Archiginnasio* (Piazza Galvini 1): formerly a university building; by Terribilia in 1562–3. On the 1st floor there is the fine *Anatomical Theatre* (1638–49) with carvings by Levanti and Gianotti. *S.Maria della Vita* (Via Clavature 10): built in 1687–90, with a dome of 1787. Fine terracotta Pietà (after 1485) by Niccolò dell'Arca (to the right of the high altar).

Environs: The *Santuario della Madonna di S.Luca* (Monte della Guardia): The sanctuary houses a Byzantine image of the Madonna, said to have been painted by St.Luke. The hermitage was founded in 1160. The church was built when the complex was expanded; it was then restored in 1306 and 1481. The present centrally-planned structure with its large crypt was designed by C.F.Dotti in 1723–57. The façade, the arched passage and the tribune were added in 1774. Note: The *Virgin of the Rosary*, an early work by Reni (3rd altar on right); the shrine's original image, a 12C *Byzantine image of the Madonna*; *Christ appearing to Mary* by Guercino (sacristy, left side). The former monastery of

Bologna, Museo Civico, bust of Lucius ▷ Verus

S.Michele in Bosco is known to have been a hermitage as early as 1085. The monastery was burnt down in 1430, rebuilding began in 1437 but was not completed until the early 17C. The façade, probably by Peruzzi, was built in 1523. He also designed the portal. The portal below the portico (1525) is the work of Formigine. The sacristy, which takes up half of the left side of the church, is probably the church of 1437. The large choir was used as a church for the monks. Inside, note the following: the *organ* (1524) by Facchinetti with a case by Raffaele da Brescia (entrance wall); *tomb of Ramazzotto de' Ramazzotti* (1525/26) by Alfonso Lombardi (to the right of the entrance); *frescos* by Bagnacavallo (rear wall of sacristy); *tombstone of Antonio da Budrio* (1435) by Jacopo della Quercia (left-hand passage before the sanctuary); *frescos* by L.Carracci, Reni and others (cloister); the *library* decorated in the 17C.

Bolsena 01023
Viterbo/Latium   p.414☐G 8

S.Cristina (collegiate church): Founded in the 11C. The elegant façade was donated by Cardinal Giovanni de' Medici (later Pope Leo X). The tympanum of the middle portal has a terracotta in the manner of della Robbia *(Madonna and Child between St.Christina and St.George)*. An 11C portal with a door lintel showing a relief of *The Wise Virgins and the Epiphany* leads from the left aisle of the simple basilica with its nave, two aisles and three apses into the *Cappella del Miracolo*. This is a simple centrally planned baroque chapel (1693) built over the underground site of a miraculous event (in 1263 the communion wafer miraculously emitted blood over the altar). The *marble altar* has a blood-stained appearance. The *altarpiece* by Francesco Trevisani depicts the miracle. On the left side of the chapel, steps lead down to the *grotto of St.Christine*. The initial section leading to the catacombs of St.Christine may originally have been a grotto dedicated to Apollo. To the right is the *Chapel of St.Michael,* where there is a large altar

panel with the *Martyrdom of St.Christine* by Giovani della Robbia. Opposite this is the saint's altar (also known as 'delle 4 colonne', owing to the four columns bearing the 9C ciborium). At the rear is a relief from the della Robbia school; in front of this is the basalt slab with which the saint was to be drowned in the lake by order of her father, Urban the Prefect. Miraculously the slab floated on the water and drifted to the shore with the saint. Legend has it that the depressions in the basalt are the saint's footprints. At the back of the grotto, there is the entrance to the catacombs themselves. There is a *monument* (1892) *to St.Christine*, with a painted statue by Giovanni della Robbia, and a Roman *sarcophagus of the martyr*.

Also worth seeing: *Castle* (13/14C); today the *Museo Civico*. Ancient finds. *Palazzo Cozza-Spada* with good Mannerist frescos.

Bolzano/Bozen 39100
Bozen/South Tyrol-Trentino   p.410☐F 2

The *Via dei Portici*—the old heart of the town—was the commercial centre of Bolzano even in the Middle Ages. Under its roofed arcades, the tradesmen could carry on their business in any weather. 12&13C walls are still to be found here. The fine stuccoed façades (e.g. No. 46) are 17&18C. The *Palazzo Mercantile* (No. 39; built by Giovanni and Giuseppe Delai in 1705-16) is a striking baroque mansion set amidst medieval surroundings.

Cathedral (Piazza Walther): The present church stands on the foundations of an early Christian cemetery church dated 400. A church with two aisles was consecrated *c.* 1180, and its façade is incorporated in the present W. front. The two E. towers were built towards the end of the 13C. In 1295 a Lombard workshop began building the basilica, which has a nave and two aisles and was completed in 1340. From 1345 onwards the nave was altered by German builders to make it the *earliest hall church in the Tyrol*. The hall choir with ambulatory and stellar ribbed vault (built 1380–1420 by Martin Schiche from Augsburg) is regarded as the most mature Gothic building in the Tyrol. In 1499, a portico was built on to the W. façade, which has a rose-window. The steep roof (1473–88) has glazed, coloured tiles. The N. tower was destroyed by fire in 1499 but rebuilt (1500–19) in splendid late Gothic style by Hans Lutz of Schussenreid to a plan by Burkhard Engelberg from Augsburg. Note the Gothic *Leitachertörl* gate on the N. side of the church, with figures on consoles; probably by M.Schiche. At the E. end of the choir there is a *lady chapel*, built by Jos. Delai 1743–5 as a small centrally planned building. Inside, the most impressive features are a fine *sandstone pulpit* (1513/14, by Hans Lutz and his workshop), important tombstones, the *early-Gothic frescos* in the late-Romanesque S. bay of the choir, the remains of 14C frescos on the S. wall, and the early 15C frescos on the W. wall of the nave.

Franciscan church (Via Francescani): The monastery was founded in 1224; the church was begun in 1291. In 1450–4, a hall with a nave and two aisles and a lozenge-type net vault was built from a room which previously had a flat roof. The tall *chancel*, with impressive key stones decorated with reliefs, is regarded as one of the finest works of the Order in the Tyrol. *St.Mary's chapel* (1340), on the N. side of the chancel, has a fine carved, winged altarpiece (1500) by Hans Klocker from Brixen. To the N. of the church there is a Gothic (partly late-Romanesque) *cloister* with frescos from the 14–17C.

Dominican church (Piazza Domenicani): In 1272, the Regensburg Dominicans founded a monastery which was abolished in 1785. However, the church, which was built in 1275 as a flat-roofed hall church (and was originally part of the monastery), is still important. In 1498 it was rebuilt as a late-Gothic hall church with stellar vaulting. The Gothic chancel was rebuilt in the baroque style in the 18C. Frescos of the early Bolzano school (1400) survive in the nave of the church. Note in particular: *St.John's chapel* built on to the chancel and painted all over in the 1st half of the 14C (the scenes from the life of Mary are by the school of Giotto). Also of interest is the late Gothic

Bolzano, cathedral, pulpit

Bolzano, cathedral

cloister with St.Catherine's chapel. The cloister also has 14C frescos (and some from the 15&16C).

Also worth seeing: The small church of *St.Johann im Dorf*, with a tower above the chancel, is entirely covered inside with frescos and dates from the early 14C. The church of *St.Martin in Kampill*, dates from *c.* 1300; it too has a tower above the chancel and is painted all over. The Romanesque church of *St.Vigil unter Weineck (St.Vigil under Weineck)*, built *c.* 1200 is decorated inside and out with frescos (*c.* 1400. The high baroque domed *Heiliges Grab* church (church of the Holy Sepulchre) on the Kalvarienberg was built by Peter and Andreas Delai (1683/4).

City Museum (Sparkassenstr. 14): A good overall view of artistic developments in the South Tyrol. The carved altar of St.Barbara by Hans Klocker (1490) is of particular interest.

Environs: A feature of Bolzano's surroundings are the numerous castles, which were originally fortresses. The most important is **Burg Runkelstein/Castel Róncolo:** Built in 1237 on a crag at the end of the Sarntaler gorge; restored after 1385 and *c.* 1500. Excellent frescos reflect late 14C court life. Nearby, the 12C Romanesque **Burg Ried. Haselburg** castle, originally dating from the 1st half of the 13C, has 16C frescos in a room in the residential part of the castle. Two of the rooms of **Burg Maretsch/Castel Mareccio,** built *c.* 1200 and rebuilt in 1560–70, contain battle scenes and allegories (1570). The **ruined castle of Rafenstein,** originally 13C, was rebuilt in the 16&17C. The Bolzano suburb of **Gries** is most pretty, with its *old parish church*, whose Romanesque walls were added to in the 15C (chancel) and 16C (stellar vault over the nave and porch). The fine late-Gothic *Erasmus chapel* with its richly arched portal was built on to the S. side of the chancel in *c.* 1519. It now houses one of the most important late-Gothic carvings in the Tyrol, the *Coronation of the Virgin*, an altarpiece (1470–5) by M.Pacher. It also contains a fine, full-size Romanesque *crucifix*. The splendid *Benedictine monastery of Gries*

(main square) was originally built for Augustinian canons in the 15C. It was abolished in 1807; when the Benedictine monastery at Muri in Switzerland was abolished in 1841, the monks from there settled in the monastery in Gries. The collegiate church of *St.Augustine,* built in 1769 – 71 by Josef Sartori of Sacco in Lombard baroque style, is particularly interesting. Fine ceiling frescos and the panels of the marble altars are by M.Knoller (1771-3). The altar carvings are by Johann Schnegg and Kaspar Schonger. Other churches worth seeing in the area: **St.Georgen am Kofel** (1400), **St.Jakob im Sand,** with its late Gothic winged altar, and the late Romanesque church of *St.Mauritius* in **Moritzing,** which has been rebuilt in baroque style with a tower above its chancel (frescos of St. Christopher from the late 14C). **Sarentino/Sarntheim** with the 13C castle, *Burg Reinegg.* To reach the pretty village of **Fiè/Völs** travel W. out of Bolzano on the road to Blumenau along the Isarco, turn S. at Schlernbach and follow the Schlern for a short distance. The *parish church of the Assumption* was built in 1515–30 by Sigmund. The nave vault dates from 1550, and the baroque imperial roof on the tall W. tower from 1703. Note the W. and S. portal, the ribbed vault and a fine crucifix (1200) in the sanctuary. Also of interest: the 12C two-storeyed *cemetery chapel of St.Michael* (the inside dates from 1500) the hall church of *St.Peter am Bichl,* built *c.* 1200 and to the W. of the town on a hill inhabited even in prehistoric times, (net vault 1498, S. portal 1530, winged altarpiece 1510); *St.Constantine* (1506) with a painting by J.A.Mölk on the high altar (1762); the castle of *Burg Prösels/Castel Presule,* built *c.* 1500 (castle chapel 1525) on a hill above the village.

Bomarzo 01020

Viterbo/Latium   p.414☐G 8

A small town picturesquely sited on a rock,

Gries (Bolzano), Pacher altar in the ▷
Erasmus chapel

Bolzano, Dominican church, 14C frescos

with the **Palazzo Orsini** towering above it. Today, part of this cluster of buildings is used as the *town hall*, and here there are frescos by the school of Pietro da Cortona (drawing room on the 1st floor). From the piazza (16C *parish church*), just beside the castle, there is a magnificent view of the Tiber valley and the castle-like village of **Mugnano**. Bomarzo is known chiefly for its **Parco dei Mostri** (grotto, stone monsters). This park is the brain child of Vicino Orsini. The most famous feature is the *Orco* (mouth of hell), an enormous mask with an open mouth in which stone benches invite the visitor to sit down; colossal figures of the *Gigante*.

Bominaco 67020
Abruzzi   p.416□I 9

Until 1423 there was an important abbey

on the hill above the town and the town's two oldest churches belonged to this abbey.

S. Pellegrino: This church, rebuilt in 1263, retains ancient features. Inside, 13C frescos including *Life of Christ* and *6 scenes from the Life of S. Pellegrino.*

S. Maria: Built in the early 12C, it has three apses decorated with plant friezes. Inside, some remains of frescos, and also a *pulpit* decorated by reliefs. The *Paschal candelabrum*, a *ciborium* and the *abbot's throne* date from the same period.

Bonnánaro 07043
Sássari/Sardinia   p. 422□C 12

Francesco Carboni (1746–1817), scholar and friend of Pope Pius VII, came from Bonnánaro. Implements typical of early

Bominaco, S. Pellegrino, 13C frescos

Bronze Age culture were discovered in burial grottoes in the fields of Corona Maltona. Archaeologists refer to this as the 'Bonnánaro culture' and date them to the early nuraghic period.

Environs: Via **Borutta** leads to the Benedictine monastery church of *San Pietro di Sorres,* regarded as one of the finest of its kind in all Italy. This masterpiece (1170–90) of black and green basalt, red tachylite, white shell limestone and grey slate was built by Magister Marianus, who added to an earlier building. Façade, apse and adjoining monastery have the black and white stripes typical of this region and there are coloured square and circular inlays in the blind arches on each of the three storeys at the front. A two-arched window opens above the red and white arch of the portal and there is a circular window below the gable arcade. The nave, two aisles and the apse have groin vaults.

S. of **Cherémule** there are numerous 'witches' houses' close together (some with wall patterns), several Roman tombs and a wide cave. On the left of this, at the front, there are bas-reliefs of some 20 human figures with flowing hair and long garments, and a shallow water basin. *c.* 1,000 ft. to the SW, somewhat out of the way, is a ruined burial cavern. At the back, in the right-hand corner, reddish-brown painted human figures in linear style are still just visible. Nearby **Thiesi** has a Gothic-Catalan church with a magnificent architrave on the portal and rose-window above it; there is also a modern painting of the town's history by a local painter on the parish house. Only Antonio Piga (Via Umberto 21) can lead the visitor to a *two-chambered tomb,* which has an enormous red symbol of a bull's head on one wall and yellow spirals on a blue background on the ceiling—this is unique in Sardinia. In front of it there is a relief with a text as yet undeciphered. The tallest church tower in Sardinia, in slim neoclassical style, was added to the *parish church* in 1870. In an isolated spot 2 km. to the S. of the bridge over the source of the Coghina there stands the enormous *Dolmen Sa Coveccada*, which is clearly on the verge of ruin, to judge by the cracks in the massive wall and ceiling slabs. The impressive *King's Nuraghe* (Sa Dumu de Su Rei) and *Sant'Antine*, inhabited from the 9–5C BC, is today saved from collapse only by massive supports in the main entrance. In spite of this the mutilated nuraghe, with its triangular ground plan, central tower with spiral staircases, two-storeyed wall passages and inner courtyard, will transport any visitor back into remote antiquity.

Bonorva 07012
Sássari/Sardinia   p.422□C 12

Bonorva lies off the main road. The restored village church still contains parts of the 16C Aragonese-Gothic building.

Environs: To the N., beyond the railway,

Bonnánaro, S. Pietro di Sorres

lies the well-preserved *Tres Nuraghi*. Along the old SS 131 and in the valley of the Riu Mulinu there are numerous *domus de janas*, some of which are still inhabited and used as shepherds' houses. Some especially large houses, which date back to 3000 BC, show the signs of having been treated with DDT several times in the fight against malaria. 1,000 ft. to the E. of the market place, on the opposite slope, there is a *nuraghic well*, with a rectangular surround and long benches in the vestibule. 5 km. further to the E. (to the S. there are many, mainly ruined domus de janas), past the country church of *Santa Lucia*, the tachylite rock walls of *Sant'Andria Priu* are reached. Although this wall is broken in several places and many tombs have collapsed with it, 17 burial chambers still survive. However, since 1968 the sacred wall paintings and ornaments have been destroyed almost beyond recognition by human folly. NW of Bornova, W. of the SS 131, **Cossoine**, with a 16C *late Gothic church* (carefully worked façade and an octagonal campanile). To the NW, the 4 km. climb to the *Chiesette di Santa Maria Iscálas*, is worth the trouble. It is a combination of late Byzantine and early Romanesque structural forms, particularly in the domical vault and the apse. 8 km. W. of Bonorva, Camaldolensian monks, using Santa Maria del Regno in Ardara as a model, built the single-aisled country church of *San Nicolò di Trullas* (1114 onwards). Built of limestone, the portico and apse are decorated with ornamental tiles. The massive *Nuraghe Scolca* occupies a dominating position. Around **Pozzomaggiore** (fine Catalan-Gothic village church of *San Gorgio* with campanile of 1570 or later) there are several *giants' tombs* and insignificant *stumps of nuraghi*, the best-preserved being *Ala* in the fields of Badda Arrozza. **Pádria** stands on the site of the Roman Gurulis Vetus. The school houses a small *local museum.* The church of *Santa Giulia* (1520 or thereafter) is a well-known example of the advance of Catalonian architecture in Sardinia. The façade is framed by two diagonal projections and, half-way up, there are small arcades.

Bosa 08013
Nuoro/Sardinia   p.422☐B 12

It was not until the 12C that the Malaspina (counts from Pisa), put a stop to the predatory incursions of the Saracens and Normans by building the *Castello di Serravalle* in 1112–1221. Present-day Bosa grew up under the protection of this castle. The tanners' houses with their typical double gables were built along the Temo. Of the Castello di Serravalle, the curtain wall and three towers have survived. The upper part of the tallest tower is open on the inner side, like the contemporary defensive towers of Oristano (q.v.) and Cagliari (q.v.).

Cathedral of S.Pietro (extra Muros): The oldest Romanesque church in Sardinia. Built using ancient Roman materials in 1073 by Lombard workmen under Bishop Costantino de Castra. By *c.* 1250 an apse, a short square campanile, side aisles and a Gothic front to the façade with a round window and a frieze of animal motifs had been added by the Cistercian monks of S.Maria di Garavata, Bosa.

Note the portal's marble architrave, Romanesque leafed capitals, pointed arches with turned columns, and small stylized trees, figures of saints, Madonna and Child, Peter and Paul between them; a small bellcote above the gable has unusual, knotted columns, found elsewhere only at Zuri (q.v.).

Environs: Further N. stands the Genoese (Doria) castle, *Monte Leone Rocca Doria*. The weathered, late Romanesque church of *S.Stefano* has two aisles and two dissimilar apses. In contrast, the *Nuraghe Nuradeo*, with its triangular plan and three outer towers connected to the two-storeyed central tower, is very well preserved. To the E., 1 km. to the W. of **Suni** *is the peculiar corridor nuraghe of Seneghe* (7/6C BC). To the SE, **Flussio** is a main centre for the weaving of baskets from dried asphodel strips. To the W. of **Tresnuraghes** stand two monoliths; legend has it that these are a peasant and his team, who were turned to stone by St.'Mark for being disobedient. **Cúglieri,** the Roman Gurulis Nova, is dominated by the dome and twin towers of the cathedral of *S.Maria della Neve*. The tourist office has a small, interesting col-

Bonorva, S. Nicolò di Trullas

Thiesi (Bonnánaro), Sant'Antine

lection of finds from Cornus (q.v.). To the S., near the town, are the Neolithic, painted *tombs of Serrugiu*. Carefully worked from a layer of tachylite, they have simple decorations. On the N. slope of Monte Turonari, on a tachylite rock, is the 12C *Castell Etzu*, originally held by the Giudicato of Torres and later by Pisa. By following tracks across the fields to the E. of and above the town, the visitor comes to the *necropolis of Monte Ruja* and the ruined, early Christian *basilica Columbaris* (4/5C). Further S., the 16C *Torre Su Puttu* dominates the two small bays (Koracódes) used by the Carthaginians, who built the town of Cornus on the plateau above. According to Livy, this town continued to grow after it was taken by the Romans in 215 BC.

Bovino 71023
Foggia/Apulia   p.416☐L 10

Cathedral of S.Maria Assunta: Consecrated in 1231 after the previous, 10C Byzantine building had fallen into disrepair. Drastically altered in the early 14C,

Bosa, S. Pietro extra Muros

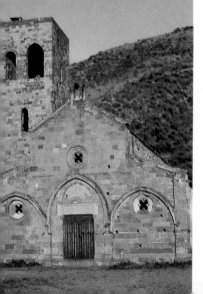

it was destroyed by an earthquake in 1930 and has since been completely rebuilt in its original form. Inside there are columns, arcades and masonry from the original building. In the 17C the semicircular apse was replaced by a rectangular choir with a tunnel vault. *S.Marco*, a single-aisled hall church with a tunnel vault, is an extension of the right aisle.

Also worth seeing: *S.Pietro*, a restored Romanesque church; the *castle*, with a splendid view.

Environs: *c.* 10 km. SE, **Deliceto** has a massive castle (defensive tower from the Norman-Hohenstaufen period).

Bra 12042
Cuneo/Piedmont   p.412☐B 4

Bra has been known since the 12C. The town was first held by the Asti, then the Visconti, the French, the Spanish and finally, from 1552 onwards, it was in the possession of Savoy. It is the home town of Giuseppe Benedetto Cottolengo (1786–1842) who, in 1828, founded in Turin the 'Little House of Divine Providence' for the needy.

The following are worth seeing: *S.Andrea* (Piazza Caduti per la Libertà): A baroque church (1682) ascribed to Guarino Guarini. The magnificent interior is to a plan by Gian Lorenzo Bernini. *S.Chiara* (Via Barbacana): built by B.Vittone in 1742. 15C *Casa Traversa* (Via Papera): decorated with terracottas. *Museo di Storia e d'Arte* and *Museo Civico 'Craveri'* (Via Craveri).

Environs: Pollenzo: a Roman town dating from 170 BC; in 101 BC it was a stronghold against the Cimbri. In 1295 it was destroyed by the Asti. Remains from Roman times include: the *forum*, the *temple*, the 6,000 seat theatre and the 17,000 seat *amphitheatre*; all the buildings are from the 1&2C AD.

Bracciano 00062
Rome / Latium   p.414 □ G 9

Bracciano stands by the lake of the same name and dates back to Etruscan times. First mentioned in 1234 as the castle of the prefects of Vico, it was held by the Orsini from 1419 onwards, and from 1696 by the Odescalchi.

Castello Orsini: Between 1470 – 85 Napoleone Orsini and his son Gentile Virginio took part of the existing prefects' castle and expanded it into one of the most brilliant examples of military architecture in central Italy. In 1494, during Charles VIII's Italian campaign against Alexander VI, Charles waited here for Alexander's troops.
Ouside: Simple, irregular pentagon, with elegant, cylindrical towers and a projecting entrance section, which has an impressive *fresco*, ascribed to Antoniazzo Romano and his school. The splendid SE *courtyard*, with a colonnaded passage and loggia, and the splendid *outside staircase*, are both well worth seeing. Inside: Stuccoed *library* (Room I) and *studiolo* (Room II) are decorated with frescos by Taddeo Zuccari. In Room III, the so-called *bed chamber of Umberto I*, there is a splendid *wooden ceiling* painted by Antoniazzo Romano, and a 15C *four-poster bed*. In Room IX there is a painted *wooden ceiling*, Antoniazzo's earliest work. Room IV contains parts of a *triptych* by the Umbrian school. Room V has frescos in the manner of Pisanello, with typical early 15C subject matter—*rural life and hunting, scenes from 'Fontaines de Jovence'*. The *Sala degli Orsini* (Room VII) has family portraits and marble busts of P.G.Orsini and his wife Isabella de' Medici by Gian Lorenzo Bernini. *Arsenal* (Room XIII) with fine tournament armour. *Etruscan finds.*

Also worth seeing: The parish church of *S.Stefano has a triptych by Salvator Rosa* in the left transept and *portraits of the Orsini family with Saints,* ascribed to Domenichino.

Brescia 25100
Brescia / Lombardy   p.410 □ E 3

Probably of Ligurian origin, the settlement was the capital of the Gallic Cenomani (4C BC). Under Augustus, the Colonia Civica Augusta Brixia was an important centre because of its position on the Alpine road (remains of the Roman buildings still testify to this). After the barbarian invasions it was a ducal seat and the favourite residence of Desiderius in the 8C. Brescia became a free city in the early 12C, and in 1167 it joined the Lombard League. Seriously unsettled by the factional disputes between the Guelphs and the Ghibellines, Brescia fell to the Scaligeri in 1332, to the Visconti in 1337 and finally to Venice in 1426, remaining under Venetian rule until 1797. In 1849, during the Risorgimento, the famous '10 days of Brescia' occurred when 22-year-old Tito Speri led a rebellion against the Austrians.

Piazza del Duomo: The town's political centre up until the 15C. The E. side of the square is occupied by the Rotonda, the

Bracciano, Castello Orsini

Duomo Nuovo and the Broletto. The square has two fountains (the S. one is by A.Calegari, 1754).

Rotonda/Old Cathedral/Winter Cathedral: A conglomeration of what was originally four buildings: the basilica of S.Maria Maggiore (6/7C); above this the centrally-planned building, the so-called Rotonda (modelled on S.Constanza, Rome), with a gallery on eight pillars (late 11C); adjoining it the crypt of S.Filastrio (9–11C); and above it the 16C transept with choir.

Duomo Nuovo: Begun by G.B.Lantana in 1604 as a replacement for the Lombard summer cathedral. Façade (1728–58) by G.B.Marchetti. The plan is based on a Greek cross, with an elongated choir. The tall dome (1825) is by L.Cagnola. *Decoration:* Sacrifice of Isaac, by Moretto (1st altar on right); l'arca dei SS.Appolonio e Filastrio, 1510 (3rd altar on right); statues and busts of various saints by A.Calegari (*c.* 1740).

Broletto: Seat of the medieval town council. Rectangular structure with courtyard,

begun towards the end of the 12C, finished *c.* 1250 (E. section). N. side dates from the 14C (under Bishop Maggi). The Loggia delle Gride opens towards the square. The campanile (1187–1234) is known as the Tor del Pégol.

Piazza della Loggia: Brescia's new political centre from the late 15C onwards. On its W. side are the *Palazzo del Comune* and the *Loggia;* on its S. side, the *Monte di Pietà*, and in the E., the *Torre dell'Orologio.*

Loggia: Modelled on a Sala della Ragione of Terraferma (Vicenza and Padua), and built in two phases — 1492–1508 and 1516–74. The model is probably by the

Brescia, La Rotonda 1 ramps **2** sarcophagus of Bishop B.Maggi (1308, Bonino Campione) **3** pavement drawing with the outlines of the basilica of S.Maria Maggiore **4** tomb of Bishop Lambertino Baldovino (1349, B.Campione) **5** access to the crypt of S.Filastrio **6** remains of the 6C mosaic pavement **7** painting by F.Maffei (procession transferring the relics of Saints from Brescia, attended by C.Borromeo, 1581) **8** three pictures by Moretto, 1533 (St. Luke, St. Mark, the sleeping Elijah) **9** Ascension, altarpiece by Moretto, 1526; underneath are choir stalls by A.da Soresina, 1522 **10** cathedral treasure (behind the altar)

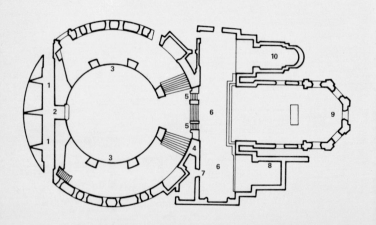

Vicenzan artist T.Formentone to plans by Bramante. The ground floor is an open hall (based on the classical Roman basilica). The top floor has pilasters and thick window frames. A frieze and balustrade run across the top of the loggia.

Monte di Pietà: Right wing built by Filippo de' Grassi in 1484–9, left wing built in similar form in 1597–1600 by P.M.Bagnadore. In the centre there is an archway with an elegant loggia. In 1485, numerous Roman inscriptions were set in the façade by order of the town council. This was the first collection of stone monuments in Italy for which there is documentary evidence.

Torre dell'Orologio: A copy of the clock tower in Venice. The *Porta Bruciata* stands to the left of the row of arches. It is the remains of the gate tower which burnt down in 1184 and was part of the town's oldest W. wall.

Piazza della Vittoria: In 1927, Marcello Piacentini won a competition for the design of this square. On the W. side, the *Palazzo dell'I.N.A.* with the *Torrione* (197 ft. tall, originally dedicated to Mussolini), and

to the N., the massive *Palazzo delle Poste*. The E. end of the square is formed by the *Torre della Vittoria*, in front of which stands the *Arengario*, with reliefs of scenes from Brescia's history. The arcaded market place lies behind the tower. This square was designed as a traditionally Italian square with a political function.

Madonna del Carmine (Contrada del Carmine): Begun in 1429. The façade has a heavily articulated double portal and gables crowned by splendid ornamental brick pinnacles. The interior was originally austere but received a baroque conversion in 1620/1. *Decoration:* Frescos by Foppa (1475, 3rd chapel on right); high altar-piece by Pieter de Witte (1596), a highly agitated 15C terracotta Entombment. The two *cloisters* with frescos of the order's history are particularly interesting.

Madonna delle Grazie (Via Calatafimi): 1529. Portal from a church destroyed in 1517. The inside of this pilgrimage church, which has a nave and two aisles, is richly stuccoed and has fine paintings by Moretto and Maffei. To the left of the church is the elegant *Renaissance cloister*.

Brescia, rotonda

S.Maria dei Miracoli (C.Martiri d.Libertà): A centrally planned building with four domes in the Venetian Renaissance style. It was built in 1488–1581 over a lady chapel—traces of which are found in the façade.

S.Francesco (Via S.Francesco d'Assisi): 1254–65, complex façade. The inside of the basilica, which has a nave and two aisles, has rich 14–16C decoration including paintings by Romanino and Moretto (with sumptuous frames) and, on the high altar, a panel by Romanino in a frame by Lamberti (16C). Well-furnished sacristy (processional cross by F.Croci, 1501). The *Grande Chiostro* (Guglielmo Frisone, 1394) is amongst Italy's finest.

S. Giovanni Evangelista (Contrada di S.Giovanni): Dates from the 4C. The inside of the building of 1140–7 was altered in 1651–74. *Furnishings:* numerous important works by Moretto and Romanino, including Massacre of the Innocents by Moretto (3rd altar on right); following the 4th altar comes the baroque *Cappella della Madonna del Tabarrino* by A.Calegari; the sanctuary has a wooden cross (1480) and some works by Moretto; the *Cappella del SS.Sacramento* (1509–10, left transept) has works by Moretto and Romanino.

Museums (Via dei Musei): Situated close together, Brescia's museums provide an excellent summary of the key phases of Brescia's cultural development. The Roman finds are housed in the *Capitoline Temple*, while the other objects (early Christian, Lombard, medieval and modern documents) are in the secularized convent churches of *S.Giulia* and *S.Salvatore*. *Excavations:* Those areas of the Roman town excavated since 1823 include the *Capitoline Temple* (AD 72, inscription) with three cellae (dedicated to Jupiter, Juno and Minerva). In front of it there is a pronaos with eight columns. The museum is housed in the cella and contains *Vittoria*, a famous Roman statue from the 1C BC, which shows Greek influence and is similar to the Venus of Capua. Under the *pronaos* there is a shrine from the Republican period. It is the oldest known shrine in the Po valley and has fine floors. The remains of the *Roman theatre* (2C AD) lie beside the Capitoline Temple. E. of the excavations is the *former Benedictine convent of*

Brescia, rotonda

S. Giulia. Tradition has it that Ansa, the wife of the Lombard King Desiderius, founded the convent (originally dedicated to St.Michael), in 753. The convent enjoyed an excellent reputation in the Middle Ages (9 empresses or queens, and over 100 princesses, are said to have retreated into it). It was dissolved in 1797. The only buildings in this extensive group to have survived largely intact are the churches of *S.Salvatore*, *S.Giulia* and *S.Maria in Solario*. In 1967, restoration uncovered parts of the 12C façade of the convent. S.Giulia today houses the *Museo Civico dell'Età Cristiana*, which has a unique collection of early Christian and medieval objects and tombs. They include the Querini diptych, a 5C diptych by Boëthius, a 4C reliquary (the earliest known ivory work), the cross of Desiderius, the tomb (1510) of Count Martinengo, and rare medals by Pisanello. *S.Salvatore:* Inside, 13 Roman columns with ancient and Roman capitals and remains of 9C frescos. The side aisles give access to the 8C *crypt*. The cloister houses the town's *Natural History Museum*. *S.Maria in Solario:* An octogonal building with dome from the 11/12C. The church probably derives its name from a Roman altar with the inscription 'Deo Soli Res Publ.' The oratory has three apses and frescos by 16C Brescian artists. Since 1964, the W. cloister of *S.Giulia* has housed the *Civica Galleria d'Arte Moderna*, with 19C works (R.Vantini, A.Canova, Angelica Kaufmann, B.Thorvaldsen, L.Bartolini, M.D'Azeglio and others), and also one of the most important private Italian collections, the *Collezione Achille Cavellini* (works by Capogrossi, Tobey, Schwitters, Baumeister, Fautrier and others). Next to this museum there are excavations of a Roman *domus* with mosaic floors and interesting 2C wall paintings. The *Pinacoteca Civica Tosio Martinengo* originates from the collections bequeathed to the town by Counts Tosio and Martinengo. Apart from works by Raphael, Tintoretto, Veronese and Hayez, the gallery offers a representative cross-section of the 15&16C Brescian school of painting, whose major figures include Romanino, Savoldo, Moretto and Foppa.

Also worth seeing: *Civica Biblioteca Queriana* (Via Mazzini): Founded by Cardinal Querini and open to the public since 1750. Over 1000 early printed books,

Brescia, cathedral square

handwritten volumes and manuscripts, totalling some 300, 000 volumes. *Teatro Grande* (Via Cavalotti/Corso Zanardelli), founded by the Accademia degli Erranti in 1619. Rebuilt in 1739. Elegant late 18C premises. *L'Ateneo di Brescia* (Via Tosio), the former *Pal. Tosio* (early 19C): seat of the Academy of Fine Arts. *S.Maria Calchera* (Via Trieste) has paintings by Moretto. To the left of the church, the *Palazzo Bruni-Conter* (1730), whose courtyard has garden *trompe-l'oeil*. *SS.Afra e Eufemia* (at the E. end of the Corso Magenta), 1776, with 15C choir and crypt. On the 1st altar on the left is a picture by Veronese, (Martyrdom of St.Afra). In the *Palazzo Gambara* (Via Calerari 30) there is a *trompe-l'oeil* on the walls of the staircase (1770). The rooms contain paintings by Moretto and others. *S.Angela Merici* (Via E.Crispi/Piazza Moretto): Built above an early Christian cemetery and altered in 1580-1603. Inside, the 'Baptism of St.Afra' by Bassano il Giovane (on the right), and a 'Transfiguration' by Tintoretto (behind the high altar). *SS.Nazaro e Celso* (Corso G.Matteotti) has fine works by Moretto,

Brescia, Way of the Cross by Girolamo Romanino in the Pinacoteca Civico Tosio Martinengo

Olivieri, Titian, Romanino and Pittoni. *Cimitero* (Via Milano, towards Bergamo): Built in strict classical forms to plans by Vantini; Italy's first monumental cemetery. *SS.Faustino e Giovita* (Via S.Faustino), monumental 17C building. The basilica, which has a nave and two aisles has a processional standard by Romanino, and at the 2nd altar on the right, a crib by L.Gambura. In its present form the extensive *castle* dates from the 2nd half of the 16C. *S.Pietro in Oliveto* (E. of the castle) dates from 1122, but was founded as early as the 8C. The church has an interesting single-aisled interior.

Environs: Montirone (12.5 km. towards Cremona): *Palazzo Lechi,* built in 1738–46 by A.Turbino for Count Lechi in Lombard-Venetian baroque style. The court of honour is separated from the Italian park and garden by an elegant railing. Excellent frescos throughout, with landscapes by Zucarelli in the central part. On the guest floor there is an Assunta by Pittoni and a portrait of Count P.Lechi by Rosalba Carriera. The upper rooms are painted throughout with magnificent architectural frescos (those in the gallery are by Carlo Carloni da Scaria). Fine *collection of paintings* (A.Turchi, G.Romano, Frangipane, Domenichino, Salvator Rosa, Simon Vouet). The elegant *chapel* has frescos by F.Savanni and an altarpiece by Pittoni. The most interesting part of the palace is the *Scuderie* (stables), which are among the best of their kind: the boxes are separated by 24 columns with Olympian Gods. The ceiling fresco of the chariot of the sun is by P.Scalvini. In June 1805 Napoleon stayed as a guest in the Palazzo Lechi. **Montichiari** (20 km. towards Mantua): Picturesque location on the last spurs of the Lake Garda moraines. *Former castle* of the Counts of Bonoris. *Parish church* (1729–60), built to A.Marchetti's plans, with a dome visible from afar and a sumptuous façade. Inside, frescos by P.Scalvini and statues by A.Calegari. The church of *S.Pancrazio* (2nd half of the 12C) stands on the outskirts of the town. The impres-

Brescia, Temple of Vespasian ▷

sive, severe interior comprises a nave and two aisles (columns and pillars alternate). Remains of 14C frescos.

Bressanone/Brixen 39042
Bolzano/South Tyrol-Trentino   p.410☐G 1

Bressanone, the oldest town in the Tyrol, was made a diocesan town in 990 instead of Sabiona. It grew in importance as an ecclesiastical centre—an importance which it still retains—and it is also a commercial town on the route leading over the Brenner to the S.

Cathedral of the Assumption: A Romanesque cathedral built in 1200. The nave is Romanesque but the choir was altered in Gothic style in 1472. In 1745–55 it was then rebuilt in baroque style by Jos.Delai. The lower, massive sections of the two impressive W. towers are Romanesque; the delicate cupolas and lanterns were only completed in the 17C. A memorial stone to the German minnesinger *Oswald von Wolkenstein* (1408) is fixed to the wall on the outside of the so-called summer sacristy, N. of the cathedral. Inside, the church has a single aisle and a tunnel vault, but its basic heaviness is enlivened and brightened by its rich baroque decoration, particularly the very fine *ceiling frescos* (1748–50) by P.Troger. The complex *marble altars* (mid 18C), are by Theodor Benedetti and Franz Faber. The *pulpit* of 1753 is by Josef Wieser of Bressanone. In the right transept there is a fine *statue of the Madonna and Child* (1st half of 16C) by Hans Leinberger. The cathedral *cloister* is regarded as one of the finest of all cloisters. Walls and vaults of the round-arched arcades, which are supported by double columns, are almost completely covered with frescos. Some of the early Gothic frescos, which date from 1330, have been uncovered—they decorated the cloister before it was vaulted—the later frescos date from between 1390 – 1510. The painters were Hans von Bruneck and Konrad von Brixen. Adjoining the cloister, SE of the cathedral, **Diocesan Museum** is worth seeing and houses the valuable cathedral treasure.

Liebfrauenkirche (St.Mary's Church): This church was built in the 12C to the W. of the cloisters. The cross vault and side aisle were added in the 14C; the baroque decoration in the 17C. Fine Romanesque frescos can still be seen in the Gothic vaults.

St. Johannes (adjoining the cathedral cloister to the S.: Originally a baptistery, it dates from the 13C. The cross vault above the square nave is 14C. The upper sections of the nave wall are painted with frescos from 1250, the lower sections have paintings dating from 1410. The choir has early Gothic frescos of 1330, which were restored in the 19C. Apse frescos date from 1420.

Bishops' Castle: The layout and corner towers of this High Renaissance building (designed by the court architect Albrecht Lucchese in 1591-1600), survive from the original structure of 1270. The W. wing was rebuilt in baroque style in 1710, incorporating a chapel (the ceiling painting by Caspar Waldmann dates from *c.* 1710). On the 1st floor of the castle there are 24 bronzed terracotta statues (similar to the figures in the Innsbruck court church) by the Bressanone court sculptor Hans Reichle. He also executed the medallions in the arched galleries.

Also worth seeing: *Town parish church of St.Michael:* The tower dates from 1459 and the remainder of the church from *c.* 1500; the inside was rebuilt in baroque style in 1757 (ceiling frescos, 1758, by Jos.Hauzinger from Vienna); on the altar there is a large group of figures (1460) showing Christ bearing the Cross. *Heiliges-Kreuz-Kirche (church of the Holy Cross):* In 1764 Franz Singer built this late baroque church on to the façade of the seminary (with baroque library). Inside, the rocaille work and ceiling frescos (1764) are by Franz Anton Zeiller. Fine wrought-iron *window grilles, oriel windows, arcades* and *inn signs* may be admired in the old part of town. Particular attention shoud be paid to the curved

Bressanone, frescos, cathedral cloister ▷

façade of the *Gorethaus* (Pfarrplatz 1), built in 1581, with delicate Gothic and Renaissance grilles, oriel windows and a fine arcade.

Environs: Near Bressanone, towards Brenner, **Novacella/Neustift** has a foundation of Augustinian canons, dating from 1141 and rebuilt after 1190. However, the existing complex, with its courtyard and library consists of 17&18C buildings. In the courtyard there is a *well*, with an octagonal well house decorated with paintings by Nikolaus Schiel (1670). The *Collegiate Church of Our Lady* was rebuilt in 1190 after a fire. In 1468 a three-aisled choir with granite ashlars and a roof of coloured, glazed tiles was built; Jos. Delai rebuilt the interior in baroque style in 1734–8. The beautiful rocaille work, which gives the church a bright and serene appearance, is by Anton and Augustin Gigl from Innsbruck, and the fine windows are by Matthäus Günther (1735 – 43). The *tower chapel* still contains frescos of 1460, by Master Konrad of Bressanone, and in the *old sacristy* there are paintings of 1470 by M. Pacher. The church entrance has a Pietà (*c.* 1400). In 1695/6, G.B. and Simon Delai added a square, centrally planned building with an octagonal dome and lantern to the N. of the nave. This is the *Chapel of the Virgin Mary*, with stucco work by Carlo Conseglio and frescos in the dome by Kaspar Waldmann. The *cloister,* built *c.* 1200 (ribbed vaults 1370), adjoins the church to the S. Frescos on the walls date from 1330 and 1490, some are by F. Pacher. The *tombstones* include the fine, deeply carved white marble tomb of Oswald von Säben (d. 1465). The *St. Michael chapel,* an unusual two-storeyed rotunda built *c.* 1200 stands to the SW, in the courtyard. The small church of *St. Jakob* in **Afers** has interesting wall paintings from the mid 15C.

Brindisi 72100

Brindisi/Apulia   p.418☐P 11

Known as Brundisium in classical Antiquity, it has always been a port for traffic to the E. (Greece and Egypt). Under Rome it was the end of the 'Via Appia', and in the Middle Ages it was a stopping-place for the Crusaders' fleets. The Roman poet Virgil died here in 19 BC.

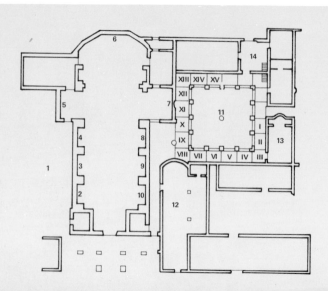

S.Giovanni al Sepolcro (Via S.Giovanni a.S.): The history of this round church is quite obscure; in the 13C it belonged to the Knights of the Holy Sepulchre. The roof is not original, and the building was probably domed. The *portal* (fine capitals and shafts) appears too large for the church. *Inside* it is not in fact circular and there may once have been a narthex against the straight wall. Eight columns with capitals, some of which are ancient.

S.Benedetto (near to S.Giovanni, key in the house beside the church): Remains of an 11C Benedictine convent. The church appears as a solid block with tiny windows. Originally it had three domes, but these were replaced in the 15C by a Gothic ribbed vault. The campanile is 11C, and the nave has a fine Byzantine *portal*. Beside the church is the Norman *cloister* of the former convent; some columns with fine animal carvings are worth seeing.

Colonne Romane (Via Regina Margerita): Brindisi's landmark. Tradition has it that the column, which is 62 ft. tall and dates from the classical Roman period (its 'sister' fell down in 1528 and is now in the

Novacella (Bressanone), inner courtyard with well of the Augustinian convent

Bressanone, cathedral of the Assumption,

Bressanone, cathedral 1 old cemetery **2** side altar with altarpiece by Jos.Schöpf **3** altar with altarpiece by Chr.Unterberger **4** altar with altarpiece by F.Linder **5** altarpiece by P.Troger, 1753 **6** high altar by Th.Benedetti with altarpiece by M.Unterberger, 1752 **7** altar with altarpiece by F.Unterberger **8** altar with altarpiece by Chr.Unterberger **9** altar of St.John with altarpiece by G.Cignarolli, 1756 **10** altar with altarpiece by Jos.Schöpf **11** cloister with 15 arches **I** frescos by Rupert Botsch, 1492 **II** Leonhard of Bressanone, 1462 **III** L. of Bressanone, 1470 **IV** H. of Brunico, 1417; wall frescos, 1330 **V** Leonhard of Bressanone, 1472 **VI** painter of the Pacher school, 1482 **VII** Pacher school, c. 1500, and L. of Bressanone, c. 1450 **VIII** painter of the Bohemian school, c. 1400, and vault paintings by L. of Bressanone, 1464–77 **IX** frescos, c. 1400 **X** wall frescos, c. 1390, vault frescos, c. 1410 **XI** frescos, c. 1410 **XII** wall frescos, c. 1405, vault frescos, c. 1390 **XIII** frescos, c. 1390, 1410 and 1426 **XIV** Leonhard of Bressanone, 1463 **XV** Leonhard of Bressanone, 1456 **12** Liebfrauenkirche (St.Mary's church) **13** church of St.Johannes **14** diocesan museum. Former canon's building. The museum contains Gothic paintings and sculpture, religious folklore, a collection of cribs, and the famous cathedral treasure with the eagle chasuble (c. 1000)

Novacella, Oswald von Säben

Brindisi, S.Maria del Casale

Piazza S.Oronzo in Lecce), marked the end of the 'Via Appia'; it has a marble capital with busts of Roman gods. Beside the column, to the left, is the house (with an inscription) where Virgil is said to have died (see above).

Also worth seeing: *Cathedral* (Piazza Duomo): Norman; completely rebuilt in baroque style. *S.Lucia* (Via S.Lucia) with 12C frescos in the crypt. Near the cathedral, the *Provincial Archaeological Museum. Castle*, built by Frederick II in 1233; 13C *Porta Mesagne*.

Environs: About 3 km. towards the airport is the church of *S.Maria del Casale*, a single-aisled Lombard-Gothic building built *c.* 1320. Geometric patterns of multicoloured stone on the façade, and inside there are early 14C Byzantine frescos.

Brisighella 48013
Ravenna/Emilia-Romagna   p.414□G 6

Brisighella stands on three hills. Prehistoric and Roman finds have been uncovered nearby. *Castrum Brasichellae* was strengthened at the end of the 13C and was then held by a number of rulers. *Collegiata SS. Michele e Giovanni Battista* (Piazza Carducci): Altered several times in the 17C. *S.Maria degli Angeli:* Built 1518–25, with *stucco decoration* of 1634 and a *Sacra Conversazione* (1520) by Marco Palmezzano in the choir. *Palazzo Municipale* (Piazza Marconi): 1824–8, with a small archaeological *museum. Torre dell'Orologio:* Built 1290, rebuilt 1850.

Environs: *Pieve del Tho* (or *S.Giovanni in Ottavo*): A church built *c.* 1100 on Roman foundations; last restored in 1959. The portal lunette has a medieval sculpture (? 8C). Inside: some Roman fragments have been incorporated; early 15C frescos, an 18C statue, and 16C paintings.

Tèside (Brunico), chapel of St.George, ▷
frescos by Leonhard, 1559

Brunico/Bruneck 39031
Bolzano/South Tyrol-Trentino   p.410 □ G 1

Churches: The parish church of *Unserer Lieben Frau* (Our Lady) was built in 1851-3 (choir walls date from 1515). It has a stone Pietà (1400) and a large wooden crucifix (1500). *St. Katharina auf dem Rain* (St. Catherine in the Field) was built in 1345 and rebuilt in baroque style in the 17C. It houses a Pietà and a group around the Cross (1450). The neo-Gothic *Ursulinenkirche* (Ursuline church) was built in 1411–27. The late baroque *Spitalkirche zum Hl. Geist* (hospital church of the Holy Ghost) (1759/60) has a harmoniously designed interior with altarpieces by Joh.Georg Grasmayr and fine rocaille work. *St.Nikolaus* in Stegen (14&15C) contains a baroque high altar, a pulpit dated 1600 and transept windows by Hans von Bruneck (1410), and also a Virgin of the Protecting Cloak in the nave by S. von Taisten, dated 1481.

Also worth seeing: Beside the parish church, the *Ragan Residence* of 1680; in the E. of the old part of town, the 16&17C *Sternbach Residence* with a room frescoed by Kaspar Waldmann (1715). *Schloss Bruneck* stands high on a hill. Built in 1251 as a bishops' castle and extended in 1330 and 1519. The 13C *Lamprechtsburg* stands on another hill.

Environs: Casteldarne/Schloss Ehrenburg (W. of Bruneck): A complex with Romanesque, Renaissance and baroque elements. **S.Sigismondo/St.Sigmund:** A village in the Puster valley with the fine 15C late Gothic parish church of *St. Sigmund*, whose high altar (1430) is one of the most important Tyrolean Gothic works. **Valdaora di Mezzo/Mitterolang** (to the SE of Bruneck): The church of *St.Agydius*, originally built *c.* 1400, has a high altar with a very fine altarpiece depicting the Adoration of the Magi, probably painted by Marx Reichlich in *c.* 1490. **Tèsido/Taisten** (E. of Bruneck): The parish church of *St.Ingenuin und Albuin* was rebuilt in baroque style (1767–8) on Gothic foundations by F.Singer from Götzens. It retains the Gothic buttresses of the nave, vault and spire and there are paintings by F.A.Zeiller.

Burgúsio with the Marienberg monastery

Budrio 40054
Bologna/Emilia-Romagna   p.410☐F 5

S.Lorenzo (Piazza Filopanti): Rebuilt in the 17C and completed to plans by Torreggiani. The campanile dates from the 15C. Inside, paintings by Mastelleta, Alessandro Guardassoni, Gaetano Gandolfi etc.

Pinacoteca Civica 'Inzaghi' (Via Mentana 9): Italian paintings from the 15–18C — an especially fine *Madonna and Child with St. Roch and St. Sebastian* by Dosso Dossi (1489/90 to c. 1542).

Also worth seeing: *Palazzo Comunale* (Piazza Filopanti): 15C, much restored. *S. Agata* (Via Marconi), 15C, rebuilt by Tubertini in 1792. *S. Domenico* (or the Chiesa del Rosario), built in the 17C with a painting (early 17C) by Tiarini.

Burgúsio/Burgeis Mais 39024
Bolzano/South Tyrol-Trentino   p.410☐E 1

Still a town of narrow alleyways and medieval farmhouses. In the 13C Romanesque parish church of *St. Maria*, the nave was extended to the W. in the 15C and a stellar vault was added. The left, side altar has a notable Pietà, dating from c. 1400. The chapel of *St. Michael* (by the cemetery) is also 13C. The Romanesque church of *St. Nikolaus* has a flat wooden ceiling and, in its apse, 13C Romanesque frescos survive. The *prince's castle*, on a rock above the Adige, is also 13C whilst the façade facing the courtyard has 16C paintings. *St. Stefan of Marienberg*, high above the Fürstenburg, is originally 8C.

Benedictine Abbey of Marienberg (Monte Maria): This abbey, which is visible from afar and stands on a steep height, was originally founded in the 11C by the masters of Tarasp in Scuol (Engadin). It was moved to St. Stefan in 1146 and to Marienberg in 1150. Most of the present-day abbey is 16&17C. The collegiate church of *Our Lady*, completed in 1201, was largely rebuilt in baroque style in c. 1645. The church façade still has an interesting Romanesque portal with columns and a fine stone Madonna (1400). The crypt, completed 1156, has excellent Romanesque frescos dating from c. 1160; together with Hocheppan, this is the earliest fresco cycle in the S. Tyrol.

Environs: Málles Venosta/Mals: *St. Benedikt* (in the N. of the town) dates from the 9C, and the tower is 12C. Remains of Carolingian stucco work can still be seen in the three altar niches of the E. wall. The frescos on the N. wall of the nave and on the altar wall (also Carolingian, 800–814) are among the best in the German-speaking area. The 19C parish church of *Mariae Himmelfahrt* (the Assumption) has a fine Gothic tower dated 1523–31. The cemetery chapel of *St. Michael*, a two-storeyed structure of 1509–16 with a net vault on the upper storey, has an altar dated 1600. Only the 12C Romanesque tower survives from the former church of *St. Johann* (now a house). *St. Martin* dates from the 12&16C. In the middle of the town, next to the parish church, are the ruins of the 12C *Fröhlichsburg*. **Láudes/Laatsch** (SW of Mals): The small two-storeyed church of *St. Leonhard* was built by Peter Koffel in 1408. The lower storey has a gap where the road passes through, and the upper storey has a Gothic winged altar (1490). The frescos on the outside are c. 1410, while those inside date from 1609. **Tárces/Tartsch** (SE of Mals) has a Romanesque church. *St. Veit am Tartscher Bühel*. Further to the S., at the entrance to the Tauferer valley leading to the Ofen Pass, lies **Glorenza/Glurns,** which was made a town in 1304. With its wall, parapet walk, arrow slits, moats and towers, the town is the only one in the Tyrol to have its defences intact. The parish church of *St. Pankraz* is mainly 15C. There are 16C houses with arcades. **Sluderno/Schluderns** (E. of Glurns, at the end of the Münstertalstr.): The parish church of *St. Katharina* was originally built by Andre Bichler in 1493–1509 and contains the notable tomb of Jacob VII Trapp, carved in white marble by Wolf Verdross in 1573. The church of *St. Michael* (by the cemetery) dates from *c.* 1500. The *Churburg* castle, dating from the 13&14C, has a fine arcaded courtyard (1525–35; groin vault and round arches; paintings *c.* 1580), a splendid, beautifully decorated interior and an interesting armoury. All in all, one of the most important S. Tyrolean castles to have survived intact. S. of Schluderns, **Montechiaro/Lichtenberg** with the 14&16C parish church of the *Hl. Dreifaltigkeit* (Holy Trinity), and the beautifully situated early 13C castle of *Burg Lichtenberg*. SE of Lichtenberg, at the outlet of the Sulden valley, the visitor comes upon **Prato allo Stelvio/Prad** with *St. Johannes,* a 13C Romanesque church with Gothic frescos dating from 1400, as well as **Agumes/Agums** and the *parish church of St. Georg* (1493).

Busseto 43011

Parma / Emilia-Romagna   p.412 ☐ E 4

Rocca (Piazza Verdi): This castle was probably constructed in 1250 and rebuilt in the 16C; the façade was altered in the 19C.

S. Bartolomeo (Piazza Verdi): Begun in 1436, rebuilt in the 18C, with the Gothic façade remaining intact: 16C frescos (4th chapel on the left) and rich *church treasure.*

Vila Pallavicino (Corso Pallavicino): Built in the 16C, perhaps by Vignola, with *stucco and fresco decorations* from the 17&18C. Houses the *Museo Civico* with paintings from the 15–18C and a fine Verdi section.

S. Maria degli Angeli (Corso Pallavicino): Not completed until 1470–2, with a *terracotta Pietà* (*c.* 1500) by Guido Mazzoni (next to the 4th chapel from the left) and, in the adjoining monastery, *books of antiphons* from the 15&16C.

Verdi's birthplace (in Roncole Verdi) and the **Villa Verdi di S. Agata,** the composer's impressive home, a little way outside the town.

Burgúsio, Marienberg monastery, fresco, 12C

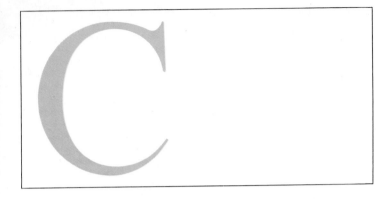

Cagli 61043

Pesaro and Urbino/Marches   p.414□H 7

Cathedral: The building was altered in 1790 but the portal of 1424 by Antonio di Cristoforo da Cagli still survives.

Chiesetta della Misericordia: The façade has a 14C *Madonna of the Protecting Cloak*, and inside there is a 15C *terracotta Madonna*; the frescos in the sanctuary are from the same period.

Also worth seeing: Remains of the Roman *Ponte Mallio* next to the new bridge across the Torrente Bosso. Frescos by Giovanni Santi, Raphael's father, in *S. Domenico* and in the portico of the *Palazzo Comunale*.

Cágliari 09100

Cágliari/Sardinia   p.422□C 14

Cágliari, the main town of Sardinia 'between the sea and the mountains' is amongst the oldest towns in Europe to have been inhabited without a break. It is also one of the most beautiful harbours in the Mediterranean. Subject, over the years, to Carthage, Barcelona, Pisa, Naples and Byzantium, it was probably founded by Phoenicians from Tyre at the same time as Carthage. Originally known as 'Carel' (Car means 'fortified town'), it became Caralis, Kalaris, Calaris, Caller and then finally Cágliari. The Romans finally established themselves there in 238 BC.

S.Saturnino: One of the oldest Romanesque churches, it dates from the 5/6C and, although damaged by English bombs in World War 2, it is still standing. The entrance to this impressive basilica (which is under a preservation order), is in the Piazza San Cosima (only open at certain times). The tunnel vault supported by four columns, has been rebuilt. The ground plan is a Greek cross. Benedictines from Marseilles extended it to the E. An early Christian burial ground (2–5C) has been uncovered in this apse.

Castle: Pisa built powerful fortifications on the hill on which the castle stands and since then the upper town has been called after the Sardinian name for them, 'Casteddu'. In 1305/7, Giovanni Capula strengthened the defences by building the massive towers of *San Pankrazio* and *the Elephant*.

Cathedral: Begun in 1250; extended 1274–1300. In 1312, it gained a *marble pulpit* supported, on lions by 'Master Gugliemo' (of Innsbruck) from the cathedral in Pisa, an unusually good early

Romanesque relief in the Pisan style (1159–62). The pulpit was split in the baroque period and since the end of the 17C, two of the lions have lain at the side of the marble balustrade of the choir. The others are by the stairs leading up to the prefecture, a castle formerly belonging to the House of Savoy (1799–1814). Since 1933, the cathedral façade has been altered in the style of Pisa and Lucca, using old plans and materials. The *crypt* has three burial chapels with Sicilian baroque stucco. *Sacristy* and *chapterhouse* are Catalan-Gothic and house the *cathedral treasure* and panel paintings of the Neapolitan and Flemish schools.

La Purissima: At the lower end of the Via La Marmora is the newly restored, late Catalan-Gothic church of La Purissima (1554), which has side chapels, fine groin vaults with painted stars, a 16C crucifix, a small organ of 1758 and a triptych of 1593.

National Archaeological Museum: The museum on the Piazza Indipendenza owes its origins, in 1806, to a bequest by Viceroy Carlo Felice: 1st room: Old Sardinian finds. 2nd room: Punic finds. 3rd room: Punic-Roman finds. 4th room: Roman-Greek finds. 5th room: Christian remains. 6th room: Coin collections. 7th room: Early medieval art. On the top floor there is a small picture gallery with works by Italian, Spanish and local painters of the 15&16C.

Also worth seeing: *S.Agostino* (1580), in the Spanish classical style, partly to plans by Bramante. *S.Eulalia* and *S.Giacomo* in Catalan Gothic style (16C). The baroque church of *S.Michele* (magnificent sacristy with famous stucco by Colombino and Altomonte). Basilica of *S.Domenico*, a modern building (1954) by R.Fagnoni on the old substructure of the nave designed by Nicolò Fortiguera (1254), whose *rosary chapel* and *cloister* have survived. The Sardinians greatly venerate the 14C *Chiesa della Madonna di Bonaria* at the beginning of the Via Milano (the Madonna is the patron saint of both the island and sailors), and the 15C *Chiesa de S. Ignazius von Làconi. The town hall* stands out on the Via Roma, opposite the harbour. It has been rebuilt in Aragonese Gothic style following the damage of 1943 (the original

Cágliari, cathedral, foot of the marble pulpit

builder was Crescentino Caselli). With its spacious halls, it dominates the character of this boulevard. The ground floor has brightly painted frescos by F.Figari, a 16C triptych of the councillors by Pietro Cavaro, and the famous *Flemish tapestry* by Franz Spierink, representing Caesar's triumph. The entrance to the *amphitheatre*, Sardinia's most important monument from the Roman period, lies at the N. end of the Viale Fra Ignazio da Làconi. The arena is open to the SW and is still used for opera. Its rows of seats (1/2C) were hewn from the limestone and it had a capacity of 10,000 spectators.

Environs: Quartu Sant'Elena, situated on the 'fourth mile' of the Roman road through the 'Sarrabus'. The *Chiesa dei Cappuccini* dates from the 13C and has blind arcades and a strange, square apse. The *cemetery church* is also 13C. The sacristy of the *parish church* has a large 16C altarpiece of Saints and Prophets, probably by Antioco Mainas. A well-preserved *corridor tomb* (technically known as 'Is Concas' and known in the vernacular as 'San Pietro in Paradiso') lies just to the right of a new road, 8 km. from the S.S.

125 near Ponte Piscina Nureddu. **Sinnai** (the name refers to forced settlers) is known for its characteristic 'foreign' wickerwork (made of straw, with brightly-coloured wool weaving). To the N. (W. of the suburb of Pirri), the ruins of the 13C Pisan fortification of *S.Michele* (rectangular layout, with three towers and a ditch) are to be found. In **Sestu,** on the 'sixth mile' of the Roman Caralis-Turris road, the late Gothic parish church is less interesting than the *Chiesa S.Gemilano,* an Arab building in 13C Romanesque style which has just two aisles and Oriental decorative motifs. In **Assémini** (NE), beside the 13C late Gothic *parish church* with its highly decorated façade and cupolas above its side chapels, particular attention should be paid to the *Oratorio di S.Giovanni,* which is the best-preserved Sardinian building from the 9/10C. Its ground plan is a cross-in-square (unique for Sardinia) and there is a small dome at the intersection of the vaults. In the E. of the village of **Uta,** standing isolated beside the cemetery, the Romanesque *Chiesa S.Maria* has survived intact. It has a nave and two aisles, arches on columns, and is built of varying shades of reddish sandstone. Regarded as the

Cágliari, archaeological museum

Chiesa della Madonna di Bonaria

finest country church in Sardinia, it was built (1135–48) by monks from Marseilles in co-operation with French, Tuscan and Arab builders. N. of the S.S. 130, at **Villaspeciosa** is the *Chiesa S.Platano*, which was first mentioned in 1141 as being in the possession of the monks of S.Victor from Marseilles. Typical of the buildings constructed by these monks, it is divided into just two aisles (cf. Sestu; very rare in Sardinia). Each aisle ends in an apse and aisles are separated by paired clusters of columns. The Byzantine origin of **Villasor** is testified to by a tablet (today in the National Archaeological Museum, Cagliari). The *village church* still has late Gothic structural features. The fine campanile was added in the 15/16C. There is a peculiar early 15C fortified tower with battlements. *S. Leonardo,* the 16C parish church of **Serramanna**, has lost nearly all its Gothic characteristics. Inside, two lions flank a richly decorated portal. In a field 3 km. to the W. of Serramanna there is a *Perda fitta*, a granite block aligned to the E. with 10 'buttonholes' arranged vertically and two 'eyeholes' on top. It is thought to be an early form of the 'dea mater mediterranea', dating from between

the end of the 4th millennium BC and the beginning of the 2nd millennium.

Caltagirone 95041
Catania/Sicily   p.420☐K 17

This town dates from an ancient settlement (Stone Age burial grounds have been uncovered in the area). The name is derived from the Arabic 'Kalat-el-Geluna'. It was conquered and settled in 1030, and became Norman in 1090. In 1693 the town was destroyed in an earthquake.

Cathedral of S. Giuliano (Piazza Umberto I): Founded under the Angevins and completely rebuilt in 1818. Modern *façade and campanile* dating from 1956. Inside: nave, two aisles and dome. The decoration includes a fine 15C. *wooden crucifix* on the altar in the left aisle.

Chiesa del Gesù (near the Piazza Mercato): Jesuit church dated 1570, with fine late 16C *façade*. The single-aisled interior has fine *marble altars* in the side chapels. The 3rd altar on the right has paintings by

Cágliari, corridor tomb near Ponte Pascina Nurreddu

Polidoro da Caravaggio ('Nativity' and 'Annunciation', 16C.) Beside the church is the old *Jesuit college* of 1570; formerly the university, today it is the *Palazzo degli Studi*. In the courtyard there is an ancient *relief* (Archaic, early 6C BC).

S.Giacomo (Corso Vitt. Emanuele): Built under the Normans in 1090, and rebuilt after the earthquake of 1693. Inside: nave, two aisles, and numerous works by the Gagini. Note the silver *reliquary of St. James* in the 'Capella del Sacramento' (N. and G. Gagini, late 16C.).

S.Giorgio (Via L.Sturzo): Founded by the Genoese in 1030, rebuilt 1699. Inside, a *painting of the Trinity'* (2nd altar on the left), attributed to the Flemish painter Roger van der Weyden, and a holy-water stoup of 1552. Only the campanile, which has been restored, survives from the original building.

S.Maria del Monte (at the end of the Scala): Built in the 12C; rebuilt in the 16&17C. The façade is late 16C and the fine campanile is 18C. Inside, the nave and two aisles have fine double columns. The

Caltagirone, view

high altar has a painting of the Madonna in Byzantine style.

Museo della Ceramica ('Il Teatrino', Giardino Pubblico): This museum surveys ceramic art from its beginnings (prehistoric finds, classical Greek vases) through the Middle Ages up to the present (everyday Sicilian pottery).

Corte Capitaniale (beside the cathedral): 16/17C palazzo, with fine portals, by Antonuzzo and G.Dom. Gagini.

Also worth seeing: *Chiesa del Salvatore* (Via L.Sturzo), an octagonal building with three 18C apses. *Chiesa del Rosario* (opposite the above) with remnants of a majolica floor and a statue of the Madonna by Antonello Gagini (1542). The *Scala*, a magnificent flight of steps dating from 1608, connects the upper and lower towns. *Museo Civico* (Via Roma, in the former prison built by the Bourbons in the 18C.) with numerous modern paintings.

Environs: About 20 km. to the E., **Grammichele,** built in 1693 on a hexagonal plan after the earthquake (the centre of the town is a hexagonal piazza with six streets leading from it). The *Chiesa Madre (S. Michele),* 1724–57, stands on the piazza.

Caltanissetta 93100

Caltanissetta/Sicily   p. 420K 17

Cathedral of S.Maria la Nova e S. Michele (Piazza Garibaldi): Built 1570–1622 and damaged in World War 2. *Façade* with a fine baroque portal and campaniles on both sides. Laid out on a Latin cross ground plan, the church has a nave, two aisles, and a broad dome. The entire nave is decorated with *frescos* and *stucco*, both dated 1720, by the Flemish artist W.Borremans.

S.Agata (also the *Collegio,* Corso Umberto): A Jesuit church, begun in 1605 on a Greek cross groundplan and centrally planned. There are fine marble inlays on the richly decorated altars; in the left aisle there is a marble pala by Ignazio Marabitti (1719–97). The 1st side chapel on the left has *frescos* by W.Borremans.

Also worth seeing: *S. Domenico* (Via S. Domenico): 15C; rebuilt in baroque style in the 18C, with a fine façade (the 'Misteri' figures used in the procession are kept in the church). *S.Maria degli Angeli* (Via degli Angeli): fine Gothic portal well worth seeing. *Castello di Pietrarossa* (by S.Maria d.A.): destroyed in the 16C, it is unclear whether it is of Saracen or Norman origin (in 1373 a meeting of the Sicilian barons was held here). *Museo Civico* (Via N.Colajanni): with archaeological finds from Sabucina (see below).

Environs: About 3 km. to the N., the **Badia di S.Spirito:** Norman, built by Count Roger on the occasion of his victory over the Arabs; consecrated in 1153. The interior is single-aisled and the apse has 15C *frescos*. To the right of the main portal is a Romanesque *font*. About 6 km. to the N. are the **excavations of Sabucina:** In 1962 work began on uncovering a Sican-Greek town from 6–4C BC; *remains of the town's fortifications*, among other things have survived. Some 4 km. to the S., on Monte Gibil-Gabel, are the ruins of the **ancient town of Nissa**, where excavations of *streets* and *remains of houses* (chequer-board plan, streets at right angles) have been excavated.

Camerino 62032
Macerata/Marches   p.414□H 7

Cathedral: Rebuilt by Carlo Maratta in 1806–32, following an earthquake. Inside there is a 14C *wooden crucifix* and, in the crypt, the *sarcophagus of S.Ansovino* with scenes from his life.

S.Venanzio: The old portal from the 2nd half of the 14C survives from the church, which was rebuilt in 1875. The lunette contains the *Madonna and St.Porfirio* and the architrave bears *Christ with the Apostles*.

Also worth seeing: The former church

of *SS.Annunziata* with 15C paintings. In the former church of *S.Francesco* there are frescos dated 1462, probably by Girolamo di Giovanni. The *Palazzo Comunale* has a bust of Urban VIII by Bernini. The Piazza Cavour has a *bronze statue of Sixtus V* by Tiburzio Vergelli (1587).

Environs: The *Villa Maddalena*, built in the 17C, contains another bust of Urban VIII by Bernini.

Campione d'Italia 22060
Como/Lombardy   p.412□C 2

Pilgrimage church of **Madonna dei Ghirli:** Several flights of steps lead up from the lake to the church in theatrical, baroque style. The façade with the triumphal arch dates from its rebuilding in the 18C; the main body is 14C. There are frescos in the arcaded passages flanking the church. In the right arcade there is a fresco of *The Last Judgment* (1400) by Franco and Filippolo de Veris. The interior is single-aisled and there are 14C frescos by a Lombard artist greatly influenced by Giotto.

Campobasso 86100
Campobasso/Molise   p.416□K 10

This, the chief town of the province, was formerly the seat of the counts of Molise. The old town lies at the foot of the castle; the new town in the plain was founded in 1814.

Castello Monforte: Built in 1549 by Cola di Monforte on the ruins of castle destroyed by an earthquake in 1546; today the castle houses a *war memorial*.

S.Giorgio: The portal is probably as early as 12C: the sacristy frescos are *c*. 1400 and the altar dates from 1629.

Also worth seeing: The churches of *S. Bartolomeo* and *S.Leonardo* with 13C portals. *S.Antonio Abate* was built in 1572. At the Porta S.Antonio, remains of the medieval *town fortifications* still survive. The *Museo Provinciale* contains archaeological finds, medieval weapons and seals.

Cannóbio 28052
Novara/Piedmont   p.412□C 2

Santuario della Pietà (By the lake shore): Begun in 1522 and enlarged by St.Carlo Borromeo in 1571, it is a domed building in Bramante's style. The octagonal dome was built to plans by Pellegrino Tibaldi. The façade, decorated with statues, is from 1909. There is a fine *altar* by Gaudenzio Ferrari; in the predella there is a silver *Pietà* of 1522, which is said to have miraculous properties.

Also worth seeing: S. Vittore (Via L.Meschio): A collegiate church begun in the 11C and rebuilt in 1730; classical façade. *S.Marta* (Via Mantelli): restored in 1581, with a Mannerist *Madonna and Child* by Camillo Procaccini on the high altar. *Palazzo della Ragione* (Via L.Meschio): built by Mayor Ugolino Mandello in 1291–4, and partially rebuilt in the 17C.

Environs: Càrmine Superiore with the small, old church of *S. Gottardo* (1332–1431); old frescos.

Canosa di Púglia 70053
Bari/Apulia   p.416□M 10

Cathedral of S.Sabino: Consecrated in 1101, extended by three bays in 1689. The only cathedral in Apulia with five domes (three over the transept, two over the nave). Unfinished 19C façade. Inside: 18 ancient columns; the bishop's throne and the pulpit are masterpieces of Apulian art. *Throne:* Carved between 1078 – 89 by Romualdo (inscription on the right side of the throne); the animal motifs (elephants and eagles) show traces of Arab influence.

The *pulpit*, the oldest surviving one in Apulia, is a splendid structure, especially the eagle supporting the lectern. The right transept leads to the 'Tomba di Boemondo': *Tomb of Bohemond*, the son (d. 1111) of Robert Guiscard; magnificent two-leaved bronze door with Saracen ornamentation in the rosettes (niello technique).

Also worth seeing: *Basilica di S.Leucio* (Colle SS. Angeli): remains of an early Christian basilica on the foundations of a Roman temple. *Battisterio di S.Giovanni:* A baptistery from the 5/6C. Remains from the Roman period: *Amphitheatre:* (near the railway station), *Arco Romano* (road to Foggia), *Roman bridge* across the Ofanto, *Roman chamber tombs* (Ipogei Lagrasta) and *ancient sarcophagi* on the Torrente Lamapopoli. *Museo Civico* with antique sculptures.

Environs: Canne della Batteglia, *c.* 20 km. towards Barletta. Generally thought to be the site of the famous battle of Cannae in 216 BC, between Hannibal and the Romans. *Antiquarium, ruins of the medieval town.* To the left of the road to Canosa is a large *menhir*.

Canossa
Reggio Emilia/Emilia-Romagna   p.412□E 5

The castle of Canossa was built in 940. In the 13C it came into the Pope's hands and was destroyed by Ottavio Farnese in 1537. Excavations begun in 1877 uncovered the original castle and the ruins of the church of S.Apollonio. The castle is best known as the place where, in 1077, at the instigation of the Countess Matilda, Pope Gregory VII lifted the excommunication of Emperor Henry IV.

Castle Museum/Museo Naborre Camparini: Contains mementos of the chief participants in this historical event, and also finds from excavations (including the old *font* from *S.Apollonio*) and early 12C *castings of capitals decorated with figures* from S.Maria in Toano.

Capestrano 67022
L'Aquila/Abruzzi   p.416☐I 9

S.Pietro ad Oratorium, in the environs of Capestrano, was founded in the 8C and rebuilt in *c.* 1100. The *portals* and frescos depict the *24 elders of the Apocalypse*. The *ciborium* is 13C.

Capo di Ponte 25044
Brescia/Lombardy   p.410☐E 2

Against the magnificent background of the Concarena range, on a steeply towering rock, stands the church of **S.Siro** (16C campanile). This simple 11/12C building has a nave, two aisles, three apses and an irregular groundplan. Fine Romanesque *portal; Font.*

San Salvatore (1.7 km. towards Edolo). This church, still referred to as 'il Monastero', is the remnant of a Cluniac monastery from the end of the 11C. It has a nave, two aisles, a transept and a choir with three apses. Burgundian influence is apparent in the decorative elements.

Environs: The *Parco Nazionale delle Incisioni Rupestri* at **Naquane** contains an important series of rock engravings. Produced over a period of *c.* 2,500 years, the engravings cover Neolithic, Etruscan, Latin and Roman times. Four main periods can be distinguished. The 1st period, until *c.* 2200 BC, has schematic figures, sundials, people praying, and geometric drawings; the 2nd period, 2200-1800 BC, has traces of drawings, while the 3rd period (1800-1000 BC) has weapons and animals; the 4th period, after 1000 BC, has not only representations of animals, weapons and humans, but also drawings of buildings and everyday scenes. **Bienno:** The 14/15C church of *S.Maria Annunziata* has a single aisle and three bays. Decoration: altarpiece by Fiamminghino (1632), an Annunciation, frescos in the nave and vault of the sanctuary by Romanino (Life of the Virgin Mary, *c.* 1540). **Breno:** The single-aisled *Cathedral of S.Salvatore* has a splendid baroque portal. Inside: an early work by Romanino, *Virgin and Saints; Transfiguration* by

Canosa d. P., Tomba di Boemondo

Tomba di Boemonda, door

Palma il Vecchio, and an *Annunciation* by Fiamminghino. Tall, elegant *campanile* (1673). The single-aisled church of *S. Antonio* (1334–59) is one of the few purely Gothic buildings in this area. *Frescos* by Romanino.

Edolo: The sanctuary of the 15/16C church of *S. Giovanni Battista* has frescos of the life of John the Baptist (1530–2).

Caprarola 01032
Viterbo/Latium   p.414☐G 9

A small village which Pope Paul II took from the Anguillara in 1465. Sold by Julius II to the Farnese in 1504. Except for the Villa Farnese, it reverted to the Papacy in 1649.

Palazzo Farnese: Pier Luigi Farnese had a pentagonal castle built by Antonio Sangallo the younger, in co-operation with Peruzzi. The massive foundations surrounded by a fosse were completed under Pier Luigi's son, Cardinal Alessandro Farnese, who inherited the estate. A compe-

Caprarola, castle 1 vestibule with coat of aarms and views of towns held by the Farnese, Federico Zuccari, c. 1567–9 **2** Salone di Giove (hall of Jupiter) with painted views by Vignola **3** Sala della Primavera **4** Sala d'Estate **5** Sala d'Autunno **6** Sala d'Inverno **7** colonnaded courtyard **8** Scala Regia with grotesques and landscapes by Antonio Tempesta, 1580–3

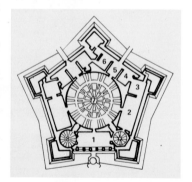

tition for its extension as a summer residence was won by Jacopo Barozzi da Vignola who, between 1559 and his death in 1573, almost completed the work. Montaigne visited the castle in 1580 and found it complete, including the garden.
Outside: The *Via Nicolai* rises steeply towards the villa and ends in an oval forecourt, in front of the rusticated entrance to the 'Cantine' (cellar). Broad ramps curve around this 1st forecourt up to the 2nd one, which is trapezoidal. The entrance opens above a niche set in a structure very like a triumphal arch. At this point the old fosse has been filled in and staircases on either side of the niche lead up to the rustic entrance. Its simplicity contrasts strongly with the lavish complexity of the ascent, which surmounts three stages of terraces. The pentagonal villa stands on foundations intended for a fortress and consists of three clearly distinguished storeys.
Inside: The circular innner courtyard is of unusual balance and beauty. The ground floor is an arcaded courtyard with rusticated masonry, and the *piano nobile* is a loggia with Ionic semi-columns; finally comes the plain attic-like top storey. The *scala regia*, one of Vignola's most important works, is a monumental spiral staircase borne by 30 paired Doric columns. The walls are decorated by landscapes and grotesques. Not only is the Villa Farnese of great importance for Mannerist architecture, but the richness of its frescos also makes it one of the finest buildings from the 2nd half of the 16C. Besides glorifying the Farnese family, the frescos reveal the tastes, interests and understanding of an intellectually complex transitional phase in the history of ideas. Federico and Taddeo Zuccari were responsible for most of the decoration but Giacomo Bertoia, Giovanni de Vecchi and the architect Vignola also worked as architectural painters.
Park and casino: The park is terraced and divided into *upper and lower gardens*. Ravine-like paths, hidden grottoes and splashing rivulets midst shady groves, are typical of the hermetic nature of a typical

Caprarola, Charles V and Cardinal Alessandro Farnese, painting by the Zuccari

FRANCISCVS·GALLIARVM·REX·CAROLVM·V·AVGVSTVM
COMPRIMENDAE·DEFECTIONIS·CAVSA·IN·BELGAS·PROFICISCENTEM
ET·ALEXANDRVM·FARNESIVM·CARDINALEM·MAGNIS
DE·REBVS·LEGATVM·LVTETIAE·PARISIORVM
AMPLISSIMO·APPARATV·SVSCIPIT·ANNO·SALVTIS·ↃↃDXL

Mannerist garden. The main attraction of the water systems installed in the upper gardens in 1620 is the so-called 'Catena', a water staircase of dolphins, with a flight of steps, rusticated walls and grottoes on either side. It is fed by the *Fontana dei Fiumi*, a fountain surrounded by river gods. Behind it is the *Palazzina* (Casino), the former summer residence of Cardinal Alessandro Farnese and today that of the Italian President. It is a delicate building with an airy double loggia by Vignola.

Church of S. Teresa: Masterpiece of the architect Girolamo Rainaldi, with a *Virgin and Saints* on the high altar ascribed to Guido Reni; the painting on the left side altar is by Giovanni Lanfranco.

Capri 80073

Naples/Campania   p.418□ K 12

Capri is one of the most famous islands in the Mediterranean and even in antiquity it was visited for its scenic beauty. The Roman emperors Augustus and Tiberius had

villas there (see below). It was also inhabited in Palaeolithic times, as the finds in the *Grotta dei Felci* on the S.side of the island show.

Capri: former **Cathedral of S. Stefano** (on the Piazza Umberto I): Until 1818 is was the seat of a bishop but today it is only a simple parish church. In 1683, an earlier Gothic building was altered in the baroque style of Capri. A flight of steps leads up to the *façade* with pilasters, volutes and a curved gable. Interior with a nave and two aisles, domes over the crossing and the aisles; fine *stucco*. Note in particular the *marble floor* in front of the main altar (ancient fragments from the Villa Jovis).

Certosa di S. Giacomo (in the S.of the town): A Carthusian monastery founded 1371–4 and destroyed several times in the course of centuries; dissolved in 1808. Restoration began in 1933. The *church*, a single-aisled hall church with fine cross vaulting; semicircular apse (externally polygonal with tracery window); a large rose-window and a Gothic portal from the 14C. Next to it is a *cloister*, which has ancient columns with capitals. To the S. is the

Caprarola, Palazzo Farnese

Renaissance *large cloister* (1563). Small *archaeological museum*.

S.Costanzo (on the road from the port to the town): Oldest church on the island. 11/12C exterior built on a central plan in the Byzantine style (drum pierced by eight Romanesque windows), extended *c.* 1330 (two-storeyed entrance to the N. and a square sacristy to the S.—the orientation of the church was turned through 90 °). Inside, the vaults are supported by ancient columns.

Villa Jovis (E. tip of the island): Built in the 1C AD for Emperor Tiberius; excavated in 1932–5. Ground plan: Four wings around a square courtyard (with cisterns underneath). To the W., the *service rooms and staff quarters;* to the S.the *baths;* to the E., the state rooms with a semicircular *tribuna* above the rocky precipice; to the N., the Emperor's *private apartments*.

Anacapri: S.Michele (Piazza S.Nicola): Built by D.A.Vaccaro in the early 18C. Fine façade. A vestibule leads into an octagonal central area with four side chapels, rectangular sanctuary and short transepts. Above

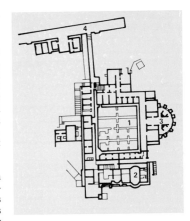

Capri, Villa Jovis 1 cisterns **2** baths **3** public rooms **4** covered walk

the main room is a chapel. *Majolica pavement* of 1761 ('Paradiso terrestre' by Leonardo Chiaiese).

Also worth seeing: Two more Roman Imperial villas (*Villa of Damecuta*, Anacapri

Capri, view

Capri, Certosa di S. Giacomo

& *Palazzo a Mare*, Marina Grande). *Baths of Tiberius* (next to the Palazzo a Mare,). *Scala Fenicia* (Phoenician stairway) from the Marina Grande to Anacapri. The numerous grottoes, particularly the *Blue Grotto, Grotta dell' Arsenale, Grotta del Castiglione, Grotta di Matromania,* all of which were used as nymphaeums in classical times. The vantage point of *Punta Tragara* is in the SE of the island.

Capua 81043

Caserta/Campania   p.416☐K 11

In the 9C, under the Lombards, people from ancient Capua built the present city on the site of 'Casilinum', its former river port. It has often been fought over in the course of its history.

Cathedral of SS. Stefano e Agata (Piazza del Duomo): Founded under the Lombards as early as 856 but repeatedly altered. It was damaged in World War 2 and has now been restored to its original form. It is preceded by a rectangular *atrium* with 20 magnificent columns and ancient

Capua, Museo Campano

capitals (3C AD). To the right is the massive 9C *campanile* (ancient materials were used in the building; i.e. the columns at the corners). Inside: Basilica with nave and two aisles, *monolithic columns* of granite. Note the 13C *Easter candlestick* by the last column on the right. The *crypt* beneath the choir has remnants of the cathedral's medieval pulpit. In the 4th chapel on the right is a *triptych* by Antoniazzo Romano (1489). The sacristy houses the *church treasure*.

Chiesa dell' Annunciata (Piazza Marconi): Built in the 13C, but rebuilt in Renaissance (1531–74) and baroque styles. Fine façade, *dome* designed by Domenico Fontana (1543–1607). *Roman ashlars* were incorporated on the right side. Among the items worth seeing are the 17C *ceiling paintings* (damaged in World War 2).

Palazzo dei Principi Normanni (Via G.Andreozzi): From the 2nd half of the 11C; with ancient material from the Roman amphitheatre in S.Maria Capua Vetere (see below); rebuilt under the Hohenstaufens. Only one of the four former corner towers of the building survives (with fine double-pointed-arch windows).

Museo Campano: (in the *Palazzo Antignano* with 15C Catalan-Moorish portal; Via Roma): The two departments have objects from the classical period, from the Middle Ages and modern times. On the ground floor, to the right of the courtyard, the *museum of stone monuments* is particularly worth seeing. It has a rich collection of ancient Campanian inscriptions. *Rooms 3–8* contain the finds from a shrine to 'Dea Matutina' (fertility goddess), uncovered at S.M.Capua Vetere. On the top floor: fine mosaics in *room 2*; an extensive ancient coin collection in *room 7*. The medieval department is housed from room 21 onwards: *room 23* is outstanding, with some Romanesque-Hohenstaufen sculptures from the Volturno bridge, which was destroyed.

S. Angelo in Formis (Capua) ▷

Also worth seeing: Church of *S.Salvatore Piccolo* (Via Principi Normanni) with a Lombard inscription on the architrave of the portal and fine 14C frescos in the apse. Church of *S.Caterina* (Piazza S.Francesco) dated 1383. 10C Lombard church of *S. Salvatore Maggiore a Corte* (Via Principi Langobardi). Church of *S.Marcello Maggiore* (Via Gran Priorato di Malta), founded in 851, with fine side portal. Church of *S.Domenico* (Piazza S.Tommaso d'Aquino), founded in 1258. *Chiesetta S.Michele a Corte* (Via S.Michele a.C.) with fine façade and 10C frescos in the apse. 16C *Palazzo Comunale* (Piazza dei Giudici). *Ponte Romano* across the Volturno, 2C BC, fortified in the Hohenstaufen period, largely destroyed.

Environs: About 5 km. SE, **S. Maria Capua Vetere,** the ancient Capua. The **Cathedral** *(Collegiata di S.Maria;* Piazza Matteotti) is particularly worth seeing: Originally 5C, the present structure is 18/19C. Inside there are a nave and four aisles and notable features include the 51 ancient columns and a Renaissance ciborium in the chapel at the end of the right aisle. The Roman *amphitheatre,* known as the 'Anfiteatro Campano', (Piazza 1. Ottobre 1860), is the largest to be built in classical times (1st half of 1C AD) before the construction of the Colosseum in Rome. Nearby there is a good collection of antiquities: The *Mithraeum* (Vicolo Mitreo), a shrine of Mithras from the 2/3C AD (original frescos in the subterranean hall). Remains of a three-arched *triumphal gate* erected for the Roman emperor Hadrian (2C AD; at the end of Corso Umberto I). Some 4 km. to the NE is **S. Angelo in Formis** with the famous Romanesque *basilica* of the same name; built in 1073 on the ruins of a temple of Diana. In front of the façade there is a portico with pointed Saracen arches. Inside, a nave, two aisles, three semicircular apses, and ancient columns; the 11C frescos are particularly fine (the apse has a Byzantine Christ Pantocrator).

Caravaggio 24043
Bergamo/Lombardy   p.412□D 3

This is the birthplace of Michelangelo Merisi, known as 'il Caravaggio', one of the forerunners of baroque painting.

Carpi, Piazza dei Martiri with S.Maria Assunta

Santuario della Madonna di Caravaggio: A road leads from the Porta Nuova, a triumphal arch (1709), to the Santuario, which lies outside the town. One of the great places of pilgrimage in Lombardy, Filippo Maria Visconti ordered the building of the church, which was consecrated in 1451. It was rebuilt by order of S.Carlo Borromeo to plans by Pellegrino Tibaldi. Begun in 1575, this church was not completed until the 18C. *Outside:* The church stands at the point where the three arcaded pilgrims' courtyards meet. It is a domed, centrally planned structure with large transepts and open arcades in front of them on two sides. *Inside:* Under the dome is the Tempietto with the object of pilgrimage. Excellent 19C frescos by Luigi Cavenaghi and Giovanni Moriggia (dome).

Carignano 10041

Turin/Piedmont   p.412□B 4

Originally a Roman foundation *(Carinianum)*, and later a fief of the bishops of Turin. Carignano fell to the Dukes of Savoy in 1418. The town was destroyed by the French in 1536.

Cathedral of S.Giovanni Battista: Begun by Benedetto Alfieri in 1757-67. Unusually bean-shaped basic form of the church nave.

Also worth seeing: *Spirito Santo:* Mid 17C. The dome was painted by the Giovannini brothers in 1719. *Chiesa dell' Albergo di Carità:* The church of the hospice was built to a design by B.A.Vittone and consecrated in 1749. The dome is typical of Vittone, with pendentives and a half-drum. *Santuario del Vallinotto,* built by B.A.Vittone in 1738/9.

Carpi 41012

Modena/Emilia-Romagna   p. 410□F 4/5

Carpi was first mentioned at the time of the Lombard King Astolf (8C). In the Middle Ages the town experienced dynastic quarrels and fell to the Pope in 1115. From 1327 onwards it was ruled by the Pio family from Modena, and under Alberto 'il dotto' (the learned one) and the last member of the family to govern, the town enjoyed its heyday. Emperor Charles V handed it to the Este in 1525, and they held it until 1859.

Cathedral of S.Maria Assunta (Piazza dei Martiri): The church was begun in 1514 by order of Alberto Pio to a design by Baldassare Peruzzi. Work on the chancel, interrupted in 1518, was completed in 1523. The façade was completed in 1667; the portals were added in 1701. The *interior decoration* (by Lelio Rossi), and most of the *wall paintings* (Fermo Forti and Albano Lugli) are 19C. The *altars,* most of whose paintings are 16C, display the 'scagliola' stucco technique perfected by Guido Fassi in Carpi in *c.* 1600. The *treasury* houses gold pieces (16–18C).

S.Maria (also **Sagra**, Piazza Re Astolfo): Founded by Astolfo in 751 and consecrated by Pope Lucius III in 1184. In 1515 it was given a new *façade,* a fine work to designs by Peruzzi. Features to survive from the Romanesque building include the apses, the portal with a mid 12C *Crucifixion* in the lunette, and the campanile built in 1217–21.

S.Nicolò (Piazza S.Nicolò): Church with dome over the crossing, built on the site of an earlier building. The apse and dome from the 1st phase of building (until 1507/8) are probably by a pupil of Bramante. Peruzzi was responsible for the nave, during the 2nd phase. In accordance with Franciscan tradition, there is a portico in front of the façade. Inside, paintings by artists from Bologna and Emilia (16–18C), and also the original painting in the dome by Giovanni del Sega (early 16C).

Castello dei Pio (Piazza dei Martiri): A brick building begun in the 14C on the site of an older castle; completed in the 16C. To the left of the façade, which was completed under Alberto Pio, are the *Uccelliera* (1480) and the *Torre del Passerino* (1320). In the middle of the façade is the 17C cam-

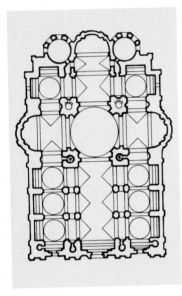

Carpi, cathedral of S. Maria Assunta: The dome, the short nave and the enormous transept make the building appear round.

panile, and to the right of it, the *Torrazzo di Galasso* (1456). The 1st floor houses the *Museo Civico* with 17&18C Carpi scagliola work, 17&19C furniture, 18C designs by the architect Girolamo Dosi, and mementoes of figures from the Risorgimento. The stately rooms on the 2nd floor include the *chapel*, the *Studio del Principe* (both 16C, with wall paintings by Bernardino Loschi) and the *Sala della Torre del Passerino* (Lombard wall paintings of court life).

Also worth seeing: *S. Francesco* (Via Trento e Trieste): rebuilt 1682; houses a sarcophagus of 1418 by a pupil of Jacopo della Quercia, and a 15C fresco of the Madonna attributed to Alberti da Ferrara. *S. Bernardino da Siena* (Via Trento e Trieste): 1620 with the Martyrdom of St. Lawrence, by Palma Giovane, S.Carlo Borromeo by Procaccini, *c.* 1600 and a painting by Stefano Lemmi, *c.* 1700). *Chiesa del Crocifisso*, now the *Santuario dell'*

Adorazione (Via S.Bernardino da Siena): Built in 1724 with a 16C terracotta Madonna by Begarelli. *S.Ignazio* (Corso Manfredo Fanti), built after 1670. *Palazzo Bonasi-Gandolfi* (Corso Manfredo Fanti 40), 18C. *Convent of S. Chiara* (Corso Manfredo Fanti), with 16C cloister. *Portico del Grano* (Corso Alberto Pio), early 16C.

Casale Monferrato 15033
Alessandria / Piedmont   p.412 □ C 4

Casale Monferrato was in the possession of the bishops of Vercelli from the end of the 9C. After gaining its freedom from Vercelli in 1196, there followed a thriving period—one which survived even its destruction by Vercelli in 1215. From 1305 onwards it was the main town of the duchy of Monferrato. The town fell to the Gonzagas in the 16C, and to Savoy in 1703. In the war between Louis XIV and Savoy, it was expanded into one of the strongest fortifications in Europe.

Cathedral/Basilica di S.Evasio: A magnificent Romanesque church, consecrated in 1107 and restored by Arborio Mella in 1859–61. The highly articulated façade leads into a narthex of five bays. This in turn is followed by a nave and four aisles. Inside, note the *statue of Mary Magdalene with Angels* by Giovanni Battista Bernero and the *tombs of the Gambera bishops and Bernardino Tibaldeschi-Orsini* by Matteo Sanmicheli.

S. Domenico (Piazza S. Domenico): A Gothic building in brick. Renaissance façade with a lunette by Matteo Sanmicheli. Inside is the *tomb of Benvenuto San Giorgio.*

Also worth seeing: *S. Caterina* (Via Trevigi): By Giovanni Battista Scapitta. Inside there is an *Ascension* by Giovanni Battista Bernero. The *Torre Civica:* Rebuilt by Matteo Sanmicheli in 1512 after a fire in 1508. The *castle* (Piazza Castello). The *Palazzo Gozzani di Treville* (Via Mameli), a building by Giovanni Battista Scapitta with a classical façade by Ottavio Bertotti

Scamozzi. The *Palazzo del Municipio* (Via Cavour) is by Filippo Giovanni Battista Robilant (1778). The *equestrian statue of Charles Albert* on the Piazza Mazzini is by Abbondio Sangiorgio.

Environs: *Santuario di Crea:* Refuge of St.Eusebius, Bishop of Vercelli (340–70) before he was pursued by the Arians. The Romanesque church of *S.Maria Assunta* was enlarged in 1483 and 1608–12.

Casamari 03020
Frosinone/Latium   p.414 □ I 10

Set in a gentle hollow of a mountain valley, this abbey is one of the most important foundations in Latium and, together with Fossanova (q.v.), one of the purest examples of Cistercian Gothic style in Italy. Its site is probably also that of the ancient *Cereatae Marianae,* the home of Gaius Marius. The abbey was founded in 1095 by a community of priests who had submitted to the rule of the Benedictine order. It was taken over by the Cistercians in 1151, and completely rebuilt subsequently. Honorius III consecrated the church in 1217.

Access to the church and the abbey is through the *Casa Abbaziale,* a gateway whose top storey originally served as the abbot's rooms. From the archway there is a fine view of the façade of the abbey church. The arches reflect the division of the church into a nave and two aisles; the powerfully proportioned nave towers above the portico and dominates the church. The W. wall has three simple window openings and a gable like the pediment of a temple. There are massive flying buttresses. All is in keeping with the freely chosen poverty of the reforming spirit which had led to the foundation of the order. Similarly the capitals of the great portal have simple foliage motifs, whilst the arches themselves are enlivened by their rich articulation. The inside is of a simple, balanced elegance, undecorated except for a triforium-like blind arcade on the wall of the nave and crocket capitals. In contrast to early monasteries (c.f. Fossanova), there

Casale Monferrato, Palazzo Gozzani

is a ribbed vault (in six sections, over the straight-ended choir typical of Cistercian buildings). The projecting transepts have two aisles of their own and there are straight-ended chapels to the E. The altar ciborium in the crossing by Carlo Rainaldi originates from the church of SS.Apostoli in Rome.

Abbey: This is S. of the church, and arranged around the cloister, whose paired columns have excellently worked capitals. A fine portal (E. side), flanked by two-arched windows leads into the chapter-house. This is divided by means of four compound piers into three aisles with ribbed vaulting and clearly shows French influence. On the N. side of the cloister a richly articulated portal, which is similar to the main portal, provides access to the church. The refectory (121 ft. long, restored 1952), is divided into two aisles by strong cylindrical columns. The abbey museum contains some finds from the ancient Cereatae Marianae and some notable baroque paintings.

Cascia 06043
Perugia/Umbria   p.414☐H 8

Situated in the mountains of Umbria, Cascia, the birthplace of St.Rita, is a place of pilgrimage.

Pilgrimage church of St. Rita: The church was consecrated in 1947. The glass coffin of the saint is in a richly decorated chapel (frescos by Ferrazi, Montanarini and others) on the N. side of the nave.

Collegiate church of S. Maria: The 11/12C building was partly rebuilt in the Renaissance. Inside: frescos by Angelucci del Frangipane and Domenico da Leonessa; a valuable ciborium (1567) by Francesco Piergentili; and also the monuments of Poli and Frentanelli in marble and mosaic.

S. Antonio: Inside the church are some frescos by Nicola da Siena (oratory) and by unknown 15C Umbrian masters.

Also worth seeing: The saint lived for 40 years in the convent of *Agostiniane di S. Rita*. Gothic choir stalls, 15C frescos, and an Ascension by Pomarancio, are the outstanding features inside the originally Gothic church of *S.Francesco* (1424), which was altered in baroque style in the 18C.

Environs: Roccaporena, the saint's birthplace with a chapel. **Logna** with *S. Giovenale*.

Caserta 81100
Caserta/Campania   p.416☐K 11

Originally an insignificant little village (La Torre); in 1752 the palace, 'La Reggia' was built along the lines of Versailles. In 1819 the name of 'Villa Reale' was changed to 'Caserta' (as in the town to the NE, the present Caserta Vecchia). **Palazzo Reale** (Piazza Carlo III): Built from 1752 on-wards in the baroque style by Carlo Vanvitelli for King Charles III of Naples and Sicily. The palace — the largest of the Neapolitan Royal Family's buildings—is immense, being 810 ft. long, 603 ft. wide, 118 ft. high and covering some 474,000 sq.ft. It has 1970 windows and over 1,200 rooms on five storeys. The outer walls are 11 ft. 6 in. thick. There are four courtyards (810 ft. x 603 ft.). The palace, with its well-preserved interior decoration, provides a history of the house of Bourbon in Naples (1734–1860). *Exterior:* The façade in brick and ashlar is very uniform. Inside, the following are particularly worth seeing: the *state staircase*, three flights with 116 steps, designed by Vanvitelli; the *palace chapel*, also by Vanvitelli (two storeys; opposite the high altar is the King's 'Tribune'), opening off the upper vestibule; on the left of the same vestibule is the entrance to the *royal chambers* (arranged symmetrically to the queen's chambers in the right wing of the palace); the *throne room* with 44 medallions of the Kings of Naples; the *court theatre* (ground floor of the W. wing; opened 1769; *c.* 500 seats, five horseshoe-shape tiers, incoporating 12 ancient columns from Pozzuoli). Behind the palace lie the **palace gardens**, which, since they cover some 300 acres and are 3 km. from the palace to the grand cascade, should be visited in a car. The way leads from the middle of the garden façade along the *Viale Mediano* to the round *Fontana Margerita*. After a sharp left turn from the palace it proceeds through the *'Bosco Vecchio'* to the *Castelluccia*, built in 1769 as a 'toy fortress' for the royal princes. To the N. is the *Peschiera Grande* (984 ft. x 393 ft.), on which sea battles were staged to please King Ferdinand IV. On to the Fontana Margerita, across the *Ponte di Ercole* along the *Canalone*, past the *Cascata dei Delfini*, the *Fontana di Eolo*, the *Fontana di Cerere* and the *Fontana di Venere* to the *Cascata Grande* with a plethora of statues (the *Aquedotto Carolino*, built in 1752-64 to supply the palace and park with water, ends here). On the E. side of the Canalone is the ingeniously laid-out *English Garden*, dating from 1782 onwards;

Cascia, polyptych in S. Giovenale ▷

many rare trees and other plants; the design of the *Bagno di Venere* is very fine.

Environs: Some 10 km. NE, **Caserta Vecchia:** The 12C cathedral of *S.Michele* (Piazza Vescovado), in Norman Romanesque style with good 13C dome. Inside: a fine 13C pulpit; the late Romanesque campanile of 1234 is worth a visit. On the outskirts of the town there are the *remains of the 9C castle*. Some 4 km. NW of the palace is **S.Leucio,** where King Ferdinand IV of Naples wished to establish a 'model town'. The church of *S.Maria delle Grazie,* a centrally planned baroque building, is worth seeing.

Cassino 03043

Frosinone/Latium   p.416□I 10

Casinum suffered devastation and destruction both in antiquity and in the early Middle Ages—at the hands of Hannibal, the

Caserta, Palazzo Reale 1 palace chapel **2** State staircase **3** throne room

Caserta, Palazzo Reale

Visigoths under Alaric, the Vandals, the Heruli and the Saracens. In World War 2 the town and monastery were turned into a bomb site. All that remained intact was the *Archaeological Area (Zona Archeologica)* with the almost circular *amphitheatre* and the tomb of the Matrone Ummidia Quadratilla. On the way to the abbey is the ruin of the *Rocca Iánula*, built by Abbot Aligerno (949–86), where Roger of Sicily kept Pope Innocent II prisoner.

Abbey of Monte Cassino: Megalithic stonework under the abbey from the 4&3C BC is the remnant of the original acropolis of Casinum, whose temple of Apollo was converted by Benedict of Nurcia into an oratory dedicated to St.Michael (529). Benedict attended to the accommodation of his pupils and brothers and in place of the old sacrificial altar on the slope of the mountain he built another oratory dedicated to St.John the Divine, which was to become the core of the later basilica. Using the 'Rule' drawn up for his monks on Monte Cassino, St.Benedict created the basis for his Benedictine order. After his death on 21 March 547 he was interred in the oratory of St.John together with his sister, S.

Scholastica, who had died 40 days before. The building constructed by Benedict was destroyed in 581 by the Lombards, before whom the monks fled to Rome with the autograph of the rule. In 717 the monastery was founded anew under Pope Gregory II and became a centre of learning. Paulus Diaconus, the historian of the Lombards, died here in 799 after several years' residence. Charlemagne visited the abbey in 787. Under Abbot Gisulfo (797 –817), a basilica (nave, two aisles) was built over the oratory of St.John. The abbey was destroyed by the Saracens in 883. The Benedictines returned to Cassino under Abbot Aligerno in 950 and founded the abbey for the third time. Abbot Atenulf (1011–22) built a church along German lines. Under Abbot Desiderius (1058–86; he became Pope Victor III in 1087), the church was again replaced by a new building based on the early Roman Christian basilicas. Pope Alexander I consecrated it in 1071. The entire complex was gradually replaced in the Renaissance. After the total destruction of 1943/4, it was completely rebuilt to its former plan, except for parts of the old crypt. *Relics of Benedict and his sister Scholastica.*

Caserta, Palazzo Reale, salon

Caserta Vecchia, with S. Michele

Castelbuono 90013
Palermo/Sicily   p.420☐K 16

Matrice Vecchia *(S. M. dell' Assunta,*
Piazza Margherita): Founded in the mid
14C. In front of the façade there is a fine
Renaissance portico and two *portals*, (that
on the left in Catalan-Gothic style). The
campanile has an octagonal spire, overlaid
with majolica. Inside: A four-aisled basilica
(the fourth aisle was added in the 16C)
with fine Romanesque *capitals*. The
easternmost aisle has a 15C *marble ciborium*; the other E. aisle has a *Madonna*,
probably by Antonello Gagini (1520). The
high altar has a fine *triptych* from the late
15C/early 16C by a Sicilian artist.

Matrice Nuova *(Natività della Vergine,*
Largo della Parrochiale): Built in 1601–9,
rebuilt after an earthquake in 1820. The
interior has a nave and two aisles. Latin
cross ground plan. The transepts are fine
stuccoed altars. There is a painting by
Giuseppe Velasquez on the 3rd altar in the
left aisle. Also a *church treasury*.

Castle: Built in 1316. Massive rectangular building with corner towers. Inside the
chapel of St.Anne has fine late 17C stucco
by Giuseppe and Giacomo Serpotta.

Castel Castagna 64030
Teramo/Abruzzi   p.416☐I 8

S. Maria di Ronzano: The church was
built in 1181 and damaged by fire in 1183
(parts of an unfinished portico can still be
seen on the façade). Frescos showing
Byzantine influence survive in the apse
and the transept: the right transept has
scenes from the Old and New Testaments; the

left one depicts the *Chosen in the lap of the patriarchs;* and the right apse has *Saints;* the main apse, *Christ blessing* and *New Testament scenes.* The *altar table* is pre-Christian.

S. Giovanni al Mavone (ad Insulam): built in the 12&13C, with 15C frescos inside.

Castel del Monte
Bari/Apulia   p.416☐N 11

This, the finest Hohenstaufen castle in Italy, is known as the 'Crown of Apulia'. It was built as a hunting lodge by Emperor Frederick II around 1240, probably to his own plans. Used as a prison for the grandchildren of Frederick II after the defeat of the Hohenstaufen by the house of Anjou in 1268. Early Gothic limestone building in the form of an equilateral octagon with eight octagonal towers. Each storey has eight rooms of equal size. (Little survives of the interior decoration and the marble wall facing). Apart from the Gothic *portal* in the form of a Roman triumphal arch, the exterior is completely undecorated. Inside there are still remains of the original drains and lavatories. The *throne room* is room 1 on the top floor.

Castel di Sangro 67031
L'Aquila/Abruzzi   p.416☐K 10

Cathedral/S.Maria Assunta: The medieval church, probably founded in the 10C, was destroyed by an earthquake in 1456. In 1727 it was rebuilt in baroque style. The façade with the two campaniles is unusual; Renaissance portal. Inside: 16C *wooden altar facing*; *Christ on Calvary* by Francesco de Mura, and 18C paintings. The 17C *font*, with a *baptism of Christ* on the lid, is preserved in the parish house.

Castelfranco Emilia 41013
Modena/Emilia-Romagna   p. 412☐F 5

The **parish church of the Assumption**

Cassino, tomb of U. Quadratilla

(Via Emilia): fine *Assumption* by Guido Reni in the apse; *St.Barbara* by Francesco Monti (left side aisle) and a *guardian angel* by Francesco Gessi (last chapel on the left) from the second half of the 17C.

S.Giacomo (Via Emilia): 17C-18C, with 17C and 18C paintings by Angelo Piò, Elisabetta Sirani and Alessandro Tiarini. The inside was restored recently.

Castelfranco Veneto 31033
Treviso/Venice   p.410☐G 3

Cathedral/S. Liberale (Piazza S. Liberale): Built by Franc. Maria Preti (1723–45) in Palladian style. The campanile was formerly a tower in the city's defences which has been rebuilt. The solemn interior is single-aisled on a Latin cross ground plan; it has a high dome and

Ionic columns. In the chapel to the right of the sacristy is one of Giorgione's most famous works, executed in 1504 or 1505. In the *Madonna and Child with St.Liberale and St.Francis*, he uniquely uses two different perspectives, one for the foreground and one for the landscape in which the Madonna sits, thus creating for the viewer an uneasy tension from an apparently calm scene. The *sacristy* has a number of good paintings, particularly frescos by P.Veronese (1551).

Castello: Built 1199–1209 in a strategic location to defend Treviso against Padua.
Casa Pellizzari (Vicolo della Chiesa 15): Giorgione is said to have lived here. The frieze painted in grisaille in the hall on the top floor is probably by Giorgione himself.

Castel Gandolfo 0040

Rome/Latium   p.414☐H 10

A little town picturesquely located on Lake Albano. It is famous for having been the summer residence of the Pope continuously since 1604. The ancient *Alba Longa*, wreathed in legend, and destroyed by the third Roman king Tullus Hostilius in *c.* 600 BC previously occupied the site of the town. In the neoclassical and Romantic periods, Castel Gandolfo was a favourite abode of German visitors to Rome (including Winckelmann, Goethe and A.Kauffmann). The Papal possessions have been extraterritorial since 1929. In the main square, the *Piazza del Plebiscito*, is the church of *S. Tommaso*, a centrally planned building by Gian Lorenzo Bernini of 1661, with stucco decoration. The picture at the high altar is by Pietro da Cortona. On the N. side of the square is the *Papal Summer Palace* (not open). The simple palace complex, built around a rectangular courtyard, was begun by Carlo Maderno under Urban VIII. Only the side facing the square is at all ornate. In the garden there is an audience building for 8,000 visitors.

Villa Barberini (Papal possession; not accessible): Built above a villa dating from the time of Emperor Domitian.

Also worth seeing: the *Emissario*, a subterranean diversion gallery to drain excess water from Lake Albano. 2.5 km. long.

Castel del Monte, castle

Castellana Grotte 70013
Bari/Apulia   p.416☐O 11

A town on the heights of the Murge, world-famous for the stalactite caves discovered in 1938 (by Prof. Anelli, 2 km. SW of the town). Along with the Adelsberg grottoes in Slovenia, these are the finest in Europe. The 'Grotta Bianca' is particularly worth seeing owing to its innumerable splendid stalactites and stalagmites. Routes are open for about 2km. *Cave Museum.*

Castellarano 42014
Reggio Emilia/Emilia-Romagna   p.412☐D 4

The **parish church of S.Maria** has the remains of a crypt with sculpted capitals and a 12C lunette. Not far from the church are medieval remains of 7 arches, which originally belonged to a Roman *aqueduct.*

Also worth seeing: *Tower and clock tower* of the castello which was almost completely destroyed in 1944. A small medi-

Castelfranco Veneto, cathedral

Castel di Sangro, cathedral

Castel Gandolfo, papal palace

eval fort. *S. Croce* (restored in 1926). The *Palazzo Comune* by Carlo Reina (1926).

Castell'Arquato 29014
Piacenza/Emilia-Romagna   p.412□E 4

Collegiata dell'Assunta: A basilica with a nave and two aisles. Built in 1122; rebuilt and restored several times. All that remains of the building on the site before the basilica — destroyed in the earthquake of 1117—is an apsidiole (baptistery) on the right side of the church. On the left side (on the Piazza Matteotti), under the 15C portico, the Romanesque *portal*, with the work of one of Nicolò's successors in the lunette, can still be seen. There are wall paintings in the 15C *Cappella di S. Caterina* (beginning of the right aisle) and baroque paintings and stucco in the Cappella di S.Giuseppe (1630, middle of the right aisle). The *baptistery* (end of the right aisle) has an 8C font and 14C wall paintings. Main altar with Romanesque reliefs, pulpit and 14C wooden crucifix in the *sacristy*.

Museo della Collegiate: Roman sarcophagi; mosaics; an 11C Byzantine woven cloth with depictions of the Eucharist; 14C-16C wooden crucifixes; 15C-17C woodwork; 16C-17C intaglio; paintings (by Traversi and Stern).

Palazzo Pretorio (now the town hall on the Piazza Matteotti): The nucleus of the palace dates from a building erected in 1293. The pentagonal tower is from the 15C, while the loggia, the covered outdoor staircase and the front structure with its portico were added in the 15C.

Castel Rigone 06060
Perugia/Umbria   p.414□G 7

This picturesquely located mountain town gives a fine view of the valley and the Apennines. Nearby is Lake Trasimeno.

Madonna dei Miracoli: This is regarded as the finest Renaissance church in the Umbrian mountain style. Building begun by Lombard craftsmen in 1494; there is a strong Tuscan influence in addition to the Lombard features. The portal and statues are by Domenico Bertini da Settignano (1512). The first bell-tower was destroyed in an earthquake and rebuilt in the 19C.

Castle: 13C.

Castel Ritaldi 06044
Perugia/Umbria   p.414□H 8

Picturesque village with 13C castle.

S. Marina: The sacristy of the parish church has a fresco by Tiberio d'Assisi (God the Father with the Virgin Mary and Saints).

S.Nicola: The portal dates from 1486; the frescoes from the Spagna school.

Environs: A kilometre away is the village of **La Pieve** and the 12C church of *S. Gregorio*, which has an interesting portal.

Castel San Pietro Terme 40024
Bologna/Emilia-Romagna   p. 410□F 5

Inhabited in prehistoric and Roman times. The Bolognans established a military base here in 1199, and in 1338 they temporarily moved their university to the town.

S. Maria Maggiore (Piazza XX Settembre): The church dates from a 13C building which was much altered in the 15C and in 1757. The (restored) campanile originates from the 13C. The façade dates from the 15C phase of the building work, and in the lunette of the portal there is a *terracotta Madonna and Child* from the school of Nicolò dell'Arca. The inside furnishings are baroque.

Piazza XX Settembre: **Colonnade** (in middle of square): Built in 1784 to designs by Giovanni Giacomo Dotti; frequently restored. **Santuario del Crocifisso**: 1602, restored in the 18C.

Castelsardo 07031

Sassari/Sardinia   p.422☐C 11

In the 12C, the Genoese family of Doria built the *Castelgenovese*, which was thought to be impregnable. However, the Aragonese starved the Doria into submission and called the maritime castle the *Castelaragonese*. The Pisans established themselves here in 1769, and since then the settlement around the mountain has been called *Castelsardo*. Narrow alleyways with a muggy sea smell lead in tight angles up to the topmost castle battlement; they also lead down to the early 15C *cathedral* with its late Gothic elements. Inside: an altar picture of the 'Master of Castelsardo' and the 'Madonna with angels playing music' (centrepiece of an altar section, one of whose wings, namely the 'Archangel Michael' can only be seen in the sacristy).

Environs: The *elephant of Castelsardo*, an eroded tachylite rock is a famous feature.

However, it is not the shape that makes it important historically, but rather the little-known *domus de janas* concealed inside it. 11 km. to the E. is **Sédini**, a village set on a steep cliff, which has *domus de janas* driven into all parts of it. The village church of *S.Andrea* still has an Aragonese-Gothic façade of 1517, and the side chapels end in fine arches. On the high altar, the Sardinian artist Lussu has painted St. Andrew after the model of Raphael. S.from here you come to the historically interesting ruined church of *S. Nicola di Silanis* (built *c.* 1220). Now overgrown, it was once one of the finest Romanesque religious buildings in Sardinia. On the return journey via the little village of **Spelunca** the traveller comes upon a *dolmen* and, on the hill above it, an unusual *nuraghe*. **Bulzi** became well-known as a result of its isolated Pisan country church (*S. Pietro di Simbranoslo dell'Immagini),* built in the 11C and altered by Benedictines in the 13C. It is an interesting mixture of early Romanesque and early Gothic forms. **Pérfugas**, formerly Erucium, further E., is interesting for several reasons. A bronze *bull* and *cow*—today in the Sanna museum, Sassari—were found here beside a nuraghe

Castell'Arquato, Palazzo Pretorio and Collegiata dell'Assunta

Castel San Pietro Terme, clock tower

Castel Viscardo 05014
Terni/Umbria   p.414☐ G 8

This village, 1640 ft. above sea level, is near Orvieto. It was originally held by the Monaldeschi della Cervara family, and later belonged to Prince Spada. 15C *castle.*

Castiglione del Lago 06061
Perugia/Umbria   p.414☐ G 7

Lying on the W. shore of Lago Trasimeno (bathing beaches), it was inhabited as early as Etruscan times. An important fortress, Castiglione was hotly contested by various princes in the Middle Ages.

Worth seeing: Well-preserved medieval castle. Inside there are fine frescos. The town hall is now housed in the *Palazzo Ducale della Corgna,* ascribed to G.Alessi. An altarpiece possibly by Raphael can be seen in the *parish church.*

Castrocaro Terme 47011
Forli/Emilia-Romagna   p.414☐ G 6

SS. Nicolò e Francesco (Piazza Garibaldi): A church with a nave and two aisles. Its date of origin is uncertain; heavily restored in 1932. Inside: an impressive panel (1506) by Marco Palmezzano showing the *Nativity* (lunette) and the *Madonna enthroned between St. Antony and St. Nicholas* (right entrance wall); *Visitation* (1611) by Francesco Longhi; Tuscan stucco relief of the *Madonna* (mid 15C); transferred wall painting (15C, right of high altar); wall painting of the *Madonna with St.Sebastian and St.Roch* (15C); baroque painting, the *Madonna del Carmine,* attributed to Cignani (1st altar on left). Silver *processional cross* (Florentine, *c.* 1450) in the treasury.

S.Nicolò (Piazza S.Nicolò): A single-aisled church. Originally 11C; late Gothic rebuilding. Inside there are 15C *wall paint-*

well. *Sas Ladas* lies a short distance away. This was regarded as an incomplete nuraghe because of the ramp up which — it used to be thought — the people dragged the stone building blocks. A few km. to the S., the old *Castello dei Doria* overlooks the village of **Chiaramonti.** To the N. of Nulvi is the *Nuraghe Alvu* which, despite its narrowness, was a formidable bastion with its central tower and four corner towers. Since 1974, the route continues from here along a new and confusing road system. 9 km. N. it reaches the red church of *Nostra Signora de Tergu.* Built of precious tachylite (the foundations are all that remain of the monastery) and beautifully situated in a newly planted acacia grove, it is regarded as a national monument. Sacred edifices have probably stood on this site since time immemorial, visible, as it is, from far away. The monastery was built in the 11C and the church in the 12C by monks from Monte Cassino.

Nostra Signora de Tergu (near Castelsardo) *Castelsardo, 'Elephant'*

ings, and also a 17C *Nativity* in the Bolognese style.

Also worth seeing: *Baptistery of S. Giovanni,* a cylindrical brick building housing a Byzantine sarcophagus. Medieval tower known as the *Torre dell'Orologio* (Via Garibaldi). Castle ruins, *Rocca*.

Castroreale 98053
Messina/Sicily   p.420☐L 16

This town, probably of Siculan origin, occupies a magnificent site up from the coast. It was formerly a favourite residence of King Frederick II of Aragon (hence its name).

Chiesa Matrice (or *Assunta,* Piazza G.Marconi): 15C, extended in the 17C. Façade with a fine *portal* dating from 1725.

Inside (nave and two aisles), the following features are worth seeing: in the nave, the baroque *marble pulpit* of 1646 and the carved *choir* (1612); in the left aisle (2nd chapel), 'S.Caterina di Alessandria' by Antonello Gagini (1534); and in the 5th chapel, a Madonna, an early work by the same artist.

Also worth seeing: *Chiesa della Candelora* (Piazza Garibaldi) with a wooden altar by G.Siracusano (1602; 'Jesus in the Temple'). Church of *S.Agata* with an 'Annunciation' by Antonello Gagini (1519). 'Torre di Federico II', a cylindrical tower, a remnant of the Aragonese *castle* rebuilt in 1324. Church of *S.Maria di Gesù* (by the cemetery) with a sarcophagus by A.Gagini (1506/7). Double *gate* in the town wall.

Environs: Some 25 km. to the NW is **Castroreale Terme:** In the S.Biagio district there are excavations of a *Roman villa* from the 1C AD (surviving features include the remains of the peristyle, floor mosaics, fragments of wall paintings, and thermal system with steam heating).

Castroví Ilari 87012
Cosenza/Calabria   p.418☐N 13

S. Maria del Castello (Via S. Maria del Castello): Begun in 1090, rebuilt in 1363 and again, in baroque style, in the 18C. The façade has two *Romanesque portals*. Above the right side portal is a 14C *bas-relief* (school of the Pisan artist Tino di Camaino). Inside, on the second altar on the left, *Madonna and Child*, 1552, by Pietro Negroni from Castroví Ilari; the *Ascension* (1560), on the high altar, is another painting by Negroni. The sacristy contains, among other items, a 17C *wooden cross* and a 14C *copper plate* with an old German inscription. From the square in front of the church there is a fine view of the Pollino range.

Also worth seeing: The 16C church of *S. Giuliano* (Via S. Maria del Castello) with Renaissance portal. The 15C *castle* (Strada Carlo Maria l'Occaso) on ancient foundations. The museum in the Biblioteca Comunale displays remains of the wall decoration of the 12C church of S. Maria del Castello.

Environs: *c.* 15 km. NW, **Morano Calabro** has some fine churches: *S. Bernardino,* 15C, with carved Renaissance pulpit; *Collegiata della Maddalena,* baroque; *S. Pietro* with a fine statue of St. Lucy by Pietro Bernini. *c.* 30 km. S. , **Altomonte** with the Gothic church of *S. Maria della Consolazione:* beautiful rose-window on the façade and, inside, 3 panels of a Tuscan polyptych, one of which (16C) is ascribed to Simone Martini, and a 14C sarcophagus of Filippo Sangineto, the founder of the church.

Catania 95100
Catania/Sicily   p.420☐L 17

The ancient 'Katane' was founded in 729BC by Greeks from Naxos (near Taormina) and developed into a centre of science and trade. It fell to Rome in 263 BC. In the Middle Ages it was of no great importance, but it recovered under the Aragonese (14C onwards). Destroyed several times by earthquakes and the eruptions of Etna (1169, 1669 and 1693).

Cathedral of S. Agata (Piazza del Duomo): Founded in 1092, and frequently rebuilt owing to earthquake damage. The three *apses* and the *transept* survive from the original building. 18C *façade* by Vaccarini (some of the lower granite columns are from the ancient theatre). On the left side of the nave is a fine Renaissance portal (*c.* 1577). The campanile dates from 1869. The ground plan of the domed cathedral is a Latin cross. It has a nave and two aisles. In the right aisle (2nd pillar) is the *tomb of Vincenzo Bellini* (d. 1835); the right transept leads to the *Cappella della Madonna* with Norman fragments. By the right wall there is a *Roman sarcophagus* (3C AD), which holds the remains of Aragonese rulers (including Frederick II, d. 1337). The chapel in the right apse houses the *relics of St. Agatha,* the church's patroness. (The rich *church treasury* is only open on 4&5 February and 17 August.) There are some more remains of the original building in the *Cappella del Crocifisso* (left transept). The *sacristy* has a fresco of the destruction caused by Etna in 1669. Between the columns of the left aisle there are *remnants of the original columns* (preceding the earthquake of 1169). The entrance to the *Terme Achelliane,* an ancient complex beneath the cathedral and the square, is at the right-hand corner of the façade. In the cathedral square, before the cathedral, is the **Fontana dell'Elefante,** an ancient elephant made of lava, with an Egyptian obelisk on its back (erected by G. B. Vaccarini in 1736).

S. Nicolò (Piazza Dante): Built in the early 18C on a Latin cross ground plan. It is the largest church in Sicily. Façade unfinished. It is domed and has a nave and two aisles. Dimensions: 344 ft. x 157 ft., height of dome 203 ft. The decoration is of no particular interest.

S.Agata (Via Vitt. Emanuele II): Masterpiece by G.B.Vaccarini; built 1735–67. Magnificent *baroque façade* and octagonal *dome*. The inside (Greek cross ground plan) has richly decorated chapels in the transepts. The *rococo choir stalls* are particularly beautiful.

Castel Ursino (Piazza Federico di Svevia; houses the **Museo Comunale**): Built by Emperor Frederick II Hohenstaufen in 1239–50, it was later the residence of the Aragonese. A square building with four wings and round towers at the corners. It survived the devastating eruption of Etna in 1669. Inside, the museum has a collection of ancient *sculpture, bronzes and paintings, especially Medieval paintings*.

Roman Theatre (Via Teatro Greco): Built on what are probably Greek walls from the 5C BC. It has a diameter 285 ft., about 7000 seats, 9 stands for spectators and 3 passageways made of lava. Not much of the orchestra and stage has been uncovered. Nearby is the **Roman Odeum,** a small theatre with 1300 seats.

Roman   Amphitheatre   (Piazza

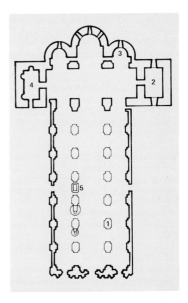

Catania, cathedral 1 tomb of V. Bellini **2** Cappella della Madonna **3** chapel of St.Agatha **4** Cappella del Crocifisso **5** remains of the original columns (before 1169)

Catania, cathedral

Stesicoro): 2C AD, used as a lava and marble quarry in late antiquity. External dimensions: 410 ft. x 344 ft. About 16000 seats. The lower passageway survives but little of the spectators' stands remains.

Museo Bellini (Piazza S.Francesco d'Assisi): Established in the house where Vincenzo Bellini, the composer (1801–35), was born; contains *mementoes* and *autographs* of the composer.

Also worth seeing: *S. Francesco* (Piazza di S.Francesco d'Assisi) with baroque façade and the tomb of Eleonora of Anjou, the wife of King Frederick II of Aragon. The 18C *S. Benedetto* (Via dei Crociferi), with splendid baroque façade. The *Chiesa dei Gesuiti* (immediately adjacent), also with a fine baroque façade. *S. Giuliano* (Via dei Crociferi), built by Vaccarini 1738–60 (the octagonal interior contains a fine painted 14C crucifix). The 18C *Chiesa della Trinità* (Via Quartatone), with a fine façade. The *Chiesa della Collegiata* (Via Etnea), 18C, with a masterly façade by Stefano Ittar (1768). The 18C *S. Agata la Vetere* (Via S.Maddalena), on the foundations of an early Christian basilica. *S.*

Maria di Gesù (Piazza S.Maria di Gesù), rebuilt in 1706, with a fine 'Pietà' by Antonello Gagini (1519, inside by a doorway on the left). *S. Maria della Rotonda* (Via Rotonda), part of what were Roman baths; converted into a Christian church. *Palazzo Biscari* (Via Museo Biscari) with fine rococo interior furnishings. *Palazzo delle Scienze* (Viale XX Settembre) with a good mineral collection. *Teatro Bellini* (Piazza Bellini), opened in 1890, one of the largest stages in Italy. *Piazza Mazzini* with 32 columns from an ancient Roman basilica. *Via Etnea* and *Via Crociferi*, fine baroque streets. *Piazza dell'Università* with the Palazzo San Giuliano and the Municipio by Vaccarini, and also the 17C Palazzo dell' Università.

Catanzaro 88100

Catanzaro/Calabria   p.418□N 14

Founded in *c.* AD 1000 during the Byzantine reconquest of Calabria by Nicephorus Phocas. In the 11C it fell to the Normans under Robert Guiscard. Emperor Frederick II Hohenstaufen handed

Cathedral square, ancient lava elephant

Catania, tomb in the cathedral

it to Pietro Ruffo, his marshal. Finally it fell to the Kingdom of Naples. Catanzaro was the administrative centre of Calabria in the Bourbon period and under Murat. The town participated with great enthusiasm in the 19C Italian Risorgimento.

Chiesa dell'Immacolata (Corso Mazzini): Rebuilt in 1765, with a magnificent baroque façade. Latin cross ground plan, a nave, two aisles and transepts with *fine altars* of multi-coloured marble.

Chiesa del Rosario (also *S.Domenico*, Via Menniti): Rebuilt in the late 16C. Single-aisled interior in the form of a Latin cross; interconnecting side chapels; a side chapel on the left has a painting commemorating the sea battle of Lepanto (1571), the *Madonna della Vittoria*. There are fine *marble altars* in the apse and transepts.

Cathedral of S.Maria Assunta e SS. Pietro e Paolo (Piazza Duomo): Built in the early 19C in neoclassical style on the site of a 12C Romanesque church which had been destroyed by an earthquake in 1783. The right aisle has an interesting *Byzantine icon.*

Museo Provinciale (in the public gardens of the Villa Trieste): It includes *a collection of ancient coins, a collection from prehistory and early history* (room 1); *Byzantine and medieval coins;* a reconstruction of the *guillotine*, on which the last executions were carried out under the Bourbons in 1821 (room II); ancient *vases* and *small objets d'art.*

Also worth seeing: *S. Giovanni* (Piazza Garibaldi), a former church of the Knights of Malta (16C). The church of *Monte dei Morti* (Via del Monte) with a late baroque portal dating from 1728. *Villa Trieste* (see above) with busts of well-known Calabrians. Fine *view from the Via Bellavista* over the Gulf of Squillace.

Environs: Some 25 km. N., **Taverna,** made famous by Mattia Preti (1613–99), the best known 17C Calabrian painter; excellent examples of his art survive in various churches: in *S. Domenico,* 'Christo

fulminante'; in *S.Nicola,* 'Madonna della Purità'; and the *Chiesa Arcipretale di S. Barbara,* 'Trinità' etc.

Cavalese 38033
Trento/South Tyrol-Trentino   p.410☐F 2

Parish church of Maria Assunta: 12C Romanesque church, in a park in the S.of the town; rebuilt several times in the 15, 16,17&19C. The fine tower was built in the early 16C, and the S. portal is also a Renaissance work.

SS. Sebastiano e Fabiano: Originally dates from 1464, the church was rebuilt in Romanesque style by Jos. von Stadl in the 19C. The baroque tower (1830) was built to a plan by Giuseppe Dalbosco.

Environs: Tésero (W. of Cavalese): The church of *S.Leonardo* occupies a splendid site in this winter health resort. It was first mentioned in 1294 and rebuilt in the 15C; the vault is 16C. The late Gothic S.portal is also 16C. The 15C *parish church of S. Eliseo* has a fine campanile, with a Gothic lower section. The upper section was built in *c.* 1800.

Cefalù 90015
Palermo/Sicily   p.420☐K 16

'Cephaloedium', as it then was, was not important in antiquity. After Arab occupation it was conquered by the Normans in 1063 and, for a time, it was the Norman kings' place of residence.

Cathedral (Piazza del Duomo): Norman Romanesque; begun in 1131 by King Roger II because of a vow, but not completed until the 13C. The first large Norman church in Sicily. The *façade*, built by a local builder in 1240, is flanked by two massive *towers*, with a 15C *loggia* running between them; fine *portal*. The three *apses* and the upper *blind arcades* are particularly worth seeing. Built on a Latin cross ground plan, it has a broad nave and two aisles.

Arab-style *arches* on *ancient columns* (the first column on the left is of cipolin) with fine *capitals*. Open *timber roof*. However, the magnificent *mosaics* in the choir constitute the main feature of interest. They are the oldest Byzantine mosaics in Sicily and were completed in 1148 by Greek craftsmen. The semi dome of the apse has a Christ Pantocrator, below which is Mary with four archangels and then the twelve apostles. The other mosaics in the choir and on the side walls are of a later date (13C). The left aisle opens into a Romanesque *cloister* (fine capitals). There is a 12C Romanesque *font* in the right aisle and in the left transept a *Madonna and Child* by Antonello Gagini.

Museo Mandralisca (Via Mandralisca): An archaeological collection (including some fine vases), a good collection of coins, and a picture gallery (with 'Portrait of an Unknown Man' by Antonello da Messina, *c.* 1470); collection of mussel shells.

Also worth seeing: Osterio Magno (Corso Ruggero)—the remains of a 12C Norman building, said to be the palace of King Roger. Remains of the old town defences (on the N., seaward side of the Piazza Garibaldi there is a tower on an ancient base). On the way up the castle hill there are the remains of an ancient temple from the 9C BC (the so-called 'temple of Diana'). Rebuilt in the 4C BC, it was later converted into a Byzantine church.

Environs: Pilgrimage church of Gibilmanna, 15 km. S., 17/18C, with a magnificent situation; one of the best-known Sicilian places of pilgrimages.

Celano 67043
L'Aquila/Abruzzi   p.414□I 9

Castle: Founded in 1392, completed in 1450 and restored after World War 2. The contrast between the closed, defended lower part and the upper sections, with windows and loggias, is particularly charming.

S. Giovanni: The church was rebuilt in 1706; and older parts and 15C frescos came to light after the earthquake of 1915. The rest of the decoration is late baroque.

Cento 44042
Ferrara/Emilia-Romagna   p. 412□F 5

First mentioned in the 8C and united with the adjacent Pieve di Cento until 1376. In 1501 the town fell to the Este through the Pope; in 1598, together with the Duchy of Ferrara, it reverted to the Papal States, which granted it the status of a town in 1754.

Picture gallery (in the *Palazzo del Monte di Pietà*, Corso Matteotti 16–18C): Important mainly for works by Guercino and other Bolognese painters (Tibaldi, L.Carracci, Calvaert).

Chiesa del Rosario (Corso Ugo Bassi): Built 1633–41, it has several works by Guercino. On the high altar is the *statue of a Madonna of the Rosary* (1626), sculpted to designs by the master, who painted the coloured mounting himself; the chapel (2nd left) which he founded in 1650 contains: a *Crucifixion* (on the altar), as well as paintings of *St. Francis*, *John the Baptist* and *God the Father* (ceiling); in the 3rd chapel on the left is an *Assumption* (1626).

Also worth seeing: *Palazzo del Governatore* (1502) and *Palazzo Comunale* (1612). *Casa Provenzali* with frescos by Guercino. *S.Biagio*, built 1742–50 to designs by Torreggiani. *S.Maria Addolorata dei Servi*, begun in 1590, largely rebuilt in 1652; painting by Calvaert and other paintings by Guercino.

Environs: Pieve di Cento: *Collegiata di S.Maria Maggiore:* After the rebuilding of 1710, all that remains of the preceding 10C building is the polygonal apse and the campanile. Some notable works of art: *Assumption* by Guido Reni, a 12C *wooden crucifix*, and *Annunciation* by Guercino. The *Palazzo Comunale* (to the left of the church) houses the *Pinacoteca Civica* and the fine 18C *baroque theatre*.

Cefalù, cathedral

Cefalù, cathedral

Cerreto Sannita 82032
Benevento/Campania   p.416 K 10

This town was probably founded on the site of the old Samnite town of Cominio Cerito. Mentioned from the 10C onwards, it was destroyed by an earthquake in 1688 and then rebuilt on a regular ground plan. Cerreto Sannita has long been a centre of applied art (weaving, ceramics). Worth seeing: the **Cathedral of SS. Trinità** 1739 (nave, two aisles, dome; the choir has fine frescos by Francesco Palumbo, 1780); the church of **S. Martino** (Piazza Vitt. Emanuele), 1702, which is approached by a broad flight of steps, and the baroque church of **S. Gennaro**. The *Santuario di Maria SS. delle Grazie* (1588) is by the *Capuchin monastery*.

Environs: *c.* 9 km. NW, **Cusano Mutri** with *SS. Pietro e Paolo* founded in the 10C

(later much altered; façade 1693); the inside has a nave, two aisles and a fine high altar, behind which are interesting figures of 1661 by Domenico de Luca. Some 8 km. SE is **Guardia Sanframondi** with the church of *S. Sebastiano* (16C portal; inside, fine stucco by D.A.Vaccaro, 1750). *c.* 8 km. SW, **S. Salvatore Telesino**, where an *abbey* of the same name was founded in the 10C. The *parish church* contains the Renaissance tomb of V.Monsorio; the high altar has a 'Transfiguration of Christ' by the school of Luca Giordano. Outside the town (SE) are the ruins of the ancient Samnite town of *Telesia* (they include the remains of an amphitheatre).

Cervéteri 00052
Rome/Latium   p.414 □ G 9

Discoveries have shown that Cervéteri

dates back to the 8C BC. In the 7&6C BC, *the Etruscan Cisra—known as Caere* by the Romans—was one of the most powerful towns in Etruria. The town, which was much larger at that time, was one of the most populous in the whole of the Mediterranean, and developed into a leading cultural centre through its trade with Greece etc. Although remaining neutral in the struggle between Rome and the Etruscans, Caere was compelled to submit to Roman domination in 538 BC. Systematic exploration of the Etruscan town, together with the surrounding necropolis was instigated by the Italian government in 1911, although there had been some earlier private excavations.

Old Cervéteri now consists of no more than some medieval buildings: the Romanesque section of *S.Maria* is 12/13C; the ancient *castle* was repaired in the Middle Ages.

The 16C **Palazzo Ruspoli** houses the *Museo Nazionale Cerite*, which opened in 1967, with finds from excavations and records.

Necropolis: The surviving sections of the necropolis which lies outside ancient Caere resemble the districts of a town, with streets and squares between the tombs. The most important area is on the tufa ridge known as 'Banditaccio' but there are also tombs on Monte Abetone. A road along the main ridge (with side roads) passes various types of tombs: from stones hollowed out to form urns for ashes to the stone houses with their chamber tombs and the earth-covered tumuli. The road leads to the 'monumental enclosure', which has been systematically explored and provides a good introduction to the tombs. One of the finest of the chamber tombs is the *Tomba dei Rilievi* (or *Tomba Bella*) which dates from the late period (4–2C BC). The inscriptions name the owners as the Matuna family; walls and pillars are covered with painted stucco reliefs of everyday objects, giving a graphic insight into the living habits of the Etruscans.

Cervia 48015
Forl ì/Emilia-Romagna   p. 410☐G 5

Only the (secularized) church of *Madonna della Neve* survives from the old settle-

Cervéteri, Tomba dei Rilievi

ment, which was rebuilt in 1698 to plans by B.Berti. Today it is one of the major resorts of the region.

Places of interest: 18C *Cathedral* (Piazza Garibaldi). *Chiesa del Suffragio* (Corso Mazzini) with a 13/14C wooden crucifix. *Santuario della Madonna del Pino* (a little way outside the town), 1487, with a 15C Venetian painting.

Environs: Pisignano: *Parish church of S.Stefano,* rebuilt in 1521, with 16C frescos (to which much has been added), and some pieces of marble unearthed in the surrounding area.

Cesena 47023
Forl i / Emilia-Romagna   p.414☐G 6

The town is prehistoric in origin; it was probably an Etruscan settlement and a Roman municipium *(Caesena)*. It fell to Theodoric in 493; in the 6C it was part of the exarchate of Ravenna. In 961 it was conquered by Berengerius II and in 1379 Pope Urban VI gave it to the Este.

Cathedral of S. Giovanni Battista (Piazza Pia): Building began in 1385 and was largely finished by 1403. The architect was Underwalden. The building was altered in the Renaissance (with the inclusion of a chapel, etc.); the sides and apse retained their Gothic form. The *façade,* which is in the style of the Venetian Renaissance, still has a Gothic portal; to the right of it is a signed 15C *Madonna* by Gottardo di Gaspare. The spire of the campanile (1456) is 17C. The inside, much restored, contains: the *sarcophagus* (1467) of Antonio Malatesta da Fossombrone by the Florentine artist Ottaviano di Antonio di Duccio (right aisle); the *marble altar* (early 16C, right side aisle); *SS. Leonard, Christopher and Eustace,* parts of a marble altar (1514) by Lorenzo Bregno (left aisle). The 17C *Cappella della Madonna del Popolo* has ceiling painting by Giaquinto and an altar by Vespignani (left aisle).

The **Biblioteca Malatestiana** (Piazza Bufalini) was built by Matteo Nuti as an extension of the mid 13C Minorite monastery of S.Francesco. The monastery remained unaltered until the end of the 17C, and was then replaced by a baroque mon-

Cervéteri, necropolis

Cesena, Rocca

astery in 1750. The reading room, built on the model of the library of the convent of S.Marco in Florence, is the oldest and most perfectly preserved example of a humanist monastery library. The library's valuable contents include numerous illuminated manuscripts from the Middle Ages and the Renaissance. Opposite the reading room is the *Biblioteca Piana* (the private library of Pope Pius VII). The *Sale della Quadreria* have 15&16C paintings and a *Sacrifice of Iphigenia* (18C), attributed to Piazzetta. On the ground floor is the 15C refectory with the *Biblioteca Comandini,* and the *Museo Storico dell'Antichità* with Roman exhibits.

Also worth seeing: *Rocca Malatestiana* (Via Malatesta Novello), begun 1379–85, continued 1429–65, and largely rebuilt 1466–76 with the aid of Nuti. The early 15C *S.Domenico* (Viale Mazzoni), rebuilt by Francesco Zondini 1706–22, with 15–18C paintings. *Teatro Comunale Bonci*

(1846). The 18C *Palazzo Romagnoli* (Via Uberti 48). *Chiesa del Suffraggio* (1689). *Palazzo del Ridotto* (Corso Mazzini), façade dating from 1782. *Town hall* (Piazza del Popolo), built 1359, altered 1474, 1557 and 1725. *S.Agostino* (Via Riceputi Savola), 1747–78.

Environs: Benedictine monastery of *Madonna del Monte.* The monastery buildings date from the 18C, but contain some older parts (1st cloister with colonnade is late 15C). The church, built in the 12C on the site of a 10C oratory, was temporarily converted into a fortress in 1356. It was given its present form by Terribilia (dome, 1568). Altered again in 1771–2, it was last restored in 1946–7 after suffering war damage. The inside is single-aisled and flanked by wide chapels, with a crypt under the sacristy. Note: the *frieze* in the nave, with 14 scenes from the Life of the Virgin Mary (1557–9) by Girolamo Longhi. *Ceiling* *painting* (1796) by Giuseppe Milani and carved *choir stalls* (1562) by G.Scalvini (in the choir). Mid 14C *fragment of a triptych* in the sacristy. Roman *sarcophagus* (1C AD) and *column with stone cross* (10C ?, crypt, altar). Numerous popular votive pictures (from the 15C onwards, in the sacristy and on the walls of the ambulatory and nave). 8 km. S.of Cesena is **Carpineta,** where the church has a signed and dated picture of the Madonna (1347) by Paolo Veneziano.

Cherasco 12062
Cuneo/Piedmont   p.412☐B 5

This Ligurian town was the Roman *Clarascum*. The medieval town was founded in 1243. Cherasco fell to Savoy as early as 1259, and in 1348 the Visconti took it over. The town reverted to Savoy in 1559 after the agreement of Cateau-Chambrésis.

S. Martino (Via Cavour): A 13&14C Romanesque church, restored in 1881. Inside, 16C fresco of the *scourging of Christ.*

S.Pietro (Via S.Pietro): The interior of this mid 13C church is baroque. The façade is Romanesque, as is the campanile, with a fresco of the Crucifixion.

S.Maria del Popolo (Via Nostra Signora del Popolo): This church was built by Sebastiano Taricco in 1693–1702. The inside is single-aisled and decorated with fine stucco.

Arco del Belvedere (Via Vittorio Emanuele II): Built by Giovenale Boetto da Fossano in 1647–88 as a memorial of the plague of 1630.

Palazzo Gotti di Salerno (Via dell' Ospedale): *Museum* and library. In addition to ancient objects, the valuable collection of coins, with 12,000 exhibits, is worth seeing.

Also worth seeing: *Palazzo Salmatoris* (Via Vittorio Emanuele II): Various peace agreements were concluded here. *Castle of*

the Visconti (Via Roma), begun in 1348 by Lodovico Visconti.

Chiaromonte 85032
Potenza/Basilicata   p.418☐N 12

Chiaramonte is one of the oldest centres in the S., rebuilt by the Normans after an earthquake in the 9C. The remains of the castle (and the enclosing walls from the 14C) occupy a dominant position in the town.

Parish church of S.Tommaso Apostolo (14C): Inside, 2 *wooden crucifixes* and 2 panels by followers of Luca Giordano are worth seeing. A Gothic remnant has been incorporated into the campanile of the church of **S. Giovanni.**

Palazzo di Giura (1st half of 18C): Standing on the site of the old castle, it contains a library and a collection of Chinese art.

Chiávari 16043
Genoa/Liguria   p.412☐D 5

The town's coat of arms includes a key, a reference to the origin of its name (*Clavarium*, that is: key to the valley). The families of Giuseppe Garibaldi and Giuseppe Mazzini came from here, whilst the Fieschi, an important Ligurian family from the neighbouring town of Lavagna, supplied two Popes, Innocent IV (1243-54) and his nephew Ottobono, who became Hadrian V (1276).

Basilica dei Fieschi: The most important—and also the best-preserved—building on the eastern stretch of the Ligurian coast. Romanesque-Gothic. Together with his nephew, Innocent IV had the church built in 1242–52. The lunette of the single portal in the fine façade has a *Crucified Christ with St.John and St.Mary, Innocent IV and Ottobono Fieschi.* The massive tower over the crossing is pierced by two rows of four-arched windows; it has an octagonal spire, with four smaller spires at the corners. Inside, there is a nave, two aisles and Gothic vaulting; apse and the two transepts have rib vaults.

Opposite the church are the remains of what used to be the splendid **Palazzo dei Fieschi** (1252). The palace fell victim to the Saracens in 1567.

Chieri 10023
Turin/Piedmont   p.412□B 4

Chieri has been part of the archdiocese of Turin since the 11C. It was a free town from the 13C onwards, and was known as the 'town of the hundred towers'. It fell to Savoy in 1418, and part of the university of Turin was moved here in 1427–34.

Cathedral of S. Maria delle Scala (Piazza Cavour): The cathedral, an important Gothic building, dates from 1405–35 and occupies the site of an 11C church, which in turn stood on the remains of a Roman temple of Minerva. It has a massive Gothic *façade* and an impressive 14&15C *campanile*. Edoardo Arborio Mella carried out restoration work in 1875–80. One peculiarity is the 13C *baptistery* built on to the S. side of the nave.

Also worth seeing: *S.Domenico* (Via della Pace), begun in 1307, dedicated in 1388. Nave, two aisles and a fine campanile dating from 1381. *S.Margherita* (Via Vittorio Emanuele II), a baroque church built in 1671 to plans by Pellegrino Tibaldi. It was restored in 1850. Built in the form of a Greek cross, it was stuccoed throughout in the 16C by G.B.Barberini. The *dome frescos* (1670) are by Gianpaolo Recchi. The *triumphal arch* (1580) near the cathedral was built in honour of Emanuele Filiberto.

Environs: The town of **Sántena** has the tomb of Cavour. The *Abbazia di S.Maria di Vezzolano* (773) was probably founded by Charlemagne. Built from 1095 onwards, it has a nave and two aisles. The façade is decorated with blind arcades and figures. The S.side was added to the clois-

ter, which has Gothic frescos including *The Three Living and the Three Dead*. The carved *rood screen* of 1189, with reliefs of the first Italian Lamentation (Burgundian early Gothic) is important, as is the brightly coloured late Gothic *terracotta triptych* (1490) on the high altar.

Chieti 66100
Chieti/Abruzzi   p.416□K 9

The ancient *Theatinum*. The Theatine order, founded in 1524, was named after this

Chieri, cathedral 1 baptistery, 1329 – 1492 **2** tombstone of Bernadino Biscaretti, 1572 **3** Doubting Thomas, 17C painting **4** polyptych, early 15C, follower of Spanzotti **5** Epiphany by Gabriele Ferrero **6** Ascension, painting **7** St. Lawrence and St.Martin, painting by Moncalvo **8** The Risen Christ, painting by Moncalvo **9** marble icon, c. 1530, by Matteo Sanmicheli? **10** chapel of Corpus Christi **11** chapel of the Gallieri **12** entrance to the crypt with nave and two aisles **13** wooden crucifix on the high altar **14** choir stalls, 15C–16C **15** Crucifixion chapel **16** way to the 1st sacristy **17** altarpiece, school of Vercelli, 1622 **18** chapel of Madonna delle Grazie by B.Vittone **19** Madonna with Saints, painting by Jan Miel, on the altar

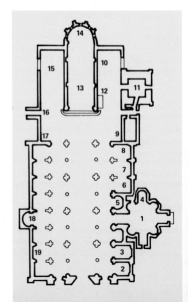

town, because one of its founders was
Bishop of Chieti.

Cathedral of S.Giustino: Modern building. The pulpit and choir stalls, and also
the stuccoed ceiling in the crypt, survive
from the baroque decoration. The 18C
altar panel shows *scenes from the life of St.
Justin.* The church treasure includes a 15C
Venetian chalice.

Three *temples* from the 2nd half of the 1C
BC survive from the *ancient Theatinum.*
Two of these three served as churches in
the Middle Ages, while one was used as a
house. A *theatre* and a *cistern* have also
survived.

**Museo Nazionale di Antichità degli
Abruzzi e del Molise** (in the Villa Comunale): Archaeological collection; particular attention should be paid to the so-called
Warrior of Capestrano, discovered in 1935,
an example of pre-Roman Picenum art of
the 6C BC.

Museo Diocesano d'Arte Sacra (near
S.Domenico): Wooden statues and remains
of frescos from the 12-17C.

Chiusa/Klausen 39043
Bolzano/South Tyrol/Trentino   p.410☐F 1

Parish church of St. Andreas: Late
Gothic church, built by Benedikt Weib-
hauser in 1480-94. Fine S.portal by Andre
Hofer (1469). Inside, net vaults with
frescos by Master Klaus. The W. gallery
dates from 1520, the late Gothic wooden
carvings from *c.* 1500. The altarpiece is by
J.G.Grasmair (*c.* 1740), with a Deposition
by P.Zeiller (*c.* 1700).

Chapel of Loreto: In 1697, Gabriel Pon-
tifeser, the father confessor of Queen Maria
Anna of Spain, advised her to found a
Capuchin monastery in his home town. In
1701 the Queen donated the so-called
Loreto treasure (paintings, sculptures, altars, chalices etc.) to the monastery and it
was housed in a room in the Loreto
chapel—built on the site of the house where
the father confessor was born.

Other churches: *Apostolic church* (*c.*
1450) with stellar vault, built on to the
front of a house; high altar dating from

Chieti, national museum, Hellenistic bed in bronze

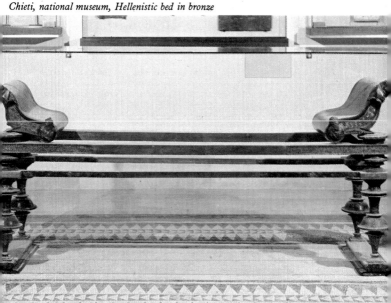

Chieti, cathedral

1770. The former *parish church of St. Sebastian* was built in 1208–13 as a two-storeyed centrally planned building modelled on the Church of the Holy Sepulchre in Jerusalem.

Burg Branzoll: This 13C castle located above the town was rebuilt in the 19C.

Environs: Castle and convent of Säben/Sabiona: The castle rock of Sabiona was the original diocesan town from the 5C onwards, preceding Bressanone (967). (Remains of an early Christian church of 574, stemming from this period, are still extant). The bishops' castle burned down in 1535; the 13C Kassian tower and the circular wall have survived. In 1681 the ruins were extended to form a Benedictine monastery. On the site of the former palace, Giovanni Battista Delai built the Lombard baroque *monastery church* (1691–1707). To the S. of it, Giacomo and An-drea Delai built the *Church of our Lady*, an octagonal centrally planned building with dome and lantern. The *Kassian chapel* has an altarpiece by Franz Sebald Unterberger from the 1st half of the 18C. The originally Romanesque *Chapel of St.Mary* was rebuilt in the 17C. On the altar is a sculpture of the Madonna and Child (1500). The *Church of the Holy Cross* on the highest point of the rock was originally 7C but rebuilt in the 17C. The interior, where the walls are covered with painted canvases, is original. The crucifixion on the high altar is by Master Leonhard of Bressanone and dates from the mid-15C. **Villandro/Villanders:** This little town to the S. of Chiusa is situated high above the Isarco valley. Note *St.Michael* (by the cemetery), a two-storeyed 14C building, and the *parish church of St.Stephan*, built in *c.* 1500. To the S. is **Barbian/Barbiano**, with the late Gothic church of *St.Ingenuin und Albuin* (1500), with a fine high altar

Chiusa, view with Branzoll castle and Säben monastery

and side altars from the same period. **Tre Chiese/Dreikirchen** (above Barbiano): three picturesquely located *St.Nikolaus* of 1400 with a fine altar (1500); *St.Gertraud,* also 1400, with notable frescos from the same period; *St.Magdalena* with a richly carved and painted, winged altarpiece from the time when the chapel was built. **Waidbruck/Ponte Gardena:** Still further to the S., above the Isarco valley (at the entrance to the Grödner valley); with the 12C *Castle Trostberg,* altered in the 15,16&17C; the banqueting hall has stucco from 1606. From Waidbruck the visitor can reach **Ortisei/St. Ulrich in Gröden,** the main town of the Grödner valley. Its population was originally Rhaetian and became known for its woodcarving. Note the *parish church of St. Ulrich,* a late baroque building from the 18C; and the 14C church of *St. Jakob* with original choir painted throughout in *c.* 1460, and a nave vaulted in the 17C. Further uphill,

along a steep mountain road, is **St. Christina/S.Cristina** with the 17C *Fischburg* castle. A road leads E. from Klausen to **Villnöss/Funes** with the church of *St. Jakob am Joch,* built *c.* 1500, with a very fine winged altarpiece (1517) on the high altar.

Chiusi 53043
Sienna/Tuscany   p.414☐G 7

The old Etruscan town of *Chamars* was the most famous of the 12 towns of the confederation and reached its zenith in the 7 – 5C BC. It was allied with Rome *(Clusium),* in the 4C and was then occupied by Goths and conquered by the Lombards. The town is built on the site of a military camp. Parts of the subterranean labyrinth of Etruscan tunnels are still used today as cellars underneath the private houses. The fortress walls and the alleyways of the once-mighty town are medieval.

Cathedral of S. Secondiano: Founded in the 6C, rebuilt in the 12C. The inside of the church is basilican, with 18 columns and an open roof truss. In the 19C the walls were decorated with paintings, which were made to look like mosaics in order to emphasize the basilican character. In the right aisle there is an alabaster *font* with a figure of John the Baptist by Andrea Sansovino. The 12C *campanile*, which was altered in the 16C, conceals an underground *cistern*, probably from the 1C AD. The inside is hewn from tufa and has two aisles and two false domes which are perforated in order to let in water from above.

Museo Nazionale Etrusco (Piazza della Cattedrale): Contains finds from the surrounding area, including Etruscan objects (from tombs), Greek ceramics, sarcophagi and sphinxes in stone. Particular mention should be made of a *large earthenware sarcophagus*, with remnants of painting and a representation of the deceased on the lid; numerous strangely shaped *Etruscan urns*, an alabaster urn with the portrait of Lars Sentinates Caesa from the Tomba della Pellegrina; and the *fragment of a head of Dionysus*.

Chiusi, Etruscan urn, 6C BC

The *Etruscan tombs* are close to the town and three are of particular importance. The *Tomba della Pellegrina* is from the period between the mid 3C and the mid 2C BC, discovered in 1928. Its cruciform ground plan is a transitional form, half-way to the later tombs with niches. There is also the early 5C *Tomba della Scimmia* or *di Poggio Renzo*. Dug into the tufa, it lies in the shade of cypresses, and its well-preserved wall paintings make it the most interesting tomb in the burial ground. It was discovered in 1846 and opened to the public as early as 1873. The 27 steps dating from this period lead down to the Etruscan door. Then follow three more (Etruscan) steps leading into the 1st chamber which is 8 ft. 10 in. high. Its tufa walls are completely covered with wall paintings. Among the *dancing scenes* and *athletic competitions* there is also a *picture of a she-ape (scimmia) tied to a tree*, which gave the tomb its peculiar name. There are *Gorgons' heads* on the ceiling. This room leads to another room with paintings of *naked youths* and others. The other burial chambers accessible from here do not contain paintings, but only tufa benches around the sides. The *Tomba del Granduca* or *della Paccianese:* is so-called because it was discovered in 1818 on land owned by the Grand Duke (granduca). A small chamber dug out of the tufa from the 3–2C BC, it contains eight cinerary urns with reliefs of the family of Pulfua Peris. A little further away is the *Tomba Bonci Casuccini* or *del Colle*, with an *original Etruscan door* and painted frieze (chariot race and banquet).

Cingoli 62011

Macerata/Marches   p.416☐H 7

Cathedral: An enormous 17C building.

Chiusi, wall painting in Etruscan tomb from the 5C BC

Inside there is a painting by Pier Simone Fanelli, and in the sacristy a *polyptych* by Antonio da Fabriano.

S.Domenico: Inside, a *Virgin of the Rosary* by Lorenzo Lotto, dated 1539; the fifteen small symbols in the rose bush represent the mysteries of the rosary.

S.Esuperanzio: Remains of frescos survive in this church built in 1278; a *Flagellation of Christ* by Sebastiano del Piombo is preserved in the parish priest's house.

Also worth seeing: The *Palazzo Municipale,* built in the 13C and rebuilt in 1531. Numerous old houses.

Ciriè 10073
Turin/Piedmont   p.412□B 4

Cathedral of S.Giovanni Battista: The cathedral was begun in *c.* 1300. The frescoed portal is 15C. Note the *Madonna* (1519) by Defendente Ferrari.

Also worth seeing: *S.Martino di Liramo,* a small Romanesque church (10–11C) with frescos from the same period. *S.Giuseppe,* a baroque building dating from 1632, with rich stucco and marble decoration. The *Confraternita del Sudario* has a painting by D.Ferrari (1516). *S.Maria di Spinariano,* outside the town, is decorated with frescos by Magister Domenico della Marca d'Ancona (late 15C).

Citerna 06010
Perugia/Umbria   p.414□G 7

In the northern Tiber valley. Its castle, which was half destroyed in World War 2, offers a magnificent view of the valley. The

Romans called the town Civitas Sobariae. The town was held by the Byzantines and in the Middle Ages there was an important fortress here.

S.Francesco: Built in the 14C and rebuilt in *c.* 1508. Inside, frescos by Raffaellino del Colle (Christ) and Luca Signorelli (Madonna and Child with Angels).

Also worth seeing: The 15C *Palazzo Vitelli,* and the Renaissance fireplace in the *Prosperi House.*

Cittadella 35013
Padua/Veneto   p.410☐G 3

This town, with its elliptical and largely intact wall, was founded and fortified in response to the defences of Castelfranco. It stands at an important crossroads.

Parish church: A fine neoclassical building by Ottavio Bertotti Scamozzi from the late 18C. In the sacristy, a painting, the *Disciples at Emmaus,* by Jacopo Bassano.

Città della Pieve 06062
Perugia/Umbria   p.414☐G 8

The birthplace of the painter Pietro Vannucci, known as il Perugino, it lies close to Perugia.

Town wall: The well-preserved medieval wall is worth seeing. The 14C castle, partly rebuilt during the Renaissance, is regarded as one of the best examples of military architecture in the entire region.

Cathedral: Built in the 11/12C, partly rebuilt in the late 13C and in the 17C. Note the Romanesque façade and the Romanesque-Gothic tower. In the baroque interior there are two paintings by Perugino: 'Baptism of Christ' and 'Mary and Child surrounded by Saints'. There are also frescos by Pomarancio, Perugino and Alfani. Underneath the apse is a crypt,

which does not, however, appear to be early Christian as was formerly thought.

Oratorio S.Maria dei Bianchi: Inside is one of the finest works by Perugino (Adoration of the Magi). The original working contract concluded between the artist and his home town is interesting both historically and psychologically.

S. Agostino: The 13C church was later rebuilt. It contains works by Pomarancio and Savini.

S.Francesco: This church is today usually known as the *Santuario Mariano.* Built in the 13C, it was later partially rebuilt. Inside, it has a fresco by Pomarancio of the Whitsun story.

SS.Pietro e Paolo: The former church of S.Antonio Abate. The sanctuary has a fresco of St.Antony by Perugino.

S.Maria dei Servi: Like S.Agostino, this church is 13C and was later partially rebuilt. Inside is a fresco of the Entombment by Perugino.

Palazzo Mazzuoli: The 16C former Palazzo della Corgna is attributed to Alessi.

Also worth seeing: There was a small but important school of painting in Città della Pieve in the second half of the 13C. Some of its works include: the Crucifixion (known as Pianto degli Angeli) which can be seen in the *Oratorio S.Bartolomeo*; the fresco in the church of *S.Maria Maddalena,* which is similar in style, and the frescos in the small 14C church of *S.Maria degli Angeli,* 3 km. from the town.

Environs: Panicale: The fresco by Perugino in the church of *S.Sebastiano* (death of the Saint with dancing executioners) is of particular interest here. The visitor should also see the medieval town centre with the simple, graceful *Piazza Mazzini* (16C fountain). **Monte Giove:** This, the most isolated castle in Umbria, was held by the Gattamelata family and now belongs to Marchese Pisciatelli, who has restored it beautifully.

Città di Castello 06012
Perugia/Umbria   [h3p.414☐G 7

This town was founded by the Umbrians and known as Tifernum. During the Roman Empire it was called Tifernum Tiberinum. Pliny the Younger praised the town and the area highly. The Lombards called it Castrum Felicitatis. It was a free town in the 12C, and as such it had to defend its independence against Perugia, the Pope and Arezzo. The town's name changed repeatedly during the following years. Thus, Castellum Felicitatis Civitas Castri became Civitas Castellana, Civitas Castelli and finally Città di Castello. The citizens called themselves Tifernati. In 1422 the town fell to the famous condottiere Braccio Fortebracci da Montone, whose family was dislodged by the Tifernati in 1428. The town successfully opposed the domination of the condottiere Niccolò Piccinino (1440), and in 1474 the citizens fought heroically against the army of Pope Sixtus IV. However, the rise to power of the Vitelli family had already begun at that time, and they turned Città di Castello into a thriving cultural centre. They brought some great Florentine artists to the town, including the young Raphael and Luca Signorelli.

Cathedral: The building dates from the 11/12C and was rebuilt in the 15&16C. The campanile (11&12C) was built in the so-called Ravenna style. On the left side is a fine Gothic portal with bas-relief. The building as a whole has a certain stylistic resemblance to the contemporary Florentine architecture of Sangallo. The baroque façade (1632) is by Francesco Lazzari, and its upper section has remained incomplete. Inside, note the fine *coffered ceiling* (18C), the dome (rebuilt 1789), the Corinthian *capitals,* the fresco by Marco Benefial in the choir, the fine 16C *choir stalls* in the sanctuary, and the Transfiguration of Christ by Rosso Fiorentino in the left aisle.

Cathedral museum: The valuable treasure of Canoscio exhibited here was discovered in 1935 in the place of the same name. The church utensils from the 5&6C are amongst the few known examples of their kind. In addition: 12C altar cloth and a Madonna and Child by Pinturicchio.

Cittadella, view

Palazzo dei Priori/del Comune: This 13C palace stands directly beside the cathedral. It was built to plans by Angelo da Orvieto. Inside, the upper storeys contain the town archive, with valuable 12C manuscripts and Roman tomb inscriptions.

S. Francesco: The originally Gothic building (13C) was partly rebuilt in the early 18C. Apart from the fine *Cappella Vitelli* (first chapel on the left by the architect G.Vasari), the interior is baroque. The chapel has a Coronation of the Virgin, a panel painted by G.Vasari for Gentilizia Vitelli. The *Cappella di S.Giuseppe* has a copy of Raphael's famous painting the 'Marriage of the Virgin' (commissioned by the Albizzini family). Next to the church is the charming *Piazza Raffaello Sanzio*.

Palazzo Vitelli a Porta S.Egidio: This palace was built in the 16C to plans by G. Vasari. Its fine rooms are stuccoed to designs by Cristoforo Gherardi. It is unfortunately not possible to visit the palace at present. However, the *pavilion* behind the palazzo may be viewed.

Palazzo Albizzini: This simple but elegant 14C palace was built in the Tuscan style and contrasts admirably with the adjacent Palazzo Vitelli.

Palazzo Vitelli alla Cannoniera: This palace, which contains the *picture gallery*, was built by order of Alessandro Vitelli in the 1st half of the 16C. The façade was designed by Antonio da Sangallo the younger and by Pier-Francesco da Viterbo. The rear façade of the palace leads into an atrium and is decorated with fine graffiti by Vasari. Frescos by Raffaellino del Colle and Cola dell'Amatrice are to be seen in the rooms and lobbies. The gallery displays paintings, choir stalls, pieces in gold, bronzes, etc. Important works include ones by: Ghirlandaio (Coronation of the Virgin), L.Signorelli (St.John and the Baptism of Christ, and also the Martyrdom of St. Sebastian), Raphael (Creation of Eve), Andrea della Robbia (Assumption), Stendardo (Creation of Eve, and Crucifixion).

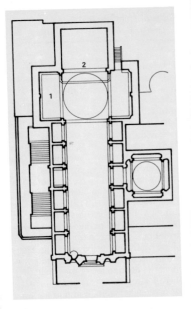

Città di Castello, cathedral 1 Transfiguration of Christ by Rosso Fiorentino 2 choir stalls

S. Domenico: This imposing Gothic building (late 14C, early 15C) stands beside the Palazzo Vitelli alla Cannoniera, and has a particularly fine portal. Inside, there are 15C paintings in Umbrian-Sienese and Umbrian-Marches styles.

Also worth seeing: *Palazzo del Podestà* or *del Governo:* Attributed to Angelo da Orvieto. The façade facing the Piazza Matteotti is baroque, while that on the Corso Cavour retains the original Gothic structure and is now being restored. *S.Maria delle Grazie:* This church was begun in the 14C and rebuilt in 1587. There is a Gothic portal on its left side. Inside is a Death of the Virgin by Ottaviano Nelli and others.

Environs: Civitella Ranieri, near Umbertide: Surrounded by thick foliage, this fine 15C castle is now privately owned and can only be viewed from the outside.

Città di Castello, Civitella Ranieri

Città Sant'Angelo 65013
Pescara/Abruzzi   p.416☐K 6

Collegiata/S. Michele: Only the portal with its pointed arch (1326) survives from the old church. The baroque interior contains the *sarcophagus* of *Bishop Amico di Buonamicizia*, (d. 1467); the marble reliefs with crosses and plaited bands incorporated in the pilasters are from a 9C pulpit.

Cividale del Friuli 33043
Udine/Friuli   p.410☐I 2

In Roman times, this town, known then as 'Forum Iulii', was an important municipium. Under the Lombards it was the seat of a duke (6–8C) and thereafter it was the residence of the patriarchs of Aquileia (until 1238). Cividale del Friuli has been Venetian since 1419; its buildings and museums make it one of the outstanding towns in Friuli.

Cathedral of S. Maria Assunta (Piazza del Duomo): Built over a very long period (begun in 1458 on the ruins of an earlier Romanesque-Gothic structure; Pietro Lombardo supervised the building from 1502 onwards; consecrated in 1529; baroque alteration from 1767). The *façade* is in two sections, a lower one with 15C Gothic portals and pointed arches and an upper Renaissance one. Adjacent to it is the massive 17C *campanile*. The interior has a nave, two aisles and no transept. The *altars* by G.Massari (1686–1766) are of particular interest. Inside, above the main portal, is a wooden *equestrian statue* of Marcantonio da Manzano who was killed in 1617. On the main altar is a late 12C gilded *altar front*. In the left choir chapel is a painting by Pordenone (1539; 'Noli me tangere'). There is a fine 13C Romanesque *wooden crucifix* on the wall in the left aisle. To the right of the choir is the entrance to the crypt (tomb of the Patriarch Paulinus, d. 802). Rich *church treasure*. The right aisle leads to the **Museo Cristiano** with two Lombard masterpieces: the *Ratchis-Ara*, a panelled 8C altar, and the *Callixtus baptistery*, a font from the same century (columns from late antiquity, 5/6C capitals, magnificent reliefs on the sides).

Tempietto Longobardo (access from the Piazzale S. Biagio): It is really an oratory to St. Mary. Its architecture and original early medieval decoration (sculptures, paintings) make it one of the most important buildings in Friuli. Probably built in the 2nd half of the 8C. The original exterior has disappeared. Inside: square ground plan, with a sanctuary (one nave, two aisles) built on to the E. The main area has a groined vault. Half way up the walls there are original *remains of frescoes*. The sanctuary has fine *columns*, some with ancient capitals. The *stucco decorations* on the walls (above the frescos) are the main work of art in the church and date from the time of the building's construction. Particularly well preserved on the W. wall are six female figures above a richly decorated stucco arch, with a splendid *round-arched window* between them. Fine wooden 15C *choir stalls*. In the left aisle of the sanctuary is the *sarcophagus of Piltrudis*, the church's founder. (The church was closed in 1976 because it was in danger of collapse.)

Museo Archeologico Nazionale (in the Palazzo Nordis, Piazza del Duomo): Contains archaeological finds, the following of which are outstanding: ground floor, room I: *Roman finds* (including inscriptions referring to the Roman 'Forum Iulii'); room II: *sarcophagus of Gisulphus* (7C) and remains of a large *floor mosaic* from the 2C AD; upper floor, room II: the 13C *veil of Beata Benvenuta Boiani* and other ancient *finds;* room III: an important *collection of small Lombard works of art* (includes the contents of the above-mentioned tomb of Gisulf); room IV: the *Pax of Duke Ursus*, an excellent 8/9C Lombard gold piece and the *psalter of St. Elizabeth*.

Also worth seeing: 15C church of *SS. Pietro e Biagio* (Piazzale S. Biagio), a cru-

Città di Castello, terracotta by Andrea della Robbia in the picture gallery

ciform building (15C frescos in the right side chapel). Church of *S.Francesco* (Piazza S.Francesco), a 14C Gothic hall church. 16C church of *S.Maria dei Battuti* (Borgo di Ponte), with a fine Renaissance choir. *Monastero Maggiore* (founded in the 8C; Via Monastero Maggiore) with the *Chiesa S.Giovanni* (first building *c.* 7C, present one 17C). 18C *Palazzo Brosadola* (Piazza S.Francesco), with important frescos by the local artist Francesco Chiarottini (1748–96). *Palazzo dei Provveditori Veneti* (Piazza del Duomo), built in the 16C to plans by Palladio. *Palazzo Municipale* (Piazza del Duomo), originally built in the 14C. 15C *Ponte del Diavolo* over the Natisone. *Ipogeo Celtico* (Via Monastero Maggiore), probably Celtic burial chambers, built into the bluffs of the Natisone river (inside, there are unusual heads on the walls).

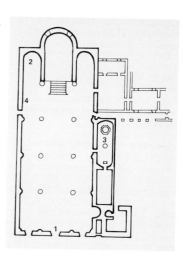

Cividale, cathedral 1 equestrian statue of M.da Manzano **2** Noli me tangere, by Pordenone **3** Museo Cristiano **4** Romanesque wooden crucifix

Civita Castellana 01033

Viterbo/Latium   p.414☐G/H 9

Conquered and destroyed by the Romans as early as 395 BC. In 293 BC the town took part in the Etruscan rebellion against Rome. The Romans responded to a further rebellion during the 1st Punic War by destroying the town once again and forcibly

Città Sant'Angelo, Collegiata S.Michele

moving it to a less well protected place, *Falerii Novi*. Constant raids in the 8C forced the inhabitants to return to the original site, with its better defensive position. The town was in the possession of the Savelli in the 11C, and it later fell to the Pope. Sixtus IV gave the town to Cardinal Rodrigo Borgia (later Pope Alexander VI), who began building the Rocca. Today it is the seat of a bishop.

Cathedral of S. Maria: This basilica, which had a nave and two aisles, was begun in the 12C, but with the alteration of the aisles into chapels (1736–40) it became a single-aisled hall church. A fine graduated portico stands in front of the W. façade. The middle section still towers upwards and opens in the style of a triumphal arch. The entablature of the side openings rests on Ionic columns modelled on ancient architecture. Some strips of Cosmati work have been inlaid for specific purposes (e.g. as a frieze in the entablature and to accentuate the pilaster shafts). Designed in 1210 by Jacopo de Lorenzo and Cosma (Roman marble craftsmen), the portico is a successful reworking of ancient models and as such is a key work of what

Cividale, Callixtus baptistery

is known as the Proto-Renaissance. The elegant proportions of the *portals* behind the portico are accentuated by Cosmati work frames. The middle portal, flanked by lions, has a Cosmati work tympanum by Lorenzo, decorated in the form of a half rose. The tympanum of the right portal, with a *mosaic picture of Christ blessing* is by Jacopo di Lorenzo. The elegant baroque interior dates from 1736–40, although the Cosmati work floor and some rediscovered remains of 13C frescos have survived. In the *old sacristy* are fragments of marble screen with Cosmati work (1237) by Deodato and Luca, the sons of Cosma II, the original Cosmati artist. The 7/8C *crypt* is on the site of an ancient shrine. 2 fine *ciboria* (mid 15C) from the school of Duccio di Bartolomeo.

Rocca: Cardinal Rodrigo Borgia (as Pope Alexander VI, 1494–1500) had this pentagonal Renaissance fortress built on the foundations of some 9C fortifications. Julius II added the octagonal inner tower, designed by Antonio da Sangallo the elder. The courtyard is surrounded by two storeys of pillars and arcades.

Environs: Falerii Novi: Cf. the history of Civita Castellana. The remains of the theatre on the forum, and also of the baths, lie next to the impressive ruins of the Roman walls, which are 2,300 yards long and have 50 towers and 9 gates. The semi-ruined 12C Romanesque church of *S. Maria di Falleri* is particularly interesting. Near to Ponte Terano there is a group of Etruscan tombs.

Civitavecchia 00053
Rome/Latium   p.414☐G 9

The most important seaport in Latium and the main departure point for Sardinia. The port of Civitavecchia was founded by Trajan as *Centumcellae*. It was conquered by Byzantium in 537/8, by the Saracens in 828, and, from the 15C onwards, it became the main port of the Papal States.

Cividale, Tempietto Longobardo

Cividale, cathedral museum, detail of Ratchis altar

Forte Michelangelo: An impressive Renaissance harbour defence. It is 328 ft. x 269 ft., compact in appearance and faced with travertine. Begun under Julius II by Bramante in 1508 on the ruins of the ancient port, it was subsequently continued by Antonio Sangallo; Michelangelo completed it in 1557 under Paul III. It has round corner bastions and the centre of the seaward-side is strengthened by a massive, projecting, polygonal bastion.

Clusone 24023
Bergamo/Lombardy   p.412☐E 3

S.Maria Assunta: Built at the end of the 17C to plans by G.B. Quadrio. The inside is single-aisled and richly decorated, with eight magnificent altars. Outstanding items include: a *crucifix* by Andrea Fantoni

(1st altar on right); *statues of St.Louis and St.Roch* by Fantoni (4th altar on right); an *Ascension* by S. Ricci (sanctuary); and a *Madonna and Child with Saints* by D.Carpinoni (3rd altar on left).

L'Oratorio dei Disciplini (1450): Frescos dating from 1485 on the outside: *Triumph of Death* and *Dance of Death*. Subject matter and style indicate Tuscan influence. There are more frescos inside (*Life of Christ*, 1471).

Palazzo Fogaccia: An unfinished late 17C palace with a gallery and drawing rooms, frescoed throughout in the early 18C.

Environs: Rovetta, birthplace of the Fantoni family of artists (17C). *Parish church of 1661 with Apotheosis of the Saints* by G.B.Tiepolo.

Codróipo 33033
Udine/Friuli   p.410□H 3

Codróipo is a lively commercial town at the centre of the plain of Friuli. The town takes its name from the nearby Roman crossroads (quadrivium: four ways). The 18C **parish church** is worth seeing (inside, a 16C *wooden crucifix* on the 2nd altar on the left is of particular interest; it was borne before condemned criminals in Venice who were on their way to be executed).

Environs: Some 3 km. SE, **Passariano** with the famous **Villa Manin,** one of the finest villas in Friuli. Built *c.* 1738, it was the residence of Lodovico Manin, the last Doge (1789–97). Napoleon stayed here for a few days in 1797 whilst discussing the treaty of Campo Formio (named after a village near Udine now known as Campoformido). The main building has a simple façade, and inside there is a three-storeyed main hall. It is flanked by *farm buildings* (the so-called 'barchesse', with round arches), each of which is connected by a gateway to the circular, arcaded *stables.* On the S. side of the complex there are two towers; the octagonal *chapel* lies to the E. (inside it there are fine marble works by Giuseppe Torretti). The adjacent *park* contains many works by the same artist (statues, herms, vases, mainly with mythological scenes). The Villa Manin today houses an institute engaged on cataloguing the cultural possessions of Friuli. *c.* 10 km. S., **Varmo:** The church of *S.Lorenzo* has a fine triptych (1526) by G.A.Pordenone.

Cogne 11012
Aosta/Aosta   p.412□A 3

S.Orso: The architectural style and decoration of the parish church show foreign influence. There are two particularly fine wooden *altars* with carved columns, the so-called 'Ritz altars'.

Also worth seeing: The *Castello Reale* beside the church was handed to Savoy in

Civita Castellana, cathedral

1191; in 1873 it was the hunting lodge of Victor Emmanuel, and today it is privately owned.

Colle del Gran San Bernardo
Aosta/Aosta   p.412□A 2

Colle del Gran San Bernardo is the highest pass in the Swiss Alps, the summit being 8,100 ft. above sea-level. The road tunnel 'La galleria del Gran Bernardo', which also has a pipeline running through it, is 5.8 km. long and was opened in 1964. It is one of the oldest Alpine passes and was probably crossed by Hannibal in 218 BC, and subsequently by the Salassi, the Romans, Charlemagne in 775, and Henry II in 1077.

The **Hospice:** built by Bernardo di Mentone in 1035 – 49 and extended several times. It encloses a small **baroque church** (1678). In 1831–7 a well-stocked *museum* was set up here; it includes a library with over 30,000 volumes.

Cómiso 97013
Ragusa/Sicily   p.420☐L 18

Possibly on the site of the town of Kasmenai, founded by Syracuse in 643 BC. It is known for the so-called 'Pietra di Cómiso', an excellent limestone for building.

Chiesa Matrice (*S.Maria delle Stelle:* near the Piazza Municipio): Originally built in the 15C, rebuilt in baroque style after the earthquake of 1693. Fine *façade,* and *dome* decorated with columns. Laid out with a Latin cross ground plan, it has a nave and two aisles. Fine *pointed arches* on columns. 17C painted *ceiling.* There is a *Madonna* (Gagini workshop) on the altar in the right transept.

S.Francesco (also *dell'Immacolata,* Via Ippari): Built in the 13C; the apse was added in 1517. The single-aisled interior contains fine *altars.* The *choir* (the so-called 'Cappella Naselli') with the *tombs of the Counts Naselli* is particularly interesting. It is square with a richly decorated dome and displays a number of stylistic influences — from Byzantine through Arab and Gothic to Renaissance. To the left of the sarcophagus is a *Madonna* attributed to Antonello Gagini (1478–1536). There is a fine 15C *cloister.*

Also worth seeing: 18C church of *SS. Annunziata* with a fine baroque façade. *Castle of the Naselli* (built in the 13C and extended in the 14–16C) with a massive octagonal tower containing remains of 14C frescos (there may previously have been a Byzantine baptistery here). *Scuola d'Arte* with a fine marble horse's head (probably 5C BC). *Biblioteca Comunale* with a mosaic floor (2C AD).

Environs: Some 20 km. SW, the excavations of the Greek town of **Camarina** (598 BC, founded by Syracuse). The surviving monuments from the Hellenistic-Roman period include the remains of a *Temple of Athene* and the remains of *streets.*

Como 221100
Como/Lombardy   p.412☐D 3

The early Iron Age necropolis shows that Como's origins lie in early history. The Gallic *Oppidum* of the Orobians became a Roman colony in 89 BC under the name *Novum Comun,* and in 49 BC Caesar granted it Roman civic rights. The regular design of the 'Castrum' is still discernible on the map of the town of Como today. After suffering greatly from the barbarian invasions, it became part of the Duchy of Lombardy and had its first heyday under the Franks. Emperor Frederick Barbarossa confirmed the independence of Como in the Peace of Constance in 1183. After an unsuccessful attempt to found a republic under the patronage of St.Abondius, the town fell to Francesco Sforza in 1450.

Cathedral district: The *Torre del Comune,* the *Broletto* and the *Cathedral* form the public centre of the town.

The Broletto: Seat of the Podestà. The construction of this city tower was begun in 1215. The ground floor is an open hall with four arcades. The upper storey has three three-arched windows. The alternating red and white marble strips are a distinctive feature. The balcony, from which public announcements were proclaimed, was added in the 15C.

Cathedral: The church of S.Maria Maggiore was completely rebuilt from 1396 onwards. Work was restarted in 1426 after some interruptions. The façade was begun in 1455 and the apses in 1513. The right transept was completed in 1627–33, and the left transept in 1653–69. The dome was built in 1731–44 to a design by Filippo Juvarra. *Outside:* The façade has four pilaster strips with numerous niches occupied by statues. These strips end in turret-like pinnacles. The niches and the rose-window

(1486) give particular emphasis to the central section. Sculptures: In the tympana (from left to right): *Adoration of the Shepherds, Adoration of the Magi, Presentation in the Temple.* The central doorway is unique for a church portal in being flanked by statues of two ancient figures, *Pliny the Elder* on one side and *Pliny the Younger* on the other, a mark of the town's respect for two of its most famous sons. Above the middle portal there is a *Madonna with four Saints;* in niches on either side of the rose- window there is an *Annunciation,* and above the window, a *seated Evangelist.* At the very top is a *Christ with two Angels.* The portals on the N. and S.sides are also interesting. The former has a *Flight into Egypt* in the lunette, and the *Virtues,* (1491) in the arch; whilst the latter has a *Visitation* with an excellent surround.

Inside: Ground plan on a Latin cross, nave and two aisles, transept with choir ending as apses with half-domes.
Decoration: Between the pillars and on the W. wall there are nine 16C *tapestries* from Ferrara, Florence and Antwerp. Two magnificent 17C *organ fronts.* The *altar of St. Abondius* with scenes from the life of the Saint. *Sacra Conversazione,* a masterpiece by Luini. The *Marriage of the Virgin* (by Ferrari). The *font,* a tempietto (1592) with eight Corinthian columns. The *S.transept,* dedicated to the 'Assumption', displays rich baroque decoration (1689). The *cathedral treasure* is preserved in the canons' sacristy.

Cathedral environs: At the N. end of the *Piazza Grimoldi* is the much-restored *Bishop's Palace* of 1013. The best overall view of the choir and dome of the cathedral may be had from the *Piazza Verdi.* The late classical *Teatro Sociale* (1811–3), with its distinguished Corinthian portico, is also on the Piazza Verdi. Opposite the choir is the former *Casa del Fascio (Caserma delle Guardie di Finanza,* built by Giuseppe Terragni in 1932), one of the most impressive buildings of Italian rationalism.

S.Fedele (Via Vittorio Emanuele): Built, probably in the first half of the 12C, on the site of a church dedicated to St.Euphemia. Basilican ground plan and front elevation; the choir has three apses. Simple Romanesque façade with rose window dating from 1509. The exterior of the polygonal choir is highlighted by a surrounding dwarf gal-

Como, cathedral

Como, cathedral, façade

lery. On the left side of the choir is a simple portal crowned by an open pediment. To the sides of the portal are Romanesque reliefs with large figurative scenes (probably 11C).
Inside: The nave has three bays and is divided by arcades with galleries above them. There are two continuous dwarf galleries, one above the other in the main apse of the chancel. The apse calotte is by Guglielmo Beltrami, and is decorated throughout with frescos of the *Martyrdom of S. Fedele*. In the side apses are two 9C *marble lions* which serve as supports for holy-water stoups.

S. Abbondio: A church built in the 11C by Benedictines on the site of a church dedicated to the Apostles Peter and Paul. Elements of Rhenish, Norman, Cluniac and Italian architecture have found a happy synthesis here. It has a nave and four aisles but no transept and the choir has markedly elongated central section. The towers on either side of the nave rise above the side apses. Five pilaster strips with half columns in front of them subdivide the simple W. façade, which has only one portal.

Decoration: The choir has 14C frescos of a christological cycle. The influence of Sienese-Umbrian painting on the Lombard masters is unmistakable.

Museo Civico: The former *Palazzo Giovio* today houses the Museo Civico. A mainly archaeological collection.

Also worth seeing: *Torre di Portal Vittoria,* the best-preserved gate from the former town defences (1192). The *façade of S. Cecilia,* which is included in the elegant façade of the Liceo-Ginnasio Volta (1812). *Casa di A.Volta,* the house of the famous physicist. The picturesque shore promenade with the *Tempio Voltiano,* a monument to Volta. The *Monumento ai Caduti* (Vle Puecher), an unorthodox war memorial by the futurist architect Antonio

Como, cathedral **A** S.portal **B** N. portal **1** altar of St.Abondius **2** 'Sacra Conversazione' by Luini **3** 18C marble group, with St.Isidore **4** Cappella dell'Assunta (chapel of the Virgin Mary) **5** sanctuary with baroque high altar, 1728 **6** canon's sacristy (cathedral treasure) **7** Cappella del Crocifisso, 1665, with altar of the crucifixion (15C crucifix) **8** Deposition by Tomaso Rodari, 1498 **9** 17C organ front **10** 17C organ front **11** Betrothal of the Virgin Mary, Ferrari **12** baptistery

Como, S. Abbondio

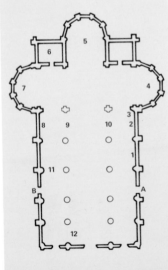

Sant'Elia. *Villa Olmo* (on the W. shore, towards Cernobbio), built for Pope Innocent XI in 1782.

Environs: *S. Carpoforo:* Built in the 11&12C on the site of what is probably the oldest church (4C) in the area around Como. The choir and campanile are of interest. **Cernobbio:** *Villa d'Este,* built for Cardinal Tolomeo Gallio in 1589. Since 1873 it has been used as a hotel. The rooms on the ground floor are decorated with fine works of art. There is a splendid *park.* Occupying a unique site in **Tremezzo** are the park and the *Villa Carlotta,* named after Charlotte of Saxe-Meiningen. The early 18C villa houses a splendid art collection (Canova, Thorvaldsen, Hayez). **Bellagio:** Apart from the 12C church of *S. Giacomo* there are two villas worth seeing. The *Villa Melzi* (near the beach) has a park containing ancient statues. The villa itself contains a valuable collection of paintings. The *Villa Serbelloni* is on the hill behind the town. There was probably a villa on this site in Roman times (Pliny the Younger). The present building dates from the 16&17C. It also has a splendid park. *L'Abbazia di S. Pietro sopra Civate:* In 722,

Desiderius, the last Lombard king, in gratitude for his son's salvation made a vow to convert the oratory on the Pesura into a monastery. The two surviving buildings are 11C. *S. Pietro al Monte:* is single-aisled, with an atrium and semicircular apses. On the outside there are pilaster strips and Lombard bands. Above the entrance by the E. apse there is a relief of Christ with Peter and Paul. Inside: the narthex (which lies within the apse) has 11C frescos of Byzantine influence: *Saints,* the *Heavenly Jerusalem, Angels, Rivers of Paradise,* and on the wall above, the *Apocalypse.* The nave has 15C *frescos.* 11C *altar with ciborium* (the altar in S. Ambrogio, Milan, is modelled on it) has a christological cycle and is a very great rarity. Under the E. apse is a crypt with a nave and two aisles (11C capitals with figures and stucco). The *Oratory of S. Benedetto* is a centrally planned building with three apses and 11C frescos at the altar (Deesis, Benedict and Andrew).

Conegliano 31015

Treviso/Veneto   p.410☐G 3

Cathedral/S. Maria dei Battuti: Built

S. Pietro al Monte near Como, frescos, 11C

Como, Sant'Apollonia, 14C

its wooden ceiling, is painted throughout with 15/16C frescos of subjects from the New Testament.

Conversano 70014
Bari/Apulia   p.416☐O 11

Cathedral of S.Maria Assunta: Building began in Romanesque style in the 12C. The building was completely rebuilt in 1359–73, but the Romanesque structure was preserved. The *W. façade* with its Romanesque portal is particularly worth seeing. Restoration work was carried out in 1912.

S.Benedetto: The oldest church in the town and formerly part of a Benedictine monastery. Built as a church with three domes on the site of an earlier building destroyed by the Saracens. Consecrated in 1108. Much has been altered in the course of time (E. apses broken off, a baroque campanile added, baroque interior). Traces of the original building survive to the left, on the outside of the building. The small *campanile* with its domical vault is original (cf. the 'Tomba di Rotari' in Monte S.Angelo). The *lions* on the Renaissance side portal are also Romanesque. Some remains of the *mosaic decoration* survive inside, particularly on the walls of the nave. Beside the church is the Romanesque *cloister*, which is well worth seeing. It has a trapezoidal lay out and fine capitals with animal and plant motifs. On the N. side is the entrance to the church's *crypt*, which is all that remains of the earlier building (see above).

Also worth seeing: *S. Caterina* (on the other side of the railway): A centrally planned building on a Syrian model (dome with octagonal drum, four apses); *castle* with three square towers; *remains of megalithic walls* (near to S.Benedetto).

Environs: Some 10 km. E., **Polignano a Mare**, splendidly situated on a cliff above

in 1354 by the Flagellants of the *Scuola di S. Maria dei Battuti*, which had been founded in Conegliano in 1271. The school building stands in front of the cathedral. Its magnificent façade was frescoed by Pozzoserato (1593). Beneath the timber ceiling there are medallions showing the scourge—the symbol of the brotherhood. The frescos are mainly of scenes from the Old Testament. The façade itself has seven triple-arched windows and two doorways with iron balconies. The campanile was not built until 1497. Inside (nave and two aisles) was thoroughly restored in 1956 – 62 and, amongst other things, it contains two good paintings: *St. Francis and Saints* (1545) by F.Beccaruzzi, and the large altarpiece, the *Virgin and Child Enthroned with Saints and Angels* (1493) by Cima da Conegliano. The late 14C *Sala dei Battuti* is worth a visit and can be reached by a staircase next to the campanile. This enormous hall, with

Tremezzo (Como), Villa Carlotta ▷

the sea (there are some splendid *grottoes* on the bluff, chiefly the 'Grotta Palazzese'). *c.* 11 km. NW is **Rutigliano** with the 12C Romanesque church of *S. Maria della Colonna*, which has a fine portal and a polyptych by Vivarini (1450); Norman *tower*, 98 ft. tall. About 15 km. N., by the sea, **Mola di Bari** has a 13C Romanesque *cathedral* rebuilt in the Renaissance, and a *castle* (also 13C).

Copertino 73043
Lecce/Apulia   p.418☐P 12

In this little town on the Salentine peninsula stands one of the largest and most splendid **castles** in Apulia. It was built from 1540 onwards for Alfonso Castriota after Ferdinand I of Naples had given him Copertino as a token of gratitude for assistance rendered against the Angevins. A fortified Angevin building was incorporated in the castle, which is trapezoidal, with four wings; the longest frontage being about 393 ft. The *main portal* is in the form of a Renaissance triumphal arch and has busts of people historically important to Copertino. The *chapel* has 16C frescos.

Environs: *c.* 3 km. NW is **Leverano**, with the tallest and best-preserved Hohenstaufen-Norman *tower*. 118 ft. high, it dates from 1220.

Copparo 44034
Ferrara/Emilia-Romagna   p.410☐G 4

The **Palazzo Comunale** (Piazza della Libertà): The Este building of 1540-7 was converted into the Palazzo Comunale in 1895. The brick tower at the back is part of the original construction.

S. Pietro: Built in the late 16C. It dates from a 12C foundation and has been altered several times. The 14C campanile was rebuilt after war damage. There are two restored paintings by Scarsellino (*c.* 1600) inside the church.

Corciano 06073
Perugia/Umbria   p.414☐G 7

S. Maria: This 13C church is well worth a visit. It was altered in the 19C. Inside,

Bellagio (Como), Villa Melzi

it contains Perugino's Assumption of the Virgin and the Annunciation and Birth of Christ, one of the finest works of the ageing master.

S. Francesco: Umbrian-Gothic. Inside, there is a panel from the Caporali school.

Corfinio 67030
L'Aquila/Abruzzi   p.416□I 9

In 1928, the town of Pentima was renamed after the ancient *Corfinium*.

Basilica di S.Pelino (or *Valvense*): This early Christian building was destroyed by the Saracens in 881 and by the Magyars in 927. It was rebuilt 1075–1188, repaired in 1255, and altered in baroque style in 1680–1718. The rectangular pulpit, which has an ornamental relief on the balustrade, was built in 1182–8. The columns of the pulpit are decorated with coloured inlay. The left aisle has remains of 15C frescos. The *Oratorio di S. Alessandro* was built from 1075–1102 using the remains of ancient and early- Christian buildings. The altar shows Burgundian influence.

Cori 04010
Latina/Latium   p.414□H 10

One of the oldest towns in Italy. Its origin is reputed to go back to Dardanos the Trojan. It was a municipium under Augustus. The medieval character of this little town —with its narrow alleyways, some of which are vaulted over (the Via del Porticato is especially picturesque), and the flights of steps to the houses — has survived well. There are numerous remains of a cyclops wall surrounding the town and dating from the 5&4C BC.

Collegiate church of S. Maria della Pietà (*c.* 1600), with interesting 12C *Easter candlestick*. A base of stylized lions supports four clustered columns.

S.Oliva: A group of churches consisting

of a medieval church and a 15C church. The older church has medieval frescos, while the more recent one contains frescos in the style of Michelangelo (1553). The newer church was begun in 1477. Its apse has a fresco of the Umbrian school (1507). Elegant 15C Renaissance cloister. The town contains the remains of two Roman temples: the **Temple of the Dioscuri Castor and Pollux,** rebuilt shortly after 89 BC. At the highest point above the town is the **Temple of Hercules,** built between 89 and 80 BC. The portico is supported by eight massive Doric columns. The church of S.Pietro was destroyed in World War 2, but the tower at the back of the temple has survived.

Correggio 42015
Reggio Emilia/Emilia-Romagna   p.410□F 4/5

Correggio, inhabited by the Romans but otherwise not mentioned until the 10C, became the seat of a count in 1452 and acquired the status of a town in 1554. When the last Correggiescho was deposed by Emperor Ferdinand II in 1630, the town be-

Conegliano, castle

came part of the Duchy of Modena. The great painter Antonio Allegri, known as Correggio, was born here in 1489.

The **Palazzo dei Principi** (Corso Cavour): Built in 1500 by order of Franziska of Brandenburg on the site of an earlier building. In the courtyard are a *fountain* (1507) and a 4C *marble lion*. The building contains the *Biblioteca Civica* (valuable 16C manuscripts and editions), the *Archivo Storico e Notarile* and the *Museo Civico.*

S.Quirino (Piazza di S.Quirino): Built in 1513–87 to a design by Vignola. The 14C campanile was originally a tower belonging to the castle. Inside: nave and two aisles, and a crypt which was rebuilt in the 19C. In the treasury there is a valuable late 14C bone reliquary from the Embriachi school.

Also worth seeing: *S. Francesco* (Via Roma), 1470; frequently modified and restored. The choir has capitals attributed to Antonio da Reggio. The mid 16C church of *S. Giuseppe Calasanzio* (Piazza Garibaldi) has paintings of the Emilian school. Next to it is *S. Chiara*, built after models by Borromini, with a façade dated 1666.

Corridónia 62014
Macerata/Marches   p.414☐I 7

S. Agostino: Inside the church are a *Madonna* (1372) by Andrea Bologna and *Madonna del latte* by Carlo Crivelli.

Pinacoteca: Paintings include some by Crivelli and Vivarini.

Environs: Monte S.Giusto: There is a Crucifixion by Lorenzo Lotto (1531) in the church of *S. Maria Telusiano.* Its twin church, *S.Claudio al Chienti* was founded in the 11C and restored in 1928. The two churches, built one on top of the other, share the same ground plan, which shows Byzantine influence—almost square, with three apses on each side of the choir and one apse on each flank. The upper church was originally entered from the corner towers in the façade, while today steps lead to the terrace above the portal of the lower

Corfinio, basilica di S. Pelino

church. *S.Maroto:* 13C, restored in 1956. It is centrally planned, with a dome and four chapels. Inside, there is a Byzantine Madonna from *c.* 1200.

Cortemaggiore 29016
Piacenza / Emilia-Romagna   p.412 □ D 4

Cortemaggiore, called *Curtis Maior* by the Romans, fell to ruin after the Carolingian period. It was rebuilt in its regular form by Gian Ludovico and his son Orlando Pallavicino from 1479 onwards.

Collegiata S.Maria delle Grazie (Piazza dei Patrioti): This church was begun in 1481 to designs by Gilberto Manzi. The three apses (in the sanctuary and the left and right transepts) are from an older building; the façade was not built until 1881. The campanile is 16C. Inside (one nave, two aisles), there is a *crypt* underneath the sanctuary; also the *Pallavicini monuments* (1499), and two panels painted by Filippo Mazzola depicting the *Resurrection* (1523).

Franciscan church (Via Garibaldi): Built in 1490, with a nave, two aisles and a modern campanile. The chapel in the right aisle has 16C *wall paintings*; the chapel to the left of this has some well-restored *wall paintings* (1530) by Pordenone (*c.* 1483–1539). On the first floor are a *Deposition* by Pordenone and *wall paintings* by a successor of De Mio (late 16C).

Cortina d'Ampezzo 32043
Belluno / Veneto   p.410 □ G 1/2

The main town of the Dolomites, it lies in the broad Ampezzo valley, surrounded by the tremendous peaks of the fissured limestone massif (Monte Cristallo 10,551 ft., Sorapis 10,515 ft., Croda da Lago 8,888 ft.).

Parish church of SS. Filippo e Giacomo (between the Piazza Roma and the Piazza Venezia): This church was built in the 13C and subsequently rebuilt several times. Inside, it is single-aisled, and the ceiling vault has been painted throughout by F.A.Zeiller (1773). There is a fine paint-

Cori, temple of Hercules

Cori, Easter candlestick, 12C

ing (1679) by A. Zanchi on the high altar, and a tabernacle (1724) by A. Brustolon on the first side altar on the left.

Cortona 52044
Arezzo/Tuscany   p.414☐G 7

On a spur of the Alta S. Egidio (near the Umbrian border and not far from Lake Trasimene), some 1,640 ft. up. One of the oldest towns in Italy, it was founded by the Umbrians and then conquered by the Etruscans, becoming one of their strongholds (it was one of the twelve cities of their confederation). A period of Roman rule followed and, in the Middle Ages, it fell to Florence. Cortona was the home town of the painter Luca Signorelli and of the painter and architect Pietro Berrettini, known as Pietro da Cortona.

Fortezza Medicea: Built 492 ft. above the town on the ruins of the Etruscan wall. The remains of the ancient acropolis can still be seen to the E. and they offer a magnificent panoramic view.

Correggio, orphanage (Mantegna)

Cathedral of S. Maria: Built on the site of a Romanesque church by Giuliano da Sangallo or his followers. The interesting 16C *portal* is by Cristofanello. The *campanile* (1566, by Francesco Laparelli), with its two stories of two-arched windows, is from the same period. The cathedral's interior, originally Renaissance, is attributed to Giuliano da Sangallo and was rebuilt at the beginning of the 18C; the painting dates from 1887.

S. Domenico (a little way outside the town): Simple early 15C façade, with Gothic portal. Inside: *Madonna and Child with Angels and Saints* by Luca Signorelli, and an *Annunciation* by Palma il Giovane.

S. Francesco: Begun by Fra Elia Coppi in 1245; rebuilt in the 17C. The left side wall survives from the original building. The inside is single-aisled, and there are three Gothic chapels. The marble tabernacle on the high altar contains a *relic of the Holy Cross*, and in the apse there is the Romanesque-Gothic *tomb of Ranieri Ubertini*.

Santuario di S. Margherita: The present building, dating from 1856 (campanile, 1650), marks the spot where Saint Margaret died in 1297. The sanctuary contains the *tomb of the Saint* in a Gothic sarcophagus of 1362, by Angelo and Francesco di Pietro, with reliefs of scenes from the life of the Saint. The lid of the sarcophagus is borne by two angels. There is also a fine 14C *wooden crucifix*.

S. Maria Nuova (to the N., a little way outside the town walls): Begun by Cristofanello in the 16C and completed by Vasari.

Museo Diocesano (Piazza del Duomo 2): Housed in the former *Chiesa del Gesù*, which consisted of two churches, one above the other, connected by staircases. The lower church, painted throughout in 1555 to a design by Vasari, has beautiful *intarsia choir stalls* (1517) by Vincenzo da Cortona. The main exhibits in the museum are works by Tuscan artists: an *Annunciation* by Beato Angelico, and paintings by the Lorenzetti brothers and by Luca Signorelli.

Etruscan Museum (in the Palazzo Pretorio): Roman busts from the 1–3C AD, amphorae, ivories, bronzes, a fine collection of Etruscan and Roman coins, as well as finds from Cortona and the surrounding area. Particular mention should be made of the famous Etruscan sixteen-branched bronze candelabra from the end of the 5C BC.

Remains of the Etruscan wall, which was formerly 2,600 m long, can be found all over the town: in the Piazza del Mercato, Porta S.Maria and near to the Porta Colonia, where the medieval wall was built on the Etruscan wall.

Environs: *Madonna del Calcinaio:* A centrally planned Renaissance church with an octagonal dome of simple, clear design. Built in 1485–1513 to sketches by Francesco di Giorgio Martini. The *stained glass in the rose-window of the façade* (1516) is a masterpiece by Guillaume de Marcillat.
Castiglion Fiorentino (N. of Cortona, half way to Arezzo): This town may possibly be the ancient *Castula*, or even *Arretium fidens*. It is mentioned as *Castillione Aretino* in 1014, and since 1384 has belonged to Florence. The town is surrounded by a battlemented wall. *S. Francesco:* From the second half of the 13C; Romanesque but Gothic influences already apparent. Fine façade with a tall two-arched window and a round window. Inside: a painting of *St.Francis* by Margaritone d'Arezzo, interesting from the iconographical point of view; a fresco *(Madonna and Child)* by a follower of Baldovinetti; and a *singers' pulpit* (1546) in the left side aisle.
To the left is the monastery, and 26 *episodes from the life of St.Francis* can be seen in the lunettes of the arcaded passage. The *collegiate church* has a fresco of the *Lamentation* by Luca Signorelli (just after 1502), and another of the *Adoration of the Shepherds* by Lorenzo di Credi. *Madonna della Consolazione:* An octagonal Renaissance church with a *Madonna and Child* attributed to Luca Signorelli or Angelo di Lorentino. The *picture gallery* in the *Palazzo Comunale* has a small collection of Florentine masters of the 15&16C. *Castello di Montecchio Vesponi:* The old 11C 'Cas-

Cortina d'Ampezzo, view

Cortona, Palazzone

Madonna del Calcinaio (Cortona)

trum Montis Giusponi'. The old walls, 774 ft. long, and the 13C square towers of the fortress, have survived.

Cosenza 87100

Cosenza/Calabria   p.418☐N 14

This town is located at the confluence of the Busento and the Crati. The ancient Consentia was Roman from 204 BC onwards; Roman colonists settled there in the 1C BC. Alaric, king of the Visigoths, is said to have been buried here in the bed of the Busento in AD 412 (poem by August von Platen). After the Saracens destroyed the town, it was Normanized under Robert Guiscard in *c.* 1000. As the main town in northern Calabria, it later came under Aragonese and Bourbon rule.

Cathedral (Piazza del Duomo): Begun in

Cortona, Museo Diocesano, Presentation in the Temple by B.Angelico

the mid 12C in Romanesque style, but soon destroyed in an earthquake. Consecrated in 1222 in the presence of Emperor Frederick II of Hohenstaufen. Rebuilt in baroque style in the 18C. The façade (1831) is neo-Gothic. After restoration, the façade and interior have today been returned to their original condition. There is a fine *rose-window* and three pointed-arch *portals*. Inside (nave, two aisles) there are fine *Romanesque capitals*. Raised choir. The *tomb of Isabella of Aragon* (the wife of the French king Philip III), who died in Cosenza in 1271, is in the left transept. This tomb (1275) is the work of a French artist. The tomb of the German king Henry VII, who died in 1242 and was also buried here, has been lost. There is an *Immaculate Conception* by Luca Giordano in the first chapel on the left. The *cathedral treasure* in the *Archbishop's Palace* behind the cathedral is worth seeing. It includes a richly decorated

12C Byzantine *reliquary cross*. Tradition has it that this belonged to Frederick II.

S. Domenico (Piazza Tommaso Campanella, at the confluence of the Busento and the Crati): Mid 15C with a late Gothic façade and a 17C baroque dome. The single-aisled interior is very spacious; it was completely rebuilt in the 18C *(stucco)*. The *Cappella del Rosario*, with the altar of the 'Madonna delle Febbre' (fine marble), is particularly interesting.

S.Francesco di Paola (Corso Plebiscito): Restored in the early 18C; damaged by an earthquake in 1854. Inside (single-aisled), to the right of the entrance, is the baroque *marble tomb of Cesare Gaeta* (1593); the high altar has a Madonna and Child *triptych* (1st half of 16C) in the Neapolitan style.

S. Francesco d'Assisi (Via Grotte S.

Francesco d'Assisi): Possibly founded as early as 1217; rebuilt in the 15C, using the previous nave as the transept of the new church. The inside has a nave and two aisles, and is in the form of a Latin cross. Of particular interest is the *Cappella di S. Caterina*, with gilded carvings and a painting by Willem Borremans ('The Life of the Saint', 1705). Fine *cloister* adjoins the church. Beside the church are remains of a Roman wall and of a medieval apse.

Castle (on the Colle Pancrazio): The central part of the building is probably pre-Norman. After it had been destroyed in an earthquake, it was rebuilt and extended by Emperor Frederick II Hohenstaufen (his additions include a *polygonal tower*). Subsequently repeatedly altered by the Angevins and Aragonese.

Museo Civico (Piazza XV Marzo, in the former church of *S. Chiara*): Gives a good general view of Calabrian culture and folklore (small *objets d'art* etc. found during excavations in the town). 13C *bas-relief of St. Francis*, from the church of S. Francesco d'Assisi. In the same building, next to the city library, is the *Accademia Cosentina*,

founded in the 16C and still in existence today.

Also worth seeing: *S. Maria di Gerusalemme* (also called Chiesa delle Cappucinelle, Via Vitt. Emanuele), 16C, with a fine façade. The picturesque *old part of town* between S. Francesco d'Assisi and the Corso Telesio.

Crema 26013
Cremona/Lombardy   p.412 ☐ D 3

Cathedral of S.Maria Assunta: Built by craftsmen from Como in 1284–1341 and one of the best examples of 13C Lombard architecture. A tall *false façade* has three arches, two-arched windows and a central rose-window. A dwarf gallery gives extra emphasis to the gable. Today, the inside is free of its baroque accretions. The left aisle contains a 15C *panel of St. Sebastian, St. Roch and St. Christopher,* by V.Civerchio; the right aisle has a late work by Guido Reni, *The Redeemer comforting St.Mark in prison.* The *crypt* dates from 1513.

Crema, S.Maria della Croce

Crema, cathedral

S.Trinità (Via XX Sett.): Built by Andrea Nono in 1737-9, it is a splendid example of baroque church architecture; two façades of vigorous design.

S.Maria della Croce (at the end of the Viale della Stazione): Built in 1493-1500 in the tradition of Bramante, to plans by G.Battagio. Cruciform, centrally planned (octagonal) church, heavily articulated both inside and out.

Palaces: *Palazzo Terni de' Gregori* (early 18C). *Palazzo Vimercati Sanseverino*, built in 1590-1623, a spacious complex with interesting arrangement of portal and windows. 18C *Palazzo Premoli*. Today, the 17C *Palazzo Benzoni* is a law court.

Museo Civico (Via Dante 49): Housed in a former Augustinian monastery, this is a regional museum with an archaeological and historical section and *picture gallery* attached.

Environs: Soncino (23 km. towards Brescia): Continually fought over by Bergamo, Crema and Milan until, in 1448, it was finally taken by Milan. In 1473 the Sforzas had the *Rocca* built. This fortress has two curtain walls and sturdy protective towers. The *Casa degli Azzanelli* (Via 4 Novembre) is a 15C residential house; its façade is decorated with terracottas. The *Casa degli Stampatori* (Via Lanfranco) housed the first printing press on Italian soil to print works in both the Hebrew language and alphabet. The Nathans—German Jews who later took the name of the town—brought printing to the town in the 15C; today *Soncino Bibles* are in the Vatican and the British Museum. A little way outside the town, towards the River Oglio, is *S.Maria delle Grazie*, built in 1492-1528 as a Carmelite church: The single-aisled interior is flanked by 10 side chapels and the influence of Alberti and Bramante is apparent. The fresco on the triumphal arch, and also parts of the frescos in the sacristy, are by G.Campi (1530). **Castelleone:** *S.Maria di Bressanoro:* This votive church, one of the oldest churches in the area, lies N. of the Treviglio-Cremona railway line. The building (1460) came about as a result of a vow sworn by Bianca M.Visconti.

Cremona, cathedral, façade

Cremona, baptistery

Cremona 26100
Cremona / Lombardy   p.412☐ E 4

This town, founded by the Gallic Cenomani, became a Roman colony in 218 BC. It was a flourishing community until it was destroyed under Titus in AD 70. In 553 the Byzantines founded a new town beside the old one. Agilulfo conquered the town in 603. It enjoyed new prosperity in the 7&8C, under the protection of its bishops. The city-state was constituted in 1098 as a consequence of the first Lombard league of cities. In the 13C the town was divided between the Guelphs and the Ghibellines. Power finally passed to the Visconti in 1334. Charles V occupied the town in 1535 and this led to a period of Spanish rule lasting 172 years, followed by Austrian rule until 1796. After the Napoleonic occupation, the troubles of the Revolution and another period of Austrian rule, Cremona became a part of united Italy in 1860.

The Town: The ancient system of streets is still discernible in the town centre, with the *Decumanus maximus* (Via Jacini, Via Mazzini) and the *Cardo maximus* (Corso Campi, Corso G.Verdi). In the same way, the angular arrangement of the medieval new town is apparent in the district around S.Agata and the Pal. del Popolo. The focal point of the town is formed by the *Piazza del Comune* with its cathedral and the *Torazzo* (a striking landmark visible from afar), the *Baptistery*, the *Palazzo Comunale* and the *Loggia dei Militi*.

Cathedral: A basilican building with a nave, two aisles, a gallery, a widely projecting transept, which itself has three aisles (very rare), and a choir with three apses. There is a 12C W. façade (subsequently much altered) and the transepts also have façades. W.façade: two dwarf galleries, one above the other, and higher up still, a large rose-window (1274). The gable has niches with figures, and also volutes (1491). The central point of the façade is the *Porta Reggia* (late 13C) with a fine series of figures (including depictions in the manner of Antelami, 1220–30). The *Portico Bertazzola* (1492-1525, Lorenzo Trotti) extends on either side of the Porta Reggia. The transept façades (13/14C) are of brick

Cremona, Palazzo del Comune

Cremona, cathedral A *Porta Reggia, frescos on the walls of the nave:* **a** Crucifixion (Giovanni A. da Pordenone, 1521) **b** Entombment (Giovanni A. da Pordenone, 1522) **c** Resurrection (Bernardino Gatti, 1529) **d-g** all by Boccaccio Boccaccino **d** Joachim's dream and the meeting with St.Anne, 1515 **e** Nativity and Betrothal of the Virgin Mary **f** Annunciation and Visitation **g** Adoration of the Shepherds and Circumcision **h** Adoration of the Magi and Sacrifice in the Temple (Gian F.Bembo, 1515) **i** Flight into Egypt and Massacre of the Innocents (Altobello Melone) **j** Dispute in the Temple (Boccaccino, 1518) **k** The Centurion (Antonio Campi, 1575) **l** The Risen Christ between Saints and symbols of the Evangelists (Boccaccino, 1506) **m** Ascension (altarpiece by Bernardino Gatti, 1575) **n** Entry into Jerusalem (B.Campi) **o** Last Supper (A.Melone, 1517) **p** Washing of the Apostles' feet, and Gethsemane (A.Melone, 1517) **q** Arrest of Christ and Christ before Caiphas (A.Melone, 1517) **r** Christ before Pilate and Flagellation (Girolamo Romanino, 1519) **s** Crowning with Thorns and Ecce Homo (Girolamo Romanino, 1519) **t** Way of the Cross (Pordenone, 1520) **u** Sudarium of Veronica (Pordenone, 1520) **v** Crucifixion (Pordenone, 1520) *Other decorations:* **1** 'Sacra Conversazione' by the Schizzi family (altarpiece by Pordenone) **2** A miracle of St.Eusebius (sculpture by Alessandro Arrighi, 1650) **3** Crucifixion with Saints and Pope Gregory XIV, by an artist from Cremona (Lucca Cattapane, 1593) **4** Roman holy-water stoup **B** *Canons' sacristy,* frescoed throughout with false perspective architecture (Antonio Galli) **5** Visitation (altarpiece by G.Gatti, 1583) **6** Wooden crucifix by Giacomo Bertesi **7** Annunciation by Malosso, 1594 **8** Ecstasy of St.Benedict (Gian Angelo Borroni, 1747) **C** *Large sacristy* (splendid coffer-work ceiling) **9** tomb of Cardinal Francesco

Sfondrati (G.B.Cambi, to designs by Pizzafuoco) **D** *chapel of the Sacrament* with pictures by Borroni: (Emmaus, Christ and Magdalena, 1747) Bernardino Campi: (Washing of the Apostles' feet, offering of Melchizedek, Raising of Lazarus, 1569), Giulio Campi: (Magdalene, Last Supper, shower of manna, 1569) **10** above, story of Esther (Giulio Campi, 1567) **11** access to the crypt (one nave, two aisles), containing the ark of St. Marcellinus and St.Peter, 1506 **12** Pietà (Tomaso Amici) **13** St. Facius feeding the poor (relief by Amadeo, 1482) **14** and **15** pulpits by Luigi Voghera, 1815, with 16C reliefs **16** Crucifixion (Boccaccino, 1510) **17** organ with 2 singers' pulpits (to designs by Campi and Bembo, 16C) **18** baroque high altar (G.B.Zaist, 1723) with the ancient mensa **19** carved choir stalls with inlay work (1490) **E** *chapel of Madonna del Popolo:* rich stuccoes by Bombarda to designs by Dattaro, 1555. Pictures by B.Campi (Herod's feast, John the Baptist in the wilderness, Beheading of John the Baptist, 1569), G.B.Trotti (Resurrection, Descent of the Holy Ghost) **20** Archangel Michael (altarpiece by Giulio Campi, 1566) **21** Entombment (A.Campi, 1566) **22** Madonna and Child with Saints (Bernardino Ricca, 1525) **23** 4 marble reliefs by Amadeo dating from 1484 (including Noli me tangere) **24** polyptych by Genovesino (1645) depicting the story of St.Roch **F** *reliquary chapel* of the 'Holy Thorn' **G** *cathedral treasure* (especially 15C gold works) **25** votive picture: Virgin Mary with Saints and Pope Gregory XIV (L.Cattapene 1593) **26** Holy Family and God the Father, sculpture group by G.Bertesi, 1657 **H** chapel of Madonna delle Grazie (altarpiece by A.Massarotti, 1670) **I** Camposanto (cemetery dating from 1130): it gives access to the early-12C mosaics (scenes from 'Psycomachia' by Prudentius) of the devastated church of St.Ambrose.

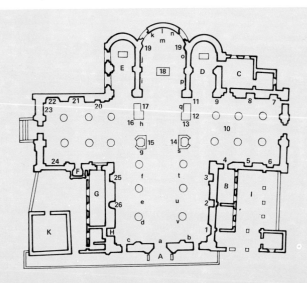

with 12C sculptural decoration incorporated in the N. portal. Decoration: Unique in its abundance. The inside of the cathedral is a fine example of a late medieval interior, even though some of the features are 16C. The interior also provides a good general view of the development of the 15/16C Cremona school of painting, founded by Boccaccio Boccaccino. Several pillars are hung with splendid *tapestries* from the workshop of Jean Raes of Brussels, after cartoons by the school of G.Romano. Five large tapestries show the life of Samson; the two small ones depict the parable of the vineyard and the sermon by the Sea of Galilee.

Torre Campanaria, known as the **Torazzo:** A six-storeyed tower, 364 ft. tall and the town's landmark. At the top it has two arcaded, octagonal storeys.

Baptistery: 1167, octagonal, much altered in the 16C. Inside is a font by L.Trotti (1520–7).

Palazzo del Comune: 1206–46. Open hall with five arcades and a council chamber above. In the 13C it was the seat of the Ghibellines (the party of the aristocracy). Altered several times in the following centuries. In front of the middle pillar is the so-called *Arrengario,* the speaker's platform.

Loggia dei Militi: A hall with two arcades, dating from 1292, with three-arched openings in the main storey. Formerly the residence of the commanders of the town guard.

S. Abbondio (Via Amati): A single-aisled church built in 1579 with excellent decoration by O.Sammacchini (frescos), as well as an altarpiece by Giulio Campi (1527). The cloister is modelled on that of Bramante's in the monastery of S.Maria della Pace, Rome.

S. Agata (Piazza Garibaldi): Founded in 1077, rebuilt in 1496. A cruciform ground plan with a nave and four aisles. Excellent decoration, splendid classical façade with a hexastyle portico (Luigi Voghera, 1845).

S. Agostino (Via Plasio): This church (built 1339–45; thoroughly restored 1951–2) contains frescos (third chapel on the

Cremona, S. Abbondio, cloister

right) by Bonifacio Bembo dating from 1452.

S.Lucca (Corso Garibaldi/Porta Milano): In front of this 13C church is an octagonal building in the style of Bramante.

S. Pietro al Po (Via Cesari): This 11C church was completely rebuilt in 1575. The splendid interior has frescos by A.Campi and G.B.Trotti. There is a Feeding of the Five Thousand by B.Gatti (1552) in the refectory of the adjoining monastery.

Palazzo del Popolo (Piazza Garibaldi): 1256; seat of the Guelph party and centre of the medieval new town.

Further palaces worth seeing: *Pal. Raimondi* (Corso Garibaldi) with severe façade (1496). The two storeys are articulated with double pilasters and rustic work. *Pal. Fodri* (Corso Umberto), with an elegant arcaded courtyard and terracotta frieze (early 16C). *Pal. Stanga* (Via Palestro), 16C arcaded courtyard with rich terracotta decoration. *Pal. Pagliari* (Via A.Manzoni), 16C. *Pal. Affaitati Magro* (Via Ugolani Dati), 1561,

by Dattaro, with a gorgeous staircase by Arrighi.

Museums: *Museo Civico* with a well-stocked *picture gallery,* an archaeological collection, cathedral treasure, ceramics, Cremona terracottas. *Museo Stradivariano:* with exhibits (designs, models, implements) relating to the violin-maker, and manuscripts by Amilcare Ponchielli.

Teatro Ponchielli (Corso Vitt. Emanuele): Classical building by Luigi Canonica in 1808, with a portico in front.

Environs: S. Sigismondo (2.5 km. towards Casalmaggiore): The new building, begun by Bartolomeo Gadio in 1463, was founded by Bianca Maria Visconti in memory of her marriage here to Francesco Sforza. S.Sigismondo is the most important Renaissance religious building in Lombardy before the time of Bramante. Cruciform ground plan. The inside is single-aisled, flanked by interconnecting chapels. It is richly decorated throughout with frescos by Antonio, Bernardino and Giulio Campi, Gervasio and Barnardino Gatti, Boccaccino, and Natali. **Quinzano**

Cremona, Mus.Civico, 'vegetable bowl' by Arcimboldo; Stradivarius violin

Pizzighetone (Cremona), view

influence (Annunciation, Nativity, Adoration of the Magi). By the river Adda is the *tower* in which François I of France was held prisoner from 28 February to 8 March 1525 after the battle of Pavia. Mementoes of him are preserved in the two medieval houses opposite S. Bassano.

Crotone 88074

Catanzaro/Calabria   p.418□O 14

Crotone was built on the site of the large Greek town of Croton, founded by the Achaeans in 710 BC. After the victory over Sybaris, it was for a time the most powerful Greek town in southern Italy. It was famous for its athletes, who were often victorious in the Olympic games. Pythagoras from Samos settled here in 532 and founded his famous school of philosophy. The town was conquered by Rome in 277 BC and was of no importance after that. Practically nothing has survived of the buildings from the town's great past. The 15/16C **cathedral** (nave, two aisles), and also the 16C **castle** on the site of the ancient acropolis, are both worth visiting; the castle houses the interesting **Museo Civico** with ancient finds from Croton and its environs (including *fragments of the Temple of Hera* at Cape Colonna—see below—and of the *Temple of Caulonia*, coins, vessels).

Environs: Some 11 km. SE, at **Cape Colonna** there is *the ancient shrine to Hera Lacinia* from the 6/5C BC (formerly the main shrine for the inhabitants of the Gulf of Taranto). Most of the columns of the temple were still upright until the beginning of the modern age but they have since been destroyed by pillage and earthquakes and now only one still stands (Doric order, over 26 ft. high and 20 flutes on the shaft).

Cuneo 12100

Cuneo/Piedmont   p.412□B 5

Cathedral of Nostra Signora del Bosco (Via Roma): The cathedral, originally built in the 12C, was rebuilt in 1662 and re-

d'Oglio (23 km. towards Brescia): At the entrance to this town is the cemetery with the 18C church of *S.Maria Assunta*. Only the apse in Cremona style survives from the 12C building. In the town is the *Piazza Garibaldi* with interesting 19C arcades on the E. side by Rodolfo Vantini. The 15–18C *parish church* is finely decorated. **Verolanuova** (25 km. towards Brescia): In the church of *S. Lorenzo* (tall dome with large bronze angel) are two major works by G.B.Tiepolo (Manna from Heaven, Sacrifice of Melchizedek, 1738–40), both strikingly large. **Pizzighetone** (20 km. towards Pavia): parish church of *S.Bassano*. After the destruction of Lodi Vecchio in 1158, the population who had been expelled from that town settled here. The basilica (nave, two aisles) dates from this period; part of it was rebuilt in 1741. There is a fresco of the Crucifixion by B.Campi inside by the entrance. In the third chapel on the left there are reliefs showing French

stored in the 18C. The classical façade (1865) is by Antonio Bono. Notable features inside include the *dome frescos* by Giuseppe Toselli (1835), the fresco by Andrea Pozzo in the apse, and the *choir stalls*.

Also worth seeing: *S. Chiara* (Via Cacciatori delle Alpi), designed by Francesco Gallo and built in 1712–19. The inside is single-aisled, and the dome has frescos by Giovanni C. Aliberti. *S. Francesco* (Piazza Giovanni Vincenzo Virginio), built in 1227, Romanesque-Gothic. The 14C façade has a fine *marble portal* (1481). The campanile dates from 1399. *S. Ambrogio* (Via Roma), built by Francesco Gallo in 1703–43. The façade dates from 1870–80; inside there is an interesting crucifix. *Santuario di S. Maria degli Angeli* (Viale degli Angeli), a pilgrimage church (1415) with 15C frescos. The remains of Angelo Carletti (1411 – 95), the patron saint of Cuneo, are here in a crystal urn. The cloister has fine *frescos* and the *monument to Duccio Galimberti, the national hero. Municipio* (Via Roma): The town hall is the former Jesuit monastery (1631); magnificent outdoor staircase; façade dating from 1776. The 17C *Palazzo Audifreddi* (Via Cacciatore delle Alpi), with the *Museo Civico*.

Environs: Two shrines to the Virgin Mary: the *Santuario della Madonna della Riva,* founded in 1492, destroyed in 1744, rebuilt in 1799, and the *Santuario della Madonna dell'Olmo,* built in 1606 on the site of a church dating from 1445.

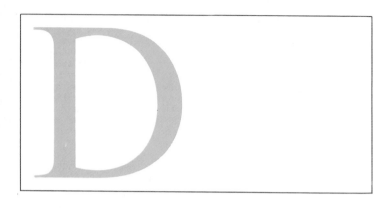

Deruta 06053
Perugia / Umbria   p.414□H 8

This town is known for its ceramic workshops.

and S. Romano), by G.B.Caporali (St. Jerome and St. Antony) and by D.Alfani (Virgin with St. Francis and St. Bernard). There are also some late 13C paintings in the sanctuary.

Palazzo Comunale: This now houses the *picture gallery*. Fine façade with three two-arched Romanesque windows and a lion of travertine stone. The portico has Roman

Deruta, majolica votive tablets in the church of Madonna di Bagno (environs)

Domodóssola, view with collegiate church

and medieval inscriptions. On the upper floor there are panels and oil paintings, and also Etruscan vases and majolicas. Note some works by Niccolò Alunno (e.g. Madonna with Saints, St.Antony), as well as some 18C paintings.

Domodóssola 28037

Novara / Piedmont   p.412 ☐ C 2

Domodóssola is the border station on the Simplon railway. In pre-Roman times it was called *Oscela Lepontiorum* and was the main town of the Leponti. The town became Roman in 24–12 BC under the name of *Domus Oxulae*. It was taken by the Lombards in the 1C, fell to the diocése of Novara in 1014, then to the Visconti in 1381, and finally taken over by Savoy in 1748. Since 1944 it has been the centre of the Val d'Ossola.

SS. Gervasio e Protasio (Piazza della Chiesa): A collegiate church with a nave and two aisles. Built in 1792–8 to a design by Matteo Zucchi. The façade was completed in 1954. The doorway has a portico with 15C frescos: the *Trinity with angels playing music*, attributed to Fermo Stella; in the lunette of the doorway is a Romanesque relief of the *Madonna and Child*. The paintings in the interior are mainly by Lorenzo Peretti and Tanzio da Varallo.

Also worth seeing: Palazzo Silva (Piazza della Chiesa), dating from 1519 and rebuilt in 1640. Inside are some fine marble chimney pieces, Roman memorial stones and a collection of costumes. *Palazzo di S. Francesco* (Piazza della Convenzione): The remains of a church of the same name, dating from 1331, were incorporated in this building. Inside there is a *Museum of Natural History*, founded by G.G.Galetti (1869). The *Collegio Mellerio Rosmini* (Via Rosmini) houses the *Museo del Sempione*, a museum with a collection devoted to the history of the Simplon tunnel. Beside it is the 15C chapel of the *Madonna della Neve*, rebuilt in the 17C. On the outer wall is a 15C bas relief of the Madonna and Child. There are fine paintings inside, including a triptych by the school of G.Ferrari.

Dorgali 08022
Nuoro/Sardinia   p.422☐D 12

This little tourist town, with its narrow alleyways of shops, is like an island within an island. The sombre house fronts (some of which still have a small loggia above the entrance), and also the costumes, facial appearance and physical build of the inhabitants, differ conspicuously from the rest of Sardinia — apart possibly from the 'maureddus' of the South West. Dorgali is said to have been founded by Drugal, the Saracen pirate. Alien, Saracen influences occur not only in the guttural language, but also in the handicrafts (weaving, embroidery, gold and silver work, and pottery), which are still very much alive.

Dorgali, entrance to caves

Environs: Within this 'island' there lies the still more isolated valley of **Cala Gonone**. These nuraghi were inhabited at an early period. The *nuragic village of Arvu*, with the remains of some 100 round huts, had some massive defensive nuraghi to the S.at the bottom of Monte Tului and on the ridge between Monte Bardia and Monte Irveri. Apart from the much-praised *Grotta de Bue Marino*, the limestone massif, which is riddled with large caves, also contains an immense number of other nuraghi (there are monk seals in the caves). Many sea birds, including cormorants, build their nests on the inaccessible rock walls, some of them 2,000 ft. high, to the S.of the Gulf of Orosei. Numerous Eleonora's falcons (*Falco eleonorae*) also live here. Large vultures from the Sopramonte occasionally come circling as far as here. The *Grotta Nova*, which lies hidden some 550 ft. above sea-level, is worth visiting with a guide. It rivals the *Grotta Ispinigoli* (E. of 'Spiritu Santu'), which was enlarged in 1975, in the radiant splendour of its alabaster stalactites. More famous than this is the ice-cold karst spring of *Sorgente su Gologone*, which is intended to fill the still hotly-disputed Cedrino dam reservoir. A cart track leads from here through the high Lanaito valley into the middle of the wildest cave region in Sardinia (Sa Oche, Corbeddu, Su Bentu and Monumentale). The last two of these had to be blocked up, because the alabaster-coated stalactite formations were being knocked away. The caves are now only accessible with a guide. To the E., almost at the end of the valley, is Monte Tiscali. Its peak has caved in to form a deep, inaccessible depression, which the last nuraghe dwellers used as a refuge from the Romans. It has still not been properly investigated despite the various clay fragments which have been found. The disorderly excavations of treasure seekers are unfortunately causing increasing damage.

Eboli 84025
Salerno/Campania   p.418□L 11

S. Pietro alli Marmi: Norman-Romanesque; built in the 13C. The three semicircular apses and the campanile survive from the original building. The inside is basilican with a nave, two aisles and fine columns and capitals, some of which are ancient. There are medieval *frescos* in the right apse. Beside the high altar are wooden statues by Giacomo Colombo (1690). The crypt contains the 13C *relics of St.Bernier.*

Collegiata S.Maria della Pietà (Corso Umberto I): Built in 1782. Inside it has a Pietà by G.Colombo (1698). 14C *wooden statue of St.Vitus.*

Also worth seeing: The 14C church of *S. Francesco,* with fine 16C frescos. The *Castello dei Colonna,* rebuilt in the 18C.

Environs: Some 10 km. NE, **Campagna** with *S. Maria della Pace.*

Égadi, Isole/Aegadean Islands
Trapani/Sicily   p.420□G 16

This archipelago off the W. coast of Sicily consists of the islands of **Lévanzo, Favig-**

nana and **Marettimo.** It was the scene of the Roman naval victory over the Carthaginians in 241 BC, which led to the Roman domination of Sicily.

Lévanzo 91010: 9 prehistoric *grottoes.* The most interesting of these is the *Grotta dell'Genovese* in the NW of the island, with Stone Age rock drawings of humans and animals.

Favignana 91023: The largest island (7.3 sq.m.) in the archipelago. It also has some *grottoes* with prehistoric finds. The medieval *Forte S.Giacomo,* today a prison; the 18C *Castello Florio;* the *Forte di S.Caterina.* The island is known for its tuna fishing, which takes place in May.

Marettimo 91010: A prison island under the Bourbons (part of the *subterranean dungeon* still survives). The *Grotta del Presepe* in the S.of the island is worth seeing for its fine stalactite formations.

Egna/Neumarkt 39044
Bolzano/South Tyrol/Trentino   p.410□F 2

Parish church of St. Nikolaus: The more recent Egna/Neumarkt district rose from 1190 onwards to the S.of the older Villa/Vill quarter. The parish church has a 13C tower with a spire of 1630, while the choir is from 1400. The 15C nave was rebuilt in the 17C.

Unsere Liebe Frau in der Vill: The choir (1412), by Master Konrad of Egna is regarded as a masterpiece of early Tyrolean Gothic. The fine nave was begun in 1460 by Master Hans Feur from Sterzing, continued by Andre Hofer and completed in 1504 by Peter Ursel from Termeno. Inside, the most notable features are the richly decorated *tabernacle* (1500) and a double tombstone thought to be the only object to have survived from the former Roman settlement of Endidiae.

Also worth seeing: The alleyway which runs at right angles to the Brenner road which has medieval character, with its arcades and houses crowded together. Note the two mansions, *Griesfeld* (mid 17C; today used as a hospital) and *Longo* (18C).

Environs: On the road to Salorno, the Romanesque church of *St.Florian* and the *Klösterle,* ruins of a former 12C pilgrims' hospice which provided accommodation for the numerous pilgrims to Rome and Jerusalem. **Pinzano/Pinzon** (NE of Egna): *St.Stephan:* The tower is Romanesque, the octagonal spire is *c.* 1500, the choir—by Master Konrad from Egna—is 1410 and the nave dates from 1500. The *Loreto chapel* was added in *c..* 1720. The choir has stained-glass windows dating from 1480. There is a very beautiful high altar—one of the best late Gothic winged altars in the Tyrol. It is the work of Hans Klocker from Bressanone, who was a pupil of Pacher, and it dates from *c.* 1500. **Ora/Auer:** To the N. of Egna, with the late Gothic church of *St.Daniel am Kiechlberg* (1400) high up. It is thought that the Roman *Endidiae* was situated on the hill of Castelfeder. Today, the ruins of the medieval castle of the Lords of Enn are to be found there.

Elba (I)
Livorno/Tuscany   h3]p.414□E 8

This, the largest of the Tuscan islands, is 10 km. from the mainland and can be reached from the nearby port of Piombino. The island is rich in high-grade ores, a feature for which it was praised by Virgil. The ore obtained from here was worked by the Etruscans in the furnaces of Porto Baratti. Greeks from Syracuse occupied the island in the 5C, and Romans founded colonies here. After Napoleon's abdication Elba became part of the Grand Duchy of Tuscany in 1815, and finally joined the Kingdom of Italy in 1860. The main town is:

Portoferraio 57037 ('iron port'): Located on the tip of a neck of land in the N. of the island, it existed as early as the 4C. 40 air raids caused extensive destruction in 1943/4. The fortifications of this important trading centre were built in 1548 under Cosimo I. They comprise: the *Forte della Stella* (1540-8), an irregular five-sided star (with a splendid view) and the *Forte del Falcone* (1548), on a tongue of land by the sea. The *Chiesa della Misericordia,* from 1566 and each year on 5 May a requiem is said for Napoleon here. The French emperor's bronze death mask can be seen here in a sarcophagus.

Casa di Napoleone: Napoleon's former residence, where he stayed with his small retinue when he was not living in one of his two other villas. The items on display include furniture of the period, mementoes of Napoleon, and caricatures and a bust of Napoleon by François Rude.

Villa Napoleonica di S. Martino, Napoleon's summer residence. Close by is the *Villa Demidoff* with the *Pinacoteca Foresiana* (art from the Napoleonic period, and also the work of Antonio Canova, Guido Reni and Salvatore Rosa).

Environs: Porto Azzurro: Small fishing town in the W. of the island, with a fortress (1603) from the time of Philip III of Spain. *Marciana Marina:* A small port whose houses (with flights of steps), make a pic-

---

Castelfiorentino (Empoli), Madonna and Child by Cimabue in S. Verdiana

turesque impression. The 12C cylindrical tower, known as the *Medicea* or *Saraceno*, was built by Pisa. *Marciana:* lies inland, to the S.of the port of the same name, on the slope of Monte Capanne, and is overlooked by a castle which today is a ruin. *Madonna del Monte:* Some 2,057 ft. up with a 15C painting of the Madonna which has miraculous properties. The small island of *Capraia*, the 'island of goats' lies to the N. of Elba. It is a picturesque and mountainous island with a single — inhabited — town, also known as Capraia, which is dominated by an early 15C Genoese fortress. On *Monte Christo* (S.of Elba) there are the ruins of the *Monastery of S.Salvatore e S.Mamiliano*, abandoned in 1553. Underneath the monastery is the *Grotta di S.Mamiliano*, today a chapel. Mamiliano was Bishop of Palermo and is said to have died here in the hermitage in the 5C.

Empoli 50053
Florence/Tuscany   p.414☐F 6

Empoli lies on the Arno to the W. of Florence. From the late 8C it was known as a fortress, *Empoli Vecchio*, but it was not mentioned as a town until 1119.

Collegiata S.Andrea (main square): The church was built in 1093 on the site of an older building which probably dates back to the 5C. The façade, with white and green marble facing, is modelled on the Florentine Romanesque church of S. Miniato al Monte in Florence. The upper part, consisting of rectangular sections and a gable, was not added until 1736 (by Ferd.Ruggeri); the interior furnishings are 18C.

Museo della Collegiata (next to the Collegiata S.Andrea): The first room which the visitor enters on the ground floor is the *baptistery*, which has a fine *font* in the shape of a marble vase. Dated 1447, it is from Donatello's workshop. The 1st room contains an interesting painting of the old town, *St.Nicholas liberating Empoli from the plague* by Lorenzo di Bicci. In the 2nd room there is a triptych of the *Madonna and Child with Saints* (1404), by Lorenzo Monaco, and an *Annunciation* (1447) by Bern. Rosselino.

Certaldo (Empoli), Palazzo Pretorio

Empoli, Collegiata, Pietà

S.Stefano, (near to the *Porta Pisana,* 1487, which was made a memorial to the siege of the town by neighbouring Pisa in 1530): The church, built by the Augustinians in the 14C, was severely damaged in 1944. Inside, nave and two aisles, the remains of frescos are worth seeing, as are the sinopias in the chapels, which were painted over by Masolino da Panicale in *c.* 1424. He also painted the fresco (1424) in the lunette above the entrance to the sacristy, as well as the remains of frescos to be found at the side.

Environs: Castelfiorentino: A settlement of Roman origin on a steep slope in the Elsa valley to the S. of Empoli. *S. Francesco:* Begun in 1213, with a very tall façade incorporating coats of arms. *S. Verdiana* (behind S. Francesco): Fine baroque façade and a campanile dating from 1805. Adjoining it is a small museum with Florentine works of art. **Certaldo,** a little further S. in the Elsa valley. Boccaccio's birthplace. The town wall dates from 1293 and includes the castle. *Casa del Boccaccio* (in the street of the same name): A medieval building with a tower; the loggia on the top floor has a splendid view. The poet is said to have lived here, and he definitely died here. Today it houses the *Centro Nazionale di Studi sul Boccaccio.* His tomb is in the church of *SS. Michele e Jacopo. Palazzo Pretorio* (or *del Vicariato*): Rebuilt in the 15C, with a battlemented façade decorated with coats of arms and terracottas. Charming courtyard with a cistern decorated with numerous polychrome coats of arms (both stone and terracotta) from the 16–18C. **San Miniato,** the former imperial palace of Frederick Barbarossa, picturesquely situated on a hill above the Arno W. of Empoli on the road to Pisa. A massive tower is all that survives of the castle built in 1240. *S. Domenico* (also known as *SS. Jacopo e Lucia de Foris portam*): Built in 1330; the façade has remained in the rough. There are 18C frescos on the interior walls, and the triumphal arch bears 14C frescos by a Florentine artist. *Cathedral:* 12C, rebuilt several times since then. The 13C Romanesque brick façade is decorated with majolica; the massive campanile was part of the old castle. **Cás-**

cina, site of the Pisan defeat at the hands of the Florentines in 1364. This historical event was depicted in the famous cartoon by Michelangelo, who executed it for the Palazzo Vecchio in competition with Leonardo (Battle of Anghiari). *S. Maria:* 12C façade in the purest Pisan style; strict architectural forms in the basilican interior. **S. Casciano in Val di Pesa:** A typical town of the Tuscan hill country. Of interest is the *Chiesa della Misericordia* (formerly known as S. Maria del Prato), a Tuscan-Gothic building dating from 1335 and rebuilt in the late 16C. Inside the church is a *panel with the Crucified Christ* by Simone Martini, and a *pulpit* with reliefs by Giovanni di Balduccio. **Impruneta:** The church of *S. Maria dell' Impruneta,* consecrated in 1054, contains the *Capella della Madonna* to the left of the high altar, with terracottas by Luca della Robbia.

Enna 94100

Enna/Sicily   p.420☐K 17

Settled by the Greeks from Gela in the 7C BC. Because of its central position, the ancient 'Henna' was described by the poet Callimachus (3C BC) as the 'navel of Sicily'. (It is also known as the 'balcony of Sicily'.) Even in pre-Greek times it was the centre of the cult of Demeter. In the early Middle Ages it was a Byzantine stronghold against the Saracens, under whose dominion the Latin name 'Castrum Hennae' became 'Casa Janna' which, as 'Castrogiovanni', was the town's official name until 1927. It reached its zenith under the Hohenstaufens and Aragonese.

Cathedral (Piazza Mazzini): Begun in 1307 and rebuilt in the 15C after a fire (only the transept and apses survive from the original building). A fine *baroque façade* reached by a flight of steps. Sturdy *campanile.* On the right side is a *Renaissance portal* which is worth seeing. Inside: nave and two aisles and a Latin cross ground plan. *Pointed arches* with squat *columns* of black basalt (the bases and capitals are richly decorated; the first two columns are by Gian Dom. Gagini, 1560).

The nave has an original carved *wooden ceiling* (16C). The *cathedral treasure* and the *Museo Alessi* are in a modern building behind the cathedral.

Castello di Lombardia: A Hohenstaufen building converted and extended under Frederick III of Aragon in the early 14C. Irregular ground plan; six towers out of 20 survive. There are three inner *courtyards* (the third contains the remains of the church of *S.Martino*) and the *Torre Pisana,* the highest part of the fortress, which is one of the island's most important medieval castles.

Tower of Frederick II (in the Giardino Pubblico): The last remnant of a 13C castle belonging to Frederick II Hohenstaufen. 79 ft. high, octagonal, with three storeys. Fine view.

Also worth seeing: Church of *S.Chiara* (Piazza Colajanni), 1725, single-aisled, today a memorial to the fallen. *S.Francesco d'Assisi* (Piazza Vitt. Emanuele), originally 14C, with fine 15C campanile. The 18C *S.Cataldo* (Piazza Matteotti), has a beautiful marble altar (1562), probably by Gian Dom. Gagini. *Museo Alessi* (Via Roma, see above) with a collection of ancient coins that is well worth seeing. *Rocca di Cerere* (rock of Ceres, underneath the Castello di Lombardia) with the few remains of the ancient temple of Ceres.

Environs: Calascibetta (derived from the Arabic 'Kalat-Shibet') lies to the N., on a hill opposite Enna: The *Chiesa Matrice (S.Pietro),* originally 14C but subsequently completely altered, has a fine marble font and a rich church treasure. To the N. of the town (by the road to *Petralia*) is a prehistoric burial ground *(Necropoli di Realmese)* from the 9–7C BC. There is another burial ground (7–5C BC in the district of *Valle Coniglio.* Myth has it that the **Lago di Pergusa,** some 8 km. S., is the place where Hades abducted Persephone, the daughter of Demeter. On the S.side of the lake a *cave* is the supposed scene of the event.

Eolie, Isole/Aeolian Islands
Messina/Sicily   p.420☐K/L 15

This archipelago lies to the N. of Sicily and is also known as the Lìpari Isles. It consists of seven larger islands (from the W.: Alicudi, Filicudi, Salina, Lìpari, Vulcano, Panarea, Stromboli) and ten small uninhabited islands.

Lìpari 98055: The castle, in its present 16C form, is worth seeing; a Greek tower from the 4/3C BC and some 13C fortifications have also survived. The main town, also known as Lìpari, has a Norman Cathedral, *S. Bartolomeo:* rebuilt in the 13&17C; façade 19C. Beside the two churches of *S. Immacolata* and *S. Addolorata,* there is a prolific *excavation site* with remnants of buildings from the Bronze Age (17C BC) to the Roman period (2C AD). The extremely interesting *Archaeological Museum,* with finds from Lìpari and the other islands, stands near the cathedral. Near to **Canneto** (N. of Lìpari) are two large rivers of obsidian (red volcanic glass). There are hot springs (62° C) near to **Piano Conte** (to the W.).

Vulcano 98050: In ancient times it was thought to be the island of Hephaestus. The *main crater* has been in the 'solfatara state' for about 100 years. The N. part of the island, known as the *Vulcanello,* did not rise from the sea until 183 BC.

Stromboli 96050: One of the few active volcanoes in Europe. The *crater* is worth the climb.

On **Salina** there are *remains of Roman houses* (S.Marina Salina), on **Panarea,** excavations of a *Bronze Age village* (14C BC), and on **Filicudi,** *remains of prehistoric settlements.*

Herculaneum, Casa Sannitica

Herculaneum, Casa di Nettuno e Anfitrite

Ercolano/Herculaneum 80056
Resina

Naples/Campania   p.418☐K 11

The eruption of Vesuvius in AD 79 destroyed this Italic town along with Pompeii
and Stabiae, burying it under molten lava
which cooled into a rock-hard mass. Excavations have been carried out since the
early 18C but systematic work began in the
20C (in the S.part of the ancient town; the
town centre itself is underneath the modern town of Resina—see below. In contrast
to Pompeii, rows of multi-storeyed houses
have survived in Herculaneum.

Baths (Insula 6): Divided into a *men's section* (reached from Cardo III) and a
women's section (reached from Cardo IV).
The central peristyle has survived and
opens, on the left, to the *apodyterium* (un-

dressing room), flanked by the *tepidarium*
(warm bath) and the *frigidarium* (cold
bath). There is a fine mosaic on the pavement of the warm bath. Beside it is the *caldarium* (hot bath), whose vault has caved
in.

Casa del Tramezzo di Legno (Insula 3):
The façade, with two doors and five windows, has survived up to the top floor
(some charred beams of the 2nd storey are
still visible). Inside there is a *Tuscan atrium*
and, in adjacent rooms, *furnishings* (including a bedstead and crockery) have survived.

Casa della Gemma (on Cardo V): Fine
atrium, in characteristic Roman style (central section is open to the sky): the basin
is a so-called 'impluvium'). The triclinium
has well-preserved *floor mosaics*.

Casa Sannitica (Insula 5): Well-preserved
house from the 2C BC. The articulation of

the top storey is worth viewing from the atrium.

Casa dei Cervi (Insula 4): Laid out in three sections (service rooms, garden, and terrace). The rooms to which the roofed atrium leads include the large *dining room* ('triclinium') with murals in the late style. The villa is named after the marble deer found in it. There is a spacious garden.

Casa del Rilievo di Telefo (on Cardo V): Reconstructed atrium. Fine *peristyle garden* with a basin in the middle (laid out as a 'hanging garden' with vaults underneath). Numerous rooms which were once finely decorated (including marble-faced walls and floors, particularly in the rooms overlooking the shore).

Also worth seeing: *Casa del Bicentenario, baths, Casa del Albergo, Casa dell'Atrio a mosaico, Casa dell'Erma di bronzo, Casa d'Argo, Casa di Nettuno e Anfitrite, Palestra,* etc.

Environs: In **Resina,** the site of the ancient Herculaneum, there are two fine late baroque villas: *Villa Campolieto,* built by L.Vanvitelli in *c.* 1760–70, and the *Villa Favorita* dating from 1768. Some 2 km. NW, **Pórtici** with the *Palazzo Reale* (built 1738–52; formerly contained the royal antique collections with the finds from Herculaneum; cf. Goethe's Italian Journey) and some good baroque villas on the Corso Garibaldi (including the *Villa Menna, Villa Buono, Villa Lauro-Lancellotti*).

Este 35042
Padua/Veneto   p.410☐G 4

Cathedral of S. Tecla (Piazza S. Tecla): Redesigned, 1690–1708, by Ant. Gaspari after an earthquake in 1688. Very interesting interior—elliptical ground plan, with chapels all around. Beautiful and elegant interior furnishings: on the right, a 15C pulpit survives from the original church; splendid painting by Giov. Battista Tiepolo in the apse—*St. Tecla requesting the town's release from the plague, 1630* (1759).

Beata Vergine delle Consolazioni (above the Via Alessi): Built in 1505; campanile from 1598. Single-aisled interior: the *Cappella della Vergine* (at the end on the left), has a beautiful Roman mosaic pavement and a fine altarpiece by Cima da Conegliano, *Madonna and Child* (1504).

Castello Carrarese: Founded by the Este family in 1050, and rebuilt in 1339 by a member of the Carrara family. The monumental walls, battlemented towers and garden make a picturesque impression.

Museo Nazionale Atestino (*Palazzo Mocenigo,* in the grounds of the Castello): The finds from the area around the town are so rich that the collection is one of the most important in Italy.

Fabriano 19100
Ancona/Marches   p.414□H 7

The town became independent in the 14C and simultaneously enjoyed a cultural flowering. One aspect of this was an important school of painters, whose major figure was Gentile da Fabriano, known by the name of his home town.

Cathedral of S.Venanzo: 13C building; rebuilt in 1617 and restored in 1920. The paintings are mainly from the 17C. In the nave there are two paintings by Salvatore Rosa; the 4th chapel on the left has a *Crucifixion, Mount of Olives* and *The Arrest*, by Orazio Gentileschi (1620); frescos on the vault of the *sanctuary* are 18C; the apse has a *Madonna and Saints* dated 1549 by Battista Franco, known as Semolei. Of the old decorations, frescos by Allegretto Nuzi survive in a side room to the right of the choir.

S.Benedetto: Dates from 1290; rebuilt in 1590 and 1749. The altar cross is 15C. The frescos in the apse are probably by Simone de Magistris (1590). The first altar on the right has a painting of *St.Carlo Borromeo* by Orazio Gentileschi.

S.Lucia (also known as *S.Domenico*): Built in the 14C, and rebuilt in 1745; the façade was not finished. Inside there is a *Madonna* (1359) by Francescuccio Ghissi. The chapel of St.Ursula has frescos by followers of Allegretto Nuzi.

S.Maria Maddalena: The high altar has a *Mary Magdalene* by Orazio Gentileschi; in the nave there is an *Annunciation* by the master of S.Biagio in Caprile.

S.Nicolò: 13C; rebuilt in the 17C. The second chapel on the right has a painting of *John the Baptist* by Andrea Sacchi. The third chapel on the right has a painting of *St.Michael* by Guercino. In the sanctuary there is a *Madonna* by Romanelli.

SS.Biagio e Romualdo: Built in the 13C; rebuilt in 1748. The 16C cloister has survived.

Also worth seeing: *S.Onofrio*, a centrally planned building; in a side room their is a large 15C cross. The *Palazzo del Podestà* was built in 1255 at the point where the four old quarters of the town meet. In front of it is a *fountain* in the style of the *Fontana Maggiore* in Perugia. The *Palazzo Vescovile*, dating from 1545 and rebuilt in the 18C, houses the *Pinacoteca Comunale* with paintings by Allegretto Nuzi, Simone de Magistris, Orazio Gentileschi and Flemish tapestries.

Environs: Campodónico: The former

Fabriano, Palazzo del Podestà

abbey of *S.Biagio in Caprile* is a little way outside the town. The frescos by the so-called master of S.Biagio in Caprile have been removed and taken to Urbino. **Genga:** *S.Clemente* has a triptych by Antonio da Fabriano. *S. Vittore delle Chiuse:* Founded in the 11C, restored in 1925–32; the campanile is 15C. This centrally planned building of reddish stone was inspired by Byzantine models.

Faenza 48018
Ravenna/Emilia-Romagna   p.410□G 5

Founded by the Etruscans, it became Roman and bore the name of 'Faventia' from the 3C BC onwards. During the Middle Ages it was for a time a free city. In the 15&16C it became famous for its majolica products (called 'Bianco di Faenza', from the town's name). Severe damage in World War 2.

Cathedral of S. Pietro (Piazza della Libertà): Built in 1474–1513 to plans by the Tuscan artist Giuliano da Maiano on the site of an older early Christian building. Consecrated in 1581. It is one of the most important Renaissance churches in Romagna. Complex façade with a flight of steps. *Inside:* Nave and two aisles, Latin cross ground plan, pure Tuscan style. There are eight chapels in each side aisle. The Cappella di S.Savino to the left of the choir has the famous *Arca di S.Savino* by Benedetto da Maiano (*c.* 1475; arca means tomb). There is a fine *Madonna and Child* (Innocento da Imola, 1526) in the fourth chapel on the right. The fifth chapel on the right has the 15C Tuscan *Arca di S. Terenzio.* In the eighth chapel on the left there is a beautiful 15C Renaissance *marble tomb.*

S. Maria Vecchia (Piazza S. Maria foris portam): Built in the 17C on the remains of an early medieval church. The campanile (8C; very well worth seeing) survives from the original building: octagonal ground plan, with single and double arched windows. The belfry has a complex arrangement of three arched windows and columns, some of them old. Inside are some fine columns from the late classical period.

Ceramics Museum (Museo delle Ceramiche, Via A.Campidori): Founded in 1908; its two floors provide a thorough survey of ceramics from all parts of the world and periods. Local majolica is particularly well represented.

Art Gallery and Museo Civico (Via S. Maria dell'Angelo): The collections date back to 1805 and the gallery offers a good insight into the painting of Romagna.

Also worth seeing: 13C church of *S. Francesco* (Piazza S. Francesco) with the richly decorated *Cappella della Madonna della Concezione.* Church of *SS.Ippolito e Lorenzo* (Via Ippolito) with an early medieval crypt (fine capitals). Church of *S. Bartolomeo* (Corso Matteotti), dating from 1209; the apse and tower survive from the original building (today the church is a war memorial). 18C church of *S. Agostino* (Corso Matteotti), with some remains of the earlier, 14C building. *Piazza del Popolo,* the town's historical centre, with the 12C *Palazzo del Podestà* (on the left of the cathedral) and the 13C *Palazzo del Municipio* (on the right, interesting interior). *Fontana Monumentale* (in front of the cathedral), baroque, by D.Paganelli (*c.* 1620).

Fano 61032
Pesaro and Urbino/Marches   p.414□H 6

Cathedral: The church was built from 1113–40 and restored in 1925. The *portal,* with Cosmati work, dates from the original phase of building, as does the *pulpit,* which has been reconstituted from the old parts. There are frescos of the Glorification of the Virgin Mary (1612) by Domenichino, in the *Cappella Nolfi.* The *Madonna* by Lodovico Carracci (to the right of the sanctuary) is also from 1612.

S. Domenico: This 13C church was rebuilt in baroque style in 1703–14. Inside: *Birth of John the Baptist* by Federico Zuccari and *St. Thomas Aquinas* by Palma il Giovane.

S. Maria Nuova: 16C building with a *Madonna and Saints* and an *Annunciation* by Perugino and a *Visitation* by G.Santi.

S. Pietro ad Vallum: Designed by Giovanni Battista Cavagna in 1610–13 but not completed until 1696; restored in 1966. *Ceiling painting* by Ant. Viviani of 1620 and, from the same year, an *Annunciation* by Guido Reni (first altar on the left). The *wooden bust of St.Peter* has a Roman bronze head and is attributed to Daniele da Volterra.

Arche Malatestiane: The church of S. Francesco was destroyed by an earthquake in 1930; the portico with the *tombs of the Malatesta,* Paola Bianca (d. 1378) and Pandolfo III (d. after 1427), has survived.

Arco di Augusto: Built in honour of Augustus in the 2C AD, and rebuilt in the 4C. The top storey was shot away in 1463; the town side was restored in 1625.

Logge di S.Michele: Built in 1495 using stones which had fallen from the arch of Augustus. Next to it is the *façade* (1503) of *the former church of S.Michele.*

Basilica Vitruviana: Built by Vitrivius Pollio, the architect who worked under Augustus. This basilica was intensively studied during the Renaissance, because it was his only surviving work. Vitruvius wrote ten books on architecture, which are the most important source books for Roman architecture.

Case Malatestiane: The most ancient section (with the museum entrance) was built in 1413; 16C loggia. Inside, the *Museo Civico Malatestiano* has Roman sculptures, medieval seals, weapons, coins, faience and paintings.

Also worth seeing: *Fontana Fortuna* on the Piazza XX Settembre; the original figure by Ambrosi (1593) is preserved in the museum. *Palazzo della Ragione,* begun in 1299; the tower was built in 1739, while the battlements were not added until 1862. *Palazzo Montevecchio,* built by Arcang. Vici in the 18C. *Rocca Malatestiano.*

Farfa Sabina 02030
Rieti/Latium   p.414□H 9

Abbazia di Farfa: In 680, Thomas of Maurienne (Savoy), supported by Pope John VII and the Duke of Spoleto, Faroald II, founded a new abbey on the ruins of a 6C abbey, which had been destroyed in the Lombard invasion. The strategic importance of this monastery ensured for it the highest possible protection. Apart from its Papal privileges, Charlemagne conferred the status of an imperial abbey upon it. The strict spirit of Benedictine life, combined with the rise in secular power, led to the monastery experiencing a heyday under the Carolingians, reaching a zenith in 890 under Abbot Peter. The Saracen invasions caused a temporary decline. As a

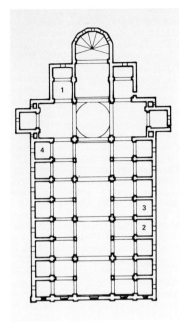

Faenza, ceramics museum

Faenza, cathedral 1 Capella di S.Savino (Arca di S.Savino) **2** Madonna and Child by Innocento da Imola **3** Arca di S.Terenzio **4** 15C marble tomb

result of the rule of Otto I and the acceptance of the Cluniac reform, the monastery enjoyed a new flowering under Abbot Hugo (997–1039). Gregory of Catino wrote his most important works here; the famous Farfa school of writing began with him. After the Concordat of Worms (1122), the abbey was subjected to Papal jurisdiction, and as a result gradually declined. It was dissolved in 1862 and re-established in 1919. Since 1928 it has been an Italian national monument.

The Carolingian church was replaced in 1492 by a new building whose Gothic portal shows northern influence. It is a Renaissance basilica with columns, a nave, two aisles and a Gothic choir. The Romanesque *Lombard cloister* is of interest, and

so is the 17C *Great Cloister*. In a side room there is a Roman *battle sarcophagus* from the 3C AD.

Feltre 32032
Belluno/Veneto   p.410 ☐ G 2

Cathedral of S.Pietro: 15C church, by the old town wall near the Porta Pusterla. The only Gothic part to survive is the polygonal apse. The church has been rebuilt several times, and was restored both outside and in during the 19C. There is a beautiful tombstone relief (1473) in the wall of the campanile (bottom left), which was built in 1392 and extended upwards in 1690. The inside is decorated with fine works of art, particularly by P.Marescalchi (2nd and 4th altars on the right). In the *Archivio Capitolare*, a fine carved wooden *Byzantine cross* from 542 is preserved; it has 52 panels illustrating scenes from the New Testament.

Baptistery of S.Lorenzo: Italian Gothic from the 14C; frequently rebuilt. It possesses a very lovely *Renaissance portal* (right side) and a 17C portico in front of the façade. Inside, the *altarpiece* by L.Bassano and the Gothic *font* (1399) are of interest.

Chiesa di Ognissanti: (crossroads of Borgo Ruga): 14C. In the sacristy there is a 14C painting of *Christ appearing to St. Antony and St.Lucy* by Lorenzo Luzzo (also known as Il Morto da Feltre).

Palazzo Comunale (Piazza Maggiore): A heavy rusticated loggia, probably by Andrea Palladio, opens into the mid 16C-building (upper section designed in the 19C). The 1st floor has an 18C theatre. The **Palazzo del Municipio,** in the right corner leading to the Palazzo Comunale, was formerly the seat of the Venetian town council. Inside there is a large old council chamber with wooden beams, frescos and coats of arms.

Also worth seeing: The handsome *Via Mezzaterra*, leading to the Piazza Maggiore, has houses and palaces with frescoed 16C façades, and also the Renaissance-style marble portal of the church of *S.Giacomo Maggiore* (Nos. 9, 19, 35, 41). On the Piazza Maggiore: a fine *fountain* (1520), redesigned to plans by Tullio Lombardo, and the church of *S.Rocco* (1599). Adjoining this to the W. is the *Piazzetta della Legna* with the *Monte di Pietà* which has sgraffito decoration. The fresco of the Pietà may be by L.Luzzo. *Museo Civico* (in the Palazzo Villabrunna, Via Lorenzo Luzzo, No. 23): The collection of paintings is particularly interesting and includes Venetian artists of the 16,17&18C (Gentile Bellini, L.Luzzo, Cima da Conegliano, Pietro Marescalchi, Marco Ricci and others).

Environs: *Santuario dei SS. Vittore e Corona:* This church (1096), on the slopes of Monte Miesna 1,129 ft. up, was built in its present form in the first half of the 12C. The façade, massive in its lower part, is decorated with chiaroscuro frescos. Inside: The square apse has an elegant gallery with slender marble columns. The *frescos* decorating the walls and pillars are also of note. In the apse, on a particularly finely-

Fano, Rocca Malatestiano

worked stone base (1440), is the *sarcophagus of the martyrs*. The splendid *tomb of Giovanni da Vidor,* the founder, is in the sacristy. The monastery (rebuilt in 1495) adjoins the church on the right, and has a small frescoed 18C cloister.

Ferentillo 05034
Terni/Umbria   p.414☐H 8

A picturesquely situated village. The church of *S.Maria* (13–15C) has a ciborium of 1489 and 16C Umbrian frescos. The church of *S.Stefano* has a fine collection of mummies.

Environs: S.Pietro in Valle: This abbey is set in the woods of Monte Solenne, 6.5 km. from Ferentillo. Founded in the 8C by order of Duke Faroaldo II, it is the only surviving building from the Duchy of Spoleto, and it provides a unique record of early medieval art and culture. Features that have survived from the original church include: the ground plan, the three apses, the transept, the tiburium, and parts of the coarse mosaic pavement behind the high

altar. The altar cloth (an interesting item from the barbarian invasions) is signed by an 'Ursus magester' and has an inscription by Hildericus, Duke of Spoleto. On the walls are some remains of strange *Roman paintings* of scenes from the Old Testament, an attempt, preceding Cavallini, to break away from the influence of Byzantine art. On the walls there are also some fine ornamental items, medieval architectural fragments and inscriptions. Five magnificent 3C *Roman sarcophagi* have scenes from mythology (hunting and harbour scenes). The figures of St.Peter and St.Paul at the church door are 11&12C; the 13C campanile has interesting 8C marble fragments.

Ferentino 03013
Frosinone/Latium   p.416☐I 10

The ancient *Ferentinum* of the Hernici. It was taken by Rome in 361 BC and destroyed by Hannibal after the battle of Cannae (211 BC). The seat of a bishop from AD 487 onwards, and a frequent abode of the Popes. The two southern town gates, the

Feltre, Piazza Maggiore

Ferentillo, marble tomb, 8C

Ferentino, Porta Maggiore

Porta Sanguinaria and the *Porta Maggiore* or *Porta di Casamari*, deserve particular attention.

Cathedral of S. Ambrogio: 11C basilica with a nave, two aisles, a simple façade with three portals, and an E. section with three apses. Inside, pillars alternate with ancient columns (Corinthian capitals) along the length of the nave. The *mosaic pavement* is by Magister Paulus, one of the earliest Roman masters of this technique (1116). Above the central altar is a *ciborium* with a palm-leaf frieze based on ancient models by Drudo da Trevio (13C). The *bishop's throne* and the turned *Easter candlestick* with Cosmati work decoration (12C) are also worth seeing. There is a 9C *ciborium* in the sacristy.

Also worth seeing: *S. Maria Maggiore:* Built in the 13C under the influence of the Cistercian Gothic style of Fossanova, and dominated by a polygonal tower over the crossing. The *Mercato Romano,* a well-preserved Roman market from the time of the Roman republic.

Fermo 63023
Ascoli Piceno/Marches　　　　　　p.416□I 7

Cathedral: On a hill above the town. Begun by Giorgio da Como in 1227. The rose-window and portal in the façade date from 1448; the bronze relief with the Madonna is from 1761. Nave and choir were rebuilt by Cosimo Morelli in 1781–9; only the W. wall with the atrium survives from the old building. In the atrium is the *tomb of Giovanni Visconti da Oleggio* (1366). There are 14C frescos of saints on the lower ground floor of the tower. Inside the church there is an 11C Byzantine *icon, the Mother of God* (fourth chapel on the right). Beside the steps in front of the choir is a *mosaic pavement* from the earlier, 5C building (excavations are being carried out under the church). The *chasuble of St. Thomas à Becket* (1170) can be seen in

Ferrara, Palazzo di Schifanoia ▷

the sacristy; it is a partial copy of a royal mantle of 1116 and has an Arabic inscription.

S.Agostino: Mid-13C building; altered a century later. Inside are 13–15C frescos. The *Chapel of Thorns* has a fine *grille* and a 14C *reliquary*.

S.Monica (originally a baptismal chapel): Late 14C frescos, with scenes from the life of John the Baptist.

Palazzo Comunale: By the portal, there is a *Statue of Sixtus V* by Accursio Baldi (1590). Built 1446–1525, it houses a *picture gallery*, with: various works by Cola dell'Amatrice; *Life of St.Lucy* by Jacobello del Fiore; a *polyptych* dated 1369 by Andrea da Bologna and a *Nativity* by Rubens, dated 1608.

Museo Civico: Archaeological finds, crafts, town history.

Also worth seeing: *Roman Baths:* AD 41–68. *Palazzo Arcovescovile:* built in 1392; rebuilt several times, most recently in 1741. Houses a picture gallery. *Palazzo degli Studi,* built by Girolamo Rainaldi in the 16C, today houses an important *library;* the Assumption of the Virgin on the façade is by Paolo di Venezia (1587); the busts of Popes are the work of Valsoldo (1617).

Ferrara 44100

Ferrara/Emilia-Romagna   h3|p. 410☐G 4

Ferrara, first mentioned in the 8C, was the seat of a Lombard duke. In 774, after the death of the last Lombard king, the town fell via Charlemagne to the Popes who, towards the end of the 10C, entrusted it to counts of Tuscany. Ferrara, being a free state, was a member of the Lombard league in the 12C. In 1240 it fell to the Este under whom it flourished as a centre of humanism.

Cathedral (Piazza della Cattedrale): Begun in 1135 and almost completed in the late 13C (basilica with a nave, four aisles, and galleries). The oldest section of the building is the façade. In 1498/9 Biagio Rossetti gave the church a new apse. The most major change to the building's design came in 1712–18, but the original propor-

Ferrara, cathedral

Cathedral, portal

tions were restored in 1925. The *campanile* was built in 1451–1595, probably to designs by Alberti. The lower section of the central portal of the façade bears important sculptures (*c.* 1135) by Nicolò; in the upper section there are sculptures and reliefs from the late 13C and early 14C. Fragments of the old building, and also a 5C *sarcophagus*, stand in the narthex. As a result of the 18C alterations, the interior appears to be divided into a nave and two aisles. Decoration dates from 1880–90. Note the following: *Apostles and Redeemer*, mounted terracottas (early 16C) by Alfonso Lombardi; *Calvary altar* (1678) by Carlo Pasetti; *St.Maurelius* and *St.George* (1450–6); bronze statues by Domenico Paris (all in the right transept); *six busts of apostles* by Lombardi (left transept); *Madonna and Saints,* (1524) by Garofalo (3rd altar on the left).

Museo del Duomo: Outstanding items include: a *sarcophagus* and other 8C fragments; 12C *marble slabs*. *Madonna del Melograno* (1408) and *St.Maurelius*, two statues by Jacopo della Quercia; *St.George* and an *Annunciation* (1469), two organ wings by Cosmè Tura; illuminated *graduals* (1473–1535); 8 *Dutch carpets* (1551–3) to designs by G. and C.Filippi.

Castello Estense (Corso Martiri della Libertà): A square fortress surrounded by a moat. One of the best-preserved dynastic medieval castles. Begun in 1385 it was finished in the 16C. The *Torre dei Leoni* was built from parts of the 13C town wall. The interior retains the original *ceiling decoration* by Camillo, Sebastiano and Cesare Filippi. Also worth seeing: detached *frescos* (Loggetta degli Aranci), attributed to Girolamo da Carpi or S.Filippi. Subterranean *dungeons*.

Casa Romei (Via Savonarola 30): One of the most important 15C secular buildings in Italy. Built in *c.* 1445 for Giovanni Romei. Camillo Filippi was largely responsible for the decoration of the interior of this building, which is set around 2 courtyards. The *Studio of Giovanni Romei* and the *Cappelletta delle Principesse* are particularly beautiful. The rooms contain frescos (chiefly 14C) removed from secularized or destroyed churches in Ferrara, and also sculptures (including some by Alfonso Lombardi) from the Renaissance.

Ferrara, Castello Estense

Ferrara, Palazzo dei Diamanti

Palazzo di Schifanoia (or Scandiana, Via Scandiana 23): Begun in 1385 as a single-storeyed building, and rebuilt in 1466–93 by Rossetti, who made it the major example of Renaissance architecture in Ferrara. Antonio di Gregorio and Ambrogio da Milano built the two-storeyed *marble portal* in *c.* 1470. Inside is the *Museo Civico di Schifanoia*. The *Salone dei Mesi* contains one of the most lavish of secular Renaissance fresco cycles. The museum also has: a *terracotta Madonna* (1460) by Dom. Paris; fine illuminated *graduals* (2nd half of the 15C) of the Ferrara school; Etruscan, Roman, Renaissance and baroque sculptures; an important coin collection.

Palazzo di Ludovico il Moro (Via XX Settembre 124): Threatened with ruin, it was (not altogether successfully) repaired in 1930–5. The visitor passes from the splendid courtyard into two rooms decorated throughout with fine frescos by Garofalo. On the first floor is the *Museo Archeologico Nazionale* with finds from the burial ground of Spina, excavated in 1922 –35. There is a collection of Greek vases in addition to some Etruscan and Greek inscriptions and ceramics.

Palazzo dei Diamanti (Corso Ercole d'Este 21): Begun by Rossetti *c.* 1492, slightly altered in 1565, with an entrance portal (1642) and corner pilasters by G.Frisoni. Today the *Pinacoteca Nazionale* is housed here. Outstanding items in this important collection, which offers an incomparable view of Ferrarese painting in the 14–17C, include: the *Arrest* and *Martyrdom of St.Maurelius* (1470) by Cosmè Tura; *Death of the Virgin Mary* (1508) by Carpaccio; *Madonna* (1525) and *Sacra Conversazione* by Garofalo; *Sacra Conversazione, Polyptych, John on Patmos, Portrait of Ghillino Malatesta,* all by Dosso Dossi;

Ferrara, cathedral museum, 'September'

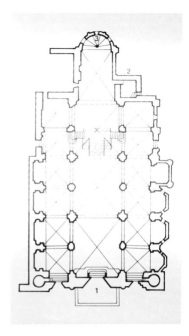

Fidenza, cathedral 1 main portal with reliefs **2** baroque E. tower with medieval sculpture **3** apse with 'Last Judgement', 13C

Martyrdom of St.Maurelius (1634) by Guercino. In the palace: *Museo Boldini* and *Civica Galleria d'Arte Moderna.*

Also worth seeing: *Palazzo Comunale* (Piazza della Cattedrale): 1243, modified in 1375, 1475–81 (Rossetti); restored in 1924–6. *S.Paolo* (Piazzetta Schiatti): built by Schiatti in 1575, with an elegant interior and paintings from the 16&17C. *S. Francesco* (Via Savonarola): 1341, rebuilt by Rossetti in 1494, with façade and interior furnishings from the 16C, works by Alfonso Lombardi, and a 5C sarcophagus. *Chiesa del Corpus Domini* (Via Campofranco), 14&15C. *S.Maria in Vado* (Via Borgo Vado), rebuilt by Rossetti in 1495 –1518, with a Byzantine Madonna and decoration from the 15-17C. *Monastery of S.Antonio in Polesine* (Via Ghilisieri) with a public church (15C, with a baroque interior), and the monks' church (13-15C wall paintings). *S.Francesca* (Via XX Settembre 49), 1619–22, with a Crucifixion by L.Carracci. *Palazzo Paradiso* (Via Scienze), baroque rebuilding of a 14/15C building with the *Biblioteca Comunale Ariostea*. *Chiesa del Gesù* (Piazza Torquato Tasso), 1570, with a terracotta Deposition (1485) by G.Mazzoni. *Palazzo Naselli-Crispi* (Via Borgo dei Leoni 18-20), built by Girolamo da Carpi in 1537. *Palazzo Prosperi-Sacrati* (Corso Ercole I d'Este 23), with a fine *portal* (1506-16) attributed to Antonio Lombardi. *Casa di Ludovico Ariosto* (Via Ariosto), built in *c.* 1500, the house of the famous poet, with contemporary furnishings and a small library. *Palazzina di Marfisa* (Corso della Giovecca 174), 1559, with notable marble portal and beautiful Renaissance furnishings. *Chiesa dei Teatini* (Via Palestro 54), 1653, with a

Presentation in the Temple by Guercino. *Palazzo Roverella* (Corso della Giovecca 47), 1508 (by Rossetti?), one of the most successful Renaissance buildings in Ferrara.

Ficulle 05016
Terni/Umbria   p.414□G 8

Ficulle is still partly surrounded by a medieval town wall with towers.

Collegiata di S. Vittoria: This church was built to a design by Ippolito Scalza.

S. Maria Vecchia: The Gothic portal is worth seeing, as are the remains of 15C frescos in the interior.

S. Sebastiano: Early Renaissance.

Fidenza 43036
Parma/Emilia-Romagna   p. 412□E 4

Cathedral of S. Donnino (Via Don Minzoni): A pilgrimage church mentioned as early as the 9C. A second building was constructed in the early 12C. The cathedral you see today, with a nave, two aisles, a long choir and no transept, was probably begun towards the end of the same century. The upper section of the façade is still unfinished but the cathedral is principally important for the fine carved ornament on the lower part. The *reliefs in the main portal* and the figures in the two side niches are in the style of Benedetto Antelami. There are some other interesting medieval sculptures by the baroque E. tower and in the apse. Inside: a notable late 13C wall painting and a valuable *church treasure.*

Also worth seeing: *Gothic town gate* (not far from the cathedral). Secularized church of *S. Giorgio* (Via Goito) with a Gothic façade, remains of 14&15C frescos and what is now a baroque interior.

Finale Emilia 41034
Modena/Emilia-Romagna   p. 410□F 4

Fortified by the Lombards, it later fell to

Fidenza, cathedral, holy-water stoup

the bishops of Modena, to whom it belonged in the 13C. The Este held it in the 14C. Raised to the status of a town in 1779.

Collegiata dei SS.Filippo e Giacomo: The church still has the campanile and the apses from the original 15C building. Inside there are 16-18C religious festive decorations, 18C silverwork and some notable 16-18C paintings.

Also worth seeing: *Castle* (Rocca), begun in 1402 and extended in 1425-30, with an elegant inner courtyard. *S. Agostino* with a Madonna and Child and St.Lawrence by Guercino.

Firenze/Florence 50100

Florence/Tuscany   p.414 ☐ F 6/7

Florence, the capital of the province of the same name and of the region of Tuscany, has 461,000 inhabitants, is the seat of an archbishop and is a university city. A number of important institutions, including the German Institute of Art History, are based here. The museums of Florence are among the most important in the world. Crafts, pure and applied, which have flourished since the Middle Ages (chiefly wool and silk processing and leather goods; later, terracotta and china), have been accompanied by thriving mechanical and chemical-pharmaceutical industries which grew up in the 19C.

History: There are traces of a settlement as far back as the 10/9C BC, but the Etruscans as usual preferred a higher site, and founded Fasula. This, as the Roman Faesulae, was the sister town and rival of Florentia, which was laid out on the bank of the Arno by Sulla in 80 BC as a colony for veterans. The Via Cassia linked both towns to the main route system of the Roman Empire (Florentia was, in addition, situated on a river). With the appointment of the Corrector Italiae, who was an administrator for Tuscany and Umbria under Marcus Aurelius or Diocletian, the town acquired a role which, where Tuscany was concerned, it was not to enjoy again until the Middle Ages. The square Roman settlement was expanded in the 8/9C by the addition of the triangle facing the bank of the Arno. This core, together with the road system running parallel to what were the Decumanus and Cardo, still form the basis of Florence's town plan. Archaeological research has shown that until the Ponte Nuovo was built in 1218-20, the sole link with the other side of the Arno was the Roman bridge, the Ponte Vecchio; the Ponte di Rubaconte (1237) and the Ponte S. Trinità (1252) were built shortly after.

The rise of the city of Fiorenza (later Firenze) began under the Frankish Countess Mathilda (d. 1115). The plundering of the rival town of Fiesole in 1125 led to an influx of people and accelerated the further development of the community. Florence was one of the main towns in central Italy at the beginning of the 13C, despite the incessant power struggles between the Ghibellines (adherents of the Emperor) and the Guelphs (the party loyal to the Pope). After ten years of popular government, with four consuls, Manfred, the King of Sicily, helped the Ghibellines to gain the ascendancy (Montaperti, 4 September 1260). With the help of the powerful guilds, the Ghibellines were toppled and a Republican people's government appointed in 1284. The Signoria, an executive council, consisted of the representatives (Priori), of the educated classes (Arti Maggiori), and of the tradesmen's guilds (Arti Minori). There was a separate citizens' army led by Gonfalonieri and victories were gained over Pisa and Arezzo, where the Ghibellines had taken refuge. In 1434, further internal unrest brought Cosimo (1434-64: 'Pater Patriae'), and with him the rich merchant family of the Medici, into power. It was under Cosimo and Lorenzo 'il Magnifico' (the Magnificent; 1464-92) that Florence became a leading centre of the arts and sciences. The Medici were dislodged in 1494 and the Dominican monk Savonarola, the opponent of Medici domination, was burned at the stake in 1498. The Medici were reinstated in 1512 with the aid of Spanish troops but they were exiled again in 1527-30. After taking the town in 1530, Charles V appointed Alessandro

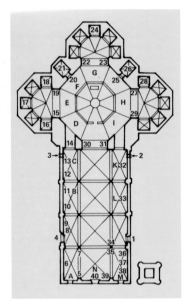

de' Medici as hereditary Duke; he was assassinated in 1537. In 1569, Pope Pius V confirmed the appointment of Cosimo I, who was Alessandro's successor, as the Grand Duke of Tuscany. In 1737, after the Medici family became extinct, they were succeeded as Grand Dukes by the house of Lorraine in the person of Francesco of Lorraine. With the exception of the Napoleonic period (1801–14), Lorraine retained the title until 1860. While the new Italy was being formed, Florence (1865–71) was the young kingdom's temporary capital.

Cathedral district: The cathedral square and the Piazza S. Giovanni surround the religious centre of the town, with the baptistery, cathedral and free-standing campanile. The W. end of the two squares, which make a single unit, is formed by the Palazzo Arcivescovado. In 1895 the Palazzo was moved back 164 ft. and the number of bays on the S. side were increased from 8 to 11 (the rear and side façades were completely rebuilt in the process). The court-

Florence, cathedral 1 Porta del Campanile with Annunciation group **2** Porta dei Canonici **3** Porta della mandorla with the Virgin Mary bestowing the Girdle on St. Thomas (masterpiece by Nanni di Banco) **4** Porta della Balla **5** panel painting of St. Catherine, school of Bernardo Daddi **6** statue of Joshua (probably a portrait of the humanist Poggio Bracciolini; the head is a work by Donatello) **7** niche with St. Zenobius (trampling on Pride and Cruelty) by G. del Biondo **8** bust of the organist Antonio Squarcia by Benedetto da Maiano **9** Niccolò da Tolentino on horseback, fresco by Andrea del Castagno **10** Giovanni Acuto (John Hawkwood) on horseback, fresco by P. Uccello **11** statue of King David by B. Ciuffagni **12** panel with St. Cosmas and St. Damian by Bicci di Lorenzo **13** Dante and the 'Divine Comedy', design by Baldovinetti, execution by Dom. di Michelino **14** ascent to the dome **15** St. Thomas by Vinc. de' Rossi **16** panel with St. Joseph by L. di Credi **17** marble altar by Buggiano, 1447, with bronze grille by Michelozzo **18** incomplete Pietà, late work by Michelangelo, c. 1550/3 **19** statue of St. Andrew by A. Ferrucci **20** door lunette with terracotta of the Resurrection by Luca della Robbia, 1444; the bronze door, 1445–69, was contributed to by Michelozzo and Maso di Bartolomeo **21** Sagrestia Nuova (or 'delle Messe') with splendidly inlaid cupboards (G. and B. da Maiano and others), fine marble fountain by Buggiano, 1440 **22** statue of St. Peter by B. Bandinelli **23** statue of St. John by Ben. da Rovezzano **24** bronze shrine to St. Zenobius by Ghiberti under

the altar, 1432–42; candlestick angel by Luca della Robbia, c. 1450 **25** door lunette with Ascension by Luca della Robbia, c. 1450 **26** Sagrestia Vecchia (or 'dei Canonici') **27** statue of St. James the Less by G. Bandini **28** Giottesque fresco fragment of 'Madonna del Popolo' **29** statue of St. Philip by G. Bandini **30** statue of St. James the Greater by J. Sansovino **31** statue of St. Matthew by Vinc. de' Rossi **32** bust of the philosopher Marsilio Ficino by A. Ferrucci, 1521 **33** niche figure of Isaiah by B. Ciuffagni, 1427 **34** descent to the Cripta di S. Reperata **35** Gothic holy-water stoup, c. 1380 **36** Tondo with a half-figure of Giotto by Benedetto da Maiano, 1450 **37** statue of a prophet by Nanni di Banco, 1408 **38** bust of Brunelleschi by his pupil A. Cavalcanti, known as il Buggiano, 1466 **39** tomb of Antonio d'Orso by Trino di Camaino **40** clock with prophets painted by P. Uccello **Stained-glass windows** (designers): **A** St. Stephen, flanked by two angels (L. Ghiberti) **B** window dating from 1395; **C** (Agnolo Gaddi) **D** Nativity of Christ (Paolo Uccello) **E** Lamentation (Andrea del Castagno) **F** Resurrection (Paolo Uccello) **G** Coronation of the Virgin Mary (Donatello) **H** Prayer on the Mount of Olives (Ghiberti) **I** Presentation in the Temple (Ghiberti) **K** (Agnolo Gaddi) **L** window with six Saints (Agnolo Gaddi) **M** St. Lawrence with angels (Ghiberti) **N** Assumption of the Virgin Mary (Ghiberti)

Florence, cathedral

yard is a high baroque imitation of Mannerism by Ciurini, who completed the palace (begun in 1582) in 1727. In the courtyard is the entrance to the church of *S. Salvatore nell'Arcivescovado*, first mentioned in 1032. Encrusted façade on the Piazza dell' Olio. Interior decoration of 1737, with architectural painting by D.Ferretti and V.Meucci. To the S., on the right, by the entrance to the Via Calzaiuoli, is the *Loggia del Bigallo*, which was built in the mid 13C as the original seat of the Misericordia and from 1425 onwards was the seat of the Compagnia di S.M. del Bigallo. Founded by St.Peter the Martyr, this was a charitable community caring for the sick. Some of the frescos are old; the loggia bears early 16C tabernacles containing a statue of the Madonna (1359–64), flanked by angels. To the left is the *Misericordia* (Arci con fraternità della Misericordia). The building has been extended many times and from 1567 onwards was the seat of the confraternity which is the oldest charitable fraternity for nursing epidemics and which was founded in response to the great plagues. The chapel has a blue-and-white terracotta panel in the manner of A.della Robbia, 1480/90. In the main house (permission required) there are late works by Benedetto da Maiano (*c.* 1495/7): Madonna and Child in marble; the flanking terracotta angels are from the della Robbia workshop; statue of St.Sebastian. The cathedral museum is to the E. of the cathedral (see under museums).

Baptistery/Baptisterio di S. Giovanni:
The baptistery stands on the site of earlier buildings (including Roman), one of which was mentioned in 897. It is known that in 1060 Pope Nicholas II consecrated a foundation stone for today's domed 8-sided building, which Dante refers to as 'bel S. Giovanni'. By 1128 it was already in use, and it was completed *c.* 1150. *Exterior:* This is original except for the rectangular choir chapel dated 1202 (originally semi-circular) and the marble facing of the corner pillars by Arnolfo di Cambio (1296). The building is the result of an early concern with things ancient (in addition to the use of ancient materials, ancient structural elements are also imitated). It is the model

of the Proto-Renaissance. The fact that the three-storeyed building is totally covered with strictly geometric panels of green and white marble increases the layered effect of the wall and enriches the proportional relationships. Round arches alternate with aedicule windows: the earliest example of the Tuscan window arrangement which was recommended in the Renaissance. The bronze doors to the S., N. and E. are the climax of the rich external decoration. The oldest door, the *S. door* has 2 x 14 reliefs in a quatrefoil frame by A.Pisano (1330–6). These were cast by Leonardo d'Avanzo the Venetian and mounted opposite the cathedral façade in 1338. In 1452 they were moved to the S. portal (the Renaissance frame is by V.Ghiberti; 1453–61). Except for the two lower compartments, the subject matter of this door is St.John the Baptist, the patron saint of the baptistery. They are Giotto-like in style. Above the portal is a group of sculptures by V.Danti (Beheading of John the Baptist, 1570). The *N. door*, (1403–24) is by L.Ghiberti (the result of a competition in 1401). The quatrefoil frames, although stylistically outdated, were obligatory. The scenes (starting at the bottom, from left to right) are: the Fathers of the Church, the Evangelists, and the New Testament. Above the door is a sculpted group: John the Baptist teaching the Pharisees and Levites (F.Rustici, 1506–11). The famous *E. door* (facing the cathedral) is L.Ghiberti's most mature work (1425–1452). Michelangelo called it a 'gate of paradise'. Ten panels have scenes from the Old Testament; relief strips of the border have alternating figures in niches and medallions with heads, following the divisions of the compartments of the doors. The door frame is from the Ghiberti workshop. There is a Baptism of Christ above the portal, which was completed by A.Sansovino in 1505 (except for the angel, which is by Spinazzi, 1792, a substitute for a clay figure by V.Danti). There is also a tabernacle supported by columns. *Inside:* The double-shelled dome consists of eight sections braced against each other, making it possible to pierce the

Baptistery, 'gate of Paradise'

wall extensively. The dome, 84 ft. in diameter is very much in the spirit of late classical buildings. The 14 column shafts of the lower order, and also the four exemplary capitals of the N. and S.wall, are in imitation of the classical style. The much-restored *pavement* resembles a carpet and is an example of medieval Tuscan inlay work. The rich *marble facing* of the walls culminates in the splendour of the enormous mosaic vault (early 13C to *c.* 1330). Another prominent feature is the *tomb* of Antipope John XXIII by Donatello and Michelozzo (*c.* 1425). The statue of Mary Magdalene is one of Donatello's most important late works (before 1455).

Cathedral of S.Maria del Fiore: In order to counterbalance the massive new monastery buildings, the cathedral of S. Reparata, itself only mid 12C, was pulled down, and work on a new building began under Arnolfo di Cambio in 1296. Work proceeded slowly as a result of several interruptions. In 1334-7, Giotto was involved as architect, working chiefly on the campanile. The vault of the nave was completed in 1378, the vaults of the aisles in 1380. The E. end was built in 1380-1421 (three apses, transept and and choir), and the drum is probably also from this period. F.Brunelleschi won the competition for the dome in 1420; the dome was completed in 1436, although the lantern was not finished until 1461, after Brunelleschi's death. The cathedral was consecrated by Pope Eugene IV on 1 January 1436. The façade, which had become out of date, was demolished in 1587 and not replaced until 1871-87 (E.De Fabris).
Outside: Lavish façade, designed by Emilio de Fabris and built in 1871-87, with a series of statues and mosaics. The cathedral's massive exterior—the portals and the E. end in particular—became the place where the monumental sculpture of the Renaissance developed dramatically. Of especial importance is the *Porta della Mandorla* (see ground plan: 3). The central motif in the gable is an alto relievo of the Madonna of the girdle, a masterpiece by Nanni di Banco (1414-22). The lunette has a mosaic of the Annunciation by D. and D.Ghirlandaio (1491). On either side there

is a statue of a prophet; that on the right has strong Gothic characteristics and is regarded as the earliest, definite work of the youthful Donatello. The octagonal dome over the crossing is interesting. It has two shells and rises to an overall height of 351 ft. (stairs at the end of the left aisle). Note the 'exedrae' (also by F.Brunelleschi and typical of Renaissance architecture), the magnificent drum, most of which is clad in marble, and the buttresses (pierced by round arches) of the lantern. These buttresses continue the ribs of the dome. The rich marble facing (green 'verde di Prato', red 'rosso di Maremma' and white 'bianco di Carrara'), together with the decorative theme, date from the initial phase under A.di Cambio.
Inside and decoration: Basilica (nave, two aisles) in the shape of a Latin cross (length 502 ft., maximum width *c.* 295 ft.). The nave appears short, with its four widely spaced pillars. It leads to the octagonal area beneath the drum. The transepts and the sanctuary at the E. end extend off this octagonal area. Each contains five chapels and ends in an apse. The simple vertical arrangement of the Gothic nave includes a balcony instead of a triforium, which continues beneath the dome. The domed sacristies lie between the transepts and the choir; there are organ lofts above their entrances. The inlaid marble pavement was completed by G. and F.da Sangallo to a design by Baccio d'Agnolo. Glass windows were made to designs by Ghiberti (some of them were executed by the German artist Nicolò di Piero Tedesco), Donatello, Uccello and others. The cathedral contains, amongst other pieces: the painted *equestrian statue* of Giov. Acuto by P.Uccello (10), which introduced the equestrian statue of antiquity to the Renaissance; a *Pietà by Michelangelo* (18) — a late work which is among his most dramatic pieces (intended for the chapel containing his own tomb. Broken to pieces by Michelangelo, it was restored by his pupil Tib. Calcagni, who completed Mary Magdalene); in addition, there are the decorations of the two *sacristies* (21 and 26), the *bronze shrine* of St.Zenobius by Ghiberti (24), and the remains of the *bishop's tomb* by Tino di Camaino for Antonio d'Orso (39). The

Cripta di S.Reparata (34) has remains of the old cathedral of S.Reparata; excavations were carried out in 1966.

Campanile: The slim tower, 278 ft. high and with octagonal clasping buttresses, was begun by Giotto in 1334 (lower part of the 1st double storey), continued by A.Pisano after Giotto's death in 1337, and completed by F.Talenti in 1359 after Pisano's death (1348). With its coloured marble facing, it is one of the finest bell-towers in Italy. The sculpted decoration with reliefs and figures in niches (moved to the cathedral museum—q.v.—and replaced by casts) depict a scholastic programme of world history and of the life and sufferings of Christ, making the tower one of the masterpieces of Italian sculpture between 1340 and 1440 (A.Pisano and his school; L.della Robbia).

SS. Annunziata (Environs): This N./S.-oriented church stands on the *Piazza della SS. Annunziata*, one of the finest Renaissance squares. It is dominated by the equestrian statue of Grand Duke Ferdinando I, which stands on the axis of the road leading to the cathedral. The last work of G.da Bologna, the statue was com-

pleted by P.Tacca in 1608. Also by Tacca, to the design of Bernardo Radi, are two symmetrically arranged fountains with bronze sea monsters. The colonnade of the *Ospedale degli Innocenti*, runs along the right side of the square and is balanced on the left by a façade (1516–25) modelled on it by A.da Sangallo the Younger, with the assistance of B.d'Agnolo. In 1419, the silk-weavers' guild founded the *Foundling Hospital* (Patronage of the Innocent Children of Bethlehem), which was designed by F.Brunelleschi. He built the middle section (nine arches) of the famous colonnade, which is the first example of columns and arches framed by a large order of pilasters, and is one of the major achievements of the early Renaissance. Some terracotta medallions with babies in the spandrels are early works by A.della Robbia and were mounted in 1463 (the other four are imitations dating from 1845). The hospital has a *gallery* with 15&16C works, including an Adoration of the Magi by D.Ghirlandaio (1488). At the end of the Via dei Servi, on the left, is the *Palazzo Riccardi Manelli* (formerly Grifoni), built in 1557–75 by B.Ammannati for Ugolino Grifoni. The *Palazzo della Crocetta*, today the Museo Ar-

'Gate of Paradise', detail

cheologico (q.v.), was built in 1620 for the Archduchess Maria Magdalena of Austria; it stands on the Via della Colonna, to the left of the hospital.

Church of SS. Annunziata: Built in 1250 as the oratory of the Servites living in the settlement founded on Monte Senario in 1234. The miraculous completion of Friar Bartholomew's fresco by an angel (1252) made the oratory into a popular shrine for the people. After some extensions which quickly became necessary, the church was rebuilt from 1444 onwards by Michelozzo, beginning with the laying of a foundation stone for the circular tribune which was completed in 1477 with the assistance of L.B.Alberti. The church and atrium date from 1453 and the portico was completed in 1604. Rich baroque decoration. Behind the portico with its seven bays is the *atrium* (Chiostrino dei Voti; roofed in 1833) with interesting high Renaissance and early Mannerist *frescos* by A.del Sarto and his school; Visitation, by Pontormo, 1516; Marriage of the Virgin, by Fraciabigio, 1513; Birth of the Virgin, signed by A.del Sarto himself; Coming of the Magi, 1514, and scenes from the life of St.Filippo Benizzi (left side wall) of 1509/10 (exception: Vision and Investiture of the Saint by C.Rosselli, 1475). Oldest fresco: Nativity of Christ by Alessio Baldovinetti (1460–2). *Church:* The aisles of the 14C basilican building were subdivided by Michelozzo so as to resemble chapels. Rich, baroque flat ceiling, completed in 1669. The original choir was demolished and, with the assistance of L.B.Alberti, replaced by a rotunda on the model of the classical Minerva Medica in Rome. To the left of the entrance is the *Cappella dell' Annunziata* with a marble tabernacle (1447-61) in honour of the miraculous 14C Florentine Annunciation fresco. Note the marble Pietà by B.Bandinelli (chapel by the right transept); Trinity with Saints, a detached fresco by A.Castagno (1454/5; by the altar of the second chapel on the left); Resurrection by A.Bronzino (c. 1550; first chapel to the left of the E. chapel of the tribune). The *Cappella di San Luca*, a 'painter's chapel', has works by Michelangelo's followers and is notable for

its unique decoration. The ceiling has a Vision of St. Bernard by L.Giordano (c. 1650). The lunettes of the *cloister* (Chiostro dei Morti), which is entered from outside the church, are frescoed with scenes from the history of the Servite order. These frescos are major works by the early 17C Tuscan school (Mascagni, Poccetti, Rosselli etc.). Over the door into the church is the *Madonna del Sacco*, a masterpiece by A. del Sarto (1525).

Badia: The Benedictine abbey (Badia) was founded in 978 by Willa of Tuscany (mother of Duke Ugo, whom Dante in his Paradise wrongly described as the founder). It is the oldest monastery within the city walls and the only imperial abbey in Florence. The Ottonian church (969–78) was rebuilt by A.di Cambio (1284–1310) and turned through 90° by Segaloni from 1627 onwards. The monastery was dissolved in 1810. At the entrance, on the left, is a Vision of St.Bernard, an important early work by Filippino Lippi (c. 1480). Among the most important decorations are works by Mino da Fiesole (a relief of the Madonna with St.Lawrence and St.Leonard from 1464-9), the tomb of Bernardo Giugni (c. 1468) and a monument to Count Ugo (1469-81), who died in 1001. The atmospheric *Chiostro degli Aranci* (c. 1400) has remains of frescos by A.Bronzino and the remains of a tabernacle attributed to B.Rossellino. The lower ground floor of the *campanile* is probably Ottonian.

S.Croce: The expansive *Piazza di S.Croce* (1865, monument to Dante), which dates from the Middle Ages and has always been the unofficial meeting place of the people of Florence, is on the site of the ancient amphitheatre. On its E. side is the church of S.Croce, the greatest of the Franciscan churches. According to Vasari, it was begun by A.di Cambio in 1294 on the site of an earlier building of 1228. The transept was completed towards 1300, while the church's consecration, in the presence of Pope Eugene IV, did not take place until 1443. The door to the sacristy corridor, and the *Medici chapel* at the end of it, are an early masterpiece by Michelozzo, c. 1455. The façade dates from 1853-63, the campanile from 1847. Radical alterations to the decoration were made by Vasari (stone altar tabernacles in the aisles; removal of the choir stalls from the nave). Simple *exterior;* on the N. flank there is an arcade with a marble tomb, *c.* 1330, from the school of Tino da Camaino (at the E. end). The clearly conceived, broad *interior* is basilican, with a nave, two aisles, and transepts at the end surrounded by chapels. The row of chapels to the E. flanks the projecting polygonal apse (good stained glass). Dimensions of the church: Length approx. 377 ft.; overall width of the nave and two aisles approx. 124 ft., transept approx. 243 ft.

Decoration: Numerous *tombs* (in addition to the 276 tomb-slabs of distinguished Florentine families set into the pavement) and *cenotaphs* (sepulchral monuments) make this into a kind of pantheon of Italian culture. Particularly important from the art historical point of view is the tomb executed by B.Rossellino in 1444/5 for *Leonardo Bruni* (1369 - 1444), the humanist, historian and Chancellor of the Florentine Republic. This was the prototype Florentine Renaissance grave. Other important monuments include: one of the most beautiful of Renaissance tombs—that of Carlo Marsuppini (1398 - 1453), humanist and Chancellor; a major work (1455–66) by D.da Settignano; the *tomb of Michelangelo,* designed by Vasari, completed in 1573; also the *tombs of Galileo Galilei* (1737), of *Machiavelli* (1787), and of *Gioacchino Rossini,* the composer. One of the most important sepulchral monuments of Italian classicism is the work of A.Canova in 1810 for Vitt. Alfieri. In 1829 Dante was given a cenotaph. Major pieces of *Florentine Renaissance sculpture* include: the graceful and delicate marble relief of the Madonna and Child in the almond-shaped wreath of angels by A.Rossellino (1478, part of the tomb of Francesco Nori). The altar tabernacle with the Annunciation of 1435 by Donatello for the Cavalcanti family—one of his major works. The wooden crucifix in the *Bardi Chapel* at the N. end of the transept, also by Donatello. The octagonal *marble pulpit* with five scenes in relief from the life of St.Francis is by B.da Maiano (1472-6). The rich array of *frescos* from the Duecento makes it possible to study the development of Florentine painting from the generation before Giotto up to the stirrings of the early Renaissance. The simple paintings in the spandrels of the eastern chapels in the transept are the oldest frescos. A follower of Cimabue (or Cavallini) painted the frescos in the *Velluti Chapel:* scenes from the legend of St.Michael (the altar has a polyptych, from Giotto's later years). Giotto's mature period is represented by the frescos in the *Peruzzi Chapel* with scenes from the lives of the two Saints John (after 1320). These were immediately followed by the frescos in the *Bardi Chapel,* scenes from the life of St. Francis (the altar panel is attributed to Barone Berlinghieri). The frescos (1332–8) in the *Baroncelli Chapel* are amongst the major works of Taddeo Gaddi, Giotto's most faithful pupil; the Madonna of the Girdle is by B.Mainardi (1480); the Baroncelli tomb is by Giov. di Balduccio of Pisa, who came from the same workshop as Tino di Camaino. From approximately the same time are the frescos by Bern. Daddi (*c.* 1330) in the *Pulci-Beraldi Chapel* and those by Maso di Banco (*c.* 1340) in the second *Bardi Chapel.* The increasing process of individualization and differentiation in the 2nd half of the century can be observed in the frescos of the legend of the Holy Cross by A.Gaddi in the *Castellani Chapel* or chapel of the sacrament (*c.* 1385) and in the *sanctuary.* The *Rinuccini Chapel* is at the E. end of the 14C *sacristy* (fine 15&16C cupboards; terracotta bust of Christ by Giov.della Robbia); it is decorated with fine frescos by G.da Milano (*c.* 1366). Beautiful wrought-iron grille with consecration inscription. The altarpieces in the aisles are good examples of Florentine Mannerism at the time of Vasari; Santi di Tito (Crucifixion, Resurrection, Supper at Emmaus); Jac. Coppi del Moglio (Ecce Homo); B.Naldini (Deposition). The entrance to the monastery cloisters (with a museum) and to the Pazzi Chapel is beside the church façade. The irregular first cloister was formed from the fusion of two Trecento cloisters and is enclosed by arcades (14C arcade flanking the church; loggia on the right *c.* 1400). Opposite the entrance:

Pazzi Chapel: Begun by Brunelleschi in 1430, and commissioned by Andrea de' Pazzi as the monument to the Pazzi and simultaneously as a chapterhouse. It is a harmonious masterpiece of the early Renaissance, with terracotta decoration by L.della Robbia. The wooden doors are the work of G.da Sangallo (1470–8). Off the first cloister is the entrance to the *monastery museum*, the former refectory (Museo dell'Opera di Santa Croce). The main work in this collection is the gilded bronze statue of St. Louis, one of the first figures by Donatello to be completely committed to the Renaissance (*c.* 1430). The second cloister *(Chiostro Grande)*, one of the finest of Renaissance cloisters, was designed by Brunelleschi and completed, probably with the assistance of Bern. Rossellino, in 1453, after Brunelleschi's death. The portal (*c.* 1450) is by B.da Maiano.

S. Lorenzo: The present building, the plans for which existed in 1419, was erected on the site of the early Christian basilica of Ambrosiana (consecrated by St.Ambrose in 393) and of the subsequent 11C Romanesque building. Giov. de' Medici originally employed the young and still unknown Brunelleschi to build the sacristy, but he was finally given the commission for the entire building (*c.* 1419/20), along with the chance to redesign it. The *Old Sacristy* and the *choir chapel* were completed in 1428. On Brunelleschi's death in 1446 his pupil Manetti undertook the completion of the nave; the dome was built to his own plan and completed in 1469. The façade designed by Michelangelo (model dating from 1517) was left unexecuted. However, in 1521, Pope Leo X commissioned Michelangelo to complete the *New Sacristy* and furnishings, as a burial chapel. From 1524 onwards he worked on installing the *Biblioteca Laurenziana* in the monastery cloister built by Manetti in 1457. The *Cappella dei Principi* adjoining the choir of the church was planned by Vasari in 1561–8. The foundation stone was not laid until 1605. Dome completed in the 19C.
Church of S.Lorenzo: Simple exterior with rich graduation around the transepts; the façade has been left in the rough. The *in-terior* was conceived as a flat-roofed columned basilica in strict application of the metrical system. The articulation of the choir is repeated in the walls of the aisles and the front elevation. This, combined with the balanced proportions, makes the church a model of Renaissance architecture. The two *pulpits* by Donatello and his pupils (see plan 3, 15) match the architecture in importance; the design of the cantoria (1) is attributed to Donatello. Filippo Lippi's altar diptych (4) is *c.* 1440. The altarpieces by R.Fiorentino (16) and A.Bronzino (4) are important Mannerist paintings. The *Old Sacristy,* one of the key buildings of the early Renaissance, is a square domed room with a small adjoining altar-room. Original twelve-sided cupola. The decoration (see plan), executed by Donatello in 1435 after the completion of the building, deserves particular attention. The two-sided tomb of the sons of Cosimo il Vecchio Medici (10) is an early masterpiece by Verrocchio. The *New Sacristy* is by Michelangelo but was completed with alterations. He was responsible for the calotte (modelled on the pantheon) and the twelve-sided lantern. The monumental figures by Michelangelo are among the most important accomplishments of European art: the tomb of Giuliano de' Medici, Duke of Nemours (d. 1516), son of Lorenzo il Magnifico, has the recumbent figures of Day and Night. The tomb of Lorenzo de' Medici, Duke of Urbino (d. 1519), grandson of Lorenzo il Magnifico, has the recumbent figures of Morning and Evening. The sculptural decorations were begun by Michelangelo in 1521 with the Madonna Enthroned on the entrance wall. The flanking figures of St. Cosmas and St. Damian are by his pupil R.da Montelupo, after Michelangelo. Fresco sketches by Michelangelo were discovered near the New Sacristy in 1976. The *Cappella dei Principi* (Chapel of the Princes) is the third funerary chapel of the Medici, with six of the Grand Dukes of Tuscany; two of the tombs have colossal figures by P.Tacca. The domed building is richly articulated and is inlaid with precious stones. *Biblioteca Laurenziana:* Founded in 1444 with the extensive library of Cosimo I and finally housed in the building, begun by

Michelangelo in 1524, over the W. side of the two-storeyed cloister built by Manetti. The vestibule, with its complex staircase and columns recessed into the walls, is an influential early masterpiece of Mannerist architecture. Reading desks by Michelangelo.

San Marco (church and monastery): Originally a Vallumbrosan monastery taken over by the Sylvestrines. In 1436 it was transferred to the Dominicans of Fiesole. Then, in 1437–52, it was rebuilt by Cosimo il Vecchio with the aid of the architect Michelozzo. Subsequently the monastery became one of the leading spiritual centres in Florence. Savonarola was the prior of the monastery; Fra Angelico (in whose memory a special museum was established in 1919, based on pieces from Florentine collections), became the monastery's most famous member. Archbishop Antoninus (canonized in 1526) worked from San Marco as a Dominican. A fine funerary chapel was built by Giov. da Bologna in 1578–89 for Antoninus. The present-day design of the façade dates from 1777/8. The interior is still Gothic in character. The decoration includes the

Florence, S. Lorenzo 1 cantoria designed by Donatello (attributed) **2** fresco with martyrdom of St.Lawrence by A.Bronzino 1565–9 **3** pulpit by Donatello, c. 1460, and his pupils Bellano and Bertoldo (initial temporary installation in 1515) **4** chapel of the Martelli with a monument to Donatello (1896) above his tomb in the floor; altar diptych with a predella by Filippo Lippi, c. 1440; sarcophagus by Niccolò Martelli, school of Donatello **5** Sagrestia Vecchia, to a design by Brunelleschi, 1420 – 29, with decoration by Donatello (4 stucco medallions from the story of John the Evangelist; 4 painted terracottas with the Evangelists); at the altar, to a design by Donatello, is a triptych from the school of Taddeo Gaddi, and in the middle of the sacristy is a sarcophagus of the parents of Cosimo il Vecchio (Giov. Bicci de'Medici and Piccarda Bueri) **6** Porta degli Apostoli; bronze door with 20 figures by Donatello **7** Porta dei Martiri (bronze door with pairs of martyrs), 10 panels by Donatello; above the two doors are painted terracotta reliefs showing the Medici family patrons **8** marble basin from the Donatello workshop **9** terracotta bust of St. Lawrence (or St.Leonard), attributed to Donatello **10** tomb for Piero and Giovanni de' Medici (sons of Cosimo il Vecchio) by A.Verrocchio, 1472 **11** altar from the school of Ghirlandaio **12** crucifix by Baccio di Montelupo **13** altar, late 15C; Roman sarcophagus used as the tomb of Niccolò di Tommaso **14** marble tabernacle by Desiderio da Settignano **15** pulpit by Donatello, c. 1460, and his pupils Bellano and Bertoldo (initial temporary installation in 1515) **16** altarpiece with the Betrothal of the Virgin by R.Fiorentino, 1523. Newly discovered fresco design(s) by Michelangelo in the lower storey of the Medici chapel. Special permission is required to visit it.

Pazzi chapel

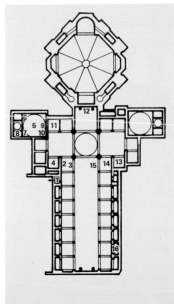

massive cross in the style of Giotto on the W. wall, a Madonna by Fra Bartolommeo (1509), and a number of major pieces of late Mannerist Florentine painting, as well as works by Giov. da Bologna and his followers. *Chapel of St.Antoninus* frescos by A.Allori, antependium and bronze candelabra by Giov. da Bologna. The *sacristy* built by Michelozzo in 1437–43 shows the influence of Brunelleschi. The recumbent bronze figure of St.Antonino in the sanctuary is by Giov. da Bologna (cast by Dom. Ortigiani). The *monastery* was restored and partly expanded by Michelozzo in 1437–52. The frescos by Fra Angelico are among the most important decoration from the time of its restoration. In the small *refectory* is a Last Supper by Dom. Ghirlandaio. There are also works by Fra Bartolommeo, painter and monk (a portrait of Savonarola, and frescos, in the priory). The *monastery library* was built by Michelozzo.

Santa Maria Novella (church and monastery): The Dominican order's most important seat in Florence. Today's church was begun in 1246 on the site of a 10C oratory and largely completed in 1360. The façade was finished from 1350 onwards (its

Synagogue, 19C

articulation is by Alberti, who worked on it from 1456). Outside, there are family tombs in the form of grave niches ('avelli').

Richly designed choir. The interior is a pillared basilica with ribbed vaults; the transept has choir chapels in the Cistercian tradition. This area, with its simple solemnity, is one of the most beautiful Gothic church interiors in Italy. One of the most important features is the *fresco* donated by the Gonfaloniere and painted by Masaccio in 1425. It shows the founders kneeling in front of a Renaissance room with a tunnel vault. This fresco ranks with the wooden *crucifix* by Brunelleschi in the *Gondi Chapel* just to the left of the main choir and designed by G.da Sangallo in 1508. The ceiling frescos of *c.* 1270 are related to the mosaics in the baptistery dome. In the *Strozzi Chapel* (in the end wall of the left transept) are frescos by Nardo di Cione, dating from *c.* 1357; the altar by Andrea di Cione (known as Orcagna) dates from 1357. In the sacristy by Jacopo Talenti is an early masterpiece by Giotto (a painted crucifix above the entrance door). The lavabo is by Giov. della Robbia (1498). The sanctuary has the famous fresco cycle by Dom. Ghirlandaio dating from 1485–90 (pupils working on it included the young Michelangelo). There are some important Mannerist paintings, including the last work by A.Bronzino, the altarpiece in the Gaddi Chapel. *Cloisters: Chiostro Verde*, built after 1350, possibly by J.Talenti, and called the *Green Cloister* after the frescos painted by P.Uccello in 'Terra Verde' on the E. wing (most of them have been removed and are exhibited in the refectory). These frescos by Uccello date from after 1447 and are outstanding examples of the new style of the early Renaissance. The so-called *Spanish Chapel* is to the N. of the Chiostro Verde. Begun in 1348 and completed in 1355, it is at one and the same time a chapterhouse and the burial place of the founders' family (Buon Amico di Lapo Guidalotti). The wall paintings by Andrea da Firenze, completed in 1365, are one of the finest examples of Trecento painting in Florence. The *Chiostro dei Morti* has the Strozzi funerary chapel with frescos by the Orcagna circle of artists.

S. Maria del Carmine: This church of the former Carmelite convent was largely destroyed by fire in 1771 and rebuilt in 1782. Fortunately, the *Brancacci Chapel* with the superb frescos by Masolino and Masaccio (1424–7) has survived. The cycle was only completed (lower panel on the left and right walls) in 1483–5 by Filippino Lippi. Apart from the frescos (1394) by Bicci di Lorenzo and a crucifix by the followers of Cimabue in the sacristy, the dome fresco (1682) by Luca Giordano, in the Corsini chapel, is also of interest.

S. Miniato al Monte: Splendidly located on a hill in the outskirts of Florence. A masterpiece of the Florentine Proto-Renaissance, mentioned as early as Carolingian times. It was originally built as a shrine over the tomb of Minias the Christian, who was beheaded in *c.* 250 under Emperor Decius. In 1018, it was a Cluniac Benedictine abbey; the abbey church was probably completed in 1207. The polychrome decoration inside dates from *c.* 1323. The monastery and church passed to the Olivetans from 1373 onwards. In 1460 Manetti built the funerary chapel of Cardinal Jacopo of Portugal, who was a member of the Portuguese royal family and died in 1459. The church suffered during the wars of the 16C and there were several restorations in the 18&19C. The campanile was rebuilt in 1524–7 after falling down. The splendid *façade* is overlaid in white and green, the richness of the decoration progressively increasing from the lowest of the three zones to the topmost. The lower ground floor is *c.* 1075. The impressive *interior* is a columned basilica with a nave, two aisles (some of the capitals are ancient), and a magnificent open roof truss. The choir lies above the 11C hall crypt, which projects like a stage (seven aisles with ribbed vaults, some of the columns are ancient; remains of frescos by Taddeo Gaddi?), and is partitioned off by a choir arch and a transenna (*c.* 1200), with a richly overlaid *pulpit*. The apse has a *mosaic of Christ Pantocrator*. The chapel of the Cardinal of Portugal, attached to the left aisle, was modelled on the Old Sacristy of S. Lorenzo by Manetti. The Cardinal's tomb is by Ant. Rossellino, who worked on an ancient porphyry model. Magnificent pavements imitate ancient models. Picturesque *cloister* with much-weathered frescos by the Uccello circle of artists on

S. Lorenzo, tomb of G. de Medici

S. Maria Novella

the N. side. The former *Bishop's Palace* (a summer residence) was altered in the 16C and today is used as a concert hall.

Or S. Michele: Probably by Arnolfo di Cambio. Built as a hall for the sale of grain on the site of an 8C oratory. Destroyed by a fire in *c*. 1304 and rebuilt to its present size from 1307 onwards. The market hall was vaulted in 1357; the open arcades were closed in 1367–80, and a miraculous image (originally attached to an outside pillar) was brought inside the building. The *figures* in the pillared niches form a rich source of study of early Renaissance sculpture, having pieces by Lorenzo Ghiberti, Nanni di Banco and Donatello. The most recent work is the Incredulity of St. Thomas, by Verrocchio in 1465–83, reputedly with the assistance of the young Leonardo da Vinci. The decoration is *c*. 1400. *Glass paintings* of the miracles of the Virgin. The *painting in the vaults* depicts the history of the world and God's intervention. In the centre of the hall/church stands the *altar tabernacle* of the S. aisle built by Orcagna in 1359 in order to house the old, miraculous image. The altar is formed by a marble screen of 1366 surrounded by bronze railings. The altarpiece is by B.Daddi.

Santo Spirito: A splendid example of Renaissance architecture. Completely rebuilt by Brunelleschi on the site of an Augustinian church which had existed since 1250 (altered several times). Work on the foundations began in 1436 but it was not completed until 1487; the campanile was finished in 1543. In 1489–92, Giuliano da Sangallo and Cronaca added an octagonal sacristy. The dome over the crossing was not finally completed until 1601–2, when a lantern was built. In the late 16C, Ammannati and others added the cloisters to the existing medieval building. Owing to unresolved artistic questions, the façade was left plain. The side walls are enlivened only by some extended windows. The side aisles continue around the entire building, except for the façade. Each bay ends in an apsidiole vaulted with a calotte to form a chapel. The reduction of all decorative features means that the grand effect of the ar-

chitectural elements is the primary and dominant feature. Features: *marble Pietà* by Nanni di Baccio Bigio after the Michelangelo Pietà in St. Peter's, Rome (16); polychrome and gilded wooden statue of St.Nicholas of Tolentino after a model by J.Sansovino (15); the Apparition of the Madonna before St.Bernard, by Perugino, is a copy of the original in the Alte Pinakothek gallery in Munich (13); Polyptych by Maso di Banco (11). The structure and decoration of the Cappella Corbinelli are both by Andrea Sansovino (7). Opposite is a panel of the Madonna and Child with Saints presenting the donors, an early work by Filippino Lippi (14). The sacristy (4) is particularly fine.

Other churches worth seeing: *S.Felice* with a magnificently balanced façade in the manner of Brunelleschi. Inside there is a painted crucifix by Giotto's followers and a triptych by Neri di Bicci, 1467. The church of *S. Gaetano* (Piazza degli Antinori) has a Martyrdom of St.Lawrence by Pietro da Cortona. *S. Maria degli Angeli* (Via degli Alfani, on the corner of the Via del Castellaccio): A centrally planned building which has remained incomplete (16 sides on the outside, 8 sides on the inside), probably inspired by Roman buildings from classical times. *Ognissanti* (All Saints' Church) has some fine decoration, including frescos by Ghirlandaio. The vestibule of the sacristy has a crucifix by the school of Veit Stoss; there is a monumental Christ in the sacristy itself. The refectory has a Last Supper dated 1480, a masterpiece by Ghirlandaio. On the right wall of the refectory hangs a Botticelli masterpiece (*St.Augustine in his Study*) and on the left wall a companion to it by Ghirlandaio (*St.Jerome in his Cell*, 1480). The *Chiostro dello Scalzo* (Via Cavour 69; entrance charge) has frescos by Andrea del Sarto dating from 1515 to 1526. The church of *Santa Trinità* dates from the 13C and was completed in the 16C. A fine pillared basilica with a nave, two aisles, accompanying side chapels, and five rectangular choir chapels in the transepts. There

S.Miniato al Monte ▷

is an important fresco cycle by L.Monaco, *c.* 1422-5, in the *Bartolini Chapel*. The *Sassetti Chapel* has frescos by Ghirlandaio (1479-86). The tomb (1455/6) of Benozzo Federighi is Lucca della Robbia's most important work in marble. *Synagogue* in Moorish style, built by M.Treves and V.Micheli in 1872-4.

SECULAR BUILDINGS:

Galleria dell' Accademia (entrance in the Via Ricasoli): Famous sculptures by Michelangelo, including the original of *David* (formerly in the Piazza della Signoria) and the four slaves or prisoners (unfinished), originally intended for tomb of Julius II. Good collection of Florentine paintings.

Piazza della Signoria: Developed as a secular centre worthy of the city's increasing importance. The *Palazzo Vecchio* or Palazzo della Signoria which dominates the square was the original seat of the former city government, the Signoria. On the S. side is the Loggia dei Lanzi. Of the old buildings surrounding the square, the *Tribunale di Mercadanzia* (old merchants' court) of 1359 on the E. side, and the *Palazzo Uguccioni* of *c.* 1550 on the N. side, have survived. The square is decorated with important pieces of Florentine sculpture, including *Neptune Fountain* by Bart. Ammannati and his school (1563-75); the twelve bronze figures at the edge of the pool are artistically important. Some 33 ft. from the fountain is a *granite disc* on the site of the pyre on which Savonarola was burned with his companions on 23 March 1498. The *equestrian monument to Cosimo I de' Medici*, is an important late work by Giov. da Bologna. Opposite the Uffizi is the marble group *Hercules and Cacus* by B.Bandinelli (1533). In front of the Palazzo Vecchio is a copy (1905) of the famous *David* by Michelangelo; original in the Galleria dell'Accademia (q.v.) since 1873. The bronze group of *Judith and Holofernes* is a dramatic late work (*c.* 1455-60) by Donatello with excellent reliefs on the base. Next to it is a copy of the *Marzocco lion* (original in the Museo Nazionale).

Palazzo Vecchio or *della Signoria:* Tradition has it that the central section of this massive but elegant building was built from 1299—1314 by Arnolfo di Cambio as the residence of the Priori delle Arti and

S.Miniato al Monte

the Gonfaloniere. The block-like character of the building is emphasized by its
battlemented gallery above two storeys
with regularly arranged rows of double-
arched windows. The rusticated Palazzo
underwent several phases of building before attaining its present size and extent,
although this is not apparent from inside.
The slender tower, 308 ft. tall, was the
landmark of Florence in 1310, and is solid
up to the battlements. It is richly decorated
with historical and mythological frescos
and tapestry cycles from 1537 onwards
when it was the Palazzo Ducale under
Cosimo I. In 1565, when it was the Grand
Duke's residence, a gallery was built connecting it with the Palazzo Pitti. From
1848 onwards it was a temporary seat of the
Italian Government. *Inside:* The entrance
leads into the small courtyard designed by
Michelozzo in 1470. This has a *porphyry
fountain basin* with the famous 'Putto with
Dolphin' ('Socratic Eros'), a cast of a
masterpiece by Verrochio (1476). The
frescos on the upper parts of the walls were
painted on the occasion of the marriage of
Grandprincipe Ferdinando to Johanna of
Austria in 1565. The stairs restored by
Vasari lead up to the *1st floor: Salone dei*

Florence, Santo Spirito 1 copy of the Risen
Christ by Michelangelo (S.Maria Sopra Minerva,
Rome) by T.Landini **2** entrance to the sacristy **3**
ante-room of the sacristy by Cronaca, 1492–4, to
plans by Giuliano da Sangallo; coffer-work vault
with mythological figures and scenes; the capitals are in part attributed to A.Sansovino **4** sacristy, 1489–92 to plans by G.da Sangallo, the
dome and lantern on a model by A.da Pollaiuolo
and Salvi d'Andrea, 1495–6; capitals by A.San-
sovino; altar by A.Allori, 1596 **5** Madonna Enthroned with Saints, school of Fra' Bartolomeo,
to the right is a bust of G.Montorsoli by
Tom.Cavalcanti, c. 1560 **6** Trinity being revered by
St. Catherine and Mary Magdalene, by Franc.
Granacci **7** Cappella Corbinelli; the architecture
and rich sculptured decoration are an early work
by A.Sansovino, 1492; this is the most interesting of the decorations **8** Nativity of Christ, school
of Dom. Ghirlandaio **9** Adultress, by A.Allori,
1577 **10** altar with martyred Saints by A.Allori,
1574; the predella shows the Palazzo Pitti before
its expansion **11** polyptych by Maso di Banco **12**
behind the bronze grille: marble sarcophagus of
the Florentine Neridi Gino Capponi, 1388–1457,
attributed to Bernardo Rosselino, 1458 **13** copy
by F.Ficherelli of the Virgin Mary appearing before St. Bernard by Perugino in the Alte
Pinakothek gallery in Munich **14** Madonna and
Child with the boy St.John, with St.Martin and
St.Catherine presenting the founders to them; a
work by Filippino Lippi, c. 1490 **15** statue of St.
Nicholas of Tolentino; it is unclear whether the
statue is a copy of a Sansovino; to the side are
painted angels by Franciabigio **16** copy of the
Pietà by Michelangelo in St. Peter's, Rome, by
Baggio Biccio, 1549 **17** stained-glass window of
the Descent of the Holy Ghost, to a design by
Perugino

S. Miniato al Monte, Manetti chapel

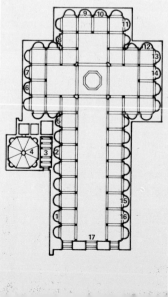

Cinquecento, 174 ft. long, 72 ft. wide (height increased by 23 ft. to 59 ft. at Michelangelo's suggestion), by Cronaca, 1495. It was the assembly hall of the Consiglio Maggiore until the latter's dissolution in 1530; today it is a concert hall. Some preparatory cartoons are all that remain of the original frescos by Leonardo da Vinci (Battle of Anghiari) and Michelangelo (Battle of Cascina). Battle paintings by Vasari have survived. The 39 compartments of the richly decorated ceiling show scenes from the history of Florence and the Medici family. On the N. side is the so-called *Udienza*, the imposing audience hall from the time of Grand Duke Cosimo I. Michelangelo's marble group, 'Victory', stands in a niche on the opposite narrow side. To the right of it is the entrance to the *Studiolo di Francesco I de' Medici* (study) by Vasari; frescos by Vasari and his school on the subject of man and nature. The corner niches have statuettes by Giov. da Bologna and others. Opposite the entrance to the Studiolo, the visitor may enter the *Quartiere di Leone X*. Only the *Sala di Leone X* is open; it has frescos glorifying this important Pope. The *2nd storey* contains the *Quartiere degli Elementi*

S. Trinità, Sassetti chapel

with five rooms and two loggias by Giov. Battista del Tasso (*c*. 1550). The design is by Vasari in co-operation with Cristoforo Gherardi. The *Quartiere di Eleonora di Toledo* for the wife of Grand Duke Cosimo I includes rooms originally intended for the Priori and designed by Vasari (1559–62). The associated private chapel was frescoed by Bronzino in 1540. The main room on the 2nd storey is the *Sala dell' Udienza*, originally the Republic's audience chamber. The very splendid ceiling is by Giuliano da Maiano with others and the magnificent marble doorways (1476–8) are by his brother Benedetto. The Sala dei Gigli (Hall of Lilies), which was partitioned by Benedetto da Maiano, has a fresco by D.Ghirlandaio (1481–5). In the *mezzanine* is the *Quartiere del Mezzanino*, extended by Michelozzo for the Priori; important art collection.

Loggia dei Lanzi: An airy, open arcaded hall, built by Benci di Cione and Simone Talenti in 1374–81 for public ceremonies of State. It earned its present name under Cosimo I when it was the guard room of the German mercenaries (Lanzichenecchi). The spandrels, with reliefs of the Virtues on a blue enamel background, date from 1384–9 and are to a design by Agnolo Gaddi. The hall is richly decorated with ancient and Mannerist sculptures, notably: the *Rape of the Sabine* (under the arch to the right of the entrance), a marble group by Giov. da Bologna dating from 1583; the pedestal has excellent bronze reliefs. *Perseus with the Head of the Medusa*, a bronze statue by Benvenuto Cellini, 1545–54 and one of his masterpieces (under the arch to the left of the entrance). Inside: *Hercules fighting Nessus the Centaur*, 1599, by Giov. da Bologna (an ancient copy of a 4C BC Greek sculpture) and *Menelaus with the body of Patroclus*.

Uffizi: In 1560 Cosimo I commissioned Giorgio Vasari to build an administrative building for the Grand Duchy of Tuscany. Making use of older buildings, Vasari built two long, symmetrical wings along the sides of a narrow street-like square; the three stories have colonnades on the ground floor. A building with a portico faces the Arno, the other end opens on to the Piazza della Signoria. It was completed in 1580 under A.Parigi and B.Buontalenti. The top storey was a statue gallery as early as the time of Buontalenti; the gallery attained its present size in 1658. Since 1852 it has been the Tuscan State Archive, and has also housed many administrative institutions. The art collection is one of the world's greatest. The **Galleria degli Uffizi** has 44 exhibition rooms, mostly devoted to the history of Florentine painting and these adjoin a gallery containing sculpture, which surrounds the entire Uffizi complex. Other Italian schools and also the Dutch masters are represented. Major works held by the Uffizi include: Duccio, Rucellai Madonna; Giotto, Madonna enthroned with Angels and Saints; Cimabue, Madonna in Maestà; Simone Martini, Annunciation and Saints. The early Renaissance is represented by: P.Uccello, The Battle of San Romano; Piero della Francesca, Portrait of Federico di Montefeltro and his wife; Botticelli's masterpieces: Birth of Venus, Primavera. Major works of the High Renaissance include: Michelangelo, the Doni Tondo

'with the Holy Family'; Raphael, Leo X with the Cardinals Giulio de' Medici and Luigi de' Rossi; Leonardo da Vinci, Annunciation, Adoration of the Magi; Andrea del Sarto, the Madonna delle Arpie. Masterpieces of Venetian painting include: Giorgione, Infant Moses brought to Pharaoh; Titian, Venus and Cupid, The Venus of Urbino. Florentine Mannerism is represented by Rosso Fiorentino, Parmigianino, Bronzino; Major baroque works: Caravaggio, Young Bacchus, The Head of Medusa; G.M.Crespi, Massacre of the Innocents. Non-Italian schools: Flemish and Dutch artists: Roger van der Weyden, Hugo van der Goes, portraits by Rembrandt and Van Dyck, Rubens, portrait of Isabella Brant; German school: Albrecht Dürer, Adoration of the Magi, portrait of his father; Lucas Cranach the Elder, Adam and Eve; Albrecht Altdorfer, Two panels showing the life of St.Florian; Johann Liss, Toilet of Venus. A group of sculptures, Niobe, and the Medici Venus, are two of the most important works from classical times. There is a fine collection of artists' self-portraits, including ones by Raphael, Titian, Bernini, Rembrandt and Velazquez.

Loggia dei Lanzi

Loggia dei Lanzi, Perseus by Cellini

Bargello (Palazzo della Podestà): Begun in 1255; Vasari cites Lapo Tedesco as the architect. Initially the seat of the Podestà, from 1574 onwards it housed the police and became known as the Bargello. Restored in the 16C by Baccio d'Agnolo and Giuliano da Sangallo. From 1859 onwards it has been a *Museo Nazionale*, taking in sculpture and pieces of decorative art from the Uffizi collections, a fine collection of arms from the Medici and an important collection of sculptures. Of these, some works by Michelangelo are outstanding: Bacchus drunk, a youthful work from 1494; the marble tondo of the Madonna and Child with the infant St.John (1504); an Apollo (David) and the bust of Brutus. Important works by J.Sansovino, and in particular by Giov. da Bologna. In the Salone del Consiglio Generale there are some pieces by Donatello, including both the original of the St.George of Orsanmichele and the magnificent bronze David. The

Bargello also houses the famous Carrand Collection of important pieces of decorative art (gold, enamel and ivories).

Palazzo Davanzati (Via di Porta Rossa 9): Important example of secular Florentine architecture of the Trecento; a tall, four-storeyed façade to which a loggia was added in the 15C. Since 1950 it has been a State museum with excellent furniture (medieval nobleman's town house).

Palazzo Medici-Riccardi (Via Cavour, corner of Via dei Gori): Built in 1444–52 by Michelozzo for Cosimo il Vecchio. In 1459/60 B.Gozzoli frescoed the chapel. After being sold to Francesco Riccardi in 1659, it was extended by seven bays on the Via Cavour, although the existing scheme was retained. The main staircase was added in 1715. As State property, it has been the seat of the prefecture since 1814. The building is one of the crowning achievements of early Renaissance palace architecture in Florence. Note the differences in the three storeys; the completely independent articulation of the rusticated ground floor with rough bosses on the stonework contrasts with the two upper storeys, which are related to one another by their window arrangement. A massive cornice unites the whole. The square inner courtyard is one of the finest examples from the Renaissance; the original statues have been replaced by antiquities from the Riccardi collections. The design of the ornamental garden is from the Riccardi period. The *Medici Museum* has been housed here since 1929.

Of especial historical importance is the *chapel*, whose interior by Michelozzo gives an impression of the original lavishness of the palace decoration as a whole. The frescos are by Benozzo Gozzoli.

Palazzo Pitti and the Boboli Gardens: The central structure survives from the original palace built in 1457–66 by Luca Fancelli for Luca Pitti, scion of one of Florence's richest families. It was acquired in 1550 by Eleonora di Toledo, the wife of Cosimo I, and from 1560 onwards it was altered by Ammannati and the courtyard side was extended. From 1592 onwards

Palazzo Pitti

G.Parigi and his son Alfonso added three window bays to the left and right to extend it to its present size. The addition of the terrace wings projecting to the W. was begun in 1764 and completed in 1819. This step-by-step extension is matched by the decoration, with Mannerist (Poccetti) and baroque (Giovanni da San Giovanni, F.Furini, Pietro da Cortona, and others) frescos and Italian Romantic works. In 1860, together with the picture gallery which had been significantly expanded by the Medici, it passed to the crown of Italy. Vittorio Emanuele II resided here (1865-71), during the period when Florence was the capital of Italy. Further collections (see below) were established in addition to the gallery of paintings. The three-storeyed, roughhewn façade becomes progressively lighter from storey to storey. The three sides of the courtyard with their rusticated Doric, Ionic and Corinthian orders make the courtyard one of the most original

pieces of Mannerist architecture, and at the same time provide a successful link with the equally Mannerist Boboli Gardens.

Boboli Gardens: Laid out in 1560 they are amongst the finest gardens in Italy. They were begun by Tribolo; Ammannati designed the amphitheatre which extends from the courtyard of the Pitti. The *Grotta Grande*, on which Buontalenti worked from 1556-92, consists of three chambers, the first of which has copies of Michelangelo's 'Slaves'. Up the hill is the *Neptune Fountain*. The *Giardino del Cavaliere* contains the *Monkey Fountain* with a Cupid by Pietro Dacca. Note the *Fountain of Oceanus* by Giov. da Bologna, on an island in the middle of a pool.

The collections in the palace: *Galleria Palatina:* The exhibits are arranged in the manner of a prince's collection. The highlights of the picture gallery are 13 paintings by Raphael, 12 by Titian, 8 by Tintoretto and 16 by A.del Sarto. Also represented are Rubens, Van Dyck, Guido Reni, Bronzino, Velazquez etc. There is a notable **porcelain collection** on the mezzanine. The *Museo degli Argenti* (royal silver room) has valuable gold and silver objects, including the almost complete archbishop's treasury brought from Salzburg by Ferdinando III in 1814. On the 2nd floor is the *Galleria d'Arte Moderna* (founded in 1860), decorated chiefly with 19C Tuscan paintings. The rooms of the *Appartamenti ex Reali* are also open and are magnificently furnished. They were used as official apartments by the Medici and the Dukes of Lorraine, and later by Vittorio Emanuele II. The so-called *Meridiana* of 1776, a favorite residence of Vittorio Emanuele II during his stay in Florence, displays a part of the Contini-Bonacossi Collection, containing some major Italian and Spanish works (Duccio, Veronese, Giov. Bellini, Zurbarán, Velazquez, Goya and others). Adjoining the palace is the *Museo delle Carozze* with a collection of magnificent coaches from the 18&19C.

Palazzo Rucellai (Via della Vigna Nova 18): Probably designed by Leon Battista Alberti (between 1446 and 1451) for the rich Florentine merchant Giov. di Paolo Rucellai; built largely by Bernardo Rossellino. The entire hewn-stone façade is articulated by pilasters, in a way which was quite new and which was to be very influential. In the square, on the right, is the Loggia dei Rucellai, built by Alberti in *c.* 1460 as the family's formal hall.

Palazzo Strozzi (Piazza Strozzi): This most typical of all palaces of the Florentine Renaissance was begun by Benedetto da Maiano in 1489, on a model by Sangallo the Elder, for Filippo di Matteo Strozzi. Continued by Cronaca until 1536 after the death of the owner (1491) and of the architect (1497). Splendid courtyard, designed by Cronaca.

Ponte Vecchio: In contrast to the Ponte Trinità, the famous Ponte Vecchio was spared destruction during World War 2. Tradition has it that an earlier, Etruscan, structure already existed. The first stone bridge of 1080 was rebuilt in 1170 and 1333 after floods. Agnolo Gaddi is said to have reconstructed it in 1345. It has borne

Palazzo Medici-Riccardi

shops since the 13C. By order of Grand Duke Ferdinando I, the only trades people still allowed to establish themselves there were goldsmiths (1593). On the E. side, Vasari built the corridor connecting the Uffizi to the Palazzo Pitti.

Also worth seeing: The *Loggia del Mercato Nuovo* (New Market; on the Via Porta Rossa at the corner of the Via Calimala): In 1547, Cosimo I had a loggia of twelve bays built over the original silk and gold market (today it is a market for straw). The *Palazzo Gondi* (Piazza S.Firenze 1), begun by Giuliano da Sangallo in 1490 and not completed until 1874. Magnificent colonnaded courtyard. The *Palazzo Pandolfini* (Via S. Gallo 74). This building owes its alien Roman character to a design by Raphael for Giannozzo Pandolfini, the Archbishop of Troia.

Museums: *Museo dell'Angelico*: See San Marco. *Museo Archeologico* (Piazza della SS. Annunziata). Housed in the Palazzo della Crocetta, which was built in 1620, probably by Giulio Parigi for Grand Duchess Maria Maddalena d'Austria. Important mainly for its Etruscan collection. The ad-joining *Museo Egiziano* (Egyptian Museum) is the most important in Italy after Turin. There are some excellent Etruscan bronzes in the *Etrusco-Greco-Romano Museum*. *Museo degli Argenti:* see Palazzo Pitti. *Museo delle Carozze:* see Palazzo Pitti.

Casa Buonarroti (Michelangelo's house; Via Ghibellina 70): This house was acquired by Michelangelo and remained in the possession of his family until 1858 (Cosimo Buonarroti). It houses important work (sculptures and drawings by Michelangelo, and the decorations of 1620). *Museo Nazionale:* cf. Bargello. *Museo dell'Opera del Duomo* (cathedral museum): Major pieces of sculpture, such as the cantoria by Luca della Robbia and the one by Donatello. Works by Arnolfo di Cambio, Andrea Pisano (some to a design by Giotto). 16 statues from the niches in the campanile, including Donatello's Habakkuk. Important works in gold. Altarpieces. *Museo dell'Opera di Santa Croce:* see Santa Croce. *Museo delle Porcellane:* see Palazzo Pitti. *Museo degli Strumenti Musicali Antichi* (historical musical instruments), in the Conservatorio Musicale Luigi Cherubini (Via degli Alfani 80,

Uffizi, Battista Sforza and Federico da Montefeltro by Piero della Francesca

where there is also the *Biblioteca Musicale* with autographs by Monteverdi, Rossini, Carissimi, Cherubini and others). Instruments by Antonio Stradivari, Nicola Amati and others.

Cenacoli (refectories): *Cenacolo di S. Apollonia:* Refectory of the Benedictine convent of S. Apollonia, which was founded in 1339. The refectory has a Last Supper, and above it a Crucifixion, Resurrection and Entombment by Andrea del Castagno; these are in the process of being restored (1984). *Cenacolo di S. Salvi* (museum of Andrea del Sarto; Via di S.Salvi): refectory of the Vallumbrosanan abbey of San Salvi, partially destroyed in 1529, with Last Supper by Andrea del Sarto dated 1519.

Theatre: Teatro Comunale (Via Magenta): Only the classical façade survives from the original theatre, which suffered fire and devastation by war. The hall with its 2000 seats is used for performances in the 'Maggio Musicale Fiorentino', apart from the usual concert and opera season. **Teatro alla Pergola** (Via della Pergola): Built in wood by Ferdinando Tacca in 1656. Adapted from the Grand Ducal courtyard and altered in 1681–94. Rebuilt in stone in 1755, and again in the 19C. The pergola is famous for its operatic performances; since the early 20C it has chiefly been used for the performance of plays.

Environs: On the way to Fièsole, the *church of S.Domenico,* begun in 1406 and completed in 1435; extended in the 17C whilst being rebuilt. In the first chapel on the left of the single-aisled hall there is an altarpiece by Fra Angelico (*c.* 1430). In 1501 Lorenzo di Credi replaced the original gold background with the present one. There is also a fresco of the Crucifixion by Lorenzo di Credi in the monastery's chapterhouse. The visitor may descend to the **Badia Fiesolana** nearby. Until 1028 it was Fièsole's cathedral; it was then taken over by the Benedictines, extended, and left to the canons of San Frediano in Lucca in 1442. In 1459 these canons began to rebuild it in Renaissance

style. The 12C Romanesque façade survived. The high altar is to a design by Pietro Tacca, 1612. Fine marble basin dating from 1461. **Fièsole:** Of Etruscan origin with remains of buildings possibly from the 7/6C BC. First mentioned in 225 BC. Known as Faesulae under the Romans, it was the centre of the area with capitol, forum, temples, theatres and baths. Invaded by the Goths in 405, besieged and starved into submission by Belisarius in 539–40. From 1125 on it was gradually but completely overshadowed by Florence. The most important buildings include the *Cathedral of San Romolo,* begun by Bishop Jacob of Bavaria (1024–8). Rebuilt from 1256 onwards. Distinctive tower dating from 1213. The inside is a Romanesque basilica with a nave and two aisles. To the right of the choir is the Cappella Salutati with the tomb (1464) of Bishop Leonardo Salutati by Mino da Fièsole. The high altar has a triptych by Bicci di Lorenzo (*c.* 1440). The sacristy contains a reliquary bust and a splendid mitre of Bishop L.Salutati. The church of *San Alessandro* stands on the site of a temple of Bacchus, which was converted into a Christian church under Theodoric. Much altered in the 11C. A basilica with a nave, two aisles, and 16 columns which may originate from the temple of Bacchus. On the ancient acropolis there is the church of *San Francesco* (a Franciscan church since 1407) with an altarpiece by Perugino dating from 1502 (2nd altar on the left) and a Madonna by Piero di Cosimo dated *c.* 1480.

Of *Roman Fièsole,* the *theatre,* dating from the time of Claudius and Septimius Severus, has survived, as have the nearby baths, which were enlarged under the Emperor Hadrian. There is a *Roman temple,* not completely excavated until 1918, when an earlier Etruscan building also came to light. Between the temple and the baths is an Etruscan wall and gate. The *museum of the excavations* has some good finds (stele with funerary banquet, dance, and animal fights dating from *c.* 460 BC; the head of the Emperor Claudius and others). Near Fièsole is the *Villa Medici,* built by Michelozzo for Cosimo il Vecchio in 1458-61. It was here that Lorenzo il Magnifico met his literary friends, including

Uffizi, Birth of Venus by Botticelli

Poliziano. To the NE of Florence *c.* 0.5 km. along the Via G.d'Annunzio after Converciano, there is a turning for **S.Martino a Ménsola,** a 9C abbey church. Rebuilt in Renaissance style in 1460, it retains parts of the 11C Romanesque building. In the right aisle there is a good triptych by Taddeo Gaddi. Nearby is the **Villa I Tatti,** acquired in 1905 by the art historian Bernard Berenson, who filled it with his rich library and art collection. The collection contains some notable paintings, mainly of the Florentine school from Giotto to the early 16C. The route continues via Ponte a Ménsola to **Settignano:** the birthplace of several Renaissance artists, such as the sculptor Desiderio da Settignano, the Rossellini, and Luca Fancelli the architect. The 15C *parish church of the Assumption of the Virgin* has a terracotta from the school of A.della Robbia behind the high altar. Small ciborium to a design by D.da Settignano. On the stretch of road towards Terenzano is the **Villa Gamberaia,** one of the finest of 16C villas. 3.5 km. SE of Florence, **Badia di Ripoli** with the abbey of Ripoli, a Benedictine foundation dating from 790 with the 11C abbey church extended in 1598. At a distance of 4 km. stands the church of *S. Pietro a Ripoli,* which is mentioned as early as the 8C. Fine interior with a nave and two aisles. Above Bagno a Ripoli and Ponte a Ema is the church of *S. Caterina dell' Antella,* built in 1387 and then decorated with frescos of the life of St.Catherine by Spinello Aretino. In L'Antella itself is the fine Romanesque church of S.Maria. **Villamagna** with the beautiful Romanesque church of *S.Donnino,* mentioned in the 8C and built in the 11C. **Galluzzo:** The *Certosa del Galluzzo* was begun in 1341 and has a large picture gallery which, in addition to the five frescoed lunettes by Pontormo (1522–5), contains a panel attributed to Masolino.

Foggia 71100
Foggia/Apulia　　　　　　　　　　　p.416□M 10

Cathedral of S. Maria Icona Vetere
(Piazza De Sanctis): Begun in *c.* 1175 by
William II of Sicily on the lines of the cathedral of Troia with its Tuscan influence
(high blind arcades on the façade and side
walls), rebuilt under Frederick II, destroyed by the earthquake in 1731 and
reconstructed in baroque style. The lower
parts of the W. façade and nave walls are
original. In 1953 a previously covered
Romanesque *portal* on the N. aisle was revealed (Tuscan: black-and-white patterned
archivolt); the subject matter of the scenes
is a matter of dispute. Inside: the heart of
Emperor Frederick II was formerly in a
sarcophagus above the main portal until
1731 (the body is in the cathedral of
Palermo). In a chapel there is the painting,
The Madonna with the seven veils, which
has miraculous properties (found in Foggia). The crypt has capitals by Nicola di
Bartolomeo da Foggia (13C).

Musei Civici (*Palazzo Arpi* on the Piazza
Nigri): Museum of archaeology and folk-

lore, gallery of modern paintings
(19&20C). The main object of interest is
an *arch with eagle consoles* on the right side
of the Palazzo Arpi—it is the last remnant
of the imperial palace (begun in 1223 and
destroyed in 1731).

Foligno 06034
Perugia/Umbria　　　　　　　　　　p.414□H 8

Foligno is on a plain, in contrast to almost
all the other towns in Umbria. The commercial and industrial area (paper factories,
mills, steel industry, etc.) lies around the
junctions with the autostrade to Rome,
Florence and Perugia. Founded by the
Umbrians, it was known as Fulginia by the
Romans and suffered greatly during the
barbarian invasions. The town's heyday
began with the Trinci family's rise to
power (14–16C). During this period there
developed a local but important school of
painting in Foligno, whose most important
member was Niccolò Alunno. On 11 April
1472, the first printed edition of the *Divine Comedy* by Dante Alighieri appeared
in one of the town's printing shops.

Foligno, cathedral portal

Foligno, cathedral 1 copy of Raphael's
'Madonna di Foligno' **2** Cappella del Sacramento
by A.da Sangallo the younger **3** crypt, 12C **4** copy
of Bernini's baldacchino in the Vatican

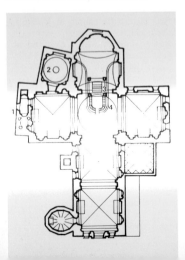

Cathedral of S.Feliciano: Built in 1133 to plans by Master Atto. The beautiful Romanesque N. façade was built by Rudolfo and Binello in 1201. It shows stylistic elements typical of churches in the South of France. The cathedral was much altered in the 16&18C. Inside, the door jambs, and the bas-reliefs of Frederick Barbarossa and Bishop Anselm, are noteworthy. It also contains the 'Martyrdom of S. Messalina from Foligno' by Enrico Bartolomei (1850) and the 'Holy Family' by G.A.Lazzareni. The sacristy has tempera paintings by Niccolò Alunno and two busts attributed to Bernini. In the right transept there is a St.Francis by Tizzoni, a painter from Foligno. Above the high altar is a copy of Bernini's baldacchino in St. Peter's, Rome. In front of the baldacchino is a 14C grille. Stairs lead to the 12C crypt, which is richly decorated with inscriptions and coats of arms. In the *sanctuary:* Apotheosis of S. Feliciano and Triumph of Religion. Left transept: copy of the 'Madonna di Foligno' by Raphael. Antonio da Sangallo the Younger designed the *Cappella del Sacramento.*

Palaces: *Palazzo Comunale* (Piazza della Repubblica): Built in the 13C, rebuilt from 1546 to 1620 and later redesigned in neoclassical style. It has some beautiful 17C rooms. The *Sala del Consiglio* contains a 16C fireplace and some frescos by Piervittori. The tower dates from the 15C. *Palazzo Orfini:* This was where the *Divine Comedy* was first printed. Note the portal of 1515. *Palazzo delle Canoniche:* The square next to the cathedral was originally Gothic in character but there have been extensive neoclassical alterations. *Palazzo Pretorio:* All that survives from the first building is an elegant loggia with late Gothic frescos.

Palazzo Trinci/Picture Gallery (Opening times in summer: 9 a.m.–12 noon, 4 p.m.-6.30 p.m.; in winter: 9 a.m.–12 noon, 2 p.m.–4.30 p.m.; Sundays and holidays: 9 a.m.–12 noon): The palace was built between 1389 and 1407. The façade was altered in the 19C. The elegant courtyard has fine Gothic staircases and windows. The chapel was painted throughout by Ottaviano Nelli; the *Hall of the Free Arts and the Planets* was painted all over by a 15C painter from Fabriano; and the *Hall of the Giants* is by the school of Nelli. Important

Foligno, Piazza

works in the *picture gallery:* Benozzo Gozzoli (Angel of the Annunciation), Niccolò Alunno (Stigmata of St.Francis), Lattanzio di Niccolò Alunno, Pierantonio Mezzastris, Bernardino di Mariotto, Dono Doni. The *archaeological museum* displays Roman and Byzantine sculptures and tombstones. Of especial interest is a stone tablet depicting the games in the Circus Maximus, in high relief.

S. Maria Infraportas (Piazza S. Domenico): Romanesque from the 11&12C, with a massive campanile. Inside there are three Crucifixions. The first is attributed to Mezzastris, the second to an artist of the school of Alunno, the third to a painter from Foligno who was influenced by the Sienese style. The Cappella dell' Assunta has 12C Byzantine frescos.

S.Domenico: Built in 1251 on the Piazza of the same name. Note the fine portal and the elegant 14C Gothic campanile.

S.Niccolò: Built in the 13C and subsequently altered. Beautiful 15C portal.

S.Salvatore: Its harmonious 14C façade in red and white, with three pointed arch portals and an elegant campanile makes an immediate impression. Inside (altered in the 18C) it has Flemish tapestries.

S.Maria in Campis: Restored after the earthquake in 1832 and the damage inflicted during World War 2. Inside are frescos by P.A.Mezzastris, a pupil of Gozzoli and painted in Umbrian-Sienese style, and also some frescos from the school of Giotto.

Oratorio della Nunziatella: The frescos by Perugino and Lattanzio di Niccolò are of particular interest.

Folklore: The *Giostra della Quintana* (horsemen's game in 17C costume) is held here annually on the second Sunday in September.

Environs: Abbazia di Sassovivo: This Benedictine abbey was founded in *c.* 1000.

The *cloister,* to plans by Master Pietro de Maria (1229), is especially fine.

Follina 31051
Treviso/Veneto   p.410☐G 2/3

Abbazia di Follina: A lay brotherhood, the Humilati, founded the abbey in 1146 and later adopted the monastic discipline of the Cistercians. When it was rebuilt in the early 13C, the basilica was given a larger interior—nave, two aisles and round pillars. Restored several times; the most recent occasion involved work on the lovely late Romanesque cloister (1268). The impressive effect of the church's Romanesque and Gothic interior is the result of its flat, clear surfaces with painted friezes, the widely spaced arches of the arcade, as well as the high open roof truss. In the right aisle is a fresco of the *Madonna and Child* (1507). The high altar retable has a sandstone *statue of the Madonna and Child* (14C). The right aisle leads to the cloister, which has two rows of columns of different shapes. Nearby is the monastery building.

Foligno, Palazzo Trinci

Fondi 704022

Latina/Latium   p.416☐I 11

The plan of the town has clearly preserved the classical rectangular ground plan with two main axial roads typical of towns founded by the Romans. There is a well-preserved *town wall*, about a mile long, with pre-Roman polygonal masonry and four gates, the best of which is the *Portella*.

Cathedral of S.Pietro: Built in the 4&5C on the site of a heathen temple, rebuilt in 1130–6; extensively restored in 1936. The façade is in travertine stone with a Gothic portal whose lintel bears a relief of *Christ blessing between Apostles and Angels*. The campanile dates from 1278. Inside: a pillared basilica with a nave, two aisles and a raised sanctuary which ends in three square apses. The furnishings are more important than the architecture. The *pulpit* (1278) is the work of Giovanni di Nicola: it has Cosmati work and columns borne by lions and rams. The *Chapel of the Cross* has the *canopied tomb of Cristoforo Caetani*, built by his son Onorato II. Lions bear three female figures (personifications of *Strength, Love* and *Prudence*), and above them the sarcophagus has an image of the deceased. Above the canopy there is a *Crucifixion with St.John and the Madonna*. Along the right wall, underneath the *triptych* by Antoniazzo Romano, there is a mosaic *marble throne* from the 12&13C. The *altar triptych* (1499) is by Cristoforo Scacco.

S.Maria Assunta: Rebuilt by Onorato II in 1490, with the exception of the Gothic tower, and consecrated in 1508. The central portal (there are three in all) has Renaissance decoration and a marble group in the tympanum, *Madonna and Child with St.Catherine and the Founder*. Inside: an extensive pillared basilica with a nave and two aisles, on a cruciform ground plan. There is an elegant Renaissance ciborium dating from 1491 in the left transept.

Palazzo del Principe: The architect of the palace (built for Onorato II in 1466–77) was the Catalan Matteo Forcimanya. He determined the building's character, which owes much to the Gothic style, while the decorative elements are Catalan Gothic.

Castle: This massive square of walls with three cylindrical corner towers was built in the 13–15C. It was under the protection of Count Onorato I that Robert of Geneva was elected here as Antipope Clement VII. This led to the Great Schism of the West. Near the castle is the *Torrione*, a cylindrical tower on a square base.

Fontanellato 43012

Parma/Emilia-Romagna   p. 410☐ E 4

Castle (Rocca): One of the best-preserved castles in Emilia. Built in the first half of the 15C, it was turned into a luxurious residence in the 16&17C. The beautifully furnished living quarters have 16 – 18C paintings. The recently restored wall paintings of Diana and Actaeon by Parmigianino (1503 – 40), are of great importance.

Also worth seeing: *Santuario della Madonna del Rosario,* 1634–41, with statues (on the modern façade) and a 17C high altar; the inside was decorated in the 18C.

Forli 47100

Forlì/Emilia-Romagna   p.414☐G 6

A prehistoric settlement, colonized by the Romans in the early 2C BC under the name of *Forum Livii*. In the early Middle Ages it was part of the Exarchate of Ravenna. From the 11C onwards it was a free town. In 1480 it passed to Girolamo Riario, whose widow was overthrown by Cesare Borgia in 1500. Between 1504–1796 and 1814–19, the town was part of the Papal States.

S.Mercuriale (Piazza Aurelio Saffi): This church, initially a 4/5C basilica, received its present name in the 7C when the relics of St. Mercuriale were moved here. The present church was built after a fire in 1173. The three apses, the crypt and the portico of the basilica (one nave, two aisles) were torn down in the 14C. The chapels at the sides and in the apses were added in the 16C. A marble portal with a lunette relief (*c.* 1230) has survived from the façade of the original building. Of particular interest inside: Venetian *nave pavement* (14C); *Crucifixion* (*c.* 1500) by Palmezzano (left); *tomb of Barbara Manfredi* (d. 1466), a work by the youthful Francesco di Simone Ferrucci. *Sacra Conversazione* by Palmezzano. *Cappella di S. Mercuriale* (1598) with the original decoration; Carved *choir stalls* (1532–5) by Alessandro Begni. *Chapel of the Sacrament* with wall and other paintings from the 14C and 16–18C: *Left side chapel* with a *passage* (1536) by Giacomo Bianchi and an *altarpiece* by Palmezzano.

Cathedral of S. Croce (Piazza del Duomo): A 12C church, most of which was rebuilt in the 15C. The present design of the nave, and also the classical façade, date from 1841. The inside was painted throughout in the 19C. Notable features inside: octagonal *Chapel of the Sacrament* (1490; middle of the right aisle); *Font* (1504) with reliefs by Tommaso Flamberti (right aisle); Romanesque *crucifix* (end of the left aisle); *Cappella della Madonna del Fuoco* (left aisle), 1619 – 36, by Dom. Paganelli, with late 18C *marble decoration*, *ceiling fresco* (1681–1706) by Carlo Cignani and early 14C *Madonna* (one of the first of woodcuts) on the altar.

Istituti Culturali e Artistici del Comune (Corso della Repubblica 30): A building from the first half of the 18C, with a façade dating from 1827. Exhibits from the Renaissance and the baroque: *sarcophagus of Marcolino Amanni* (1458) by Antonio and Bernardo Rossellino. 2 *Dutch tapestries* (late 15C), to designs by Wolgemut and Dürer. *Christ's Nativity* and *Christ on the Mount of Olives* by Fra Angelico. In the same building: *Galleria d'Arte Moderna, Galleria delle Ceramiche, Museo Etnografico Romagnolo,* and the interesting *Museo Archeologico.*

S. Maria dei Servi (Piazza G.B. Morgagni): Originally a building from the 2nd

Fontanellato, castle, room of Diana

half of the 12C, rebuilt in 1645; it was given its present form in 1750. Notable features: *tomb of Numai* with reliefs (1502) by Giovanni Ricci (beginning of right aisle); 15C *choir stalls* (sanctuary). *Fresco of the Crucifixion* (1st half of the 14C), ascribed to Giuliano da Rimini; *Madonna* (2nd half of 14C) by Guglielmo Organi and *wall paintings* (late 13–17C, all in the chapter-house, end of the left aisle).

Chiesa del Carmine (Corso Mazzini): Completely redesigned by Merenda in 1735. The *marble portal* (1464–5) by Marco Cedrini was moved here from the cathedral in 1915. The campanile, begun in 1498, is decorated with ornamental terracottas. Inside there are good 17&18C paintings.

Also worth seeing: *Palazzo del Municipio* (Piazza Aurelio Saffi), 1359, with a portico dating from 1459 and a façade of 1826. *Palazzo del Podestà* (Piazza Aurelio Saffi), built by Riceputi in 1459-60, and restored in 1912 and 1926. *Chiesa della Trinità* (Piazza Melozzo degli Ambrogi), built 1782–8 on the site of an earlier building dating back to the 4C. *Rocca di Ravaldino* (Via della Rocca), built from 1472–82. *S.*

Biagio (Piazzetta S.Biagio), with paintings by Palmezzano and Guido Reni.

Environs: *S.Maria delle Grazie di Fornò*, begun in 1450 and drastically restored in 1853-7. Gothic statue of the Madonna, remains of the original paintings of 1500. On the altar is the Byzantine icon. Behind the altar is a marble *Trinity* in relief attributed to A.Rossellino. *S. Maria in Acquedotto:* This building, restored from 1925-34, was erected in the 12C, on the site of a Byzantine basilica. The campanile is *c.* 1300.

Fornovo di Taro 43045
Parma/Emilia-Romagna   p. 412□ E 5

Parish Church/Assunta: Built in the 11C, probably on the remains of a Roman basilica. There are interesting remains of sculptures on the façade (Romanesque sculptures and 2 reliefs from the 13C), on the portal of the right side, and in a niche on an apse (13C *pilgrim*). Inside: note the marble relief of the *Life of St.Margaret*, from the first half of the 13C, by a follower

Forlì, picture gallery, tomb by Rossellino

of Benedetto Antelami; *Cappella della Madonna* (1626), with paintings and stucco.

Environs: Torrechiara: The castle was built in 1448–60 and its rooms are decorated with fine 14–16C and 18C paintings.

Fossa 67020
L'Aquila/Abruzzi   p.414□I 9

S.Maria ad Cryptas (or delle Grotte): Outside the town. Built in the second half of the 13C on Cistercian lines (i.e. with a square end to the choir, tunnel-vaulted nave, groin-vaulted choir). Inside is a 13C fresco cycle: beginning at the choir arch on the left of the nave is a series of *scenes from the New Testament,* and on the right, *Old Testament scenes.* On the W. wall is the *Last Judgement,* and in the choir, *Christ's Passion and Apostles.* The New Testament cycle commencing with the *Epiphany* was added in the 15C.

Also worth seeing: The parish church of *S.Assunta* has a 14C tabernacle, frescos

from *c.* 1500 and a processional cross dated 1557.

Fossacesia 66022
Chieti/Abruzzi   p.416□K 9

Environs: *S. Giovanni in Venere:* This monastery flourished in the Middle Ages. The church, dedicated to John the Baptist, was built in the 8C on the ruins of a temple to Venus Conciliatrix and rebuilt in 1165. In the lunette of the main portal (1225–30) is *Christ between the Virgin and John the Baptist,* and on the side portal are *David, Zachariah,* a *Visitation* and *John the Baptist before Herod.* The inside has a pointed arch tunnel vault, and in the side apses are frescos by Luca di Pallustro (1190).

Fossano 12045
Cuneo/Piedmont   p.412□B

The town was founded by the Guelph party in 1236. It fell to Savoy in 1314. The birthplace of the painter Bergognone (Am

Forlì, S.Mercuriale. Right: picture gallery, Mount of Olives by Beato Angelico

brogio da Fossano), the most important exponent of Lombard painting before Leonardo da Vinci.

Castello dei Principi d'Acaja (Piazza Castello): Built in 1314; a square medieval castle with four corner towers.

S.Maria Nascente e S.Giovenale (Via Roma): The cathedral was built by Mario Ludovico Quarini in 1778–91.

SS.Trinità (Piazza dei Battuti Rossi): Built by Francesco Gallo in 1730–8. The single-aisled church is decorated with baroque frescos and has a fine campanile.

Fossanova 04010
Latina/Latium   p.414 □ I 10

Abbazia di Fossanova: Formerly a Cistercian abbey. The church is the first and the most important example of Cistercian-Gothic in Italy. The abbey was founded by the Benedictines in the 9C and taken over by the Cistercians in 1133. The church was begun in 1187, probably by

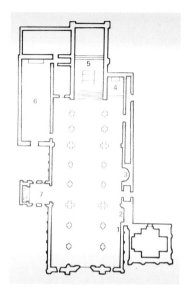

Forlì, S. Mercuriale 1 Crucifixion, c. 1500, by Palmezzano **2** tomb of Barbara Manfredi (d. 1466) **3** Sacra Conversazione by Palmezzano **4** Cappella di S. Mercuriale, 1598 **5** choir stalls, 1532–5 **6** chapel of the sacrament **7** 1st side chapel

Fossacesia, S. Giovanni

masons from the mother house of Clairvaux in Burgundy; it was consecrated by Innocent III in 1208. The monastery (the church was used as a stable from 1812 onwards) was transferred by Leo XII to the monks of Trisulti in 1826, and finally to the Franciscan order. Thomas Aquinas died here on 7.3.1274, on his way from Naples to the Council of Lyons.

Monastery church: The ascetic rules of building applied by the Cistercians gave rise to an architecture whose beauty derives from clear design and harmonious proportions. Both outside and inside, the church of Fossanova is the classic example of the early Gothic Cistercian architectural style. *Outside:* Basilican design with towering nave, is clearly revealed by the simple *façade.* The staggered portal, with its columns and the tympanum consisting of a semicircular window above a door lintel decorated with Cosmati work, has a frame resembling an aedicule. The top storey is dominated by the massive rose-window. *Inside:* Despite the clearly discernible Gothic design, the massiveness of the structural elements gives an impression of Romanesque severity. The nave and two aisles are separated by massive pillars; the dividing arches are borne by semi- columns with crocket capitals.

Monastery building: Except for the S. side, which was rebuilt in 1280–1300 in elegant Gothic forms with the assistance of Roman stonemasons, the capitals in the cloister display typical Burgundian forms of the transitional period between the Romanesque and the Gothic. Opposite the entrance is the *refectory,* a single-aisled room which is supported by 5 arches and has a staircase leading to the *dormitory.* On the E. flank is the splendid, almost square *chapterhouse.* To the E. of the monastery is the *pilgrims' hostel,* with the room where Thomas Aquinas died.

Fossombrone 61034
Pesaro and Urbino/Marches   p.414☐H 6

The ancient *Forum Sempronii.*

Cathedral of S. Maurenzio: Altered in baroque style in 1772–84. In the *canons' sacristy,* a relief of the *Madonna and Saints* by Domenico Rosselli (1480) survives from the altar of the old building. There is a *Madonna with Saints* by Taddeo Zuccari in the *Oratorio della Grotta* underneath the church.

Corte Alta: This castle above the town was extended in 1464–70 on the instructions of Federico di Montefeltro. Inside: an old *theatre* and the *Museo Civico Vernarecca* (paintings, drawings).

Cittadella: This five-storeyed building above the castle has a chapel with 15C frescos.

Also worth seeing: *Palazzo Vescovile:* In the chapel is a *Crucifixion,* a fresco dating from 1493; Palazzo Comunale. *Palazzo Albani* or *Corte Rossa* (town house). Both 16C.

Environs: Furlo: The abbey of *S. Vincenzo al Furlo* was founded in the 8C. In 1271 a new church was built, the first bay and the right aisle of which have not survived. The *Galleria del Furlo* is a tunnel built by the Emperor Vespasian in AD 76/7.

Frascati 00044
Rome/Latium   p.414☐H 10

Frascati dates from 1191, when the neighbouring town of Tusculum (see Environs) was destroyed by order of Pope Celestine III. Its expelled inhabitants settled around the churches of S.Maria and S.Sebastiano. The town wall was built in the 14C. The villas which make Frascati famous date from two different phases of construction, one Mannerist (2nd half of the 16C) and one baroque (1st half of the 17C). The *Villa Aldobrandini* should not be missed not only is it easily accessible but it is also particularly beautiful. Although the repu

Fossanova, abbey cloister.

Frascati, Villa Aldobrandini

Frascati, abbey

tation of Frascati is based mainly on the villas in the environs, the following are also well worth a visit.

Cathedral of San Pietro: Nave and two aisles, built by Girolamo Fontana in 1698 –1700 on a Greek cross ground plan. The interior decoration is by Carlo Rainaldi and Prospero de Rocchi. Near the main entrance is the *Monument to Charles Edward Stuart* (1788); on the third altar on the right is a *Virgin of the Rosary* in the manner of Domenichino; the second altar on the left is a *baroque altar with a 14C panel of the Madonna.*

Chiesa del Gesù: This single-aisled Jesuit church has an elegant façade faced in travertine and attributed to Pietro da Cortona. Inside, a white marble strip leads up to a black marble disc, from which point the false dome painted by Antario Colli should be viewed. The frescos by the three altars and in the sanctuary are by A. Pozzo.

Town park: Formerly the park of the Villa Torlonia, destroyed by bombing in 1943/4; the casino has survived. The park contains a series of fountains, the *Teatro delle Acque.*

Villa Aldobrandini (or **Belvedere**): Building was begun in 1598 by Giacomo della Porta, and completed after his death by Carlo Maderno in 1602–4. The work was carried out rapidly, and the most important architects of the time were employed. As a result, the villa became the model for other ones around Frascati. The gardens are crossed by a strictly arranged pattern of paths. The exedra of the nymphaeum is cut into the side of the hill and has apse-like niches containing statues. The central niche has a figure of Atlas. There is a garden room on the left of the nymphaeum and a chapel of St. Sebastian on the right, as well as frescos by Domenichino.

Capuchin Monastery of S. Francesco (1575) with the painting of *St. Francis Receiving the Stigmata* by Paolo Brill.

To the left of the Via Car. Massaia is the **Villa Lancellotti** (Piccolomini): a typical villa in a valley, the park landscape blending with the architecture. Two inside rooms have ceiling paintings by Annibale Carracci; nymphaeum of 1620.

Villa Falconieri: The first of Frascati's villas. Built by Alessandro Ruffini in 1545–8. The *casino* was enlarged by Francesco Borromini for the Falconieri, from 1650 onwards. The inside is richly decorated with *frescos* by Carlo Maratta and others. The *lion gate*, attributed to Borromini, leads to the pool with cypresses, which A. Böcklin used as a motif on several occasions.

Villa Mondragone: Built by Martino Longhi the Elder in 1573–5 and 1577 for Cardinal Marcus Sitticus of Hohenems. Gregory XIII, a friend of the Cardinal's, frequently stayed here. It was here that the Pope, on 13.2.1582, sanctioned the Gregorian calendar named after him. The magnificent but ruined nymphaeum is by Fontana.

Other villas: *Villa Vecchia* (mid 16C; acquired by Cardinal M. Sitticus of Hohenems in 1567 and rebuilt by Vignola). *Villa Borghese:* built in 1604/5 on the lines of Mondragone. *Villa Torlonia:* The nymphaeum, whose basic features have survived, is a masterpiece by Maderno. *Villa Grazioli:* Frescos by Domenichino, Annibale Carracci and the Zuccari circle of artists.

Environs: Tusculum (*c.* 6 km.): Telegonus, the son of Circe and Odysseus, is the legendary founder. The name, however, suggests an Etruscan origin. Cicero, Lucullus, Caesar, Tiberius and others had property here. The Counts of Tusculum (10–12C) dominated Rome, and many of them became Popes. The town was completely destroyed under Pope Celestine III in 1191. The *ancient ruins* (amphitheatre, foundations of Tiberius's villa, the water

pipes and cisterns and the well-preserved Greek theatre) bear witness to the town's great past. **Grottaferrata** (*c.* 6 km. away): *Abbazia di Grottaferrata*, establishment of the Greek Basilian monks, founded by St. Nilus in 1004. The builder was St. Bartholomew, a pupil of St. Nilus. The early Romanesque church has a nave and two aisles and was consecrated by Pope John XIX in 1025. It was in 1473, under Cardinal Giuliano Della Rovere, that Giuliano da Sangallo fortified it as a castle. Magnificent 12C *campanile*. *Church of S. Maria:* The pronaos has a Byzantine-style *marble portal* with a pair of intarsia doors from the late 11C. Tympanum with mosaic of Christ between the Virgin and John the Baptist. The *font* is borne by four winged lions (10&11C) and is decorated with reliefs. The interior is 18C baroque. There are fragments of a Cosmati work floor. The wall with the triumphal arch has a mosaic of Pentecost and above it are remains of frescos from the same period (13C). *Cappella di San Nilo:* with frescos by Domenichino (1609/10; life of St. Nilus and St. Bartholomew). The altarpiece of the chapel is by Annibale Carracci. *Museum:* archaeological finds (Attic tomb stele from the 5C BC with a youth reading; stole of the Eastern church, with depiction of the life of Christ in silk interwoven with gold threads). **Rocca di Papa** (*c.* 12 km.): Highest of the Castelli Romani, at the foot of Monte Cavo. Mentioned as a Papal castle in 1181. The church of *Santa Maria Assunta* (1664–1753) was rebuilt in 1815–45 after an earthquake: the altarpiece in the right transept is by C. Giaquinto (1739); the plaster model of the marble Pietà in the cathedral is in Münster is by G. Th. Achtermann. **Marino** (*c.* 10 km.): This little town above the northern shore of the Lake Albano is known for its full-bodied wines. It was built in the vicinity of the ancient *Castrimoenium*, and can be traced back to the 11C. Held by the Colonna from 1419 onwards. The interior of the church of *Madonna del Rosario* (1713), a building reminiscent of 17C northern Italian architecture, is notable. There is also the late Renaissance church of *Santa Maria delle Grazie* with the altarpiece depicting *St. Roch* (attributed to Domenichino). The

Fountain of the Four Moors on the Piazza del Plebescito (1642) commemorates the battle of Lepanto, at which Marc Antonio Colonna was in charge of the Papal fleet.

Fratta Polesine 45025

Rovigo/Veneto   p.410☐G 4

Villa Badoer: This splendid villa was built in 1568-70 by Andrea Palladio, the important and highly influential architect from Padua. The raised central section is preceded by a *portico* and stands at the top of a large flight of steps. Colonnades on the right and left lead to the annexes at the sides. Finally, there are two fountains with figures. Inside are parts of frescos by Giallo Fiorentino.

Also worth seeing: Parish church of *SS. Pietro e Paolo* (1552, rebuilt in 1682); very fine 18C interior decoration. *Villa Bragadin-Mischiatti* (not far from the Villa Badoer): a very beautiful villa in Palladian style.

Gaeta 04024
Latina/Latium   p.416☐ 11

Cathedral of SS.Erasmo e Marziano:
Rebuilt several times; all that survives of
the original bishop's church from the 11C
is the magnificent *campanile*. It has a massive basement storey with monolithic
columns and Roman remains. The three
upper storeys have slender two-arched
openings by Nicola di Angelo, a Roman
marble craftsman (1148–74). Beneath the
ornate top of the tower there are blind arcades. Inside, the most important feature
is the *marble Easter candlestick* in the form
of a column—11 ft. 6 ins. tall, it has reliefs
of the life of Christ and St.Erasmus. At the
high altar is the *Banner of the battle of
Lepanto* (1570). To the right of the high
altar is the *Martyrdom of St.Erasmus,* by
C.Saraceni. There is a *bronze pulpit* (1692)
in the richly stuccoed and decorated 17C
crypt. *Diocesan museum:* Fine fragments of
an ambo from the old cathedral; 11C *exultet roll; Pietà* by Quentin Massys;
Madonna with Saints by Seb. Conca.

The **medieval quarter** extends between
the cathedral and the church of **S.
Catarina** (with a painting of the *Madonna
del Silenzio* by Luca Giordano in the sanctuary, on the left).

Chiesa dell' Annunziata: Dates in its
present form from the 17C, although the
portal on the left side, and the structure of
the single-aisled interior survive from the
original building of 1320. Lavish baroque
decoration: the first altar on the right has
a *Nativity of Christ,* and the first on the left
has a *Crucifixion* by Luca Giordano. The
choir has an *Epiphany* and a *Presentation
of Christ in the Temple* by Seb. Conca.

Castle: 8C; extended and enlarged by
Frederick II (1227), Charles II of Anjou
(1289), Alfonso I of Aragon and Charles V
(1536). It consists of two massive, towered
blocks, the upper one is the *Castello
Aragonese,* and the lower is the *C.Angioino.*

Torre d'Orlando: High up on Monte
Orlando. It is the tomb of Lucius Munatius
Plancus, one of Caesar's most important
commanders in Gaul. The monument (22
BC) consists of a round arch 46 ft. tall, 305
ft. in circumference, faced in travertine,
and crowned with a Doric frieze.

The **Mausoleum of Lucius Sem-
pronius Atratinus**, situated near to
Chiesa degli Scalzi, is similar in type to the
Torre d'Orlando. Atratinus (73–20 BC) was
the commander of the fleet of Mark Antony (38–4 BC), and consul in 34 BC.

Santuario della SS.Trinità (also known
as *della Montagna spaccata:* cracked mountain). Tradition has it that cracks appeared

as a result of the earthquake after Christ's crucifixion. The shrine, founded in the 9C, was soon visited by innumerable believers. There are several paintings by Seb. Conca in the adjoining Benedictine monastery. Near to the shrine are the remains of the *villa of Lucius Munatius Plancus* (cisterns).

Environs: Fórmia (*c.* 6 km.): One of the most important stations on the ancient Via Appia. It is famous for being the site of Cicero's villa. The ancient monument, about 2.5 km. outside Fórmia in the direction of Itri, is thought to be the *Tomba di Cicero* (Cicero's tomb). **Itri** (*c.* 11 km.): Picturesque little town overlooked by an interesting ruined castle. **Sperlonga:** Picturesque little fishing town on the site of the Greek settlement of *Amynklai*. The Roman villa of *Ad speluncas* (grottoes) gave the town its present name. It was on the instructions of Emperor Tiberius that the Greek sculptors Athanodorus, Hagesandros and Polydoros (famous for their Laocoön in the Vatican) built a natural theatre in the largest grotto in AD 4 – 26. The grotto villa of Tiberius was excavated after 1957. There are sculptures from the villa in the *national museum* within the villa precincts.

Galeata 47010

Forlì/Emilia-Romagna   p.414 ☐ G 6

Palazzo Polesterile, formerly **Palazzo Comunale** (Via Zannetti): At the right corner of the Palazzo façade there is a *column* with a Byzantine cross (probably 10C). The Palazzo houses the *Museo Civico Domenico Mambrini* with various exhibits: Prehistoric and Roman *(bronzes* and *ceramics),* Medieval and Modern objects and 15&16C *paintings.*

Abbazia di S.Ellero: The abbey on the nearby hill was founded by St.Ellero in the late 5C. The church was rebuilt in the 17C, but still preserves the Romanesque *portal* and some *sculptures* and *architectural remains* incorporated in the façade. The inside has notable 11&12C sculptures: *St. Ellero on horseback* (3rd altar on the left); *Madonna and Child* (2nd altar on the right) and a carved *marble sarcophagus* (in Byzantine style) of *St.Ellero* in the crypt.

Gallipoli 73014

Lecce/Apulia   p.418 ☐ P 12

Worth seeing: 17C baroque *cathedral,* with fine choir stalls by Antonietta da Pace; *castle,* 13–17C, just to the left of the bridge from the mainland; *Fontana Ellenistica* at the mainland end of the bridge, baroque fountain (1756) with three Hellenistic reliefs; *Town museum* (near the cathedral), with vases and other items.

Environs: *c.* 17 km. to the SE is **Casarano:** The *Chiesa di Casaranello* has a dome over the crossing and 5C Byzantine mosaics (key in the house beside the church). About 15 km. to the NE is **Galatone,** with the baroque church of *Santu-*

Gaeta, cathedral, Easter candlestick

Gaeta, 'Annunciation' by Giovanni da Gaeta (Diocesan Museum)

IHESIC FRI IVILANVS BORCA PRIOR
MARIE INPENSVIS PAIR STA
II M CCCC VI DIE XXV

STA MARGARITA STA CATE

Nardo (Gallipoli), Osanna

Villa in Lazise (Garda)

ario del Crocifisso. About 20 km. to the N is **Nardo** with a 12C Romanesque-Gothic *cathedral* and the 16C church of S. Domenico with a Hosanna (1603). Some 25 km. to the NE is **Galatina,** with the late 14C *S. Caterina di Alessandria*: a Gothic Franciscan church with a Romanesque portal and 15C frescos.

Gandino 24024
Bergamo/Lombardy   p.412☐E 3

Basilica of S.Maria Assunta: Originally built in 1423, rebuilt by G.Maria Bettera di Gandino in the 2nd half of the 17C. Basilican ground plan with centralized features; richly decorated. Note the use of local stone in the building. The *portal* dates from 1712. There is a 14C *font* in the modern baptistery to the right of the church.

Museo della Basilica: Built in 1928 in order to house the basilica's rich treasure (Flemish tapestries, vestments, the 15C cross of Matrenyanos de Filippis).

Garda 37016
Verona/Veneto   p.410☐E 3

This, the main town on the E. shore of Lake Garda, shelters at the head of a bay. The winding streets of the *old town,* with the remains of the old town fortifications, are worth looking round, as is the parish church of **S.Maria Maggiore** (one nave, two aisles), with Roman and Lombard decorative panels on the outside. Note also the Venetian **Palazzo del Capitano** (in the harbour square) and the Camaldolensian monastery of *Eremo,* situated above the town on the site of the medieval castle *(Rocca).*

Lazise (Garda), Scaliger castle

Environs: At the N. end of the bay of Garda is the romantic **Cape of S. Vigilio** with the *Villa Guarienti* (1570). *c.* 8 km. to the N. is **Torri del Benaco,** with an early medieval castle. Some 28 km. to the N. is **Malcésine,** in a magnificent location with an old *Scaliger castle* (13/14C). About 4 km. to the S. is **Bardolino** with the Romanesque churches of *S. Severo* (11C) and *S. Zeno* (9C). *c.* 9 km. to the S. is **Lazise** with a 13C *Scaliger castle* and a well-preserved surrounding wall. About 18 km. to the S. is **Peschiera del Garda,** with a massive *fort* from the Venetian period, enlarged by the Austrians in the 19C.

Gardone Riviera 25083
Brescia / Lombardy   p.412☐ E 3

Vittoriale: A complex of several buildings and gardens. It was built for Gabriele d'An-

nunzio, the poet, writer and war hero. The idea of the 19C artist's villa was here taken up anew and given an unorthodox interpretation. There are a number of notable battle trophies, apart from the thousands of *objets d'art*. The poet is buried in the *mausoleum.*

Gavi 15066
Alessandria / Piedmont   p. 412☐ C 5

S. Giacomo: This Romanesque parish church, built from 1172 onwards, has a nave, two aisles, and a deeply set portal with a *Last Supper* on the architrave. The inside has beautiful Romanesque columns with richly carved capitals.

The castle: A massive Genoese fortress, built in 1626–39.

Gela 93012

Caltanissetta/Sicily   p. 420☐K 18

Gela is one of the oldest Greek colonies in
Sicily. Founded by people from Rhodes
and Crete in 688 BC, it enjoyed a heyday
under the tyrant Hippocrates (498–491
BC) but it was later surpassed by Syracuse.
It was destroyed by Carthage in 405 BC,
and in 1233 Frederick II Hohenstaufen re-
founded it as 'Terranova', its name until
1927.

Greek town fortifications (in the W. of
the town, off via Corso Vitt. Emanuele and
Via Mazzini): Remains in good condition:
walls from the late 5C BC are up to 26 ft.
high and originally extended 12 km. Uncovered in 1949–54, they consist of carefully dressed limestone tufa blocks with
rounded edges. After destruction at the
hands of the Carthaginians in 405 BC,
bricks were used to repair it in the 4C BC.

Museo Nazionale (Corso Vitt.
Emanuele): Houses *finds from the excavations* at *Gela* and the *Prov. Caltinissetta* (terracottas, vases, bronze statues and a

valuable coin collection). Some *Silenus
masks* in red clay (5C BC) are particularly
worth seeing. To the S.of the museum (site
of the ancient acropolis) are the remains of
two *Doric temples* (5C BC), one column of
which has been re-erected). There are also
remains of *houses* from the 4C BC standing
on older prehistoric shrines and dwellings.

Also worth seeing: *Chiesa Matrice*
(Piazza Umberto I), 1766–94, with neoclas-
sical façade dating from 1844; remains of
Hellenistic *baths* from the 4C BC.

Environs: *c.* 14 km. to the N., at the foot
of **Monte Disueri,** is the island's second
largest *Siculian burial ground.* About 21
km. to the NW is **Butera** with a large
burial ground (prehistoric to Hellenistic;
finds in Gela), and an 11C Norman *castle.*
21 km. to the E. is the 14C **castle of Fal-
conara.**

Gemona del Friuli 33013

Udine/Friuli   p.410☐H 2

During the Middle Ages, Gemona was in-

Gardone Riviera, Vittoriale

dependent but subject to the overlordship of the Patriarch of Aquileia; from 1420 onwards it belonged to Venice. The town, at the centre of the terrible earthquake of 1976, was severely damaged. Of the once-famous **Cathedral of S.Maria Assunta** (Via G.Bini), only the foundations still remain. Begun in the 13C, it was consecrated in 1337. There were notable Romanesque sculptures on the façade. Particularly interesting features inside were a carved *antependium* by A.Moranzone (1391), the remains of a Roman *tomb altar from Aquileia* and a *bell* from 1423. Also worth seeing the Renaissance **Palazzo del Comune** (Piazza del Municipio), built in 1502, with a fine façade.

Environs: *c.* 3 km. to the W. is **Osoppo,** also devastated in 1976. There was a beautiful *altarpiece* (Madonna enthroned) by Pellegrino da S. Daniele, dating from 1494/5, in the church of S.Maria di Neves. About 8 km. to the N. is **Venzone,** also a victim of the 1976 earthquake. The chief object of interest was the 13/14C *Cathedral of S.Andrea* (Piazzetta del Duomo): Outside, the late Romanesque *reliefs* on the portals were particularly fine. Opposite the

Gemona, cathedral (before the earthquake)

cathedral, note the *Cappella di S.Michele* of 1250 (inside, 22 mummified corpses), and, on the Piazza Municipio, the *Palazzo Comunale* (built in 1400) has fine windows. Some 10 km. to the SE is **Tarcento,** damaged in the earthquake of 1976, with the 18C *Palazzo Frangipane* and the remains of the 13C *Castello di Coia.*

Genova/Genoa 16100
Genoa/Liguria   p.412☐ C 5

Genoa, the main town of the province, and also of the region of Liguria, is superbly situated on the Gulf of Genoa and, as 'Greater Genoa', it stretches for some 30 km., from Voltri to Nervi. There are seaside resorts on either side of the city. The *Riviera di Ponente* extends as far as Ventimiglia and the border with France and the *Riviera di Levante* reaches as far as La Spezia.

Genoa is an archepiscopal seat and, since 1812, has also had a university. However, its chief feature is that it is today the largest maritime and trading port in Italy and, together with Marseilles, it is the most important Mediterranean port. The oldest sections of the *Porto Vecchio* harbour basin were built in *c.* 1250. At its W. corner is the *Lanterna* (1543). This, the city's landmark, is the oldest surviving lighthouse (first mentioned in 1316) in Genoa.

History: Inhabited as early as the Ligurian period, when it was in contact with the Mediterranean peoples; it was enlarged into a Roman municipium after 205 BC. As a result of centuries of dispute (with the Saracens among others), Genoa increased its strength in the 12&13C and became a maritime power which participated both victoriously and profitably in the 1st Crusade. In 1284 it gained the upper hand over Pisa, its rival in the Tyrrhenian Sea. Genoa took possession of Corsica, Sardinia and Elba, declared some Greek islands (Rhodes, Samos, Lesbos and Chios) to be its principalities, and founded colonies on the Black Sea. The power of Venice also had to face the rivalry of Genoa but weakened by bitter and lasting feuds within its own walls, Genoa lost the naval battle of Chioggia to Venice in 1381. Genoa also lost important trading colonies and had to endure foreign rule (e.g. that of France). Under Andrea Doria the city experienced a new heyday (1528), but this was brought to an end by France (1684) and by Austria (1746), and then once again by France under Napoleon (1796). From 1815 onwards it was part of the kingdom of Sardinia, which was incorporated into the kingdom of Italy in 1860. During the Risorgimento Genoa was once again able to play a historically important role, in the form of the secret society of the 'Carbonari', which opposed the rule of the Habsburgs. The revolutionaries Mazzini and Garibaldi also operated here. The former city republic became part of the Republic of Italy in 1946.

Cathedral of S.Lorenzo: The black-and-white-striped marble façade shows Tuscan-Pisan influence, and is most impressive in its austerity. The three portals were not added until the 13C, and, together with the rose-window, they betray French Gothic influence. The *Martyrdom of St.Lawrence* is depicted in the architrave of the middle portal, while the tympanum shows a *Majestas Domini* with the symbols of the four Evangelists. On both sides of the door there are reliefs from *childhood of Christ* (left) and *tree of Jesse* (right). It was a bishop's church as early as 985. The façade was not completed until 1100, the portals were added later still; the campanile dates from 1522.

At the right corner of the façade there is a 13C figure which became famous under the name of *Arrotino* (knifegrinder). The dome over the crossing is by Galeazzo Alessi (1567). The solemn interior is divided into a nave and two aisles. The Gothic vaults are supported by richly decorated Corinthian columns. The contrast of black and white is continued inside. The frescos on the vaults above the high altar depict the *Last Judgement* and the *Martyrdom of St.Lawrence* (Lazzaro Tavarone, 1622). To the left of the sanctuary is the *Cappella Lercari* with an altar by Carlo Barabino and ceiling frescos by G.B.Castello; the wall frescos are by Luca Cambi-

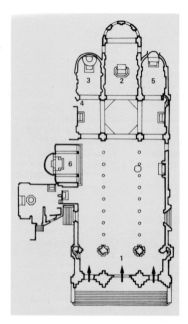

Genoa, Cattedrale di S. Lorenzo 1 portals 2 high altar / sanctuary 3 Cappella Lercari 4 entrance to the treasury 5 Cappella Senarega 6 Cappella di S. Giovanni Battista

aso (c. 1560). The entrance to the treasury is to the side of this chapel. In the right side apse, also known as the *Cappella Senarega*, are frescos by Giovanni Andrea Carlone showing *scenes from the life of S.Sebastian* (c. 1560); there is also the *Crucifixion with the Virgin Mary, St.John and St.Sebastian,* a brilliant painting by Federico Barocci (1596). Particularly beautiful is the **Cappella di S.Giovanni Battista,** where the ashes of the 'Baptist' are preserved. The chapel was built by Elia and Giovanni Gaggini in 1451-65, and a conspicuous feature is its glorious marble front. It also houses excellent sculptures by Andrea Sansovino (*Madonna, John the Baptist,* 1504). The **treasury** has some sumptuous works, Byzantine gold pieces such as the *Zaccaria Cross,* the *cope of Pope Gelasius* (1118), and the famous *Sacro Catrino,* a vessel made of Roman glass (1C).

SS.Ambrogio e Andrea (also known as *Chiesa del Gesù;* Piazza Matteotti): The Jesuit building (1589–1606) replaced a very old church which was used by Milanese bishops as an alternative church in the 6&7C. Apart from the beautiful *wall and ceiling frescos* by Giovanni Carlone, the richly stuccoed interior (one nave, two aisles) also has some fine paintings: *Assumption of the Virgin* by Guido Reni, *Circumcision* (high altar) by P.P.Rubens, and *St.Ignatius healing a man possessed*, also by P.P.Rubens (1620; one of his masterpieces).

SS.Annunziata del Vastato (Piazza della Nunziata): This church was originally built in the 13C and rebuilt between 1591 and 1620 with the assistance of the Genoese Lomellini family. The magnificent building, in typically Genoese baroque style, is richly decorated inside. In 1843 an elegant neoclassical colonnaded portico was added to designs by Carlo Barabino. The basilican interior, with its nave and two aisles, is magnificently stuccoed and has frescos by G.B. and G.Carlone. It is probably the city's most brilliant church interior. There are numerous pictures by famous artists such as Luca Cambiaso, Bernardo Strozzi and Giov. Andrea Ansaldo; particularly important are the *carved wooden groups of figures* by A.Maria Maragliano, the Genoese artist.

SS. Cosma e Damiano: Genoese-Romanesque. The main points of interest here are the severe structure (1188) and the equally severe interior.

S.Donato (Piazza S.Donato): This church, in a purely Romanesque style, is one of the city's oldest (12C). The building was enlarged in the 13C. The tall *octagonal tower* is of particular interest. Inside, at the end of the left aisle, is a triptych by Joos van Cleve (1485).

S. Giovanni di Prè (Piazza della Commenda: entrance from the Salita S. Giovanni): There was a church on this site as early as the 7C. Until 1098, it contained the ashes of John the Baptist, which are now in the cathedral. This severe Romanesque-Gothic church from the 12C was altered several times before being restored in 1870. The extensive interior, with its nave and two aisles, has an *oratory*, also with a nave and two aisles, which is of interest.

Genoa, SS.Annunziata del Vastato, dome

Campanile of S.Agostino

S.Maria Assunta di Carignano

S.Maria Assunta di Carignano (Piazza Carignano): This very fine building, with its central dome and the towers above the façade, was begun by Galeazzo Alessi in 1552 and completed in 1603. From here there is a particularly fine view of the city.

S.Maria di Castello (reached by going up the *Salita di S.Maria di Castello* from the Piazza Embriace with the interesting 12C *Torre degli Embriaci*): The church stands on older foundations and was built as a basilica. Altered in the 12C using some of the old parts. In 1442 it passed to the Dominicans, who were responsible for some of the extremely rich decoration inside, particularly the paintings by Pier Francesco Sacchi (3rd chapel on the right) and Giovanni Mazone (3rd chapel on the left). There are some fine wooden sculptures by Leonardo Riccomanni (1452) on the door of the sacristy. From here the visitor passes into the interesting 15&16C

Dominican convent, with its three cloisters and frescos. There is a small *museum* with works by Lodovico Brea, L.Riccomanni and Maragliano and frescos by Justus von Ravensburg and C.Braccesco (15C).

S.Matteo (Piazza S.Matteo): Romanesque-Gothic church, with a beautiful black-and-white-striped façade from the 13C. Built by Martino Doria in 1125. Inscriptions on the white marble strips on the front commemorate this family's glorious deeds. The brilliantly stuccoed interior (one nave, two aisles) has marble columns and is still purely Gothic in its architecture. At the high altar is the *sword of Andrea Doria*, and in the crypt is his *tomb*, designed by Giov. Angelo Montorsoli (16C). There is a charming little cloister (1310) on the left of the church.

S.Siro (Via S.Siro): The eventful history of this ancient church began in the late 4C

Villa Bombrini, 16C

when it became Genoa's first cathedral. From the 10C onwards, S.Lorenzo became the city's main church. S. Siro was the property of the Benedictines in the early 11C, and in 1575 it passed to the Theatines who rebuilt it in 1586-1613. The right portal in the façade dates from the 16C. The inside, which is richly decorated with frescos, is baroque and has paintings of the Ligurian and Genoese school.

S. Stefano (Piazza di S. Stefano): This church is one of the oldest in Genoa (12C), but was severely damaged during World War 2. The crypt, which is divided into a small nave and four small aisles, is even older (*c*. 10C). Christopher Columbus was baptized in the church. A rose-window above the portal of the particularly tall façade admits light to the interior. The raised *sanctuary* is a rare feature for a Genoese religious building. There is an excellent *choir-gallery* by Donato Benti and Benedetto da Rovezzano (1499) on the inside wall of the façade. Of the numerous paintings, a large panel by Giulio Romano deserves particular attention.

The Via Garibaldi and its palaces: This narrow street is one of the most beautiful streets in Italy. Known as the 'Street of Palaces', it is also one of the city's finest sights. It was formerly called *Via Aurea* and was built in 1550 to plans by Galeazzo Alessi. Starting at the W. side of the *Piazza Fontane Marose* (q.v.), it is lined by the following buildings: *Palazzo Cambiaso* (No.1) by G.Alessi (1565), today the seat of the Bank of Naples. *Palazzo Gambaro* (No.2), fine portal to designs by Giovanni Ponzello (1565). *Palazzo Parodi* (No.3), an elegant loggia and interesting frescos, by Franco Lercari (1567-81). *Palazzo Correga-Cataldi* (No.4) by Giov. Battista Castello (1558), seat of the Genoa Chamber of Commerce; richly gilded and stuccoed gallery by

Lorenzo De Ferrari. *Palazzo Spinola* (No.5), second half of the 16C; notable frescos by Calvi and Lazzaro Tavarone; today it is the seat of the Banca d'America e d'Italia. *Palazzo Doria* (No.6) by G.B.Castello (1563). Its façade dates from the 17C. Inside is a very fine marble fireplace, also designed by Castello. *Palazzo Podestà* (No.7), designed by G.B.Castello (1583); a fine inner courtyard. *Palazzo Cattaneo Adorno* (Nos.8 – 10), double portal from the late 16C. No.10 has fine frescos by L.Tavarone.

Palazzo Doria Tursi or **Palazzo Municipale** (No.9). Begun by Rocco Lurago in 1564. Since 1848 it has been the city hall. A majestic building, its *portico* has five large frescos by L.Tavarone. In the *Sala del Consiglio Generale* there is a fresco by Francesco Gandolfi (1862) showing Columbus at the Spanish court after the discovery of America. The *Sala del Sindaco* has a famous *bronze tablet* with a Roman inscription (117 BC) and *3 letters by Columbus*. The *Sala Rossa* has 17C Flemish tapestries to designs by Jordaens, and also the *Guarneri violin* of Niccolò Paganini.

Palazzo Bianco (No.11): Built in 1565 by

G.Orsolino and D.Ponzello. Rebuilt and enlarged in 1711 and restored after 1942, it gives a good impression of Genoese baroque. Since 1884, the palace has housed the *Galleria di Palazzo Bianco*, one of the city's most important collections of paintings. The main focus is on the painters of the Genoese and Ligurian school (15-17C). There are also some fine works by Filippino Lippi, Giovanni Pisano, Veronese, Palma il Vecchio, Pontormo; painters of the Spanish school, Murillo and Zurbarán; as well as Flemish artists such as van Dyck, Rubens, van der Goes, G.David, Metsys and others.

Palazzo Rosso (No.18): This magnificent building belonging to the Brignole-Sale family was built by the Lombard architect Matteo Lagomaggiore in 1671 – 7; completely restored in 1953-60. The important collection of paintings *(Galleria di Palazzo Rosso)* takes up some 100 rooms. The gallery also houses prints, drawings, coins, small sculptures, a collection of maps, as well as an important ceramics collection (with examples by Albisola and Savona), and a collection of cribs with wooden figures, mainly Genoese from the (17&18C).

Palazzo Durazzo Pallavicini

The Via Balbi and its palaces: The Via Garibaldi ends at the *Piazza della Meridiana*. The *Palazzo della Meridiana* (No.1) and the *Palazzo Brignole* (No.2) stand on this square and the Via Cairoli (1778) leads from it to the Via Balbi, also lined by palaces. One of the finest is the **Palazzo Durazzo Pallavicini** (No.1), begun by Bartolomeo Bianco in 1618. This magnificent though severe building is enlivened by a tall portal decorated with coats of arms, balconies and arcades. The solemn impression is intensified by a splendid staircase with columns (outer courtyard). The brilliantly furnished halls (17&18C) have beautiful paintings by Rubens, van Dyck, Tintoretto, Veronese, Ribera, Guercino, Segantini, Strozzi, Perin del Vaga and others; there are also ceramics and porcelain.

Palazzo dell'Università (No.5): An impressive building to plans by B.Bianco (1634–6). The Jesuits taught philosophy and philology here; the Medical Faculty was added in 1682. The palace possesses what is probably the most beautiful courtyard and garden in Genoa. Some outstanding works of art include the *six allegorical bronze statues* (1579) by Giambologna in the *Aula Magna*—these were formerly part of the tomb of Luca Grimaldi. The richly furnished *university library* is housed in the former church of *SS. Gerolamo e Francesco Saverio*, nearby, which has excellent frescos by Domenico Piola in the former sanctuary. The library has over 350,000 volumes, over 1,000 early printed works and some 3,000 manuscripts.

Palazzo Reale (No.10): Built by Giov. Angelo Falcone and Pier Franc. Cantone towards the middle of the 17C. Carlo Fontana made major alterations in 1705 when the building took on its present appearance. Originally in the possession of the Balbi family, it passed to the Durazzo family, became a royal residence in 1824, and today houses a splendid collection of paintings, in the unique state-rooms (Reni, Guercino, van Dyck, Giordano, Roos, Guidobono, Strozzi and others). The *Galleria degli Specchi* is outstanding. It is frescoed throughout by Domenico Parodi and contains *The Rape of Proserpine,* a virtuoso marble group by Franc. Schiaffino. There is a fine *Crucified Christ* by van Dyck in the *Saletta dei Fiamminghi.* The

Palazzo Municipale

Palazzo S. Giorgio

Palazzo Rosso, Sala della Primavera

complex also includes the garden, which has a view of the harbour, and the *Teatro Falcone* which was totally destroyed in 1944 and has been rebuilt in modern style.

Other palaces and museums: Palazzo Doria Pamphilj (Piazza Principe): This enormous complex is a combination of two buildings and was intended as a counterpart to the showpiece of the rival Fieschi family in Carignano. Andrea Doria acquired the existing buildings in 1521 and had them decorated by Perin del Vaga, a pupil of Raphael, and by Giov. Angelo Montorsoli (work continued until 1547). The *Loggia degli Eroi* (with portraits of the Doria family) and the *Sala dei Giganti* are outstanding – both are richly decorated throughout with frescos by del Vaga. The palace is adjoined by a beautiful *garden*, laid out to plans by Giov. Ponsello and enlivened by two 16C fountains. Charles V (1533), Napoleon (1805), and later Vittorio Emanuele I and Giuseppe Verdi (1877), stayed in this palace as guests.

Palazzo Ducale (Piazza Matteotti): The former residence of the Doges is particularly attractive for its elegant façade with well-balanced arrangement of columns and two fine inner courtyards (in the right-hand one there is an elegant *fountain* by Giov. Mazetti, 1642). The palace had to be restored in the early 19C as a result of a fire in 1777.

Palazzo S.Giorgio (Piazza Caricamento): On a picturesque square, this interesting palace has an old, Gothic section, with fine three- and four-arched windows. Built in *c.* 1260; in 1571, rebuilt in Renaissance style. From 1407–1797, it was the seat of the powerful Banca di S.Giorgio.

Palazzo Spinola and the Galleria Nazionale di Palazzo Spinola (Piazza Pelliceria No.1): In the middle of the old town near the harbour. Formerly belonged to the Grimaldi. The 16C façade was rebuilt by the Spinolas in the 17C, and at the same time a rich collection of paintings was installed. Apart from the superb furnishings, attention should also be paid to the excellent frescos by Tavarone, De Ferrari and Galeotti. The numerous important paintings include *Madonna praying* by J.van Cleve, *Ecce homo* by Antonello da Messina, *Holy Family* by P.P.Rubens, and *Boy with dog* by A.van Dyck. There is a ceramics collection, most of which comes from Savona.

Museo di Architettura e Scultura Ligure (*S.Agostino*, Piazza Negri): 13C; former church with fine façade and campanile decorated with ceramics. Simon Boccanegra, the first Doge, was elected here in 1339. Today it houses the museum, which has sculptures and fragments of frescos from the 10–18C.

Museo E.Chiossone (Piazza Mazzini-Villetta Dinegro): Houses an extraordinarily interesting collection of Oriental art (from the 3rd millennium BC up to the 19C).

Palazzo Rosso, bed chamber

Squares worth seeing in the town: In the *Piazza Acquaverde* stands the enormous monument to Columbus of 1862. *Piazza Corvetto:* A beautiful, extensive square with the *Villetta Dinegro* and its magnificent garden with the *marble Mazzini monument.* **Piazza Dante:** Columbus is said to have spent his childhood in the *Casa di Colombo.* The 18C house is overgrown with ivy. The original house was destroyed in 1648 when the city was being bombarded by the French fleet of Louis XIV. Behind it is the 12C *Chiostro di S. Andrea*, an old Benedictine cloister with figures on the capitals. The best-preserved section of the old city wall includes the *Porta Soprana* (1155).

Piazza de Ferrari: A bustling square at the centre of the city, the Piazza de Ferrari is a starting point for numerous sightseeing tours. The *Piazza Matteotti*, the *Piazza S. Matteo* and the *Cathedral of S. Lorenzo*

are all close by. The centre of the square is occupied by a large shell-shaped *fountain* by Crosa di Vergagni (1936). The *Teatro Comunale dell'Opera* (1828) is the most important of the major buildings around it. On the NE side is the bronze *equestrian statue of Garibaldi* by Augusto Rivalta (1893). To its right is the *Accademia Linguistica di Belle Arti* (C.Barabino, 1831), with good Genoese paintings on the first floor. To the SE is the *Borsa*, a splendid building whose style owes much to the baroque. The busy *Via XX Settembre* begins here. Laid out between 1892 and 1905, it has a large number of arcades, magnificent buildings, and shops.

Piazza Fontane Marose: This is not merely the point where the famous *Via Garibaldi* begins; the square itself is surrounded by such beautiful palaces as the black-and-white-striped *Palazzo Spinola* (No.6) with its four-arched windows (15C), the *Palazzo Negrone* (No.4; 16/17C), and the *Palazzo Pallavicini* (No.2) dating from 1575.

Piazza S.Matteo: This most picturesque square has remained almost unchanged up to the present day and, together with the church of *S.Matteo* (q.v.), it gives a particularly good impression of old Genoa. In particular, it evokes memories of the ancient Doria family, who owned the surrounding houses (Nos. 15, 16, 17) dating from the 13C to the 15C. The Renaissance palace, the *Casa di Andrea Doria* (No.17) was presented to Doge Andrea Doria by the Republic of Genoa in 1528 in recognition of his services.

Also worth seeing: *Camposanto di Staglieno* (up the Bisagno valley). This, one of the most famous cemeteries in Italy, takes the form of a series of terraces on a slope. It was laid out in 1844–51 as a large rectangle with its paths forming a cross. The *tomb of Mazzini* is some way up the

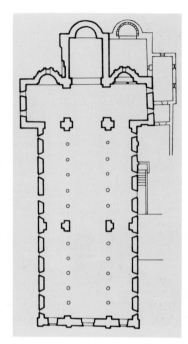

Gerace, cathedral of S.M.Assunta 11C, originally Byzantine-Norman

Genoa, painting by Francesco Gamba in the Galleria d'Arte Moderna di Nervi

hill, beside the *Boschetto dei Mille*. *Torre del Popolo* (1307), on the Via Tommaso. The 12C battlemented *Torre degli Embriaci* on the Piazza Embriaci, near to S.Maria di Castello, is built of heavy ashlars. *The house where G.Mazzini was born* (Via Lomellini, No.11) is a museum. It contains documents and mementoes of this leading figure of the Risorgimento, a library with some 30,000 volumes devoted to the Risorgimento and a large collection of manuscripts by Mazzini, Garibaldi and others. The *Via S.Luca* is one of the oldest streets in the old town. *Portici di Sottoripa:* Here, beneath the dark, low arcades which begin immediately behind the harbour, a great deal of local colour can be seen, particularly in the many small 'trattorie' with their special fish dishes. The *Loggia dei Commendatori Gerosolimitani* (Piazza della Commenda) was originally 12C but now dates from 1508 and is Genoa's first Renaissance building, note the particularly beautiful campanile. The *Piazza Banchi* was formerly the grain market and was once completely surrounded by loggias. On it there now stand the *old Borsa*, the *Loggia dei Mercanti* (1570–95) and the church of *S. Pietro di Banchi*, which is interesting for its style and for its fine decoration inside (frescos by T.Carlone, A.Ansaldo, P.G.Piola and others).

Gerace 89040

Reggio Calabria / Calabria   p.420 / N 15/16

Cathedral of S.Maria Assunta (Piazza Vittorio Emanuele): The largest church in Calabria. Consecrated by Robert Guiscard in 1045, rebuilt in the 13C under the Hohenstaufens, and also after the earthquake of 1783. Building began in Byzantine style (in the crypt) but the nave is Norman. The interesting *E. end* has three semicircular apses (the left one is set further back). Laid out as a Latin cross, the inside has a nave and two aisles, with two arcades of 10 marble and granite *columns*. These are arranged in two groups and some are ancient and come from Locri. Some have no fluting and there are fine capitals. There is a beautiful 14C *tomb* in the right transept. The entrance to the *crypt* is in the left transept.

S.Francesco (Via Cavour): Built in 1252

Gioia del Colle, castle

in Romanesque style and later altered. A fine Arab-Norman Gothic portal. Inside, the *tomb of Nicolò Ruffo* (d. 1372) in late Pisan style is well worth seeing. The *high altar* has fine 16C marble inlay work.

Also worth seeing: The Byzantine church of *S. Giovanello*, with three apses; *remains of the castle*, with a splendid view of the sea.

Gioia del Colle 70023
Caserta/Apulia   p.416☐ N 11

Castle: The name 'gioia' refers to the building's use as a hunting lodge. Built in the early 12C by Riccardo Siniscalco, a son of Drogo de Hauteville. The ground plan is irregular, and consequently it is thought that the complex has been enlarged. The oldest part is probably the SE tower. It is likely, but has not been proved, that Frederick II was involved in the building. There were four towers until the 17C, when the N. and NW towers were destroyed by earthquake and fire. The castle was not rebuilt until 1834. The castle

has had a variety of owners and the original interior furnishings have been completely lost. It has been State-owned since 1967, when restoration work began.

Environs: On *Monte Sannace* (c. 6 km. away) are the excavations of an Apulian town (6–4C BC), whose name is not yet known.

Giove 05024
Terni/Umbria   p.414☐ G 8

Palazzo Mattei: This imposing palace was originally a fortress and was rebuilt in the early 17C. It was owned successively by the Anguillara and Farnese families and finally by the Mattei family. Frescos by the school of Domenichino can be seen in several of the rooms.

Gorizia/Görz 34170
Görz/Friuli   p.410☐ I 2/3

Gorizia was held by the Patriarchs of Aquileia from 1001 onwards. From 1500

Grado, baptistery with Roman sarcophagi

–1919, being the seat of a count, it was an Austrian province. It was at the centre of the battles of Isonzo in World War 1. Part of the town had to be ceded to Yugoslavia after World War 2.

Cathedral of SS. Illario e Taziano (Piazza del Duomo): Built originally in the 13C, rebuilt in the 14C (the rebuilt section is today the chancel). Enlarged in baroque style in 1688–1702 (there are now a nave and two aisles, and the nave has been lengthened). The façade is 19C. After suffering severe war damage the church was restored in 1927. Inside: beautiful columns of dark marble, and galleries above the aisles. 17/18C *stucco and marble works* at the altars. The *pulpit* (1711) is worth seeing. The *chancel*, which dates from the original building, is Gothic. There is a cenotaph to the last count of Gorizia (d. 1500) in the *chapel of the sacrament* in the extension of the left aisle. The *Acatius chapel* in the extension of the right aisle has fine late Gothic vaults and 15C frescos. The outstanding features of the rich *church treasure* are the items from the old church treasure of Aquileia. Here, the works worth seeing include: a reliquary bust of St.Hermagoras, dating from 1340, two valuable bishop's crooks and a silver gilt processional cross dating from 1261.

Castle: A medieval building (10C), it was rebuilt in 1508/9 during a brief Venetian interlude (the alterations included the erection of the *surrounding walls*). Five *corner bastions* have survived. A large *Lion of St.Mark* (1509), the symbol of Venice, above the entrance gate. The *clock tower* is a dominant feature. Opposite is the 12/13C *palace*, formerly the residence of the counts of Gorizia. It has fine Romanesque windows. The castle courtyard contains the 15C *house* where the Diet of Gorizia was held. The remains of the foundation walls of the medieval *castle keep* have survived. The *interior* of the castle is worth seeing (furniture, fabrics, 17C weapons; the 'Hall of the Counts' is particularly fine).

Also worth seeing: The church of *S. Spirito* (on the castle hill), built in 1414,

with fine Gothic oriel windows on the right flank and 15C frescos. The 17C Jesuit church of *S. Ignazio* (Piazza della Vittoria), with a fine baroque fresco of St. Ignatius of Loyola (1721) in the interior. The *Palazzo Attems* (Piazza de Amicis), built in Palladian style in the 18C. It houses the province museums: a picture gallery and a war museum. The *Museo Storico* on the castle hill, with an interesting folklore collection.

Environs: Some 15 km. to the SW is **Gradisca,** a former Venetian fortress built to counter the Habsburg threat. The *fortifications* (15–17C), with their massive towers, have survived. The 16C *Cathedral of SS.Pietro e Paolo,* with a fine façade dating from 1752, is also worth seeing. About 14 km. to the W. is **Cormons,** a former Lombard fortification against the Slavs, with some fine churches including the baroque *Cathedral of S.Adalberto* and the 15C *S. Giovanni Battista,* which has good frescos.

Grado 34073
Gorizia / Friuli   p.410 □ I 3

Grado was the port of Aquileia in ancient times. Owing to the protected position of Grado in the lagoon, the inhabitants of Aquileia fled to here at the time of the Hun invasions. After the assault by the Lombards in 568, the Patriarchs of Aquileia finally took up residence here, and Grado enjoyed its heyday under the name of 'Aquileia Nova'. From the 12C it was overshadowed by Venice.

Basilica di S.Eufemia (Piazza dei Patriarchi): A new building was consecrated here in 579; it had been erected on the remains of two older churches (see below). *Dedicatory inscription of the Patriarch Elias* in the pavement of the nave. This is a colonnaded, arcaded basilica of the Ravenna type. Fine round-arched windows all round the outside. The campanile is 15C. The interior, restored after World War 2, has a nave and two aisles, but no transept. 20 columns with fine capitals, some of them ancient. The *pavement mosaics* (6C; about 9,680 sq.ft., with geometric patterns) are especially fine. The foundations of the oldest of the earlier churches have been uncovered beneath the floor. There is a fine *holy-water stoup*, made from an ancient capital. There is also an interesting 14C *pulpit* on the left of the nave, and a 14C silver *retable* behind the high altar. 12/13C *frescos*, including one of Christ blessing, in the apse. The right aisle leads to the *diaconicon* with its fine pavement mosaic (6C) and to the *pastophorion* in the right apse, also with a 6C pavement mosaic. There is a collection of early Christian architectural fragments in the *Cella Trichora* at the end of the left aisle. Between the basilica and the baptistery there is a small collection of Roman *stone monuments*. Part of what was a very rich *church treasure* has survived.

Baptistery (to the left of S.Eufemia). Built in the 5C; the ground plan is octagonal. Each of the eight sides has a round-arched window on the outside. There is a semicircular apse on the E. side. Remains of the original *mosaic pavement* have been uncovered inside. The *font* and the *altar in the*

apse have been reconstructed using some old parts.

S.Maria delle Grazie (Piazza dei Patriarchi): Built, probably *c.* 400, as a basilica with a nave and two aisles on the site of a simple, earlier building. The apse is screened off by a transenna, so that the ground plan is rectangular. The façade has a massive tripartite window. The interior had its baroque features removed after 1920. Fine *columns* with some interesting Byzantine capitals. The right aisle has an original *mosaic pavement*, with geometric and vegetable motifs. There are two fine *windows* (5&6C) in the apse. The enclosure of the choir has been reconstructed, with some original parts from the 6&9C. The aisles lead to the prothesis and the diaconicon behind the apse; they contain remains of the old *pavement mosaics*.

Also worth seeing: *Basilica di Piazza Vittoria*, built on the foundations of a 5C

Grado, Basilica di S.Eufemia **1** pulpit, 14C **2** pala, 14C **3** 12/13C frescos in the dome **4** Cella Trichora **5** pastophory **6** baptistery

Grado, S.Eufemia, pulpit

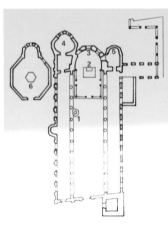

single-aisled early Christian church. The remains of the pavement mosaic have survived.

Gravedona 22015
Como/Lombardy   p.412☐D 2

S.Maria del Tiglio/Church of Queen Theodolinda: Built by the Maestri Comacini in the mid 12C on the site of an early Christian baptistery. A centrally planned building with a porch, which opens at the bottom of the campanile, and apses on three sides. The clover-leaf-shaped apse opposite the porch is flanked by two smaller apses. There are dwarf galleries running around the inside of the building.

Basilica of S.Vincenzo (next to S.Maria del Tiglio): This church, early Christian in origin, was built in 1072 and much altered in the 17/18C. The crypt, with its nave and six aisles, survives from the Romanesque church.

S.Maria delle Grazie (above the town):

A single-aisled building with six bays and a chancel with three apses (1467); the open roof truss is supported by flying buttresses which descend a long way. Frescos by local artists. The cloister is interesting.

Environs: Abbazia di Piona (on the opposite shore of the lake): A Cluniac house. The church of *S.Nicolao* from the 2nd half of the 11C. The cloister (1252–7) is a fine example of the transition from the Romanesque to the Gothic.

Gravina di Púglia 70024
Bari/Apulia   p.418☐N 11

This town owes its name to the deeply-carved eroded gullies which, in the W. part of the Murge, are known as 'gravina'. Churches and dwellings were built in the grottoes in the early Christian period.

Cathedral of S. Maria Assunta: Founded in 1092 as the town's main church, succeeding S.Michele (see below) in this role. Begun in Romanesque and ex-

Gravedona, S.Maria del Tiglio

Grosseto, S.Francesco, crucifix

Grosseto, cathedral

tended in Gothic style in the early 15C. It was rebuilt during the Renaissance after a fire in 1470. Beautiful *choir stalls* inside.

Rione Fondovico: Oldest part of town. Byzantine grotto church of *S.Michele,* formerly the town's main church. It has a nave and four aisles, with pillars. The sanctuary has four apses and is cut entirely out of the living tufa rock. Hardly anything has survived of the 10–14C frescos. Nearby, *S.Vito Vecchio,* another grotto church, has a small *museum* displaying detached frescos from the Byzantine period which have been restored.

Castle (key in the *Palazzo del Comune*): The ruins of a hunting lodge of Emperor Frederick II. Only a few remnants survive of the tower over the entrance gate. There is a large vaulted *cistern* underneath the inner courtyard and the foundations of stables and other rooms also remain.

Also worth seeing: *S.Sebastiano,* with a 13C cloister (capitals with fine animal and plant motifs). *S.Maria delle Grazie,* early 17C; *S.Sofia; S.Maria dei Morti.*

Grosseto 58100
Grosseto/Tuscany   p.414☐F 8

Cathedral of S.Lorenzo: Built in *c.* 1300 on the ruins of an older church (1190– 1250); the *façade,* which is Romanesque in style with alternating layers of red and white marble, was restored by Caldana in 1840–5. The pilasters have capitals with the symbols of the four Evangelists by Sozzo di Rustichino, the architect of the cathedral. Inside: a Renaissance *dome* of 1540, rebuilt in baroque style, and restored, not very successfully, in 1858–65. Notable features: a *large font* by Antonio Ghini (1470); a *large 15C wooden cross* from the Siennese school in the *Cappella del SS.Sacramento,* and a 16C *marble ciborium* in the ante- room of the sacristy. The *campanile,* built originally in 1402, has single-arched, two-arched, three-arched and five-arched open windows, one above the other.

S.Francesco: 14C, with a crucifix (1289) by Duccio di Buoninsegna.

Museo Archeologico in the *Palazzo del Liceo,* in the old town centre. Finds from the environs are on display here. They come from Roselle and the necropolis of Poggio Buo. There are also finds from the Villanova culture, fragments of Etruscan tomb stele from the 6C BC, and a winged marble siren from the 2C BC.

Museo Diocesano di Arte Sacra (above the cathedral sacristy): The museum, totally bombed out in 1943, displays pieces of art from the churches and cathedral of Grosseto. They include some of the earliest works of the master of S.Pietro Ovile: *Madonna and Child with bird,* a *Crucifixion* by the followers of Simone Martini, and *Madonna with Cherries,* one of the masterpieces of Sassetta.

Palazzo della Provincia: Rebuilt in the

20C in Sienese Gothic style on the site of the former Palazzo Aldobrandeschi.

Monument to Leopold II (Piazza Dante Alighieri): Built by Luigi Magi in 1846 to commemorate the conquest of malaria.

Defensive Wall: Hexagonal, with bastions, it surrounds the old town in a manner similar to Lucca, so that Grosseto is known as 'Little Lucca'. The wall, built on top of the old 14C walls, was erected by Francesco I in 1574 to a design by Baldassare Lanci. In 1835, Leopold II had the glacis and the bastions converted into streets and gardens.

Environs: Roselle: The sulphur springs, which were known in antiquity as the *Terme di Roselle*, lie 6 km. to the N. of Grosseto and there is still a thermal bath there today: the *Bagno Roselle*. The *ruins of Roselle* (or *Rusellae*): one of the 12 towns of the Etruscan Confederation, it was subjugated by the Romans and completely destroyed by the barbarians. The town wall, over 1.75 miles long, is still intact and includes the remains of 6 gates. Inside the walls are the remains of a Roman *amphi-theatre* from the imperial period, and also some Roman buildings. **Marina di Grosseto,** a small seaside resort situated on the bay, with a beach of fine sand. **Castiglione della Pescaia,** a small harbour lying a little to the N., between the sea and Poggio Petriccio, and overlooked by a massive castle. At the foot of Poggio Petriccio is the medieval quarter of *Castiglione Castello*, surrounded by a wall which is reinforced by numerous towers. This town is thought to be the Etruscan *Hasta,* and also to be the *Portus Traianus* of the Romans. **Roccalbegna:** A town set in picturesque countryside with the 13C Romanesque church of *SS. Pietro e Paolo.* Two panels from Ambrogio Lorenzetti's late period, the *Madonna and Child* which is part of a *Maestà, and St. Peter and St. Paul,* are worth seeing. **Pitigliano:** To the SE of Grosseto. An unusually picturesque little mountain town, surrounded by deep ravines. The houses of this settlement are clustered around the tufa outcrop in fortress fashion and the Romans stored the local wines in the tufa caves. It was originally an Etruscan settlement, and was thereafter under Roman domination. The town's fate was later closely related to that of the Or-

Sovana (Grosseto), Tomba Ildebranda

sini family. The *Palazzo Orsini*, built in the 14C. The *cathedral* (SS.Pietro e Paolo) has a baroque façade. The *column* with the bear of the Orsini (1490) stands in the Piazza. The *synagogue*, built by Vicolo Manin. A Jewish community settled in Pitigliano in the 15C. The former Hebrew school today houses some remains of the collection of the Museo Civico: Etruscan finds and other excavations. Nearby, to the N. of Poggio Strozzoni (one Orsini is said to have strangled his wife here!), are the ruins of the *Villa Orsini*, with its former garden: benches cut from tufa, and 2 gigantic figures, also hewn from the rock, and referred to by the people as 'Orlando and his wife'. **Orbetello**, located at the tip of a neck of land in a lagoon of the same name which teems with fish. Part of the town wall dates back to the Etruscans, and another part to the fortifications begun under Philip II in 1557. A roadway, 2 km. long, runs between the two lagoons to what was the island of Monte Argentario, from whose peak there is a magnificent view as far as Corsica. Porto S.Stefano, on the N. side of the island, has a ferry service to the Isola del Giglio. The *cathedral* was built in the 14C on the site of an older church. The *Antiquarium Civico* (in the *Palazzo della Pretura*, Via Ricasoli), with implements, burial objects from Etruscan and Roman tombs in the environs, and architectural and sculptural fragments: tufa *sphinxes*, 7&6C BC, Orbetello ceramics and bronze statuettes. A *canal* connects the two lagoons and the Etruscan wall runs along its edge, changing direction at the end of the canal. **Cosa (Ansedonia):** S. of Orbetello, on the border with Latium, and situated on a hill overlooking an isthmus. Cosa is an ancient town, formerly a Roman colony, built in 273 BC on the site of an older settlement. The new settlement of *Ansedonia* was taken by Charlemagne, occupied by the Saracens in the late 10C, and completely destroyed by the Sienese in 1330. The site was reconstructed after the excavations of 1948. The best-preserved parts are the town walls with their 18 towers, and the *Porta Romana*. The town was originally laid out in a grid pattern, with a *forum,* a basilica, 2 temples, and an *acropolis* on somewhat higher ground. The remains of the *capitol* are at the highest point of all, from where there is a a wonderful view of Orbetello, the lagoon and the island of Giannutri. A number of other sites lie in the vicinity. The *Tagliata Etrusca* is a deep channel cut 50 to 65 ft. into the rock and intended to prevent the harbour from silting up: it is a masterpiece of Roman engineering. There is also the *Bagno* or *Spacco della Regina*, a fortified natural rift in the earth whose purpose is still not clear. **Sovana:** A small medieval town on the border with Latium. This Etruscan foundation enjoyed its heyday in the 7&6C BC. Items of interest, apart from the excavations in the surrounding area, are the superb ruins of the *Rocca Aldobrandesca* built in the 13–14C and destroyed again in the 17C. The *cathedral* (SS. Pietro e Paolo) dates mainly from the 12&13C, and is a reconstruction of an older 9–11C building. The façade and vaulting are 14C Gothic but despite the rebuilding it remains a Romanesque church with a crypt (nave and four aisles). The remains of an Etruscan temple from the 3&2C BC were discovered in 1905 in the N. part of the cathedral, and are now housed in the archaeological museum in Florence. Environs of Sovana: *Etruscan necropolis* (can only be visited with a guide). Most of the tombs are from the 4&3C BC: unique and particularly rich architectural decorations are cut into the tufa. *Grotta Pola*, a tomb with interesting use of columns; *Tomba Ildebranda*, the most interesting of the sites: it is a temple with columns whose capitals take the form of human heads between leaves (2C BC).

Gualdo Tadino 06023
Perugia/Umbria   p.414☐H

Cathedral: Of the original 13C building only the exterior survives unaltered. The interior was altered several times—most recently in the 19C. Beside the cathedral is a *fountain,* designed in the 16C by Antonio da Sangallo the elder.

S.Francesco: This fine Gothic church has

been restored in the original style. It now houses the town *picture gallery* (opening times: 9 a.m.–1.30 p.m.; 4 p.m.–7 p.m.). The most important works include: Niccolò Alunno (Madonna and Child with Saints), Matteo da Gualdo (triptych and others), Sano di Pietro (Coronation of the Virgin).

Palazzo Comunale: Built in the 18C on the remains of the 15C Palace of the Guilds and the Priors. The front of a Roman sarcophagus has been incorporated in a wall in the town hall.

Rocca Flea: This well-preserved castle was built by Frederick II Hohenstaufen and enlarged in the Renaissance.

Gualtieri 42044
Reggio Emilia/Emilia-Romagna   p.412☐E 4

Palazzo Bentivoglio (Piazza Bentivoglio): Begun in the early 16C to designs by G.B.Aleotti, it was the residence of a lord until 1634; part of it was pulled down in 1750. Part of the interior is today still decorated with late 16C wall paintings.

Piazza Bentivoglio: *Torre del Comune,* early 17C, by Aleotti; *S.Maria della Neve,* early 17C, rebuilt in 1773–83 after suffering flood damage.

Guardiagrele 66016
Chieti/Abruzzi   p.416☐K 9

This was the home of Nicola di Guardiagrele, the most important 15C goldsmith in the Abruzzi.

S.Maria Maggiore: The campanile in the middle of the façade was built in 1110–1202, but the *portal* is 14C. The portico has frescos of *S.Cristoforo* by Andrea Delitio (1473), and a portal dating from 1578. There is a 16C *Madonna* in the baroque interior of 1706–8; the *church treasure* includes a *silver cross* by N.di Guardiagrele (1431).

Guastalla, Ferrante Gonzaga

Guastalla 42016
Reggio Emilia/Emilia-Romagna   p.412☐E 4

Guastalla, founded by the Lombards as a stronghold in 603, became the first free town in Emilia in 1116. The seat of a duke from 1626 onwards, the town had a court frequented by writers and scholars, and was held by a branch of the Gonzagas from 1539–1746. Then, in 1748, it became part of the duchy of Parma and Piacenza. Napoleon presented the town to his sister Pauline in 1806, and from 1814 onwards it belonged to the Duchess of Parma. It fell to the duchy of Modena in 1848.

Cathedral of S.Pietro (Piazza Mazzini): Built by Francesco da Volterra, and consecrated in 1575. The façade—altered in 1810—dates from 1719. Most of the decoration is 17C.

Piazza Mazzini: *Statue of Ferrante Gon-zaga*, by Leone Leoni, 1564; 15C *Palazzo Gonzaga*, with grotesque decorations by Bernardino Campi (1586).

Also worth seeing: *Biblioteca Maldotti* (Corso Garibaldi 54): Valuable editions and manuscripts, and also a museum with 17–19C portraits of the Gonzagas and local figures. *S. Maria Annunziata*, or *dei Servi* (Via Prampolini), built by Volterra in 1598 and altered several times, with a painting by G.M.Crespi (4th altar on the left).

Environs: A little way outside the town is the **Basilica delle Pieve.** Begun in *c.* 915, consecrated in 997, almost completely rebuilt in the 13C. Last restored in 1926 –31, after being rebuilt several times. The interior (one nave, two aisles) has three apses and a framed late 15C *terracotta Madonna* which is attributed to Guido Mazzoni.

Gubbio 06024

Perugia/Umbria   p.414☐H 7

Gubbio, which lies on the steep slope of

Monte Ingino, is regarded as one of the best examples of a medieval town in Italy. In contrast to Assisi, the medieval architecture here makes an impression that is both sparse and bold.

History: The town is said to date from the Umbrian settlement of Iguvium. Later, under the name of Eugubium, it became a flourishing Roman municipium. The inhabitants left the valley in the 10C at the suggestion of Bishop Ubaldo Baldassini, and built the new Gubbio on a steep slope. The Gabrielli family took possession of this powerful free town in 1350 but were then expelled by Cardinal Albornoz in the name of the Pope. In order to avoid the Pope's claim, Gubbio voluntarily surrendered to the Dukes of Urbino, who brought the town the splendour of a court. However, Gubbio became a Papal possession in 1631. It has been part of the Italian State since 1860.

Palazzo dei Consoli: This, one of the finest palaces in Italy, was built by Matteo Gattapone in Trecento style in 1332-7 and is a successful amalgam of Gothic vigour

Gubbio, Palazzo dei Consoli

and massive Romanesque sparseness, with an additional trace of delicacy. The windows and portal are by Angelo da Orvieto. The high arches, which form the artificial basement of the building and of the piazza, are an admirable feature. The interior is distinguished by a sober ceremoniousness and now houses the *archaeological museum*. The exhibits include the famous *Eugubian Tables* (3&2C BC; 7 tables in the original Umbrian language and in the Umbrian-Etruscan alphabet, the others in the Umbrian-Latin alphabet). The tables were discovered in the Roman amphitheatre in 1444. The *picture gallery* on the second floor contains works by Guido Palmerucci (Madonna and Child), Tommaso Nelli (Virgin of Mercy), and Bernardino Nucci (tabernacle with Apparition of the Holy Ghost).

Palazzo Pretorio: The present town hall is opposite the Palazzo dei Consoli. Built in 1349 in Umbrian Gothic style to designs by Matteo Gattapone, it was later partly restored. The palace today houses the *town archive*. Behind the palace, an elegantly curving staircase (late Renaissance-baroque) leads to the lower street.

Palazzo del Bargello: Elegant early 14C Gothic building, with a fountain, also Gothic in style (behind the Palazzo dei Consoli).

Palazzo del Capitano del Popolo (Palace of the Tribune of the People; on the Largo Lazzarelli): This palace is regarded as a model of home-bred 13C architecture.

Palazzo Ducale (above the Piazza della Signoria): Built in 1476 at the behest of Federico da Montefeltro (the substructure is early medieval, while the front with the large hall is 12–13C. The arcaded courtyard is in typical Urbino Renaissance style and is worth a visit. Inside, the bright, elegant rooms have magnificent fireplaces.

S.Giovanni (Piazza S.Giovanni): Built in the early 13C, the church is the first example of Gothic architecture in the typical local style. Inside, the influence of the Cistercians is noticeable in the architecture and decoration. The façade dates from the first few years of the 14C. The only Renaissance work to note is a fine *majolica font* in the Gothic chapel.

Gubbio, Palazzo dei Consoli

S. Agostino: This 13C church was originally also built in a predominantly local Gothic style, and was much altered in the 16–18C. Inside there are frescos of the Last Judgement and the life of St. Augustine by Ottaviano Nelli, Gubbio's greatest painter.

Cathedral: Begun in the 13C. There are five conspicuous bas-reliefs, depicting the Evangelists with the Lamb, on the Gothic façade. A Gothic *sarcophagus* and the baroque *chapel of the sacrament* are captivatingly beautiful features of the simple interior. Frescos by Dono Doni.

S. Francesco: This, possibly the finest church in Gubbio, in the local Gothic style, has three apses and a fine two-arched portal. There is a fresco by Ottaviano Nelli, of the life of the Virgin, in the left apse of the church, which has a nave and two aisles. Francis of Assisi tamed a wild wolf in Gubbio and tablets depicting the wolf commemorate the event.

S. Pietro: This is the oldest church in the town. It was built in the 8&9C and partly rebuilt in the 13C. The interior dates from the 16C. Fragments of the original structure, for example late Romanesque acanthus capitals, may be seen on the façade. Two splendid Renaissance organs.

S. Secondo: The *cloister* of this 12/13C church is especially splendid. The funerary chapel has some peculiar frescos by Giacomo Bedi, another painter from Gubbio. The frescos depict the story of St. Sebastian and others.

Local Events: The *Corsa dei Ceri* is held each year on 15 May. The youths of the town have to run along carrying heavy wooden structures from the Piazza up to Monte Ingino. The *Tiro della Balestra* (crossbow contest) is held on the Piazza della Signoria in medieval costumes on the last Sunday in May.

Also worth seeing: For those interested in local art history, the works of Domenico di Cecco (Pietà) in the church of *S. Maria della Piaggiola* will be of interest. His gaunt figures are typical of this region. The large *Roman theatre* was probably built in the 1C. The church of *S. Domenico* was originally Gothic but was later rebuilt. Its monastery has a false triptych by Giacomo Bedi, while the Confraternità dei Bianchi has an impressive Passion of Christ by the same artist. In the church of *S. Maria Nuova* is the 'Madonna del Belvedere', Ottaviano Nelli's masterpiece. The medieval *Tiratoio dell'Arte della Lana* (wool factory), is on the Piazza S. Francesco.

Environs: Down the hill outside the town is the old 15C **water pipe,** which was still working during the last war. The basilica of St. Ubaldo, from where there is a very fine view, stands on Monte Ingino (2,950 ft.). On Monte **Cucco,** the grotto of the same name, with its interesting karst features, is worth visiting.

Gubbio, view

Gúspini 09036
Cágliari/Sardinia   p. 422| |B/C 13|

S. Nicola di Mira: Built in 1611, it is single-aisled, with a timber ceiling and two side chapels. The ground plan is a Latin cross. Further chapels were added as early as the mid 17C, and also a tunnel vault made of brick. In the 18C, Sardinian builders added the square campanile, the sacristy and a 7th chapel. The façade is crowned with battlements which are characteristic of late Gothic churches in central and southern Sardinia, and also a famous, delicately traceried *rose-window* above the portal.

Environs: There are several prehistoric remains along the edge of the mountain range: *menhirs* (e.g. the well-known 'Sennoreddas'), *giant's tombs* (in the Capra and Pauli Planu [marshy plain] areas), *nuraghi* (Bruncu s'Orku has a nuraghe with a central tower, a surrounding wall and as many as seven outer towers) and insignificant remains of small Roman settlements. The best way of obtaining information on these sites is to ask peasants or in the 'Pro Loco' of **Gonnosfánádiga**. To the N.: The large, devastated *Nuraghe Melas* stands on a hill to the W. of the Casa Scano. Opposite, the *Nuraghe Saurecci*, with several towers, is the second defensive fortress. With its massive surrounding wall, it dominates the route from Capo Frasca. Further to the NW, by the Stagno di San Giovanni, all that remains of a pre-Roman settlement which was later known as Neapolis is the little church of *S. Maria di Neapolis*, and also some fragments of a Roman road and a water pipe. The Capo Frasca peninsula has interesting prehistoric remains and is a military area closed to the public. In the W. mountainous region, just below the peak of Monte Arcuentu, there is a prehistoric *cistern well* along with some scanty remains of walls. The trip across the mining region, through Montevecchio, Ingurtosu, Cantoniera and Biddardi, passes many pits, ore dressing floors and ore smelting works. Some of these date back to the Phoenicians, although today they are almost all in ruins after being revived during the Middle Ages.

Gúspini, deserted medieval Pisan buildings for washing ore

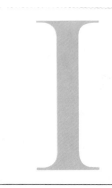

Iesi 60035
Ancona/Marches p.414☐ I 6/7

Birthplace of Emperor Frederick II (b. 1194) and of Pergolesi the composer (b. 1710; annual music festival).

Cathedral: Rebuilt in 1732–41; the façade was not built until 1889. Inside there are

Iesi, cathedral, interior

two *lions on columns* from the portal of the medieval church, and also the *tomb of Angelo Ripanti* (1512). The frescos in the dome spandrels date from 1750.

S. Marco: This church outside the old town was built in the first half of the 13C and restored in 1854. Inside, there are 14C frescos in the apse and the right aisle; the remaining paintings are 19C. In the left aisle is the *Nolfi monument,* dating from 1513.

Palazzo della Signoria: Built by Francesco di Giorgio Martini in 1486-98, while the portal dates from 1588. Inside is a *picture gallery* with paintings by Lorenzo Lotto: *Entombment* (1512), a *Madonna with Saints* and an *Annunciation* (1526), an *Annunciation* (1530) and, last but not least, *scenes from the life of St. Lucy* (1529/30). The *museum* houses archaeological finds, medieval sculptures, and a *Nativity of Christ* by L.della Robbia.

Environs: Chiaravalle: The Cistercian abbey of *S. Maria in Castagnola* was founded in 1126. The church was rebuilt in 1688.

Iglésias 09016
Cagliari/Sardinia p.422☐ B 14

Ore-bearing rock containing lead, tin and

silver was mined by the Carthaginians and Romans in open-cast diggings in an area near to Iglésia, which did not at first exist as a town. It is not until the 13C that Pisan documents mention a mining village here, called 'Villa di Chiesa'. In 1258, the Pisans, with the aid of miners from the Tyrol and Tuscany, converted the deserted, mainly open ore pits into 'modern' mines with long blasted galleries. They brought with them a new specialist language and working regulations which were written down in the 'Breve di Villa di Chiesa in Sigero', Italy's first mining regulations. It was in a foundry of 'Villa Ecclesiae' that the Pisans struck the beautiful silver coin of their republic, bearing the Hohenstaufen eagle. Not only the *fortifications* of the present-day Iglésias, some of which are still visible, but also all the religious buildings from the 2nd half of the 13C, date from this Pisan period. From the open main square, the Piazza Quintino Sella, amidst the narrow winding alleyways, the visitor can see *Salvaterra Castle,* restored by the Aragonese in 1325, the *Porta Castello* with some sections from the old Pisan walls, and also, high up the mountain, the *Chiesetta Nostra Signora del Buon*

Camino—the renovated church looks better from the square than it does close to. The visitor crosses the pedestrian precinct of the Via Matteotti to enter the Piazza la Marmora, and then passes along the Via Centrale to the Piazzetta del Municipio with the single-aisled late Romanesque cathedral of *S. Chiara* (1285/8). This has small side chapels and an attached campanile in a different style. The bell itself was cast by A.Pisano in 1337. The simple façade only has a small rose-window above its portal and, on the gable, some blind arcades, some of which were added later. The interior was altered in Catalan style in 1576–88 and a fine stellar vault was added. 100 yards to the S., down a winding alleyway, lies the restored 15/16C *Chiesa di S. Francesco.* This too is single-aisled, and has side chapels beneath Gothic arcades built at various different times. The nave supports a peculiar Gothic wooden ceiling. The almost plain façade has only three small rose-windows. Although it was built at the same time as the cathedral, the *Santuario* [pilgrimage church] of *Nostra Signora di Valverde,* next to the cemetery at the SE end of the Viale Valverde, is today somewhat neglected but displays a clearly

Chiaravalle (Iesi), cloister

Gothic architectural style. The interior was altered in 1592 in Catalan late Gothic style.

Museum: The *Istituto Tecnico Minerario*, with the adjoining *Museo di Mineralogia* (permission to visit the museum is granted by the 'Preside' of the institute), is worth a visit.

Environs: Villamassargia, famous for its late Romanesque church of *Nostra Signora del Pilar,* built by Arzocco di Gana in 1307 (emphatically simple façade, undecorated portal, open rose-window, high blind arcades, and tower-like structure with two belfry windows). On the other hand, the actual village church, *Madonna delle Neve,* is late Gothic (16C). The remains of a Genoese fortress destroyed by the Aragonese may be seen near the parish church of the town of **Domusnóvas,** which is being completely rebuilt. The Carthaginians built furnaces for smelting silver in the ore-bearing region to the N. and these continued to be used by the Romans. In dry periods it is possible to drive through the former stalagmite grotto of *S. Giovanni,* some 3 km. above the town. 2,620 ft. in length, there are the remains

Iglésias, Tempio d'Antas

of a neolithic cyclops wall 430 ft. along it and, after 1,570 ft., a long cave branches off to the left. To the N.: 3 km. to the N. of Arcu Genna Bogai, the head of the pass, turn right on to an improved highway and, after another 2 km., the *Tempio d'Antas* stands up a hill to the left. In 1977, this religious site, a virtual ruin whose origin is in dispute, was finally restored, fenced in and closed off. This striking Roman temple was, according to an inscription on the beam above the columns, built at the beginning of the 3C AD. It was erected on the site of a Punic shrine to the god Sid (7C BC). Parts of the old structure of this shrine can still be seen underneath. The steps, portico and inner room form a rectangle at whose entrance there stood two columns with Doric capitals (after Lilliu). To the W.: Far above **Monteponi** there is an enormous open-cast pit. Access is difficult but the mining terraces and the small drifts can still be seen here and there. The Carthaginians, and later the Romans, made Sardinian slaves dig up the entire mountain, starting from its top. Some 12 km. to the SW is the large 'hill' of the *nuraghic settlement of Serrucci,* which also included some smaller watch-tower nuraghi in forward positions. The 'hill' proves to be a heap of debris; its sides have remains of nuraghic walls standing at several points. The village, which is well fenced in and closed off and consists of some 100 round huts, extends mainly towards the SW. It is so covered in scrub as to be almost unrecognizable. To the N. of Gonnesa, at 65.5 km., a road leads on through the mining villages of Nebida and Masua via **Acquaresi,** the highest pit-head village. From here on the road surface is very bad as far as the Cala Domestica. The ruins of what was an *ore dressing floor* are to be found here. NW of this, by the coast, there is a massive medieval *watch-tower* whose entrance is halfway up the building (today, access is by an iron ladder).

Imola 40026
Bologna / Emilia-Romagna   p. 410 ☐ G 5

Imola, which may be Etruscan in origin,

Imola, Rocca

is probably identical to the Forum Cornelii which was founded by the Romans in 82 BC and which was part of the Exarchate of Ravenna until 754. Enlarged as a fortress by the Lombards, it fell to the Carolingians and then to the Pope. A free town from 1084 onwards, it suffered several battles and changes of ruler before finally falling to the Papal States in 1503. Severely damaged in World War 2, it is today an important centre of industry and trade.

Cathedral of S. Cassiano (Piazza del Duomo): Built in 1187-1271, rebuilt by Cosimo Morelli in 1781. Only the campanile, 1473-85, with its baroque upper part, dates from an earlier period, whilst the façade is from 1849. The classical interior contains: A 15C *wooden crucifix* (2nd chapel on the right). 16C *Assumption of the Virgin,* by Giacomo Bertucci (3rd chapel on the left). Early 16C *font* (in front of 1st chapel on left). The *treasury* houses an il-luminated *book of antiphons* and a *paten* (? 11C) on a 15C Florentine pedestal. *Reliquary of St. Cosmas,* 1387, by Romolo di Senuccio.

Palazzo Vescovile (Piazza del Duomo): Founded in 1188, rebuilt by Morelli in 1766, with a façade dating from 1845. The building has interestingly decorated rooms and houses the **Museo Diocesano d'Arte Sacra**. Outstanding exhibits: *Byzantine sarcophagus.* Two *Romanesque lions* and *female figures,* both from the old cathedral. Mid 14C *Madonna with donor,* attributed to P. and L.Veneziano. Mid 14C *St. Catherine,* with a bishop Saint, ascribed to Vitale da Bologna. 15C *Madonna and Child,* from the Vivarini school. *Sacra Conversazione* by Palmezzano.

Istituti Culturali del Comune (in the *Palazzo dei Musei,* a monastery rebuilt in the 17/18C. The museum on the ground floor has departments of prehistory, natural science, numismatics and ceramics. The visitor ascends from the *Museo del Risorgimento*, up the staircase built in 1749–61 to designs by Torreggiani, to the *library* which has some valuable 13–15C manuscripts. The *picture gallery* has 15–18C paintings, including ones by Garofalo, L.Carracci, S.Filippi, Girolamo da Carpi and G.M.Crespi.

S.Domenico (Via Quarto): This single-aisled building with side altars was rebuilt in the 18C. The *polygonal apse* restored in 1955, a *chapel*, and the *portal of the façade* (1340, by Giacomo di Cereto), are all from the previous building (14C). Notable features inside: 15C *column with stone crucifix* (to the right of the entrance). *Martyrdom of St.Ursula*, 1600, by L.Carracci (high altar). *Choir stalls*, 2nd half of the 16C (sanctuary). *Monument*, 1341, by Bitino da Bologna (ante-room to the right of the sanctuary). Chapel to the right of the sanctuary (dating from the earlier church and restored in 1936–7), with *remains of 14&15C frescos*, and the mid 15C *polyptych* by Giovanni da Riolo. The late 15C *former monastery*, with its two cloisters, is situated to the left and right of the church.

Chiesa dell'Osservanza (Piazza Bianconcini): Built in 1467–73. The *portico*, which has 3 sarcophagi built into its walls, was completed in 1483. The double-aisled interior was completely rebuilt in 1930, but retains the much-weathered early 16C *Tribune of Pope Julius II* (left of W. wall) and a *fresco of the Madonna*, 1473, by Guidaccio (left wall). The sacristy leads to the left *cloister* (1487; restored in 1907) and the *Cappella della Madonna delle Grazie*, which has a dome painted all over (Zampa, 1768) and a painting of the Madonna by Guidaccio. To the left of the church is a small *garden* with a reconstruction of the tribune of Justus II and, in an aedicule, an early 15C *terracotta Pietà* (the Christ is modern).

Palazzo Comunale (Piazza Matteotti): The façade and the interior of the building (12C) were rebuilt by Torreggiani in the 18C, and altered again by Morelli in 1771.

Restoration undertaken in 1935 uncovered remnants of the Romanesque building—see the portal on the right flank. 18C interior decoration.

S.Maria in Regola (Via Cosimo Morelli): Rebuilt by Morelli in the 2nd half of the 18C. Only the fine campanile, 1180–1 with 13C additions, survives from the earlier building. The enormous square interior is flanked by chapels; the decoration is modern. Notable features include: the 18C Dutch *Sacra Conversazione* (1st chapel on left). White marble *sarcophagus*, 1372, with *relics of St.Sigismund* (2nd chapel on left, underneath the altar). *Byzantine transennae* (6C) and *stone cross* (10/11C; high altar and behind it). A 17C *cloister* survives from the former monastery.

S.Maria dei Servi (Piazza Mirri): Built in the 2nd half of the 14C, much altered in 1500–2; beautiful *portal in the façade* dating from 1505. 18C *campanile*. The single-aisled interior has splendid *side altars* with 16C wooden frames, and its furnishings include three late 17C *paintings* by M.Viani (2nd altar on right; right wall of sanctuary; 2nd altar on left), and a Byzantine *painting of the Madonna* (in a 17C frame, at the high altar).

Also worth seeing: *S. Agostino* (Via Emilia). A single-aisled building rebuilt by Morelli in the 18C, with decoration mainly from the same period. The *Palazzo Sersanti* (Piazza Matteotti), built by Giorgio Fiorentino in 1482, restored in 1925. *Chiesa del Suffragio* (Piazza Matteotti), 1585, with some paintings from the 16C and early 17C. *Palazzo Paterlini*, formerly *Sforza* (Via Cavour 84), built in 1480–2 to designs by Giorgio Fiorentino. *S.Maria del Valverde* (Via Orsini), 13C, rebuilt and enlarged by F.Ambrosini in 1617, with a painting of the Madonna, dating from the 2nd half of the 15C and attributed to Berruguete, and a picture of S.Carlo by L.Carracci. *Castle* (*Rocca*; Piazzale Giovanni dalle Bande Nere), 1259, extended in 1332–6, strengthened in 1422–73 and 1499. *Porta Montamara* (Viale Aurelio Saffi), only remnant of the old town wall, restored in 1924.

Environs: 6 km. towards Bologna, the Santuario della Madonna del Piratello, built in *c.* 1491, with a *campanile* from the early 16C. The interior was restored in 1833 and includes a *ciborium* of *c.* 1494 (high altar) and a mid 15C stone *Virgin* (behind the high altar).

Imperia 18100

Imperia/Liguria   p.412☐ B 6

This, the main town of the province, dates from 1923, when localities *Oneglia* and *Porto Maurizio* were joined together. The beautiful old town centre of Porto Maurizio has survived around the extensive *Piazza Parrasio,* the highest point of the town.

Basilica of S. Maurizio (Piazza del Duomo): The enormous church, built by Gaetano Cantoni in classical style in 1781–1832, dominates the square, and it is probably the largest church in the whole of Liguria. The façade is flanked by two campaniles, and in front of it there is a portico with 8 Doric columns. The octagonal building supports a dome crowned by a lantern. The interior appears bright and spacious, one reason for this being its unusually high Corinthian columns. The vaults are coffered. Inside, the numerous works of art blend in with the overall design, and they reflect the taste of the 19C.

Also worth seeing: Underneath the 18C *convent of the Poor Clares* (Via S.Caterina) there is a fine, extensive, arcade, built on the remains of medieval fortifications and offering a view of the sea. *S. Pietro:* a charming 18C building with staircase, colonnaded portico and small campanile. Napoleon, among others, stayed in the 17C *Palazzo Castaldi-Lavagna* behind S. Pietro. *S.Giovanni Battista* (Oneglia, Via S.Giovanni): a baroque church with works by Maragliano, Filippo Parodi, Greg. De Ferrari and Salvatore Revelli.

Environs: Montegrazie (*c.* 8 km.): The Gothic pilgrimage church of *Nostra Signora delle Grazie* (1450), not far from the town, has a beautifully articulated façade, and inside, with its nave and two aisles, there are some splendid 15&16C frescos. **Moltedo** (about 7 km.): The parish church of *S.Bernardo* (1642) has a *Holy Family* painted by van Dyck.

Irsina 75022

Matera/Basilicata   p.416☐ M/N 11

Until 1895, this town was known as Montepeloso. Excavations have shown that *Irsus,* the original settlement, must have been 6.5 km. to the SE of the present site. In the early 11C, Montepeloso was one of the strongholds of Byzantium against the Normans, but it was destroyed by Roger in 1133.

Cathedral of the Assumption: Dating from the 13C, it was rebuilt in 1777. The façade is undecorated, and the simple campanile has pointed two-arched windows. Inside: a nave and two aisles, separated by pillars, dome over the crossing. The first chapel on the right has a *font* (1761) on a column with a capital of white stone dating from 1453. Other notable features: a 16C polychrome *marble statue of St. Euphemia,* and an *Ecce Homo* by a 16C Neapolitan painter. In the *crypt* there is a *marble basin* which may be part of the baptism font dating from 1110. The *sacristy* has 16&17C reliquaries and embroideries.

S.Francesco: Rebuilt in 1531 in the style of a 12C building. There are two small 13C columns in the façade, which dates from 1717.
Inside: A nave with side chapels and a transept. The *frescos in the crypt* are worth seeing. The late 14C wall paintings are by a Neapolitan artist and his assistants; they show *scenes from the life of Christ* and the *Virgin.*

Museo Ianora (Piazza del Popolo 12): This collection, devoted to the history of Irsina, is housed in a 17C palace.

Also worth seeing: *Grotta di S. Lucia,* with wall paintings.

Ischia, castle

Ischia, view

Ischia (I) 80070
Naples/Campania   p.416□ I/K 11

The island of Ischia, which is volcanic in origin, lies to one side of the Gulf of Naples. In the 8C BC it was the first place where Greek colonists settled in Italy. The Greeks called it Pithecusa, the Romans Aenaria. Since the 19C it has been much frequented for its radioactive mineral springs (acting against gout and rheumatism).

Castello d'Ischia: Some remnants of the 14C *cathedral* (interesting crypt with beautiful groin vault; remains of 14C frescos) survive on the 330 ft. high *trachyte peak*. In the Middle Ages it was an important refuge from raiding pirates. The way leads from here to the ruin of the 16C chapel of *S. Pietro a Pantanello* (hexagonal ground plan). There are also the ruins of the *Immacolata* (18C) and a *convent of the Poor Clares*. The *Maschio*, a 15C castle, stands on the peak.

Ischia Ponte: The 14C cathedral of *S. Maria Assunta* is worth seeing (inside there are fine stucco decorations and, in the transept, a fine 13C wooden crucifix), as is the baroque *Palazzo Arcivescovile* (1738–41) with a fine early Christian sarcophagus in the bishop's ante-room on the first floor.

Ischia Porto: Church of *S. Pietro* dating from 1781; fine façade; oval ground plan, two side chapels, round but flattened apse. Corinthian pilasters with continuous entablature all around the interior. Flat dome. The *Museo dell'Isola*, with its geological and archaeological displays, has been attached to the church since 1947.

Lacco Ameno: 18C church of *Madonna delle Grazie*, with an original façade; single-aisled interior, with three side chapels to

Issogne, castle

the left and three to the right; there is a dome above the transept and another over the chancel. On the 1st pillar on the right is a Roman Hercules herm, and on top of it there is a holy-water stoup.

Forio: The *Torrione*, the town's landmark, is a round watch-tower dating from 1480. The church of the *Madonna di Loreto* was originally founded in the 14C by fishermen from Ancona. Inside there are a nave, two aisles, a dome above the crossing, a polygonal apse, and some very fine stucco and marble works. The many *substantial houses* from the 16–18C give the town a picturesque appearance.

Issogne 11020
Aosta/Aosta   p.412☐B 3

Castello di Issogne: A Renaissance cas-

tle on the Dora Baltea, built in its present form by Georges de Challant in 1480. The most splendid of the Savoyard residences, it is today used by the regional government. The building is simple on the outside, having no defensive towers, and consists of three wings surrounding a square inner courtyard with a beautiful fountain; a garden adjoins the fourth side of the courtyard. Splendid interior decoration, including some 15C frescos, which are among the finest in the Aosta valley: the hall is outstanding.

Ivrea 10015
Turin/Piedmont   p.412☐B 3

Ivrea, known as *Eporedia* by the Romans, was founded in 100 BC. It later became the seat of a Lombard and then a Frankish duchy; in the 9C, it was the seat of a mar-

Ivrea, castle

quis. Independent in the 12C, it fell to William VI of Monferrato in 1266, and was first taken over by Savoy in 1313. The carnival tradition goes back to Barbarossa's times. Olivetti is based in Ivrea.

Cathedral (Piazza del Duomo): The 4C cathedral was rebuilt in the 11C and again in the 18C; the façade is late classical, dating from 1854. The towers, and the crypt with its Roman columns, remained unaltered. There is a fragment of a 12C fresco in the ambulatory, while the sacristy contains a painting by D.Ferrari dating from after 1500. The altarpiece is by Claudio Beaumont.

Also worth seeing: *S. Bernardino* (Via Jervis): 15C, with scenes from the life of Christ by Giovanni Martino Spanzotti.

Casa di Credenza (Piazza Marsala): in the 13C, the ruling nobles assembled here; the present brick building is 16C Gothic. *Castello delle Quattro Torri* (Piazza Castello): 1358; the fourth tower was destroyed by an explosion in 1676. The *Giardino Pubblico* has the campanile of the former church of S.Stefano (1041). *Casa Tagliati* (Via Bertinatti 4): 12C castle with tower. *Roman bridge.* The *Seminario Vescovile* (Via Arborio), 1715–46, was built to plans by F.Juvarra; it has a fine courtyard with mosaics from the 10C cathedral. *Municipio* (Piazza Vittorio Emanuele): 1758, with fine clock tower and the *Museo Civico P.A.Garda.*

Environs: Remains of *amphitheatre* (late Roman). The *Serra d'Ivrea,* is the largest glacial moraine in Europe.

Lagonegro 85042

Potenza/Basilicata p. 418☐M 12

There was a settlement here in prehistoric times, as the excavations carried out in 1914-15 on the slope of Monte Alpe have shown. The site of *Nerulum* in antiquity, the town was called *Lagolibero* in the 16C, when it was part of Lauria.

Churches: S. Nicola: Parish church extended in 1779-1839; fine *silver bust of St. Nicholas of Bari* by C.Frezza (1756). The **Madonna del Sirino** (on the Piazza Grande) is adjacent to a small chapel, which has a beautiful Romanesque portal with lions. **S.Anna:** 1665 with a good façade; 17&18C furnishings. **S.Nicola,** high up on a cliff; until 1839, the parish church. Mona Lisa del Gioconda is said to have been buried here in 1505,

Palazzo feudale: castle ruins on a rocky peak, with a picturesque flight of stairs of 1603. Particularly fine view of the town and Monte Sirino.

Environs: Lauria: Old houses in the town have ornate wrought iron balconies from the 17C. The upper part of town is known as *Castello* after the remains of the former castle and contains the remains of the medieval wall. *S.Maria dei Martiri* has a Deposition by a 16C Neapolitan painter. The *parish church*, with 15C campanile, contains 16C *wooden statues of the Madonna and St.Nicholas.* The lower part of Lauria is called *Borgo. S.Giacomo Maggiore* has carved choir stalls from 1554.

Lagopésole 85020

Potenza/Basilicata p. 416☐M 11

Lagopésole is the largest and last castle built by Frederick II of Hohenstaufen. The

Lagopésole, castle, rock mask

castle was begun in 1242 and completed after Frederick's death and differs from the other fortresses he built in Southern Italy. It has a rectangular layout with 4 corner towers, each of which originally contained a hall. The large courtyard has a roofed-over fountain, and the small courtyard has a tower crowned with battlements; they are separated by a wall across which a covered passage leads from the living apartments in the W. to the church.

Lanciano 66034
Chieti/Abruzzi   p. 416□K 9

One of the most interesting towns in the province. Known as *Anxanum* in antiquity, it was renowned in the Middle Ages for its varied industries—textiles, ceramics, forged iron workings—as well as for its famous fairs.

Cathedral (S. Maria del Ponte): The church, standing above three arches of the Ponte di Diocleziano, was enlarged in 1389, in the 15C, and—in neoclassical style—in 1785–8. The terracotta figure of the *Madonna del Ponte*, originally mounted on the church's outer wall, was moved inside after an earthquake in 1088.

S.Maria Maggiore: Built in 1227 on the ruins of a Temple of Apollo, it was extended in the 14& 15C. The wonderful *portal* with rose-window was built by Francesco Petrini in 1317. In the sacristy there is a *silver cross* by Nicola di Guardiagrele (1422).

Also worth seeing: *S.Nicola da Bari* has a 16C panel of the Madonna between St. John the Evangelist and St. Nicholas of Bari. *S. Agostino* has work by Nicola di Guardiagrele.

L'Aquila 67100
L'Aquila/Abruzzi   p.416□I 9

The main town of the province, it was founded towards the mid-13C by uniting neighbouring settlements for the purpose of achieving greater security. Emperor Frederick II, to whom a military base in the N. of the kingdom of Naples was very

Lagopésole, castle

Lanciano, cathedral

welcome, granted the new town certain privileges and, by providing the symbol of the eagle, also gave the town its name. Disputes over the Kingdom of Naples' hereditary succession governed the fate of L'Aquila during the following centuries. In 1703, an earthquake destroyed large parts of the old town.

S. Bernardino: with the tomb of S. Bernardino of Siena, a well-known Franciscan priest who died in L'Aquila in 1444. The church and monastery were built in 1457–72, and the *façade*, which has sturdy cornices and pairs of columns, was by Cola dell'Amatrice in 1527. The nave has a baroque *wooden ceiling* by Bernardo Mosca with paintings of the life of the saint by Girolamo Cenatiempo. There is a *Resurrection* and *Coronation of the Virgin* on a *terracotta altar* with polychrome glaze, by Andrea della Robbia (second chapel on the right). The fifth chapel, the *Cappella di S. Bernardino* is *S. Bernardino's mausoleum*. Built by Silvestro dell'Aquila in 1505, it has a modern sarcophagus (the old sarcophagus was taken away in 1799, during Napoleon's conquest of the town). Silvestro dell'Aquila also made the *wooden figures* on the main altar in the chancel, which was was built after the earthquake of 1703. The *monument of Maria Pereira Camponeschi*, the church's foundress dates from 1496, and is to the left of the high altar. Also by Silvestro dell'Aquila, it shows the foundress with her daughter, who died at the age of 15 months. To the right of the high altar is *Mount Calvary* by Rainaldo Fiammingo.

S. Maria di Collemaggio: Begun in 1287. In 1294, Pietro da Morrone had himself crowned Pope Celestine V here. 15C *façade* of red and white stones in a geometric pattern, the main features being horizontal friezes, three portals and three rose-windows. The portals, which date from 1440, are graced with decorated columns, and the middle portal has figures in wall niches. Interior restored in baroque style after 1706. The *mausoleum of S. Celestine*, built by Girolamo da Vicenza in 1517, is in the last chapel on the right, next to the high altar. Restoration revealed 14C

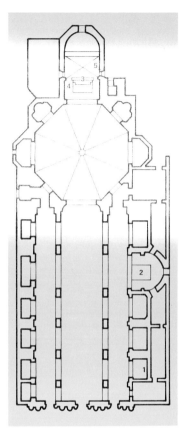

L'Aquila, S. Bernardino 1 altar by Andrea della Robbia **2** tomb of St. Bernard **3** high altar **4** tomb of Maria Pereira Camponeschi **5** Mount Calvary by Rinaldo Fiammingo

frescos on the flanks, and 16C frescos on the entrance wall, including a *Crucifixion* by the architect Cola dell'Amatrice (1517).

Castle: Begun in 1530 and designed by Pirro Luigi Scrivà. It is built around a square courtyard and has four wings with corner bastions, which end in a sharp angle; the whole is surrounded by a deep moat. Formerly the castle was used as a barracks and a stronghold for the viceroy's troops; today it houses the *Museo Nazionale Abruzzese*. Standing just before the gate to the old town the castle presents a solid and massive appearance.

Museo Nazionale Abruzzese: Mainly collections of paintings and sculpture from the 12 – 18C, which have come from churches in the Abruzzi. Among some of the finest things are: *Carved wooden doors* from S. Maria in Cellis at Carsoli (1132) and from S. Pietro at Alba Fucense; *frescos* dating from 1237, from S. Maria di Cartignano at Bussi; *carved and painted Madonnas* from the 13-14C; a *painted bone reliquary* from the cathedral at Penne; a *processional cross* by Nicola da Guardiagrele dating from 1434; *Sebastian* and a *Madonna* by Silvestro dell' Aquila. The numerous 15 – 18C altar panels include paintings by Lambert Lombard and Rinaldo Fiammingo. The massive *skeleton of Elephas Meridionalis* is in a room in the corner bastions.

Also worth seeing: *Cathedral:* with the reconstructed *monument to Cardinal Amico Agnifili* by Silvestro dell' Aquila. *S. Domenico:* begun by Charles II of Anjou

in 1309 and restored after 1703; next to it is the old *residence of the Anjou. S. Giuseppe del Minimi:* also restored after 1703; above the font is a *baldacchino* by Silvestro dell' Aquila (1447) and there is an *equestrian statue* of Ludovico Camponeschi by Gualtiero d'Alemagna (1432). *S. Maria Paganica* has a portal dating from 1308. *Le Cancelle* is a group of 15C houses, whose surviving shops keep up the impression of an old business street. *99 Cannelle* is a fountain with 99 pipes, which was begun in 1272; it commemorates the legend according to which L'Aquila was founded by uniting 99 villages, each of which had its own quarter in the town, where there was both a piazza and church.

Environs: Bazzano: One of the villages whose unification led to the formation of L'Aquila. *S. Giusta:* 9C building; restored 13C. The three-storeyed façade of 1238 has columns, a rich carved portal and two rose-windows. Inside, on the entrance wall, there are 13&14C frescos. The pulpit is typical of the area, being rectangular, supported by columns, with a semicircular projecting lectern, and reliefs on the parapet. In the *Confessio* there are the remains

L'Aquila, Basilica S. Maria di Collemaggio

of the early Christian church, including a *grotto* in which St. Giusta is said to have suffered martyrdom. **Pagánica:** *Santuario della Madonna d'Appari:* 16C building; inside there are frescos of the same date. **S. Vittorino:** *S. Michele:* Consecrated in 1170 and restored in 1528. Inside there are 12C reliefs of the *Martyrdom of S. Vittorino* and 13C frescos in the apse. Nearby is the *Amiternum* of antiquity, which was the home of Sallust the historian. Virgil mentions it, describing it as an important Sabine town already extant when Aeneas arrived in Italy. The Romans conquered Amiternum in 239 BC. A *theatre*, an *amphitheatre* and an *aqueduct* have survived in good condition.

Larino 86035
Molise/Campobasso   p.416 ☐ L 9/10

Cathedral/Assunta and S.Pardo: Consecrated in 1319. The façade has a *rose-window*, and above it a Lamb surrounded by symbols of the Evangelists'. The portal of 1319 by Francesco Petrini is flanked by gryphons and lions and has the *Crucified Christ between the Virgin and St. John* in the lunette. The interior has a nave and two aisles and was restored in 1950–5. The main altar and bishop's throne are marble. In the left aisle there are two fine paintings, *Immaculate Conception* by Francesco Solimena and *S. Pardo* by Luca Giordano. Further there are remains of 14C frescos, 16C *wooden reliefs* of the *transferring of the bones of S. Pardo* and the *Last Supper* and a 17C *silver bust of S. Pardo.*

Also worth seeing: The Roman *amphitheatre* and *thermal springs.* The *Palazzo Comunale* with mosaic floors from the 3C BC.

La Spezia 19100
La Spezia/Liguria   p.412 ☐ D 6

Praises of the Gulf of La Spezia have been sung by many poets, including Petrarch, Dante, Shelley, d'Annunzio among others. Today La Spezia, the capital of the province of the Riviera di Levante, is a modern town lying on the Gulf. It is also a diocesan seat. Since 1929, the naval har-

L'Aquila, castle

L'Aquila, Fontana delle 99 Cannelle

bour has given the town a particular character. Today it is an important industrial centre.

Cathedral of S. Maria Assunta: Severely damaged in 1943, restoration of the building is largely complete. Only the sacristy and the campanile have remained unchanged. The original church was built in 1271 and was at that time outside the town walls. It was torn down in 1436 and rebuilt shortly thereafter. Inside there are a nave and four aisles and numerous 15–17C works of art, of which only a few are mentioned below: *The Feeding of the Five Thousand,* by the Ligurian artist Giov.Batt. Casoni; the *Coronation of the Virgin with Saints,* polychrome terracotta by Andrea della Robbia; and *The Assumption of the Virgin* by Dom. Fiasella, in the chancel.

Museo Archeologico Lunense (in the *Museo Civico, Palazzo Crozza*): The *Sezione Ligure* houses Italy's most important collection of figure stele, which come from Lunigiana and date from the Bronze and Iron Ages. The exhibits, some 9,000 in number, include a golden *Byzantine necklace* from the 5C BC, Etruscan-Roman ceramics and bronzes, Roman mosaics, and a fine *bust of the young Augustus.*

Also worth seeing: *Museo Tecnico Navale* (go through the main entrance to the vast complex of *arsenals,* on the *Piazza Dom. Chiodo*). Here, there are both historical and more modern models of ships, ships' charts, weapons and mementoes. The *Castello di S.Giorgio* was founded by Niccolò Fieschi and restored in 1371. In the early 17C, the city of Genoa financed the building of the castle's massive walls.

Latisana 33053
Udine/Friuli   p.410□H 3

Latisana has probably been inhabited since Roman times. From 1186 onwards, the patriarchs of Aquileia granted it in fee to the counts of Gorizia.

Parish church of S.Giovanni Battista: Consecrated in 1760. The 2nd altar on the right has a *Pala* with a 'Baptism of Christ' by Paolo Veronese of 1567—probably one of his most important works. The third altar on the right has an interesting *wooden crucifix* by Andrea Fosco of 1566.

Environs: In the Pineta district of Lignano, which is c. 16 km. to the S.there is the 14C church of *S.Maria di Bevazzana.* The church was on the mouth of the River Tagliamento until 1967, when it was moved here. Inside are fine 15C frescos.

Lecce 73100
Lecce/Apulia   p.418□P 12

Lupiae of antiquity is today the main town of the so-called 'Terra d'Otranto'. The town is well worth visiting for its independent baroque style (15–17C), or 'barocco Leccese'; Gregorovius called it the 'Florence of the Rococo'.

SS. Nicola e Cataldo (Campo Santo): Formerly a Benedictine church and the most interesting church in Lecce for the

La Spezia, museum, stele

student of architectural history. Built in 1180 by Tancred, the last Norman king of Sicily, it is the only building in Lecce from the Norman-Hohenstaufen period. The *main portal* is the original Romanesque and has the founder's dedicatory inscription on the architrave. It is divided into three parts and in places Arab, antique and Byzantine influences can be picked out. On the right side there is a simpler Romanesque portal. The layout is a mixture of a centrally planned and a longitudinally planned building. *Interior:* The narrow nave and two narrow aisles display French-Gothic influence; the nave is barrel-vaulted and there are beautiful capitals. Windows in the dome let in light. From the adjoining *cloister* you can get to the *roof terrace*, which gives a fine view of the 12C octagonal *dome*.

S. Croce (Piazza della Prefettura): The town's most striking baroque church. It was founded by Walter di Brienne in 1353. Both church and the adjoining Celestine monastery were rebuilt from 1549 onwards and were not finished until *c.* 1700—the façade was only finished in the early 19C. The baroque church was designed by G.Riccardi and G.Zimbalo and is the imaginative culmination of the 'barocco Leccese'. Adjoining the church on the left is the **Palazzo della Prefettura**, which is the former monastery (see above) and has a splendid *baroque façade*. The *Museo Castromediano*, the province's museum, occupies the N. wing and other parts; finds include ancient vases, terracotta and coins.

Piazza del Duomo: An enclosed square, which gives the impression of an inner room (like St. Mark's Square in Venice). The *Cathedral of S.Oronzo* was originally begun in 1114. In 1659–70, it was completely rebuilt in baroque style by Giuseppe Zimbalo, known as Zingarello. The campanile is 230 ft. tall, in four stages and two façades, one Renaissance and one baroque. Adjoining it on its right are the *Bishop's Palace* (portico with half-columns) and the *priests' seminary* (built in 1709), both of which have richly decorated façades. The seminary's courtyard has an extremely richly decorated *baroque fountain*.

Next to the seminary are the ruins of the *Roman theatre*.

Piazza S.Oronzo: The centre of the modern town. On the S.side there are excavations of the ancient *amphitheatre* from the 1&2C AD. Formerly it had 25,000 seats; now it is 16 ft. below the present floor level. *Roman column* (cf. Brindisi) with S. Oronzo, the town's patron saint. On the W. side is the so-called *Sedile*, a loggia dating from 1592, formerly a town hall; next to it is the portal of the church of *S.Marco* dating from 1543.

Also worth seeing: *S. Matteo*, built in 1710, with a splendid baroque façade. *S. Angelo*, baroque façade, with a 12C ciborium in the sacristy. The *Chiesa del Rosario, Chiesa del Carmine and S.Chiara*, all have fine baroque façades. The *Palazzo del Seggio*, has Gothic arcades. The *Porta Napoli* (Via Principe di Savoia) is a triumphal arch dating from 1548, built in honour of Emperor Charles V. 16C *castle*, built on a Norman castle.

Environs: 3 km. outside the town are the excavations of **Rudiae**, of antiquity, the

Lecce, SS. Nicola e Cataldo

home of the poet Ennius (239–169BC). Some 20 km. to the NW is **Squinzano:** The former Basilian monastery of *S.Maria delle Cerrate*, it was founded in the 13C by Tancred the Norman, and has remains of a Romanesque cloister. Today, a Greek dialect is still spoken by some people in the towns of *Calimera*, *Martano* and *Carpignano* (cf. Otranto).

Lendinara 45026
Rovigo/Venice   p.410[?1 F 4

Cathedral of S.Sofia (Via S.Giuseppe): Beautiful, expansive interior of nave and two aisles. Renovated in the 18C; campanile built in 1797–1857. Richly carved *marble altars*. On the 1st and 3rd altars on the right are the paintings *St. Peter and St. Paul* by Ant. Zanchi, and on the 2nd altar on the right, *Descent of the Holy Spirit* by Dom. Maggiotto. Frescos are by Giorgio Anselmi (1795). In the sacristy, there is a fine picture of *Madonna and Child with Angel making music* by Dom. Mancini (1511).

The church of **S.Giuseppe** (with a baptistery) has 17C paintings of the Bologna school, and a late-15C terracotta *Madonna and Child*.

Santuario della Madonna dei Pilastrello (Via del Santuario): Originally 16C; redesigned in the 18C. The *Capella del Bagno*, in part original 16C, has a nave and two aisles and a basin with miraculous water for bathing the sick; also good paintings. Adjoining the chapel is the *Salone del Pelligrino*, which has pictures by Angelo Trevisani, Tomm. Sciacca, Ant. Celesti etc.

S.Biagio (Riviera S.Biagio): Classical 19C church, built according to Palladian architectural principles; portal from 1531. The altarpiece is a *Visitation* of 1525, by Seb. Filippi da Lendinara and it is well worth seeing for its delicate background landscape.

Also worth seeing: In the *Palazzo Comunale* (Piazza Risorgimento) a splendid wooden grille by the Lorenzo brothers and Cristoforo Canozzi (1450).

Lentiái 32020
Belluno/Veneto   p.410 ☐ G 2

Parish church of S. Maria Assunta: Late 15C, with a broad façade; further enlarged in 1568 and restored in the early 20C. The church together with its massive campanile dominate the main square of the town. The interior is splendid; the nave is vaulted by a heavy coffered ceiling painted with scenes from the *Life of the Virgin* by Cesare Vecellio, in 1577–9. In the left aisle there is a *Baptism of Christ* by Palma il Giovane; behind the high altar there are parts of a valuable *polyptych* from Titian's workshop.

Lentini 96016
Syracuse/Sicily   p.420 ☐ L 17

Founded in 729 BC—at the same time as Catania—by Greeks from Taormina on Naxos and called 'Leontinoi'. Lentini was the home of Gorgias, the famous sophist (485–380 BC), and of Jacopo da Lentini (13C), one of the first poets to write in Italian.

Chiesa Madre S.Alfio (Piazza Duomo): Built after 1693 and restored in the 18C, when the façade was given its present lovely appearance. The interior is fine and has a nave and two aisles. In the right aisle there is a 19C silver *figure* of St.Alfius. An early Christian *crypt* from the 3C is reputed to be the burial site of St.Alfius, the church's patron saint. The chapel to the left of the chancel has a Byzantine icon, the 'Madonna del Castello', which is possibly 9C.

Archaeological Museum (Via Piave): Houses the excavation finds of Leontinoi. *Room I* has Bronze Age ceramics (from the 20C BC onwards). *Room II* has ceramic ar-

Lecce, S. Croce

chitectural fragments from the remains of a temple from the 8–6C BC. *Rooms IV* and *V* have finds from burial grounds, as well as fine vases.

Also worth seeing: *Chiesa della Fontana* (Via Roma), 18C; a 13C capital makes a beautiful holy-water stoup. The *Grotto di S.Mauro* has Byzantine frescos.

Environs: Excavations of **Leontinoi** can be seen in the S.of the town, along the Via Regina Margherita. Parts of the *town defences,* dating back to the 7C BC, have survived. There is also a *necropolis* (6C BC or later), which lies outside the S.gate (the so-called 'Porta Siracusana'). On the Colle Metapiccola, a *prehistoric settlement,* with remains of houses from the 11C BC, has been uncovered.

Leonessa 02016
Rieti/Latium   p.414 □ H 8

A little town founded in 1228. In 1539, Charles V gave it as dowry on his daughter Margaretha's second marriage, which was to Ottavio Farnese. The town abounds in medieval houses and houses from the 16&17C which give it great character.

Church of S. Francesco (Via Cucci): Mid-15C. Early-16C terracotta *crib* with a polychrome frame and many figures. Fine Gothic *portal* of 1356 came from the torn-down *church of S. Donato.* Nave and two aisles and the octagonal pillars have 14C *votive frescos.*

Also worth seeing: *S.Maria del Popolo* (Corso S.Giuseppe da Leonessa): Begun mid-15C and completed much later; 18C interior renovation. *S. Pietro* (above the Piazza del Municipio): 15C, with a fine portal of 1467.

Lèrici 19032
La Spezia/Liguria   p.412 □ D 6

Castello: On a neck of land on rising ground. First built in the early 13C by the Pisans and conquered by Genoa as early as 1256. Genoa extended it and added an imposing pentagonal tower. The main body of the massive building, retaining walls and bulwarks, were not built until 1555. A small courtyard and the *Chapel of S.Anastasia* lie within the walls.

Also worth seeing: The parish church of *S. Francesco* (Via Petriccioli): a baroque building of 1632 – 6; façade restored in 1962. The single-aisled interior has numerous valuable works of art, chiefly from the 16&17C. *Casa di Andrea Doria* (Via Doria No.3): The powerful Genoese of the same name stayed here in 1528 when he changed his political allegiance, leaving the services of the French king François I to join Charles V.

Environs: **S.Terenzo**, some 12 km. away, became well-known mainly because famous figures such as Lord Byron, Shelley and Böcklin. stayed here. The late medieval *Castello* was restored in the 15& 16C. The parish church of *S.Maria dell'Arena* is nearer the sea and has fine sculptures.

Lèuca 73030
Lecce/Apulia   p.418 □ P 13

Cape of S.Maria di Leuca, the SE tip of Italy, where the Ionian Sea and the Gulf of Taranto meet. The name is derived from 'akra leuka', ancient Greek for the white limestone rocks. The church of *S.Maria de Finibus Terrae* is on the cape itself. Inside, to the right of the entrance, there is an altar, which came from the previous building, a classical Temple of Minerva. From the *lighthouse,* and in clear weather, the view stretches as far away as Albania.

Environs: Some 7 km. to the N. is **Patù**: 'Le Centopietre' is a building which as yet has not been clearly identified; it could be a prehistoric shrine, a Greek tomb, or an early medieval church. Externally, it is a stone box; internally, it is divided up by pilasters and columns. The roof is made of stone slabs. On the W. wall there are remnants of 14C frescos—13 saints can still be made out. Opposite this building stands the 12C church of *S. Giovanni,* which is a mixture of Byzantine and Apulian-Romanesque.

Lévanto 19015
La Spezia / Liguria   p.412   D 6

Parish church of S. Andrea: The most important church in this very old town. Fine Pisan-Gothic *façade* on which white marble alternates with dark stone. The interior was originally single-aisled (mid-13C); two more aisles were added in 1463.

Loggia del Comune (near the town park): 13C; arches with Romanesque capitals.

Also worth seeing: The *Casa Restani* (near the parish church): originally a 13C house; an arcaded passage and a four-arched window have survived from that time.

Environs: *Monterosso, Vernazza, Corniglia, Manarola, Riomaggiore.* The area called *Cinque Terre* stretches as far as La Spezia and provides an excellent idea of the former isolation of these medieval localities.

Licata 92027
Agrigento / Sicily   p.420 □ K 18

Licata was founded by Agrigento in the 3C BC; traces of the ancient settlement of 'Phintias' can be seen on a hill in the W. of the town. In 256 BC Licata was the scene of the Romans' great naval victory over the Carthaginians in the battle of Eknomos. On 10 July 1943 American invasion troops landed here from Africa and advanced north.

S. Domenico (Corso Roma): 1618 with two fine paintings of 1611 by F.Paladino 'S. Antonio Abate' on the right, and 'SS. Trinità' on the high altar).

Licata, castle

Chiesa del Carmine (Corso Roma): 18C; narrow baroque façade; fine cloister in the adjoining monastery.

S. Maria la Vetere has a *bronze crucifix,* which formerly belonged to S. Carlo Borromeo.

Chiesa Madre (Corso Vitt. Emanuele): 1508. Inside is the interesting *Cappella del Crocifisso* with carving from 1705 and a wooden crucifix, which survived the Turkish conquest of the town in 1553.

Also worth seeing: The 17C *Castle of S. Angelo,* fine view.

Environs: About 10 km. to the NW, near to **Torre di Gaffe,** are the remains of the 15C *Castelazzo di Palma.* On a hill in the W. the remains of the ancient Greek town of *Phintias* are visible. There are two further hills with ruins of ancient towns.

Livorno, cathedral

Livorno, Monumento dei 4 Mori

Livorno 57100
Livorno/Tuscany   p.414□ E 7

Livorno was first mentioned in 904. The
town fell to Genoa in the late 14C and was
bought by Florence in the 15C.

Cathedral of S. Francesco d'Assisi:
Built in 1594–5 to a design by Bern. Buontalenti, and finished by Aless. Pieroni in
1606. There is an interesting portico in the
form of a loggia, which has 3 arches, supported by two columns with a single capital. Above this loggia there is a terrace. The
rest of the façade is flat with a window and
a pediment.

S. Giulia: A little church behind the cathedral. A panel of *St. Giulia and 8 scenes
from her life* on a gold background is attributed to the school of Giotto.

S. Ferdinando (or *Chiesa della Crocetta*)
Built in 1707–14 to a design by Giov. Batt.
Foggini. It has the finest interior in
Livorno with elegant stucco and marble
statues.

Museo Civico 'Giovanni Fattori' (in
the middle of the park of the Villa Fab-
bricotti): This collection was brought together in 1896 and includes prehistoric
remains, Etruscan and Roman finds, the
work of early Italians such as Neri di Bicci
Cima da Conegliano etc., paintings by
Giovanni Fattori, a 19C painter born in
Livorno, and paintings by Modigliani
himself born in Livorno (1884).

Aquario Comunale 'D.Cestoni': Fish
other marine life and a museum of natural history.

Monumento dei Quattro Mori (built in
honour of Ferdinando I): So called after the

4 chained, naked negroes around the base; they were cast from bronze by Pietro Tacca in 1626. Above them stands the marble statue of Ferdinando I Medici, by Giovanni Bandini (1595).

Fortezza Vecchia: A massive brick fortress towering above the water and dating back to the 9C. It was built by Antonio da Sangallo il Giovane in 1534.

Torre del Marzocco: An octagonal tower, built by the Florentines in 1423 on top of the old Pisan tower of 1154.

Fortezza Nuova, (in the S. Marco district): Late 16C; partly destroyed.

Viale Italia: A Lovely route to the sea with villas, palazzi and gardens.

Locri 89044
Reggio Calabria/Calabria   p.420☐N 16

Locri Epizephyrii was founded in the 7C BC by Locrians from Greece and was so-called due to its site on the promontory of Zephyrion. Here in *c.* 660 BC Zaleukos was the first to codify a Greek town's laws. Ionians emigrated from Samos to Locri in the late 5C BC. During the Peloponnesian War (431–404 BC), Locri was an ally of Syracuse. In 275 BC, after being conquered by Rome, it lost all importance. Saracens destroyed the city in the 7C AD; subsequently the inhabitants founded Gerace.

Zona degli Scavi di Locri Antica: Remains of the *town wall*, which were originally *c.* 7.5 km. long. Behind the Antiquarium (see below) are the remains of an *Ionic temple* (5C BC) and of a *Doric temple* (7C BC). Further inland, near the Casa Marafioti, there is a *late Doric temple.* A *Graeco-Roman theatre* can be seen nearby in the Località Pirettina. Occupying a gully between Mannella and Abbadena there is a *shrine to Persephone,* in which many votive offerings have been found (see below). Foundations of a *Temple of Athene* have been found nearby. There are also several *burial grounds,* including Siculan from 10–9C BC, Greek and Roman. The *antiquarium* at the entrance, by road SS. 106, is also worth a visit. It has finds from tombs in Locri's burial grounds: ceramics and bronzes from the 9–8C BC; fragments from the various temples in the excavation area; terracotta votive gifts and coins.

Lodi 20075
Milano/Lombardy   p.412 D 4

After Lodi Vecchio (the Roman 'Laus Pompeia') had been completely destroyed by the Milanese, Barbarossa founded a new Lodi in 1158. It was designed as a fortified town with straight streets opening on to the cathedral and market squares. During the Middle Ages, Lodi was constantly feuding with Milan. The Adda bridge was stormed by Napoleon.

Cathedral (Piazza della Vittoria): Begun in 1160 and completed in the 12C; completely restored in 1958–65. The façade is no longer original; the rose-window dates from 1506. The building is basilican in plan with 6 bays and there is a choir with 3 apses.

The 'Incoronata' (a pilgrimage church near the cathedral): Built by G.Battagio and G.Dolcebuono in 1488–90. It is a two-storeyed, octagonal structure with a spherical dome. The Chapel of St.Paul contains four *paintings* of Christ's childhood by Bergognone. The *Cappella Maggiore* has a 'Coronation of the Virgin' by A.Piazza (1519).

S. Cristoforo: Rebuilt by Pellegrino Tibaldi in 1564–86.

S.Francesco (at the end of the Via XX Sett.): Begun in the 1290's; the façade is incomplete. A preliminary bay is followed by 3 bays based on the metrical system, there is then a transept and chancel. The church has the tombs of many of Lodi's distinguished families. There are numerous *frescos* by local Lombard painters of the 14&15C. Fine *wooden door.*

S.Agnese: 14C; The 1st altar on the right has a *polyptych* (Virgin and Child with Saints) by A.Piazza dating from 1520. 15C *crucifix* in the apse.

Museo Civico (Corso Umberto I): The museum is housed in the former monastery of S.Filippo. Valuable 17–19C *ceramics collection* from local workshops. On display are *archaeological finds, weapons, and paintings.*

Ospedale Maggiore: Begun in 1459 and extended in 1571 to plans by Pellegrini. The *façade* dates from 1792. Fine *arcaded courtyard.*

Broletto (Piazza Broletto, to the left of the cathedral): The ruins of the former Palazzo Comunale from the 13C.

Environs: Lodi Vecchio (6 km. to the W.): *S.Bassiano*, founded in the 4C. The Romanesque building was redesigned in Gothic-Lombard style in 1322. The façade is tripartite and has open double-arched windows above the aisles and a rose-window. **S.Angelo Lodigiano** (12 km. towards Pavia): Before the town came under the rule of the Visconti in the 13C, it was a fief of the bishops of Lodi. The latter issued the order to build the *Castello*, which was given its present form by the Regina della Scala in 1370. The castle is used as an institute and as the *Museum Gian Giacomo Morando Bolognini* (the Bolognini had the building restored at the beginning of the century). The museum is a fascinating example of a patrician interior from the 15–16C, containing furniture, pictures, weapons, and an extensive library. The castle courtyard has a beautiful fountain.

Lomello 27034

S.Maria Maggiore: Impressive early 11C Romanesque building. Today, the W. section is in ruins; the campanile survives. Inside, the basilica has a nave, two aisles and a transept. There is an alternation between round and rectangular pillars for the flying buttresses supporting the open roof truss. Beneath the apse there are the remains of a *crypt*. The exterior masonary of the E. end is interesting.

S.Angelo Lodigano (Lodi), castle

Baptistery of S. Giovanni ad Fontes
(next to S.Maria Maggiore): 5C; top part
8C. Four rectangular niches alternate with
four semi-circular ones; octagonal dome.
Inside: remains of a *font*.

Lonigo 36045
Vicenza / Veneto   p.410 F 3

Santuario della Madonna dei Miracoli
(along the Via S. Bonifacio): After a miraculous event, a chapel of the Virgin was
enlarged (1488–1501) into a church with
an adjoining *Olivetan monastery* . The
building was probably designed by
Lorenzo da Bologna and the plans carried
out by A.Lamberti. The façade is late 15C
and richly decorated with many votive
panels (15&16C); there is a vestibule. Then
comes the old chapel with the miraculous
image. The church itself is single-aisled
with ribbed-vaulted bays; the choir with
a polygonal end. The walls have pilasters
with stylized capitals. The church was
painted throughout in the 18–19C. Opposite the main entrance is the *Cappella di
S. Francesca Romana.*

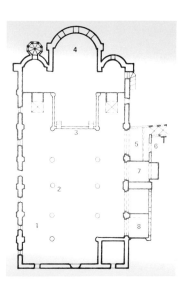

Lodi, cathedral 1 Vistarini tomb, 16C **2** S.
Bassiano, 1284 **3** Last Supper (Romanesque
sculpture) **4** inlay work by Fra' Giovanni da Verona
5 remains of a 'Last Judgement' (fresco, late 14C)
6 access to the Cortile dei Canonici **7** miracle of
the snow, by G.C.Procaccini **8** baptistery: tomb
of Bassiano da Ponte (A.Fusina); L'Assunta,
polyptych by M.Iazza, Massacre of the Innocents, polyptych by C.Piazza, 1529.

Lodi, S.Francesco

Lodi, cathedral, portal, Eve

Lodi, S. Filippo (18C; fine decoration with frescos by Carloni)

Rocca (along the Via Garibaldi): Built 1576-8, to plans by Vinc. Scamozzi, on the site of an older castle. The building is formidable in appearance; only on the S.side is it more varied by gables.

Loreto 60025

Ancona/Marches   p.414☐ I 7

A much-visited place of pilgrimage. Legend has it that after the conquest of Palestine by the Moslems the house in which the Virgin Mary was born was transported here by the angels.

Santuario della S.Casa: Church above the shrine of S. Casa, with nave and two aisles and Latin cross ground plan. The different styles visible in the building are evidence of the long period of construction in which many artists were involved.

Reconstruction began in 1468, when Baccio Pontelli added wall passages in the transept and apse to protect against raids by pirates. Giuliano da Sangallo built the *dome* in 1498-1500. The *façade* dates from 1571-87. The campanile by L.Vanoitelli was built in 1750-4. The *bronze statue of Sixtus V* by Antonio di Bernardino Calcagni stands in front of the façade and dates from 1589; on the pedestal, besides the *Virtues,* there are reliefs of the *Expulsion of the money-changers* and *Christ's entry into Jerusalem,* as well as depictions of the *The transportation of S. Casa.* The façade has a *Madonna* of 1583 by Girolamo Lombardo (1583) and three wonderful *bronze doors.* The left door of 1596 by Tiburzio Vergelli has *Scenes from the Old and New Testaments.* The middle door of c.1600 by Antonio di Girolamo and his brothers Pietro, Paolo and Giacomo Lombardo has *Scenes from the Life of Adam and Eve* and incidents of *ecclesiastical history.* The right

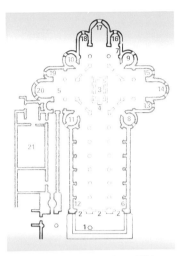

Loreto, basilica 1 statue of Sixtus V **2** bronze portals **3** S.Casa **4** altar **5** candlestick **6** tabernacle **7** tomb of N.Caetani **8** sacristy of St.Mark **9** sacristy of St.John **10** sacristy of St.Luke **11** sacristy of St.Matthew **12** font **13** Swiss chapel **14** Spanish chapel **15** chapel of the Duke of Urbino **16** Polish chapel **17** German chapel **18** Canadian chapel **19** Slav chapel **20** French chapel **21** treasury

Loreto Aprutino, S. Maria in Piano

portal was built at the same time and has scenes from *the New Testament* and from the *Life of the Virgin* by Calcagni, Seb. Sebastiani and Tarquinio Giacometti. Inside, under the dome of the crossing stands the *S. Casa*, which is surrounded by a 16C marble screen designed by Bramante. The house has bronze doors. The inside, blackened by candle soot, has 14C frescos and a cross. *Reliefs on the doors* date from 1568–76 and are the work of Girolamo and Ludovico Lombardo, T.Vergelli and A.Calcagni. On the S.side, there are *Scenes from Christ's Childhood, Annunciation, Adoration of the Shepherds, Adoration of the Magi and Dispute in the Temple.* On the N. side there are scenes from the Passion: *Mount of Olives, Flagellation, Road to Calvary* and *Crucifixion.* The cycle of marble reliefs on the outer walls begins on the N. side with the *Nativity of the Virgin* and the *Betrothal of the Virgin.* On the W. side comes an *Annunciation, Visitation* and *Estimation,* and

on the S., the *Nativity of Christ* and the *Adoration of the Magi.* The cycle ends in the E. with the *Death of the Virgin* and the *Transportation of the Santa Casa.* These reliefs are attributed to Baccio Bandinelli, Raffaello da Montelupo, Andrea Sansovino, Tribolo, Francesco da Sangallo the Younger, and Domenico Aimo. The *bronze tabernacle* and the *monument of Niccolò Caetani* are by T. Vergelli and A.Calcagni, while the *five-branched candlestick* is by the Lombardi brothers (*c.* 1550). Octagonal rooms in the corners of the transepts were planned as four sacristies dedicated to the Evangelists. Only the two sacristies on the right side were completed; the *sacristy of St.Mark,* in the W., has a *dome with painted angels and prophets* by Melozzo da Forl i (after 1477). A Passion cycle was planned for the walls but only *Christ's Entry into Jerusalem* was actually painted. In 1479, Luca Signorelli painted the E. *Sacristy of St. John* with angels, Evangelists and

Church Fathers; on the walls are the *Apostles with Doubting Thomas* and the *Conversion of Saul*. The same artist was also responsible for the frescos in the vault of the nave, which have been painted over more than once. The paintings in the *choir chapel* are by Ludwig Seitz (d. 1908).

In front of the basilica is the **Piazza della Madonna** with a *fountain* to a design by C.Maderno and Giov. Fontana. The *Palazzo Apostolico* was begun by Bramante, and continued by Antonio Sangallo the Younger and Luigi Vanvitelli.

Loreto Aprutino 65014

Pescara/Abruzzi   p.416☐ I 8

Environs: *S.Maria in Piano:* Founded in the 9C and renovated in 1280; façade restored in 1956. The portal is dated 1559 and the portico 1560. The 15C campanile is decorated with coloured majolicas. Inside there are remnants of frescos: *Lives of Saints* on the long walls date from the 14&15C and the entrance wall has a 15C *Last Judgement*.

Lucca 55100

Lucca/Tuscany   p.414☐ E 6

A town in the NW of Tuscany. The old town is particularly fine having numerous churches and being surrounded by the ramparts of the town defences. Originally it was an Etruscan settlement and then Ligurian; the town became Roman in 180 BC. Lucca was involved in various wars and subjected to different rulers, e.g. under the Lombards in *c.* 570, but it became a free state in 1115. The 12&13C were Lucca's heyday. It then became dependent upon the Scaligers and upon Pisa, only regaining its freedom under Charles IV. After four centuries of peace, Lucca was occupied in the early 19C first by Napoleon and then by Austria. World War 2 caused severe damage in the town.

Cathedral of S.Martino: Probably begun by S.Frediano in the 6C. It was built by Bishop Anselmo da Baggio (later Pope Alexander II) in 1060 and restored in the early 13C. The church is outwardly Romanesque and has a fine asymmetrical

Loreto, Santuario della S.Casa   *Loreto, sacristy of St.Mark*

façade in black and white marble, with three-storeys of arcades. Particularly worth seeing are the *Deposition* in the lunettte of the left portal by Nicolò Pisano, the paintings of *4 scenes from the life of St.Martin,* and the expressive reliefs of *the months* in the narthex. The inside, much restored in the 14C & early 15C, has a nave, two aisles and a transept, which itself has two aisles. There is a fine polychrome marble floor with geometric patterning by the school of Civitali (e.g. *Judgement of Solomon* by Antonio Federighi). On the inside of the narthex there is *St.Martin on horseback with the beggar* by a Lombard-Luccese craftsman of the early 13C (this is copied on the arches of the narthex). The left aisle has an octagonal tempietto, the *Tempietto del Volto Santo* by Matteo Civitali dating from 1482–4. The little marble temple contains a crucifix, the *(Volto Santo)* from the 11C or 12C; Christ is clothed in a splendid garment with gold embroidery. In the arches around the tempietto there are figures of prophets, after Byzantine models. The *Volto Santo* is one of the most famous works of this kind and was mentioned by Dante in his *Inferno.* The altar itself is 18C and was possibly by Filippo Juvara (1725).
The Cappella del Santuario, in the left transept, has a *Madonna and Child with Saints* by Fra Bartolommeo (1509). In the middle of the same transept is the *Tomb of Ilaria del Carretto,* who died in 1405. This, a beautiful work by Jacopo della Quercia, dates from 1408 and shows Paolo Guinigi's second wife as a young woman resting on the sarcophagus, while at her feet is a little dog to symbolize loyalty. The same craftsman also made the *statue of St.John the Evangelist,* which stands by the left pillar of the *Cappella della Libertà,* a chapel to the immediate left of the *sacristy,* whose name commemorates the liberation of Lucca from Pisan domination. The monumental altar by Giambologna (1579) is also interesting, having a view of Lucca in the predella. Other fine features include: *stained-glass windows* (1485) by Pandolfo di Ugolino da Pisa in the choir; the *marble screens,* composed of fragments of the old choir screens, by the school of Matteo Civitali; the *tomb of Pietro da Noceto* (Pope Nicholas V's secretary) by Matteo Civitali,

which dates from 1472 and is a typical 15C Florentine tomb. The right aisle has a *Last Supper* and an altarpiece by Tintoretto of 1592. In the *sacristy* there is a particularly beautiful panel by Domenico Ghirlandaio, the *Martyrdom of St. Clement and St. Sebastian, Entombment,* and other scenes. The 13C *campanile* with single- and four-arched windows.

S.Michele in Foro: A typical example of 12C Pisan Romanesque found in Lucca. The very high façade dates from the early 13C, when there was a plan for the height of the church to be raised; it is possible that Giudetto da Como—who also worked on the cathedral's façade—contributed to the rich façade decoration. All the columns of the 4 rows of arcades are worked in very different ways; some are flat, some with reliefs, some rather Lombard and some are inlaid with coloured marble. The pediment is crowned by an enormous (more recent) marble statue of the *Archangel Michael fighting the Dragon.* At one corner there is a statue of the *Madonna and Child* by Civitali (1480). The colonnade on the left flank is 14C. The *campanile* stands by the arm of the transept and has 12C rows of arches. The apse is clearly of Pisan origin. There are locked gates across the transepts. On the right there is a fine portal with a richly decorated 12C architrave. Inside: Nave and two aisles with classical capitals. The 16C vault has a band of frescos. Most interesting: a panel by Filippino Lippi of *SS Jerome, Sebastian, Roch and Helena;* a terracotta *Madonna and Child* by Andrea della Robbia, and a 13C painted *wooden crucifix.*

S.Frediano: In the N. of the town. Built from 1112–47, above an 8C basilica, which was revealed during excavations in 1950 (results of these excavations can be seen near the font). In the 13C, the height of the building was increased. The façade is simple with 3 portals, pilaster strips and a colonnaded gallery. Side wings were added later. The façade has a Byzantine mosaic of the *Ascension* attributed to Berlinghiero

Lucca, cathedral

Lucca, cathedral 1 St. Martin on horseback, Lombard-Luccan artist, early 13C 2 altarpiece, Dom. Passignano, 1594 (Nativity of Christ) 3 altarpiece, Federigo Zuccari, 1595 (Adoration of the Magi) 4 altarpiece, Tintoretto, 1592 (Last Supper) 5 altarpiece, Dom. Passignano, 1598 (Crucifixion) 6 marble inlay work, Ant. Federighi (Judgement of Solomon) 7 pulpit, Matteo Civitali, 1494–8 8 sacristy; attributed to Bart. di Giovanni (Madonna and Child with Saints, story of St. Peter); panel, Domenico Ghirlandaio (martyrdom of St. Clement, Entombment, martyrdom of St. Sebastian, Conversion of Paul) 9 tomb of Pietro da Noceto, Matteo Civitali, 1472 10 tomb of Dom. Bertini, Matteo Civitali 11 Capp.del Sacramento; 2 angels, Matteo Civitali, 1477 12 Capp.; altar of S.Regolo, Matteo Civitali, 1484 13 sanctuary; marble screens, Matteo Civitali, choir stalls, Leon. Marti, 1452; stained-glass window, Pandolfo di Ugolino da Pisa, 1485 14 Capp.della Libertà, altar by Giambologna, 1579 15 sculpture of John the Evangelist by Jacopo della Quercia 16 Capp.del Santuario; altar, Fra Bartolomeo, 1509 (Madonna and Child Enthroned with St. Stephen and John the Baptist) 17 tomb of Ilaria del Carretto, Jacopo della Quercia, 1408 18 altarpiece, Jacopo Ligozzi, 1596 (Visitation) 19 Tempietto del Volto Santo, Matteo Civitali, 1482–4, crucifix, 11/12C, small altar, attributed to Fil.Juvarra, 1725; outside the Tempietto: St. Sebastian, Matteo Civitali, 1484 20 altarpiece, G.B.Paggi (Annunciation) 21 fresco, Cosimo Rosselli

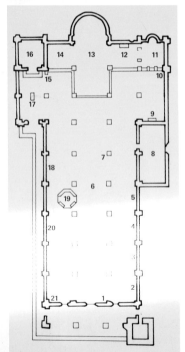

Berlinghieri. Inside, the basilica is sober with a nave and two aisles, which are divided by columns. The inner wall of the façade has frescos, including *Madonna and Saints* by Amico Aspertini, a *Visitation* and *Peter and Paul* by a 15C Florentine artist. The finely carved *font* in the right aisle is mid-12C; around its circular basin there is a relief of 10 *stories of Moses*. The figures are in a style found on Roman sarcophagi; these were copied by the craftsman Master Roberto in the late 12C and executed by the circle of artists surrounding Master Biduino. The font in use today is a marble tabernacle by Matteo Civitali (1489). The *Cappella Trenta*, the 4th chapel in the left aisle, has an altarpiece by Jacopo della Quercia in the form of a Gothic *polyptych* with a predella dating from 1422, in which the figures of the *Madonna and Child with four Saints* are hewn from a single huge block of marble. The much-damaged *tomb of Lorenzo Trenta and his wife* is set into the floor in front of the altar. On the wall opposite there is an altarpiece by Francesco Francia, *Immaculate Conception and Saints*. Further features of interest include two glazed terracottas by Andrea della Robbia (next to the older baptismal font), *Annunciation* and *St.Peter the Martyr*.

S. Giovanni (actually 2 buildings): The church of *S.Reperata* or *S.Pantaleone*, and the *Baptistery of S. Giovanni*. Only the main portal and the right side have survived from the 12C church; the rest of the building dates from 1622. On the architrave of the Gothic portal there is a *Madonna between two Angels and Apostles* by Master Villano (1187). The basilica has a nave and two aisles and rows of columns; one of the capitals of the columns is Roman, the others are Romanesque. Passing under an arch, you come to the *baptistery*. Here too, there are two fonts, one ancient and one more recent — 15C Tuscan in origin.

Chiesa del Salvatore (also called *Misericordia*): 12C; the upper section is neo-

Lucca, S.Michele in Foro

Lucca, cathedral of S.Martino. Volto Santo (11/12C)

Lucca, cathedral of S.Martino

Gothic and dates from the 19C. The portals by the Pisan master Biduino are of interest: the main portal has *scenes from the life of St.Nicholas* by a follower of Biduino, and the right portal has the *Baptism of St.Nicholas* by the master himself.

S. Maria della Rosa: 1309; enlarged several times. Along the side there is a Pisan-Gothic row of arches. Renaissance portal by the school of Matteo Civitali.

S.Giusto: 12C; simple, severe façade with blind galleries and three portals. The left portal has the simple Pisan feeling for design, while the middle portal displays the richer style of Lucca.

S.Alessandro: Also 12C. An example of Luccan architecture, which has survived in excellent condition. The marble façade is grey with white stripes. The portal has a 13C relief of *Pope Alexander.*

S.Paolino (also *SS Paolino e Donato*): Built in 1522 on the site of a Roman building, which was possibly a temple. Behind the altar, there is a pre-Christian *sarcophagus* with a *Good Shepherd* relief; inlaid *choir stalls* by Salimbene Magni (1563).

S.Maria Forisportam (also *S.Maria Bianca:*) So-called because it was 'outside the (Roman) walls' of the town. Mainly 13C —the upper section dates from the 16C— with Pisan influence visible in the columns and colonnades. The lunettes of the 3 portals have reliefs from the 12& 13C. Inside there are paintings by Guercino—*Assunta with Saints* and *St.Lucy.*

Opera del Duomo (in the Palazzo delle Poste e Telegrafi, Piazza degli Antelminelli 5) with the *Tesoro del Duomo* (cathedral treasure): The most precious item is the *Cross of the Pisans*, a sumptuous work from 1424–39, in the form of a silver tree with gold decoration. Most of the other items in the collection are Gothic and Renaissance church treasures.

Museo Nazionale di Villa Guinigi (Via

Barga (Lucca), cathedral, pulpit

della Quarquonia): A municipal museum with art from the Middle Ages and mementoes of Boccherini and Puccini. There are also Etruscan vases (including one depicting *Theseus*), mosaics, Roman marble sculptures, burial objects in the form of jewellery from Etruscan graves, marble sculptures from the façade of the church of S. Michele, and terracottas by della Robbia. Mention may also be made of a sacristy bench of 1488 by Crist. da Lendinara from the cathedral. The exhibits in the *picture gallery* include a *Croce dipinta* by Berlinghiero Berlinghieri, and the work of 15C artists.

Birthplace of Giacomo Puccini in the Via di Poggio, in front of the church.

Pinacoteca Nazionale (in the *Palazzo della Provincia*): Begun in 1578 by Ammannati, who built the left section and the portal. The other wing was added in 1728 when Francesco Pini adapted his style to that of the Ammannati section. The palace is built above the *Fortezza Augusta*, which was built in 1322, above the Castruccio Castracani, after a design by Giotto. A picture gallery, in the left wing, has paintings from the Renaissance up to the 19C, and derives partly from items in the collection of Duchess Marie-Louise dating from 1819. Mention should be made of: a *painted wooden cross (Croce dipinta)* by Berlinghiero Berlinghieri; *Holy Father with Mary Magdalene and St. Catherine* by Fra Bartolommeo, from 1509; and paintings by Beccafumi, Andrea del Sarto, Pontormo and others.

Palazzo Mazzarosa (Via S. Croce 64): 17C; in the courtyard there is a small collection of sculptures, including a Roman sarcophagus with a relief of Venus and Adonis. In the palace there is a fine collection of art.

Palazzo Gigli (today the Cassa di Risparmio): Early 16C. Ascribed to Matteo and Nicolò Civitali.

Palazzo Mansi (Via Galli Tassi): 17C; gallery of Italian painters (Francia, Domenichino) and numerous Dutch artists (Terborch, van Dyck, Breugel the Elder).

Palazzo Pretorio (Piazza S. Michele): Be-

Lucca, S. Frediano

Lucca, S. Maria Forisportam

gun in 1492 to a design by Matteo Civitali and completed by his son Nicolò; enlarged in 1588. 17C clock on the façade.

Villa di Paolo Guinigi (Via Guinigi, to the S.of the amphitheatre): A brick building of 1418, with loggia and rows of arches. Since 1968 it has housed the **Museo Nazionale di Villa Guinigi.**

Roman amphitheatre (Via Fillungo, near to the Piazza S.Frediano): Parts of the ring, and 2 rows of 54 arches, are still visible. An arch leads into the amphitheatre, which today houses a picturesque market. Surrounding houses are built on the foundations of the building, which dates from the 2C AD.

Teatro Romano: Remains, which have only recently been uncovered in excavations, can be seen in the houses on the Via S.Sebastiano and in the adjoining Piazza delle Grazie. The campanile of the former church of S.Agostino stands on a row of arches which was formerly part of the Roman theatre.

Town wall: Built in 1504–1654, with 11 bastions and a platform. The traveller is advised to take a walk along the 'Giro delle Mura' some 40 ft. up, because of the magnificent view over the whole town with its numerous churches. Town gates include the *Porta dei SS Gervasio e Protasio*, also known as dell'Annunziata, in the SW, on the Via S.Croce. It was built in 1260, even earlier than the surrounding wall, and is flanked by 2 distinctive semi-round towers. The *Portone dei Borghi*, in the N., along with part of the surrounding wall dates from 1260. It is Pisan in form with two cylindrical towers.

Environs: Viaréggio: NW of Lucca; with a sandy beach 20 km. long, has been famous as an elegant resort since the 2nd half of the 19C. Viaréggio's carnival procession, with its enormous phantasy shapes and splendid masks, is one of the best known in Italy. The *Premio Viaréggio* for literature is awarded here each August. On the nearby *Lago Massaciuccoli* is the *Villa Puccini*, where the composer and his wife are buried. **Pietrasanta:** Inland, to the N. of Viaréggio; the main town of Versilia. The town is important for its marble industry. Founded in 1242–55, it enjoyed a brief hey-

State library, Codex Latinus

Lucca, S. Frediano, font

day in the 1st half of the 14C; after which the population declined and the town became of less importance. Remains of a former fortification, the *Rocchetta* or *Rocca Arrighina*, still survive. The *cathedral of S.Martino*, dating from 1330, with its incomplete red *campanile* from the 15–16C, is worth seeing. In the *baptistery* of 1608 (beside and to the right of the cathedral) there is an interesting *font*. Designed by Donato Benti in 1509, the shell with the tempietto is by Fabrizio Pelliccia and Orezio Bergamini (1612). **Bagni di Lucca:** an agglomeration of several small spas to the N. of Lucca. They existed as early as the 11C (the *spa of Corsena)* and enjoyed a surge in popularity during the early 19C. Lucca's aristocracy, members of the ruling European families, and many literary figures, stayed here. The main baths are the *Bagni Caldi*, which are visited from May to October and derive their water from the salty sulphurous springs. The *Ponte a Seraglio* is picturesquely located on the bend of a small river. **La Villa** consists of not only the modern section of town, but also the old *Corsena* district with the Romanesque church of *S. Pietro*. **Lima** offers a splendid view from its high tower. **Barga** is further N. in the Serchio valley. Its for tifications were built under Barbarossa in 1186. The town was placed under Floren tine protection in 1341. The 9C *Ca thedral/S. Cristofano* is a fine sight to see extended in the 12C (façade) and 14C. Side chapels were added later. The Lombard Romanesque façade has interesting con soles with both human and fabulous being in the 2 rows of arches. The Lion door ha a relief of a *wine harvest*. Interesting *pulpi* Also worth seeing in the church: late-12C *S.Cristoforo;* 15C *Croce dipinta;* and a *view of Barga*, which is the background to a 16C painting of *St. Joseph* by Baccio Ciarpi. *Convent of St.Clare*: Founded in 1456 with a large *Assumption of the Virgin* by the della Robbia school at the high altar; fine mid 17C inlaid *choir stalls*. From the *Piazza L'Arringo* there is a magnificent panorama particularly of the mountains. **Castel nuovo di Garfagnana**, is still further N. in the fertile hill country of the Garfag nana. The old castle of *La Rocca* was built in the 12C with an irregular ground plan later enlarged. The poet Ariosto lived her from 1522–5. The ruins of the old castl of *S.Nicolao* can be seen to the N. The 16C border fortress, *Montalfonso*, built by A

Lucca, Palazzo Mansi

fonso II of Ferrara, stands half an hour's journey to the W.

Lucera 71036
Foggia/Apulia   p.416☐, L 10

Cathedral of S. Maria (Piazza del Duomo): Built 1300–17 by Charles II of Anjou on the ruins of a Saracen mosque. The architect was Pierre d'Angicourt. It has a nave, two aisles, three Gothic portals, and a beautiful apse. 14C *cenotaph to Charles II of Anjou*. 14C wooden *crucifix*. 15C *frescos*. The *altar table* is reputed to have come from the Hohenstaufen castle, the Castel Fiorentino (see below).

Castle: Begun by Frederick II in 1223. Excavations have revealed earlier Roman and Byzantine buildings. After the downfall of the Hohenstaufen, Charles I of Anjou enlarged it; subsequently it fell into complete ruin and was used as a quarry. The ground plan is an irregular pentagon and the wall is some 2,950 ft. long. There are 24 *defensive towers*, including two round towers called the 'lion's tower' and the 'lioness's tower'. The Hohenstaufen palace buildings occupy the NE corner in the form of a *keep* but only the ground storey has survived: this, a square building with four wings (165 ft. by 165 ft.), has a truncated pyramid-shaped top. In the courtyard *remains of the fountain* have survived. *Excavation* has been in progress since 1964 and the foundations of a Gothic church can be now be seen.

Museo Civico 'Giuseppe Fiorelli' (Via de Nicastri): With finds mainly from the ancient Luceria. A *statue of Venus* (1C AD) and a grey limestone *negro's head* are particularly fine.

Also worth seeing: *S.Francesco* (Via Zuppetta): 14C with 14, 15&18C frescos. A (restored) Roman *amphitheatre*, from 1C BC lies on the outskirts of the town and is indicated by signposts. It is 430 ft. long and 325 ft. wide.

Environs: Remains of the Hohenstaufen

hunting lodge, the **Castel Fiorentino** are some 20 km. to the NE, near the *Masseria Petrulli*,; Frederick II died here.

Luco dei Marsi 67056
L'Aquila/Abruzzi   p.416☐ I 9

The ancient town of *Lucus Angitiae.*
S.Maria delle Grazie: Outside the town on the site of the old temple of Angitia. It was severely damaged in the earthquake of 1915. The 13C portal is framed by fluted columns decorated with shells, blossoms and palm leaves.

Lugnano in Teverina 05020
Terni/Umbria   p.414☐ G 8

Collegiata S.Maria Assunta: This 12C church is a fine example of the independent development of Romanesque architecture in S. Umbria. The graceful two-arched rose-window, and the symbols of the Evangelists, are reminisent of Spoleto's architecture of the same date. The sumptuous sculptures, influenced by Guglielmo and Antelami, are also typical of the region. The inside has a nave and two aisles.

Lugo 48022
Ravenna/Emilia-Romagna   p.410☐G 5

Lugo was founded by the Romans but did not become important until the Middle Ages, when the castle was built by bishops from Ravenna. Destroyed by the Count of Curvio in 1218 and rebuilt in the early 14C, the town came into the possession of the Este in 1377. Together with the duchy of Ferrara, it passed to the church in 1598. In 1796 it was severly damaged when there was insurrection against French occupation.

S. Francesco (Via Codazzi): Previous building of 1227–34; in 1764–84, Cosimo Morelli redesigned the building in classical style. It is single-aisled, with a dome and a narthex of three bays. Restoration of 1969 uncovered Romanesque remains on the S.side, and also parts of the original portal with its peaked arch. The *cloister,* on the S.side, was built in 1471 and has been restored. Inside: the 1st chapel on the left has a 15C wall painting of the *Virgin sheltering supplicants under her cloak*; there are several 18C *paintings* by Benedetto del Buono. In the treasure chamber there are 14C *reliquaries.*

Rocca (Piazza Martiri): Most of the castle was restored in the mid-16C. The battlemented cylindrical *main tower* (restored) to the rear, and the left outer wall survive from the 14C building. In the courtyard there is a *fountain* with the Este coat of arms. Exhibits in the *museum* include a 7C soldier's helmet of the Ravenna type.

Also worth seeing: *S. Francesco di Paolo* (Corso Garibaldi): 1890, with 7 framed terracotta statues (late 15C, Ferraran, 2nd chapel on right); Romanesque Madonna (3rd chapel on left). *Chiesa della Croce Coperta* (Str. Cotignola): 15&16C votive wall paintings (again mostly Ferrarese in style), and a 14C marble Madonna on the main altar. *Chiesa del Carmine* (Piazza Trisi): restored mid-18C, with a fine 18C organ by Callido; stucco, some of which is by Trentanove; and paintings from 16–18C. The enormous *monument to Fran-cesco Baracca* (Piazza Battisti and Piazza XX Settembre) is also fine.

Luni 19030
La Spezia/Liguria   p.414☐ D/E ◖

Both excavations and written documents testify to the town's very interesting history. Luni, possibly Etruscan in origin, was a Roman colony as early as 177 BC. The town's name came from the cult of Luna, the moon goddess—documents relating to this cult can be seen in the *Museo Nazionale*. The Greek historian Strabo described the large harbour of *Luni,* which existed in Roman times and was important for the transport of marble quarried in the surrounding area (Carrara). Luni became a diocesan seat in the 5C AD, and so it remained until 1204.

Amphitheatre: Probably built around 1C AD; sandstone faced with marble. From what remains it has been deduced that the amphitheatre could hold some 6,000 spectators.

Also worth seeing: The foundation walls of a temple of Diana and of a house dating from the time of the Roman republic. Pitchers from a granary. The remains of a lighthouse. Parts of the town wall, of a town gate and of a 5C basilica.

Macerata 62100

Macerata / Marches   p.416☐I 7

Cathedral (Piazza S.Vincenzo Strambi): The present building was erected by Cosimo Morelli in 1771–90. Incomplete façade. The restored *campanile* dates from 1478. Inside, there is a 'Madonna with Saints' at the 2nd altar on the right, and

Macerata, Loggia dei Mercanti

a 'Madonna with Saints' by Allegretto Nuzi, 1369, in the *canons' sacristy.*

Biblioteca Comunale (Piazza Vittorio Veneto): It houses the **Pinacoteca** with paintings by Crivelli, Maratta, Andrea Boscoli.

Also worth seeing: Basilica della Madonna della Misericordia (1797). Chiesa S. Giovanni (1621). *Palazzo del Governo* (Piazza della Libertà), 17C, with a portal dating from 1509. Next door is the *Loggia dei Mercanti*, 1504/5. *Sferisterio* (Piazza N.Sauro; 1820–9), a stadium for ball games and equestrian sports.

Environs: S.Maria delle Vergini (above the town): A pilgrimage church founded in 1581, it is centrally planned with good frescos by Baglione and Gasparini.

Montecassiano (a few km. to the N.): *S. Assunta,* 15C, with an altar from the Robbia workshop dating from 1527. The *Palazzo Municipale,* built by Antonio Lombardo in the 15C, houses a collection of paintings. There are also numerous interesting *old houses.*

Santuario di Macerata: The sanctuary houses a revered *wooden Madonna,* for which a chapel was built as early as the 14C. A centrally planned building on the ground plan of a Greek cross with bevelled corners and dating from the 2nd quarter of the 16C houses this chapel, which was faced on the inside in 1585–90 and the outside in 1696.

Macomer 08015
Nuoro/Sardinia   p.422□C 12

The present site of this little town, with its gloomy old centre, is just to the SW of the Roman *Macopsissa*, as milestones on the town's outskirts show. Only in its tower (1573), in its façade, and in the ribbed vault of a chapel, does the inelegantly restored *village church of S.Pantaleo* still show some 16C Catalan Gothic traces. However, Macomer is surrounded by innumerable *pre-nuraghic and nuraghic buildings*.

Environs: The *Nuraghe S.Barbara* stands just to the N. of the new SS 131, near to the 16C chapel of *S.Barbara*. This nuraghe has a rectangular substructure, which is otherwise unknown in this design, with its 4 hollow chambers for defence. The round central tower, which dates from 1000 BC, has a spiral staircase leading to the upper platform where there were probably formerly either one or two further vaults. Three nuraghi form a conspicuous defen-

sive barrier to the W. of the road from Bortigali to Mulárgia. The most interesting is the *Nuraghe Orrolo*, only accessible by foot (45 min.). Almost at the upper end of **Silanus** there stands the Cistercian church of *S.Lorenzo* (1150–60), which is single-aisled. In the 14C, the apse and façade were strengthened in Pisan style and blind arcades were added, while the interior was decorated with coarse frescos. To the S., on the far side of the new road, there is a series of closely grouped buildings which are millenia apart in date. These are: firstly, the early Romanesque 11C *Chiesetta S.Sabina,* which is divided into two parts but is a continuous structure on the inside; it is partly late Romanesque and partly early Gothic in style (a round main building with a pointed dome, an apse, and a porch with a round arch). Secondly, the *Nuraghe Sarbana,* which still has two storeys. Built of dark basalt covered with yellowish-red lichen, it has an inner staircase in good condition. Nearby there are also a vaulted *nuraghic (?) well* and a *giant's tomb.* Above the road is the 'Madrone' (141 ft.), one of the tallest Sardinian *nuraghic towers*. A conspicuous feature of the S.end of the town of **Bolótona** is the fenced-in small 13C

Silanus (Macomer), S.Sabina

church of *S. Bachisio*, with its later Aragonese decorations on the portal, the windows, and on the splendid rose-window. To the S.: To the E. of the railway near **Bórore,** there are two striking *giant's tombs* with high, free-standing round-arched stele. One of these is near to Imbertighe, which is the ruin of a nuraghe, and the other is close by the little church of S.Bainzu. The church of *S.Maria degli Angeli* (1483) in **Santu Lussurgiu** houses a beautifully painted 16C wooden statue of the Madonna and Child. If one drives a further 10 km. (almost as far as Sindia), and then turns S.and then E. along a dirt road, one reaches the grandly designed but ruined Cistercian abbey of *S. Maria di Corte,* built by St.Bernard from 1147 onwards at the request of the Giudice Gonario of Torres. Restoration has been in progress here since 1975.

Manfredonia 71043
Foggia/Apulia   p.416□M 10

Manfredonia was founded in 1256 by Manfred, the son of Emperor Frederick II,

Bolótana (Macomer), S.Bachisio

Manfredonia, S.Maria

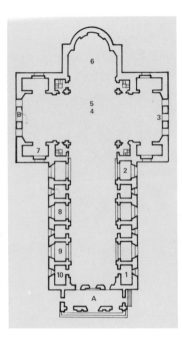

Mantua, S.Andrea

in place of the malaria-ridden town of Sipontum (see below), and was populated with the remaining inhabitants of that town. Completely destroyed by the Turks in 1620, it was later rebuilt on a chessboard-like ground plan. As a result only insignificant parts of the old town still survive. (*S. Domenico* with a Gothic portal; a *castle* from the Hohenstaufen-Angevin period).

S.Maria: A former cathedral, consecrated by Pope Paschal II in 1117. A square, centrally planned building with a dome and surrounded by columns with archivolts (Pisan influence, cf. Troia Cathedral). The *portal* is in typical Apulian-Romanesque style: columns supported by lions are topped by a canopy borne by animals. Above the door there was formerly an *eagle*, a remnant from the 11C pulpit and today housed in the *Castello Svevo* in *Bari*. The inside was completely changed in the

Mantua, S.Andrea A façade with portico **B** portico (incomplete) **1** baptistery (structure still in its original state). Decorations: **3** tondi, 2 of them by Correggio (Holy Family and Entombment), Ascension, school of Correggio **2** Longinus chapel, frescos to designs by G.Romano **3** tomb of Bishop Andreasi **4** Confessio **5** Paradise fresco by Anselmi, 1777–82 **6** apse fresco by Anselmi (martyrdom of St.Andrew) **7** tomb of Strozzi on the left wall of the chapel **8** frescos by Lorenzo Costa il Giovane (Nativity and Adoration of the Magi) **9** Madonna Enthroned with Saints, panel painting by Lorenzo Costa the elder **10** tomb and bust of Mantegna

16C. An interesting *crypt* (20 columns, the dome resting on the four central columns). Next to the crypt are the remains of an early Christian church and of some catacombs, and also a small *museum* with finds from the ancient Sipontum.

S. Leonardo: Built at the same time as S. Maria, this was formerly in the commandery of the Teutonic Order of Knights.

A building with three domes (the middle one is missing today) with octagonal drums. Decorated with pilaster strips on the outside. A nave, two aisles, three apses, and half-tunnel vaults in the aisles. The *portal on the N. flank* is particularly interesting (the main portal is undecorated). It is one of the gems of Apulia: with columns borne by lions and a canopied gable supported by gryphons. On the doorposts and in the frieze on the arch there are plant-like reliefs with S-shaped leaves; as well as hunting and lyre-playing centaurs and other animals. There is a 'Maiestas Domini' in the tympanum. In the panel under the gable archivolt there is a mutilated group of three figures: St.Leonard, the patron saint of the church and of prisoners, is on the right.

Maniago 33085
Pordenone/Friuli   p.410 □ H 2

Cathedral of S.Mauro (near the Piazza Italia): This lies in what is, so far, the oldest known parish of the former bishopric of Concordia Sagittaria, near Portogruaro.

It was built in 1468 in late Gothic style on the site of an early medieval structure, from which some fragments of sculpture survive on the façade. That *façade* has a beautiful rose-window and a portal with a pointed arch. In the right aisle there is a 17C wooden altar with a pala that is attributed to Amalteo and there are 16C frescos by the same artist in the ribbed vault of the sanctuary and in the apse.

Also worth seeing: The remains of the *castle*, mentioned as early as the 9C, stand above the town. The *Piazza Italia* has the Loggia Comunale and a fine fountain.

Mantova/Mantua 46100
Mantua/Lombardy   p.410 · E/F 4

This town is of Etruscan origin. Under Augustus it was a veterans' colony but after the collapse of the Roman Empire, the Goths, Byzantines, Lombards and finally the Franks followed in succession. Around 1000, power was held by the Attoni family of Canossa, whose last and most famous member was Countess Matilda (1046–

Mantua, Piazza delle Erbe

Mantua, Palazzo Ducale

Mantua, Palazzo Ducale, Francesco II d'Este in bronze, by Mantegna

1115). In the 12&13C, Mantua, being a free town, was a member of both Lombard Leagues. During the struggles between the Guelphs and Ghibellines, the Bonacolsi family ruled the town for 55 years, beginning in 1273. After this, Luigi Gonzaga seized power in 1328. In 1433, Emperor Sigismund elevated the Gonzagas to the rank of marquises. and Charles V made them dukes in 1530. The rule of the Gonzagas in Mantua ended in 1707, and the town came under the Habsburgs. From 1796-1814, as a result of Napoleon's activities, it shared the fate of other Italian towns and states, being incorporated firstly in the Cisalpine Republic, then the Italian Republic and the Kingdom of Italy. In 1814 Mantua once again came under Austrian rule, until it was finally absorbed into a united Italy in 1866.

S. Andrea: The campanile, dating from 1413, survives from the earlier churches. Work on the present one began in 1472 and the façade and portico were in position by 1490. S.Andrea is the key building in the development of baroque church design. Leone Battista Alberti's plan of 1470 harks back to classical Roman spatial forms of a monumental character. The layout is cruciform, with a dome above the crossing. The traditional subdivision into nave and aisles is abandoned in favour of a single continuous space. Instead of the aisles, large chapel areas of different sizes adjoin the main space in a rhythmic sequence (a-b-a). The arrangement of the chapels follows the pattern of small and large bays in the tunnel-vaulted main area, the walls of which are no longer subdivided by columns, but by colossal pilasters. The same articulation is continued on the façade and portico.
Decoration: The *tomb of Andrea Mantegna* (1506) is in the first chapel on the left; the panel painting of the *Virgin Enthroned with Saints* by Lorenzo Costa il V. (1525) is in the next chapel. The *mausoleum of Bishop Andreasi* (1549) is at the end of the S. transept, the *Confessio* is in the middle of

Palazzo Ducale, Cardinal Gonzaga, by Mantegna

the crossing, and underneath it is the crypt where the *blood of Christ* is preserved. The Mannerist *Strozzi mausoleum* (1598) is in the left-hand chapel of the N. transept.

Rotonda di S. Lorenzo (Piazza delle Erbe): A centrally planned church built by Countess Matilda of Canossa in the late 11C. The circular interior has 10 round pillars; the ambulatory has a gallery above it. Radically restored in 1908.

Cathedral of S.Pietro: The Romanesque campanile, the outer wall of the S.row of chapels (Gothic), and the *Cappella dell' Incoronata* (1480) survive from earlier churches. The new one, begun in 1545 to plans by Giulio Romano, is one of the most convincing examples of Mannerist architecture. Behind the massive baroque façade (1756) there is a highly articulated spatial layout, based on early Christian basilicas in Rome: the raised nave is flanked by two aisles on each side. These are divided from one another by rows of Corinthian columns with continuous architraves. There are two rows of chapels adjoining the outer aisles and the rhythmically alternating vaults of these give the impression of further aisles.
Decoration: The outstanding features of the richly decorated interior are: a 5C *marble sarcophagus* between the 1st and 2nd chapels on the left, a 14C *fresco of the Crucifixion* in the 3rd chapel on the left, and the *painting of the apse* by Domenico Fetti.

Palazzo Ducale (13–18C): The *Corte Vecchia* was used by the Gonzagas as a family seat from 1328 onwards. It consists of the *Palazzo del Capitano* and the *Domus Magna*, both built by the Bonacolsi in the late 13C. These two palaces were extended over the centuries into one of the largest and, formerly, one of the richest residences of a ruling house in Europe. The most important periods in the building are: the 14/15C *Castello di S. Giorgio*, the *Basilica of S. Barbara* (1562–5) which served as the court church, the *Piazza Castello*, the *Cortile della Cavallerizza* and the *Giardino Pensile* (late 16C). Inside, the palace is one of the most comprehensive museums of the art

of interior decoration, with apartments from very different periods, some of them exquisitely designed, fresco cycles (particularly Mantegna's *Camera degli Sposi* and the *frescos by Pisanello*, curiosities such as the *horses' staircase* and the *apartments of the court dwarfs*, etc.

Palazzo del Te: Built for Federico II Gonzaga in 1525–35. The building, sculptures and paintings are by Giulio Romano, assisted by Primaticcio, Fermo da Caravaggio and others. Built around the four sides of a square courtyard, the front façade and those facing the courtyard are of severe design, whereas the garden side is more festive. A typical feature of Giulio Romano's style is his Mannerist interpretation of the classical architectural motifs of the Renaissance. The Palladian motif of the garden loggia extends across the entire E. front. The garden ends in a large exedra with seats. The rooms inside the palace are decorated with mythological scenes. The tour, beginning at the N. Loggia (which is now the entrance), proceeds E.: *Horses' Hall, Hall of Psyche, Room of the Winds, Eagle Room, David's Loggia, Stucco Hall, Hall of Caesar, Giants' Hall,* three smaller rooms and the S.Loggia.

Palazzo della Ragione (1250), on the S.side of the *Piazza delle Erbe*, with a 15C portico in front of it. Together with the *clock tower* (1473) to the W., and the **Palazzo del Podestà** (1227) to the NE, it forms the centre of Mantua. The 13C statue of the seated Virgil, who was born in Mantua, occupies a niche facing the *Piazza Broletto*. On the SE side of the palace, the .Via Ardigo is spanned by an arch which leads to the *Arengario* (1300), which has a loggia and three-arched windows.

Teatro Scientifico (Piazza Dante): A theatre with a brilliant tradition (comedies by Plautus performed at the court in 1501, Monteverdi's 'Orfeo' in 1607, etc.) The first academy in Mantua was founded in 1562. Its purpose was to cultivate ancient theatrical tradition in the sense of the

Mantua, Castello di San Giorgio t

Mantua, Palazzo del Te

Renaissance concept of humanism. The 'Accademia dei Timidi' commissioned the present building in 1767, and it was completed in 1769, the architect being Antonio Galli Bibiena. It is one of the most splendid baroque theatres. **Teatro Sociale** (Piazza Marconi): a classical building dating from 1822, with a rich and refined interior.

Also worth seeing: *S. Sebastiano* (Largo XXIV Maggio): A brilliant design by L.B.Alberti (1460). The first Renaissance building to use a Greek cross plan. A clear, centrally planned structure with a façade based on an ancient model. The *Casa di Andrea Mantegna* (1476) is diagonally opposite. It is a strictly cubic building with an original round courtyard; the design is probably by Mantegna himself. The *Palazzo di Giustizia* (Via Poma), built for the Gonzagas in 1620. A monumental façade with caryatids on the piano nobile. In the same street is the *Casa di Giulio Romano*, the house where the artist lived. Built in 1544 to his own plans, it is one of the better examples of Mannerist architecture. The church of *S.Barnaba* dates from the 18C in its present form; façade by A.Bibiena. *Palazzo Sordi* (Via Pomponazzo), built in 1680: the façade, courtyard and stairs are of gorgeous baroque design, and the rooms are richly furnished. The *Palazzo dei Rabbini* (Via Bertani 54) and the *synagogue* (Via Govi 1) are two interesting 18C buildings in the former *Ghetto*. The *Palazzo Canossa* (Piazza Canossa), a magnificent baroque complex with a staircase that is worth seeing.

Environs: S.Benedetto Po (20 km. towards Modena, via Carpi): *Abbazia di Polirone*, one of the most important Benedictine abbeys in N. Italy. Founded in 1007 as a result of a grant of land by Count Tebaldo di Canossa. The first church (1020–40) was replaced in 1445 by a new building commissioned by the Gonzagas, the major benefactors of the monastery. The monastery building also dates from this period. Giulio Romano added the exterior facing in 1544-7. The inside, where Gothic parts are still apparent, was richly decorated. G.Romano designed the main façade, with its portico and a large loggia above it. There are 32 terracotta statues (in niches) by A.Begarelli; they depict patriarchs, Church Fathers, and Saints. There are also 10 paintings from the Romano school with scenes from the Old and New Testaments. To the left of the sanctuary is the 11C *chapel of the Immaculata*, the original burial place of Countess Matilda of Canossa, a generous benefactress of the monastery. The empty *sarcophagus* of Matilda is in the atrium leading to the sacristy, to the right of the sanctuary. The *sacristy* is to plans by G.Romano, as is its decoration. In front of the sanctuary there are pavement mosaics dating from 1151, with the cardinal virtues in the middle. Three *cloisters*: Chiostro di S. Benedetto (1246, altered in the 15C), Chiostro di S.Simeone (1458), and Chiostro Reale e degli Abati with a late-15C monumental staircase altered in the 17C. **S.Maria delle Grazie** (after travelling 9 km. towards Cremona, turn right towards Curtatone). Built by Francesco I Gonzaga in 1399–1406 as a votive church celebrating Mantua's release from the plague. Large portico in front of the church, which is single-aisled but which has numerous chapels to the sides. A picturesque interior in the Spanish baroque style.

Maratea 85046
Potenza/Basilicata   p.418 □M 13

S. Maria Maggiore: It has a medieval campanile and a 15C portal with marble angels.

Chiesa del Rosario: *Madonna and Saints* by Matteo Simonelli.

Chiesa dei Francescani: It has 17C choir stalls and, adjoining the church, a

monastery of the same name and dating from the same period.

In the upper part of town, known as *Castello*, is the **parish church:** it has a *marble ciborium* dating from 1519 and a fine 17C *relief of the Annunciation*.

Marsala 91025
Trapani/Sicily   p.420 H 16

Marsala is the westernmost town in Sicily. The ancient 'Lilybaeum' was the first, and, later, also the last, stronghold of the Carthaginians in Sicily. It was an important harbour under the Saracens ('Marsa Ali', meaning 'Harbour of Ali'). It saw the start of the 'Risorgimento', with the landing of Garibaldi's 'Thousand', which was to result in the country's unification. It is also known for the production of sweet wine.

Cathedral of S.Tomaso di Canterbury (Piazza della Repubblica): Built under the Normans; the *façade* is 17C. It was rebuilt after being destroyed in World War 2. It has some fine 16C works by the Gagini family of sculptors (the sanctuary has sculptures of *St.Vincent* and *St.Thomas*, among others). The church treasure includes some fine 16C Flemish *tapestries*.

Edificio Termale (by the sea, near the Viale Piave): A Roman bath (3C AD). Beautiful *pavement mosaics* with animal scenes (the best is the 'mosaico delle belve', showing beasts hunting). Remains of the *baths* and their associated structures survive. The complex was part of the Roman town, of which some remains have been uncovered.

Also worth seeing: There is a Punic-Roman *necropolis* in the N. of the town, between the Viale d.Fante, the Via Cappucini and the Piazza Porticello.

Environs: 8 km. to the N., on the island of **S.Pantaleo**, are the remains of the ancient Punic town of *Motya* (8C BC, *Mozia* in Italian); the island can only be visited by permission of the island's administrative office (Marsala, Via Garraffa). Excavations in all parts of the island; museum.

Marzabotto 40043
Bologna/Emilia-Romagna   p.412□F 5

A little way outside Marzabotto, in the park of the *Villa Aria*, there is an important **excavation**, on the site of an Etruscan town (Misa ?), founded in the late 6C BC and destroyed by the Gauls in the mid 4C BC. The finds are housed in the *Museo Etrusco Pompeo Aria*.

Maser 31010
Treviso/Veneto   p.410□G 3

Villa Barbaro (now known as Volpi di Misurata): This villa, which stands on a gentle rise and whose whole layout is deliberately aimed at achieving a harmonious unity with its surroundings, is one of the outstanding villas of the Veneto. Andrea Palladio worked on this project in 1560–1, probably in close collaboration with his employers, the brothers Daniele and Marc Antonio Barbaro, both of whom had received a humanist education. The sculptures and stuccoes are by A.Vittoria, while the frescos were painted by P.Veronese.

The projecting middle section has four Ionic columns bearing a pediment, and is flanked by *loggias* on both sides. The two dovecotes adjoin each end of these loggias. At the rear there are: a *nymphaeum* with fountains; sculptures of Olympian gods; and a *grotto of Neptune*. The magnificent *frescos* in the individual rooms (vestibule, Stanze del Cane, del Lucerna, Centrale 'dell'Olimpo e dell'Eternità', di Bacco, del Tribunale d'Amore) are *trompe l'oeil* and depict mythological and allegorical figures, man in nature and in his family, animals and landscapes, and architectural elements. The iconographical programme of the scenes places the world of the gods, the natural course of events, and human life, in a richly interrelated system of all-embracing harmony. In the road, diagonally opposite the entrance to the villa, is the **Temple to Marc Antonio Barbaro.** Built by Palladio in 1580, it is a domed, round building with a fine portico borne by Corinthian columns. The brilliantly articulated interior, whose floors are inlaid with pebbles, matches the exterior.

Maser, Villa Barbaro

Massa 54100
Massa/Tuscany   p.412☐E 6

This, the main town of the province, lies
amidst hills on the little river Frigido in
the NW of Tuscany. Massa is known to
have existed since 882, but did not become
important until the decline of Luni. Its
heyday was in the 11C but subsequently
it was governed by Lucca, Pisa, Milan and
Florence, and was much coveted as a possession owing to its importance as a centre of the marble industry and as a harbour
(Marina di Massa). The old town of *Massa
Vecchia* lies at the foot of the fortress of
Malaspina. New Massa *(Massa Nuova* or
Massa Cybea) was not built until 1557. It
is arranged on a systematic plan, with wide
streets and large squares.
Old Massa is defended by walls, some bastions of which and the *Porta Quaranta* still
survive. At the highest point there stands
the *Rocca,* only recently restored.

The **Cathedral** (S.Pietro e S.Francesco)
was altered by Giacomo Malaspina in the
15C and has a modern façade of Carrara

Maser, chamber of Bacchus, P.Veronese

Massa, Rocca

marble. Besides the many altars along the side of this single-aisled church, there is also a *fresco by Pinturicchio* on the baroque altar of the Cappella del SS. Sacramento.

S. Maria degli Ulivi, in the industrial quarter of Marina di Massa, is worth seeing for a wooden carving of St. Leonard by Jacopo della Quercia.

Environs: Carrara: Situated at the foot of the Apuan Alps, amidst olive groves and vineyards. The town's importance and wealth derive from the nearby marble quarries in the Apuan Alps and from the associated industry. There are two schools in Carrara: the *Scuola del Marmo* where the purely technical aspects are taught to those in industry, and the *Accademia di Belle Arti*, for artistic training. The latter was founded in 1769 and can be visited by permission. A collection of ancient marble stones; splendid library. *Cathedral:* It originates from the 11C, its apse was extended in the 13C, and it took on its present form in the 14C. The white and grey marble facing completely covers the building. The façade, with its ground level arcade, is Pisan Romanesque up to the 1st storey and Gothic above. Inside: The nave and two aisles are separated by columns with differing capitals. There is a 14C *marble Annunciation* (artist unknown — French influence) in the right aisle. The fine, polychrome 16C *marble pulpit* is by two local artists, Domenico del Sarto and Master Nicodemo. The hexagonal *font*, supported by a single block of marble and topped with a hexagonal dome-shaped cover (1527), is an interesting feature of the oratory-cum-baptistery. The *campanile*, from the 2nd half of the 13C, has single-arched, double-arched, three-arched and four-arched windows. It is crowned by a spire, and offers a panoramic view from on top. An excursion may be made to the *marble quarries*, many of which are at altitudes of up to 3,250 ft., in the Apuan Alps. The *marmor lunensis* (so called after the port of Luna) was quarried by the Romans in the three valleys of Carrara: *Fantiscritti, Collonata* and *Torano*. Carrara has some 400 marble quarries. They are the most important in the world and produce marble of differing qualities and colours (white, black, yellow and greenish veins). A marble railway *(Ferrovia marmiferi)* was built in 1876 – 91, leading from the sea through the town of Carrara to the terminus of Ravaccione. **Castelnuova Magra** (N. of Carrara): Two items worth seeing in the parish church are a 17C *Crucifixion* by Anthony van Dyck, and a *Mount Calvary* ascribed to Pieter Bruegel. **Sarzana** is situated at the NW tip of Tuscany, on the border with Liguria and on the edge of the fertile Magra valley. It formerly belonged to the bishops of Luni. In the 13C it was ruled by Pisa, Genoa and Florence before finally falling to Genoa. The *Fortezza di Sarzanello* was built by Castruccio Castracani in 1322 on the site of the former 'Castrum Sarzanae' which has been known since 963. It was from here that the various families ruled the town. The *Cathedral of S. Maria Assunta* was built in Romanesque-Gothic style after the bishop of Luni moved here. The upper section of the façade is the work of Lorenzo Riccomanni, while the latter statues date from 1735. The *Assunta* behind the altar, and another altar figure dating from 1463, are also the work of Lorenzo, in co-operation with Francesco Riccomanni. In the left chapel is a *Croce dipinta* by Master Guiglielmo dating from 1138, a masterpiece of primitive Tuscan painting. **Pontrémoli:** This, one of the centres of the northern district of Lunigiana, is surrounded by hills covered with sweet chestnut trees. Owing to its favourable location (it was mentioned as a stop on the *Via Francigena* as early as 990), it was fought over on various occasions by the power-hungry aristocratic families of Genoa and Florence. It was not until 1322 that Castruccio Castracani built the *fortress*, known as the *Cacciaguerra*.

Massafra 74016
Taranto/Apulia   p.418 | O 11

The old and new quarters of this hill town are separated by the 'Gravina di San Marco'. The town is known for its grotto churches, of which there are 28 in all.

Grotto church of S. Antonio Abate (V. Vittorio Veneto): Located underneath the Ospedale Matteo Pagliano, it was originally two cultic rooms with an entrance of its own. The right-hand half is divided by two pilasters into a nave and an aisle and has a semicircular apse with a rectangular niche; the left half is an irregular square with a raised altar on the rear wall. Only some remnants (including a painting of Pope Urban V, 1362–70) survive from the 14–15C Byzantine-style *frescos.*

Grotto church of La Candelora (E. slope of the Gravina di S. Marco, reached from V. Frappietri): The façade has been destroyed; of particular interest is the *ceiling* with its various structures (gable roof, ribbed vault, stellar dome vault, lens-shaped dome). There are *frescos* in the arcade niches: the best and oldest are on the right, narrow side of the first niche and depict the Purification of the Virgin Mary and the Presentation in the Temple.

Also worth seeing: On the slope of the *Gravina della Madonna della Scala* is the grotto church of the same name, with an ancient, miraculous image painted on stone; there are also the frescoed grotto churches of *Maria della Buona Nuova* and *S. Simone a Famosa* (key obtainable through the 'Pro Loco' in the town hall). The 13C *castle.*

Environs: Some 10 km. to the NW is **Mottola:** Again, there are many grotto churches in the area around this town; they include *S. Angelo,* with two rooms above one another, each with a nave and two aisles.

Massa Marittima 58024
Grosseto/Tuscany   p.414☐F 7

This is the main town of the Maremma, and has been a mining centre, particularly of silver and copper, since ancient times. The many medieval buildings in Massa Marittima date from the town's zenith but during the 16&17C it gradually declined in importance and the population was decimated by malaria. It is picturesquely situated on a hill between the valleys of Pecora, Zanca and Noni, and is made up of the *Città Vecchia,* the old, lower town with its

Massafra, castle

mainly Romanesque architecture, and the *Città Nuova,* the newer town set higher up with its Gothic arches. In the old part of town there are numerous gates with the town's coats of arms and the symbol of Siena, to which Massa was allied. The *Fortezza dei Senesi* was built by the Sienese in 1337. It is now partly destroyed, because sites were required for building in 1744 and 1845.

Cathedral: Dedicated to the Assumption of the Virgin and to St.Cerbone. Building began in the Pisan style in the 1st half of the 13C. In 1287–1304, a Pisan architect lengthened the structure towards the sanctuary and the apse. The façade makes a splendid impression, with the warm golden hues of its stone, and it stands at the top of a high flight of steps. The lower section of the façade has 7 blind arches, the portal bears a *relief of the story of St. Cerbone's life,* and in the upper part of the façade there is a loggia with 10 arches borne by interesting columns which stand on the back of a kneeling man and on horses and gryphons (attributed to followers of Giovanni Pisano). The multicoloured marble is white, red and green.

Inside the church are a nave, two aisles and fine capitals on columns of differing heights. On the inside wall of the façade, note the 14C coloured stained-glass *rose-window* depicting *St. Cerbone before Pope Vigilius.* The following are also worth seeing: The *baptistery* with a rectangular font made of travertine and *reliefs,* particularly those of *the life of St.John the Baptist* from the vision of Zachariah until the Saint's beheading, and individual depictions of Christ, John the Baptist, Isaiah, etc., by Giroldo da Como (1267). The marble tabernacle in the middle of the font dates from 1447 and bears patriarchs and prophets in 12 niches. The figure of the Baptist himself crowns the whole. In the left transept is the *Cappella della Madonna* with a notable *Madonna delle Grazie,* which was painted in *c.* 1316 and betrays the influence of the 'Maestà' by Duccio di Buoninsegna. In the church's left aisle are a 4C Roman sarcophagus and a 14C fresco of the Madonna and Child with Saints. Access can be obtained to the subterranean rooms of the cathedral *(Cappella delle Reliquie),* which house the beautiful and valuable church treasures, including the *Reliquary of St. Cerbone,* a 16C Sienese gold piece

Massa Marittima, Palazzo Pretorio

S. Galgano (Massa Marittima), abbey

in the shape of a Gothic temple. Underneath the apse there is a room with the *Arca di S. Cerbone,* the marble sarcophagus; it rests on columns and pilasters showing 8 scenes from the legend of the Saint, and on the lid are a further 10 relief medallions. This masterpiece of 14C sculpture is attributed to Goro di Gregorio, 1324.

S. Agostino: A Romanesque-Gothic church, begun in 1299–1313, with an unfaced travertine façade. The side walls have pointed arch windows, and the Gothic apse is polygonal. The interior is single-aisled and the apsidal chapel has a 15C *marble ciborium,* while in the chapel to the left of the sanctuary there is a terracotta of the *Madonna and Child* by a 15C Florentine artist.

Palazzo dell'Abbondanza: Located a little way below the *Palazzo Vescovile,* it has an ancient fountain, the *Fonte pubblica,* underneath the 3 pointed arches of the façade.

Palazzo Pretorio: (or *dell' Podestà*): A Romanesque building dating from *c.* 1230, with 30 coats of arms (1426–1633) on the façade, which opens out into a beautiful row of Romanesque two-arched windows from the 2nd storey onwards. The original battlements no longer survive.

The **Palazzo Comunale** actually consists of 3 buildings. The middle section from the 14C, built by the Sienese architects Stefano di Méo and Gualtiero di Sozzo; the left-hand building, whose lower section dates from 1344, has a later upper part and a 13C tower. On the tower, at ground-floor level, there is a relief of the *Sienese she-wolf* by Urbano da Cortona, 1468. The inside of the Palazzo has 16C ceiling frescos on the 1st floor and, on the right wall, the *Madonna Enthroned,* a famous work by Ambrogio Lorenzetti (*c.* 1330).

Museo Archeologico (in the Palazzo delle Armi, a Renaissance building): Etruscan and Roman finds, vases, cups and coins are exhibited, as are pieces of majolica from Faenza and Gubbio, and also Sienese school panel paintings (*St. Gabriel* by Sassetta).

Environs: S. Galgano A deserted Cistercian abbey at the foot of Monte Siepi of 32 km. along the road to Siena. The tremendous ruins are all that remain of one of the most characteristic examples of the Cistercian Gothic in Italy after the abbey of Fossanova. The church dates from 1224. The 16C monastery building is also in ruins despite attempts to restore it.

Matélica 62024
Macerata / Marches   p.414 H 7

S. Francesco (Via S. Francesco): This church was rebuilt in the 18C and restored in 1925. Its 13C portal survives. Inside, the 2nd altar on the right has a *Madonna with St. Catherine and St. Francis* by Marco Palmezzano, 1501. The 4th and 5th chapels on the left have an *Adoration of the Magi* and a *Stoning of St. Stephen,* dated 1569 and signed by Giovanni Francesco and Simone de Magistris. By the old *cloister* there is a *chapel* frescoed by Simone de Magistris (?).

Museo Piersanti (Via Umberto I; visits by request): A 15C *triptych* with the Madonna, by Arcangelo di Cola da Camerino. A *crucifix* by Antonio da Fabriano, dated 1452 and signed. Seven *paintings of Saints* by Jacopo Bellini.

Also worth seeing: The *cathedral* (Corso Vitt. Emanuele), built by C. and G.B. da Lugano in 1474. *S. Agostino* (14C), with a fine Romanesque portal.

Matera 75100
Matera / Basilicata   p.416 N 11

This, the main town of the province, occupies an unusually picturesque location on the rocks above a deep gorge; typical rock dwellings, the so-called *Sassi,* and the *Castle Tramontana.*
The settlement goes back to palaeolithic times. It declined in influence under the Greeks, was destroyed by the Franks in 867 and was rebuilt in the early 11C under the

rule of Byzantium. Matera was part of Apulia in 1663, and later became part of Basilicata, of which it was the capital until 1806. The town is the seat of an archbishop.

Castle Tramontana: Built by Giovanni Carlo I in the late 15C. Externally it has two cylindrical towers, and in the middle of the courtyard there is another and much sturdier tower.

Cathedral: This building dates from 1268–70 and is in Apulian Romanesque style. The prominent middle section of the tripartite façade has a rose-window borne by the *Archangel Michael* and three other *figures of angels*. On the right flank there are two splendid portals, one of them with a Basilian monk in the tympanum, while the other is the *lions' portal*. The interior has a nave and two aisles and is built on a Latin cross. It still has columns from the original building, but the rest of it derives from the baroque rebuilding. The *ceiling frescos in the nave* date from the 18C, the pulpit from 1722. An *Assumption of the Virgin* from the Venetian school (1627); a *crib* with polychrome stone figures by Altobello Persio and Sannazaro d'Alessandro (1534), and the *Cappella dell'Annunziata* in the left aisle are all worth seeing. The small church of *S.Maria di Costantinopoli* is particularly interesting. It stands in a small courtyard which is reached from the above-mentioned chapel and it has a fine Romanesque portal. The campanile, 171 ft. tall, with three storeys of two-arched windows, was built at the same time as the church.

S.Domenico: Dating from the 1st half of the 13C, it was enlarged in the 17C; a nave and interconnecting side chapels. Inside are a *copy of Raphael's Holy Family* and a *Madonna and Child* by Stefano da Putignano (1518).

S.Francesco d'Assisi: Built at the beginning of the 13C above an underground church, dedicated to St.Francis in 1218, decorated in baroque style in *c.* 1670. This is also the date of the façade, the nave with its side chapels, and the stucco decoration.

Note: the 16C *holy-water stoup*, and *part of a polyptych* by Bartolomeo Vivarini. *SS.Pietro e Paolo*, the underground church has 11C frescos in the 3rd chapel on the left.

Chiesa del Purgatorio: Dates from 1747. Numerous macabre figures on the tall façade.

Palazzo Giudicepietro: The diamond-shaped ashlars of the exterior are an interesting feature.

Museo Nazionale Ridola (in a former convent of the Poor Clares): Founded by Domenico Ridola. Apart from its archaeological collection, the museum also houses ethnological exhibits and a gallery. The *archaeological department* is worth seeing.

Environs: *Rock churches* near Matera. The rock churches, of which there are some 130 in all, date from the time of the monks' migration in the 11C. *S.Maria de Idris* (in the Sasso Caveoso in the town) is hewn almost entirely from the rock itself and has frescos from the 14,15&16C. Near the altar is the descent to the underground church of *S.Giovanni M.Errone* (also S.Pietro), excavated entirely in the rock. It dates from 718, has a nave, two aisles and frescos in Byzantine style dating from 1190 and before. *S.Pietro Caveoso:* Built in 1656 on the site of an earlier building, and restored in 1752. The façade is baroque. A 17C stone font, and a 16C polyptych. *S. Pietro Barisano* (in the Sasso Barisano): This church is partly hewn from the rock and dates back to the 12&13C. The campanile and façade are 17C. Inside there are a nave and two aisles with pilasters; a Romanesque *font* and the 16C *altar of the Crucifixion* are of interest. *S. Barbara:* A small Byzantine church, excavated wholly out of the rock. Inside there are 13C frescos and an iconostasis, and behind the latter is a throne of stone. Nearby is the small underground church of *Cappuccino Vecchio* divided into two aisles by a central wall. Among the rock churches in the environs

Matera, town

of the town, the following are worth mentioning: *S. Gregorio* on the road to Altamura. *S. Pietro in Loma* on the road to *Laterza*. The *Chiesa allo Iazzo Gattini*, opposite the town. *Madonna delle Tre Porte*, decorated with frescos from various periods. *Chiesa della Madonna della Croce*, with 15C frescos. *S. Falcione*, with 13C Byzantine style frescos. *S.Maria della Valle*, cut entirely from tufa, with a Romanesque façade by Leonio di Táranto (1280). It has four aisles and some frescos dating from 1640–90. The *Grotta dei Pipistrelli*, a natural cave, is the most extensive and interesting of the caves in the Bradano valley and was inhabited even in neolithic times. Underneath this large grotto there is another, the *Grotta funeraria*, where 40 skeletons have been found. The *castles* between the Basento and the Bradano are, in many cases, built above old fortifications that have fallen into ruins or been forgotten. They are mostly of Norman-Swabian origin, subsequently rebuilt by the Aragonese and the Angevins, and form a continuous chain of defensive castles against Saracen invasions, mainly in the 15&16C. *Lago di San Giuliano:* Formed by damming the river Bradano to the SW of Matera. **Timmari,** an important centre of archaeological excavations, lies to the N. of the lake.

Mazara del Vallo 91026
Trapani/Sicily   p.420□H 17

This was a Phoenician harbour in ancient times. In 1097 it was the site of the first Norman parliament in Sicily.

Cathedral of S.Salvatore (Piazza della Repubblica): Founded by the Normans (1073), but only completed in the late 17C. The *E. end,* with remains of the original structure, is worth seeing. The façade, completed in the early 20C, has a fine *portal* with a relief, dating from 1584, of 'Count Roger defeating a Muslim'. The inside has a nave and two aisles, with a dome over the crossing. The nave, aisles and transepts are richly decorated and include: works by the Gagini family of sculptors, e.g. the late-15C *marble sarcophagus* by D.Gagini in the right transept, and a *group of figures* (1532–7) by Antonello and Antonino Gagini in the sanctuary. The entrance to the *Aula Capitolare*, with its

Matera, rock church

Roman sarcophagi, is beneath a marble arch (1523).

Also worth seeing: *S.Nicolò Regalo* (Molo G.Caito), 12C Norman, with a square ground plan, three apses and fine blind arcades. *S.Veneranda* (Piazza S.Veneranda), 1714, with a rich baroque façade. The 14C *S.Caterina* (Via S.Giuseppe), rebuilt in baroque style in the 17C, also with a fine façade. The *Museo Civico* has a Roman collection.

Medicina 40059
Bologna / Emilia-Romagna   p.410 □G 5

Medicina is mentioned as early as the 9C. Emperor Frederick I raised it to the status of a free commune.

Parish church of S.Mamante (Piazza Garibaldi): Built by G.A.Ambrosi in 1734–9, with 17&18C decoration. The campanile is one of C.F.Dotti's masterpieces.

Also worth seeing: *SS.Francesco e Anna*

(Via Saffi), 17C, with classical portico. *Chiesa dell'Assunta,* designed by Torreggiani, completed in 1753. *S.Maria del Carmine,* 17&18C. *Palazzo della Partecipanza* (Via Pillio) with a large staircase possibly by Dotti. The *clock tower,* with a statue of the Virgin Mary by A.Piò stands in the Via della Libertà. The 18C former *Palazzo del Podestà,* recently altered. The 17&18C *Palazzo Comunale.*

Melfi 85025
Potenza / Basilicata   p.416□ □M 11

Castle: Built by the Normans, partly rebuilt before 1228–9, altered in the 16C. Four synods were held in the castle from 1054 to 1101, and the First Crusade was proclaimed from here. Today it houses a collection of the most recent finds from the pre-Roman period.

Cathedral of the Assumption: Guglielmo il Malo commissioned it in 1155. It has a baroque façade, and its campanile, which dates from 1153, has withstood every earthquake. The emblem of

Melfi, castle

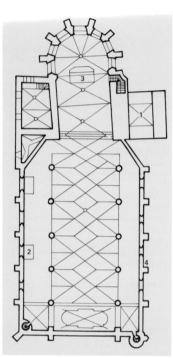

Merano, cathedral/parish church of St. Nicholas 1 High Gothic tower with porch dating from 1350, with early-15C frescos **2** Assumption of the Virgin, painting by M.Knoller **3** high altar **4** St. Nicholas, tabernacle figure, 1350

the Normans of Sicily is to be seen above the two-arched window of the campanile.

Palazzo del Vescovado: A bishop's palace with a fine baroque fountain in the courtyard. The famous *sarcophagus of Rapolla*, a masterpiece from the Roman imperial period discovered in neighbouring Rapolla in 1856, is worth seeing.

Environs: Note the following grotto churches: *Madonna delle Spinelle*, excavated from the tufa, with arches and a dome. Signed frescos by Guglielmo from the late 12C. *Santa Margherita*, entirely excavated from the tufa, with 13C frescos depicting Christ, the Madonna, and Saints.

Merano/Meran 39012
Merano/South Tyrol-Trentino   p.410☐F 1

From 1280–1420, Merano was the capital of the Tyrol and the residence of the ruling lords. The inner town, with its arcaded alleyway, parish square, grain market square and the town gates (the Passeirer, Bozner and Vintschger gates), still retains its medieval character.

Parish church of St.Nicholas: The fine chancel and the lower section of the tower were built in 1302–76 as an extension of an older church. The nave was built between 1340 and 1420, but was not vaulted until 1448–80. Finally, in 1617, the Gothic tower was crowned with an octagonal upper section and a spire of original style. Note the fine high Gothic *porch in the tower* dating from 1350, with important early-15C frescos. There is a fine St.Nicholas in a tabernacle (1350) on the outer S.wall of the nave. Late Gothic buttresses were added to this wall between 1450 and 1480. Much of the original decoration of the hall church, which has a nave, two aisles and a net-type ribbed vault, was unfortunately altered in the 19C. Outstanding features: the *sandstone pulpit* dating from 1500, the altarpieces—the work of Martin Knoller (c. 1800)—of the *side altars*, the *crucifix* (1510) in the chancel arch, a small altar with *St. Ursula* (1500), and an early-16C *St. Nicholas*. The *frescos* in the nave date from the 16C and were restored in the 19C. The S.wall of the nave has interesting 15C *stained-glass windows*.

Barbara chapel (beside the parish church): A two-storeyed, centrally planned octagonal building, with a spire, dating from the 1st half of the 15C; formerly a crypt chapel and cemetery chapel. There is a Pietà (1500) in the crypt chapel.

Hospital church of the Holy Ghost: This church was built between 1425 and 1450, probably by Stefan von Burghausen, and is almost identical to the church of the Holy Ghost in Landshut. The *exterior frescos* are early 15C. The portal (1440) has

Merano, view

a Gothic *tympanum* with a Holy Trinity and the two founders, and also some neo-Gothic statuettes. The uniform inside, which has a nave, two aisles and a fine ribbed stellar vault, is one of the most beautiful Gothic church interiors in the South Tyrol; its Gothic furnishings frequently have neo-Gothic additions. Thus, the neo-Gothic high altar has the wing of an altar built by Jörg Lederer in 1520. The *frescos* on the vault above the high altar date from 1480; there is a large 14C *Crucifixion*, along with other Gothic pieces.

Castello Principesco: The rooms of this small castle built by Duke Sigmund der Münzreiche in 1480 still retain their Gothic furnishings and there are paintings in the courtyard. The castle chapel has frescos dating from 1480 and restored in the late 16C.

Zeno Castle: This impressive ruined cas-tle above the Passer gorge dates from the 12C. From 1288–1300, the rulers of the Tyrol used it as a residence along with Castel Tirolo. It has an interesting late-13C two-storeyed *chapel*.

Town Museum: This houses collections devoted to geology and folklore, significant Gothic and baroque works of art, and paintings by Friedrich Wasmann, who lived in Merano.

Also worth seeing: The 12C Roman-esque church of *Maria Trost* in the Unter-mais district of town. The 14C apse was rebuilt in baroque style in the 17C. The Romanesque frescos on the inside of the triumphal arch, and also on the nave walls, are of interest. 14C frescos in the choir, on the vault and outside; late baroque frescos (c. 1780) on the nave vault, triumphal arch and chancel vault. The frescos on the fa-çade and in the portico date from the 19C.

Tésimo (Merano), parish church of the Assumption, stained-glass window (1520)

Leon castle near Lana (Merano), 13C

Environs: The environs of Merano are rich in history, with castles from the Romanesque and Gothic periods. **Tirolo/Tyrol and the Castel Tirolo:** Firstly, the village of Tirolo. This lies on the Kiechelberg and has the Romanesque and baroque *parish church of St. John the Baptist*, and the 15C church of *St. Ruprecht*. The route then leads on to the *ancestral castle of the Counts of the Tyrol.* Built in 1140, it stands on a high crag. The region takes its name from this castle and it was used by the Tyrolean counts as their residence until 1363. The castle was restored after 1900. Note: the white marble *round-arched doorway*, with its splendid reliefs, which leads to the main residence. It dates from *c.* 1170 and shows the influence of Lombard architectural sculpture. The two-storeyed *chapel* has a round apse, is covered with frescos from the 2nd half of the 14C, and has another richly decorated portal. **Schenna/Scena** (at the entrance to the Passeier valley): *St. Martin* (*c.* 1200). *St. Johann,* a fine Gothic Revival church dating from 1869; the tomb of Archduke Johann (d. 1859) and his wife. *St. Georg,* round Romanesque church from the 13C, with frescos dating from 1400. *Scena castle* (*c.* 1350). **Riffian/Rifiano** (N of Merano): *Parish church of the Mater Dolorosa* (a baroque church with Rocaille stuccoes dating from 1772 and the dome frescoed by Jos. Strickner, *c.* 1775. *Cemetery chapel of Our Lady* (two-storeyed chapel dating from 1400, with interesting frescos [1415] by the Merano painter Wenzel throughout the interior). **Gratsch/Quarazze** (W. of Castel Tirolo): *St. Peter* in Gratsch is one of the region's oldest churches (originally 10C). The church, altered in the Gothic period, still has numerous 11C frescos both outside and in. **Lana** (in the Adige valley, S.of Merano). The *parish church of the Assumption,* with a net vault and a tall free-standing tower to the SE, is in Niederlana and was built from 1483 onwards, probably by Hans Hueber. The attraction of the church is its 46-ft. tall *high altar,* the largest and one of the most important South Tyrolean altars,

Lana (Merano), parish church, high altar

Castel Tirolo (Merano)

with 33 carved figures, including a Peter and a Paul of about life-size. The altar was made from 1503–11 by Hans Schnatterpech with the aid of the carver Bernhard Härpfer, while the paintings on the wings are by Hans Schäuffelein. *chapel of St. Michael* (in the graveyard): Late Gothic chapel of 1520, with 18C frescos. The 13C *chapel of St. Margaret* was rebuilt in baroque style in the 17C. The three apses have frescos dating from 1220, restored, though not very well, in the 19C. There are three castles near Lana: *Braunsberg*, the *ruin of Brandis*, and *Leonburg* (all 13C). The village of **Tésimo/Tisens** is on the way from Oberlana to the Gampen pass. Its *parish church of the Assumption* was built in 1520–30 and the nave was vaulted in *c.* 1600. It has fine glass windows in the chancel. The two-storeyed graveyard chapel (1480–90) contains frescos by a painter of the Bolzano school. The 13C *St. Hippolyt* stands alone on a hill (the in-

terior is 17C). **Grissiano/Grissian** lies near to Tésimo and has the small hall church of *St. Jakob* (1142), whose nave was vaulted in the 17C. Note the Romanesque frescos (*c.* 1200) in the apse and the E. wall of the nave. **Senale,** with whose hospice a pilgrimage church was associated as early as the 12C, is to the S.of the Gampen pass. The present building of Our Lady in the Forest is a hall church by Hans Hueber, with a nave and two aisles. The *cemetery chapel* contains a fresco and a relief dating from *c.* 1500.

Messina 98100
Messina/Sicily   p.420│ │M 16

In 730 BC, Greeks from Chalcis on the island of Euboea founded this settlement on a site where there was probably previously a Sicel town. The original name of 'Zan-

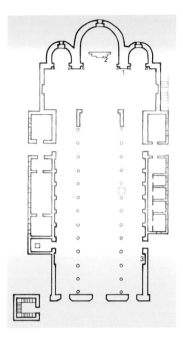

Messina, cathedral

Messina, cathedral of S. Maria 1 tomb of Archbishop G.de Tabiatis **2** high altar with Byzantine painting **3** late Renaissance portal by Caravaggio

cle' means 'sickle' (shape of the harbour). Refugees from Messenia occupied it in 493 BC and renamed it 'Messana'. The conflict between Rome and Carthage flared up in the 3C BC, and the Romans subsequently conquered the island of Sicily.

Cathedral of S.Maria (Piazza Duomo): Begun under the Normans in the early 12C, and consecrated in 1197 under Emperor Henry VI Hohenstaufen. It burned down in 1254 and was added to in different styles (Gothic, Renaissance) during the following centuries. Completely destroyed in 1908, but rebuilt in the old Norman style in 1919–29 using many of the original parts. Destroyed once again by bombs

in 1943, when many works of art were lost for good. Exterior: The lower section of the *façade* is original and has three Gothic portals, the middle one being particularly beautiful. There is a *late Renaissance portal* by Polidoro da Caravaggio (1573–1610) on the right flank, and also some fine *windows* with Catalan Gothic double arches. There are three fine restored *apses*. The campanile (completed in 1933), with the world's largest *astronomical clock*, is also interesting. Inside: Almost all the features are copies of the destroyed originals, e.g. the *mosaic* in the choir (originally 13C); on the high altar is a copy of the *Madonna della Lettera*, a Byzantine painting. In the 1st chapel of the right side aisle there is a *Statue of the Baptist* by Antonello Gagini (1525), and between the central and the right apse is the *tomb of Archbishop G.de Tabiatis* by di Gregorio, the Sienese artist (1333). There is an interesting and very rich *treasury*.

S. Annunziata dei Catalani (Via Garibaldi): Built by the Normans in the 12C; partially rebuilt owing to an earthquake. A fine 13C *façade* with three portals. The apse and the dome over the crossing survive from the original building, and the multi-coloured *round arches* should be seen. Inside there is a beautiful *holy-water stoup*. Beside the church is a *statue*, by A.Calamecca (1572), of *Don Juan d'Austria*, who was victorious at the battle of Lepanto.

Museo Nazionale (Via della Libertà): It houses the remains (paintings, sculptures), surviving from after 1908, of many churches in Messina. Outstanding exhibits include: in the garden in front of the museum, a *Neptune* (1557) from the Neptune fountain in the Piazza Unità d'Italia (by G.Montorsoli); *room II* has the famous 'Triptych of St.Gregory' by Antonello da Messina (1473; badly damaged in 1908); *room V* has two paintings by Michelangelo da Caravaggio ('Adoration of the Shepherds', 'Resurrection of Lazarus', 1604–9); *rooms VII–IX* have a collection of antique and Byzantine architectural remains and ceramics.

Also worth seeing: 13C church of *S. Francesco d'Assisi* (Via S. Francesco d'Asissi), Gothic, rebuilt after 1908 with some parts (apse and right-side portal) from the old building. The 13C *S. Maria Alemanna* (Via S.M.Alemanna). The *cemetery*, one of Italy's finest. *Fontana di Orione* in front of the cathedral, and *Fontana del Nettuno* (Piazza Unità d'Italia), splendid fountains by G.Montorsoli (1547–50). A trip around the *Viali di Circonvallazione*, with its fine views, is well worthwhile.

Metaponto/Metapontum 75010

Matera/Basilicata   p.418□N 12

A tourist resort (Lido di Metaponto) with a sandy beach running from the mouth of the Brádano to that of the Basento. It has a glorious past and was one of the most important towns of Magna Graecia. Metapontum was founded in the 8C as a Greek colony and reached its zenith in the 5C BC. It subsequently came under Roman administration and was destroyed by the Arabs. Pythagoras probably died here (*c*. 480 BC) after leaving Crotone.

Messina, S.Annunziata dei Catalani

Antiquarium: Finds from the ancient Greek colony, with maps of Magna Graecia and the Greek colonies on the Ionian coast. Painted terracottas from the temple. Reliefs from the 5&4C BC (Athene, Dionysus etc.), silver coins, funerary objects (statuettes, jewellery).

Tavole Palatine: Remains of a temple said to have been dedicated to Hera (6C BC). The temple was built 3 km. outside the ancient town, on the remains of an older shrine. Of the 36 original columns (6 on each short side and 12 on each long one), only 15 are still standing. Note the architrave at the N. corner. The capitals are archaic Doric. There are some Hellenistic *burial chambers* on the site.

Torremare: The remains of the medieval fortifications, and also some houses, are still visible.

Agora: The centre of ancient Metapontum. The *theatre,* and also the 6C BC Doric *temple of Apollo Lycius,* both stand on a rise.

Milano/Milan 20100
Milan/Lombardy   p.412☐D 3

In 222 BC, when they crushed the Gallic Insubres, the Romans — probably along with destroying the Etruscan Melpum — took a settlement founded by the Celts. Mediolanum acquired Roman civic rights in 89 BC. Under Augustus, it was the main town of the XI trans-Padus region and was already the largest town in Northern Italy. Milan started upon one of its periods of prosperity when, as a result of the new division of the empire by Diocletian, Maximian raised Mediolanum to the status of capital of the Italo-African part of the empire. The Edict of Milan (freedom of belief for Christians) was issued by Constantine and Licinius in 313. When the imperial officer Ambrosius was appointed bishop of Milano in 370, the town became an ecclesiastical metropolis of prime importance (resolution of the conflict with the Arians; Ambrosian Liturgy). The Ostrogoths completely destroyed Milan in 539 and it fell to the Lombards in 569. It was not until the Ottonian period that the

Metaponto, Tavole Palatine

town once again gained a leading role in Lombardy. For a long time, the Milanese bishops also remained the political leaders of the city. In 979 there was an insurrection against the archbishop. The 'Pataria', a people's movement, joined with a reforming papacy to oppose the rule of the archbishop and of the aristocracy (immediate cause of the Investiture Contest). The citizenry (from 1097 onwards there were consuls) also began to defend itself successfully against outside interventions. Although the town was destroyed in 1162, Barbarossa was defeated at Legnano in 1176 and had to concede a large degree of independence to Milan in 1183 (the Lombard League). The Visconti emerged victorious from the struggles between the Ghibellines and Guelphs. It was under Visconti domination that Milan attained the peak of its political power. The Sforza followed in 1450. By this time the population of Milan already exceeded 100,000. The building activities of the Visconti (dukes since 1395) and of the Sforza had a decisive influence on the appearance of Milan; the cultivation of the arts had become a tradition for both families (Petrarch, Leonardo da Vinci, Bramante and others). France's invasion of Italy, and the fall of Lodovico Sforza in 1499, ended this, probably Milan's most significant, period. Finally, in the dispute between the Emperor and the French throne, the town and duchy fell in 1545 to Philip II of Spain, the son of Charles V. Milan remained under Spanish rule until 1714. Domination passed (1714) from the Spanish to the Austrian Habsburgs in the War of the Spanish Succession. Milan once again came to life intellectually in the 18C. The expectations originally aroused by the Revolution were not fulfilled during the period of French rule, which lasted almost 20 years (1796–1815). Milan became the capital of the Cisalpine Republic in 1796, and of the Regnum Italicum in 1805 (extensive building by Napoleon) with the Viceroy Eugène Beauharnais. After 1815, with the restoration of Austrian rule, Milan was the capital of Lombardy-Venetia. The first signs of autonomy came under Viceroy Maximilian of Austria. In the decades after 1815, Milan had also become one of the centres of the Risorgimento (the 'Cinque Giornate', an insurrection against the Austrians in 1848), and it was finally wrested from the Austrians in 1859. Since 1861 it has been part of a united Italy. Milan remained the 'Capitale morale' of the country even after the complete unification of Italy (1870). It was here that the most important political movements - Liberalism, Socialism,Catholicism - had their origin. The city developed into the economic centre of the new State. Fascism and the Resistenza (resistance movement) also began in the capital of Lombardy.

The city's development and its appearance: Little has survived from the Roman and early Christian periods but what has is impressive, particularly in the district of S.Lorenzo. Medieval buildings, such as S.Ambrogio, S.Eustorgio, and the Broletto, are a feature of the city. The undertakings of the Visconti and Sforza (city walls, castle, churches such as S. Maria delle Grazie or S.Satiro, Ospedale Maggiore) considerably altered medieval Milan. There are still a large number of 18C buildings: Palazzo Reale, Palazzo Litta, Teatro alla Scala, Via Manzoni and there was intense building activity under Napoleon: completion of the cathedral, the Foro Buonaparte project, the Arena, restoration of the city gates, l'Arco della Pace, numerous new palaces (Via Monte Napoleone, Via Monte di Pietà, etc.). The city's complexion changed completely in the late 19C. Several areas on the outskirts were included in the city in 1873. Large blocks of flats from that period still characterize whole residential streets. The building of the Galleria, and the redesign of the Piazza del Duomo, completely altered the city centre. Parks were laid out or extended. The Cimitero Monumentale was laid out in 1866. Extensive building began again in the 1920s: Stazione Centrale, Centro degli Affari, Piazza Diaz, Piazza S. Babila, thoroughfares such as the Corso Matteotti, Via V.Pisani, the laying out of the Piazza della Repubblica, and the fair ground. The serious war damage has t

Milan, cathedra

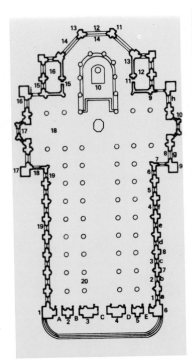

Cathedral

Milan cathedral. Exterior: A–E 19C bronze portals **1–19** gigantic statues on the pillars of the exterior **Interior: a–i** windows from the 15/16C **1** tomb of Archbishop Aribert (10C), with an 11C crucifix above it **2** tomb of Archbishop Ottone Visconti (13C) **3** tomb of Marco Carelli (1406) **4–6** altars designed by Pellegrini **7** tomb of Gian Giacomo Medicis (L.Leoni, 1560) **8** Madonna (14C) **9** St.Bartholomew (M.d'Agrate, 1562) **10** sanctuary with high altar and choir (Pellegrini) **11** sacristy door (Hans von Fernach, 1393) **12** S.sacristy **13** statue of Martin V (1424) **14** medal commemorating the church's consecration **15** sacristy door (14C, G.da Campione) **16** N. sacristy **17** altar of 'Madonna dell'Albero' **18** Trivulzio candlestick (13C) **19** altar design by Pellegrini **20** baptistery (Pellegrini)

day been for the most part repaired. Important modern buildings include the Torre Velasca and the Pirelli sky-scraper, in addition to the extensive rebuilding.

Cathedral: Dedicated to the Nativity of the Virgin. The 4C summer cathedral of S.Tecla stood on the area of the Piazza del Duomo until 1461. The octagonal baptistery and the winter cathedral of S.Maria Maggiore (9C) were to the left of it. The construction of the present cathedral began in 1386 on the same site and French and German architects were involved. The Solari supervised construction in 1459–76 and they were followed by G.Antonio Amadeo in *c.* 1500. P.Tibaldi took over in 1567, and the design of the crypt is due to him. The spire was added in the 18C. It was only under Napoleon (1805–9) that the front, which Tibaldi conceived as a two-towered baroque façade, was completed in Gothic form. The basilican cathedral has a nave, four aisles, and a broad transept and is one of the largest of churches. 135 pinnacles crown the buttresses and there are over 2300 statues ('giganti') on the exterior. The decoration of the cathedral is mainly 16C. The cathedral treasure is housed in the crypt.

S. Ambrogio

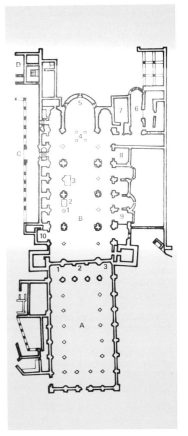

S. Ambrogio (Piazza S. Ambrogio): Built from 379–86 as a martyrs' basilica on an early Christian cemetery. Originally dedicated to St. Gervase and St. Protase, and dedicated to Ambrose after his death in 397. The apses and the preliminary bay are *c.* 950. Rebuilding of the bays of the nave, the towers and the atrium was begun after 1080. In 1492, Bramante began building the *Canonica*, another monastery courtyard. The baroque alterations were removed in 1857. In the 1950s, owing to war damage, the whole complex was thoroughly, and splendidly, restored. In front of the church there is an *atrium* in the form of an arcaded courtyard (this is very rare). The galleried church has four bays and is laid out on a metrical system. The last bay has an octagonal tower. There is no transept. The heavy vault dates from the last third of the 12C. Note the following features: The *Pergamo*, a pulpit assembled from older parts in *c.* 1200, with a

Milan, S. Ambrogio A atrium **1–3** portals **1** in the architrave: early Romanesque sculpture (S. Ambrogio) **2** wooden doors (scenes from the life of David, 18C, to 4C models) **3** door frames: 8–10C sculptures **B** basilica **1** column with brazen serpent, Byzantine, 10C **2** plinth of a column of the 4C basilica **3** Pergamo; under it is an early Christian sarcophagus (with a depiction of a marriage), 4C **4** ciborium and paliotto **5** apse: choir stalls, 1469, with scenes from the life of St. Ambrose; in the middle is a 9C cathedra; mosaic of Christ in the apse calotte **6** Sacello di S. Vittore in Ciel D'Oro: 5C mosaics on a gold and blue ground (St. Ambrose and other Saints) **7** Sacrestia delle Messe, two frescos by Tiepolo, 1737 ('Martyrdom of St. Victor' and 'Shipwreck of St. Satiro') **8** altarpiece and frescos by Lanino **9** panel painting by Gaudenzio Ferrari **10** 'The Risen Christ', fresco by Bergognone, 1491 **C** Portico della Canonica **D** Museo di S. Ambrogio

Last Supper (underneath this is an early Christian sarcophagus). The *ciborium* dates from after 1196: 4 Roman columns with 9C capitals support a baldacchino with Lombard-Byzantine reliefs. The antependium of the high altar dates from as far back as the 9C: gilded reliefs with a christological programme and scenes from the life of St. Ambrose.

S. Eustorgio (Piazza S. Eustorgio/Porta Ticinese): Founded in the 6C. The 11C building was completely destroyed by Barbarossa in 1164, when the relics of the Magi were removed to Cologne. The new building was altered several times, taking on its final form in 1278. The chapels on the S.flank are later. It has a nave and two aisles, and is 8 bays long. The church was used by Milanese families as a burial place (Visconti, Bricio, Torelli and others). *Features:* In the 4th chapel on the right is the *tomb* of Stefano Visconti (1327) by G.di Balduccio, and above it is the fresco of St. George by a Lombard artist. The *high altar* has reliefs with the story of the Passion (14C). To the right of the sanctuary is the *Chapel of the Magi* (ancient sarcophagus). A door to the left of the sanctuary leads to the only surviving Roman and early Christian *cemetery* in Milan. Past the left of the sanctuary is the *Portinari Chapel,* built by Michelozzo in 1462–8 for the Florentine banker Pigello Portinari. This is the first and one of the most beautiful Renaissance religious works in Milan. The space is arranged in the same way as the Old Sacristy of S. Lorenzo in Florence: a square, domed room with an adjoining rectangular altar area. The *drum* has a painted stucco frieze (angels with festoons). The *frescos* (1466–8, probably by Foppa) depict the four Latin Fathers of the Church, the Annunciation, the Assumption of the Virgin, and scenes from the life of St. Peter Martyr, to whom the chapel is dedicated. The *Arca di S. Pietro,* at the entrance to the altar area, was made in 1336–9 by Giovanni di Balduccio from Pisa. Eight statues (the virtues) bear the *sarcophagus,* which is crowned by a pyramidal structure with a baldacchino. On the sarcophagus, there are reliefs with scenes from the life of St. Peter Martyr, and statues of Saints. The upper part has figures symbolizing the hierarchy of Heaven. Beneath the baldacchino there are statues of Christ, Dominic, Peter Martyr, and the Madonna.

S. Ambrogio, Pergamo, c. 1200

S. Eustorgio

S. Fedele (Piazza S. Fedele; behind the town hall): Begun in 1569 by Pellegrini as a Jesuit church, by order of St. Carlo Borromeo; not completed until the 19C. The façade, with its plethora of sculpture, is interesting in proportion. The inside is single-aisled, and follows the arrangement of Jesuit churches (the model is Il Gesù, Rome). The furnishings date from the 16 –19C.

S. Lorenzo Maggiore (Corso Porta Ticinese/Piazza Vetra): The most important remnant of Roman and early Christian Milan. 16 marble columns (Corinthian capitals) stand in front of S. Lorenzo and were used here in the 4C as part of the church's atrium. Their origin is uncertain but they are said to be late imperial. It is a centrally planned building based on Byzantine models It stands on Roman remains, and was built in the late 4C. Following its devastation, Martino Bassi rebuilt it in Renaissance form from 1574 onwards by order of Carlo Borromeo. However, the attached buildings *S. Aquilino* and *S. Ippolito* date from the early Christian period, while *S. Sisto* is 6C. The present façade dates from 1894; the canon's

buildings which abut on both sides are from 1626 – 32. Radical restoration in 1937/8.

S. Maria delle Grazie (Corso Magenta): Founded in 1463 by Count Gaspare da Vimercate. The church has a nave, two aisles, nine bays accompanied by chapels, with a transept and graduated choir, and was built by G. Solari in 1466 – 90. The monastery buildings were completed as early as 1469. In 1492, the chancel and the transept were torn down by order of Lodovico il Moro in order to make room for a centrally planned building. Bramante was awarded the commission. Two apses directly adjoin a domed space, and a choir bay is inserted between the 3rd apse and the dome. The fourth arm (not built) was intended to replace the nave. The clear architectural forms of the interior (painted) are in striking contrast to the small divisions of the outside of the drum. Lodovico wanted to be interred here together with his wife Beatrice. Their graves are today in the Certosa di Pavia. The *cloister* and the *old sacristy* are also the work of Bramante. The refectory houses the celebrated *Last Supper* by Leonardo da Vinci.

S. Maria delle Grazie

S. Maria della Passione (Via Conservatorio): Built by G.Battagio in 1482–5 as a centrally planned church on a Greek cross, while the dome (1530) is by C.Lombardo. In 1573–91, the ground plan was changed, to plans by M.Bassi, into a Latin cross (nave and two aisles; flanked by semi-circular, projecting chapels). The fine *decoration* includes: a series of paintings by D.Crespi (scenes from the Passion) beneath the dome on the left. The left-hand organ front is also by Crespi. On the right is the tomb of Archbishop Birago, the founder of the church (1495). There are works by B.Luini and Bergognone in the right transept and there is a Last Supper by G.Ferrari in the left transept.

S. Maria presso S. Celso (Corso Italia): Begun by Dolcebuono in 1490, continued (with altered plan) by Solari and Amadeo, completed in 1505. The atrium, 1514–26, is by Cesariano, while the façade was built in 1570 to plans by G.Alessi. It has a nave, two aisles, a transept, a dome over the chancel, and an ambulatory. Splendid *decoration:* There is an Assumption of the Virgin (statue by A.Fontana, 1586) to the left of the crossing; the choir stalls are to designs by G.Alessi, 1570. There is a Baptism of Christ by G.Ferrari in the 4th arch of the ambulatory. The 1st chapel on the left has a work by Bergognone. There is a 'Holy Family' by P.Bordone on the altar of the right transept. The entrance to *S. Celso*, an early 12C church, is just to the right of the transept.

S. Maria presso S. Satiro (Via Torino): The former baptistery, the Cappella della Pietà, still survives from the original church founded by Archbishop Ansperto

Milan, S. Lorenzo A portico **B** central area **C** ambulatory **D** atrium **E** chapel of St.Aquilinus **F** sacristy **G** baptistery **H** towers **I** Cappella Cittadini **K** chapel of St.Hippolytus **L** foundation walls of a Romanesque chapel **M** chapel of St.Sixtus **1** baroque high altar with marble spoils from the basilica **2** remains of mosaics (late-4C): 12 tribes of Israel and the 12 Apostles; heads of the patriarchs and names of the Apostles (above the entrance); head of an old man (right) **3** Roman portal (1C AD) **4** mosaic (late-4C), Translation of Elijah **5** silver shrine of St.Aquilinus **6** entrance to the substructure **7** mosaic (late-4C), Christ and the Apostles **8** marble sarcophagus of Galla Placidia, 5C **9** Deposition, fresco, late-13C **10** tomb of Giovanni del Conte, 1568, and above it are remains of 11C frescos **11** remains of ancient flooring **12** contemporary copy of Leonardo's 'Last Supper'

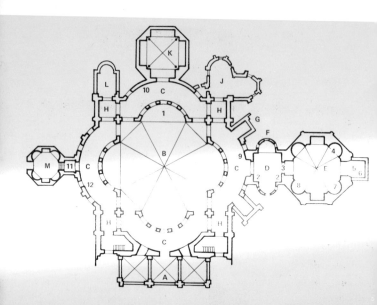

in the 9C. The church of 1242 was replaced from 1478 onwards by a new building by Bramante. It was extended once again in 1482 under the supervision of Amadeo to plans by Bramante (baptistery). The façade was only completed in the 19C. The interior (one nave, two aisles), with its large, tunnel-vaulted transept and its false sanctuary, creates the impression, despite its small surface area, of a wide basilica in the ancient Roman tradition (painted ceiling panels, perspective drawing in the chancel). The *baptistery* is one of the finest arrangements of space of the early Renaissance.

S.Simpliciano (Corso Garibaldi/Piazza S.Simpliciano): Founded by St.Ambrose in the 4C on the site of an early Christian cemetery. The present church is the result of several extensions of the 12C Romanesque one. Since 1967, some questionable restoration, aimed at recreating the church's original appearance, has been in progress. Chapels open on both sides of the interior (one nave, two aisles) which is hall-like, the vaults being of equal height. The transept has two aisles and there is a dome over the crossing; the chancel is flanked by

two chapels whose vaults project into the transept. The apse calotte has a fresco by Bergognone (Coronation of the Virgin, 1514). The sacristy adjoins the left transept but its entrance is at present obstructed. Two *cloisters* abut on the E. of the church; the smaller dates from 1449, and the large one, with its clear forms, was built in *c.* 1550 to designs by V.Seregni.

Castello Sforzesco: The *Rocca Viscontea* of Galeazzo II Visconti was destroyed by the people in 1447 during the Ambrosian Republic, and, from 1450 onwards, Francesco Sforza had this powerful castle built. The main tower dates back to the brief involvement of Filarete (1452–4). The castle consists of a large front courtyard (the Piazza d'Armi), a stronghold (refuge of the Sforzas; the so-called Rocchetta [1468–71]), and, opposite the Rocchetta, the Corte Ducale (1472) with an Italian garden, for use as a residence in peaceful

Milan, S.Maria presso S.Satiro 1 nave **2** transept **3** sanctuary **4** Cappella della Pietà: Pietà group of figures in painted terracotta by Ag.de Fondutis; remains of 10C Byzantine-style frescos **5** sacristy or baptistery: terracotta frieze (putti, angels, male busts) by Ag.de Fondutis

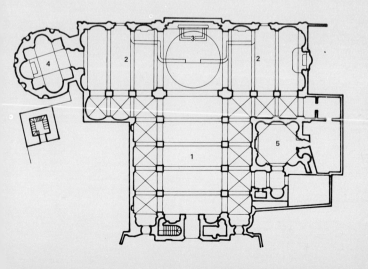

times. The marriage of Gian Galeazzo Visconti to Isabella d'Aragon was celebrated in 1488, and in 1491 that of Lodovico to Beatrice d'Este was also solemnized. The six bastions built under the Spaniards were razed by order of Napoleon. The castle had become so ruined by the late 19C that the possibility of demolishing it was considered, but it was then decided to thoroughly restore it (1893–1911). The castle today houses the *City Museums*. The Filarete *tower*, and the fine inner courtyard of the *Rocchetta*, are the most interesting features besides the museums.

The Piazza Mercanti and Via Mercanti District: The former political centre of medieval Milan. The *Broletto Nuovo* or *Palazzo della Ragione* (1228–33) stands on the side leading to the Via Mercanti; there is an open, arcaded hall on the ground floor. The *Scuole Palatine* (1645) forms the E. side of the square. To the S. is the *Loggia degli Osii* dating from 1316. Opposite the Broletto, in the Via Mercanti, is the *Palazzo dei Giuriconsulti* (1560–5); the lawyers' school which played a major role in the city and the duchy.

Palazzo Reale (S.of the cathedral): The Broletto Vecchio stood here until 1138. Built by Piermarini for the Austrian governor in 1788 on the site of an older Visconti residence (14C). Gorgeous rococo and Empire rooms.

Ospedale Maggiore: The extensive hospital founded by Francesco Sforza in 1457 lies between Via F.Sforza and Festa d.Perdono (today part of the university is housed here). Eight smaller courtyards are grouped around a large central one. The S.side was begun by Filarete and Solari in 1465. The central section of the façade with its portal, and also the church, are by Ricchini (1624–49). The exterior, with its

Milan, S.Maria delle Grazie A B so-called Tribuna **C** sanctuary **D** Chiostrino **E** old sacristy **F** chapel of the Madonna delle Grazie **G** entrance to refectory **H** refectory **1** tomb monument to the Della Torre family, 1483 **2** frescos by Gaud. Ferrari, 1542 **3** chapel with rich stucco decoration, 16C; frescos by Giovanni De'Mio **4** and **5** intarsia choir stalls, 1470–1510, with sgraffiti above them (depictions of Dominican Saints, and medallions of the Evangelists and church fathers) **6** bust of Lodovico il Moro, 15C **7** miraculous image **8** private chapel of the Conti; bronze grille, 18C **9** Crucifixion fresco by D.Montorfano, 1495 **10** Last Supper by Leonardo da Vinci

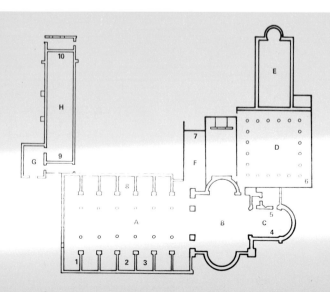

terracotta facing, became the model of many Milanese façades.

Palazzo Marino (Piazza della Scala). Built for Marini from Genoa in 1558–60 (fine courtyard). Since 1861 it has been the town hall; in 1888–90 the building was enlarged and the façade completed.

Baroque palaces: *Pal.Clerici* (Via Clerici), early 18C. Spectacular staircase; frescos by Tiepolo in the Galleria degli Arazzi. The late-17C *Pal.Dugnani* (Giardini Pubblici), today a school. There are frescos by Tiepolo in the middle room. *Pal.Litta* (Corso Magenta), built in 1648 for Count Arese, the President of the Senate; the façade dates from 1752–63. *Pal.Sormani/Biblioteca Comunale* (Via F.Sforza/Corso di Porta Vittoria), with well-articulated façade (1736, F.Croce). *Pal.Trivulzio* (Via Piatti/near the Via Torino), built by G.Ruggeri in 1707–13. In the courtyard is a 15C portal from the Pal.Mozzanica.

Teatro alla Scala (Piazza alla Scala): Built by Piermarini in 1775–8 on the site of the church of S.Maria della Scala. The elegant façade is crowned by a tympanum (chariot of Apollo). In 1946 the inside was restored in its old form after being damaged in the war. Probably the world's most famous opera house, it has staged numerous premières and there is probably no other theatre that is associated in such a way with the names of important composers, singers and conductors (Rossini, Bellini, Donizetti, Verdi, Ponchielli, Puccini; Toscanini; G.Pasta, Malibran, Callas).

19C and 20C Milan (see the section devoted to the city's development and its appearance): *Galleria Vittorio Emanuele II:* Built in 1865–77 as an arcade of shops between the Piazza del Duomo and Piazza della Scala. Designed by Guis. Mengoni, it is cruciform in plan and has an iron and glass roof. The lunettes have mosaics symbolizing the four continents, the arts, agriculture, science and industry. The arcade leading to the Piazza del Duomo (laid out by G.Mengoni in 1865) opens through a large triumphal arch. Dedicated to the first King of United Italy, it was intended as a monument to the new State and, as a moral and political symbol, was deliberately built next to the cathedral. The

La Scala 1859, Museo teatrale alla Scala

Piazza Cordusio is surrounded by large insurance offices and the Post Office, built in 1897–1901. *Via Dante,* impressive late-19C street. *Foro Buonaparte,* built under Napoleon, while the buildings in the 'Viennese ring road style' date from the end of the 19C. *Cimitero Monumentale* (near the Stazione Garibaldi), designed in 1866 by C.Maciachini in Lombard Gothic style. *Stazione Centrale,* built by U.Stacchini in 1907–31. The large arrivals hall is designed as a showpiece and some of its decoration is martial in character. Soaring skywards next to the station is Milan's largest building, the elegant *Grattacielo Pirelli,* built in 1955–9 by a group of architects, including Nervi, for the Pirelli company. Since 1978 it has been owned by the Regione Lombardia, a fact that is seen by many as symbolizing the end of Milan's prosperity. The *Torre Velasca,* a tower of flats and offices, was built by a team of architects in 1958.

Museums: *Civica galleria d'arte moderna* (Via Palestro, 16): Marino Marini collection and Grassi collection, with works chiefly by French Impressionists. *Civica raccolta di stampe/Achille Bertarelli* (Castello Sforzesco): Interesting and extensive exhibits devoted to local history. *Civiche raccolte di archeologia classica e romana* (Corso Magenta, 15): Local Roman finds in addition to Greek and Etruscan items. *Civiche raccolte di archeologia paleontolica ed egizia* (Castello Sforzesco) with a Neolithic department (Lagozza culture) and the very important Egyptian department. *Civiche raccolte di arte applicata e incisioni* (Castello Sforzesco): ceramics, ivories, glasses, gold objects, furniture, porcelain and so forth. *Civico gabinetto dei disegni* (Castello Sforzesco): Graphics collection with sheets from the 15 – 20C; the 17C 'Lombard group' is the outstanding feature. *Civico museo d'arte antica* (Castello Sforzesco): Sculptures from the early Christian period up until the 16C (Michelangelo's 'Rondanini Pietà'), paintings from the 14–18C (Bellini, Mantegna, Foppa, Correggio, Tintoretto, Tiepolo, Guardi). *Civico padiglione d'arte contemporanea* (Via Palestro, 16) with Italian Futurist pieces. *Collezione 'G.e I.Jucker'* (Via Macchi, 28)): 19C paintings, particularly works by Fattori. *Museo civico di storia naturale* (Corso Venezia, 55), museum of natural history. *Museo degli strumenti musicali* (Castello

S.Maria delle Grazie, Last Supper by Leonardo da Vinci

(forzesco): A good collection of musical instruments. *Museo del Duomo* (Piazza del Duomo, 14): Significant collection of stained glass and sculptures from the 14–20C, paraments from the 15-20C. *Museo di Milano* (Via Sant'Andrea, 6): Museum of the history of Milan. *Museo di Sant'Ambrogio* (Piazza S. Ambrogio, 15): fabrics from the 4–12C, 17C tapestries, early Christian objects (bed of St. Ambrose), 14/15C frescos. *Museo 'Poldi Pezzoli'* (Via Manzoni, 12): Originally the bequest of a 19C private collector, it has an excellent collection of 15–19C paintings, weapons, tapestries, furniture, small sculptures, etc. *Museo teatrale alla Scala* (associated with the theatre): The theatre's development from its beginnings until today, with mementoes from the rich history of the opera house. *Pinacoteca Ambrosiana* (Piazza Pio IX, 2): Pictures by Lombard and Venetian artists of the 15–18C, and an important collection of drawings. *Pinacoteca di Brera* (Via Brera, 28): Housed in the magnificent Palazzo di Brera, built for the Jesuits in 1651-1773. The statue of Napoleon I by Thorvaldsen (1809) stands in the inner courtyard, which is surrounded by two Palladian galleries. Founded in 1803 as a teaching collection for the academy of arts, the core of the gallery's collections came mainly from secularized churches and from acquisitions in Rome. It is one of the most important art collections in Italy. At the moment only some of the rooms are open.

Also worth seeing (in the immediate vicinity of the cathedral): *Piazza Belgioioso* with the *Pal. Belgioioso* (1772-81, Piermarini) and the *Casa di Manzoni*, where the writer died in 1873. *Casa degli Omenoni* (between the Piazza Belgioioso and the church of S. Fedele), which the sculptor built in 1565; Mannerist palace with an elegant façade (giant caryatids). *S. Gottardo in Corte* (near the Pal. Reale), dating from 1336, with an elegant campanile. *Piazza Fontana:* On the W. side, the archbishop's palace, whose 15C core was faced by Piermarini in 1784 – 1801; to the E. is the former *Pal. del Capitano di Giustizia* (1586). *S. Carlo al Corso* (Corso Vitt. Emanuele): Centrally planned church built in 1832-47 with a colonnaded portico. The 11C *S. Babila* (Piazza S. Babila), altered several times since then, restored in Romanesque form in 1853-1901. *S. Nazaro*

Maggiore (Corso di Porta Romana/Ospedale Maggiore). Built for St. Ambrose on the site of an early Christian cemetery. Rebuilt in the 11C. *Via A.Manzoni* with 18&19C palaces; in the lower half there is the church of *S.Francesco di Paolo*, a notable 18C building. (In the Brera district): *S.Maria del Carmine* (V.P.Veterᴏ): 1400 to 1456; inside is the magnificently decorated Cappella della Madonna del Carmine (1616–76 to plans by Quadrio). *S.Marco* (Via Fatebenefratelli): 13/14C; completely rebuilt in baroque style in 1691-8. Finely decorated (the S.transept has the 13C tomb of the Blessed Lanfranco, and in the sanctuary is the baptism of St.Augustine, dating from 1618). Verdi's 'Messa da Requiem' was first performed in the church on the occasion of the funeral of Manzoni. *S. Angelo* (Via Moscova): Franciscan church built in 1552-84, with 16&17C decoration.

Environs: Saronno (23 km. towards Varese): NE of this town is the pilgrimage church of the *Madonna dei Miracoli*, begun by G.A.Amadeo in 1498 (façade by Pellegrini, 1596-1612). Basilican structure with a dome in the style of Bramante over the crossing. Rich baroque decoration. The frescos throughout the church are outstanding: dome (choir of angels, G.Ferrari, 1534), dome tondi (Genesis, G.Ferrari, 1545); the *Cappella della Madonna* has frescos by Bernardo Luini, 1525 (Adoration of the Magi, Sacrifice in the Temple, Sibyls). In the corridor leading to the chapel there are two paintings by Luini (Marriage of the Virgin, and Dispute in the Temple). **Melegnano** (16 km. towards Lodi): Famous for two battles, that of 13/14 September 1515 in which Marshal Trivulzio, commanding the army of François I of France, routed the troops of Massimiliano Sforza, and the battle of 8 June 1859 when the French troops defeated the Austrians in one of the most important battles in the fight for Italy's unity. The church of *S. Giovanni Battista*, built in 1418 and altered in baroque style in 1618. In the *baptistery* (1st chapel on the right) there is a 'Baptism of Christ' by Bergognone, 1506. The 15C *Broletto* is opposite the church. The *castle* was built by Ber-

nabò Visconti in 1350. On the edge of th town is the *Ossario*, which commemorat the battle of 1859. **Legnano** (some 30 km towards Varese): The battle in which th cities of the Lombard League managed defeat Emperor Barbarossa took place he on 29 May 1176. The basilica of *S.Magn* A centrally planned building on a Gree cross plan, with an octagonal dome an drum, both dating from 1504, in the sty of Bramante (the campanile dates from 1752). Inside, behind the high altar, is polyptych by B.Luini (1523) in a splendi frame; the frescos on the entrance arch ar in the sanctuary are by Lanino (1560-4 The *Monument to the Battle of Legnar* (1900) stands in the Corso Italia. The *M seo Civico* is of local interest and has i teresting 2C silver cups with Cybele Outside, to the E., is the **Abbazia** **Chiaravalle**, founded in 1135 by Berna of Clairvaux. This is the most importan Cistercian Gothic building in N.Ital (tower over the crossing). **Abbazia d Viboldone**, Benedictine abbey begun i 1176 (frescos by the school of Giotto).

Milazzo 98057
Messina/Sicily   p.420□L 1

Founded as 'Mylai' by Greeks from Zar cle (Messina) in 716 BC, it was the scen of the famous Roman naval victory over th Carthaginians in 260 BC, the first suc victory gained by Rome. Garibaldi's trium phant advance through Sicily ended her on 20 July 1860.

Castle: Built in the 13C by Empero Frederick II Hohenstaufen on the site c an older building from which the *mai tower* probably derives. 14C Gothic *porta* Magnificent view.

Also worth seeing: *Duomo Vecchio* in th so-called 'Città Murata', built in the lat 16/early 17C, but in ruins today (with in teresting remains of the old building) *Duomo Nuovo* (Via Umberto I) contain four pictures by Antonello de Saliba (16C *Burial grounds*, some of them prehistoric have been uncovered in all parts of th own and those dating from the 14/13C BC near the Via Porticello N. of the castle, and the 10–8C BC near the Piazza Roma are outstanding. 8/7C BC *Greek tombs,* with ceramics, have also been discovered.

Environs: Rometta lies some 25 km. to the E., in the mountains. It has a Byzantine church (*Chiesa del Salvatore*—a centrally planned building) and the remains of a Hohenstaufen castle.

Minturno 04026

Latina / Latium   p.416 □ I 10

Cathedral of S. Pietro (Corso Vitt. Emanuele): 11C building, enlarged in the 13&14C. Further alterations in the 17C. The arches of the *portico* vary in form and the entrance one is original. Romanesque *tower*. Note the: *Easter candlestick* with fine mosaics, and a Roman base and capital. The *pulpit* of 1260 is also decorated with mosaics. The polychrome reliefs show scenes from the story of Jonah; the left-hand one has a lion on the inside. The pulpit is by Giovanni di Nicola or

Peregrino da Sessa. The *chapel of the sacrament* of 1587 is profusely decorated with stucco and coloured marble.

Castle (Piazza Roma): Built under the Dell' Aquila, converted as a residence. Thomas Aquinas visited the castle in 1272, and Alfonso of Aragon stayed there in 1452. Despite the damage sustained in World War 2, some picturesque corners of the *Quartiere Medioevale* have survived.

Environs: Minturnae. An important inland harbour on the Garigliano, it was an important town of the Ausonians, who were allied to the Samnites. The town suffered a severe defeat in 315 BC, when the Ausonians were beaten in the Samnite Wars with Rome. A Roman colony was established under Caesar and Augustus. The surrounding area became increasingly marshy, and this and the barbarian invasions—it was probably destroyed in 580–90 by the Lombards—led to the town's downfall. Excavations have revealed the town's *wall*. The town lay on the river bank and had two *gates*, at opposite ends of the town, on the Via Appia. The excavations have also revealed the wall surrounding the

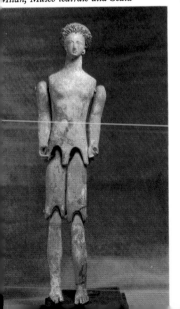

Milan, Museo teatrale alla Scala

Milan, Castello Sforzesco

first Roman settlement of 296 BC. *Remains of the Republican and Imperial Forum* (with *baths*), numerous *temples,* the oldest being 6C BC and dedicated to the Italic Dea Marica. The most important monument is the *theatre,* which dates from the 1C AD. There was room for 4,600 spectators, and it had an orchestra and a raised stage. Since 1961, classical works have been performed here during the summer. On the way to Minturnae are some remains of the ancient *aqueducts.*

Mirabella Eclano 83036
Avellino/Campania   p.416□L 11

Aeclanum, lying on the ancient Via Appia, was, in antiquity, one of the most important towns in the region of the Hirpini.

Chiesa Matrice S. Maria Maggiore: Enlarged and rebuilt in the late 19C. The campanile, rebuilt in 1930 after the last major earthquake, has a Roman inscription on its base. Notable features inside are the *painted wooden ceiling* (1749); a beautiful mid-12C *wooden crucifix* (clear southern French influence) in the right transept. The *church treasure* includes the surviving fragments of two 11C *exultet rolls.*

Environs: Some 3.5 km. SW is the **necropolis of Madonna delle Grazie** from the 2nd millennium BC (rich finds of Stone Age tomb furnishings; receptacles, stone tools). Some 3 km. NE, on the *Passo di Mirabella,* are the ruins of the ancient **Aeclanum** (see above); the excavations include the remains of the *baths* and the *foundations of private houses;* there is a small *antiquarium* nearby.

Mirándola 41037
Modena/Emilia-Romagna   p.412' .F 4

Mirándola, which belonged to the Abbazia di Nonantola under the Lombards, became a free commune at the end of the 12C. It was ruled by the Pico family from 1311 onwards. One of the members of this

family was Giovanni II, known as Pico della Mirándola (1463–94), the famous scholar and philosopher. The Picos, who were dukes from 1619 onwards, ruled until 1707, when Emperor Joseph I of Austria deposed the last duke and transferred the dukedom to Rinaldo d'Este.

Places of interest: *S.Francesco* (Via Vo turno), rebuilt in the 15C, it has tombs of the Pico family, including a work by Paolo di Jacopo delle Masegne. *Chiesa del Gesù* (Via Verdi), 17C, with the Circumcision Christ, 1690, by I.Monti. The *Collegiata,* a restored church dating from 1477, and the *Oratorio del Sacramento,* with a 17 Madonna by A.Tiarini stand on the Piazza della Conciliazione. *Museo Civico* (Via Verdi), with prehistoric and Roman finds and also 16&17C paintings. The *Palazzo del Comune* (Piazza Grande), whose Renaissance design has been restored.

Modena 41100
Modena/Emilia-Romagna   p.410□F

Modena, built by the Romans as Mutina in 183 BC on the site of a prehistoric and Etruscan settlement, has been the seat of a bishop since the 3/4C. Under the Lombards and Franks the town was the seat of a count, and its walls were built in 891. It was held by the Canossa family in the 10C and from the 12C onwards it was a free town. In 1288 it fell to the Este, and from 1598 onwards it was their main residence. In 1452, together with Reggio nell'Emilia, it was raised to the status of a duchy by Emperor Frederick III. The Este ruled continuously until the arrival of the French in 1796; the duchy passed to Francis IV of Austria-Este in 1814. Today Modena is an archbishopric and a university city, and also an important industrial and trading centre and the capital of the province of the same name. Important artists from Modena: Tommaso da Modena (1325/6 before 1379), Guido Mazzoni (c. 1450 1518), Nicolò dell'Abate (1509/12–1571).

Cathedral of S. Geminiano (Piazza Grande): As early as 400, there was a burial chapel here containing the relics of St. Geminianus. Between 752 and 780 the relics were transferred to a second building but this collapsed in c. 1000. The present cathedral, which is one of the finest and best-preserved Romanesque buildings in Italy, was begun in 1099 and was largely complete in 1130–40. However, it was not consecrated until 1184. Lanfranco, of Lombardy, was the architect and master builder; his successors up until 1323 were also Lombard builders. In the 13C, the sanctuary and transept were heightened, as were the aedicules above the two E. staircase turrets, and the *Porta Regia* (2) was built. The *campanile*, known as called 'La Ghirlandina', had a storey added in 1261, but was only completed in 1319 when Arrigo da Campione crowned it. The rose-window and the 2 side portals (c. 1200) of the *façade* are by Anselmo da Campione; the central portal is a masterpiece by Wiligelmus, the sculptor. The four reliefs, with their scenes from Genesis, are amongst Italy's oldest Romanesque sculptures. The two outer ones were moved from their original position in c. 1200, when the side portals were built. All the carved decoration on the façade is by Wiligelmus or his school, with the exception firstly of the lions supporting the columns of the two-storeyed porch (19C restorations), and secondly of the Christ Enthroned (c. 1200) above the rose- window. There are numerous *capitals*, also from the school of Wiligelmus on the right flank. The *Porta dei Principi* (1) — restored after the war — is by the master of S. Geminiano, a follower of Wiligelmus; the *Porta Regia* (2), which is by a Lombard workshop, has a statue of St. Geminianus (1376) by G. Paruolo in its aedicule. The *exterior pulpit* (3), 1501, is by Jacopo da Ferrara, while the four *reliefs* of scenes from the life of St. Geminianus (4), 1442, are the work of Agostino di Duccio, a pupil of Donatello. The *Porta della Pescheria* (5) on the left flank was built by a follower of Wiligelmus in 1120–30. The inside of the basilica has a nave and two aisles, but was not given its present groin vault until the 15C; its capitals are from the school of Wiligelmus. The *pulpit* (6), built by Enrico da Campione in 1322, has late-14C terracotta statues, as well as paint-

Modena, cathedral of S. Geminiano

Modena, cathedral of S. Geminiano, foot of the pulpit

ings dating from c. 1380 attributed to Cristoforo da Modena. The pillar of the pulpit bears a *Madonna* dating from 1414. On the 1st altar on the left (7) is an early-15C *terracotta panel*, in the form of a polyptych and ascribed to Michele da Firenze. There is a *painting* by Dosso Dossi (1522) at the 2nd altar (8). The fine *tribuna* (9) bears reliefs that were restored in 1920 but which originally date from 1160–80, and were the work of Anselmo da Campione and three other masters. The associated *ambo* (10), 1208–25, is the work of Master Bozarinus and his fellow-artists. There is a 14C *wooden crucifix* above the tribuna. In the *crypt*, which has Lombard capitals, 1099–1100, there are a *font*, 1587 (left apse), the *tomb of St. Geminianus* (central apse), and *terracotta statues*, 1485, by Guido Mazzoni (right apse). There are fragments of 13–15C *frescos* in the right apse (11) of the church, while the sanctuary has intarsia *choir stalls* (12), 1465, (restored in 1971) by Cristoforo and Lorenzo da Lendinara. The left apse (13) has a *fresco of the Madonna*, attributed to Cristoforo da Modena, at the altar; 15C Tuscan *relief of the Madonna* on the left; *statue of St. Geminianus*, ascribed to Agostino di Duc-

cio (right). On the left side are a *polyptych* (14), 1384, by Serafino Serafini, and a *monument* (15) of N.Cavallerino, probably to designs by Giulio Romano. The *sacristy*, 1477 (entrance in left apse), has intarsia *benches*, 1474, by Bernardino da Lendinara, and four *intarsia panels* of the Evangelists, 1477, by C.da Lendinara. There are thirteen *Dutch tapestries* 16C, in the chapter house. The treasury has an 11/12C *portable altar;* the archive in the chapter house has eight sumptuous illuminated manuscripts originating from c. 1130. The **Museo Lapidario del Duomo** (Via Lanfranco 6) has eight fine *metopes, c.* 1130, and *fragments* from various phases of the cathedral's construction.

S.Bartolomeo (Via dei Servi): Built for

Modena, cathedral 1 Porta dei Principi **2** Porta Regia **3** external pulpit, 1501, by Jac. da Ferrara **4** reliefs, 1442, by Ag. di Duccio **5** Porta della Pescheria **6** pulpit, 1322, by E.da Campione **7** terracotta panel, early-15C, by M.da Firenze **8** painting, 1522, by D.Dossi **9** choir screen **10** pulpit by Bozarinus **11** fresco fragments, 13–15C **12** choir stalls, 1465 **13** Madonna fresco, attributed to C.da Modena **14** polyptych, 1384, by S. Serafini **15** monument, c. 1530, N.Cavallerino

Modena, cathedral, polyptych

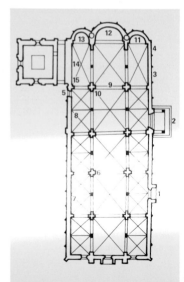

the Jesuits by P.G.Soldati in 1607, it has a façade dating from 1727, and contains *frescos* by Andrea Pozzo (1642–1709) in the chancel and apse, an *image of the Saint* by G.M.Crespi on the left wall of the sanctuary, and other *paintings* from the 1st half of the 17C.

S. Pietro (Via S. Pietro): Originally a Benedictine foundation. Rebuilt by P.Barabini in 1476–1506. The church has a nave and four aisles, and its 3 marble portals were added in 1549. The decoration on the inside of the *rose-window*, 1555, is probably by some of Begarelli's fellow-artists. The six *statues* in front of the nave pillars were sculpted by Begarelli personally. The contents are mainly 16C, note: the *organ* by G.B.Fracchetti (left of entrance) with organ panels, 1546, by the Taraschi, displayed in the left and right aisles. *Calling of St. Peter*, 1557, by G.Romanino (left wall of sanctuary). *Madonna with St.Jerome and St.Sebastian*, late 15C, by Francesco Bianchi Ferrari (3rd chapel on left).

Palazzo dei Musei (Largo Porta S. Agostino): Built by P.Termanini in 1753, it houses several museums. The **Galleria Estense** is one of the most important collections in Italy and comprises part of the magnificent art collection owned by the Este. The 1st section contains Etruscan, Greek, Roman and Romanesque sculptures, 12&13C Arabian and Persian vases, and a sumptuous collection of Italian and French ivories and enamels. The *Pinacoteca*, which offers a broad survey of northern Italian painting from the 14C up until the 18C, has works by artists including Tommaso and Barnaba da Modena, Giovanni di Paolo, Cosmè Tura, Veronese, Tintoretto, Bassano, Dosso Dossi, Correggio, the Carracci, Guercino, Reni, Domenichino, Strozzi, Rosa and Guardi. The **Museo Estense** contains medallions (by Pisanello and others), small bronze statues and bronze reliefs (Sansovino, Giovanni da Bologna, Adriaen de Vries, etc.) and terracotta and marble sculptures (by G.Mazzoni, Begarelli, Bernini and others). The **Museo Civico** has: Romanesque frescos from churches in Modena; 14&15C Byzantine, Tuscan and Modenese panel paintings; statuettes of terracotta and wood; reliquaries; works by Dosso Dossi and Begarelli; 18&19C Italian porcelain;

Modena, Palazzo Ducale

Modena, Biblioteca Estense

and departments for musical instruments, arms and ethnography. The **Biblioteca Estense,** one of the richest collections of manuscripts in Italy, has codices of great historical, literary and artistic significance. In addition: the *Galleria Campori* (small collection of baroque paintings). *Galleria Poletti* (19C art). *Civica Biblioteca di Storia dell'Arte Luigi Poletti* (important library of art history). *Museo del Risorgimento* with interesting exhibits.

Palazzo Ducale (Piazza Roma): One of Italy's lárgest palaces, begun by B.Avanzini in 1634 on the site of a castle (1291), but not completed until the late 19C. The *façade,* by Avanzini, has marble statues, 1560, by Prospero Spani, on both sides of the portal. The fine *courtyard* is the work of Padre Guarini. The *interior decoration* dates from *c.* 1700. Today the seat of the military academy, this building also houses a *library,* a *pantheon* and the *hall of the gold medallions.*

S. Domenico (Piazzale S. Domenico): Redesigned by G.A.Torri as an oval, domed church in 1708–31. Its 18C contents include a terracotta group by Begarelli.

Modena, Galleria Estense, Minerva

S.Maria Pomposa or S.Sebastiano (Via Castel Maraldo): 1717 – 19, contains 17&18C paintings by B.Cervi and F.Vella.

S.Agostino (Largo Porta S.Agostino): In 1663, the original building dating from 1235 was enlarged to house the Este tombs and monuments. Some remains of the original structure are visible on the left flank. The single-aisled interior was richly decorated in 1662 and contains a *stucco group of the Descent from the Cross* by Begarelli (1st altar on right), and a fragment of a *fresco of the Virgin* by Tommaso da Modena.

S.Francesco (Largo S.Francesco d'Assisi): Built in 1244 and restored in 1828-9, with furnishings and decorations mostly from the 19C, it contains a *terracotta Descent from the Cross,* possibly dating from 1523, by Begarelli (rear of left aisle).

S.Biagio (Largo Porta Bologna): A single-aisled, domed church largely rebuilt in 1661, with a *Crucifixion,* 1543, on its left flank. It also has some notable 15–17C decoration.

S.Vincenzo (Corso Canal Grande 75): A single-aisled, domed church built in 1617, with a transept and six side chapels. Largely destroyed in World War 2, and now almost completely restored. The façade dates from 1761, the decoration and furnishings mainly from the 17&19C. The sacristy contains a *Crucifixion* and *Descent from the Cross* by a follower of Tommaso da Modena.

S.Giovanni Battista (Piazza Matteotti): 17C, with a fine, polychrome *terracotta Descent from the Cross* by Guido Mazzoni (15C).

Palazzo dell'Università (Via dell'Università): This was built by A.Tàrabusi in 1774 for the re-opening of the university, which, according to documentary evidence, dates from as early as the end of the 12C. Today it houses a *zoological museum.*

Modena, Galleria Estense, El Greco ▷

Palazzo Comunale (Piazza Grande): Begun in 1194, restored in 1378, almost completely rebuilt in 1624, and in the 18C it was extended at the sides and towards the rear. The *clock tower,* built in 1552 and restored in 1669, has a female figure, probably 13C, at the right-hand corner, and inside are beautifully furnished *16&17C rooms.*

Módica 97015
Ragusa/Sicily   p.420☐L 18

Módica is on the site of the ancient Sicel town of Motyka (known as Mohac under the Arabs), and has a magnificent situation on either side of the river Módica.

S. Maria Betlem (Via Marchese Tedeschi): Built in the 15C, and restored after the severe earthquake of 1693. A fine *façade* in late Renaissance style, completed in 1821. The interior is basilican and has a nave and two aisles. Of particular interest is the *chapel of the sacrament* (right aisle, entered through a beautiful portal with a pointed arch): Built in the late 15/early 16C, late Gothic and early Renaissance styles (Arab-Normaan influences are also discernible). The altar has a fine painted stone 16C 'Madonna and Child'.

Chiesa Madre S. Giorgio (Corso Garibaldi): Built by Rosario Gagliardi in 1702–38; fine façade with five portals. The interior (one nave, two aisles) has rich *stucco* and an *altarpiece* by Alibrandi (1513; 'Life of St.George'; his *relics* are in a silver urn in the chapel on the right).

Chiesa del Carmine (near the Corso Umberto I): 15C, with an interesting façade which has a Gothic portal and a rose window. The inside has a basilican ground plan and contains a marble group by Antonello Gagini (1478–1536).

Also worth seeing: The 16C church of *S.Pietro,* a basilica with a nave, two aisles, a fine façade, and a Madonna from the Gagini workshop in the 2nd chapel on the right. The church of *S.Maria di Gesù* was destroyed in the 15C and has a Catalan Gothic portal that is worth seeing. The adjoining former monastery, now a prison, has a 15C cloister.

Environs: Some 12 km. SW, **Scicli,** with the 18C *Chiesa Matrice,* splendid façade; *S.Bartolomeo* (18C) with a painting of the 'Descent from the Cross' by Mattia Preti, the greatest Calabrian painter (1613–99); *Chiesa del Carmine* with an 18C façade by Gagliardi. *S.Maria la Nova,* with work from the Gagini workshop. Some 10 km E., the **Cava d'Ispica,** with numerous Sicel burial grounds, cave dwellings, 4&5C Christian catacombs, and Byzantine rock shrines.

Módica, Chiesa Madre S. Giorgio

Molfetta 70056
Bari/Apulia   p.416☐N 16

Cathedral of S. Corrado (Duomo Vecchio, on the harbour): Building began in 1150; a mixture of Byzantine and Romanesque elements. It is generally regarded as the most important domed church in Apulia. There are three domes above the nave the middle one is elliptical, the outer two round; each of the first two is surrounded by an octagonal drum, whilst the last one has a square drum. They all have a pyramidal roof. The façade has two towers of half size, and there are two campaniles by the apse. The semicircular apse is concealed by a wall. The interior is asymmetrical. The floor level of the transept was lowered—as can be seen from the pedestals of the pilasters supporting the dome over the sanctuary—after the crypt beneath the sanctuary was filled in because of water seepage.

Also worth seeing: The 17C cathedral of *S.Maria Assunta* (Corso Dante) with its splendid baroque façade, and the church of *S.Bernardino* (near the Piazza Garibaldi) with a painting by Ribera.

Environs: 6 km. SE, on the coast,

Mondovì, Santuario di Vicoforte **1** chapel of the sanctuary, a baldacchino with columns surrounded by a gallery **2** chapel of St.Benedict with the tomb of Margherita di Savoia-Gonzaga, 1589 – 1655 **3** chapel of St. Francis de Sales **4** chapel of St.Joseph **5** chapel of St.Bernard with the tomb of Charles Emmanuel I

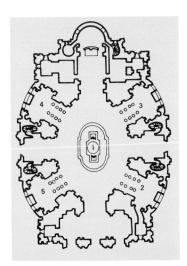

Giovinazzo, with a Romanesque *cathedral* dating from 1283, altered in baroque style in the 17C (interesting apses, fine portal).

Castello Reale: This former royal castle (13C, rebuilt in the 15C, and, in baroque style, in the 17C) overlooks the town.

Also worth seeing: *S. Francesco* (Piazza Vittorio Emanuele II), a 13C foundation, rebuilt by Filippo Castelli in 1789 in neo-baroque style. *S.Maria della Scala* (Piazza Vittorio Emanuele II), founded in 1230, a four-aisled Gothic church dating from 1330–6. Its fine contents include: a polychrome terracotta Pietà dating from 1400 and the 'Assumption of the Virgin' by Claudio Francesco Beaumont and Giandomenico Molinari (1766).

Mondovì was founded as Monte di Vico in 1198. After power had changed hands several times, the town fell to Savoy in 1396. From 1472 onwards it had a number of important printing presses. The 'Summa Confessiones', a text by St. Antonius, appeared here on 24 October 1472 and was the first book printed in Piedmont. The university was founded in 1560 and was transferred to Turin in 1566. The battle of Mondovì, fought by Napoleon, took place on 22 April 1796.

S.Donato (Via Del Belvedere): The baroque cathedral was built by Francesco Gallo. A fine *portal,* decorated with statues. The church is richly adorned with *frescos* and *reliefs.*

Also worth seeing: *Chiesa della Missione,* dedicated to St. Francis and St. Saverio (Piazza Maggiore), built by Giovenale Boetto and others in 1664–78. The impressive baroque façade leads into the single-aisled interior with the important frescos by A.Pozzo, 1679. Beside the Chiesa della Missione is the *Palazzo di Giustizia*, the former Jesuit college, built in 1713–16 by Antonio Falletti, a fellow-artist of Francesco Gallo. *S. Filippo* (Via S. Giuseppe Cottolengo), built by Francesco Gallo in 1734–50. *SS.Pietro e Paolo* (Piazza S.Pietro): Built in 1489, frequently enlarged and altered, notably in 1611. Beautiful baroque façade. *Belvedere* (Via del Belvedere), splendid view, with the 14C *Torre dei Bressani*, which was formerly the campanile of a Gothic church and contains 15C frescos.

Environs: Santuario di Vicoforte, also *Santuario Basilica Regina Montis Regalis*. The pilgrimage church was built in 1596 –1731, while its neoclassical façade dates from 1883. The church is in the form of a large ellipse set between four corner towers. The large elliptical *dome* by Francesco Gallo is a dominant feature. Inside, in the middle of the church, is the Chapel of the Holy Sacrament to a design by Francesco Gallo. The four radiating *chapels* contain tombs of the House of Savoy.

Monfalcone 34074
Gorizia / Friuli   p.410☐I 3

Legend has it that Monfalcone was founded by the Greeks and fortified under Rome. From 1420–1797 it was a Venetian enclave in Austrian territory, and until 1915 it was Austrian.

Castle (Rocca): Built by the Romans, enlarged by the Venetians in 1420, damaged in a pirate raid in 1615, and damaged again in 1915 (see above). Sturdy square *central tower*, surrounded by a low *outer wall*.

Also worth seeing: *Cathedral of S. Ambrogio* (Piazza Unità d'Italia), founded in the 14C, completed in 1767, rebuilt in 1926–9 after being destroyed in World War I. *Panzano*, the site of the ancient settlement (archaeological finds) lies in the S. outskirts of the town.

Environs: Some 5 km. SE, near the mouth of the Timavo, are the remains of *Roman baths*. About 6 km. SW, **S. Giovanni al Timavo,** with the rebuilt 15C Gothic church of *S. Giovanni* (inside are the remains of an early Christian basilica). Some 7 km. SE, **Duino,** with a *ruined castle* dating from the 11C and destroyed in the 16C, and the beautiful 14C *castle* of the princes Thurn and Taxis, where Rainer Maria Rilke wrote his famous 'Duineser Elegies' in 1912. **S. Canziano** (S.Kanzian) is some 5 km. SW: near the parish church and the Protus chapel are some *early Christian excavations* (including walls, floor mosaics of a basilica). About 7 km. N., **Redipuglia,** with a war memorial to some 100,000 Italian soldiers who fell in World War 1 (battles of Isonzo).

Monópoli 70043
Bari/Apulia   p.416☐O 11

S. Maria Amalfitana (Via Amalfitana): Sailors from Amalfi built this church in the early 12C above a Basilian grotto (the right

S. Giovanni al Timavo (Monfalcone)

aisle leads to the crypt). The most interesting feature of the church is the exterior of the E. end, which has a very high central apse and ornate windows. Inside: A pillared basilica with a nave and two aisles but no transept.

Cathedral: Founded in 1107, but thoroughly altered in baroque style in 1742–70. The sacristy contains some remains of the portal from the old cathedral: parts of a surround, and two fine capitals. The apse contains a 12C Byzantine Madonna.

Castle: Built under Frederick II, and rebuilt in the 14&15C.

Environs: The turn-off for the 11C **Cripta di S. Procopio** (three rooms, frescos) is 4 km. along the road to Brindisi (in the *L'Assunta* district). Near the *Masseria Seppannibale* is the ruined church of the same name. Romanesque and square in form, it is the only building in Apulia known to have two domes. 15 km. SE, on the coast, are the excavations of the Greek town of **Egnatia** (Greek: 'Gnathia'), which the Roman poet Horace recorded in his writings. It is known mainly for its distinctive ceramics.

Monreale 90046
Palermo/Sicily   p.420 □ I 16

Cathedral of S.Maria la Nuova: This is the most important Norman building in Sicily. Begun by William II (the Good) of Sicily in 1174 and rapidly completed. Exterior: The façade is flanked by two sturdy *towers*, (the left one incomplete); 18C *colonnaded portico*. The façade and the splendid *apse* have interlaced pointed *blind arcades* of pale calcareous tufa and black lava. The main portal (in the portico of the W. façade) has the famous *bronze door* (1186) by Bonanno Pisano which is set in a richly decorated *pointed archway* (the portal of Pisa Cathedral, 1180, was the model for the door): 40 panels with scenes from the Old and New Testaments (inscriptions in Sicilian dialect). The portal on the left flank (the *portico* is the work of Gian. Dom. and Fazio Gagini and dates from 1569) has a *bronze door* by Barisano da Trani (1179, 28 panels with Saints). Inside: A basilica

Monreale, cathedral, cloister

Monreale, cathedral

with a nave, two aisles, the beginning of a transept, and three apses; it is 335 ft. by 131 ft. A square *sanctuary* with marble

Monreale, cathedral 1 door by Bonanno Pisano **2** door by Barisano da Trani **3** mosaic of Christ **4** Cappella del Crocifisso **5** entrance to the cloister **6** cloister

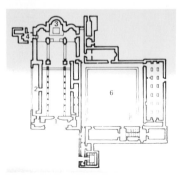

screens. 18 *ancient columns* with splendid capitals, some with ancient motifs, bearing pointed arches in the Arab manner. Open *timber ceiling*. The *pavement* is original and is made of marble, granite and porphyry. The walls are completely covered with unique *mosaics* (completed in 1182, 68,172 sq.ft. in area): scenes from the Old and New Testaments; the central apse has a *Christ Pantocrator*, and beneath this is the *Madonna with Angels and Apostles*. On the left of the sanctuary is the *Coronation of William II by Jesus*, and on the right is the *Presentation of the Church to the Virgin*. The beginning of the right transept contains the *tombs of the Norman Kings William I* (d. 1166) and *William II* (d. 1194), the latter in a marble sarcophagus dating from 1575. The *Cappella S. Benedetto* with its rich 18C marble decoration, is entered from here. To the left of the sanctuary are the *tombs of Margaret of Navarra* the wife of William I, and of their two sons

Monsélice, Villa Duodo

Roger and *Henry*. In an urn on the altar is the *heart of Louis IX (the Saint)* of France (d. 1270). The left choir chapel leads to the *Cappella del Crocifisso* with beautiful marble reliefs dating from 1688. Behind this is the *cathedral treasury*. The entrance to the exceptional Romanesque *cloister* lies to the right of the main façade. The cloister is the finest of its kind in Italy, and forms part of the adjoining former Benedictine monastery. 154 ft. by 154 ft., it has covered walks on all sides, 228 *twin columns* and a *fountain*.

Monsélice 35043

Padua/Veneto   p.410☐G 4

Duomo Vecchio (S. Giustina): This Romanesque-Gothic building (1256) stands at the end of the picturesque, gently rising Via del Santuario. The *façade* bears pilaster strips (the portico is 15C) and a 13C battlemented *campanile*. There is an open roof truss above the single-aisled interior, which is undecorated and creates a severe impression. The interior ends in 3 choir chapels. There is a 15C *polyptych* of the Venetian school on the high altar.

Santuario delle Sette Chiese with the Villa Duodo: The path leading up the hill behind the cathedral (from here there is a superb view towards Rovigo and the Apennines) is lined by seven chapels and ends in the *Villa Duodo*. It was intended to serve as a kind of pilgrimage where indulgences were granted in imitation of the seven pilgrimage churches of Rome. V.Scamozzi designed the villa (completed in 1611, extended in the 18C). The small church of *S. Giorgio* has a particular charm.

Castello or Ca' Marcello: This fortress, built in the 13C, became the residence of

Ezzelino da Romano, and was enlarged several times. Its present owners restored it in 1935–9. In addition to a magnificent collection of medieval and Renaissance furniture, there is also an interesting and unique set of 14C fireplaces.

Also worth seeing: *Torre Civica* (1244, another storey added in 1504) in the Piazza Mazzini, with the town's coat of arms. The delicate loggia of the *Monte di Pietà* stands on the same square. The ruins of the *Rocca* (fine view).

Montagnana 35044

Padua/Veneto   p.410 □ F 4

Duomo S.Maria (now the parish church, Piazza Vittorio Emanuele II): The high façade of the present parish church, which was built in 1431–1502 on the site of a Romanesque building, faces the town's broad main square. The plans are probably by Sansovino — the beautiful *marble portal* (1527), in particular, bears his stamp. The splendid, tall, single-aisled interior is tunnel vaulted. Above the crossing there is a dome resting on pendentives. Note the design of the two apses of the transept with their shell vaults. The *sanctuary* is particularly beautiful. The large *fresco* is probably by G.Buonconsiglio, while the *high altar* is attributed to Sansovino (1555). The *altarpiece* (1555) is by P.Veronese.

Town fortifications with the Castello degli Alberi: The town's fortifications, enlarged by F.da Carrara in the 14C, are amongst the few to survive almost undamaged today. A wide, deep moat entirely surrounds the most impressive walls, with their 24 polygonal *towers* and four fortified bastion-like gates (*Porta Vicenza, Porta Padova* with *Torre Ezzelina*, 13C, *Porta XX Settembre* and *Porta Legnano* with *Castello degli Alberi*).

Also worth seeing: *S. Benedetto* (Via S. Benedetto), 17C, restored in the 18C, with baroque interior. *S. Francesco* (Via S. Francesco) with 15C campanile of brick and fine interior decoration. The *Villa Pisani* (Porta Padova), 1560, to designs by A.Palladio with two-storeyed portico. Inside there are statues of the four seasons by A.Vittoria (1566–77). The *Palazzo del Mu-*

Montagnana, Porta Legnago

nicipio (Via Carrarese), 16–18C, to plans by M.Sanmicheli.

ment by the painter Francesco Bassano the Younger (late 16C).

Montanaro 10017
Turin / Piedmont   p.412   B 4

Montanaro, today an agricultural centre, was held by the bishops of Vercelli in the 11C. It subsequently fell to the Abbazia di Fruttuaria, and then to Savoy in 1433.

Chiesa dell'Assunta: This parish church is the work of Vittone (1758–65); the sacristy has sumptuous *cupboards* carved by P.A.Actis to plans by Vittone.

S.Marta: The oratory beside the church, in Piedmontese high baroque style, was built in 1741–70 and is another work by Vittone. To the left of it is the elegant **campanile,** built in 1770–2 to plans by Vittone and Quarini.

Also worth seeing: The *Castello,* newly founded in 1353, and later converted into a villa. The *Palazzo Comunale,* designed by Vittone, 1769.

Environs: S.of the town, near the cemetery, is the church of *S.Maria di Loreto,* 1681–4, to plans by Guarino Guarini.

Montecchio Maggiore 36075
Vicenza / Veneto   p.410 F 3

Villa Cordellina-Lombardi: Built in 1735–60 to plans by the Venetian architect Giorgio Massari. The main building is in the style of the Palladian villas (at the front is a colonnaded portico with a pediment). The frescos in the two-storeyed central hall are by Giov. Battista Tiepolo (1743; scenes from ancient history).

Also worth seeing: Above the town are the so-called *Castelli di Giulietta e di Romeo,* 2 medieval castles.

Surroundings: Arzignano: The *parish church of Ognissanti* has a notable *Entomb-*

Montefalco 06036
Perugia / Umbria   p.414☐H 8

S. Agostino: The finest feature of this Gothic church (13&14C) is its beautiful portal with a pointed archway. Inside there are frescos on the right (Madonna and Child; Umbrian school showing Sienese influence; early 15C) and left (Madonna della Misericordia; early 15C, by Giovanni di Corraduccio from Foligno) sides of the entrance. The last chapel but one on the right has frescos by the school of Benozzo Gozzoli; the Madonna and Child in the last chapel is probably by Mezastris; on the left side is the 'Niche with Crib' by Giovanni di Corraduccio from Foligno; the late-14C 'Coronation of the Virgin' is attributed to A.Lorenzetti. The 15C Madonna and Child with St. Augustine and St.Nicholas is probably by Ugolino di Gisberto. There are Umbrian late Gothic paintings (early 15C) in the sacristy, in the vault and in the lunette.

S.Chiara: Extensively altered in the 17C. Note the frescos (1333) in the Cappella Santa Croce.

S.Franceso (the town's picture gallery): This 14C church houses a fine collection of Umbrian and Tuscan paintings. In the first vault on the right side: the chapel of St.Jerome by B.Gozzoli (*c.* 1452). In the second one: frescos by a painter influenced by Mezastris; 'John the Baptist' and 'St. Jerome' by Francesco Melanzio, a painter from Montefalco. Third vault: the famous 'Madonna del Soccorso' by F.Melanzio. Fourth vault: frescos dating from *c.* 1440 by an artist who was obviously much influenced by Ottaviano Nelli. Fifth bay: frescos from the early 15C (transition to the international Gothic style). The central apse is decorated with frescos by B.Gozzoli. On the walls there are scenes from the life of St. Francis. In the vault: Triumph of St.Francis and other Saints. By the windows there are figures of Saints, including

St.Chiara from Montefalco. The medallions underneath the window depict Dante, Petrarch and Giotto. The left apse has 14C frescos. The frescos on the left of the nave comprise: a niche with the Madonna, Saints, Raphael, and Tobias, all by F.Melanzio; panel with the Madonna and 4 Saints, also by F.Melanzio; St. Illuminata, with St.Vincent and St. Nicholas, are by Antoniazzo Romano. Madonna and Child with five Saints, by F.Melanzio (St.Severo is a self-portrait of the painter). The baroque chapel has a canvas by Fantino of Bevagna. The niche with St.Anthony is attributed to Mezastris, and the one with St.Andrew is by Tiberio d'Assisi. The famous crib is by Perugino.

S.Illuminata: The beautiful portal was built in 1500. The frescos inside are the work of F.Melanzio and Bernardino Mezastris.

S.Fortunato (outside the town walls): The original building dates from the 5C; it was partially rebuilt in the 15&18C. The beautiful portico is 15C. However, when the church was altered, the builders managed to preserve the magic of the early Christian church. The *chapel of the rose,* with frescos by Tiberio d'Assisi, is to the left of the portico. There is a fresco by B.Gozzoli above the portal, and to the right of the portal is St.Sebastian, also by T.d'Assisi. The sober, single-aisled interior has an interesting altar with a St.Fortunatus by B.Gozzoli.

Montefiascone 01027
Viterbo/Latium   p.414☐G 8

A little town situated on a hill above Lake Bolsena on the site of the Etruscan shrine of Voltumna, which was a meeting place of the Etruscan confederation. During the period of the barbarian invasions it became a place of refuge. The town achieved independence in the 12C and was able to preserve it despite the attempt by Pope Paul III to make it into the seat of a Farnese duchy. It was severely damaged by earthquakes in 1695 and 1783. Its muscatel wine, known as 'Est, est, est', is renowned.

Cathedral of S. Margherita (Piazza S. Margherita): The *dome,* which was not

Montefalco, S.Francesco, Gozzoli frescos

completed until last century, was built by C.Fontana above the centrally planned, octagonal building which was begun in 1519 and is attributed to Michele Sanmicheli. The twin-towered façade dates from 1840 –3. Magnificent interior (the *frescos* are 19C).

S.Flaviano (close to the town, on the road to Orvieto): One of the most original medieval churches in Italy. Its design is in the tradition of two-storeyed churches which began with the Palatine chapel in Aachen. The lower church was begun in 1032 on the site of an earlier building, possibly dating from the 6C. The upper church was completed in the 12C. Restoration in the early 14C and in the 17C. A simple exterior—an old house adjoins the left flank —but the *façade* is somewhat more ornate. There is a *Renaissance loggia* above the graduated Gothic portal. A small campanile has been added on the left. *Lower church:* A pillared hall with a nave, two aisles, and ribbed vaults. The choir is formed from the aisles which continue around the end of the nave like an ambulatory, off which three semicircular apses radiate. The entrance to the upper church rises between two pairs of columns, arranged so as to give the appearance of a crossing. The nave wall continues as a double arcade and is supported by engaged columns. *Upper church:* A basilica with a nave, two aisles and an open roof truss. By the papal altar is the *Throne of Urban IV,* dating from 1262. The capitals are of extraordinarily rich design. There are numerous frescos, mainly 14C, on the walls. Those in the apse are 16C. To the right of the entrance is the *tomb slab of Bishop Johannes Fugger* from Augsburg.

Monteleone di Spoleto 06045
Perugia/Umbria   p.414□H 8

Lying 3, 209 ft. above sea-level, Monteleone has some beautiful, small 15&16C palaces along its main street. The Gothic church of *S.Francesco* is also interesting. Two discoveries have made this region famous: in 1902 a waggon was found here

which probably dates from the 6C BC and is now in the Metropolitan Museum in New York. A little later, 44 well-like tombs were discovered on the Colle del Capitano. These are of great importance for research into the prehistory of Italy.

Environs: Villa S.Silvestro: This is in the immediate vicinity of Monteleone, next to the remains of a Roman temple (3,300 ft. above sea- level).

Montepulciano 53045
Sienna/Tuscany   p.414□G 7

A walled town situated picturesquely on a rounded hill-top between the Valdichiana and the Valle dell'Orcia. The town was inhabited in the Etruscan period, and was later allied with Siena and Florence alternately. The fortifications were built by Antonio Sangallo the Elder by order of Cosimo I.

Cathedral: Built in 1592–1630 to plans by Ippolito Scalza on the site of the old parish church. Restored in 1888. The incomplete campanile (2nd half of the 15C) survives from the earlier building. The façade is still in the rough. It has three portals and windows, and stands at the top of a high flight of steps. The inside, with its nave and two aisles, is harmonious and simple. There are interesting fragments of the *tomb of Bartolomeo Aragazzi,* the secretary of Martin V, scattered around the church. They are attributed to Michelozzo. There is a drawing of a reconstruction of the tomb (1885) in the Sala Capitolare, which also houses the designs of the façade. The tomb was taken apart in the 18C. The recumbent figure of the deceased is to the left of the central portal, and two reliefs from the tomb are attached to the first two pillars above the holy-water stoup. Behind the high altar there is a triptych by Taddeo di Bartolo, 1403, of the *Assumption of the Virgin,* an *Annunciation,* and a *Coronation,* with *Scenes from the Passion* and *Scenes from the Old Testament.*

S.Agostino with a magnificent Florentine

Gothic façade by Michelozzo. The portal is framed by fluted pilasters and its round forms are in imitation of the Gothic. The tympanum has a terracotta relief by Michelozzo: *Madonna with John the Baptist and St.Augustine*. There are four statues in niches with pointed arches above this, and, higher still, a rose-window. Inside, the church is single-aisled with a *Crucifixion* by Lorenzo di Credi and a *painted wooden cross* by Pollaiuolo.

S.Biagio (actually *Madonna di S.Biagio*) is a little way outside the town. A purely Renaissance building with a central dome, it is a rival to the elegant Chiesa della Consolazione in Todi. Begun in 1518 to a design by Sangallo the Elder, the church was completed in 1545. Over the centuries, the travertine has gradually turned golden, giving the church its splendid appearance. The orders on the two towers, which almost adjoin the façade, pass from Doric through Ionic and Corinthian to Composite (the right tower was not completed). The powerful exterior articulation is repeated on the inside. The sanctuary has some slightly annoying baroque decoration, comprising gilded stucco and frescos

Montepulciano, S.Biagio

attributed to Zuccari. In the left chapel there is an *Annunciation* by Lippo Memmi, a pupil of Simone Martini (2nd half of the 14C).

Palazzo Comunale: This late-14C building is a three-storeyed, battlemented palazzo.

Palazzo Contucci (or *del Monte*): Like the above palazzo, this is in the town centre near the cathedral. It was begun by Antonio da Sangallo the Elder in 1519 and completed by Baldassare Peruzzi. The top storey was not added until the baroque period. The great hall inside was painted throughout by Andrea Pozzo.

Palazzo Tarugi (or *Nobile*): Ascribed to Vignola, a 16C architect. It has one arcade at ground-level and another on its top storey surrounded by a balustrade.

Museo Civico (in the *Palazzo Neri Orselli*): Built in Siennese Gothic style. Note the following works of art on the 1st floor: a *Coronation* ascribed to Angelo Puccinelli, a *Madonna and Child* by a follower of Duccio, a *St.John* and other works by Andrea della Robbia (*St.Stephen, St.Bonaventure, St.Catherine, St.Bernard, Annunciation*, etc.), and works by his school.

Environs: *Monte Oliveto Maggiore (Abbazia):* An extensive and isolated abbey NW of Montepulciano. The monks turned the barren chalky soil into a productive oasis —this district was formerly known as the *deserto di Accona.* Together with two nobles from Siena, Bernardo Tolomei (1272-1348) founded a kind of hermitage here, on his family's land. Later, the community of monks adopted the rule of St.Benedict. Apart from the church, built in 1400-17, and its Gothic façade, the *cloister (Chiostro Grande)* of the monastery is also worth seeing. The cloister was built in stages (1426-74) and, in c. 1500, was decorated with complete series of Renaissance frescos. The fresco cycle depicts scenes from the *Legend of St. Benedict.* It was painted by Luca Signorelli who worked here in 1497-8, and also by Sodoma who was active from 1505. Nos. 21–29 are by Signorelli, and the rest are by Sodoma. The church contains a *Road to Calvary* by Sodoma (one of his masterpieces) and a set of *intarsia choir stalls* by Fra Giovanni da Verona. **Sinalunga:** Located in the heart of the Valdichiana, to the N. of Montepulciano. Known as *Asinalunga* from 1197 onwards, it belonged alternately to Sienna and the Medici. Garibaldi was taken prisoner here in 1867, after one of his attempted marches against Rome. The sole item of interest is the *Collegiata* (S. Martino), built from the materials of the destroyed castle. The single-aisled interior, with its side chapels, has a *Madonna with Saints,* a panel by Sodoma.

Monte Sant'Angelo 71037

Foggia/Apulia   p.416 □ M 10

Monte S.Angelo contains the most important and oldest shrine of St. Michael in Italy. The church was built by Bishop Laurentius of Siponto in the late 5C after shepherds had seen a vision of the Archangel here.

Grotto of St.Michael: A stair cut out of the natural rock leads down to the grotto. At the entrance to the grotto there is a Romanesque portal with the oldest surviving *bronze door* in Apulia (cast in Constantinople in 1076 at the expense of the Pantaleon of Amalfi; the donor's inscription is at the bottom of the right leaf of the door): The 24 niello-work panels in praise of the angels are nailed to wood. The most interesting items in the grotto itself are: the *altar of St.Francis* behind the portal on the right (Francis of Assisi visited the grotto); a *bishop's throne,* the oldest surviving one in Apulia, to the left of the main altar; immediately to the left of this is an *altar of the Virgin Mary.* There are two old reliefs of St.Michael on the wall to the left of the entrance. During restoration, a Mithras stone was discovered under the high altar, and this proves that the grotto was used as a cultic site in pre-Christian times. Above the grotto there is an octagonal, four-storeyed *campanile* (1273–81).

Tomba di Rotari: 12C. The name is a corruption of 'Rodelgrimus' (inscription to the left of the entrance). The building's function is unclear (baptistery, campa-

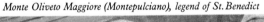

Monte Oliveto Maggiore (Montepulciano), legend of St. Benedict

nile?). A square substructure bears an octagonal and then elliptical dome. Inside there are fine *capitals* with biblical scenes, and, at the transition between the lower storey and the dome, *reliefs* depicting 'Lust'. Directly adjoining this is an apse, the last remnant of the Romanesque church of *S. Pietro*.

Also worth seeing: (beside the Tomba di Rotari) *S. Maria Maggiore*, built in 1170 on the site of an earlier building; portal dating from 1198, façade in the Tuscan style. The *castle* has a Norman core, which was enlarged and added to under the Hohenstaufens and the Aragonese ('Torre dei Giganti', pentagonal main tower).

Environs: Some 25 km. W., **S.Giovanni Rotondo:** 'Padre Pio' (now dead), who bore the stigmata, worked here. A side trip may be made to **Vieste** and **Peschici**, two picturesque little towns on the E. coast of Monte Gargano.

Montescaglioso 75024
Matera/Basilicata   p.416□N 11/12

SS. Pietro e Paolo: This 17C parish church was built at the highest point of the village and contains Venetian paintings. Next to it is the interesting **Abbey of S. Angelo,** a former Benedictine monastery which today houses public offices and schools, and was originally a Norman foundation (first mentioned in 1079). The abbey has two *cloisters* with outstanding portals. Some interesting structures survive from the original building: the *campanile* with its *double-arched window,* and the high *dome* of the church, both part of the 1st cloister; and the fine *Renaissance windows* and the carved *fountain* are features of the second cloister. The Hellenistic *colossal statue of Telamon* was discovered in the environs of Montescaglioso in 1925, and is today exhibited in the museum of Reggio Calabria.

Environs: Bernalda: A town to the S.of Montescaglioso in the S. Basento valley. The finds from a Lucanian and Greek set-

tlement testify to the town's long history. Nearby are the 11C *ruins of Camarda.*

Monza 20052
Milan/Lombardy   p.412□D 3

The site of a Celtic settlement, Monza, known as Modicia by the Romans, became a royal summer residence under the Lombards. Queen Theodolinda commissioned numerous buildings in the late 6C. Emperor Berengarius chose it as his residence in 918. It became a free imperial town at an early date and was frequently pitted against Milan, finally coming under Milanese rule in 1324.

Cathedral of S. Giovanni Battista: Probably founded during the reign of Theodolinda. It was completely rebuilt in the 13C and enlarged once again in the 14C. The façade was begun in 1370–96 under the supervision of Matteo da Campione, but not completed until the late 19C. A basilican structure with a nave, two aisles, a transept and a choir with chapels on either side. The aisles are flanked by chapels, most of them interconnected to create the impression of a church with a nave and four aisles. *Contents:* Apart from the few remaining Gothic items (*Evangelist pulpit, frescos* in the chapel of Theodolinda), the interior is dominated by 18C paintings, some of which are not very successful. The *baptistery* is by Pellegrini. *Chapel of Theodolinda:* Frescos dating from 1444. The *Iron Crown* is preserved in the altar tabernacle. The queen's relics are said to be preserved in the *sarcophagus* behind the altar. *Cathedral treasure:* In addition to the Iron Crown, which probably dates from as late as the 9C, there are other priceless items: gold pieces from the 5C (presented by Theodolinda) to the 11C, tapestries, medieval religious objects and valuable documents such as the purple codex.

Villa Reale: Built by G.Piermarini in 1777–80 for Archduke Ferdinand of Austria. A classical villa with a park laid out in 1806 for Eugène Beauharnais. In the park is the Mirabello horse racecourse, and the motor racing circuit.

Museums: *Museo Serpero* (cathedral treasure). *Civica Galleria d'Arte* (in the Villa Reale): paintings from the 16–20C. The *Museo civico dell'arengario* (in the Arengario), with an archaeological department.

Also worth seeing: *The Arengario*, the town hall dating from the 13C, built on the model of the Palazzo della Ragione in Milan. On the S.side is the *parlera*, a balcony from which the laws were proclaimed. *S. Maria in Strata* with a façade of 1398.

Mortara 27036
Pavia/Lombardy   p.412□C 4

Basilica of S.Lorenzo: A building with a nave and two aisles, built in 1375–80,

Monza, cathedral 1 Tempietto (baptistery) **2** organ gallery (Evangelicatorio) **3** chapel of Theodolinda (iron crown) **4** entrance to the cathedral treasury **5** cloister

probably by Bartolino da Novara. The façade is tripartite and is decorated by a frame of three terracotta strips. Decoration: the right aisle has frescos by Gaudenzio Ferrari (1524); in the 1st chapel on the left there is a richly carved, gilded crib by Lorenzo da Mortara (1490).

S. Croce: The late-11C church was replaced in 1596 by a new one to plans by Pellegrini.

Environs: The abbey of *S.Albino* (2 km. towards Pavia), a 5C foundation rebuilt under Charlemagne and again in the 11C. *S.Maria del Campo*, founded in the 12C. The present building dates from 1400. The multi-coloured façade is painted to appear like marble. Inside, by the sanctuary, is a fresco depicting the Carolingian battle of Mortara.

Murano 30121
Venice/Veneto   p.410□G 3

This town is built on an island to the N.

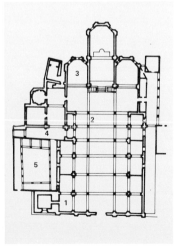

Monza, cathedral

of Venice and mainly owes its reputation to the Venetian glass industry, which was transferred here by Venice in 1292.

S.Pietro Martire: This pillared basilica, with its nave and two aisles, was built in 1348 as a Dominican monastery church, and was rebuilt in the style of the Venetian Renaissance after a fire in 1474. The portal, the round-arched windows and the campanile (modern roof) were also built at that time. In the much-restored arcaded courtyard is a marble cistern dating from 1347. Inside, the *paintings* are of particular interest: there is a large panel painting of the Assumption of the Virgin from Giovanni Bellini's workshop dating from *c.* 1510 in the right aisle. Just to the left of it is a masterpiece by Bellini dating from 1488, whose colours have, unfortunately, been inadequately restored. In the right aisle there is a painting by Jacopo Tintoretto of the Baptism of Christ. In the left aisle there are two paintings by Paolo Veronese: St. Agatha in prison and St. Jerome in the wilderness, both dating from 1566. In the *sanctuary* there are enormous 18C pictures by Bart. Letterini, and behind the high altar a 16C Descent from the Cross by G.Porta. The *Cappella de Sacramento* has a Renaissance altar.

S.Maria degli Angeli: A nuns' convent and church, founded in the 12C, rebuilt in the 16C and desecrated during secularization. The inside of the church dates from *c.* 1500, but was completely built over and disfigured in the 19C. The following are still of interest: the *coffered ceiling* with the Coronation of the Virgin, Saints and Prophets, painted by Nicolai Rondinelli in *c.* 1500; the *baroque altars* with scagliola inlay work; an altarpiece of the Glorification of the Virgin, painted by Palma Giovane in the late 16C; and the *tomb* of Senator G.Batt. Perandas, sculpted by A.Vittoria in 1586/7.

SS. Maria e Donato: This church was originally built in 999 and dedicated to the Virgin Mary. A new building was begun in 1111 and was dedicated to St.Donato in 1125 after his relics had been brought here from Cefalù. The whole building was altered in baroque style under Bishop Marco Giustinian (d. 1735), whose tombstone is set in the floor of the cathedral; all the baroque additions were later removed. The

Monza, Villa Reale

baptistery was torn down in 1719, but the walls of its replacement still retain some remains of the original one. It also houses, from the late classical period, the *sarcophagus* of a Roman family. This was used as a font during the Romanesque period. The *campanile* is 12C. The church, a cruciform basilica with a tripartite sanctuary, was built of brick and has a simple front and plain side walls. However, its main feature is the wall of the apse. This has two rows of arcades and a frieze of terracotta slabs in between. The upper part of the wall has been extended to form an ambulatory. The two rows of columns and arches are reminiscent of the outer chancel wall of St. Mark's. The nave has an early-15C Venetian vault and the church has a coloured mosaic pavement with numerous figures. This dates from 1140 and is similar to the pavement of St.Mark's. The interior makes a bare impression despite the beautiful marble columns. *Contents:* 14C wooden Venetian altarpiece of the Virgin. There is a votive picture by Lazzaro Bastiani (1484) above the door to the baptistery. In addition, in the left aisle, there is a gilded and painted relief crown of St. Donato (1310); it is attributed to Paolo

Veneziano and is probably the earliest example of Venetian painting. The apse contains a mosaic of the Virgin praying (1st half of 13C). Fragments of late-14C frescos.

Also worth seeing: The *Fondamenta Novagero* is opposite SS.Maria e Donato. The *Palazzo Da Mula* (on the Fondamenta Vetrai, opposite the Ponte Vivarini): The house and garden are a good example—indeed the only such example surviving in Murano—of a summer villa in the Venetian Renaissance style. The palace dates from the 15C and was rebuilt in the 16C; fragments of 12&13C Venetian-Byzantine reliefs were incorporated in the late Gothic front. *Palazzo Trevisan* (No. 34 on the Fondamenta Novagero): a 16C Venetian palace.

Museo Vetrario di Murano (in the Palazzo Giustinian): Venetian glass was much in demand as early as the 13C. However, the earliest surviving examples date from the 2nd half of the 15C. Venetian glass (mirrors dating from the 15C) was world-famous, but it increasingly lost ground from the end of the 16C onwards. However, the mechanization of glass production

Murano

Murano, Museo Vetrario di Murano

in the 2nd half of the 19C opened up new opportunities and led to a resurgence of glass manufacture in Murano.

Muro Lucano 85054

Potenza/Basilicata   p.416 □M 11

Cathedral: Built in 1009 (or possibly earlier), it suffered greatly from an earthquake in 1694 and a fire in 1707, and consequently was almost completely rebuilt in 1725-8. It contains a 17C *wooden pulpit*.

Also worth seeing: *San Marco,* which contains a 17C *panel* ascribed to Giovanni Lanfranco. *Santa Chiara:* Interesting 17C *wooden altars* painted in green and gold. Remains of a *Romanesque-Gothic monastery* near to the church of *San Antonio.* The *castle* dates from pre-Norman times; the top storey was destroyed in the earthquake of 1694.

Napoli/Naples 80100
Naples/Campania   p.416☐ K 11

Naples was founded as 'Parthenope' by Rhodians in the 8C BC. It was enlarged by settlers from Cumae in the 7C BC, and from Chalcis in Euboea in the 5C BC. It was allied to Rome from 326BC onwards, but always retained a relatively large degree of independence. It became Norman in the 12C, and then passed to the Hohenstaufens. From the time of the Angevins (13C) onwards it became the capital of the Kingdom of Sicily, and from 1503–1707 it was the residence of the Spanish viceroys. It was Habsburg from 1713 onwards, and fell to the Bourbons in 1748 (until 1860).

Cathedral of S. Gennaro (Via del

Naples, Castel del Ovo

Duomo): Built 1294 – 1313 in French-Gothic style, on a site formerly occupied by other buildings, some of which were early Christian. It has been much restored and altered, especially after the earthquake of 1456. The complex consists of three buildings: the *cathedral* itself, *S.Restituta* attached on the left, and the *Cappella del Tesoro* on the right. In the 19C, the façade was completely restored after the model of the cathedrals of Siena and Orvieto; the middle portal, dating from 1407, is all that remains of the original building. Inside, there are a nave, two aisles, a broad transept, and three polygonal apses. Nave and aisles are separated by rows of eight pointed arches. Baroque *wooden ceiling*. The *sanctuary* which originally had a ribbed vault, was restored in baroque style in the 18C. There is a fine 12C Sicilian-Arab *cross reliquary* in the 4th chapel on the right. The richly decorated *Cappella Minutolo*, on the far side of the choir, has a retable dating from 1301 behind the main altar and a 15C triptych on the side altar. From the left aisle there is access to the basilica of *S. Restituta*, which may have been built as early as the 5C. It has a broad nave, no transept, and a fine triumphal arch on free-standing columns. The *Cappella della Madonna del Principio* (left aisle) has a mosaic of the Madonna and Child dated 1322 in the apse. In adjoining chapels there are two 12–13C marble slabs with reliefs. Access to the 4C baptistery of *S.Giovanni in Fonte* via the right aisle of the basilica. The baptistery is square, has a round dome and extensive remains of original mosaics. The *crypt*, beneath the cathedral's main apse, was built in the 15C to house the relics of St.Januarius, the church's patron saint, who died in 305. A colonnaded hall, it has a nave, two aisles and semicircular niches at the sides. From the cathedral's right aisle you can get to the *Cappella S.Gennaro* (also called simply *Il Tesoro*). Built in 1608–15, it contains Naples' most valuable relic, the *skull of St.Januarius* and *two ampoules of his blood*, which liquefies each year on certain dates. At the end of the right aisle a door opens into the *Piazzetta Sisto Riario Sforza* with the *Giglia di S. Gennaro*, a column in memory of the city's patron saint, built in 1631 after an eruption of Vesuvius.

S. Anna dei Lombardi (Piazza Montoliveto): Begun in Catalan Gothic in 1411,

Naples, National Museum of S. Martino, Tavola Strozzi, 1464

and later frequently restored and enlarged, particularly during the Renaissance. Simple façade with a portico flanked by projecting *side chapels* with early Renaissance decorations. There are still some remnants of the original Gothic building, e.g. the *pointed-arched windows*, on the nave walls. The interior was originally a hall type of church with side chapels and a rectangular chancel. The chapels to the sides of the portico are early Renaissance and architecturally of great interest. On the left is the *Cappella Piccolomini*, and on the right is the *Cappella Mastrogiudice;* each square with a dome. The *Cappella Tolosa*, behind the last chapel in the left aisle, has a beautifully designed dome. Furnishings: The *wooden doors* of the main portal date from 1510. The 1st chapel on the left has the *marble tomb of Maria of Aragon,* completed by Benedetto da Maiano in the late 15C—a masterpiece among princes' tombs in Naples. The 1st chapel on the right (the 'Cappella Mastrogiudice,' mentioned above) has a massive *Altar of the Annunciation* of 1489 by Benedetto da Maiano (it has more recently been suggested that it is an early work of Michelangelo). The main chapel

in the chancel has a very fine set of 16C *choir stalls* by Giovanni da Verona. To the right of the chancel, access is gained to the *Cappella della Pietà*, which has a fine *terracotta Pietà* of eight figures by Guido Mazzoni (d. 1518). The *sacristy*, known as the old sacristy, has inlaid *cupboards from the 15C.*

Santissima Annunziata (Via Santissima Annunziata):A fire led to rebuilding (from 1760 onwards) on the ruins of the original Gothic church. The dome was built from 1774–81. The façade is slightly concave and bears Ionic and Corinthian columns. 16C bell-tower. The single-aisled interior is long (245 ft.) in proportion to its width (50 ft.), and is divided into a nave, area under the dome and a choir. In all there are 44 marble columns with Corinthian capitals. The ceiling is barrel-vaulted. The drum of the dome consists of eight arches on double columns. At the high altar there is an *Annunciation* by the painter Francesco de Mura (1696–1784). The furnishings of the *sacristy* date from the 16C and include a majolica floor, gilded oak cupboards and a carved altar. The *crypt* by Vanvitelli lies beneath the crossing. It is

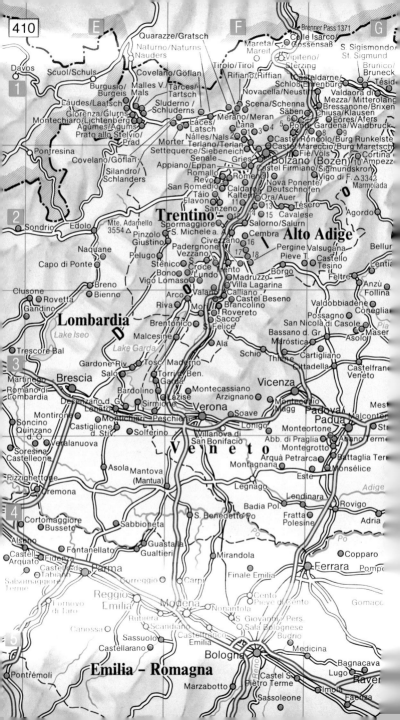

Austria

Lienz
Spittal
Villach
Klagenfurt
St. Veit a. d. Glan

n Candido/
ichen
bbiaco/
blach

Friuli

Vigo di Cad
Pieve di Cad
Zúglio
Tolmezzo
Pontebba
Malborghetto
Tarvisio/Tarvis
Predil
Jesenice

Venezia Giulia

Venzone
Gemona d. Friuli
Osoppo
Ragogna
Maniago
Tarcento
Colloredo di Monte Albano
Tricesimo

Yugoslavia

Kranj
Ljubljana (Laibach)

Valeriano
Spilimbergo
Barbeano
Villalta
S. Daniele d. Friuli
cénigo
Martignacco
Udine
Cividale d. F
prio
San Martino al Tagliamento
Mereto di Tomba
Pordenone
Torre
Codroipo
Mortegliano
Cormons
Gorizia
ciile
Versutta
Medea
Gradisca
Prodolone
Passariano
Castions
Palma nova
Redipuglia
Vito al Tagliamento
Varmo di Strada
Monfalcone
Sesto al Reghena
Cordovado
San Canzian
San Giovanni al Timavo
Oderzo
Latisana
Aquileia
Duino
Lignano
Castello di Miramare
viso
S. Donà di Piave
Sabbiadoro
Lignano Pineta
Grado
Trieste
Eraclea
Cáorle
Muggia
Koper

rano
Torcello
urano
enezia (enice)

ADRIATIC SEA

Gulf of Trieste

Rijeka

Kvarner

ggia
omarina
to Dubrovnik
to Rijeka
to Pula

Po Delta
to
ano
vvia

1 Tésimo/Tisens
2 Grissiano/Grissian
3 Méltina/Mölten
4 Sarentino/Sarntheim
5 Tre Chiese/Dreikirchen
6 Villandro/Villanders
7 Barbiano/Barbian
8 Ortisei/St. Ulrich
9 Funes/Villnöß
10 S. Cristina/St. Christina
11 Termeno/Tramin
12 Vigo di Ton
13 Pinzon/Pinzano
14 Egna/Neumarkt
15 Segonzano
16 San Mauro di Pinè
17 Montagnaga di Pinè
18 Madrano

KEY

⊚	Town described in text
	Motorway
	Main road
	Secondary road
	Railway
–··–··–	National boundary
– – –	Regional boundary
– – –	Ferry
✈	Airport

N
50 km

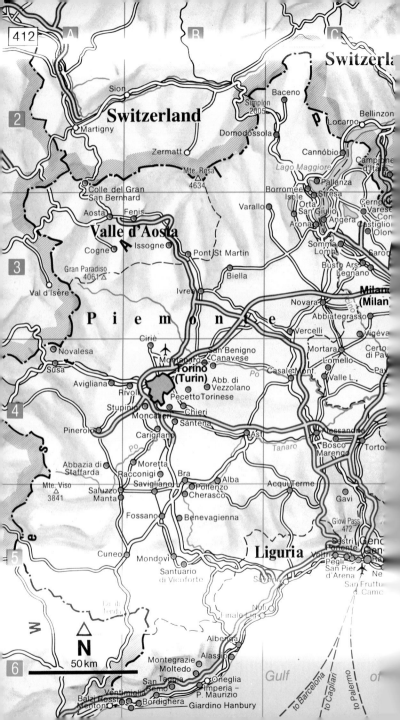

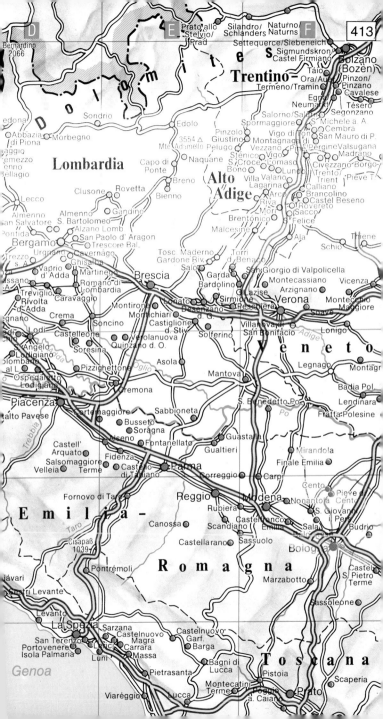

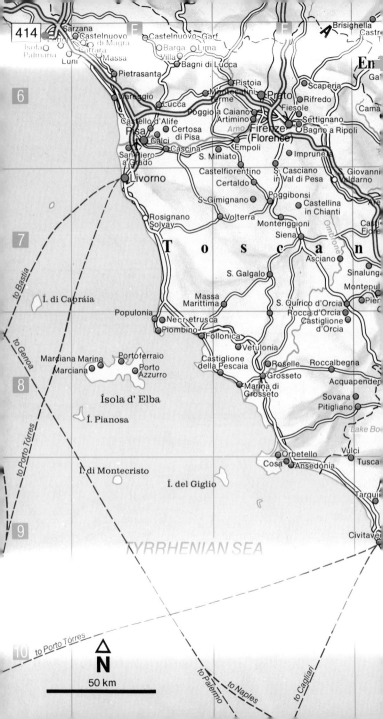

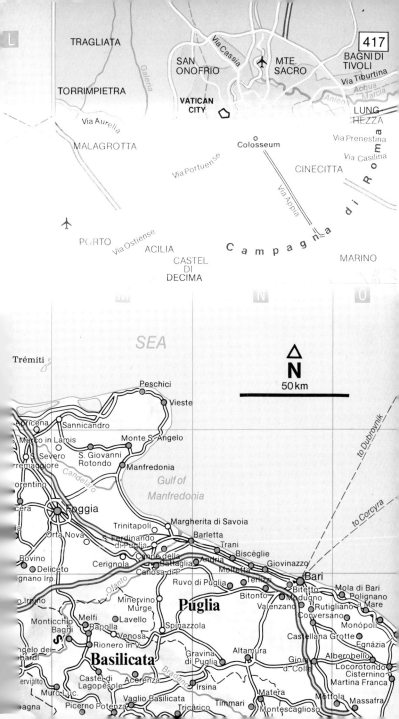

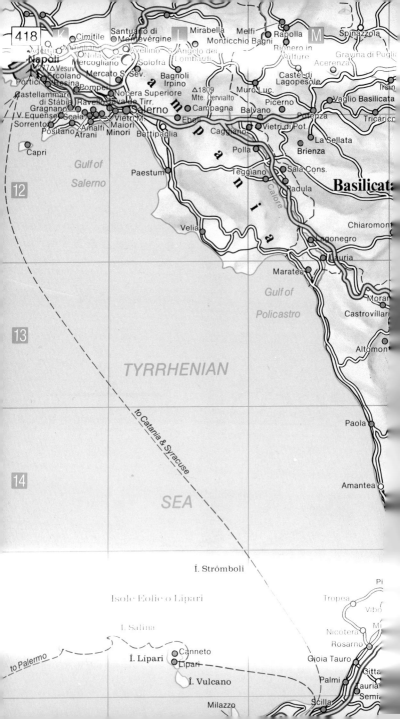

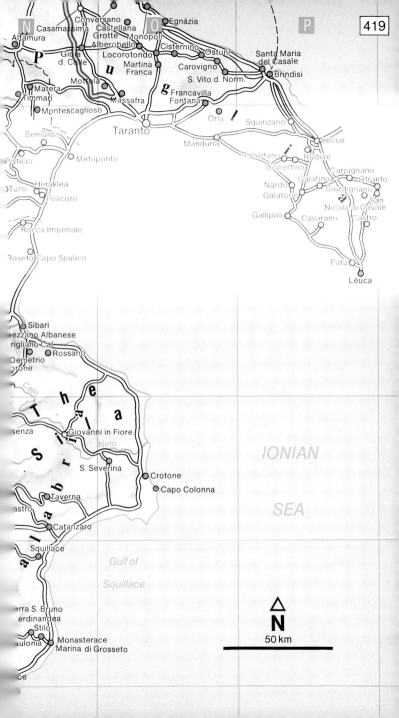

N

O

P

Casamassima
Conversano
Castellana Grotte
Egnázia
Altamura
Monopoli
P
Gioia d. Colle
Alberobello
Cisternino
Ostuni
u
Locorotondo
Carovigno
Santa Maria del Casale
Martina Franca
Matera
Mottola
g
S. Vito d. Norm.
Brindisi
Timmari
Massafra
Francavilla Fontana
Montescaglioso
l
Bernalda
Taranto
Orìa
Squinzano
Manduria
Lecce
Pisticci
Metaponto
Leverano
Rudiae
i
Heraklea
Copertino
Carpignano
Tursi
Policoro
Nardò
Galatina
a
Otranto
Galatone
Giurdignano
San Nicola di Casole
Rocca Imperiale
Gallipoli
Casarano
Castro
Roseto Capo Spulico
Patù
Lèuca

Sibari
Spezzano Albanese
Corigliano Cal.
Rossano
Demetrio Corone
Catrì
T h e
Cosenza
S i l a
Giovanni in Fiore
Neto
IONIAN
S. Severina
Calabria
Crotone
Capo Colonna
Taverna
SEA
Castro
Catanzaro
Squillace
Gulf of
Squillace
Serra S. Bruno
Ferdinandea
Stilo
Monasterace
Caulonia
Marina di Grosseto

△
N
50 km

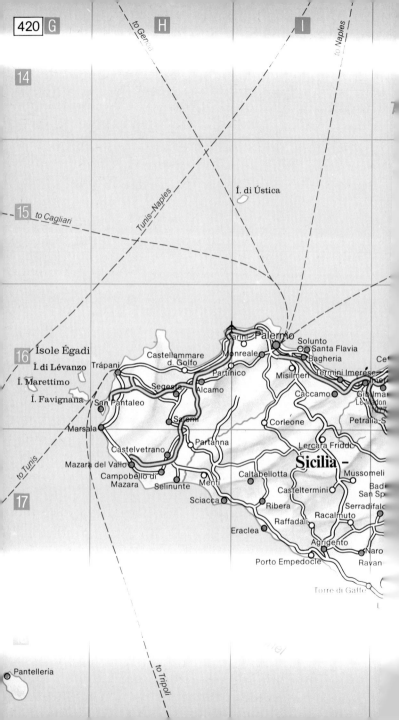

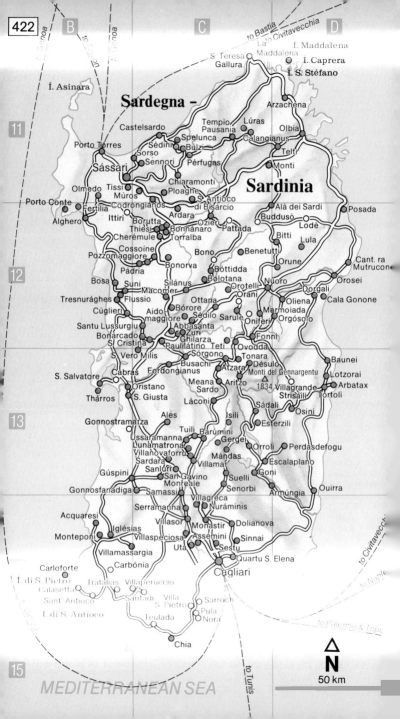

a hall with nave, two aisles, and a flat dome on 16 granite columns.

SS.Apostoli (Via SS.Apostoli): One of the finest baroque churches in Naples. Rebuilt in 1626 – 32 above an older church; the dome was built at the end of the century. Sober façade with an *external staircase* of 1685. The single-aisled interior has four chapels on each side, a transept and a semi-circular apse. Particularly imaginative *carved decorations* (especially in the crossing). *Vault frescos* were painted by G.Lanfranco in 1638–46. The 'Cappellone dell' Annunziata' in the left transept, has a fine *altar wall* by Francesco Borromini.

S. Chiara (Piazza Trinità Maggiore): Gothic, built in 1310–1330; damaged by an earthquake in 1456 and restored in the 16–17C. From 1742-7 it underwent a complete baroque alteration under D.A.Vaccaro. It was destroyed in World War 2 and later rebuilt in the orginal Gothic form. Exterior: The façade is divided in two by a cornice. The upper storey has a fine *rose-window;* the lower one has a *marble portal,* and a pointed-arched *portico.* The outer walls of the nave have buttresses, and the choir is lower than the nave. The church has a massive *campanile* whose foundations are 14C, the other storeys being later; a Gothic inscription is preserved on the basement storey. The inside takes the form of a single-aisled hall-type church, which is very long in proportion to its width; there are side chapels but no proper choir. Behind the S.transverse wall, which is perforated by a beautiful tracery window, is the *choir of the order of St. Clare.* It has a nave and two aisles, and forms a rectangle lying across the main axis of the church; side aisles have ribbed vaults. From here the nuns of the adjoining convent would take part in divine service. The church is particularly rich in fine tombs, especially those of the Angevin dynasty. The *tomb of Robert I* (d. 1343) is behind the high altar. The tomb of his son, Charles of Calabria (d. 1328) is to the right, against the wall of the choir and was carved by Tino da Camaino. The *tomb of Mary of Valois* is on the right. There are more Angevin tombs in side chapels. The famous *Chiostro delle*

Maioliche, has colourful majolica tiles. The cloister of the convent, it was built in the 14C and restored from 1739–43.

S. Domenico Maggiore (Piazza S. Domenico Maggiore): Gothic, built from 1289 - 1324, next to a somewhat older church; later repeatedly restored and altered after suffering damage from earthquakes and fire. Its present form dates from the 19C. The façade is not uniform in style, having Gothic windows and a baroque portico. The portal is 14C and has fine old *wooden doors.* The choir has no windows or other external decorations. Basilican interior with a nave, two aisles, pointed-arched *arcades* and a baroque *wooden ceiling.* The aisles have ribbed vaults. The choir has a polygonal apse, and two chapels on each side. The 7th chapel on the left has the *Altar of Maria delle Neve* by G.da Nola (1536). The first chapel of the left transept has a fine *Annunciation* by Titian, which dates from after 1557. The chapel to the left of the choir contains the*Flagellation of Christ,* a famous work by Caravaggio dating from 1607. The main chapel in the choir has a marble *Easter candlestick* of 1585 with nine allegorical statues by Tino da Camaino (14C). The 7th chapel on the right leads to the sacristy which has a splendid *ceiling fresco* by Francesco Solimena ('Triumph of True Belief', 1709). The 6th chapel on the right leads into the so-called *Cappellone del Crocifisso,* which has a 13C Crucifixion and 'Entombment' (probably Neapolitan, 15C). The right transept leads to the old *Dominican church.* By the altar in the right chapel is the oldest surviving portrait of St.Dominic (late 13C).

Gesù Nuovo: Built by Jesuits from 1584 –1601 in the courtyard of the *Palazzo Sanseverino,* which was the source of the church's ashlar façade. The damaged dome was restored in the 18C. The interior of this basically centrally-planned building, has a dome above the crossing, tunnel-vaulted transepts, and small additional cupolas above the corner rooms; the nave has been extended by an additional bay. Inside, on the entrance wall, there is a famous *fresco,* the 'Expulsion of Heliodorus' by Fr.

Naples, cathedral

Solimena, 1725. The altar in the 2nd side chapel on the right has a *Visitation* by Massimo Stanzone (1585–1656).

S. Giovanni a Carbonara (Strada Carbonara): Built by Augustinian monks in the early 15C. A magnificent *external staircase* leading up to the church was built by F.Sanfelice in 1708, in the style of the 'Spanish Steps' in Rome. The *main portal,* on the S.side of the church, has a pointed arch and is decorated with the coat of arms of the Durazzeschi Angevins. Inside the single-aisled hall church, there is an open rafter roof; a fine *triumphal arch* and a square choir with a ribbed vault. On the N. wall of the nave there is the splendid 15C *marble tomb of Giovanni Miroballo* from Naples. A passage leads from the left side of the choir to the *Cappella Caracciolo di Vico,* built in 1516 – 57 in fine Renaissance style. A round chapel, it has a coffered cupola, and Doric columns on the walls. The choir of the church contains the massive late Gothic *tomb of King Ladislaus* (d.1414), a Durazzeschi-Angevin. The *Cappella della Natività della Beata Vergine* is in the extension of the choir. Built in 1427, it has a round ground plan (polygonal from the outside), and fine peaked-arched windows. On the walls there is a 15C *fresco cycle* of scenes from the life of the Virgin Mary by L.da Besozzo of Milan. Remains of a beautiful majolica floor survive. The *Renaissance monument* to *Sergianni Caracciolo del Sole,* the chapel's founder (d. 1432), is opposite the entrance. The *Cappella del Crocifisso* is to the left of the church's main entrance; it dates from 1533 and is named after a Crucifixion (by Giorgio Vasari?). In the E. is the 15C *Oratorio di S.Monica,* which has a fine late Gothic portal. The lower church, *S. M.Consolatrice degli Afflitti* is 17C.

S. Lorenzo Maggiore (Piazza Gaetano): Regarded as the town's finest Gothic church. Begun in 1270, using the walls of a dilapidated early Christian building, it was completed some 50 years later. (*Remnants of floor mosaics* survive from the earlier building.) In subsequent years it was much altered. From the late 19C onwards the original building was reconstructed. The Gothic choir, and the portal with a *wooden door* of 1325 (in the baroque façade of 1743), survive from the old building. The campanile was built in 1487–1507. Inside, the single-aisled hall church is very wide; there are side chapels and an open roof truss. A triumphal arch separates the transept from the nave. The Gothic *choir* is splendid, having a nave, two aisles, a polygonal apse, and a ring of chapels. On the right of the choir, is the *tomb of Katharine of Austria* (d. 1323; the wife of the Angevin Charles of Calabria), which is very probably by Tino da Camaino. There is a fine, life-sized 14C *wooden crucifix* just to the right of the entrance to the church. The marble *high altar* is by Giovanni da Nola. Of the 14C *frescos* in the transept and choir, only remnants survive. The 17C *cloister* is also of note.

S. Maria del Carmine (Piazza del Carmine): Built by Carmelite monks in the

S. Chiara, Chiostro delle Maioliche

13-14C as a hall church with an open rafter roof; later radically altered, particularly in the 18C, when the interior was restored in baroque style. The façade dates from 1766. The *campanile*, 246 ft. high and a Neapolitan landmark, dates, in its present form, from the 17C. It has a classical articulation in four storeys (rusticated, Doric, Ionic and Corinthian), and an onion-shaped spire. The interior is single-aisled with side chapels. Splendid polychrome *marble* on the walls. Remnants of the original, polygonal design are still visible in the apse and transept. Between the 4th and 5th chapels on the left there is a *marble statue of Conradin, the last Hohenstaufen king,* which was designed by Thorvaldsen in 1836. Behind the high altar, there is a fine 14C Gothic *wooden crucifix.* Also behind the high altar is the *Madonna della Bruna,* a late Byzantine icon.

S.Maria di Donnaregina (Largo Donnaregina): Gothic, built in 1307-18 with the assistance of Queen Mary of Hungary, wife of Charles I of Anjou; later repeatedly altered. The interior is single-aisled, and mostly two storeyed. The choir has ribbed vaults, a polygonal conclusion, and fine peaked-arched windows. The *tomb of Mary of Hungary,* along the left wall of the nave, is a masterpiece by Tino da Camaino (1325-26). The *Cappella Loffredo,* to the right, has remnants of 14C mural paintings. The nuns' choir is covered throughout with frescos, the most important of which are the *Last Judgement,* probably by P. Cavallini, *c.* 1308, on the entrance wall, and *Christ's Passion* by the same artist on the long wall to the left.

S.Maria la Nova (Via S.M.la Nova): The oldest Franciscan church in Naples. Originally 13C, it was rebuilt in 1596-9 (parts of the original structure can be seen in the nave). A double staircase leads up to the

Renaissance façade, which has Corinthian pilasters and a pediment. A single-aisled hall church, it has side chapels and a coffered ceiling (1598–1600). There is a dome above the transept and, next to this, there is an angular choir with a barrel vault. To the right, on a pillar of the crossing there is a painted wooden figure, '*Ecce Homo*', by Giovanni da Nola. The 2nd chapel on the left, the 16C *Cappella di S. Giacomo della Marca*, has fine *frescos* of 'Scenes from the Life of St.John the Baptist' by Luca Giordano (1632–1705). The 4th chapel to the left of the nave contains the famous *Eustachius altar* by Giovanni da Nola. In the chapel to the left of the choir is a fine 15C miraculous image of the *Madonna delle anime purganti*, covered with votive gifts. The Cappella S.Giacomo leads into the *Little Cloister*, which is 15C. From here you can get to the *refectory*, which was part of the former monastery and has a fine ribbed vault. The *Large Cloister* is accessible from the outside, and is of interest for its rococo decorations.

Castel Nuovo (Piazza del Municipio): A city landmark. Built in 1279–84 under Charles I of Anjou; extended under subsequent Angevin rulers. Giotto painted the palace chapel in 1328–33. Renovation of the ruined building carried out by the Aragonese included the construction of the triumphal gate. The building was enlarged into its modern fortified form from 1503 onwards, under the Spanish viceroys. In the 20C restoration has been extensive. The ground plan is an irrregular four sided building with massive *corner towers*. Exterior: The main entrance, with the famous *Renaissance triumphal arch*, is on the W. side, facing the town. The triumphal arch (between the *Torre della Guardia* and the *Torre di Mezzo*) was built from *c.*1450 onwards in honour of Alfonso I of Aragon. Numerous important contemporary craftsmen contributed to its construction, including Francesco Laurana, Paolo Romano and Mino da Fiesole. It was completed in 1466. The *Torre Beverello*, in the NE corner, is the main tower of the whole complex. The lake side, to the E., is richly articulated and concluded by the *Torre d'Oro*, which used to be the kings' treas-

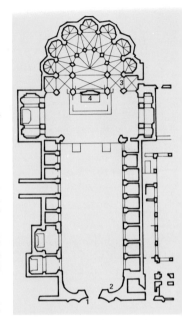

Naples, S.Lorenzo Maggiore 1 Gothic wooden door **2** wooden crucifix, 14C **3** tomb of Catherine of Austria **4** altar of Giovanni da Nola

ure chamber. The S.side has today been restored to its former state and has *a wall passage and battlements*. Inside the castle. The E. section is especially worth seeing. On the left is a 15C *open-air staircase* leading up to the *Sala dei Baroni*, built in 1452–7. To the right of the portal there is a beautiful *balcony window*. The extensive interior (85 ft. long and 92 ft. high) has a unique *stellar vault*. The Renaissance *Porta del Trionfo* has a frieze of the triumphal procession of Alfonso I. Almost nothing survives of the original furnishings. The 'Sala dei Baroni' is adjoined on the right by the *chapel*, founded in 1307. It has a fine 16C Renaissance portal, and above this is a large Gothic-Catalan rose window. A single-aisled structure, it has an open roof truss and a rectangular chancel with a ribbed vault. Nothing has survived

S.Maria di Donnaregina, nuns' choir

of the frescos by Giotto, mentioned above. On the left of the choir, there is a marble Renaissance tabernacle (15C). The chapel is adjoined on its right by the *Palace of the Spanish Viceroys* (16C; restored).

Castel del Ovo (at the S.end of the bay with the harbour): Built as an island in the 1C BC, but today connected to the mainland by a causeway. Formerly owned by Lucullus, the Roman bon viveur. Enlarged into a fortress under the Normans, it was mainly used as a prison by the Angevins. Notable features inside include an early medieval *colonnaded courtyard* and the church of *S. Salvatore,* which probably dates from the 7C. Unfortunately these are not accessible as it is a military zone.

Castel Capuano (Via dei Tribunali): Founded in the 12C under the Normans; enlarged and converted into a law court under the Spanish viceroys in the 16C. A four-winged building with a fine *main façade*. Inside, notable features on the 1st floor are the *Sala della Corte d'Appello* and, in particular, the *Cappella Summaria* with a fresco cycle by the Spanish artist P.Ruviale (1527–54) of scenes from the Passion.

Castel S. Elmo (at the top of *Monte Vomero*): Built under the Angevins in 1329–43 as a fortified seat, and converted into a fortress under the Spanish Habsburgs (Charles V). The ground plan is a six-pointed star; the surrounding wall has a wall passage and embrasures. Inside arsenals have been cut in the rock.

Palazzo Reale (Piazza del Plebiscito): Work on the building, intended as a residence for the Spanish viceroys, began in 1600 to plans by D.Fontana, but proceeded only very slowly. It was radically restored in the 19C after a fire. Exterior: An immense main façade with three storeys and 21 windows. The ground floor originally had a continuous pillared portico, which was later altered for structural reasons, and was divided in traditional manner into three orders of pilasters (Doric-Ionic-Corinthian). Passing through a vestibule you come to the square inner courtyard with a two-storeyed *portico*. Turning left, there is the massive *staircase*, originally 17C, with two flights of stairs leading to the upper storey. From here the historic rooms can be visited. Of particular interest are: The *court theatre* dating from 1768, at the N. end of the front building. There are fine tapestries in the adjacent *middle hall*. *Room No. 11* has a lovely painting, the 'Return of the Prodigal Son' by the Calabrian artist Mattia Preti (1613–99). Since 1927, the rear section of the palace has housed the *national library*, which has a rich stock of manuscripts, papyri, early printed books, etc.

Palazzo Cuomo (Via del Duomo): Built in 1464–90; it was torn down and reconstructed stone for stone. Since 1880, it has been a museum. The façade is Gothic-Catalan, intermingled with early Renaissance features. There are two storeys. Some of the the *windows* on the 1st

Naples, Castel Nuovo 1 Torre della Guardia 2 Torre di Mezzo 3 triumphal arch 4 Sala dei Baroni 5 Porta del Trionfo 6 chapel 7 viceroys' palace

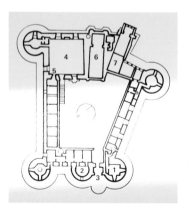

storey are Gothic (on the S.side), and some are Renaissance (main façade). Exhibits in the *Museo Civico Filangieri* include: a *terracotta bust of Ferdinand I of Aragon* by A.Canova (1804), in the entrance hall and the *'Capa di Napoli'*, a woman's head of ancient origin; on the first floor there are some good *pictures* by G.Ribera and Mattia Preti.

Palazzo Carafa di Maddaloni (Via S. Biagio dei Librai): Built in 1466 in late Gothic-Catalan style intermixed with early Renaissance features. Exterior: Walls with rectangular ashlars; broad *portal* with beautifully carved wooden doors, above which there is an entablature with two late classical *busts of emperors*, and a *statue of Hercules* between them. Inside is a *vestibule* in Gothic-Catalan style. An *ancient marble column* can be seen on the left of the passage leading to the courtyard.

Porta Capuana (Piazza Porta Capuana): Built as a city gate in 1484–8 by the Florentine artist Giuliano da Maiano. It is one of the most interesting buildings of its kind in Italy. The gate arch is framed by two *round towers*, called 'Onore' and 'Virtù'. The outer wall is marble and decorated with *reliefs*. There is a fine *archivolt* around the arch through which the traffic passes. Above the high frieze, with *figures of Saints* by Giovanni da Nola, there is a massive *cornice*.

Zoological Institute (in the *Villa Comunale*, along the so-called 'Riviera di Chiaia'). With the world-famous **aquarium,** founded by Anton Dohrn from Stettin in 1870. The *frescos* throughout the common room are the work of the German painter Hans von Marées (1837–87) and have made the institute famous.

Teatro S. Carlo (by the Palazzo Reale): One of the largest theatres in Europe. Built in 1737, reputedly in eight months, at the instigation of King Charles III. In 1762, under G.M.Bibbiena, the stage facilities

Naples, Castel Nuovo

were renovated and the acoustics improved. Operas by Rossini, Bellini and Donizetti had their premières here. Exterior: The lower storey has a *loggia* with five pillars and Ionic columns; above the entablature there is a massive *pediment*. The interior was rebuilt in 1816 after a fire. The stage measures *c.* 108 ft. by 112 ft., and the auditorium, which holds some 3,000 people, is *c.* 89 ft. by 74 ft. In their present form the *interior furnishings* date from 1841.

Fontana del Nettuno (Piazza G.Bovio): This is regarded as the finest fountain in Naples. It was originally erected by the harbour in 1600–1, and was subsequently moved several times until it came to occupy its present position in 1898. It is the work of the Tuscan artists M.Naccherino and P.Bernini; C.Fanzago made some additions in the mid-17C. There is noticeable Florentine influence in the architecture (the so-called 'Fontana isolata'). A structure in three stages, each stage has a different ground plan. At the bottom, there is a basin in the shape of a clover-leaf, in the middle there is a round platform and the top is quatrefoil. The fountain's figures are mythological, including Neptune and other sea creatures.

National Archaeological Museum (in the *Palazzo degli Studi;* Piazza del Museo Nazionale): One of the world's most important museums of antiquities. Ground floor: The chief features of the entrance hall are the beautiful *Roman portrait statues.* Room 1 and the following rooms have Roman *copies of Greek sculptures*, including the 'Doryphoros' in Room 3, after the original by Polyclitus. Room 13 has the 'Farnese Heracles', a copy by Lysipp. Room 16 has the 'Farnese Bull' from the baths of Caracalla in Rome. Beginning in Room 30 there is a rich *collection of Roman portraits*, including a colossal likeness of Caesar in Room 40. There are notable *mosaics* in the mezzanine, where 'Alexander in battle' in Room 61 is especially famous. On the right of the upper storey there is a *collection of bronze statues from Pompeii and Herculaneum,* and beginning in Room 66 there is a unique *collection of ancient paintings,* the most interesting being those from the ancient towns of Pompeii, Herculaneum and Stabiae, which were buried during the eruption of Vesuvius in 79 AD. There are *ancient glass vessels* in Room 84 and the following rooms.

S.Maria la Nova

National Museum of Capodimonte (in the *Palazzo Reale* di Capodimonte): Palace built in the 18–19C. The *museum with 19C paintings* occupies the 1st, and partly the 2nd floors (mainly Neapolitan painters). There is a splendid *collection of weapons* and an important *porcelain collection*. The famous *picture gallery* is on the 2nd floor. Particularly worth seeing: Room 2 has famous *tapestries* depicting the battle of Pavia, which were designed by Bernart of Orley (1488–1541). Room 4 has the painting *St.Louis of Toulouse crowning Robert of Anjou king of Naples* by Simone Martini (1317). Room 5 has a *Crucifixion* by Masaccio (1426). In Room 10 there is a *portrait of Cardinal A.Farnese* by Raphael (1510–12). Room 15 has *paintings by Correggio,* including the so-called 'Gipsy Madonna' dating from 1515. Room 19 is devoted to *Titian.* Room 20 has pictures by Pieter Bruegel the Elder, the *Blind leading the*

blind and *The Misanthropist* (1568). Room 45 has *paintings by Francisco Goya,* 'Charles IV' and 'Marie-Louise of Parma', from the late 18C. Rooms 68–71 on the 1st floor house the *porcelain collection,* which is well worth seeing and includes items from Vienna and Meissen.

National Museum of S. Martino (next to the Castel S. Elmo): Since 1866 it has been housed in the former *Carthusian monastery* which dates from 1325. It contains paintings, sculptures, small works of art and other items of local Neapolitan history. Approaching through the *Little Cloister,* the visitor first enters the *Maritime Museum* (Rooms 1–4 with some fine old models of ships). Room 7 has the *'Tavola Strozzi'* dating from 1464. Rooms 32–40 house a *collection of local interest* showing the folklore, festivals and customs of Naples. Room 42 and the following rooms house the *picture gallery;* in Room 43 there is a fine 14C Florentine triptych. In Rooms 62–64 there is the *collection of sculptures:* Room 63 contains two works by Tino da Camaino, 'Madonna and Child, seated' and 'St. Dominic'. The *collection of applied art* is housed in Rooms 72–78. The fine

17C furnishings of the former **monastery church** make it worth a visit.

Also worth seeing: Churches: *S. Angelo a Nilo* (Piazza S. Domenico Maggiore): 15C, with the impressive Renaissance tomb of Cardinal Brancaccio from the workshop of Donatello, 1427–8. *S. Eligio* (Piazza del Mercato): founded in 1270, one of the oldest Gothic churches in Naples. The late-16C *S. Filippo Neri* (Via dei Tribunali), has an important painting by Luca Giordano, 'Christ driving the money-changers from the Temple' (1684, on the inner entrance wall). *S. Francesco di Paola* (Piazza del Plebiscito): 19C, built in the style of the Pantheon in Rome. In the square outside, there are two equestrian statues by Canova. *S. Gennaro extra Moenia,* underneath the Capodimonte, is one of the city's oldest churches (5C), and has extensive early Christian *catacombs.* The entrance hall of the 17C *S. Giorgio Maggiore* (Via del Duomo) was the apse of a previous (early Christian) basilica. *S. Giovanni Maggiore,* in the old harbour quarter, near the Via Mezzocannone has an early Christian apse (6C). *S. Gregorio Armeno* (Via S. Gregorio) is 16C with fine baroque fur-

National Archaeological Museum, mosaic from Pompeii

Naples, S.Anna dei Lombardi, Cappella Piccolomini

Naples, Palazzo Reale

nishings. The 14C *S.Maria dell'Incoronata* (Via Medina) is a two-aisled vaulted basilica. *S.Maria Maggiore* (Via dei Tribunali) is 17C, with a fine portal (the rest of the building is a war ruin). *S.Maria del Porto*, at the foot of the Posilippo is 16C, with the Renaissance tomb of the humanist Jacopo Sanazarro (1458–1530). *S.Paolo Maggiore* (Piazza S.Gaetano)is 16C and one of the city's finest early baroque churches; built on the site of an ancient temple. The 14C *S.Pietro a Maiella* (Via S.Pietro a.M.), has fine 17C ceiling paintings by the Calabrian artist Mattia Preti. The *Cappella Sansevero* (Via Fr.de Sanctis)is 17C; fine baroque form. The 15C *SS.Severino e Sossio* (Via B.Capasso) has lavish 16C furnishings. *S.Maria di Piedigrotta* is the scene of a famous public festival on 7 September. **Palaces:** The 16C *Palazzo Cellamare* (Via Chiaia) has a fine portal and an interesting chapel. The *Palazzo de Sinno* (Via Roma), has an unusual 18C stairwell. The *Palazzo Donn'Anna* (Via Posilippo), 17C, is magnificently located by the sea. The 16C *Palazzo Gravina* (Via Montoliveto) has a façade which is worth seeing. The 19C *Villa Pignatelli-Acton* (Riviera di Chiaia) houses a fine porcelain collection. The *Palazzo Sanfelice* (Via Arena della Sanità is 18C, with a fine stairwell. The *Palazzo Spinelli di Laurino* (Via dei Tribunali), *c.* 1500, also has a fine staircase. **Other things of interest:** The *Fontana dell' Immacolatella* (Via Nazario Sauro), an early 17C fountain, and the *Fontana di Montoliveto* (Piazza Montoliveto) from 1668. The *Piazza Dante* was built by Vanvitelli in the 18C. *Villa Comunale*, the former royal park, has many 19C fountain figures. The *Museo Nazionale della Ceramica 'Duca di Martina',* in the beautiful *Villa Floridiana* on the S. slope of M.Vomero, has a splendid porcelain collection. The *Conservatorio di Musica* (Via S.Pietro a Maiella) has an extensive collection of items relating to music. The *Academy of Art* (Via Bellini) has 19C Neapolitan paintings and sculptures.

Environs: Some 11 km. to the W. is **Camaldoli**, with a 16C *monastery*.

National Museum, bust of Caesar

Naples, National Museum of Capodimonte, wall tapestry of the battle of Pavia designed

Narni 05035
Terni / Umbria   p.414□H 8

This town lies on a spur of lias stone below the olive trees. From the hill there is a view along the extensive valley of the wild Nera. This is the home town of Erasmo da Narni, known as Gattamelata, the condottiere. The modern town centre, the so-called Narni Scalo, is today in the valley. The first settlement dates from the Umbrian foundation of Nequinum. Later, under the Romans, it was an important strategic centre, especially at the time of the war between Vitellius and Vespasian, and also during the barbarian invasions. The Spanish army destroyed the municipal archive in 1527.

Cathedral: One of the most important Romanesque religious buildings in south-ern Umbria. It dates from the 12C. The close connection with Rome is visible here too. The mosaic of Christ inside the church is the oldest mosaic in the whole of Umbria and points to the influence of Latium. The *chapel of Bishop Cassius* and his wife Fausta, dating from 558, is part of a rare work of early Christian architecture. The church narthex is 15C.

Also worth seeing: *S. Maria in Pensole,* in the same style as the cathedral and an equally important example of independent local Romanesque art. The *Palazzo del Comune* (13–16C) today houses the town's picture gallery, whose exhibits include two valuable works: a Coronation of the Virgin, by Ghirlandaio, and an Annunciation, by B.Gozzoli. The *Loggia dei Priori,* the priors' hall, is attributed to Matteo Gattapone from Gubbio. The *fountain* in the Piazza del Comune (14C) is an imitation of the fountain of Perugia. *Castle:* Built un-

by Bernart of Orley (1488–1541)

der Cardinal Albornoz in the 14C and later enlarged by Pope Pius II. The *Bridge of Augustus* fell down in the 7C, was restored, and fell down again in 1053. Interesting remains of the foundations are all that can be seen today.

Naro 92028
Agrigento/Sicily   p.420 □I 17

Chiesa Matrice (SS. Annunziata, Via Lucchesi): A baroque building founded in 1619. Inside there are a nave, two aisles and fine *stucco*, including a *Madonna* of 1534 by Vincenzo Gagini (2nd altar on the right), and a *font* of 1424.

S.Caterina (Via Cannizaro): Built by the Chiaramonte (see below) in the 14C. Fine *baroque façade*. Inside there are a nave, two aisles, three apses with beautiful Gothic arches, remains of 15C *stucco decoration*, and a *font* dating from the time of Aragonese rule.

S.Francesco (Piazza Garibaldi): Founded in 1635, with an ornate *baroque façade* in the Spanish manner. The interior is single-aisled with fine frescos. Items of interest include an 18C silver statue, the *Immacolata*.

S.Agostino (Piazza P.Favara): Lavish 18C *baroque façade*. Fine 15C marble *holy-water stoup*.

Also worth seeing: The late-16C *Santuario di S.Calogero*, with a fine baroque façade. The 14C *Matrice Vecchia* has a good portal and rose-window. The 13–14C *Castle of the Chiaramonte* is a massive well-preserved square building. In the Contrada Canal Baglio is the *Grotta delle Meraviglie*, an early Christian catacomb.

Naturno/Naturns 39025
Bolzano/South Tyrol-Trentino   p.410☐F 1

Parish church of S. Zeno: Naturno is a village of some size built along a main road, in the lower Val Venosta or Vintschgau valley. S. Zeno was originally a Carolingian church, the remains of which can still be made out in the substructure of the tower. There are remains of Romanesque frescos dating from 1230. The modern church was built in 1475 and its interior was restored in 1760. Frescos dating from 1500 are on the outer walls.

S. Prócolo: Built in the 8C and given a tower in the 12C. On the S.outer wall there is a fresco cycle dating from 1400. Of greatest interest are the 8C frescos inside the church.

Environs: Castello Taranto/Castle Dornsberg/Tarantsburg: Originally 13C, the present building is early Renaissance from the 16C and stands on the S. bank of the Adige. **Láces/Latsch** (further up the Adige, in the W.): The *hospital church* was built in various phases during the 14, 15& 16C; the portal dates from 1517. Net vault with frescos from 1600. The high altar by Jörg Lederer is from 1517, and the remaining furnishings are 17&18C. The late Gothic *parish church of St. Peter and St. Paul,* dating from the early 15C, has neo-Gothic decorations inside. The *graveyard chapel* has a carved door of 1500 and an altar dating from 1681. The church of *Our Lady of Bichl* was built in 1450 (the tower is from a previous 13C building). The side chapel dates from 1680 and the furnishings are from the 15, 16&18C. The *former church of St.Nicholas,* today used as a depot for the fire brigade, was built by the Knights of St. John in *c.*1200, and vaulted in the 17C. The late-16C *Mühlrain residence,* with its 17C façade and the 17C *Chapel of St.Anna,* is also worth seeing. **Morter:** Further to the W. is Goldrain. The traveller continuing southwards from here into the Martello valley soon comes to the village of Morter with the *parish church of St.Dionysius* dating from 1500, the Romanesque church of *St.Vigilius* from 1180 (with a Crucifixion dating from 1420 above the portal and a winged altar of 1600), and the 8C chapel

Naples, National Museum of S. Martino, Recumbent Madonna

of *St.Stephen*, which stands above the castle of Obermontani and is decorated throughout with 15C frescos. 14C groin vault. The ruins of the *Castle of Obermontani*, picturesquely located on a rounded rocky peak, date originally from the 13C (restoration in progress since 1960). Manuscript I of the the Nibelungenlied, dating from 1323, and the Titurel manuscript, both come from the former library of the castle. **Silandro/Schlanders:** Silandro lies in the other direction, W. along the Adige, at the opening of the Schlandernau valley. Silandro is the main town of the central Val Venosta and has fine old houses; *Schlandersberg castle* towers above the town. The late Gothic *parish church of the Assumption of the Virgin*, with its high tower, was built in *c*. 1500. In the 18C it was lengthened westwards, given new vaults and furnished inside. The sumptuous frescos are by Jos.A.Mölk. The *Chapel of St.Michael* by the graveyard dates from 1500, and the *hospital church*, which also has vault frescos by J.A.Mölk (1760), was originally built in 1514. There are also frescos dating from 1516 on its walls; it was later restored in the baroque style. **Covelano/Göflan:** On the other side of the Adige, opposite Silan-dro, we find the town of Covelano, with the Gothic church of *St.Martin* from the 2nd half of the 15C. Its tower is from the original 12&13C building, and the Romanesque door dates from *c*. 1290. Inside there is an altar by Jörg Lederer (1515). The stone Pietà in the predella dates from about 1400. The *Chapel of St. Walpurgis* above the church of St. Martin dates from the 15&16C.

Nepi 01036
Viterbo/Latium   p.414   G 9

This originally Faliscan settlement was called 'Nepet' by the Etruscans. Furius Camillo conquered it in 383 BC. From the 5C onwards it was the seat of a bishop and was united with the bishop's seat of Sutri in 1435. Destroyed by Albuin in AD 568, it began to flourish again in the 9C. Part of the Etruscan *town wall* has survived and this can be seen to follow the example of the Greeks, making use of longitudinal and transverse blocks (stretchers and binders). Also *remains of the Roman wall*. The *Rocca* was built by Rodrigo Borgia in 1450.

Naples, Palazzo Reale di Capodimonte, Napoleon room

The cathedral (Assunta, Via Matteotti): Built in the 9C, enlarged in the 12C, destroyed in 1798 and restored in 1831. With its nave and four aisles, it preserves only scant traces of its Romanesque past. *Triptych* by Giulio Romano. The 12C *crypt* has a nave, 8 aisles and 3 apses.

Palazzo Comunale (Piazza Umberto I): Begun by Antonio da Sangallo, and completed in 18C baroque. The colonnaded hall has a *fountain* attributed to Bernini.

Environs: Castel S.Elia (2.5 km.): A rural settlement with the remains of medieval fortifications. Modest Etruscan tombs. From the village the traveller descends to the **Basilica di S. Elia**, an important building architecturally. Tradition has it that it was built in the 8C or 9C above a hermitage founded by St. Benedict. The present structure dates from the 11C and is a simple basilica with a nave, two aisles and a semicircular apse adjoining the transept. Columns and capitals are taken from ancient buildings. In the nave and transept there are remains of a *Cosmati floor*. The *pulpit* comes from the previous building. The *high altar* has a Cosmati wreath and

Naturno, ruined castle of Obermontani

a fine ciborium. The *frescos* in the apse and transept are important. Dating from *c.* 1200, they are typical of the 12C Roman school, formed by the brothers Johannes and Stephanus, and Nicolaus, Johannes' nephew.

Nervi 16167
Genoa/Liguria   p.412□C 5

Museo Giannettino Luxoro (Villa Luxoro, Via Aurelia, No. 29): A splendid collection of paintings, Genoese furniture, clocks, silverwork, copperware, majolica, silver holy-water fonts from the 18C, ceramics from Savona, and Genoese crib figures by Antonio Maria Maragliano, Gagini, Pittaluga and others.

Galleria d'Arte Moderna (*Palazzo Serra,* Parco Municipale): Since 1928, the 17C Palazzo Serra has housed a large-scale exhibition of 19&20C Italian and Ligurian painting.

Nettuno 00048
Roma/Latium   p.414□H 10

Nettuno may possibly have been a Saracen foundation which fell to the Monastery of Grottaferrata in 1163. The Frangipani were followed as owners by the Borghese.

Features of interest: *Medieval town wall.* The *fortifications* were built by Antonio da Sangallo and Baccio Pontelli in 1496–1503 on the instructions of Pope Alexander VI (Borgia).

Environs: Torre Astura (approx. 12 km.): This massive castellated tower stands in the sea and is connected to the mainland by just a stone bridge. It is of historical importance for Conradin of Swabia (Hohenstaufen) fled here after defeat at Tagliacozzo, only to be delivered up to Charles of Anjou by Giac. Frangipani.

Nicosia 94014
Enna/Sicily   p.420□K 17

The ancient town of Herbita once occupied this site. Under the Normans it was inhabited by Lombards and Piedmontese, who have left their mark on the local dialect.

Cathedral of S. Nicola (Piazza Garibaldi): Founded in the 14C; the façade with its fine portal and the campanile with Gothic blind arcades, both survive from the original building. The façade has 16C statues of the four cardinal virtues. Fine 15C portico on the left side. Latin cross ground plan and, inside, nave and two aisles, which have been restored in the baroque style. In the nave there is a marble pulpit of 1566 by the school of Gagini. The chapel to the left of the high altar has rich marble inlay. The font is also from the Gagini workshop.

S. Maria Maggiore: Founded in 1267, destroyed by a landslide in 1757, and only rebuilt in the 19&20C (consecrated in 1904). Magnificent baroque portal. The inside has a nave and two aisles, and on the right of the choir there is an interesting triptych by Antonello Gagini (1499–1512), and the so-called 'Throne of Charles V', reputedly used during the emperor's visit in 1535. The choir also has a beautiful 16C holy-water stoup.

Also worth seeing: *The church of S. Vincenzo* with Borremans frescos dating from 1777. The *Chiesa del Carmine* has an Annunciation by Antonello Gagini of 1527. Remains of a Norman castle.

Environs: The small mountain town of **Troina**, 30 km. to the E, probably occupies the site of the ancient Enghion. *Remains of the ancient walls.* The *Chiesa Matrice* is of Norman origin.

Nocera Umbra 06025
Perugia / Umbria   p.414 □ H 7

A small health resort, with a beneficial climate, lying in the mountains of E. Umbria. Discoveries of 1895 include the remains of Roman bridges, and a Lombard necropolis with 367 tombs. These finds are on display in the Museo delle Terme in Rome and they indicate that this little town was formerly an important strategic centre.

Cathedral: As with so many similar

Láces (Naturno), high altar by Jörg Lederer

buildings, this took several years to complete. A small cathedral, it was built in the 11C and restored in the 15C. The fine portal has late medieval decorations.

Picture gallery: Housed in the former church of S.Francesco (opening hours: 9 a.m.–1 p.m.). Important works include: a polyptych of 1483, by Niccolò Alunno; and St.Anne meeting St.Joachim, by Matteo da Gualdo.

S.Filippo: An architectural curiosity. It was designed by the architect Luigi Poletti (1792–1869), who had destroyed several medieval buildings to rebuild them in the neoclassical style. In this case Poletti built the 19C church in Gothic-Romanesque style!

Tower of the Trinci: Originally 11C; it later became part of a castle which came into the possession of the famous Trinci family from Foligno.

Nola 80035

Naples/Campania   p.416□ K 11

Nola was an Oscan foundation, later coming under Etruscan domination. It became Roman in 313 BC. The Roman emperor Augustus died in Nola in AD 14. It became a diocesan seat at a very early date. Nola was destroyed by Genseric the Vandal in 455 during the barbarian invasions. It was the home town of the sculptor Giovanni da Nola (1488–1558) and of the Dominican monk Giordano Bruno.

Cathedral of S. Felice (Piazza del Duomo): Gothic, built in c. 1400, and rebuilt in 1878–1909 after a fire. The façade has a *portico* with Ionic columns. Inside there are a nave, two aisles and fine Renaissance columns. The pulpit has *reliefs* and is thought to be an early work of Giovanni da Nola. *Giovanni da Nola's tomb* is in the 'Cappella di S.Paolino'. The *crypt* is especially worth seeing. At the beginning of the stairs there is an early medieval *canopy*; the 13C Byzantine relief of *Jesus and the Apostles* is also noteworthy.

To the left, behind a railing, are the *relics of S.Felice,* who founded the church and was the first bishop of Nola.

Also worth seeing: The 18C baroque church of *S.Chiara* (Via Tommaso Vitale). Adjoining it is the 14C building of the same name, with remains of 14C frescos on the walls. The church of *SS.Maria della Misericordia* (Piazza Giordano Bruno) has a fine Romanesque-Gothic campanile. The 15C *Chiesa dell'Annunziata* (Piazza dell' Collegio) has a notable 16C panel painting of the 'Annunciation' by C.Scacco, on a gold background. The *Palazzo Orsini* (Piazza Giordano Bruno) dates from 1461. Fine portal; some ancient fragments of a former building have been incorporated into the wall.

Environs: Directly to the N. of Nola, above the autostrada, is **Cimitile:** The present town developed from the early Christian 'coemeterium' (martyrs' graveyard) of Nola. There is a whole *complex of early Christian and medieval basilicas* which is worth seeing: *S.Felice in Pincis* has notable remains of the 5C mosaic decorations. To the N. is *S.Paolino,* of which only bits of the nave still stand; in the 14C, the apse was converted into a chapel in itself, *S. Giovanni.* To the S. of this is the 8C *SS. Martiri,* with the remains of a fresco cycle of the story of the Passion. Some 6 km. to the W. is **Marigliano** with the fine church of *S.Maria delle Grazie* (also known as *Collegiata*). It dates from 1494 and has paintings by D.A.Vaccaro and Luca Giordano.

Noli 17026

Savona/Liguria   p.412□C 5

Cathedral of S. Pietro: Only the surrounding walls of the original 13C church survive; 17C baroque rebuilding. Inside (nave and two aisles), these alterations find expression mainly in the pulpit and at the high altar. The cathedral has a valuable *church treasure:* a Gothic *reliquary* (1430) and a 15C *pallium of St.Eugenius* (bishop and the town's patron), a *marble urn,* and a silver *processional cross* (1417).

S.Paragorio (near the railway station): An old bishop's church from the beginning of the 12C (restored in 1888); magnificently situated not far from the sea. The façade has pillars and double arcades. Beside the apse is a low tower with a spire. The nave has massive, tall pillars and wooden rafters; the two side aisles have groin vaults. Aisles and the nave each end in an apse. Opposite the choir, there is a 13C *bishop's throne* in wood. Underneath the 3rd arch on the right there is an impressive painted *wooden cross (Volto santo,* 12C). The body was originally clothed in fabric. Sanctuary niches are decorated with 15C frescos. *Crypt.*

Also worth seeing: *Casa Repetto.* A fine house from the beginning of the 14C, standing just to the right of the cathedral in the Piazzetta Praga. *Casa Pagliano* (Corso Italia): 14C, built in natural rock and stone; restored. From the Corso Italia you can get to the extremely picturesque *Piazza del Milite Ignoto,* with the *Torre del Comune.* Here begin the arcades of the *Loggia della Repubblica Nolese,* which lead along the Corso Italia as far as the Piazza Dante. There is a plaque in memory of Giordano Bruno, a Renaissance natural philosopher. In the *Via Colomba* there are medieval houses, especially the 13C *Casa Maglio,* and also the *Torre del Canto,* the town's highest tower. The Via Colomba also leads to the *Porta di S.Giovanni* by the old town wall. There are two very picturesque streets, which are spanned in places by arches, namely, the *Via Silvano Acerbo* and the *Via Antonio da Noli.*

Environs: *Castello di Noli* (on Monte Ursino). The remains of the massive 13C fortress lie within the castellated walls (which have square towers); there is a still older tower from the 11C and this is round.

Nocera Umbra, cathedral

Noli, S.Paragorio

Nonantola 41015
Modena / Emilia-Romagna   p.410 □ F 5

Nonantola, a town of Roman origin, suffered greatly in the battles of the barbarian invasions; it then fell to the Lombards. In 756, the relics of St.Sylvester, the Pope, were placed in the monastery which had been founded in 751-2 by Anselm, the Lombard leader. Destroyed by the Hungarians in 899, it was rebuilt in the 11C and rapidly became important, both culturally and politically. In the 12C the monastery was a moving spirit pressing for church reformation. Its downfall began in the 14C. It lost its independence in 1449 and was then disposed of as a benefice by the Popes. In 1821 it became a part of the archdiocese of Modena.

Abbey church: Built in 1121 above an earlier building, which had been destroyed in the earthquake of 1117. The 17&18C additions were removed in 1913-21. A brick building in three storeys, it has a 12C *portal* with fine reliefs of 1121, by pupils of Wiligelmus. Inside: a *painting of S. Carlo Borromeo,* of 1612, by L.Carracci, and *wall paintings,* from the late 15C, by a master from Modena (both in the right aisle); in the left aisle there is a *font* with ancient fragments. The *high altar* has a polyptych of 1460, by Michele di Matteo Lambertini, and slabs of 1568-72, by Silla Longhi. The *crypt,* which was filled in in *c.* 1500 and rebuilt in 1913 - 21, still retains some Romanesque columns and capitals. The contents of the treasure chamber and the archive include a 10C *cross reliquary,* with a foot, dating from 1678, an 11C Byzantine *Staurothek,* an 11C *Gradual,* and a 12C illuminated *Gospel.*

S.Michele (in the N.): Founded in the 9C, rebuilt in 1000 after the Hungarians destroyed it. The basilica has a nave and two aisles and was redesigned in the baroque style in 1790 (see the façade); partial restoration 1918-21.

Norcia 06046
Perugia/Umbria   p.414 | H 8

A remote town, surrounded by mountains. The home town of St.Benedict (6C), the reformer of European monasticism, and his twin sister St.Scholastica. The town has been Christian since 250. Today, Norcia is still surrounded by a wall, which has survived well.

S.Benedetto: Tradition has it that this church was built in the 6C on a piece of land belonging to the Saint's parents. The building has been restored several times. The façade dates from the late 14C. The statues of the twin Saints stand on both sides of the beautiful Gothic portal. Work by the best two local painters of the 16&17C, Michelangelo Carducci and Filippo da Liagno, can be seen within.

Cathedral (S.Maria Argentea): Built in 1560 and restored in the 18C. Inside, the Madonna of the Rosary is an example of 16C Abruzzi-Umbrian art.

Castellina: This imposing castle was built from 1554-63 to plans by Vignola. It stands on the site of a Roman temple dedicated to the goddess Fortuna Argentea. The castle now houses a picture gallery (opening hours, May to September: 10 a.m.-12.30 p.m., 3.30 p.m.-6 p.m.; October-April: 10 a.m.-12.30 p.m., 2 p.m. -4 p.m.; closed on Mondays). Important works: Resurrection of Christ (Niccolò di Siena), Madonna and Child with Saint (Antonio da Faenza), Coronation of the Virgin with Saints (16C, Jacopo Sciliano). Also on view: the gold and silver reliquary of St.Benedict, which is decorated with enamel and is 15C Venetian-Gothic in style, and two ceramic statues ascribed to Giovanni della Robbia.

S.Agostino: Fine façade, with Gothic portal. The interior has 15&16C frescos; the fresco of St.Sebastian shows the influence of Mantegna. Walnut choir stalls are a typical example of local 17C wood-carving.

S.Francesco: Gothic with local characteristics predominating.

Tempietto: A little temple begun in 1354 to plans by the architect Vanni Tutie. The building is a primitive interpretation of the Gothic style.

S.Scholastica: The oldest church in Norcia, partly proto-Romanesque.

Environs: Particularly fine landscape is offered in the following towns: Forche Canapine, Monte Vettore, Valle del Corno and Piani di Castelluccio. Campi is one of the resorts of cultural interest. The church of S.Salvatore has a unique 14C façade. Inside there are many frescos, mainly by Sparapane. The parish church has a cross by Petrus Pictor (1241). The Benedictine abbey of *S. Eutizio*, near Piedivalle, is of great importance in the study of the art of the area. A Romanesque church, it was begun in 1190 to the plans of Maestro Pietro and extended in 1236.

Notaresco 64020
Teramo/Abruzzi   p.416 ⃞│8

S.Maria di Propezzano: Founded in 715 after the appearance of the Virgin Mary. The present building was built around 1300. The façade, which faces S.has a rose-window with terracotta decorations. There are knotted columns on the *Porta Santa,* which was built by Raimondo di Poggio in the early 14C. Inside, frescos date from 1499.

S. Clemente al Vomano: A monastery founded in the early 9C, rebuilt in 1108, and restored in 1926. The church portal dates from 1108. Inside, there are nave and two aisles and capitals from the first half of the 12C. The mid-12C *ciborium*, which is decorated with stucco, is the work of Roberto di Ruggero; the altar *antependium* shows Byzantine influence. The *frescos* in the left aisle date from 1419, and the *wooden statue of Clement V* in the right side apse is 15C.

Noto 96017
– Syracuse/Sicily   p.420 ⃞L 18

Cathedral of S. Nicola di Mira e S. Corrado (Piazza Municipio): Baroque, completed in 1776. The façade rises above a wide *external staircase*. Inside: nave, two aisles and a dome. The *Romanesque lions* on both sides of the main entrance are worth seeing. Richly decorated *side chapels*.

Noto, S. Chiara

Chiesa di S. Chiara (Corso Vitt.Emanuele): Built by Rosario Gagliardi in 1730. The interior is of particular interest, being elliptical, with lavish *stucco and marble decorations*. The 2nd altar on the left has a *Madonna and Child* by Antonello Gagini.

Chiesa del Crocifisso (Piazza Mazzini): Completed in 1715, it has a fine façade, with splendid column-bearing *Romanesque lions* at the portal. Inside, nave, two aisles and an especially interesting *Madonna and Child* ('Madonna delle Neve') of 1471 by Francesco Laurana (the altar in the right aisle). This is the artist's only dated work in Sicily. The left transept has the richly decorated *Cappella Landolina*.

Palazzo Villadorata (Via Nicolaci): Built in 1737, it has an especially fine façade and *portal*. The baroque *balconies* on the first floor are original.

Also worth seeing: *Church of S.Domenico* (Piazza XVI Maggio), built by Rosario Gagliardi in 1727, with a fine façade. The early-18C church of *S. Francesco* (Corso Vitt.Emanuele) has an ornate baroque façade. Next to it is the beautiful baroque monastery of *SS.Salvatore* with the *Museo Civico* (Piazza XVI Maggio), which houses a collection of prehistoric and ancient finds.

Environs: Some 16 km. NW is **Noto Antica**, the ancient predecessor of modern Noto (surviving remains include *parts of the town walls* and of the *castle*). About 26 km. to the NW is **Castelluccio,** which gave its name to a Sicilian prehistoric epoch (a *settlement from the 2nd millennium BC* has been uncovered). About 10 km. to the S.is **Noto Marina** with *excavations* of the ancient town of *Eloro.* Formerly an outpost of Syracuse, it dates back to the 7C BC; items excavated include remains of walls, and temple fragments.

Nova Ponente/Deutschnofen 39050
Bolzano/South Tyrol-Trentino   p.410☐F 2

Nova Ponente, St. Helena

A winter resort beautifully situated on a plateau to the E. of the Isarco. The *parish church of St.Ulrich and St.Wolfgang,* which was rebuilt in 1455–98, has a Romanesque tower and inside, net and stellar vaulting. The choir dates from 1500. The neo-Gothic high altar has 4 fine reliefs, which were taken from the wings of an old altar of 1422 (Nativity of Christ, Adoration of the Magi, Presentation in the Temple, Death of the Virgin). The isolated small 13C church of *S.Helena* is situated high up and has beautiful frescos dating from 1410 both outside and inside.

Environs: Vigo di Fassa: Travelling along the Dolomite route you pass through Nova Levante/Welschnofen, which according to tradition was founded by the Lombards, and crossing the Karer Pass you enter the Fassa valley. The town of Vigo di Fassa occupies a steep slope above the valley, and the church of *S.Giuliana* stands in a delightful spot just outside the town. In 1519, the church was enlarged into the one you see today. Inside, the 15C vault paintings are very beautiful, as is a carved Gothic altar of 1517.

Novara 28100
Novara/Piedmont   p.412☐ C

S.Maria Assunta (Piazza della Republica): A cathedral, with a nave and two aisles, built in 1865–9 to plans by A.Antonelli above an earlier 12C building. The *choir* of 1831 was built by Stefano Melchioni and the *portico* dates from 1854–6. The *campanile* has a Romanesque substructure and is topped by a dome by A.Antonelli, who was also responsible for the *high altar,* which has a baldacchino on six columns. The bronze *relief on the high altar* is by B.Thorvaldsen; the 2nd altar on

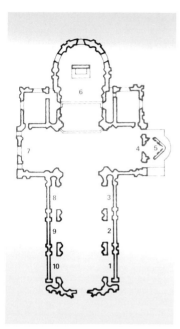

Novara, S. Gaudenzio

Novara, S. Gaudenzio 1 Deposition, by Moncalvo **2** Circumcision, painting by Fiammenghino **3** Crucifixion, painting by G.Ferrari **4** stairs to the Cappella dello Scurolo **5** Cappella dello Scurolo, 1674–1711; in the vault is a fresco (Triumph of St.Gaudentius) by Stefano Legnani; the large octagonal urn of silver and crystal contains the relics of St.Gaudentius and is by Castelli **6** baroque high altar, to the left of it is a baroque cathedra **7** St. Gaudentius, painting by Pelagio Palagi, 1833 **8** frescos by Stefano Legnani and B.Lanano **9** polyptych by G.Ferrari, 1516 **10** murder of Sennacherib, painting dating from 1627–29

the right has the *Betrothal of St.Catherine*, 1525–30, by G.Ferrari. In the *cloister* of the adjacent *bishop's palace* there are items of archaeological interest. The *library* in the chapter house is one of the richest in Piedmont. The octagonal *baptistery* stands in front of the cathedral entrance. A centrally planned 5C building, rebuilt in the 12&17C and restored in 1960. Inside: ancient columns, polychrome terracottas, and Romanesque frescos (1070).

S. Gaudenzio (Via Gaudenzio Ferrari): The town's most important building. A single-aisled church, it was begun by P.Tibaldi in 1577, and completed in 1659. The *domed tower*, 397 ft. tall, was built by A.Antonelli in 1875–8. The *campanile* is by B.Alfierei, 1753–86. Inside are numerous *frescos* and paintings by G.Ferrari.

Also worth seeing: *Ognissanti* (Via Silvio Pellico): built in *c.* 1050, altered in the 18C and recently restored to its former Romanesque form. Inside there are frescos, and the remains of frescos, from about 1400. *S.Pietro al Rosario* (Piazza Gramsci) is a baroque church with an elegant façade; inside, frescos by Fiammenghino, 1630. *S. Marco* (Via Carlo Negroni): built in 1607–17 to a design by Lorenzo Biraghi and restored in 1955; façade decorated with statues. Inside, vault frescos by Moncalvo, paintings by D.Crespi, etc. *Palazzo di Giustizia* (Via Amico Canobio): formerly the Palazzo Fossati, restored in the 18C. The portico has double columns; the 11C loggia at the rear was restored in the 14C and has vestiges of 15C terracotta decoration. *Casa dei Medici* (Via A.Canobio): 16C, atrium with stucco, pretty inner courtyard. *Casa della Porta* (Via Canobio N. 6): a palace of Romanesque origin, converted in the 15C. *Broletto* (Piazza della Repubblica): consists of four 13 – 17C buildings grouped around a courtyard. Restored in 1920–30. The *Museo Civico* with a local archaeological collection occupies the building. The Broletto also houses the *Galleria d'Arte Moderna*.

Núoro 08100

Núoro/Sardinia   p.422 □C 12

Núoro lies at the 'heart' of the Barbagia region and is the 'secret capital' of Sardinia. Indeed, people from all over Sardinia are encouraged to participate in the annual procession—now usually held on the last weekend in August. The 19C cathedral of *Santa Maria della Neve* stands on the square of the same name. Inside there is a good 17C painting of the Crucified Christ by A.Tiarini (to the right of the choir).

Environs: A little to the E. of the Casa della Deledda, on the Viale F.Ciusa, is *Nostra Signora della Solitudine*, in rural surroundings. This old country chapel, which houses the tomb of Deledda, dates from 1615, although it was only decorated from 1955 onwards. The pilgrimage church of *Madonna de su Monte* stands on Monte Ortobene amidst mighty chestnut oaks. The Sardinian procession in traditional costumes, referred to above, leads here. *Fonni* is still the most glorious village in Barbagia; there are many nuraghi in the immediate vicinity. A beautiful rustic path leads across a courtyard and up to the church of *Nostra Signora dei Martiri* (with a mobile [!] 17C Madonna). The route SE, towards 'Sardinia's Dolomites', the 'Punta sos Nidos' (4,426 ft.), and the 'Punta Corrasi' (4,800 ft.), takes you to **Oliena**, one of the last genuine villages in the interior. It has a rather special wooden framework into which cows were harnessed when being shod. The only religious treasure of note is the *triptych* by an unknown 15C Sardinian painter, which is preserved and protected in the sacristy of the 17C parish church. *Santa Maria Maggiore* is a rather crude Gothic church from the 15C.

Núoro, cathedral

Oderzo 31046

Treviso/Veneto   p.410□H 3

Cathedral of S. Giovanni Battista: Gothic, built in the 14C on the site of a previous early-medieval building. The side chapels were added in the 17C. In the 20C the cathedral was restored to its original form. Exterior: A simple façade with a fine *Renaissance portal* of *c*. 1500; flat pilaster strips on the outer walls. The dome is unfaced. Inside it is a single-aisled hall church, with a slightly raised choir and rectangular side chapels. Noteworthy furnishings include: some of the original *late Gothic wall paintings* (very fine friezes with medals). The entrance wall has frescos by J.Veneziano dating from 1606 (of the bishops of Oderzo). There is an ancient *floor mosaic* in the choir chapel. The *Cappella di S.Francesco*, to the left of the choir, has fine pictures by P.Amalteo (*c*. 1550; scenes from the life of John the Baptist). In the chapel to the right of the choir there is a picture (the Infant Christ) by A.Bellunello dating from 1477. On the left wall of the nave there is a 14C relief of the Madonna.

Also worth seeing: *Museo Civico* with objects from the Roman Opitergium (including floor mosaics from a late-antique villa).

Offida 63035

Ascoli Piceno/Marches   p.416□I 8

S.Maria della Rocca (on a hill at the end of the Via Roma): The reconstruction of the double church began in 1330. The upper church has 14C *frescos*, those in the choir are 15C. A portal underneath the apse leads to the lower church, where there are mid-14C *frescos* and a *Depiction of St. Catherine* dated 1423.

Palazzo Comunale (Piazza Vitt.Emanuele II): 15C façade, 14C tower with Ghibelline battlements. Inside: a *picture collection and archaeological finds*.

Olbia 07026

Sassari/Sardinia   p.422□D 11

Nuraghic remains found in the surrounding area suggest that there were sporadic settlements here at an early date (with a shrine, Cabu Abbas?).

S.Simplicio: This is indisputably one of the finest religious buildings in Sardinia. Severe granite ashlars form the wall. The simple pilasters are connected by double arches at the height of the alternating capitals. A tripartite colonnade gives a pleasant, more varied appearance to the façade above the simple arches of the portal. Above the right aisle a bellcote rises, with an open peal of bells. The darkened interior is divided into a nave and two aisles by granite pilasters with columns and wild capitals. Near the entrance, Roman urns and milestones with inscriptions are firmly fixed into the masonry on both sides.

Environs: Hardly anyone can find the *Nuraghic castle of Cabu Abbas,* because the directions have usually been copied wrongly. Inconspicuously situated in the NE mountain crest, it was probably intended to be scarcely visible from below. There are two large gates with enormous architraves. The topmost tower has evidently been destroyed. Remains of steps lead into a rectangular room, to the side of which is a deeper hole worked in stone. Journeys of discovery are best directed to the previously neglected W. Towards **Telti,** there is the deserted Roman *Castra mansio Gemellae.* There are sparse *nuraghic remains* near **Alá dei Sardi** and **Monti.**

Oria 72024
Brindisi/Apulia   p.418☐ O 12

Castle: Only the square tower and some adjoining buildings date from the Hohenstaufen period. Enlarged into a fortress under Charles I of Anjou (see the *Torre del Cavaliere* and *Torre del Salto*). It changed hands frequently during the following centuries and was once owned by the Borromei of Milan. Under the inner courtyard (Piazza d'Armi), right next to the Torre del Salto, you can get to the oldest building in Oria: *SS. Crisante e Daria,* a Byzantine grotto church and the sole example of a so-called 'basilica aperta' in Apulia. Its ground plan is that of a basilica with a nave and two aisles; there are five domes. Only insignificant parts of the Byzantine frescos have survived. Above the church are the remains of an upper church torn down under Frederick II.

Environs: Francavilla Fontana (about 6 km. NW) with the splendid *Palazzo Im-*

periali (building continued from 1450 until the 18C), today the town hall; **Manduria** (*c.* 11 km. S.with the remains of a *megalithic wall* (5–3C BC), especially near the *Chiesa dei Cappucini.*

Oristano 09025
Cágliari/Sardinia   p.422☐ B 13

The history of Oristano really begins with the Phoenician and later Punic, Roman and Byzantine town of Tharros, which, despite its strong defences, was plagued by Saracen raids. The town's indigenous inhabitants left it in *c.* 1000 and initially moved 'somewhere up-country'. From *c.* 1070 onwards a new town of Oristano was built on the lower Tirso, almost exactly on the site of the Roman military camp of Othaca.

Cathedral (cannot be missed from the Via Cagliari, the N./S.access road): A peculiar bulbous dome with unusual, distorted faces around the top of the hexagonal tower. The chancel section has been severely disfigured. It was begun in the 12C but was pointlessly blocked up after 1733. The adjacent *bishop's palace* contains a 12C Pisan altar. There are fine Gothic windows on the 14C tower and in a chapel. The apse retains the 13C'substructure. The *interior* is single-aisled and has several side chapels, a large dome and a massive chancel (12/13C Romanesque lions on the baroque grille). Just to the right of the chancel there are sections of a Tuscan Romanesque pulpit by Nino da Pisa (early 12C), with the famous Pisan *bas reliefs* on their inside. The colourful 14C marble statue of the 'Madonna del Rimedio' stands on the altar. On the right wall of the chapel there is a clear, but little mentioned, inscription which ends with some hourglasses. It is thought to be the *oldest piece of writing* in the Sard language. The chancel has a large painting by S. Conca (17/18C). The 1st chapel to the right of the entrance contains an *Annunziata,* a brightly painted 14C wooden statue known as the Madonna with Three Faces (an early work by Nino Pisano).

S. Giusta (Oristano), portal, detail

Chiesa di S.Francesco (at the beginning of the Via Sant'Antonio): The front of this small classical church retains some Cistercian Gothic ornament (1250–80). Inside, an extraordinarily expressive *wooden crucifix* is, in all the guides, said to be of 14C Spanish origin. However, it definitely derives from the 'Rhenish school of woodcarving'. The *sacristy* contains a panel of *St. Francis,* an early work by P.Cavaro (16C), and a 14C *marble statue* of a bishop (Nino Pisano, 14C). The *reliquary* is a local piece of work.

Also worth seeing: On the N. edge of the town, the Via Tharros runs E. to the park-like *Piazza Roma.* In 1291, Giudice Marino II commissioned the massive, square *Torre di S.Cristoforo* on the site of the Porta Manna. The Torre has a belfry with an old bell dating from 1230. The *Corso Umberto* leads to the *Piazza Eleonora,* with its unsuccessful monument, and also to the *town hall.* The latter contains an important archive of documents from the Aragonese period (1479–1720), and also a small *picture gallery* (16C retable by P.Cavaro, and a 15C Catalan triptych on a gold ground).

Museum: 100 yards to the SW, to the left of the Via Vittorio Emanuele, is the *Antiquarium Arborense.* This small museum of local history and culture displays valuable finds from the town's early history, including a *Dea Mater Mediterranea,* scarcely 1½ inches high, found by a shepherd boy in 1976.

Environs: Santa Giusta (3 km. S.): On a hill, the church of the same name was built in Pisan/Lombard Romanesque style in 1135–45. Despite Arab influence in the decorative motifs, this is Sardinia's best, consistent, example of this architectural style. There are lions above the portal under the flat architrave. The round arch above them contains a conspicuous cross of dark trachyte. Pilaster strips lead up to the high blind arcades. The powerful campanile with its double-arched windows has been well restored. Columns of marble and granite divide the interior into a nave and two aisles. Some of the capitals are of classical simplicity, while others are Romanesque with fabulous beings. On the left of the apse is a 15C marble tabernacle by A.Brebno. **Fordongianus:** Earlier, when known as *Forum Trajani*, it guarded the Tirso bridge and was an important fortified strongpoint against the 'Barbarici' mountain shepherds. Today it lies isolated. Only the pillars of the old *Roman bridge*, underneath the present Tirso bridge, still bear witness to the Roman domination. The thermal springs below Fordongianus were, under Punic and subsequently Roman occupation, enlarged into the *Aquae Hypsitanae* (sulphur springs of 40–60°C). 2 km. SW is the *Chiesetta S.Lussurgiu* (also *San Rossore*, so called because of its red trachyte), which was founded by monks from Southern France shortly after 1100. In *c.* 1250 a Gothic façade was added, and in the 15C a Catalan one (fine blind arcades along the sides and on the apse). The pecu-

Oristano, baroque portal by Vitu Sotto

liar early Christian *crypt* (4/5C) is a lon[g] catacomb with a tunnel vault and ancien[t] Christian walled-in sarcophagi, ending i[n] a semicircular apse. The broad plain an[d] the mountains to the E. are positivel[y] strewn with the *remains of nuraghi* an[d] *stone castles*. Of interest are the *Nuragh[e] Pizzinnu* near Milis (central tower wit[h] small outer towers), and *S'Uraki* to the W[.] of **San Vero Milis** (massive central towe[r] polygonal rampart with towers and re[-] mains of dwellings). Magnificent gateway[s] to estates are typical of this region. Littl[e] known examples include the *baroque gat[e-] way*, with its wrought-iron gate, of *Vit[u] Sotto* (some 430 yards N. of the church [of] *Madonna del Rimedio*), and the earlier ga[te] to the Villa of the Marchese Francesco Boy[l] di Putifigari. These two gates spawne[d] numerous, though more modest, imit[a-] tions. **Bonárcado** (on the SE slope o[f] Monte Ferru): The Romanesque *Chies[a] S.Maria* stands above the old town, wit[h] its steep alleyways lined by sombre basa[lt] houses. This church was formerly part o[f] a Camaldolese monastery attached to th[e] abbey of 'Santi Zeni e Romualdo' in Pis[a.] The main building and lower tower da[te] from the 12C. Arab stonemasons com[-] pleted the work in 1242, incorporatin[g] (this is quite clear in the apse) some Moo[r-] ish elements, the first in Sardinia. The soli[-] tary **San Salvatore** offers somethin[g] special (key from the attendant): A *pr[e-] Christian temple* with a sacred well (4[00] BC?). It lies underground and has ai[r] shafts because of the violent sandstorm[s] blowing from the dunes to the W. Th[e] tunnel-vaulted, cruciform crypt has som[e] additional chambers and a font. 3 m. S[.] is *S.Giovanni in (di) Sinis*. Easy to overloo[k,] it is probably the oldest church in Sardini[a] and is a 5C equal-armed Byzantine cruc[i-] form structure with a dome. In the 9/10[C] Benedictines from Marseille altered it i[n] rugged, massive Romanesque style. A *fo[nt] with a blue ground is certainly of later dat[e.] It bears a large fish. The violent sea win[d] has badly affected the church exterior. Fu[r-] ther to the S., **Tharros** has been excavat[ed] from the sand dunes. It is a typica[l] Phoenician-Punic port, being situated b[e-] hind a wall across an isthmus, with a ha[r-] bour on both sides of it. The town was lat[e]

Oristano, S. Giovanni in Sinis

built on by the Romans, but its inhabitants deserted it in the Middle Ages. Today, it provides more information about the Carthaginians than their North African home or other sites in Sardinia. Tharros is now divided into districts safeguarded by several barbed-wire fences, but is nevertheless worth seeing with a knowledgeable guide. New remains of the *defensive wall* have recently been uncovered inland, and a *font,* probably Christian (with a step for immersion purposes) has also been discovered.

Orroli 08030

Núoro/Sardinia   p.422 □ C 13

The sombre old part of the town has houses and stables, often still surrounded by walls, of dark basalt, as is the village church (1582), with its highly original campanile.

Environs: A protective barrier of *24 nuraghi* was built in *c.* 1000 BC on the plateau to the W. of the Lago di Flumendosa basso. The *Orrubiu* (also *Arrubiu,* i.e. red mountain) is the most extensive and impressive of these, covering over 21,500 sq.ft. (enlarged in the 8/7C BC). It is in very poor condition and little remains of a complex that consisted of a central tower with several storeys, a three-stage (?) inner defensive cordon, and an outer wall with five large towers and smaller, flanking outworks. The 16C parish church of *S. Sebastiano* in **Escalaplano** is one of the few churches in Sardinia to have been built during the Italian Renaissance. Around the village there are *domus de janas,* particularly in the Sa Fossada area. To the S. are the remains of a *nuraghic well* (Sa Fuenta Coberta). The village of **Armúngia,** which is still inhabited, is unusual in having a nuraghe beside the municipio. A steep, winding road leads to *Esterzili,* a

Tharros (Oristano), excavations

shepherd's village, and then becomes even steeper as it continues in a series of sharp bends across the saddle of Monte Santa Vittoria. 7 km. to the SE (on foot) is the rectangular nuraghic temple of *Domu d'Urgia*, which is today abandoned to ruin. The historically important *Pranu Murdegu* area is equally neglected.

Orta San Giulio 28016
Novara / Piedmont   p.412☐ C 3

S.Maria Assunta (Via Caire Albertoletti): parish church, founded in 1485, rebuilt in the 18C. *Facade* with steps, porch with columns and marble portal, 11C, with Renaissance decoration, restored in the 20C. Fine *paintings*.

Palazzo della Comunità (Piazza Motta),

1582, arcade, outdoor staircase, turret; inside there is a room with a baroque fresco.

Environs: Sacro Monte d'Orta (1.5 km.): Dedicated to St.Francis. Begun in 1590 and completed in the 17&18C. It consists of *20 chapels* scattered over the mountain. These contain frescos and terracottas of scenes from the life of the Saint. Early baroque. The frescos are by Morazzone, Nuvolone, Fiammenghino and others. The sculptors include Prestinari and Bussola. **Isola S.Giulio** (Lake Orta): The ancient **Basilica of S. Giulio,** one of the most important Romanesque buildings in the province of Novara. Dating from the 6C, it was completed in the 11C but in its present baroque form it is 18C. The capitals in the side aisles, and also the 11C campanile, are Romanesque. Inside, a 12C Romanesque *pulpit* with the symbols of the Evangelists and fantastic animals by Guglielmo di Volpiano. Numerous *fresco*

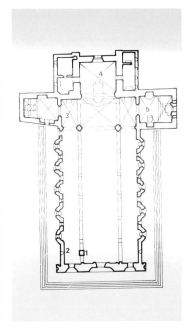

Orta San Giulio, Pal. d.Comunità

from the 15C (mainly the school of G.Ferrari) and 17C.

Orvieto, cathedral 1 Gothic font **2** Madonna by Gentile da Fabriano **3** Cappella del Corporale with Pietà by I.Scalza **4** choir stalls **5** chapel of Madonna di S. Brizio

Orvieto 05018

Terni/Umbria   p.414□G 8

Built on tufa, Orvieto, one of the largest cities in Umbria, resembles a fantastic island. It was a centre of Etruscan culture before the birth of Christ, but its name has remained unknown, as has its name under the Romans. It was not until the early Middle Ages that Orvieto was mentioned in writing as 'Urbs Vetus' or 'Urbibentus'. The city's unique situation soon made it the favourite refuge of the Popes. In 1157 an agreement was signed between the Pope and the free town of Orvieto, under which the Pope undertook to observe the city's independence. In return, the inhabitants ackowledged his desire to have a residence

in the city. The feast of Corpus Christi was established by Pope Urban IV in 1263. Despite this, Pope Martin IV was driven out of the city in 1282 because of the large number of French whom he had brought with him. Conditions among the citizens were also not always peaceful: there were frequent fights between the Monaldeschi, Filippeschi and Alberici families, with the whole city becoming involved. The city certainly benefited economically from the Popes' presence. At the time when Thomas Aquinas and Bonaventura da Bagnoregio were teaching at the 'Studium', the city became a cultural centre. Churches and palaces were built during this period. In *c.* 1450, Orvieto finally accepted direct Papal protection in order to escape the war, and it remained in the Papal States until 1860. In the course of the city's history, thirty-seven Popes lived in the fortified castle.

Cathedral: An architecturally unique building, Pope Nicholas IV laid its foundation stone to commemorate the miracle of Bolsena. The initial architect was probably Arnolfo di Cambio. He was followed by Ramo di Paganello from Sienna, who evidently made alterations to Arnolfo's design. The present façade is attributed to Lorenzo Maitani from Siena, architect from 1308–30. The splendid bas reliefs beside and between the portals are also by him and his fellow-workers (his son Vitale and Nicola di Nuto). They depict Scenes from Genesis; Prophets; the Life of Christ and the Last Judgement. The symbols of the Evangelists on the façade are also by L.Maitani. The tympanum of the main portal has a 'Madonna and Child' by Andrea Pisano. In the centre of the rose-window there is a 'Portrait of the Saviour' by Giovanni di Stefano from Siena. The square frame of the rose-window has 52 marble heads from the 4C; to the sides there are 12 prophets from the 14–16C, and above the rose-window, the twelve Apostles. The mosaics are 14C, but have frequently been altered since. Inside, the Latin cross ground plan is a conspicuous feature of the church, which has a nave and two aisles. The columns and side walls consist of alternating layers of black basalt and pale limestone. The transept displays very strong Gothic stylistic forms, while the nave is still partly characterized by a classical rhythm. To the right of the nave there are 16C holy-water stoups by A.Federighi. On the left: a Gothic font begun by Luca di Giovanni from Siena and continued by Jacopo di Piero Guidi from Florence and others. Side wall: a Madonna by Gentile da Fabriano. The apse is decorated with frescos by Ugolino di Prete Ilario and Pinturicchio. The left transept has the Cappella del Corporale, where the blood-stained cloth of Bolsena is preserved in a sumptuous reliquary, the work of Ugolino di Vieri (1338). On the chapel walls are frescos by Ugolino di Prete Ilario, which were reworked in the 19C. The large apse window by Giovanni Bonino from Assisi is to drawings by Maitani, who was in turn influenced by Simone Martini. However, the finest part of the cathedral is the *Cappella Nuova* and the right transept. In 1447, Beato Angelico painted the two vaults, depicting Christ in Judgement with Angels and Patriarchs. The work was continued in 1499 by Luca Signorelli, who created one of the most famous apocalyptic cycles. It shows the End of the World, the Sermon of the Antichrist (on the left, portraits of Signorelli and Beato Angelico), the Assembly of the Blessed, the Blessed entering Heaven, the Damned, the Resurrection of the Body. On the lower part of the wall there are medallions with portraits of poets. The fine marble Descent from the Cross by Ippolito Scalza is opposite the *Cappella dei Corpi Santi.*

Palazzo dei Papi: The 13C palace is built of tufa and is now the *Museo dell'Opera del Duomo.* The major exhibits include: Etruscan finds, and paintings by Andrea Pisano

Orvieto, cathedral, reliquary

Orvieto, cathedral

Orvieto, cathedral, Cappella Nuova, frescos

Cathedral, façade, detail

(Madonna and Child), Nicolò Nuti (Christ blessing), Simone Martini (Madonna and Child), Ippolito Scalza (St. Thomas) and Francesco Mochi (Angel of the Annunciation).

Palazzo Faina: This palace houses the interesting *Etruscan Museum* and stands opposite the cathedral.

S. Andrea: Stands on the Piazza della Repubblica. It was built in the 12C on the site of a 6C church (the remains can be seen in the underground passage). It was altered once again in the 14C. The twelve-sided campanile is partly influenced by the Lombard style, and partly by Roman military architecture of the Augustan period (e.g. the two polygonal towers by the Porta Venus in Spello). Inside is a 13C marble pulpit; the tomb of Magalotti in the style of Arnolfo di Cambio, with a fresco attributed to Ambrogio Lorenzetti.

Palazzo Comunale: This palace originates from the 13C and was rebuilt by Ippolito Scalza in 1573–81.

Palazzo del Popolo: This palace is to the NW of the Piazza della Repubblica. It is in Romanesque-Gothic style, on the model of the Palazzo della Ragione. The exterior is typical of the secular architecture of the times, with a large external staircase; inside there is a large hall.

S. Domenico: The first building dates from the 13C and was frequently altered thereafter. It contains the tomb of Cardinal de Braye by Arnolfo di Cambio, a masterpiece of Italian Gothic sculpture.

S. Giovenale: This church was built around 1000. However, the frescos by unknown local painters date from the 14&15C.

Maurizio: This charming 14C statue stands on a small tower on the Piazza del Duomo and strikes the hours.

Cathedral

Pozzo di San Patrizio: In 1527 Clement VII gave instructions for this well on the N. edge of the town to be built to plans by Antonio da Sangallo the younger. The well has two concentric staircases (248 steps leading to the bottom, 203 ft. down). It was intended to serve as a reservoir in the event of the city being besieged. Nearby is the fortress built by Cardinal Albornoz.

Necropolis: This Etruscan burial site from the 6C BC is a little way outside the centre, in the S. part of the city.

Etruscan temple: Near the well.

Osimo 60027
Ancona/Marches   p.414□I 7

Cathedral of S. Leopardo (Piazza del Duomo): The first church was built in the 4C AD on the remains of an ancient temple to Aesculapius. It was rebuilt in the 8&13C, and was last restored in 1956. In front of the 16C *façade* is a *portico* built of older structural components, 13/14C. The inside was altered in the 19C and ha columns from a 13C pulpit in front of th choir. In the crypt, an ancient sarcopha gus serves as the *altar table*, and the retabl with reliefs of the Magi and Moses, Noal and Jonah dates from the 6C, while the in scription is from 1751. The capitals ar from the 11&12C. Older fragments wer used for the *sarcophagus* of *Bishop Ber venuto*, who died in 1281.

The former **baptistery** is now the **mu seum** (Piazza del Duomo): the *font* b Paolo and Tarquino Iacometti dates from 1627.

Also worth seeing: *S.Giuseppe da Copei tino* (Piazza Gallo), 13C. *Palazzo Munici pale,* 1675, with the 13C Torre Civica.

Ostia 00050
Rome/Lazio   p.414□G 1

Roman tradition has it that Aeneas lande at Ostia. King Ancus Marcius is the town legendary founder. More recent researc

Orvieto, Palazzo dei Papi

has produced the date of 338 BC for the town's origin. Ostia was the main base for Roman maritime power in the period around 300 BC. The town wall, which was built when Ostia was founded, was rebuilt under Sulla (1.5 miles around). As early as the reign of the Emperor Augustus, deposits from the Tiber caused the coast to silt up, and this made it necessary to draw up new plans for the harbour. Emperor Claudius put these plans into effect on the right bank of the Tiber (work completed in AD 54). For the same reasons, Trajan had a pentagonal artificial basin built to the N. of the harbour in AD 103. This basin held up to 200 ships and was open towards the sea. The first and most serious reason for the town's decline was the decision by Constantine, in 314, to give administrative independence, and thus also genuine independence, to Portus Romae, which had, until then, been a part of Ostia. The collapse of the Empire, and the downfall of the city of Rome, meant that the harbour no longer had a function to fulfil and the town fell into disrepair. In *c.* 830, Pope Gregory IV founded a new settlement only a few hundred yards up the course of the Tiber as it ran prior to 1558).

Ostia Antica: In order to secure the mouth of the Tiber against marauding seafarers, a massive *Castello* was built here. Julius II, when still a cardinal, built a triangular castle with corner towers and included a tower erected under Martin V. Julius's architect, Baccio Pontelli (1483–6), incorporated the latest military developments of his period and made the castle into one of the first modern fortresses. Remains of frescos by Baldassare Peruzzi in a *bath for the soldiers* which still survives. Today the fortress is a storehouse for the excavations.

Ostia Scavi: The first excavations were carried out under Pius VII in the early 19C, and in 1855 under Pius IX Continuous, systematic and scientific excavation began in 1909 and the results give an exact picture of the town and its life. They also make it possible to follow the development of the Roman town beyond the example of Pompeii. Apart from the traditional Republican types of house (Pompeii), there are also 'Insulae', rented town houses with several storeys. Such houses are frequently combined into 'Caseggiati'.

Ostia, excavated mosaic

Ostia Antica, view

Sights: The **Via delle Tombe,** with numerous tombs from the Republic and Empire, runs parallel to the Via Ostiensis which ends at the Porta Romana. The town is entered through the **Porta Romana,** which was built in the Republican period and was decorated in the 1C AD. The *Piazzale della Vittoria* is at the beginning of the *Decumanus Maximus,* the main street, which is about 4,000 ft. long and is lined by the major public buildings. In the Piazzale is the **statue of Minerva Victoria.** Discovered in 1910, it is based on a 4C BC model in the manner of Scopas, and was part of the decoration of the town gate in the Imperial period.

Opposite are the **Terme dei Cisiarii** (of the coachmen), which were subsequently installed in a storehouse (Horrea) of the 1C BC. The floor mosaics depict the everyday life of Ostia. Further along the Decumanus, on the right, are the **Terme di Nettuno,** begun under Hadrian, with notable floor mosaics devoted to Neptune. A street just before the baths, the Via dei Vigili, leads to the *Caserma dei Vigili,* the firemen's barracks, 2C AD, with the *Caesareum* dedicated to the cult of the emperors, situated at the end of the street, on the left. To the N. of the theatre is the **Piazzale delle Corporazioni,** the commercial centre of Ostia, where more than 70 business houses had offices. The *arcade* in front of the offices which line the square has mosaic floors reflecting the far-flung trading links of Ostia. The *ruins of the Temple of Ceres* are in the centre of the square.

To the W. of the Piazzale is the **House of Apuleius,** a splendid house with an atrium, remains of columns, and mosaics. Abutting on this is the best-preserved of the town's 18 known temples to Mithras, known as the **Mithraeum delle Sette Spere,** after its surviving mosaics. Towards the Decumanus are four small *tem-*

ples from the 2C BC built on a single foundation.

In the **Via dei Molini,** which branches off to the right, are an enormous *granary* and *cereal mills* A side street, the **Via del Balconi** (V.di Diana), is lined by two-storeyed houses. The balconies of the *Casa di Diana,* a business and residential house, are evidence for their use in antiquity. Opposite this is the *Thermopolium,* a tavern with well-preserved original furnishings.

Forum, centre of the town's public life, with the mighty *Capitolium,* the main temple dedicated to Jupiter, Juno and Minerva. The imposing brick core of this (time of Hadrian) has survived. The remains of the *Temple of Rome and Augustus* (1C BC), built entirely of marble, with the statues both of Rome as Victory, dressed as an Amazon, and of Victory, are opposite the Capitolium. The *Baths* (2C, extended in the 4C) are on the E. side, the *Basilica* for public meetings is on the W. side, the *Curia* is to the N., and the *Tempio Rotondo* (3C AD) is to the W.

Towards the Tiber, to the W. of the Cardo, is a small *market square* surrounded by shops, and next to this is the **Horrea Epagathiana et Epaphroditiana,** a vast warehouse with a portal and a two-storeyed arcaded courtyard. Close by is the 4C **Domus di Amore e Psiche,** a house arranged around an inner courtyard.

Between the *Via della Foce* and the *Cardine degli Aurighi,* which both branch off from the Decumanus, are the **Baths of the 7 Sages** with rich frescos and mosaics, and the **Insula degli Aurighi** (house of the chariot drivers). These present a single façade to the street. On the Decumanus is the **Basilica Cristiana,** originally a bath, converted into an early Christian church in the 2–4C AD. The **Schola di Traianum** was the shipowners' seat.

Near the *Porta Marina* is the **Casa delle Muse** with a restored pillared arcade around the inner courtyard, and good frescos. Behind this is the **Casa a Giardino,** a residential complex without any shops, built around a garden. A good example of Roman domestic life. By the *Porta Laurentina* is the triangular *Campus Magnae Matris,* completed under Antoninus

Pius, with shrines of Oriental cults. The harbour facilities were uncovered in very recent excavations.

The **Museo Ostiense,** located E. of the Cardo, towards the bank of the Tiber, with its own access road, contains the most important finds from Ostia and its burial grounds.

Environs: Isola Sacra (2 km. towards Fiumincino): Laid out under Trajan, it was the necropolis of the Imperial harbour of Portus.

Ostuni 72017
Brindisi/Apulia   p.418☐ I O 11

Cathedral: Built in late Gothic style in 1470–95. Pre-baroque façade. A nave and two aisles, each of which has its own portal and rose-window in the façade. There are blind arcades on the façade and on the flanks.

Also worth seeing: *S.Spirito* dating from 1637 (Piazza XX Settembre), with scenes from the life of the Virgin on the Renaissance portal. *Vito Castello,* a bishop's palace on the site of the Norman castle torn down in the 16C.

Environs: Some 8 km. SE, **Carovigno** has remains of a *megalithic wall* and a 15C *castle.* Some 15 km. SE, **San Vito dei Normanni:** On the road to Brindisi a turning leads to the grotto churches of *S. Biagio* and *S.Giovanni,* with their interesting 12/14C Byzantine frescos.

Otranto 73028
Lecce/Apulia   p.418☐P/Q 12

Otranto is the easternmost town in Italy. Under the Byzantines it was the secular and ecclesiastical metropolis of Salento but under the Normans it was replaced by Lecce. In 1480 it was taken by the Turks ('sacco di Otranto', massacre of 800 inhabitants) and since then it has been of only secondary political importance.

Otranto, cathedral, mosaic pavement

Cathedral of S. Annunziata: A colonnaded Romanesque basilica with a nave and two aisles, begun by Bohemond in 1080 (see Canosa di Púglia). Crypt consecrated in 1088, nave completed after 1150. Baroque portal, and above it a late Gothic rose-window. Inside, the 17/18C baroque decoration have largely been removed, except for the coffered ceiling. Colonnaded arcades, some of whose capitals are ancient. The main feature of artistic interest is the *mosaic pavement*, extending across the entire interior: it was laid down by Pantaleon in 1163–6 (there is an inscription near the depiction of the building of Noah's Ark). A tree grows out of the back of two elephants (near the main portal) and extends towards the apse, with branches to left and right. Pictures of animals, fabulous beings, heroes (including Alexander the Great), Bible stories, signs of the zodiac, and much more. To the right of the chancel is the *Cappella dei Martiri*, containing the remains of 560 of the town's inhabitants who were executed in 1480 (see above); the execution stone is under the altar. Underneath the church is a *crypt* which is well worth seeing. The entrance is in the right aisle, and it has 42 columns of many different stones (marble, porphyry, granite), and also different types of capitals—Roman, Byzantine and medieval; remains of Byzantine frescos.

S. Pietro: 10/11C; the only cruciform Byzantine church with a dome in Apulia to have survived completely undamaged. Cylindrical dome, three semicircular apses. The interior is decorated throughout with 11–13C *frescos* of the Church Fathers and Saints; scenes from the Life of Christ; Old Testament scenes (Adam and Eve). The dome shows a Christ Pantocrator.

Also worth seeing: *Castle*, built by the Aragonese in 1485–98 around a Hohenstaufen core; bastions were added by Charles V. Nearby, *S. Maria dei Martiri* commemorates the victims of the 'sacco di Otranto' (see above).

Environs: Some 5 km. along the coast road leading S.is **S.Nicola di Casole**, the remains of a *Basilian monastery* important in the 13C (today it is a farm, but it is open). Some 10 km. W., in **Giurdignano**, the grotto church of *del Salvatore* (three domes, 8C), a beautiful *menhir* and a *dolmen tomb* near the village; some 15 km. NE, **Carpignano** with the grotto church of *SS. Cristina e Marina* (oldest known frescos in Apulia, 10&11C). Some 16 km. S., **Castro**, with the stalactite caves of *Grotta Romanelli* and *Grotta Zinzulusa*, which are of palaeontological interest.

Ottana 08020
Núoro/Sardinia   p.422 □ C 12

S. Nicola: This massive Romanesque building of dark and greenish-violet trachyte was built in 1140–70 as a bishop's church on the lines of S.Maria of Regno in Sardara (q.v.). The sides bear pilaster strips and high up, beneath the roof, plain

Ottana, S. Nicola, triptych

blind arcades. At the E. end is a small, rudimentary, converted campanile. The W. side is all the more decorative by contrast, with its three rows of blind arcades, all adorned with inlaid tiles. A fine double-arched window over the portal relaxes the otherwise uniform severity.

Environs: To the S., the edge of the mountainous country is full of the *remains of nuraghi* and *domus de janas*. In the Bingas valley there is a massive, upended Neolithic slab, which has clearly been worked on its lower side. Known as the *Altare de Lógula*, it is possibly a dolmen. The *Barbagia Ollolai*, which always resisted the Romans, begins on the hill of **Sarule**, known for its recently discovered old carpet patterns. The 16C late Gothic village church of *San Gavino* still has its massive campanile and a beautiful Gothic rose-window over a Renaissance portal. The single-aisled interior has pointed arches, while the

side chapels have Gothic ribbed arches; the Gothic stellar vault survives above the choir. **Teti,** known for the 'Warrior of Teti' (National Archaeological Museum in Cagliari), which was, however, found in the nuraghic refuge of Abini, 11 km. to the N. In **Orotelli,** which was a bishopric before Ottana, the *Romanesque church* (1200 –25) was later altered on the lines of S. Nicola in Ottana. 10 km. N. of Ottana, the old *Bagni Oddini* baths (sulphur spring at *c.* 36°C) above the Roman bath were restored in 1977 and can now be used again. A little to the N. of the Contoniera di Tirso, there are 3 historic buildings standing close together: *Nuraghe Lucca, old church* (15C), and the modern church of *Madonna della Neve*. After 8 km., on the E. edge of the Gocceano, with its nuraghi, and to the W. of **Bottida,** there stands the *ruined fortress of Burgos*. Built from 1130 onwards on a steep granite hilltop, it was a key military position in the decades of struggle between the Giudicati of Arborea and Torres, as well as having an eventful history in other ways. The fortress fell into disrepair in the 16C, and treasure seekers moved in and laid waste to it. To the W. of **Benetutti,** the beautiful *Nuraghe S'Aspru* is worth visiting, and the massive *Nuraghe Boes* to the NW of Nule is also of interest. Nule, famous for the recent development of its old carpet patterns, has the unspoiled 13C *Chiesetta di S.Paolo* on the W. edge of town.

Ozieri 07014

Sassari/Sardinia   p.422☐C 12

Mentioned as a town in 1838, Ozieri, whose name derives from the Roman 'octo', is surrounded by pastures and fields on the almost treeless 'Tola' plain. The town is shaped like an amphitheatre open towards the W., with steep steps rising on all sides from the main square, the *Piazza Cantareddu.* Like the houses in Orgosolo, the houses here have loggias supported by columns.

Cathedral: Originally 16C, it is situated in the upper town at the top of a beautiful, wide flight of steps. When G.Cima carried out his neoclassical alterations in the 19C, he did not touch the Aragonese Gothic transept. In the *sacristy,* an altarpiece with several wings depicts the story of the 'Madonna di Loretto'. It is definitely the work of a 'master of Ozieri' (*c.* 1540), who belonged to the Hispano-Flemish school but is unknown. The Spanish crucifix in the *Chiesa S. Lucia* is given an earlier date (1380/5).

Environs: The digging of caves was, in the distant past, rendered easier by the splintery slates and limestones in the granite of the environs. The most significant of these caves is that of *San Michele,* discovered in 1914 and the centre of the *San Michele culture.* This, the most highly developed aspect of the Sardinian neolithic period, is named after the cave. The *domus de janas* are also typical, and are interconnected at several points inside. Some details of the caves and of the unique ceramic finds can best be seen in the museums. The *Grotta del Carmine,* with similar finds, is to the N., by the church of the same name. The unique twin towered *Nuraghe Burghidu* is some 11 km. to the N.

Padova/Padua 35100
Padua/Veneto   p.410☐G 3

In Roman times, when known as 'Patavium', it was one of the most important towns in northern Italy. In the Middle Ages it was a free town and opposed the Hohenstaufens. From 1405 onwards it was subject to Venice. Padua was the home town of the Roman historian Livy (59 BC –AD 17) and the town where St. Anthony of Padua (1195–1231), the famous preacher of penitence, was active, although he was a native of Lisbon. The famous university was founded in 1222.

Cathedral of S.Maria Assunta (Piazza Duomo): This Renaissance cathedral was rebuilt in 1551–82 but it originally dates from the 9C and was also rebuilt in the 12C

Padua, S. Giustina

after being destroyed. Enlarged in the 17C (side chapels, drum of the dome). The façade is of unfaced bricks. The chancel has three apses and sturdy pilasters. Inside: the nave consists of two cruciform structures, each with a dome, one behind the other; the bays having alternating domes and tunnel vaults. The transepts end in apses. Interesting *contents:* On the left of the right transept is the tomb of Cardinal Zabarella (1427) with beautiful figures (Virgin, Saints). There is a 13/14C painting of the Madonna in Byzantine style in the apse of the same transept. The tomb of Bishop Barocci (d. 1507) by Tullio Lombardo is on the right of the left transept; on the left wall there is a fine late Gothic tomb (*c.* 1420). There are some notable paintings (including: Scenes from the Life of St. Sebastian, 1367; a Flight into Egypt, by Fr.Bassano) in the *Sagrestia dei Canonici* to the left of the chancel. The entrance to the *crypt,* where the altar table is an ancient sarcophagus, is to the right of the chancel.

Baptistery (N. side of the cathedral): An earlier baptistery was rebuilt in 1260; the new dome was painted after 1370 by the Florentine artist Menabuoi.

The portico dates from approximately the same period. The baptistery is decorated outside with pilaster strips and friezes of round arches. The interior is square in shape, with a massive dome on pendentives, and the altar area also has a dome. The building's main decorations are the *frescos* by Menabuoi: Christ Pantocrator surrounded by Angels and Saints in the main dome, whilst in the drum there are scenes from the Old Testamnent, and the pendentives bear frescos of the Evangelists. On the walls there are scenes from the New Testament (note the Crucifixion above the triumphal arch). The Descent of the Holy Ghost is painted on the small dome. The altar has a *polyptych,* also by Menabuoi, of the Virgin Enthroned and John the Baptist.

Cappella degli Scrovegni also known as the *Arena chapel,* since it stands on the floor of the ancient amphitheatre on the Corso Garibaldi. Built by Enrico Scrovegni in 1303–5. A simple brick building, with few features on the outside. The inside is a long tunnel-vaulted rectangle; there is a low polygonal chancel with a ribbed vault. The chapel contains the famous *fresco cycle* by Giotto (painted *c.* 1305/6; the largest and most important surviving work by this artist): the Story of the Virgin and the Life of Christ are depicted on the side walls in three rows one above the other, beginning at the top front right and ending at the bottom front left. The Last Judgement is on the entrance wall, and the frescos on the triumphal arch include God the Father Enthroned. At the

Padua, S.Antonio (Il Santo) 1 burial chapel of St. Antony **2** Cappella della Madonna Mora **3** Cappella del Beato Luca Belludi **4** High altar with work by Donatello **5** Cappella del Tesoro **6** Cappella di S.Felice **7** Cappella del Sacramento

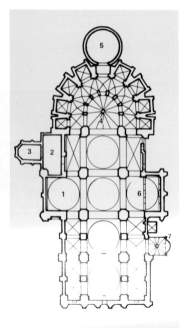

altar is a fine *Gothic statue of the Madonna* by G.Pisano. In the apse, paintings of Saints by Menabuoi. The *sarcophagus* of Enrico Scrovegni, the founder of the church (see above; d. 1336), is behind the altar.

Chiesa degli Eremitani (SS. Filippo e Giacomo, Piazza Eremitani): Built by Augustinian hermits from 1276 onwards as a Gothic monastery church, and completed in the mid-14C. Destroyed by bombs in 1944 and rebuilt as a copy of the original in 1946–50. The façade is divided in two: a lower section of round-arched niches on either side of the portal, and an upper one with pilaster strips and a rose-window, crowned by a gable. The *side portal* dating from 1442 is especially interesting. It is an early Renaissance work by the Tuscan artist Baroncelli. The interior is single-aisled, with three rib-vaulted choir chapels; the vaulted wooden ceiling has been reconstructed in its original form. There are four side chapels to the right of the nave. Just in front of the choir, on the right, is the entrance to the *Cappella Ovetari*, which contains the remnants of the famous fresco cycle painted by A.Mantegna in 1448–56

(only two scenes, the Assumption of the Virgin and the Martyrdom of St. Christopher, survive; the rest was destroyed in 1944, see above). Other features: a 14C painted *crucifix* by Guariento di Arpo on the high altar. 14C *Gothic wall paintings,* including a Madonna by Menabuoi, in the Cappella Sanguinacci to the left of the choir. On the side wall to the left of the nave is the *Renaissance tomb* of M.M.Benavides by B.Ammannati (1546).

S.Antonio/Il Santo (Piazza del Santo): A pillared basilica built in 1232–1307 to commemorate St.Antony of Padua; a stylistic mixture of Romanesque, Gothic and Byzantine structural forms. The *Cappella del Tesoro* was added in 1690–1739. 375 ft. long and 180 ft. wide, the ground plan displays a mixture of French and Italian influence. The nave and two aisles with a wide transept are typical of the churches of the Italian mendicant orders, whilst the connecting bay and the polygonal choir are French. The classical complex with its 5 domes (see S.Marco in Venice) has been lengthened by 1 dome in each direction (the dome over the crossing is conical, the choir dome has Gothic ribs). Lombard-

Il Santo, Miracle of the Donkey by Donatello

style façade, with blind arcades below, and above them a dwarf gallery with fine capitals. The outer walls of the nave and transept are of brick, and the choir also has dwarf galleries. Inside there are a number of interesting works of art: in the left transept, through an arched entrance, is the so-called *Cappella dell'Arca del Santo*, the chapel containing the tomb of the Saint, built in 1500–46; the Saint's relics are in the altar (many votive gifts); on the walls there are 16C high reliefs of scenes from the Saint's life by J.Sansovino, T.Lombardo and others. The *Cappella della Madonna Mora*, with a fine late Gothic tomb on the right, and a marble Madonna (1396) on the front wall, is entered from here. On the left is the passage leading to the *Cappella del Beato Luca Belludi* dating from 1382, with frescos by Menabuoi. The high altar bears some famous Donatello bronzes (1446–50): on the front the so-called *Man of Sorrows* and angels playing music, the retable has the Miracle of St. Antony, above this is the Virgin Enthroned, and beside her are St.Francis and St.Antony. There is an Entombment on the rear. The choir leads to the magnificent baroque *Cappella del Tesoro* (see

above). The *Cappella di S.Felice* (right transept) houses a masterly *fresco of the Crucifixion* by Altichiero Altichieri (1377 –9). Some interesting *Renaissance tombs* in the nave. On the right, at the beginning of the ambulatory, is the entrance to the 13C *Chiostro del Capitolo* with its fine early Christian sarcophagi. The SE corner leads to the 15C *Chiostro del Noviziato*.

In the immediate *vicinity of the basilica* are: In the square in front of the church, Donatello's famous *equestrian statue of Gattamelata* (his real name was Erasmo da Narni, a Venetian condottiere; his tomb is in the Cappella del Sacramento by the right aisle). Executed in 1447-53, it is the first bronze Renaissance monument of its kind. On the right of the church is the *Scuola del Santo* dating from 1427; an interesting feature on the upper storey of the chapter house is the 16C *fresco cycle* (including 'St. Antony having a new-born child testify to his mother's innocence', by Titian, 1511). The *Oratorio di S. Giorgio* dating from 1377, with walls frescoed by Altichiero Altichieri (1378–84), is to the left of the Scuola.

S.Giustina (Prato della Valle): A Roman-

Gattamelata statue by Donatello

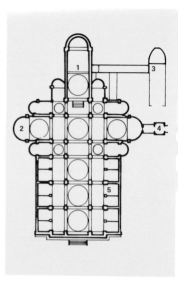

Padua, S.Giustina 1 choir stalls and painting by Veronese (Martyrdom of St.Justina) **2** sarcophagus of Luke **3** Coro Vecchio **4** Sacello di S. Prosdocimus **5** death of St. Scholastica, by L.Giordano

esque Benedictine church rebuilt from 1521 onwards in High Renaissance form, and completed after 1580, V.Scamozzi being one of the artists. This is the largest Renaissance church in the Veneto (364 ft. long on the inside, 249 ft. wide at the transept). It consists of two sections, firstly the nave and crossing, and secondly the chancel, and is a cruciform, domed basilica. Inside: a nave with two aisles and three domes, and six chapels in each of the aisles; a large square crossing surmounted by a dome, with three domed chapels on each of three sides (the chapels end in apses; the longer central chapel has a monks' choir). Interesting *contents:* behind the high altar is P.Veronese's Martyrdom of St.Justina (1575), and the choir has magnificent carved *choir stalls* with scenes from the Old and New Testaments — the work of the French artist R.Taurigny, 1558–66. The relics of St.Luke the Evangelist are in an alabaster sarcophagus (fine 14C reliefs) in

the apse of the left transept. A passage leads from the left-hand chapel of the right transept to the the so-called *Coro Vecchio* (the monks' choir of the earlier Romanesque building, see above), with fine 15C choir stalls. The entrance to the *Sacello di S. Prosdocimo,* an early Christian cruciform, domed basilica, is in the right transept; the altar has a 5/6C relief depicting St.Prosdocimus, the 1st bishop of Padua. The 'Death of St. Scholastica' by Luca Giordano is in the 4th chapel on the right. There are three cloisters from the 15/16C to the S.of the church.

Palazzo della Ragione (between Piazza delle Erbe and Piazza delle Frutta): The medieval town hall, also known as *Il Salone,* is today used as a concert hall. An earlier building (a law court) was converted

Gattamelata statue by Donatello

Il Santo   *Cappella degli Scrovegni* ▷

in 1306, at which time the assembly hall on the upper floor was frescoed throughout by Giotto; rebuilt in 1420–35 after a fire, with the addition of the arcades to the long sides). The exterior has two-storeyed loggias and a ridged roof. The interior is an enormous room (about 260 ft. long, 89 ft. wide, 89 ft. high) with *frescoed walls* (the lower zone dates from the 14C, some of the work being by Menabuoi; the upper zone was repainted after 1420, the artists including G. and N.Miretto); they depict the *cycle of months,* with an average of 26 pictures per month. On the W. wall is a wooden copy of the Gattamelata horse dating from 1466. The 16C *Palazzo del Podesta,* the modern town hall, with a fine inner courtyard, is to the E. of the Salone. On the N. side is the *Palazzo del Consiglio* (1283), with a fine front on the Piazza delle Frutta.

Museo Civico (Piazza del Santo): The collection was begun in 1880 (prehistoric and archaeological department on the ground floor, picture gallery on the upper floor). Interesting paintings include: room 1: Giotto, crucifix from the Cappella dei Scrovegni (see above). Room 2: 15/16C Venetian masters, including Fr.Morone, G.Bellini. Room 7: Paintings by J. and D.Tintoretto, P.Veronese and others. The N. wing houses 17/18C Venetian paintings (note the works by G.B.Piazzetta and G.B.Tiepolo).

Also worth seeing: Church of *S.Francesco* (Via S.Francesco), dating from 1416. 18C church of *S. Lucia* (Via S. Lucia). 16C *Scuola di S.Rocco* (near the above church). Church of *S. Maria del Carmine* (Piazza Petrarca), *c.* 1500. Late-14C church of *S. Maria dei Servi* (Via Roma), with a fine portico. 14C church of *S.Nocolò* (near the Via Dante), with an altarpiece by G.D.Tiepolo (1777). Church of *S.Maria in Vanzo* (Via Seminario) dating from 1436,

with fine paintings, including an Entombment by J.Bassano, 1574. Church of *S. Sofia* (Via Altinata), founded in the 9C, with fine Byzantine capitals inside. *Piazza dei Signori* with the 16C church of *S. Clemente*, the *Loggia del Consiglio* (built 1496–1533) on the S.side, the *Palazzo del Capitano* on the W. side (built in 1599–1605 as the residence of the Venetian governor of the city). *Liviano* (Piazza Capitaniato) with the *Sala dei Giganti* and the *Loggia Carrarese* (1343). The *university* (known as the Palazzo del Bò, Via 8.Feb.) with a splendid 16C Renaissance courtyard; to the S.is the *Piazza Antenore* with the tomb of the mythical founder of the city, Antenor (1283/4). *Caffè Pedrocchi* (Via 8.Feb.) dating from 1831, an artists' meeting place. Numerous palaces from all periods. Of the city gates, the 13C *Porta Altinata* (Via Altinate) is the most interesting. Remains of the ancient Roman *Ponte di S.Lorenzo* below the Riviera dei Ponti Romani.

Environs: Some 15 km. SW, **Montegrotto Terme,** a much-frequented spa. About 15 km. W., the 11C **Abbey of Praglia** (notable 15C church; a fine 16C fresco of the Crucifixion by B.Montagna in the monastery refectory; the *Cortile Pensile,* a cloister dating from 1495, and the monastery library are also interesting). In **Monteortone,** a few miles to the SE of Praglia, is the 15C *Santuario della Madonna della Salute* (the choir has famous frescos by J.da Montagnana, 1497).

Paestum 84063

Salerno/Campania   p.418□L 12

Paestum was originally known as Poseidonia when it was founded in *c.* 600 BC by Greeks from Sybaris in the Gulf of Tarento. It was taken over by Lucanians in the 4C BC and from 273 BC onwards it was under Roman rule. After being destroyed by the Saracens in the 9C, the town was deserted by its inhabitants, who founded Capaccio, some 15 km. inland. It was plundered once again by the Normans under Robert Guiscard and the town fell into complete oblivion until the 18C, one reason being its site in a malaria-infested lowland. The ruined temples of Paestum make it one of the most

Padua, Scuola del Santo, Titian fresco

interesting towns to visit in Magna Graecia.

The so-called 'Basilica': Oldest temple in Paestum, mid-6C BC; the name was arbitrarily chosen in the 18C, and today it is fairly certain that the building was devoted to Hera. A peripteral form with 9 by 18 baseless columns; dimensions 177 ft. by 77 ft. The column shafts swell considerably, and the capitals are bulbous. A two-aisled cella with a pronaos 'in antis'. Some of the metopes survive above the architrave on the inside. The roof has not survived. There is a *sacrificial altar* (71 ft. by 20 ft.) on the E. side in front of the temple; beside it is a *bothros*, a square shaft for the remains of the sacrifices.

The so-called 'Temple of Neptune': Actually dedicated to Hera Argiva; the most beautiful and best-preserved temple in Paestum. Built in the classical Doric style in *c.* 450 BC. A peripteros on a stylobate of three steps with 6 by 14 columns; the dimensions are 197 ft. by 79 ft. The columns are of travertine and as a result they are much eroded in parts. The capitals are well preserved. A three-aisled cella with an opisthodomos and pronaos, both 'in antis'; two orders of columns one above the other in the cella. In front of the temple are the remains of two *sacrificial altars*.

Forum: A rectangular structure (490 ft. by 87 ft.) built in the 3C BC on the site of the old Greek Agora. Originally surrounded by a splendid arcade with late Doric columns. On the N. side is the so-called *Tempio Italico* from the 3C BC, probably dedicated to the Olympian triad of Jupiter, Juno and Minerva; today some of the columns are in Salerno, where they have been used in other buildings. Just to the right is the so-called *Teatro Greco*, a circular structure, possibly used as a meeting place. The *Via Sacra*, uncovered in 1907, the processional street of the ancient town, runs past the W. side of the forum.

Sacello Sotteraneo: A shrine to Hera from the 6C BC uncovered only in 1954 (dimensions 13 ft. by 10 ft. by 7 ft.). Built of limestone blocks, roofed with clay bricks. White stucco decoration inside; the important finds, including iron spears, bronze vessels, some still filled with honey,

Paestum, museum, Tomba piccola

Paestum, Temple of Neptune

and a magnificent Attic vase with black figures, are in the museum.

Temple of Ceres: Actually dedicated to Athene; built in the late 6C BC in the Archaic-Doric style. The peripteros has 6 by 13 columns (dimensions 108 ft. by 48 ft.). Much of the entablature survives. Rectangular cella with pronaos (this is where the oldest Ionic columns on Italian soil were found). Remnants of the *stucco* and of the original *painting* survive.

Museum: A modern building dating from 1952 and housing the finds from Paestum, the surrounding burial grounds and the shrine to Hera at the mouth of the river Sele (see below). Outstanding exhibits: six *metopes* from the above Heraion (6C BC) in room I on the ground floor; room II has some more metopes from the Heraion; the last one on the right, a warrior brandishing a lance, is especially fine (*c.* 490 BC).

A *metope frieze* from the above Heraion on the outer walls of the central hall. On the left wall of room III, the central room, there is a fine *clay statue of Zeus* from the 6C BC; to the left of it is a *female bust* (also 6C BC). The *finds from the subterranean shrine to Hera* in Paestum are just to the left of the entrance; there are also some fine *Greek vases* and the *Tomb of the Diver* (5C BC), with the only surviving classical Greek wall paintings.

Also worth seeing: The *Roman amphitheatre* (today it is cut in two by the SS 18). *Foundations of houses of the Greek town* (laid out like a chessboard). A tour may be made around the *town walls* (total length almost 3 miles), which are mostly very well preserved, some dating from the Greek period; the *Porta Marina* is of considerable interest.

Environs: Some 12 km. N. is the *Shrine*

of *Hera Argiva* on the Sele river, uncovered in 1934–40 (research is still in progress). Founded in the 7C BC. The *foundations of the large Temple of Hera* from the 6C BC survive (pseudoperipteros; dimensions 128 ft. by 62 ft.; the metopes are in the museum). The *remains of the oldest Temple of Hera* in the shrine are immediately to the N.; the metopes found here are also in the museum of Paestum.

Palazzolo Acreide 96010
Syracuse/Sicily   p.420☐ L 18

Founded as 'Akrai' (see below), by Syracuse in 664 BC. One of the few Greek colonies in inland Sicily.

Archaeological zone of Akrai. *Greek theatre:* 3C BC, built from the living rock; very well preserved. It held some 700 spectators (an indication of the ancient town's small population), 12 rows of seats, stage restored by the Romans. The *floor surface of the orchestra* is well preserved. To the right of the theatre are the foundations of the **Bouleuterion** (town hall), a rectangular building. *Latomia l'Intagliata* and *Latomia l'Intagliatella* (behind the theatre): quarries with rock caves from the Greek period. It was a place of hero worship in ancient times (*reliefs* on the walls of the second quarry), and was used for cultic purposes in the early Christian period too.

Also worth seeing: The *Chiesa dell' Immacolata* (Corso Vitt. Emanuele III; in the town), with a fine Madonna by Francesco Laurana (1470). In the archaeological zone there are: the remains of a *Temple of Aphrodite* (above the quarries), the *Templiferali* (SE of the theatre; another place of hero worship), the *Santóni* (about ½ mile SE of the theatre; rock sculptures used in the cult of Cybele), and the *antiquarium* at the entrance.

Environs: Some 4 km. SE (road to Noto) is **Eremo di S.Lucia** with early Christian excavations (*tomb, rock basilica*).

Palermo 90100
Palermo/Sicily   p.420☐I 16

Palermo was founded by the Phoenicians and was known as 'Panormus' ('Good Harbour') by the Greeks. The main town of the Carthaginians in Sicily, it became Roman in 254 BC. During the period of the barbarian invasions it was Ostrogoth until AD 535, but was then recaptured by Belisarius for Byzantium. It fell prey to the Saracens in the 9C, and was Norman from 1072 onwards; in 1194 it fell to the Hohenstaufens by inheritance. In 1266, after the downfall of the Hohenstaufens, it was ruled by the Angevins who were expelled in 1282 in the famous rebellion of the *Sicilian Vespers* and replaced by the Aragonese. Various rulers then followed. The Bourbons were expelled by Garibaldi in 1860.

Cathedral of S.Maria Assunta (Piazza d.Cattedrale): Consecrated under King William II of Sicily in 1185 (nothing survives of the earlier buildings, a Byzantine church and a mosque). The structure was altered repeatedly in the following centuries, and the dome was only added in the 18C. Much of the original building remains at the *E. end* (Arab-Norman structural elements in the three apses and the two towers). The *W. end* is in Gothic and baroque styles; the façade dates from the 14/15C, and the 12C campanile is con-

Palermo, cathedral 1 tombs of Norman and Hohenstaufen Kings and Emperors **2** chapel of St. Rosalia

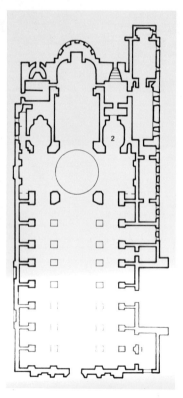

Palermo, cathedral, sarcophagus

nected by arches to the body of the church. *S.side:* 15C porch; a verse from the Koran on a column, late Gothic decoration on the gable; early-15C portal with carved wooden leaves. *Interior:* Completely altered in the late 18C. To the left of the entrance, at the end of the right aisle, a double chapel, houses the famous Royal Tombs: the *sarcophagi of Roger II of Sicily* (d. 1154); *his daughter Constance* (d. 1198); her husband, the German *Emperor Henry VI* (d. 1197); their son, *Emperor Frederick II Hohenstaufen* (d. 1250). To the right of the choir is the *Cappella di S.Rosalia,* the town's patron saint (her relics are in a silver urn). The *crypt* (two aisles, a part of the original Norman structure) includes the *tomb of Walter of the Mill* (Gualterio Offamilio), the archbishop of Palermo and founder of the cathedral. The church contains a number of *sculptures* by Antonello Gagini and a *Madonna* by F.Laurana.

La Martorana (S.Maria dell'Ammiraglio, Piazza Bellini): Built in Byzantine-Norman style in 1143 by George of Antioch, the admiral of Roger II (hence the church's name). The campanile is 12C. A cruciform, domed basilica with three apses and a *narthex* reaching as far as the tower (Renaissance alterations). The Byzantine-style *mosaics,* laid down at the time of the church's building, are the main object of interest: to the right of the entrance Roger II is shown being crowned by Christ, and on the left George of Antioch appears at the feet of the Virgin Mary. Christ Pantocrator, surrounded by angels, appears in the dome; on the drum there are Old and New Testament scenes (Prophets, Apostles).

S.Cataldo (Piazza Bellini, beside the Martorana): First mentioned in the 12C. Arab-Norman style with three domes. Inside, a nave, two aisles and three apses. Fine *ancient columns,* with Arab-style arches above them. The original *pavement mosaic* survives; the walls are bare, and the architecture makes a strong impression in consequence.

S. Giovanni degli Eremiti (Via dei Benedettini): In 1132 Roger II built on to an existing mosque. The ground plan is T-shaped. There are two domes above the nave, a dome above the middle of the transept, and another dome above the right

Palermo, cathedral

transept, while the campanile (also domed) rises above the left transept. The church interior has no windows. The right transept joins the former mosque (a two-aisled rectangular room), and the side wall of the former mosque courtyard forms the right wall of the church (beautiful arches). The *cloister* is very atmospheric (13C; pointed arches on double columns; exotic plants.)

Cappella Palatina (in the Palazzo dei Normanni, Piazza d.Parlamento): Consecrated in 1140 as a court chapel under Roger I; its purely Norman style survives. A basilica (one nave, two aisles) with *Corinthian columns,* some of them ancient and Arab-style pointed arches. A raised choir with three apses, and a dome above it. The choir is separated from the nave by a *marble transenna.* There are *mosaics* on all the walls and in the dome (12–14C; Christ Pantocrator and Biblical scenes). The *ceiling* is colourfully painted and decorated in Arab style. An interesting *mosaic pavement.* The *throne of Roger I* is in the nave, and there is a richly decorated Easter candlestick to the right of the choir, beside a fine ambo decorated with mosaics. The *tomb of the Norman king, William I* (the Bad) is in the crypt.

S.Giovanni dei Lebbrosi (Via Salv. Cappello; on the outskirts): One of the oldest Norman churches in Sicily. Founded by Roger I in 1070, and completed in the 12C (a lepers' hospital was added at the same time; hence the name of the church). The campanile is modern, in the Arab style. The interior is a basilica with a nave, two aisles, a hemispherical dome and three apses. The remains of an Arab building (*Castello d'Iethria*) are to the right of the church.

S.Spirito (Chiesa del Vespro, Cimitero d. S.Orsola): It became famous as the place where the 'Sicilian Vespers' rebellion began in 1282. Founded by Walter of the Mill (see Cathedral) in c. 1178; later taken over by the Cistercians; restored in the 19C. Pointed blind arcades (black lava used as decoration) on the flanks. The interior has a nave, two aisles and three apses; open timber ceiling with remains of the old

paintwork. Fine 16C sarcophagi in the chancel.

S.Domenico (Piazza S.Domenico): 14C, with fine baroque façade. One nave, two aisles, and the ground plan is a Latin cross. Inside, interesting *tombs* of famous citizens of Palermo, including the politician Francesco Crispi (1819–1901) in the chapel to the right of the choir. The entrance to the fine 14C *cloister* is to the left of the church. On the E. side (Via Bambinai) is the *Oratorio del Rosario di S. Domenico* with notable *stuccoes* by the local artist Giacomo Serpotta (1656–1732); the *Madonna del Rosario* by van Dyck (c. 1628) is on the high altar.

S. Giuseppe dei Teatini (Corso Vitt.Emanuele): Built in 1612–45; 18C *dome,* roofed with majolica in various colours; the *drum* is decorated with double columns. The interior has a nave and two aisles, and each of these is separated from the next by 14 marble columns. The ground plan is a Latin cross. Beautiful *stucco* and *frescos* (restored after war damage) on the ceiling of the nave. The *Chiesa della Madonna della Provvidenza* occupies the crypt under the church.

S.Francesco d'Assisi (Piazza S.Francesco d'Assisi): Built in 1255–77 and later frequently rebuilt and altered. A fine early-14C Gothic *portal* on the façade, with an interesting rose-window above it. Remains of the original structure along the flank and in the apse. Inside it is a hall church with a nave and two aisles; fine *arcades* and *sculptures* from the Renaissance (some by Domenico Gagini, 1420–68, at the main entrance and in the 1st chapel on the left; a richly decorated arch, 1468, by Francesco Laurana and Pietro de Bontade in the 4th chapel on the left). To the left of the church (Via Immacolatella) is the **Oratorio di S.Lorenzo** with its masterly stucco (1698–1710) by Giacomo Serpotta; the 'Nativity of Christ' by Caravaggio (1609) is on the altar.

Palermo, S.Giovanni degli Eremiti, cloister

Chiesa del Gesù (Piazza Professa): Begun in 1564; the first Jesuit church in Sicily. Enlarged after 1600 (side chapels); 17C *baroque dome;* severely damaged in World War 2. *Late Renaissance façade.* The ground plan is a Latin cross, and there are a nave and two aisles. Rich *marble decoration* and *stuccoes* throughout the church. Next to the church, on the right, is the *Casa Professa,* and the entrance to the **city library,** founded in 1760.

S. Maria del Carmine (Piazza d.Carmine): One of the finest baroque churches in Palermo. Founded in 1626, *façade from the early 19C. The late-17C dome is covered with majolica.* The interior (one nave, two aisles) is in the form of a Latin cross. Note the chapels at the ends of the transepts, with their fine *stucco* by Giuseppe and Giacomo Serpotta (1683–4).

Palazzo dei Normanni (Piazza d.Parlamento): Converted from the Arab emir's palace into the palace of the Norman kings; today it is the seat of the regional parliament of Sicily. The façade facing the square dates from 1616; remains of the original Norman structure survive on the right (*Torre Pisana,* also known as *Torre di S. Ninfa,* a sturdy, four-storeyed tower). Inside, a fine 17C *courtyard with loggias* and, on the 1st floor, the *Cappella Palatina.* On the top floor, the *Hall of King Roger,* decorated with 12C mosaics (animal, plant, and hunting scenes) is well worth seeing. Immediately beside the palace is the *Porta Nuova* (or *Porta d'Austria*), the W. end of the old part of Palermo; it was built in 1535 in honour of Emperor Charles V of Habsburg.

Palazzo Zisa (at the end of the Via Whitaker): Norman pleasure palace; the name comes from the Arabic 'aziz', meaning 'beaming, shining'. Begun by William I of Sicily (1154–60), and completed by his son William II. Arab and Near Eastern stylistic influences are apparent. Rectangular ground plan, and rectangular towers on the narrow sides; blind arcades on the exterior. Inside, the square *fountain hall* is of great interest: three exedrae, fine stalactite vault. Above the fountain there are *mosaics* with hunting scenes and plant ornament.

Palazzo La Cuba (Corso Calatafimi):

Palazzo dei Normanni

Built by William II of Sicily in 1180 as another pleasure palace in Arab-Norman style (its form and style are closely related to the Palazzo Zisa). The dome from which the building takes its name no longer survives. There are fine *blind arcades* on the exterior. Inside there is a single *hall;* only a few fragments survive from the original stalactite vault.

La Cubula (Corso Calatafimi, Villa Napoli): Built by William II; Arab-Norman pavilion; a cube with four pointed arches, surmounted by a red hemispherical dome.

Palazzo Chiaramonte (or *lo Steri*, Piazza Marina): Built in 1307–80; it is one of the most notable Gothic palaces in Sicily. Three storeys, with fine Gothic windows on the top storey; surmounted by inlaid limestone tufa and black lava. Inside, the *Great Hall* has a fine late-14C *wooden ceiling* with paintings in the Moorish-Sicilian manner.

National Archaeological Museum (Piazza Olivella): One of the most important museums in the whole of Italy.

Founded in the 19C and housed in a former monastery. Among the chief attractions are the *water spouts from Himera* (5C BC) in *room 8* on the ground floor. *Room 10* has the famous metopes from the temples of Selinunte. *Rooms 11–14*, ground floor, house the Etruscan collection. The 1st floor includes the *Sala dei Bronzi* (No. 7) with the 'Ram' (3C BC, from Syracuse) and 'Heracles fighting a stag' (Roman, from Pompeii). *Room 8* displays terracottas from Selinunte; Roman sculptures in *room 11*. The *prehistoric collection* is at the start of the 2nd floor and is followed, in *rooms 13–15*, by a most interesting collection of Greek vases.

Galleria Nazionale della Sicilia (in the Palazzo Abbatelli, Via dell'Aloro): A museum of non-classical art, the chief feature being a collection of Sicilian painting from all periods. In *room 2*, the 'Triumph of Death' by an unknown 15C master is outstanding. In *room 4* is the 'bust of Eleonora of Aragon' by Francesco Laurana (1471). *Rooms 5 and 6* are devoted to the Gagini family of sculptors. *Room 10*: 'Virgin of the Annunciation' by Antonella da Messina (1473), Sicily's most important painter.

La Martorana, dome mosaic

Metope from temple of Selinunte

Also worth seeing: The Church of *La Magione* (Piazza Magione) is a 12C Norman building. The *Chiesa dell' Olivella* (Piazza d.Olivella) is 16C, with fine frescos and marble inside. *S. Zita* (Via Squarcialupo): 14C, with altar wall by A.Gagini (1517); next to this is the *Oratorio di S.Zita* with fine stucco decorations by Serpotta (*c.* 1700). *S. Maria della Catena* (Corso Vitt.Emanuele): 15C; portals by Vincenzo Gagini. *Convento dei Cappuccini*, the Capuchin monastery, on the W. fringe of the town has thousands of mummified bodies in the subterranean passages. The 14C Gothic *Palazzo Sclafani* (Piazza della Vittoria), has a beautiful façade and portal. The late-15C *Palazzo Aiutamicristo* (Via Garibaldi), has a fine courtyard. The late-19C *Teatro Massimo* (Piazza G.Verdi) is one of the largest theatres in Italy. The *Diocesan museum* (in the Palazzo Arcivescovile by the cathedral) includes some works of art brought from devastated churches in Palermo. *Galleria d'Arte Moderna* (Piazza Ruggero VII, in the Politeama Garibaldi) has works mainly by Sicilian artists. *Museo Etnigrafico Siciliano Pitrè* (in the grounds of the castle, La Favoritá, in the N. of the city), with collections of folk items. *Puppet museum* in the Palazzo Fatta (Piazza Marina). Some fine baroque squares: *Quattro Cantio, Piazza Pretoria* with a fine 16C fountain, and *Piazza Bellini*.

Environs: At the foot of Monte Grifone is the church of **S.Maria di Gesù** with a splendid view of the *Conca d'Oro.* In the N. of the city is *Monte Pellegrino* with the *grotto of St.Rosalia,* the city's patron saint (converted into a church in 1625). The remains of the *Favara* castle, in which Emperor Frederick II enjoyed staying, are in the S.of the city, near to Vicolo Castellacio.

Palermo, crypt of Capuchin convent

Palestrina 00036
Rome/Latium   p.414☐H 9/10

The origins of the antique Praeneste, which existed as early as the 8C BC, lie in mythology. In 499 BC, the city passed from the Latin league of cities to the Romans. During the civil wars the city was on the side of Marius, whose opponent, Sulla, destroyed the city in 82 BC, putting the inhabitants to death. The temple of the goddess Fortuna Primigenia, and also the oracle, were spared, and then enlarged in order to appease the deity. The medieval Palestrina occupies the entire former temple district, and was built above the city of Praeneste which was destroyed during the battles with the Lombards. Since 1630 it has been in the possession of the Barberini family. The city is a bishopric, and also the birthplace of Giovanni Pierluigi da Palestrina (1524–94), the great composer.

Temple of Fortuna Primigenia: This temple complex ascends a slope in 4 terraces, with an upper and a lower shrine. The temple is known from classical sources e.g. Cicero and Livy. Reconstruction only became possible as a result of the excavations of 1952-5. The complex of buildings constructed by Sulla in the lower shrine, the oracle grotto (Antro delle Sorti) of the 4C BC, and the 3C BC Temple of Juno, are all beneath the cathedral and the adjoining bishops' seminary. The *oracle grotto,*

n the shape of a clover-leaf, with some remains of the 2C AD floor mosaic, and the
apsidial hall, can both be reached from a
gate to the left of the seminary. The upper
shrine was built above a massive symmetrical system of ramps, in a number of terraces, interconnected by means of
staircases. A broad *forecourt,* terminated by
open colonnaded halls, expands towards
the mountain into a 'stairway exedra' which
leads up to the statue of Fortuna Primigenia. The semicircular shape of the
monumental stairway has survived in the
concave sweeping façade of the **Palazzo
Colonna-Barberini,** which was built in
the 11C and largely restored in 1493. Since
1955 it has housed the **Archaeological
Museum** with finds from the temple district. Among its most important items are
some engraved bronze mirrors and the Nile
mosaic (both the supposed origin of this
mosaic, viz. the apsidial hall in the lower
shrine, and its date – between the 1C BC
and the period around 200 AD – are
disputed).

Environs: Castel San Pietro Romano
(3 Km.). Picturesque location, with the
ruins of a 14C fortress. Panoramic view as
far as Rome. **Genazzano** (8 Km. E.).
Birthplace of Oddone Colonna (Pope Martin V) and of Prospero Colonna, Charles
V's military commander. Many of the
city's medieval buildings have survived.
The church of *S. Croce* has 13C frescos.
The *Santuario della Madonna del Buon
Consiglio* preserves the original of a famous
miraculous picture which, according to the
legend, was transferred from Scútari in
1469 by miraculous means. There are Roman remains nearby. Especially noteworthy is the *Casa Apolloni,* which has an
external staircase and an ornate 14C façade
with double-arched windows. Oddone
Colonna is thought to have been born in
this house. The *Castello Colonna* was restored by Oddone Colonna in the 15C and
enlarged by order of Cesare Borgia.

Palmanova 33057
Udine/Friuli   p.410□H 2/3

Built by Venice in the late 16C as a bulwark
against Austria. A fortified city (in part
colonized with pardoned criminals), it was
long regarded as the strongest European

Palestrina, archaeological museum, mosaic

fortress. The French conquered it in 1797, and it was Austrian until 1866. The city is worth seeing for its *overall layout:* planned as a regular nine-sided figure, there is a six-sided central square (see below), from which six streets radiate; ring roads further subdivide the town.

Piazza Grande: City centre, in the middle is a hexagonal *fountain* dating from 1602. There are eleven *statues* of Venetian 'generali provveditori' in the square. On the S. side there is a seven-arched *loggia* from the late 16C–early 17C. On the N. side is the *cathedral,* begun in 1615 but not consecrated until 1777; Longhena and Scamozzi jointly designed it.

Also worth seeing: The fortified *city walls* with broad bastions and *city gates* (built in 1603 – 5 and designed by Scamozzi).

Environs: Some 12 km. W. is **Castions di Strada:** The Romanesque church of *S.Martino* contains (early medieval) 12C frescos. The church of *S.Maria delle Grazie* has fine frescos by the Venetian G.Negro (1534; scenes from the lives of St.Blasius

and St.Mary Magdalene). About 17 km NW is **Mortegliano:** The 19&20C ca thedral of *SS.Pietro e Paolo* has a splendid carved altar by Giovanni Martini (late Gothic, 1526). Some 15 km. E., on a hil near **Medea,** is the *Ara Pacis,* an enor mous monument to the dead dating from 1950.

Palmi 89015

Reggio Calabria/Calabria   p.418□M 1

A little town at the foot of Monte S.Elia (1,900 ft.; from the peak there is a superb view of the coast; in clear weather two vol canoes, Stromboli and Etna, are visible). The **Museo Calabrese di Etnografia e Folclore** in the Palazzo di Città is well worth seeing. It gives a comprehensive sur vey of Calabrian folklore.

Environs: On the coast about 10 km. to the N. is **Gioia Tauro,** the antique Matauros, the home town of the ancien Greek poet Stesichoros (640–555 BC); the *burial ground* was excavated some years ago It is one of the most important trading

Palmanova, view

centres for olives in Italy. Some 5 km. SE, on the slope of the Aspromonte, is **Seminara** (destroyed in an earthquake in 1908, but rebuilt): It was at one time the most powerful fortress in southern Calabria.

Palombara Sabina 00018
Rome/Latium   p.414 ☐ H 9

First mentioned in the 11C. Owned successively by the Savelli, Colonna and Torlonia families. The central point of the settlement is the *Castello Savelli*, a 16C structure incorporating a 9C tower. Near to this town is the abbey (today a ruin) which was founded by Basilian monks in the 9C and taken over by the Benedictines. The Romanesque church of **S. Giovanni in Argentella** forms part of the complex. It is a basilica with three apses; before the façade there is a *narthex* where a Byzantine fresco (Madonna and Child) may be seen along with Roman and medieval fragments. The main apse has an *arched frieze* on pilaster strips. Inside, the basilica's columns, which are spoils from the 9&10C, form irregular aisles. *Frescos* date from *c.* 1400. There is an *iconostasis* in Cosmati work in the right aisle. The *ciborium* is new, with castings from the 9/10C.

Pantálica
Syracuse/Sicily   p.420☐ L 18

From the 13–18C BC, under the name of 'Hybla', this was the centre of a Siculan kingdom, which at this time was almost free of Greek influence. Almost nothing has survived of the prehistoric settlement, except for a so-called 'Anaktoron' (mansion) from the 12–11C BC in the S. of the plateau. The extensive **burial grounds** around the town are very impressive (approx. 5,000 tombs forming the largest known Siculan burial place). Individual and family graves are dug into the rock walls, and rich finds of weapons, domestic utensils etc. have been made in them (see the museum in Syracuse). During the Middle Ages some of the graves were

remodelled into residential caves and chapels. Most important: the *Necropoli di Filiporto* (in the W.) from the town's late period (9–8C BC); the *Necropoli N-W* (12 –11C BC); the *Necropoli Nord* (12–11C BC and the largest burial ground in Pantálica); finally, the *Necropoli della Cavetta* (in the S., 9–8C BC, with many graves).

Pantelleria 91017
Trapani/Sicily   p.420☐G 18

This island, 32 sq. miles in area, with its active volcanoes and hot steamy springs, lies half way between Sicily and Africa. The ancient *Cossyra* was an important base for the Carthaginian fleet. There are Stone Age excavations near *Mursia* in the SW of the island. Nearby are the so-called 'Sesi', neolithic tombs resembling nuraghi.

Paola 87027
Cosenza/Calabria   p.418☐M 14

Birthplace of St. Francis of Paola (1416–1506), founder of the mendicant order of the Minims, and 'Apostle of Mercy'.

Santuario di S. Francesco (2 km. N. of the town): Monastery founded by St. Francis in 1435; contains the basilica of *S. Maria degli Angeli*, whose façade is Renaissance below and baroque above; fine late-15C portal. The interior is asymmetrical, with two aisles. In the right aisle is the late-16C *founder's chapel* in late Renaissance style, with a dome and marbles of various colours; 15/16C *cloister*.

Also worth seeing: A small 10C *Byzantine church*, with 14C frescos, in the Guadimiri area of town.

Parma 43100
Parma/Emilia-Romagna   p.410☐E 4

A Roman colony since 183 BC. Important in the Middle Ages for its wool-weaving mill and its university. It was under Milanese rule from 1346 to 1512, and then became part of the Papal States. Under the Farnese from 1545–1731, it was then Bourbon until 1859, with few interruptions.

Cathedral of S.Maria Assunta (Piazza del Duomo): After being destroyed by an earthquake, it was rebuilt in the 12C as a Lombard Romanesque pillared basilica; extensions around the side chapels were carried out in the following centuries. Massive campanile, built in 1284–94, 207 ft. tall (with a bell dating from 1393). The façade has three dwarf galleries, one above the other. The *central portal*, by G.da Bissone, 1281, is especially fine. The outer walls and apses are also richly articulated; a dome over the crossing borne by an octagonal drum. Inside: a nave and two aisles, and the ground plan is a Latin cross. The transepts and choir are raised (underneath them is the crypt, see below). There are women's galleries above the arcades of the nave, and noteworthy capitals on the pillars. Decoration: the chief work of art is the *dome fresco* by Correggio (1526–30; Assumption of the Virgin). On the right of the right transept, a relief by B.Antélami (1178), on a pulpit, depicts the Deposition. In the choir there is a marble bishop's throne with reliefs by Antélami (including the Conversion of St.Paul). The left aisle leads to the *crypt* with its fine medieval columns; on the floor of its nave are the remains of an early Christian *mosaic.*

Baptistery (to the right of the cathedral): Built in 1196–1260 in Romanesque-Gothic style (the last architect was Antélami). Built of red marble from Verona, it is octagonal, with arcades on the outside surmounted by 5 rows of loggias (4 open, 1 blind). Note in particular the three *portals*, decorated with biblical scenes by Antélami: the *Porta della Vergine* (N.), with the Virgin Enthroned in the lunette; the *Porta del Giudizio Finale* (W.), with Christ in the lunette; the *Porta della Vita* (S.; with the Tree of Life in the lunette). Inside there are outstanding works by Antélami: reliefs of New Testament scenes (including the Flight into Egypt) over the portals. There are 12 reliefs depicting the *Twelve Months* in a circle on

the floor. 12/13C *frescos* (including a Madonna and Child) on the walls. *Font*

S. Giovanni Evangelista (Piazzale S. Giovanni): Originally founded in the 10C and completely rebuilt in Renaissance form in 1498–1520 by the architect B.Zaccagni. Magnificent baroque façade by S. Moschino (1604–7); the campanile dates from 1614 and is also baroque. Interior: a nave and two aisles, with a Latin cross ground plan and a dome over the crossing. 6 side chapels on each flank. Fine Renaissance capitals on the pillars. The church's major works of art are the *frescos* by Correggio. The Vision of John the Evangelist at Patmos (1520–3) is in the dome, and 'John the Evangelist writing the Apocalypse' is in the left transept (above the door to the right of the altar). Also note: frescos dating from 1530 by Correggio's pupil Parmigianino in the right transept. The choir has a copy by C.Aretusi (1587) of the lost Correggio fresco of the *Coronation of the Virgin.* Frescos by Correggio (angels, putti) were recently uncovered on the choir vault. Frescos by Parmigianino (including St.Agatha, 1522–4) in the 1st and 2nd chapels in the left aisle. To the left of the church is the entrance to the *Benedictine monastery* (founded in the 10C) with three interesting *Renaissance cloisters;* two fine frescos by Correggio (Sacrificio Romano) in the chapterhouse. The Borgo Pipa leads to the famous *Storica Farmacia di S.Giovanni Ev.* (an old pharmacy): Established in the 9/10C; three rooms (Sala del Fuoco, S.dei Mortai, S.delle Sirene) with original Renaissance furnishings.

Chiesa della Madonna della Steccata (Strada Garibaldi): The best-known church in Parma. Built in Renaissance style by B. and G.F.Zaccagni in 1521–39 (modelled on St.Peter's in Rome). The ground plan is a Greek cross with an extended W. arm; square chapels in the corners. Contents include: *frescos* by Parmigianino (figures from the Old Testament) on the triumphal arch; frescos in the dome by B.Gatti (Ascension, 1560). The apse of the choir con-

Parma, baptistery, piece by Antélami

tains a *bronze statue* of the Risen Christ by A.Spinelli (1563). To the left of the entrance is the *tomb* of Count Neipperg (1775–1829), the morganatic husband of Marie Louise, Napoleon's widow.

Camera del Correggio (Via M.Melloni): In the S.Paolo monastery; painted throughout in masterly style by Correggio in 1518–19. Includes the famous *Putti del Correggio*.

Palazzo della Pilotta (Piazza Marconi): A brick building begun in 1593 but not completed. Contains the *Museo Nazionale*, the *Galleria Nazionale*, the *Biblioteca Palatina* and the *Teatro Farnese*. *Museo Nazionale d'Antichita:* devoted mainly to antiquities, carvings, furniture and coins. *Galleria Nazionale:* a rich collection of important paintings by major artists, especially Correggio. Of particular interest: room VII contains the Madonna del S. Gerolamo and the Madonna della Scala, by Correggio. There are also masterpieces by Parmigianino, Fra Angelico, Giulio Romano, Tiepolo, Canaletto, El Greco, Hans Holbein the younger (in room XIX: Portrait of Erasmus of Rotterdam) and

many others. The *Biblioteca Palatina* dates from 1769 and has an exceedingly rich collection of manuscripts, autographs, early printed books and other works. Contains the complete works of the famous poet G.B.Bodoni (1740–1813) in the Museo Bodoniano. *Teatro Farnese* (on the 1st floor): Built of wood from 1618–28 by G.B.Aleotti, a pupil of Palladio (modelled on the 'Teatro Olimpico' in Vicenza). With its 4,500 seats, it was the largest theatre in the world at that time (285 ft. long, 105 ft. wide, 75 ft. high).

Also worth seeing: Church of *S.Pietro Apostolo* (Piazza Garibaldi), founded in the 10C. Church of *S.Francesco del Prato* (Piazzale S.Francesco), with a fine Gothic rose-window on the façade dating from 1461. Church of *SS. Trinità dei Rossi* (Strada Garibaldi) with interesting carvings inside. Church of *S.Alessandro* (Piazzale A.Barezzi), rebuilt by B.Zaccagni in 1507. Church of *SS.Annunziata* (Strada M.d'Azeglio) with an elliptical ground

Parma, cathedral 1 Deposition by Antelami 2 bishop's throne

Parma, cathedral, bishop's throne

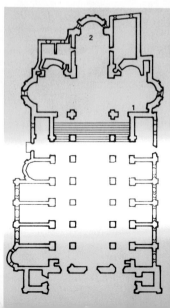

plan. The church of *S. Sepolcro* (Strada della Repubblica), with a beautiful 17C carved baroque ceiling. The 18C church of *S. Antonio Abate* (Strada della Repubblica), designed by F. Bibiena, with a notable interior. The 17C *Palazzo del Municipio* (Piazza Garibaldi). *Parco Ducale* (across the Ponte G. Verdi), laid out in the 16C, with the Palazzo Ducale. The *university* (Strada dell'Università), founded in the 11C; the building is 16C.

Museums: *Museo Glauco Lombardi* (in the Palazzo di Riserva, Piazzale Marconi), an art collection with 18/19C works. The *Pinacoteca Giuseppe Stuard* (Strada da Cavestro), with a good collection of paintings (chiefly by early Tuscan artists). *Museo di Arte Cinese* (Viale S. Martino) with a collection, unique in Italy, of Chinese objects.

Paternò 95047
Catania/Sicily   p.420☐L 17

Castle: Built in 1073 by the Normans under Count Roger, rebuilt in the 14C and restored in the 20C. Massive cube-like building in good condition. On the ground floor there is a *chapel* with remains of frescos. The stairway to the upper storeys runs inside the thick outside walls. Beautiful *windows* on the 1st and 2nd floors (with a view of Etna).

Also worth seeing: The church of *S. Barbara*, an 18C centrally planned building with a large dome and a Madonna from the Gagini workshop inside (1st altar on the right); *Chiesa dell'Abbadia*, a Benedictine church, with the 16C 'Madonna d'Itria'.

Pavia 27100
Pavia/Lombardy   p.412☐D 4

This city, known as Ticinum by the Romans, was an important centre in the time of Augustus. The Ostrogoth king Theodoric chose it as one of his favourite residences. In 572, after 3 years of siege, the city fell into the hands of the Lombards, who made it their capital. It continued to be the capital and the place of coronation of the Regnum Italicum up into the 11C.

Parma, baptistery, portal lunette

The city was first called Papia in the 7C. Pavia became a free commune as early as the beginning of the 12C, but initially pursued a largely imperial policy (Barbarossa was crowned in S.Michele in 1155). It later came under Visconti rule (1359). One famous event was the battle of Pavia in 1525, at which Francis I of France was captured.

Cityscape: The regular layout of the streets, the heritage of the Roman 'castrametatio', is still a feature of the centre of Pavia. Apart from the historical monuments, Pavia also has an abundance of interesting quarters with streets of houses, many of them well preserved, from the period between the Middle Ages and the baroque (especially around S.Teodoro, S. Michele and the Collegio Castiglione and the Piazza della Vittoria).

Cathedral: In 1488, work was begun on gradually tearing down the two Romanesque cathedrals (the winter and summer cathedrals) in order to build a new one. The main apse and the sacristies were built in 1507, the sanctuary in 1586, the drum of the dome in 1762-8, and the dome was completed in 1884. The façade was faced in 1898, and it was only in 1936 that the transepts were finished. It is thought that Bramante, Leonardo da Vinci and Francesco Giorgo were involved in the project. The cathedral is an immense, centrally planned building with apses of equal size on three sides, and it is only on the 4th side (the façade) that it is elongated.

S. Teodoro: 12C brick building with tripartite façade. A basilican structure with a nave, two aisles, a false transept, a dome, three apses and a crypt. Inside, it has interesting 13/14C frescos. On the rear wall of the left aisle is a view of Pavia dating from 1522.

S.Michele: Several kings and emperors were crowned in this church, which is Lombard in origin. The present structure dates from after 1117 (earthquake). The metrical layout has a nave, two aisles and a gallery (but no clerestory), with a large transept and an elongated choir (crypt).

Octagonal dome over the crossing. The late-12C façade stands out in front of the church: the front is divided into three sections by clustered semi-columns; there are three portals and a dwarf gallery runs along the top of the gable. The central section is emphasized by a group of windows. On the lower section of the façade there are several horizontal relief strips (chimeras, animals, humans). *Contents:* an arch decorated with sculptures in the right transept, and a silver cross from the 2nd half of the 10C in the chapel before the sanctuary. In the sanctuary are the remains of a 12C mosaic pavement. The altar table dates from 1386. In the apse there is a fresco of the Virgin Mary by a pupil of Bergogno (1491).

S.Pietro in Ciel d'Oro: The Lombard foundation was replaced by the building consecrated in 1132: a nave and two aisles, extending for five bays, with a false transept (octagonal dome above the crossing) and a choir with three apses and a crypt. Radically restored in 1875-99. The façade is similar to that of S.Michele. *Contents:* above the high altar is a three-tiered tomb, the *Arca di S.Agostino*, a Lombard work displaying the clear influence of the Campionese school (in the lower section). The *crypt* contains the tomb of Boethius, Theodoric's adviser (454-526), who was executed.

S.Maria del Carmine (Via Roma): The building of this Carmelite church began in 1390. A basilican structure with a nave and two aisles (metrical system) 4 bays long and a transept with 3 bays; 5 choir chapels. Each of the aisles is flanked by 8 chapels. The *façade* is superbly articulated throughout. There are good 15&16C *furnishings* in the elegant interior.

University: Founded in 1361 (the core dates from the 14/15C), greatly enlarged by Piermarini in the reign of Maria Theresa and by Pollak in the reign of Joseph II; subsequently enlarged again under Napoleon and Francis I. Elegant inner courtyards, large grand staircase and Aula Magna

Parma, baptistery, dome fresco

(1788). The *Ospedale S.Matteo* (1449) is also in the university district.

Castello Visconteo: Built in 1360–5 by Galeazzo II Visconti. An extensive square structure with a large inner courtyard. One of the finest fortresses in Lombardy.

Museums: In the castle: *Archaeological Museum, Sculpture Museum* (exhibits from the Lombard and Romanesque periods and the Renaissance), *Museo del Risorgimento. Pinacoteca Malaspina* (Piazza Petrarca): paintings by Italian, German, Flemish and Lombard artists.

Also worth seeing: *Ponte Coperto.* This

Pavia, cathedral **1** Adoration of the Magi, by Daniele Crespi **2** chapel of S.Siro (Madonna and Child with S.Siro), relief by Tommaso Orsalino, 1653 **3** Madonna of the rosary, Bernardo Gatti, 1532 **4** pulpit with reliefs (life of S.Siro), by Siro Zanelli, 1672 **5** apse with richly carved choir stalls from the 18C **6** chapel of S.Alessandro Sauli, rich baroque marble decoration **7** canons' sacristy **8** chaplains' sacristy **9** Madonna and Child with St.Antony and St.John the Baptist, by C.Sacchi **10** altar of the Blessed Sacrament, 17C, figures by Tommaso Orsalino **11** and **12** recent structural elements

covered medieval bridge across the Ticino was rebuilt in 1951 after the war. *S.Maria in Betleme* (on the other bank of the river): 12C, the spatial arrangement is similar to S.Teodoro. *Collegio Borromeo* (by the Porta Nuova): founded in 1561; the magnificent complex originates from plans by Pellegrini. *Palazzo Municipale* (Piazza Municipio): baroque building dating from 1728–30. *S.Maria di Canepanova* (to the left of the town hall): octagonal, domed structure built by Amadeo in 1492–1507, one of the cathedral architects, probably with the assistance of Bramante. *Collegio Ghislieri* (N. of the town hall): an endowment by Pius V (1567) for students. Opposite this is the *Collegio Castiglione* dating from 1429 (altered in the 18C), in the square is a statue of Pius V, and on the E. side is the façade of the former church of *S.Francesco da Paolo. Collegio Cairoli* and *S. Francesco* (next to the Collegio Castiglione): the Collegio was founded as a priests' seminary by Emperor Joseph II, and built by Piermarini and Pollak. S. Francesco (1230–98) with a notable apse. *Piazza della Vittoria:* this market square, laid out in 1357, is N. of the cathedral; on its S.side is the Broletto (a medieval town

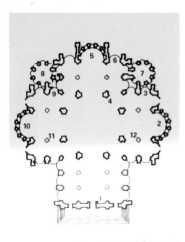

Pavia, S.Michele

house) from the 12C, with loggias dating from 1563. *Palazzo Botigella* (Via Cavour No. 30): probably designed by Bramante. *Tre torri* (Piazza Leonardo da Vinci): three well-preserved medieval fortified tower houses. *S.Lanfranco* (2 km. outside the city, on the Via della Riviera beginning S.of the railway station): an 11C foundation. In the 12/13C church is the *Arca di S.Lanfranco* (a bishop who died in 1198) by Amadeo (1498). A sarcophagus resting on 6 columns, with a graceful tabernacle above it.

Environs: Certosa di Pavia (7 km. towards Milan): Situated on the edge of the park of Pavia castle, it was begun in 1396 as a mausoleum for Gian Galeazzo Visconti and his family. Architects from the Milan cathedral stonemasons' lodge were appointed to carry out the work, which was interrupted in 1402 on the death of Gian Galeazzo. Building was resumed in 1426 –62, and completed in 1450–73 under the Sforza. After this the façade was begun under the supervision of Solari, and later Amadeo (completed in the 2nd half of the 16C). The spacious complex includes: the church, in front of which is an atrium (piazzale) with visitors' quarters (17C); on the S. side of the church is the splendidly designed *Chiostro della Fontana* with a refectory to the W. and a new sacristy to the E.; adjoining this is the *chapter courtyard* with the chapter house; the *library* is to the S.of the Chiostro della Fontana. From here the visitor passes into the *Chiostro Grande* with the cells of the Carthusian monks, whilst the *Palazzo Ducale* extends along its N. side. The *church* has a nave, two aisles, an extensive transept, a tower over the crossing, and a large choir. The sides of the nave are flanked by large chapels. The *façade* is heavily ornamented with a rich programme of figures. **Montalto Pavese** (about 30 km. S.: The castle dates from 1595; well-furnished rooms with numerous paintings by Genoese artists; garden laid out in early baroque style.

Pegli 16155
Genoa/Liguria   p.412☐C 5

Villa Doria (Piazza Bonavino, No. 7): This fine 16C building belonged to Andrea Doria. Since 1928, the **Civico Museo**

Pavia, Ponte Coperto with cathedral

Navale (maritime museum) has been housed here. It concentrates mainly on the history of seafaring: models of ships from

Certosa di Pavia, monastery church 1 polyptych (God the Father by Perugino and the church fathers by Bergognone), 1499 **2** Ambrose by Bergognone **3** Ecce Homo by Bergognone (above the door lintel) **4** marble cenotaph for Lodovico il Moro and Beatrice d'Este (Gian Cristoforo Solari, 1497) **5** so-called reliquary altar by D.Crespi, 1625; in front of it are the bronze candelabra by Annibale Fontana, 1580 **6** frescos in the apse calotte by Bergognone (Coronation of the Virgin with Saints and Francesco Sforza and Lodovico il Moro) **7** the scourging of Christ (copy by T.Orsolino of a Michelangelo) **8** tympanum with the temptation of St.Antony **9** Old Sacristy (pendent capitals, intarsia, 16C) **10** triptych (of hippopotamus teeth) with miniatures of scenes from the Old and New Testaments, workshop of Embriachi, early 15C **11** sanctuary (gorgeous choir screen, late 16C), richly carved choir stalls with inlay work (designs by Bergognone, 1498), very rich decoration from the 16/17C, frescos by D.Crespi, 1630 **12** lavabo; inside is the lavabo with reliefs by A.Maffioli da Carrara, 1489 **13** fresco in the apse calotte by Bergognone (Gian Galeazzo and his sons presenting the model of the Certosa to the Virgin Mary) **14** mausoleum of G.G.Visconti, 1497, mainly designed by G.Cr.Romano **15** entrance to the New Sacristy **16** entrance to the Chiostro Piccolo **17** Madonna and Child by Bergognone (above the entrance) **18** panel painting dating from 1491 (Bergognone), S.Siro and other Saints **19** polyptych by Macrino d'Alba, 1496

different centuries, charts, maps, and also nautical instruments.

Villa Durazzo Pallavicini (Via Ignazio Pallavicini, No. 11): Built in 1837–46, the villa houses the **Museum of Ligurian Archaeology,** which deals with prehistoric Liguria (palaeolithic and neolithic periods), and displays finds from Ligurian caves (Grimaldi, Finale). There are also finds from Genoese tombs (under the Piazza De Ferrari).

Penne 65017
Pescara/Abruzzi   p.416□ I 8

Cathedral of S.Maria degli Angeli and S. Massimo Martire: This church was built on the site of a temple of Vesta and rebuilt in the 11&14C, altered in baroque style in 1660, and rebuilt in 1955 after being severely damaged in World War 2. Inside: a *wooden cross* (c. 1300), a *font* (1655), a silver *processional figure of S.Massimo* dating from 1762; the *altar of Bishop Oderisio* (1117) has been reassembled. In the *crypt* are columns from ancient buildings, with 11C capitals, and also remains of 13&14C frescos.

S.Giovanni Evangelista: The *campanile* built in the 2nd half of the 15C has majolica decoration on its windows. Inside are a 16C *Madonna* and a *processional cross* by Nicola da Guardiagrele (1450).

Also worth seeing: *Porte S.Francesco* dating from 1780. The church of *S.Maria in Colleromano,* built in the first half of the 14C, enlarged in the 16C, and given a new façade in 1792, stands outside the gate. The façade was restored in 1960. 15&16C frescos.

Perugia 06100
Perugia / Umbria   p.414 G 7

The capital of Umbria, it was praised by

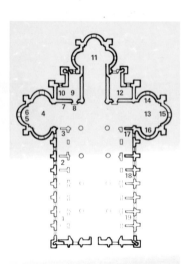

Certosa di Pavia

Goethe for its situation. It unites the advantages of city life with the quiet life style typical of the whole region. Perugia is Umbrian in origin and did not finally become Etruscan until the 4C BC, subsequently attaining great power. In 310 and 295 BC Perugia, together with other Italian cities, fought against Rome, but Perugia was defeated. The enmity between Perugia and Rome disappeared when Hannibal, on 21 June 217 BC, inflicted a crushing defeat on the Roman army at Lake Trasimene. Perugia thereafter became a Roman municipium. Octavian destroyed Perugia in 41–40 BC. The emperor subsequently made peace with the city which was then named 'Augusta Perusia'. The city remained independent in the early Middle Ages, and was only held briefly by the Lombards. However, it was then destroyed by King Totila. The city was especially favoured by Henry VI, who acknowledged Perugia's claim to dominion over the adjoining lands (1186) and promoted its rise to power within Umbria. Perugia also maintained very good relations with the Pope, but without relinquishing its preference for independence. The city had become a free community in the 12C. The 14C was the city's period of power and cultural splendour, but also of bloody battles lasting into the 16C. Pope Paul II took the troubled city in 1540 and ordered the 'Rocca Paolina' to be built as a symbol of his power. The Rocca was destroyed by the population in 1859. Perugia became part of the Italian State on 14 September 1860.

1st Tour: On the left-hand side of the main street, the *Corso Vannucci,* called 'il Perugino' after Pietro Vannucci, there stands the old *exchange* (Collegio del Cambio) in front of the Piazza IV Novembre. The fresco cycle by Perugino (1496–1507), the wood carvings by Domenico del Tasso (1491–3), and the door by Antonio Bencivenni da Mercatello (1501), are artistically important. Next door is the *Collegio della Mercanzia* (Chamber of Commerce). The Gothic, wooden decoration in the large hall is interesting (1403). On the corner leading into the Corso Vannucci/Piazza IV Novembre is the *Palazzo dei Priori,* one of the finest palaces in the whole of Italy,

with Tuscan-Venetian stylistic elements The portal leading to the Corso Vannucc is an example of Sienese art (Gano d Siena, 1340); the tympanum has a St.Lou from Tolosa, St.Lawrence and St.Ercolan The elegant arcade and flight of steps a on the side facing the Piazza. Above th portal are the symbols of the city (the gr phon) and of the Guelph party (the lion It leads into the medieval city council ha the *Sala dei Notari*, with its impressiv round arches and frescos from the scho of Cavallini (Bible stories, legends, fair tales, coats of arms). The third floor hous the *Galleria Nazionale dell'Umbria,* one the most important art galleries in Italy an certainly the most important in Umbri (opening times: 9 a.m.-2 p.m.; 9 a.m. p.m. on public holidays; closed on Mo days). The collection comprises work from six centuries. In view of their larg number, only some of the artists can b mentioned: Pietro Vannucci il Perugin Bernardino Betti, il Pinturicchio, Bea Angelico, Benozzo Gozzoli, Piero dell Francesca, Luca Signorelli, Barolome Caporali, Arnolfo di Cambio, Agostino Duccio, Duccio di Buoninsegn Benedetto Bonfigli and others. In th Piazza IV Novembre is the *Fontana Ma giore,* a masterpiece of Italian Gothic scul ture, built to plans by Nicola and Giovan Pisano and Fra Bevignate. The bas relie on the upper basin (figures from biblic and secular history) are attributed Giovanni Pisano, the nymphs to Arnol di Cambio. Symbols of the twelve month are to be seen on the lower basin.

Cathedral: It is dedicated to St.Lawrenc Work on the building was begun in 134 and completed in 1430. It is one of the fe hall churches in Italy. The façade is incon plete. The statue (1553) of Pope Julius I by Vincenzo Danti, a pupil Michelangelo, is on the side facing th Piazza. The campanile was designed Valentino Martelli. Inside: an altar b Agostino di Duccio (left aisle), a banner Berto di Giovanni showing a view of Per gia from the year 1526, the Madonna del Grazie by Giannicola di Paolo, the Desce from the Cross by Federico Barocci, an the fine choir stalls by Giuliano da Maian and Domenico del Tasso (1491). In the adjoining cathedral museum—*Museo dell' Opera del Duomo*—the visitor should see the 'Madonna Enthroned with Saints and a Donor' by Signorelli.

Loggia Braccio Fortebraccio: This is in the Piazza IV Novembre, to the right of the statue of Julius III. A 15C work by Fieravanti.

Via della Maestà delle Volte: This medieval street just to the right of the Loggia has the church of the same name (façade originally by Agostino di Duccio, 1590), redesigned by Martelli, with a beautiful fountain.

Continuing down the street, the route leads to the *Arch of Augustus:* the base is Etruscan (3C BC), the upper section is Roman, and the loggia is 16C. Opposite this is the *Palazzo Gallenga*, an 18C building, now the seat of the *Italian university for foreigners* which was founded in 1925 and has become the most famous of its kind in Italy. Past the Palazzo Gallenga, at the end of the Corso Garibaldi, stands the interesting church of *S.Angelo*, the most important palaeo-Christian building in Umbria

after S.Salvatore in Spoleto. It is a round building from the 5&6C, somewhat restored in the 14C. Returning along the same street, the 13C church of *S.Agostino* is on the left. It has a splendid early-16C choir, probably built to plans by Perugino, while the frescos are by Pellino di Vannucio (1377). The *Cappella del Buio* is in the style of Brunelleschi but designed by Francesco di Guido da Settignano. The *Via Pinturicchio* begins opposite the Palazzo Gallenga. Pinturicchio lived in No. 7. The church of *S.Maria Nuova* lies at the end of this street. Inside, the wooden choir is in the Gothic style of the Marches. The route passes through the Porta Pesa and along the Via Brunamonti to the 13C church of *Madonna di Monteluce* which was altered in the 15C—the portal was left untouched. The sacristy contains remains of 14C frescos by Fiorenza di Lorenzo. Not far from S.Maria Nuova is the church of *S.Severo* with a fresco by Raphael (Trinity and Saints, 1505), and underneath this is a row of Saints by Perugino. Returning to the Palazzo dei Priori along the Via dei Priori (behind the palace), there are 14&15C houses and the 12C Torre degli Sciri. Beside the *Porta Trasimena* is the elegant

Perugia, Palazzo dei Priori

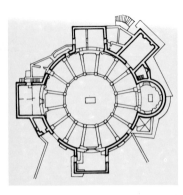

Perugia, S. Angelo The exterior of the 5/6C rotunda is sixteen-sided, and its interior is reminiscent of S. Stefano Rotondo in Rome

Oratorio della Madonna della Luce with its Renaissance façade (1518). The frescos on the ceiling are by B.Caporali. Passing to the right of the church and down to the Piazza S.Francesco al Prato, there is another gem of the Renaissance, the *Oratorio di S. Bernardino*. The building, clearly influenced by Donatello and L.B.Alberti, was built by Agostino di Duccio from 1457 to 1461. The altar inside the church is an early Christian sarcophagus (4C). Beside this church is that of *S.Francesco al Prato*. The building dates from the 13C. The façade was rebuilt in 1927 and is a faithful copy of the original. Between the Oratorio and the church of S.Francesco there is a small chapel where the condottiere Braccio Fortebraccio da Montone is buried. The tomb of the jurist Bartolo da Sassoferrato is also to be seen here, as is a banner by Bonfigli which was painted on the occasion of the plague in 1461. Returning to the Via dei Priori, the route leads past No. 5, Via Deliziosa (on the right), where Perugino lived. Further along on the left is the baroque church of *S. Filippo Neri* with a façade by Tommaso Stati from Cortona (1647–63). The interior is the work of Paolo Marucelli from Rome and the architectural style is clearly Roman in inspiration (S.Andrea della Valle, S.Susanna). Next to it is the *Oratorio di S. Cecilia*,

designed in 1687 by Pietro Baglioni, a pupil of Borromini.

2nd Tour: This tour begins at the *Piazza Matteotti*, with the 15C *Palazzo del Capitano del Popolo*. The Via Marzia leads to the Etruscan *Porta Marzia* (3&2C BC) and then to the entrance of the famous *Rocca Paolina*, which was built by Antonio da Sangallo the younger, on the instructions of Pope Paul III, on what was then a residential quarter. Today it serves as a passageway to the sunken, subterranean, medieval town. From here turn left into the Viale Independenza and after a few minutes the route comes to the uniquely beautiful church of *S.Ercola* (13&14C), a church with a tower, very rare in Italy. It is not known whether this is the result of northern influence or whether it is the result of local necessity. Inside: 17C frescos by Andrea Carlone from Genoa, and the altar is a very fine Roman sarcophagus from the 2C. Then turn into the Corso Cavour, on the left of which is the church of *S. Domenico*. The original hall church was begun in 1305, part of it later caved in, and it was rebuilt by Carlo Maderno in 1632. Inside, the basic structure of the cruciform building, 397 ft. long, with a nave and two aisles, has survived despite this rebuilding. The fine apse window is one of the largest in Italy. The splendid tomb of Pope Benedict XI is attributed to the school of Arnolfo di Cambio owing to its similarity to the tomb of Cardinal del Braye in Orvieto. Note also the altar by Agostino di Duccio, and the frescos, in the chapel of St. Catherine, by two 14C Umbrian painters who were evidently influenced by Giotto and Sienese art, and also by artistic tendencies in the Marches and Emilia Romagna. The former monastery of this church houses the *National Archaeological Museum* of Umbria (opening times: 9 a.m.–2 p.m.; closed on Mondays). This important collection has a rich prehistoric section (Umbria, Tuscany, Marches and Abruzzi) and an Umbrian-Etruscan Roman one. The museum is of particula

Perugia, Galleria Nazionale dell Umbria, painting by Pinturicchi

interest to specialists. Further along the Corso Cavour the route reaches the *Porta Romana* or *Porta S. Pietro*, a monumental work by Agostino di Duccio (2nd half of the 15C). Here, the influence which Leon Battista Alberti (Malatesta temple in Rimini) exerted on Agostino di Duccio is apparent. Here too is the church of *S. Pietro* with a monastery attached to it. This church was built in *c.* 1000 in the style of a Roman abbey church. It was frequently rebuilt over the centuries, but it still gives an impression of integrated harmony. The elegant campanile was built in 1468 to a design by B. Rossellino. Some columns from the original church may still be seen in one of the cloisters (17C). The church entrance is decorated by a beautiful 16C portal. Inside there are paintings by Antonio Vassilacchi (school of Tintoretto, 'Life of Christ and Saints'). In the right transept, among other items, are two panels by Eusebio da Sangiorgio. The works in the left transept include a Pietà by Perugino, another panel by Eusebio da Sangiorgio, and a copy of the Deposition by Raphael (the original is in the Borghese Museum, Rome). On the same side is the Vibi chapel by Francesco di Guido da Set-

tignano in the style of Brunelleschi; it contains a sumptuous tabernacle by Mino da Fiesole. Among the items in the sanctuary is one of the finest set of choir stalls in Italy. Dating from 1535, it is the work of Stefano and Damiano Zambelli to drawings by Raphael. In the sacristy there are paintings by Perugino and valuable miniature books.

S. Giuliana: 13C, with a 14C façade. The fine 14C cloister is attributed to Matteo Gattaponi.

S. Prospero: Documents show that the church existed as early as the 8C. The tunnel vault and the fine ciborium with its marble decorations are both interesting and so are the frescos by Bonamico, which are thought to be an initial attempt to break away from Byzantine influence.

Tomb of the Volumnii: A little way outside the city centre is a well-preserved Etruscan burial site from the 2C BC which was accidentally discovered by a peasant in 1840. The tomb is a reconstruction of a dwelling of that period. One room contains the 'family group': Aruns Volumnius, Veilia Volumnia, children and grand-

Perugia, Collegio della Mercanzia, Great Hall

children, and finally Publius Volumnius, a Roman citizen of the 1C BC, seized by homesickness on his deathbed. On the upper storey is a small museum with objects found in the 38 Etruscan tombs in the town of *Palazzone.*

Tomba di S. Manno: This is another Etruscan burial site (3C BC) with tunnel vaults (Roman influence) and a long inscription.

Tomb of Sperandio : This Etruscan tomb from the 4C BC is near the villa of the same name. Magnificent jewels (now in the State museum in Florence) and fine sarcophagus (in the museum of Perugia) were discovered here.

Customs and Public Events: The *Sagra Musicale Umbra,* an international festival of sacred music, is held in the second half of September. *Umbria Jazz* is held from late July until early August, usually on the Piazza IV Novembre. The *Theatre in the Square* is held in the first 10 days of August in the squares and monasteries of the town. The exact dates are obtainable from the tourist office.

Environs: Magione: Fine 15C castle of the Knights of Malta; note the towers and the beautiful inner courtyard. **Passignano sul Trasimeno:** It was between this little town and Mount Gualandro (near Tuoro) that, on 21 June 217 BC, Hannibal inflicted a crushing defeat on the army of Consul Gaius Flaminius. Swords and the remains of bones were still being found in the area up to a few years ago. Some of the names in this region, such as Ossaia (charnel-house), Sanguineto (flow of blood), and Sepoltaglia (gravemakers), still refer to this battle. **Maggiore:** An island in Lake Trasimene with the 14C Gothic village church of *San Michele Arcangelo.* Inside there are 15C frescos and a fine crucifix by B.Caporali; there is a fine 15C house in the village; the *Villa Isabella,* a former monastery, with frescos by Sano di Pietro, Caporali and others, is in the S.part of the island. **Montalera:** This beautiful castle (originally 13C, later altered) stands on a hill near Panicale. **Fontignano:** The church contains Perugino's tomb, the artist having died here of the plague in 1523. **Pretola** offers some good examples of the local, rural style of building, with its distinctive features (a tower house with a mill).

Perugia, S. Angelo

Perugia, Porta Marzia

Perugia, Collegio del Cambio, audience room

Pesaro 61100
Pesaro/Marches   p.414☐H 6

Cathedral: The façade is 13C. Inside there is an exposed *pavement mosaic* from the earlier 5/6C AD secular building. Its subject matter includes the *Return of Helen from Troy to Greece.*

S.Agostino: The *portal* dates from 1413. Inside is an *Annunciation* by Palma il Giovane (third altar on the right). The *choir stalls* have 16C intarsia, with landscapes, still lifes, and town views.

S. Francesco: The *portal* with the Madonna and Saints, and also an *Annunciation*, dates from 1356–78. The interior was altered in baroque style in the 18C, and restored in 1948. 14&15C *frescos* on the

entrance wall and the aisles. The *sarcophagi* of Paola Orsini (d. 1371) and the blessed Michelina (1536).

Palazzo Ducale: This building was begun by Alessandro Sforza in the mid-15C and enlarged by Girolamo and Bartolomeo Genga in the 16C. Some of its rooms were painted throughout in the 16C, including the *bathroom of Lucrezia Borgia.*

The **Palazzo Vincenzo Toschi-Mosca** houses the *Musei Civici.* The main works in the picture gallery are the paintings by Giovanni Bellini, the so-called *Pala di Pesaro*—a Coronation of the Virgin (1473–4), a Crucifixion (1459), a head of John the Baptist, and a God the Father (1502); there are some friezes from the Palazzo Ducale at the entrance. The other highlights of these collections are the local majolicas, the industry having been established here since the 16C.

Perugia, The Magi, by Perugino

National Archaeological Museum, Perugia

Museo Oliveriano: Inscriptions, archaeological finds, more recent coins, and small sculptures.

Also worth seeing: *Rocca Costanza*, completed in 1505.

Environs: *Villa Imperiale* (privately owned, can only be visited upon request): From 1469 onwards, a new, larger villa was built for the Sforza on the site of an existing one. Francesco Maria I della Rovere, the Duke of Urbino, had the new villa enlarged by Girolamo Genga in 1530. The arrangement of the individual components of the structure is determined by the villa's site on a hill: the lower storey has only one wing; the central storey has, in addition, a courtyard and a second wing; on top there is only one wing, and behind it the courtyard; above the second wing there is a terrace, and behind this a garden. Inside, the decoration of 16C frescos has largely survived. Painters such as Dosso Dossi, Bronzino, Girolamo Genga, Perin del Vaga, and Camillo Mantovano, painted *scenes from the life of Duke Francesco Maria I della Rovere,* and there are also architectural and landscape paintings, mythological and allegorical pictures, including the famous *Calumny,* probably by Raffaello del Colle. **Montefiorentino:** *Chapel of Count Oliva,* built by Francesco di Simone Ferruci in the second half of the 15C: a centrally planned building on a square ground plan. On the altar inside is a *Madonna with Dominican and Franciscan Saints* by Giovanni Santi, Raphael's father, dated 1489. Tombs and a beautiful majolica floor date from the same period. **Gradara:** This fortress, built in the 13C by the Malatesta, was rebuilt by the Sforza in the 15C. The courtyard has *frescos* by Girolamo Genga, and there is a terracotta altar by Luca della Robbia in the chapel. *Also worth seeing:* the 14C town walls.

Pescara 65100
Pescara/Abruzzi   p.416☐ K 8

This is the ancient *Aternum*, known as Pis-cara by the Lombards. The town was al-most completely destroyed several times, most recently in World War 2. It is the birthplace of the poet Gabriele d'Annun-zio, and a museum has been set up in the *house of his birth*.

Main places of interest: *Palazzo del Governo* and the *Tempio Nazionale della Conciliazione*.

Pescocostanzo 67033
L'Aquila/Abruzzi   p.416☐K 9

Collegiata of S.Maria del Colle: This church built in the 11C was rebuilt in 1466, and enlarged in 1558 and also in the 17&18C. The façade and *portal* are 16C. Inside, the *wooden figure of the Madonna del Colle,* in a painted niche, dates from the 13C, while the *panel of the Virgin Mary be-tween St.Margaret and St.Apollonia* and the *pulpit* are 16C. The decorations are chiefly baroque: the *grille* in front of the chapel of the sacrament was built in 1699–1717 by Francesco di Sante di Rocco and his nephew Ilario. The painted and gilded *wooden ceiling* in the nave was designed by C.Sabatini from 1670–82. The ceilings of the aisles date from 1742-3. The *holy-water stoup* borne by a bronze eagle is dated 1610, and the *organ* is from 1619.

Petralia Sottana 90027
Palermo/Sicily   p.420☐K 16

Chiesa Matrice (S.M.Assunta): Rebuilt in 1633–81; a notable façade by G.Palazotto (1686–1754). On the left flank there is a 16C *portal* in Catalan Gothic style. Inside are a nave and two aisles, and the ground plan is a Latin cross. Monolithic columns. Fine *marble works* on the altars (including the 'Infant Christ', attributed to Antonello Gagini, 1478–1536, on the right of the nave). In the left aisle is an interesting 15C *triptych*. A notable *church treasure* in the sacristy.

Pesaro, Palazzo Ducale

Also worth seeing: Church of *S. Maria della Fontana* with a 16C Catalan Gothic portal. The baroque church of *S. Francesco*, with a fine wooden pulpit inside. The *Chiesa della Trinità* with a pointed arch portal (15C) and, in the apse, a notable altar by Gian Dom. Gagini (1503–67).

Environs: Some 5 km. SE is **Petralia Soprana** (3,763 ft.), the highest-lying town in Palermo province. Of interest are the church of *SS. Pietro e Paolo* (with two beautiful 15C Catalan Gothic portals), and *S. Maria di Loreto* (a centrally planned 17C building; inside, behind the high altar, is a marble pala attributed to Dom. Gagini, 1420–92).

Petrella Tifernina 86055

Campobasso/Molise   p.416□K 10

S. Giorgio: This church founded in 1165 was consecrated in 1217, altered in baroque style in 1732, and restored in 1955. An inscription on the portal, which bears the prophet Jonah, names a certain *Magister Epidus* as the builder and gives the date 1211.

Environs: *S. Maria della Strada:* This mid-12C church has not suffered any major changes on the outside, but groin vaults were added inside after the earthquake of 1456. The right portal shows *Alexander the Great's ascension in a chariot borne by gryphons*. Inside are a 15C *tomb*, a 16C *wooden cross*, and the figure of the *Madonna della Strada*, painted over more than once in the course of time.

Piacenza 29100

Piacenza/Emilia-Romagna   p.412□D 4

Piacenza, which is prehistoric in origin, was colonized by the Romans in 218 BC and, as the municipium of Placentia, attained great military importance as a base used against the Gauls. The town fell to the Lombards in 568 and to the Franks in 774, later it became a free community and,

as a member of the Lombard league, took part in the struggle against the Hohenstaufens. After changing hands several times, it passed to the Papal States in 1512 before being united with Parma in 1545 to form the duchy of Parma and Piacenza.

Cathedral (Piazza del Duomo): Begun in 1122 on the site of an earlier building destroyed in the earthquake of 1117, it was not completed until 1233. Somewhat altered in the 16C, and restored in 1897–1901. The campanile, 1333, had a revolving *copper angel* by Pietro Vago added in 1341. The *middle portal* of the façade was rebuilt in 1563 (the 2 lions and both columns date from this period); the zodiac on the front of the arch, and the 4 reliefs, are modern works. The carved decoration of the *side portals* (2nd half of the 12C) are by followers of Nicolò. In the aedicule of the portal of the left transept (12C) is a 14C statue of the Madonna, while the portal of the right transept has 12C reliefs. The *central apse* also has 12C reliefs, in the style of Nicolò. One result of the long period over which building continued is that the lower sections of the interior show Romanesque forms and the

Pesaro, birthplace of Rossini

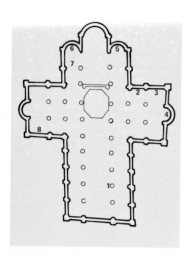

Piacenza, cathedral 1 frescos, 14&15C **2** Crucifixion fresco, late-15C **3** Bolognese wall painting, 14C **4** wall painting, late-15C **5** frescos, 14C **6** fresco fragment, late 14C **7** story of St. Martin by Procaccini and Fiamminghino (vault) **8** fresco of Saints, late-14C

upper parts Gothic. On the inside of the façade are some more 12C *reliefs*, and in the lunette are some from the 15C. Also note the: 14&15C *frescos* (1). *Painting of the dome* by Guercino (begun by Morazzone in 1625/6). Late-15C *fresco of the Crucifixion* (2). 14C Bolognese *wall painting* above a Gothic *tomb* (3). Late-15C *wall paintings* (4). 14C *frescos*, with many 19C additions (5). *St. Jerome* by Guido Reni (sacristy). In the chapter house archive are 13–15C *antiphonaries* and a *triptych, c.* 1390, by Serafino Serafini. 2 *pulpits* assembled from old reliefs (above the entrance to the crypt). In the sanctuary is a Gothic *altarpiece*, 1479 (behind the high altar). The *choir stalls*, 1471, are by Giangiacomo da Genova, and their *paintwork* is by Procaccini and L.Carracci. Late-14C *fresco fragment* (6). *Story of St. Martin* by Procaccini and Fiamminghino (7). Late-14C *fresco of Saints* (8).

S. Antonino (Piazza S.Antonino): In the 4–9C it was a cathedral. The present church dates from a building constructed in the early 11C and consecrated in 1041. Laid out as a Greek cross, the left arm of this church pointed southwards and was lengthened in the 13C when 2 aisles were added to it. The façade of the resulting basilica was added on the W. front. In front of the old façade (now the left transept), Pietro Vago built a *portico* known as 'Paradiso' which still encloses the Romanesque portal with sculptures by a follower of Nicolò. Work continued on the aisles in the 15&16C; the sanctuary was altered in the 16&17C. In the 17C, the chapels on the right of the church, and also those on both sides of the façade, were built, and the interior was altered in baroque style. Work carried out in the 1920s restored the old form almost entirely. The decoration is almost exclusively baroque. The *museum* in the sacristy includes reliquaries and illuminated manuscripts. A *cloister* (1492).

S. Savino (Via Giulio Alberoni): This church, which has today a nave and two aisles, was consecrated in 1107 and replaced a previous building destroyed by the Magyars in 924. The campanile is 13C and the façade dates from 1721. The interior still retains its original appearance and contains some fine features: 12C *mosaic floor* (sanctuary). 12C *wooden crucifix* (above the high altar). Early-15C Lombard *fresco fragment*, (left wall of sanctuary). 4 *reliefs of the Apostles*, late 12C (above the entrance to the crypt). The *crypt*, with its beautiful floor, one of the finest 12C mosaics. In 1960, Paduan wall paintings dating from the 12C were uncovered in the cell of the campanile.

Palazzo Farnese (Piazza Cittadella): Begun by F.Paciotti in 1558, continued by Vignola from 1564 onwards, not completed until 1602. The recently restored rooms house the important collection of the **Museo Civico**. The *Archaeological Museum* contains Etruscan, Roman and medieval mosaics and marble sculptures. The *picture collection* includes a fresco cycle removed from S.Lorenzo and dating from *c.* 1350 to 1450, and also works by Botticelli, Veronese, Altdorfer, Pordenone, Corneille de Lyon, Mengs, and S.Ricci.

Piacenza, Piazza dei Cavalli with Palazzo Comunale

The museum also has a *department of sculpture and objets d'art.*

S. Sisto (Cantone S. Sisto): Built by A.Tramello in 1499–1511. The sanctuary was rebuilt in 1576, the façade not until 1596, further alterations in 1755. Almost all the decoration is 16C. At the high altar is a *copy of the Sistine Madonna* (now in the picture gallery in Dresden), painted by Raphael for this church. To the right of the church is the former *Benedictine monastery* (2nd half of the 16C), with a cloister. The *campanile* dates from 1506–7.

Madonna di Campagna (Piazzale della Crociata): A Renaissance church built by Tramello in 1522–8 as a centrally planned building, and much altered in 1791 by the addition of the chancel. The numerous paintings inside are from the 16–18C. Of particular interest: The *painting of the dome*, begun by Pordenone in 1528–31,

completed by Soiaro in 1543. *Wooden statue of the Madonna,* probably mid-14C (aedicule of the high altar). 16C *choir stalls* (sanctuary). *Frescos* by Pordenone (1st and 2nd chapels on the left; left of the entrance).

Palazzo Comunale (Piazza dei Cavalli): Begun in 1280, it is an outstanding monument to secular Lombard architecture. The *marble dragons* on the pillars of the ground floor arcade, and the 13C Lombard *statue of the Madonna,* up in a niche between the 4th and 5th windows, are of particular note. Of the painting, which originally covered the entire building, only a few remains on the right flank are still visible.

Piazza dei Cavalli: In front of the Palazzo are *equestrian statues* of two Farnese dukes, dated 1620 and 1625, masterpieces by Francesco Mocchi; the pedestal reliefs are also by him.

Also worth seeing: *S.Francesco* (Piazzetta S.Francesco), begun in 1278, with a notable portal and 15–17C decoration. *S. Vincenzo* (Via G.B.Scalabrini), a domed building with a nave and two aisles, built in 1595–1617, with an incomplete façade and rich 18C painting. *S. Giovanni in Canale* (Via della Beverova), founded in 1221, given a new apse in 1522, and restored in 1956 and thereafter (when the 17&18C alterations were removed). It contains 15–18C furnishings and an early-14C Veronese sarcophagus (right aisle, between 3rd and 4th chapels). *S. Sepolcro* (Via di Campagna), built by Tramello in 1513–33, with two 15C cloisters in the former *Olivetan monastery* which adjoins the church. *S. Eufemia* (Via S. Eufemia), built in the 11C, altered in 1739 and restored in 1904, with baroque altars along the aisles. *Palazzo Radini Tedeschi* (Via Citadella), designed by Vignola, with a large 16C drawing room decorated by T.Zuccari. The 15C *Palazzo dei Tribunali* (Via Giordano Bruno 7), built by G.Battagio and decorated by Agostino de Fondutis in 1485, with a fine marble portal at the rear. *Palazzo Governatore* (Piazza dei Cavalli), restored in classical forms in 1781. *Palazzo Vescovile* (Piazza del Duomo), 15C, with a façade dating from 1858 and wall paintings on the 1st floor by Procaccini, L.Carracci, Cignani and others. *Galleria d'Arte Moderna Ricci-Oddi* (Via S.Siro 13), an important modern museum building (G.Arata, 1931), with 19C Italian art.

Environs: Collegio Alberoni: Located on the city's outskirts, with an interesting *art collection*. Particular exhibits: Ecce Homo by Antonello da Messina, Madonna Enthroned by Jan Provost. Works from the schools of D.Bouts, G.David, Veronese and Raphael. Dutch tapestries, 15–17C.

Pianella 65019

Pescara/Abruzzi   p.416☐ K 9

S.Angelo/S.Maria Maggiore: The nave and the two aisles of this church built in the 12C all end in richly articulated semicircular apses. In the portal are *the Virgin Mary between John the Baptist and John the Evangelist, Peter, Paul, Nicholas and two patriarchs;* above these is a 13C *rosewindow.* Inside is a *pulpit* with reliefs of the

Piacenza, Museo Civico, Paul III, S. Ricci

symbols of the Evangelists (12C). The main apse displays *Christ with four angels* and the *Apostles*, a 12C fresco; votive pictures from the 14/15C.

Piazza Armerina 94015

Enna/Sicily   p.420☐K 17

Cathedral of S. M.Assunta (Piazza Duomo): Built in 1604 on the site of an earlier building; the *baroque portal* dates from 1719. The *campanile*, in Catalan Gothic style, is from the original building (1420). The chief items of interest in the single-aisled interior are a *processional cross* of 1485 (chapel to the left of the sanctuary) and the *Madonna delle Vittorie* (Byzantine; in the tabernacle of the high altar): a gift from Pope Nicholas II to Count Roger I at the Council of Melfi in 1059.

Also worth seeing: The church of *S. Pietro* (Viale Gen. Cascino), late Renaissance, with a fine coffered ceiling (17C). Church of *S. Giovanni di Rodi* (Piazza Umberto I; 13C) with a Gothic portal. *Palazzo Trigona* (near the cathedral; 18C) with a fine baroque front.

Environs: Some 6 km. SW *(Contrada Casale)* is the main attraction of Piazza Armerina, namely the **Villa Romana del Casale:** excavations (most recently from 1950 onwards) of a *villa* whose former owner is still not known despite many hypotheses. Built in the early 4C AD. The centre of the complex is a large fountain courtyard in the form of a peristyle, grouped around which are some 50 rooms (including: throne room, large triclinium, baths). Sicily's most magnificent mansion dating from Roman times. The *floor mosaics* in all parts of the villa, covering a total of some 37,500 sq.ft., are incomparable: they show motifs from mythology and daily life. *Room 26,* with the large *hunting mosaic,* and *room 28* with the famous *bikini-clad girls,* are outstanding. Some 15 km. NE (near *Serra Orlando*) are the excavations of the ancient town of **Morgantina** (excavation work by Americans since

1955): It existed from the 5C BC until the beginning of our era. Items uncovered include the *agora* (with the remains of a speaker's rostrum), a *theatre,* foundations of *temples and houses,* and extensive remains of the *town wall,* 6.2 miles long.

Picerno 85055

Potenza/Basilicata   p.418☐M 11

This town extends along the ridge of a mountain in the NW of Basilicata. Lying at an altitude of a little above 2,300 ft., it is characterized by the cylindrical, battlemented medieval tower and by the parish church. The town has many picturesque little alleyways and old houses with beautiful portals. The town centre is still reminiscent of the medieval *Picernum,* although the settlement suffered greatly from the earthquake of 1857.

Parish church of S.Nicola, with a fine 16C altar panel.

Cappella dell'Assunta (near the main square). This church dates from the 14C;

Piacenza, S. Antonino

a portal with a sharply curving arch and reliefs of Roman figures wearing togas.

Piedimonte d'Alife 81016
Caserta/Campania   p.416□K 11

S. Tommaso d'Aquino (Piazza Ercole d'Agnone): Built, along with a monastery, by Dominicans in 1414. It was a reconstruction of an older church of S. Pietro, and was built on the ruins of an ancient Roman temple. The portal is from the earlier building; some fragments of the temple survive on the foundations of the *campanile* which is covered with majolica. Completely rebuilt in the 17C. The 16C wooden *choir stalls* in the apse are an interesting feature of the single-aisled interior.

Also worth seeing: 15C church of *S. Biagio* (Via D'Agnese), with fine late Gothic portal and notable 15C frescos inside, with scenes from the Old and New Testaments. *Santuario della SS.Annunziata* (Via Vallata) dating from 1640; inside there is rich stucco decoration, gilded wooden altars and 17&18C paintings. S. Maria Maggiore, 18C (Via D'Agnese). *Palazzo Ducale,* restored in the early 18C, with a fine façade including pointed arch windows and two portals. *Museo Alifano* in the disused monastery near S. Tommaso (see above), with exhibits from the fields of archaeology and local history.

Environs: Some 7 km. N. is **Castello d'Alife** with the remains of a Norman *fortress* (two massive cylindrical towers, connected by a wall, still survive).

Pienza 53026
Siena/Tuscany   p.414□G 7

Pope Pius II, born here as Enea Silvio Piccolomini, gave Bernardo Rossellino the commission to build the city, and he began the task in 1459. At the same time, cardinals, bishops and nobles began building themselves palaces and houses in the Pope's new summer residence, which was at that time also an administrative centre. Owing to the death of Pius II in 1464, this unique example of uniform design remained incomplete. Pienza is a dead city today.

Cathedral, dedicated to the Assumption and built in 1459–62 on the site of a Romanesque parish church. The serious-looking façade has a high base, pilasters with columns at the sides above which there are three arches and a triangular gable with the Pope's coat of arms. The interior is a hall church with a nave and two aisles (a type of church which had aroused the enthusiasm of Pius II on his journeys beyond the Alps). Interesting contents: *Madonna and Child with Saints* at the altar of the 1st chapel. In the lunette is a *Pietà* by Matteo di Giovanni, who also executed the *Virgin Enthroned* above the door to the *campanile*. In the 2nd chapel is a 15C *marble altar* by Bernardo Rossellino with the gilded *reliquary bust of St.Andrew,* the city's patron. In the *crypt* is a *font* of travertine to designs by Rossellino.

Palazzo Piccolomini, just to the right of the cathedral. This palace is one of Rossellino's (1459–62) masterpieces, inspired by the forms of the Palazzo Rucellai in Florence. The building has an almost square ground plan and a fine inner courtyard with sgraffiti which leads to a garden. The rooms of Pope Pius II, fine portraits (including *Johanna of Austria* by Bronzino; *Pius II* above the bedroom door), and mementoes of Marshal Ottavio Piccolomini.

Museo Diocesano di Arte Sacra with a display of art treasures from the churches of the diocese.

Environs: *S.Anna in Camprena,* a church founded by Bernardo Tolomei in 1324. The refectory with the *frescos by Sodoma* dating from 1502–3 (*Descent from the Cross, Mary, St.Anne* and others) is worth seeing here. **Abbadia S.Salvatore:** This, once

Piazza Armerina, Villa Romana ▶

the richest abbey in Tuscany (Abbazia di S.Salvatore) is to the S.of Pienza and was founded as a Benedictine monastery in 743. It was then occupied by the Camaldolese, and from 1228 onwards by the Cistercians, who remained here until the monastery was dissolved under Leopold I in 1782. They did not return until 1939. The monastery is closed today. The *church* dating from 1036, with a 16C cloister, may be visited. The church interior, altered in the 16C, has a single aisle and a raised sanctuary where there is a *wooden cross* from the 2nd half of the 12C, and also a fine set of 15C intarsia *choir stalls*. The so-called *crypt* is actually the 1st church, dating from the 8C (today it is below ground level). **S.Quirico d'Orcia:** In a beautiful location on the hill between the Valle dell'Orcia and the Valle dell'Asso. Note the *Collegiata* or *Pieve di Osenna (SS.Quirico e Giulitta),* a building dating from before the end of the 12C, and now much restored. Unique *portals:* there is a *Romanesque arcaded portal* on the simple façade, and in the architrave is a relief of the Battle of the Giants. The right side portal, dating from the 2nd half of the 13C, is *Lombard* and is attributed to Giovanni

Piazza Armerina, Villa Romana

Pisano. The third portal is *Gothic* and was built in 1298. Inside the church is a fine set of intarsia *choir stalls* by Antonio Barili (1482–1502). **Castiglione d'Orcia:** This fortified town is at an altitude of almost 2,000 ft. Notable features here are the *parish church* with a painting by Pietro Lorenzetti (*Madonna and Child,* in the chapel), and two others of the Sienese school (*Madonna and Child with four Saints* and *Madonna and Child with two Saints).* **Rocca d'Orcia** is only 1 km. further on, almost opposite S.Quirico. Its charm lies not only in its medieval buildings, but also in its ruined tower (*Rocca d'Orcia,* also known as *Rocca di Tentennano).*

Pieve Tesino 38050
Trento/South Tyrol-Trentino   p.410□F/G 2

Parish church of the Assumption (Assunta): Gothic church with a rich church treasure (14C chalice; 17C monstrance; 15&16C liturgical vestments).

Environs: Castello Tesino: On a hill (with a prehistoric settlement) above the town is the church of *SS.Ippolite e Cassiano* (1436). Its interior walls were frescoed throughout at the time when the church was built. **Borgo Valsugana** with the baroque parish church, *della Natività della B.V.,* built by Bernardo Pasquali in 1698. However, an earlier building was mentioned as far back as 1207. The campanile dates from 1748–58 (the roof from 1815/16).

Pinerolo 10064
Turin/Piedmont   p.412□A 4

Pinerolo owes its mild climate to its sheltered location and is referred to as the 'Nice of Piedmont'. It was first mentioned in the second half of the 10C. In the 13C this strategically important town became the residence of a branch of the counts of Savoy, and came under French rule several times between the 15&17C. Since 1748 it has been a bishop's seat.

Cathedral of S. Donato: The cathedral was founded in 1044. The present Gothic structure dates from the 15&16C. The plain tripartite façade, whose portals are crowned by tympana with conspicuously pointed gables, is a typical feature of Gothic buildings in Piedmont.

Also worth seeing: *S. Maurizio*, mentioned as early as 1078. The Gothic building (1470) has a nave and four aisles, and was restored in 1897. The campanile was built in 1326–36. Inside are *frescos* by the Pozzi brothers, and also a depiction of the *Birth of the Virgin Mary* by C.F.Beaumont.

Pinzolo 38086
Trento/South Tyrol-Trentino   p.410□E/F 2

In the cemetery in the N. of the town is the interesting *funeral chapel of S. Vigilio,* originally built in *c.* 1000, rebuilt in the 15C, and enlarged and vaulted in 1515. The particular charm of this little church lies in its frescos (those on the W. façade are 12C&14C; those on the lower S. wall are 16C; those inside the church date from the 1st half of the 16C). The two upper friezes on the S. wall are the work of S.Baschenis, 1539. About 2 km. to the NE of Pinzolo, situated high up, is the church of *S.Stefano,* with frescos by Simone Baschenis (1519).

Environs: Giustino (SE of Pinzolo): The *parish church of S. Lucia* was built in the 14C, rebuilt in the 16C and restored in the 19C. It has a fine carved high altar dating from the 1st half of the 16C. **Pelugo** (SW of Pinzolo at the opening of the Val di Borzaga): The village church of *S. Antonio Abate* has frescos by Dionisius Baschenis (1493).

Piombino 57025
Livorno/Tuscany   p.414□ E 8

Originally the Roman town of *Porto Falesia* belonged to Pisa in the 13C and then had a varied history after Pisa declined in

power, being fought over as a coastal base. At the Congress of Vienna, having previously been part of Napoleon's empire, Piombino was finally awarded to the Grand Duchy of Tuscany.

Parish church (S.Antimo): Built by Gambacorti in 1374 (on the façade, only the pointed arch survives from the original building). An interesting building, with two aisles of different lengths and a *font* by Andrea Guardi (1470). Just to the left of the entrance is a font which is no longer in use today. The modern font is on an Etruscan column bearing traces of a hunting relief.

Environs: Populonia: This town occupies a somewhat elevated site. Known in the Iron Age (in the 9C BC), in the early 3C BC it was the Etruscan settlement of *Pupluna* but by the 4C it was almost completely deserted. Various finds from the Etruscan and Roman periods may be seen in the *Museo Etrusco*. A fine panoramic view from the medieval **Rocca** which has a cylindrical battlemented tower, and also a square tower. The associated Etruscan port of *Porto Baratti,* on the Gulf of the

Pienza, view

same name, consists only of a few houses. It was of great importance for the iron trade from Elba even in Roman times. The Etruscan burial grounds located around the anchorage are well preserved, owing to the slag which was later deposited on top of them, and when they were discovered in 1908 they were in good condition, with all the funerary objects intact. The graves from the period between the 9&3C BC are well-preserved. They are tumuli with pseudo-domes. Examples are the *Poggio della Porcareccia* next to the chapel of S. Cerbone and, further towards the mountain, the individual tombs *(Le Grotte)*, which are dug into the tufa. Numerous small graves of the Villanova culture have been found in the *Poggio delle Granate* between the road and the sea. **Follónica:** A modern bathing resort, with a beach of very fine sand, on the gulf of the same name. The *Carnevale maremmano* is held here every year. **Vetulonia:** Located inland to the E. of Follónica, it is built on the acropolis of the Etruscan *Vetluna* (later called *Colonna*), which was one of the ancient cities of the Etruscan Confederation. The finest funerary objects are housed in the Archaeological Museum in Florence; on the site itself, the only interesting feature is the differing shapes of the various tombs. These are graves *(cucumelle)* and pits which have been dated with certainty as belonging to the beginning of the Etruscan heyday in Italy (7C BC) and were excavated in the late 19C: *Poggio alle Birbe, Colle Baroncio* or *Poggio alla Guardia*. The main attraction is the *Tumulo della Pietrera* (about 3 km. from Vetulonia). This is a tomb with a dome, and its design and surrounding wall are reminiscent of the tomb in Mycenae. Underneath the main room, which has a dome and rises to a height of 36 ft. and a width of 16 ft., there is another and older room with a dome.

Pisa 56100

Pisa/ Tuscany   p.414 E 6

Pisa is thought to have been founded as a Greek colony in the 7C BC, or even the 6C BC. It became a Roman colony in 180 BC,

and in the early 11C it increased in importance and it became a major trading and maritime power which was constantly fighting against Venice and Genoa. In the 12&13C it rose to the peak of its power and also enjoyed its artistic heyday. After an eventful history it fell to Florence.

The cathedral square (also called the 'Piazza dei Miracoli'), with the cathedral, the baptistery, the campanile and the camposanto, is the focus of cultural interest. There are also some remains of the battlemented *city wall* from the period after the mid-12C.

Cathedral: This, one of the major works of Italian architecture, is a typical example of the Pisan Romanesque architectural style. Founded in 1063, built by Buscheto and Rainaldo, consecrated (while still incomplete) by Pope Gelasius II in 1118. The *façade,* frequently imitated in the neighbouring towns (Pistoia, Lucca), was begun in the early 13C. Above a tall blind arcade with projecting columns are 4 open galleries, each shorter than the last. It is faced with white marble, and the decorations consist of inlaid marble, and mosaics of marble and glass stones. The arcade continues along the sides of the building. An elliptical *dome* dating from 1380. The *bronze doors* on the façade are from the workshop of Giambologna and date from after the fire of 1595. At the top of the gable is a *Madonna* by Andrea Pisano (the two angels are from the workshop). The *Porta di S.Ranieri* in the side facing the campanile is the entrance to the cathedral. Its bronze doors, dating from 1180, are the work of Bonanno Pisano and show interesting Hellenistic and Roman influences (life of Christ). The interior has a nave and four aisles and is 312 ft. long. (The transept, which has three aisles, is 105 ft. long.) The wide, solemn nave, separated from the side aisles by 68 ancient columns (these are spoils of war), is given an Oriental appearance by the black-and-white strips of marble. The most important art work is the *pulpit* by Giovanni Pisano, which stands next to the left pillar of the dome and was made between 1302 and 1311. (It was taken apart in 1599 and not re-assembled until

1926. Those parts which were lost have been reconstructed.) Some of the 6 columns are borne by lions, and some are themselves formed from figures. They support the main body of the pulpit, whose parapet, with its reliefs (birth of John the Baptist, scenes from the life of Christ, Last Judgement) presents the entire extraordinary richness of Giovanni Pisano's artistic creativeness, especially his dramatic expressiveness. In the right transept is the *tomb of Henry VII of Luxembourg* (Emperor Arrigo in Dante's 'Paradiso') by Tino di Camaino (1315). In the middle of the nave there hangs the *bronze lamp* by Batt. Lorenzi (1587), also known as 'Galileo's lamp', because its oscillations are said to have drawn Galileo's attention to the movement of a pendulum. In the sanctuary, at the high altar, there is a *Crucified Christ* by Giambologna, the apse has some paintings of saints and also some scenes by Beccafumi and Sodoma, and there are some saints by Andrea del Sarto on the pillars. The *fresco in the dome* dates from the 1st half of the 17C. The remains of the *cathedral treasure* are preserved in the sacristy. They include a small ivory Madonna by Giovanni Pisano dating from 1299.

Campanile, also known as the 'Leaning Tower' owing to its marked deviation from the vertical (height to the N.: 181 ft. 2 in., to the S.: 178 ft. 10.5 in.). The cylindrical tower was begun in 1173 but when work on it had reached the 3rd floor, it was interrupted for about a century owing to soil movements. Building resumed in 1275 with an attempt to correct the inclination which had already occurred. Today there is no danger of the ground subsiding any further; cement is injected to support the building. The tower has a tall blind arcade like that of the nearby cathedral. Above this, 6 rows of open galleries run around the building and at the top there is a cylindrical bell chamber. The beautiful *portal* dating from 1173/4 depicts various animals and monsters. The *terrace*, from which Galileo conducted experiments on gravity (law of free fall), is reached by climbing 294 steps.

Baptistery: A cylindrical structure with a conical dome, standing in front of the cathedral façade. Begun in 1152 under the supervision of Diotisalvi, and continued in the mid-13C (Nicola Pisano was put in charge of the building in 1260, and was

Piombino, Etruscan tomb in Populonia

also responsible for the Gothic additions —there is a break in style between the early, tall blind arcade like that of the cathedral, and the gallery zone above them). In 1284, Giovanni Pisano was given the task of decorating the baptistery. The dome is an addition dating from 1358, and the building was completed at the end of the 14C. The main portal, opposite the cathedral façade, has a *copy of a Pisano Madonna* (the original is in the Museo del Opera). Some of the sculptures inside the baptistery have been removed from the outside of the building. They are attributed to Nicola Pisano, his son Giovanni, and his workshop. The octagonal *font* (1246) in the middle is an interesting feature, as is the hexagonal *pulpit* by Nicola Pisano, begun in 1260 (signed and dated). The pulpit is of the Apulian type and here, too, the main body of the pulpit rests on columns (with a central column), some of which are borne by lions. Above the three-lobed arches are the rectangular *relief panels* of the parapet, showing scenes from the life of Christ. Here, the figures are of a splendid plasticity, and the scenes are densely crowded. Apart from Nicola himself, his son Giovanni and Arnolfo da Cambio contributed to this work.

Camposanto (cemetery to the left of the cathedral): A rectangle with an open passage running around a square lawn rather like a cloister. In 1203, Archbishop Ubaldo de Lanfranchi ordered earth to be brought here from the hill of Golgotha in Palestine, and the burial place was built by Giovanni di Simone in 1278. There are interesting old *sarcophagi*, *sculptures* and *frescos* along the walls (many of the art treasures were destroyed by a direct hit in 1944—the damage to the frescos dates from this period). The outstanding frescos are the *Triumph of Death* (just to the left of the entrance) in 3 scenes, with the well-known depiction of the bodies of three kings in various stages of decomposition; the artist is still in doubt (Andrea or Nardo Orcagna, Pietro Lorenzetti or Francesco Traini). On the N. wall are the *Creation of the World*, Siennese school, 1390, and 23 large *scenes from the Old Testament* by Benozzo Gozzoli painted between 1468 and 1484 and now much

damaged, together with an *Adoration of the Magi,* also by Gozzoli, above the Cappella Ammannati.

Museo dell' Opera del Duomo with sculptures by Giovanni Pisano, frescos, a David and Goliath by Gozzoli, and a bronze gryphon, which is a rare Arab work from the 10C.

S.Caterina (Piazza S.Caterina): Built by the Dominicans between 1251 and the early 14C. With a characteristic Pisan *façade* (the blind arches are 13C, and above them are 2 rows of graceful Gothic galleries from 1330). Inside, to the sides of the high altar, is an *Annunciation* by Nino Pisano (marble, remains of the mount and gilding).

S.Francesco (Piazza S.Francesco): Begun in 1211; the lower section of the façade dates from the 1st half of the 14C, while the upper section was not completed until 1603. The *chapter house* of St. Bonaventure, with the frescos by Pietro Gerini dating from 1392, is worth a visit.

S.Michele in Borgo (Via Borgo Stretto): Thought to have been built in 990 on the site of a temple of Mars. The 14C Pisan *façade* by Fra Guglielmo Agnelli shows the transition from Romanesque to Gothic forms. Above the 3 *portals* there are 3 *open galleries,* note the inlaid marble decoration. The interior was originally frescoed throughout (some remnants survive), and on the lunette of the portal is a mid-13C *fresco* of St.Michael.

S.Stefano dei Cavalieri: in the Piazza of the same name, which once formed the old town centre. The church (1565 – 9) and campanile (1570–2) are to designs by Giorgio Vasari. Inside are works from the 16–18C, including a *holy-water stoup* to drawings by Vasari, and an *altarpiece* (1st altar in the right wing) with the stoning of St. Stephen, also by Vasari (1571).

S.Maria della Spina (Lungarno Gam-

Pisa, Leaning Tower

bacorti): A jewel of Pisan Gothic architecture. The church, in which a thorn from Christ's Crown of Thorns is preserved as a relic (Spina means thorn), was raised by 3 ft. in 1871 because of the danger of flooding. This small church is an oratory which was enlarged in 1323 and is richly decorated with figures and Gothic architectural ornamentation (gables, turrets, crockets, niches etc.). The *figures above the façade* are from Nino Pisano's workshop, and the crowning central Madonna and Child is a copy of the original in the Museo Nazionale. The *figures in niches* (Christ and the Apostles) at the sides are the work of followers of Giovanni Pisano. The masterpiece by Nino Pisano, *The Madonna and Child,* is now in the Museo Nazionale.

S.Paolo a Ripa (Piazza S.Paolo a Ripa): A church, built in the 11&12C on the site of an earlier building dating from 805. The façade is early 12C and there are 3 open *galleries* above a closed substructure. The forms of the cathedral are repeated on the left side of the transept.

Università degli Studi or 'Sapienza' (to the right of the Arno, Via XXIX Maggio): A university is mentioned as early as the 12C. The building is 15C, with mid-16C alterations carried out under Cosimo I (fine Renaissance courtyard) and a façade dating from 1907–11. The *library* has a rich collection of valuable manuscripts. The *museums and collections from the individual faculties* adjoin the main building. Galileo was Professor of Mathematics here from 1610 onwards.

Museo Nazionale di S. Matteo (Lungarno Mediceo): A former Benedictine convent, it became a prison in 1860, and now houses a valuable *collection of Tuscan paintings and sculptures* from the 12–15C, as well as ancient sarcophagi and some Flemish masters. On the *ground floor* note a sibyl from the baptistery, by Giovanni Pisano, and other sculptures and structural fragments from the baptistery and the cathedral; a 'Croce dipinta' by Giunta Pisano, works by Donatello, Verrocchio, Desiderio Settignano, the school of della Robbia, and others. On the *upper floor* is a splendid polyptych by Simone Martini dating from 1319.

Palazzo dei Cavalieri or 'della Carovana'

Pisa, cathedral with baptistery

on the square of the same name. Standing just to the left of the church, it is a three-storeyed palace with a 19C *flight of steps* in front of its splendid *façade* (1562) in the style of Giorgio Vasari, completely covered with sgraffiti, and 6 niches with the *busts of the Grand Dukes of Tuscany* (Cosimo I – Cosimo III).

Domus Galileiana (Via S. Maria 18): Contains mementoes of Galileo Galilei and an extensive library with old editions of his works.

Also worth seeing: *Palazzo Gambacorti* (Lungarno Gambacorti) in the 14C Pisan Gothic style. *Logge di Banchi* (Piazza XX Settembre), 1603–5, the former wool and silk market.

Environs: S.Piero a Grado: A mid-11C Romanesque building in the direction of Marina di Pisa (about 5 km.) and built on the site of an earlier basilica from the 6&7C. (Remains of this building can still be seen.) A former pilgrimage church. There are majolica tondi in the white and black tufa of the outer walls. The interior, which has a nave and two aisles separated by columns, follows the layout of the extensive ancient basilica. Above the arcade of the nave there is a broad zone with *frescos* from the 2nd half of the 13C, attributed to Deodato Orlandi. Lower row:

Pisa, cathedral 1 tomb of Matteo Rinuccini and bronze crucifix, P.Tacca, 1582 2 frescos, Pisan school, 15C 3 altar; Madonna delle Grazie, Andrea del Sarto and G.A.Sogliani 4 altar with marble urn and God the Father in the lunette by Bart. Ammannati 5 Capp.di S.Ranieri, chapel and sculptures by B.Lorenzi and others 6 tomb of Henry VII, Tino di Camaino 7 Porta di S.Ranieri 8 sacristy and treasure chamber with Madonna by Giov. Pisano, 1299 9 dome, frescos, Orazio and Girol. Riminaldi, 1631 (Ascension), and floor dating from the 13C 10 sanctuary; bronze candlestick, Giambologna, 1602; intarsia choir stalls, late-15C, rebuilt in 1616 11 St.Agnes, Andrea del Sarto 12 Madonna and Child, Sogliani 13 St. Catherine and St.Margaret 14 St.Peter and John the Baptist, Andrea del Sarto 15 high altar, 1773, bronze candlestick, Giambologna 16 apse; angel by D.Ghirlandaio; Deposition, Sodoma, 1540; panel with various Old Testament scenes by D.Beccafumi 17 Byzantine panel, 13C 18 tomb of Archbishop d'Elci, G.B.Vaccà 19 Capp.del Sacramento, by B.Lorenzi, sculpture by Franc.Mosca, 1563; altar after G.B.Foggini, 1685; mosaic, 14C (Annunciation) 20 marble altar by Stagio Stagi 21 altar, Batt. Lorenzi, 1592 22 altar, Vent.Salimbeni 23 altar by Passignano 24 altar by G.B.Paggi 25 pulpit, Giov. Pisano, 1302–11

Pisa, cathedral, pulpit by G.Pisano

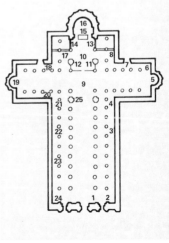

Popes from Peter to John XVII (1003); middle row: Life of Peter; upper row: the wall of heavenly Jerusalem. **Certoso di Pisa** (about 14 km.): A magnificent 14C monastery complex (open to visitors), located near *Calci* in the area of *Monte Pisano*. This complex, with its church, monastery, hostel and the monks' cells, was largely rebuilt in the 17C. The main façade dates from the 18C, and the church with the double flight of steps of its marble façade is baroque in character (inside are 18C *frescos* and a marble partition between the vestibule and the monks' choir). The monastery (1636–51) is surrounded by monks' cells and has a courtyard with a picturesque *fountain* with several basins, dolphins and an angel. The nearby *parish church* in **Calci,** an 11C Romanesque building with a Pisan façade, is also worth seeing.

Pisticci 75015
Matera/Basilicata   p.418☐N 12

This town is situated on the summit of a hill planted with olive trees, and from its

Pisa, cathedral, Porta di S. Ranieri

castle (of which only remnants survive) there is a fine view of the Basento valley. Its ceramics factories are rooted in the traditions of the region.

Chiesa Madre, or *SS. Pietro e Paolo,* built in 1542 on the ruins of an earlier building dating from the 12C (only its campanile surivives).

Torre Bruni: The remains of an ancient cylindrical tower near to Chiesa Madre.

Pistoia 51100
Pistoia/Tuscany   p.414☐ F 6

Pistoia is a city lying in the foothills of the Apennines to the NW of Florence. Documents show that it was a settlement as early as the 3C BC. Pistoia (the Roman 'Pistoria') enjoyed its heyday in the 12C, but suffered greatly in the Middle Ages from the struggle between the Guelphs and the Ghibellines, falling to Florence in 1351 and thereby losing its independence.

Cathedral (Piazza del Duomo): The original building is 5C, and the present structure, in the Pisan Romanesque style, dates from the 12/13C. In 1311, a portico with arches of differing widths was added to the façade with its 3 rows of loggias. A coffered tunnel vault, decorated with *terracottas* by Andrea della Robbia, forms a porch for the tympanum of the main portal. The terracotta of the *Madonna and Child* in the lunette itself is also his work (1505). The interior, with its nave and two aisles, is both simple and impressive. Visible remains of the 13&14C frescos. The famous *silver altar of St. James* in the Cappella di S. Jacopo (off the right aisle) is worth seeing. The small figures, of which there are 628 in all (busts and standing figures, either on their own in pointed niches or in groups), are by various artists from several different centuries, and they reflect stylistic developments within Florentine Gothic. ('The Virgin Mary

Pisa, cathedral

Pisa, cathedral, tomb, Tino di Camaino

Pisa, Museo N., Madonna by Nino Pisano

with the Apostles', 1287, is the earliest panel, further sections were added up until 1456, and there were other additions later.) Jacopo di Ognabene worked on the altar from 1361–4, and 2 half-length prophets (on the left) are the work of the young Brunelleschi. 9 main scenes from the life of the Saint by Leonardo di Giovanni (1367–71). In the chapel to the left of the choir, between John the Baptist and St. Zeno, is a Madonna and Child Enthroned, the *'Madonna di Piazza'*, which was designed and begun by Verrocchio, and completed in 1485 by his pupil Lorenzo di Credi. The monumental *tomb of Cardinal Niccolò Forteguerra*, at the beginning of the left aisle, dates from 1419–73 and is also the work of Verrocchio and Lorenzo di Credi, as well as other pupils of Verrocchio. The *font* beside and to the left of the main portal is the work of Andrea Ferrucci da Fiesole to a design by Benedetto da Maiano (2nd half of 15C).

The octagonal Gothic *baptistery* opposite the cathedral was built between 1338 and 1359 to drawings by Andrea Pisano and faced with white and green marble.

S.Andrea (Via S.Andrea): One of the most interesting churches in Pistoia. The Pisan *façade* has a blind arcade faced with green and white marble, but is incomplete. The *main portal* has a statue of St.Andrew after the manner of Giovanni Pisano, and in the architrave is a relief showing the Procession and Adoration of the Magi by Gruamonte and his brother Adeodato (1166). The capitals are by the contemporary, but cruder, artist Enricus. The most important item of furnishing in the interior with its nave and two aisles is the *pulpit* by Giovanni Pisano, 1298–1301. The structure of this pulpit, one of his masterpieces, follows that of the pulpit built by his father Nicola in Pisa. The wooden, gilded Crucified Christ at the 3rd

Pisa, Oratorio di S. Maria della Spina

Pisa, S. Paolo a Ripa

altar on the left is also by G. Pisano. The 14C *font* is in the style of Pisano.

S. Giovanni Fuorcivitas (Via Cavour): As its name suggests, this church was formerly outside the city walls. The present structure, built in the mid-12C on the site of an earlier building from the early 8C, was only completed in the 14C by an artist from Como. The flanks have stripes of green and white marble with high blind arches and above them 2 rows of arches progressively decreasing in size. The portal has a fine *architrave relief* of the Last Supper by Gruamonte dating from 1162. In the middle of the single-aisled interior is the *holy-water stoup*, an early work by Giovanni Pisano. On the right wall is the *pulpit* by Fra Guglielmo da Pisa, a follower of Nicola Pisano. The rectangular main body of the pulpit adjoins the rear wall and is borne by two columns resting on walking lions; its reliefs show scenes from the lives of the Virgin Mary and Christ. There is a large *polyptych* (1353–5) by Taddeo Gaddi on the main altar. Another interesting altar has a glazed terracotta Visitation. This is attributed to Andrea della Robbia or Paolino del Signoraccio.

S. Maria delle Grazie or *del letto* (Piazza S. Lorenzo): Built in 1452–69 to a design by Michelozzo, with a simple façade and a fine portal.

S. Bartolomeo in Pantano (Piazza S. Bartolomeo in Pantano): This, the city's oldest Romanesque church, has a Pisan façade but is incomplete. On the main portal is a *relief* of Christ and the Apostles by Gruamonte (1167). The models for its figures derive from Roman sarcophagi. The *pulpit* inside, built by Guido da Como in 1250, is a work from the Romanesque period in Pistoia, before the influence of Giovanni Pisano made itself felt.

S.Pietro Maggiore (Piazza S.Pietro Maggiore): A former 13C church with a Pisan type of façade (blind arcade, strips of white-and-green marble). The articulation of the *architrave* of the main portal, with the individual figures standing in the niches, is reminiscent of Roman sarcophagi and is the work of Buono di Bonaccolto (2nd half of the 13C).

S. Maria dell' Umiltà (Via della Madonna): Built by Ventura Vitoni in the style of Brunelleschi on the site of the old church of S.Maria Forisportam. A fine 18C *portal* on the façade, which is still unclad. Note the octagonal *vestibule*, with 8 *frescos* (1494).

Palazzo del Podestà or *Pretorio* (Piazza Duomo): Dates from 1367; side wings only added in the mid-19C. The *courtyard*, with its broad arcades on massive pilasters, with numerous terracotta reliefs, marble objects and frescos, is worth a visit.

Palazzo del Comune (Piazza Duomo): A massive building erected by the Guelphs in 1294, with an *arcade* at ground level, *double-arched windows* on the first floor, and slightly pointed *three-arched windows* on the top one. Beside and to the left of the main window, a black *marble head* is set in the wall. It is said to be that of Filippo Tedici (who betrayed the city during its occupation in 1315), and also that of Musetto (king of Majorca in the early 12C). The Medici coats of arms are above the window. The rooms of the Palazzo are decorated with 15&16C *frescos*. The chief exhibits in the **Museo Civico** on the top floor of the Palazzo are 14–16C *Florentine and Sienese works of art* and a comprehensive *medal and coin collection* (dating from 741 to 1878).

Ospedale del Ceppo (Via F.Pacini): So called after the tree stump (Ceppo), in which the alms for the institution were collected. An interesting feature of this 13C or 14C building is the Florentine-style *portico* which dates from 1514 and was decorated with glazed *terracottas* from the school of della Robbia. The 'Coronation of the Virgin Mary' above the left side portal dates from 1510 and is thus the earliest work. In the spandrels of the arches are *medallions* with the coats of arms of Pistoia, the Medici and the hospital, and also scenes from the life of the Virgin Mary.

Pisa, Palazzo dei Cavalieri

The *frieze* above them depicts the acts of Mercy alternating with the Virtues.

Environs: Montecatini Terme: To the W. of Pistoia, half way to Lucca. This, well-known resort, owes its fame to the sulphur and soda springs which have made it into the most modern and most frequented spa (with mineral water cures and baths) in Italy. The healing waters were known as early as the 14C. Today the town consists of modern sanatoria, recreation centres and luxury hotels, but it also has both early and late 18C buildings. A funicular railway runs from the Viale Diaz up to *Monte Alto.* **Póggio a Caiano:** Half way along the road to Florence; it is also easily reached from Prato. The villa is one of the most splendid Medici country seats in the environs of Florence. Lorenzo il Magnifico ordered it to be built to a design by Giul. da Sangallo (1480–5). His son, Pope Leo X, organized the artistic decoration: above the loggia is an 'Etruscan' *frieze* with white figures in relief on a blue ground. The *salone* is decorated with frescos by Andrea del Sarto and Allori, and also has a charming bucolic scene by Pontormo (in a lunette). A spacious, shady *garden* adjoins the villa.

Artimo: has the **Villa di Artimino,** situated near to Carmignano. It is one of the finest Medici villas, built by Bern. Buontalenti in 1594 for Ferdinand I. The beautiful *garden* is especially worth visiting.

Policoro 75025
Matera / Basilicata   p.418□N 12

Parish church: Contains a 13/14C *wooden carving* of the Madonna and Child.

Palazzo Municipale: The *archaeological collection* is housed here. It comprises clay statuettes, marble figures and panels with inscriptions, and also vases from the excavations in Heracleia.

Environs: Eraclea (Heracleia; travel a few km. W. along the old road to Tursi, then turn right): Founded by Taras and Thourii in 433 BC; it included the port of Siris. In the late 5C and early 4C BC, Heracleia had important workshops for proto-Italic vases and for the minting of coins. The town declined in importance after allying itself to Rome in 272 BC. The first settlement was on the hilly slope to the W.

Pistoia, cathedral

Pistoia, baptistery

of the castle, and it was further expanded in the valley between the acropolis and the road from Policoro to Tursi. The necropolis was to the S.of the settlement. Of the ancient town, some *walls and houses,* with inscriptions, can still be seen. It was only recently that the whole complex was detected by means of aerial photography. The hill on which the *acropolis* stands is still strewn with remains of walls and architectural fragments. Among the most important finds are the *Tavole di Eraclea,* 2 bronze panels from the late 4C on which decrees are inscribed. Today the panels are in the museum in Naples. The other finds (small objects, mainly vases with rare mythological motifs) are preserved in the *National Museum della Sirtide* in Policoro, and also in the *antiquarium* on site. **Tursi** (a few km. inland, to the W. of Policoro). The *cathedral* has a 15C portal, and inside is a 14C triptych of 'Madonna della Icona'. There are 9&10C frescos in the crypt.

Polla 84035
Salerno/Campania   p.418□M 12

S.Antonio da Padova: A 16/17C baroque building. In front of the façade is a three-arched portico; the portal dates from 1541. Notable features of the single-aisled interior are the *ceiling paintings* by Michele Regolia dating from 1666 and the *frescos in the dome* by Dom. Sorrentino, and also a *wooden crucifix* by the Sicilian artist Fra Umile da Petralia (1636). Fine carved 17C *choir stalls.*

Also worth seeing: Roman remains in the parish of S.Pietro: The *Mausoleum of Gaius Ucianus,* and a *milestone* with an inscription dedicated to P.Popilius, the builder of the Via Popilia (the road from Capona to Reggio Calabria). *Grotta di Polla,* where prehistoric objects were discovered.

Environs: Some 6 km. NW is the famous **Grotta di Pertosa,** which has been the subject of investigation since 1897 (it was inhabited from the Stone Age up until the Middle Ages). About 8 km. N. is **Caggiano,** with a Norman castle in good condition.

Pompei/Pompeii 80045
Naples/Campania   p.416□ K 11

Originally founded by the Oscans, Pompeii came increasingly under Roman rule in the 3C BC and developed into a flourishing provincial town. It was first destroyed by an earthquake in AD 63. Together with Herculaneum and Stabiae, it was completely buried by the eruption of Vesuvius in AD79. The town was entombed under a layer of ashes and pumice stone up to 23 ft. thick. Excavation work on the town has been in progress since the 18C and has been systematically pursued since 1869; some 60% of the area of the town has so far been uncovered.

Pistoia, cathedral, silver altar of St. James

Pistoia, S.Andrea, pulpit by G.Pisano

Finds from earlier excavations are in the National Archaeological Museum of Naples. However, since 1911 the objects have been kept on site. The excavations provide a splendid general view of Roman life (especially domestic).

Forum: On the site of the town's oldest settlement. Originally designed as a colonnaded court. On the N. side is the *Temple of Jupiter* (it served the cult of the so-called 'Capitoline Triad' of Jupiter, Juno and Minerva) dating from the 2C BC, in typical Roman architectural style. Opposite it is the *Macellum*, the building housing the meat market. On the W. side is the large *Temple of Apollo* in Roman-Etruscan style, built in the 2C BC.

'Forum Triangulare' (E. of the forum): Only remnants (including four capitals) survive from this, an Archaic-Doric temple from the 6C BC. It is the oldest building in Pompeii. Additional religious buildings were erected on this site in the 3C BC.

Theatre (next to the Forum Triangulare): Built into the slope in the Greek manner (constructed in the 2C BC, enlarged in the Roman imperial period). Some 5,000 seats; there are three doors in the rear wall of the stage. Immediately behind this is a large square used as a school for gladiators in the 1C AD. Beside the theatre is the small **Odeion** (formerly roofed, it has above 1,000 seats).

Thermae Stabianae (Via dell' Abbondanza): The oldest baths in Pompeii, they included an open-air swimming bath. The real thermal baths are behind the E. colonnaded front: separate entrances for men and women; between these is the heating system. There then follow in succession the *apodyterium* (undressing room) and on the left the *frigidarium* (cold bath), *tepidarium* (warm bath), and *caldarium* (hot bath). The remains of the warm air heating system are visible. Some of the original murals in the women's section have survived.

House of Menander (to the right of the Via dell'Abbondanza): Named after a picture of the Greek poet Menander in a niche of the peristyle. Well-preserved wall paintings (flying swans in the entrance hall; landscapes in the atrium; scenes from the Trojan War in the room to the left). Two well-preserved bronze bedsteads in a small room in the SE corner; theatrical masks on the tables.

House of Julia Felix (Via dell' Abbondanza): The owner rented out some parts of this house for festivals (particularly the ornamental garden; in front of this a spacious hall adjoining the public rooms). This hall gives on to the private rooms of the lady of the house (the pictures discovered there are in the Louvre in Paris). The house also contained baths.

Amphitheatre (SE corner of the town): Built in c. 80 BC; the oldest complex of its kind. Dimensions 446 ft. by 341 ft.

Pistoia, S.Andrea, main portal

Pistoia, Temptation by Niccolò Tommaso

0,000 seats. Very simple design (for example, there are no underground animal cages or water pipes for sea battles and the ke). In front of the amphitheatre is a large *palaestra* (460 ft. by 425 ft.), which was sed for the athletic training of the young.

House of M.Lucretius Fronto (on the Via Stabiana): Very well preserved. Fine *wall paintings* (landscapes, mythological scenes) in the tablinum. The paintings (including the legend of Theseus) in the adjoining cubucula (dormitories) are also worth seeing.

House of the Faun (between Vicolo di Mercurio and Via della Fortuna): One of the largest villas in Pompeii (260 ft. long, 115 ft. wide). Famous for its *mosaic floors* (cf. the National Archaeological Museum in Naples); the so-called 'Battle of Alexander', discovered in the room with the red capitals, is especially fine.

House of the Vettii (Vicolo di Mercurio): One of the best-preserved houses in Pompeii. The splendid façade on the street, and the sumptuous interior furnishings, bear witness to the owners' wealth. The peristyle has been reconstructed from original parts (the plants in the inner courtyard are also arranged in an ancient pattern; most of the objects are original).

Villa of the Mysteries (outside the excavation site proper; can be reached by the street to the right of the railway station; signposts): It contains the finest *wall paintings* from classical times. The cycle of pictures, approx. 55 ft. long, in the large triclinium, showing scenes from the Dionysiac mysteries, is particularly worth seeing; it dates from the 1C BC. The figures are almost life-size.

Antiquarium (beside the Porta Marina): Built in 1861 to house the finds. Contains objects from the pre-Samnite period until the downfall of the town: architectural fragments, statues, portraits; objects of everyday life. Particularly impressive are the plaster casts of buried humans and of a chained-up dog which was surprised by the eruption of Vesuvius.

Also worth seeing: *Basilica* by the forum; *House of Loreius Tiburtinus; Casa delle Venere; Temple of Fortuna Augusta; House of the tragic poet; House of Pansa; the Lupanar; Casa del Centenario; House of the silver wedding; House of Sallust; House of the surgeon; Building of Eumachia* (office and trading hall of the dyers, washers and cloth merchants); *Temple of Isis; Casa degli Amorini Dorata* and many others; remains of the *town wall;* the *roads* with ancient stepping stones for road crossings and wheel marks; *necropolis* outside the Porta di Nocera; *Villa of Diomedes*.

Environs: Some 8 km. S.is **Castellammare di Stabia** with a notable small collection of ancient objects ('Antiquarium Stabiano', Via Marco Mario), containing the finds from the town (especially the fine wall paintings); in the district of Pianoro di Verano, above the town, are two Roman villas on which systematic excavation work has been in progress since 1950 (the so-called *Villa di Arianna* and *Villa di S. Marco*). Some 10 km. S.is **Gragnano** with the fine 16C *Chiesa del Corpus Domini* and a massive 10C *castle* (splendid view of the Gulf of Naples).

Pomposa 44020
Ferrara/Emilia-Romagna   p.410☐G 4

Abbazia di Pomposa: Probably founded by the Benedictines as early as the 7C, first mentioned in the 9C. In 981 the abbey was described as being dependent on the monastery of S.Salvatore in Pavia, and in the late 10C it was already in the possession of the archbishops of Ravenna. Because it enjoyed both imperial and papal privileges, it developed in the 11C into an important centre of intellectual and cultural life. Its decline, resulting from the fact that the region had become unhealthy, be-

gan in the late 13C, and almost a[ll the] monks had moved to Ferrara by 149[...] ter this the abbey came to be own[ed by] Cardinal Ippolito d'Este, and in th[e ...] it was placed under the administrat[ion of] the bishop of Comacchio. Seculariz[ed by] Napoleon, it later regained its reli[gious] character as a result of restoration w[ork in] the late 19C. The complex of build[ings,] one of the most important Roman[esque] works of art in Italy, consists of the ch[urch,] the monastery buildings and the law [court.] The *campanile* dates from 1063. A[ddi-] tions were made as early as 1150 to th[e ...] *portico,* with its rich ornamental and f[igura-] tive decoration. The frescos w[hich] decorated its interior have been det[ached] and are now on display in the sma[ll mu-] *seum.* From the right flank of the co[mplex] the visitor enters the 9C *church,* a ba[silica] (one nave, two aisles) of the Ravenna[...] The side apses were not added unt[il the] 12C; the right side apse was torn do[wn in] the baroque period. The columns [of the] arcade are Roman and Byzantine s[poils.] The *pavement,* most of which sur[vives,] consists of several sections ranging [from] the 7C to the 11C. At the beginning [of the] nave are 2 *holy-water stoups,* the righ[t one] built from a Byzantine capital, the le[ft one] a 12C Romanesque work. The mi[d-13C] Bolognese *wall paintings* are especiall[y fine.] The *frescos* in the aisles also date fro[m the] 14C but are not in the Bolognese sty[le. In] the Gothic *cloister* to the right [of the] church, the only remnants surviving [from] the 12C are the corner pillars. The [*chap-] ter house* is to the E., with 13C porta[ls,] double windows, and significant [early] frescos inside. In the large room to the [W.] of this is the *museum,* which house[s the] frescos removed from the atrium, an[d ...] fragments from various periods o[f the] monastery's history. In the *refectory* o[n the] S.side of the cloister are some furthe[r ...] wall paintings, the work of artists [from] Rimini (1316–20). The *law court* to t[he W.] of the monastery buildings was [...] shortly after 1000 and extensively al[tered] in 1396. The exterior has subsequ[ently] been restored to its old form.

Pompeii, Villa of the Mys[teries]

Pont-Saint-Martin 11026
Aosta/Piedmont   p.412□B 3

Pont-Saint-Martin: Note the *ruined castle* above the town, built in 1214 as the castle of the Lords of Bard and destroyed at an early date. The chapel of *S.Rocco* with medieval frescos. The *Castello Baraing*, a fine neo-Gothic building belonging to the doctor and philanthropist Baraing (1827 – 94). The intact *Roman bridge* (1C BC) over the Lys, 105 ft. long, 16 ft. wide, 92 ft. high.

Pópoli 65026
Pescara/Abruzzi   p.416□ I 9

Taverna Ducale: This building was probably built by Giovanni Cantelmo (1333 – 77) as a storehouse for the ducal tithes, and was later used as an inn. A second Taverna was added in 1574, and both buildings were handed to the university in 1680. On the façade are the coats of arms of the Cantelmo and related families.

Pordenone 33170
Pordenone/Friuli   p.410□H 2

Pordenone was a busy trading centre as far back as Roman times; in the Middle Ages, under the name of 'Portus Naonis', it was a fortified settlement, and was Austrian from the 10–16C. In the 16C it was the seat of an 'Accademia Liviana'.

Cathedral of S.Marco (Piazza S.Marco): Begun in the 13C, building continued over a very long period (the chancel is 15C, the portal 16C, baroque alterations in the 18C). The façade is incomplete; there is a fine Renaissance portal dating from 1511. The *campanile* (1291-1347) is one of Italy's most impressive. There is a *'Tiburio'* (octagonal, decorated with blind arcades) above the crossing. The interior has not yet been completely restored (it is being returned to its original late Gothic condition). In the 1st chapel on the right is the *Madonna della Misericordia* by Giovanni Antonio Pordenone (1515). On the SW pillar of the crossing are some very fine frescos by the same artist (1515-23; poor state of

Pompeii, House of the Faun

repair). Behind the high altar is another masterpiece by Pordenone (*Priests being consecrated by St. Mark,* c. 1534, incomplete).

Palazzo Comunale (Corso Vitt. Emanuele II): Built in Gothic style from 1291-1365. A fine *arcade* of pointed arches; on the top floor, interesting *double-arched windows.* The *central tower* (16C) is based on the clock tower in St. Mark's Square, Venice.

Pinacoteca Civica (in the Palazzo Ricchieri, Corso Vitt. Emanuele II): A good collection of paintings from the Venetian and Friuli schools. A 'Pala di S.Gottardo' by G.A.Pordenone (1525) is outstanding.

Also worth seeing: Church of *S.Giorgio* (Largo S.Giorgio) with a peculiar campanile from 1852. Church of *S.Maria degli Angeli* (Via del Cristo), with a portal of 1510 and fine 15C frescos inside. 13C *castle* (Piazza dei Grani), formerly one of the most important in Friuli.

Environs: Torre, a suburb to the N. of the city, with the 13C church of *SS. Ilario e Taziano* (inside is a notable pala by Pordenone dating from 1520).

Porto Tórres 07046
Sassari/Sardinia   p.422☐B 11

San Gavino: This, the largest Romanesque church in Sardinia, deserves a visit. An inscription from the 7/8C commemorates the victory of the Sards over the Lombards. The early Christian rite was transformed during the long period of construction of this massive basilica (beginning in the early 12C). The priest then began facing eastwards to perform his celebrations, so that apses and chancels were required at the opposite end. The nave accordingly became very long and there was no façade in the true sense. Consequently attention was lavished on the side portals. The island's most valuable stones were brought here as building materials: marble, granite, porphyry and trachyte. The impressive length of this church is enhanced by the use of columns to divide the interior into a nave and two aisles.

Pompeii with Vesuvius

Pompeii, Cave canem

Pompeii, baths, caldarium

Environs: The Romanesque church of
S. Michele in Plaiano, built in the Pisan-
Lombard style, stands 12 km. from the E.
fringe of Porto Tórres. This long, narrow,
single-aisled building has no apse today.
The blind arcades of its N. front show Arab
decorative forms added at a later date. The
route leads through **Sorso** (after La Marmora, one of the most beautifully built villages in Sardinia) to **Sénnori,** with the
Nuraghe Sa Pattada, which is of little significance. The nuraghi in the deserted
plain of Nurra are also relatively insignificant. The mysterious *Monte d'Accodi,* 8 km.
to the S.of Porto Tórres, is unique in the
entire W. Mediterranean. It consists of the
massive remains of the platform of a rectangular, raised *Stone Age altar,* which can
only be compared with the 'Ziggurat' in
Mesopotamia. The rude stone structure
does not yet display the skill shown by the
builders of the nuraghi. It has been clearly
established that building began in about
3000 BC. In the SW corner is a long *menhir,* which has an almost square cross-
section. According to local shepherds, it
was formerly the architrave of a wide entrance (?).

Portovénere 19025

La Spezia / Liguria   p.412 □ D 6

S. Lorenzo (collegiate church): Situated
high up on a slope, it was originally built
in the Romanesque style and consecrated
by Pope Innocent II in 1131. It has been
altered on several occasions, for example
during the Gothic period, and once again
in the 16C (restored in 1931-8). The
façade has light-and-dark stripes and a
Gothic central portal, and is framed on
each side by two smaller portals, the left-
hand one being Romanesque. The campanile built in 1494 replaced the older one

Pompeii, Casa della Venere

which was destroyed in a bombardment. The glorious interior has a nave and two aisles. Some of the arches are double arches, and it has Doric marble columns. To the right of the entrance is a *font* with Romanesque decoration (12C). Above the somewhat raised sanctuary, the dome, restored in the 16C, is borne by pilasters. There are impressive traces of frescos in the right aisle. The numerous works of art from the 15&16C Tuscan school include: the *Madonna Bianca*, a small painting on parchment (in the chapel to the right of the high altar), and a *triptych* from the 2nd half of the 15C (high altar). There are 10&11C *reliquary caskets* in the sacristy.

S.Pietro: This uncommonly charming little church built in the Genoese Gothic style in 1277 stands at the end of a promontory. The entire façade is covered by the typical light and dark stripes (completely restored in 1931–5). The interior, on a rec-

tangular ground plan with a semicircular apse, still shows some traces of the earlier marble floor from a church built in the 6C.

Castello: There was already a Roman and a medieval fortification on the site before Genoa constructed this splendid, strategic castle in the 16C. A gigantic bulwark was built as a reinforcement in the 17C.

Calata Doria (reached from S.Lorenzo via the Via Capellini): Tall, narrow houses, some as early as the 13C, and some fortified, make a vivid and picturesque impression.

Environs: Isola Palmaria with the *Grotta dei Colombi* (above the *Grotta Azzurra*), has numerous prehistoric traces, especially of Stone Age man. A particularly fine type of marble is quarried on this island—splendid landscape. **Isola del Tino:** The ruins of the old abbey of *S. Venerio*

Pomposa, Abbazia di Pomposa

(mid-11C). **Isolotto del Tinetto:** Here we find the remains of an old 6C hermitage, and also a small church with monks' cells.

Posada 08020
Nuoro/Sardinia   p.422□D 12

This, the entrance to the Posada delta from the sea, was guarded even in pre-nuraghic times by cave-dwellers based in the rocky hills, as is proved by the numerous burial sites (particularly in the 'Gasile Orgolesu' area, and also to the SW, on the other side of the main road). To the W. of the delta, the Romans built the military base of *Fer-ronia*, whose ruins can be seen from the tower of the *Castello della Fava*, built to the E. of and above the actual town of Posada. This steep-sided 12C fortress was — together with the massive Saracen tower at Sa Caletta—used by the Giudici of Ottana

(and Torres) to guard the coast. Some scant remains of a small nuraghic settlement are to be found above *Siniscola,* on the peak of Cupetti; there are also traces of Roman buildings here.

Environs: *Burial caves,* and even semi-ruined *Tombe di giganti,* are to be found all over the wild granite plain NW of the Monte Alto. This region is so isolated that a special dialect has survived in **Bitti** to this day. The only church of particular interest is to be found above **Lula:** this is the little church of *S. Francesco,* said to have been founded by a bandit suffering from pangs of conscience. Like a castle, it is surrounded by a wall containing small individual lodgings which are inhabited by entire families for days at a time during the 'great pilgrimage' in early May. Beside this are the pits and caves of the *de sos Enattos,* where lead and zinc were prospected for. Dating from the 4/5C, they were used until the 16C and are now ruined. The remains of a small nuraghic village are to be seen to the E. of the *Nuraghe Loddone.*

Possagno 31054
Treviso/Veneto   p.410□G 3

Birthplace of Antonio Canova, the famous sculptor (1757–1822).

Tempio Canoviano (church of S. Trinità) Built by G.A.Selva and A.Diedo in 1819 – 32, it was founded by Canova for his home town. The exterior is a mixture of the Pantheon in Rome and the Parthenon in Athens: the main building is circular, and in front of it is a portico with two rows of Doric columns; there are 7 metopes with reliefs by Canova on the frieze (the remaining 20 panels are empty). Inside, the height and diameter of the dome area are equal (both about 92 ft.); the dome is coffered (cf. the Pantheon); chapel niches are cut into the wall which is about 13 ft. thick. Notable features: *1st chapel* on the right, with a picture by Luca Giordano; at the sides are plaster models by Canova for the metope reliefs (see above). There is a 17C altarpiece by Palma il Giovane in the *3rd chapel.* The main chapel has a *Lamenta-*

tion of Christ by Canova, dating from 1797–9. In the chapel to the left of this is the *tomb of the artist* (the sarcophagus is Canova's own work; underneath, on the right, is a self-portrait of Canova dating from 1812).

Canova Museum (next to the house of his birth): Built in 1834–6; includes models (chiefly of clay and plaster) for the marble originals, plaster casts of originals, and some original sculptures. Outstanding individual exhibits: plaster model of *Daedalus and Icarus;* designs for the *Amor and Psyche;* original model of the recumbent figure of Paolina Bonaparte. The *house where he was born* contains his tools and his death mask.

Potenza 85100
Potenza / Basilicata   p.418 ☐ M 11

The town was founded by the Romans some 460 ft. below the present settlement, at a road junction between the river Gallitello and the temple of Bethlehem (according to another theory, the ancient Potenza was in Serra di Vaglio). After an eventful history (plundered by Alaric's Goths in AD 402, incorporated by the Lombards into the duchy of Benevento in the 6C), the town developed further up the hill, on its present site. Potenza subsequently experienced frequent changes of ruler. Although it has often suffered earthquake damage, the town has been rebuilt again and again.

Cathedral of S. Gerardo (Largo del Duomo): (S. Gerardo of Piacenza was the bishop of Potenza); Built in 1197–1200, enlarged in 1250, rebuilt by Antonio Magri, a pupil of Vanvitelli, in 1783–99, restored after the earthquake of 1930. Only the apse and the round windows of the façade survive from the original building. The stone portal is from the 18C building. Inside, the ground plan is a Latin cross, and the tall dome has modern frescos by Mario Prayer. There is a *Romanesque sarcophagus* in the chapel of S. Gerardo in the right transept, and the *ciborium* with its fine 18C marble

Pordenone, Palazzo Comunale

inlay work is in the chapel of the sacrament in the left transept.

S. Francesco (Piazza M. Pagano): Built in 1274 (restored in 1937). There are fine 15C *Renaissance portals* on the façade, and the left aisle has pointed arches. There are further pointed windows on the *campanile.* Inside: *Marble tomb of Donato de Grasis* (d. 1534) in Renaissance style. 13C Byzantine panel of the *Madonna of the Earthquake* at the high altar. Another good altar, early 16C, with an *Adoration of Christ and Saints.* A rather poorly preserved fresco of *St. Sebastian* in the left transept.

S. Maria del Sepolcro (Viale Ciccotti): Built in 1266, rebuilt in 1490 and 1650. Two-aisled interior. The left aisle is narrower and dates from the 17C rebuilding, as does the fine gilded *coffered wooden ceiling.* The right aisle has a baroque altar which has stucco decoration and houses the *relic of the Holy Blood*. The apse is covered by a ribbed dome. Other items worth seeing: A *Madonna with St. Francis and St.Roch* from the school of Raphael. *Angel appearing to the Shepherds*, 17C, by Giuseppe Ribera (also attributed to Pietro Nivelli). A *Madonna* of the Venetian school.

Chiesa della Trinità (Via Pretoria): 13C, rebuilt after the earthquake of 1857. Inside are *panels* from the 16, 17&18C.

San Michele (Via A.Rosica): 11&12C Romanesque building with a fine 15C *predella of a polyptych* (Christ among the Apostles, on a gold ground).

Museo Archeologico Provinciale (Viale Lazio): The museum was founded in 1899 by Lacava and De Cicco, two archaeologists. Apart from the rich *archaeological collection*, it has an *ethnological department* and a *gallery*. The most interesting items are the finds from ancient Lucania, from the prehistoric up to the imperial period. Weapons and utensils from Venosa and Vietri, sculptures and terracottas from Potenza (relief of a Roman

temple), Metapontum (marble tempietto, Doric capitals), Lavello and Váglio Basilicata. **Museo Lucano** (Via Malta): work by local shepherds; note the *wood carvings*.

Teatro Francesco Stabile (Piazza Mario Pagano): Built by Giuseppe Pisanti in 1811.

Parco di Montereale: A beautiful garden with a panoramic view on the summit of the hill of the same name.

Environs: Váglio Basilicata (14 km. to the E.): Located on a plateau at a height of 3,000 ft. to the N. of Potenza. The *excavations* (some finds are in the Archaeological Museum in Potenza) and the *remains of the neolithic settlement* are of interest. In the 16C Váglio passed to the Salazar family, whose most famous member was Francesco di Salazar, the 'Count of Váglio'. He incited parts of Lucania, Apulia and Calabria to rebel against Spanish rule, and for this he was beheaded in Barletta. The former monastery church of **S. Antonio** (17C wooden pulpit and 5 gilded carved altars of the 15&17C) is in the oldest part of town. The 2 *fountains* at the entrance to the town, and a *Palazzo* with a fine Renaissance portal, are also worth looking at. The chief items brought to light by *excavations* in the surrounding hills were prehistoric remains (in the *wood of Rossano*, on *La Serra*, and in the highest part of the plateau, which extends as far as Potenza). The *remains of a settlement* which was enclosed by a wall 5 miles long still survive (built in 1000 BC, inhabited until *c*. 500 BC). **Brienza:** Medieval foundation on a hill, with a beautiful setting and a broad panoramic view. The remains of an Angevin castle (rebuilt in 1571) dominate the site.

Porto Tórres, S. Gavino

Pozzuoli 80078

Naples/Campania   p.416 □ K 11

Founded by Samian Greeks in the 6C BC under the name of 'Dikaearchia'. From 194 BC onwards it was a Roman colony ('Puteoli') and developed into a flourishng Roman town (important port). It fell into ruin in the early Middle Ages after being looted in the course of the barbarian invasions. Centre of the 'Phlegraean Fields'.

Cathedral of S. Proculo (Via del Duomo): Located on the site of ancient cultic buildings. Built in the 11C on the ruins of a temple of Augustus; radically restored in baroque style in 1634. Rebuilt after the fire in 1964. Six massive ancient Corinthian columns on the façade (founder's inscription on the frieze). A further Roman inscription above the portal. In the single-aisled interior is the *tomb of the composer G.B.Pergolesi* (1710–36).

The so-called **'Serapeum'** (by the harbour): Public market hall dating from the 1C BC. A square courtyard surrounded by colonnades. A building with fountains formerly stood in the centre. Behind the four columns of Cipollino marble is a *Cella* with a semicircular apse (a statue of Serapis was found here in 1750, hence the name of the hall). The corner rooms are equipped as *latrines*. The floor of the hall is today once again below water level, be-

cause the ground rises and falls periodically due to the volcanic activity of the entire region. The *Antiquario Flegreo* has been in the N. wing since 1953, with finds from Pozzuoli and its environs.

Flavian Amphitheatre (entrance in the Corso Terracciano): Built under the Emperor Vespasian (AD 69–79). It is the third largest amphitheatre of classical times, coming after those in Rome and Capua. (489 ft. by 380 ft. on the outside, 35,000 seats.) The outer walls have been almost completely pulled down (used as building materials). Originally designed for the staging of sea battles.

Also worth seeing: *Via Campana* in the NW of the town with numerous *Roman tombs*. *Piscina Cardito* (Via Vecchia di S. Gennaro), a Roman cistern. *A small amphitheatre* from the 1C BC on the railway between Via Solfatara and Via Vigna. Solfatara (the elliptical crater of a volcano with a diameter of 2,530 ft.; approached from the Via Solfatara).

Environs: Some 8 km. NW is **Cumae,** the ancient Greek Kyme, the first Greek

Portovénere, S. Lorenzo

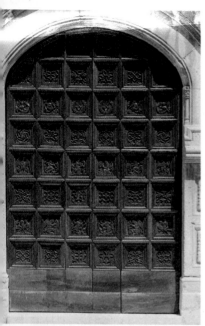

Potenza, S. Francesco, portal

Pozzuoli, Serapeum

settlement on the Italian mainland (8C BC). The *acropolis* survives (with some 5C BC fortifications) with the remains of the *Temple of Jupiter* (half way up, on the right, is a *Temple of Apollo*). The *cave of the Cumaean Sibyl* (revered as a prophetess in ancient times) is at the foot of the hill. The so-called *'Cripta Romana'*, which is a tunnel from the Augustan period, the *Arco Felice*, which is a Roman arch from the 1C AD, and the *necropolis*, are also worth looking at. Some 8 km. to the W. is **Baia,** a famous spa in the classical period. Significant remains of the *Roman baths* and of the impressive Temple of Mercury survive. Some 10 km. to the SW is **Bacoli** with the remains of the so-called 'Piscina Mirabile' (at the S.end of the town), which is the largest *cistern* of Roman classical times, with a capacity of some 425,000 cu.ft., and the *Cento Camerelle*, which is a two-storeyed water reservoir. S.of Bacoli is **Cape Miseno** with a splendid view of the Gulf of Naples (in the nearby small town of *Miseno* are some Roman ruins, including the remains of a theatre and of baths). Some miles offshore from Cape Miseno lies the island of **Procida**, whose main town is also known as Procida. Note

the so-called 13C 'Terra Murata', the *cas-tle* of the town, and the 17C church of *S. Michele*, with a ceiling painting by Luca Giordano.

Prata d'Ansidonia 67020

L'Aquila/Abruzzi   p.416□ I 9

S.Nicola: This baroque church was built on the site of an earlier 13C building. Inside is a *pulpit* dating from 1240, which was brought here from S.Paolo di Peltuino in 1796. The *parapet* of the pulpit rests on six columns and is decorated with rosettes.

Environs: *S. Paolo di Peltuino:* Ancient capitals were re-used in this church, rebuilt in the early 12C. There are also old frescos and Byzantine-style reliefs.

Prato 50047

Prato/ Tuscany   p.414□ F 6

Piazza del Comune: Cathedral: In the 10C it was still the parish church of S.

Stefano. The present building dates mainly from the following centuries. The façade and the right flank were built by Guidetto da Coma in 1211 in the style of Pisa and Lucca, while the 5 later chapels (the crypt being eliminated), were added in the 1st half of the 14C to a design that followed the tradition of G.Pisano. On the *façade* (stripes of green and white marble), attention should be paid to the *lunette of the portal* with a white, glazed terracotta (Madonna and Child) by Andrea della Robbia, 1489. The famous *outdoor pulpit* on the right corner of the façade, the 'Pergamo del Sacro Cingolo', is a true masterpiece. It is so called because of the relic carefully preserved inside the church, the sacred girdle of Mary, which is displayed here on high festivals. The simple, round pulpit which encases the corner of the façade is by Michelozzo, while the reliefs of dancing putti (originals now in the Museo dell' Opera, see below), are among the most outstanding works of Donatello and date from 1434–8. The interior (one nave, two aisles) of the cathedral, with heavy columns of dark green marble, was not vaulted until 1676. The only decoration in the nave is the chalice-shaped *pulpit* by

Pozzuoli, Serapeum 1 tholus **2** cella **3** latrines **4** Antiquario Flegreo

Pozzuoli, sulphurous vapours

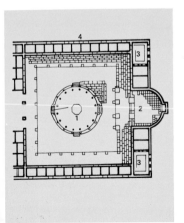

Mino da Fiesole and Ant. Rossellino, dating from 1473. The reliefs are arranged in a circle and show: Herod's Feast and the Beheading of John the Baptist, by Mino da Fiesole; the Annunciation, Stoning and Burial of St. Stephen, by Rosselino (the base with sphinxes and the shaft are by fellow-artists). The choir has one of the most interesting 15C Florentine *fresco cycles,* a masterpiece by Fra Filippo Lippi, painted with the assistance of Fra Diamante between 1452–66 (Lippi lived in Prato for a long period). The ceiling of the choir shows the Evangelists (the design for the central glass window is also by Lippi), the frescos on the right wall display the life of John the Baptist and are arranged in 3 zones, and on the left wall is the story of St. Stephen. The large *bronze cross* (1653) by Ferdinando Tacca is by the high altar. The chapel to the right of it is decorated with 15C *frescos,* some of which (Nativity of the Virgin, Presentation, etc.) are attributed to Paolo Uccello or his followers. In the chapel to the left are early-15C *frescos* by Agnolo Gaddi. Also note: the *tomb of Fil. Inghirami* (d. 1480), attributed to Simone di Niccolò de Bardi, a Madonna and Child enthroned, *Madonna dell'Olivo,* by

Benedetto da Maiano (1480), and a fine *wrought-iron grille* dating from 1348 beside and to the right of the main portal. The *Cappella del Sacro Cingolo* (just to the left of the entrance) has frescos by Agnolo Gaddi and assistants (1392–5) which depict the legend of the Holy Girdle which was presented by the Virgin to Thomas the Apostle at the moment of her Assumption and was found in Palestine by a citizen of Prato. On an altar is a Madonna and Child by G. Pisano dating from *c.* 1317.

S. Maria delle Carceri (Piazza S. Maria delle Carceri): Built in 1484 – 95 by Giovanni da Sangallo on a Greek cross ground plan, with a central dome and drum. The façade is faced with multi-coloured marble but is incomplete. The magnificent interior is a fine example of the harmonious proportions of a Renaissance building. It has *terracottas* (white on a blue ground) by Andrea della Robbia in the frieze and on the coffered ceiling; the furnishings date from *c.* 1490.

S. Francesco (Piazza S. Francesco): A late-13C brick structure. The *façade* with its marble facing of green and white stripes

Prato, Piazza del Comune

is simple in design, and has a main portal, a rose-window and a gable. The notable *tomb of Gimignano Inghirami* (d. 1460) is attributed to Bern. Rossellino. Passing through the 15C *cloister*, the visitor comes to the *chapter house* with the frescos by Niccolò di Pietro Gerini, *c.* 1395.

Prato, cathedral **1** outside pulpit, Donatello and Michelozzo, 1434–8 **2** wooden crucifix, school of G.Pisano **3** tabernacle with Madonna dell' Olivo, Benedetto da Maiano, 1480 **4** altar panel, Filippo Lippi, 1452 (Death of Jerome) **5** Capp.del Crocifisso; frescos by A.Franchi, 1873–6; wooden crucifix, 12C **6** Capp. dell' Assunta; frescos, attributed to Andrea di Giusto, 15C (scenes from the life of St.Stephen, Marriage of the Virgin) and to Paolo Uccello, 15C. **7** high altar, bronze crucifix, F.Tacca, 1653, and stained-glass window, Lorenzo da Pèlago, 1459, and frescos, Fra Filippo Lippi and Fra Diamante, 1452 – 66 **8** chapel; frescos, attributed to Agnolo Gaddi, early-15C (legend of St.James the Great and of St.Margaret of Cortona) **9** chapel; tomb of Filippo Inghirami (1480), attributed to Simone di Niccolò de Bardi; detached fresco, 14C **10** sacristy; remains of the decoration, 14C **11** Capp.del Sacramento; panel, Zanobi Poggini, 1549 **12** bronze candlestick, Maso di Bartolomeo **13** pulpit, Mino da Fiesole and Antonio Rosselino, 1473 **14** Capp.del Sacro Cingolo, 1385–95; grille, Maso di Bartolomeo, 1438–67; frescos, Agnolo Gaddi and assistants, 1392–5, (Legend of the Holy Girdle of the Virgin Mary); figure, G.Pisano, c. 1317

S.Domenico (Piazza S.Domenico): Built between 1283 and 1322 to the plans of 2 Dominican monks, and partially altered by G.Pisano. The incomplete façade with a notable marble portal has—like the left flank of the church—a continuous row of columns with tomb niches. The single-aisled interior was altered in the mid-17C after a fire.

Palazzo Pretorio (Piazza del Comune): This massive cube-like structure was built in two phases, as is clearly apparent, during the 13&14C. The battlements and tower date from the 16C.

Galleria Comunale (housed in the Palazzo Pretorio). One of the region's major collections, mainly Florentine masters from the 14&15C. A 14C *Maestà*, and the *frescoed tabernacle* (Madonna and Saints) by Filippino Lippi (1498) which was attached to the artist's mother's house, are both on the ground floor. On the 1st floor: the original of the small *Bacchus* (1665) by Ferd. Tacca (the fountain on the square in front of the palace is a copy), and a *Legend of the Holy Girdle*, ascribed to Bern. Daddi, as well as another *Madonna* by Filippino

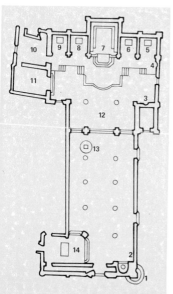

Prato, cathedral, cloister

Lippi. Baroque painting is displayed in the so-called 'Green Room'.

Museo dell'Opera (by the cathedral): Exhibits works by Donatello and from the schools of Lippi, Lorenzo Monaco, Botticelli, and some attributed to Uccello.

Castello dell'Imperatore (Piazza S. Maria delle Carceri): formerly known as the 'Fortezza'. Unique in northern Italy, it was probably built here, by the old city wall, by Apulian masters in 1237–48. Frederick II Hohenstaufen commissioned this square fortress, which has corner towers and Ghibelline battlements and resembles buildings of his in southern Italy.

Environs: Villa Pratolino-Demidoff (15 km N. of Florence). The unusually large garden (625 acres) with the former Medici villa (already a ruin in the 18C) is hidden behind a long and high wall. Count Demidoff occupied the house of the Medici pages. The visitor is conducted through the *park* by a gamekeeper specially appointed for the purpose (it is difficult to obtain admission). The park contains Giov. da Bologna's enormous, bearded *Apennino* crouching beside a pond. **Rifredo:** To the NW of this town is the Medici villa of **'La Petraia'**, which is worth visiting for its magnificent *garden*. The fine *fountain* by Giambologna, with a goddess wringing out her hair, was taken from the nearby Villa di Castello and now stands in the terrace gardens, which are half cultivated and half overgrown, against a backdrop of Florence. In 1575, Bernardo Buontalenti converted the villa itself from a castle into a Renaissance-style pleasure seat for Cardinal Francesco de' Medici. When Florence was the capital of the kingdom of Italy (1864–70), the villa was the residence of Victor Emmanuel II (hence its other name of 'Villa Reale di Petraia'). To the NE of Rifredo is the **Villa Medicea in Careggi**, built by Cosimo il Vecchio (he died here in 1464). His grandson Lorenzo il Magnifico also lived in the villa, dying here in 1492. The original design still survives, and the *frescos* by Bronzino and Pontormo are worth seeing. **Scarperia:** A town 30 km. N. of Florence, with the remains of a *wall*, which the Florentines built in 1306 to protect their city. Note the

Prato, cathedral, outside pulpit

Prato, Palazzo Pretorio

Oratorio della Madonna di Piazza with the remains of 14C frescos inside, a 15C marble tabernacle by Jacopo del Casentino, and further torsos of Saints and Prophets by the same artist. *Palazzo Pretorio:* A bishops' palace built in 1306, with a battlemented façade and a tower.

Predappio 47016
Forl i / Emilia-Romagna   p.414□ G 6

In the environs of Predappio Mussolini's birthplace, are:

S.Cassiano in Appennino: An 11C cemetery church (one nave, two aisles), much rebuilt in 1934. Some remains of the Romanesque carvings survive on the outside of the central apse.

Rocca della Caminate: Built in the 11C, possibly on the site of a Roman fortress, 15C towers. Severely damaged in the earthquake of 1870, the castle was much restored in 1927 to form a residence for Mussolini.

Pula 09010
Cágliari / Sardinia   p.422□ C 14

Pula is the centre of a coastal plain, once feared for its malaria and its oppressive heat. Apart from a nuraghe that still survives on the NW edge of the town, Pula has no sights worth mentioning.

Environs: Nora: The first Roman foundation in Sardinia (238 BC). There was originally a Phoenician port here. Typically, it had a harbour on both sides, and access from the mainland was guarded. It fell to Carthage in *c.* 500 BC. Excavations from 1952 onwards uncovered parts of a Punic harbour underneath the Roman town. The Punic section consists of houses with herringbone floor patterns, a Carthaginian shrine with a snake relief, a temple to the goddess Tanit, a pre-Punic well, and some scant but traceable remains of two *late Carthaginian shrines* of different sizes, the only examples of their kind in Europe. The Punic jewellery found in the tombs is much the same as that in the tombs of Cágliari. Some of it is of massive

Nora (Pula), scarab

Nora (Pula), Punic column

gold, and there are also worked *scarabs* from Egypt. The Romans started by enlarging Nora into their most important military base: they built paved roads with water pipes and drains running under them, splendid houses with mosaic pavements and heating installations, temples, theatres, warm baths and workshops. By the 9C, Nora had fallen into ruin, part of it had been torn down for other buildings in Pula and Sarroch, dunes had passed over it, and the sea had flooded it in the E. The well-kept excavations can be visited freely.

To the NE: Near to Sa Grux' e Marmuri, buildings from three different periods stand strangely juxtaposed: a *country church,* a *ruined nuraghe,* and the coastal watchtower of *Antigori.* The *parish church* of **Sarroch** has a 13C holy-water stoup. Between Sarroch and the Saracen tower of *Torre Zavorra* there are two nuraghi (*Domu s' Orku;* these are of different sizes and dates, 16/15C and 9/8C BC). The late-13C *parish church* of **Villa San Pietro** derives its particular charm from its Arab decorated arches.

Racconigi 12035

Cuneo/Piedmont   p.412 □ B 4

Castello Reale (Piazza Carlo Alberti): Built from 1681–1834. There was originally a monastery on this site, and later a square medieval castle with four corner towers. Emmanuel Philibert wanted to convert it into a villa. The *garden front* (1681) is by G.Guarini while the *front façade* was built in 1755 to plans by Giovanni Battista Borra. In 1834 the two *classical wings* at the front were added by Ernesto Melano. The *garden* was laid out to designs by Le Nôtre.

S.Giovanni Battista (Via S.Giovanni): A sumptuously decorated baroque church by Francesco Gallo (1719–30).

Ragusa 97100

Ragusa/Sicily   p.420 □ L 18

Cathedral of S.Giovanni Battista (new town, Piazza S.Giovanni): Baroque, built in 1706-60. Splendid *façade*. The interior has a nave and two aisles, the ground plan is a Latin cross, and there is a large dome. Fine *stucco and marble* in the chapels. There is a notable *crib* with clay figures at the altar in the right transept.

S.Giorgio (Ibla, near the Piazza Duomo): Built in 1744-75, with a splendid *baroque façade* by Rosario Gagliardi. The neoclassical dome dates from 1820. The inside (one nave, two aisles) has fine modern *painted-glass windows*. Valuable *church treasure.*

Also worth seeing: Church of *S.Maria delle Scale* (new town, Via XXIV Maggio), rebuilt after 1693, with some remnants from the original 15C church (portal, Gothic pulpit). Church of *S.Giuseppe* (Ibla, Piazza Pola) with a fine baroque façade. *S.Giorgio Vecchio* (Ibla, near the Villa Comunale), with a 15C Catalan Gothic portal that is worth looking at. *Museo Archeologico* (new town, near the Villa Margherita), with ancient finds from the province of Ragusa.

Randazzo 95036

Catania/Sicily   p.420 □ L 16

S.Maria (the principal church since 1916; Via Regina Margherita): Built in the Norman-Hohenstaufen style in 1217-39, and later repeatedly altered. The building materials include lava. The three fine *apses* and the notable *portal* on the right flank (Catalan Gothic, 16C) survive from the original building. The façade and campanile were rebuilt in the 19C. On the left flank is the *Tribonia* from the 16C (sacristy). The interior is basilican with a nave, two aisles, and monolithic columns of lava. Fine *sculptures*, some from the Gagini workshop. There is a 13C Byzantine-style fresco above the side portal. *Church treasure.*

S.Nicolò (Piazza di S.Nicolò): 14C, rebuilt in 1583. The fine *apse* and the *transept* are original; the *façade* (decorated with lava) is 17C. The interior has a nave, two aisles and a high dome; the ground plan is a Latin cross. On the left wall of the right transept is a fine *marble relief* by Antonello and Giac. Gagini (1535; scenes from the Passion). At the altar of the left transept is a *relief* of the life of St. Nicholas by A.Gagini (1523). A late Gothic *font*.

S. Martino (Via Umberto): Built in the 13/14C, and later completely rebuilt. Destroyed in World War 2. The façade is 17C; a splendid 14C *campanile* with two-coloured decoration (limestone and lava). The interior has a nave and two aisles, with fine *capitals* on the columns. To the right of the main portal is a *font* of red marble (1447), which is well worth seeing, and a 14C late Gothic *holy-water stoup*. Beautiful *marble work* by Vinc. Gagini ('Madonna delle Grazie') in the right transept. The *polyptych* is attributed to Antonello de Saliba. There is a 15C Gothic *marble tabernacle* in the left apse. A rich *church treasure.*

Also worth seeing: *Palazzo Finocchiaro* (Via Duca degli Abruzzi) dating from 1509, in Gothic-Renaissance transitional style, with a fine façade. The *Palazzo Scala*, a former royal summer residence, now dilapidated (Via Umberto V). *Via degli Archi* with a notable entrance arcade.

Rapallo 16035

Collegiata/SS. Gervasio e Protasio (Piazza Cavour): The present church has been rebuilt and altered on several occasions. It is predominantly early 17C (there

was already a church on the same site in the 12C, and this in turn stood on ancient walls). Its classical marble façade dates from 1857, its dome from 1929, and its modern bronze door from 1957. The campanile was built in 1753. Inside there is a fine 18C *crucifix* (2nd chapel on the right). *The Miracle of S.Biagio* (last chapel on the right), a painting by Domenico Fiasella. A 16C *Annunciation* (6th chapel on the left).

Castello: This 16C building bears witness to the violent struggle between the maritime powers of Pisa and Genoa. In the 11&12C, Rapallo was also involved in the struggle.

Also worth seeing: The church of S Francesco (1575) with its painted façade and 'Christ's Crowning with Thorns', fine carving by Maragliano to the left of the high altar. **Ponte Romano** (on the Corso Colombo), also known as 'Hannibal's bridge', because it is said to have once been used by him.

Environs: Monastery of Valle Christi (some 2.6 km. to the N.): Ruins of a Cistercian monastery built in 1204. The pilgrimage church of **Madonna di Montallegro**, at an altitude of 2,000 ft. (about 11 km. to the NE, can be reached by car or cableway) was built in 1557 (restored in 1907) and has numerous interesting paintings. **S.Michele di Pagana** (half way towards S.Margherita): This church with its baroque campanile contains numerous 17C paintings, in particular one by van Dyck in the left chapel: *Crucifixion with St. Bernard, St. Francis and a founder.* **Villa Spinola** (1.5 km. further on towards S. Margherita): The Treaty of Rapallo between Germany and Russia was concluded here in 1922.

Rapolla 85027

Cathedral: Completed in the mid-13C; a fine *portal* (1253) and two *reliefs* by Sarolo da Muro Lucano on the *campanile*, which is by the same artist and dates from 1209.

Chiesa del Crocifisso: Hollowed out of the volcanic tufa. 14C *frescos* (Christ Enthroned, Madonna, St.Benedict, Robert of Anjou and Sancia of Aragon).

Ravello 84010
Salerno/Campania   p.416 □ K 11

Cathedral of S.Pantaleone (Piazza Vescovado): Founded in 1086 and rebuilt in the 18C. The main portal has a Romanesque *bronze door*, which is well worth seeing (it was made by Barisano da Trani in Apulia in 1179). It has 54 panels with scenes from the New Testament (Passion). The campanile dates from the 13C. Of particular interest is the *ambo*, built in 1272 by another Apulian artist (Nic. da Foggia). To the left of it is a small *ambo* dating from 1130, with fine mosaic decoration. To the left of the high altar is a *chapel* with the Saint's blood.

S.Giovanni del Toro (Via S.Giovanni del Toro): Built in the 11C and rebuilt in the 18C. Fine pointed windows on the façade. The campanile is in Arab-Sicilian style. In the interior, which has a nave and two aisles and is divided by ancient columns, the 12C *ambo* on the right of the nave should be noted. The *crypt* has 14C *frescos*.

Palazzo Rufolo (to the right of the cathedral): Built in the Arab-Norman style. The square *courtyard*, with splendid Oriental arcades, is particularly beautiful. Next to it is the *garden* of the palace, with subtropical plants. It is said that in 1880 Richard Wagner found the inspiration here for 'Klingsor's Magic Garden' in his opera Parsifal.

Also worth seeing: The 12C church of *S.Maria a Gradillo*, with a fine façade. The *Villa Cimbrone*, with the 'Belvedere Cimbrone' (splendid view of the Gulf of Salerno).

Environs: Some 1 km. to the NW is **Scala**, with the 12C cathedral of *S. Lorenzo;* the Romanesque portal and the church treasure are of interest. There is a 13C wooden Crucifixion at the high altar of the crypt.

Rapallo, Valle Christi monastery

Ravello, Palazzo Rufolo

Ravenna 48100
Ravenna/Emilia-Romagna   p.410□G 5

In classical times it was situated on a lagoon and it was the base for a Roman fleet (it was known as 'Portus Classis' under Augustus). Under the Emperor Honorius the seat of government of the Western Empire was moved here from Milan in AD 404, owing to Ravenna's protected location. It then enjoyed its first heyday under the rule of Honorius and his sister (425–50). In the course of the barbarian invasions, the town was taken by Odoacer of the Heruli and by Theodoric the Ostrogoth (493 – 526; Dietrich of Bern in the German heroic saga). The town flourished again under his rule and in the following Byzantine period under the Emperor Justinian, 527–65. It lost much importance after the Lombard conquest in 751. Ravenna's important early Christian churches make it one of the most interesting towns in Italy.

S.Vitale (Via S.Vitale): The court church of Amalaswinta, the daughter of Theodoric the Great. She succeeded him in 526, the year of his death. Construction was begun by Archbishop Ecclesius, but the church was only consecrated by Archbishop Maximian in 546, after the Byzantines had annihilated the Goths. It is the first centrally planned, domed building in the West, and was the model for Charlemagne's palatine chapel in Aachen. A brick building, with massive buttresses outside; the campanile is 17C. Inside, the floor is lower than the surroundings, so that ground water sometimes penetrates. A two-storeyed structure, with a women's gallery. The dome is of clay amphorae, and its frescos date from 1780. The *choir* with its splendid Byzantine capitals and, above all, its *mosaics* is of especial interest. On the left of the apse is *Emperor Justinian with his retinue,* and on the right is *Empress Theodora with her retinue;* in the semi-dome is Christ with Archbishop Ecclesius (with a model of the church) and St.Vitalis, the patron of the church. There are Old Testament sacrifices above the arcades of the choir. Half left, opposite the choir, are the remains of the former *narthex,* and in front of it are remnants of the original *mosaic pavement.*

Tomb of Galla Placidia (next to S. Vitale): Built in *c.* AD 440, probably as a memorial chapel for martyrs (Galla Placidia herself died in Rome). the ground plan is cruciform, with an elongated W. arm. The building appears to be very low today because the floor has risen. The architrave of the portal has classical Bacchic ornamentation. The finest features are the *mosaics* inside (the oldest in Ravenna, they are entirely in the Roman, not yet in the Byzantine style): on the entrance wall is *Christ the Good Shepherd;* whilst on the opposite side the subjects include *St.Lawrence* with the attributes of his martyrdom (the gridiron on which he was roasted to death). Note also the *doves* drinking water (symbols of life). The dome is of lustrous blue, with some 800 stars. In the centre and in the side arms are late classical *sarcophagi* (tradition has it that they are those of Galla Placidia and her son).

Ravenna, San Vitale

San Vitale, Empress Theodora

S.Apollinare Nuovo (Via di Roma): A basilica with a nave and two aisles, built by Theodoric in 500–4 (its original name was *S.Martino in coelo auro*). After the destruction of the Ostrogoths, the church was given a new name (its present one) in 560, and went over to the use of the Catholic rites (during which there was a so-called 'damnatio memoriae' of Theodoric, with all traces of him being removed, see below). The apse was destroyed by an earthquake in the 8C. Of the original *mosaics*, only those on the walls of the nave survive. There are three rows of mosaics one above the other. At the very top, on the left, are the miracles and parables of Christ (beardless Christ), and on the right is the Passion (bearded Christ; these mosaics are from the time of Theodoric). In the middle, there are 16 Saints on the left, and 16 on the right. At the bottom, on the left, is a procession of virgins from Classis, the port of Ravenna; their garments bear clavae, symbols of rank. In the mosaic of the palace of Theodoric, the persons between the arcades (they probably included Theo-

doric) were removed in the course of the above-mentioned 'damnatio memoriae', and replaced by curtains (some hands still survive on the columns). In front of the choir, on the left, are the 'Magi' (much restored in parts), and on the right is Christ Enthroned with Angels. The *ambo* dates from the period of the church's building. There is a mosaic (possibly of Theodoric the Great) on the right entrance wall.

Cathedral of S.Orso (Piazza Duomo): The oldest church in Ravenna, built by Bishop Ursus in the 5C. Replaced by a new baroque building in 1734, the architect being Fr. Buonamici. The *crypt* and *campanile* (9/10C) survive from the original building. *Inside:* A basilica with a nave, four aisles, and a dome over the crossing. On the right of the nave is the famous *marble ambo* of Bishop Agnellus (556–68), re-assembled from the original parts (decorated with animal scenes). There are also some beautiful early Christian *marble sarcophagi* (2nd chapel on right; right transept). In the *Cappella del SS.Sacramento* (left transept), built by C.Maderna in 1612, are frescos by Guido Reni dating from 1620.

Ravenna, S. Vitale 1 apse with mosaics **2** narthex

San Vitale ▷

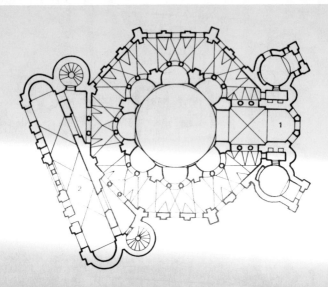

Orthodox Baptistery/S. Giovanni in Fonte (beside and to the left of the cathedral): Built by Bishop Ursus in the 5C on Roman foundations (possibly an ancient bath). An octagonal ground plan; fine *marble inlay work* on the inside walls. Ancient holy-water stoup (from a temple of Jupiter); the font is 16C. The main decorations are the Roman-style *dome mosaics* which date from the time of the building's construction. Some of them have been extensively, but poorly restored. They depict the baptism of Christ in the river Jordan by John the Baptist (Christ is undressed, and the river god Jordan [!] is handing Christ a towel); underneath are the Apostles (still without haloes) in a circle.

Arian Baptistery/S. Maria in Cosmedin (entrance from the Via Paolo Costa): Built in *c.* 500, reconsecrated in the orthodox (Catholic) rite by Bishop Agnellus in 561. Octagonal ground plan, also built on ancient Roman foundations. Of the original mosaic decorations, only the *dome mosaic* survives: its theme and arrangement are identical to those in the Baptistery of the Orthodox: Christ's baptism in the Jordan (the heathen river god Jordan appears here too!); the Apostles' ha[is new.

S. Francesco (Piazza S. Francesco): A ba silica built in the 5C under Bishop Neo (449–52), and almost completely rebui in *c.* 1000. In 1261 it was taken over by th Franciscans and given its present name. I 1321, Dante was buried in the N. wall (hi tomb has disappeared today; the poet's re mains were not re-discovered until 1865, Rebuilt after severe war damage. The cam panile dates from the 9C. Inside (one nave two aisles), all that survives of the origina 14C frescos is a man's head (possibly tha of Dante). Fine ancient columns.

S. Giovanni Evangelista (can be reache from the Viale Farini): A basilica founde by Galla Placidia (see above) in 425. De stroyed in World War 2, but rebuilt in it original form. The campanile dates fron the 9/10C. A particularly fine Gothic *po tal* at the front of the building (14C); depicts St. John leaving his shoe behind fo Galla Placidia. The interior has a nave an two aisles. The original mosaics in the aps are lost. On the walls of the aisles are th remains of the *mosaic pavement* datin

San Apollinare in Classe

from 1213 (scenes from the 4th Crusade, 1202–4; some are very primitive).

Mausoleum of Theodoric/Rotonda
(reached by the Vecchia Via del Cimitero): Built in *c.* 520, probably by Syrian artists working for the king of the Ostrogoths. A two-storeyed round building, built from blocks of Istrian limestone. The lower storey is in the form of a Greek cross. The *dome* is worked from a single block (the material is again limestone from Istria; *c.* 36 ft. in diameter, *c.* 11 ft. 10 in. high, *c.* 3 ft. thick, weight *c.* 300 tons), but it was cracked when being put in position. The questions relating to its transport and installation are as yet unresolved but it still has the hooks it was carried by. The decoration (pincer ornaments) reveals Germanic influence. The upper storey (reached by a staircase added later) has a *porphyry sarcophagus* but the body of Theodoric was removed from the mausoleum soon after his death, in the course of the Byzantine 'damnatio memoriae'. His golden armour was discovered during construction work in the 19C, but was stolen from the museum in 1924.

Museo Nazionale di Antichità (near S. Vitale): Housed in the former monastery of S. Vitale, it contains Roman, Byzantine and early Christian finds (inscriptions, architectural fragments, sculptures, ivory carvings, etc.).

Museo Arcivescovile (near the cathedral): Its most valuable item is the *ivory throne* of Archbishop Maximian (526–56), a carved Egyptian work showing scenes from the life of the Old Testament Joseph and from the life of Christ. From here the visitor passes into the *Oratorio di S. Andrea*, formerly the private chapel of the Archbishop's Palace (built in *c.* 500): In the atrium is a *mosaic of Christ,* showing Christ as warrior on a lion and snake; in his hand is a book with the sentence 'Ego sum via, veritas et vita: I am the way, the truth and the life'. The Lamb of God, borne by four angels, appears in the vault of the chapel proper.

Also worth seeing: Church of *Spirito*

Ravenna, S. Apollinare in Classe **1** Maximian's altar of the Virgin Mary **2** Felicola altar **3** mosaic area

Mausoleum of Theodoric

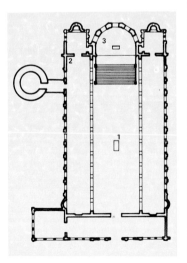

Tomba di Dante

Tomb of Galla Placidia

Santo (near the Arian Baptistery), built in *c.* 500, but completely altered; inside is a 7C *ambo*. The church of *S. Agata* (Via G.Mazzini), built in *c.* 470, and also completely altered; inside, interesting columns and a fine pulpit. The 5C church of *S. Croce* (near the tomb of Galla Placidia), rebuilt in 1602. The late Renaissance church of *S.Maria in Porto* (Via di Roma); there is a fine loggia (the so-called *Loggia del Giardino*) in the adjoining monastery. *Palace of Theodoric* (corner of Via di Roma and Via Alberoni), possibly the remains of the guard-house of the real palace. *Palazzo Veneziano* (Piazza del Popolo), with 8 late classical columns (on the very right is a capital with the monogram of Theodoric). **Tomba di Dante** (in the Zona Dantesca), dating from 1780; inside is a relief of Dante by Pietro Lombardo (1435-1515), and below it is the urn containing the poet's remains; there are fine late classical sarcophagi on the square around the

Tomba. *Rocca di Brancaleone* (in the NE of the town), a fortress built by the Venetians in 1457. *Accademia di Belle Arti* (Via A.Baccarini), including the famous Renaissance statue of Guidarello Guidarelli by Tullio Lombardi (1455-1532). The *Biblioteca Classense* (Via A.Baccarini) includes in its rich collection a *text of Aristophanes* from the 10C, an autograph by Dante, *letters from Cicero* and Byron, etc.

Environs: About 6 km. S.is **S.Apollinare in Classe:** The largest and best-preserved of the basilicas of Ravenna. Funerary church of Apollinaris, the first bishop of Ravenna. Begun in 535, consecrated in 549; restoration work from 1904 onwards. 10C campanile. There is a *narthex* in front of the church. Inside are a nave, two aisles, and fine ancient columns; the only surviving *mosaic decoration* is in the apse. The half dome of the apse has Christ as the 'Good Shepherd' (a cross with 99 stars), and below this is the church's patron Saint with the faithful (depicted as sheep). Above the triumphal arch we see Christ Pantocrator, surrounded by six sheep on each side (symbols of the Apostles). Also worth seeing: the 6C *altar of the Virgin Mary* of Archbishop Maximian in the nave; the 9C *Felicola altar* at the end of the left aisle; early Christian and early medieval *sarcophagi* in the aisles. Note the *crypt.*

Reggio di Calabria, bronze mirror

Recanati 62019
Macerata / Marches   p.414 □ I 7

Cathedral (at the end of the Via Falleroni): Rebuilt in the 14C, with a later façade; the interior decoration dates from the 18C, except for the ceiling (1620). In the sacristy are the *tombs of Angelo Cino,* d. 1412, and *Pope Gregory XII,* d. 1417.

S. Domenico (Piazza Leopardi): Rebuilt in the 14C. *Portal* to a design by Giuliano da Maiano, 1481; at the second altar on the left is *St. Vincent Ferrer* by Lorenzo Lotto, c. 1515.

Palazzo Comunale (Piazza Leopardi): This building dates from 1898 and houses the *pinacoteca* with paintings by Lorenzo Lotto: a polyptych (1508), a Transfiguration of Christ (1512) and an Annunciation (1528). There are also a St. Augustine by Ludovico di Magno da Siena, 1395, and a Madonna with Saints by Pietro Paolo Iacometti.

Also worth seeing: *S. Agostino* (Via Calcagni) with a portal of 1484 to a design by Giuliano da Maiano. *S. Filippo* (Corso Persiani), built in 1665. The 18C *Palazzo Leopardi* (Piazza del Sabato del Villaggio).

Reggio di Calabria 89100
Reggio Calabria / Calabria   p.420 □ M 16

Reggio di Calabria was founded in c. 720 BC by Greek settlers from Chalcis. Along with Zancle (later Messina), it controlled the straits between the mainland and Sicily. It was allied to Athens in the 5C BC,

while from 270 BC onwards it was a confederate of Rome. In the 1C BC it received new impetus as a Roman municipium. During the barbarian invasions it was taken by Visigoths and Ostrogoths. In 1059, after a Byzantine and Saracen interlude, it became Norman under Robert Guiscard. The Aragonese made it the capital of Calabria.

Cathedral (Piazza Duomo): Rebuilt in the neo-Romanesque style. On the flight of steps are fine *statues of Paul the Apostle* and *St. Stephen of Nicaea* (the first bishop of Reggio) by Francesco Ierace (1854–1937). With its spacious interior (one nave, two aisles), it is one of the largest churches in Calabria. The left aisle leads into the *Cappella del SS. Sacramento* with its rich 17/18C marble decoration. There is a *pulpit* in the nave. *Church treasure.*

Chiesa degli Ottimati (Piazza Castello):

Also rebuilt after the earthquake of 1908. Notable remains of the *mosaic pavement* and some fine *columns from the Norman period.*

Museo Nazionale (Piazza de Nava): The city's main feature of interest. An archaeological museum for Calabria and Basilicata, it is one of the most important museums in southern Italy. It includes a *prehistory department* (Stone, Bronze and Iron Age finds from Calabria). The main emphasis is placed upon the *classical collection* with finds from the cities of Magna Graecia in southern Italy. The items from Locri include the remains of an equestrian group, splendid vases, weapons and jewellery. Finds from Reggio, Medma (near Rosarno), Croton, Caulonia and others, and the two bronze statues from Riace are now also housed here. There is also a rich collection of *coins* from Magna Graecia. In addition, the museum has a *department of medieval and Renaissance art* and a *picture gallery,* which includes two fine paintings by Antonello da Messina, 1430–79.

Also worth seeing: *Castle* (Piazza Castello) with two massive Aragonese round towers (15C; never destroyed by an earthquake). Remains of the *Greek city wall* (Mura Greche) from the 4C BC, and of *Roman baths* (with floor mosaics) on the Lungomare Matteotti.

Environs: Some 25 km. to the N. is **Scilla,** the ancient Scyllaeum, site of the Homeric monsters Scylla and Charybdis (on the opposite, Sicilian side). The *castle* occupies a fine site overlooking the sea.

Reggio Emilia 42100

Reggio Emilia, prehistoric in origin, was settled by the Romans in the early 2C BC under the name of 'Regium Lepidi'. The city went through an extremely turbulent period, changing hands frequently, in late antiquity and the early Middle Ages, before becoming a free community in the

12C. The Este ruled from 1290–1306, and again from 1409 until the French arrived in 1796. An independent republic was proclaimed, but the city was nevertheless later incorporated into the kingdom of Italy, and fell to the Austrian branch of the Este family in 1815.

Cathedral (Piazza Vittorio Emanuele): Founded in the 9C, extensively rebuilt in c. 1285 and 1311, and repeatedly altered since then. The medieval apse was replaced by a choir in 1508, and the *façade* was begun to designs by P.Spani in 1554. The *main portal* was completed in 1555, and the *figures of Adam and Eve*—also by P.Spani—were added above it in 1557. The two figures in the niches to the sides of the portal are by pupils of Spani. It was only possible to face the lower section of the façade with marble. There is a *Madonna with two founders* by B.Spani in the niche of the octagonal tower. The cathedral has a nave, two aisles and three domes. Inside, the sculptures by Bartolomeo Spani (1468–1539) and his nephew Prospero (1516–84) are the main feature of interest. The *pulpit* of 1780 uses four reliefs by B.Spani (1st pillar on left). *Tomb of Count Orazio Malaguzzi* (d. 1498) by B.Spani (3rd chapel on right, left wall). *Tomb of Girolamo Fossa,* 1562, by P.Spani (near the right entrance portal, right aisle). *Tomb of Bishop Ugo Rangoni,* 1561–6, a masterpiece by P.Spani (right wall of the chapel to the right of the sanctuary). *Ciborium,* begun by P.Spani in 1577 and completed by pupils in 1586 (altar of the chapel to the left of the sanctuary). *Tomb of Bishop Bonfrancesco Arlotti* (d. 1508) by B.Spani (left wall of the chapel to the left of the sanctuary). *Monument to Cherubino Sforzani* by P.Spani (left of entrance). Some works in the rich *church treasure.* Other fine items include a *Deposition, c.* 1600, by Palma Giovane (2nd chapel on right). Remains of a *Roman mosaic* (crypt, right of entrance). *Choir stalls,* 1460 (sanctuary). *Painting of the main dome,* 1779, by F.Fontanesi. *Altarpiece* by Guercino (4th chapel on left).

S.Prospero (Piazza S.Prospero): Built in 1514–27 on a 10C foundation; the façade was added in 1748–53. The campanile, 1536–51, remained incomplete. Note the *tomb of Lodovico Parisetti,* 1555, by P.Spani (right wall of right transept). *Painting of the sanctuary,* 1597–8, mostly by Procaccini. *Choir stalls,* 1546 (sanctuary). *Christ bearing the Cross,* 1581, by P.Spani (left transept, altar). *Tomb of Ruffino Gabloneta* (d. 1520) by B.Spani (left wall of left transept).

Madonna della Ghiara (Corso Garibaldi): Begun by A.Balbo from Ferrara in 1597 on the site of a medieval Servite church, and only completed in 1619 under his follower Pacchioni, to whom it owes its dome and its rich stucco decoration (not finished until 1650). The side entrances date from 1631, and the central portal from 1642. The fine, rich baroque contents include two outstanding altarpieces: *Crucified Christ* being comforted by an angel, by Guercino (1), and *St. George and St. Catherine* by L.Carracci (2). The

Madonna was painted by Lelio Orsi in 1569 and is the reason why the church was built. Since 1596 it has been on a rich altar in the right transept (3).

Musei Civici (Piazza Cavour): Housed in the former Minorite monastery. In the first few rooms are Roman and medieval mosaics, a wooden model of the cathedral façade by P.Spani, a sumptuous late classical gold treasure, and finds from the tombs of the necropolis of Goleto. The adjoining rooms contain the *Museo Spallanzini di Storia Naturale* (bequeathed by the great 18C naturalist), and the *Museo del Risorgimento.* The *collection of sculptures* has marble works from the Roman period up until the 18C, while the *Museo Chierici di Paletnologia* has a rich prehistory collection. On the 1st floor is the *picture gallery,* chiefly 14–19C Emilian paintings.

Civica Galleria Anna e Luigi Parmeggiani (in the *Palazzo Parmeggiani,* Corso Cairoli 2). This building has a notable 15C *Spanish portal* which was brought from Valencia. The collection includes 16–18C *Spanish portal,, gold items,* and *small sculptures* from the 13–16C.

Reggio Emilia, Madonna della Ghiara 1 crucifixion (Guercino) **2** SS. George and Catherine (L. Carraci) **3** Virgin Mary (Lelio Orsi)

Reggio Emilia, Cathedral

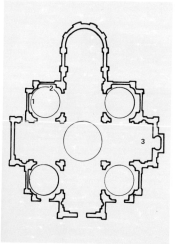

S. Giovanni Evangelista (Piazza S. Giovanni): Mid-16C. The *painting inside* is by T.Sandrini and S.Badolocchio, and there are *paintings* by Tiarini and P.Guidotti as well as a late-15C mounted terracotta *Deposition*.

S. Girolamo (Via S.Girolamo): Built by G.Vigarini in 1646, it consists of a lower church, an upper church and a rotunda.

SS. Pietro e Prospero (Via Emilia a S. Pietro): 1586–9. The dome dates from 1629 and the façade from 1782. Most of the baroque decoration was replaced when restoration work was done in 1929–30.

S. Giorgio (Via Farini): In 1734, Torreggiani added the dome and transept to the church of 1638. The campanile dates from 1675–8; rich baroque decoration.

S. Agostino (Via Bardi): Dating from the 15C and altered several times, it still retains the original polygonal apse and the campanile (1452). The interior was refurbished by G.Vigarini in 1651–66. The façade dates from 1746.

Monumento dei Concordii (Parco del Popolo): A splendid Roman tomb from the 1st half of the 1C.

Palazzo Comunale (Piazza Vittorio Emanuele): Begun in 1414 and frequently altered and enlarged since then. The façade dates fom the 2nd half of the 18C, while the tower (much altered) is from the end of the 15C.

Palazzo Vescovile (Piazza Vittorio Emanuele): Rebuilt by B.Avanzini in the 17C, the *courtyard* and *portico* (left) being by B.Spani. The *façade*, restored in the late 19C, includes the late-15C front of the baptistery.

Environs: A little way outside the town is the so-called *Mauriziano*, the beautifully furnished residence of Ariosto.

Ribera 92016

Agrigento/Sicily   p.420□ I 17

Environs: Some 25 km. to the N. is the splendidly situated town of **Caltabelotta**, which was already inhabited in classical times. In 1302, Frederick II of Aragon and

Rieti, S.Agostino

Charles Valois concluded a peace treaty here under which Sicily passed to Aragon ('Sicilian Vespers' revolt, 1282). The remains of a 12C *Norman castle* located high above the town are worth seeing; from here the visitor may obtain one of the finest panoramic views in Sicily. Some 20 km. to the SE are the excavations of the ancient town of **Heracleia Minoa/Eraclea Minoa** where the Platani flows into the sea. Founded by Selinunte in the 6C BC, it was destroyed in the 1C BC; excavation work since 1951. The *theatre*, the remains of the *town wall*, and the *antiquarium* at the entrance to the excavation site, are all worth seeing.

Rieti 02100
Rieti/Latium   p.414 □H 9

The ancient Reate was the capital of the Sabines; from 288 BC onwards it was Roman. The town was destroyed by the Normans in 1149 and rebuilt with the aid of Rome. Gregory IX received Frederick II and his son Conradin (1234) here, and also canonized St. Dominic. It was also the place where Nicholas IV crowned Charles II of Anjou.

Cathedral of the Assumption (Assunta; Piazza Battisti): On the site of an early church dedicated to the Virgin Mary. Begun in 1109 and consecrated in 1225. Altered in baroque style in 1639. Romanesque *campanile* dating from 1252, built by masters Andrea, Pietro and Enrico and restored after the earthquake of 1898. The *central portal* of the Romanesque façade has a later portico (1458) and is richly decorated. To the left of it are fragments of reliefs and the remains of a medieval fresco. A notable feature of the baroque interior is the *4th chapel* of the left aisle, with works by G.L.Bernini, C.Fontana and others. The statue of St.Barbara at its altar dates from 1657 and is by G.Mari to a design by G.L.Bernini. The *hall crypt* dating from 1157 has a nave and two aisles with 16 columns. The last column on the right has an inscription in honour of Emperors Valentinian, Valens and Gratian (373).

Palazzo Vescovile (Piazza Vittori): A bishop's palace built by master Andrea in 1283 and enriched in 1288 by a fine *loggia* facing the Piazza Vittori (a plaque commemorates the marriage of Henry VI Hohenstaufen to Constance, celebrated in Rieti in 1185). On the ground floor is a magnificent two-aisled *arcade* with a Gothic ribbed vault ('Volte de Vescovado'), and on the upper floor there is a massive *hall* (154 ft. x 46 ft.).

Museo Civico (Piazza Vitt. Emanuele II): A museum housed in the *Palazzo Comunale* (built in the 13C, refurbished in the 18C), with numerous finds and paintings from the circle of Antoniazzo Romano, including a dated and signed *triptych* by that artist.

Also worth seeing: *S. Francesco* (Piazza S. Francesco), begun in 1245 and completed in the 2nd half of the 13C. The 13C church of *S. Agostino* (Piazza Mazzini), with the Romanesque portal of the earlier building and a fresco of the Sienese school, dating from 1354, in the lunette. The church of *S. Pietro Apostolo* (Via Roma) dating from 1153, with a Romanesque portal and intarsia doors from the mid-15C. The magnificent 16/17C *Palazzo Vecchiarelli* (Via Roma 57), with a picturesque inner courtyard. Boniface VIII commissioned the vaulted *Arco del Vescovo* (at the start of the Via Cintia) in 1298. Well-preserved 13C *city walls*.

Environs: Convento di Greccio (about 17.5 km.): This is the most important of the four Franciscan monasteries in the environs of Rieti where Francis of Assisi lived and worked. Founded in 1260, it has retained its original Franciscan simplicity in spite of the later alterations. The *Cappella di S. Luca* commemorates the occasion when St. Francis installed the crib on Christmas night, 1223. The 13C *oratory* and *dormitory* of St.Bonaventure.

Rimini 47037
Forlì/Emilia-Romagna   p.414 □H 6

From 268 BC it was the Roman colony of

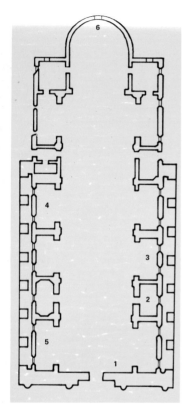

Rimini, Tempio Malatestiano **1** tomb of Sigismondo Malatesta **2** fresco by Piero della Francesca **3** tomb of Isotta degli Atti **4** bas reliefs by A.di Duccio **5** Arca degli Antenati e dei Discedenti **6** Vasari picture

example in the history of art of a classical building becoming the model for a Renaissance structure. There are six massive arcades on either side. The campanile dates from the 15/16C. The *interior* is single-aisled, with four side chapels on each side. Note the *tomb* of Sigismondo Malatesta (see above; d. 1468) on the right of the entrance wall. In the 2nd chapel on the right is a painted *fresco* depicting Sigismondo, by Piero della Francesca (1451). In the 3rd chapel on the right (Cappella d'Isotta) is the *tomb* of Isotta degli Atti, the third wife of Sigismondo; on the wall on the right is a painted *crucifix* dating from 1310. The 4th chapel on the left has *bas reliefs* by A.di Duccio (1418 until after 1481); subjects include the artes liberales. In the 1st chapel on the left is the famous *Arca degli Antenati e dei Discedenti*, also by Duccio (1454). The apse has a painting by G.Vasari of St.Francis receiving the stigmata (1548).

Also worth seeing: Church of *S.Agostino* (Via Cairoli), 1247, with a fine campanile and medieval frescos in the apse. Church of *S.Giuliano* (Via S.Giuliano), rebuilt in the 16C, with a painting by Paolo Veronese in the apse (martyrdom of St.Julian). *Arch of Augustus* (Corso di Augusto), built in 27 BC by the Emperor Augustus as part of work on the Via Flaminia. *Bridge of Tiberius* across the Marecchia, completed in AD 20. The Romanesque-Gothic *Palazzo dell'Arengo* (Piazza Cavour), 1204. *Museo e Pinacoteca Comunale* (Via Gamalunga), with an archaeological department and some fine paintings.

Rionero in Vúlture 85028

Potenza/Basilicata   p.416☐M 11

Near the main square of this town is the *Casa dei Fortunato*, a splendid example of the residence of a rich family. Rionero is a centre for excursions into the beautiful surrounding region, which is rich in archaeological sites *(Paduli, Passo di S. Francesco, Cappella del Priore)*.

Environs: S.Antonio Abate: A Benedic-

'Ariminum' (the final station on the Via Flaminia). From the 13C onwards it was held by the Malatesta, and from 1528 it was part of the Papal States.

Tempio Malatestiano/S.Francesco (Via IV Novembre): Built in Gothic style in the 13C, and rebuilt in early Renaissance style in 1447–56 (under Sigismondo Malatesta). The façade was designed by Leon Battista Alberti (1404–72) in the style of the Arch of Augustus (see below). This is the first

Rimini, Arch of Augustus

tine foundation. The simple Gothic skeleton is clearly apparent despite the earthquakes of 1316, 1615 and 1851 and the resultant restorations. The façade with its campanile is a recent recontruction. **Monticchio Bagni** (5 km. to the S.: Situated 1,770 ft. up the W. slope of Vúlture, its mineral springs have made Monticchio into a spa. From here a road and a cable-car lead up to Monte Vúlture. **Monte Vúlture** (4,350 ft.): An extinct volcano. Its slopes were inhabited even in the Stone Age. From its summit there is a fine panoramic view which includes the two lakes that have formed in extinct craters. On the shore of the 'Lago Grande' are the ruins of the *Benedictine monastery of St. Hippolytus,* whose first building dates back to the 11 or 12C. The monastery of *S. Michele di Monticchio* (or *del Vúlture*) stands in an isolated site on a crag above the lakes. It has an 18C church and, cut into the rock, the earliest chapel of S. Michele, with a square main room and a small exedra. Some of the Byzantine frescos (Deësis) have been obliterated.

Riva 38066
Trento/South Tyrol-Trentino   p.410☐F 3

This small town at the N. end of Lake Garda has a fine harbour with arcades and a clock-tower, and attracts numerous tourists. *La Rocca,* the former castle of the Scaligers, dates from the 12–15C and is surrounded by water. The Romanesque church of *S. Tomaso* was built in 1184, and its choir and sanctuary contain 14C frescos. The church of the *Inviolata,* N. of the town on the road to Arco, is also significant. The octagonal interior of this church (1603), which has a square exterior, is extraordinarily richly decorated. The black, red and gold stucco work is by Davide Reti (1609), the frescos are the work of Martino Teofilo Polacco (c. 1610), and the fresco of the Madonna at the high altar was painted by Mangiavino in the 16C. On the side altars, one of the altarpieces, with crucifix, is by Guido Reni (early 17C), while the other three are the work of Jacopo Negretti, known as Palma Giovane (1544–1628).

Environs: Arco (to the NE of Riva): This small, old town with its 12C castle (ruined since 1703) was painted in watercolour by Albrecht Dürer as early as 1495.

Rívoli 10098

Turin/Piedmont   p.412 ☐ B 4

Castle: Located above the town, the castle has retained its original 12C square ground plan. Destroyed by fire in 1691, it was partially rebuilt in the Piedmontese high baroque style in 1711–13 to plans by Michelangelo Garove, and, from 1715 onwards, by F.Juvarra. The stucco work inside is by C.Papa and P.F.Somazzo, and the painting by G.B.Van Loo, A.Malatto and others.

Also worth seeing: *S.Maria Assunta,* also known as *S. Domenico* (Via Marchetti), a collegiate church from the 13&14C, altered in baroque style by Mario Ludovico Quarini in the 18C. Beside and to the left of the baroque front there stands the 14C Lombard Gothic campanile. The 17C *S. Croce* (Via S.Croce), with a sumptuous organ by Stefano Maria Clemente.

Rocca Imperiale 87074

Cosenza/Calabria   p.418 ☐ N 12

This little town lies on the border of Calabria and Lucania. On top of a hill above the town is the **castle,** built by Emperor Frederick II Hohenstaufen along the lines of Lagopesole near Potenza and of Lucera near Foggia in Apulia; altered by the Aragonese. *Parish church* with a 17C carved polyptych and a 13C campanile.

Environs: Standing on Capo Spulico, on the coast some 15 km. S. , is **Caste Roseto.** Dating from the 16C, it has batt lemented *towers* and a fine site overlook ing the sea. 3 km. inland is the village o **Roseto Capo Spulico,** with a medieva *wall,* most of which survives.

Roma/Rome 00100

Rome/Latium   p.414 ☐ G/H 9/1

I. INTRODUCTION

History: As early as *c.* 1000 BC there wa a Latin settlement (Roma Quadrata) on th Capitoline Hill; at the same time there wa probably also a bridge to the island in th Tiber below. Evidence suggests there wa a Sabine settlement on the Quirinal an Esquiline hills from the 8C. The two settlements merged in *c.* 600 BC and on the plain in the middle of the 3 hills (the Forum), was incorporated in *c.* 500 BC, which could be considered as the date o the emergence of Ancient Rome. The legendary date of Rome's foundation by Romulus and Remus in 753 BC seems to be an amalgam of these dates. The Etruscan kings were driven out in 510 BC, leaving their social structure as a legacy to the Roman republic of the Patricians. Rome's supremacy was extended in the course of the 4C BC and the successful conclusion of the Punic Wars (201 BC) was the beginning of Rome's rise to become the ruling power of the Mediterranean world. By this time Rome was a highly developed military and bureaucratic state. In the last century BC Rome was shaken by civil wars and conspiracies. The age of the Republic finally came to an end with the murder of Caesar in 44 BC. The empire became an institution under Augustus, whose reign was known as the Golden Age and under whom the city achieved a size it was to remain at for centuries. The Julio-Claudian House followed Augustus up to AD 69, when it was succeeded by the Flavians. The succession of Adoptive Emperors began in AD 96. In 193 Septimius Severus established a new dynasty. The 'Second Flavians' ruled from 305 to 330, when

Arco (Riva), castle

Constantine transferred the seat of government to Constantinople. In 395 the Empire divided into western and eastern. The last Western Roman Emperor, Romulus Augustulus, was removed by Odoacer. Rome was sacked many times in the course of migrations and the centres of the Empire had meanwhile become Constantinople (East Rome) and Ravenna. Rome gradually declined and its population dwindled; only 25,000 remained, compared with up to 1.5 million at the time of the Emperors. The sole authority, the Papacy required the help of Pepin, King of the Franks (753), in order to create a secure basis for its display of power. The Papacy's swift rise to political power came when it linked itself spiritually with the Emperor—in 800 Pope Leo III crowned Charlemagne. The Investiture contest (Gregory VII) provided the high point of this power. With Innocent III the Papacy attained the summit of its world power. In the mid-12C the citizens of Rome vainly attempted to establish a city state (Cola Rienzi). Martin IV reinstated the senate in 1284. Exile in Avignon and the schism (14&15C) took Rome once more to the the very edge of collapse. Only under Martin V did Rome start to rise again. The Renaissance Popes may have laid the foundation stone of present-day Rome but it was the Popes of the 16–18C, following the Counter-Reformation, who gave the city its real character. Spiritual and political upheavals at the end of the 18C—which altered the historical landscape of Europe— also had a serious effect on Rome and the Papal States. The Papacy faced a grave crisis, when, in 1798–99, the 'Roman Republic' was proclaimed and French troops occupied the city. Pius VI was taken to Valence (France) and Napoleon declared Rome the titular capital of the 'King of Rome' (his son). It was not until the Congress of Vienna in 1815 that Rome was reinstated as capital of the restored Papal States. The Pope was again forced out of Rome by the revolution of 1848. In 1850 Pius IX succeeded in returning to Rome with the help of French troops from Gaeta. It was not until 1870, when Napoleon III was forced to withdraw his French protecting force from the city, that Rome was able to realize the aims of the Risorgimento by becoming capital of unified Italy. On the 20 September 1870 Italian troops marched into the city through the Porta Pia. The Pope withdrew into the Vatican as a 'voluntary prisoner'.

The topography and development of the city: The seven hills of historical Rome are surrounded by a tight loop of the Tiber. Up until the late 19C there was only the Trastevere district and the Borgo di S.Pietro (Castel Sant'Angelo, Vatican) on the other side of the Tiber. It was not until the beginning of this century that Rome extended beyond the Aurelian Wall of the late Imperial Age. Within the Servian Wall (378 BC) lay the Capitol (Campidoglio), the Palatine (M. Palatino), the Esquiline (M. Esquilino), the Viminal (M. Viminale), the Quirinal and, right in the S., the Aventine (M. Aventino). The Aurelian Wall (AD 271) incorporated the following areas into the city boundaries: the Caelian (M. Celio) in the S., M. Pincio in the N., the Campus Martius, stretching W. to the Tiber, Pagus Janiculensis (Trastevere) on the other side of the Tiber, as well as M. Testaccio S.of the Aventine. The Janiculum (Gianicolo) and the Ager Vaticanus, with M. Mario behind it to the NW, were not incorporated into the city until the expansions begun in 1870. From Julius II onwards the Popes began to radically alter the medieval structure of the city: the Via Giulia was built; the hills were incorporated into the planning of the city (layout of the Via Sistina) and the seven main churches were connected under Sixtus V. The most decisive alteration of the city's medieval character was the building of St.Peter's, the dome of which can be seen for miles; domes of baroque churches also dominate the city's skyline. Above all, the layout of the town was characterized by its squares. From the 16C on a series of villas (originally over 20) were built around the town. After 1870 new quarters were planned (N. of the meadows around the Castel Sant'Angelo,

Rome, view of the Tiber with St.Peter's and Castel Sant'Angelo, painting by Vanvitelli

round the Stazione Termini and the Piazza Vittorio Emanuele), new roads were opened (Corso Vittorio Emanuele), new bridges built, the Tiber was regulated and pretentious administrative buildings, ministries and monuments were erected. The population increased rapidly, passing one million in 1930. Mussolini tore into the city structure too (Via dei Fori Imperiali, Corso del Rinascimento, Via della Conciliazione). In the N. of Rome the Foro Italico and in the S. the satellite town EUR were built..

II. MONUMENTS

The ancient monuments: In the Middle Ages the ancient monuments were used as quarries (the Colosseum) or converted into fortresses (Theatre of Marcellus). In the course of the 16C an increased interest in antiquity developed, but at this time it was limited principally to the excavation of sculptures. It was not until the late 18C that research and conservation of the remaining monuments began (Winkelmann). Self-contained excavation areas are now the Forum Romanum, the Imperial Fora and the Palatine.

Ara Pacis Augustae and Mausoleum of Augustus (Via di Ripetta): Built by Augustus to celebrate his pacification of the Provinces in 13 BC (excavated 1903–37). The sacrificial altar inside is enclosed by a surrounding wall. The outside of this enclosure is decorated with a garland frieze in the lower half and a relief of a procession in the upper half. The inside has a sort of paling with a garland frieze.

The Popes
The following is a selection of the most important figures in the history of the Papacy (including popes who played important roles in the development of Rome). All the popes are listed from the 17C onwards. The dates given are the beginning and end of each pontificate.

Peter (Apostle)	+64 or 67
Clement I (the first Roman pope)	88–97
Sylvester I	314–335
Liberius	352–366
Leo I the Great	440–461
Gregory I the Great	590–604
Honorius I	625–638
Stephen III	752–757
Leo III	795–816
Clement II (Suidger of Bamberg)	1046–1047
Nicholas II (Gérard de Bourgogne)	1059–1061
Gregory VII (Hildebrand of Sovana)	1073–1085
Urban II (Odo of Châtillon)	1088–1099
Alexander III	1159–1181
Innocent III	1198–1216

Innocent IV	1243-1254
Martin IV	1281-1285

'French' Popes

Clement V	1305-1314
up to	
Gregory XI	1370-1378

Popes of the Great Schism

Rome

Urban VI	(1378-1389)
Boniface IX	(1389-1404)
Innocent VII	(1404-1406)
Gregory XII	(1406-1415)

Avignon

Clement VII	(1378-1394)
Benedict XIII	(1394-1423)

Pisa

Alexander V	(1409-1410)
John XXIII	(1410-1415)

Rome

Martin V (Colonna)	1417-1431
Nicholas V (Parentucelli)	1447-1455
Pius II (Piccolomini)	1458-1464
Sixtus IV (della Rovere)	1471-1484
Innocent VIII (Cibo)	1484-1492
Alexander VI (Borgia)	1492-1503
Pius III (Todeschini-Piccolomini)	1503
Julius II (della Rovere)	1503-1513
Leo X (Medici)	1513-1521
Clement VII (Medici)	1523-1534
Paul III (Farnese)	1534-1549
Paul IV (Caraffa)	1555-1559
Pius IV (Medici)	1559-1565
Gregory XIII (Boncompagni)	1572-1585
Sixtus V (Peretti)	1585-1590
Clement VIII (Aldobrandini)	1592-1605
Paul V (Borghese)	1605-1621
Gregory XV (Ludovisi)	1621-1623
Urban VIII (Barberini)	1623-1644
Innocent X (Pamphilj)	1644-1655
Alexander VII (Chigi)	1655-1667
Clement IX (Rospigliosi)	1667-1669
Clement X (Altieri)	1670-1676
Innocent XI (Odescalchi)	1676-1689
Alexander VIII (Ottoboni)	1689-1691
Innocent XII (Pignatelli)	1691-1700
Clement XI (Albani)	1700-1721
Innocent XIII (Conti)	1721-1724
Benedict XIII (Orsini)	1724-1730
Clement XII (Corsini)	1730-1740
Benedict XIV (Lambertini)	1740-1758
Clement XIII (Rezzonico)	1758-1769
Clement XIV (Ganganelli)	1769-1774
Pius VI (Braschi)	1775-1799
Pius VII (Chiaramonti)	1800-1823
Leo XII (Genga)	1823-1829
Pius VIII (Castiglioni)	1829-1830
Gregory XVI (Cappellari)	1831-1846
Pius IX (Mastai-Ferretti)	1846-1878
Leo XIII (Pecci)	1878-1903
Pius X (Sarto)	1903-1914
Benedict XV (della Chiesa)	1914-1922
Pius XI (Ratti)	1922-1939
Pius XII (Pacelli)	1939-1958
John XXIII (Roncalli)	1958-1963
Paul VI (Montini)	1963-1978
John Paul I	1978
John Paul II	1978

The Emperors

The Julio-Claudian House

Octavianus Augustus	27 BC-AD 14
Tiberius	14-37
Caligula	37-41
Claudius	41-54
Nero	54-68

The Flavians (69-96)

Vespasian	69-79
Titus	79-81
Domitian	81-96
Trajan	98-117
Hadrian	117-138

The Antonines (138-192)

Antoninus Pius	138-161
Marcus Aurelius	161-180

The Severans (193-235)

Septimius Severus	193-211
Caracalla	211-217
Diocletian	284-305
Maximian	285-305

The 'Second Flavians' (305-363)

Constantius I Chlorus	305-306
Constantine the Great	312-337
Constantine II	337-340
Julian the Apostate	361-363
Honorius	395-423
Romulus Augustulus	475-476

The **Ara Pacis Augustae** is one of the most important political and religious monuments from the early Imperial Age. Beside it stands the **Mausoleum of Augustus.** The circular ring of stones was covered by a mound of earth (like an Etruscan tomb). In front of it there were two obelisks.

Basilica di Porta Maggiore (Via Prenestina, 17/Porta Maggiore): This subterranean complex dates from the 1C AD. It was discovered in 1917 and as yet its significance is not clear. In ground plan it is similar to that of a Christian basilica with a porch. Walls and ceilings are covered with stuccoes of mythological scenes and landscapes.

Circus Maximus (below the Palatine): The remnants of Rome's largest circus, probably dating from 329 BC, lie in the valley between the Palatine and the Aventine.

Domus Aurea (NE of the Colosseum): After the burning of Rome (AD 64), Nero had an extensive villa laid out with numerous buildings, an artificial lake (see

Colosseum), game enclosures, vineyards etc. The over-costly project ruined the state's finances and the villa was converted into functional buildings by Nero's successors.

The Fora and the Palatine: The Forum Romanum: The marshy area between the Capitoline and the Palatine was drained in *c.* 510 BC under the Etruscan King Tarquinius Superbus. By the 5C the rectangular area—at first composed of holy shrines, but later including secular complexes as well—had already become the religious and political focus of the city. Originally the Forum was also involved in trading, but as it took on a bigger role in representative government, the former role was assumed by the various markets. Julius Caesar had the Forum rearranged and built on the last empty sites. From Augustus onwards buildings contributing to the divinity cult of the Caesars and closely linking the function of the Forum with that of the Imperial house, were either built or renamed. The Forum declined following the barbarian invasions. Rapid dwindling of the population left the area around the Forum so empty that it was referred to as the Campo Vaccino (Cow Pasture). Some buildings, such as the Curia and the Temple of Antoninus and Faustina, remained structurally untouched as they were converted into Christian churches. There have been systematic excavations since 1870.

Details of the excavations (entrance on the Via Fori Imperiali): On the Palazzo Senatorio (in the W.) the arches of the *Tabularium* (State archives of the Roman Republic) can be seen. Below these are 3 Corinthian columns, which are the remains of the Temple of Vespasian (AD 79). In front of this stands the *Arch of Septimius Severus* which was dedicated to the emperor by the Senate and people in 203. Reliefs celebrate the emperor's military campaigns. The three-arched structure was the prototype for many triumphal arches. To the left of the arch is the orator's tribune, the *Rostra*, named after the ships' beaks, or rostra, captured and brought back to Rome. Slightly raised, in the SW cor-

1503 – 1513
JULIUS II
DELLA ROVERE

1513 – 1521
LEO X
MEDICI

1534 – 1549
PAUL III
FARNESE

1585 – 1590
SIXTUS V
PERETTI

1592 – 1605
CLEMENT VIII
ALDOBRANDINI

1605 – 1621
PAUL V
BORGHESE

1623 – 1644
URBAN VIII
BARBERINI

1644 – 1655
INNOCENT X
PAMPHILJ

1655 – 1667
ALEXANDER VII
CHIGI

ner of the excavation area are 8 Ionic columns belonging to the *Temple of Saturn* (remains of the 4C building). The State treasury was housed here. The S. side is bordered by the *Basilica Julia,* begun by Julius Caesar and completed under Augustus. In front of the basilica stand the *Column of Phocas* (608) and the bases of two equestrian statues *Equus Domitiani* and *Equus Traiani.* Below the church of SS. Luca e Martina (N. side of the Forum) is the *Curia.* This tall brick building was formerly the senate house. Inside there are *marble balustrades* from the time of Hadrian, reliefs of which show the emperor addressing the people, a seated statue of Trajan and reliefs of the burning of tax documents. On the Comitium, or area in front of the Curia, is the *Lapis Niger,* which traditionally marks the tomb of Romulus. Adjoining the Curia to the E. is the *Basilica Aemilia* (1C BC). The Forum is bordered to the E. by the *Temple of Julius Caesar,* next to which stand the remains of the *Temple of Castor and Pollux,* —3 Corinthian columns from the building of AD 6. S. of the temple is *Santa Maria Antiqua,* which was built in the 8C and includes the vestibule (or library) of the Augustan complex on the Palatine. The wall paintings are interesting—an 8C christological cycle (many times painted over). Below the Palatine the *House of the Vestals* extends to the E. In front of it is the round *Temple of Vesta,* in which the eternal fire was guarded and the Palladium (by tradition said to come from Troy) preserved. The remains date from the last period of construction under Septimius Severus. Opposite the House of the Vestals is the *Temple of Antoninus and Faustina* (2C), in front of which are the foundations of the *Regia* (the official residence of the Pontifex Maximus). Next to the temple is a *round building,* which was dedicated to Maxentius's son, who died when young (309). The largest structure in the Forum Romanum excavation area is the *Basilica of Maxentius.* This was begun by the latter in 306 and completed by Constantine. SE of the basilica (next to the 13C church of S. Francesca Romana), at the start of the Via Sacra, stands the *Arch of Titus,* built after his death in AD 81. It is single-arched with reliefs of Titus's victory over the Jewish people.

The Palatine (Entrance to the right of the Arch of Titus, via the Clivus Palatinus) This was the first hill of Rome to be settled and was built over with private houses during the republican era. The emperors then had large palatial complexes built there. In the 16C a garden and casino were laid out by Vignola for Cardinal Farnese, under which lies the greater part of the, as yet still unexcavated *Domus Tiberiana.* To the S. of this lies the *Domus Livia,* the simple architecture of which contains wall paintings of the greatest importance: Illusionistic wall arrangement in the 2nd Pompeian style. To the E. of the House of Livia is the *Domus Flaviana* with the imperial representation rooms. Grouped around a peristyle (with labyrinth) are a dining hall and nymphaeum (in the S.; court room, Aula Regia and lararium (N.). The imperial living quarters of the *Domus Augustana* adjoin the Domus Flaviana to the E. The Palatine is concluded to the E. by the *Stadium of Domitian* and the *Palace of Septimius Severus.*

Fori Imperiali (on both sides of the Via dei Fori Imperiali): Julius Caesar had a new forum laid out to the N. of the Forum Romanum (some remains of which can be seen behind the church of SS. Luca e Martina). Augustus, Vespasian, Nerva and Trajan also created new fora. The best excavated of the Imperial Fora, the *Forum of Trajan,* is dominated by *Trajan's Column* (in front of the churches of Nome di Maria and S. Maria di Loreto). A ribbon of reliefs, 670 ft. long, depicting Trajan's Dacian campaigns winds around the column. The NE side of Trajan's Forum is bordered by the *Mercati Traianei,* a large, central market-place (entrance in the Via IV Novembre). In the Middle Ages the Priory of the Knights of Malta was built on the remains of the Temple of Mars Ultor in the *Forum of Augustus.* The *Fora of Nerva and Vespasian,* adjoining to the E., are unexcavated. In the *Forum Boarium*

Capitol, Marcus Aurelius

(Piazza Bocca della Verità), ancient Rome's cattle-market, there is a rectangular temple with Ionic columns from *c.* 100 BC); this is one of the best-preserved temples and was probably dedicated to *Fortuna Virilis.* Inside there are 9C wall paintings. Beside this is a round, marble temple (2C BC), at one time thought to be dedicated to *Vesta.* At the end of the forum (below the Palatine) is the *Arch of Janus* (4C). Open on all sides, it was used as a meeting-place by traders. Beside it, to the left, is the smaller *Moneychangers' Arch,* which moneychangers dedicated to Septimius Severus in 204. The nearby church of S.Maria in Cosmedin was also built inside one of the Forum buildings. Between the Forum Boarium and the Theatre of Marcellus lay the *Forum Holitorium,* the vegetable market, the remains of which (a colonnade) are near the church of S.Nicola in Carcere.

Burial Monuments: *Pyramid of C. Cestius* (Porta S. Paolo): At the height of Rome's fascination with things Egyptian under Augustus, Caius Cestius, praetor and tribune of the people, had this monument built for himself on the road to Ostia (11 BC) W. of the pyramid is the *Prot-*

estant Cemetery with the tombs of famous non-Catholic foreigners (e.g. Keats and Shelley).

Catacombs (from the Latin ad Catacumbas, an open field on the Via Appia Antica): Extensive subterranean network of burial tunnels, which in parts is quite complicated. It was used primarily by Jews and early Christians, whose religion prohibited the cremation of their dead. Originally it was designed for the poorer sections of society, but from the 3C even bishops were laid to rest here. During the persecution the catacombs provided sanctuary for the Christians, as they were protected from Roman law. 11 catacombs have so far been researched, the most important being the catacombs of *St. Calixtus* (cf Via Appia Antica), *St. Domitilla* (Via delle Sette Chiese), *SS. Pietro and Marcellino* (Via Casilina) and *Priscilla* (Via Salaria).

Colosseum (Via dei Fori Imperiali): Begun by Vespasian in AD 70 on the site of the artificial lake of the Domus Aurea (q.v.) and completed by his successor, Titus, in AD 80. It was properly called the *Am-*

Capitol

phitheatrum Flavium. Four storeys rise above an oval ground plan; the storeys, which have a succession of barrel and groin vaults, form the substructure of the audience tiers. Ambulatories provide access to the interior. In the centre of the complex is the arena, where gladiator fights, sea fights and drama were staged. The structure of the exterior became the prototype for architectural arrangement from the Renaissance onwards. The 3 storeys of arcades have Doric, Ionic and Corinthian semi-columns and the unarched 4th storey has Corinthian pilasters. The Colosseum held around 50,000 spectators.

Arch of Constantine (by the Colosseum): Built for the emperor by the people and Senate (Senatus Populusque Romanus) in memory of his victory of Saxa Rubra (312). The arch follows the example of the Arch of Septimius Severus. Reliefs glorify the virtues of the emperor (below) and depict hunting and sacrificial scenes (above, from an older arch of Trajan).

Theatre of Marcellus (Via del Teatro Marcello): Augustus dedicated this theatre, built 17–13 BC, to the prematurely-deceased son of his sister Octavia. In the Middle Ages it was made into a fortress (which Peruzzi later converted into a Renaissance palace). Originally the theatre had a capacity of *c.* 14,000 seats. (cf. Porticus Octaviae.)

Pantheon (Piazza della Rotonda): A round temple built by Agrippa in 27 BC in connection with his baths. It was rebuilt under Hadrian following a fire in 118. Given to the Pope by Phocas in 608, it became a church dedicated to all martyrs. From the 16C famous individuals were buried here; after 1870 it served as tomb for the Italian royal household. The temple's diameter is the same as its height. The walls have two shells; the inner shell is broken alternately by rectangular and semicircular niches (wall sections between the niches are also hollow). The sole source of light is a round opening in the dome. Originally the dome was gilded and the ceiling of the portico (with 16 Corinthian columns) was clad with bronze. Since the 16C the Pantheon has been repeatedly used as a model for other buildings.

Porticus Octaviae (near the Theatre of

Capitoline she-wolf, Musei capitolini

Triumphal Arch of Septimius Severus

Marcellus): Remains of a temple complex, restored by Augustus in 27 BC and dedicated to his sister. Behind the arch lies the old ghetto.

Baths: Roman baths were generously laid-out swimming baths of occasionally extraordinary proportions. In the centre of the complexes were vaulted buildings—the largest in antiquity—built of brick and faced with marble. Grouped around these were open rooms with pools and sports areas. Larger baths also had libraries. The complexes had underground heating systems (hypocausts) and warm air was conducted into the rooms through wall pipes (tubuli). The sequence of the baths was dictated by the order of the rooms: from changing cubicles, through cleansing pools, to lukewarm baths (Tepidarium), hot baths (Caldarium) and then cold baths (Frigidarium). The *Baths of Caracalla* (Via delle Terme di Caracalla): Begun under Septimius Severus in 206 and completed by Caracalla in 217, the complex could hold 1600 bathers. Apart from the baths there were libraries, galleries and a stadium. The *Baths of Diocletian* (Piazza della Repubblica): The largest Roman baths, built from 298–305. When the Pope gave the dilapidated building to the Carthusians, the order commissioned Michelangelo with the conversion of the surviving central rooms (Tepidarium) into a church, *S.Maria degli Angeli*, (1536–66) The interior is a good example of an impressive Roman building (along with the Basilica of Maxentius in the Forum Romanum and the Pantheon). In the choir, there is a fresco by Domenichino. Housed in the other rooms of the baths is the *Museo Nazionale*.

Via Appia Antica: Built by the censor Appius Caecus in 312 BC, the 'Queen of Roads' leads to Capua and then on to Brin

Arch of Constantine

lisi. As burial within the town was forbidden by Roman law, the arterial roads were littered with graves. The road starts at the Circus Maximus (by the old Servian Wall). The first section (up to the Porta S. Sebastiano) has the *Tomb of the Scipios* (in front of the Porta S.Sebastiano), which is the oldest tomb monument in Rome. The Aurelian Wall (208-282) is broken here by the *Porta Appia* (now the Porta S. Sebastiano). The *Catacombs of St.Calixtus*, from the 1C AD, lie on the Via Appia. The *Papal Crypt* and the 5 sacramental chapels with 3C frescos are worth seeing. Above the catacombs stands the *Basilica of S. Sebastiano*, one of Rome's seven major churches. Built *c.* 370, it was originally dedicated to saints Peter and Paul; baroque conversion in the 17C. The single-aisled interior contains a large glass display case of relics. On the left side of the road is the *Temple of Romulus*, adjoining which is the *Circus of Maxentius* and, a little further on,

the tomb of *Caecilia Metella*, the best-preserved of the tomb monuments. A circular building from the time of Augustus, it was converted into a castle in the Middle Ages.

Churches: Basilicas—the first large buildings in Christendom—made the most decisive contribution to the development of western church architecture. The centrally-planned building could only be integrated into the Christian liturgy in the form of a baptistery (or a memorial or tomb building). With the crises of the Papacy, the centre of church architecture in the Middle Ages was not in Rome. It was not until the Papacy was strengthened, and after the Council of Trent in particular, that extensive building of new churches got underway in Rome. A new style developed which was closely tied to the Counter-Reformation and the baroque was born in Rome. Individual architectural elements were no longer observed in isolation; architecture and decoration had converged into unity. The use of light became an important compositional element and the interiors of churches became more spacious.

S. Agnese fuori le Mura (Via Nomentana): Founded in the 4C by Constantia, daughter of Constantine. The much-converted building was built under Pope Honorius in the 7C. A colonnaded basilica, it has a nave, two aisles, a series of galleries and a semi-circular apse.

S. Agostino (Piazza S. Agostino): The old church (the present transept) was extended in 1479–83. The interior was renovated in 1750. The church contains some interesting art: the Madonna del Parto by Sansovino, 1518 (near the middle portal); Isaiah, a fresco by Raphael of 1515 (3rd pillar on the left); the Madonna di Loreto by Caravaggio, 1605 (1st chapel, left); St. Anne with the Virgin and Child by Sansovino, 1512 (2nd chapel, left); the high altar is attributed to Bernini; the Chapel of St. Agostino (right transept) has paintings by Guercino; and there are fine tombs.

S. Andrea delle Fratte (next to the Palazzo Propaganda Fide): Nave converted in the late 16C, in the style of Il Gesù. Transept, dome and campanile built by Borromini in 1653–56. The two marble angels in front of the choir were made by Bernini in 1667–70 for the Ponte Sant'Angelo.

S. Andrea al Quirinale (Via de Quirinale): One of the major works of Roman baroque architecture. Built by Bernini, 1658–70. In lay-out it consists of a succession of ovals. Lavish sculpted decoration. The choir (with the Martyrdom of St. Andrew) is accentuated by Bernini's use of light.

S. Andrea delle Valle (Corso Vittorio Emanuele / near the Piazza Navona): Begun in 1591 by the della Portas, the building was continued by Maderno and completed in 1665 by C. Rainaldi. The principal church of the Theatines, the design further develops the early baroque style of Il Gesù. G. Lanfranco's dome painting (Glory of Paradise, 1621–25) became the model for baroque dome painting. The three frescos in the apse are by M. Preti (Life of St. Andrew), from 1650–1.

Colosseum

SS.Apostoli (Piazza dei SS.Apostoli): The Colonna family church. Founded in the 6C and rebuilt by F. and C.Fontana, 1702–8. Façade by Valadier, 1827; arcaded portico with beautiful grilles. The ceiling fresco is a masterpiece by Baciccia, 1707. The tomb of Clement XIV, Canova's first Roman work (1789) can be seen at the end of the left aisle.

S.Carlo ai Catinari (Piazza B.Cairoli): Built by R.Rosati, 1612–20 (façade by Soria, 1635–8). Greek cross ground plan; well-lit dome. The *Cappella di S. Cecilia* (3rd right) is a *tour de force* of late baroque interior architecture in which light is employed to maximum effect (Gherardi, 1692–1700).

S.Carlo al Corso (Via del Corso): Begun in 1612 by O.Longhi; finished in 1672. The dome—one of the finest in Rome—is by Pietro da Cortona, 1668. The interior, in the form of a Latin cross, with nave, two aisles, transept and ambulatory, appears most spacious. On the high altar there is a work by C.Maratta, 1685–90.

S.Carlo alle Quattro Fontane (Via delle Quattro Fontane/Via del Quirinale): Built by F.Borromini, 1638–41 (façade 1665–8). The intersection of the two streets was architecturally enhanced by four fountains. *Façade:* The concave-convex-concave movement of the lower floor is surmounted by the triple concave wall of the upper storey, in the middle of which there is a baldacchino crowned by a medallion. The interior is remarkable for the feeling of spaciousness achieved in the smallest of spaces (colossal arrangement): The area covered by the dome inscribes an elongated rhombus, the corners of which are cut off by two circles (the entrance and the altar area) and two ellipses (the side altars). Side chapels. Two-storey arcaded cloister.

S.Cecilia in Trastevere (Via di S.Cecilia): Founded in the 5C; rebuilt in the 9C and

Rome, Pantheon A pronaos (portico) **B** rotunda **1** antique bronze door **2** fresco of the Annunciation (Mezzolò da Forlì), in front are two angels (attrib. Bernini) **3** tomb of Victor Emmanuel II **4** high altar with 'miracle' icon (entrance to the Cappella Reggia on the left) **5** monument to Cardinal Consalvi (Thorvaldsen, 1824) **6** tomb of Raphael, above it the 'Madonna del Sasso' **7** tomb of Umberto I and tomb of Queen Margherita **8** tomb of B. Peruzzi

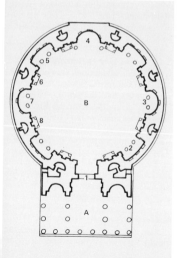

St. Agnes, catacombs

Pyramid of Cestius

restored many times thereafter (baroque interior). *Furnishings:* Beneath Arnolfo di Cambio's *ciborium* (1293), in the Confessio, lies the reclining figure of Cecilia by Maderno. In the apse there are 9C *mosaics of Christ*. The entrance to the ancient Calidarium is in the right aisle. (St. Cecilia, a patrician lady, who died for her Christian faith, was kept in her own calidarium in the hope that she would be killed by the excessive heat. Unharmed by this experience, she had her head cut off.)

S.Clemente (Via S.Giovanni in Laterano): In 1084 the Normans destroyed a basilica, which had itself been built above a Roman house of the 4C. Pope Paschal II had a smaller basilica built higher up in 1099, and this was subsequently altered many times. Converted to baroque by C.S. Fontana in 1715–19. The ruined lower rooms were discovered in 1857. *Upper church:* The sequence of rooms occurring in an early Christian basilica has been maintained despite the later alterations; 12C atrium with prothyros (main door) and cleansing fountain (18C). 18C façade. The interior has a nave, two aisles, an arcade of antique columns and, in the middle of the nave, 6C *choir screens* (from the lower church), Cosmatesque *paschal candlesticks* and an *altar with a baldacchino* (relics of St. Clement). There are 12C mosaics on the triumphal arch and in the apse. In the apse there is a *Bishop's throne* and *stalls for the clergy*. The church's pavement is one of the earliest examples of Cosmati work. The *Cappella di S. Caterina* has frescos, generally attributed to Masolino, which are of great interest to the student of art history. *Lower church:* Columned basilica with a wide nave and two aisles. Very important 11&12C frescos. *Mithraeum:* Beneath the lower church are the remains of a Roman house with religious rooms (sacrificial altar, bust of Alexander).

S.Costanza (Via Nomentana): Constantine's daughter, Constantia, had this circular building built as a mausoleum in the 4C. It later served as a baptistery and, from 1254, as a church. In front of the building there is an atrium with niches. The interior is now free from all later additions. The dome is supported by a circle of 12 pairs of columns. There are niches on the walls of the ambulatory and 4C mosaics in the ambulatory vaults.

S. Croce in Gerusalemme (Piazza S. Croce in Gerusalemme): One of Rome's 7 principal churches. According to legend Constantine had the relics of the Cross (brought from Palestine by his mother St.Helena), preserved in a hall in the Sessorian Palace. In 1144 Pope Lucius II had a basilica built within the 4C palace walls. The whole complex was altered to baroque by D.Gregorini, 1743–50. Inside there is the 12C pavement in Cosmati work. There are 15C mosaics in the *Chapel of St.Helena* (to the right of the apse).

Il Gesù (Piazza del Gesù): The Jesuits' mother church. Founded by Cardinal Alessandro Farnese. Begun by Vignola in 1568

Forum of Trajan

and completed in 1584. The façade was designed by G.della Porta. *Interior* converted to baroque in the 17C. Latin cross ground plan, with transept and dome over the crossing, in the manner of S.Andrea in Mantua. Longitudinal plan, even in the arrangement of the chapels, which are all interconnected. The source of light —from the nave vault and the dome—is most important. The decoration (nave vault fresco by Baciccia) gives the originally austere interior a brighter character. The altar at the end of the left aisle is a triumphal tomb monument to Ignatius Loyola by A.Pozzo (1700).

S.Giovanni in Laterano and *Scala Santa* (Piazza S.Giovanni in Laterano): The palace of Plautius Lateranus came into the posession of the Imperial House through Fausta, wife of Constantine, in the 3C. Constantine presented the complex to Pope Melchiades. The palace served as papal residence up to the exile in Avignon. S. Giovanni in Laterano is still the titular church of the Bishop of Rome and thus the highest-ranking of the Catholic churches and the first of the 4 Basilicae maiores. Originally it was dedicated to the Redeemer, later to John the Baptist and John the Evangelist. A columned basilica, it was the first monumental building in Christendom and was built with Imperial means. Following an earthquake, it was rebuilt in 905 and magnificently furnished in 1288-92. The church was burnt down several times and declined during the Pope's exile in Avignon. Later restorations radically altered the basilica: the side portico dates from 1585; Borromini converted the church to baroque from 1650; in 1733-6 a façade by A. Galilei was added; in 1886 the choir was enlarged. The main façade has colossal pilasters. Borromini's conversion of the nave preserved its basilican character but gave it a new rhythm by combining the arcade pillars into blocks of pillars linked by pilasters. Figures of the Apostles occupy dynamically conceived niches. The *cloister*, completed in 1230, is similar to that of S. Paolo fuori le Mura. The *baptistery* of Giovanni in Fonte (the very first and the prototype for all succeeding baptisteries), was probably built over the nymphaeum of the 3C Lateran Palace. It was converted to baroque under Urban VII in the 17C. The *Lateran Palace* was built in its existing form under Sixtus V., who also had the *obelisk* (from the Circus Maximus) set up in front of it. NE of the palace lies the holy shrine of SS. Salvatore della Scala Santa, built by D. Fontana in 1585 over the remains of the 4C papal palace. The building contains the *Holy Steps*, which by tradition were brought from Jerusalem by St. Helena. On the upper floor is the former *pope's private chapel* in 13C Cosmati work. Known as the *Cappella Sancta Sanctorum*, it contains precious relics (e.g. an image of Christ). On the outside of the E. wall there are the remains of the former papal palace's dining hall.

S. Ignazio (Piazza S. Ignazio): Built from 1626–85, together with the Jesuit college.

A. Pozzo's *nave and dome frescos* are important examples of trompe l'oeil ceiling painting; the 'Triumph of Faith' is set in the framework of fantastic mock-architecture. The right transept has a relief by Le Gros, the 'Glory of St. Aloysius Gonzaga' (1699), and in the left transept there is a relief of the 'Annunciation' by Valle (1750).

S. Ivo alla Sapienza Corso del Rinascimento): Former university. The two wings of the university palace and the two-storey arcaded courtyard laid out under Sixtus V (by G. della Porta, 1587), flank the *Cappella di S. Ivo alla Sapienza*, a unique masterpiece by Borromini (1642–60). The courtyard assumes the function of an atrium. The focal point is not the church's façade but its spiralling dome. Centrally-planned hexagonal interior.

SS. Luca e Martina (Via del Foro Romano): The upper church of S. Martina, rebuilt by Pietro da Cortona 1634–50, is a domed, centrally-planned building over a Greek cross ground plan. The basic form of the architecturally important façade is dictated by the concave conclusion of the interior. The vertical emphasis of the two-

S. Giovanni in Laterano

storey façade is also exemplary (pilasters on the outside, columns inside). The *interior* is remarkable for its clear design; the walls are articulated with pilasters and columns in between which there are niches.

S.Luigi dei Francesi (Piazza S.Luigi dei Francesi): The French national church was begun in 1518; façade by G.della Porta. The interior (nave and two aisles) was converted to baroque in the 18C and contains interesting *tombs*. The church's most important possession is Caravaggio's picture cycle of the *Life of St.Matthew*, 1599-1602, painted for the Contarelli chapel (last in the left aisle).

S. Maria in Aracoeli (near the Campidoglio): Tradition has it that the Tiburtine Sibyl prophesied the coming of Christ to Augustus on this site. In 1250 the 6C church was replaced by a building in the style of the Mendicants. In 1348 the people of Rome commissioned the church's monumental staircase in thanks for deliverance from the plague. Lavish *furnishing:* To the right of the main entrance is the tomb of Cardinal d'Albret by Andrea Bregno (1465); the 1st chapel on the right has frescos of the 'Life of St.Bernard' by Pinturicchio (1486); on the transept pillars there are two ambones from *c.* 1200; at the high altar a 10C Byzantine icon; *the tomb of St.Helena* lies in an aedicule in the middle of the left transept; the tomb of Cardinal d'Aquasparta (1302) is at the end of the transept, where there is a fresco by P. Cavallini.

S. Maria in Campitelli (Piazza Campitelli): Built at the instance of Alexander VII by C.Rainaldi, 1663-7, as a votive church for the 'Madonna in Portico', following the plague of 1656. The church is Rainaldi's masterpiece. *Interior:* The clever use of rows of Corinthian columns in the nave produces an elegant interior with an interesting perspective effect. The 'miraculous' image is at the high altar in the semicircular apse.

S. Maria in Cosmedin (Piazza Bocca della Verità): Built over a 4C market building in the 12C. An arcaded basilica, it has a nave, two aisles, a choir with 3 apses, an unvaulted crypt and a portico. Beneath the portico is the famous *Bocca della Verità* (the Mouth of Truth), an antique Triton mask.

S.Ignazio, dome fresco by A. Pozzo

Fine marble Cosmati work, including: pavement, choir, pulpits, bishop's throne and paschal candlestick. There are important *remains of 12C frescos* in the nave. The *crypt*, Rome's first unvaulted crypt, has a nave and two aisles.

S.Maria Maggiore (Piazza S.Maria Maggiore): The 4th of the basilicae maiores and one of the 'Seven Churches' of Rome. The

S.Giovanni in Laterano, A basilica 1 portico with benediction loggia **2** Porta Santa **3** Cappella Torlonia (last of Rome's family chapels, 1830) **4** Cappella Massimo (G. Della Porta, 1570) **5** Boniface VIII proclaiming the first holy year (1300), fresco by Giotto **6** cenotaph of Sylvester II **7** tomb of Alexander III **8** organ (1598) **9** portico by D. Fontana (16C) **10** tomb of Innocent III **11** Papal altar (1397) with confessio **12** tomb of Leo XIII (1907) **14** Cappella Colonna (G. Rainaldi, 1625) **15** old sacristy **16** altar of the Holy Sacrament **17** entrance to the cloister **C Cloister** (1215–32) with numerous Cosmati works and fragments from the older basilica **18** chapel (1675) **19** chapel (O. Longhi) **20** Cappella Corsini (A. Galilei, 1732–5) **21** statue of Cardinal R. degli Annibali (Arnolfo, 13C) **B Baptistery 1** octagon (baroque conversion under Urban VIII) **2** Cappella del Battista (5C) **3** Cappella di S.Rufina (the old narthex, converted into a chapel in 1154) **4** Cappella di S. Venanzio (4C) **5** Chapel of St.John the Baptist (bronze door of 1196) **D Lateran Palace E obelisk**

origin of this Christian basilica is disputed; it is said to have originated under Liberius (4C) or Sixtus III (5C). The early Christian building was later altered and totally encased in the 17&18C. In 1288 a small transept was added and the apse restored; in 1377 the campanile was rebuilt. From 1550, a series of chapels were added along the aisles. In 1670 C.Rainaldi encased the choir area and created the great staircase. From 1741–50 F.Fuga added the two-storey portico with benediction loggia. The obelisk in front of the apsidial façade was set up by Sixtus V in 1587, (having been brought from the Basilica of Maxentius on the orders of Paul V in 1613). The interior has maintained its original character despite all the later additions. Most important features inside are the *mosaics*, the *Sistine Chapel* and the *Cappella Paolina*.

S.Maria sopra Minerva (near the Pantheon): Rome's only sizeable Gothic church. Begun in 1280 above the remains of a temple; completed in 1450. Basilican layout, with nave and two aisles, in the tradition of Italian churches of the Mendicant order. The interior was restored in the 19C. The church served as a burial place for Ro-

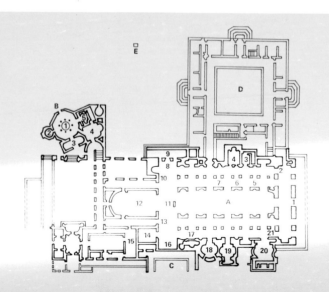

nan families. *Furnishings: Cappella Al-dobrandini* (6th chapel on the right): Architecture by G.della Porta and Maderna; altarpiece by Barocci; Aldobrandini tomb by G. della Porta. *Cappella Carafa*, last chapel in the right transept, with frescos by F.Lippi, 1492. The body of St. Catherine of Siena lies under the high altar. On the left in front of the choir, is a statue of 'Christ as Hercules' by Michelangelo (1521). In front of the church there is an elephant (by Bernini, 1667) with an obelisk on its back.

S.Maria della Pace (see Squares).

S.Maria del Popolo (Piazza del Popolo): Built from 1472–7, it has one of the earliest Renaissance façades in Rome. The interior, with nave and two aisles, was altered in the 17C; the aisles are flanked by chapels. *Decoration:* In the Cappella Della Rovere (1st on the right) there are frescos over the altar; the next chapel is the funerary chapel of the Cybo family, well-designed by C.Fontana, (1682). The apse has frescos by Pinturicchio and the tombs of cardinals Della Rovere and Sforza, both by A.Sansovino. The chapel to the left of the apse has two paintings by Caravaggio. The Cappella Chigi (2nd left, opposite Cappella Cybo) was designed by Raphael and has the tombs of the Chigi family. Figures by Bernini and Lorenzetto occupy 4 niches.

S.Maria in Trastevere (Piazza S.Maria in Trastevere): Probably Rome's oldest church. Dedicated to the Virgin in the 3C, it took on its present form around 1140. It was later altered many times, but without detriment to the character of the building. The basilica has a nave and two aisles (columns with an architrave), side chapels and a front portico. Fine *apse mosaics:* upper part (1140), lower part, with Christ and the Virgin Mary (1291). Cappella Avila (5th left) by A. Gherardi (1680).

S.Maria in Vallicella (Piazza della Chiesa Nuova/Corso Vittorio Emanuele): Built above an earlier building from 1575–1605. Monumental basilica, it has a nave, two aisles, transept and dome. Frescos by Pietro da Cortona. High altar paintings by Rubens (1608). Altarpiece in the Cappella Spada by Maratta (architecture by Rainaldi). In the left transept there is a

Isola Tiberina

painting by Barocci. The *Oratorio dei Filippi* adjoins the church on the left. The monastery, with the little oratory, received a new façade by Borromini in 1640. Two courtyards, a sacristy and a refectory adjoin the monastery.

S. Maria della Vittoria (Piazza S. Bernardo): Built 1605–26, probably to de-

signs by C. Maderna. On the altar in the Cornaro Chapel (4th left) is Bernini's celebrated 'Ecstasy of St. Theresa', (1646).

S. Paolo fuori le Mura (Via Ostiense):
The 3rd of the basilicae maiores. In 386 a basilica was built over the spot in which St. Paul was reputed to have been buried in AD 67. Another building followed in the 5C and of this there remain some mosaics of the triumphal arch. The Benedictine convent on the S. side was built in the 10C. The apse mosaics were restored in the 13C; the wall paintings in the nave some time later. In 1750 a portico was added to the façade. The fire of 1823 almost totally destroyed the church. The reconstruction, finished under L. Poletti in 1854, is a copy of an early Christian basilica. The monumental columned atrium was not completed until 1925. *Furnishings:* 5C frescos on the triumphal arch; 3C altar with ciborium (papal altar); 12C paschal candlestick. The 12C cloister has 13C Cosmati work. On the church's walls there are medallions of all the popes.

S. Pietro in Montorio (Via Garibaldi/Gianicolo): A single-aisled

S. Maria Maggiore, A portico (Fuga, 1743–50) **1** statue of Philip IV of Spain (G. Lucenti, 1692) **2** Porta Santa **B** nave (ceiling gilded with the first gold brought from America) **3** monument to Clement IX (Rainaldi, 1671) **4** monument to Nicholas IV (D. Fontana, 1574) **5** 5C mosaics with scenes from the Old and New Testaments **C** aisles **D** baptistery (F. Ponzio, 1605) **E** sacristy (F. Ponzio) **F** Cappella di S. Michele (15C frescos) **G** memorial column to the conversion of Henry IV of France **H** reliquary chapel (F. Fuga, 1750) **I** Sixtine chapel (Domenico Fontana, 1585) begun for Sixtus V **1** crib of Christ **2** ciborium of 1590 **3** tomb of Pius V (D. Fontana) **4** tomb of Sixtus V (D. Fontana) **K** baldacchino **6** statue of Pius IX (1880) **7** tomb of Bernini **L** transept with mosaics on the triumphal arch (Sixtus III) **M** apse with 13C mosaics **N** Cappella Paolina (1611 by F. Ponzio for Paul V Borghese) **1** high altar with 9C icon **2** tomb of Paul V (F. Ponzio) **3** tomb of Clement VII (F. Ponzio) **O** Cappella Sforza (G. Della Porta. 1564 –73) **P** Cappella Cesi (1550) **a** column with a statue of the Virgin Mary **b** obelisk

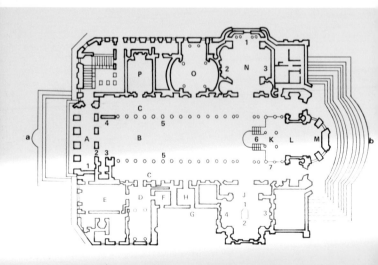

church. The Cappella Raimondi (2nd left) was built to designs by Bernini in 1646. In the church's courtyard is Bramante's *Tempietto* of 1502, on the supposed site of St. Peter's martyrdom. The tempietto is circular and in the form of the ancient memorial and funerary buildings. Crypt and chapel within.

S.Pietro in Vincoli (Piazza S.Pietro in Vincoli): An early Christian basilica which has been restored many times, most recently in the 18C. The *chains of St.Peter* are to be found at the high altar. The *tomb of Julius II* is in the right transept; when the tomb planned for St.Peter's was left unfinished, Pope Paul III had 3 of Michelangelo's statues, *Moses*, *Rachel* and *Leah*, set up around a wall tomb. (Julius II lies without a memorial in St.Peter's). The *tomb of Nicholas of Cusa* is in the left aisle.

S.Sabina (Piazza Pietro d'Illiria/ Aventine): The best example of a 5C basilica with nave and two aisles. The portico's wooden door is extremely old, dating from *c.* 430. Inside: *choir gallery* (8–11C) and an interesting *cloister* (13C).

S.Susanna (Largo S.Bernardo): An 8C basilica, altered in the 15C, with an important façade by C. Maderna, 1603.

Palaces and Squares:
The development of Rome's palaces was closely connected with the arrangement of its squares, particularly in the baroque period. Here too the Roman baroque shows itself to be a style concerned with the effects of space. Rome's baroque squares are characteristically enclosed (c.f. S. Maria delle Pace, c.f. S. Ignazio) and flights of steps are a constantly repeated motif (c.f. S.Peter's). Travertine is a characteristic building material of this period and it is often used for façades. The yellowish tone of this stone helps soften the impact of the sheer face and mass of the buildings.

Palazzo Barberini and Piazza Barberini: The *Palace:* Urban VIII acquired the Pal. Sforza, and had it converted by Maderna, Bernini and Borromini from 1625–33. The building has two wings and a forecourt (trapezoidal), around which there are 3 flights of steps. The main building's façade is similar in structure to that of an amphitheatre and windows on the top

Santa Sabina

storey are narrowed to give a *trompe l'oeil* perspective. The *Piazza:* Originally built up with low houses; in the centre of the square is Bernini's *Fontana del Tritone* (1643).

Palazzo Borghese (Piazza Borghese): The palace was initially built for a Spanish cardinal in 1590. In 1605, it came into the possession of Paul V, who had it extended by F.Ponzio. Garden courtyard by C.Rainaldi (1690).

Palazzo della Cancelleria (Piazza della Cancelleria): Built for Cardinal R.Riario, 1483–1511, it later came into the possession of the Curia. The Roman Republic assembled here in 1798–9; Napoleon resided here, and it was the seat of the Roman Republic of 1848. It is now an extraterritorial possession of the Vatican. The façade has 3 storeys and is very long, with rhythmically grouped wall pilasters. Three-storeyed arcaded courtyard. Incorporated within the palace is the church of *S. Lorenzo in Damaso*.

Palazzo Colonna (Piazza dei SS. Apostoli/Via della Pilotta): This palace was

Piazza Navona

built by Martin V and made into an extensive complex in the 18C (see museums).

Palazzo Doria (Via del Corso): Originally built in the 15C, but converted and extended many times in the following centuries. The rococo façade (1743) on the Via del Corso adjoins the church of S.Maria in Via Lata (1660). Interesting 16C *courtyard* (see museums).

Palazzo and Piazza Farnese: The *Palace:* Begun in 1514 by A.da Sangallo the Younger, continued by Michelangelo (upper storey) and completed by G.della Porta. The palace later came into the possession of the Bourbons and is now the French Embassy. The free-standing 4-sided building has 4 completed façades and an inner courtyard, which has orders reminiscent of the Colosseum. An upper storey *loggia* opens onto the garden side. Admittance is limited to the gallery, which was painted by Annibale Carracci and has mythological scenes within a complicated architectural framework (1597). In all, it is the finest example of a Roman Renaissance palace. Its beauty is all the better appreciated for the regular structure of the piazza on which it stands; 2 large baths (from the Baths of Caracalla) converted into fountains dominate the square.

Palazzo Massimo alle Colonne (Corso Vittorio Emanuele): Built on top of an old palace by B. Peruzzi in 1534–6. The extensive portico under the flat façade leads to a series of courtyards linked by loggias. In the courtyard there are antique spoils.

Palazzo Spada (Piazza Capo di Ferro): Built for Cardinal G.Capodiferro and later acquired by Cardinal B.Spada. It is now the seat of the Italian Council of State. The building has 4 sides around a courtyard. Façade and courtyard are lavishly decorated with reliefs and statues. In a 2nd courtyard there is Borromini's *trompe l'oeil* perspective colonnade, 1635. (see museums)

S.Pietro in Vincoli, Moses by Michelangelo

Fontana di Trevi

Palazzo Vidoni Caffarelli (Corso Vittorio Emanuele, near S.Andrea della Valle): Built to a design of Raphael (1515). Heavily rusticated ground floor, above which the piano nobile has double Doric half-columns.

Piazza Campidoglio: The Capitoline square lies in a hollow between two rises of the Capitoline Hill. In antiquity the Tabularium stood on this spot. The square was laid out from 1538 by Michelangelo, who was commissioned by Paul III. Michelangelo altered the orientation of the square, so that it no longer led towards the forum but to the then-inhabited city and towards St.Peter's. The trapezoidal square has a star-shaped pattern, in the middle of which stands the equestrian statue of Marcus Aurelius—the only surviving antique equestrian statue in Rome (the statue was believed to portray Constantine). The base of the statue was made by

Michelangelo. The two palaces at the sides, the *Palazzo dei Conservatori* (right) and the *Palazzo del Museo Capitolino* (below the church), are colossally arranged over two storeys. On the E. side is the *Palazzo Senatorio*, behind which some remains of the Tabularium can be seen. At the foot of a flight of steps is a *fountain* with the river gods of the Tiber and the Nile and Minerva. The spaces between the palaces have flights of steps. The 4th side of the piazza is concluded by a *series of figures*: the two Dioscuri (horse breakers), colossal figures found in the ghetto, the 'Trophies of Marius', the statues of Constantine the Great and Constantine II, as well as two milestones from the Appian Way. The Palazzo Senatorio was designed by G.della Porta and G.Rainaldi (1582–1605); the Palazzo dei Conservatori was designed by Michelangelo and executed by G.della Porta; the museum palace was built some 100 years later.

Monument to Victor Emmanuel II

Piazza Colonna: Named after the Column of Marcus Aurelius (2C). In front of the column there is a *fountain* by G.della Porta. On the N. side is the *Palazzo Chigi* (1562, G.della Porta); on the S. the *Pal.Buffalini* (16C); on the W. side (see Piazza Montecitorio) the *Pal. Wedekind* (1838) with a portico of 16 antique temple columns (from Veio); on the E. side (Via del Corso) the *Galleria Colonna*, a shopping street completed in 1625.

Piazza Montecitorio: Adjoining the Piazza Colonna to the W., it is dominated by the *Pal. Montecitorio*, the seat of the Italian parliament. Begun by Bernini in 1650 and completed by C.Fontana in 1694. The window ledges are of interest, being of solid rock (Mons Citorius). The obelisk, which came from the Campus Martius was set up in 1792.

Piazza Navona: A baroque adaptation of the ancient Stadium of Domitian, which occupied the site in the 1C. Tower houses were built along the surrounding walls of the stadium from the 13C. The square was already important in 1477, when the Capitoline market was transferred here. Games and festivals were held in the piazza. The square achieved its final form under G.B.Pamphilj, who became Pope Innocent X in 1644. The Pamphilj family enlarged their private palace, laid out the fountains and had the church of S.Agnese rebuilt. In the middle there is a fountain with an obelisk; there are also fountains at both ends in place of the ancient starting and finishing posts of the race track. The *buildings:* On the W. side: *Pal. Pamphilj* (1644–50) by G.Rainaldi; frescos inside by Pietro da Cortona. The church of *S.Agnese* is a centrally-planned building (Greek cross ground plan) with a pointed dome by Borromini. Lavish furnishings. The *Collegio Pamphilj* adjoins the church. The foundations of the stadium are visible outside the N. curve. On the E. side is the former *Collegio degli Spagnoli* with the former Spanish national church of *S. Giacomo* (choir towards the piazza). On the S. side are the *Pal. de Torres* and the massive *Pal. Braschi* (see museums). The *Fountain of the Rivers* by Bernini (1647–49) is in the middle of the square. This cleverly-conceived rock structure is surmounted by an obelisk, which is itself crowned by a dove (the Pamphilj family emblem). At the S. end of the square is the *Fontana del Moro*, also by Bernini, and at the N. end the *Fountain of Neptune*, which was not built until 1878. The square was famous for its August *races* well into the 19C.

Piazza del Popolo: The *Porta del Popolo* (restored to designs by Michelangelo in the 16C) was the busiest entrance to Rome until the 19C. The piazza was rearranged by Valadier in the 19C. In the centre is an obelisk (from the Circus Maximus). On the N. side is the church of *S. Maria del Popolo*. The Via del Corso, Via del Babuino and Via Ripetta radiate from the piazza to the S. Between these streets are the churches of *S. Maria dei Miracoli* (1662–81, Rainaldi and Fontana) and *S. Maria in Monte Santo* (1662–75, Rainaldi) respectively.

Piazza del Quirinale: *Pal. Quirinale:* Former papal summer residence to which almost all of Rome's important architects contributed (1574–1730). Stretching behind the palace (now the seat of the Italian president) are extensive gardens. In front of the palace is an *obelisk* set up under Pius VI and statues of the Dioscuri, brought from the Baths of Constantine under Pius VII. The E. side of the piazza is occupied by the *Pal. della Consulta*, built by F. Fuga, 1732–4 (now an administrative court).

Piazza di Spagna: A long and rather irregularly-shaped square, at the S. end of which is the *Collegio di Propaganda Fide*, built for the Congregation for the Spreading of the Faith, set up in 1622. The façade which looks on to the piazza side is by Bernini, the one on the Via Propaganda by Borromini. In the lower half of the square is the *Column of the Immaculate Conception*, an antique column erected in the 19C. On the W. side is the Spanish Embassy, the *Pal. di Spagna*, from which the

Stazione Termini

square derives its name. In the narrow middle section of the square is the *Fontana della Barcaccia*, a boat-shaped fountain by P.Bernini. Leading up to the church of *SS. Trinità dei Monti*, from the continuation of the Via Condotti, are the Scalinata di Spagna, the *Spanish Steps* (1723–25 by De Sanctis). The steps, used as a resting place and a social meeting point, are composed of several flights, interrupted by landings and a large terrace. At the top the steps open onto a little square with an obelisk (from the garden of Sallust). The church of *SS. Trinità dei Monti*, with twin towers was founded by the French in 1495–1585. Fine furnishings.

Piazza Venezia: In the 19C two palaces were torn down to make way for the Victor Emmanuel Monument. The *Pal. delle Assicurazioni Generali di Venezia* was built to complement the *Pal. di Venezia*. The Victor Emmanuel Monument (built by G.Sacconi, 1885–1911) rises in the S.and is the new termination of the magnificent old Roman boulevard, the Via del Corso. An open colonnaded hall rises from a massive base in the style of an ancient sacrificial altar. In front of this, on a pedestal, is the Altare della Patria with the equestrian statue of Italy's first King; numerous reliefs on the base. The *Palazzo and Palazzetto di Venezia* were begun in 1455 for Cardinal Pietro Barbo, who became Paul II, and completed in 1491 under his nephew, Cardinal M. Barbo. Until 1797 it was the Embassy of the Venetian Republic and then the Austrian Embassy (until 1916). It served as Mussolini's residence until 1943. The courtyards of the Palazzo and Palazzetto are linked by arcades. (see museums).

Villas: From the 16C villas were built in the immediate vicinity of the city e.g. the Villa Suburbana (Villa Giulia) and later further out e.g. Tivoli. By the 18C Rome was surrounded by a wreath of villas and gardens built by the papal families. The most important villas are: The *Villa Borghese*, built for Cardinal Scipione Caffarelli Borghese with extensive gardens (altered in the 19C), 1613–17. The *Villa Doria Pamphilj* (Gianicolo), laid out with a casino for Camillo Pamphilj by Algardi in 1644. The *Villa Giulia* (see museums). The *Villa Madama*, a villa complex from the high Renaissance, was begun in 1516

Stadium (Stadio Flaminio)

S. Maria in Cosmedin, Mouth of Truth

Apollo, Villa Giulia

for the future Clement VII (Medici) to designs by Raphael and altered by A. da Sangallo the Younger. The *Villa Medici* (Pincio), built in 1544 has a lavishly decorated garden façade (with spoils) and a delightful 16C garden. (see *Pal. Quirinale.)*

Fountains: *Fontana dell' Acqua Felice* (Piazza S.Bernardo), a three-arched structure—rather like a triumphal arch—with sculptures of Moses, river gods and lions. Built under Sixtus V by D. Fontana (1585 – 87). *Fontana dell' Acqua Paolo* (Gianicolo), a cascade; built by F. Ponzio and G. Fontana for Paul V. *Fontana dei Quattro Fiumi* (see Fountain of the Rivers, Piazza Navona). *Fontana delle Tartarughe* (Piazza Mattei/Ghetto), a Mannerist shell fountain with sculptures (1581–84). *Fontana di Trevi* (Piazza di Trevi), the largest of Rome's fountains, with lavish array of figures in front of a palace; clever use of perspective. Laid out under several popes (see the inscriptions), and completed in 1762. The narrow square is further accentuated by the skilfully arranged columned façade of the church of *SS. Vincenzo e Anastasio* (Martino Longhi the Younger, 1650) which occupies a site at the intersection of two streets.

Rome in the 19&20C: The building work which began in 1870–1 decisively altered the structure of papal Rome which had developed over the centuries. The Corso Vittorio Emanuele II was opened, the Victor Emmanuel monument was erected, new districts were developed on the sites of former villas, the main station and the ministries (Via XX Settembre) were built, the old Tiber harbour (Ripetta) was removed and the river was regulated. *19C Monuments: Victor Emmanuel Monument* (see Piazza Venezia). *Pal. della Giustizia* (near the Castel Sant'Angelo), one of the major buildings dating from the period of Italian industrialization (1889 – 1900). *Monumento di Garibaldi* (Gianicolo), an equestrian statue of the national hero (1895). *Monuments of the 20C: The Foro*

Coronation of the Virgin by Raphael, in the Vatican

Brutus, Musei capitolini

Laocoön, Vatican

Italico, the sports complex in the N. of the city, built in 1928. Next to it is the *Olympic Stadium.* The satellite town *EUR* in the S. of Rome, built for an exhibition planned for 1942, with the *Heroes' Palace.* After the war a few important model buildings appeared: *Stadio Flaminio* (Viale Tiziano, in the N. of the city), a multi-purpose stadium built by Nervi for the Olympic Games of 1960. *Stazione Termini* (main station), begun in 1938 and completed in 1950 by a team of architects.

Museums: *Galleria Colonna* (17 Via Pilotta) with 15–18C paintings. *Galleria dell'Accademia Nazionale di San Luca* (77 Piazza dell'Accademia di San Luca) with art of the 17–20C. *Galleria Doria Pamphilj* (1a Piazza del Collegio romano), one of the most important private collections with works by Titian, Raphael, Caravaggio, Bernini and Velasquez; interesting interior. *Galleria Nazionale d'arte moderna* (131 Viale delle Belle Arti) with works by Italian painters of the 19&20C. *Galleria Nazionale di Palazzo Barberini* with Italian painters from the 12–17C, inc. Pietro da Cortona (ceiling paintings), Caravaggio and Raphael. *Galleria Nazionale di Palazzo Corsini* (10 Via della Lungara) with 17&18C works. *Galleria Spada* (Palazzo Spada), a private collection with works from antiquity up to the 18C. Interesting 17C interior. *Musei Capitolini* (Piazza del Campidoglio), a Sculpture collection (dying Gaul, She-Wolf, Brutus, Capitoline Venus) and picture gallery. *Museo Barracco* (168 Corso Vitt. Emanuele), a 19C private collection (Assyrian, Egyptian, Greek and Roman sculptures). *Museo della Città Romana* (15 Piazza Agnelli; EUR), traces the history of Rome's development as a city. *Museo di Goethe* (18 Via del Corso) with documents concerning his travels in Italy. *Museo del Palazzo di Venezia:* Sala del Mappamondo, with a collection of weapons, tapestries, silver, ceramics etc. *Museo di Roma* (10 Piazza San Pantaleo), the City museum, with F.E.Roessler's scenes of Rome (19C). *Museo e Galleria Borghese* (Via Pinciana), the former private collection of the Borghese family and one of the most important museums in the world. Apart from antique sculptures there are works by Bernini (David, Rape of Proserpine), Canova (Paolina Borghese), paintings by Raphael, Caravaggio, Lotto, A. da Messina, Veronese, Correggio etc. *Museo Etrusco di Villa Giulia* (9 Piazzale Villa Giulia) — the Etruscan museum is now housed in the villa (with 2 courtyards) built for Pope Julius II by Vignola and Ammanati (1551 – 3). *Museo Napoleonico* (Piazza Ponte Umberto I) with mementoes of the Bonaparte family.

Also worth seeing: Near the Piazza Navona: *Pal. Madama* (Seat of the Senate): Built for the Medicis in the 16C; baroque façade of 1649. *S.Maria della Pace*, one of the most inspired of baroque buildings; church façade by Pietro da Cortona, 1656 – 7. Fine stucco decorations; high altar by C. Maderna, frescos by Raphael. Two-storey cloister (to the N.) by Bramante. *Pal. Pio* (towards the Piazza Farnese): Baroque palace built above the Theatre of Pompey. W. of the Campo dei Fiori, picturesque market with monument to Giordano Bruno. The *Via Giulia*, linking the Vatican with the Farnesina, was laid out under Julius II. Numerous palaces and the church of *S. Giovanni dei Fioren-*

tini (16–17C). **Tiber Island and Church of S.Bartolomeo**: 17C building with the relics of Bartholomew the Apostle. **Old Ghetto:** The Jewish Quarter stretches between the Tiber Island and Largo Argentina; *synagogue* 1889, *Portico d'Ottavia*, *Pal. Mattei* (17C), *Fontana delle Tartarughe*, *Pal. Santa Croce*, 15C with rusticated ground floor. (Via S. Maria del Pianto), the church of *S.Maria del Pianto* (17C) and the *Pal. Cenci.* **Largo Argentina:** Excavations of temples from the time of the Republic: *Teatro Argentina* (1830); *S.Francesco alle Stigmate* (1721). **In the vicinity of the Pantheon:** *S.Maria Maddalena* with rococo façade of 1734. **Piazza S.Ignazio:** *c.* 1700. **Piazza Pietra:** The remains of a temple can be seen along the side of the modern exchange building. **In the vicinity of the Piazza di Spagna:** *Pal. Zuccari* (Via Gregoriana) with Mannerist façade (giants' mouths). *Café Greco* (Via Condotti), 18–19C tea house with a long tradition. *Pincio* (above the Piazza del Popolo): Park with casino, laid out at the beginning of the 19C by Valadier. **Via Vittorio Veneto:** Bernini's *Fontanella delle Api* stands at the beginning of this magnificent 19C boulevard. Beneath the

Sistine Chapel, Death of Moses by Signorelli

church of *S.Maria delle Concezione* (Martino Longhi il Vecchio, 16C) is the famous Franciscan cemetery. **In the vicinity of the Colosseum:** *SS.Giovanni e Paolo:* A basilica built above a Roman house in the 5C; converted to baroque in 1718. *S. Gregorio Magno:* Founded in the 6C by Gregory the Great; façade and atrium by G.B.Soria, 1633; interior rearranged by F.Ferrari, 1725–34. *S.Stefano Rotondo* (Via di S. Stefano Rotondo): round building from the 5C. **Aventine:** *S.Alessio* and *S. Anselmo:* S.Alessio: 9C basilica renovated by De Marchis in 1750. The *Villa del Priorato di Malta* is an extraterritorial possession of the Grand Master of the Knights of Malta, as is the church of *S.Maria del Priorato,* rebuilt by Piranesi, 1765. **Trastevere:** The *Farnesina* (Via della Lungara): Built by B.Peruzzi for A.Chigi in 1508–11, with frescos by Giulio Romano, S.del Piombo, Raphael and Sodoma. **Outside the walls:** *S. Lorenzo fuori le Mura* (Piazza S. Lorenzo): An early Christian basilica (one of the 7 churches of Rome); later altered, badly damaged during the war (now restored). Beside it is the monumental Roman cemetery, the *Campo Verano* (19C). *Porta Pia* (Via XX Settembre), built in 1561 to designs by Michelangelo.

IV. THE VATICAN

A. From the Castel Sant'Angelo to St.Peter's: The ancient *Pons Aelius,*—for centuries the only bridge to St.Peter's—was converted to baroque by Bernini, 1669–71; 10 angels, bearing the instruments of Christ's suffering, are symbols of the stations of the Cross, the altar of St. Peter being the symbolic Golgotha. The **Castel Sant'Angelo:** Originally Hadrian's Mausoleum (2C) and included within the ancient fortifications of the city at an early date. In the Middle Ages the popes managed to gain possession of it. In the 13C the papal fortress was connected to the Vatican by a passage, the Passetto. Alexander VI (15C) built the four bastions. The loggia— the earliest in Rome — was opened under Julius II. The castle provided the popes with a place of refuge, a treasury and a prison (untill 1901). The building has housed a *museum* (with a col-

lection of arms) since 1934. The *Via della Conciliazione,* was built from 1936–50, as a monument to the reconciliation of the State and the Church, a medieval quarter being sacrificed to make way for it. Only the church of *S.Maria in Traspontina* (16 –17C), the *Pal. Torlonia* (15C) and the *Pal. dei Penitenzieri* (15C) were left standing. Of the old streets leading to St.Peter's, the *Borgo S. Spirito* remains. The hospital, founded in the 8C, was rebuilt in the 15C. The church of *S.Spirito in Sassia* was built by A.da Sangallo the younger (16C).

B. The Vatican State. The conclusion of the *Patti Lateranensi* of 1929 ended the dispute between the Pope and the Italian State, which had begun with the occupation of Rome in 1870. The Lateran Treaty made the Vatican a sovereign state. The Vatican State includes the Vatican City, St.Peter's, St.Peter's Square, the Vatican Palace, the museum buildings and the walled Vatican Gardens, as well as the extraterritorial posessions of S.Giovanni in Laterano, S.Maria Maggiore, S.Paolo fuori le Mura, the Catacombs, a few palaces and the summer residence in Castel Gandolfo.

C. St.Peter's and St.Peter's Square: *History:* In antiquity the site was occupied by Rome's largest cemetery. Nearby and to the left was the Circus of Nero, where St. Peter the Apostle was martyred in AD 64 (or 67). He was buried in the nearby cemetery and his grave very quickly became a place of worship for the early Christians. The first church of St.Peter was built by Constantine the Great in 324. The old building of St.Peter's, which had become lavishly furnished in the course of the centuries, had become so dilapidated by the 15C that a new building was considered. In 1452 the choir and transept were renovated. It was not until 1506, under Julius II, that work began on a new building. Originally designed by Bramante as a pure centrally planned building, the plans were altered to a longitudinal building when Raphael took over. A final decision was not reached until Michelangelo simplified

David by G.L. Bernini, Galleria Borghese

Bramante's designs, made them more colossal and actually resumed building (1546–57). After Michelangelo's death, G.della Porta, Vignola and Fontana completed the building in 1590. The centrally planned building did not fulfil the liturgical requirements of the Council of Trent, however, and Paul V commissioned Maderna with the lengthening of the nave.

Work on extending the building started in 1607 and it was consecrated by Urban VIII in 1626.

St.Peter's Square: By Bernini for Alexander VII, 1656–67. The *benediction loggia* (in the middle of the façade) and the windows of the palace from which the Pope gives his blessing, had to remain visi-

St. Peter's, **A** portico **a** benediction loggia **b** Porta Santa **c** 'Door of the Holy Sacrament' **d** central door (from Old St.Peter's, 1435, Filarete) **e** 'Door of the Dead' (Manzù) **f** entrance to Vatican Palace **g** equestrian statue of Constantine (1670, Bernini) **h** equestrian statue of Charlemagne (18C) **B** nave **1** Pietà (Michelangelo, 1500) **2** 'column of Christ' **3** monument to Leo XII (1836) **4** monument to Christine of Sweden (C. Fontana) **5** monument to Pius XI (1949) on the left **6** tomb of Innocent XII **7** monument to Matilda of Canossa (Bernini) **8** chapel of the Most Holy Sacrament: decoration by Borromini, altarpiece by P. da Cortona, ciborium by Bernini **9** monument to Gregory XIII (Rusconi 1720) **10** tomb of Gregory XIV **11** Madonna del Soccorso (12C from Old St.Peter's) **12** tomb of Gregory XVI (1854) **13** tomb of Benedict XIV (1759) **14** tomb of Clement XIII (1788 Canova) **C** dome area **15** Papal altar with baldacchino (Bernini, 1624–28, under Urban VIII) **16** Confessione (Maderna) with statue of Pius VI (Canova) in front of entrance to tomb of St.Peter **17** St.Longinus (Bernini, 1639) **18** St.Helena (A. Bolgi, 1639) **19**

St. Veronica (F. Mochi, 1646) **20** St. Andrew (F. Duquesnoy, 1640) **21** Cattedra di S.Pietro: containing the Throne of St.Peter, supported by four Fathers of the Church; behind it is the window of the Holy Ghost (all by Bernini, 1656–65) **22** monument to Urban VIII (Bernini, 1642) **23** monument to Paul III (G.della Porta, 1575) **24** tomb of Alexander VIII **25** altar of Leo the Great (relief by Algardi, 1650) **26** tomb of Alexander VII (Bernini, 1672) **27** tomb of Pius VIII (1853) and entrance to the sacristy of St.Peter's **D** sacristies (C. Marchionni, 1776–84) **28** altar of Gregory the Great **29** tomb of Pius VII (Thorvaldsen, 1823) **30** statue of St.Peter (13C, Arnolfo) **31** monument to Leo XI (Algardi, 1642) **32** tomb of Innocent XI (C.Maratta, 1679) **33** Choir chapel **34** tomb of Innocent VIII (A. Pollaiuolo, 1498) **35** monument to St. Pius X (1923) **36** on the right, monument to John XXIII; altar table with tomb of St. Pius X; on the left, monument to Benedict XV **37** monument to the last Stuarts (Canova, 1817) **38** stair up to the roof and to the dome **39** Baptistery **E** Scala Regia (Bernini).

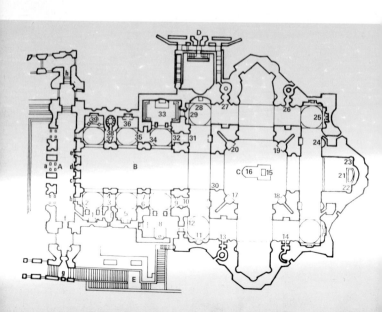

ble to all in the square. Bernini solved this problem by dividing the square into two halves, the *Piazza obliqua* and the *Piazza retta*. The *colonnades* of the oval part of the square form a visible barrier, but do not entirely cut the square off from the outside world. In the centre stands the *obelisk* (which has stood in the piazza since Sixtus V brought it here in 1596), with Maderna's *fountains* to either side. The second (trapezoidal) part of the square is connected to the church and also contains the entrance to the papal palace on the right side (bronze gate, behind which is the Scala Regia). The steps in front of St.Peter's optically shorten the distance to the church and add to the façade's impression of height. **Interior:** The religious and artistic centrepiece of the interior is the tomb of St.Peter over which rises Bernini's baldacchino with the papal altar. Other furnishings: see plan. The **Vatican Palace** and **Gardens** are not open to the general public, with the sole exception of the *Campo Santo Teutonico* (left of St.Peter's), a cemetery used by Germans since the 8C.

D. The Vatican Museums (entrance on the Viale Vaticano): The formation of the Vatican Collections began in 1503, when Julius II displayed the statue of Apollo, followed by that of Laocoon in 1506. The library was laid out in the mid-16C. When Clement XIV inherited several collections of antiques in 1770, a systematic extension of the Vatican Museums was ordered. Now incorporated into the museums are the Raphael Stanze and the Sistine Chapel. The most important sections (in the same order as the guided tour): *Museo Pio-Clementino* (Belvedere Torso, Laocoön group, Apollo Belvedere). *Museum Chiaramonti*. *Museo Gregoriano Etrusco* (Etruscan Museum). *Antique vase collection. Map gallery:* With a view on to Bramante's Belvedere Court (left) and the Vatican Gardens with the Casino Pio IV (right). *Stanze di Raffaello and the Logge di Raffaello:* (School of Athens and Disputà). View from the loggia into the courtyard of the Vatican Palace. The *Chapel of Nicholas V* (frescos by Fra Angelico). *Appartamento Borgia* (frescos by Pinturicchio). *Sistine Chapel:* Meeting place of the Conclave and the Pope's private chapel. 15C cycle of frescos on the lower part of the walls (Botticelli, Signorelli, Perugino, Ghirlandaio and Rosselli) and the celebrated frescos of

St.Peter's Square

Rossano

Michelangelo, which were painted in two periods (1508 – 12, ceiling and window arches; 1534–41 the Last Judgement). Next is the *Vatican Library* (treasure of Sancta Sanctorum, fresco of the Aldobrandini Marriage, the Salone Sistino—after Sixtus V). *Picture Gallery* (Raphael, Leonardo). *Former Lateran Collections*.

Rosciano 65020
Pescara/Abruzzi   p.416☐ I 9

S.Maria Arabona: Built in 1208 on the site of an altar to the Goddess Bona. It is the earliest Cistercian building in the area (rectangular termination to the choir, pointed arch vault). The monastery was in use up to 1587; the church was restored in 1952. Inside, to the left of the high altar is a 13C *tabernacle* with floral reliefs and a *paschal candlestick* on two dogs and a lion

(a 2nd is lost) and around the shaft of which winds a vine; birds and grapes in the capital. The main apse has a *votive fresco* by Antonio da Atri, 1373.

Rosciolo de'Marsi 67050
L'Aquila/Abruzzi   p.416☐ I 9

S.Maria delle Grazie: Built in the 13C; extended in the 15C. The right portal comes from the older building; the *main portal* on the left, is by Giovanni and Martino (1446). Inside: *remains of frescos*.

Environs: S.Maria in Valle Porclaneta (3 km. N.): Built before 1080 (the former monastery is in ruins); altered in the 13C (polygonal choir). Façade with portico. To the right, above the portal, there is a *Madonna* by Master Niccolò, whose own *tomb* is within. The *pulpit* is by Ruberto di Ruggero and Nicodemo da Guardiagrele, 1150, and the *iconostasis* and the *ciborium* are from the same period. The beautiful *frescos* on the walls date from the 14&15C.

Rossano 87067
Cosenza/Calabria   p.418☐ N 13

S.Marco: Stands in an exposed position on a sheer cliff at the SE edge of the town. 10C, pure Byzantine; square ground plan, five domes and three semicircular apses. Central dome supported by four pillars. Inside: Byzantine *fresco remains*. 16C campanile.

Museo Diocesano (*Episcopal Palace*): The most important exhibit is the 6C 'Codex Purpureus', a Greek bible manuscript of 188 pages, with silver lettering on purple parchment with 12 miniatures.

Also worth seeing: Cathedral of *S.Maria Assunta* (modern façade): On the left of the nave, there is a baroque altar with the much-visited 'Madonna Achiropita', an early medieval fresco (8–9C). (Achiropita means 'painted not by humans' but by anels' hands'). *Chiesetta della Panaghia* (near cathedral): 12C, Byzantine, with semi-circular apse and remains of frescos. *S. Bernardino:* 15C; beautiful façade. *S. Domenico:* 17C with beautiful 18C wood carvings.

Environs: *c.* 15 km. W. is **Corigliano Calabro**, now an agricultural centre (the name is perhaps derived from 'chorion helaion', meaning 'olive-land'). Church of *S.Antonio da Padua:* 16–18C; dome faced with different coloured majolica tiles. A side road (sign-posted) between Corigliano and Rossano leads W. to the monastery church of **S.Maria del Patir** (or Patirion): Remains of a Basilian monastery from the early 12C (declined in the 15C; dissolved 1806). Church with nave, two aisles and three apses in Byzantine style; 15C main portal; beautiful *capitals* within and a most remarkable 12C *mosaic pavement* towards the back of the church (with animal motifs). About 25 km. NW of Rossano in the 'Piana di Sibari' are the remains of the Greek town of **Sybaris** on the bank of the Crati (signposted). It was important in the 6C BC but destroyed by Croton in 510 BC; There have been American excavations over the last 20 years of the Greek, and later Roman town (regular guided tours). S.of Sybaris is the site of the Greek town of *Thourioi*.

Rovereto 38067

Trento/S. Tirol-Trentino   p.410□F 3

This town, which was settled in prehistoric times, was important under the Romans. In the 13C the little town acquired its massive fort, which occupies a steep crag. Rebuilt in the 15C, it has been a *Historical Museum* since 1921 (historical weapons).

Parish church of S. Maria del Carmine: A baroque building of 1674–8 with façade by Giuseppe Antonio Schiavi (1750). Late 15C cloister has frescos of 1559. High altar of 1700 by Cristoforo Benedetti and unusual grisaille painting by Giorgio Wenter Marini (1923).

Also worth seeing: *S.Marco,* 1450–62. Converted in 1603; side chapels added in

Rossano, Codex Purpureus, Fol. 7

Rovereto, view

Rovigo, castle tower

1834. Baroque stucco by Pietro Calori (1900). *S. Maria delle Grazie*, a beautiful centrally-planned building of 1728. The *Madonna del Monte*, a 17C pilgrimage church, lies in the NW of the town.

Environs: Sacco (SW of Rovereto on the Adige): the baroque *parish church of S. Giovanni Battista* has an excellent façade by Antonio Giuseppe Sartori (1754). Originally dating from the 12C, the church was rebuilt in 1658 and enlarged in 1754. The lavishly furnished *Cappella dell' Annunziata* dates from 1645. **Brancolino** (NW of Rovereto): *S. Maria*, originally 13C, was enlarged in 1514 and gained its present form in the 17C. Stucco and architectural ornamentations by Pietro Antonio Sorisena (1672–3); oil paintings (of the same date) by Pompeo Ghitti. **Villa Lagarina** (further N.): The *Chiesa dell' Assunta*, a 12C parish church was rebuilt in 1620. Inside stucco and vault frescos are

by G.A. Baroni (1759). The Cappella Rupert is interesting and richly furnished; it was built as a funerary chapel in 1621 to a design by Santino Solari. **Valano** (W. of Villa Lagarina, on the other side of the Adige): The little church of *S. Rocco* was built around 1500 (following the enlargement of a preceding building). Still further N. along the Adige lies **Calliano** with the former fortress of Trento, the 13C *Castel Pietra* with a medieval Great Hall (in the S. of the town on a massive crag). The castle was altered from the 14–17C. Of particular interest are the series of frescos around the 2nd storey of the Great Hall (c. 1470). **Castel Beseno:** The largest castle in Trentino, situated on a high rocky plateau. It results from the 14C combination of three older castles. The oldest part of this massive ruin dates from the 12C. The imposing complex was rebuilt in 1513 by Count Trapp, following a fire. Scant remains of a 15C fresco cycle. **S. Felice:** SW

Rovigo, Accademia dei Concordi, Death of Cleopatra by S. Mazzoni

of Rovereto. The 13C *parish church of SS. Felice e Fortunata* was enlarged in the 16C and converted in the 18C. Of particular interest is the side chapel, the *Cappella di S. Felice* 1717–19, which has a very beautiful baroque altar containing the funerary urn of the saint. **Brentònico:** Further S. lies Brentònico with the *parish church of SS. Pietro e Paolo*, referred to as early as the 12C; given its present form in 1584–93. Of interest is the crypt with columns and figured capitals from the 10 or 11C.

Rovigo 45100

Rovigo/Veneto   p.410☐G 4

A provincial capital, it lies in the fertile Polesine region between the the Adige and the Po. The town is first mentioned in documents of 838, and was already fortified in the 10C. The Este family ruled the town apart from a few interruptions, until it was annexed to Venice in 1482.

Cathedral of S. Stefano (Piazza del Duomo): Founded in the 10C and altered several times in the course of the following centuries. The mainly baroque building has a beautiful, well-lit, single-aisled interior with a dome over the crossing (Latin cross ground plan). The three side chapels are interconnected. Inside the most important furnishings are the *bronze lamps*.

Chiesa della Beata Vergine del Soccorso or **'la Rotonda'** (Piazza XX Settembre): A beautiful, balanced, though somewhat austere building with an octagonal ground plan, built by F. Zamberlan, a pupil of Palladio, in 1594–1602. The *campanile* of 1655 has 6 storeys and was built to designs by B. Longhena. The extremely festive interior achieves its effect through the use of lavish furnishings and large 17C *paintings*.

Porta S.Bortolo (Piazza Roma): The last remnant of the defensive walls. This beautiful, double battlemented gate was built in 1482–6, following the annexation of Rovigo to Venice. 16C *Coat-of-arms of the Donà delle Rose family*.

Palazzo del Municipio, formerly the *Loggia dei Notai* (Piazza Vittorio Emanuele II): The 16C palace (restored 1765) has three large arcades, above which there is an elegant *loggia* with a Madonna by G. Mauro (1590). In the large room on the 1st floor there is an excellent painting (*Pietà*) by F.Maffei, as well as other paintings. The *Torre dell'Orologio*, on the left, was built in 1763.

Palazzo dell'Accademia dei Concordi (Piazza Vittorio Emanuele II): This building of 1814 contains the Academy's *Library*, and **Picture Gallery**. The Academy was founded by Humanists in 1580. Of great interest is the collection of paintings on the 1st and 2nd floor: 'Virgin and Child' by G. Bellini, 'Christ Carrying the Cross', attributed to Bellini; 'Birth of Christ', 'Visitation of Mary' and others by G.B. Pittoni; 'St.Francis of Paola' by G.B. Piazzetta; 'Portrait of Antonio Riccoboni' by G.B. Tiepolo; and 'Portrait of Giulio Contarini da Mula' by A. Longhi.

Also worth seeing: *S. Francesco:* Romanesque-Gothic parish church built in 1300–1430 with a campanile of 1520. *S. Bartolomeo* (Piazzale S.Bartolo): 15C, beautiful brick campanile of 16C. Inside: barrel-vaulted with baroque stucco in the side chapels. Nearby is the *monastery of the former Olivetan church*; Renaissance cloister. *Palazzo Roncale* (Via Laurenti), built in 1555 to designs by M.Sanmicheli and fronted by a pillared portico with widely-spaced arches. *Palazzo Roverella* (Piazza Vittorio Emanuele II): Begun by Cardinal Bartolomeo Roverello in 1475, but not completed until the 16C. On the Piazza G.Matteotti in the Giardino Pubblico, two massive towers, the *Torre Donà* and the

Torre Mozza, which belonged to the 10C fort are still standing. Palazzo Angeli (No. 28,Via Angeli): Built by F.Schiavi in 1780 with frescos inside by G.B.Canal. The *Seminario Vescovile* (No. 89, Viale Tre Martiri) has a painting collection of remarkable quality as well as a very fine library.

Rubiera 42048
Reggio Emilia/Emilia-Romagna   p.410☐E/F 5

Places of interest (on the main street): *Parish church of SS.Donnino e Biagio,* with reliquary and ciborium by F.Spani, 1517. *Palazzo Sacrati:* former town hall. *castle.*

Environs (3 km.N.): **SS. Faustino e Giovita:** Romanesque church with 13C fresco of the Virgin and 16C paintings of patron saints from the Garofalo School.

Ruvo di Puglia 70037
Bari/Apulia   p.416☐ 11

Cathedral of S.Maria Assunta: Begun in Romanesque style in the 13C; in the 16C a row of chapels was added to both sides of the nave (hence the disparity between height and width of façade). Façade: simple with three *portals*, all without architrave and tympanum—the middle one is particularly richly decorated, while the right one may date from an older building. Rose-window with date (1237); along the edge of the roof there are round arches on consoles with human and animal heads. On the E. side there are three apses; the campanile may once have been a defensive tower.

Museo Jatta (Piazza Giovanni Bovio): Unusual *collection of about 1700 antique vases* from Ruvo and the surrounding area (Founded in 1810 by the Jatta brothers).

Environs: *c.* 6 km. E. is **Terlizzi:** The *Oratory of the Madonna del Rosario* has a beautiful Romanesque portal.

Sabbioneta 46018
Mantua / Lombardy   p.410☐B 4

Description: The walls were laid out by Vespasiano Gonzaga and include six bastions and two gates; they enclose a rectangular grid of streets, with two squares where most of the important buildings are situated.

Historic buildings: The *Palazzo del Giardino* (Piazza Castello): On the right hand side of the street are the remains of the castle which was destroyed in 1794. The left-hand side of the palazzo is connected to the right corner of the square by the *Galleria degli Antichi* (1568). Inside there are a number of frescoed rooms with mythological themes (including frescos by Bernardino Campi). There is a small, mirrored room with pastoral scenes. The gallery of antiquities (1583–4) used to contain a collection of Roman busts put together after the Sack of Rome (1527); today this is housed in Mantua. The *Palazzo Ducale* (Piazza Garibaldi) was built in 1568, and has a façade from 1586. The most interesting features are the Galleria degli Antenati (gallery of ancestors) and the four remaining statues of the Gonzagas as knights (from an original 12). The *Chiesa della Incoronata* (W. of the Palazzo Ducale) is an octagonal church dating from 1586 – 8 which contains the mausoleum of Vespa-

siano Gonzaga by G.B.Della Porta (1592), with a statue (1588) of Vespasiano Gonzaga by L.Leoni. The *Teatro all'Antica* (Via Vespasiano Gonzaga) is also known as the *Olimpico* theatre and was built in 1588–90 by V.Scamozzi. Apart from the Teatro Olimpico in Vicenza, this is Italy's most important 16C theatre.

Also worth seeing: The parish church of *S.Maria Assunta* (Piazza Garibaldi, 1581); the fifth chapel on the right (1773) is by A.Bibiena. Some of the *town walls* are still standing, including the two gates, the Porta della Vittoria and the Porta Imperiale.

Environs: Villa Pasquali (just past the Porta Imperiale on the route to Mantua) has a splendid baroque parish church built by A.Bibiena in 1765–84.

Sacile 33077
Pordenone / Friuli   p.410☐H 2/3

This is first mentioned in the 8C BC, and was ruled by the Patriarchs of Aquileia from 1077 onwards. In 1419 it fell to Venice. During the Renaissance its literary standing was such that it was known as the 'Second Padua'.

S.Nicolò (Piazza del Duomo): This was built at the end of the 15C on the site of a pre-Romanesque structure. It has a fine

Renaissance façade, and an interior with a nave, two aisles, arcades with pointed arches, and an open roof. The wall by the entrance has an *epitaph* for the son of a Turkish sultan who died here in exile in 1454.

Also worth seeing: The 14C church of *S. Gregorio* (Via Roma); the *Chiesa della Pietà* (Via della Pietà), an early 17C, centrally planned church; the 15/16C frescoed *Palazzo Ragazzoni-Flangini* (Viale Zancanaro).

Environs: *c.* 11 km. N. of **Polcenigo** is one of Friuli's oldest churches, *S.Floreano*, with a Romanesque apse and vestibule and fine 13/14C frescos in the interior.

Salemi 91018
Trapani/Sicily   p.420☐H 16

This is known to modern historians for the 'Proclamation of Salemi', with which Garibaldi won control of Sicily for Victor Emmanuel in 1860.

Castle (Piazza Alicia): This dates from the

Salerno, cathedral, ambo

time of Emperor Frederick II Hohenstaufen (1220 – 50), and was restored in 1950. It has a trapezoid ground plan and three of the four original corner towers are still standing — Garibaldi planted the Italian flag on the round tower (see above).

Also worth seeing: the Cathedral (17/18C) has a *Statue of St. Julian* on the second altar on the right which is attributed to Francesco Laurana, a *font* from 1464 by Dom. Gagini, and a fine *processional cross* (1386) in the sacristy.

Salerno 84100
Salerno/Campania   p.418☐L 11

This was originally a Greek settlement, but became celebrated in the Middle Ages for its medical school. It flourished under the Lombards, Normans and Hohenstaufen, but was closed down by Murat in 1812.

Cathedral of S. Matteo (Via Duomo): Built in 1076 – 85 under the Norman Robert Guiscard; since then it has been extensively rebuilt, although its original form has recently been restored. Steps lead up to the arcaded *atrium* (138 ft. by 131 ft.) in front of the cathedral. The arcade is borne by 28 ancient columns from Paestum and houses 14 ancient *sarcophagi*. The central portal of the cathedral façade has famous *bronze doors*, which were made in Constantinople in 1099 and have 54 panels. There is a 12C campanile. The interior is basilican with a nave, two aisles and three semicircular apses. Note the large 13C Norman *mosaic* of the Evangelist Matthew over the entrance portal. The first chapel on the right has a *St.Januarius* by F.Solimena. The last pair of columns in the nave before the choir have highly decorated 12C *ambones*, and there is an *Easter candlestick* from the same period near the right hand one. The right apsidal chapel contains the *tomb of Pope Gregory VII* (d. 1085), the main opponent of Em-

Salerno, cathedral

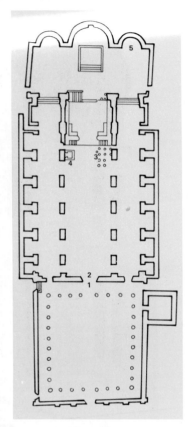

Salerno, cathedral 1 bronze door, 1099 **2** mosaic of St. Matthew, 13C **3** pulpit, 12C; Easter candlesticks **4** pulpit, also 12C **5** tomb of Gregory VII, mosaic of the Archangel Michael, 1260

peror Henry IV in the Investiture Contest; the apse itself contains a *mosaic* of the Archangel Michael in Byzantine style (1260). The crypt contains the *relics of Matthew the Evangelist*, which have been housed in Salerno since 954.

S.Giorgio (Via Duomo): A 17C baroque building with an interesting portal. It is single-aisled with *frescos* and *stucco*, much of which is by Angelo Solimena (1675). Ex-

amples of his work include a painting of St. Michael above the fourth altar on the right and frescoed scenes from the lives of various saints (1680, youthful works) in a *chapel* to the left of the church. There is also an interesting baroque *wooden pulpit*.

Museo Provinciale (Via S. Benedetto): Opened in 1927, this houses the *archaeological finds* from Salerno and its environs, which include the 'Ager Picentinus'. Note the huge bronze *head of Apollo* from the 1C BC.

Also worth seeing: The *Chiesa de Crocifisso* (Piazza Matteotti) is pre-Romanesque in origin, with 12C Romanesque frescos in the crypt. The 13C *bishop's palace*, or Episcopio, is to the right of the cathedral, and still contains some ancient fragments. There are the remains of an 11C *aqueduct*, which can be reached from the Via Arce. The *cathedral museum* (Via Mons. Monterisi) has a fine 12C altar frontal (Paliotto), and paintings by Caravaggio, Giordano and Vaccaro. The *biblioteca provinciale* (Via dei Mercanti) has a fine collection of manuscripts and incunabula. To the NW, above the town, are the ruins of a Lombard *castle*, enlarged under the Normans, which afford a splendid view.

Environs: *c.* 5 km. W. is **Vietri sul Mare**, with its parish church of *S. Giovanni Battista*. This has a fine 16C *polyptych* under the fourth arch on the right; *c.* 9 km. NW is **Cava de'Tirreni**, with the 17C church of *S.Francesco*, which has a high altar with rich marble intarsia; some 4 km. to the SW is the 11C Benedictine monastery of *SS Trinità della Cava*, whose church (also 11C) has a fine 13C ambo attached to the last pillar in the nave. To the left of the church is the entrance to the *monastery*, which has a fine 13C cloister and interesting museum, archive and library. *c.* 19 km. NW is **Nocera Superiore**, with the early Christian church of *S. Maria Maggiore*, which was rebuilt in the 19C; it has a round ground plan and a huge font in the centre. *c.* 2.5 km. NE is the 12C *Santuario di S. Maria Materdomini* which has a fine portico with three arches in front of the façade.

Salò 25087
Brescia/Lombardy   p.410☐E 3

Cathedral: (Annunziata) This was built
in 1453–1502; the (uncompleted) façade
and Renaissance portal date from 1509. It
has a nave and two aisles with five bays and
a strikingly high arcade. The choir has
three apses and a much-extended sanctuary. *Decoration:* Decorated vaulting by
T.Sandrini (1591), work by Zenon
Veronese (1502–37) in the first four chapels
on the right; on the left of the baptistry is
a Madonna with saints by Romanino from
1529, and between the first and second
chapel on the left is a polyptych by
P.Veneziano. The fourth chapel on the left
houses a 'St.Antony of Egypt with St.Roch
and St.Sebastian' by Moretto.

Also worth seeing: The *Palazzo della
Magnifica Patria,* (1524), and the *Palazzo
della Podestà,* which was renovated in 1905,
are both on the Lungolago Zanardelli. The
Cimitero, which is on the route to Porto
Portese, was laid out to plans by Rodolfo
Vantini.

Environs: Toscolano-Maderno (10 km.
N. of Salò): The Romanesque church of
S.Andrea in Maderno has a façade with
half-columns and arches. The interior has
been restored to its original form.
Toscolano was the Roman settlement of
Benacum, which was the centre of the
Riviera Bresciana (on the west bank of
Lake Garda) during the 1&2C AD. The
church of *SS.Pietro e Paolo,* which was be-
gun in 1584, has some fine 16C sculptures.
Behind it is the campanile (1727) and the
chapel of the *Madonna del Benaco,* and to
the right is the site of the excavation of a
Roman villa (mosaics).

Salorno/Salurn 39040
Bolzano/Trentino South Tyrol   p.410 F 2

Parish Church of St.Andreas: This was
built in 1628–40 in sedate Lombard baroque; the chapel of St.Joseph by the cemetery is in the same style, and dates from
1650. The *pagan temple,* as it is known, is
a 16C castle cellar built against a cliff and
contains vaulting supported by rows of
columns. The ruins of the 13C *Haderburg,*

Salorno, view

which was extended in the 14&16C, are situated on a steep, high, inaccessible cliff. The castle was built on the site of an earlier one which was mentioned as early as the 11C.

Environs: S. Michele all' Adige/St. Michael on the Adige (S. of Salurn): The

parish church of St. Michael, formerly the *church of the Augustinian canons,* was founded in the 12C, although the present church was built by G. Borghetti and St. Panizza in 1686–98 after the original one was destroyed in a fire. The interior contains some interesting stucco; the frescos in the dome are by F.W. Ruprecht, and those in the nave and the altarpieces are by G. Alberti. **Cembra** lies on the route from Lavis (which is between Salorno and Trento) to Cavalese, and contains the church of *S. Pietro,* with its original 14/15C campanile. The church itself dates from 1516 and has net vaulting and a painted interior. The most interesting features are the plant motifs (1549) in the vaulting and the fresco of the 'Last Judgement' on the north wall (1759), which is by V. Revisi, a pupil of Tiepolo. Further along the Cembratal (Val de Cembra) towards Cavalese is **Segonzano,** a collection of several villages. The parish church of *SS. Trinità* is a 15C building, rebuilt in the 19C, with a 17C carved high altar containing a 16C shrine with a group of carved figures. **Vigo di Ton** (S. of Salorno, NW of Mezzolombardo): The 13C *Castle Thun,* rebuilt in the 16C, has some fine 16/17C furnishings; the parish church of the *Assunta* dates from the 13, 16&18C, and has an altarpiece on the left side-altar by F. Guardi. **Spormaggiore** is on the route from Mezzolombardo to Malveno; the imposing 14/18C ruins of the *Castello di Belfort* lie in between Spormaggiore and Cavalese.

Salsomaggiore Terme 43039
Piacenza/Emilia-Romagna   p.412 E 4

Castello di Tabiano (c. 5 km. E.): This is a 12C castle which was destroyed in 1150, then rebuilt and converted into a private residence in the 18C. The *small church*

has been restored, with its Romanesque exterior preserved.

Bargone (c. 5.5 km. E.): 12C *castle* with a 16C Renaissance courtyard. **Scipione** (3.3 km. NW): 12C *castle.* **Vigoleno** (11 km. W.): A 12C *castle* which was destroyed in the 14C and then rebuilt. The Romanesque church of *S. Giorgio* (12C?) has an early 13C relief in the lunette above the portal, and the interior contains the remains of some 15C frescos.

Saluzzo 12037
Cuneo/Piedmont   p.412 A/B 5

S. Assunta (Piazza Risorgimento): This is a late Gothic cathedral, built between 1491 and 1501. It has an unfinished façade and a *portal* decorated with statues and a baroque door, and frescos in the lunettes. The campanile is baroque (1711), and the interior has a nave, two aisles, a polygonal apse and clustered pillars; it is one of the largest interiors in Piedmont. The *decoration* includes four pieces of a polyptych from around 1500.

S. Giovanni (Via S. Giovanni): A typical example of local medieval architecture. It was built in French Gothic style, being begun in 1330 and completed in 1504. The façade is incomplete, the campanile is from 1376, and the apse from 1463–1504. In place of the transept, there is a *Loreto chapel,* which has three aisles and dates from 1655; the choir contains a highly sculptured *tabernacle* and carved wooden *choir-stalls.* A niche on the left hand side contains the tomb of the founder, Ludovic II, who died in 1508. The Gothic *cloisters* with coloured terracotta date are 15C, and a Renaissance portal leads through to the *chapter house,* which contains the *tomb of Galeazzo Cavassa di Carmagnola* and some 16C frescos.

Also worth seeing: The *Casa Cavassa* (Via S. Giovanni) is an elegant Renaissance residence dating from around 1500, with furniture and paintings from the same period. It houses the town *museum.* The *castle* (Piazza Castello) was built by Tommaso I, the Marquis of Saluzzo, in 1170, and rebuilt in 1826. The Confraternità della Misericordia (1761).

Environs: Manta (*c.* 4 km. S.! The *castle* was built in the 14C by Tommaso III di Saluzzo, and was extended in the 15C. It has a number of fine rooms, including the 'Sala baronale custodisce' with its extraordinary fresco cycle from the early Piedmontese Renaissance, which still has elements of French Gothic. **Abbazia di Staffarda** (*c.* 10 km. NW): This Cistercian abbey is one of the most important in Piedmont. It was founded in 1135, destroyed in 1690, and later restored. Its founder was Manfred I of Saluzzo. The Gothic *Ospizio dei Pellegrini* has survived, and now serves as a restaurant; just to its left is the Gothic *Loggia del Mercato*, an open arcaded loggia. The *church* has a Romanesque façade and a 15C Gothic portico, with an interior which is pure Cistercian. It consists of a nave and two aisles, and contains a 15/16C German polychrome wooden crucifixion with Mary and John. There are paintings (1531) by Ottone Pascale on the high altar, and the French

Gothic wooden pulpit is from 1400. The *monastery* near the church has a well-preserved Gothic chapter house.

San Benigno Canavese 10080

Turin / Piedmont   p.412 □ B 4

Abbazia di Frutturia: This Cluniac monastery was founded by St.William of Volpiano in 998 and consecrated by Emperor Henry II in 1003. In 1014 King Arduin laid the Holy Roman Empire's insignia on the altar. The monastery remained important until 1477, after which it suffered a decline; it was captured by Victor Amadeus in 1710, and in 1749 Carlo Vittori Amedeo delle Lanze became abbot. He rebuilt the church and the monastery in rococo style. *S.Maria Assunta*, which is today the parish church, was built by Quarini in 1750–60 to a design by Vittone. The classical façade is preceded by a portico with Corinthian columns, and the interior includes fine stucco medallions of the Stations of the Cross by G.B.Bernero. Only the Romanesque campanile still stands from the old abbey's residence; it has an

Saluzzo, Casa Cavassa

11C Ottonian fresco of the 'Madonna and Child', which shows the Byzantine influence typical of the period.

San Candido/Innichen 39038
Bolzano/Trentino South Tyrol   p.410□G 1

Collegiate Church of St.Candidus and St.Corbinian: This early 13C church is one of the most unusual and important Romanesque buildings in the South Tyrol. The campanile, which is attached to the façade, dates from 1320–5, the vestibule and its gallery are from 1465, and the auxiliary saints' chapel is from 1524. The portals are especially fine: the *south portal* has a Lombard relief (1250) by Master Friedrich in the tympanum, and above it is a fine fresco (1480) by Michael and Friedrich Pacher. The interior is plain but striking. The vault of the crossing has *frescos* of the Creation (1270), and there is a *crucifixion* (1200) on the high altar. The painted *organ* is from 1629. The 12C *crypt* was altered in the 13&19C before being restored in 1967/8. There is a *niche* on the W. of the church containing frescos (1450) by Master Leonhard of Brixen.

Parish Church of St.Michael: Only the *round tower* with its baroque cupola survives from the original Romanesque church, which was rebuilt after a fire in 1760 in Tyrol late baroque style to a design by Rudolf Schraffl. The *frescoed vaulting* and *decorative painting* are by Christof Anton Mayr and date from 1760.

Funerary chapels: In 1653 two chapels were added in imitation of the Church of the Holy Sepulchre in Jerusalem and the Chapel of Grace at Altötting in Bavaria. The early 16C reliefs are of especial interest.

Environs: Dobbiaco/Toblach: Toblach is 5 km. E. of San Candido, on the watershed between the Rienz and the Drau, and has the *parish church of St. John the Baptist*, an impressive late baroque church built by Rudolf Schraffl in 1769–82. The frescos on the ceiling and the altarpiece

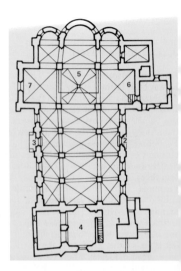

Innichen, Collegiate church **1** campanile **2** S. portal with fresco by the Pachers **3** Romanesque N. portal **4** W. portico **5** presbytery with Romanesque Crucifixion at the high altar **6** S. transept, statue of the Virgin, 15C **7** N. transept with Renaissance altar and three reliefs by Michael Parth, around 1520

(1769) are by Franz Anton Zeiller, the sculpture on the high altar is by Johannes Perger (1774) and the pulpit, which dates from 1769, is by Franz Singer. The five *chapels of the Stations of the Cross* around the church are by Michael Parth from 1519, and have interesting reliefs.

San Daniele del Friuli 33038
Udine/Friuli   p.410□H 2

This is the centre of the 'Anfiteatro morenico del Tagliamento', and it was an independent commune in the Middle Ages; it became Venetian in 1420, although under the control of the Patriarchs of Aquileia.

Cathedral of S. Michele (Piazza del Duomo): Now 18C baroque, it was originally 14C. It has a fine *façade* (1707) with

Toblach (Innichen), parish church

Innichen, Collegiate church

steps leading up to it, and an unfinished 16C *campanile*. The interior consists of a nave and two aisles, with domes over the crossing and the nave. There is a fine *font* (1509) in the left aisle, and an interesting painting by Pordenone (*Holy Trinity*, 1535) on the first side altar on the left. Rich *church treasury*.

S. Antonio Abate (Via Garibaldi): This is a late Gothic building dating from the second half of the 15C, with a heavily decorated *façade* and a portal from 1470. The interior is single-aisled, with an open roof and three apses, a splendid *fresco cycle* by Pellegrino da S. Daniele which was painted in 1497–1522 and includes depictions of Christ, the Evangelists, prophets and saints; it is one of Friuli's finest examples of high Renaissance painting. There are some older, 15C *frescos* on the left wall, which include the Nativity of Christ. There is a wooden *pietà* (1488) in the main

apse, and to the right of the entrance is a 15C Venetian *carved wooden altar*.

Palazzo del Municipio (Piazza del Duomo): This 15C palazzo houses the *Biblioteca Guarneriana*, which was founded by Guarnerio d'Artegna in 1464 and contains an extensive Renaissance collection, including a number of manuscripts. The *Archivio Comunale*, which is attached, contains old documents, some from the 13C.

Also worth seeing: The church of *S. Daniele* (castle hill) was originally 10C, but is now 18C baroque (with a 12C Romanesque relief in the apse); the church of the *Madonna della Fratta* (Via Cavour) has a fine Gothic façade dating from 1470.

Environs: Villalata is some 13 km. S. and has one of the finest 12C *castles* in Friuli. **Valeriano** is 9 km. W., with the church of *S. Stefano*, which includes the oldest sur-

viving work by Pordenone (1506). The
14/15C church of *S.Maria dei Battuti* has
numerous works (1524) by Pordenone;
Ragogna is 5 km. NW and has the remains of an early medieval *castle*.

San Demetrio Corone 87069
Cosenza/Calabria   p.418☐N 13

Church of S.Adriano: This is inside the
Palazzo del Collegio Italo-Albanese, a former
Basilian monastery founded by St.Nilus
of Rossano. It is an 11/12C building with
a nave, two aisles and fine capitals. There
are 13C Byzantine style *frescos* of saints
over the arches and the *font* (which was
originally a Byzantine capital) and Norman
mosaic pavement with animal motifs are
also of interest.

Environs: Acri is some 15 km. S., on the
probable site of the ancient Pandosia, although some say it was Acheruntia. It has
a few interesting churches: *S.Maria Maggiore*, with ancient foundations, was originally Romanesque although totally rebuilt
in the 18C; *S.Francesco di Paola* is 16C, and
the *Chiesa dell'Annunciata* is baroque, and
has a fine carved wood portal. There are
also the ruins of a *castle*.

San Fruttuoso di Camogli 16030
Genoa/Liguria   p.412☐C/D 5

**Abbazia di San Fruttuoso di
Capodimonte:** This Benedictine monastery was attached to the monastery of
Monte Cassino and founded in 984 in ful-
filment of an old pledge: in 711 Bishop
Prosper of Tarragona promised to build a
monastery and a church to house the relics
of S.Fruttuoso, a martyr from Tarragona
who died in 275. It was severely damaged
by the Saracens, but rebuilt by the
Benedictines and flourished in the 13C under the protection of the Doria family. Destroyed again by the Saracens, it began to
decline in the 15C. It comprises a church,
a small cloister and the 13/14C *abbey building*, which has a fine façade with arched

windows. The high church interior, with
its nave and two aisles, has traces of the
church which was built in 984. The new
church and façade had to be set back some
16 ft. The small *cloister*, which can be
reached from the right aisle, also contains
some relics of the original structure. The
elegant *loggia* leads through to the *Doria
tombs*.

San Gimignano 53037
Siena/Tuscany   p.414☐F 7

13 out of a total of 56 *towers* are still standing, and their attempts to outdo each other
give the city its characteristic skyline. Prehistoric finds from the surrounding area
suggest that this was once the site of an
Etruscan settlement.

Cathedral/Collegiata (Piazza del
Duomo): This is a 12C Romanesque building dedicated to the Assumption; its basilican ground plan was altered into the shape
of a Latin cross by Giuliano de Sangallo
in 1456. The plain façade dates from 1239,
and the 14C walls and vaulting are fres-

S.Fruttuoso di Capodimonte 1 church **2** abbey **3** cloister **4** loggia

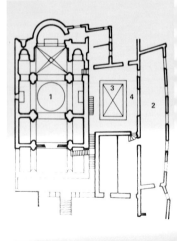

coed, with a *Last Judgement* on the inside wall of the façade. To the right of this, in the nave, is *Hell*, with *Paradise* on the left; the frescos are by Taddeo di Bartolo and date from 1393. Underneath the Last Judgement is a *Martyrdom of St.Sebastian* (1465) by Benozzo Gozzoli; the *frescos on the pillars* (Augustine, Bernard, Jerome) are also by Gozzoli and date from the same year. The walls of the right aisle show 14C New Testament scenes by Barna Senese. The *Cappella di S.Fina*, a local 13C saint, is especially interesting. Beneath the seventh arch on the right, it is in pure Renaissance style by Giuliano and Benedetto da Maiano (1468). The splendid *dossale* (1475) has two frescos by Domenico Ghirlandaio and his assistants (1457), including one of his masterpieces, St.Gregory telling St.Fina of his approaching death, and the funeral rites of the saint. There is a wooden *Annunciation* (c.1421) by Jacopo della Quercia on consoles on the inside of the façade.

S. Agostino (Piazza S.Agostino): This is in the NW of the city, and can be reached by way of the Via S.Matteo, which is lined by a number of medieval buildings, includ-ing some towers. It was built in Romanesque/Gothic transitional style in 1280–98, and has a slender campanile. The *Cappella di S.Bartolo*, which is just inside on the right by the main portal, has an impressive *marble altar* with Renaissance figures and reliefs by Benedetto da Maiano (1494). The high altar in the sanctuary contains a panel painting of the *Coronation of the Virgin and Saints* by Piero del Pollaiuolo (1483), and there are frescos on the chancel walls by Benozzo Gozzoli and his assistants.

Museo d'Arte Sacra dell'Opera della Collegiata: The *Palazzo della Prepositura* (Piazza Pecori) has a collection of works of art from the cathedral and other churches; it also houses the old Museo Civico.

Palazzo del Popolo/Palazzo Nuovo del Podestà: This was begun in 1288 and extended in 1323. Its battlemented façade bears *coats of arms*, and the *Torre Grossa* (177 ft. high), offers a splendid view. The courtyard is picturesque, and has a 14C *cistern*. The finest work of art is in the room where Dante addressed the Podestà and the Consiglio Generale in 1300. There is a

San Gimignano

fresco by Lippo Memmi (1317), a *Maestà* (Madonna and child enthroned with saints) based on that by Simone Martini in the Palazzo Pubblico in Siena. The **Pinacoteca Civica**, which is housed in the palazzo, contains works by Gozzoli, Pinturicchio, Filippino Lippi etc.

Fonti: This 12–14C structure consists of ten round and pointed arches on pillars and columns. It lies just outside the *Porta delle Fonte.*

The **Porta S.Matteo** at the end of the Via S.Matteo is Sienese and dates from 1262. The **Porta S.Giovanni** is at the other end of the city, on the street of the same name. It also dates from 1262, but is more interesting. The small church of the *Madonna dei Luni* was built on in 1601.

Also worth seeing: *S.Jacopo,* 13C by the Porta S.Jacopo; *S.Lorenzo in Ponte* (Via del Castello), 1240; the *Piazza del Cisterna.*

Environs: Poggibonsi is E. of S. Gimignano on the road from Florence to Siena. As 'Podium Boniti' it was one of Tuscany's strongest fortresses, until it was destroyed by Guy de Montfort in 1270. It was rebuilt in 1478 under Lorenzo il Magnifico to a design by Giuliano da Sangallo, but was left unfinished. The *Palazzo Pretorio* is a Gothic building with stone coats of arms on the exterior wall and a battlemented medieval tower. The monastery of *S.Lucchese* is on a hill just outside the town; it was once a Camaldolese house, but was taken over and extended by the Franciscans in 1213.

Monteriggioni: This is further S. than Poggibonsi on the road to Siena, and stands on a mound with a *surrounding wall* some 230 ft. in circumference. Built 1213-19 and 1260-70, this is defended by 14 towers.

San Ginesio 62026
Macerata/Marches   p.414☐ J 7

Collegiata (Piazza Gentili): This is a Romanesque building which was altered

in the 15C; the upper section of the façade, which shows German influence, is by Enrico Alemanno and dates from 1421. The interior contains a German *Pietà*, and a *Madonna* by Pietro Alemanno (1485) in the choir.

Also worth seeing: There is a Madonna by Federico Barocci in the church of *S. Gregorio* (Via Brugiano). *S.Agostino* (Via Umberto I) has a picture of the battle between S.Ginesio and Fermo in 1377. *S. Francesco* (Via Cucchiari) has a fine Romanesque portal from the original building (1240). The *Museo Comunale* (Piazza Gentili) is housed in the former church of S.Sebastiano. The *Ospedale dei Pellegrini* has a 13C loggia.

San Giorgio di Valpolicella 37010
Verona/Veneto   p.412☐ F 3

Pieve di S.Giorgio: This was built at the end of the 11C as a basilica with two choirs (an E. one with three apses, and a W. apse entered through a new portal). The nave is much higher than the two aisles; there is no transept and the roof has an open truss. The W. apse contains the remains of some 12C paintings, such as a *Christ Pantocrator* in a mandorla. Since 1923 the high altar (E. apse) has borne a reconstructed 8C *ciborium* (combination of early Christian motifs and Lombard decorative forms on the slabs of the arcades). The S.side of the nave leads out to an early 12C Romanesque *cloister,* whose NE inner wall has three slabs from the original ciborium set in it.

San Giovanni in Persiceto 40017
Bologna/Emilia-Romagna   p.412☐ F 5

Points of interest: The *Palazzo Municipio* has a John the Baptist by Francesco Francia; the *Collegiata di S.Giovanni* has a St. Antony of Padua with the Infant

San Gimignano, Pinacoteca Civica Taddeo di Bartolo

Christ by Guercino, and a Virgin with St.Roch and St.Sebastian by Francesco Albani. The 13C *Palazzaccio* was once the residence of the Abbot of Nonantola.

Environs: Sala Bolognese has the fine 11C parish church of *S.Biagio*, which was restored in 1924.

San Leo 61018
Pesaro and Urbino/Marches   p.414□G 6

Fortress: This huge medieval building is where Cagliostro was imprisoned and died in 1795.

Cathedral: This was built in the 13C on the foundations of a Roman Temple of Jupiter. The columns inside have Roman capitals, and the *crucifix* in the apse dates from 1209.

Pieve (S.Leo): This was built from old materials in the 8/9C, and was altered in the 11&18C. Some of the interior columns and pillars have Roman capitals, and there are Byzantine captials on the ciborium

San Marino, Palazzo del Governo

(881) on the high altar. The first chapel in the *west crypt* was built by St.Leo in th 4C.

San Marino 47031
Republic   p.414□G/H

This tiny republic has been independen since 1631; its most interesting features ar the *Palazzo del Governo*, which has som interesting rooms, and the three fortresse which dominate the skyline—*Guaita* (11C) *Fratta* (13C) and *Montale* (13C). Th church of *S.Francesco* (1361), and the *Pa lazzo Valloni*, with its *museum* and *pictur gallery*, are also worth a visit.

San Pier d'Arena 16149
Genoa/Liguria   p.412□C

Palazzo Scassi (Piazza Montano, oppo site the Giardino Pubblico): The architect G.Alessi, known for his work in Genoa completed this harmoniously propor tioned building in 1560 (it was restored in the 19C). The façade is especially fine. G.A.Carlone painted the ceiling of the por tico (*Samson strangling the lion*); the other ceilings are by B.Castello.

San Remo 18038
Imperia/Liguria   p.412□B 6

S.Siro, the collegiate church (Piazza S. Siro): This 13C Romanesque/Gothic church was built on the site of an earlier structure, and was later subject to baroque alterations before being restored in its origi nal style in 1902. The façade is separated into three sections, and has a large Gothic *portal* with a rose-window above it. The Gothic lunettes contain 13&16C figures.

Madonna della Costa (Piazza Castello): This is a beautifully-situated baroque church with a *frescoed dome* by G.A.Boni and a small *panel painting* on the high altar, a 'Madonna and Child' by N. da Voltri (*c.* 1401).

S.Stefano (Piazza Cassini): This was restored in 1733 and 1881, and contains a fine painting by D.Piola.

Also worth seeing: The palm- and oleander-fringed *Corso dell' Imperatrice*, named in honour of a visit by the Russian Tsarina Maria Alexandrovna, has a **Russian Orthodox Church** near the Casino Municipale; its golden dome recalls its Moscow model.

San Severino Marche 62027
Macerata/Marches   p.414☐H 7

S. Agostino/New Cathedral (Via Salimbeni): A 13C church rebuilt in the 15C, with a 19C interior; the portal dates from 1473. The first altar on the right has a *crucifix* from 1473, and the second has a *Madonna with saints* by Antonio and Giovanni Gentile (1548). There is a *Madonna* by Pinturicchio in the sacristy.

S.Lorenzo in Doliolo (left at the end of the Via Salimbeni): An 8/9C church rebuilt in the 11C, the period from which

the *portal* dates. The campanile is 14C, and the choir modern. The interior contains the remains of some 14C *frescos*.

Old Cathedral (in the medieval upper town): A 10C building which has been altered subsequently; the campanile is 14C. The first chapel on the left contains *frescos* by Lorenzo and Jacopo Salimbeni from the early 15C, and the *choir stalls* date from 1483. Much of the stonework of the *cloisters* has been destroyed by earthquakes.

Also worth seeing: Piazza del Popolo: The *clock-tower* contains the 18C *Chiesetta della Misericordia*. The *Palazzo Municipale* was built in 1764 and houses the *Pinacoteca*.

Sant'Agata de'Goti 82019
Benevento/Campania   p.416☐K 11

Cathedral of S.Maria Assunta (Piazza S.Alfonso): Founded in 970, rebuilt in the 12C and altered in baroque style in 1723 –34. There is a portico in front of the façade with 12 ancient columns and capitals,

San Marino

and a fine Romanesque central portal. The interior consists of a nave and two aisles, and is sumptuously decorated with baroque *stucco-work*. The raised choir still has remnants of its original *mosaic pavement*. The *crypt*, which is under the choir, has 12 ancient columns and some fine 14C *frescos*, with scenes from the Passion, apostles, saints and a pope.

S.Menna (Piazza Trieste): This was begun under Count Robert of Capua, and consecrated in 1114; it has a fine Romanesque *portal*. The interior has a nave and two aisles, which are separated by old columns, some of whose capitals are Romanesque and some even older. The remains of the 12C *mosaic pavement*, with geometrical patterns, are visible most clearly in the apse.

Chiesa dell'Annunziata (Largo Annunziata): This is a Gothic building with a fine marble *Renaissance portal*. The interior is single-aisled and has the remains of 15C *frescos* on its walls. The apse contains an interesting 15C *diptych* ('Annunciation').

Also worth seeing: The church of *S.*

Francesco (near the Piazza L.Viscardi) contains the interesting *Renaissance tomb of Lodovico Artus* (d. 1370). There is a prehistoric *necropolis* on the outskirts of the city which dates from the 19/18C BC. It is near the villages of *Presta* and *S.Pietro*, and some of the finds are on display in Benevento and Naples.

Environs: Airola is *c.* 9 km. SE, and contains the 16C *Chiesa dell'Annunziata* by Luigi Vanvitelli. The interior has a nave and two aisles and contains some fine marble pieces; there are two works by Fr. de Mura in the sacristy (a fresco of the 'Assumption of the Virgin' (1727) and an 'Addolorata').

Santa Maria a Piè di Chienti
Macerata/Marches   p.414□I 7

This church was founded in the 8/9C, and rebuilt around 1100; the façade was altered in baroque style in the 18C, and the church was restored in 1927–8. The rear of the fine, originally Romanesque church is divided into two sections, and the ambulatory with radiating chapels off the choir shows French influence.

Sant'Antioco 09017
Cágliari/Sardinia   p.422□B 14

Originally founded by the Phoenicians in the 7C BC, who began the dyke connecting it to the main island of Sardinia, this was eventually completed by the Romans. Some remains of the early work on the dyke can still be seen from the Roman bridges. There are two *stele* ('Monk and Nun') in the south of the island; God is said to have turned them to stone as a punishment for their illicit love affair. The Benedictines from S. Vittore, near Marseilles, completed a bishop's church in 1102 on what is now the Piazza de Gasperi, but their leader transferred them to Tratalias (q.v.) before the Normans arrived. Sant'Antioco was not safe again until, in the 16-18C, the Aragonese built a fortress with

Tratalias (Sant'Antioco), Santa Maria

numerous towers on the old acropolis of Sulcis out of rubble from Roman remains. The parish church of *Sant'Antioco* was destroyed and rebuilt several times; it has some interesting ancient sections near the entrance, especially the *catacombs* under the right transept, and Roman and Punic *coffin tombs* with offerings such as slippers, Roman and Byzantine stucco-work, remains of early Christian (?) columns around a stone altar, and a chapel with huge columns and Romanesque (?) capitals. Further S.are the *Catacomba di Santa Rosa*, who, according to tradition, is the Mother of Sant'Antioco. Passages were later cleared under what is now the NW of the city, where the *Punic/Roman necropolis* (3–5C BC) lies. They also contain some scanty remains of the *antiquarium*, which includes mostly mass-produced Carthaginian religious figures, funerary stele and hideous faces of the idols Tanit and Bes. Further N. is the well-guarded *tophet*, which contains hundreds of urns, often still lidded, containing the ashes of first-born children burnt as sacrifices to Tanit or Baal. Outside the enclosure is the original *sacrificial stone*, on which three children could be slaughtered simultaneously.

Environs: The 17C Saracen tower in the NW of the island made **Calasetta** a sanctuary in the 18C for Ligurian exiles; it was built in the style of an African colonial settlement, a character which it has maintained. **Carloforte**, the main town of the nearby island of *San Pietro*, is built around the old watch-tower of *San Vittorio*. The Romans maintained the small stronghold of *Accipitrium Insula*. 6 km. NW of Santadi, past the nuraghic remains of *is Pireddas*, is **Villaperuccio**. 3 km. N., on the E. side of the valley of the Canale el Gabriela, are a number of *domus de janas* with huge vestibules, which have only recently been discovered. The fortress of *Carropu* has yielded string ceramic fastenings and obsidian pieces, which date from the same period as the finds in the cave on the island of Santo Stefano (q.v.). Opposite, on the mainland, **Tratalias**, has Pisan Romanesque *Chiesa S. Maria* (1156 –1213), with interesting inscriptions dating back to the time of the Giudici. There are some distinctively Gothic elements: over the façade's main portal is a bas relief of two lions (?) from 1234? with intertwined tails. The nave is raised and has a well-preserved rose-window. Unlike any

Sant'Antioco, Punic sacrificial altar

Santa Severina, view

other church in Sardinia, there is a flight of steps high up on the gable, which must once have led inside to the gallery. 7 km. past the reservoir at Monte Pranu, near **Santadi**, is the site of the Carthaginian fortress of *Pani Loriga*.

Sant'Arcangelo di Romagna 47038
Forlì/Emilia-Romagna   p.414□G 6

Worth seeing: The *triumphal arch* (Piazza Gangarelli) was built by C.Morelli in 1772. The 19C *Palazzo Comunale*, also on the Piazza Gangarelli, has a painting of the Virgin (1385) by Jacobello di Bonomo. The 18C *Collegiata* by G.F.Buonamici has some baroque paintings and a 14C Riminesque panel of the *Crucifixon*. The *castle* in the Via della Cella was probably begun in the 14C; its rooms are well-preserved and contain some 17C pieces of furniture.

Environs: *S.Michele*, 1 km. to the S., is a 6C single-aisled structure whose poor condition prompted its restoration in 1968–70. The campanile is Romanesque.

Santa Severina 88070
Catanzaro/Calabria   p.418□O 14

This town's name is probably derived from the old Enotrian settlement of 'Siberene'. It was taken by the Normans under Robert Guiscard in 1073–4 after it had been held first by the Saracens and then the Byzantines. In the 15C a number of Albanians immigrated, and in 1783 part of the town was destroyed by a large earthquake.

Cathedral of S.Anastasia: This is a 13C building which has since been much altered; only the central portal still stands from the original façade, and the building's appearance dates from 1705. The interior was altered in the early 20C (although there is an interesting 17C *marble pulpit*). The *baptistry*, entered through the left transept, is basically 8/9C Byzantine, round in shape, with four arms.

S.Filomena: This Norman church has a square ground plan, three semicircular apses and a cylindrical dome. Oriental influence is clear in the 16 pillars on the E. side. There are two fine *portals*, and the crypt (*S.Maria del Pozzo*) was previously a cistern.

Also worth seeing: The *castle* was built by Robert Guiscard on Byzantine foundations; the 17C *Chiesa Addolorata* was built on the remains of the 'Cattedrale Vecchia', a pre-Norman basilica; the former *Quartiere Grecia* to the E. of the city (abandoned in 1783) has some interesting church ruins, including the *Chiesa del Ospedale* with a Byzantine-Norman apse.

Sant'Elpidio a Mare 63019
Ascoli Piceno/Marches   p.414□I 7

Collegiata: The high altar is an old Roman sarcophagus.

Chiesa della Misericordia: The *frescos* (1603) are by Andrea Boscoli, and include scenes from the life of the Virgin, figures from the Old Testament and personifications of the Virtues.

Also worth seeing: The *Palazzo Comunale* has a polyptych by Vittorio Crivelli; much of the *city wall* has survived.

San Vincenzo al Volturno
Campobasso/Abruzzi   p.416□K 10

This was founded at the beginning of the 8C, and its Benedictine abbey became, during the course of the century, one of the largest and most powerful in the land. The monastery and church, however, were severely damaged by 9C earthquakes and Saracen raids, and the new 13/14C structures were flattened by a further earthquake in 1349, after which the monastery declined in importance. The *church* was rebuilt in 1953–8, and the 14C sanctuary contains some pieces of stone flooring from the original building. A little way away is the *crypt* of the now-destroyed *church of S.Lorenzo in Insula*, which survived the destruction and has 9C frescos displaying Byzantine influence.

San Vito al Tagliamento 33078
Pordenone/Friuli   p.410□H 3

In the Middle Ages, S.Vito was a fortified and under the control of the Patriarchs of Aquileia; it came under the sway of Venice in 1420, but retained its rights under the Patriarchate. During the Renaissance it became known for its school of painting, which included Andrea Bellunello (1445 –94). Today it is an agricultural and industrial centre.

Cathedral of SS. Vito, Creszenzio e Modesto (Piazza del Popolo): This was built in 1745 in baroque style on the site of an old Romanesque building, to which the campanile (completed by G.A.Pordenone, 1491) belonged. The interior contains work by A.Bellunello (a *Madonna* on the left, 1488) and Amalteo.

Also worth seeing: The church of *S. Maria dei Battuti* (Via Bellunello) has a fine Renaissance portal (1493) and frescos by Pomponio Amalteo (*c.*1540) inside; the church of *S. Lorenzo Salvaroli* (Via P.Amalteo) has a fresco by A.Bellunello on the triumphal arch (St. Vincent Ferrer, 1481) inside on the right, and the tomb of Amalteo. There are remains of the old *city fortifications*, including the *Torre Raimonda* with its small *museum*.

Environs: Some 10 km. S.is **Cordovado**, with the interesting *Chiesa della Madonna* (1603), which is octagonal and centrally planned. **Prodolone** is about 2 km. N., and its church of *S.Maria delle Grazie* contains some interesting frescos by P.Amalteo (1539 and later). Some 6 km. N. in **Versutta**, the church of *S.Antonio Abate* has fine 14/15C frescos, some in Tuscan style. About 12 km. N. is **S. Martino al Tagliamento**, where there is a St. Christopher by Pordenone outside the *parish church*, and a pala by Amalteo inside.

Sanzeno 38010
Trento/South Tyrol-Trentino   p.410□F 2

Parish church of SS.Sisinio, Martirio e Alessandro: Bishop Vigilius of Trento ordered a church to be built on the site where the missionaries Sisinius, Martyrius and Alexander were martyred in 379. The present building is a Gothic hall church built in 1465–86 on the site of the original church. The 12C campanile is still standing, and the *Cappella Santi Martiri* built on to the right transept of the church is 13C and contains some Romanesque frescos. The *W. portal* is also of interest: it is Renaissance, but Romanesque in style.

Environs: S.Romedio: The pilgrimage church of *S.Romedio*, 3 km. E. of Sanzeno, is charmingly situated on a crag. According to legend, the nobleman Romedius founded a hermitage here, and a Brotherhood of S.Romedius is known to have been here since the 12C. The complex, which is on several levels and which has a number of chapels, was built at various different times. The most interesting feature is the *Cappella di S.Nicolò*, which has a portal dating from 1200 with contemporary frescos above it. There are also 13C fresco remains in the chapel of St. Romedius. **Romeno** is N. of S.Romedio, and includes the church of *SS. Tomaso e Bartolomeo* (1187), which is in a farmstead on the edge of the village, the site of a previous Antonine monastery and a hospital. One of the rooms still has Romanesque frescos and the church, built on what was a Roman building, has Romanesque frescos dating from around 1200. **Romallo**, NW of Romeno, contains the church of *S.Biagio*, which has an interesting 11/12C crypt. **Revò** (SW of Romallo) has a late Renaissance patrician's house the Casa Thun, which was built around 1610 and is decorated both inside and out with charming frescos by Balthasar Rester. **Táio**, S. of Sanzeno, is an isolated and picturesque village; 4 km. SE of it is *Castle Bragher*, which was built in 1270 and extended in the 16/17C. The sumptuously furnished rooms on the first and second floors are of particular interest.

Sanzeno, S. Romedio

The mid-15C *castle chapel of S.Celestino* has an important fresco cycle by Leonhard of Brixen (1461). **Flavon** is SW of Táio, on the opposite side of the river Noce. Its parish church of the *Natività di S. Giovanni Battista* was originally 13C but was rebuilt in the 16C. It has a Gothic campanile and a cycle of frescos by Battista Baschenis (1485).

Sardara 09030

Cágliari/Sardinia   p.422□C 13

S. Gregorio: This late Romanesque church was built in 1300–25 and is a good example of the transition to Gothic, with its slender, soaring façade, pointed arches above the portal, two rows of blind arcades, and two elongated windows in the small, decorated campanile. The interior is single-aisled and contains a *baroque wooden statue* of San Bartolomeo.

S.Anastasia: The foundations and even the façade of this chiesetta contain stones from nuraghi and Byzantine fragments. Nearby is a temple with a well which has false vaulting over the original (9/8BC) sanctuary.

Environs: The water of the *Terme di Sardara (S.Maria de is Acquas)* has healing powers attributed to it; there is a church and small bathing pool under huge eucalyptus trees 2.5 km. S. of Sardara. The area 3.5 km. S.is dominated by the *Castello di Monreale*, an old border fortress used by the Giudicato of Arborea against Cágliari. The only point of interest in the mountainous area around Sardara is the *Nuraghe Ortu Comidu*, which has five towers and wells; it is some 2.5 km. E-SE of the river valley. **San Gavino Monreale** contains the church of the same name, which is in the upper village and has an old apse from 1378. The main church is *S.Chiara*, which is 16C late Gothic. The monastery of *S. Lucia* dates from 1850, and its church and cloister have been restored. It includes some intact Sardinian wood-carving from the 17C. There are some 1–3C Roman tombs in the neighbourhood. The town of

Sanluri is 8 km. SE, and the 14C *Castelle di Eleonora d'Arborea* is in its centre. It includes a collection of medieval weapons, also some valuable exhibits from the time of Napoleon, and manuscripts by d'Annunzio and contemporary paintings. The 16C *parish church* of **Samassi** has a Catalan Gothic campanile and is celebrated for its unique ribbed vaulting. The beautiful Romanesque *Chiesetta S. Gemiliano* is further up the hill. The decorative motifs on the round arches of the façade and on the apse are late 13C, and are among the earliest examples of Gothic. The small, simple Romanesque church of *S. Pietro* (1250–70) in the village of **Villamar** is still almost entirely original (although an aisle and a small campanile have been added). The apses are unequal, and there is a large altar with P.Cavaro's celebrated retable (1518) and masterly Gothic decoration in the 16C interior. **Lumanatrona** is dominated by the massive 16C *village church*, which contains a fine altarpiece by a pupil of P.Cavaro. Some 1.5 km. to the S. of **Ussaramanna**, several strikingly large *domus de janas*, some with windows, have been hewn out of a projecting flat rounded hummock. To the W. of **Villanovaforru**, excavations of the *Genna Maria* nuraghic castle and settlement, on the mountain, were still in progress in 1978. **Ales** was the seat of a bishop as early as 1182. After 1650, D.Spotorno built an almost undecorated, 'worthier' *cathedral* above the old Romanesque basilica. The exterior of the cathedral has two campaniles and a balustrade above the portal, and inside there is much marble and stucco decoration, as well as some beautifully carved wooden stalls. There is a statue showing Peter with a thrusting harpoon.

Sársina 47047

Forlì / Emilia-Romagna   p.414 □ G 6

Sársina was inhabited by the Umbrians, and the Romans conquered it in 266 BC. In the Middle Ages the bishops held the title of Dukes of Bibio until the 14C, from which time onwards the city changed hands several times.

The cathedral (Piazza Plauto): A church with a nave and two aisles, probably of Byzantine origin, rebuilt in *c.* 1000, and frequently altered since. Traces of a torn-down portico survive on the façade, and *Roman* and *medieval fragments* are on display outside the building. There is a Romanesque *pulpit* in the choir.

Museo Archeologico Sarsinate (Via Cesio Sabina): It contains a small prehistoric department and an interesting collection of Roman finds from this region.

Also worth seeing: At the edge of the city is the *tomb* (early Augustan age) of *A.Murcius Obulaccus, the Roman*.

Sarzana 19038

La Spezia / Liguria   p.414 □ E 6

Cathedral of S.Maria Assunta (Piazza Nicolò V): The present building, which was later twice enlarged, once in 1474 and again in the late 17C, was built shortly after 1204 on the site of the ancient former parish church. Various artists worked on the beautiful *marble façade*. The *portal* was built by M.De Vivaldo in 1355, and he may also be responsible for the entire lower section of the façade. The upper section with the Gothic rose-window (1474) is the work of L. da Pietrasanta. Of the statues, that of Pope Nicholas V (in the middle) is of especial significance, because he was born in Sarzana. On the right is the magnificent 13C *campanile*, which has a careful, precise design with four rows of two-, three- and four-arched windows. The excellent impression created by the *interior* with its nave and two aisles is partly the result of the wide-spanning arches and of the tall octagonal columns. The richly carved baroque *wooden ceiling* (1662–70) is by P.Giambelli. The chapel of the right transept has the *altar 'della Purificazione'* (Purification of the Virgin Mary) with the marble work by L.Riccomanni di Pietrasanta. This altar is important both artistically and from the art history point of view, and combines Gothic stylistic elements with Tuscan Renaissance features.

The middle section containing the actual image may be by D.Sarti (1642). The counterpart, in the chapel of the left transept, is the *altar 'dell'Incoronazione'* (Coronation of the Virgin Mary), a marble work, also by L.Riccomanni. To the left of the sanctuary is the *Cappella del Crocifisso* (of the Crucified Christ). This contains the precious 'Cross of master Guglielmo' (1138). The church contains some paintings by D.Fiasella, who is also known as 'il Sarzana', after his birthplace. At the high altar there is also an important painting by F.Solimena with *depictions of Pope Clement, Philip Neri, St.Lawrence, and John the Evangelist.*

Also worth seeing: S. Andrea. Mentioned from 1135 onwards, rebuilt several times, restored in 1928. There is a fine 16C *font* by G.Morello, decorated with putti and garlands, in the single-aisled, tunnel-vaulted baroque interior. *Palazzo Picedi-Benetti* (Via Mazzini No. 5) with 18C wrought-iron window grilles. *Palazzo Magni-Griffi-Lamotte* (Via Mazzini No. 22), fine *marble staircase.* Set on a hill, the *Fortezza di Sarzanello* dates back to the 10C. Its ownership changed more than once, a fact which can to a large extent be seen from the walls. Built in the 14C on an old, Roman site, and rebuilt by Genoese princes in the 16C. A deep moat surrounds the massive castle.

Sássari 07100
Sássari/Sardinia   p.422 □ B 11

The foundation stone of Sássari was laid by the Romans to the S.of the plain. They gave it the name of castrum fluminaria. The Byzantines, who called the village Tatthari, allowed it to fall into disrepair. The name later developed into Sacer, when it was a settlement for refugees escaping from the dangers of the wet valleys around the present cathedral. The city's leaders oscillated between the various powers and this is reflected in the variety of architectural forms. There was much baroque rebuilding and today there is a great deal of cement. Only in 1836 was the city able to

extend beyond the constricting walls, and consequently its narrow streets today pose problems for traffic. However some old sections have been demolished in the name of progress (for example the Aragonese castle of 1330, which was pulled down in 1877) and there are modern suburbs containing some ugly high-rise buildings. Nearly all the churches were also subjected to a baroque 'revision'.

Cathedral of S.Nicola: Its many phases of construction reflect the city's history: Pisan (13C), particularly on the N. side; Catalan Gothic (14/15C); baroque inside; Spanish late Gothic in its gorgeous tripartite façade with portico (18C). The interior is single-aisled. Some of the side chapels have ribbed arches, and others are cruciform and have domes. The 'Madonna del Bosco' at the high altar is a 16C Sardinian copy of a work by an unknown 14C artist from Florence. The font in the late baroque Piedmontese style is also of interest. The *cathedral archive* includes the 'Madonna col Bambino' processional banner and the sudarium of St.Veronica (16C). Several fine paintings, including the 'Madonna dell' Umiltà' and the 'Sacra Famiglia', are preserved in the *Aula.*

Also worth seeing: From the cathedral the visitor passes 160 yards to the NE along the Via S.Caterina to the church of *S. Caterina* (1580), whose front was — as usual—unfortunately completely altered in baroque style. Inside, a central dome and a groin vault, and on the left is the 'Trinità', a late imitation in the local baroque style. The nearby Corso Vittorio Emanuele leads 550 yards SE direct to the church of *S. Antonio Abate* (1707, also known as *Chiesa dei Servi di Maria*). The baroque alterations were all for the worse. 450 yards to the W. is the *Santissima Trinità,* which also suffered from its baroque reconstruction. Just to the N. is the *Fonte Rosello,* a square baroque fountain (1606) with animal heads spouting water, and above this is the equestrian statue of St.Gavinus with flags. There are a large number of small churches, but the only other one really worth mentioning is *S. Maria di Betlem* on the Corso Vico, 400

yards S. of the railway station. It has retained its plain Romanesque façade (13C)
with its Pisan-Lombard portal and rose-
window. Rebuilding inside resulted in a
ribbed vault in 1465, and subsequently
(19C) also in an apse with a dome. Here
too there is a 'Madonna col Bambino', but
this is a 12C Gothic wood carving, and opposite is a terracotta statue of the Pietà in
the 16C Aragonese style. In the sacristy is
a 'Madonna in gloria e quattri Santi' by
S. Cavedone.

Libraries/Museums: *University library:*
It possesses the *Carta de logu* of Eleonara
of Arborea, which is the most valuable
written document in Sardinia, and also
texts by locally important Sardinians. *Picture gallery:* A collection of paintings from
Sardinia. *Sanna museum* with a unique display of Sardinian arts and crafts. *Mostra
Artigianato Sardo* (Viale Mancini): An extensive exhibition from the whole of
Sardinia, located SW of the city park (Giardino Pubblico). It provides an unusual impression of genuine folk art in Sardinia, an
art which is today alive again. This exhibition is usually only open from the end
of May onwards. *Sanna archaeological museum* (Via Roma): It gives a good overall
view of the strange history of the 'forgotten island'.

Environs: Along the Viale San Pietro, almost within the SW fringe of the city, the
visitor arrives at the *Chiesa di S. Pietro di
Silki,* a very strange building: The ground
floor, including the tower, is severely
Romanesque (13C), but above this level the
building was altered completely in the
14C. The interior has Gothic vaults in the
first and third chapels on the left, and the
first chapel also contains the 'Madonna
delle Grazie', a 14C Catalan Gothic carved
group. There is a gilded altarpiece on the
high altar. The small single-aisled Romanesque church of *S. Michele di Plaiano* (about
9 km. towards Porto Tórres) was built in
1082. After the apse was destroyed the nave
remained standing and, after being temporarily owned by the monks of St. Zeno,
it was repaired in 1120 by Pisan stonemasons who were working on San Gavino (see
Porto Tórres). Some 330 ft. NW of **Tissi**

Sássari, cathedral

railway station, some old *burial caves* have
been dug out of the slope, and in one of
them an enormous round-arched stela has
been chiselled out as in Imbertighe. Near
to **Muros** is the *Casa de Turricula,* which
has been dated at about 1500 BC by the
radiocarbon method. It is an important
building of the Bonnánaro civilization.

Sassoferrato 62039
Macerata/Marches   p.414☐H 7

Lower town (Borgo): **S. Maria del Piano**
(Piazza Gramsci): The façade is dated
1618. Inside, there is a *Nativity of Christ*
in the first chapel on the left, and in the
second chapel a *Madonna with Saints* by
Paolo Agapiti, 1511–18. The fourth chapel
has a 14C *fresco* by Baronzio, and in the
fourth chapel on the right there are a 15C
Cross and *two miracles of St. Nicholas of*

Tolentino by Giovanni Guerrieri, 1614.
S.Croce (a little way outside): Built in the
12C using ancient remains. There is a
polyptych by Giovanni da Pesaro at the
altar, and in the 1st chapel are 14C *frescos*.

Upper town (Castello): In the
Franciscan monastery is an early-15C
polyptych with Doubting Thomas, by Zan-
nino di Pietro. The *cloister* has frescos by
Tarquinio Salvi, father of Sassoferrato.
A.Francesco: 14&15C *frescos* in the apse,
and a 14C *cross* at the high altar. **Palazzo
Municipale** (Piazza Oliva), built in the
14C and rebuilt in the 16C. Next to it is
the **Palazzo dei Priori,** with the *Museo
Civico* inside.

Sassuolo 41049
Modena/Emilia-Romagna   p.410☐E/F 5

Sassuolo, a free commune belonging alternately to Bologna and Modena, changed
hands from the late 12C onwards before
coming into the possession of the Este in
1417. In 1599 it once again fell to the Este.
The town belonged to this family until
1859.

**Objects of interest: Palazzo degli Es-
tensi** (now a military academy; Piazzale
della Rosa): Built by B.Avanzini in 1634
using the castle which had already been
rebuilt in the 15C. Inside there are good
baroque *stuccoes and frescos*. **S. Giorgio**
(Piazza Martiri Partigiani): A richly decorated baroque church with a dome.

Savigliano 12038
Cuneo/Piedmont   p.412☐B 5

Savigliano was founded in 981. It was part
of the Lombard league until the 13C, and
from 1238 onwards it was under the protection of Emperor Frederick II. It fell to
Savoy as early as 1349. The battle of
Savigliano, between the Austrians and the
French, took place on 4 November 1799.

S. Andrea (Via S. Andrea): Collegiate
church, 1402, rebuilt in 1699-1757, the

work of Andrea Vaj. The interior has a
nave, four aisles, and an ambulatory. The
foundation of the *campanile* is decorated
by a fresco dating from *c.* 1300.

Also worth seeing: *S.Pietro dei Cassinesi*
(Piazza Moleneri), a 16C abbey church.
Palazzo Cravetta (Via Jerusalem), with a
fine inner courtyard dating from 1620.
Museo Civico in the former Franciscan
monastery.

Savignano sul Rubicone 47039
Forlì/Emilia-Romagna   p.414☐G 6

Savignano is not definitely mentioned until 1150, when it is stated to be a possession of the archbishops of Ravenna. It fell
to the Malatesta of Rimini in 1261, and to
the Papal States in the late 15C.

Objects of interest: *Fish market* (Corso
Vendemini), 1710. *Palazzo Comunale*
(Piazza Borghese), late 16C. *Rubiconia
Simpemenia Accademia dei Filopatridi,*
with a large and important library. *S.Lucia,*
built by Theodoli in 1730, with 18C decoration in the single-aisled interior.

Savona 17100
Savona/Liguria   p.412☐C 5

This, the main city of the province and a
bishop's seat, has an important harbour
(the fifth largest in Italy) and a strong industry. In the past, the city was called Savo
oppidum alpinum by the Romans. It was
threatened by its close proximity to the
Guelph city of Genoa, which gained the
upper hand in the dispute and, in 1528,
conquered the Ghibelline city of Savona.
The area of interest from the cultural point
of view is concentrated around the harbour
where, despite the devastation suffered in
World War 2, splendid buildings dating
from the Middle Ages up until the baroque
may be found in the narrow streets.

Sassuolo, Palazzo degli Estensi ▷

Savona, Pinacoteca Civica, Crucifixion by Donato de Bardi

Cathedral of S.Maria Assunta (Piazza del Duomo): Built in 1589–1604 on the site of a Franciscan church, its marble façade is now in 19C baroque style. The dome also dates from last century, whereas the campanile has remained unaltered since 1611. The interior (one nave, two aisles) is a treasury of important works of art. The baptistery has a beautifully worked *font* (probably 12C), with a Renaissance marble mount, and to the right of the portal is a *marble crucifix* by A.Molinari (1499), who was also responsible for the *marble pulpit* in the nave. In the sanctuary, with its baroque high altar, there is a splendidly carved and inlaid set of *choir stalls* (*c.* 1500), on which several artists worked (Pope Julius II bore half the expense). The second side chapel on the left has 2 coloured, carved wooden groups of figures, the so-called 'casse', by Maragliano and Runggaldier.

Cappella Sistina (beside the cathedral): This building was founded by Pope Sixtus IV in memory of his parents (*c.* 1480). The harmonious stuccoed interior (1764) contains a fine *tomb*, the work of M. and G.De Aria (1490). There is a good 18C *organ* on the pulpit.

S.Giovanni Battista (Via Paleocapa/Via Mistrangelo): The animated *baroque façade* (1735) is part of a former Dominican church dating from 1567. Numerous good paintings (C.G.Ratti, P.G.Brusco, F.Schiaffino, D.Piola and others), note-in particular a fine triptych by van Hoogstraaten behind the high altar.

Palazzo della Rovere (Piazza della Rovere): This monumental, unfinished building by G.da Sangallo has a large courtyard and was built in 1495 by order of Cardinal Giuliano della Rovere, later Pope Julius II.

Pinacoteca Civica (*Palazzo Pozzobonello*, Via Quarda Superiore No. 7): This collection gives a good impression of the *15–17C Genoese school*. The *ceramic collection* is of particular charm. In the two rooms (I and II) by the entrance there are a number of outstanding works of art by artists such as L.Brea, G.Mazone, V.Foppa, D.de Bardi. Room V has some good works by D.Fiasella.

Also worth seeing: *SS.Annunziata* (Via Paleocapa), late 15C, with beautifully carved choir stalls. The *Oratorio di S. Maria di Castello* (Piazza Sisto IV) has the excellent, winged altarpiece 'Madonna and Saints' (high altar), 1490, by L.Brea (right-hand section) and V.Foppa. *Torre del Brandale*, mentioned in the 12C. *Torre di Leon Pancaldo*, 1312 (restored several times). The 17C *Palazzo Vescovile* (above the Via A.Aonzo): Pope Pius VII was held here during his captivity (1809–12). *Fortezza Priamar* (Viale Dante Alighieri): A Genoese fortress (1542–3), for which older buildings, including the cathedral at that time, were demolished.

Art and customs: The unusual Good Friday procession, takes place every two years and can look back on a long tradition (16C). Large wooden figures, the so-called 'casse', are carried through the streets on the shoulders of the participants. The figures are by artists such as A.M.Maragliano, G.Runggaldier, St. Murialdo, A.Brilla).

Environs: Pilgrimage church of **Nostra Signora di Misericordia** (about 7 km.). This basilica, built in 1536–1633, has an elegant, interestingly articulated façade by T.Carlone (1609–11) in front of it, and contains a wealth of works of art. The ceiling paintings in the nave are by B.Castello, as are the frescos in the dome. Note the *Visitation of the Virgin Mary*, 1664, a marble relief by the school of Bernini (3rd chapel of left aisle). A *crucifix* which is now kept in the sacristy is probably by G.A.Ponselli. The marble front of the crypt, with *putti* by P.Orsolino and the *statue of Madonna di Misericordia*, 1560, also by Orsolino. In the *museum* beside the church is a valuable *church treasure* with excellent wood carvings by Ligurian artists. In the same town are the 17C *Palazzo dell'Ospizio*, and the *Cappella di Poggio*, 1680, with frescos by B.Guidobono.

Scandiano 42019
Reggio Emilia / Emilia-Romagna   p.410□E 5

Clustered around a castle founded in 1262, Scandiano has had a turbulent history.

Objects of interest (in the Piazza Duca d'Aosta): *S. Giuseppe*, with an 18C façade and baroque decoration. The parish church of *S.Maria* includes a 14C mounted wooden Madonna of the Rosary. The *castle*, 1262, rebuilt in the Renaissance.

Schio 36015
Vicenza / Veneto   p.410□F 3

Cathedral of S.Pietro (Piazza A.Rossi): A baroque church begun in 1741. *Double outdoor staircase* before the façade which dates from 1805 and has a massive *portico*

along classical lines. The *interior* was originally single-aisled with side chapels. In 1879 these chapels were interconnected and converted into aisles. The walls are in classical style (semi-columns, round-arched arcades). Tunnel-vaulted nave. In the sacristy is the *Sacra Conversazione* by Palma Vecchio (1520).

S.Francesco: Built in late Gothic style in 1436–42. In front of the façade is a *loggia* with round-arched arcades. The single-aisled *interior* has an open roof truss and was expanded in the 16C by the addition of a further aisle (created by interconnecting the side chapels). The side aisle is separated from the nave by pointed arches and has a groin vault. Fine *choir stalls* (1504); the *frescos* on the ceiling, depicting the life of St.Francis, are by Francesco Verla. On the front wall of the side aisle are the surviving fragments of a 16C *sgraffito* of a female martyr.

Environs: Some 10 km. E., **Thiene** with the notable *Castello Porto-Colleoni*, built mainly in the 15C (late Gothic/early Renaissance).

Sciacca 92019
Agrigento / Sicily   p.420□H 17

Cathedral of S. Maria Maddalena (Piazza Don Minzoni): Norman, 12C; the *E. end* is original. Completely redesigned in baroque style in the 18C. A fine 16C *façade* with figures by Antonino and Gian Dom. Gagini. Inside there are a nave and two aisles. In the right apse is a *marble tabernacle* by Antonino Gagini (Renaissance, 1581; St.Peter and St.Paul, story of the Passion).

S. Margherita (Via F.Incisa): Built in 1342 and rebuilt in 1594. The left side portal, which is by Francesco Laurana in early Renaissance style, is well worth seeing. The single-aisled interior has fine 17C stucco.

Steripinto (Corso Vitt. Emanuele): A palace built in 1501 in Sicilian-Catalan style.

Sciacca, Castello Luna

A very fine façade, a Renaissance portal, and two-arched windows.

Also worth seeing: *Chiesa del Carmine* (Via F.Incisa; 17C) with a splendid Gothic rose-window. *S.Maria delle Giummare* or *di Valverde* (near the Via Valverde): its core is Norman, but it was rebuilt in Catalan Gothic style in the 16C, and it has an interesting front. *Castello Luna* (Via Castello; 14C). *Casa Arone* (Via F.Incisa; 15C).

***

Segesta 91013
Trapani/Sicily   p.420☐H 16

The origin of the inhabitants of 'Egesta', the ancient town of the Elymni on Monte Barbaro, has not been conclusively determined. The town was the cause of the Sicilian expedition by the Athenians in 415

BC during the Peloponnesian War. The downfall of the town began after the expansion of Carthaginian power in Sicily in 409 BC. Two recently excavated *Doric buildings* (6&5C BC) are all that remains of the town, apart from the two structure described below.

'Temple of Artemis': Begun in Doric style in *c.* 425 BC, but never completed (only the peripteros of columns, the entablature and the triangular pediments are complete; the military events described above probably caused the work to be broken off). The ground plan is peripteral with 36 columns (about 30 ft. tall). The dimensions are approximately 200 ft. by 85 ft. The columns are still unfluted, and the stylobate is incomplete. The roof and cella are entirely absent. The bosses used in transport are still present on the stone blocks of the substructure. According to more recent research work, the building

Segesta, Temple of Artemis

was not a temple in the usual sense, but a kind of 'pseudo-temple', a peripteros of columns surrounding an indigenous shrine.

Theatre: Reached by a path that passes by a tower from the old town defences. The best-preserved Hellenistic theatre in Sicily (3C BC). Built into a mountain slope in typically Greek manner. 207 ft. in diameter, seven wedges, divided into two circles, for spectators.

Segni 00037
Rome/Latium   p.414□H 10

Colonized by Tarquinius Superbus, Segni was one of the first Roman municipia. Part of the *cyclopean city wall*, which is about 2 km. long and dates from the 6/5C BC,

has survived. A bishop's seat since the 5C AD. It was a church possession up until the 16C and it was here that Alexander III canonized Thomas à Becket. The city was extensively plundered by the Spaniards in the war between Paul IV and Philip II (1557). 'Opus signinum', the technique of building walls that uses broken materials, derives its name from Segni.

Cathedral: A Romanesque structure rebuilt in 1626–57. The additions to the façade are by Valadier, 1817; part of the campanile is still Romanesque. Inside, note the *Madonna and Saints* by Pietro da Cortona, the altarpiece in the right transept. *Glorification of the Cross*, by Borgognone, in the left transept.

Porta Saracena: A Cyclopean gate. The lintel is formed by monoliths about 10 ft. in length.

Selinunte
Trapani/Sicily   p.420☐H 17

The ancient 'Selinus' (from the Greek for a wild celery plant growing there) was founded in 628 BC by Megara Hyblaea (near Syracuse), and was the most westerly Greek colony in Sicily. It was a flourishing town in the 6&5C BC and it took part in the Peloponnesian War (431–404 BC). It was destroyed by the Carthaginians in 409 BC, and was of no importance from then onwards. In the early Middle Ages, those of the temples that were still standing (see below) were devastated in an earthquake. The archaeological zone is divided into two sections: the E. district (temples G, F, E), and the W. district (acropolis with temples D, C, B, A, O), separated by the Gorgo di Cotone. To the W. of the Modione is another small temple district.

E. district: Temple G: A Temple of Apollo, it is one of the largest classical temples (360 ft. by 160 ft.). Built in the Doric style (late archaic-early classical) in 550–480 BC. The ground plan is peripteral with 8 by 17 columns; a pronaos and an opisthodomos; the cella has three aisles, each with 10 columns. Enormous *capitals* (with a surface area of about 172 sq.ft.!).

Temple F: A Temple of Athene, severely damaged. Built in 560–540 BC in the high archaic-Doric style. The peripteros has 6 by 14 columns, and measures 200 ft. by 79 ft. The pronaos has two rows of columns. The surviving *metopes* (battle of the giants) are in the Palermo museum.

Temple E: A Temple of Hera. Re-erected in 1959, apart from the pediments. One of the finest classical temples. Built in the Doric style in 490–80 BC. 230 ft. by 92 ft. The peripteros has 6 by 15 columns. Pronaos and opisthodomos; the *base of the cultic statue* survives in the cella.

W. district: Intersected by two roads running N.-S. and E.-W. **Temple O:** Same dimensions as temple A (see below). Built in the early 5C BC. Only the foundation walls survive.

Temple A: The name of the god venerated here is unknown. Built at the same time as temple E. 131 ft. by 52 ft. The peripteros has 6 by 14 columns. Pronaos and opisthodomos. In the wall between the pronaos and the cella there was originally a spiral staircase leading up to the roof. Outside and to the E. of the temple is a *propylon* with 22 monolithic Doric columns dating from after 480 BC.

Temple B: Dates from the Hellenistic period (4C BC). It has no peripteros of columns. 26 ft. by 16 ft. Traces of the ancient paintwork are seen in the plaster work of the walls.

Temple C: Temple of Heracles. A landmark of Selinunte. The oldest temple in the acropolis, built in 580–570 BC in the high archaic-Doric style. 210 ft. by 79 ft. with a very deep pronaos, which is quite out of proportion. The peripteros has 6 by 17 columns (the distances between them vary), of which twelve were re-erected in 1929, some with the entablature. *Metopes* in the museum of Palermo. To the S. of the temple is a high archaic *megaron*.

Temple D: The name of the god venerated here is unknown. Built in 570–554 BC in the high archaic-Doric style. The peripteros has 6 by 13 columns, and the cella is very narrow. To the NE are the *remains of an archaic temple*.

Shrine of Malophoros (on the other side of the Modione, the classical Selinus): A shrine of Demeter ('Malophoros' means 'the fruit-bringing woman'). The temenos measures about 200 ft. by 160 ft., surrounded by the propylon from the 5C BC and by the Temple of Demeter (a megaron without a peripteros of columns, 65 ft. by 35 ft., with a cella and pronaos). At the N. wall is a *temple of Zeus Meilichios*.

Also worth seeing: *Remains of the ancient fortifications* at the N. gate. *Necropolis* to the W. of the shrine of Demeter.

Selinunte, temple C ▷

Environs: Some 15 km. to the NW, near Campobello (*Rocche di Cusa, Grandi Cave*), are the ancient *stone quarries*, which were used to build the temples of Selinunte. Some 15 km. to the N. is **Castelvetrano** with some interesting churches (including *S. Domenico*, 16C, with rich stucco and fresco decoration; *Chiesa Madre*, 16C, with Renaissance portal and stucco by Serpotta), and an *Archaeological Museum*.

Senigallia 60019
Ancona / Marches   p.414☐H 6

Cathedral (Piazza Garibaldi): Rebuilt in 1790. The façade is 19C. The previous Byzantine building was used by Sigismondo Malatesta as a stone quarry for the Tempio Malatestiano in Rimini.

Chiesa della Croce (Via Fagnani): Begun in 1576, rebuilt in 1604–8; inside, at the high altar, is an *Entombment* by Federico Barocci, with the Palazzo Ducale of Urbino depicted on it (1579–82).

S.Martino (Via Marchetti): Built in 1740; inside, at the 2nd altar on the right, is a *St.Anne with Mary and the child Jesus* by Guercino, and there is a *Madonna with Saints* by Palma Giovane at the 3rd altar on the left.

Also worth seeing: *Fortress* (*Rocca;* Piazzale Vitt. Veneto), and *city walls* dating from *c.* 1500. The 17C *Palazzo Municipale* (Piazza Roma). *Neptune fountain* (Piazza Roma), with an ancient figure.

Environs: 3 km. W., **S. Maria delle Grazie**, which Giovanni della Rovere ordered to be built by Sabatino da Fabriano in 1491. *Tomb of the Duke* and *Madonna* by Perugino.

Senorbi 09040
Cágliari / Sardinia   p.422 IC 13

There are few items of cultural significance in the village itself, apart from the 18C wooden statues by G.A.Lonis in the *parish church*. A little to the N. we find the Romanesque chapel of *S.Mariedda* and, a good 2 km. to the NW, the ruins of the *Chiesa della Madonna d'Itria*. Senorbì, nonetheless has a claim to history. The incomparable marble *Dea Madre Mediterranea* (17 in. tall, *c.* 200 BC) was discovered in the Turriga district. It is the largest of some 50 similar Sardinian sculptures. Today it is to be found, along with many others, in the State Archaeological Museum in Cágliari.

Environs: In **Dolianova** (to the S., the church of *S.Biaggio* in the S.part, which is partly late Gothic but was then 'beautified', pales into insignificance beside the *Basilica S. Pantaleo* which stands on the NW edge and was built in 1170–1289 in Romanesque and Gothic styles, but without any stylistic inconsistency. On this site there was originally an early Christian church, and later a Byzantine church. The new façade, with its portals and sculptured friezes, is particularly splendid. The decorative motifs on the blind arcades, on the campanile and on the apse reveal Arab influence. Next to the large side portal there are also a *Roman sarcophagus* under a richly decorated canopy and a 5C *immersion font*. The interior is divided into a nave and two aisles by massive round arches on powerful pilasters with Byzantine fragments. Some 3 km. to the W. of Dolianova, a track leads across the fields to the neglected shepherds' church of *S.Maria Simbranos*. On its front there is a *sundial* on a coloured stone mosaic. The W. side has a long *flight of steps*, and at the rear there are two apses. **Monastir**, with the 16C late Gothic church of *S.Pietro*, derives its name from the Camaldolese monastery, the ruins of which are 3.5 km. to the S.4 km. to the E. we find the remains of the 12C *Castell Baratuli* and the *Castello di Balardi* of the Giudici of Cagliari. **Villagreca** is a late foundation by Greek settlers who fled from the Peloponnese via Corsica to Montresta near Bosa in 1750, and from there to this present site in *c.* 1800. It is only on the campanile, below the strange dome, that the simple village church of Villagreca displays some rococo decorative motifs. 2 km. to the N. is the *early nuraghe of Sa Korona* (dating from shortly before 2000 BC). To the N.: **Suelli,** a bishop's seat in the Middle Ages, has the 16C late Gothic parish church of *S. Giorgio,* which still has some simple Romanesque sections from the 13C and, on the high altar, a retable of the 'Mother of God with St.Peter, St.Paul and the holy bishop George' by the brothers Paolo and Michele Cavaro (1533–5). The adjoining *bishop's chapel* has a wrought-iron grille and a painted wooden altar, two pleasing 18C Sardinian works. 4 km. to the N. is the *Nuraghe Piscu.* To the NE: Excavations at *Pranus-Mutedda* near **Goni** have revealed a *burial site* which was partly a shaft-type tomb cut out of the rock like a hypogeum, and partly a dolmen situated above ground level.

Sepino 86047

Campobasso / Molise   p.416 □ K 10

The Roman *Saepinum* was built after the violent battles of the second Samnite war (326–304 BC). After invasions by the Saracens in the 9C, the Roman town was deserted and the new Sepino founded. Systematic excavation work has been in progress here since 1950. The items uncovered include a *water mill.* On the *Porta di Boiano,* flanked by two round towers, is an inscription naming Tiberius and Drusus as the builders.

Sermoneta 04010

Latina / Latium   p.414 □ H 10

Cathedral of S. Assunta (Via S.Maria): A basilica which has a nave and two aisles and was much disfigured by later alterations (transition from Romanesque to Gothic). Built in the 13C above the ruins of a Temple of Cybele. A splendid *campanile* with five storeys opening through double-arched windows. Inside is a panel, transferred on to canvas, the *Madonna degli Angeli,* by Benozzo Gozzoli. The Cappella Maggiore has 16C *frescos* of scenes from the life of the Virgin Mary. By the altar is a *marble throne* taken from a Roman altar.

Dolianova (Senorbi), S. Pantaleo

Ninfa (Sermoneta)

Castello Caetani (Via della Fortezza): All that has survived of the first of the two Annibaldi is the unpretentious old core of the castle, and a tower known as 'Maschietto'. The castle was enlarged under the Caetani in the early 14C. It is also to them that we owe the interesting *frescos* of the 'Camere Pinte'. An act of deceit brought the castle into the possession of Alexander VI. In 1500, with the assistance of Antonio da Sangallo the elder, he converted it into a modern fortress. Cesare and Lucrezia Borgia lived in the *Casa del Cardinale* which was built at that time.

Environs: Ninfa (about 10 km. NW): An abandoned medieval settlement. In the 12C it was a feudal possession of the Frangipane, and was destroyed by Barbarossa's troops. After it was rebuilt, the Colonna took possession of it in 1294. Pietro Caetani acquired it in 1298. Its decline began in the 17C and continued until its last inhabitant deserted it in 1680. It has remained untouched since then, and the *surrounding wall*, the *castle*, *churches* and *palaces*, and the *squares* and *towers*, have all survived as ruins exposed to destruction. **Norma** (about 8 km. N.): From the village of Norma, some of whose medieval features still survive, it is possible to reach the **ruins of the ancient Norba** (popularly known as **'Civita'**). Legend has it that Norba was founded by Heracles, and it was later occupied by the Volsci. The surviving sections include the massive *town walls* dating from the 4C BC, the *ruins of the Temple of Diana*, and the *Great Acropolis* (2C BC), surrounded by an opus incertum sacred precinct. The *'small acropolis'* has been converted into a church. **Abbazia di Valvisciolo** (12 km. NW): Founded by Greek monks in the 8C, and rebuilt by the Templars in the 13C. *Abbey church*, a typical example of the use—which began in Fossanova—of the Cistercian Gothic style in smaller church buildings. This church, which has a plain façade decorated by a rose-window, was built in *c.* 1240. A pillared structure with a nave, two aisles, and a rectangular apse flanked by two chapels. There is a square *cloister* with fine capitals in the *monastery*, which was restored in 1959–62.

Serradifalco 93010

Caltanissetta/Sicily   p.420☐K 17

An old feudal possession of the princes of Serradifalco, situated in a sulphur-rich area. Some 8 km. NE of the town, turn off to the left and continue to the **archaeological zone of Vassallaggi:** Excavation work was only begun a few years ago (the *finds* are in the *national museum of Agrigento*). The remains are from a town founded by Agrigento in the 6C BC. The surviving items include the remnants of the *town defences,* of an *archaic shrine* and of *houses* (5&4C BC). An extensive *necropolis* dating from the 5C BC has been uncovered.

Serramonacesca 65020

Pescara/Abruzzi   p.416☐K 9

S. Assunta: The portal and floor, which date from 1275, were brought here from S. Liberatore a Maiella.

Environs: S. Liberatore a Maiella (about 1.5 km. S.). One of the oldest Benedictine abbeys, it was already in existence in the 9C. Destroyed by an earthquake in 990, it was rebuilt in 1007 by the monk Teobald from Monte Cassino. The façade was rebuilt in the 16C. The *side portals* dating from 1080 have survived.

Serra San Bruno 88029

Catanzaro/Calabria   p.418☐N 15

This town in the mountains of Calabria, altitude 2,635 ft., originated from the Carthusian monastery of St. Stephen of Bosco. Bruno of Cologne (1032–1101), founder of the Carthusian order, built a hermitage here in 1091. It was in the possession of the Cistercians up until the 16C. It then returned to the Carthusians and was rebuilt, possibly with the assistance of Palladio, the great Renaissance architect from Vicenza.

Certosa di Serra S.Bruno (a little way outside the town): Rebuilt in the 18C on the ruins of the original building (see above). The surrounding wall has round corner towers. Inside are the remains of the old monastery (including the façade of the church, and parts of the nave and the two aisles; the arcades in the cloister date from the 17C). Next to it is the *Nuova Certosa* (early 20C). Nearby is the church of *S. Maria del Bosco*, where St.Bruno died. A *statue of the Saint*, the object of a pilgrimage held on Whit Monday each year, stands in a pool.

Also worth seeing: *Chiesa Matrice* or *S. Biagio* (18C), with a fine baroque façade, four marble figures (formerly in the Certosa, by David Müller, 1611) with bas reliefs on the base and a carved baroque pulpit in the interior. *Chiesa dell' Addolorata* with a notable ciborium (C.Fanzago, 1631) at the high altar.

Sessa Aurunca 81037
Caserta/Campania   p.416□I 11

Cathedral of S. Pietro (Piazza del Duomo): Completed in Romanesque style in 1113, but later much altered. Some of the materials used in its construction were ancient, being taken from Roman buildings in the town. In front of the façade is a magnificent three-arched 13C *portico* in the Campanian style; the archivolt of the middle arch is particularly fine. Three *portals*, the middle one more beautiful than the other two, lead into the church. The so-called 'Portale dell'Episcopio' is to the left of the portico. Some remains of the original Romanesque are still discernible on the right flank of the cathedral (viewed from the Via Spine). Inside, a basilica with a nave, two aisles, fine monolithic columns and good capitals. The nave has a notable 13C *mosaic pavement* (with geometric patterns showing Oriental influence). There is a splendid 13C *pulpit*, with fine mosaic, under the sixth arch on the right. Just to the right of the pulpit is an *Easter candlestick* from the same period. To the right of the choir is the *Cappella del Sacramento*

with a painting by Luca Giordano (1632 -1705; 'Comunione degli Apostoli'). The *crypt* has 20 columns and is under the choir.

Also worth seeing: The church of *S. Giovanni* with paintings by the school of Solimena (1717). 18C church of *S. Germano* with beautiful baroque interior. The baroque *Chiesa dell'Annunziata*, a cruciform domed structure. The so-called *Basilichetta*, the remains of a church founded in the early Christian period. *Fontana dell'Ercole* on the Piazza Umberto I. In the W. of the city are the remains of the *Roman theatre*, of a *cryptoporticus*, and of *ancient baths*.

Environs: Some 12 km. to the NE is **Roccamonfina** with the *Santuario di Maria SS.dei Láttani*, a 15C pilgrimage church (the most noteworthy feature is the cloister dating from 1440 in the adjoining Minorite monastery). Some 12 km. to the SE is **Carinola** with a 11C *cathedral* which is worth looking at (notable portals in Romanesque-Gothic style) and some fine 15C Palazzi (*Casa Novelli*, Corso Umberto. *Casa Martullo* and the former *Palazzo Ducale*, Vico de Sole).

Sesto al Reghena 33079
Pordenone/Friuli   p.410□H 3

Abbazia di S.Maria in Sylvis: A monastery founded by Benedictines in 730-5 on the site of a Roman settlement. In the Middle Ages it was one of the richest and most powerful monasteries in Friuli (with possessions reaching as far as Carnia and Istria). From the 15-18C it was a commendam of rich aristocratic families from Venice. It consists of a *circuit of walls* (originally with seven towers; the *gate tower* dates from the 10/11C). This circuit surrounds the Romanesque *abbots' chancellery* (in the W.), the *campanile* (whose substructure is 11C), the *abbots' residence* (in the E.; the present building is 16C), and the church with its annexes.

Abbey church: The basic Romanesque

Sestri Levante, view

form dating from the 10/11C survives; partly rebuilt in the 14C; there are a nave and two aisles, and the E. section, under which there is a crypt, is raised. The transept is barely discernible. The choir has three apses (square ended on the outside). Open roof truss. The aisles are separated by round arches borne alternately by columns and pillars. There are fine round-arched windows in the clerestorey. The archivolt of the main apse is supported by two ancient Roman columns. The interior was originally painted throughout; the surviving remnants are mainly on the entrance wall and in the choir and their subjects include the *Annunciation and Nativity of Christ, and scenes from the lives of Saints*, probably painted by Paduan artists in the 1st half of the 14C. A beautiful *crypt* (entrance beside the stairs leading to the choir) with a nave, two aisles, and good, but unfortunately frequently altered, 10C capitals. Against the walls there are stone

benches from the period of the church's construction. In the nave is the richly decorated *marble sarcophagus of St. Anastasia* (8C, Lombard), and in the left apse is a fine *Annunciation* (a 14C Lombard marble relief).

The church's annexes: In front of the church there is a complex consisting of three buildings: To the left of the entrance is a 12C *loggia* decorated with frescos. Above the portal, which dates from *c.* 1450, there are *frescos* from the 12/13C (including the Archangel Gabriel). Adjoining this is a *vestibule* (with a 15C wooden ceiling), standing on the foundations of the original church (14C frescos, and in the adjoining room to the left is a *collection of stone monuments*). Then there is a Romanesque *atrium*, divided in three by pillars (only part of the round arch survives), and decorated on its S. side with two fine *Romanesque windows* (one of them has five arches, the other has four). *Architectural fragments* and detached *frescos* are on display in the aisles. The upper storey of the vestibule and atrium is a large room (formerly it was used, among other things, as a dormitory for pilgrims) with fine 11C *windows*.

Sestri Levante 16039
Genoa/Liguria   p.412☐D 5

Parish church of S.Maria di Nazareth (Piazza Matteotti): Baroque church dating from 1604–16, while the colonnaded portico in the classical style was not built until 1840. There is a fine 16C *Madonna* above the middle portal. Extraordinarily rich 18C interior with a number of important Ligurian works of art. *Assumption of the Virgin*, 1762, a marble group by F.Schiaffino at the high altar. *Virgin with St.Lawrence and John the Baptist*, by L.Tavarone (2nd side chapel on the left). *Death of St.Joseph*, by O.De Ferrari, 1654 (3rd side chapel on the left). *Descent of the Holy Ghost* by D.Fiasella (4th side chapel on the left). There is a valuable 18C *silver monstrance* in the sacristy.

Pinacoteca Rizzi (Via Cappuccini No. 10): Valuable collection of paintings, with works by Tiepolo, Raphael, Rubens, Zurbaran, El Greco, Reni, Magnasco and others.

Also worth seeing: *S. Pietro in Vincoli*, 1640, a Capuchin church with a bright and elegantly stuccoed sanctuary. Good paintings by Cambiaso, Fiasella and others. There are early-18C silver liturgical implements in the sacristy. *Chiesa dell' Immacolata* (with a Capuchin monastery), 1683. Its single-aisled interior has two beautiful works by D.Piola, and two more by Fiasella. The small Romanesque church of *S. Nicolò* (1151) was formerly a parish church. The façade had to be rebuilt in the mid-15C, and is beautifully articulated. There is a campanile. *Torretta:* It was from here that G.Marconi, the physicist and radio engineer, conducted his first short-wave experiments.

Sestri Ponente 16100
Genoa/Liguria   p.412☐C 5

Parish church of the Assunta (Via Sestri/Piazza Baracca): This church was built in 1620 (the façade was restored in 1934). Its value in terms of art lies chiefly in its wealth of *paintings* in the spacious interior. Special mention should be made of the *frescos* by G.Benso, depicting the 'Assumption of the Virgin', 1635, and by G.A.Ansaldo (in the apse and sanctuary), and also to the works by the Ligurian artists Fiasella and Piola.

Siena 53100
Siena/Tuscany   p.414☐F 7

This medieval city extends over three hills in delightful Tuscan countryside and its artistic wealth makes it one of the most interesting cities in Italy. Two conflicting legends tell of a foundation by the Senones (Gauls) or by Senio, son of Remus. Either way, 'Sena' certainly existed in Etruscan times. It became Roman during the Republican era, and Augustus established the military colony 'Sena Julia'. Having suffered, under the Ghibellines, constant power struggles with Guelph Florence, the town achieved prosperity and an artistic flowering in the Middle Ages (high points in the 13&14C). On the 2 July and 16 August of each year, the famous 'Corsa del Palio', a medieval race, is held.

Cathedral (Piazza del Duomo): Dedicated to the Assumption, it was built on the site of an older church. Begun in the mid-11C and largely complete by 1215 (dome 1259–64, apse from the same time later destroyed). It has a nave and two aisles, and is entirely clad in marble (Giovanni Pisano began the statuary of the façade—now in part in the nearby Museo dell'Opera—in 1284–99. Construction was interrupted in 1339 by the adoption of a colossal scheme to turn the existing church into just a transept of a new, larger one. This plan was abandoned due to errors in the statics calculations, the enormous costs and the plague of 1348. (*Remains of the Duomo Nuovo* to the S. of the present church.) The original plans for the new building, preserved in the Museo dell' Opera, show a total length of 359 ft. 5 in. The upper half of the façade of the old building, begun by Pisano, was completed by Giovanni di Cecco in 1376 along the lines of Orvieto cathedral. The white marble façade, decorated with red and green marble and adorned with lavish statuary is one of the most lively and beautiful of Italian creations. (The Venetian mosaics in the gable fronts are to designs dating from 1878.) The left flank adjoins the archbishop's palace, while the right is banded with black and white marble, interrupted by tall Gothic windows and the square, Romanesque *campanile* (1313), also clad in bands of marble with window openings—single-arched at the bottom and increasing to six arches at the top. (It may be climbed, but the Torre del Mangia affords a better view.) The splendid *interior* has black and white banded walls with pilasters and 14C vaulting, painted in blue with gold stars. A *cornice* with, in all, 172 terracotta busts of popes and lords, from the 15&16C runs between the arcade and the vault in the nave. The *marble pavement* is remarkable for its 56 designs with 'sgraffiti' and intarsia work depicting coats-of-arms and figurative scenes almost exclusively by Sienese artists (40 altogether, including Matteo di Giovanni, Ant. Federighi, Pinturicchio, Beccafumi); dating from between 1369 and 1547 (some replaced by copies, the originals being in the nearby museum). The principal feature of the interior is the *pulpit* in the left transept by the dome. The work of Nicolà Pisano, his son Giovanni, Arnolfo di Cambio and pupils (1256–8), it is octagonal and supported by 9 columns of porphyry, granite and green marble, some resting on lions. The central column is surrounded by 8 figures (personifications of grammar, astronomy, music, etc.). The white marble reliefs of the surround show the Life of Christ and the Last Judgement with figures of prophets in between. *Libreria Piccolomini:* Entrance in the left aisle with Pinturicchio's fresco 'Coronation of Pius III on 8 Oct. 1503' above. The two marble arches of the entrance are by the Sienese artist 'Il Marrina'. Cardinal Franc. Piccolomini, later Pius III, commissioned this

Siena, cathedral

room to house the library of his uncle Aeneas Silvius (Pius II). Its walls were frescoed by Pinturicchio and his pupils, 1502–9 with 10 scenes from the Life of Pius II. Also worth seeing: *Piccolomini Altar* (left of the library entrance): a three-tiered Renaissance piece with figures in niches by Andrea Bregno, 1503. 'Madonna and Child' in the central, upper niche by

Jacopo della Quercia. *Tomb of Cardinal Riccardo Petroni* on the left wall of the Cappella di S. Ansano (left transept) by Tino di Camaino, 1317/18, in Gothic style. Four caryatids support the sarcophagus with reliefs, over which lies the dead cardinal beneath a curtain held aside by angels. *Cappella di S. Giovanni Battista*, Renaissance structure of 1482, frescoed by Pinturicchio (portrait of Alberto Arringhieri as a young and as an old man, 1504, Birth of John the Baptist, John the Baptist in the Wilderness), a font by the school of Federighi, after 1484, and a bronze statue of John the Baptist, one of Donatello's last works, 1457. The wooden *choir stalls*, carved in 1362–97, were decorated with intarsia work by Fra Giovanni da Verona, 1503. The central section dates from 1567–70 and is based on drawings by Riccio. The round *choir window* (1288) to cartoons by Duccio is of Italian workmanship (oldest example of such a glass window produced in Italy) with scenes from the Life of the Virgin.

Baptistery (entrance from the Piazza S. Giovanni by the apse): The polygonal *font* by Jacopo della Quercia (1417) is one of the

Siena, cathedral 1 campanile portal with tomb of Bishop Tomaso Piccolomini del Testa, Neroccio, 1484/5 **2** Capp. della Madonna del Voto or Chigi, Benedetto Giovanelli, 1661; altarpiece with Madonna del Voto, attrib. Guido da Siena, 1260 (?) **3** sanctuary; marble altar, Baldassare Peruzzi, 1532; bronze ciborium, Vecchietta, 1467–72; choir stalls, side parts by F. and G. di Francesco del Tonghio among others, 1362–97 with additions by Fra Giovanni da Verona, 1503, middle part by Teseo di Bartoline and B. di Giovanni after Riccio, 1567–70; window after Duccio, 1288 (scenes with the Virgin, saints and Evangelists) **4** sacristy and entrance to chapterhouse **5** pulpit, N. and G. Pisano, A. di Cambio among others, 1265–68 **6** Capp. di S. Giovanni Battista, Giovanni di Stefano, 1482; frescos, Pinturicchio, 1504 (2 paintings of Alberto Arringhieri, Birth of John the Baptist and John the Baptist in the Wilderness) **7** Piccolomini Library; fresco, Pinturicchio, 8 Oct. 1503 (lunette: coronation of Pius III); inside: frescos, Pinturicchio and pupils, 1502–9 **8** Piccolomini altar, Andrea Bregno, 1503

Cathedral, Libreria Piccolomini

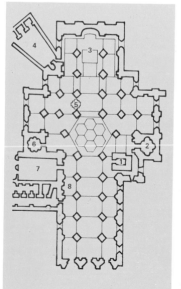

most beautiful works of the 15C and is from the transitional period between the Gothic and the Renaissance. It has gilded bronze reliefs by Ghiberti, Donatello, Jacopo della Quercia and Giovanni di Turino. The *marble ciborium* in the middle is a late work by Jacopo della Quercia. The vaults and walls of the baptistery, also called S.Giovanni, are covered with mid-15C *frescos* by Vecchietta, Michele di Matteo and Benvenuto di Giovanni.

S.Agostino (Prato di S.Agostino): Built in 1258, rebuilt in the 15C and again in the 18C. Inside, note, on the right wall, a *Crucifixion* by Perugino, 1506; in the immediately adjacent *Cappella Piccolomini* a fresco by Ambrogio Lorenzetti (Maestà) and the dramatic Massacre of the Innocents (1482) on the left wall by Matteo di Giovanni. On the right wall is a panel with the legend of Agostino Novello by Simone Martini (*c.* 1330). At the altar is an *Epiphany* by Sodoma. The very recently (Feb. 1978) discovered late 15C *frescos* by Siena's universal genius Francesco di Giorgio depict the 'Annunciation to Joachim', 'Birth of Mary' and 'Adoration of the Shepherds'.

S.Maria dei Servi (formerly *della Concezione*; stands at the top of a flight of steps on the Piazza Alessandro Manzoni): 13C basilica, extended in the 14&15C. The superb Romanesque *campanile* with 4 rows of wall openings (single to quadruple) affords a fine view. Transept and apse are high Gothic; the interior, with a nave, two aisles, a sanctuary and four chapels, is attributed to Baldassare Peruzzi or Porvina and is Renaissance in style. In the 2nd chapel of the right transept there is a fresco of the *Massacre of the Innocents* by Pietro Lorenzetti. At the altar is a *Madonna and Child* by Lippo Memmo (*c.* 1317).

S.Francesco (Piazza di S.Francesco): An extension of a smaller church carried out in 1326. Main building to plans by Franc. di Giorgio, 1475, followed by baroque alterations, 1655. On the left wall of the 1st chapel of the left transept is the detached fresco of the *Crucifixion* by Pietro Lorenzetti, *c.* 1331. On the right wall of the 3rd chapel, from the same period, is the detached fresco of *St.Louis of Anjou* by Ambrogio Lorenzetti, whose *Madonna del Latte* (Virgo lactans) is in the adjacent monastery.

Cathedral   *Baptistery, font (Ghiberti)*

Pinacoteca Nazionale (Via S.Pietro, 29): Housed in the *Palazzo Buonsignori*, one of the most beautiful private palaces in Siena, dating from the early-15C. On display are paintings from the late-12 to mid-16C, representing all the major artists with the exception of Simone Martini. Note: parts of a polyptych by Duccio (?), the famous 'Madonna of the Franciscans', another panel by Duccio. Works by Guido da Siena, Ambrogio and Pietro Lorenzetti (including an Annunciation, one of Ambrogio's masterpieces), an important Crucifixion (1440) by Giovanni di Paolo, as well as works by Sodoma and others.

Museo dell'Opera Metropolitana (in the Duomo Nuovo, cathedral square): On the ground floor are figures from the cathedral façade by Giovanni Pisano, *c.* 1290. On the upper floors are the plans of the proposed extension of the cathedral and drawings for the pavement 'sgraffiti' and mosaics. The museum's main attraction, apart from a wooden *Crucifixion* by Giovanni Pisano (Room II) and a *triptych* of 1342 by Pietro Lorenzetti (2nd floor), is Duccio's *Maestà* from the former high altar of the cathedral (displayed there, 1311–1505). This masterpiece by Duccio, with its harmonious mixture of Byzantine, Gothic and Florentine elements, more or less marks the beginning of the Sienese School, which played a leading role in Italian painting from the 14C onwards. **Museo Etrusco Senese** (Via della Sapienza, 13): Consists mainly of finds from the immediate vicinity.

Santuario Cateriniano (near the Fonte Branda; Vicolo del Tiratoio): The home of the saint (Caterina Benincasa—who had a vision of her mystical marriage with Christ—1347–80, canonized 1461, joint patron saint of Italy since 1939) can be viewed.

Piazza del Campo or simply 'Il Campo': This beautiful scallop-shaped square lies at the point where the city's three hills meet, with the *Fonte Gaia*, a rectangular fountain open on one side with rectangular reliefs on the three walls by Jacopo della Quercia (original in the Palazzo Pubblico, copy by Tito Sarrocchi, 1868).

Palazzo Pubblico, formerly the seat of the Signoria and the Podestà, this, the most

Flight into Egypt by Giovanni di Paolo, Pinacoteca Nazionale

elegant Gothic palace in Tuscany (1297–1310, extended in the 14C) is built of stone on the ground floor, the other storeys being of brick, as is the 296 ft. high *Torre del Mangia*, rising to the left. Built by the Rinaldo brothers in 1338–48, it has a distinctive stone top and bell-chamber. At the foot of the tower is the *Cappella di Piazza* (fresco by Sodoma), added in 1352 after the great plague. A second, symmetrical wing was added to the central part of the palace in 1680/1. In the vestibule, in the Sala d'attesa, there is a *Coronation of the Virgin*, a masterpiece by Sano di Pietro (1445). The next room has a fresco of the *Resurrection* by Sodoma (1537). On the 1st floor, on the left wall of the 'Sala del Mappamondo' (named after the lost map of Ambrogio Lorenzetti) is a *fresco* by Simone Martini depicting the enthroned Madonna and Child, surrounded by apostles and saints, 32 figures in all. Also by Simone Martini in the same room is the famous *monumental fresco of the Sienese general Guidoriccio Fogliani* on horseback, 1328. On the arcade wall are two *frescos* (1529) by Sodoma. On the right in the 'Sala della Pace' is the greatest medieval cycle of secular *frescos*, painted by Ambrogio Lorenzetti in 1338–40. Opposite the window is *'Good Government'* filled with scenes from medieval life and symbols. In the 'Cappella' and 'Anticappella' there are *frescos* (1407–14) by Taddeo di Bartolo (scenes from the Life of Christ and the Virgin, gods, philosophers, rulers etc).

Museo Civico (in the Palazzo): Houses (in the loggia on the top floor of the palazzo) the surviving *original parts of the Fonte Gaia* (the copy of which is in the square). This fountain was built by Jacopo della Quercia together with Franc. di Valdambrino, in 1409–19. There are also the *remains of an enormous fresco* by Ambrogio Lorenzetti (Madonna and Child, 1340).

Also worth seeing: Palazzo Sansedoni (on the Campo): Brick building of 1216 with 14C extensions and a tall *tower*, which once rivalled the Torre del Mangia. **Palazzo Chigi-Saracini** (No.89 on the Campo): 14C, extended in the 18C. Now seat of the Accademia Musicale Chigiana (founded 1930). **Palazzo Piccolomini-Adami** (formerly *Chigi* in the Via del Capitano near the Campo): 16C, with interesting *frescos* by the Flemish painter Bar-

Fonte Branda

Pinacoteca, Lucretia

ent of Orley. **Palazzo del Capitano di Giustizia** (adjacent, No.15): Late 13/early 14C, battlemented. **Palazzo Tolomei** (No.11, Piazza Tolomei): The oldest private palace in Siena, dating from 1205–67. **Palazzo Salimbeni:** 14C Gothic building on the piazza of the same name, where the **Palazzo Spannocchi,** begun by Benedetto da Maiano in 1470, with beautiful inner courts, also stands. **Palazzo Piccolomini** (Via Banchi di Sotto, on the corner of Via Rinaldini): The façade is reminiscent of the Palazzo Rucellai in Florence. Built in 1469, probably to designs by Bern. Rossellino. **Logge della Mercanzia** or *dei Mercanti,* or *di S.Paolo* (near the Campo, at the start of the Via di Città): Built in Gothic-Renaissance transitional style to designs by Sano di Matteo, 1417–28. Top storey 17C. **Logge del Papa** (Via di Pantaneto): Built in Renaissance style to drawings by Ant. Federighi by Pope Pius II in honour of his family. **Fonte Branda,** a well, referred to as early as 1081, extended in 1198 and given its present form by Giovanni di Stefano in 1246: three large battlemented arches cover the water basin. It can be reached by the **Via Galluzza,** one of Siena's picturesque old streets with medieval houses; and then down the Via di Fonte Branda. **Via Sallustio Bandini,** another typical 13C street, at the edge of the city, behind the university (one of the oldest in Italy). **Porta Camollia:** 14C city gate, rebuilt in 1604, at the end of the street of the same name with the greeting 'Cor magis tibi Sena pandit' (Siena offers you its whole heart).

Environs: Abbazia di Torri (*c.* 18 km. S., near Rosia): Torri has an abbey from the 2nd half of the 11C. Unique *cloister* dating from the same time. **Asciano** (*c.* 20 km. SE): Picturesque medieval town in the upper Ombrone valley with the interesting *Collegiata S.Agata,* a beautiful 11C Romanesque church in travertine. Interesting single-aisled plan with three apses. *Museo di Arte Sacra,* left of the church (admission by the parish priest) with a collection of important 14&15C Sienese paintings from the surrounding churches, including a polyptych by Matteo di

Giovanni and a masterpiece by Ambrogio Lorenzetti: 'St. Michael slaying the Dragon'. **Castellina in Chianti** (*c.* 21 km. N.): Important wine-growing centre (Chianti!) in characteristic Tuscan countryside on a hill between the Arbia, Elsa and Pesa valleys.

Siracusa/Syracuse 96100

Syracuse/Sicily   p.420☐M 18

Founded by Corinthians on the island of Ortygia (now the Old Town) in 734 BC, it developed into one of the most important Greek colonies in Sicily. In ancient times it was mostly ruled by tyrants (Gelon, 485 – 78 BC, Hieron I, 478 – 46 BC, Dionysius I, 406–367 BC). It played a decisive role in the Peloponnesian War (5C BC) and it was the home of the famous scientist Archimedes (287 – 212 BC). Its supremacy in Sicily came to an end following its conquest by Rome (212 BC).

Old Town (Ortygia): Cathedral of S. Maria del Piliero (Piazza Duomo): Formerly a Temple of Athene from the 5C BC, it was converted to a church in the 7C. By closing the peripteros, removing the cella walls and breaking through the flanks a basilica with a nave and two aisles was created. Remains of the Doric temple (6 x 13 columns) include the cella walls, two columns of the opisthodomos, almost all the columns of the peripteros, remains of the stylobate and fragments of the entablature. In the 12C the clerestory was added to the nave. 18C *baroque façade.* Inside, note, in the right aisle, first chapel, a Norman *marble font* (13C); adjacent is the *Chapel of St.Lucy* (patron saint of the city) with lavish baroque decoration. At the end of the right aisle is the *Cappella del Crocifisso* with a picture by Antonello da Messina ('St.Zosimus'). An ancient part of the entablature serves as the table of the high altar. The apse of the left aisle is all that remains of the original Byzantine church. A few statues by Gagini (left aisle, apse).

Siena, Palazzo Pubblico ▶

Siena, castle, 14/15C

Temple of Apollo and Artemis (Largo XXV Luglio): Oldest temple in Sicily (late 7/early 6C BC, high archaic style). Peripteros with 6 x 17 columns, measurements of 195 ft. x 80 ft. At the front are two rows of columns, pronaos with columns 'in antis'; cella with nave and two aisles. Some of the columns are unfluted monoliths. After its conversion it was used as a Byzantine church, mosque, Norman church and Spanish barracks.

Castello Maniace (Piazza Federico di Svevia): Named after a Byzantine general who liberated Syracuse from the Arabs in 1038. Built around 1240 by Frederick II Hohenstaufen. Square (171 ft. x 171 ft.); four round corner towers. The interior (entrance through a beautiful Gothic *marble portal*) is partly original (*fine windows, vaults*).

National Archaeological Museum

(Piazza Duomo, soon to be in the Villa Landolina, Via Augusto von Platen): One of the most important of its kind in Italy. Of particular interest: *archaic kouroi;* the *Landolina Venus* (2C AD); an *Ephebus torso* (c. 500 BC); a *bust of Augustus;* the *sarcophagus of Adelfia* (4C AD). *Prehistoric collection;* beautiful *vases. Collection of Greek-Sicilian coins.*

Museo Nazionale Bellomo (Via Capodieci): Housed in the *Palazzo Bellomo* (13C). Collection of medieval and modern art. *Annunciation* by Antonello da Messina (1474).

Also worth seeing in the Old Town: The church of *S.Pietro* (Via S.Pietro), early Christian, 14C alteration (remains of frescos); *Chiesa del Collegio* (Via Landolina), baroque, 17C, with beautiful façade and lavish interior; *Fountain of Arethusa* (along the Via Picherale from the cathedral square): Mythical site of the nymph Arethusa's metamorphosis (tropical aquarium nearby).

New Town (Neapolis): S. Giovanni Evangelista (Tyche district, left of the Viale Teòcrito): Built by the Normans on the site of the tomb basilica of St.Marcian, first Bishop of Syracuse (martyred, 4C), which was destroyed by the Arabs in 827. Of particular interest is the *Crypt of St.Marcian* (entered from the church): Originally a centrally planned building; there are *remains of frescos* and beautiful *capitals* depicting the Evangelists. Next to the church are the extensive early Christian *Catacombs of S. Giovanni.*

Archaeological Zone (Parco Monumentale della Neapoli; entry from the Viale Rizzo): **Greek Theatre:** Largest theatre in the ancient world (diameter 465 ft.; 61 rows of seats, hewn out of the living rock; held about 15,000), dating from the 5C BC. The stage is largely destroyed; the marble facing of the orchestra and the first 11 rows of seats are partly preserved. Converted in Hellenistic and Roman times (installation of two tunnels to the sides of the orchestra). Above are two large *porticoes* and a *nymphaeum;* adjacent to the left is the ancient *Street of Tombs* (rock tombs).

Syracuse, cathedral

Syracuse, Museo Nazionale Bellomo

Latomia del Paradiso: Ancient quarry with sub-tropical vegetation. About 135 ft. deep. To the left of the entrance a path leads to the *Ear of Dionysius,* a cave narrowing towards the top with very good acoustics (named by Caravaggio, 16C). The tyrant Dionysius is supposed to have spied upon enemies of the state imprisoned in the quarry from here. To the right is the *Ropemakers' Grotto* (still a ropemakers' workplace). Adjacent are two further quarries (*Latomia di S.Venera* and *Latomia Intagliatella*).

Altar of Hieron: Built by the tyrant Hieron II (306–215 BC) for state sacrifices. The massive foundations (665 ft. x 77 ft.), hewn out of the living rock, survive.

Roman Amphitheatre: Built in Augustan times. Hewn out of the rock in the Greek tradition (except the S.side), meas-

uring 470 ft. x 400 ft. In the middle there is a cistern.

Also worth seeing in the New Town: Church of *S.Lucia* (Piazza S.Lucia), originally Byzantine, later repeatedly altered, with a painting by Caravaggio (Burial of St.Lucy, 1609) in the apse (the church also provides access to early Christian *catacombs*); *Latomia dei Cappucini* (Piazza Cappucini), probably used to imprison captive Athenians (see above, Syracuse in the Peloponnesian War); *Ginnasio Romano* (Via Florina), remains of a complex from the 1C AD (theatre, temple, portico); *Foro Siracusano* with the remains of the ancient Agora; *Villa Landolina* (Via von Platen) with the tomb of the German poet August von Platen (d. 1835 in Syracuse).

Environs: To the S.of the city, on the other side of the river Ciane ('Cyane' in antiquity; still planted with papyrus), upon a hill, are the remains of the **Temple of Zeus** (mid-6C BC), two columns of which are still standing; to the NW of the city (c. 9 km.) stands the **Castle of Euryalus,** a superbly preserved fortress within the ancient city walls (built from 402–397 BC as a defence against the Carthaginians; the war machines constructed by Archimedes were set up here during the siege by the Romans). The *towers* and the *subterranean passages* (hewn out of the rock) are of interest.

Sirmione 25019
Brescia/Lombardy   p.410☐E 3

Rocca Scaligera: Fortress with a multitude of towers, an intact curtain wall and a fortified harbour (for the Lake Garda fleet). Built under Mastino I della Scala (13C). Inside is a lapidarium (Roman and medieval finds).

S.Maria Maggiore (15C): The altars have paintings by 16C Venetian artists. **S. Salvatore** (above Porta Valentino), the church's three apses are 8C; Carolingian

and 13C frescos. **Collina di Cortine** (on the right outside the town) splendid park with 19C villa (now hotel). **S. Pietro in Mavino** (on the 325 ft. high hill of the peninsula) founded in the 8C; the present building (1341) replaced an 11C one.

Grotte di Catullo: Ruins of a 1C AD Roman villa, traditionally held to be that of the poet Catullus. The villa takes up the whole of the end of the promontory. Similar in plan to the Villa Jovis (Capri). Adjoining the older villa is a second one of large proportions (800 ft. x 350 ft.). The north part is completely uncovered and the best preserved.

Environs: Lonato (15 km. towards Brescia). *Cathedral,* dedicated to John the Baptist, built to designs by Paolo Soratini, 1738–80. Large-scale front façade and a dome (similar to those in Brescia and Montichiari), which dominates the townscape. Inside, 16–18C paintings. Next to the cathedral, the *Piazza Martiri della Libertà* with the town hall (18C) and in front of it a column with the lion of St.Mark, symbol of Venice, under whose rule the town remained until 1797. **Desenzano** (10 km.

Syracuse, Castello Maniace

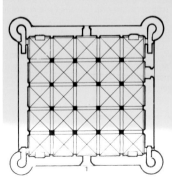

Syracuse, Castello Maniace 1 Gothic entrance portal

from Sirmione): *Parish church of S.Maria Maggiore:* Late-16C, nave and two aisles and superb decoration: three *panel paintings* by Celesti (in the apse) with the Life of Mary Magdalene and an *altarpiece* by Gian Domenico Tiepolo 'Last Supper' (2nd chapel on the right). *Villa Romana:* excavations of a Roman villa of the 2&4C. *(mosaic pavement).* **Santuario di S.Luigi** (in Castiglione delle Stiviere): St. Louis Gonzaga, who died in 1591 with a reputation as a mystic, was born in Castiglione in 1568 (canonized in 1726 by Benedict XIII). His brother Francesco had a church built for him as early as 1612 (completed 18C). The *fresco* by Giorgio Anselmi in the dome depicts the Death and Apotheosis of Louis Gonzaga. Behind the splendid high altar *skull of the saint,* to the right of which, in a side room, are *mummies of the Gonzaga family.* **Solferino** (SE of Desenzano): The site, with **S. Martino** (della Battaglia), some 10 km. N., of the decisive battles on 24 June 1859—following Palestro Magenta, Malegnano, Varese, Treponti and Salò—which finally assured victory for the Piedmontese together with the French over the Austrians. *Memorials:* The church of S. Pietro, which serves as an Ossario (charnel-house); 'La Spia d'Italia', a tower (1022), houses mementoes and a museum.

Solofra 83029
Avellino/Campania   p.418 □ L 11

Collegiata S. Michele: 16C. Splendid 17C baroque façade, with interesting central portal. Campanile of 1564. Most of the interior (nave, two aisles) was painted by G.T. and Fr. Guarino in the 17C (on the nave ceiling, decorated with gilded and carved wood, there are 20 *Deeds of the Archangel* by the former; the latter painted 21 *scenes from the New Testament* on the ceiling of the transept). In the apse is a painting by G.B. Lama in two parts (above *Coronation of the Virgin,* below *Orchestra of Angels,* 1598), between which is a *Statue of St.Michael,* 15C *diptych* on the left.

Also worth seeing: *Palazzo Ducale* (next to the Collegiata), late 16C with beautiful portal and square inner court.

Environs: *c.* 16 km. SW **Mercato San Severino** with the 17C *Chiesa dei Minori*

Syracuse, National Archaeological Museum, bronze horse, 8C BC; athlete, 460 BC

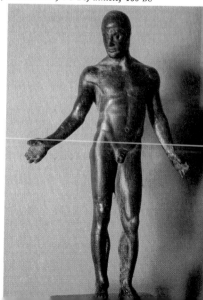

Syracuse, ancient street of tombs

Osservanti, the *Palazzo Municipio*, built to plans by Carlo Vanvitelli.

Sondrio 23100

Sondrio/Lombardy   p.412☐D 2

Collegiata (on the S.edge of the old town centre): The church, dedicated to St. Gervase and St.Protase, was built at the start of the 18C (G.P. Ligari). The single-aisled interior contains paintings by G.P. Ligari (on the pillars between the 1st and 2nd chapels on the left and right), as well as two large-scale paintings by G.Parravicini, the theme of which is the martyrdom of the patron saints.

Also worth seeing: *Museo Valtellinese di Storia e Arte* (Via 4 Novembre) with an important collection of local arts and crafts. A few palaces with interesting rooms. *Pal. Sassi* (Via Quadro 27), *Pal. Sertoli* (Piazza Crispi 8), *Casa Carbonera* (Via Angelo Custode 5) with loggias (18C) in the inner court. *Cinema-Teatro Pedretti* (Piazza Garibaldi) by Luigi Canonica, 1810. *Madonna della Sassella* (2 km. on the main road to Cólico): 15C pilgrimage church set amidst vineyards. The high altar has a 'Nativity of Christ' by Gaudenzio Ferrari, 1534; interesting frescos by A.Passeri, 1511 (in the sanctuary).

Environs: Morbegno (c. 30 km. W. of Sondrio): Parish church *S.Giovanni Battista*, 1680–1714, façade not completed until 1779. Spacious interior. High altar by Carlo Buzzi, apse frescos by Ligari. In the 2nd chapel on the left a painting by G.B. Pittoni. The Gothic church of *S.Antonio* with baroque façade and campanile contains (3rd chapel right) a work by B. Luini of 1520 (Life of St.Martin of Tours). Towards the cemetery is the pilgrimage

Sirmione, Rocca Scaligera

church of the *Assunta* (begun 1418, completed end of 16C). Single-aisled interior with 18C frescos. The high altar is a splendid carved work by the sculptor Angelo Maino in collaboration with the painter Fermo Stella, both under the direction of Gaudenzio Ferrari (1515–26). Early 18C frame. In the middle of the altar is a 15C fresco (Madonna and Child).

Soragna 43012
Parma/Emilia-Romagna   p.412□ E 4

Soragna, a settlement originating around the 9/10C castle, fell, in 1347, to the Lupi family, who called themselves the Marchesi of Soragna. In 1709 their fief became a principality of the Holy Roman Empire.

Castle: The original fortress was converted into a luxurious residence for the Lupi family in the 16C. The impressive rooms display fine *frescos* and *paintings* of the 16–18C.

Sorrento 80067
Naples/Campania   p.418□ K 12

Sorrento originated as a Greek foundation of the 6/5C BC. Even in ancient times (then called 'Surrentum') it was visited as a health resort. In the Middle Ages it was a constant bone of contention (battles against the Byzantines, Lombards, Saracens and Normans, among others). Home of the poet Torquato Tasso (1544–95).

Cathedral of SS. Filippo e Giacomo (Largo Arcivescovado): Built in the 15C on the walls of an earlier building, constantly altered later. Neo-gothic façade, 1913–26; the campanile has a passage from the

11/12C (antique columns at the sides). On the right side of the church is a marble *Renaissance portal* (1479). Interior: pillared basilica with nave and two aisles. On the left of the nave is a *bishop's throne* (1573) with a beautiful marble baldacchino, built of ancient fragments of masonry; *pulpit* from the same period. In the right aisle are the remains of 11/12C marble *choir screens*.

S. Antonio (Piazza S. Antonio) Probably the oldest religious building in the city; rebuilt in the 17C. In front of the façade is a three-arched 12C *portico*; on the right side is an interesting 12C *portal* (made of antique materials). Interior: basilican with nave and two aisles; beautiful antique granite columns. Note the 18C *crib*. The early medieval *crypt* was completely altered in the 18C.

Museo Correale di Terranova (Via Correale): Opened 1924; containing antique and medieval sculptures and a good collection of craftwork. Of particular interest: *Room II,* dedicated to *Torquato Tasso* (with a few autographs of the poet); Room IV contains the *Sorrentine base* from Augustan times (beautiful reliefs); Room VI with

Sirmione, Grottoes of Catullus

remarkable remains of *medieval choir screens*. On the upper floors are the *craft collection* and *painting section*.

Also worth seeing: *Cloister of the Franciscan monastery* (Piazza F. Saverio Gargulio) from the 14C. *Sedile Dominova* (Via S. Cesareo), a loggia with 15/16C dome. 13C *Palazzo Venier* (Strada Pietà) with beautiful façade.

Environs: *c.* 15 km. NE is **Vico Equense** with the originally Gothic *Chiesa dell'Annunziata (still containing remains of the early medieval choir screens).*

Spello 06038

Perugia/Umbria   p.414 □ H 8

1,055 ft. above sea-level, at the foot of Mount Subasio. Roman walls and well preserved gates, which cloak the otherwise medieval town with antiquity.

Porta Venere: Dating from the time of Augustus, very well preserved with two 12-cornered towers, typical of the military architecture which can be found in the structure of many Umbrian campaniles. The **Porta Consolare** from the same period is also most interesting. It has three tomb statues from an earlier epoch. The third important gate is the **Porta Urbica.**

S. Maria Maggiore 12/13C church with 17C façade and ornate portal. Interior: the *Baglioni Chapel,* decorated by Pinturicchio, 1501 (the Annunciation includes a self-portrait of the artist), the pavement is of Deruta majolica; Perugino frescos (Madonna Enthroned with Dead Christ, 1521); tomb of Caius Titienus Flaccus. Housed in the church is the *Town Museum,* containing numerous works: C. Lamparelli, Descent from the Cross, Death of Joseph; Paolo Vanni da Perugia (1391), Large cross in silver and enamelled copper.

Also worth seeing: *Arch of Augustus;* church of *S. Andrea,* with Pinturicchio's Madonna and Child with Saints; *Palazzo Comunale* (Piazza Maggiore) with beautiful loggia (1270) and many Roman fragments in the vestibule; painting by Perugino in the church of *S. Girolamo; Casa della Confraternita* (15C).

Spezzano Albanese 87019

Cosenza/Calabria   p.418│ N 13

This town is at the centre of the colony founded by Albanians fleeing to Calabria from Epirus (northern Greece). Many Albanians found refuge in Calabria (which was the least populated area in the kingdom of Naples) following the death of their leader Georg Kastriota Skanderbeg (1400 –68), who was supported by Alfonso I of Aragon in the struggle against the Turks.

Environs: In the vicinity of the town are excavations of prehistoric *burial grounds* from the 8C BC (by *S. Lorenzo* and *Torre Mordillo;* another by *Cicapesce* SE of the town). A *Hellenistic town* was uncovered in 1963.

Spilimbergo 33037

Pordenone/Friuli   p.410☐H 2

Spilimbergo was founded in the 11/12C by the German lords of Spengenberg. There has been a famous Mosaic School here since 1921.

Cathedral of S. Maria (Piazza del Duomo): Begun (1284) in Romanesque style, consecrated in 1359; one of the most important Romanesque-Gothic churches in Friuli. Of particular interest on the outside is the *N. portal* ('Porta moresca', 1376). The façade has seven beautiful *Romanesque windows;* on the E. wall of the nave are *blind arcades. Campanile,* formerly a tower of the adjacent castle. Interior, nave, two aisles, wide pointed arches. Restored timber ceiling. The main decoration of the church are the *frescos,* the most beautiful being in the sanctuary, 14/15C. In the left and right aisle and on the entrance wall hang the leaves and balustrade of the old *organ* (painted by Pordenone, 1524; the or-

gan itself is now in the church of SS. Giuseppe e Pantaleone). In the 'Cappella del Rosario' (right aisle), behind the altar, are beautiful early 14C *frescos* (bishops, saints); the superb *marble work* is by G.A. Pilacorte (1498). In the left aisle there is a beautiful *font* (1492), also by Pilacorte. Romanesque *crypt* with *marble triptych* (1472) and the *tomb of Walterpertoldo IV of Spilimbergo* (d. 1382).

Castle (Piazza del Duomo): Founded in the 8C, extended in the 14C; later repeatedly rebuilt after being destroyed. Consists of several Gothic and Renaissance palaces grouped in a semi-circle: (from the right) *Palazzo Dipinto* (14C) with beautiful façade (frescos, double and triple-arched windows); *Palazzo Spilimbergo-Ciriani* (16C), of particular interest inside are the decorations by Giovanni da Udine; *Palazzetto di Troilo; Palazzo Tadea* (16C).

Also worth seeing: Church of *S. Giovanni Battista* (Via Mazzini), 14C, completely altered in the 18C, with beautiful ceiling painting to designs by G.B. Tiepolo; church of *SS. Giuseppe e Pantaleone* (Via Mazzini), 14C, rebuilt in the 18C, with

Sorrento, gulf from the S. and Vesuvius

beautiful choir stalls, 1477 (formerly in the cathedral), and the old cathedral organ (1525; two panels painted by Pordenone).

Environs: *c.* 5 km. SW, **Barbeano:** The church of *S.Antonio Abate* contains beautiful Gothic frescos (G.F. da Tolmezzo, 1484).

Spoleto 06049
Perugia/Umbria   p.414☐H 8

The city is probably of Umbrian origin, although the name suggests Etruscan roots (Etruscan spur meaning town). Spoleto was the Umbrian city which put up the fiercest resistance to the Carthaginian Hannibal. During the Roman era it was a 'municipium'. The mother of the emperor Vespasian, Vespasia Polla, came from Spoleto. After the Goths and the Byzantines Spoleto became the centre of the great Lombard duchy of the same name. In 1155 the city was destroyed by Barbarossa's troops and so almost all traces of earlier epochs have been destroyed. In 1185, as a peace offering, Barbarossa gave the city the icons, which are still preserved in the cathedral. At the end of the 13C the Pope gained control of Spoleto, which had formerly been a free commune. From 1324 to 1359 Spoleto was made subject to the city of Perugia. Cardinal Albornoz seized the city for the Pope and had the castle built in 1362. Lucrezia Borgia is supposed to have been named as representative of the Pope (15C). During the Risorgimento there were such patriots as Pompeo da Campello and Luigi Pianciani (who later became Mayor of Rome). On the 17 September 1860 Spoleto became part of the Italian State.

Cathedral: Consecrated in 1198. The colossal campanile dates from the 12C. The mosaic on the façade is the work of a Byzantine called Solsternus, 13C. The façade is a remarkable example of the classical tenets of harmony. The Renaissance portico was added by Ambrogio Barocci from Milan and Pippo da Firenze (in

Spoleto, cathedral 1 Bernini: bust of Urban VIII **2** frescos by Filippo Lippi **3** tomb of Filippo Lippi **4** frescos by Pinturicchio

Spoleto, cathedral

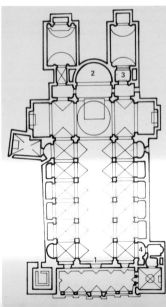

Bramante's style), 1491 – 1504. Interior (renovated by Luigi Arrigucci in the 17C): the Eroli Chapel with frescos by Pinturicchio, the Orsini tomb and the tomb of Filippo Lippi (designed by his son Filippino Lippi with inscription by Agnolo Poliziano commissioned by Lorenzo il Magnifico); Filippo Lippi's frescos in the apse (1466-9). Also: Crucifix by Alberto Sozio (1187), paintings by Annibale Carracci, bust of Pope Urban VIII by Bernini, altars by Giuseppe Valadier and finally the above-mentioned icon (most probably 12C), a gift from Barbarossa.

S.Salvatore: This basilica (4C) stands just outside the town. It is one of the oldest Christian buildings in Europe and a very rare example of the classical European architecture of that time, independent of the Roman style of basilica. The sanctuary, with its groin vault, seems to be one of the first attempts to vault a basilica. This church had a considerable influence on the later S.Umbrian architectural style. Ornate capitals and delicate decoration inside.

S. Ponziano: This remarkable Romanesque structure is not far from S.Salvatore.

The portal has Cosmati work motifs and fine stonemasonry. Interior (rebuilt, 18C): Crypt with old frescos and finds of archaeological interest.

Ponte Sanguinario: This is an excellent example of Roman civic architecture during the Empire.

Amphitheatre: Not far from the Ponte Sanguinario (in the Via dell'Amfiteatro) stands this badly damaged amphitheatre (2C). King Totila converted it into a fortress, hence some coarsely walled-up arches. Cardinal Albornoz (14C) used the amphitheatre as building material for the city's castle.

S.Gregorio Maggiore: This church is to the right of the Porta Garibaldi. Originally an early Christian building, it was totally converted in 1079 – 1146, the façade is 12&14C. A heavy Lombard influence is evident in the Romanesque interior, with a nave and two aisles. This is particularly apparent in the sanctuary (with an extra storey) and in the crypt; note the 12&15C frescos.

S. Salvatore

S.Eufemia: This 12C church, which has remained Lombard in style, is in the archbishop's palace (15C, near the cathedral). Unusually for central Italy, the interior has beautiful galleries above the aisles and alternate columns and pillars. Also of interest inside: beautiful Romanesque altar and 15C triptych. Those interested in the Lombard period should note that the remains of a majestic early medieval building have recently been discovered beneath the palace.

Palazzo Comunale: This building is very near S.Eufemia. It dates from the 12C and was rebuilt in the 18C. The tower survives from the original building. Below the palace lies a beautiful Roman house (most likely the dwelling of Vespasia Polla) with floor mosaic, bronze and marble decoration and frescos. The picture gallery is now housed on the first floor of the palazzo. (opening hours: summer: 8 a.m. to 12 noon, 4 p.m. to 8 p.m.; winter: 8 a.m. to 12 noon, 3 p.m. to 5 p.m.) Important works: crucifix from the 2nd half of the 13C from the School of Simone and Machilos, crucifix by the Master of Cesi, triptych by Niccolò Alunno, Antonello Saliba da Messina (Madonna with the Keys), Giovanni Spagna (Madonna and Child with Saints), also works by Guercino, Paolo Antonio Barbieri, Mola and Sebastiano Conca.

Museo Civico: This large former palace (14C, Via del Duomo 31), was probably created by Gattaponi. (Visitors must apply to the custodian of the Caio Melisso Theatre.) Principal works: the Lex Spoletina, 3C BC, Christian art of the 4C, sarcophagus of Ponzia Romana (12C), sarcophagus of St.Isaac, also a marble head from the 5C BC, probably depicting the God Clitumnus.

Piazza del Duomo: The fountain is a Roman sarcophagus from the Empire.

Palazzo Arroni (formerly Racani): This 16C palace built in Tuscan style has architectural elements by Bramante and Laurana.

Arch of Drusus: Erected following a victory over the Germans (23 BC), it is not far from the picture gallery. The arch was originally the entrance to the forum. Near

S.Eufemia

the arch is the church of S.Ansano, which was built on a Roman temple.

Fonte di Piazza: This impressive fountain, dating from 1748, was based on contemporary Roman examples. The remains of a Roman **theatre** (1C, diameter of 242 ft.) were recently excavated beyond the Piazza della Libertà.

Palazzo Collicola: This early 18C palace, on the piazza of the same name, now houses the *Gallery of Modern Art*. The gallery contains works by numerous contemporary painters and sculptors, such as Corsi, Garelli, Guttuso, Fabbri, Mandelli, Marcucci, Vespignani and many others.

S.Filippo Neri: Built in Roman Jesuit church style by the architect Loreto Scelli of Spoleto, 1640-66.

Palazzo Pianciani: The Piazza Pianciani was named after this 18C palace.

S.Domenico: 13C, with red and white striped façade. Among other things, it contains a large crucifix (14C, local school),

many 14&15C votive frescos and an altarpiece by Giovanni Lanfranco.

S.Giovanni e Paolo: Most probably built on the foundations of an older church. The frescos date from the same period (12C) and depict the Life of Thomas à Becket. Some of these frescos may be by Alberto Sozio; at any rate the influence of the painting of Latium is apparent here. Note the *Torre dell'Olio* (13C) and, in the nearby Via di Porta Fuga, the medieval and Renaissance buildings.

Porta Fuga: 12C. According to legend Hannibal was put to flight here. The gate was built on older antique remains.

City Walls: A polygonal layer from the 6 –5C BC, a second one with square stones from the 3C BC, the third from the 1C BC.

S.Pietro: This fine church just outside the city was begun in the 5C and acquired a lavishly articulated façade in the 12&13C, upon which plants, animals, rural scenes etc. are superbly depicted. Clear Lombard-Provençal influence, as well as classical lines — a constant feature of the Spoleto

Castle

area. On the upper part of the façade is the Provençal fable of Reynard the Fox, as well as scenes from the Gospel and stories from medieval encyclopaedias (Physiologus).

Ponte delle Torri: This imposing bridge (672 ft. long, 270 ft. high) was built to designs by Matteo Gattapone (1362–70), probably on the foundations of a Roman bridge. The two pillars in the middle are hollow and can be used as towers.

Castle: Built 1359–62 by Matteo Gattapone at the instance of Cardinal Albornoz. It consists of two very beautiful courts, surrounded by a wall with six towers, one at each corner and one in the middle of both of the longer sides.

Also worth seeing: *S. Paolo inter Vineas.* This church was consecrated by Pope Gregory IX as late as 1234, although the building is considerable older. The airy Romanesque church was altered in the following centuries, particularly in the 18C. *S. Agata* with an adjoining monastery was built on the Roman theatre in the Middle Ages. The *Caio Melisso Theatre* was rebuilt in 1880 by the Mantiroli, replacing the old

Spoleto, S. Pietro

Teatro de'Nobili (19C). The famous Teatro de'Nobili was one of the first Italian theatres. The church of the *Madonna di Loreto* is one of the finest examples of Umbrian architecture from the time of the Counter Reformation. It was built to a design by the Florentine Annibale Lippi in 1572. The church of **S. Niccolo** (14C) was built together with the lower-lying church of S. Maria della Misericordia and its monastery. The beautiful Gothic portal is of interest. The interior of S. Niccolo is worth seeing for its beautiful gallery. An unusual but harmonious structure connects the choir of the main church and the apse of the lower one. Many scholars resided at S. Niccolo, including Martin Luther in 1512. The Teatro Nuovo was built to a design by Ireneo Aleandri between 1854–64. The stucco and the portraits (Rossini, Alfieri, Goldoni, Metastasio) are by A. Bagioli. The productions of the 'Teatro Lirico Sperimentale' take place here every year.

Events: Festival dei Due Mondi (Festival of the two Worlds), annually between the 15 June and 15 July.

Environs: S. Giuliano: Built on an older 6C church at the end of the 12C. The church of **S. Giacomo** has many frescos by Giovanni Spagna (Life of St. James, and others). These were painted in 1526–8 and are unique in their spontaneous, graceful, narrative expressiveness. **S. Anatolia di Narco:** (or **Castel S. Felice**): Note the beautiful Romanesque church of S. Felice (2nd half of the 12C). **Fonti del Clitunno** (Spring of Clitunno): A famous site distinguished by its romantic natural beauty. The well-preserved temple (5C) is of both artistic and historical importance and it contains the oldest Christian paintings in Umbria.

Squillace 88069

Catanzaro/Calabria   p.418| |N 15

Squillace has been the seat of a bishop since the 4C. It was the home of the important statesman and writer of late antiq-

Fonti del Clitunno (Spoleto), ancient temple

uity Magnus Aurelius Cassiodorus (*c.* AD 490–583): secretary of the Ostrogoth king Theodoric and compiler of a 'History of the Goths'. Cassiodorus concerned himself with the preservation of manuscripts. Two monasteries were established in Squillace after 540 ('Castellense' and 'Vivarium'). The town is interesting for its **cathedral** (*S. Trinità*), with a nave and two aisles, rebuilt in the 18C following an earthquake (beautiful marble work inside) and the ruins of the **castle** (inner part 9C; splendid view). Below the castle is the (supposed) **birthplace of Cassiodorus** (15C inscription, now in the Palazzo Comunale).

Environs: *c.* 12 km NE, on the coast, is the 'Roccelletta del Vescovo di Squillace', the ruins of the once mighty church of **S. Maria della Roccella**. Date of construction not yet known with certainty (additions date from early Christian to Norman times, 11C); single-aisled basilica, Latin cross ground plan with three semicircular apses. The ground plan of the crypt correponds to the choir and transept of the upper church. Remains of ancient buildings nearby served in part as building material.

Stilo 89049

Reggio Calabria / Calabria   p.418☐N 15

La Cattolica (above the town): One of the most important buildings, in terms of art history, in Calabria. Well-preserved Byzantine cruciform domed church from the 10C. (Models in Greece and Anatolia): Square ground plan; five domes, the middle one of which is larger; three apses, domes with cylindrical drums. Two-arched windows in the apses. Main dome supported by four antique columns. *Remains of frescos.*

Stilo, La Cattolica

Subiaco, Monastero di S. Benedetto

Also worth seeing: *Cathedral* (Piazza Duomo) with 14C portal (in the wall to the left of the portal is an antique statue); inside is a painting ('St.Francis of Assisi'), attributed to Mattia Preti (1613–99).

Environs: *c.* 22 km. W., **Ferdinandea,** summer residence of the Bourbon king Ferdinand II (late 19C); the palace contains a small *museum* (mementoes of Garibaldi, etc.), nearby *remains of an iron foundry. c.* 15 km. E. on the coast near **Monasterace Marina** are the remains of the Magna Graecian town of **Caulonia** (excavations since 1912): Founded 7C BC; parts of the *town walls* and the foundations of a 5C BC *Doric temple* are amongst the surviving sections. Finds from Caulonia include polychrome terracotta fragments.

Stresa 28049
Novara/Piedmont   p.412☐C 3

Isola Bella (on Lago Maggiore between Stresa and Pallanza): Beginning in 1632, an uninhabited island was developed into the site of a magnificent villa and garden. The island was named Isola Bella in honour of Isabella d'Addas, the wife of Carlo III Borromeo. *Palazzo Borromeo,* begun in 1632 (façade not completed until 1958, using old plans). Special permission has to be granted to see the *picture gallery* (paintings by Bergognone, Bellini, Bordone, Carracci, Tempesta). *Garden:* One of the most splendid Italian gardens of the 17C, it extends over 10 terraces linked by flights of steps (1632–71).

Environs: Pallanza: On the N. side of the Golfo Borromeo on Lago Maggiore; Roman origin. The area was the private possession of the Julio-Claudian emperors in the 1C, and of the bishops of Novara in the Middle Ages, finally falling to Savoy in 1743. Now part of Verbania. *S.Lionardo* (Piazza Garibaldi): 16C parish church, rebuilt 19C. 200 ft. campanile, begun in 1520, completed in 1589 by P.Pellegrini. *S. Remigio:* 12C Romanesque church, 15&16C frescos inside, Madonna (1528). *Palazzo Pretorio* (Piazza Garibaldi): Now

Stresa, Lago Maggiore

the town hall. *Palazzo Dugnani* (Via Cavour): 18C, with the *Museo Storico Artistico e del Paesaggio.*

Subiaco 00028
Rome/Latium   p.414☐H 9

Antique Sublaqueum originated on the edge of three artificial lakes laid out by Nero, where he had his villa built. Even before then four aqueducts carried the water of the Anio to Rome. Benedict of Nursia (Nurcia) settled in the valley around 480. He and his numerous pupils established 13 monasteries (of which only the Monastero S. Scolastica survives).

Monastero di S. Scolastica: In 937 Leo VII gave the monastery Subiaco Castle with its surrounding estates. Heyday 11–13C. In 1464 the Germans A. Pannartz and C. Schweynheim built Italy's first printing works. Bomb damage to the church façade and the *1st cloister* (16C) was repaired. The *2nd cloister* of 1052 was rebuilt in the 14C. On the entrance side is a splendid *arcade* in German late Gothic style (15C). Let into the inner wall is a *Romanesque column* with a Cosmati work capital. The church, consecrated by Benedict VII in 980, was rebuilt under Cistercian Gothic influence in the 13C. By the (original) portal is a 14C *fresco.* Entrance via the Romanesque *campanile* (1052/3), superb in its simplicity. On the tower buttress is a *stone relief* of an animal and an inscription. 11C *frescos* in the passage. Classical interior (1769–76). Choir vault with early 15C *frescos.* The sacristy (altarpiece attributed to C. Maratta) leads to the *Grotto of St. Scholastica* (frescos (1426) in the *Cappella degli Angeli*). The *3rd* (Cosmati work) *cloister* was built in 2 phases: S. side by Master Iacopo (around 1200), the rest by his son Cosma the Youn-

Subiaco, Monastero di S. Benedetto

ger and the latter's sons, Luca and Iacopo (1227–43). *Archive* and *library*.

Monastero di S.Benedetto *(Sacro Speco):* The cave (Sacro Speco) used by St. Benedict as a hermitage for three years has developed into this picturesquely built monastery on and in the cliff, which, in its present form, is mainly 13C. Cistercian Gothic style, upper church with 14C alterations. The monastery is particularly important for its painted decoration—it is a veritable gallery of medieval Italian *fresco painting* (9–15C). The earliest fresco, dating from around 800, is in the 'Grotta dei Pastori' and depicts a *Madonna and Child with Saints.* The 'Cappella di S.Gregorio Magno' (Cappella degli Angeli) contains Byzantine *frescos* of the Roman school (12C). At the chapel entrance is the *Portrait of St.Francis,* painted in 1224 during the saint's lifetime. The lower church contains *frescos of the 13C Roman school,* partly from

the 1st half of the 13C (same period as Pietro Cavallini). The *frescos* of the 'Cappella della Madonna' (with the Scala Santa leading upwards) are from the 14C Sienese school. The same hand is responsible for a part of the *upper church frescos.* The 'Sala del Capitulo Vecchio' contains *frescos* by the school of Perugino.

Also worth seeing: Church of S. Francesco: Built in 1327 above the old oratory of S. Pietro al Deserto. Simple Franciscan structure; *triptych* by Antoniazzo Romano (1467). 3rd chapel on the left with *frescos* attributed to Sodoma, as is the chapel altar, with the *Nativity of Christ.* **Church of S.Andrea:** Massive façade of 1765, rebuilt after bombardment, with two low, flanking towers. Domed church with classical interior. *Miraculous Draught of Fish* by Sebastiano Conca. In the sacristy a *Madonna and Child* by C.Dolci and valuable *paraments.* **Castello**

Sulmona, cathedral

Abbaziale: Built in the 11C by Abbot Giovanni, later seat of the commendatory cardinals of the abbey. 1755 under Pius VI.

Sulmona 67039
L'Aquila/Abbruzzi   p.416□I 9

The ancient Sulmo was the home town of the Roman poet Ovid.

Cathedral: Built on the ruins of a Temple of Apollo and Vesta. Rebuilt 1078–1118, destroyed by repeated fires and earthquakes, and most recently during World War 2. On the baroque façade is a *portal* by Nicolo Salvitti, flanked by lions, 1391. The baroque interior dates from 1726. *Tombs of Bishop Bartolomeo de Petrini and his sister,* 15C. The 11C crypt contains a bishop's throne and a 12C *Byzantine*

Madonna. The church treasure includes a silver bust of St. Panfilo by Giovanni di Marino di Cicco, 1458-9, a silver gilt chalice and a bishop's crook by Ciccarello di Francesco di Bentivegna, late 14C.

Church and palace of the Annunziata: Former seat of the Confraternità della Penitenza, a brotherhood founded in 1320. The church, also founded in 1320, was rebuilt in 1710, following several earthquakes. The palace façade has *portals* from various periods, the left one is late Gothic (1415), the middle one (1483) shows traces of the early Renaissance, while the right one (1533) is late Renaissance. The *clock* is 18C. Inside the palace is the *Museo Civico:* archaeological finds, a painted wooden tabernacle (1435) by Giovanni da Sulmona, 14&15C processional crosses.

Also worth seeing: Roman *gate* and *aqueduct.*

Environs: Badia Morronese: Pietro da Morrone, who, as Pope, chose the name Celestine V, lived here in the 2nd half of the 13C. In 1293 it became the principal abbey of the Celestine Order, which was dissolved in 1807. The church of *S.Spirito*, entry from the Cortile dei Platani, was built at the instance of Celestine V in the 2nd half of the 13C. The façade and most of the decoration are 17&18C. The Cappella Caldora contains the sarcophagus of Restaino Caldora-Cantelini, made in 1422 by Gaultiero d'Alemannia (Walter of Munich?); the frescos are attributed to Giovanni da Sulmona. **Shrine of Hercules Quirinus** (right next to the abbey; known as the 'Villa of Ovid') 1C BC. **S. Onofrio** (lying a little higher up): Celestine V's hermitage, where he lived following his abdication; in his cell there are frescos by Gentile da Sulmona.

Susa 10059

Turin/Piedmont   p.412 □ A 4

S. Giusto (Piazza S. Giusto): Gothic cathedral built on the remains of a Romanesque Benedictine monastery in the 1st half of the 11C. The lower part of the campanile preserves its Romanesque structure and frescos. Inside, note the carved wooden *choir stalls*, 13&14C, and the *Cappella di Rocciamelone* with a Gothic bronze triptych, 1388. In the sacristy is *Nativity of Christ* by D. Ferrari.

Also worth seeing: Arco di Augusto (Via degli Archi): This marble triumphal arch was built for Augustus by Cottius in 8 BC. The frieze reliefs portray the conclusion of the federal agreement. **Porta Savoia** (Parco di Augusto), a double gate in the town walls with Roman and medieval remains. **S. Francesco** (Via Rosaz), founded in 1247 in honour of St.Francis, who visited the town in 1213. The late Romanesque façade has a Gothic door surmounted by canopies. The interior is a round-pillared basilica with nave, two aisles and polygonal apse. In the right aisle are 13&14C frescos of the four Evangelists,

among others. **Palazzo di Città** (Via Palazzo di Città), housing the *Museo Civico*, which includes Roman inscriptions, reliefs and tombstones. The **Castello** dates back to the 10C.

Environs: Novalesa (*c.* 8 km.): *S.Stefano di Novalesa*, the parish church, has a treasury, which includes the valuable silver reliquary of St.Eldrado, 14C. *Abbazia di S. Pietro e Andrea*, founded by Benedictines in 726 and Charlemagne's base during the Lombard campaign in 774. The monastery church was rebuilt by Victor Amadeus II in 1712. Four further chapels date from the 11C, S.Maria Maddalena, below the monastery, S.Pietro and S.Salvatore behind it and S.Eldrado with 14C frescos, which relate the legend of St.Eldrado, 11C (prin-

Susa, cathedral **1** remains of the antique 'Porta Sacoia' **2** entrance to the campanile **3** Romanesque campanile, 11C, the most beautiful in Piedmont **4** baroque altar with triptych by A. Bergognone **5** way to the ancient baptistery, 9&10C **6** Cappella della Madonna del Rocciamelone, altar 1358 **7** choir stalls, 13&14C, from the church of S. Maria Maggiore in Susa **8** sacristy with church treasure

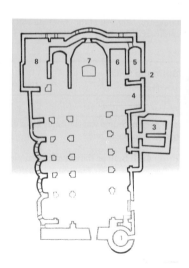

cipal saint of the region) and of St.Nicholas of Myra.

Sutri 01015
Viterbo/Latium   p.414☐G 9

This legendary Pelasgian foundation was an important Etruscan centre (name derived from Suturina, Etruscan for Saturn). 391 BC Roman, AD 728 given to Pope Gregory II by the Lombard king Liutprand, thereby becoming the basis of the future church state. Council town. Frederick Barbarossa met Hadrian IV here. Remains of the medieval *town walls* with several towers are preserved.

Cathedral of S.Maria Assunta: Romanesque, greatly altered in the 17&18C. Interior with nave and two aisles, altered in the 18C. Nave with *Cosmati work pavement*. Altar in 2nd chapel on the left with *Christ Blessing* (13C). Lombard *crypt* with nave and six aisles.

Madonna del Parto (key kept by cathedral sacristan): Former Etruscan tomb with a nave and two aisles, at the *Villa Staderini*. Converted into a mithraeum, then into a church. *Frescos* in the vestibule (Archangel Michael), behind the altar and on the walls. At the villa entrance ruins of the medieval *castle* ('Charlemagne's Castle') can be seen.

Amphitheatre: An oval, carved out of the tufa. Date of construction disputed (Etruscan or time of Augustus).

Environs: Bassano Romano (6 km.) with the *Palazzo Anguillara*. Palace of the Giustiniani (now Odescalchi), extensively renovated in the 16&17C, with important late Mannerist frescos (B.Castello, Albani, Domenichino). Elegant portal by Vignola.

Susa, view

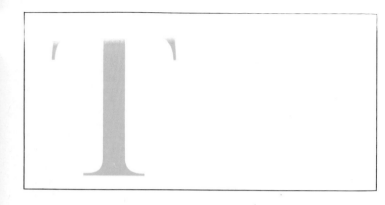

Taggia 18011
Imperia/Liguria   p.412□ B 6

**Parish church of SS. Giacomo e
Filippo** (Piazza Card. Castaldi): This
single-aisled church, reconstructed in
1675–81, houses some fine works of art
(*Madonna di Taggia* by Salvatore Revelli).
To the right of the entrance is a *bust in
memory of the artist* by S.Baratta. There are
also good works by L. and G.Cambiaso.

S. Domenico (Piazzale S. Domenico):
Built in 1460, well restored in 1935. There
are 2 fine 16C reliefs above the portal. A
very distinguished, restrained, single-
aisled interior, framed by Gothic chapels.
Several brilliant *sculptures* by L.Brea (1st,
2nd and 3rd chapels, and in particular, on
the right of the high altar, the 'Madonna
of Mercy with Saints', 1483; the large altarpiece of the 'Baptism of Christ', 1495, to
the left of the sanctuary), and also a very
impressive 15C *crucifix* of Spanish origin
at the altar to the right of the sanctuary. A
15C *cloister lies to the right of the church and
the monastery* was an important cultural
centre.

Also worth seeing: *Madonna del Cannetto*
(to the left of the Piazza Revelli): A picturesquely situated Romanesque church
with Gothic *portal* and *campanile* and the
remains of a 12C *crypt* and of a still older

little *lower church.* The 16C frescos inside
are by G.Cambiaso. Ruins of the 12C *castle* and of the massive 16C *ramparts.*

Tagliacozzo 67069
L'Aquila/Abruzzi   p.416□ I 9

Palazzo Ducale: Work was begun by the
Orsini in the 14C. On the first floor is a
loggia with a fine coffered ceiling and 15C
frescos. The *frescos* in the *chapel* next door
are attributed to Lorenzo da Viterbo.

Also worth seeing: *S. Francesco,* 14C,
with a 16C wooden crucifix. *Piazzetta Ar-
goli* and *Piazza dell'Obelisco.*

Taormina 98039
Messina/Sicily   p.420□L 16

It was founded as 'Tauromenium' in the
4C BC on the site of an older Siculan settlement and colonized by Greeks from the
devastated town of Naxos (see below).

Cathedral of S. Nicola (Piazza del Municipio): Built in the 13C on the foundation of a former basilica, and later
repeatedly rebuilt. Beautiful façade
(*Renaissance portal* dating from 1636, *rose-*

Taormina, Teatro Greco with Etna ▷

Taormina, Palazzo dei Duchi

window). Fine portals on both flanks. Inside, a nave, two aisles, fine marble columns, and richly decorated altars (on the 2nd altar on the left is a *polyptych* by Antonello de Saliba, 1504).

Teatro Greco (Via del Teatro Greco): This is the chief object of interest in Taormina. Built in the 3C BC, and converted under the Romans (2C AD) for use in animal-baiting and gladiator fights. The diameter is 358 ft. at the widest point. The auditorium is built into the living rock in the classical Greek manner. The lower part of the stage and the *parascenia* (areas for actors to the sides of the stage), are very well preserved. The columns in front of the stage wall were added in the 19C. A double portico ran around the top of the auditorium *(cavea).* From the theatre there is a famous *view* of Etna and the coast. To the right of the theatre are a small *antiquarium* and the *remains of a small classical temple.*

Naumachia (Via Naumachia): Remains of a Roman cistern, with careful brickwork. The front is 400 ft. long.

Palazzo dei Duchi di S. Stefano (Vico Spucha): Built in Gothic style in *c.* 1330. A square ground plan, fine double-arched windows. On the ground floor there is an interesting room with a *ribbed vault* and a *central column* of granite.

Also worth seeing: 17C church of *S. Pancrazio* (reached by Via Guardiola), built on a classical temple of Sarapis. Church of *S. Caterina* (Corso Umberto I) with a fine statue of St. Catherine (1493). The former church of *S. Agostino* (Piazza 9 Aprile; today it is the *library*) dating from 1448; fine portal with a pointed arch. The Roman *odeon* (Via Teatrino Romano) from the imperial period. The Giafari district contains the remains of a Roman *aqueduct* still used today, the so-called 'Piscina Mirabile'. The Roman *baths* (near the Teatro Comunale). The 15C *Palazzo Corvaia* (Piazza Vitt. Emanuele), Gothic, with a fine façade. *Palazzo Ciampoli* (Corso Umberto I) dating from 1412, in the Catalan Gothic style (on the left side is a portal, the last remnant of a large courtyard). The 14C *Badia Vecchia*, a Gothic building to the right of the Via Dionisio Primo. *Castle.*

Environs: Some 5 km. S. is *Capo Schisò* with the excavations of the ancient town of **Naxos,** the oldest Greek settlement in Sicily (founded in 735 BC by Chalcidians from the island of Euboea). The surviving items include sections of the *town walls* (6C BC, and parts are older still; built from blocks of lava), and the *remains* of some *shrines* (especially in the S. section of the excavation site) and of some *brick kilns* from the 6C BC. Remains of houses in the N. part. Some 20 km. to the NE, high up the mountain, is **Forza d'Agrò** with the former Basilian church of the *Triade*, which is well worth seeing. It was built in Norman style in 1171/2 and has a domed campanile. Inside is a notable late-15C painting by Ant. Giuffrè ('Abraham entertaining the three archangels'). 16C ruined castle.

Taranto 74100
Taranto/Apulia   p.418☐O 12

Taranto, which is probably a Cretan foundation, was settled in 708 BC by Spartan colonists. In the 4C BC it was the most important city in Magna Graecia. It became Roman in 272 BC, then Byzantine, and was destroyed by the Saracens in the 10C. The town enjoyed a resurgence from 1080 onwards under the Normans. It later became part of the kingdom of Naples and shared its fate.

Cathedral of S.Cataldo (at the end of the Via del Duomo): Situated on the site of the ancient acropolis and of an early Christian church from the 4C. The present building was erected in 1071 on the walls of a church used as a mosque by the Saracens (it is now the crypt and is in the form of a Greek T). The dome, with its round drum, displays Byzantine influence. The three aisles were added after 1150 (the entrance being moved to the opposite side), and three bays were added in the 16&18C. Notable features inside include the *capitals* (some of them antique Corinthian) of the arcade, and the remains of the original *mosaic pavement*. The splendid late baroque *Cappella di S.Cataldo*, with the tomb of the city's patron saint (vault frescos by P.de Matteis, 1773), is at the front of the cathedral on the right. The crypt (see above) has fine 12C Byzantine frescos. *Treasury.*

National Archaeological Museum (Museo Nazionale, Corso Umberto in the new town): Together with the National Museum in Naples it is the most significant museum in southern Italy. It provides a very good impression of the culture of Magna Graecia. Apart from a *collection of early ceramics* is also has a very extensive *collection of vases* with outstanding examples of ancient pottery. Particular attention should be paid to an Attic black-figured skyphos (cup-like drinking bowl) depicting the battle between Heracles and Antaios and Hermes' theft of the cattle. Other important items: The 'Sala degli Ori' with its *ancient jewellery* (6–3C BC). The *coin collection* which includes mintings from Magna Graecia. The *sarcophagus* of the winner of the fourth Panhellenistic Games.

Also worth seeing: The late-11C *S. Domenico Maggiore* (rebuilt in 1302, Romanesque façade, baroque outdoor staircase). *Oratorio della Santissima Trinità* (Via del Duomo): the remains of an ancient temple (6C BC) in the inner courtyard are the only notable evidence of classical times in the old city. On the Canale Navigabile is the *Castello S. Angelo,* built by the Aragonese in 1480 on Byzantine, Norman and Hohenstaufen foundations. It has four wings and four round towers. In the new city, to the N. of the Mar Piccolo, are the remains of a Roman *aqueduct.*

Tarquinia 01016
Viterbo/Latium   p.414☐G 9

This town, which was founded in mythical times by Tarchon, the son or brother of Thyrrenus (Greek Thyrrhenoi = Etruscans) on the hill still called 'La Cibita', already existed at the time of the Villa Nova culture (9C BC) and developed into one of the leading Etruscan centres with a strong influence on Rome (it gave the city of Rome a royal dynasty in Lucius Tarquinius). Conquered by the Romans in 311 BC. It was a bishop's seat in the 5C AD. From the 7C onwards Corneto replaced Tarquinia, which was gradually abandoned. As a city republic, Corneto allied itself to Pisa in 1174 and took the name of Tarquinia in 1922. Apart from the Etruscan remains, the *towers* (of which there are 18, some of them partly demolished; the foundations of 20 more towers also exist) make Tarquinia one of the most interesting towns in Latium.

Palazzo Vitelleschi (Museo Nazionale Tarquiniense; Piazza Cavour): Built for Giovanni Vitelleschi in 1436–9 in a transitional style between Gothic and Renaissance. Apart from surviving decorative fragments (in the vestibule of the chapel there are 15C *frescos,* and also a

Madonna and Child by Fra Filippo Lippi, 1437), it also houses one of the most important *Etruscan collections.* The exhibits provide an impression of the Villa Nova culture (10–8C BC) until the downfall of Etruscan culture in the 2C BC. *Tomb paintings* (6–2C BC, including those from the famous Tomba 'del Triclinio'.

S. Maria di Castello: The most important medieval building in the town, constructed in 1121–1208. The façade has three portals, the middle one is by Pietro di Ranuccio Romano (1143). Basilican interior, with a nave, two aisles and a ponderous ribbed vault. The dome over the crossing fell down in the earthquake of 1819. Some important Cosmati works *remains of the floor* and the *altar ciborium* by Giovanni and Guittone Ranucci (the sons of Nicola Ranucci), 1168. The *pulpit* by Giovanni di Guittone, 1209. The octagonal *font* in the right aisle is said to have been hewn from an ancient tomb.

Also worth seeing: The medieval *cathedral,* altered in 1642, on the Piazza Duomo, with frescos (1508) by Antonio da Viterbo in the choir. The church of *S. Pancrazio* (Via S. Pancrazio) is from the transitional period between Romanesque and Gothic (13C), with three semicircular apses, decorated with a Norman zigzagged band on the outside. There is a medieval quarter around the *Palazzo dei Priori* (near S. Pancrazio).

Environs: Necropolis: *Remains of the town wall* have survived from the Etruscan Tarquinia. The *Ara della Regina,* probably a temple foundation, has a magnificent (restored) staircase. The *necropolis on the so-called 'Monterozzi',* used from archaic times until the early Roman period, with a wealth of different types of tombs. The rich *painted decorations* are particularly significant and typical of Tarquinia.

Tarvisio Alto has a **parish church** (1445), with a fine Gothic window and 15C frescos

on the façade; inside there are 15C *frescos* of the Tolmezzo school; 16C *choir stalls.* There are ancient Roman *tombstones* behind the church.

Environs: Some km. to the SW of Tarvisio is a cableway to the **Santuario di Monte Lussari** at an altitude of some 5,900 ft., a pilgrimage church mentioned as early as 1360. About 10 km. W. is **Malborghetto** with an old *fortress* and the *Palazzo Canal* (1550, Renaissance). Some 22 km. W. is **Pontebba,** where the church of *S. Maria Maggiore,* a late Gothic building dating from 1504 with a massive *campanile,* is worth seeing. (In the choir is a very fine winged altar by S. V. Maller, 1517).

Cathedral of S. Clemente (Piazza del Duomo): Built under Norman rule in 1116, rebuilt in the 17C to plans by A. Vaccaro. Restored after severe damage in World War 2. The façade has a portico and there are two granite sphinxes (from the Roman imperial period) either side of the middle portal. Ancient marble fragments on the foundation of the massive campanile. The interior is basilican with a nave, two aisles and beautiful granite columns and Corinthian capitals, some of them ancient. Two *holy-water stoups* fashioned from ancient capitals at the entrance. A fine 13C *pulpit* under the 6th arch on the right. There is a 14C painted *crucifix* by the Neapolitan artist Roberto Oderisi behind the high altar. Stairs lead from the left aisle to the *crypt of St. Paris* (a Roman *sarcophagus* at the beginning of the stairs).

Also worth seeing: Church of *S. Benedetto* (Via S. Benedetto), originally 8C, with fine ancient columns inside. 14C church of *S. Francesco* (Piazza Municipio), with rich decoration. Church of *S. Caterina,* a fine 18C baroque building. *Chiesa della Madonna della Libera* with a fine Gothic campanile. *Archbishop's palace* (near the cathedral), with many ancient spoils (including the columns either side of the portal).

The *Loggione,* a 14C building upon ancient walls. Remains of the *Roman theatre* in the *Le Grotte* quarter.

Environs: Some 10 km. SE, **Calvi Risorta:** In the Calvia Vecchia district there are the remains of the ancient town of *Cales* (theatre, amphitheatre, baths, tombs) dating from the 2C BC–1C AD.

Teggiano 84039
Salerno/Campania   p.418□M 12

Cathedral of S.Maria Maggiore: Built in the 13C on the foundations of what was probably an early Christian church. Destroyed by an earthquake in 1857. The apse bears a fine *Romanesque relief,* framed by two ancient columns. On the façade there is an interesting *portal* (1279) by Melchior of Montalbano and on the right flank there is a fine *Renaissance portal* (1509). Inside (one nave, two aisles) note: a *marble pulpit* (1271) with the symbols of the four Evangelists; next to it is an *Easter candlestick,* also by master Melchior (lion as stylophore). There are also a number of 14&15C *tombs.*

Also worth seeing: Church of *S.Andrea,* built on the remains of a classical Temple of Juno, with two fine 14C triptychs inside. Church of *S.Angelo,* built on the ruins of the classical Roman theatre (part of the ground plan survives): Inside, behind the high altar, there are four 11C Romanesque reliefs (symbols of the Evangelists); the crypt—some of its columns are ancient—is worth seeing. The church of *S. Pietro,* built into the classical Temple of Aesculapius, with the *Museo Civico* (chiefly ancient finds). *Chiesa della Pietà* with a fine Renaissance cloister. *Oratorio del'Crocifisso* with a Romanesque portal. The church of *S.Marco* (about 4 km. outside the town to the W.) with a Roman mosaic; not far from this are the remains of a *Roman bridge.*

Environs: Some 11 km. E., **Sala Consilina** with the beautiful baroque church of *S.Pietro* (1765), and the *Palazzo di Alberico Grammatico,* also baroque (1722). Some 20 km. SE, **Padula** with the well known charterhouse, the *Certosa di S.Lorenzo,* founded by Tommaso Sanseverino in 1306, and extensively altered in baroque style in the 17/18C. The church, with a portal dating from 1374, is especially worth seeing. In front of it is an atmospheric cloister. There are also the remains of a Romanesque cloister by the kitchen wing. A large cloister (about 160,000 sq. ft.) dating from 1690. The *archaeological museum of western Lucania* is today housed in the adjoining rooms.

Tempio Pausania 07029
Sássari/Sardinia   p.422□C 11

The façade, with its little campanile, of the *Oratorium S.Pietro* is the only part that is still to some extent 15C, with an Aragonese portal and Romanesque pendentives. The only features of the adjacent cathedral that are still 15C are the portal and campanile. Its interior has very fine carved wooden rococo altars (chestnut wood).

Environs: The *Nuraghe Majori* is signficant for its late form, with two chamber passages for defence. 9 km. N., and some 4 km. E. of the chapel of *S.Pietri di Ruda,* there is another unusual nuraghe, the *Nuraghe Izzana* on the sides of the Vignola valley with a triangular (!) ground plan. It has a well-preserved vault. **Calangianus:** The *parish church* has a 16C retable by A.Lusso. On Monte Deo there are *tombe di giganti* and a nuraghe of the same name. Both these are built of layers of flat granite splinters.

Teramo 64100
Teramo/Abruzzi   p.416□I 8

Cathedral of S. Assunta and S. Bernardo:
The new cathedral was erected in 1158 on the site of a building pulled down in 1155, and a new, larger choir was added to it in the 14C. It was altered in baroque style in 1739, but these changes were

removed in 1932-5. The lower part of the façade dates from the 12C, while its upper section and the portal, which includes an inscription for Diodatus Romanus dated 1332, are 14C; the Archangel Gabriel and the Madonna of the Annunciation are the work of the goldsmith Nicola da Guardiagrele. In the transept there is an *aedicule* by Antonio da Lodi, dated 1493. The raised choir has a masterpiece by Nicola da Guardiagregle, the silver *antependium* executed for Giosia de Acquaviva in 1433 -48: in the middle it shows Christ blessing, surrounded by the Evangelists and Church Fathers, and at the sides, in four rows one below another, we see: Christ's childhood, Christ's works, the Passion and, at the very bottom, scenes from the time between the Entombment and the Coming of the Holy Spirit; the enamels on the intersections between the individual reliefs show Apostles and Prophets. On the right wall is the *polyptych* by Jacobello del Fiore, dated 1450. There is a painting by Seb. Maieski, 1622, in the *sacristy*.

Also worth seeing: A *Roman theatre* and an *amphitheatre* to the SE of the cathedral. A Madonna attributed to Silvestro dell' Aquila in the church of *S. Madonna delle Grazie. S. Getulio* has the remains of the old cathedral.

Terlano/Terlan 39018
Bolzano/South Tyrol-Trentino   p.410☐F 1

Parish church of the Assumption: This town on the Adige harbours a real gem in its parish church (originally 13C, enlarged, extended, and expanded anew in the 14C). The *Coronation of the Virgin*, which was originally above the W. portal and now stands on the N. side altar, is from the school of Pacher (1380). Some captivating features of the interior are the fine *groin vaults and the wall paintings* (late 14C; those on the E. wall of the side aisle are *c.* 1450) which decorate all the inside walls and the ceiling. The larger *campanile*, located opposite the small Romanesque campanile, was rebuilt in 1891-3 to the old design and with the old materials.

Also worth seeing: *The Maultasch ruins* from the 12-16C.

Environs: Settequerce/Siebeneich (2 km. from Terlano in the direction of Bolzano): The pretty little baroque church of *St.Anton* by the Deutschhaushof courtyard was built by Johann and Peter Delai (1689-98). The altar with columns (1699) is from the workshop of Cristoforo Benedetti. 5 km. NW of Terlano, towards Merano, is *Vilpian*, from where the road leads SW to **Nalles/Nals** with the 13C *Schwanburg* castle, rebuilt in the 16C. From Vilpian we can also climb to the picturesque little village of *Meltina/Mölten*, the Roman Maletum. *Parish church of St. Maria* and *Church of St.Anna* with Gothic sculptures.

Termini Imerese 90018
Palermo/Sicily   p.420☐I 16

Cathedral of S.Nicola di Bari (Piazza Duomo): The original structure was rebuilt in the 17C. The façade is modern (completed in 1912), and there are niches with *figures of Apostles* from a Renaissance altar (early 16C). Ancient fragments are incorporated in the campanile. Inside (one nave, two aisles), there are fine Renaissance pieces on the altars (including a *wooden crucifix* dating from 1511 in the 6th chapel on the left).

Villa Palmieri (entrance in Via Garibaldi): A garden with remnants of the Roman town *(Basilica, Curia);* the Via Anfiteatro, with remains of the ancient *amphitheatre* (it formerly held 4,000 spectators), begins here.

Museo Civico (Via del Museo): The *collection of antiquities,* with finds from Himera, is worth seeing.

Also worth seeing: *S. Maria della Misericordia* (Via Mazzini), baroque, with a fine Renaissance triptych by Gaspare da Pesaro, 1453. *Belvedere Principe Umberto* (reached by the Via Belvedere), built on the site of the ancient forum, with remains of the old *castle* (splendid view). *Riparo del Castello* (below the castle), with Stone Age excavations. *Baths* (Piazza Bagni), built on Roman and Arab foundations.

Environs: Some 15 km. to the E. are the remains of the ancient town of **Himera/Imera** (near *Buonfornello*) to the left of the railway: Founded in 648 BC by Messina, it was the most westerly Greek colony on the N. coast of Sicily. The poet Stesichorus (*c.* 640–555 BC) lived here for many years. The site of the famous victory of the Greeks over the Carthaginians in 480 BC, it was destroyed by Carthage in 409 BC. The items excavated include the remains of a *Doric temple* (with a peripteros of 6 by 14 columns, 184 ft. by 72 ft.; built after 480 BC as a token of victory in the above-mentioned battle). Some 11 km. S. is **Cáccamo** with a splendidly situated 12C *castle* (the 'Hall of Conspiracy' is worth seeing. It was here, in 1160, that the barons rebelled against the Norman king William I). The cathedral, originally Norman, (1090; in the right transept, reliefs attributed to Fr.Laurana; the marble portal leading to the sacristy is probably by Dom. Gagini).

Teramo, cathedral

Termoli 86309

Campobasso/Molise   p.416 □ L 9

Cathedral of S.Basso: Built in the 6C on the ruins of a Roman temple, repeatedly rebuilt—most recently in the 18C—and restored in 1932–5. The *façade* was built by Alfano da Termoli in the mid-12C, while the top section dates from the 15C. The crypt has a 10&11C *mosaic pavement.*

Also worth seeing: the *castle* built by Frederick II.

Terni 05100

Terni/Umbria   p.414 □ H 8

Probably founded by the Sabines, and called Interamna Nahartium by the Romans, Terni played an important part in the early history of Umbria. However, as a result of its position in the plain and the danger of epidemics (it was in a malarial region), the town's historical and economic development was much hampered in the past. Terni, the former 'Cinderella of Umbria', did not come into its own until the late 19C. Today the town is an important industrial centre. Terni's hydroelectric power stations (Galletto, Monteargento, Recentino, Papigno-Velino, Cervara, delle Marmore, Nera Montoro, Papigno-Penna Rossa) form the largest interconnected hydroelectric system in the Italian peninsula. The town's coat of arms is a pictorial representation of the town's past: a hero slaying a dragon whose poisonous breath is polluting the town.

S.Francesco: This Gothic-Romanesque church was begun in 1265 and enlarged in the 15C. The campanile (1445) was designed by Angelo da Orvieto. Inside, the

Terlano, parish church, portal

Cáccamo (Termini Imerese), castle

Paradisi chapel was decorated by Bartolomeo di Tommaso da Foligno in the 15C.

S. Salvatore: This church consists of a rotunda, a portico and the Manassei chapel. The history of the rotunda is unclear. Some regard it as a Roman temple dedicated to the sun, while others consider it to be a building from the pre-Christian period. The most recent opinions are that it is 11C. Whatever the case, considerable remains of a Roman building have been brought to light underneath the church. The portico is 12C. Inside, the Manassei chapel has frescos by an Umbrian artist of the first half of the 14C, and also a Crucifixion attributed to a pupil of Giannicola di Paolo (early 16C).

S. Pietro: It has a fine apse with a polygonal ground plan and Gothic windows. The campanile dates from 1430. Inside there are remains of 13&14C Umbrian frescos. The best of these is possibly the Dormitio Virginis by an unknown early-15C artist.

Cathedral: Originally Romanesque, it has been frequently altered over the centuries. Inside there is a fine crypt. The organ was built to a design by Bernini.

S. Lorenzo: This church was built in the 13C above a Roman building (Temple of Mars?) and enlarged in the 17C. Note the graceful façade.

Roman amphitheatre: Built by order of Faustus Titius Liberalis in AD 32. It held ten thousand spectators.

Palazzo Spada: This is the last work of Antonio da Sangallo the younger, who died in Terni in 1546. This severe building, which resembles a fortress, reflects Terni's insecure past. The halls inside are decorated with frescos from the 16–19C. The most important of these are those by the Zuccari brothers in the main salon.

Also worth seeing: *Palazzo Bianchini-Riccardi*, by A.da Sangallo, *Palazzo Mazzancolle* (14C), *Palazzo Montani* (17C) and the *Carrara, Gazzoli* and *Manassei* palaces from the 18C. The Palazzo Carrara houses the prehistoric and archaeological collection, and also the town's picture gallery, which includes works by Giovanni Spagna, Domenico Alfani, Francesco Melanzio, Arrigo Fiammingo, and Gerolamo Troppa. The Marriage of St.Catherine by Benozzo Gozzoli (1466), and a Crucifixion by Niccolò Alunno are outstanding.

Environs: Carsulae is regarded as the most important archaeological centre in Umbria for Roman finds. The town is mentioned by Tacitus and Pliny the Younger, and reached its zenith in the 1-3C AD, being destroyed by the Goths in the 6C. The sights are: the triple *archway*, of which only the middle vault survives, the *forum* with two twin temples, the *basilica* of the forum, the *amphitheatre*, the *theatre*, a massive building with a circular ground plan, the ancient *Via Flaminia*, and remnants of domestic buildings. There is also the very interesting church of *S.Damiano*, built in the early Middle Ages on the Roman ruins. *Sangemini:* Known for its mineral water springs. *S.Francesco:* This church with its fine Gothic portal was built in the 15C. Inside are frescos from the 15&17C. *Palazzo del Popolo:* In the medieval quarter, with a picturesque tower and a fine flight of steps. *Oratorio di S.Carlo:* With two notable Umbrian frescos from the first half of the 15C, and also a 14C ciborium. *S.Giovanni:* A parish church with a fine façade and Romanesque portal, as well as mosaics. *S.Niccolò* (privately owned) contains the only known fresco by Rogerio da Todi (1295). **Cesi:** This medieval village lies among olive groves. The church of *S.Maria* houses an interesting local work, a panel of the Madonna and Child with Angels and Saints by the Maestro di Cesi (1308). The small 11C Romanesque church of *S.Angelo*, partly altered in the 13C, is also of interest. There are Roman fragments in the walls of the former Romanesque church of *S.Andrea* (1160). *S.Antonio:* This church has a fresco by Giovanni di Giovannello di Paulello from Narni. On **S.Erasmo** are an old polygonal wall and the 12C church of *S. Erasmo*. **Cascata delle Marmore:** A waterfall 7.5 km. E. of the town, drops a total of 540 ft. The beautiful play of the water is the work of the Consul Manius Curius Dentatus, who dammed the waters of the river Velino in 271 BC and channelled them into the bed of the Nera in order to prevent the area from becoming a swamp. **Lago di Piediluco:** Surrounded by greenery, this lake is well off the beaten track. The village of the same name has a 14C *castle* and the 13C church of *S. Francesco* with 14C paintings. **Stroncone:** A picturesque, small medieval town with fine view of the Terni valley, and an imposing baroque fountain in its main square. **Otricoli:** The 13C church of *S. Maria* has been almost completely rebuilt. Inside is a painting attributed to Rinaldo da Calvi. Note the ruins of a Roman *amphitheatre* and baths. The famous Zeus of Otricoli, now in the Vatican Museums, was discovered here in the 18C. Otricoli was originally an Umbrian foundation; and was called Ocriculum by the Romans.

Terracina 04019

Latina/Latium   p.416☐I 10

Cathedral of S. Cesario: Built on the former forum (today the Piazza del Municipio) opposite the *ruins of the temple of the triad of gods* Jupiter, Juno and Minerva (three cellae; 1C BC) and on the site of a Temple of Rome and Augustus (used as an early Christian church). Consecrated in 1074, altered in the 12C and (inside) in the 18C. The *façade* stands at the top of 18 temple steps with a portico of 6 ancient columns resting on Romanesque lions. Decorated with a 12C Sicilian-Norman mosaic frieze. 13C *campanile*. An *ancient sarcophagus* in the portico. The interior, with its nave and two aisles, was altered in the 18C. The original 13C *floor*, the *Easter candlestick*, and the *pulpit* with its lion columns dating from 1245 (all Cosmati work) have survived.

Also worth seeing: The *Chiesetta dell' Annunziato* stands by the ascent to the Temple of Jupiter. Cistercian Gothic style; there are 13C frescos inside. At the heart

Tivoli, Villa d'Este, park

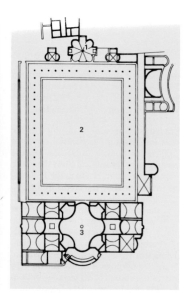

Tivoli, Villa Adriana, Piazza d'Oro 1 vestibule **2** courtyard with peristyle **3** central room

of the modern town hall is the *Torre Frumentaria*, a medieval tower, which houses the interesting *Archaeological Museum*.

Environs: Temple of Jupiter Anxur on *Monte S.Angelo* (3 km. by car). Enormous foundations, which the visitor can walk through (the intersecting tunnel vaults are an early form of groin vault), including the entrance to the former oracle, an extensive terrace on which there stood a temple cella measuring 46 ft. by 43 ft. The *remains of ancient ramparts* around the former temple complex.

Tindari 98060

Messina/Sicily   p.420□ L 16

The visitor first drives to the famous **shrine of the Black Virgin of Tindari,** a Byzantine work which is venerated as miraculous. The church is possibly the site of the ancient acropolis of Tyndaris (see below) and there is a *portal* of 1598 with unusual sculptures. From the church the way leads over the Via Teatro Greco to the excavations of the ancient town of **Tyndaris** in a magnificent position above the sea: founded by Syracuse in 396 BC, its population came from Messina. The reason for the town's downfall is not known. Remnants of the Hellenistic-Roman town survive and have been excavated: *Greek theatre* (3/2C BC, 28 rows of seats, diameter of 207 ft.) rebuilt by the Romans for gladiator combats and animal-baiting. The so-called *gymnasium*, a forum basilica from the late imperial period (82 ft. by 89 ft., originally three-storeyed). Remains of *paved roads* and *houses*. A *bath* (3C BC, with fine pavement mosaics). Significant remains of the *town walls* (the so-called 'Mura Greche', especially on the road lead-

Tivoli, Villa Adriana

ing to the shrine and along the Via Teatro Greco). A *museum* at the entrance to the excavation site proper.

Environs: Patti (about 10 km. E). *Cathedral of S.Bartolomeo:* Built in the 18C in a dominant position above the town. In the right transept, by the wall, is the sarcophagus of Adelaide of Montferrat (d. 1118), the mother of the Norman king Roger I. A Madonna by Antonello de Saliba.

Tivoli 00019
Rome/Latium   p.414□H 9

Roman historians describe the ancient Tibur as a town of the Siculi. It was Roman in 380 BC, and flourished under Hadrian. It was an independent imperial

city from the Middle Ages until 1816, and was then part of the Papal States. It is an old bishop's seat.

Cathedral: Only the 12C portico and the campanile survive from the Romanesque building. The pillared basilica (one nave, two aisles) was rebuilt in *c.* 1650. The 13C *Deposition* in the 4th chapel on the right, and the 12C *triptych* with the Redeemer seated between Mary and John in the 3rd chapel on the left, are outstanding.

Villa d'Este: This site, originally occupied by a Benedictine monastery, was acquired by Cardinal Ippolito d'Este (the son of Duke Alfonso and Lucrezia Borgia) in 1550 and converted into one of the most important Mannerist villas. Pirro Ligorio probably began building it *c.* 1560. Alterations were made in later centuries. After 1803 it was owned by the Austrian Habsburg- Este (until 1914 it belonged to

Franz Ferdinand, the heir to the throne who was murdered in Sarajevo). It has been Italian State property since 1918. The long, three-storeyed palace, with its two-storeyed front on the town side, is decorated with frescos by L.Agresti, the two Zuccari, and others. However, these are of less significance than the Mannerist *garden*.

Temple of Vesta (Via della Sibilla): A round temple from the 2C BC. 10 of its original total of 18 Corinthian columns have survived. The incorrect designation 'Temple of Sibyl' actually applies to the neighbouring rectangular temple, which has a portico with four Ionic columns. The round temple was a frequent subject of paintings from the period around 1800.

Villa Gregoriana (Largo S.Angelo): Built on the original course of the Aniene, whose waters were diverted through two rock tunnels *(Traforo Gregoriano)* in 1826–35, owing to the floods. From here waterfalls drop a total of 520 ft. The two upper terraces of the park offer a good view of the *Cascata grande* (350 ft.). In the park are the *Sirens' grotto* and the *grotto of Neptune*.

Also worth seeing: Church of *S.Giovanni Evangelista* (Viale Trieste. The choir has a fresco cycle attributed to Antoniazzo Romano. There are 12/13C frescos in the apse of the Romanesque church of *S. Silvestro*.

Environs: Villa Adriana (about 6 km. to the S.: A sumptuous villa which the Emperor Hadrian ordered to be built for himself from AD 125 onwards on the plain in front of the Sabine hills. Apart from the service buildings, the villa comprised temples, nymphaea, sporting facilities, a theatre, a library, a round hall for lectures and discussions, gardens and fish ponds. The complex fell into disrepair after the time of Constantine, and was used as a quarry in the Middle Ages. Systematic excavation of the site, which has belonged to the Italian State since 1870, only began in 1950. Since the Renaissance, the ruined villa has stimulated the imagination of architects. The most interesting sections include the *Piazza d'Oro* (an open colonnaded hall with attached garden rooms, around a courtyard), and the so-called *Teatro Marittimo* (a circular villa on an artificial island surrounded by a moat).

Todi, cathedral

The *'Canopo'* (the statues, discovered in 1950-5, are in the *museum* adjoining the villa). The canal is a replica of the one at the Sanctuary of Serapis in Egypt and leads to the *Serapeum*. **Tomb of the Plautii:** 2 km. from the Villa Adriana, on the *Via Tiburtina* and beside the Ponte Lucano over the Aniene, this is a round tomb in the manner of that of Caecilia Metella on the Via Appia Antica (1C). Inscriptions refer to the Plautii, a family of Etruscan origin.

Todi 06059
Perugia / Umbria   p.414 □ G 8

This beautifully situated little town offers an extensive view of the Umbrian countryside. Todi was originally founded by the Etruscans (Etruscan: tular, border and tud, community, town), then became Roman (Tuder), and was a flourishing free commune in the Middle Ages. Todi was the home town of the mystical poet Iacopone da Todi.

Piazza del Popolo: This square is one of

the finest in Italy—a miracle of urban architecture.

Palazzo del Popolo: This, the oldest palace (13C), together with the Palazzo del Capitano del Popolo, forms the present town hall. It was built by Lombard artists. The fine staircase should be noted.

Palazzo del Capitano: Built in the last decade of the 13C, it is rather Gothic in character. The museum and picture gallery (opening hours: In summer: 9 a.m.–12 noon; 4 p.m.–6 p.m. In winter: 10 a.m.–12 noon; 3 p.m.–6 p.m.) are housed in the present *Palazzo Comunale*. The museum has Etruscan and Roman collections. The picture gallery includes works by Giovanni Spagna (Coronation of the Virgin) and Giambologna (Deposition).

Palazzo dei Priori: Begun in 1283, the palace was continued in the 14C. Pope Leo X had the Renaissance windows built in 1513. The eagle (the town's symbol), which dates from 1339 and is the work of Giovanni Gigliacci, may be seen on the façade.

Todi, Palazzo del Popolo

Cathedral: Begun by Lombard artists in the 12C, it was repeatedly redesigned up until the 17C. The interior is basilican, but is nevertheless distinguished by its severe Gothic style. It has a Gothic high altar with a cross, and the fresco on the inside of the façade depicts the 'Last Judgement' by Ferraù da Faenza who was influenced by Michelangelo. The apse has fine 16C choir stalls by the brothers Antonio and Sebastiano Bencivenni, who came from the Marches. The adjoining small museum has 14C statues of the Pisan school. There are some very fine Gothic capitals in the cathedral.

S. Fortunato: Begun in 1292, building dragged on into the 15C. This hall church is considered to be the finest in Umbria (the other two are S. Domenico and S. Lorenzo in Perugia). The fine, though incomplete, façade is original and was built by Santuccio da Fiorenzuola from Spoleto and Bartolo d'Angelo. The three portals, with the central one being outstanding, are faced with marble and are reminiscent of

Todi, S.Fortunato 1 choir stalls 2 tomb of Jacopone 3 Masolino da Panicale

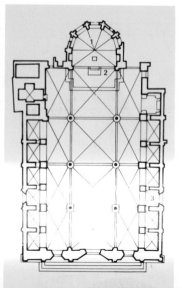

the cathedral in Orvieto. Inside: 'Madonna and Child' (on the right) by Masolino da Panicale; fine choir stalls by Antonio Maffei from Gubbio; tomb of Iacopone da Todi (1230–1300) in the crypt.

S. Maria della Consolazione: Located a little way out of the centre of town, this is the most unusual building in Umbria and is a supreme achievement of the regional style. The church is attributed to Bramante (begun in 1508 and completed in 1607). It is reminiscent of the splendour of the great 16&17C churches. However, the impression is tempered by the serene, simple Umbrian countryside. The interior is majestic and luminous. Apart from Bramante, other artists working on this church were Cola di Caprarola and Lombard artists collaborating with Sangallo, Vignola, Alessi and Scalza.

Also worth seeing: *Palazzo Atti* (1552). The church of the *Crocifisso* by G.D.Bianchi and Ippolito Scalza. The fountain of *Scarnabecco* with arcades (1241) by Podestà Scarnabecco from Bologna. The very well-preserved medieval *town wall* extending from the church of the *Consolazione* as far as the Porta Romana. The 11C church of *S. Niccolò* is the oldest religious building in Todi and was built on the ruins of a Roman amphitheatre. The apse of this church connects it to the adjoining 14C church. The church of *S. Filippo Benizzi* is octagonal and was built during the Renaissance. The portal dates from the baroque. *S. Ilario* was consecrated in 1249. The campanile is in the Umbrian Romanesque style. The remains of an Etruscan town wall can still be seen within the Roman town wall.

Tolentino 62029
Macerata/Marches   p.414☐I 7

Cathedral: The new building dates from around 1830, with a medieval campanile. Inside, a 15C German *Pietà* survives from

Tolentino, S. Nicola ▷

the previous building, as does the *inlay work* of the old choir stalls built in 1426. Behind the altar, on 13C columns, there is an *early Christian sarcophagus* from the 4C AD, where the relics of Catervo and Settima, the city's patron and his wife, are preserved. On the front there are reliefs of the Good Shepherd, Peter and Paul, and the Magi.

S. Nicola da Tolentino: St. Nicholas of Tolentino, the Augustinian hermit, lived here from 1275 until his death in 1305. After his canonization in 1446, the church, originally dedicated to St. George, was renamed in 1476. The 13C structure was rebuilt in the 16C, the apse was added in 1510 and the side chapels in 1503–1634, while the façade dates from 1628 and was increased in height in 1757–67. The *portal* by Nanni di Bartolo, showing St. George and the Madonna between St. Augustine and St. Nicholas of Tolentino, is signed and dated 1432. The interior decorations are 16C, the ceiling is from 1628, while the apse and the chapel of the sacrament were decorated in the 19&20C. On the right of the 1st chapel is a *St. Anne* by Guercino, there is a 14C *recumbent Madonna* in the

4th chapel, and on the left of the 4th chapel is a 15C *stucco relief of the Madonna*. The chapel of St. Nicholas has a *sarcophagus* installed in 1474, and its walls are covered by an outstanding *fresco cycle* by a painter from Rimini. Completed in 1348, it shows the life of St. Nicholas. Above, there is a Life of Christ, probably by Giovanni Baronzio. There are scenes from the Life of the Virgin in the lunettes, and Evangelists, Church Fathers, and Virtues are depicted in the vault. The arms of the Saint were venerated in the *Cappella delle SS. Braccia*, a 15C extension of the old sacristy. In 1926 the arms were placed in the crypt with the other mortal remains. The statues in the niches are symbolical, and the paintings depict miracles. The miracle in Genoa was painted by Carracini, and that in Venice by Matthias Stomer. The 13C *cloister* was rebuilt beside the church in 1640–7, and the frescos are also 17C. There is an *oratory* on the E. side.

Environs: Chiaravalle di Fiastra: A Cistercian abbey founded in 1142. A typical Cistercian church with a rectangular choir and plain capitals. The vault reveals a change in plan: work began on a tunnel

Torcello, S. Fosca

vault, but from the end of the 13C onwards a ribbed vault was built.

Tolmezzo 33028
Udine/Friuli   p.410☐H 2

This, the main town in NW Friuli (Carnia), was fortified because of its position on the road to Carinthia. In the Middle Ages it was a commune under the Patriarchs of Aquileia. It became Venetian in 1420. Art historians know it for the 'school of Tolmezzo' (15/16C; its most important representatives were Giovanni Martini and G.da Tolmezzo, 1450–1510).

Cathedral of S.Martino (Piazza XX Settembre): A single-aisled hall church built in the 18C, with a modern façade. Notable contents: *Renaissance holy-water stoup* to the right of the entrance (16C, B.da Bissone). On the walls there is a fine *picture cycle* by Nicolò Grassi (1682–1748).

Museo Carnico delle Arti e Tradizioni populari (in the *Palazzo della Comunità Carnica,* Piazza Garibaldi): A rich collection of regional folklore and applied arts.

Environs: About 10 km. N., **Zúglio,** the capital of Carnia in Roman times. The *ancient excavations* to the NE of the village are especially worth seeing: remains of the forum with basilica and temple (1C AD). Further excavations are still in progress (baths in the district of *Vieris;* a temple, probably from the Republican period, in the district of *Ciamo Taront;* an early Christian basilica, with remains of the pavement mosaic, in the *Ciampon* district. Also worth seeing to the NW of the village, on the Monte S.Pietro, is the 7C church of *S.Pietro;* inside is a magnificent carved altar by Domenico da Tolmezzo (school of Tolmezzo, 15C).

Torcello 30100 Venezia
Venice/Veneto   p.410 ☐G 3

To the NE of Venice, in the extreme N. of the lagoon, is the island of Torcello. Colonized in the 7C, it was of great importance in the 9–14C and was independent until the 14C when it lost its power to Venice. The island fell into oblivion in the 18C, when the diocesan seat was moved

Torcello, Palazzo del Consiglio

Torcello, cathedral with S.Fosca

from Torcello to Burano. The chief feature is the Piazza (10 minutes' walk from the landing place) with its monumental buildings: S.Fosca, the cathedral of S.Maria Assunta with its campanile, the Palazzo dell' Archivio and the Palazzo del Consiglio. The last two are today used as museums.

Cathedral of S. Maria Assunta: The church was founded by Ravenna in 639. Some remains of the round baptistery built

Turin, cathedral **1** mausoleum of Giovanni d'Orliè de la Balme, around 1493 **2** Madonna and Child, painted terracotta, mid-14C, on the altar **3** chapel of SS.Crispian and Crispiniano **4** Madonna with Saints, painting by Bartolomeo Caravoglia, around 1665, on the altar **5** Birth of Christ, painting by Giovanni Comandù, 1795 **6** marble bust of Domenico della Rovere, founder of the church **7** entrance to sacristy **8** high altar **9** chapel of the Holy Shroud (Cappella della S.Sindone), built by G. Guarini **10** altar with the Holy Shroud, by Antonio Bertola

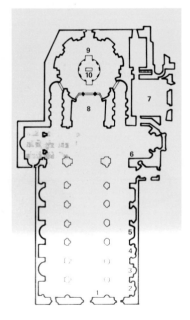

at that time are today to be found in the W. front of the church. In the 9C the crypt that still survives today was built, as were the two side apses. The cathedral was enlarged in the 11C by the addition of a new building. The cathedral structure is a colonnaded basilica with a tall nave, two aisles and an open roof truss, but no transept. The building is supported inside by marble columns with very fine capitals. An interesting *iconostasis*, which probably dates from the 11C and whose lower section bears large, excellently carved Byzantine reliefs (the slab with the pair of peacocks is especially fine). Again in the 11C, the floor of the church was inlaid with geometric patterns. However, the *mosaics* are the church's main attraction. The early-13C Madonna and Child is in the central apse above the apostles (12C). In the S.part of the choir there is a mosaic based on those in San Vitale in Ravenna, but probably 12 or 13C. On the W. wall there is a mosaic arranged as six rows of pictures depicting Christ in Judgement. Most of it probably dates from the 2nd half of the 12C. In 1929, all the baroque additions were removed from the altar which was restored to its original 7C condition. There is a synthronon arranged around the bishop's throne. The holy-water stoup by the main portal probably dates from *c.* 1100. The campanile is 11C.

S. Fosca: This cruciform, centrally planned brick building was erected in the 11C as a church in memory of St.Fosca, who was martyred in Ravenna. A portico borne by columns was added at the front in the 12C. The central area of the plain interior is a cube but appears round. The ceiling is flat. The area is bounded by eight columns with fine capitals, behind which there are niches. The sanctuary occupies the triple apse to the E. The modern altar by S.Fosca dates from 1935, and the figure of the recumbent Saint on the S.side of the church from 1407.

Museo dell'Estuario: This museum contains some important paintings, sculptures and pieces of handicraft etc., from classical times up to the 16C. It is housed in the Palazzo dell'Archivio and the Palazzo del

Consiglio, which date mainly from the 13&14C.

Torino/Turin 10100
Turin/Piedmont   p.412□B 4

Turin, the capital of Piedmont, is the fourth largest city in Italy after Rome, Milan and Naples; and its large car factories give it considerable economic importance. The centre, with its regular grid of streets, betrays the Roman origin of the city, which is now dominated by the baroque buildings of G.Guarini and F.Juvarra, and by tall modern ones. In ancient times Turin was the Celto-Ligurian settlement of Taurasia, which was destroyed by Hannibal. Augustus enlarged it into the legionary base camp of Augusta Taurinorum. It was later the main town of a Lombard duchy; and then, from 800 onwards, the seat of a Frankish margravate. From the 11C it was in the hands of the counts of Savoy. During this period it was of little importance, but this began to change when Turin, after the departure of the French who had held it since 1502, became the residence of the house of Savoy in 1562. Savoy fought the French again when it opposed Louis XIV in the War of the Spanish Succession from 1706 onwards. In 1720 Turin became the capital of the so-called kingdom of Sardinia, and after the Napoleonic wars it became the focal point of Italy's endeavours to achieve unity, which were promoted by Camillo Benso, Count of Cavour (1810–61), who came from Turin. In 1861–5, Turin was the capital and the seat of the court of the kingdom of Italy.

S.Giovanni Battista, the Cathedral (Via XX Settembre): Built by the Florentine artist Meo dei Caprina in 1492 – 8 in Renaissance style. The *marble façade* has three sculpted portals. The free-standing *campanile* beside and to the left of the façade dates from 1470, and was completed by F.Juvarra in 1720. The interior (one nave, two aisles) is very simple apart from the decoration of the side chapels. There is an *altarpiece* by Defendente Ferrari in the 2nd chapel of the right aisle. Behind the high altar is the *Cappella della SS.Sindone*, a circular room with a tall dome by G.Guarini, 1694. The white *monuments to the house of Savoy*, which King Charles Albert erected in 1842 for four of his ancestors, contrast with the dark brown marble of the chapel. The coffin-like urn above the altar contains the so-called *shroud of Turin*. This was brought from Cyprus to Chambéry in 1452 and has been preserved in Turin since 1578. Tradition has it that it was Christ's burial shroud (with impressions of his body and face).

Santuario della Consolata (Via Consolata): An image of the Virgin Mary has been preserved in this shrine of the Virgin since the time of St. Maximius (4C). G.Guarini built the baroque church in 1679–1703, and its *interior decoration* is by F.Juvarra, 1714. The classical façade, with its portal borne by four columns, dates from 1860. Beside the shrine is the only *Romanesque campanile* in Turin. Dating from the 11C, it was formerly part of S. Andrea, the church of the Benedictine monastery. The monastery was occupied from 942 onwards, but is ruined today. Inside the church are the *marble statues of Queen Maria Teresa* and *Queen Maria Adelaide* by V.Vela, 1861.

S. Lorenzo (Piazza Castello): Begun in 1634, from 1660 the work was supervised by G.Guarini and is his main achievement. The hall-like *interior* has a splendid *dome*. The choir, with its fine *high altar*, has a smaller dome. The first altar in the main area has a *Crucifixion* by Andrea Pozzo, 1677–9. Fine intarsia *choir stalls*, 1730, by Carlo Maria Ugliengo.

Other churches: *SS. Martiri* (Via Garibaldi): The most splendid church in Turin, begun by Pellegrino Tibaldi in 1577. The *frescos* of the single-aisled interior were renovated by Luigi Vacca in 1836. The *frescos* by A.Pozzo on both sides of the organ are original, however. *S. Filippo Neri* (Via Maria Vittoria): with a mid-19C classical entrance hall in the Corinthian style by Giuseppe Talucchi. Work on the church to Guarini's plans continued from 1679 onwards, and was completed by Juvarra in 1714. The *oratory of S. Filippo*, a design by Juvarra, stands beside the church. *S. Massimo* (Via S. Massimo): A single-aisled neoclassical church by Carlo Sada. *S. Croce* (Piazza Carlo Emanuele II): a single-aisled structure, built in 1718 – 30 to a design by Juvarra, with a baroque *campanile*. The classical façade is mid-19C. The most important feature is the painting of the *Deposition* by Claudio Francesco Beaumont, 1731. *S. Pelagia* (beside and to the left of S. Croce): Built in 1770 to drawings by Nicolis di Robilant. *SS. Annunziata* (Via Po): Built by Carlo Morello in 1919–29 on the site of a baroque building. *Chiesa della Gran Madre di Dio* (Piazza Gran Madre di Dio): Neoclassical building by Ferdinando Bonsignore, 1818–31. *S. Maria del Monte* (Monte dei Cappuccini): Built by Ascanio Vittozzi in 1583–96, baroque interior. *S. Domenico* (Via Milano): Significant Gothic church dating from the 14&15C, with a nave and two aisles. The *campanile* was built in 1451. The *chapel of the rosary* has a painting of the Virgin of the rosary by Guercino. *Basilica Magistrale dei SS. Maurizio e Lazzaro* or *Basilica Mauriziana*, built by Carlo Emanuele Lanfranchi in 1679. The neoclassical façade is by Carlo Bernardo Mosca, 1835–6. *S. Agostino* (Via S. Agostino), built in 1555–1642, altered in baroque style in 1758. *Chiesa del Carmine* (Via del Carmine). The single-aisled interior, 1732–5, is by F. Juvarra. The façade dates from 1873. *S. Francesco da Paola* (Via Po): Early baroque church with Mannerist features. Founded by Madama Reale Maria Cristina in 1632 – 4. *S. Cristina* (Piazza S. Carlo): Single-aisled church by Carlo di Castellamonte, begun in 1637; the *front* is by Juvarra. *S. Carlo* (Piazza S. Carlo): A single-aisled church, built from 1619 onwards; the *façade* repeats the architectural motifs of S. Cristina. Ferdinando Caronesi was the builder. The *relief in the tympanum* is by Stefano Buti, and the *campanile* dates from 1779. *S. Teresa* (Via S. Teresa): This single-aisled church, whose ground plan is a Latin cross, was built in 1642–74 to a design by Andrea Castaguta. The façade was built in 1764, while the decorations date from 1878. The *tomb of Maria Cristina di Fran-*

cia is in the first chapel, and the *4th chapel* was built to a plan by Juvarra. *Chiesa della Visitazione* (Via XX Settembre), ground plan in the form of a Greek cross, built by Francesco Lanfranchi from 1660 onwards, with fine decoration inside. *S. Francesco d'Assisi* (Via S. Francesco), single-aisled, built in 1608 above a Romanesque structure. The façade and dome date from 1761. *SS. Trinità* (Via Garibaldi): Classical façade of 1830, circular ground plan, built in 1590–1606 to a design by Ascanio Vittozzi, and the *fresco in the dome* is by Francesco Gonin and Luigi Vacca, 1844–7. *Chiesa del Corpus Domini* (Via Palazzo di Città): A single-aisled church, begun by Ascanio Vittozzi in 1607–9, completed from 1609 –71. Marble *interior decoration* by B. Alfieri, 1753, *frescos* by Luigi Vacca, 1853. Beside this is the *Chiesa dello Spirito Santo* (Via Porta Palatina), built by Ascanio Vittozzi in 1610 and rebuilt by Feroggio in 1764– 7. In the *chapel of the Crucifixion* there is a wooden Crucifixion, the work of Stefano Maria Clemente.

Palazzo Madama (Piazza Castello): Its core is a medieval castle. Enlarged in 1416 by adding two sixteen-cornered towers built above the tower of the Roman E. gate, the Porta Decumana. In 1718, Madama Reale Maria, the widow of Charles Emanuel II, commissioned Filippo Juvarra (1678–1736) to build the *double staircase* and *W. façade*, which are among the most magnificent of their kind anywhere.

Palazzo Reale (Piazza Castello): The royal castle is a brick building erected in 1646–58. The pillars of the iron grille of the courtyard bear the bronze *equestrian statues of Castor and Pollux* by Abbondio Sangiorgio, 1842. By the staircase there is a fine work showing *Duke Victor Amadeus on horseback,* and also various other *statues of Savoy princes.*

Palazzo Carignano (Piazza Carignano): Built in 1680 by G. Guarini for the princes of Carignano, it has a *brick façade* divided into an upper and lower part. King Vic-

Roman gate and Roman theatre

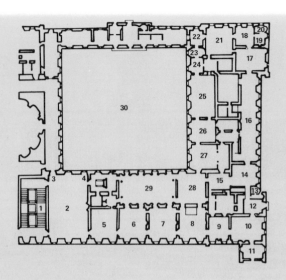

Turin, Palazzo Reale 1 staircase **2** Swiss Salon **3** entrance to Cappella della S.Sindone **4** pincer staircase (Scala delle Forbici) **5** room of the lifeguards (Sala delle Guardie del Corpo) **6** room of the footmen (Sala degli Staffieri) **7** pages' room (Sala dei Paggi) **8** throne room (Sala del Trono del Re) **9** private audience room (Sala delle Udienze Private) **10** council room (Sala del Consiglio) **11** Chinese cabinet (Gabinetto Cinese) **12** Charles Albert's bedroom (Camera da Letto di C.A.) **13** chapel (Pregadio di Carlo Alberto) **14** breakfast room (Sala della Colazione) **15** landscape room (Saletta di Paesagio) **16** dining room (Sala da Pranzo) **17** Queen's bedroom (Camera di Letto) **18** Queen's workroom (Sala del lavoro) **19** Queen's study (Studiolo) **20** Queen's chapel (Oratorio) **21** Queen's maid's bedroom (Sala delle cameriste) **22** Queen's ante-room (Sala della macchine) **23** Queen's private chapel (Cappella privata della regina) **24** cabinet of miniatures (Gabinetto delle Miniature) **25** dining room (Sala da Pranzo) **26** coffee room (Sala del Caffè) **27** reception room (Sala di Ricevimento) **28** medal room (Sala dei Medaglioni) **29** ball room (Salone da Ballo) **30** court (Cortile) with bronze equestrian statues at the gate

tor Emmanuel II was born in this building, which was the seat of the Sardinian parliament in 1848–59 and of the Italian parliament in 1861–4. The *rear façade* (Piazza Carlo Alberto) was built by Ferri and Bollati in 1864–71.

Palazzo dell'Accademia delle Scienze (Via dell'Accademia): Built by Guarini as a Jesuit college in 1679. In 1757 the semi-nary was handed over to the Academy of Sciences.

Accademia Filarmonica (Piazza S. Carlo): Distinguished by its splendid *rococo decoration*. There are *frescos* by Bernardino Galliari in the atrium.

Castello del Valentino (Giardino Pubblico), a French-style Renaissance castle

Palazzo Madama

with four pavilions. The castle was begun in 1650 for Madama Reale Christina of France, from 1860 it was an engineering school, and today it is part of the polytechnic.

Università (Via del Po): Built in 1713 by A.Ricca from Genoa. The Biblioteca Nazionale Universitaria, the well-stocked *university library*, is an important feature.

Mole Antonelliana (Via Gaudenzio Ferrari): Originally begun in 1863 as a synagogue to plans by Alessandro Antonelli, and extended upwards as a tower in 1878 –9. 540 ft. high, it was the tallest building in Italy at that time and was a landmark of Turin.

Other palaces: *Palazzo Chiablese* (Piazza S.Giovanni), built in the 17C, decorated by B.Alfieri in 1740. It was the seat of the government of Charles Emmanuel III. To-day it is the office of the Piedmontese building authority. *Palazzo del Seminario Arcivescovile* (Via XX Settembre), built in 1711–28 to a plan by Piero Paolo Cerutti. *Palazzo Graneri* (Via Bogino), built by Michelangelo Garove in 1683. *Palazzo Carpano* (Via Maria Vittoria), a significant example of Piedmontese baroque style, built in 1686 by Michelangelo Garove, with 18C additions by V.Alfieri and Francesco Martinez. *Palazzo Dal Pozzo della Cisterna* (Via Carlo Alberto), seat of the provincial government, by Francesco Valeriano Dellala dei Beinasco, while the classical façade is by Gioacchino Felice Butturini, 1783. *Palazzo della Valle* (Via Carlo Alberto), one of the finest palaces in Turin, by Juvarra, 1716. *Palazzo Weill-Weiss* (Via Bogino), built in the 18C by Ignazio Agliaudi di Tavigliano, the façade dating from 1840. *Palazzo Cavour* (Via Cavour), residence of Cavour, built in 1729 to a plan by Gian Giacomo Plantery. *Pa-*

Turin, Castello del Valentino

lazzo Solaro del Borgo (Piazza S.Carlo) by Isnardi di Carglio, rebuilt by B.Alfieri in 1753, seat of the Philharmonic society since 1839. *Palazzo Provana di Collegno*, also called *Cavalchini-Garofoli* (Via S. Teresa), built in 1698, probably to plans by Guarini. *Palazzo Lascaris* (Via Alfieri), built by Amedeo di Castellamonte in *c.* 1665. *Palazzo Avogadro di Collobiano* (Via Alfieri), where Vittorio Alfieri wrote his first novel in 1775. *Palazzo di Città* (Piazza P.di Città), built by Francesco Lanfranchi in 1659–63 and rebuilt by B.Alfieri and others. *Palazzo di Giustizia* (Via Corte d'Appello), built to plans by Juvarra in 1720, continued by B.Alfieri in 1741, and completed by Ignazio Michela in 1830–8. *Palazzo Barolo* (Via delle Orfane), begun *c.* 1639 and continued by Gian Francesco Baroncelli in 1692, while the wonderful staircase by B.Alfieri dates from 1713. *Borgo e Castello Medioevale* (Viale Virglio), built by Alfredo D'Andrade in 1884 in the style of a medieval town. *Ospedale di S. Giovanni Battista* (Via Giovanni Gioletti), a severe building by Amedeo di Castellamonte, Gian Francesco Baroncelli and Michelangelo Garove, 1680–3.

Also worth seeing: *Teatro Regio* (Piazza Castello), the façade dating from 1738 being by B.Alfieri. The interior was redesigned from 1964–72 to plans by Carlo Mollino. The *Roman theatre* on the N. side of the cathedral (Via XX Settembre) was built in 1C BC. *Porta Palatina* (Piazza Cesare Augusto), 1C BC, one of the city's gates. *Monument to C.Cavour* (Piazza Carlina), 1873, by Giovanni Duprè. *Equestrian statue of Emmanuel Philibert* (Piazza S. Carlo) by Carlo Marocchetto, 1838. *Equestrian monument to Prince Amadeus* (Corso Massimo D'Azeglio), a masterpiece by David Calandra, 1902. *Monument to Alfieri* in front of the Palazzo Madama (Piazza Castello). *Fontana Angelica* (Piazza Solferino).

Museums and libraries: *Museo Civico d'Arte Antica* in the Palazzo Madama. *Biblioteca Reale* in the Palazzo Reale. *Armeria Reale* (Piazza Reale). *Museo Nazionale del Cinema* in the Palazzo Chiablese. *Museo Nazionale del Risorgimento* in the Palazzo Carignano. *Museo di Geologia e Paleontologia* in the Palazzo Carignano. *Museo di Antichità*, *Museo Egizio*, *Galleria Sabauda*, all in the Accademia delle Scienze. *Museo di Zoologia* (Via Accademia Albertina). *Museo di Mineralogia e Petrografia* (Via S. Massimo). *Museo di Antropologia e di Etnologia* (Via Accademia Albertina). *Galleria dell'Accademia Albertina* in the Accademia Albertina di Belle Arti. *Galleria Civica d'Arte Moderna* (Via Macenta). *Biblioteca Civica* (Via della Cittadella). *Museo Nazionale D'Artiglieria* (Via della Cittadella). *Museo Nazionale della Montagna* (Via Maresco Giardino; the museum has been closed since 1974 owing to restoration work).

Environs: La Basilica di Superga, built in 1717–31 to a plan by Juvarra. It is his masterpiece. The reason for building the church on this site was the vow of Victor Emmanuel, who watched Prince Eugene

Stupinigi hunting lodge (Turin)

fighting the French here. The church has a round ground plan. The entrance is formed by a classical *portico*, reminiscent of the Roman Pantheon. It is connected to the adjoining *monastery* by two *towers*, whose arrangement reminds one of that of S.Agnese in Rome. In the inner courtyard the visitor passes through a fine *portico* to the *tombs of the kings of Savoy* from Victor Amadeus II to Charles Albert. Simone Martinez, G.B.Ravelli and Carlo Amedeo Rana were the builders (1777). From the church there is a view of the *column* commemorating Umberto I, by Tancredi Pozzi, 1900. **Stupinigi,** the hunting lodge of Victor Amadeus II, was built by Juvarra in 1729–30. The town is of ancient origin, as indicated by the Latin name Supinicum. From 1573 onwards the site was in the possession of the Mauritian order and this order handed it over to the counts of Savoy. The unusual ground plan has the castle itself—with four wings in the form of a cross—in the centre and behind the principal courtyard. The *garden* was laid out by Giovanni Tomaso Prunetto in 1739–41. The castle today houses the *Museo dell' Arredamento.* **Venaria:** Another hunting lodge of the house of Savoy. The first building was erected by Amedeo di Castellamonte in 1660. Devastated several times by the French in 1693 and 1706, the present structure (1714–28) is by B.Alfieri. It was the favourite residence of Madama Reale Giovanna Battista. **Pecetto Torinese** was established by Charles Emmanuel as a vine-growing area on 18 November 1735. This is the famous region of the vermouth of Turin. *S.Maria della Neve,* the parish church, was built by Bernardo Antonio Vittore in *c.* 1799. The tower, which remains from an earlier Romanesque building, dates from 1106. *S.Sebastiano:* This Lombard church has a nave, two aisles and a strikingly simple façade.

Torre de' Passeri 65029
Pescara/Abruzzi   p.416 ☐ I 9

Environs: S. Clemente a Casauria:
This abbey was founded in 871 by Louis
II in gratitude for his release from im-
prisonment. The monastic community
was attacked by the Saracens in 920 and by
the Normans in 1078. After being rebuilt
in the 12C the monastery again flourished,
but only a part of the damage caused by
the earthquake of 1348 was made good.
The earthquake of 1915 destroyed the
monastery completely, and the church was
restored in 1920–2 and 1932–4. In front
of the façade there is a portico with three
arches. In the *lunette* of the central portal,
Abbot Leonatus (1152–92) is seen kneeling with a model of a church in front of
St.Clement, and the story of the abbey's
foundation is told on the *architrave;* the
bronze panels on the door depict the three
castles belonging to the abbey, amongst
other subjects. Inside there is a 12C *ambo*
with rosettes, and the semicircular projecting lectern bears two symbols of the Evangelists (the second lectern with the symbols

Trani, S.Nicola Pellegrino, crypt

of the other two Evangelists has been lost).
The *Easter candlestick* is of somewhat later
date and is inlaid. The *ciborium* (same
period) with relief figures.

Tortoli 08048
Nuoro/Sardinia   p.422 ☐ D 13

The many enormous stones used in the
building of the houses prove that the
Ogliastra area around Tortoli was inhabited
in nuraghic times. The Aragonese made
Tortoli the main town of the county of
Quirra. But the area is wet and was ravaged
by malaria. As a result no cultural monuments worthy of mention have survived.
The water is now controlled by a dam on
the upper Flumendosa and this fertile district has once again become inhabitable.
Arbatax, the only safe harbour on the E.
coast, has nothing of interest apart from the
over-praised and not very extensive red
trachyte cliffs, which rise above a rubbish
tip. Arbatax means 'fourteenth tower' in
Arabic. This refers to the harbour tower,
which was a watchtower (16C). The Rio
di San Giorgio (also known as Rio Quirra)
is a massive underground karst river on the
N. edge of the trackless limestone massif
of the Quirra. Some 9 km. SE of the isolated **Perdasdefogu** ('flint'), this river,
swollen by the winter rains, has hollowed
out a gorge which is over 2,600 ft. long and
in many places over 65 ft. deep. There are
several steep drops, the 'Camellas de
Turulu', which are unique in Sardinia. The
ruins of the 13C *Castello di Quirra* stand
like an eyrie upon a steep crag further to
the S.This castle belonged to the Giudici
of Cágliari. Nearby, the 13C *S.Nicolà*, the
only Romanesque church built entirely of
brick, has round arches with a well
preserved frieze, stands by the road. To the
SW: Many bronze figures from the
nuraghic period were found in the 'Bivio
Càrmine' in the 14C. The whole region is
full of the remains of nuraghi. However,
an over-zealous priest had a bell cast from
these 'heathen gods'. The area around the
peak of the Punta 'su Scrau' on the Pizzu'
e Paceu and the start of the open Grotta di
Orroli is about an hour's drive NW from

Osini. From Ulassai, a good paved road leads to the 'Grotta de su Marmuri'. Here, the large entrance has had stairs built which extend as far as daylight reaches. To the N.: Just to the S.of **Lotzorai** is the 13C *ruin of Medusa*, the first fortress which the Aragonese were able to storm.

Tortona 15057
Alessandria / Piedmont   p.412 ☐ C 4

Although largely modern, Tortona has a number of artistically interesting monuments. Originally a Ligurian and later a Roman settlement, it was rebuilt in 1155 after being destroyed by Frederick Barbarossa.

Cathedral (Piazza Duomo): Dedicated to the Assunta and San Lorenzo, this is an imposing late Renaissance building, erected under Pope Pius V in 1574–84. The classical façade, dating from 1880, was built by Niccolò Bruno. Inside, note the baroque altarpiece by G.Battista Crespi on the high altar.

Palazzo Vescovile: This bishop's palace beside the cathedral dates from *c*. 1550, and its chapel contains a *triptych* by Macrino d'Alba (1499).

Also worth seeing: *S.Maria dei Canali* (Via Verdi), 12C, the city's oldest church. The 15C *Palazzo Guidobono* (Piazza Aristide Arzano), with the city *museum*. The 16–18C *castle* (Via Castello). A *Roman tomb*, 2/3C BC (Via Emilia). *Santuario Madonna della Guardia* (Via Emilia), 1931. Ruins of the castle (18C).

Environs: Near to Rivalta Scrivia is the *Abbazia di S.Maria*, a former Cistercian abbey, built in 1153–1250. The church, begun in 1180, was rebuilt in the 17C. The fine chapterhouse is all that remains of the abbey apart from some ruins.

Trani 70059
Bari/Apulia   p.416 ☐ N 10

Cathedral of S. Nicola Pellegrino

(Piazza Duomo, on the sea front): One of the finest Romanesque churches in southern Italy. The original part is the hypogeum of St.Leucio, the first bishop of Brindisi (7C), below the transept; in the 9C this was incorporated into a new building (S.Maria della Scala) as its crypt. When work on what is today the upper church was begun, the preceding one was used as the lower church. The patron is a pilgrim known as Nicola, who died in Trani in 1094, while the model for the church itself was S.Nicola in Bari, but considerable alterations were made during the building. The *portal* of the main façade is reached by a double stairway and underneath is an entrance to the lower church. The lower part of the façade has four richly decorated blind arcades on each side. Above these is the *central window* with beautiful elephants and a rose (not all of which survives). The main feature of the portal — which is typical of the Apulian Romanesque, but does not have an architrave or a tympanum — are the *bronze doors*. The work of Barisano da Trani (1175), they have 32 panels of reliefs—Jesus, Mary, Apostles, Saints and Biblical scenes. The *campanile* is only loosely connected to the body of the cathedral (13/14C). Being dilapidated, it was torn down and rebuilt from 1952 onwards; on the 2nd floor there is a change in style from Romanesque to Gothic, and the masonry is pierced by an increasing number of windows. A cornice protrudes a considerable distance out from the top of the transept. There is an ornate *rose-window* in the gable of the S.transept. Interior, the ciborium and pulpit were destroyed in the 18C, and only fragments survive. The early-19C baroque decoration was removed when the restoration was carried out; remains of the original mosaic pavement survive in the choir. The arcades of the nave are supported by twelve double columns. Above the side aisles there are triple-arched women's galleries and an open roof truss. The side aisles lead to the *crypt* (with splendid capitals), and from here the *lower church* is entered (it is very low, and has short, strong columns, some of them ancient). From here, access may also be gained to the *hypogeum of S.Leucio* (see above), a rectangular room which lies below sea-level and in which a passage leads around a cell (remains of frescos).

Church of Ognissanti (Via Ognissanti by the harbour): Dating from the mid-11C, it was formerly part of a Templars' hospital. It is one of the few Apulian churches whose *portico* survives (by the main façade). The double-towered façade is unfinished, and today has an open belfry. The *middle portal* is splendidly decorated; there are scenes from the Annunciation in the tympanum. Three free-standing apses (the middle one is very tall) by the choir. The interior has a very narrow and tall nave, two aisles, and an open roof truss.

S.Francesco (Via Ognissanti): Begun in 1176 as a Benedictine church, consecrated in 1184, taken over and re-named by Franciscans in the 16C. It is a three-domed church on a Byzantine model; it has the start of a portico and a campanile (pilasters on the main façade). Rectangular choir.

Also worth seeing: *S.Andrea* (Via Mario Pagani), a small cruciform domed basilica with a rectangular drum to the dome, and an interesting choir. The Romanesque three-domed churches of *S. Lucia* and *S. Antonio* on both sides of the entrance to the harbour. The baroque church of *S. Teresa*. The Hohenstaufen *castle* (1233, square four-winged building right by the sea on the Piazza Manfredi; as it is a prison, it is not open). The 15C late Gothic *Palazzo Simone Cacetta,* formerly the seat of the Venetian governors. *Villa Comunale* (public garden to the E. of the port), with some *Roman milestones* on the Via Traiana, which led from Benevento via Trani to Brindisi.

Environs: On the sea about 8 km. to the NW is **Biscéglie**, which has fine Romanesque churches, although some of them are much dilapidated and altered. 11C cathedral of *SS.Pietro e Paolo* (baroque, with a mutilated portal). The 11C *S. Adoeno,* with a 12C font and a fine rose-window on the façade (four lions on consoles). *S. Margherita,* 12C, a single-domed church with a square drum above the dome. A *castle* with a Norman core.

Trapani 91100
Trapani/Sicily   p.420☐ H 16

Cathedral of S. Lorenzo (Corso Vitt. Emanuele): Built in 1635 on an earlier building (14C). A baroque *façade* with a *portico* of 1740. The interior has a nave, two aisles and a dome. A *Crucifixion* attributed to van Dyck.

Chiesa del Collegio (Corso Vitt. Emanuele): 17C, baroque, with an especially fine *façade* (1636). Inside are a nave and two aisles, and the ground plan is a Latin cross. Fine *marble works* on the altars, and there is a notable 18C *cupboard* in the sacristy.

S.Maria del Gesù (Via S.Agostino): 15C, late Gothic façade, fine portal. The interior has a nave and two aisles. The main work of art is the *Madonna degli Angeli* by Andrea della Robbia (1435–1525) in the *Cappella Staiti;* above this is a marble baldacchino by A.Gagini (1521).

Santuario dell' Annunziata (Via Agostino Pepoli): Built in 1313–32, enlarged in the 14&17C, comprehensively rebuilt in 1760. *Façade* with a fine Gothic portal and rose-window from the time when the church was built. The interior is single-aisled, and on the right is the *Cappella dei Pescatori* (14C, octagonal dome, beautiful frescos), and on the left is the entrance to the fine *Cappella dei Marinai* (16C, Renaissance, dome). Behind the high altar access is gained to the actual 'Santuario', a splendidly decorated room (*marble arch* by Antonino and Giac. Gagini, 1531–7), with the famous 'Madonna di Trapani' (Nino Pisano or workshop).

Museo Nazionale Pepoli (beside and to the right of the above church): Housed in a former monastery. An excellent *collection of archaeological finds* (some from Monte Erice, see below).

Also worth seeing: *Il Palazzo* (Via Cas-

Trani, S. Nicola Pellegrino, portal ▸

Monte Erice (Trapani), Chiesa Matrice

the burial place of the ancient Greek hero Diomedes. It was a place of exile from classical times onwards. There are three islands: San Domino, San Nicola and Capraia. The centre of the archipelago is **S. Nicola,** with its former abbey of **S. Nicola.** This had a turbulent past: the earliest information dates from the 8C (at that time it was under the control of Monte Cassino). In the 13C, Cistercians replaced the Benedictines. The abbey was destroyed by pirates in 1343. It flourished again in the 15C under the rule of St. Frigidianus of Lucca, and was expanded into a fortress against the Turks, who besieged it in 1567.

Abbey church of S. Maria a Mare: Begun by the Benedictines in 1054, and later altered. The original area is almost square in shape and is surrounded by arcades. Outside, to the W., is a two-aisled narthex with groin vaults. The side aisles also have groin vaults. A ribbed-vaulted, rectangular choir from the Cistercian period. The *cloister* was rebuilt in the Renaissance. The interior houses the remnants of the original *mosaic pavement* (geometric patterns and animals). In the *Cappella di Cristo Grande* is a high medieval *wooden cross* in the Byzantine style. At the high altar there is a 15C Venetian *polyptych,* showing scenes from the Assumption and Coronation of the Virgin).

saretto), a beautiful medieval palace. *Palazzo della Giudecca* (Via Giudecca), a Catalan Gothic palace in the old ghetto.

Environs: An excursion along the Via Fardella may be made to *Monte Erice* (2, 464 ft.), the classical Mons Eryx. One of the most famous shrines to Venus of classical times ('Venus Erycina'). The *Castello Venere,* from which there is a splendid view, today stands on the site of the temple. There is an interesting *museum* in the town hall, and the 14C *Chiesa Matrice* (fine portal) has a 'Madonna col Bambino' attributed to Francesco Laurana.

Tremiti, Isole/Tremiti Islands
Foggia/Apulia   p.416□ L 9

This group of islands lies to the N. of Monte Gargano. According to myth, it is

Trento/Trient 38100
Trento/South Tyrol-Trentino   p.410□ F 2

This town surrounded by high mountains and located in a wide part of the Adige valley has existed since *c.* 3000 BC, when it was a pre-Aryan settlement. It was militarily important in Roman times, being the most northerly town in the homeland outside the provinces (excavations on the Dos Trento brought to light the foundations of the then acropolis). The conversion to Christianity began in the 4C, and Trento became the seat of a bishop. Under Theodoric the Goth, it became the centre of a grand duchy. Charlemagne captured it in 774, and in 952 Otto the Great incorporated it into the Holy Roman Empire.

The ecclesiastical principality of Trento was established shortly thereafter. From the 13C there were prince-bishops, one of the most important of whom was Prince-Bishop Federigo Vanga. He began the construction of the new cathedral, and caused an outer wall to be built around the city. Maximilian I was crowned Emperor in Trento in 1508. The city was further enlarged in 1514 under Prince-Bishop Bernardo Clesio, who made extensive changes to the medieval cityscape by adding wide streets, broad squares, and Renaissance palaces. From 1545 onwards the city became the seat of an ecumenical council. The rule of the prince-bishops came to an end in 1796 when the French occupied the city.

Cathedral (Piazza Cesare Battisti): The main feature of the piazza is the magnificent N. flank of the cathedral. The piazza itself has a fountain of Neptune by F.A. Giongo (today there is a bronze copy from 1942 in the square, and the stone original is in the courtyard of the Palazzo Municipio). The piazza forms the centre of old Trento and is framed by houses several storeys high with loggias and by the Palazzo Pretorio.

A building of which only traces survive was erected in the early 12C over the tomb of St. Vigilius (405). Finally, Adam of Arogno began a new building in 1212 under Bishop Vanga, and work proceeded slowly but continuously. The building was not completed until the 16C (under B.Clesio), when the crossing tower, the upper storey of the N. tower of the façade (the S.tower was never completed), the portico on the N. aisle, and the roof over the nave, were all added. The tripartite *façade* forms the W. front and was only completed in the 16C. However, the main view from the Piazza Cesare Battisti is of the *Romanesque N. side* and its 16C portico, with Romanesque lions supporting the columns. The plain S.side was built in the 14C. The E. wall with its ornate, graduated portal is very beautifully articulated. The E. window and the large rose-window in the front of the N. transept are also worth looking at. In the late Romanesque *interior*, one is surprised by the Gothic features, a soaring,

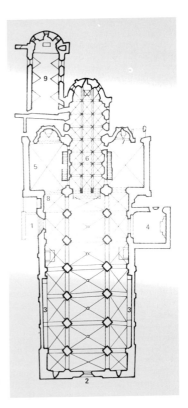

Trento, cathedral **1** vestibule, 16C, with Romanesque portal with columns **2** W. portal **3** stair in aisle wall **4** Cappella del Crocefisso, 1682 **5** frescos, 14C **6** high altar, 1743 **7** relief with Stoning of St.Stephen, 13C **8** tomb of Bernardo Clesio (d. 1539) **9** sacristy

vertical emphasis, the result, chiefly, of the tall pillars and narrow arcades. The baroque high altar by Domenico and Antonio Giuseppe Sartori (1743) appears foreign but does not jar. The stairs in the aisle walls leading up to the towers are peculiar. Notable features of the N. and S.transepts are the 14C *frescos* by various artists. On the W. wall of the S. transept there is a panel of the Crucifixion (1504; by a German painter). Below it is the tomb to Bishop Ulrich IV of Liechtenstein

(1505). Beside and to the left of this is the tomb slab of a Venetian soldier: it is the work of Luca Moro, 15C. The *bishops' tombs* on the walls of the aisles date from the 14,15&16C. In 1682, Giuseppe Alberti added the *Cappella del Crocefisso* to the S. aisle. It is square with an octagonal dome, a lantern, and a splendid marble altar which appears to form a frame for a sculptured Crucifixion by Sixt Frei from Nuremberg (*c.* 1515).

SS.Annunziata: This centrally planned building constructed by Antonio Brusinelli in 1713–15 stands opposite the cathedral behind the Piazza Cesare Battisti immediately to the right of the Via Rodolfo Belenzani; rebuilt after World War 2. There is a medieval *watchtower* diagonally opposite the church in the same street.

S.Maria Maggiore: The 1st street to the left off the Via Rodolfo Belenzani leads directly to the parish church of S.Maria Maggiore. The fine *campanile* survives from the original church of S.Maria ad Nives. The octagonal top with its dome was added in 1742. The present church was built as a uniform Renaissance structure by Antonio da Medaglia in 1520–4 under Bernardo Clesio. In 1900/1, the top part and the façade, among other sections, were restored (unfortunately not very well). The old mid-16C portal survives in the façade (the figures date from 1900). Despite this disfigurement, S.Maria Maggiore is a uniform and monumental high Renaissance building and, together with the cathedral, is among the city's most important churches. The most interesting feature in the interior of the tunnel-vaulted hall-type building, which has three chapels on each side (some with fine 16&18C paintings), is the *singers' gallery* (white marble, bearing reliefs) on the N. wall of the choir. It is by Vincenzo Grandi of Padua, 1534. Note the four large *canvases* on the entrance wall, painted by G.M.Falconetto in 1506.

S.Francesco Saverio: The enormous baroque façade of the Jesuit church of S. Francesco forms a fitting end to the Via Rodolfo Belenzani. The building was be-
gun in 1701 to plans by Andrea Pozzo, the famous architect, painter and theoretician who came from Trento. The interior has late-19C frescos. Some remains of the original paintings by Pozzo's pupil Gaudenzio Mignocchi were discovered on the inside of the entrance wall in 1954. The former *Jesuit college* with the *Biblioteca Comunale* and a State archive is adjacent.

San Lorenzo: The former Benedictine monastery church stands on the Giardino Pubblico (behind S.Francesco Saverio). A church of limestone ashlars and brick was built for the Benedictines, who were invited to Trento in 1146. Located outside the old city, it was at that time on the other side of the Adige (whose course was diverted in the 19C), opposite the Torre Vanga and connected to it by a wooden bridge. In 1235, when the Benedictines moved to S. Apollinare, the Dominicans took over the church and monastery (the monastery subsequently served as a prison, an infirmary, a shelter for the homeless, and a barracks). It was restored in 1956 (the top of the campanile above the S.side apse dates from the 18C). The chief items of interest are the E. end and the interior of the church, which has a nave, two aisles and a groin vault.

S.Apollinare (NW of the old town, on the present bank of the Adige at the feet of Dos Trento): This small 12–14C church soars upwards. Roman spoils, possibly the remains of an ancient temple, were used for its construction. The W. façade contains a Romanesque side portal. In the 19C, the originally flat end of the choir had an apse added to it. The single-aisled interior has an interesting fresco from about 1319 at its left side altar.

S.Pietro (Via S.Pietro): In the E. section of the old city is the only Gothic church in Trento. It was built by the German community in 1472 and, despite restoration in the 17&19C, it has retained its original appearance. The façade (1848) is neo-Gothic.

Trento, cathedral square with Fountain of Neptune ▷

In the N. of the choir is a *funeral chapel* from the 2nd half of the 17C.

S.Chiara e S.Michele (Via Santa Croce): In the very S. of the old city is the small church of S.Chiara, also called S.Michele, which dates originally from the 12C and was rebuilt in 1629. There is an Annunciation by G.B.Moroni (1548) on the right wall of this hall church.

Torre Civica: This imposing, medieval tower, whose foundations probably date from the period around 1000, stands directly by the Palazzo Pretorio in the Piazza Cesare Battisti. From the 12C onwards it was directly connected with the first city wall.

Palazzo Pretorio: This three-storeyed building beside the Torre was originally built in the 13C (the previous building was 12C), and was used as the bishop's residence until the latter was moved to the Castel del Buonconsiglio in 1255. The palace was rebuilt in the 16C, but was restored to its original state in 1953–63. The palace today houses the *Museo Diocesano* (with good works of art, including the cathedral treasure) and the *bishop's library*.

Castelletto: Between the cathedral and the Palazzo Pretorio (and connected to both), the Castelletto was originally built together with the Palazzo Pretorio in 1207–18 on the foundation walls of an earlier palace. The 11C chapel of St.John was on the ground floor but was destroyed in the 18C. Above it was the courtyard chapel of St.Blasius, which is today used as a *sacristy* and in which the fine 11C apse survives. The slender *campanile di S. Romedio* rises at the S. corner.

Casa Balduini (opposite the Palazzo Pretorio, on the other side of the Piazza Cesare Battisti): This building is originally Gothic, but has been much altered. Remains of late-15C frescos.

Case al Duomo (on the N. side of the Piazza Cesare Battisti): The two Case have a fresco cycle (*c.* 1530), the work of M.Fogolino. The house on the corner has

painted sculptures giving an illusion of depth.

Via Rodolfo Belenzani: The 16C *Casa Ferrari* (No. 39), the 15C *Casa Alberti-Colico* (No. 32) with its 16C frescos, and the gorgeous 16C *Palazzo Geremia* (No. 22), which was also painted by Fogolino in *c.* 1540 all lie along the road between the Piazza Cesare Battisti and S. Francesco Saverio. Opposite them is the *Palazzo Thun* (No. 19), which has been the *Palazzo del Municipio* since 1873. This 16C palace was rebuilt in 1832–5. In the courtyard there are frescos dating from 1551.

Castel del Buonconsiglio (in the NE of the old city, by the city wall): Today it is used as a museum; it houses the *Museo Nazionale* and the *Museo Risorgimento*, with prehistoric finds from the environs of Trento. In the N., with its rear by the city wall, is the *Castelvecchio* with the massive, Romanesque *Torre di Augusto*, also known as the *Torre Grande*. Built in the 1st half of the 13C, it originally served as a residence for the Podestà. The battlemented building encloses an inner courtyard, which is framed on three sides by four-storeyed loggias (late 15C) with round and pointed arches and frescoed garlands on the parapet of the upper storey. Features inside include the *Sala degli Stufi*, with a collection of 15–18C ovens; the old *chapel* with frescos dating from 1483; the *Sala dei Vescovi* with frescos by Fogolino; and what were the first private apartments of B.Clesio, on the 3rd and 4th floors. In 1528–36, B.Clesio had a new building, the *Magno Palazzo*, a gorgeous residence, built S.of the Castelvecchio. The piano nobile surrounds the lion's courtyard on three sides, and its fourth side forms the city wall. The loggia on the S. side of the courtyard has frescos by Romanino and is very fine. Inside the palace note the *atrium* with its frescos by Romanino; the *marble staircase* which was also painted by Romanino and leads to the lion's courtyard; the round *Torrione* with frescos by Fogolino and a stuccoed ceiling; the *Stua della Figure* with its rich stucco decoration; the *Camera delle Udienze* (audience chamber) with frescos by Romanino; and the *Camera del Camin-*

nero with a beautifully stuccoed and frescoed ceiling by Dosso Dossi. The *Sala Grande*, the largest room in the palace, with a coffered ceiling and *trompe l'oeil* painting by Dosso Dossi, is on the 2nd floor. There are some more *trompe l'oeil* by Dosso Dossi in the *Camera degli Scarlatti* with its scarlet fabrics. Prehistoric and archaeological collections are today housed in the S.wing of the Magno Palazzo (the library wing). In the late 17C, under Bishop Francesco Alberti-Poja, the Castelvecchio was connected to the Magno Palazzo by a building with four bays of windows. It contains two rooms with baroque stucco and paintings by Giuseppe Alberti. A multi-storeyed gallery leads from the S.wing of the Magno Palazzo to the *Eagle's Tower* (Torre dell'Aquila). In *c.* 1400, this tower was enlarged, on top of the eagle's gate in the city wall, as a private residence for Bishop George I of Liechtenstein. The central room of the tower contains the finest work in the entire Castel del Buonconsiglio. This is the famous *fresco cycle of the months*. It was painted with incredible dexterity in *c.* 1400, probably by Wenzel, a painter at the Bishop's court.

Trento, cathedral, view of apse

Also worth seeing: *Palazzo Galasso* (Via Roma, on the corner of Via Alfieri, opposite the church of S.Francesco Saverio): A monumental three-storeyed palace, built in 1603 by order of Georg Fugger of Augsburg to a design by Pietro Maria Bagnadore. Nearby, the *Palazzo Salvadori* with fine baroque façades. *Palazzo Delmonte* (Via del Suffragio, corner of Via S.Marco), a simple mid-16C building, with a fine portal and remains of 16C frescos. Near the cathedral, by the Via Calepina, are the *Palazzo Lodron* (1577), with interesting paintings dating from shortly after the building's construction, and the early-17C *Palazzo Sardagna* with late Renaissance forms in addition to baroque ones. In the Via Oss-Mazzurana (No. 65) is the *Palazzo Tabarelli*, built by Alessio Longhi in the 1st half of the 16C. The façade, with its uniform rustication, is of interest. The late baroque *Palazzo Larcher* is in the Via Mazzini (No. 10), S. of the cathedral. The *Torre Vanga*, a massive 13C tower, stands in the

Trento, cathedral, Christ Pantocrator

Trento, Castel del Buonconsiglio: arcaded court; an external view

Piazza Leonardo da Vinci, SW of the Giardino Pubblico.

Museums: Apart from the museums in the Palazzo Pretorio and in the Castel del Buonconsiglio, mention should also be made of the *Museo di Storia Naturale del Trentino-Alto Adige* with its extensive natural history collections from the area around Trento.

Environs: Civezzano (NE of Trento): The parish church of *Maria Assunta* was built by order of B.Clesio in 1512–25 in Renaissance style with features harking back to the late Gothic (tracery on the windows; campanile; interior). The altarpieces are by J.Bassano. **Pergine Valsugana/Persen:** This considerable town, which has been the centre of silver mining in the area around Trento since the Middle Ages, is E. of Trento, on the road to Padua: *Parish church of the Natività* in German late Gothic style. Baroque church of *S.Carlo* with Renaissance elements, and typically Italian Renaissance villas on the Via Maier. The 13C castle of *Castello di Pèrgine*, whose restoration was ordered by Bernardo Clesio in 1531,stands impressively to the E., on a hill above the town. To the NW of Pergine Valsugana are **Madrano**, with the baroque *parish church of the Decollazione di S.Giovanni Battista;* **Montagna di Pinè** with a notable *pilgrimage church* built by Antonio Brusinelli in 1730–40; and **San Mauro di Pinè** with the church of *S. Mauro*, which mixes Gothic and Renaissance elements and has a triptych with carved figures in the shrine (1520). **Vezzano** (the Roman Vettianum) is on the road from Trento to Riva. From here the traveller may continue to **Padergnone** with the *parish church of SS.Filippe e Giacomo*, which was rebuilt in 1630 but still has 16C frescos, and to **Madruzzo** (S. of Calavino), with the church of the

B.V.Maria di Loreto (1645) and the 12&16C castle of *Castel Madruzzo* situated high up and restored in the 19C. SE of Trento (when coming from Sarcle, do not go to Riva but continue eastwards) **Stènico** with a 12–16C castle which stands high above the town (interesting buildings and frescos). To the S.of Stènico are **Bono** with the church of *S. Felice*, which has frescos by Cristoforo Bascheni (1496), **St.Croce** (Comune Bleggio) with a *parish church*, whose crypt with its frescos (1303) is of especial interest, and **Vigo Lomaso** with the 13&15C parish church of *S. Lorenzo* and a baptistery (originally 12C), whose 8&9C stone reliefs are today in **Lundo** above the portal of the 16C church of *S. Silvestro*.

Trevi 06039

Perugia / Umbria   p.414 □ H8

Trevi dates back to an Umbrian foundation with a temple dedicated to Diana Trivia (from whom the name derives). The city was conquered by Rome in the 3C. In the Middle Ages it was hotly contested by Saracens, condottieri and others.

Town hall: Begun in the 14C and frequently altered since then (15C portico, 13C tower). The picture gallery is today housed in the town hall. Important works: Coronation of the Virgin, by Spagna; Madonna and Child, by Pinturicchio; Deposition, by the school of Sodoma. A panel with a banner by Niccolò Alunno.

Cathedral: Begun in the 11C, rebuilt in the 15C and given its present form in 1893. The three very fine apses are remnants from the original church, as is the sculpture of Emilian on the same wall. Inside, the magnificent altar of the sacrament is by Rocco da Vicenza (1522). The high altar bears a Trinity (1585), and the font also dates from the 16C.

Madonna delle Lacrime: Built in Renaissance style in the late 15C, the design being by Antonio Marchisi. The wonderful portal is by Giovanni Giampietri da Venezia. The features inside include the Cappella del Presepio, decorated by Perugino (1521), the Cappella di S.Francesco, frescoed by Spagna (1520), the Cappella della Risurrezione, with frescos by Orazio Alfani (1530).

Also worth seeing: 16C church of *S. Martino*. Inside, Madonna and Child, by Mezzastris. There is a wonderful fresco by Spagna of the Assumption of the Virgin in a chapel adjoining the church. *S. Francesco:* This 14C church was built on the site of an older one. Fine portal. Inside: Votive frescos from the 14&15C. A very beautiful 14C crucifix on the high altar. *Portico Mostaccio:* Remains of the former castle (11C).

Environs: S. Pietro in Bovara (3 km. S. of Trevi): This interesting 12C Romanesque church was restored in the 16C. The sanctuary dates from the 16C, as do the choir and the side doors. The campanile was built in 1582. Heathen decorative elements are to be found on the façade, as well as an inscription with the architect's name, Atto. The fine 16C monastery stands beside the church. **S. Maria in Pietra Rossa:** This church (one nave, two aisles) is 3 km. N. of Trevi. A large number of 14&15C votive frescos are to be seen inside. One column bears an elegant tabernacle by Rocco da Vicenza.

Treviglio 24047

Bergamo / Lombardy   p.412 □ D 3

Collegiata di S.Martino: Begun in 1008, it was first altered in 1482-1507, and again during the course of the 18C. A massive Romanesque *campanile* stands beside the broad late baroque *façade* (1740). The apse is flanked by another graceful campanile from the 14C. Inside are *frescos* from the 2nd half of the 18C (Galliari), and a *polyptych* of the legend of St. Martin by Bernardino Butinone and Bernardino Zenale (1485).

Environs: Rivolta d'Adda (about 10 km. SW of Treviglio): *Basilica SS.Maria e Sigismondo.* Built in 1088-99 by builders from

Como. The apse has semi-columns, Lombard bands, and a dwarf gallery. Picturesque market place with wide medieval arcades. *Pal. Stampa* (18C); the Stampas were the local lords from 1666 onwards. **Brignano Gera d'Adda.** *Castello Visconteo:* Originally 16C, it was turned into a splendid baroque seat by Giovanni Ruggeri in 1710. A main section and two wings enclose a *principal courtyard*. The exposed fourth side is occupied by an open *arcade* connecting the two side wings.

Treviso 31100

Treviso/Veneto   p.410□G3

A Roman foundation (Tarvisium); a bishop's seat from the 4C onwards. When it was a free town in the Middle Ages, it opposed Emperor Frederick Barbarossa; from 1344 onwards it belonged to Venice.

Cathedral of S. Pietro (Piazza del Duomo): An earlier Romanesque building was rebuilt from 1481 onwards under the supervision of P.Lombardi. The chapels N. and S. of the choir were added in the early 16C, while the nave was only completed in the 18C. The outside of the *choir* is especially fine. Some remains of the Romanesque building survive in the outer walls. In front of the façade there is a portico dating from 1836 (the steps have lions from the medieval main portal). *Inside*, a nave and two aisles. The ground plan has been developed from that of a cruciform, domed basilica. There are four domes over the nave, and another over the choir. The middle dome has a drum. Note a *sarcophagus* with reliefs of St.Theonestius, St.Tàbra and St.Tabrata (probably by T.Lombardi, 1506) in the choir. The N. side of the choir leads to the richly decorated *Cappella del Santissimo* (works by G.B. and L.Bregno, 1509–13. The vestibule has a fine painting by Fr. Bassano (Discovery of Christ's shroud). On the S. side is the *Cappella dell'Annunziata* with the following fine works: altarpiece by Titian (Annunciation); frescos by G.A.Pordenone (including scenes from the Life of Christ), both from *c.* 1520; in the ante-room, 12C Romanesque reliefs (scenes from the Life of the Virgin). Stairs at the sides of the choir lead to the Romanesque *crypt*. Notable *sacristies* (including a gilded wooden panel with a carved Last Judgement, 14C). On the N. side of the cathedral is the 11C Romanesque *baptistery,* inside which the font, the choir screens, and the 13C frescos (Madonna and Child) are worth seeing.

S.Nicolò (Via S.Nicolò): The building of this Gothic-style Dominican church began in *c.* 1300, and was largely complete by 1389 (the clerestory was enlarged in the 19C). The exterior has pointed windows, a round-arched frieze on the roof extension, and buttresses in the form of pilaster strips on the flanks and the W. end. Inside, the ground plan follows the scheme of churches of the Italian mendicant orders (basilica with a nave, two aisles, a transept, and immediately adjoining choir chapels, the three central chapels ending in apses). The wooden ceiling was rebuilt in the 19C. The nave is about 108 ft. high. Notable *furnishings:* the presbytery (fine ribbed vault) has marble *choir screens* dating from 1666 and the *sumptuous tomb* of A.d'Onigo (1490–1502). Immediately to the right of this is the *Cappella Monigo* with 14C frescos (including Madonnas). The church's oldest *frescos* (including Pope Benedict XI), dating from the early 14C, are in the chapel on the extreme right. On the 2nd pillar on the left are important frescos by Tomaso da Modena (14C, including St.Agnes). In the 2nd bay of the right aisle there is a fine painting, by Fr.Bassano, of Christ and Mary appearing to St.Dominic and St.Francis. On the S. side of the church is the former *Dominican monastery.* Its chapter house contains famous *frescos* by Tomaso da Modena.

Also worth seeing: 13C church of *S. Francesco.* Inside is a 'Madonna Enthroned' by Tomaso da Modena (to the left of the choir). 15C church of *S.Maria Maggiore,* with an early painting by the same artist (the Virgin Mary in the 'Tempietto della Madonna'). *Palazzo Comunale,* 13C,

Treviso, fresco by Tomaso da Modena ▷

Treviso, Museo Civico, Arturo Martini

with a fine exterior (partly rebuilt). Façades of *town houses* (typically, arcaded with painted upper storeys). *Porta S. Tommaso* (1518). *Museo Civico*, with an archaeological department and a picture gallery (the works by Tomaso da Modena are outstanding).

Tricárico 75019
Matera/Basilicata   p.416☐M 11

Cathedral: Built by Robert Guiscard on the foundations of an earlier building, and altered in 1638. A 13C double-arched window on the campanile. The interior of the church has a nave and two aisles, and in the sacristy there is a *fragment of a sarcophagus* from the 3C AD, with a relief of Adonis.

S. Chiara: Rebuilt in the 16C, with a fine gilded *coffered ceiling* and a 17C Neapolitan *majolica floor* in the sacristy. **S. Francesco:** This church, much altered in 1882, was originally built in the 13C. Gothic *portal*. **Monastery:** This is attached to the 15C church of *S. Antonio da Padova*. The *frescos* are worth seeing. **Castle:** Only a *tower* now survives from this Norman fortress.

Environs: Numerous remains of Lucanian and Roman settlements, for example: **Tempa dell'Altare** (3 km. away) with a *double surrounding wall* and *ancient burial sites*. **Piano della Città:** *Remains of fortifications*.

Tricésimo 33019
Udine/Friuli   p.410☐H 2

In Roman times, Tricésimo was a station

Treviso, Palazzo Comunale

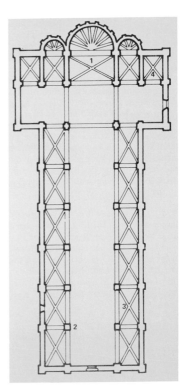

Treviso, S.Nicolò 1 tomb of A. d'Onigo **2** frescos by Tommaso da Modena **3** painting by Bassano **4** oldest frescos in the church

on the Via Iulia Augusta from Aquileia to Noricum (the name is derived from 'ad tricesimum lapidem' 'at the 30th milestone'). It was severely damaged in the earthquake of 1976. Note the church of *S.Maria della Purificazione*, rebuilt in baroque style in 1770–84, but with Bernardo Bissone's fine Renaissance portal (*c.* 1500) from the previous church being retained on the right side.

Environs: Some 4 km. W., **Colloredo di Monte Albano** with what was an interesting castle (begun in the 14C) until it was destroyed in the earthquake of 1976.

Trieste 34100
Trieste/Friuli   p.410☐I 3

Cathedral of S. Giusto (Colle di S. Giusto): Built on the site of the ancient Ro-

man capitol; two older Romanesque churches were united in the 14C (the left aisles come from the church of S.M.Assunta, and the right aisles are from S. Giusto, a centrally planned Byzantine building). Asymmetric façade with a fine Gothic *rose-window;* the *pillars of the main portal* are formed from ancient tombstones. Ancient remains (including columns and capitals) were used in the building of the massive *campanile* (enlarged in the 14C). Today the interior has a nave and four aisles (formed from the combination of the above churches); a fine *wooden ceiling* (rebuilt in the 16C). In front of the choir are the remains of the *mosaic pavement* of a 5C early

Christian basilica, and the old ground plan of S. Giusto is discernible from the apses in the right aisles. The columns have interesting *capitals*. There are *frescos* (probably from the 11C) on the right of the larger side apse, and in the dome is a 13C *mosaic of Christ*. Left aisles: a splendid late-12C *mosaic* of the *Virgin Mary with Christ* in the apse, and, below it, *mosaics with Apostles*. There is a rich *cathedral treasure* in the chapel of St. Antony. In front of the cathedral, there is a Romanesque *baptistery* on the left (with a small *antiquarium* in the portico), and the Gothic *church of S. Michele del Carnale* (with a fine crypt) is on the right.

S. Maria Maggiore (Via S.M. Maggiore): Baroque, built in 1627–82, not completed until the 18C. Fine façade, designed by Andrea Pozzo, a Jesuit. Inside, a nave, two aisles, and a dome (rebuilt in the 19C); the ground plan is a Latin cross. The altar in the right transept has the *Death of St. Ignatius* by Fr. Maffei; fresco in the apse, 1842.

S. Antonio Nuovo (Piazza S. Antonio): Built in classical style by Pietro Nobile in 1827–49, it has a picturesque site on the Canal Grande. The façade has a portico (in the style of an Ionic temple) above a flight of steps. The interior, with a massive dome on double columns, is based on a classical model. The decorations are also classical.

S. Silvestro (Piazzetta S. Silvestro): Romanesque-Gothic, built in the 11C on the site of the city's oldest Christian place of worship (which commemorates the martyrdom of St. Thecla and St. Euphemia). The *campanile* was originally a tower from the old city wall. The façade has a Gothic *rose-window*. Inside (one nave, two aisles), there are fine *capitals* on the columns, and the choir has a ribbed vault.

Roman theatre: (Via del Teatro Romano): Built in the 2C AD, and destroyed during the barbarian invasions. About 6,000 seats, and four wedges of spectators. Laid out in the classical Roman manner (semicircular cavea, stage, scenic building) with a double colonnaded portico at the top.

Castle (Colle S. Giusto): There was a fortress here even in Roman times. Begun by

Trieste, M. Civ. Revoltella, Napoleon

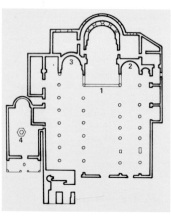

Trieste, **S. Giusto 1** remains of the 5C mosaic pavement **2** mosaic of Christ, 13C **3** mosaic of the Virgin, 12C **4** baptistery

the Venetians in 1368 as a triangular building, it was only completed in 1630 after it had been enlarged and polygonal bastions had been added by the Austrians. It was a residence of the imperial Austrian governors up until the 18C. The castle houses the **Museo Civico,** (which has, on the 2nd floor, reconstructions of the rooms of the governors).

Museo Civico di Storia e Arte (by the Cathedral of S.Giusto): The art collections of the city of Trieste are housed in this building, which also has a *prehistoric collection* with finds from the Karst district, a good *archaeological department,* and a *picture gallery* with a 14C triptych and a room with works by Tiepolo.

Orto Lapidario (beside the above museum): Designed as an open-air museum for Roman antiquities from Trieste and its environs (architectural fragments, remains of large sculptures, tombstones). At the end of the fourth terrace is a *cenotaph* to J.J.Winckelmann, who was murdered in Trieste in 1768.

Museo Civico Sartorio (Via Duca d'Aosta): Housed in the 18C Villa Sartorio, it provides a good impression of the elegant home decor of 19C Trieste.

Also worth seeing: 19C church of *S. Spiridone* (Piazza S.Antonio), an imitation of a Byzantine cruciform, domed basilica. *Roman basilica* (Colle S.Giusto), from the 2C AD. *Arco Riccardo* (Piazzetta Riccardo), a Roman arch from the 1C BC. *Palazzo della Borsa Vecchia* (Piazza della Borsa), dating from 1806, one of the city's finest classical buildings. *Rotonda Pancera* (Via S.Michele/Via della Rotonda), dating from 1818, with a fine façade. *Museo Revoltella* (Via A.Diaz), with a collection of more recent art (chiefly paintings). *Collezione Stavropulos* (Via Imbriani), with some good ancient and medieval sculptures. *Museo del Mare* (Via Campo Marzio), with an interesting seafaring section. The *aquarium* by the harbour. *Piazza Unità d'Italia,* the city centre, opens towards the harbour.

Environs: Muggia (through the southern industrial suburbs of Trieste) with the late Gothic cathedral of *SS. Giovanni e Paolo* (fine portal) and the 11C pillared basilica of *SS.Ermarcora e Fortunato* with a fine in-

Trieste, Palazzo Carciotti

terior (13C frescos, old choir screens, interesting pulpit). Some 7 km. NW is the **Castle of Miramare,** built in English-Norman style in 1856–60 for Maximilian, later the Emperor of Mexico (shot dead in 1867); it has survived intact.

Troia 71029
Foggia/Apulia   p.416☐L 10

Cathedral of S.Maria Assunta: This is one of the finest Norman-Romanesque churches in Apulia. Built in the Tuscan-Pisan style in 1093. In the mid-12C, an earlier building (probably a cruciform domed structure) was incorporated as the transept of the new church. Remains of the old building, for instance some foundations of the apse and other items in the E. transept, were discovered during restoration work. The main façade is divided in two by a cornice supported by consoles. Below, there are round, blind arcades, and a portal with a fine *bronze door*. The work of Oderisius from Benevento (1119), who employed the niello technique, it has 28 panels with saints, bishops, animal heads, and especially fine door knockers; at the bottom right, there is a dedicatory inscription (the third row, and part of the fourth, were renovated in the 16/17C). Above, in the gable, is the large and splendid *rose-window:* it is asymmetric (eleven spokes), with fantastic tracery. The rose-window is framed by animal figures on consoles. On the W. side of the nave is another splendid *portal*. The tympanum has Christ with two angels, and the bronze door (1127) was again built by Oderisius, using the same technique as in the main portal. A fine apse with round arches on double tiers of columns. Inside, fine *capitals* on the columns of the nave. The main feature is the marble *ambo:* built in 1169, it is rectangular and stands on four columns with acanthus capitals; on the left side there is a relief showing an animal fight (lion, sheep, dog: Oriental motif); the surround is framed by a tendril pattern. The lectern is very fine. It is supported by an eagle that has struck a hare (Byzantine motif). The *cathedral treasure* (sacristy) includes some particularly valuable items: three 12C exultet rolls (Easter eulogy), and two ivory receptacles with gold bronze fittings.

Trieste, Castle of Miramare

Also worth seeing: *S. Basilio:* An 11C domed church. A pagan motif survives on a column in the gallery: the garlanded bull was a symbol of the blood sacrifice in antiquity. The cathedral ambo was originally in this church.

Environs: According to a disputed theory, the battle of Cannae is said to have taken place in the *valley of Celone* below Troia in 216 BC (weapons and tombs have been discovered).

Tusa 98079
Messina/Sicily   p.420□K 16

The interesting features of this small hill town include: the **Chiesa Madre** (fine portals; inside, a *Madonna* from the Gagini workshop). There is also the **Chiesa delle Benedettini**, with a medieval portal. In the **town hall** there is an *ancient statue* from Halaesa (see below).

Environs: Some 5 km. N. are the remnants of the ancient town of **Halaesa** (founded in 403 BC, and destroyed by the Arabs).

Tuscania 01017
Viterbo/Latium   p.414□G 8/9

S.Pietro (former cathedral): A masterpiece of medieval Italian architecture. Despite extensive rebuilding in the 12C, the interior (one nave, two aisles) has preserved the basic features of the original church, built by 'maestri comacini' in the 8C. The *façade* was built in the course of the 12C changes, and has rich carved decoration (restored in 1870; the splendid rose-window was reassembled from fragments after the earthquake of 1971). A plain basilican *interior* with a transept and three apses at the E. end. The raised choir begins before the crossing. In the right aisle there is a *ciborium* dating from 1093 and in the choir another. The *ambo sides* are slabs with Lombard plaited-bands. A *stone bench for the cathedral chapter* runs around the main apse, and at the top is a *bishop's throne.* The *frescos* surviving in various places are from the 12C Roman school (with strong Byzantine influence). The *crypt* has a nave and eight aisles, with 28 columns and 12&14C *frescos.*

S. Maria Maggiore (beside S. Pietro): Built in the 8C on the model of S.Pietro, and rebuilt in the 12C with the older components being included and the spatial arrangement preserved. Consecrated in 1206. There is a free-standing Romanesque *campanile* in front of the façade, which is similar to that of S.Pietro. The *central portal* has especially rich carving. A basilican *interior* with an open roof truss. A triumphal arch with a fresco of the *Last Judgement* (14C). *Pulpit* above four stocky columns with 8/9C slabs bearing Lombard plaited-bands.

Also worth seeing: Renaissance church of *S.Maria del Riposo* (1495); fine façade with a rich portal dating from 1512. The 14C church of *S.Maria della Rosa* has a splendid high altar by Giulio Pierino d'Amelia.

U

Udine 33100
Udine/Friuli   p.410□H 2

Cathedral of S. Maria Annunziata (Piazza del Duomo): Romanesque, begun in 1225, but not finished until the 18C, when it underwent a baroque conversion. Traces of the original building can still be discerned externally (particularly in the

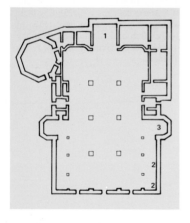

Udine, cathedral **1** Annunziata and angel of the Annunciation by Torretti **2** altarpieces by G.B. Tiepolo **3** frescos by G.B. Tiepolo in the chapel of the sacrament

choir). The *façade* has a beautiful portal. Sides of the nave also have beautiful *portals*: S., Renaissance (1525) N., Gothic, (1396). Octagonal *bell tower* (built on an old baptistery in the 15C. Inside is the *tomb of the patriarch Bertrand*, founder of the cathedral). The cathedral has nave, two aisles and directly interconnected side chapels. Lavish sculpted decoration by Giuseppe Torretti (among others). At the high altar: *Annunciation* and a painting of the *Patriarch Bertrand*; *angel candlestick* on the transept pillars and a *Madonna* in the 2nd sacristy. *Dome frescos* are by L.Dorigny (1654–1742); in the right aisle (1st and 2nd chapels), *altar paintings* by G.B.Tiepolo (1737–8); *frescos* in the *Chapel of the Sacrament* are by the same artist.

Oratorio della Purità (Piazza del Duomo): 18C chapel, formerly a theatre (plaque on façade). Unique *frescos* of scenes from the Old and New Testaments by Giovanni Battista and Gian Domenico Tiepolo (1759). Also of interest is the *font*, of 1479.

S.Maria del Castello (Colle del Castello): Built in the 13C on a much older building (possibly even early-Christian); the town's main church until 1263. Much altered until it was restored to its original form *c.* 1930. The façade has a beautiful

Loggia di S. Giovanni with clock tower ▷

Romanesque *portal*; Venetian style *campanile*. The interior has a nave, two aisles and open roof truss; part of the apse dates back to an 11C building, as do the nave walls. Of particular interest are the *frescos in the right apse* (c. 1250). Those in the main apse from the 14–15C are in bad repair. The wall of the left aisle has *architectural fragments* from the original building.

Castle (finest entrance is that over the Arco Bollani—by Palladio, 1556): Symbol of the city, it was the former seat of the patriarchs and Venetian governors and a one time seat of the Friuli parliament. In 1511, it was destroyed by earthquake and a new building of four wings was planned, although only one wing was built. Beautiful *double flight of steps*. Housed inside are 4 museums: **Museo Civico,** with an interesting *Archaeological Department* and G.A.Pordenone's *Madonna dell'Uva* (Pordenone 1484–1539). **Galleria d'Arte Antica,** a collection of paintings, the following being of particular interest: in Room 24, *Christ's Bleeding* by Vittore Carpaccio (1496) and G.B.Tiepolo's *Consilium in Arena,* (1749). The **Galleria d'Arte Moderna** has Friuli painting of the 19–20C. The **Museo del Risorgimento** (E.wing of ground floor) has mementoes of the Unification of Italy.

Loggia del Lionello/Palazzo del Comune (Piazza della Libertà): 15C, built in Venetian Gothic style on to an older building. The lower floor is a loggia; the upper floor is enclosed (like the Doge's Palace in Venice). The main façade has a *flight of steps*. Beautiful upper floor *windows*. At the N. corner there is a *Madonna* by Bartolomeo Bon (mid 15C).

Loggia (or Porticato) di S. Giovanni (Piazza della Libertà): Built in 1533–9 on the ruins of a 14C chapel; Lombard-Venetian Renaissance style. Tall central arch with single-storey arcades leading from both sides. Now a *war memorial*. Nearby to the left is the *clock tower* (Torre del Orologio) of 1527.

Palazzo Arcivescovile (Piazza Patriarcato): Seat of the Archbishop of Udine

since 1757. The oldest part was built in the 14C; extended and converted to its present form in the 18C. Massive main front. Well worth seeing inside are G.B.Tiepolo's frescos in the 'Galerie' and 'Sala Rossa'. The 'Sala Azzura' has *frescos* of 1538–9, attributed to Giovanni da Udine.

Also worth seeing: 13C church of *S. Francesco* (Via B.Odorico da Pordenone) with beautiful 14C paintings. 18C *Cappella Manin* (Via Torriani) with interesting sculpture by G.Torretti. 14C church of *S. Giacomo* (Piazza Matteotti) with lavish baroque decoration inside. 18C church of the *Madonna delle Grazie* (Piazza I Maggio) with a much-venerated picture of the Madonna (Byzantine, 14C). 16C church of *Madonna del Carmine* (Via Aquileia) with the tomb of Odorico da Pordenone (1265 –1331), a missionary in Asia. 14C church of *S. Antonio Abate* (Piazza Patriarcato) with a beautiful 18C façade. *Palazzo Antoniani* (Via Gemona), built by Andrea Palladio in 1556. 17C *Palazzo della Provincia* (Piazza Patriarcato) with beautiful frescos by Giulio Quaglia (1698). *Piazza del Mercato Nuevo* (now Piazza Matteotti), an old city quarter which has survived with its 14C lay-out and a beautiful fountain by Giovanni da Udine of 1543.

Environs: *c.* 9 km. NW is **Martignacco:** The church of *S.Nicolò* contains beautiful 14C frescos. *c.* 16 km. W. is **Mereto di Tomba:** The *parish church* has fine marble sculpture by G.Tórretti.

Umbertide 06019
Perugia/Umbria   p.414☐ G 7

Santa Croce: 18C baroque building in brick with an altar painting by Luca Signorelli (Descent from the Cross), 1515–17.

S.Maria della Reggia: 1559–1655 with octagonal ground plan.

The 14C **castle** (in the town centre) was partly converted in the 15C.

Environs: Montone: Home town of the condottiere Braccio Fortebraccio. The museum is housed in the Gothic church, *S. Francesco*. **S. Gregorio:** A Romanesque church with 13C Umbrian-Romanesque wood carvings. **S. Giustino:** With the famous *Bufalini Castle* by Giorgio Vasari (a splendid example of its kind). It is privately owned but it is possible to view the elegant Renaissance interior by appointment.

Urbania 61049
Pesaro e Urbino/The Marches   p.414□H 6

S. Cristoforo: Begun in the 10C and converted in the 16&17C. The cathedral acquired a new façade in 1870. Inside: the tomb of Agostino Chigi (d. 1651); in a side room there are epitaphs from a catacomb; the church treasury includes a vase attributed to Pollaiuolo.

Oratorio Corpus Domini: 14C; converted in the 15C. The interior was laid out in the first half of the 16C; frescos of the Holy Family (1501), Prophets and Sibyls (1530–38) are by Raffaello del Colle.

Chiesa del Crocifisso: Houses the tomb of the last Duke of Urbino (Francesco Maria II della Rovere, d. 1631). The 'Crucifixion' at the high altar and the Madonna in the 1st chapel on the right were painted by Federico Barocci.

S. Francesco: Built in 1215 and converted to baroque in 1762. The design for the portal (early 15C) is reputed to have been drawn up by Ghiberti.

Palazzo Ducale: Begun in the 14C and later greatly altered; inside there is a picture gallery.

Environs: S. Angelo in Vado: The birthplace of the painters Taddeo and Federico Zuccarri. The church of *S. Maria dei Servi* (begun in 1331) has a bronze relief of the Virgin. The *Palazzo Comunale* has an interesting Virgin Mary with Saints by Federico Zuccaro.

Urbino 61029
Pesaro e Urbino/The Marches   p.414□H 6

There was a Roman settlement here in 185 BC. The Counts and Dukes of Montefeltro

Udine, Palazzo Arcivescovile, Tiepolo fresco

ruled the city from the 12–15C. They were succeeded by the della Rovere family in 1508 and the city again became a fief of the church in 1626. Under Duke Federico II, who ruled from 1444–82, Urbino was one of Italy's most dazzling courts.

Cathedral (Piazza Duca Federico): Begun in 1474 on the site of an early medieval church, and not finished until 1534. The dome was built in 1604. The church had to be extensively rebuilt after an earthquake in 1789; the façade was completed in 1802. Inside: Martyrdom of St.Sebastian by Federico Barocci, 1557 (3rd altar on the right); St.Cecilia, also by Barocci, and Last Supper, 1599 (4th altar in the the Chapel of the Sacrament, on the left near the choir); the Adoration of the Magi (opp. The Last Supper) by Giovanni Battista Urbanelli (the grille is 15C). In the left transept: statues of Raphael and Clement XI (1710); Emperor Heraclius with the Cross by Palma Giovane, 1629 (3rd altar on the left); Annunciation by Raffaelino da Reggio, 1550 (5th altar). In the choir there is a copy of the altar of 1708 and an Assumption by Christoph Untersberger (1794). On the right by the choir, is the Cappella della Concezione (built 1516; interior arrangement 17–18C) with the Birth of Mary by Cignani and an Assumption by Carlo Maratta, (both early 18C). The fresco fragment (with Madonna) over the altar dates from the medieval building. 16C Figures of Abraham, Isaac, Daniel, Zacharias, Joseph, John the Baptist and John the Evangelist by Fabio Viviani. From the right transept you can get to the *Museo Diocesano:* Among the most important exhibits are a lectern in the shape of an eagle and a 12C staurotheque from S.Michele in Murano.
To the left of the cathedral is the *Oratorio della Grotta,* which consists of 3 chapels in cellar rooms donated to a brotherhood in 1501, 1519 and 1611. *Cappella della Natività:* Adoration of the Shepherds by Emilio Taruffi (1682); *Cappella del SS. Crocifisso* (rebuilt after 1789): Tomb of Federico Ubaldo della Rovere, who was murdered in 1623; *Cappella della Resurrezione:* a marble group, Mary praying by the dead Christ, (by Giovanni dell'Opera

but reworked sometime after 1789). It was originally commissioned by Francesco Maria II della Rovere for his own tomb, but subsequently intended for his murdered son.

S.Domenico (opp. the Palazzo Ducale): The first Dominican church was built in the 13C. The new building (1362–5) was converted to baroque in the 18C and restored in 1934 & 1966. Striking portal in the baroque façade by Maso di Bartolomeo (c. 1450). The lunette has a Madonna with Dominican saints by Luca della Robbia.

S.Francesco (Piazza della Repubblica): Built in the 14C with a single aisle; altered in the 18C. The apse has the 'Vision of St.Francis' by Federico Barocci (completed in 1567 and retouched in 1581. In 1766 an early 16C chapel was removed from the cloister and tranferred to its present position in the church, where it now serves as a sacramental chapel. The ground plan was formerly octagonal and is now square. In the *Cappella Albani* (left aisle), an early Christian sarcophagus with a relief of the Good Shepherd serves as altar.

Oratorio di S.Giovanni Battista (Via Barocci): Built in the second half of the 14C, the interior is completely covered with frescos and it has an ogee wooden ceiling. The Crucifixion scene opposite the front wall dates from 1416 and bears the signatures of the brothers Jacopo and Lorenzo Salimbeni, who also painted the scenes from the Life of John the Baptist on the right wall and both Madonnas on the left wall. The painting of the saint's martyrdom on the left wall dates from c. 1450. Frescos on the front wall are by another artist; the angels at the high altar were painted by Federico Barocci.

S.Sergio (Via Raffaelo): The city's oldest church, which was formerly a bishop's church. Inside are the remains of an early Christian font.

Palazzo Ducale (Piazza Duca Federico):

Urbino, Palazzo Ducale ▷

Urbino, Palazzo Ducale, Miracle of the Host by Uccello

In 1447, shortly after assuming power, Federico da Montefeltro began the new palace building. First the wing on the Piazza Rinascimento was built, probably by Maso di Bartolomeo. From 1465 to 1472 Luciano Laurana built the wing on the Piazza Duca Federico and the buildings behind it, around the Cortile d'onore and the Giardino pensile (hanging garden). This work was continued by Francesco di Giorgio Martini with several colleagues. The oldest wing was heightened in 1504 –8. Around the Cortile d'onore lay the public rooms, ball room, theatre, library, chancellery and throne room. Grouped around the Giardino pensile are the private rooms, those of the Duchess on the cathedral side and those of the Duke opposite, next to the public rooms (both connected to each other by a passage over the outer wall of the Giardino pensile), with the Studiolo, the Muses' temple and the Cappella, which lay in one of the round towers behind a loggia. The E. façade is set back and opens onto a public square. The W. façade with garden, terrace and loggias takes in the surrounding countryside. Rooms are well-proportioned and decoration (apart from one room which has frescos) includes door frames adorned with reliefs, mantlepieces and vaulted consoles, as well as intarsia work on the door wings and in the wall casing of the Studiolo (with figurative depictions among other things), which was partly designed by Botticelli. The palace has housed the Institute of the National History of Art since 1880 and the *Galleria Nazionale delle Marche* since 1912.

From the entrance you come to the arcaded *Cortile d'onore*, which has fresco fragments from S. Domenico and from S. Biagio in Caprile near Fabriano. In the older wing there are the four rooms of the Appartamento della Iole: In the first room (from the S. áre reliefs from the façade; in the second a painted alcove and a marble head

—probably from a Madonna by Agostino di Duccio; in the third—probably the old audience chamber—frescos of famous men were discovered beneath the plaster in 1939; the Salone della Iole is lavishly adorned with reliefs. In the wings on the Piazza Duca Federico are the throne room, with tapestries designed by Raphael, and the ball room with a Madonna and Saints by Marco Basaiti as well as a Madonna by Pietro Alemanno; in the vestibule of the Duchess' suite there is a Madonna by Giovanni Bellini (1490); stucco ceiling in the Duchess' chamber; in the bedroom a polyptych with Mary and Scenes from the Life of Christ by Giovanni Baronzio (1345), a Coronation of the Virgin and a crucifix; in the oratory is a Madonna by Allegretto Nuzi (1372), the ceiling comes from the Palazzo Corboli. In the Sala degli Angeli, the Duke's anteroom, there are blue and white reliefs on the doors which depict Athena, Apollo, Mars, Hercules and a still life, 15C wedding chest; in the bedroom there is a portrait of Duke Federico with his son Guidobaldo by Pedro Berruguete (formerly in the Studiolo), a predella with Profanation of the Host by Paolo Uccello (1466) and Last Supper by Justus of Ghent (1473-74); Salvator Mundi by Melozzo da Forlì (1466), in the dressing room is a Flagellation, from the cathedral sacristy, and Madonna di Senigallia, both by Piero della Francesca (1472-75), further on an Ideal City (c. 1470). The Cappella del Perdono was reputedly designed by Bramante. in the Muses' temple there used to be pictures of the Muses. In the Studiolo there is intarsia work on the pannelling, above which hung pictures of important men (see below). In Guidobaldo II's castle there are delicate stucco reliefs and stone intarsia work. In the Duke's audience chamber is a Portrait of a Lady by Raphael, banner paintings by Luca Signorelli, Crucifixion and Pentecost (1431)

Urbino, St. Dominic

the academy, which was founded in 1869. It is a typical town house with a shop on the ground floor.

Environs: S. Bernardino degli Zoccolanti: This *monastery,* founded in 1425, was dissolved from 1870–1933. *S.Bernardo* dates from the 2nd half of the 15C and has a rectangular choir of a later date. Inside are the tombs of Federico and Guidobaldo da Montefeltro and Elisabetta Gonzaga (1620). Next to the cloister, *S. Donato* (13C). Inside, are remains of frescos of the 15&16C and the tombstone of Guidantonio da Montefeltro.

and Titian's Last Supper and Resurrection (1542–44). The adjoining guest rooms have pictures of illustrious men, from the Studiolo, by Justus of Ghent and Pedro Berruguete (14 others are in the Louvre). On the 2nd floor there are 16C painters: Simone de Magistris, Orazio Gentileschi, Federico Barocci.

Casa di Raffaelo (Via Raffaelo): The house where Raphael was born now houses

Urgagno 24059

Bergamo/Lombardy　　　　　　p.412☐ D 3

Parish church: Built 1792–1874. It contains a late classicist masterpiece by Luigi Caguola.

Also worth seeing: Castello: The castle was begun in 1354 and converted to baroque in the 18C.

Ustica 90010

Palermo/Sicily　　　　　　p.420☐I 15

Ustica is a very fertile volcanic island about 50 km. from Palermo. In antiquity it was used for exile. No buildings have survived from the times of Roman, Saracen or Norman occupation. Of interest on the S.coast are the **Grotta dell' Acqua** and the **Grotta Pastizza** (accessible only by boat; beautiful stalactite caves).

V

Valenzano 70010
Bari/Apulia   p.416☐N 11

Church of Ognissanti (can be reached by the Via Tufaro): This, the last remnant of a Benedictine monastery, is regarded as the purest and most beautiful three-domed church in Apulia. The exterior is very simple and plain; one arch is all that survives of the portico. The domes have square drums.

Environs: Some 15 km. W., **Modugno,** with its two small Romanesque churches: *S.Pietro* in *Balsignano* (one dome, part of the apse has collapsed) and *S.Maria delle Grotte* (frescos).

Varallo Sesia 13019
Vercelli/Piedmont   p.412☐C 3

S. Gaudenzio: This single-aisled 13C church was altered in 1710. It has an extremely high substructure and is completely surrounded by an arcade. There is a triptych (1516–20) by G.Ferrari in the chancel.

S.Marco: The oldest church in the valley, it was altered during the Gothic period and an arcade was added at the front. The exterior frescos are 15C. Inside there are

frescos by G.Ferrari and his pupil G.C.Luini. The *Madonna delle Grazie* (1487–1501) has a fresco cycle by G.Ferrari. Covering almost 915 sq.ft., it dates from 1513 and depicts the Life of Christ. The adjoining monastery has a Pietà, also by G.Ferrari (a work from his youth).

Environs: Santuario del Sacro Monte: Founded in 1486, by B.Caime, a Franciscan friar (d. 1499), who named it

Varallo Sesia, S. Gaudenzio

Nuova Gerusalemme. Its 45 chapels tell the Holy Story, from the Fall of Man up until Christ's tomb, by means of painted terracotta groups and frescos. For example, the 5th chapel has a Crucifixion by G.Ferrari. The *Basilica dell'Assunta* (1614–49) has a modern façade by G.Ceruti. In the dome there is a relief of the Assumption (150 figures) by the Milanese artists Bossola and Volpini.

Varese 21100

Varese/Lombardy   p.412□ C 3

Basilica of S.Vittore: The present building, dating from 1580–1615, goes back to plans by Pellegrini. The façade, 1791, is by Polak. Inside there is a statue of the Virgin Mary, and also a fresco of the Virgin. The massive baroque campanile dates from 1617–1773.

Baptistery: Dedicated to John the Baptist, 12&13C, traces of an earlier 8&9C building. 13C *font* and 14C *frescos*.

Palazzo Estense and Giardini Estensi:

Built 1766–73 for Duke Francesco III of Modena. Today it is the town hall. The park behind it is a classical Italian baroque garden.

Museums: The 18C *Villa Mirabello*, altered according to the English taste in 1843, stands in a park, behind this baroque garden, and now houses the town's museums: *Museo del Risorgimento* and *Museo Archeologico* (warrior's tomb from Sesto Calende, 5C BC).

Also worth seeing: *Piazza Monte Grappa*, a square with porticoes and fountains. It was built in 1927–35 on the site of an old quarter of the town. The architect was Loreti. *S.Giuseppe* (Via Magatti/near to the Piazza Monte Grappa): The 17C church, with its façade dating of 1725, has excellent 17&18C decorations. The numerous *villas* and *gardens* from the late 19C and early 20C have given Varese the reputation of being a garden town, a relatively rare phenomenon in Italy.

Environs: Il Sacro Monte (8 km. to the NW, below the Monte Tre Croci): The last 2 km. of the route to the pilgrimage church

Castel Seprio (Varese), S.Maria Fuori Porta, frescos, 7C

of *S. Maria del Monte* are lined with 14 chapels. They contain life-size images of the 'Mysteries of the Rosary'. The church: From the 15C onwards a pilgrimage developed around a miraculous image from the 14C. Major extensions were begun in 1473 and were continued in the 16&17C. The 14 chapels are also 17C. Beside the church is a *museum* whose exhibits include pictures by Venetian and Flemish painters. **Castiglione Olona:** *Collegiata:* Built from 1421 onwards in Lombard Gothic style. A basilican structure, with three bays, above a tied system. The chancel adjoins the third bay. The main chancel chapel has a five-sided apse and is decorated with frescos by Tuscan painters: in the middle, the Story of the Virgin Mary by Masolino (*c.* 1428), on the right, the Life of St. Stephen by Lorenzo Vecchietta, on the left, the Life of St.Lawrence by Paolo Schiavo, and also on the left, the tomb of a Cardinal, in the Venetian-Lombard style. *Baptistery:* It houses one of Masolino's most mature works: the fresco cycle of 1435 with the story of John the Baptist. The font is modelled on that in S.Giovanni in Bragora (Venice). The *Chiesa di Villa:* Built 1430 –41. Its basic plan is taken from the old sac-risty in the church of San Lorenzo, Florence. The façade was also designed in the style of Brunelleschi. Inside is the monument to Count Guido Castiglioni (1485). *Casa Castiglioni:* This palace was built by the Cardinal and the frescos in the Camera del Cardinale and the Salone are outstanding. The fresco in the Sala del Archivio is also the work of Masolino. **Castel Seprio:** This town, formerly a Lombard castrum, may possibly date from as far back as the late Empire. It was an important fortress in the high Middle Ages. The castle was destroyed by Archbishop Ottone Visconti in 1287 but its ruins show traces of buildings dating from the 5–11C. They include the 7C *Basilica of S. Giovanni,* a 5C *baptistery,* and the 11C church of *S. Paolo* with its hexagonal plan. The early medieval church of *S.Maria Fuori Porta,* a building with a large atrium and three conchs, lies away from the hill on which the castle stands. The frescos inside are today generally thought to be 7C and are attributed to a master of Eastern origin, who was influenced by the Hellenistic tradition. The story of Christ's childhood, based on the Protevangelium of James, is depicted in two horizontal rows. **Somma Lom-**

Il Sacro Monte (Varese), S. Maria del Monte

Veji, Etruscan town

in 1566 and completely rebuilt in 1860. The partly restored rose-windows in the façade are the work of Ruggero de Fragenis (1293).

S.Maria Maggiore: Also destroyed by the Turks in 1566 and devastated by fire in 1645, it was rebuilt in 1785. The *Cappella della Spina* has a *Madonna* of Titian's school, a *Mystic Marriage of St.Catherine* ascribed to Veronese, and a monstrance from the school of Nicola da Guardiagrele.

Veji/Veio
Rome/Latium   p.414□G 9

This was probably the largest town in ancient Etruria. When the Romans conquered it in 396 BC after a ten year siege, the decline of Etruscan rule began. The town ceased to exist in the period following Emperor Hadrian. The first excavations were carried out in the 17&18C. The famous Apollo of Veji (today in the Villa Giulia, Rome) was discovered during further systematic digs carried out earlier this century. The monuments are scattered over an area which can be covered on foot in about 3½–4 hours. Worth seeing: The remains of the so-called *Temple of Apollo* (dedicated to Minerva), where the sacrificial altar survives. The *Ponte Sodo,* an Etruscan rock tunnel which secured the town's supply of drinking water during sieges. The *Grotta Campana* (key obtainable from the custodian in Isola Farnese) is outstanding. This tomb from the first half of the 6C contains what are possibly the oldest Etruscan frescos (much faded).

bardo (27 km. S.: *Castello Visconti,* extant as early as the 12C. Francesco and Guido Visconti had the castle rebuilt in 1448. In the courtyard there is a *collection of local stone monuments.* There is a maze in the garden. 2 km. NE, *Arsago Seprio: S.Vittore,* a 9C basilica with a nave, two aisles and a chancel section with three apses. The inside has a simple alternation of columns, and some of the capitals are Roman spoils. The *campanile* is also 9C. The 11/12C *baptistery* is an octagonal building with a drum, formed of small arches, in the vault. A gallery runs around the inside and there are niches.

Vasto 66054
Chieti/Abruzzi   p.416□K 9

Cathedral of S.Pietro: This church, altered in 1293, was destroyed by the Turks

Velia (ruins)
Salerno/Campagna   p.418□L 12

Some 6 km. to the NW of Ascea lie the ruins of the ancient town of **Elea** (Italian: Velia), an Italic settlement. After the loss of Alalia in Corsica in 540 BC, the Greek Phocaeans used Elea as a trading post on the route to Massilia (today Marseilles). Elea sided with the Romans from the Punic Wars onwards. In the 6/5C BC it

Velleia, excavations

was famous for the so-called Eleatic school of philosophy (Xenophanes, Parmenides, Zeno and others). Excavation work has been in progress since 1899; the items uncovered include the *foundations of some temples* (one dating from the 6C BC), the *remains of houses, thermal baths* from the Roman period (2C AD), and some *sections of the town wall*.

Velleia
Piacenza/Emilia-Romagna   p.412□D 4

This town was originally a Roman municipium (free town) and its heyday was in the 1&2C. However, it was destroyed before the end of the 4C. Today it is one of the most important archaeological centres in Emilia.

The complex consists of: A *forum;* colonnade wrongly reconstructed in the 19C; the pavement survives almost in its entirety and has an inscription with founders' names. A rectangular *basilica.* An *amphitheatre* and *thermal baths* (both very dubious 19C reconstructions). In the N. there are some buildings of unknown function. An 'antiquarium' has been built to the E.

Velletri 00049
Rome/Latium   p.414□H 10

S.Clemente: This cathedral was erected in the 13&14C on the site of a 4C building, and altered 1659–62. The Renaissance portal was built in 1512 to plans by Traiano da Palestrina. The pillared basilica, with its chancel, stands above the Romanesque crypt. There is an altar panel by Antoniazzo Romano, signed and dated 1486, in the second chapel on the right. The ciborium cover is 13C Cosmati work. Remains of 13&14C frescos are to be seen in the apse.

Museum: The most important exhibits include: the 'Madonna and Child with Angels' by Gentile da Fabriano, fragments of 12C rolls, and a good reliquary cross (11/12C).

Palazzo Comunale: Built (1573–90) by Giacomo della Porta, it was rebuilt after being bombed in World War 2. The Museo Comunale houses an important ceramics collection.

Also worth seeing: *Palazzo Ginetti:* A notable feature is the staircase by Martino Longhi the Younger, which leads to loggias.

Venezia/Venice 30100

Venice/Veneto   p.410□ G 3

Venice is thought to have been founded in 421, when a small community grew up in Malamocco under the rule of the Exarch of Ravenna. The Exarch's sphere of influence was itself part of the Byzantine Empire. From 697 onwards, the community was ruled by a 'Duca', elected by the 12 maritime tribunes of Venice, with the agreement of Byzantium; from 742 onwards he was called 'Doge'. In the 9C the seat of the Doge was moved to the area of present-day Venice. The city constantly increased in power as a result of its trading ventures with the East. The relics of Mark the Evangelist were brought from Alexandria to Venice in 828/9, and it was in honour of the relics that the work of building the church of St.Mark was begun in 830. S.Pietro in Castello was elevated to a cathedral in 827. The city's real growth into a major power began around 1000. Venetian ships took Constantinople in 1204. During the Crusades, a powerful colonial empire was developed in the Balkans, Asia Minor, Syria and Palestine. In the 13C, after some internal political disputes, Venice defended its position abroad as a seafaring and trading power in the East, particularly against Genoa. In the 14C, the city's riches led to an almost unimaginable outburst of building, with one palace after another springing up. An original architectural style developed in the 15C and went far towards giving the city its unique aura. The Venetians took control of Verona, Padua, Vicenza, Brescia, Bergamo, Cremona, Ravenna, Udine and Friuli. Wars with other major powers, as well as with the Emperor and the Pope, were conducted successfully for the most part.

The incipient stages of the early Renaissance were to be felt around 1460 and reached their peak in the 16C, especially in Venetian painting. In 1453, when Venice was the largest and richest town in Italy, the Ottomans conquered Constantinople. Then, in the 16C, the Ottoman Empire gradually seized the Byzantine possessions held by the Venetians. Venice was obliged to relinquish its supremacy as a seafaring and trading metropolis. The end of the Republic came on 12 May 1797, three days before Napoleon's troops occupied it. Lodovico Manin, the last Doge, abdicated exactly 1100 years after the State of Venice was founded. The city fell alternately to Italy, Austria and Italy again. Despite the more modern buildings dating from the 19&20C, and despite frequent predictions of its ruin, the city still makes an astonishing, fascinating impression — one that is quite strange to the visitor. It also has an extraordinary amount to offer on the cultural level. The curious quality of a large city having gondolas instead of cars and vaporetti instead of buses is particularly charming in this day and age. Venice is an important cultural centre and has a Fine Arts Academy, an Architectural Institute, a Commercial College, a State Archive, the Marciana National Library, and other libraries, museums and theatres. Since 1895 it has been the site of the art exhibitions held during the Biennale d'Arte Moderna, and since 1945 artistic events with an international stature have been held here; in particular, the festivals of music and film are of world-wide significance.

Venice, regatta, in the background S. Maria della Salute

Piazza S. Marco with Piazzetta: The Piazzetta is framed by the Doge's Palace (q.v.) and by the Libreria Vecchia di S. Marco. The two columns bear the two symbols of Venice, the lion of St.Mark and a statue of St.Theodore, who is the former patron saint of the church. Legend has it that the enormous granite columns were brought from the East to Venice by ship in 1172 and were set up as a symbol of power. The figures on the columns are also from the East. The bronze lion, to which the wings and book were added later, probably originates from 14C China, while the figure of St.Theodore was a Roman marble statue from the time of Hadrian.

The visitor passes from the Piazzetta to the actual Piazza S. Marco, which consists of an L-shaped extension of the Piazzetta and is one of the most beautiful squares in the world. At first glance it appears rectangular but it is in fact trapezoid, widening towards the magnificent façade of San Marco. At the church end the Piazza is 270 ft. across, whereas at the other it is 187 ft. The sides are 577 ft. long. San Marco formerly stood opposite S.Geminiano, which Napoleon had torn down in 1807, directing the so-called *Ala Napoleonica* (Napoleonic Wing) to be built in its stead. The Piazza is flanked on both sides by the long colonnaded buildings of the *Procuratie Vecchie* to the N. (begun in 1500, continued under B.Bon and G.Grigi in 1512, and under J.Sansovino in 1532), and the *Procuratie Nuove* to the S.(begun under the supervision of V.Scamozzi in 1583, and completed by B.Longhena in *c.* 1640). The Torre dell'Orologio, the famous clock tower, stands opposite the NW corner of San Marco. The *Merceria,* the most famous business street in Venice, begins beneath the large central arch of this tower. It is a Renaissance building and on the terrace there are two hammer-striking bronze giants (cast by P.Savini in 1497) which strike the hours. The massive, free-standing *campanile* stands at the corner of the Piazza and the Piazzetta. It was built in the 12C on 9C foundations; the spire has an Archangel Gabriel (early 16C). The tower, 312 ft. tall, fell down in 1902 but was rebuilt (1903–12). At the foot of the campanile stands the *Loggetta di S. Marco,* originally built (1537–40) by J.Sansovino and restored in 1912. Constructed of polychrome marble, it is decorated with figures and reliefs by G.Lombardi, D.Cattaneo and T.Minio.

Piazza San Marco

The 4 bronze statues in the niches are by Sansovino, as is the terracotta group of the Madonna and St.John inside the building. Outside the W. front of San Marco there are *3 flagstaffs* which flew the flags of the kingdoms of Cyprus, Candia and Morea, conquered by Venice. Their bronze bases were cast by A.Leopardi in 1505. Beside the church and to its right, in front of the S.façade, there are two marble pillars from Constantinople (*c.* 6C). The *Pietra di bando,* standing by the SW corner of San Marco, is the stump of a porphyry column plundered from Acre. It was used for the proclamation of new laws.
S.of the church, by the outer wall of the treasury (Tesoro), are the 4C porphyry reliefs of the Tetrarchs. Plundered from Constantinople, they probably represent the 4 sons of Emperor Constantine. The Piazza dei Leoncini, with the massive Palazzo Patriarcale (1837–50), opens out between the clock tower and San Marco. The two marble lions by G.Bonazza are in the foreground.

Basilica of S.Marco/St.Mark's church: 1. History: This church, probably the richest in the entire Western world, was preceded by another building, the so-called *palace chapel,* dedicated to St. Theodore. Then, in 828/9, 2 sailors brought the relics of St.Mark the Evangelist from Alexandria to Venice. These relics were buried in 836 in a church founded especially for this purpose. In 976, after this original church had been damaged, Doge Petro Orseolo I had a second one built, of which only the small walled-in crypt below the crossing, and also some traces in the masonry, still survive. Its key elements, narthex, domes and a cross-shaped layout, have survived from the building of 836. The main parts of the present-day church were built in the 2nd half of the 11C under Doge Domenico Contarini and completed in 1094. Western and Romanesque elements, such as the hall crypt beneath the sanctuary, were added to the original Byzantine model, and an original Venetian style of architecture developed. The 5 domes, which are arranged in a cross, were not raised, although the church had two storeys. A new phase of building began in 1204 and the inside was

completely covered with mosaics. The columned W. façade was built and a N. narthex. The height of the domes was increased to good effect by means of external domes. The façades of the N. and S. narthexes were decorated further in the 13&14C. The *baptistery* (31), the bronze doors of the W. front, the Gothic tracery windows on the W. and N. façades, and the Cappella di S.Isidoro (39), were all added. A further phase started in 1385, when the upper façade was crowned with late Gothic statues on the points of the arches and figures in the tabernacles. The new sacristy (36) and the Cappella di S. Teodoro were built in the late 15C, while the Cappella Zen (30) dates from the early 16C.

2. The present-day building: W. façade (the front facing the Piazza S.Marco): The lower order has 5 door-arches (1–5) with columns; the capitals are partly Byzantine and the doorways are rectangular. Between them, the walls are covered by Veneto-Byzantine reliefs from the 13C: 1st doorway (1), Porta di S.Alippio, with 13C reliefs above the portal. 2nd doorway (2; 14C), window with tracery and bronze doors from 1300 (the decoration above the door stems from the 2nd quarter of the 13C; the mosaic showing the Translation of the Body of St.Mark dates from 1728). The 3rd doorway (3) has an enormous mosaic of the Last Judgement dating from 1836 in the upper tympanum, (the reliefs on the 13C arches are reminiscent of French carved portals). 4th doorway (4), bronze doors and window with tracery as in the 2nd doorway (above them, a mosaic of 1660 showing the Arrival of the Body of St.Mark). The 5th doorway (5) is reduced in size owing to the Cappella Zen (locked door; fine inlay work and carving, no later than the 11C; above this, a mosaic, *c.* 1660, showing the Removal of the Body of St.Mark from Alexandria). The upper order of the façade rises from a terrace to which staircases (9) to the right and left of the main door (7) give access. The arches of the upper order have mosaics by A.Gaetano (1616/17); in the centre there is a large window with reliefs in the archivolt and, above this, the huge statue of St.Mark giving his blessing (*c.* 1419). There are 16C statues on the points of the other 4 arches. Below the four, outer water-carriers (*c.*1400), there are six tabernacles containing statues standing on the piers. Above the central doorway, at the feet of the figure of St.Mark, there stand copies of the 4 massive *bronze horses* which date from the Roman Imperial period. Taken to Constantinople in the 4C, they were shipped from the hippodrome there to Venice in 1204. In 1797 Napoleon's soldiers carried them off to Paris but in 1815 they were finally returned to San Marco.

S.Façade (the 1st part faces the Piazzetta, the 2nd part adjoins the Doge's Palace): Essentially, it follows the pattern of the W. façade. The wall of the 2nd part, set further forward owing to the Tesoro (32), is covered with ornament and on the lower level there is a 14C two-arched window. Before the Zen chapel was built, the archway in the 1st part (10) contained an entrance door, now walled up, leading into the W. narthex. The former door arch and the 13C mosaic in the tympanum are still inside the Zen chapel. The adjoining arch

Venice, Basilica of San Marco: 1 to **5 doorways 6** porta di S.Pietro **7** main portal **8** Porta di S.Clemente **9** Doge's monument **10** archway with columns in front of the Zen chapel **11** doorway to the baptistery **12 Porta dei Fiori 13** E. dome **14** Ascension dome **15** dome of the Pentecost **16** dome of St.John **17** dome of St.Leonard **18** Deesis, Byzantine relief, 11C **19** Madonna del Bacio, devotional relief **20** Sorrowing Christ, around 1400 **21** Altar of St.James, wall altar **22** Altar of the Sacrament, 17C, with modern baldacchino (with columns) **23** Byzantine icon in relief (Virgin Mary, 13C) **24** altar of St.Paul, counterpart of the altar of St.James (21), 15C; statue of St.Peter, 16C **25** Altar of the Virgin Mary, 1617, with Byzantine devotional picture, around 10C; next to it 3 relief icons, 13, 9&17C **26** Madonna dello Schioppo,

large, very beautiful Veneto-Byzantine relief icon, 13C **27** altar of the Annunciation, 14C; statues, 13C; painted crucifix, brought from Constantinople to Venice in 1205, miraculous properties **28** Iconostasis; built by Jacobello and Pierpaolo Dalle Masegne and their workshop above the end wall of the crypt, beautiful columns supporting figures, 1394–1404; in the midst of the superb, late Gothic marble statues there rises, above the steps, a large bronze crucifix by Jacopo di Marco Bennato **29** pulpits, built with spoils in the early 14C **30** Cappella Zen **31** baptistery **32** Tesoro/treasury **33** Cappella di S. Clemente **34** presbytery **35** Cappella di S.Pietro **36** sacristy **37** Cappella S.Teodoro **38** stair to crypt **39** Cappella di S.Isidoro **40** Mascoli chapel

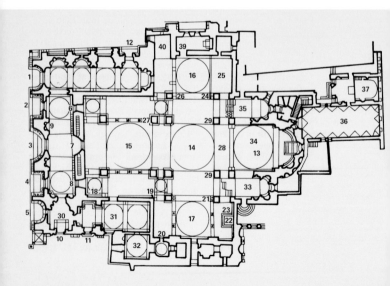

(11), comprising a door and a 14C window with tracery, leads into the ante-room of the baptistery, and to the right of it is a Gothic two-arched window. The upper order of the S.façade continues the W. façade, with its terrace, late Gothic arches crowned with figures, and figures in tabernacles. **N. Façade** (on the Piazza dei Leoncini): Like the W. façade, it consists of a lower series of arches, a terrace, and an upper order with figures on the arches and in tabernacles. The N. front forms a right angle with the wall of the Mascoli chapel (40) in the transept. The next chapel, the Cappella di S. Isidoro (39) adjoins the Palazzo Patriarcale on the E. There are reliefs, some of which are Byzantine, on the lower storey of the 1st part. The fine Porta dei Fiori (12) dates from the 3rd quarter of the 13C. Also notable are the carving of the archivolts, and the large icons in relief above the Porta and the adjoining transept wall. Features of particular interest in the upper order include the so-called Doccioni (water-carriers) on the arches, which are probably the work of P.Lamberti in the 1st half of the 15C. **Narthexes:** The W. and N. narthexes pass smoothly into one another but were built in different periods, the W.

in the 11C, the N. not until the 13C. However, the pairs of marble columns in front of the inner wall and the roof, with the domes on pendentives and tunnel vaulting in the W. section, are most probably later (probably 13C). The mosaic pavement in the W. section may be late 11C, while that in the N. section could date from the 13C. The bronze leaves of the main door, inlaid with silver, date from the 1st half of the 12C and are modelled on the Byzantine door-leaves of the Porta di S.Clemente (8). The angels to the right and left of the door arch are 12C. The St.Mark in the vault dates from the mid-16C, as do the mosaics in the Pozzo (light shaft) which are the work of the brothers Fr. and V.Zuccato. Above the Porta di S.Clemente is a mosaic by Zuccato (1532), and next to it on the right is the door to the Cappella Zen. However, the festive, rich impression made by the narthexes results from the mosaics that cover all the vaults. A 13C late Romanesque picture cycle on a gold ground begins in the S. Other features include the monuments (*c.* 1100) to Doge Vitale Michiel and his wife (9) in the W. narthex and, in the N. narthex, further 13–15C tombs, some of them with remnants of

Piazza San Marco, painting by Querena

early Christian sarcophagi. *Interior:* The inside of the church is dark, despite the 16 small, round-arched windows under the domes, the large rose-window in the S. transept, and the W. windows. Arches and columns between the pillars make it appear that the inside is divided into a nave and two aisles and they support an 11C gallery. The uneven pavement is inlaid with mosaics. The main attraction of the church, and of the narthexes, are the *mosaics,* which cover a total area of 43,000 sq. ft., the largest area of mosaics in the world. They date mainly from the 11–14C, and were restored in various places from the 15C onwards. The entire upper part of the church, the five domes, and all the tunnel vaults in between, are covered with mosaic cycles on an unbroken gold ground. The most significant cycle is that depicting the Story of Christ. Here, the east dome (13) shows Christ blessing, the Ascension dome (14) has the Risen Christ (*c.* 1200), the dome of the Pentecost (15) depicts the 12 Apostles enthroned with the Holy Ghost (*c.* 1150). The dome of St.John (16) is decorated with scenes from the Life of the Evangelist, while the dome of St. Leonard (17) has 4 saints (13&17C). The diagram of the ground plan gives details of other decoration; the *iconostasis* (28) and the *Pala d'Oro* in the sanctuary (34) are amongst main features of interest.

Cappella Zen (30): The present chapel was converted (1503/4–15, restored 1604) from an entrance to the narthex in order to provide a fitting resting-place for the tomb of Cardinal Giambattista Zeno, nephew to the Venetian Pope Paul II. The early 16C tomb, with the large recumbent figure and 6 allegories, is of interest. The altar statues and the bronze baldacchino were built by Paolo Savin and Pietro Campagnato to designs by A.Lombardi, who was also responsible for the statue of the Madonna (1515). The two lions beside the altar, the icons in relief on the wall to the right, and the standing Madonna just to the left of the altar, all date from the 13C.

Baptistery (31)/Cappella di S. Giovanni: Furnished as a baptistery in 1312–20; very fine mid 14C mosaics; hex-agonal font, probably designed by J.Sansovino in *c.* 1545 and built by T.Minio and Desiderio da Firenze, with 8 pictorial reliefs on the bronze lid. The bronze figure of the Baptist is by Segala, 1565. The two 14C tombs of Doges, the 13–15C paintings behind the altar, and the 13C fresco fragment, are all of interest.

Tesoro/Treasury (32): The thick walls of the Tesoro contain some parts dating from the 1st millennium which were probably part of a corner tower of the Doge's Palace. The church treasure was kept here from 1209 onwards. The building was altered and strengthened in the 15C. The treasury consists of 3 rooms, namely the Anti-Tesoro, the sanctuary (which has 110 reliquaries in 11 wall niches), and the Tesoro proper. Despite the looting and melting-down (1797) of some its contents, it houses over 300 precious objects and, in terms of cultural history, is one of the most important collections of treasure in the Western world. The works plundered from Byzantium during the conquest of Constantinople are of particular value among the relics, garments, gold pieces, glasses, icons in relief and other objects. Note in particular the so-called 6/7C *Throne of St.Mark,* an Alexandrian marble reliquary.

Cappella di S.Clemente (33): This was originally connected to the Doge's Palace and was reserved solely for the Doges. The 14C columned iconostasis is from the workshop of Dalle Masegne. The beautiful 12C mosaic in the apse, and the altar with 15&16C figures, are of interest.

Sanctuary (34): The old choir stalls of the choir, and the tapestries dating from 1551, are today in the Museo Marciano and Museo Correr. However, the *singing galleries,* designed by J.Sansovino in 1537 (left side) and 1541–4 (right side), are still in place. Late Gothic tabernacles, and wall retables with relics, originating from the Dalle Masegne workshop, are to be found on both sides on the pillars. On the late Gothic columned balustrades of coloured marble, to the sides of the high altar, there are 4 statues of the seated Evangelists (mid-16C) by Sansovino. The four statues of the patriarchs (on the left) were added by Gabriele Orlandini and Battista Nicolini in 1614. The high altar was rebuilt, from old parts, in 1834-6. The bronze lanterns are 16C, the baldacchino with its statues and carved columns is 13C, while the rear pair of columns possibly dates from as early as 5/6C Byzantium. Behind the altar, and on its own marble pedestal, is the famous *Pala d'Oro,* an enormous gold altarpiece which is extremely richly decorated with figures and precious stones, and dates from between 976-1345 (Byzantine and Venetian gold and enamel). In the central niche of the apse, there is a tabernacle with turned 16C columns and a bronze relief by Sansovino on the tabernacle door. The bronze door in the apse wall, leading to the sacristy, is a fine late work by Sansovino.

Cappella di S.Pietro (35): The principal feature is the iconostasis from the Dalle Masegne workshop, *c.* 1397.

Sacristy (36): A bright, broad Renaissance building dating from 1471, with 16C vault mosaics and sumptuous 15&16C intarsia cupboards. The sacristy is adjoined by two rooms, the *Sagrestia Capitolare* (with a

Nativity of Christ by G.B.Tiepolo on the altar) and the *Antisagrestia.* There is also the *Cappella di S. Teodoro* (37), which was built as a new church for the Doges in 1486.

Crypt (38): The 11C hall crypt is underneath the sanctuary of the Cappella di S. Pietro and of the Cappella di S.Clemente. To the W. of this crypt is the old, walled-up 10C crypt. The antependium on the altar dates from the 15C.

Cappella di S.Isidoro (39): The relics of St. Isidore were brought from Chios to Venice in 1125. The chapel, decorated with mosaics, was built in honour of the relics in 1354-5.

Cappella dei Mascoli/Cappella Nova (40): Built in 1430, from 1618 onwards it was dedicated to the brotherhood of unmarried men. The locked outer door leading to the Piazzetta dei Leoncini is 14C, as are the interesting altar carvings. The mosaics are 14&15C.

Museo Marciano: This museum, which has exhibits from the church treasure, is housed above the narthex.

San Marco, interior

San Marco, bronze horse and clock tower

Other churches:

S.Alvise (extreme N. of the town, on the Rio S.Alvise): A nuns' church dating from 1388. The building was altered in the 17C, and only the façade and parts of the sacristy and of the campanile survive from the original structure. The nuns' gallery, and two early works by Tiepolo on the right side, are worth seeing.

SS.Apostoli (Campo SS.Apostoli): A very old parish church, rebuilt several times. Painting of guardian angel by F.Maffei (2nd half of 17C) on the altar in the chapel to the left of the high altar; remains of frescos (1300) in the chapel to the right. The *Cappella Corner* (Venetian early Renaissance), with an altar painting by G.B.Tiepolo, was added in the late 15C.

S. Bartolomeo (SE of the Rialto): Founded in the 12C as a church for German merchants; in the 18C it was converted into a building with a nave and two aisles. It has panel paintings which are among the chief works of the Venetian early Renaissance, including 4 by Seb. del Piombo (1507–9, originally on the organ shutters).

S.Michele in Isola

S.Benedetto (further S., towards the Canal Grande): 1685. 2nd side altar on the right, St.Sebastian by B.Strozzi, a masterpiece of the Venetian baroque, and the 1st side altar on the left has an altarpiece by Tiepolo.

Carmini/S.Maria del Carmelo (in the SW of the town, near the Rio di S. Barnaba): A 13&14C columned basilica, with a nave and two aisles; the chancel, façade and interior were rebuilt in the 16C. At which point the *rich furnishings* were added. Late 16C paintings in the clerestory. In the right aisle: the medieval bronze relief with a Deposition by Francesco di Giorgio Martini; statues by Girolamo Campagna and Antonio Corradini, 1721; fine carved organs from the 16C, with paintings by Marco Vincentino and Andrea Schiavone. In the left aisle: panel painting by L.Lotto, *c.* 1523. The 15C sacristy and 16C cloister are worth seeing.

S.Cassiano: Originally 10C, it was rebuilt in the 17C as a hall church with a nave and two aisles. The campanile is 15C. Inside there are fine paintings by Marconi, A.da Messina, L.Bassano and J.Tintoretto.

S. Caterina (in the N. of the town): A nuns' church, originally 9C, rebuilt several times. 15C nuns' gallery. The high altar has a copy of a Veronese which is in the Accademia, and also paintings by Tintoretto of the legend of St.Catherine.

S. Eustachio/S. Stae (Canal Grande): Beautiful façade, 1709, by Domenico Rossi. Fine paintings inside, including ones by Tiepolo (Bartholomew), G.A.Pellegrini (Andrew), and G.B.Piazzetta (Jacob).

S.Fantin (near the Piazza S.Marco, opposite the Teatro La Fenice): A Renaissance church dating from 1507. Sanctuary to a design by J.Sansovino, 1564. Fine decoration, including the tomb of V.Dandolo, *c.* 1517, above the sacristy door, and a Romanesque font.

S.Felice (Strada Nuova): A Renaissance church, originally 10C, and restored in

Venice, S. Maria Gloriosa dei Frari 1 tomb of Pietro Bernardo (d. 1538), parts of it by T. Lombardo **2** above the portal the baroque monument to Girolamo Garzoni (d. 1688). A rectangular door with tympanum and statues from the 15C leads from outside to the church interior **3** tomb of the procurator of S. Marco, Alvise Pasqualino (d. 1522), by L. Bregno **4** altar by B. Longhena, 1663; altarpiece by Franc. Rosa, 1670 **5** bronze statuette by G. Campagna, 1593 **6** monument to Titian, who is reputed to have been buried here in 1576, by L. and P. Zandomeneghi, 1838 – 52 **7** Zeno-Valier altar with paintings and frescos by G. Salviati, c. 1560 **8** only the two gable figures and the marble statue of St. Jerome remain of the old stucco relief retable by A. Vittoria, 1560; altarpiece by Gius. Nogari, 1763 **9** tomb, 16C **10** Pesaro Altar with altarpiece by Jac. Palma **11** and **12** two baroque monuments **13** monument to Benedetto Brugnolo di Legnago (d. 1505), by Giov. Maria Mosca **14** door to cloister (closed) with decorative terracotta frieze, 1420; above it an urn with the ashes of the Count of Carmagnola, 1432 **15** wall tomb of Jacopo Marcello (d. 1484), Pietro Lombardi and his workshop **16** wall tomb of Beato Pacifico, who was, according to legend, architect of the Frari, around 1335 **17** round-arch portal to the sacristy with monument to Benedetto Pesaro (d. 1503) **18** wooden equestrian statue of the Roman Paolo Savelli (d. 1405) **19** sacristy, 1450, with Veronese vault and wall paintings; on the entrance wall a picture by P. Veneziano (Enthroned Virgin) **20** tabernacle of the relics of the Blood of Christ, 15C **21** door to the 14C chapterhouse, which contains the tomb of doge Francesco Dandolo (d. 1339) **22** relic altar, 1711 **23** altar with triptych by G. Bellini, 1488 **24** Cappella Bernardo with panel painting by B. Vivarini,

1482; on the right wall tomb with sculptures from 1370 – 80 **25** chapel of the sacrament with wall tomb of 1336 on the right and wall tomb from the mid-14C on the left side **26** Florentine chapel; national chapel of the Florentines with altar of 1436. In the middle niche of the retable is the modern-looking wooden figure of John the Baptist by Donatello, around 1516 **28** Assunta by Titian, 1516, behind the high altar, an enormous retable flanked by a pair of Corinthian columns **29** monumental tomb of doge Francesco Foscari (d. 1457), built by P. and A. Bregno in 1460 with beautiful figures and coats-of-arms of 1473 **30** monument to doge Niccolò Tron (d. 1473) by A. Rizzo with good statues by same **31** chapel of St. Francis with altar painting by B. Licinio, early-16C. 14C wall tomb on the right. Frescos by the younger Jac. Palma and by Vicentino **32** Trevisan chapel. On the right wall tomb of Melchiore Trevisan (d. 1500) with statue by L. Bregno and good frescos. Gothic sarcophagus from the mid-14C on the left, above it a fragment of a ceiling painting by Tiepolo **33** Milanese chapel. Left: On the pavement at the entrance is a tomb slab for Claudio Monteverdi (d. 1643). Altar, 1503, panel painting by A. Vivarini and M. Basaiti **34** Cappella Corner, 1422; with a font, crowned by a marble statue of John the Baptist by Jac. Sansovino, 1545. The wall frescos (around 1460) and the reliefs on the end of the bench originate from the Mantegna circle. On the altar is a triptych of 1474 by Bart. Vivarini. Window with colourful stained glass pictures from the 15C **35** the tympanum of the outer chapel portal has a most beautiful tympanum relief, c. 1440 **36** wall tomb of Generosa Orsini-Zen and her son Maffeo, beneath which are late Gothic stalls of the 15C **37** above the door to the campanile is a tympanum relief, 1390; above it a

The Frari

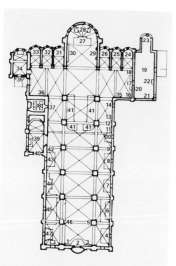

painting by P. Negri, 1670 **38** campanile **39** Cappella Emiliana (S.Pietro), 1434. Marble polyptych with figures from various periods on the altar. Niche figures, *c.* 1440. On the left, wall tomb, 1464 **40** entrance to church, statue of St.Peter in tympanum outside, painted crucifix from the late-15C, inside **41** Marble choir screens, begun under Bart. Bon, 1468 and completed by Pietro Lombardo, 1475, surrounded by choir screens; choir stalls by German wood carvers under the supervision of Marco Cozzi, 1468 **42** monument to Jacopo Pesaro with Titian painting; Pesaro Madonna, (1519–1526) **44** mausoleum of Doge Giovanni Pesaro (d. 1659), built in 1669 to a design by B. Longhena, most of the figures by M.Barthel **45** monument to Antonio Canova (d. 1822), executed by the Canova's pupils: Ferrari, Rinaldi, Zandomeneghi and Bosa, 1827 **46** two fonts with bronze figures by Gir. Campagna **47** side altar of the Holy Cross with statues by Giusto Le Court; adjacent to the right: wall tomb, 1360

1957. The altarpiece on the right side altar shows a picture by the youthful Tintoretto (*c.* 1547).

S.Francesco della Vigna (in the E. of the city): A monumental church begun in 1534 to a design by J.Sansovino and completed in 1572 when Palladio provided the façade. A panel painting of the Virgin enthroned, by Antonio da Negroponte, 1450–60, on the altar in the right transept. Left of the choir, the *Cappella Giustinian*, with fine sculptures dating from *c.* 1500, and an interesting retable, also *c.* 1500. The 5th chapel in the left aisle has an altarpiece by P.Veronese, 1562, while the 3rd chapel has ceiling paintings by G.B.Tiepolo. 15C *cloisters*, and chapels; the *Cappella Santa* opposite the transept has a painting by Giovanni Bellini, 1507.

Frari/S.Maria Gloriosa dei Frari (to the W. of the Canal Grande): Along with SS.Giovanni e Paolo, it is the most important late Gothic religious building in Venice. First built in 1338, pulled down in 1415. The present building was begun in 1340, starting with the chancel, then the transept and then the campanile in 1361 –9, while the nave was not built until 1420–43. A vaulted, columned basilica, it is an impressive brick building with a nave, two aisles, a broad transept and 7 choir chapels. The main point of interest is the *Assunta* (Assumption) by Titian (No. 28 in the plan). The monastery buildings, which are part of the Franciscan church and have 16C cloisters, today house the State Archive.

SS. Giovanni e Paolo, Colleoni monument

S. Geremia (in the N., by the Canal Grande): Built by Corbellini as a domed church in 1735.

Gesuati/S. Maria del Rosario (by the Canale della Giudecca): Designed by Massari and built by the Dominicans in 1726 –36, it has a massive, beautifully articulated façade, a bright and interesting, domed interior, and it is richly decorated (altarpieces by Piazzetta, Ricci, Tintoretto and Tiepolo, who also painted the ceiling frescos). It stands on the neck of land which ends with the Dogana.

Gesuiti/S. Maria Assunta (in the N., near the landing-stage for Murano): The Crociferi were active here from 1200 onwards but only a small oratory, decorated inside in the late 16C with a cycle of paintings by Palma Giovane, has survived from their monastery. The present church was built from 1714 onwards to designs by Dom. Rossi. The façade is particularly impressive. The inside, with its stucco and marble, its bright colours and golds, and its frescos by Francesco Fontebasso, has sculptures by G.Torretti in the niches of the pillars of the crossing, and also at the high altar. There is an altarpiece by J.Tintoretto on the altar of the Virgin in the left transept. In the last left-hand chapel of the nave is the church's main attraction: the large altarpiece of the *Martyrdom of St.Lawrence* by Titian, dating from before 1559. There are paintings by Palma Giovane and Fumiano in the sacristy.

S. Giacomo dell'Orio/S. Giacomo del Lupio: This parish church, with its picturesque site on the Campo of the same name in the NW of the city, dates from 1225 (campanile and transept). Its nave and two aisles were added in the 15C, and the fine sanctuary with its dwarf gallery was built in the 16C. The inside is decorated with works by Tizianello, Palma Giovane and L.Lotto (high altarpiece dating from 1546). In the old sacristy (1775), paintings by Palma Giovane, and in the Cappella di S.Lorenzo there are some more paintings by the same artist and an altar painting by G.B.Pittoni; in the baptistery (1566) there are works by Palma Giovane, again, and Fr. Zugno. The new sacristy has ceiling paintings by Paolo Veronese, and also houses a collection of important pic-

SS. Giovanni e Paolo, view of interior

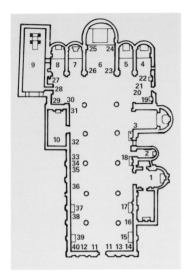

doge by G. Campagna **25** famous monument, masterpiece of the Venetian Renaissance, to Andrea Vendramin, late 15C, to design by T.Lombardo, with bas-reliefs by P. and A.Lombardo and statues by T.Lombardo **26** Gothic monument to Doge Marco Corner (d. 1368) with statue of the Madonna by N. Pisano **27** monument to Doge Seb. Venier (d. 1578) **28** monument to doge A.Venier (d. 1400) **29** wall tomb of Agnese and Orsola Venier, early-15C **30** monument to Leonardo Prato da Lecce (d. 1511) **31** marble altar, 16C; above the sacristy monument to Jacopo Palma Vecchio and Giovane (father and son), 1621 **32** above: monument to Doge Pasquale Malipiero (d. 1462) by P. Lombardo **33** monument to Senator G.B. Bonzo (d. 1508) by G.M. Mosca, 1525 **34** above: monument to Pompeo Giustiniani, 1616 **35** important monument to Doge T.Mocenigo (d. 1423), work of P.Lamberti and G.di Martino da Fiesole **36** monument to Doge Niccolò Marcello (d. 1474), work of P.Lombardo **37** altar with copy of the original Titian painting (burnt) **38** monument to Orazio Baglioni (d. 1617) **39** Renaissance altar with statue of St.Jerome, a masterpiece by A.Vittoria **40** monument, 19C, above it a late-15C monument

tures: Veronese, Buonconsiglio, Fr. da Ponte (*c.* 1570) and Palma Giovane.

S. Giacomo di Rialto (on the Canal Grande):

A domed church dating from the 12C, the Greek-cross plan, similar to that of San Marco, was retained when it was rebuilt in the 16&17C. The columns and capitals inside are 12C, while the columned W. portico is late 14C.

S.Giobbe/SS.Giobbe e Bernardino (in the NW):

Begun in 1450 as a flat-roofed building, altered and enlarged in 1470. A dome was added to the sanctuary, which contains the tomb of Doge Lod. Moro. A series of notable chapels line the N. side of the nave, the most interesting being the Cappella dei Martini (the 4th starting from the chancel), which is decorated in Tuscan style, with a dome on pendentives and patterns of glazed, coloured tiles.

S.Giorgio dei Greci (near to S.Zaccaria):

This, the church of the Greek colony, was built between 1539 and 1561 (the cupola dates from 1571, while the campanile is later than 1587). The subdivision of the interior, where there is an elongated, vaulted hall area, is in accordance with the Greek rite. The iconostasis has a fine 14C icon of Christ Pantocrator.

Venice, SS.Giovanni e Paolo/Zanipolo 1 late Gothic Cappella dell'Addolorata, converted to baroque, with wall paintings and stuccoed Soffitto by G.B. Lorenzetti, around 1639 **2** Cappella della Paolo/Hyacinth Chapel with Byzantine Madonna **3** Cappella di S.Domenico with very beautiful ceiling painting by G.B. Piazzetta, 1727 **4** Cappella del Crocifisso with baroque altar, to the right and left of which are bronze statues by A.Vittoria **5** Cappella della Maddalena with 16C altar retable **6** sanctuary with baroque high altar **7** Cappella della Trinità **8** Cappella Cavalli **9** Cappella del Rosario, 1582; burnt down in 1867 with paintings by Tintoretto, Palma, Titian and others; restored, 1913, it now contains works by Veronese and pupils; the original statues by A.Vittoria and G.Campagna survived **10** sacristy, 16&17C with ceiling painting by M.Vecellio; on the altar a painting by Palma Giovane **11** portal with the monuments to Doge Alvise Mocenigo (d. 1577) and his wife **12** monuments to Doge Giovanni Mocenigo (d. 1485) by T.Lombardo **13** monument to Doge Pietro Mocenigo (d. 1476) by P.Lombardo **14** 13C relief, epitaph to Doge Ranieri Zeno (d. 1268) **15** side altar with retable by F.Bissolo **16** early baroque wall tomb of Marcantonio Bragadin **17** side altar with very good retable, *c.* 1475–80 **18** baroque marble mausoleum for the Doges Bertuccio and Silv. Valier (d. 1658 and 1700) **19** panel painting by Alvise Vivarini (1474) and Coronation of the Virgin by G. Martini da Udine (early 16C), above it the equestrian statue of Nicola Orsini (d. 1509) **20** altar with painting by Lorenzo Lotto, 1542 **21** wall tomb, 1510, above the door **22** altar with Christ and St. Peter and St. Andrew by R. Marconi **23** monument to Doge Michele Morosini (d. 1382) **24** monument to Doge Leonardo Loredan (d. 1521) with statue of the

S.Giorgio Maggiore/S.Stefano (on the Isola di S. Giorgio Maggiore, in the S.): Built 1566–80 to a design by A.Palladio, it was originally part of an old Benedictine monastery. One of the masterpieces of 16C Western architecture, it is, despite the long sanctuary, a well proportioned building with a nave and two aisles, a transept, and a dome on a drum over the crossing. The beautiful façade was not added until 1597 –1610. Inside: Two late works by Tintoretto in the chancel (Shower of Manna and Last Supper). A wooden crucifix, 1400, in the right aisle (2nd altar) and, next to it (1st altar), a Nativity of Christ by J.Bassano. Further altarpieces by Tintoretto and his workshop and by Seb. Ricci. The late 16C choir stalls have carvings by Albert de Brulle. 4 Evangelists by Girolamo Campagna on the main altar. Today, the *monastery* houses the 'Fondazione Cini'. The *refectory* by Palladio, and the *staircase* and *library* by B.Longhena, are especially worth seeing. The 15C *dormitory* is behind the church. To the right of the church are *2 cloisters,* the rear one having been built in 1516–40 by Giovanni Buora and his son Antonio, while the front one dates from 1579–1614.

S. Giovanni in Bragora: 8C parish church; some of the columns in the present church date from this period. In 1475 –9 it was enlarged into a late Gothic basilica with a nave and two aisles, and a new sacristy was added in 1485 – 94. Inside: a large canvas by Palma Giovane on the W. wall. Remains of frescos on the wall and chancel arch. A 15C Pietà in the first side chapel on the right. There is a 15C wooden shrine on the left wall. 13C marble icons above the sacristy door. To the right of the door there are 4 15C panel paintings. The sacristy has a large wooden crucifix by Leonardo Tedesco, *c.* 1490/1. The old retable with the painting by Cima da Conegliano (Baptism of Christ, 1492–4) is on the rear wall of the apse. There are more pictures, by Bart. and Alvise Vivarini, in the chancel chapels and side chapels. The baptismal chapel has a 15C octagonal font of red marble.

S.Giovanni Crisostomo (NE of the Ri-

alto): A domed Renaissance church by M.Coducci, begun in 1497, with a very fine, clear ground plan and structure. Inside: the high altar has an altarpiece by Seb. del Piombo (1509–11). The altarpiece of the 1st side chapel on the right is by Giov. Bellini, and in the 1st side chapel on the left there is a relief of the Coronation of the Virgin by T.Lombardo (1502).

S. Giovanni Decollato: This columned basilica with a nave and two aisles stands near the Fondaco dei Turchi. It was founded after 1000. The outer walls, high clerestory, and nave columns, all survive from the 11C. The 13C remains of frescos in the N. apse chapel are interesting as the oldest surviving frescos in Venice.

S.Giovanni Elemosinario (W. of the Rialto bridge): First mentioned in 1051. Rebuilt by Scarpagnino in 1527–39 on basically the same plan. The campanile dates from 1398–1410. The dark interior has paintings by Titian (painting on high altar, 1545), Pordenone (altarpiece in the right-hand chancel chapel, 1535), J.Palma Giovane (in the left transept) and G.B.Pittoni (retable in the 18C sacristy), as well as a 14C marble Pietà on the altar of the left-hand chancel chapel, and a fragment of a relief from the 6C (?) in the left transept.

SS.Giovanni e Paolo/Zanipolo (Rio dei Mendicanti): This Dominican church, begun in 1333, is one of the most important Italian Gothic buildings. With its tall nave with two side aisles and five bays, its broad transept, and its apse with a choir and two chapels on each side, this building is the largest church in Venice and makes an imposing impression from the outside. To the right of it is the famous *equestrian statue* (1481–96) by A.Verrocchio of the condottiere *B.Colleoni.* —See figure.

S. Giuliano (N. of the Piazza S. Marco): Old parish church rebuilt in 1553, with J.Sansovino providing the plans for the fine façade and the figure above the portal. Inside, particular attention should be paid to: the statues by A.Vittoria who, together with Sansovino, is responsible for the entire building. The painting on the high altar is by Palma Giovane. The altarpiece on the 1st side-altar on the right is by P.Veronese.

S. Giuseppe di Castello (in the SE): A nuns' church restored in the 16C. Note the illusion of depth in the 17C ceiling painting, and the late 16C monument to Doge Marino Grimani and his wife on the left side-wall (design by V.Scamozzi, figures and reliefs by G.Campagna).

S. Lazzaro dei Mendicanti: This hall church stands to the N. of SS.Giovanni e Paolo. It was built as a hospital church in 1601–31 to designs by V.Scamozzi. The façade was designed by Gius. Sardi in 1673. Note in particular the late baroque tomb in the portico, the altarpiece by P.Veronese on the 1st side-altar on the right, and that by J.Tintoretto on the 2nd side-altar on the left.

S. Lio/S. Leone (to the E. of the Rialto bridge): An 11C church dedicated to Pope St.Leo and rebuilt in the 18C. Inside: Ceiling painting by D.Tiepolo. St.James, by

Titian, at the 1st side altar. On the right: the 15C Cappella Gussoni, possibly by P.Lombardo. 17C crucifixion by P.della Vecchia.

Madonna dell' Orto: This flat-roofed columned basilica, in the N. of the city, has a nave and two aisles. It was begun in 1350 and has been rebuilt several times. Its 15C façade is decorated with beautiful sculptures (12 Apostles by Paolo and Pierpaolo Dalle Masegne). The church contains the tomb of J.Tintoretto, as well as some important paintings by him (above the door to the Cappella di San Mauro and in the sacristy). There are also paintings by Cima da Conegliano and Jac. Palma Giovane (Cappella di San Mauro). A fine *cloister* and a *campanile* with a dome (*c.* 1500).

S.Marcuola/SS.Ermagora e Fortunato (in the N., by the Canal Grande): The present building (1728 – 36) was built by G.Massari using parts of older buildings. It stands on the site of an apparently very old church. Inside there are paintings in the manner of Titian and Tintoretto around the pulpits, and also a famous Tintoretto (Last Supper, in the sacristy, on the

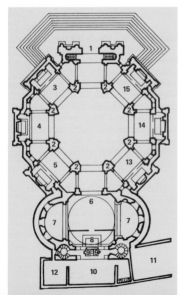

Venice, S.Maria della Salute **1** triumphal arch façade **2** colossal composite columns with statues on the volutes **3,4** and **5** altar chapels with altarpieces by Luca Giordano, from 1667 onwards **6** presbytery **7** Exedra **8** high altar with group by Justus Le Court, Byzantine Madonna and Child, bronze candelabra and Easter candlesticks, 1570. Left and right of the altar rise two campanili **9** antique columns from the theatre of Pola **10** monk's choir with carved stalls and 3 ceiling paintings by Gius. Salviati **11** Great Sacristy with works of art, which were gathered here from various churches in the 19C, inc. altar painting, a Titian masterpiece, 1511/12 with St.Mark; icon of the Virgin, 1115, in the altar tabernacle; tapestry to a design by Jacopo Bellini as antependium; 8 tondi on the walls with paintings by Titian, further pictures by Gius. Salviati and an enormous painting opp. the entrance by Jac. Tintoretto, 1561; in the antesacristy are equally important paintings and sculptures: a Pietà by Tullio Lombardo **12** Small Sacristy (usually closed) with sarcophagus, around 1500, and portal tympanum, *c.* 1443 **13** chapel with altarpiece (Miraculous Descent of the Holy Ghost) by Titian **14** and **15** chapels with paintings by P.Liberi, 1687

left) with groups of statues, some by G.M.Morlaiter.

S.Maria della Fava (E. of the Rialto): Built by Antonio Gaspari in 1711; domed sanctuary, by G.Massari, not added until 1750–53. The chief item of interest in the 1st side-chapel on the right is the altarpiece by G.B.Tiepolo. The 2nd side-altar on the left has a masterpiece by Piazzetta, *c.* 1725. Tabernacle of the sacrament with 2 angels by G.M.Morlaiter.

S.Maria Formosa: Tradition has it that this church dates from the 7C. It was rebuilt in the 11C as a domed church on a Greek cross plan. In 1493–1500, Mauro Coducci rebuilt it again as a basilica with a nave, two aisles and a transept. The beautiful façades were not added until the 16C (facing the Rio) and 17C, while the campanile dates from the 17C. Inside there are notable paintings by Bartolomeo Vivarini (1473, 1st chapel on right), Leandro Bassano (2nd chapel on right), and Palma Vecchio (*c.* 1520, 1st chapel of the right transept). The mosaics in the apse vault are to a design by Palma Giovane. On the altar of the small *Oratorio della Purificazione* are some fine marble statuettes (1400) and an altarpiece by G.B.Tiepolo.

S.Maria del Giglio/S.Maria Zobenigo: This 17C hall church is near the Teatro La Fenice, and has an imposing baroque façade to a design by G.Sardi, with figures by G.Le Court. The inside is richly decorated and the paintings include works by Gius. Salvati on the W. wall, pictures of the 4 Evangelists painted by J.Tintoretto in 1552–7 (former organ shutters) in the chancel, and an early work by P.P.Rubens in the sacristy.

S.Maria Mater Domini (SE of the Fondaco dei Turchi): A small parish church, dating originally from the Romanesque period, and rebuilt as a Renaissance church in 1502–40. J.Sansovino played a part in the enlargement of this richly decorated church.

S.Maria dei Miracoli (NE of the Rialto Bridge): The first Renaissance building in Venice, with inimitably clear, pure lines. A masterpiece of the early Italian Renaissance, it was built (1481–9) by P.Lombardo and his sons to provide a wor-

S. Giorgio Maggiore

thy resting place for the miraculous icon of the Virgin Mary, now on the high altar. It is a tunnel-vaulted hall church, with a domed sanctuary, and it is clad in polychrome marble both inside and out. The paintings, and particularly the sculptures, which are here almost overshadowed by the architecture, are of high quality (Titian workshop, Tullio Lombardo, Antonio Lombardo, Pietro Lombardo, A.Vittoria).

S. Maria della Pietà/S. Maria della Visitazione (Riva degli Schiavoni): Built by G.Massari in 1745-60. The marble façade, which joins the front of the former hospice, was only completed, to Massari's design, in 1906. The ceiling paintings inside are by G.B. Tiepolo (1754-60), the altarpiece on the late baroque high altar is by Piazzetta and G.Angeli, the marble statues on the high altar are by Gai and Marchiori, and the tabernacle angel is the work of M.Morlaiter.

S.Maria della Salute: This magnificent church, the most important Venetian baroque building, is diagonally opposite the Piazzetta, on the other side of the Canal Grande. It has an impressive façade, which stands at the top of a flight of steps. The building was founded in 1630 in thanks for deliverance from a plague and was built by B.Longhena. The outside is decorated with gables, massive volutes, balustrades and statues. The central area, which is octagonal in plan, has 8 strong pillars and is crowned by an enormous drum and dome. To the S.is the *sanctuary,* also surmounted by a drum and dome.—See figure.

S.Martino (in the E. of the city): Rebuilt in 1550 to designs by J.Sansovino, and then rebuilt again and redecorated in the 17&18C. Inside there are the notable tomb of Doge Francesco Erizzo (1633), and the altar in the large left side chapel with figures by T.Lombardo (2nd half of the 15C).

S.Michele in Isola (on the cemetery island between Venice and Murano): An early work by Mauro Coducci (1469, nave and chancel completed in 1499). The façade, which had considerable influence as

piece of monumental Renaissance architecture, was built in 1477. It has Ionic capitals and is ornamented. Inside, the main features are the rood loft and the well-carved arches. To the left of the façade is the *Cappella Emiliana,* a centrally planned hexagonal building by G.Bergamasco, *c.* 1530.

S.Moisè (to the SW of the Piazza S.Marco, by the Rio di Barcaroli): A hall church originally dating from the 8C. The present building was begun in 1632 and has a façade by A.Tremignon, 1688. There are notable paintings inside, including some by Tintoretto, and the sacristy has an interesting altar antependium by Nic. and Seb. Roccatagliata, 1633.

S.Nicolò da Tolentino (in the W., by the Giardino Papadopoli, on the Rio Tolentini): V.Scamozzi built this Theatine church in 1591-1601 (some of the plans were by Palladio). The portico is 18C. Rich decoration.

S.Pantalon/S.Pantaleone (on the Rio Ca' Foscari): Built by Fr. Comino in 1668-86 on the site of a 13C church. Inside, the vaults were painted (1680-1740) by G.Fumiani, and the high altar is by G.Sardi. Left chancel chapel: Coronation of the Virgin, paintings by Giov. d'Alemagna and Bart. Vivarini; altar: marble relief, earlier than 1400.

S.Pietro in Castello (on the Isola di S. Pietro): This, formerly the Patriarch's church, with a campanile by M.Coducci (1482 - 8), has a façade from 1596 by F.Smeraldi, based on plans by Palladio. The inside was altered by G.Grapiglia from 1619 onwards. High altar to a design by B.Longhena. In the right aisle there is a marble throne of St. Peter, *c.* 13C, with fragments of Islamic carvings. Significant paintings by P.Veronese, P.Liberi, P.Ricchi and M.Basaiti, and a statue of the Immaculata Virgin by M.Morlaiter. Mosaic icon by A.Zuccato (1570).

SS.Redentore (on the Giudecca, in the S.):After the city was freed from the plague, the Signoria gave instructions for a votive church to be built on this site in 1577–92 to plans by A.Palladio. This is a masterpiece of Western architecture in a style between Renaissance and baroque. The façade is in the manner of an ancient temple. The inside makes an inspiring impression resulting from its harmonious lines and smooth spatial articulation, with a nave, a sanctuary and a retro-choir. There is a Crucifixion by G.Campagna on the baroque high altar.

S.Rocco: The sanctuary survives from the original church (1489–1508). The present hall church was built by Giov. Scalfurotto in the mid 18C. The façade dates from 1765–77, and its upper storey has statues and a large relief by G.M.Morlaiter. Inside, fine paintings by Tintoretto, Ricci and Trevisan.

S.Salvatore (near the Teatro Goldoni): This church, which stands on the site of previous 7&12C buildings, was built by Giorgio Spavento from 1507 to 1534 with the help of T.Lombardo and J.Sansovino. The façade was built in 1663 to a design by G.Sardi. The architecturally well-balanced interior has some noteworthy pieces: sculptures and reliefs by Sansovino, G.Campagna and A.Vittoria; paintings by P.Bordone, F.Vecellio and, in particular, Titian (painting on high altar). A 14C silver reredos is sometimes displayed on the high altar. In the architecturally interesting *sacristy*, dating from the period when the church was built, the paintings give an illusion of depth.

Scalzi church/S.Maria di Nazareth (by the railway station, on the Canal Grande): This single- aisled Carmelite church was begun by Longhena in 1670, and the façade was built under G.Sardi in 1683–9. The beautiful late baroque interior formerly had ceiling frescos by G.B.Tiepolo, which were destroyed in World War 1. The splendid, theatrical high altar by G.B.Viviani and G.Pozzo has survived.

S. Sebastiano (in the W.): This nuns' church was built by A.Scarpagnino between 1505 and 1546. The oil paintings and frescos by P.Veronese (later than 1553) are the main reason for its world-wide renown. Statues on the gallery parapet by G.Campagna.

S.Simeone Piccolo (Canal Grande): Late baroque domed church, built by Giov. Scalfurotto in 1718–38; Pietà by Palma Giovane.

S.Stae/S.Eustachio (Canal Grande): A church by Domenico Rossi, built in 1709, with an imposing façade. Inside, paintings by G.B.Tiepolo, G.A.Pellegrini, G.B.Piazzetta, A.Balestra, G.Lazzarini, G.B.Pittoni and S.Ricci.

S. Trovaso/SS. Gervasio e Protasio (Campo S. Trovaso): A spacious, single-aisled church (1584–1657), with notable paintings by Tintoretto (Last Supper, *c.* 1555), M.Giambono (earlier than 1440), G.Bellini and 3 beautiful marble reliefs (*c.* 1460/70).

S.Zaccaria (E. of S.Marco): The earlier 10C building was a part of the most important convent in Venice. The crypt (10&11C) is underneath the Cappella S. Tarasio (1440; in the S., to the right of the chancel). It has 3 fine late Gothic carved altars and frescos by Andrea da Castagno, 1442. This church is one of the most notable examples of the Venetian early Renaissance. Building was begun by A.Gambello and continued from 1481 onwards by M.Coducci, who completed it in *c.* 1500. Inside, the nave has two side aisles, and its walls are adorned with 17&18C paintings showing Venetian history. The columns have early Renaissance capitals. An ambulatory with chapels runs around the sanctuary. The high altar has paintings of Christ's Passion by J.Palma Giovane. The left aisle has an altar of the Virgin Mary, with one of Giovanni Bellini's finest paintings (1505).

Palaces:
Palazzo Ducale/Doges' Palace: The Doges' Palace, the former residence of the Doges and the seat of the chief magistrates is a symbol of the power and the gorgeous opulence of the Venetian Republic. Built between 1309 and 1442 on the site of a 9C

wooden castle, it became the prime example of the Venetian Gothic style and today the façades on the Molo (the older section) and on the Piazzetta have a captivating effect. Their lower sections appear virtually weightless, with a traceried gallery standing on columns with very fine capitals, whilst the upper section has massive, marble-clad walls, Gothic windows and two balconies. At the corners of the S.wing (Molo) there are fine mid 14C statues (Drunkenness of Noah, and Fall of Man). The *Porta della Carta*, which was built 1438 – 42 under the supervision of Giovanni Bon and his son Bart. Bon, has rich ornamental carving and statues. It is the most important example in Venice of the transitional style between the Gothic and the Renaissance. The visitor passes through the *Portico Foscari* (vaulted corridor), and then through the famous *Arco Foscari* (triumphal arch, 1462–71, with figures of Adam and Eve by A.Rizzo), to reach the staircase (*Scala dei Giganti*; built by A.Rizzo from 1483 onwards, with fine reliefs; colossal statues of Mars and Neptune by Sansovino, 1554) on which the newly elected Doge was crowned. To the left of the staircase is the *Cortile dei Senatori,* the courtyard of the N. wing. This wing was begun by A.Rizzo in 1483 as a four-storeyed structure, but not finished until the 2nd half of the 16C. To the right of the Scala dei Giganti is the enormous *Cortile del Palazzo*, with a 16C bronze well-head. Here, the marble façade (330 ft. long, 4 storeys high) of the E. wing is impressive when seen from the inner courtyard. The simplest way is to go round the Doges' Palace on the official tour. The guided tour begins on the 1st floor of the E. wing at the *Scala d'Oro*, a staircase built in 1557/8 with the assistance of J.Sansovino (gilded vault decoration with reliefs by A.Vittoria). The first landing leads on to the 2nd floor, where the living quarters of the Doges are to be found. The outstanding rooms here are: the *Sala degli Scarlatti* with its marble relief and chimney-piece by A. and T.Lombardo, the *Sala Grimani* and the *Sala degli Stucchi* with 17&18C stucco. After leaving this room, the visitor will find, on his right, a little doorway on whose inner wall Titian painted the fresco of St.Christopher in 1523/4. The Doges' apartments on the opposite side today house a *collection of paintings* (including works by Quentin Massys and

Doge's Palace

Hieronymus Bosch). We return to the Scala d'Oro and pass from here to the 3rd floor. Especially worth seeing here are: the 16C *Atrio Quadrato* with its gilded ceiling painted by J.Tintoretto; the *Sala delle Quattro Porte* with another splendid ceiling, 4 doorways, and historical paintings on the walls; the *Sala dell' Anticollegio* with 4 paintings on the walls by Tintoretto and others by Veronese and Bassano; the *Sala del Collegio,* the council chamber, with paintings by P.Veronese on the gilded ceiling. From here we enter the *Sala del Senato* with its splendid ceiling, and continue into the *Antichiesetta* and *Chiesetta,* the domestic chapel of the Doges' Palace with its ante-room (altar chapel by V.Scamozzi with a marble group by J.Sansovino). The collection of weapons in the *Sale d'Armi* is a few rooms further on. We then move into the S.wings of the palace, with the *Sala di Guariento* and the *Sala del Maggior Consiglio,* which was at that time the largest hall in Italy (177 by 82 by 51 ft.) and was redecorated in 1577 (magnificent ceiling, paintings by P.Veronese, J.Palma Giovane, J.Tintoretto and others). The Paradise painted by Tintoretto (after 1588) on the wall behind the raised platform for the Signoria and the Doges' throne is the largest painting on canvas in the world. Up to 1800 persons could take part in the council meetings held here. The W. wing of the palace can be reached from here. Note the *Sala della Quarantia,* the *Sala dello Scrutinio* with the Last Judgement by Palma Giovane, and the Doges' portraits in the frieze beneath the ceiling; painted by Tintoretto, Vicentino and Aliense. On the way out, the visitor crosses the notorious *Bridge of Sighs,* which was built by A.Contin in *c.* 1600, and can see part of the old, dark State prison, begun by G.A.Rusconi in 1563, and completed under Contin in 1614. The ground floor of the S.and W. wing also houses the *Museo dell'Opera di Palazzo* (entrance at the Porta del Frumento), which originally exhibited architectural sculptures from the Doges' Palace.

Ca' d'Oro (Calle di Ca' d'Oro): Marino Contarini had this palace built in 1421–40 under the supervision of Giovanni and Bart. Bon, with assistance from Matteo Raverti. It is on the site of the old Casa Zeno dating from the 12/13C. The columns and capitals on the ground floor arches on the waterfront survive from the old building. The world-famous coloured marble façade is a masterpiece, combining Venetian late Gothic with early Renaissance (clear, simple round arch on the ground floor, rectangular windows). It owes its name to its former rich gold covering. In the palace courtyard there is a well-head by Bart. Bon (1427), decorated with very fine reliefs. In 1894 Baron Giorgio Franchetti bought the completely neglected palace, had it restored and fitted with costly old furniture, and installed in it a magnificent collection which he donated to the Italian State. The Ca' d'Oro has been open to the public since 1927, the museum being known as the *Galleria Franchetti.* It has paintings (Titian, Mantegna and Van Dyck), tapestries, sculptures and small *objets d'art,* mostly of 15&16C Venetian origin.

Other palaces: The following section discusses the most important of Venice's innumerable palaces in alphabetical order.

Doge's Palace, Fall of Man

The location is given for palaces not on the Grand Canal. *Ca' Da Mosto:* The birthplace of Alvise Da Mosto, the traveller who discovered the Canary Islands. The two lower Veneto-Byzantine storeys are 13C. *Fondaco dei Tedeschi/Trading- House of the Germans:* This, the oldest trading-house of a foreign nation in Venice, was founded in the 1st quarter of the 13C and rebuilt in Renaissance style by Giorgio Spavento and Antonio Abbondio in 1505–8 after a fire. Today it is a post office. *Fondaco dei Turchi:* This palace, built in about the mid-13C, was used by the Turks as a trading-house from 1621 to 1838. The famous and typically Veneto-Byzantine façade dates from the 13C and was rebuilt from the old materials in 1880. Today it houses the *Museo di Storia Naturale*, which is devoted to the flora and fauna of the lagoon. *Palazzo Albrizzi* (on the Campiello Albrizzi): Rebuilt in the 17C from older buildings. Inside, fine rooms with baroque stucco work. Paintings by C.Loth, P.Liberi, A.Zanchi and others; ceiling frescos by G.A.Pellegrini, sculptures by A.Canova. *Pal.Ariani:* Gothic palace from the 2nd half of the 14C, with a fine façade (today a school). *Pal. Barbarigo:* 2nd half of the 16C, with late 16C frescos on the outside by Camillo Ballin (the only surviving painted façade of any palace on the Canal Grande). The 15&17C *Pal. Barbaro* (S. Stefano) contains B.Strozzi's masterpiece, the portrait of Giov. Grimani. *Pal. Bernardo:* Built in 1442, with a late Gothic façade and a fine staircase in the courtyard. *Pal. Camerlenghi* (on the Rialto): After the Rialto fire of 1513, it was rebuilt in 1525 – 8 using parts of the former, early Renaissance palace. *Pal. Centanni/P.Goldoni* (Calle Nomboli No. 2798): Late Gothic palace in which Carlo Goldoni was born in 1707. *Goldoni Museum. Pal. Civran:* Built by Giorgio Massari in 1701. *Pal. Coccina Tiepolo* (S. Silvestro): Built by Giangiacomo Grigi in the mid-16C. *Pal. Contarini del Bovolo* (S.Luca): Late Gothic palace from the mid-15C, with an interesting staircase tower (Scala Minelli) and loggia (1499): good paintings inside. *Pal. Contarini Fasan* (also known as Casa della Desdemona): Late Gothic front from the last third of the 15C. Fine loggia on the main storey. *Pal. Contarini delle Figure* (S.Samuele): Built in 1504–46; completed by Abbondio, known as Scarpagnino. The residence of Jacopo Contar-

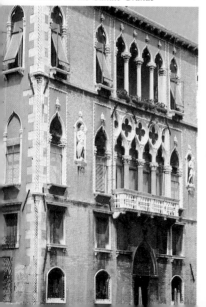

Palazzo on the Canale Grande

Canale Grande with Ca' d'Oro

ini. *Pal. Contarini dal Zaffo:* 15C building with a marble-clad façade of the Venetian early Renaissance. *Pal. Corner della Ca' Grande:* Built by Jac. Sansovino from 1537. One of the masterpieces of the Venetian Renaissance; outstanding façade. Today it houses the prefecture. *Pal. Corner Spinelli* (S.Angelo): Built in *c.* 1500 by M.Coducci. Early Renaissance façade. Interior altered by M.Sanmicheli in 1542. *Pal. Da Mula-Morosini:* 15C, with rococo decorations inside. *Pal. Dario:* Late-15C, with a marble-clad façade probably by P.Lombardo. *Pal. Dolfin-Manin:* Built from 1532 onwards to a design by J.Sansovino, with a ground floor loggia. The early classical interior furnishings, were designed for the last Doge, Lodovico Manin by A.Selva. Today the palazzo houses the *Banca d'Italia. Pal. Erizzo:* 15C. Interior altered in baroque style by G.Massari in 1717. *Pal. Falier-Bonora:* 15C, with old Venetian terrace gardens. *Pal. Flangini:* Built by G.Sardi in the 17C. *Pal. Foscari,* 15C. *Pal. Grassi:* Built by G.Massari in 1718. Large staircase with frescos by P.Longhi. *Pal. Grimani:* Begun in 1540 by Michele Sanmicheli, who built the two lower storeys and the water-gate with figures by A.Vittoria. Today it is the seat of the Corte d'Appello (Court of Appeal). *Pal. Gussoni* (S. Maria della Fava): Fine early Renaissance building by P.Lombardo, *c.* 1474–80. *Pal. Labia:* Built by A.Cominelli in 1720. The façade, to plans by A.Tremignon, dates from 1750. Inside, famous frescos by G.B.Tiepolo. The frescos were transferred to canvas in 1969–72. *Pal. Lion-Morosini:* Remains (outdoor staircase and arcaded wall) of the 13C Veneto-Byzantine palace are preserved in the Campiello del Remer. *Pal. Loredan* and *Pal. Farsetti:* The two lower storeys of the façades of the adjoining palaces are Veneto-Byzantine and date from the 13C. *Pal. Malipiero:* Built in 1622 using some older parts. *Pal. Michiel dalle Colonne:* Built in the 2nd half of the 17C, on the foundations of late Gothic buildings. *Pal. Minotti:* Erected in the 15C using some older Veneto-Byzantine parts. *Pal. Nani:* 16C. *Pal. Patriarcale* (on the E. side of the Piazzetta): Built by Lorenzo Santi in 1837–50, with an immense banqueting hall of the Doges. *Pal. Pesaro:*

Work on the first storey was completed in 1679 to a design by B.Longhena, but the upper section of the palace was not completed until 1710. Today it houses the *Museum of Modern Art* and a *Museum of Oriental Art. Ca' Rezzonico:* Begun in 1660 to a design by B.Longhena. The third storey, by G.Massari, was not added until the mid-18C. Today, this baroque palace, with its ceiling fresco by G.B.Tiepolo and its rococo furnishings, houses the *Museum of the Settecento Veneziano,* with 18C Venetian and non-Venetian works of art. *Pal. Sagredo:* Built *c.* 1400, later enlarged and altered inside in baroque style (staircase by A.Tirali, 1734; ceiling painting by P.Longhi, 1754). *Pal. Soranzo* (Campo S.Polo, No. 2169): Late Gothic façades. *Pal. Tiepolo Maffetti* (Campo S.Polo, No. 1957): Monumental late baroque building. *Pal. Treves Bonfili:* The new building dates from *c.* 1680. Inside, a work by Canova (Hector and Ajax, 1808–10). *Pal. Tron:* Late 16C. Inside, rococo decorations and paintings by J.Guarana. *Pal. Vendramin* (near S. Maria del Carmelo, Dorsoduro 3462): A 17C building. Inside, beautiful but poorly preserved rococo decoration (stucco, frescos, majolica and chinoiserie). *Pal. Vendramin-Calergi:* Begun by Mauro Coducci before 1500 and completed in 1509, probably by T.Lombardo. Extended by V.Scamozzi in the 17C. Fine Renaissance façade. Richard Wagner lived here, and died here on 13 February 1883. *Pal. Widmann-Foscari* (near S.Canciano, Cannaregio 5403–4): Built by B.Longhena in 1630, with a Renaissance façade. Inside, 17&18C frescos and stucco (privately owned). *Pal. Zenobio* (near S. Maria del Carmelo, Dorsoduro 2593–7): Built by A.Gaspari in 1680–5. An 18C loggia, and, in the grand hall, stucco works by artists from the Ticino region, and some very beautiful ceiling frescos by L.Dorigny, 1686–8. *Pal. Zorzi* (Castello 4930): Early-15C, with wall facings.

Venetian schools: *Scuola Grande della Carità* (in the Accademia): On the first floor, a large meeting-room, decorated with a carved and gilded ceiling in 1461–84, today a room exhibiting early Venetian panel paintings; next door, on the left, is a former albergo (lodging room) with a fine ceiling and Titian's 'Presentation of the Virgin' (1534–9). *Scuola Grande dei Carmini* near the Carmini church: Two-storeyed façade dating from 1668 (possibly by B.Longhena). On the first floor, a large hall with 9 splendid ceiling paintings by G.B.Tiepolo, and paintings on the walls by A.Zanchi and G.Lazzarini. 'Judith and Holofernes', by G.B.Piazzetta, is outstanding. *Scuola Grande, S.Giovanni Evangelista* (near the Frari church): Partly rebuilt in the 15C; it is one of the best works of the Venetian early Renaissance. Fine courtyard with a portal by M.Coducci. The picture cycle by Carpaccio, originally in the oratory, is today in the Accademia. *Scuola Grande di S.Marco* (beside S.Giovanni e Paolo): 15C. The façade has coloured facings and is a masterpiece of the Venetian early Renaissance. It was designed by the most important architects in the city at that time: M.Coducci, Giov. Buora, the Lombardi and possibly, also G.Spavento. The building was enlarged by J.Sansovino in the 16C. Inside there are paintings by Padovanino, Tintoretto, Jacopo Palma Vecchio, and Belliniano; a meeting-hall with a gilded and coffered ceiling and a 16C

Bridge of Sighs

chapel; a lodging-room with 16C furnishings. *Scuola Grande di S. Rocco* (Campo S. Rocco): Built 1515 – 60 by Bon Bergamasco, Scarpagnino and G.Grigi, and has a fine marble-clad façade. Very well-preserved furnishings and numerous paintings by Tintoretto (particularly in the grand hall with its very fine ceiling and its benches; also in the albergo or lodging-room). *Scuola Grande Tedesca/German Synagogue* (in the Ghetto Nuovo in the NW): Built in 1529 and partly redecorated in the 2nd half of the 17C. Hebrew merchant families settled in Venice at an early date on the island called Giudecca (meaning, Jews' Island). In 1516, these 'infidels' were settled in the Ghetto Nuovo. There had been an iron foundry here and the word 'ghetto' is derived from getto (casting). From 1541 onwards they also settled in the adjoining Ghetto Vecchio and, from 1633, in the Ghetto Nuovissimo. *Scuola Mercanti* (near Madonna dell'Orto): Built by A.Palladio in 1570. *Scuola Vecchia della Misericordia* (Rio della Sensa in the N.): The school of this confraternity, founded in 1303, was built in the 1st half of the 15C (good façade) on the Campo of the same name. *Scuola S. Angelo Raffaelo* (on the Campo SS. Apostoli): Baroque building with a painting of Christ by Titian. *Scuola di S. Fantin* (near the Teatro La Fenice): Rebuilt in 1592 – 1600 by A.Contin and A.Vittoria. Today it houses the Ateneo Veneto and the adult education centre. Façade and original decoration. *Scuola S. Giorgio degli Schiavoni* (on the Rio S. Antonio): Built by the Dalmatian confraternity. The façade is 16C. A picture cycle by Vitt. Carpaccio, 1501 – 11.

Bridges: Venice is also renowned for its *bridges*. The best-known of all is the *Rialto Bridge*, which was the only bridge across the Canal Grande right up into the 19C. There is said to have been a pontoon bridge here as early as 1181. In the 13C it was replaced by a wooden toll-bridge. In the 15C this bridge gave way to a drawbridge, which had shops standing on it. But it was only in 1588–91 that A.da Ponte and his

Museo Vetrario di Murano ▷

Rialto Bridge

Madonna and Child, by B.Cima, Accademia ▷

nephew A.Contin built the present stone bridge, which is constructed as a street with shops and has a high arch to allow ships to pass underneath. The bridge is dedicated to St. Theodore and St. Mark, who appear as reliefs on the faces of the bridge together with an Annunciation. The *Bridge of Sighs* (see the Doges' Palace) is also by A.Contin. *Ponte dei Tre Archi* (over the Canale di Cannaregio at S. Giobbe), a baroque pillared bridge with several arches.

Theatres: Venice is rich in theatres, even though, as is usual in Italy, plays are only staged there in the 'Stagione', i.e. during limited seasons, and by touring companies, since the theatres do not have permanent ones of their own. *Teatro Goldoni* (Calle Formo): 17C, with the splendid Corte del Teatro, where open-air performances are held; it is surrounded by Gothic and Renaissance buildings. *Teatro Italia* (Calle

dell'Anconeta): Gothic revival. *Teatro La Fenice* (opposite S. Fantin): The largest theatre in Venice and one of the most famous in all Italy. Built by A.Selva in 1790–2. Opera house and theatre; the main auditorium has 1500 seats. *Teatro Malibran* (Campo S.Giovanni Crisostomo): Opened under Giov. Grimani in 1678, restored in 1920. *Teatro Rossini* (Rio di S. Luca): Rebuilt by F.Costa in 1756 after a fire, and restored in 1875. *Teatro Verde* (on the Isola di S.Giorgio Maggiore): Built by L.Vietti and A.Scattolin in a beautiful park, after the manner of Greek open-air theatres.

Museums, Libraries, Archives: The *Gallerie dell'Accademia* (Canal Grande, entrance on the Campo della Carità), housed in 3 adjacent buildings: the late Gothic former monastery church of S.Maria della Carità, the former Scuola Grande della Carità (see under Schools), and the convent of the Lateran Canons, which had origi-

nally been rebuilt by A.Palladio. The *gallery of paintings* has over 800 pictures mainly by Venetian artists, including some major works. In particular there are outstanding paintings by Gentile Bellini, V.Carpaccio, Giov. Bellini, Giorgione, Titian, P.Bordone, J.Tintoretto and P.Veronese. In addition, there are fine works by Mantegna, Cima da Conegliano, Pietro Longhi, F.Guardi, Seb. Ricci, Palma Vecchio, Piero della Francesca, L.Lotto, Tiepolo, A.Canaletto and A.Vivarini. *Civico Museo Correr* (Procuratie Nuove): The Venice city museum, with historical and cultural exhibits and a collection of works by 14–16C Venetian painters. The *Museo del Risorgimento* is also here, on the 2nd floor. It has documents concerning the city's history from the end of the Republic up to the present. The building also houses the *Museo Archeologico* (see below) and the *Biblioteca d'Arte e Storia Veneziana* (see below). *Museo Archeologico* (Procuratie Nuove, on the Piazza S.Marco): A collection of antique art which, along with the Vatican treasures, is one of the oldest in Italy; it has many Greek originals. *Galleria Franchetti* (Ca' d'Oro; see Palaces). *Museo del Settecento Veneziano* (Ca' Rezzonico; see

Palazzo Rezzonico). *Goldoni- Museum* (see Palazzo Goldoni). *Pinacoteca Querini-Stampalia* (by S.Maria Formosa): A library with over 100,000 volumes, including early printed works and manuscripts, together with a collection of paintings by 14–18C Venetian painters. The art collections of the *Seminario Patriarcale* (Canal Grande): 17C monastery (with cloister). Built by B.Longhena, it houses an important collection of sculptures and paintings from the 14–18C. The *Pinacoteca Manfrediana* is on the 1st floor. *Museo di Storia Naturale* (see Fondaco dei Turchi). *Museo Storico Navale*, with exhibits on Venetian and Italian naval history, stands by the Arsenal in the NE of Venice. The *Arsenal* is an enormous complex where the Venetian fleet was fitted out. Michele Sanmicheli and A.Da Ponte were involved in building it (reliefs and statues by G.Campagna and Sansovino; two colossal iron lions from Greece on the entrance bridge). The *Museum of the Conservatory,* with old musical instruments and various documents by great musicians, including R.Wagner, is in the baroque *Pal. Pisani*, between the Canal Grande and S.Stefano. *Biblioteca Nazionale Marciana* (in the Zecca on the Piazza

Arsenal

S.Marco). The library, which was founded in 1468, has been in the former mint (Zecca) since 1905. It has 750, 000 volumes, including 3000 early printed works and some 13, 000 manuscripts, among them 1200 Greek codices. *Libreria Vecchia di S.Marco* (Piazza S.Marco): Building began in 1537 under Jac. Sansovino and was completed by Vincenzo Scamozzi in 1588. There are shops on the ground floor. The library has works from the Biblioteca Marciana, and also the books donated by Cardinal Bessarion in 1468. Its lecture rooms and reading rooms are superbly decorated by Titian, Veronese, Tintoretto and others. *Biblioteca d'Arte e Storia Veneziana* (Procuratie Nuove). *Archivio di Stato* (in the former Franciscan monastery by the Frari church): it has 15 million fascicles and documents.

Environs: Burano: The boat to Torcello (NE of Venice) stops at the island of Burano shortly before reaching Torcello. Burano is a picturesque little fishing town with a fine campanile and painted houses, and it is especially known for its pillow lace. The lacemaking school in the *Palazzo del Podestà* (Piazza B.Galluppi 4) is worth seeing. **Caorle:** Formerly a harbour N. of Venice, today a romantic fishing village with beautiful old houses. It was important as a bishop's seat after 1000. The *cathedral,* a brick basilica with a nave and two aisles, was begun in 1038 and shows similarities to the early Christian churches of Ravenna. The *Pala d'Oro,* consisting of old 12–14C Byzantine and Venetian silver work, is behind the high altar. The campanile dates from the 2nd half of the 11C. **Chioggia:** A harbour on the coast S. of Venice. Chioggia was a free town in the 11C, and always benefited from its position on the mouth of the Brenta. In the 18C, in order to protect the harbour, Venice built enormous defences, the *Murazzi,* consisting of huge flat dams of Istrian stone. Note the 17C *Palazzo Grassi* (Piazzetta Vigo) and *S. Domenico* (nearby), also 17C, with a late work by Carpaccio on the 2nd side altar and a famous 14C processional cross; the *Palazzo del Podestà* (city centre; a good painting by Jacobello del Fiore, 1436); next to the town hall, a *Gothic granary,* 1322; the baroque *cathedral* S.of the Corso, built in 1633 – 74 to plans by B.Longhena; nearby, the late Gothic brick building of *S.Martino* with a very lovely polyptych by

Strà (Venice), Villa Pisani

Paolo Veneziano (1349). **Concordia:** On the mainland, N. of Venice, was a Roman military station and an important trading-post. The seat of a bishop as early as the 4C, it was destroyed by the Visigoths in 452. There are remains of antique and early Christian buildings. The cathedral of 1466 has an apse dating from 1884 and a W. bay of 1906. The baptistery dates from as early as 1089. **Fiesso d'Arico** (on the mainland, SW of Venice, on the Brenta). It was here that rich Venetians built their huge country villas. *Villa Soranza* (on the Brenta), a typical example of a 16C mansion with frescos outside and fine stuccoes, most of them 18C, inside. *Villa Lazzara-Pisani/La Barbariga* (opposite the Villa Soranza): Inside, stuccoes and 18C chinoiseries. *Villa Torre-Donato-Olivieri,* 18C. **Malcontenta:** Between Fiesso and Venice, also on the Brenta, the *Villa Foscari/La Malcontenta,* on a canal at the mouth of the Brenta near Fusina. Only the living-quarters have survived from the villa built by A.Palladio in 1550–60. Inside, the *Sala* has frescos by B.Franco and G.B.Zelotti. The town of **Strà:** lying on the Brenta to the S.of Fiesso d'Artico, contains the *Villa Pisani,* an imposing early 18C summer residence and probably the most impressive of these villas. There are more than 30 large rooms, the finest of which is the *Sala di Ballo* (rising to a height of 2 storeys), with *trompe-l'oeil* architectural painting and an enormous *ceiling fresco* by G.B.Tiepolo (1761/2).

Venosa 85029

Potenza/Basilicata   p.416 ☐M 11

Horace was born in this region pregnant with history. The prehistoric finds in the immediate vicinity are evidence of early settlement. Venusia was captured by the Romans in 290 BC and destroyed by the Saracens in the mid 9C. Once rebuilt, it was held by various families.

Castle: The castle, with its cylindrical corner towers, was built by Prince Pirro del Balzo in 1470. Later it was destroyed. Outside there is a 19C fountain with a lion from the amphitheatre.

Cathedral: Also known as S. Andrea Apostolo. Built 1470–1502, its façade was altered and a simple marble portal added

Venosa, Abbazia della Trinità

by Cola da Conza in 1512. The interior, with its nave and two aisles, is divided by pillars. A fine marble arch (1520) leads to the Cappella del Sacramento.

Chiesa del Purgatorio: The inclusion of the campanile in the façade of the church is unusual for this region. Inside, a Madonna with S.Filippo Neri, a painting by Carlo Maratta.

Abbazia della Trinità: The Abbey of the Holy Trinity is a short way outside the town. It consists of three parts: the old church, the new one, and the adjoining abbot's residence. The church, originally founded by Benedictines, was consecrated in 1059. This first building was then enlarged in 1063 along Cluniac lines. However, this rebuilding was never completed. The abbey has been restored again today, but the monks abandoned it years ago. The façade of the old church has a fine late 13C portal flanked by two stone lions. Inside, it has a nave and two aisles, with mosaics in the apse (4&5C). The outer walls of the aisles continue as those of the new church, and so the visitor passes through a doorway to the left of the apse into the exten-sion, which also has a nave and two aisles. This can also be entered from the outside, through a portal in the left side arm of the new church. The portal has some Roman fragments. It is also noticeable how the massive stone ashlars from the nearby amphitheatre and from other Roman buildings in Venosa have been used in these churches. Interesting frescos from various periods can be seen on the pillars inside the old church, and also on the walls.

Museo Briscese (Via Vittorio Emanuele): An interesting collection of prehistoric finds from excavations in the surrounding area.

Also worth seeing: Tomb of Marcus Claudius Marcellus: Marcus Claudius Marcellus captured Syracuse, fought a battle against Hannibal near Potenza, was consul five times, and was killed near Venosa in 208 BC. His abilities earned him the title of the 'Sword of Rome'. *Jewish Catacombs:* They lie 165 ft. below the level of the road, close to Marcellus's tomb. *Roman Amphitheatre:* Situated near the Abbazia.

Ventimiglia, view

Environs: Lavello: This town, situated N. of Venosa, on the edge of the province, has a castle and a display of finds from the region, including some from the prehistoric settlement.

Ventimiglia 18039

Imperia/Liguria   p.412□B 6

Cathedral of S. Maria Assunta: This Romanesque building, dating from the 11&12C and restored in 1950, has a beautifully designed portal (*c.* 1222). Inside there is a tunnel-vaulted nave, two aisles, and a good panel painting of the 'Madonna and Child' by B.da Modena (3rd side altar on the left).

Baptistery (left of the façade): This octagonal building dates from the same period as the cathedral. It encloses the old font and incorporates remains of Lombard sculptures from the 8C, when there was a previous building on this site.

S.Michele (Via Piemonte): This early 12C Romanesque church, a Benedictine priory, stands on the ruins of a temple dedicated to Castor and Pollux. When the building was restored in 1947–59, the 16C interior with its nave and two aisles was converted back to a single-aisled structure. There is an interesting 11C Romanesque crypt.

Archaeological Museum (Piazza della Libertà), Civico Museo Archeologico G.Rossi: This museum has a particularly good collection from the excavations of Ventimiglia, including inscriptions and sculptures, an outstanding set of ancient travelling silver cutlery, as well as vessels, glasses, oil lamps and burial objects.

Also worth seeing: *Via Garibaldi* with its old houses: a bishop's residence, Loggia dei Mercanti (*c.* 1400), Teatro Civico, now the seat of the Biblioteca Aprosiana (founded in 1648), Oratorio dei Neri with pictures and frescos by A.Carrega. The so-called *Zona Archeologica* (on the Via Aurelia, towards Bordighera) is regarded as the most important burial site in Liguria. The ancient theatre (2C AD) is the best preserved feature. The extent of the Roman town is readily apparent.

Environs: Giardino Hanbury(Mortola

Ventimiglia, Teatro Romano

Inferiore, *c.* 6 km. along the Via Aurelia towards the Italian-French border): This garden was laid out by Sir Thomas Hanbury, an Englishman, in 1867. It is now State-owned and, with its *c.* 5000–6000 plant forms, it is probably one of the world's most beautiful gardens, in which sculptures blend with the luxuriant vegetation. The old Roman road can be found in the lower section. The caves of **Balzi Rossi** (*c.* 7 km. along the Via Aurelia towards Grimaldi; descend 300 ft. to the caves by lift): These reddish rocks contain caves which were inhabited in prehistoric times. They have yielded animal skeletons, tools, and parts of human skeletons of the 'Cromagnon man' type, which are now in the museum at the 'Barma Grande' grotto. **Bordighera: Museo Bicknell** with the Istituto Internazionale di Studi Liguri.

Vercelli 13100

Vercelli/Piedmont   p.412☐C 3

S. Eusebio (Piazza S. Eusebio): The cathedral (1572-1700) was built over an early Christian church. Work began in 1572 to

plans by Pellegrino Pellegrini, and from 1700 onwards B.Alfieri, who also designed the façade, took over supervision of the building. The campanile is 12C. The valuable church treasure is kept next to the Madonna dello Schiaffo (1428) in the chapel of the sacrament.

S. Andrea (Via G.Ferrari): The founder of this Romanesque church with its adjoining monastery was Cardinal Guala Bicchieri (1219 – 27). It is one of the first Cistercian churches in Italy still based on the French Cistercian architectural style. The tympanum of the main portal, and the decoration—reminiscent of a palace—of the arch soffits and side portals, are both by B.Antelami. The campanile dates from 1407. Slightly damaged in 1617, the church was restored by A.Mella in 1822–30. Some fragments of sculpture, probably by B.Antelami, are exhibited in the Museo Lapidario in the church's cloister. Inside the church there is a wooden choir by Paolo Sacca da Cremona (1511) with intarsia still lifes and townscapes. There is a wooden, painted crucifix (late 15C to early 16C) in a chapel of the transept. The typically Cistercian abbey dates from

Vercelli, S.Andrea

Verona, Ponte Scaligero

1219. It was secularized in 1802 but in 1930 monks returned to it. The Ospedale Maggiore opposite the church was founded by Cardinal Bicchieri in 1224.

Also worth seeing: *S. Giuliano* (Corso Libertà), a church with a nave, two aisles. It has a painting by Bernardino Lanina (1547). *S.Cristoforo* (Via S.Cristoforo), with paintings by G.Ferrari. *S.Paolo* (Piazzetta S.Paolo), a Romanesque church of 1260, restored in 1420 and 1786. Paintings by Bernardino Lanino, the most important pupil of G.Ferrari. *S. Chiara* (Via F.Monaco), 18C church and monastery, by B.Alfieri among others. The *seminary* by F.Juvarra has a particularly fine courtyard. *Castle* (Piazza Amedeo IX), rectangular in plan with corner towers. The portal of the Romanesque church of *S.Maria Maggiore*, which is in a ruined state today, is in the Giardino dei Marchesi di Gattinara. *Museo Civico Antonio Borgogna* (Via Borgo-gna). This is the second most important collection of Piedmontese painting, sur-passed only by that in Turin. *Museo Leone* (Via Verdi), Piedmontese paintings.

Environs: Campi Raudi: Marius, the Roman commander and consul (156–86 BC) defeated the Cimbri on this battlefield in 101 BC.

Verona 37100

Verona/Veneto   p.410☐F 3

Roman from the 1C BC and a royal seat of the Ostrogoths in the late classical period, it was ruled by the Scaligers during the high Middle Ages, held by the Visconti from 1387, and became Venetian in 1405.

Cathedral of S. Maria Matricolare (Piazza del Duomo): Built in 1139 in

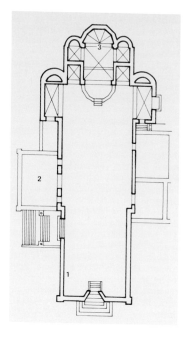

S. Zeno Maggiore, portal

Verona, S. Fermo, Upper Church 1 tomb of Rangoni di Brenzone **2** chapel of the sacrament **3** choir stalls

Romanesque style on the ruins of an older building destroyed by an earthquake. (The first church was built in the 5C, remains of the mosaic floor survive.) Altered in the 15C (nave heightened, rib vault introduced). The campanile, to a design by Sanmicheli, was not completed until the early 20C. Originally Romanesque, the façade has a two-storey porch dating from 1139. On either side of this, two knights, which are generally referred to as Roland and Oliver, paladins of Charlemagne, stand on columns. Very fine apse, with notable capitals and a good ornamental frieze on the cornice. The interior has a nave, two aisles, five bays, and beautiful Gothic capitals on the pillars. The 1st altar of the left aisle has an 'Assumption of the Virgin' by Titian (1st half of 16C). The

frescos by G.M. Falconetto (1503) on the side chapels of bays 1–3 are worth seeing. After the 4th bay, there are wide chapels on both sides with beautiful 18C baroque decoration. The tomb of St.Agatha (14C) is in the last side chapel on the right ('Cappella Mazanti'). Notable choir screens by M.Sanmicheli. The left aisle gives access to the 'Corte S.Elena', with the Romanesque church of the same name, and the 12C cloister. Near to the cathedral there is also the baptistery of *S.Giovanni in Fonte* (1122–35), with a glorious interior having a nave, two aisles and alternating supports. The nave, with its open roof truss, ends in an apse.

S.Anastasia (Piazza S.Anastasia): Begun by the Dominicans in the late-13C, the brick nave was completed in the 15C in Gothic style. The façade is unfaced but there is a magnificent portal. Inside there are a nave, two aisles and a broad transept.

The arcade consists of massive round pillars. The ceiling has a beautiful ribbed vault. Outstanding features include: the tomb of the Venetian general G.Fregoso (1565) is in the right aisle, between the 1st and 2nd pillars; the 15C Renaissance altar of the Miniscalchi family is in the left aisle (4th chapel); the 15C tomb of the condottiere Cortesia Serego from Verona is on the left of the sanctuary; on the opposite side are 14C frescos showing scenes from the Last Judgement; to the right of the sanctuary is the chapel of the Pellegrini family, with fine terracotta reliefs showing New Testament scenes by Michele da Firenze (1430–5); the 'Cappella Cavalli' with famous frescos by Altichiero Altichieri (14C) is in the right transept.

S.Fermo Maggiore (Via S.Fermo): Built from 1065 onwards over an earlier church, which today forms the lower church. The upper church was altered in the 13C: the nave with its two side aisles was converted into a hall-like area; the chancel became polygonal; the chapels to the sides of the sanctuary were closed; and other changes were also made. Completed in the 14C. The outside is not homogeneous because of the time taken over the building. The steps up to the main façade date from 1592. There is a fine portal framed by blind arcades. Access to the lower church is on the N. side, next to the rich double portal (*c.* 1400) leading to the upper church. The apses are Romanesque-Gothic. The campanile, which was completed in the 14C, has a conical roof typical of Verona. Inside: The upper church is single-aisled; the glorious mid 14C wooden ceiling in the form of a tunnel vault is outstanding. On the left wall is the tomb of Niccolò Rangoni di Brenzone (1425/6; by the sculptor Nanni di Bartolo and the painter Antonio Pisanello). After the side portal comes the chapel of the sacrament, with rich 17C decoration. The late Gothic choir stalls (15C) are behind the baroque high altar. The ground plan of the *lower church* has scarcely been altered. It basically has a nave and two aisles, but the addition of further columns has given it an additional aisle. There is a triumphal arch on ancient columns. The altar has a 14C wooden crucifix. Beautiful frescos on the 13/14C pillars.

S.Zeno Maggiore (Piazza S.Zeno): One

Piazza dei Signori

of the most important Romanesque churches in N.Italy. Built in 1118-35 on the site of an earlier building destroyed by an earthquake. Exterior: The façade (*c.* 1200) has a circular window and a glorious, typically Romanesque portal (built by Maestro Nicolao in 1135-8). The unique bronze door has 48 scenes from the Old and New Testaments. The outside walls of the church are in tufa and brick with pilaster strips, with a dwarf gallery on the S.side. The late 14C Gothic chancel ends in an apse and the campanile has a white base and a typical conical spire (building began in the 11C). Basilican interior with a nave, two aisles, and a raised chancel section (above the crypt, see below); compound piers alternate with round ones having fine capitals. The nave has a late Gothic wooden ceiling. Decoration: There is a beautiful marble font (*c.* 1200) in the right aisle. The balustrade in front of the high altar bears mid-13C statues of Christ and the Apostles. In a niche to the left of the sanctuary is a 13/14C marble figure of St.Zeno, the patron saint of the church, who was bishop of Verona in the 4C. Above the high altar is a triptych by Andrea Mantegna (1456-9), the middle panel is a Madonna and Child. The apse frescos are late Gothic. The crypt lies beneath the chancel and has a nave and eight aisles (beautiful capitals), with the tomb of St. Zeno. To the N. of the church is the cloister of a 12/13C Benedictine monastery secularized in 1773, with fine Romanesque double columns.

S. Bernardino (Vicolo Lungo S. Bernardino): Built in 1452 – 66, Renaissance portal dating from 1474/5; the side chapels on the right were built in 1486-1522. Altered in baroque style in the 17C, restored in 1931. Access to the church is gained through the front courtyard of the adjoining monastery. The façade is of unfaced brick and the portal (see above) has statues over the gable of St.Francis, St. Bernardino and St.Bonaventure. The interior is single-aisled, with an open roof truss. The chapel of the Avanzi family on the right, with its fine Renaissance paintings, including a 'Crucifixion' (1498) by Francesco Morone, is especially well worth seeing. To the right of the chancel is the entrance to the 'Cappella Pellegrini': built by M.Sanmicheli in 1529-57 on a central plan, it has a lovely cupola.

Arena

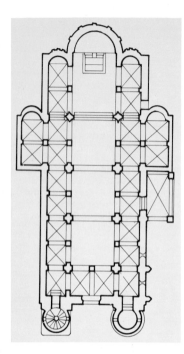

Verona, S. Lorenzo: Originally Romanesque, 12C (interior furnishings mostly destroyed in World War 2

Arena (Piazza Bra): Roman amphitheatre built in the 1C AD; incorporated into the town under Gallienus in AD 265. It was converted into a fortress during the Middle Ages and damaged by earthquake in the 12/13C (the stones were used as building materials for other houses); used as an open-air theatre since the 19C. The dimensions were originally 499 by 404 ft. (today 453 by 358 ft.), and there are 22,000 seats. Only some sections of the original outer wall survive.

Piazza dei Signori: This, in the past, was the administrative centre of Verona. It is bordered by a uniform, compact series of buildings, beginning, on the right of the entrance from the Piazza delle Erbe, with the 12C *Palazzo del Comune,* which has a Renaissance facing of 1524 and a fine inner courtyard (the late Gothic 'Corte del Mercato Vecchio'). This is connected by an arch to the *Palazzo dei Tribunali* (the tower is from the former, 14C Palazzo Grande of the Scaligers), which was the seat of the Venetian governors; the gateway, *c.* 1530, is by Sanmicheli, and there is a fine loggia dating from 1476 in the inner courtyard. To the left of Via S.Maria Antica is the *Palazzo del Governo,* the palace of the Scaligers (built after 1300; under the Venetians it was the seat of the city's Podestà), with a fine medieval façade on the Piazzetta S.Maria Antica. Adjoining the Palazzo del Governo on the left is the so-called *Loggia del Consiglio,* built in 1476–93 as the meeting-place of the city council, with a richly decorated upper storey. A *monument to Dante,* 1865, stands in the middle of the square. The visitor passes from the Piazza dei Signori along Via S.Maria Antica to the 12C church of *S.Maria Antica* with the adjoining *Scaliger tombs.* The impressive canopied tomb of Cangrande I (d. 1329), with an equestrian statue of him above it, is on the N. wall.

Scaliger Tombs

Juliet's Balcony ▷

Castelvecchio (on the Adige): Built (1354–6) by the Scaligers as, amongst other things, a refuge. The tower dates from 1375, and the adjoining bridge over the Adige was begun in 1355 and rebuilt after being destroyed in 1945. The complex is in two parts. The real fortress has powerful corner towers grouped around a courtyard, whilst the fortified residence-castle of the Scaligers is to the left. During the restoration work (1923/4), parts of other buildings in Verona were moved here; they include the late Gothic and Renaissance façade of the main courtyard. The *Civico Museo d'Arte* (Museo di Castelvecchio), with a sculpture department and a picture gallery, has been housed in the castle since 1925. Outstanding exhibits include: the Romanesque sarcophagus (1179) of St. Sergius and St.Bacchus, and the original equestrian statue from the tomb of Cangrande I della Scala (see above).

Also worth seeing: *S. Giorgetto* (near S. Anastasia, see above), 14C, with a beautiful fresco by Pisanello ('St.George', 1435, actually from S. Anastasia). The 12C *SS. Apostoli*, with a fine apse. *SS. Tosca e Teuteria* (near to SS.Apostoli), one of the oldest churches in Verona, first built in the 5C. *S. Eufemia* (Via Francesco Emilei), 13C, with remains of the original 14C wall paintings (to the left of the chancel). *S. Giorgio Maggiore* (also called S.Giorgio in Braida; to the left of the Adige, near the Porta S.Giorgio), rebuilt in the 15C; fine paintings inside, including the 'Martyrdom of St.George' on the high altar by Paolo Veronese, 1566, and the baroque bronze statues by A.Rossi (St.George and John the Baptist). The 12C *S.Giovanni in Valle*, a purely Romanesque basilica with fine late classical sarcophagi in the crypt. *S. Lorenzo* (Corso Cavour), 12C, with a beautiful interior. *S.Maria in Organo* (near the Porta Organo), rebuilt in the 15C, with splendid choir stalls (1491–9) and an interesting sacristy; in the chapel is a 15C wooden statue of Christ riding the ass on Palm Sunday. *S.Stefano* (on the left bank of the Adige), founded in the 5C, with interesting inscriptions on the façade and the fine early baroque 'Cappella degli Innocenti' on the right aisle. *SS. Nazaro e Celso*, 15C, with a notable 14C processional cross on the high altar. *S. Tomaso Cantuariense*, built *c.* 1500, with a fine late Gothic portal dating from 1464/5. The *Ro-*

Verona, production of Aida in the Arena

man theatre, 1C AD, on the left bank of the Adige. Above it, in the former monastery of S.Girolamo, is the Archaeological Museum. The *Piazza Bra* with: the 'Gran Guardia', the drill-hall of the Venetian troops (begun in 1610); the city's modern town hall; and the 'Museo Lapidario Maffeiano', a small but significant archaeological museum. *Piazza delle Erbe*, the centre of the city's life, located on the site of the ancient forum; in the middle is the 'Madonna Verona' fountain: the basin and statue are of ancient origin. The *Porta dei Borsari* (Corso Cavour) and *Porta dei Leoni* (Via Leoni) are remains of the ancient Roman city defences. *Arco dei Gavi* (near the Castelvecchio), a triumphal gate from the 1C AD. *Porta Palio* (Stradone di P.Palio), city gate built by Sanmicheli in 1542–57. *Juliet's Balcony* (access from the Via Cappello 21) on a fine 13/14C medieval house. The 16C Palazzo Bevilacqua (Corso Cavour). *Giardino Giusti* (Via Giardino Giusti 2), a beautiful garden, laid out in 18C style. *Ponte Pietra*, an ancient bridge across the Adige, rebuilt in 1945 after being destroyed.

Environs: S. Michele Extra: To the S. of Verona, with the frequently visited pilgrimage church of 'Madonna della Pace', built in the 16C to plans by Sanmicheli.

Vetralla 01019
Viterbo/Latium   p.414☐G 9

S. Francesco: This 11C Romanesque church stands on the site of an earlier 8C building. Notable features include the portal, the three apses with pilaster strips on small half columns, the nave and sacristy with their much-restored Cosmati-work floor (12/13C), and the much-faded frescos which stem from the Gozzoli school and depict the miracles of St.Francis. There is an early Renaissance sarcophagus by Paolo Romano in the sanctuary. The ciborium in the main apse is early 15C.

Environs: Norchia This Etruscan necropolis from the 5–3C BC, 10 km. from Vetralla, has interesting rock tombs which were probably part of the town of Orgola

(Etruscan: Orcle) abandoned in the 9C BC. Two 4&3C BC temple tombs with reliefs on the pediments stand in the amphitheatre. The original settlement, with the ruins of the pre-Romanesque church of *S. Pietro*, is above the Fosso di Pile.

Vibo Valentia 88018
Catanzaro/Calabria   p.418☐N 15

Collegiata S.Maria Maggiore: Built in 1680–1723 in baroque style on the foundations of a Byzantine basilica and a Romanesque church (destroyed by an earthquake in 1638). The façade is 19C, and inside there is a single aisle. The ground plan is a Latin cross and the side chapels are interconnected. Fine *stucco decoration*. The left transept has a beautiful *altar* with 16C marble statues by Antonello Gagini. Carved choir stalls in the chancel.

Castle: Built, using ancient materials, on the site of the old acropolis. The Norman tower was enlarged and strengthened under Frederick II Hohenstaufen and under the Angevins.

Excavations of ancient Hipponion: Remains of a *Doric temple* (6/5C BC) on the Belvedere Grande (excavation work since 1916). The remains of the *town wall*, with three *towers* (5/4C BC) near the cemetery. The remains of an *Ionic temple* on the rising ground of Cofino. Other remains.

Also worth seeing: The 13C *Chiesa del Rosario* with a fine baroque pulpit. The 17C *S.Maria degli Angeli* with fine paintings. *S.Michele* (16C, Renaissance) with a good portal worth seeing and an octagonal lantern on a dome. *Archaeological Museum* in the Palazzo Gagliardi with ancient finds from the town and its environs. *Roman baths* with lovely mosaics.

Environs: Some 15 km. to the NE, **Pizzo** with an Aragonese *castle* (1486) where Murat, the King of Naples (by Napoleon's grace), was shot dead on 13 October 1815. Some 12 km. to the S., **Mileto:** the first seat of the Norman king Roger I (1031–1101) before the conquest of Sicily. He is buried in the church of *S. Trinità*, the sarcophagus being in Palermo. The *remains* of the old town, destroyed by an earthquake in 1783, lie to the E. of modern Mileto. The peninsula of Tropea runs to the W. and SW of Vibo Valentia. Two towns are worth seeing: **Tropea** with a *cathedral* whose core is pre-Norman but which has been much altered in the course of time. Inside there are remains of 11C frescos and also fine octagonal columns. **Nicótera,** magnificently sited above the *Gulf of Gioia*. The town was fortified under Robert Guiscard. **Rosarno** is some 30 km. to the SW, on the site of the Locrian colony of Medma (6C BC); since 1913 there have been finds of a particular kind of terracotta.

Vicenza 36100
Vicenza/Veneto   p.410☐F 3

Cathedral of S.Maria Maggiore (Piazza Duomo): Begun in *c.* 1400, it is a Gothic reconstruction on the ruins of an earlier Romanesque building, from which the S. side portal survives. There is a long building history. The dome was not begun until the mid-16C, with the assistance of Palladio. Severely damaged in World War 2, it was rebuilt in 1946–50. Outside: The nave is late Gothic, and the chancel is Renaissance, with fine pilasters and a dome, covered with copper plates, on a polygonal drum. A Gothic façade with a portal dating from 1792 (the statues are copies of the originals dating from 1649). Inside there is a single aisle, and four bays with a ribbed vault; each arch has two side chapels. The raised chancel is reached by a red marble staircase. Decoration: A richly decorated high altar dating from 1534 (G.da Pedemuro and G.Pittoni). In the 5th side chapel on the right there is a polyptych by L.Veneziano (1356, marked Byzantine influence). The altar in the 4th chapel on the left is a fine Gothic marble sarcophagus dating from 1359. There is a late Gothic altar-piece by Antonino di Nicolò da Venezia ('Coronation of the Virgin', 1448) in the 5th chapel on the left. In the last chapel on the left note the tomb of Girolamo and Gio. Battista Gualdo dating from 1574. The entrance to the crypt, which has a fine 'Madonna Mora' on its altar (15C), is in front of the high altar.

S. Chiara (also S. Bernardino; Contrà S. Chiara): Building began in late Gothic style in 1451. Centrally planned octagonal building with outside chapels at the sides; the vault has a polygonal drum. There are fine pilaster strips at the corners; the walls are framed by pointed arch friezes. By the portal is a relief of St.Bernardino of Siena (*c.* 1500). Inside, the 15C frescos on the front wall are of note.

S. Corona (Contrà S.Corona): The first building (13C) was intended for a relic of Christ's Crown of Thorns; hence the name. The chancel and sanctuary were rebuilt in 1479–1504 to plans by Lorenzo da Bologna; repeatedly restored in the 18&19C. It is the first Gothic church in Vicenza and the influence of the French Cistercian style is discernible, e.g. in the angular chancel chapels. Outside: The nave is partly covered by later buildings; the chancel has a richly decorated terracotta cornice. The façade was rebuilt in 1888 using some old parts. Inside: a nave and two aisles; pointed arcades on massive columns; nave with ribbed vault (the bay in front of the chancel is lower than the others). A raised chancel, with access by a red marble staircase; underneath is the 15/16C crypt leading to the 'Cappella Valmarana', built in the 16C to Palladio's plans. Decoration: imposing high altar (1669–86) by Fra Giorgio Bovio; in the 5th chapel of the left aisle is a gorgeous 16C altar by Rocco da Vicenza. The 'Baptism of Christ', a masterpiece by Giovanni Bellini dating from 1500–20. In the 4th side chapel on the right is an 'Adoration of the Magi' by Paolo Veronese dating from 1573. In the right transept is the late 15C 'Cappella Barbarano' with a (restored) 15C wooden cross. There is a fine late 18C altarpiece in the 'Cappella Thiene' to the right of the sanctuary.

SS.Felice e Fortunato (Corso SS.Felice e Fortunato): First founded as early as 313 (parts of this church's mosaic floor have survived). After being rebuilt and extended several times, it was altered in baroque style in the 17C. Restoration work since 1934. Outside: 9/10C façade; the main portal and rose-window are later (12C). Above the tympanum of the portal are the remains of 12C frescos of the Last Judgement. The baptistery (c. 1400) is on the N. side of the nave; the campanile has 14C battlements (in front of it are the foundations of an early Christian baptistery, destroyed in the 9C). Beside the apse is the 5C martyrion (see above), which was used to house relics. It had a Greek cross ground plan and a semicircular apse. The interior is basilican (one

nave, two aisles); some of the columns are late classical; the chancel is raised. The 4C mosaic floor (see above) is in the front part of the nave. The crypt with the 4C tombstone of the church's patrons is under the chancel. The right aisle gives access to the small church of S. Maria Mater Domini (the ground plan is a Greek cross and there is a tunnel-vaulted narthex in front).

S. Lorenzo (Piazza S. Lorenzo): Building began in the 13C in Romanesque style, and was only completed in the 15C. The early 14C façade is in two stages. On the lower one there are pointed blind arcades and a splendid portal (1342–4) with lions as stylophores, beautiful reliefs of Apostles and Evangelists on the jambs, Virgin Enthroned in the tympanum. The upper stage has a large rose-window in the centre and 5 smaller round windows. The interior, with its nave and two aisles, is in the style of a basilica, with fine early Gothic capitals and pointed arcades; the nave and aisles have ribbed vaults. The choir chapels have polygonal apses; on the sides of the sanctuary there are still Romanesque double-arched windows from the earlier building. Interesting features include a

Vicenza, S. Corona 1 high altar by Fra Bovio **2** altar of R. da Vicenza (Bellini painting) **3** 'Adoration of the Magi' by P. Veronese **4** Cappella Barbarano

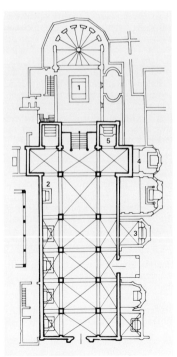

Vicenza, S. Lorenzo

black marble slab from the original altar of 1289 behind the present high altar in the choir. There are also two important monuments: to the left, that of General Ippolito da Porto, 1572; beside it, that of Leonardo da Porto, 1545. On the right in the 'Cappella della Madonna' (left of choir), is a fresco by B.Montagna ('Beheading of St. Paul', *c.* 1500). There is a fine Renaissance altar in the right transept. Late 15C cloister.

S.Rocco (Contrà S.Rocco): The building of this Renaissance church began in 1485, during a plague. It was lengthened in the 16C. Façade divided into three by pilaster strips; in the middle is a fine rose-window, and under it a round-arched portal. Note the fine polygonal apse with blind arcades and a fine cornice. The campanile dates from 1530. The inside has a single nave, with a vault tunnel; a wide gallery on round-arched arcades and octagonal pillars. The 16C high altar is in the polygonal apse; the sanctuary frescos are late medieval, restored in the 20C. There is a 15C wooden crucifix on the balustrade of the gallery, in front of a fine Virgin Mary and John the Evangelist (16C). The 2nd altar on the right has a notable 'Adoration of the Magi' by A.Galeazzi (1559). A 15C cloister.

Santuario della Madonna di Monte Berico (access via the Viale X Giugno): Built as a Gothic basilica in 1428 after a vision of the Virgin Mary. Extended by Lorenzo da Bologna in 1476–80 around a monks' chancel (for the adjoining Servite monastery); enlarged by Palladio from 1576 onwards; the present building was constructed in 1688–1703. It is a cruciform domed building, as can be seen from the outside. A dome with a massive lantern rises over the arms. Outside, particularly on the portals, there are numerous statues and reliefs from the workshop of O.Marinali (d. 1720). The old shrine mentioned above (late Gothic church; the rose-window is the only original part of the façade, everything else is restored) adjoins the church to its right. 19C campanile. The inside of the church has magnificent baroque decoration; tunnel-vaulted arms (the S.arm leads to the old basilica referred to above). Fine decoration: A masterpiece by B.Montagna ('Pietà with Peter, John and Mary Magdalene', 1500) in the chapel of the 1st bay. Fine 15C inlay work on the choir stalls. The sacristy (access via the S. aisle of the basilica), with a beautiful fresco by B.Montagna, is also worth seeing. Opposite the sacristy is the late Gothic cloister; on its E. side is the monastery refectory with a painting by P.Veronese, 'Banquet of St.Gregory the Great', 1572.

Basilica Palladiana (Piazza dei Signori): It stands on the S.side of the Piazza, which is still the centre of the town (site of the ancient Roman forum). Previously known as the 'Palazzo Pubblico', when it was used as the law courts and the assembly building of the 'Grand Council'. Building began in 1449 of a late Gothic palazzo with an open pillared hall on the lower storey and a large hall on the upper storey. In the late 15C it was surrounded with loggias. After the building's partial collapse in 1496, the reconstruction dragged on and Palladio played a key role from 1546 onwards. The basilica is one of his most important works. Completed in 1617; roof rebuilt after being destroyed in World War 2. Exterior: Columns (Doric below, Ionic above), with massive arches between them. The so-called 'Palladian motif': the coupling of columns one behind the other creates a three-dimensional effect on the façade. Paired columns at the corners.

Loggia del Capitaniato (Piazza dei Signori): This building opposite the basilica was begun in 1570/1 to plans by Palladio, and was to be the residence of the Venetian commander, but it was only partly built (of the 7 arches planned for the façade, only 3 were completed). The lower storey has massive round arches and between them 4 powerful half-columns with exuberant capitals. Stucco decoration on the walls; the right, short side has a scene showing the victory of Lepanto (1571).

Teatro Olimpico (Piazza Matteotti): Begun to plans by Palladio in 1580 and com-

Vicenza, S. Lorenzo ▷

missioned by the 'Accademia Olimpica' of Vicenza, and completed in 1583. The wings, still standing today, were built in 1584. Inside: built on an ancient model, but very freely adapted by Palladio to his own ideas. Semicircular rows of seats rise up from the orchestra and, at the top, there are columns and a balustrade (18C statues). The back of the stage is wooden and has 3 entrances through portals. Behind these the rising floor and foreshortening effects give an illusion of depth to what are supposed to be the alleys of a town. In the niches at the front there are statues of members of the Academy. Today's ceiling dates from 1914 but is a faithful copy of the original. The so-called 'Odeo', with pictures by F.Maffei (*c.* 1635) and frescos, adjoins the theatre.

Palazzo Chiericati (Piazza Matteotti, has contained the Museo Civico since 1855): Begun by Palladio in 1550, it was not completed until 1680). Beautiful front, with marked Antique influence. The ground floor of the *Museo Civico* houses an archaeological section with finds from Vicenza and its environs. The main floor has a richly endowed picture gallery (in room I note the 'Death of the Virgin Mary' by Paolo Veneziano, in the 14C Byzantine style of the Veneto; in room X, paintings by Francesco Maffei, Vicenza's most famous 17C painter).

Villa Valmarana dei Nani (Stradella dei Nani): the main house was built in 1669; the guest building (the so-called 'Foresteria'), the gate complex and the stables are of later date. The villa is famous for the extensive and well-preserved frescos by both Tiepolos, father and son, (1757) in the main house and in the Foresteria. There are 18C statues of dwarfs on the wall surrounding the villa complex. Tradition has it that a crippled daughter of the owner lived in the villa and had dwarfs as attendants. This is also the origin of the villa's name: 'nani' is Italian for 'dwarfs'.

Villa Rotonda (also Villa Capra; beside the Via dei Nani, access via Piazza Fraccon and Borgo Berga): The most famous villa built by Palladio; begun in 1550/1, but only completed at the end of the century. Square ground plan; a centrally planned building with a dome and porticoes with massive external staircases at each side.

Basilica Palladiana

Also worth seeing: *Carmine*, a 14C church on the Piazza Carmine, with fine 15C reliefs in the chapel niches. The 17C *S.Maria dell'Aracelli* (Piazza Aracelli), with an interesting façade. *S. Maria dei Servi* (Piazza delle Biade), 15C, with a fine late Gothic interior. *S. Stefano* (Contrà S. Stefano), 17/18C, built in the style of the Roman baroque churches. The 17C *Oratorio di S.Nicola* (Piazzetta S.Nicola), with significant 17C Venetian paintings inside. *Palazzo Vescovile*, the Bishops' Palace (Piazza Duomo), with the so-called 'Loggia Zeno' (late 15C) in the courtyard. The numerous palaces include: the *'Ca'd'Oro* (Corso Palladio), late Gothic; the *Casa Pigafetta* (Contrà A.Pigafetta), with a late Gothic-early Renaissance façade; the *Palazzo Thiene* (Contrada Porti) from the early Renaissance; the *Palazzo Civena-Trissino* (Viale Eretenio) and the *Palazzo Valmarana-Braga* (Corso Fogazzano), masterpieces by Palladio; the *Palazzo Barbarano* (Contrada Porti) from Palladio's late period; the *Palazzo Trissino-Baston* (Corso Palladio, today the town hall) dating from 1592, one of V.Scamozzi's main works. The *Loggetta Valmarana* (in the 'Giardino Salvi', a park), built in Palladian style in the 16C. The *Ponte S.Michele*, dating from 1619, crosses the river Retrone.

Vicovaro 00029
Rome/Latium   p.414□H 9

S.Giacomo: This octagonal Renaissance building was begun by Domenico da Capodistria in 1454. The portal is decorated by pilasters, and by niches with statues. In the tympanum there is a relief showing two members of the Orsini family.

Vietri di Potenza 85058
Potenza/Basilicata   p.418□M 12

Vietri was inhabited in prehistoric times, as is shown by finds, mainly ceramics, in the grotto of M.la Serrapola, SE of the town. The salty, sulphurous waters, which have their source to the S., are used for cures and baths for skin diseases and women's diseases.

Parish church: The Romanesque campanile has a fragment of a Hellenistic

Vicenza, Teatro Olimpico, interior

Vicenza, Palazzo del Monte di Pietà

Vigévano, Castello Sforzesco

figure, half man, half woman, built into its wall.

Environs: Balvano: Founded by the Normans, it has some interesting remains of an 11C castle, which was rebuilt in 1278.

Vigévano 27029
Pavia/Lombardy   p.412☐C 3

Piazza Ducale: This was built from 1492 onwards by order of Ludovico il Moro on the site of a medieval residential town quarter. Its design probably goes back to a plan by Leonardo (1492). Oriented on an east-west axis, it is bordered on three sides by uniformly designed arcades with living-quarters above them. Even the roads leading to the Piazza are concealed behind arcades. Its uniformity is accentuated by splendid wall paintings (restored in 1902) and strictly symmetrical paving. The narrow, concave E. side incorporates the cathedral in the symmetrical arrangement of the Piazza, although it is oriented along a different axis from that of the Piazza, and the cathedral façade becomes part of the arcade scheme of the Piazza.

Cathedral: The first phase in the building of this cathedral dedicated to St. Ambrose was in 1532–53. Work then continued, with interruptions, to designs by A.da Lonate and it was dedicated in 1612. The façade is to plans by J.Caramuel de Lobkovitz, Bishop of Vigévano, 1680. The dome was completed in 1716 and the massive campanile was built in 1497. The inside has largely retained its original appearance, despite 19C painting. The cathedral treasure includes tapestries of Flemish and local manufacture.

Castello Sforzesco: Access to this castle

is gained from the S.side of the Piazza. In 1345–50, Luchino Visconti had this former 10C stronghold converted into a stately residence. His work was continued by Gian Galeazzo and Galeazzo Maria Sforza. Building was completed under Ludovico il Moro. The marriage of Galeazzo Maria Sforza to Bona of Savoy was celebrated in the castle in 1468.

Torre del Castello: This tower rising behind the S.front of the Piazza connects the castle and the Piazza, turning the Piazza into an impressive outer courtyard. The design for this imposing entrance to the castle is ascribed to Bramante. The E. side of the spacious castle courtyard is dominated by the three-winged complex of the *Palazzo Ducale*, which was rebuilt in Tudor style in 1854–7. Covered battlements on the extension of the N. transverse wing lead to the so-called *Rocca Vecchia*, which was a barbican. A loggia in the style of Bramante joins the S.wing of the palace to the former Falconiera (falconry).

Villanova di San Bonifacio 37047
Veneto   p.410 ☐ F 3

S. Pietro Apostolo: Part of a former Benedictine abbey, it was built in the 12C on the site of an earlier building. The bell storey of the campanile and the frieze on the N. side of the exterior both date from *c.* 1400. The baroque interior dates from the 18C, as does the vaulting of the nave and aisles. The three impressive apses have a fine round-arched frieze on the outside. The façade has been partly rebuilt (the upper section is original). Inside: a basilica with a nave and two aisles; raised chancel over a crypt. Fine capitals on the columns of the nave. The central apse has an interesting mid 15C sandstone altarpiece with depictions of saints. The rear of the high altar is decorated with an 8C relief. At the beginning of the right aisle there are fine frescos (life of St.Benedict) from the end of the 14C. The crypt has a nave, four aisles and notable capitals.

Environs: Soave: (*c.* 8 km.). First men-

tioned in the 6C. The 24-tower *wall* and the *castle* (magnificent location above the town) are outstanding, as is the *parish church*, with a fine painting of the Madonna by Fr.Morone (1529), and the *town hall* of 1375.

Vipiteno/Sterzing 39049
Bolzano/South Tyrol-Trentino   p.410 ☐ F 1

Parish church of Unsere Liebe Frau im Moos (to the S., outside the town): The chancel was built by Hans and Friedrich Feur in 1420–55 in the South German Gothic style; in the typanum of the sacristy door is a stone relief of the Mount of Olives (*c.* 1450). The nave (1497–1524) was built by B.Weibhauser and H.Lutz as a hall area with a nave, two aisles and five bays. Above the German, Austrian and Tyrolean coats of arms, the tympanum of the S. portal shows the Madonna Enthroned, executed by Th.Scheiter in 1497 to a design by M.Stöberl. The baroque frescos in the nave vault, which replaces the Gothic ribs, are the work of J.A.Mölk (1753). The most interesting feature inside is the neo-Gothic *high altar*, which houses 5 large shrine figures from the former winged altar by Hans Multscher (1456–8). The busts of Christ and the 12 apostles (*c.* 1460, influenced by Multscher), and an interesting Crucifixion from the same period, are also on the chancel wall. The *tombstones* in the church and outside it are 14–16C, while the beautiful *choir stalls* are rococo. Roman tombstones may be found outside on the S.wall of the nave.

Spitalkirche zum Hl. Geist (Hospital church of the Holy Ghost, in the S.of the old town, to the N. of the town wall): In 1380, this church, with its ribbed vaulting, was added as a rectangular hall into the former burghers' hospital. The N. aisle is 17C. Inside there are frescos by Hans von Bruneck, 1420.

St.Elisabeth und Deutschhaus (St. Elizabeth and Hospice of the Teutonic Order of Knights): The hospice, founded in 1241 and standing on the Brenner road, belonged to the Teutonic Order of Knights from 1254–1813 and is today used as a hospital. It is still of interest as a group of medieval buildings. The W. wing is 15C, while the S.and E. wings date from the late 16C. In 1729–33 Jos. Delai built the associated church of *St.Elisabeth,* a centrally planned baroque building with a frescoed dome (1733) by M.Günther, who also painted the altar-piece. The rococo stucco work is by A.Gigl from Innsbruck, while the side altar is the work of Georg Trabl (1598).

Also worth seeing: *St.Margareta,* a simple baroque structure by P.Delai (1678–80); the base of the tower dates from 1330. *Ansitz Jöchlsthurn:* In the mid-15C, the Jöchl family enlarged an older house, turning it into a mansion for their own use; today it houses the law courts (the inside rooms have stellar groin vaults and in the hall on the 2nd storey has a very beautiful wooden ceiling from *c.* 1500). To the E., its chapel of *St.Peter and St.Paul* (1474) has damaged frescos (1480) by Fr.Pacher on its outside wall. It also has a late Gothic door, a late baroque high altar, and a wooden carving of the Madonna and Child, 1330.

Burg Sprechenstein (on a rocky ledge to the S.of Sterzing): Built in 1240, restored and extended in 1511–15, the Romanesque castle chapel has frescos in its apse (1515), while the late Gothic winged altar dates from 1505.

Burg Reifenstein (on Sterzing Moos, the moor to the S.of the town): The oldest section of this castle (the main castle is to the S., with the castle keep, the residence and the hall) dates from the mid 12C. It was enlarged in 1500–11. The residence has rooms with Gothic decoration, and a carved, barred door between the richly decorated Green Hall and the chapel.

Multscher Museum: It contains carved figures and painted wings from the Multscher altar in the parish church.

Environs: Colle Isarco/Gossensass: This beautiful village with its 16C houses (e.g. No. 144 and Nos. 145–8) lies to the N. of Sterzing and to the S.of the Brenner.

The parish church of the *Mariae Empfängnis* (the Immaculate Conception) is a baroque building by Franz de Paula Penz (1750–4); the N. tower dates from an older, 15C church. The vault frescos inside the church are by M.Günther (1751). The two-storeyed *Barbara Chapel,* probably built in 1510, stands beside the parish church, by the cemetery. The lower chapel serves as a crypt, and the upper chapel houses a late Gothic carved altar of 1515. **Mareta/Mareit:** This village with the parish church of *St.Pancraz,* which was built by Gallus Apeller the Elder in 1685 –95, is in the Ridanna valley to the W. of Vipiteno. The ceiling frescos (1811) are by F.Altmutter; the high altar dates from 1780, the side altars from 1740 and the altar of the side chapel from the 17C. *St. Magdalena:* This single-aisled late Gothic church, with its net vault and its isolated location on a hill outside the village, was built in 1481/2. The late Gothic carved *high altar* with its painted wings is the work of M.Stöberl from Sterzing (1509). Beside it, to its left, is the earlier high altar (*c.* 1470), which is probably by H.Harder. *Schloss Wolfsturn:* This is the only baroque castle in the South Tyrol. A very homogeneous building probably built by G.Delai between 1729 and 1740, it stands on a hill above the town. The castle chapel has rich stucco by A.Gigl and frescos by M.Günther (1738).

Visso 62039
Macerata/Marches   p.414□H 8

S.Maria: This building was begun in the 12C, but not completed until the 15C. The portal, flanked by lions, has ancient wooden door-leaves; the lunette fresco with the 'Annunciation' dates from 1441. The baroque interior is 17C, as is the wooden ceiling. Surviving older features include: A holy-water stoup. 15C frescos in the Rimini style in the chancel. An early 16C fresco by Giovanni di Pietro, known as Lo Spagna, on the 1st altar on the left. A

Vipiteno, tower ▷

Madonna from the 2nd half of the 12C on the 2nd altar on the left. The baptismal chapel has an early 12C crucifix, and also Gothic capitals.

Viterbo 01100
Viterbo/Latium   p.414☐G 8/9

San Lorenzo: The cathedral was built by Lombard architects in the 12C on the ruins of a temple of Hercules; campanile added in the 2nd half of the 14C; façade rebuilt in *c*. 1560–70. The repair of bomb damage fully restored the original three-dimensional effect of the Romanesque pillared basilica with its nave, two aisles and 20 monolithic columns with richly decorated capitals. Notable features: The E. section with its three apses. The porphyry tomb of John XXI (Pope and Doctor of the Church), called Pietro Ispano in Dante's 'Paradiso' (to the right of the entrance). 12C panel painting of Madonna della Carbonara in the left apse. Christ blessing, with Saints and the founder, 1472, by Gerolamo da Cremona, above the sacristy door.

Palazzo dei Papi: This Papal palace, which is one of the most important 13C secular buildings in Italy, dates from 1257–66 (elegant Gothic loggia, 1267). The massive hall was the scene of Papal elections in the 13C.

San Francesco: This church was built in 1236 and partially rebuilt in 1373. The repair of the damage caused in World War 2 was completed in 1953. The simple building is single-aisled and cruciform, with a projecting transept. There is only one apse. It has a Gothic two-arched window, and lies at right angles to the axis. The 15C outdoor pulpit is in memory of St.Bernardino's sermon (1426). A simple but impressive interior with important tombs, including that of Pope Hadrian V, which is regarded as one of the early works of Arnolfo da Cambio, and that of Pietro di Vico, the Prefect of Rome (d. 1268), decorated with Cosmati work.

S.Maria della Verità: Built as a Premonstratensian church in the early 12C. Taken over by the Servite order in 1262, at which time the round apse, the chapels and the Gothic cloister were added. The severe

Vipiteno, parish church, Multscher altar

damage suffered in World War 2 was repaired by 1960. A hall-like nave with an open roof truss. The frescos in the Cappella Mezzatosta by Lorenzo da Viterbo (1469) are outstanding. These were transferred to canvas when they were restored. The convent with its magnificent Gothic cloister (three sides date from the 13C, the fourth was built in the 14C) today serves as the *Museo Civico*, which houses archaeological finds, sculpture from buildings and detached frescos.

Also worth seeing: The church of *S. Maria Nuova*, built in the 12C, and freed in 1906–14 from the disfigurements of the 19C. Thomas Aquinas preached from the outdoor pulpit in 1266; above the portal is a head of Jupiter, and inside there are richly decorated chapels; a small Romanesque cloister. The 9C church of *S. Sisto*, built on a pagan temple, extended in the 12C, with interesting capitals and a high altar built of 4&5C fragments. *S.Maria in Gradi:* This church stands by the town wall and has a fine early Gothic cloister (1266 – 8). An excellently preserved medieval town quarter on the *Via S.Pellegrino*. The town has numerous fountains; the *Fontana*

Grande, begun by Bertoldo and Pietro di Giovanni in 1206 and completed in 1279, is outstanding. The partially preserved *town walls* with their 7 gates, including the baroque 'Porta Romana' of 1653 with its decoration dating from 1705.

Environs: Bagnaia (*c.* 5 km.): Famous for the *Villa Lante*, which, together with its park, is one of the most significant Mannerist villas. Cardinal Giovanni Francesco Gambara, a relative of the Farnese, had this 'Giardino all' italiana', with its strictly geometric arrangement on five terraces, laid out by Vignola in 1566–78. In the middle is the Fontana di Quadrato with four Moors, the work of Taddeo Landini, holding the coat of arms of Pope Sixtus V. The Casino Gambara has, on its loggia walls, frescos of the famous villas of Latium. Inside there are frescos by Antonio Tempesta, and also, on the upper storey, some by Raffaellino da Reggio and G.B.Lambardelli. The second Casino was built in 1585–90 by Cardinal Alessandro Montalto, a nephew of Pope Sixtus V, and has frescos by the Cavalier d'Arpino (architectural painting by Agostino Tassi), and loggia frescos by Agostino Tassi. The park con-

Vipiteno, epitaph

Reifenstein castle (Vipiteno)

tinues behind the Casini, with waterworks and grottoes (illuminated fountains, fountains with dolphins and giants). **Férento** (about 9 km.): An Etruscan centre, allied with the Romans (Ferentum) in *c.* 241 BC. The ruins of the 1C AD theatre, erroneously thought to be Etruscan, survive from ancient Ferentum. Now that it has been repaired, it is used in summer for performances of works by classical playwrights. There are Etruscan and Roman burial places in the environs and also the ruins of *S.Bonifazio* (9/10C), the former bishops' church of Ferento. **Soriano nel Cimino** (*c.* 16.5 km.): A town of Etruscan or Phoenician origin, possibly the Surrina Vetus destroyed by the Romans. In the Middle Ages it was known as Surianum. The *Palazzo Chigi-Albani:* An important work by Vignola, begun in 1562. On the left, short side is the Fontana Papacqua (= Regina delle acque). **S.Martino al Cimino** (6.5 km.): This abbey church, built in the 13C by the Cistercians of Pontigny, is one of the most progressive examples of Cistercian Gothic in Italy. The monumental façade, which was added to and partially rebuilt in the 19C, is flanked by two campaniles dating from the 14C (?). Above the gradu-

ated portal, the façade is pierced by rose-windows. The outside is buttressed. Only some parts (refectory, chapterhouse) of the monastery have survived.

Vittória 97019

Ragusa/Sicily   p.420□ K/L 18

Worth seeing: The *Chiesa della Madonna delle Grazie* (Piazza del Popolo) of 1754, with a fine baroque façade; the 18C *Chiesa Madre S.Giovanni* (Piazza F.Ricca) with interesting baroque furnishings, particularly the pulpit and altars; *Teatro Comunale* (Piazza del Popolo) with a fine neo-classical façade.

Vittorio Veneto 31029

Treviso/Veneto   p.410□ G 2

Worth seeing in the Ceneda quarter is the *Piazza della Cattedrale* with the former 16C town hall; the *loggia*, with frescos by P.Amalteo inside, is particularly beautiful. Above the town is the *Castello di S.Martino*, whose present structure dates from the

Bagnaia (Viterbo), Villa Lante, fountain

16/17C, but which was originally a Lombard fortress. Interesting features of the Serravalle quarter include the *Cathedral of S.Maria Nuova* with a Madonna and Child by Titian in the chancel, and the churches of *S.Andrea* (14C) and *S.Giustina* with the Venetian-style tomb of Riccardo VI da Camino, the town's last ruler (d. 1335). *S. Lorenzo* is another fine church with notable 15C Venetian frescos inside. The *Museo del Cenedese* in the Loggia Serravallese is worth a visit; its most valuable exhibit is a relief of the Madonna by J.Sansovino.

Vizzini 95049
Catania/Sicily   p.420☐L 18

Chiesa Matrice S. Gregorio: Built on the ruins of the *Palazzo Senatoriale* after the earthquake of 1693. The fine 15C Catalan Gothic portal on the right side is from the Palazzo. The inside (one nave, two aisles) is basilican and has two paintings by Fil. Paladino (1544–1614) that are worth seeing: the *Martyrdom of S.Lawrence* (2nd altar on the right), and the *Madonna della Mercede* (4th altar on the right).

Also worth seeing: The church of *S. Giovanni Battista* with fine stucco decoration inside. *Chiesa dei Cappuccini* with a painting by Paladino (see above) dating from 1607 ('Descent from the Cross'). The church of *S.Maria di Gesù* with a Madonna by Antonello Gagini (1527).

Environs: Some 10 km. to the W. is **Licodia Eubea** on the site of the ancient town of Euboia (founded in 650 BC); finds from *Siculan tombs.*

Volterra 56048
Pisa/Tuscany   p.414☐F 7

The Etruscan Velathri, one of the 12 cities of the confederation, was so strongly fortified that it was able to withstand two years of siege by Sulla during the Social War. From the 3C BC onwards it was the Roman municipium of 'Volaterrae'. In the medieval period it was a free state under the rule of Florence; the finest buildings date from this period.

Cathedral: This originally Romanesque 12C building was rebuilt in the second half

Viterbo, Palazzo dei Papi

of the 13C in the Pisan style, with its characteristic architectural features (blind arches, galleries). The inside, with its nave and two aisles, was altered in the 16C, when the columns were faced with stucco giving an impression of pink granite.

The walls are in black and white stripes, and the rich coffered ceiling is painted with 16C heads of Saints. The monument to St. Octavian by Raffael Cioli (1522) is in the first chapel of the right transept. The apse has wooden, Gothic choir stalls and a bishop's throne dating from 1404. The marble ciborium by Mino da Fiesole (1471) is on the high altar, and two angels by the same artist stand on 12C columns beside the altar.

The pulpit in the left aisle was assembled in the 17C from parts dating from the 12C. The rectangular front of the pulpit has reliefs by various painters. The fresco of the Adoration of the Magi, by Gozzoli, on the left wall of the Cappella dell' Addolorata, is also worth seeing.

Baptistery: opposite the cathedral, it is octagonal (only one side is faced with marble) and has a Romanesque portal. Inside there is an elegant font (1502) by Andrea Sansovino, with reliefs of Christ's baptism and of the four virtues.

S. Francesco: This church dates from the 13C, but was later almost completely rebuilt.

Cappella della Croce di Giorno: Begun in 1315, this chapel stands close to S. Francesco. There is a fresco of the Evangelists by Jacopo da Firenze on the inside of the dome, while the other frescos, by Cenni di Francesco Cenni (1410), show the Legend of the Cross (the cycle follows that by A.Gaddi in S. Croce in Florence), and scenes from the Life of Christ.

Museo Diocesano di Arte Sacra (Via Roma 1): The former Palazzo Vescovile houses art works from the cathedral and from other churches in the surrounding area.

Museo Etrusco Guarnacci (Via Don Minzoni 11): This museum houses one of the most interesting Etruscan collections (begun in 1732) in Italy. Its main feature is a collection of more than 600 cinerary urns, nearly all from the Hellenistic period (4–1C BC; the older burial grounds have been swallowed up by the 'Balze'). The urns of tufa, alabaster or terracotta often show Greek reliefs of domestic scenes, while their lids bear the typically Etruscan recumbent figures of the deceased. The urn showing 'the soul's journey to eternity' is outstanding.

Palazzo dei Priori: It stands opposite the Palazzo Pretorio in a dominant position on the Piazza dei Priori, one of the most beautiful medieval squares in Italy. Some of the tall, grey palaces are not original. The present palace was built in the 1st half of the 13C, and its well-preserved façade bears coats of arms in stone and terracotta. Inside is a fresco of St. Jerome, ascribed to Luca Signorelli. The Galleria Pittorica on the 2nd floor houses Florentine, Sienese and local paintings of the 14–17C, including a 'Deposition' by Rosso Fiorentino (1521, room I), an 'Annunciation' by Luca Signorelli (1491), a triptych by Taddeo di Bartolo, and a 'Christ' by Ghirlandaio.

Casa Ricciarelli: This palace, in the street of the same name (No. 12), retains its highly distinctive children's windows, set lower than the ordinary windows, often with grilles.

Fortezza: This fortress stands at the town's highest point and can only be visited with ministerial permission. It is one of the most powerful fortifications of Renaissance Italy. To the E. is the 'Rocca Vecchia', built in 1343 on an irregular ground plan, and rebuilt by Lorenzo il Magnifico. The tower in the middle is called 'La Femmina'. To the W. is the 'Rocca Nuova', with a square ground plan and five towers; the middle tower, called 'Il Maschio', was built by Lorenzo il Magnifico in 1472.

Mura Etrusche: The Etruscan wall, about 5 miles long, surrounds the town. (The present medieval wall is only about 2 miles long). Part of the Etruscan wall is very well preserved, particularly underneath the church of S. Chiara. The *Arco Etrusco*, or Porta all'Arco, is a part of the town wall. The posts and the three barely recognizable stone heads are Etruscan; they were re-used by the Romans when they rebuilt the gates. The wall running above is medieval. From here there is a splendid view for miles around.

Roman theatre: Some remains of the 'Anfiteatro di Vallebuona', which dates from the imperial period, are to be found in a broad meadow to the N. of the town.

Le Balze: This is a gorge situated at Borgo S. Giusto at the end of the town. Formed by washing away the soil, it has already swallowed up the oldest Etruscan burial grounds and also the earlier, 7C church of S. Giusto; the second church of the same name is today once again threatened with destruction.

Environs: Pomarance: A medieval town located near the confluence of the Possera and the Cecina. The Romanesque *parish church* of St. John is noteworthy. **Sillano** or **Rocca di Silano:** The ruins of a fortification originally consisting of three

rings, only the inner wall of which, at an elevation of 1736 ft., has survived. This was the former fortress of the bishops of Volterra. Fine view.

Voltri 16158

Genoa/Liguria   p.412 □ C 5

S. Ambrogio (Via Fra Simone da Carnoli): This 17C church houses a painting of 'St. Ambrose' by G.A.Ansaldo, the painter born in Voltri, and also a 'Nativity of the Virgin' by G.A.de Ferrari (1630). The sacristy has a 'St. Erasmus' by B.Strozzi.

SS. Nicolo ed Erasmo (above the River Léiro): This church (1652; dome, 1714) has a nave and two aisles with richly stuccoed columns. There are numerous good paintings: 'St. Lucy' and 'St. Charles Borromeo' by G.A.Ansaldo, 'Purification of the Virgin' by G.A. De Ferrari, 'John the Baptist' by L.Cambiaso, and others. G.A.Carlone painted the frescos in the Chapel of the Rosary.

Environs: Nostra Signora delle

Volterra, Fortezza

Grazie: This pilgrimage church stands at an elevation of 425 ft., and dates from 1205. It was formerly the parish church of Voltri. Rebuilt in the 18C, and restored, together with the nearby monastery, a century later. A vision of the Virgin (1748) is connected with a Genoese victory over the Austrians. The *Cappella della Madonna* contains a much venerated 16C painting by C.Odone. The Gothic interior, with its contrasting black-and-white colouring, has some further notable paintings by L.Cambiaso (high altar) and F.Floriani (to the left of the high altar). There is a 'Madonna and Child' by G.Palmieri in the sacristy. The crypt (1868) houses the tombs of the Brignole-Sale family.

Vulci

Viterbo/Latium   p.414□F/G 9

In the 6&5C BC, the Etruscan Velcha (pre-Etruscan settlement also demonstrable), one of the confederation of twelve cities, was one of the most important and richest towns in Etruria. It was not conquered by the Romans until 280 BC. However, from the 9C AD onwards it was abandoned once again.

Excavations: A rich burial ground with over 6000 graves was found here. The predatory excavations of the 18C and early 19C enriched museums in Berlin, London, Paris and Würzburg. Alessandro François, the archaeologist, carried out excavations on the instructions of the Torlonia princes and in 1857 he discovered the tomb named after him. Its famous frescos were moved to the Albani-Torlonia villa in Rome. The Coccumella, a large tumulus 490 ft. in diameter, is thought to have been a sacrificial mound. Excavation work in the area of the town was not begun until 1956, and its chief accomplishment has been to reveal the Vulci of the imperial period. To the N. of the town, the *Ponte dell'Abadia*, with its bold arch, crosses the gorge of the Fiora. It probably dates from the imperial period, on Etruscan foundations.

Volterra, Museo Etrusco Guarnacci

Glossary

Acanthus: Decorative element found especially on → Corinthian capitals; it developed from the stylized representation of a sharply serrated, thistle-like leaf.

Aedicule: Wall niche housing a bust or statue; usually with a → gable, → pillars or → columns.

Aisle: Longitudinal section of a church or other building, usually divided from other such sections by an → arcade.

Altar: Sacrificial table of Greeks and Romans. The Lord's table in the Christian faith. Catholic churches often have several side altars as well as the high altar.

Ambo: Stand or lectern by the choir screen in early Christian and medieval churches; predecessor of the → pulpit.

Ambulatory: A corridor created by continuing the side aisles around the choir; often used for processions.

Antependium: Covering for the front of the altar.

Apse: Large recess at end of the → choir, usually semicircular or polygonal. As a rule it contains the → altar.

Apsidiole: A small apsidal chapel.

Aquamanile: Pouring-vessel or bowl for ritual washing in the Catholic liturgy.

Aqueduct: Water pipe or channel across an arched bridge; frequently built as monumental structures by the Romans.

Arabesque: Stylized foliage used as a decorative motif.

Arcade: A series of arches borne by columns or pillars. When the arcade is attached to a wall (and is purely decorative), it is called a blind arcade.

Arch: A curved structure of support employed in spanning a space.

Architrave: Main stone member on top of the columns; lowest part of the → entablature.

Archivolt: The face of an arch in Romanesque and Gothic portals; often more than one.

Ashlar: Hewn block of stone (as opposed to that straight from the quarry).

Atrium: In Roman houses a central hall with an opening in the roof. In Christian architecture, a forecourt usually surrounded by columns; also known as a → paradise.

Attic: A (usually richly decorated) storey above the main → entablature; intended to conceal the roof.

Baldacchino: Canopy above altars, tombs, statues, portals, etc.

Baluster: Short squat or shaped column.

Balustrade: Rail formed of → balusters.

Baptistery: Place of baptism; may be a separate building.

Baroque: Architectural style from c.1600–c.1750. Distinguished by powerfully agitated, interlocking forms.

Bartizan: A small corner turret projecting from the top of a building.

Base: Foot of a column or pillar.

Basket arch: A flattened round arch.

Basilica: Greek hall of kings. In church architecture, a type of church with nave and two or more aisles, the roof of the nave being higher than the roofs above the aisles.

Bay: Vertical division of a building between pillars, columns, windows, wall arches, etc.

Blind arcade: → Arcade.

Blind tracery: → Tracery.

Bracket: A projection from the wall used as a support—for a bust, statue, arch, etc.

Calotte: Half dome with no drum.

Campanile: Bell tower; usually free standing.

Capital: Topmost part of a column. The shape of the capital determines the style or → order.

Cartouche: Decorative frame or panel imitating a scrolled piece of paper, usually with an inscription, coat-of-arms, etc.

Caryatid: A carved figure supporting the entablature.

Cella: Main room of ancient temple containing divine image.

Cenotaph: Monument to dead buried elsewhere.

Chapterhouse: Assembly room in which monks or nuns discuss the community's business.

Charnel house: House or vault in which bones are placed.

Choir: That part of the church in which divine service is sung. Shorter and often narrower than the nave, it is usually raised and at the E. end. In the Middle Ages the choir was often separated from the rest of the church by a screen.

Ciborium: Canopy over high altar; usually in the form of a dome supported on columns.

Classicism: Revival of Greek and Roman architectural principles.

Clerestory: Upper part of the main walls of the nave, above the roofs of the aisles and pierced by windows.

Cloister: Four sided covered walk (often vaulted) and opening inwards by arcades.

Coffered ceiling: A ceiling divided into square or polygonal panels, which are painted or otherwise decorated.

Column: Support with circular cross-section, narrowing somewhat towards the top; the type of column

is determined by the → order. → Pillar.

Compound pillar: Often found in Gothic buildings. A central shaft has attached or detached shafts or half-shafts clustered around it.

Conch: Semicircular recess with a half-dome.

Confessio: Chamber or recess for a relic near the altar.

Corinthian order: → Order with richly decorated → capitals; the base has two or more tiers and is similar to that of the → Ionic order.

Cornice: Projecting upper limit of a wall; topmost member of the → entablature of an → order.

Cosmati work: Decorative technique involving the use of marble inlay, mosaics etc.; many Roman marble workers had the family name Cosma.

Crocket: Gothic leaf-like decoration projecting from the sides of pinnacles, gables etc.

Crossing: The intersection of the nave and transept.

Crypt: Burial place, usually under the → choir. Churches were often built above an old crypt.

Curtain wall: Outer wall of castle.

Cyclops Wall: Ancient wall made of large rough blocks of stone of irregular shape.

Dipteros: Temple in which porticoes are connected by a double row of lateral columns.

Diptych: A painted hinged double (altar) panel.

Dolmen: Chamber tomb lined and roofed with megaliths.

Doric order: → Order in which the columns lack a base and bear flat, pad-shaped → capitals.

Dormer window: Window in sloping roof which projects and has its own gabled roof.

Drum: Substructure of a dome; as a rule either cylindrical or polygonal.

Dwarf Gallery: Romanesque feature; wall passage of small arches on the outside of a building.

Entablature: Upper part of an → order; made up of → architrave, → frieze and → cornice.

Exedra: Apse, vaulted with a half dome; may have raised seats.

Façade: Main front of a building, often decoratively treated.

Facing: Panelling in front of structural components not intended to be visible.

Faience: Glazed pottery named after the Italian town of Faenza.

Fan vault: Looks like a highly decorated rib vault; Concave-sided cone-like sections meet or nearly meet at the apex of the vault.

Filigree work: Originally goldsmith's work in which gold and silver wire were ornamentally soldered on to a metal base. Also used in a more general sense for intricately perforated carvings and stucco.

Finial: Small decorative pinnacle.

Flying buttress: Very large Gothic windows made it necessary to buttress or strengthen the outer walls by half-arches and arches. This support transmitted the thrust of the vault to the buttress.

Foliate capital: Gothic capital in which the basic form is covered with delicate leaf ornaments.

Fosse: Artificially created ditch; often separated castles from the surrounding land with access by a drawbridge.

Fresco: Pigments dispersed in water are applied without a bonding agent to the still-damp lime plaster. While the mortar dries, the pigments become adsorbed into the plaster.

Frieze: Decorative strips for the borders of a wall. The frieze can be two- or three-dimensional and can consist of figures or ornaments.

Gable: The triangular upper section of a wall. Normally at one end of a pitched roof but it may be purely decorative.

Gallery: Intermediate storey; in a church it is usually for singers and the organ. Arcaded walkway.

Gobelin: Pictorial tapestry made in the Gobelins factory in Paris.

Gothic: Period in European art and architecture stretching from the mid 12C to the 16C.

Grisaille: Painting in various shades of grey.

Groin vault: Vault in which two → barrel vaults intersect at right angles. The simple groin vault is to be distinguished from the rib vault, in which the intersecting edges are reinforced by ribs.

Half-timbering: Beams are used as supporting parts with an infill of loam or brick.

Hall church: In contrast to the → basilica, nave and aisles are of equal height; no → transept.

Hermitage: Pavilion in parks and gardens; originally the residence of a hermit.

Holy Sepulchre: Structure representing Christ's tomb as discovered by Constantine, who later encased it in a miniature temple.

Iconostasis: In the Eastern church, a screen of paintings between the sanctuary and the nave.

Intarsia: Inlaid work in wood, plaster, stone etc.

Ionic order: → Order in which the columns stand on a base of two or more tiers; the → capital has two lateral → volutes.

Jamb: Vertical part of arch, doorway or window.

Keep: Main tower of a castle; last refuge in time of siege.

Lantern: Small windowed turret on top of roof or dome.

Loggia: Pillared gallery, open on one or more sides; often on an upper storey.

Lunette: Semicircular panel above doors and windows, often with paintings or sculptures.

Mandorla: Almond shaped niche containing a figure of Christ enthroned.

Mannerism: Artistic style between → Renaissance and → baroque (c.1530–1630). Mannerism neglects natural and classical forms in favour of an intended artificiality of manner.

Mansard: An angled roof in which the lower slope is steeper than the upper. The area gained is also called a mansard and can be used to live in. (Named after the French architect F.Mansart.)

Mausoleum: A splendid tomb, usually in the form of a small house or temple. From the tomb of Mausolus at Halicarnassus.

Mensa: Flat surface of the altar.

Mezzanine: Intermediate storey.

Miniature: Small picture, hand illumination in old manuscripts.

Monks' choir: That section of the choir reserved for the monks, frequently closed off.

Monstrance: Ornamented receptacle in which the consecrated Host is shown (usually behind glass).

Mosaic: Decoration for wall, floor or vault, assembled from small coloured stones, pieces of glass or fragments of other materials.

Mullion: Vertical division of a window into two or more lights.

Narthex: Vestibule of basilica or church.

Nave: Central aisle of church, intended for the congregation; excludes choir and apse.

Neo-baroque: Reaction to the cool restraint of → classicism. Re-uses baroque forms; developed in the last part of the 19C as a historicizing, sumptuous style with exaggerated three-dimensional ornamentation and conspicuous colours.

Neo-Gothic: Historicizing 19C style, which was intended to revive Gothic structural forms and decorative elements.

Net vault: Vault in which the ribs cross one another repeatedly.

Nuns' choir: Gallery from which nuns attended divine service.

Nymphaeum: Roman pleasure house, often with statues and fountains.

Obelisk: Free-standing pillar with square ground plan and pyramidal peak.

Odeum: Building, usually round, in which musical or other artistic performances were given.

Onion dome: Bulbous dome with a point, common in Russia and E.Europe; not a true dome, i.e. without a vault.

Opisthodomos: Rear section of Greek temple; behind the cella.

Orangery: Part of baroque castles and parks originally intended to shelter orange trees and other southern plants in winter. However, orangeries often had halls for large court assemblies.

Oratory: Small private chapel.

Order: Classical architectural system prescribing decorations and proportions according to one of the accepted forms — → Corinthian, → Doric, → Ionic, etc. An order consists of a column, which usually has a base, shaft and capital, and the entablature, which itself consists of architrave, frieze and cornice.

Oriel: Projecting window on an upper floor; it is often a decorative feature.

Pallium: A cloak worn by the Romans; in the Middle Ages, a coronation cloak for kings and emperors, later also for archbishops.

Pantheon: Temple dedicated to all gods; often modelled on that in in Rome, which is a rotunda. Building in which distinguished people are buried or have memorials.

Paradise: → Atrium.

Pavilion: Polygonal or round building in parks or pleasure grounds. The main structure of baroque castles is very often linked by corner pavilions to the galleries branching off from the castle.

Pedestal: Base of a column or the base for a statue.

Pendentive: The means by which a circular dome is supported on a square base; concave area or spandrel between two walls and the base of a dome.

Peripteros: Greek temple in which the porticoes are connected laterally by single rows of columns.

Peristyle: Continuous colonnade surrounding a temple or open court.

Pilaster: Pier projecting from a wall; conforms to one of the → orders.

Pilaster strip: Pilaster without base and capital; feature of Anglo-Saxon and early Romanesque buildings.

Pillar: Supporting member, like a → column but with a square or polygonal cross section; does not conform to any order.

Plinth: Projecting lower part of wall or column.

Polyptych: An (altar) painting composed of several panels or wings.

Porch: Covered entrance to a building.

Portico: Porch supported by columns and often with a pediment; may be the centre-piece of façade.

Predella: Substructure of the altar. Paintings along lower edge of large altarpiece.

Pronaos: Area in front of ancient temple (also of churches); sides enclosed and columns in front.

Propylaeum: Entrance gateway, usually to temple precincts. The Propylaeum on the Acropolis at Athens, 437–432 BC, was the model for later buildings.

Prothyra: Railing before door of Roman house.

Pseudoperipteros: Temple in which porticoes are connected laterally by → pilasters and not → columns.

Pulpit: Raised place in church from which the sermon is preached. May be covered by a → baldacchino or → sounding board.

Putto: Figure of naked angelic child in → Renaissance, → baroque and → rococo art and architecture.

Pylon: Entrance gate of Egyptian temple; more generally used as isolated structure to mark a boundary.

Quadriga: Chariot drawn by four horses harnessed abreast.

Refectory: Dining hall of a monastery.

Relief: Carved or moulded work in which the design stands out. The different depths of relief are, in ascending order, rilievo stiacciato, bas-relief and high relief or altorilievo.

Reliquary: Receptacle in which a saint's relics are preserved.

Renaissance: Italian art and architecture from the early 15C to the mid 16C. It marks the end of the medieval conception of the world and the beginning of a new view based on classical antiquity (Ital. rinascimento = rebirth).

Retable: Shrine-like structure above and behind the altar.

Rib vault: → Groin vault.

Rocaille: Decorative ornaments adapted from the shell motif; chiefly late → Renaissance and → Rococo.

Rococo: Style towards the end of the → baroque (1720–70); elegant, often dainty, tendency to oval forms.

Romanesque: Comprehensive name for architecture from 1000–c.1300. Buildings are distinguished by round arches, calm ornament and a heavy general appearance.

Rood screen: Screen between → choir and → nave, which bears a rood or crucifix.

Rose-window: A much divided round window with rich → tracery found especially in Gothic buildings; often above the portal.

Rotunda: Round building.

Rustication: Massive blocks of stone separated by deep joints.

Sanctuary: Area around the high altar in a church.

Sarcophagus: Stone coffin, usually richly decorated.

Scroll: Spiral-shaped ornament.

Sedilia: Seats for clergy; usually in the wall of the S.side of the choir.

Sgraffito: Scratched-on decoration.

Sounding board: → Pulpit.

Spandrel: The triangular space between the curve of an arch, the horizontal drawn from its apex, and the vertical drawn from the point of its springing; also the area between two arches in an arcade, and that part of a vault between two adjacent ribs.

Springer: The first stone in which the curve of an arch or vault begins.

Squinch: An arch or system of arches at the internal angles of towers to form the base of a round drum or dome above a square structure. → Pendentive.

Stela: Standing block.

Strapwork: Renaissance carved work modelled on fretwork or cut leather.

Stucco: Plasterwork, made of gypsum, lime, sand and water, which is easy to model. Used chiefly in the 17&18C for three-dimensional interior decoration.

Synagogue: Jewish place of worship.

Tabernacle: Receptacle for the consecrated host.

Telamon: Support in the form of a male figure (male caryatid).

Terracotta: Fired, unglazed clay.

Thermal baths: Roman hot-water baths.

Tracery: Geometrically conceived decorative stonework, particularly used to decorate windows, screens, etc. If it embellishes a wall, it is known as blind tracery.

Transenna: Screen or lattice in openwork found in early Christian churches.

Transept: That part of a church at right angles to the nave; → basilica.

Triforium: Arcaded wall passage looking on to the nave; between the arcade and the clerestory.

Triptych: Tripartite altar painting.

Triumphal arch: Free-standing gateway based on a Roman original.

Truss frame: Frame of timbers joined together to span a gap and to support other timbers, as in a roof.

Tunnel vault: Simplest vault; continuous structure with semicircular or pointed cross section uninterrupted by cross vaults.

Tympanum: The often semicircular panel contained within the lintel of a doorway and the arch above it.

Volute: Spiral scroll on an Ionic capital; smaller volutes on Composite and Corinthian capitals.

Winged altar: Triptych or polyptych with hinged, usually richly carved or painted, wings.

Index of Major Artists

Minor Towns and Places of Interest listed in 'Environs'

Abbadia S.Salvatore → Pienza
Abbaza di Piona → Gravedona
Abbazia di Rivalta Scrivia → Tortona
Abbazia di S.Antonio di Ranverso → Avigliana
Abbazia di Sassovio → Foligno
Abbazia di Staffarda → Saluzzo
Abbazia di Torri → Siena
Abbazia di Valvisciolo → Sermoneta
Aci Castello → Acireale
Acri → San Demetrio Corone
Acquaresi → Iglésias
Aeclanum → Mirabella Eclano
Afers → Bressanone
Agumes → Burgusio
Agums → Burgusio
Aidomaggiore → Abbasanta
Airola → Sant'Agata dei Goti
Alà dei Sardi → Olbia
Ales → Sardara
Almenno San Bartolomeo → Bergamo
Almenno San Salvatore → Bergamo
Altomonte → Castrovillari
Amiterno → L'Aquila
Amiternum → L'Aquila
Anghiari → Sansepolcro
Anghiari → Arezzo
Ansedonia → Grosseto
Arbatax → Tortoli
Arco → Riva del Garda
Ariccia → Albano Laziale
Armúngia → Orroli
Artimino → Pistoia
Arzignano → Montecchio Maggiore
Asciano → Siena
Assemini → Cágliari
Assuni → Barumini
Atrani → Amalfi
Atzara → Aritzo
Auer → Egna

Bacoli → Pozzuoli
Badia di S.Spirito → Caltanisetta
Badia Moronese → Sulmona
Bagnaia → Viterbo
Bagni di Lucca → Lucca
Bagno a Ripoli → Firenze
Bagno Roselle → Grosseto
Baia → Pozzuoli
Balvano → Vietri di Potenza
Balzi Rossi → Ventimiglia
Barbeano → Spilimbergo
Barbian → Chiusa
Barbiano → Chiusa
Bardolino → Garda
Barga → Lucca
Bargone → Salsomaggiore Terme
Basilica di Superga → Turin
Bassano Romano → Sutri
Bazzano → L'Aquila
Bellagio → Como
Benetutti → Ottana
Bernalda → Montescaglioso
Bienno → Capo di Ponte
Biscéglie → Trani
Bitetto → Bari
Bitti → Posada

Bolótana → Macomer
Bonárcado → Oristano
Bono → Trento
Bordighera → Ventimiglia
Borgo → Pieve Tesino
Borore → Macomer
Borutta → Bonnánaro
Bosco di Galliera → Bologna
Bosco Marengo → Alessandria
Bottida → Ottana
Bozen → Bolzano
Brancolino → Rovereto
Breno → Capo di Ponte
Brentónico → Rovereto
Brienza → Potenza
Brignano Gera d'Adda → Treriglio
Bruneck → Brunico
Bulzi → Castelsardo
Burano → Venezia
Burgeis → Burgusio
Busachi → Abbasanta
Butera → Gela

Caccamo → Términi Imerese
Caggiano → Polla
Cala di Vela Marina → Arzachena
Cala Gonone → Dorgali
Calangianus → Tempio Pausania
Calascibetta → Enna
Calasetta → Sant'Antioco
Calci → Pisa
Caldaro → Appiano
Calliano → Rovereto
Caltabelota → Ribera
Calvi Risorta → Teano
Camáldoli → Nápoli
Camarina → Comiso
Campagna → Eboli
Camppi Raudi → Vercelli
Campobello → Selinunte
Campochiesa → Albenga
Campodonico → Fabriano
Cancello → Acerra
Canne della Battaglia → Canosa di Puglia
Canneto → Eolie, Isole
Caorle → Venezia
Capraia, Isola → Elba
Caprera (I) → Arzachena
Carinola → Sessa Aurunca
Carloforte → Sant'Antioco
Cármine Superiore → Cannobio
Carovigno → Ostuni
Carpignano → Otranto
Carpineta → Cesena
Carpoforo → Como
Carrara → Massa
Carsulae → Terni
Cartigliano → Bassano d. Grappa
Casarano → Gallipoli
Cáscina → Empoli
Caserta Vecchia → Caserta
Cassano d'Adda → Bergamo
Cassano d'Adela → Treviglio
Castel Besono → Rovereto
Castel d'Appiano → Appiano
Casteldarne → Brunico

Castelfiorentino → Empoli
Castel Fiorentino → Lucera
Castel Firmiano → Appiano
Castellammare di Stábia → Pompei
Castelleone → Crema
Castellina in Chianti → Siena
Castello d'Alife → Piedimonte
Castello di Gaglianico → Biella
Castello di Tabiano → Salso maggiore Terme
Castello Enryalos → Siracusa
Catello Taranto → Naturno
Castello Tesino → Pieve Tesino
Castelluccio → Noto
Castel Mareccio → Bolzano
Castelnuovo di Garfagnana → Lucca
Castelnuovo Magra → Massa
Castel Róncolo → Bolzano
Castel Roseto → Rocca Imperiale
Castel San Felice → Spoleto
Castel San Pietro Romano → Palestrina
Castel Sant'Elia → Nepi
Castel Seprio → Varese
Castelvetrano → Selinunte
Castiglione della Pescaia → Grosseto
Castiglione delle Stiviere → Sirmione
Castiglione d'Orcia → Pienza
Castiglion Fiorentino → Cortona
Castiglione Olona → Varese
Castions di Strada → Palmanova
Castro → Otranto
Castroreale Terme → Castroreale
Caulonia → Stilo
Cava de Tirreni → Salerno
Cava d'Ispica → Módica
Cavernago → Bergamo
Celone → Troia
Cembra → Salorno
Le Centropietre → Lenca
Cernobbio → Como
Certaldo → Empoli
Certosa di Pavia → Pavia
Certosa di Pisa → Pisa
Certosa di Trisulti → Alatri
Cesi → Terni
Cherémule → Bonnánaro
Chiaramonti → Castelsardo
Chiaravalle → Iesi
Chiaravalle di Fiastra → Tolentino
Chioggia → Venezia
Cimitile → Nola
Cisternino → Alberobello
Civate → Como
Civezzano → Trento
Civitella Ranieri → Città di Castello
Collegio Alberoni → Piacenza
Colle Isarco → Vipiteno
Colloredo di Monte Albano → Tricesimo
Concordia → Venezia
Concordia sulla Secchia → Mirandola
Contrada Casale → Piazza Armerina
Convento di Greccio → Rieti
Cordovado → San Vito al Tagliamento
Corigliano Calabro → Rossano
Cormons → Gorizia
Cosa → Grosseto